POLITICAL SYSTEMS *of the* WORLD

J. Denis Derbyshire
Ian Derbyshire

Chambers

Published 1989 by W & R Chambers Ltd
43–45 Annandale Street, Edinburgh EH7 4AZ

British Library Cataloguing in Publication Data
Derbyshire, Denis
Political systems of the world.
1. Political systems—Encyclopaedias
I. Title II. Derbyshire, Ian
320'.03'21

ISBN 0-550-21008-3

Maps by Euromap Limited
Cover design by David Sneddon

Typeset by Pillans & Wilson Specialist Litho Printers Ltd. Edinburgh

Printed in Great Britain by
Richard Clay Ltd, Bungay, Suffolk

CONTENTS

PART I: THE COMPARATIVE APPROACH

PART II: POLITICAL SYSTEMS OF THE WORLD'S NATION-STATES

PART III: TOWARDS ONE WORLD

PREFACE

There are between 150 and 200 sovereign states in the world today, the number varying according to how the word sovereign is defined. Each has its own unique ethnic and social composition and its own unique history. The interplay of these, and other, factors has created, in turn, a unique system of government. There will be similarities between different systems but, in the final analysis, each is distinctively unique.

In this book we describe these systems and try to relate them to the social and economic forces which, over the years, have fashioned them. At the same time, we have identified particular features which are common to all, or most, of them and have classified them in an attempt to make objective comparisons.

In our classifications we have looked at countries where citizens have a comparatively free choice of which group of people should control the levers of political power and those where that choice is limited. The first we have called multi-party, or pluralistic, states and the second one-party, or monistic. This is an important distinction but it is not the only criterion for deciding whether or not a political system can be said to be democratic.

As we enter the last decade of the present century we are confronted with momentous changes in all parts of the world and it is impossible to predict with certainty the extent to which they will develop. The accession to power in the Soviet Union of Mikhail Gorbachev has already had the effect of casting a stone into the apparently static pool of Eastern European politics and its ripples are spreading to other regions.

There are clear signs that politicians throughout the world are becoming aware that economic systems cannot be changed without affecting political systems. In the Soviet Union, for example, political changes have been made to facilitate economic reform. In China, on the other hand, economic change has preceded political reform with dire, if predictable, consequences. It seems certain that if people are given greater economic choice then, sooner or later, they will demand political choice as well.

In the pages that follow we have tried to provide a better understanding of political institutions and events in the contemporary world and have addressed ourselves not just to academics and professional observers of the political landscape but also to the more general reader who is looking for a serious, but not over-technical, account of global politics.

We think our approach is new in a number of ways. First, we consider all the contemporary states and not just the well known and obvious. Second, we attempt to identify connections between a country's political system and its historical, social and economic background. Third, we look in some detail at the dynamics of political systems, including the activities of parties and similar groupings, as well as the formal institutions which states have erected. Fourth, partly to make the material more manageable, but also to provide a better understanding of geographical and demographic influences, we have adopted a regional approach to our exposition of political systems. Finally, we have looked at examples of how sovereign states, either by choice or necessity, have found it increasingly profitable to co-operate with each other rather than compete.

It has been a labour of love but also, at times, one of great frustration, mainly because of the virtually impossible task of ensuring that the information about each state is still valid in a world where political change is the rule rather than the exception.

JDD and IDD
August 1989

TABLES

LIST OF MAPS

PART I

THE COMPARATIVE APPROACH

CHAPTER 1

UNDERSTANDING POLITICAL SYSTEMS

1.1 Introduction

To give a reasonably full account of the political systems of every sovereign state in the world is, by any standards, a daunting task, but having done a considerable amount of work in discovering the factual bases of these systems, we felt it would be helpful to attempt an analysis of similarities and differences to discover what lessons, if any, could be learned.

A comparative study of government is, of course, not particularly novel and many valuable books have been written in this field, some of which we identify at the end of each chapter. As far as we are aware, however, no one has attempted a comparative approach on such a wide scale and, for this reason alone, we felt the effort would be useful.

Although we believe our research to be academically valid, we have not addressed ourselves solely to academics. Indeed, we have assumed little or no prior knowledge or preparation in our readers, simply a lively interest in current affairs and a desire to be better informed about the world in which they live. We hope, however, that serious students of politics will find the book of interest and help. We have tried to keep our information as accurate and up to date as possible, but, with such a wide canvas, covering a rapidly moving scene, some changes will, inevitably, have occurred by the time the final version has been produced.

1.2 Political man

The Greek philosopher, Aristotle (384–322 BC), said that man was by nature a political animal. He argued that it was within man's natural development to live in some sort of ordered society under a system of government. In the times in which he lived the kind of community he saw as natural was the comparatively small city-state of Ancient Greece, with thousands, rather than millions, of citizens able to practise direct democracy.

In the world of today there are few communities that resemble those small communities. The Most Serene Republic of San Marino in Italy is probably the best example. It is the sole city state which survived after the unification of Italy in the nineteenth century and has the distinction of being the world's oldest republic, its independence recognised and its protection guaranteed by Italy. Because of its small population, about 20,000, San Marino is able to enjoy a uniquely intimate kind of government.

The majority of countries have considerably larger populations, of course, and their governments are more remote from the average citizen. Nevertheless, Aristotle's belief that mankind achieves natural fulfilment by living in a political community seems to have been borne out by subsequent events, as this account of the political systems of the world will try to show.

1.3 What is a political system?

So that we can better understand the nature of a political system it will be helpful if we first attempt to define certain words which are frequently used in everyday speech but whose meanings are not always clear.

We use the word government in a variety of ways. In a general sense we use it to mean an orderly way of running a community's affairs and it is possible to distinguish between local government, perhaps regional government, and national government. The absence of government is anarchy, with everyone looking after him or herself: the law of the jungle. In a more specific sense we speak of the government as a body of people who have power to make us behave in certain ways. Because they are the government they have authority as well as power. In other words, their power is legitimate. We will not concern ourselves for the moment about how this power is achieved. That is something we shall discover as we look at each country more closely.

Another word frequently used in this context is the state. Often we see it as synonymous with government, with the two words interchangeable. To some extent this is quite valid: a government department might also be called a department of state. The word should be used a little more precisely, however. Governments come and go, as we all know, but the state may be said to be permanent, comprising the whole apparatus by which a community is governed: the armed forces, the police, the civil service, the judicial system and so on.

The word can also be used to describe a country which has an independent, internationally recognised, government, such as the state of Israel or the state of Egypt. What then should we say of the United States of America? Is this another use of the word state? No, the word is applicable to nations or parts of nations. It just happens that the contemporary world consists largely of nation-states and the United States is simply a nation-state comprising fifty sub-national states. We will look at the concept of the nation-state more closely a little later.

Within the same broad context we speak of politicians. They are the people who achieve, or hope to achieve, power and, in simple terms, run the government. How do they fit into the scheme of things? Civil servants, members of the armed forces, judges and similar public servants are the permanent personnel of the state while the politicians provide the temporary element. Politicians are the people who occupy positions of power as long as they have the support of the community, or they may be the people who aspire to power but are temporarily out of office. Exactly how politicians achieve power need not concern us at the moment; this will become evident as our study proceeds. We will see that power is obtained sometimes on the basis of consent, the democratic approach, and sometimes on the basis of force, the autocratic approach.

Both the words government and state are rather static terms but if we add to them the political dimension, provided by politicians and their activities, we have something much more dynamic: a political system.

A political system can probably best be understood in demand-response terms. In the majority of countries politicians are elected to positions of power and authority, the ballot box giving the ordinary citizen an opportunity to make his or her demands known. Politicians will try to anticipate these demands by offering a 'prospectus' of what they will provide if elected – a manifesto of promises – and the elector can then choose between different manifestoes on offer. Once a political party has been elected to office it will be judged by its performance and the electorate's response to that performance will again be demonstrated through the ballot box at subsequent elections.

Not all political systems provide such an open choice through the ballot box. There are still a number where a government is imposed by force or where the opportunity to vote politicians into office is limited to a section of the population. The South African political system, for example, provides opportunities for people to elect a government of their choice provided the colour of their skin is white. If it is a little darker, their opportunities to be governed by politicians of their own choosing are more limited. If they are black then a government is imposed on them and there is nothing in the political process which allows them to express their views.

A country's political system, then, is more than its institutions and more than the formal processes of government. It includes the dynamic interplay of people's ideas and interests: the whole process of demand and response which politics represents. Even if a government is highly authoritarian, giving little room for the political process to work, there will always be at least an undercurrent of activity which expresses the true aspirations of people, however subordinated they may be by those with power and authority.

1.4 The advantages of comparing systems

The comparative approach is a particularly advantageous way of arriving at a better understanding of political systems. Not just systems in general, but also a specific one about which you may consider yourself to be very knowledgeable.

First, the comparative approach forces you to stand back and look objectively at a particular system. It should be no surprise that some of the best studies of the American system of government, for instance, have been made by people whose personal experience has been gained in a different political environment.

Second, the comparative approach alerts you to similarities in institutions and processes which make your own system more understandable.

Third, the experience of one country can be used to anticipate the effects of change in the political system of another. For example, a knowledge of the voting system in the Republic of Ireland, where a form of proportional representation operates, will enable some sort of prediction to be made of the likely impact if it were introduced into the United Kingdom.

Finally, and this is probably the greatest advantage of all, a wider understanding of how countries with different histories, different ethnic compositions, different social problems and different philosophical backgrounds have approached the basic problem of creating and sustaining satisfactory institutions and processes of government is an excellent way of stimulating interest in the political process and a greater degree of participation. It is surely a sad reflection on the state of contemporary democracies that, at best, fewer than 5 per cent of their populations can be classed as being 'regularly' active in a political sense.

1.5 The nation-state

The comparisons of political systems which will be made are based on the concept of the nation-state and Table 1 lists those which will be considered. Although today it is seen as the 'natural' political unit for most areas of the world the nation-state is a comparatively new concept. No fewer than 123 of the 165 states which will be examined are products of the present century, 74 being post-1959 creations. In the Middle East and Africa only three of the 65 were in existence before 1910 and even in Europe, where a majority of 'old' states might be expected, more than 40 per cent of them achieved full independent nationhood after the First World War.

Before the twentieth century most of the world's inhabitants were, in one way or another, in the thrall of the established Western European powers and if a datum point of, say, 1810 is taken, only 15 of today's 165 states existed in a form that might be readily recognisable today.

A nation may be described as a group of people, often from different backgrounds, and sometimes from different races, who have come to live together and have adopted a common identity. The unity of a nation is usually reinforced by a common language and sometimes a common religion. A state is the name given to the whole apparatus of government which a nation creates as the machine for operating its political system.

The nation-state is then enshrined and perpetuated by the adoption of symbols such as a national flag and a national anthem. The human apex of the nation-state is the individual designated as head of state, in the person of a king, queen or president. Sometimes the head of state is little more than a symbol of national unity, with few or no political powers. Sometimes the roles of head of state and head of government are combined but, in such cases, an attempt is usually made to differentiate between the two roles. In the United States, for example, the office of president generally attracts the respect of most citizens regardless of the personality or political views of the holder.

The nation-state manifests itself in a wide variety of different forms, ranging from the democratic to the highly authoritarian. It is this rich variety which provides the material for what will follow.

1.6 The plan of the book

The first part of the book concentrates on the comparative approach, looking first at the various constitutional forms which can be adopted for political systems and then at the philosophies or ideologies which underlie the constitutional structures. Then executives, heads of state and heads of government, and assemblies or parliaments in different countries are compared. Then, moving on to the more dynamic elements of political systems, voting methods and parties are examined.

The second part is designed to show political systems in action, giving a factual account of the political institutions and processes of each country and an objective summary of how they currently operate. Altogether 165 states are covered. They include 157 of the current 159 full members of the United Nations plus the eight independent states of Kiribati, North and South Korea, Nauru, Switzerland, Taiwan, Tonga and Tuvalu. The Byelorussian and Ukrainian Socialist Soviet Republics have been excluded since, although they are both individual members of the United Nations, they are, in reality and in a political sense, part of the Soviet Union.

The eight non-UN states have been added because all have full national sovereignties and their presence outside the United Nations organisation has no useful bearing on the subject matter of our present examination of political systems. Switzerland, for example, has chosen, on the basis of its long history of neutrality, not to be a UN member and Taiwan was a member, under the title of the Republic of China, from 1945 to 1971, when the People's Republic of China received full international recognition. South Korea has repeatedly sought UN membership since 1949, but has been rebuffed by Soviet vetoes. The four South Pacific states of Kiribati, Nauru, Tonga and Tuvalu, which attained independence only relatively recently, have determined on a neutralist course and have not yet applied for direct UN representation.

Table 1

NATION-STATES OF THE WORLD

State	Year
Afghanistan	1747
Albania	1912
Algeria	1962
Angola	1975
Antigua and Barbuda	1981
Argentina	1816
Australia	1901
Austria	1918
Bahamas	1973
Bahrain	1971
Bangladesh	1971
Barbados	1966
Belgium	1830
Belize	1981
Benin	1960
Bhutan	1907
Bolivia	1825
Botswana	1966
Brazil	1822
Brunei	1984
Bulgaria	1908
Burkina Faso	1960
Burma	1948
Burundi	1962
Cambodia	1953
Cameroon	1960
Canada	1867
Cape Verde	1975
Central African Republic	1960
Chad	1960
Chile	1818
China	2nd C BC
Colombia	1830
The Comoros	1975
Congo	1960
Costa Rica	1821
Cuba	1899
Cyprus	1960
Czechoslovakia	1918
Denmark	c940
Djibouti	1977
Dominica	1978
Dominican Rep	1844
Ecuador	1830
Egypt	1922
El Salvador	1838
Equatorial Guinea	1968
Ethiopia	11th C
Fiji	1970
Finland	1917
France	741
Gabon	1960
Gambia	1965
Germany East	1949
Germany West	1949
Ghana	1957
Greece	1829
Grenada	1974
Guatemala	1839
Guinea	1958
Guinea-Bissau	1974
Guyana	1966
Haiti	1804
Honduras	1838
Hungary	1918
Iceland	1944
India	1947
Indonesia	1949
Iran	1499
Iraq	1932
Ireland, Republic of	1937
Israel	1948
Italy	1861
Ivory Coast	1960
Jamaica	1962
Japan	5th C
Jordan	1946
Kenya	1963
Kiribati*	1979
Korea North*	1948
Korea South*	1948
Kuwait	1961
Laos	1954
Lebanon	1944
Lesotho	1966
Liberia	1847
Libya	1951
Luxembourg	1848
Madagascar	1960
Malawi	1964
Malaysia	1957
Maldives	1965
Mali	1960
Malta	1964
Mauritania	1960
Mauritius	1968
Mexico	1821
Mongolia	1921/1946
Morocco	1956
Mozambique	1975
Nauru*	1968
Nepal	1768
Netherlands	1648
New Zealand	1853/1947
Nicaragua	1838
Niger	1960
Nigeria	1960
Norway	1905
Oman	1951
Pakistan	1947
Panama	1903
Papua New Guinea	1975
Paraguay	1811
Peru	1824
Philippines	1946
Poland	1918
Portugal	1128
Qatar	1971
Romania	1881
Rwanda	1962
Sao Tome and Principe	1975
Saudi Arabia	1932
Senegal	1960
Seychelles	1976
Sierra Leone	1961
Singapore	1965
Solomon Isles	1978
Somalia	1960
South Africa	1910
Spain	1492
Sri Lanka	1948
St Kitts-Nevis	1983
St Lucia	1979

Table 1—Nation-States of the World (contd.)

St Vincent and the Grenadines	1979	Tonga*	1970	Venezuela	1830
Sudan	1956	Trinidad and Tobago	1962	Vietnam	1954/1976
Suriname	1975	Tunisia	1956	Western Samoa	1962
Swaziland	1968	Turkey	1923	Yemen Arab Republic	1918
Sweden	1523	Tuvalu*	1978	Yemen People's Democratic Republic	1967
Switzerland*	1648	Uganda	1962	Yugoslavia	1918
Syria	1946	United Arab Emirates	1971	Zaire	1960
Taiwan*	1949	United Kingdom	1707/1921	Zambia	1964
Tanzania	1961	United States	1776	Zimbabwe	1980
Thailand	1350	Uruguay	1825		
Togo	1960	USSR	1917–22		
		Vanuatu	1980		

All the states in this table, except for those asterisked, are current members of the United Nations. The dates indicate the year of each country's inception as a nation-state. This date will normally be the year in which its first constitution was adopted, which may or may not be the one currently in force. In the case of a minority of countries, particularly those with dates prior to the nineteenth century, the inception of nationhood will pre-date the adoption of the first constitution or a codified constitution may never have been adopted.

The 165 states have been grouped into nine geographical regions: Western Europe; Eastern Europe; the Middle East and North Africa; Central and Southern Africa; North America; Central America and the Caribbean; South America; Asia; and Oceania. This classification has been chosen in preference to one based purely on philosophical values, such as liberal-democratic, totalitarian and so on. Such an approach is superficially attractive but fraught with difficulties. It is, inevitably, subjective and can have the effect of distorting the profile of a political system so as to force it into one of the chosen categories. On the other hand there are, apart from convenience, some good reasons for adopting the regional approach.

First, there is an undoubted link, as will be demonstrated, between a country's geography and history and the political system it develops. A look at the continent of America, and its associated islands, will illustrate this point.

The whole of North America was at one time a British colony. The fact that Canada, which retained its connection with Britain, also retained aspects of the British constitution in its political system is understandable. Equally understandable is the recognition that the United States, which broke its link with Britain 200 years ago, chose to develop a different system which looks more guardedly at the dangers of unfettered executive power and seeks to control and restrain it. The United States constitution, therefore, reflects other influences, such as the political climate in eighteenth-century France.

The geography and social composition of North America have also had effects on the political systems of both Canada and the United States, resulting in federal structures of government which take into account the size and diversities of both countries.

Moving south down the continent, the fact that much of Central and South America were once part of a Spanish empire whereas the islands of the Caribbean came under British and French influence is, again, reflected in their political systems.

Second, there is a discernible link between a country's ethnic characteristics and the political system it develops, and these characteristics tend to be regionalised in many cases. For example, it is not surprising that the majority of Islamic states are to be found in the Middle East and North Africa.

An attempt to classify states geographically or politically is, inevitably, a somewhat arbitrary process. Where does Western Europe end and Eastern Europe begin? Should Turkey, which bestrides both Europe and Asia, be included in Europe? If in Europe, why the Western, rather than the Eastern, part?

Similar problems occur when classifications are attempted in other parts of the world. What exactly is meant by the Middle East? Should not the continent of Africa be regarded as a whole? If not, how should it be divided? Asia produces similar, and perhaps even more intractable, problems, such as that of defining boundaries. Another arises from the sheer size and complexity of the area, extending from Afghanistan in the west to Japan in the east.

One region which has been used for classification purposes is Oceania. Where exactly are its boundaries? Indeed, can it be said to exist at all? For the purposes of this book it is regarded as including Australasia and those island territories in the Pacific which do not fit easily into any other of the regional groupings which have been chosen.

The arbitrary nature of the classification is freely admitted and no apologies are offered. Without such an approach much of the material would have been less manageable and, in any event, for the majority of states alternative groupings would not have brought out so clearly the influences of history, geography and social development.

The third part of the book deals with residual territories in the world which cannot be viewed as fully fledged independent states. Into this category fall five tiny West European principalities, city and theocratic states, Andorra, Liechtenstein, Monaco, San Marino, and the Vatican City, which are closely linked to and heavily dependent for their external security upon their much larger neighbours. These have been termed semi-sovereign states. Also into this category fall the 50 overseas colonies and external dependent territories that still exist in the world of today.

This final part also looks beyond nation-states and their dependencies to regional and global groupings, recognising that the accelerated improvements in communications of all kinds, and the growing economic interdependence of countries, will inevitably cause the world to shrink in political as well as physical terms.

RECOMMENDED READING

Charlton, R., *Comparative Government*, Longman, 1986, Ch 1.

Crick, B., *In Defence of Politics*, 2nd edn., Penguin, 1982.

Dogan, M. and Pelassy, G., *How to Compare Nations*, Chatham House, 1984.

Evans, P. B., Rueschemeyer, D. and Skocpol, T. (eds), *Bringing the State Back In*, Cambridge University Press, 1985.

Hague, R. and Harrop, M., *Comparative Government and Politics: An Introduction*, 2nd edn., Macmillan, 1987, Chs 1–3.

Harding, N. (ed), *The State in Socialist Society*, Macmillan, 1984.

King, R., *The State in Modern Society: New Directions in Political Sociology*, Macmillan, 1986.
Leftwich, A. (ed), *What is Politics? The Activity and its Study*, Basil Blackwell, 1984.
Lukes, S. (ed), *Power*, Basil Blackwell, 1986.
Macridis, R. and Brown, B. (eds), *Comparative Politics: Notes and Readings*, 5th edn., Dorsey, Homewood, Illinois, 1977.
Roberts, G. K., *An Introduction to Comparative Politics*, Edward Arnold, 1986, Ch 1.

CHAPTER 2

CONSTITUTIONS

2.1 What a constitution is

A constitution can be regarded in two ways. First, it is a general statement of how a country is governed. For example, the United States constitution could be described as republican, federal and presidential, whereas that of the United Kingdom would be monarchical, unitary and parliamentary. For someone familiar with 'constitutional language' but who knew nothing about the political systems of the United States and the United Kingdom these two statements would say something, but not much.

On the other hand, for someone completely unversed in constitutional and political terminology the two descriptions would do little or nothing to advance a knowledge of the two countries. Republican, monarchical, federal, unitary, presidential, parliamentary are all words which are intended to have precise meanings within the context of an exposition of a political system.

In an even more general sense a constitution may be said to be liberal or authoritarian, using two contrasting words which can be found in any non-technical dictionary. These distinctions would probably conjure up a picture of two political systems that a layman would understand. If you had the choice, which would you prefer: liberal or authoritarian? Most people would choose the former, if only because it had a more 'comfortable' sound. But if one constitution was said to be more liberal than another or more authoritarian than another difficulties would immediately be created.

To use the word constitution in a general sense, therefore, is not particularly helpful. It is rather like saying that France has better weather than Britain. What parts of France and Britain? What times of the year? Is the weather consistent, year in and year out? Obviously, more questions are raised than answered.

In a more specific sense, a constitution is a document or set of documents describing the framework of a political system. It stipulates where power lies within a state, what the institutions of government are, how they are constructed and how they are intended to operate. In doing so, it provides what might be said to be a set of rules for politicians in a particular country to follow: what offices they can hold, how they get to office, what they can do and not do in office, how laws are made, how they are enforced, how disputes between citizens and the state are resolved.

2.2 What a constitution is not

A constitution falls far short of being an accurate description of a political system. For example, it is unlikely even to mention political parties or any other forms of organised interests. It will say how power is distributed but not how it is used.

There are several possible analogies which could be used to point out differences between a constitution and a political system but the most accurate is probably a theatrical one. A constitution can be said to be the text of a play whereas the political system is its enactment. Often a constitution even falls short of being a complete text and is rather more a plot with a cast of characters. There are two missing elements which are needed if a constitution is to become alive and translated from a written text into a live production.

The first is political activity or the interplay of power: in other words, how a head of government arrives at a position of power, how that power is used, how he and his supporters try to retain power and how their opponents try to divest them of it. This is where the activities of parties and interest groups are all important.

The second missing element is what are called constitutional conventions. These are the understandings which politicians accept as being the unwritten rules of how a constitution should work in practice. Conventions bring flexibility and reality into the political process. They allow a constitution to remain firm in its fundamentals but flexible enough to adapt to changing political circumstances.

The use of the word convention is, perhaps, unfortunate because it can have a very different meaning, particularly in the United States where it is the name given to conferences or rallies of political parties. Furthermore the combined term, constitutional convention, refers in the United States to a special meeting of state government representatives, called at the request of two-thirds of state legislatures, to draft new amendments to the constitution. A better approach would be to speak of conventional behaviour, in other words customary practices which politicians adopt because experience has shown that they make the governmental process work more smoothly. This conventional behaviour acts as a lubricant to the political system.

A constitutional convention begins life as an attempt to solve a problem or potential problem. If it is successful then it may be accepted by politicians as an agreed way of approaching a similar problem in the future. If it works successfully on a number of occasions there will be tacit agreement that it has achieved the status of a constitutional convention. It may even be written into a constitution as a formal amendment so that there will be no confusion about whether or not this, originally conventional, procedure should always be followed.

In the United Kingdom there is no legislation which says that the Prime Minister must be a member of the House of Commons but, although in the second half of the nineteenth century no fewer than six of the twelve governments were headed by peers, there has been no Prime Minister sitting in the House of Lords since 1895. A constitutional convention has established this practice. A similar convention ensures that government ministers must be members of one or other of the Houses of Parliament.

To recapitulate, a constitution provides the framework for a political system. It does not give a full, or even accurate, picture of how the system works in practice.

2.3 Written and unwritten constitutions

Most states have a basic, written document which is called its constitution. It may not be the same one which was adopted when the state first came into existence. Even if it is, it is likely to have been amended several times since its original adoption.

A minority of states do not have such a basic document. Excepting those in which the existing constitution has been temporarily suspended, of the 165 states listed in Table 1 only six fall into this category: Bhutan, Israel, New Zealand, Oman, Saudi Arabia and the United Kingdom. Because of this they are often said to have unwritten constitutions. This is not strictly true.

Although the King of Bhutan would appear to have unlimited powers, with no constitution to restrain him, there are written rules which govern procedures for elections to the Royal Advisory Council and the National Assembly and say how they operate, and the King is expected to ensure they are observed.

In the cases of the other two absolute monarchies of Oman and Saudi Arabia, fewer informal quasi-constitutional checks exist. In both countries, however, the head of state is expected to govern in conformity with the Sharia, the sacred law of Islam. In addition, in Saudi Arabia the King must retain the consensus of the rest of the extensive royal family as well as the ulema (Muslim religious jurists) and sheikhs.

Israel has no single document which it calls a constitution but in 1950 the state parliament voted to adopt one by evolution over an unspecified period of time and since then a number of laws have been passed which are regarded as being part of the constitution. The Jewish holy book, the Torah, also remains an ancient source of political authority.

When it became a fully independent state New Zealand decided to model its political system on that of the United Kingdom even to the extent of not adopting a formal written constitution. Nevertheless, there are certain pieces of legislation which are seen to have a particular constitutional significance, such as the Acts which determine the eligibility of voters and their representatives.

The United Kingdom is usually cited as the classic example of a state without a written constitution but again, as in the other three countries, there are Acts of Parliament which are regarded as being constitutionally important. The most notable is probably the 1689 Bill of Rights which established the legislative supremacy of parliament and from which the rest of the evolutionary constitution developed. In more recent years the legislation restricting the powers of the House of Lords (the Parliament Acts of 1911 and 1949), and widening the franchise (the Reform Acts of 1832, 1867, 1884, 1918, 1928, 1948 and 1970), must be regarded as being a form of constitutional amendment.

Thus it is not really accurate to distinguish between written and unwritten constitutions. A better distinction would be between codified and uncodified documents for it is certain that, although it would probably be a long and tortuous process, it would be quite possible to draw up a written, codified constitution for the United Kingdom, and for the other five countries, if it were thought useful and necessary.

2.4 What a constitution contains

Individual constitutions do vary but most contain certain basic statements about the institutions which have been created to govern a state and how they are expected to operate. Some constitutions go further and, being framed either at a state's inception or following a major political upheaval resulting in a change of regime, identify the kind of society a political system is trying to create and maintain.

The main thrust of most constitutions is to distinguish between the three basic powers of government: the power to make laws, the *legislative* function; the power to enforce laws, the *executive* function; and the power to interpret laws and adjudicate in disputes between the citizen and the state, the *judicial* function.

The United States constitution, for example, has seven main Articles:

Article 1	defines the legislative powers;
Article 2	deals with the office of President, as the nation's chief executive;
Article 3	sets out the powers of the courts, including the Supreme Court;
Article 4	deals with relations between the individual states;
Article 5	describes how the constitution can be amended;
Articles 6 and 7	deal mainly with arrangements for transforming a loose federation of states into a full union.

The constitution of the French Fifth Republic has fourteen main Titles:

Title 1	deals with the sovereignty of the Republic;
Title 2	sets out the powers and duties of the President;
Title 3	describes the role of the Prime Minister and the rest of the government;
Title 4	sets out the structure and functions of parliament;
Title 5	deals with the relationship between parliament and the government;
Title 7	sets out the composition and role of the Constitutional Council;
Title 8	describes judicial powers;
Title 10	sets out the composition and role of the Economic and Social Council;
Title 14	describes how the constitution can be amended.

The other titles deal with detailed, specific matters.

Many constitutions begin with a broad statement of the aims which they hope to achieve.

The preamble to the United States constitution of 1787 reads:

> We, the people of the United States, in order to form a more perfect Union, establish Justice, insure domestic Tranquillity, provide for the common Defense, promote the general Welfare, and secure the Blessings of Liberty to ourselves and our Posterity, do ordain and establish this Constitution for the United States of America.

The preamble to the French constitution of 1958 reads:

> The French people hereby solemnly proclaim their attachment to the

Rights of Man and the principles of national sovereignty as defined by the Declaration of 1789, reaffirmed and completed by the Preamble to the Constitution of 1946.

Most states have a Bill of Rights, guaranteeing certain basic individual rights, such as freedom of speech and freedom of assembly, either incorporated in or associated with a codified constitution. It would be possible for any state to adopt such a charter even without a codified constitution and whether or not to have a Bill of Rights has been a matter of debate for some years within the United Kingdom.

Although the great majority of states have a guarantee of individual rights either built into their constitutions or associated with them, the mere fact of there being such a written guarantee should not be assumed to mean that such rights really exist and are protected. Some of these apparent guarantees are couched in rather limited terms. The Iranian constitution, for example, states that the press is free but adds: 'except in matters that are contrary to public morality or insult religious belief'. In similar vein, Article 50 of the Soviet Union's 1977 state constitution (Fundamental Law) grants freedom of speech, of the press and of assembly, so long as it is 'in accordance with the interests of the people' and is used 'to strengthen and develop the socialist system'.

Whether or not individual rights are really guaranteed and protected needs therefore to be determined by rather more objective means than just the reading of such a guarantee in a constitution.

2.5 Rigidity and flexibility

Sometimes attempts are made to distinguish between what are seen as rigid and flexible constitutions, usually on the basis of how easily a constitution adapts to changing circumstances. If it adapts readily it is said to be flexible and if it does not it is rigid.

Perhaps understandably, an unwritten constitution suggests great flexibility. After all, there is no formal, legalistic procedure for making a change. If the political will is there then a change will take place, probably by introducing a new constitutional convention or usage, or discarding an old one. But the assumption that a codified constitution is less flexible than an uncodified one is often misleading. When a usage can be changed or discarded without any technical obstacles it seems reasonable to conclude that the politicians who might make a change will approach a proposal very warily.

If a change has to go through some elaborate, formal procedure, such as in the United States, where an amendment to the constitution has to be proposed by a two-thirds vote of both houses of Congress and then ratified by the legislatures of three-quarters of the states, it seems reasonable to assume that a lightly or poorly conceived change will get a thorough consideration before it is finally accepted. However, in a state where such a weighty, formal procedure is absent the onus is placed on proposers of change to be absolutely certain in their own minds that there will no lasting, damaging consequences. Confronted with this responsibility, it is understandable that, in more cases than not, the *status quo* will be retained and the change cautiously avoided.

This is especially the case in liberal democracies, where constitutional government, in accordance with formal rules, is most deeply embedded in the public and political psyche. An exception has been France, which has framed 17 constitutions since 1789. In newer, emergent, or one-party, regimes the process of constitution re-drafting has often been frequent, with fresh codes being introduced to meet the changed circumstances of the day. The South American states, independent since the early nineteenth century, have been particularly prominent in this respect. Venezuela, for example, has had 26 constitutions, though the present one dates back almost 30 years. The Dominican Republic has had 25; Haiti more than 20; Ecuador 17; El Salvador, Bolivia, and Colombia 16 apiece; Honduras twelve; and Brazil eight. Similarly, in communist regimes new constitutions have regularly been framed as a means of giving recognition to the advancing stages of 'socialist development' that have been attained. The Soviet Union has had four such documents, in 1918, 1922, 1936 and 1977, since the revolution of 1917. Yugoslavia has had a similar number since the federal republic was first established in 1945, while Czechoslovakia and Romania have each had three.

2.6 Separation or fusion of powers

We have already said that the main area of concern of a codified constitution will be the three main institutions of government: the legislature, the executive and the judiciary. A comparison of constitutions could attempt to discover whether these institutions are kept separate or are fused.

The best known proponent of the doctrine of the separation of powers was the French philosopher, Baron Montesquieu (1689–1755), who set out the theory in *De L'Esprit des Lois* (1748). He argued that by keeping the three institutions separate and balanced the possibility of one of them, and particularly the executive, accruing undue power, and then exploiting it to the detriment of the citizenry, would be avoided.

His views made a considerable impact and were clearly taken into account by the framers of the United States constitution. As one of them, James Madison (1751–1836), said: 'the accumulation of all powers, legislative, executive and judiciary, in the same hands . . . may justly be pronounced the very definition of tyranny.' Oddly enough, Montesquieu cited England as a country enjoying relatively great liberty because the powers of government were distributed between the legislative, executive and judicial institutions and had the effect of balancing each other. In reality, as will be seen later, a political system based on a parliamentary executive, as in the United Kingdom, creates a fusion, rather than a separation, of the legislative and executive functions.

The concept of a separation or balancing of powers is still a useful test of the degree of freedom from autocratic rule within a political system but on its own is an insufficient, and sometimes unreliable, criterion.

2.7 Unitary or federal states

A constitution invariably seeks to clarify the relationship between the government with the responsibility for the whole of a state's territory and that concerned with only part of it: in other words, central government and localised government.

Democratic government is believed to have begun in the city states of ancient Greece, and particularly the city of Athens, which, with a total population of less than 50,000, was able to practise direct and universal participation in government. In fact the very word democracy (*demokratia*), roughly meaning rule (*kratos*) by the people (*demos*), is derived from ancient Greece. In that situation democracy was direct, involving the active and personal participation in government of all adult 'full-citizens' at some time in their lives, by accepting office on a rota basis. There are still vestiges of direct democracy in those contemporary states which make use of juries in their judicial systems.

Today, of course, there are few, and no major, states small enough to enjoy direct democracy. The unusual, perhaps unique, example of the tiny Most Serene Republic of San Marino in Italy has already been noted. Elements of direct democracy also survive in several of the smaller cantons (states) in the Swiss Confederation, with the electorate, numbering at most 10,000, meeting in a public place on one day each year to select officials and vote on issues. These cases are anachronisms and the vast majority of states which claim to be democratic do so on the basis of representative, rather than direct, democracy.

Putting exceptions such as San Marino and the Swiss cantons aside, all modern states find it necessary to have institutions to administer the needs of particular localities as well as the whole population. The larger the area the more obvious the need to cater for local, or regional, as well as national interests. The extent to which power is devolved by the government in the centre to the localities and the nature of the power devolved indicate whether or not a genuinely federal system is operating.

A nation-state is one which claims sovereignty over the whole of its territory. In other words, everyone within its boundaries is subject to its laws. If a government decides to divide its sovereignty within its boundaries and pass some of it to local bodies it means the devolution of some of its law-making powers. If the central government retains the right to override these devolved powers at any time then the state cannot be said to be truly federal.

If a federal system is adopted the respective legislative powers of the governments in the centre and the localities must be clearly defined and the local governments must be protected against the erosion of those powers by central government. This can only be done successfully through the medium of a written, codified constitution. Because circumstances change, there must be provision for this distribution of legislative power to be reviewed but in a truly federal system that review cannot be undertaken arbitrarily by the central government and the process must involve the localities, either by giving them 'blocking' powers with respect to proposed constitutional amendments in their areas of concern or through the adjudicatory medium of an impartial constitutional court.

The supreme example of a genuinely federal system of government is found in the United States constitution. Section 8 of Article I sets out the powers of the central legislature, Congress, and, by implication, leaves the residue of powers to the state legislatures. Article V prescribes how the constitution can be amended, such amendments requiring the approval of three-quarters of the state legislatures, and Article III the adjudicatory authority of the Supreme Court.

This form of devolution is effected by prescribing the legislative powers of the centre and leaving the residue with the localities. Another method is to prescribe the powers of the localities and leave the residue to the centre. Virtually all the world's federal systems adopt the former approach although the Canadian constitution comes nearer to the latter, defining precisely the powers of both the federal and state governments.

When executive, rather than legislative, powers are decentralised a state is said to have a unitary constitution and of the 165 states in Table 1 the great majority are unitary, only 20 having federal structures. As with most other aspects of political systems, history, geography and culture are the strongest factors behind the choice of a federal system of government. Of particular importance, not surprisingly, is country size, with seven of the eight largest nations in the world having federal structures. Moreover, the one exception within this grouping, China, has established five 'autonomous regions', for its non-Han minority border communities, which are of a quasi-federal nature. It is for this reason that, despite their small numbers, 40 per cent of the world's population live in states with federal constitutions. The broad range of factors that have determined the existence of federal structures in these and the remaining 13 states are presented in Table 2 together with a brief exposition of the types of federal system in operation.

Table 2

FEDERAL STATES IN THE CONTEMPORARY WORLD

In brackets are the world rankings (WR) of these states in terms of population (*c* 1985) and areal size; the chief determinants of federalism and its form then follow.

Argentina: pop: 31.20m (WR 28); area: 2.78m km^2 (WR 8).
Historical, cultural and geographical: early history was dominated by a conflict between town and country, particularly the European-style sophistication of Buenos Aires and the rough, uncivilised style of the gaucho. An attempt to impose a unitary system in 1829 failed. There are today 22 provinces, each with its own assembly, governor and constitution. The five-member Supreme Court adjudges federal-state constitutional conflicts.

Australia: pop: 15.76m (WR 48); area: 7.69m km^2 (WR 6).
Geographical and historical: the size of the country and distribution of the population have created distinctive, separate communities. For example, both Darwin, in the north, and Perth, in the west, are more than 3,000 kilometres from the capital, Canberra, whereas the two largest cities, Sydney and Melbourne, are, respectively, less than 300 and 500 kilometres. Historically, throughout the 19th century the country was divided into six distinct colonies, founded separately, governed separately and bounded by largely uninhabited land. Not until 1901 did the colonies unite in the Commonwealth of Australia. The six states have their own legislatures and constitutions, with, still today, 60 per cent of the nation's population residing in their capitals. They receive the bulk of their funds in the form of annually negotiated grants from the centre, which has authority to levy income tax. Federal-state conflicts are ruled upon by the seven-member Australian High Court.

Austria: pop: 7.55m (WR 73); area: 0.08m km^2 (WR 109).
Partly historical and partly artificial: a weak federal system which had operated between the two world wars was revived, under United States influence, in 1945.

Table 2—Federal States in the Contemporary World (contd.)

There are nine states (*Länder*), each with its own assembly. The policy-framing powers residing with the state governments are however limited to the spheres of regional planning, agriculture, hospitals and electricity. Federal-state disputes are adjudged by the 14-member Constitutional Court.

Brazil: pop: 143.30m (WR 6); area: 8.51m km^2 (WR 5).
Geographical and cultural: the size of the country and distribution of the population favoured federalism. The land mass is greater than continental United States, minus Alaska. Each of the 23 states has a single-chamber assembly, elected governor and constitution. There is a 16-member Supreme Court to decide on federal-state conflicts though it is viewed as strongly susceptible to presidential influence. The new constitution adopted in 1988 will enhance states' powers and their tax-raising capabilities *vis-à-vis* the federal government, strengthening what was previously a comparatively weak federal system.

Canada: pop: 25.63m (WR 31); area: 9.98m km^2 (WR 2).
Geographical, historical and cultural: the size of the country and the wide cultural mix created strong regional differences. Historically, the nation was created by the confederation of four British colonies in 1867. Six other former colonies joined the Dominion between 1870 and 1949. The ten resulting provinces have their own assemblies and elected premiers. They can frame their own civil laws and have control of education policy. The nine-member Supreme Court rules on federal-state constitutional disputes.

The Comoros: pop: 0.47m (WR 147); area: 0.002m km^2 (WR 160).
Geographical and historical: this state is a group of three islands. Each island has its own elected governor and island assembly, with partial administrative and legislative autonomy.

Czechoslovakia: pop: 15.50m (WR 50); area: 0.13m km^2 (WR 93).
Historical and cultural: a federal system, adopted in 1968, is a means of giving recognition to the nation's Slovak minority. The country is now divided into two equal, Czech and Slovak, republics, each with its own assembly, cabinet and Prime Minister. The republics have legislative competence in the spheres of education, health, culture and local justice. The effective strength of the federal system is, however, weakened by the communist principle of democratic centralism.

West Germany: pop: 60.73m (WR 12); area: 0.25m km^2 (WR 73).
Historical and partly artificial: the Weimar Republic, carrying on earlier German Empire traditions, had a weak form of federalism which was destroyed by the Hitler regime. Under United States influence it was revived in 1945 as a means of providing a check against the possible future abuse of central authority. There are, exclusive of West Berlin, which is outside the jurisdiction of the Federal Republic, ten states (*Länder*), each with its own constitution, elected assembly and government headed by a minister-president, and substantial civil service. The states have powers in education, police and local government matters and have local taxation powers, raising and collecting property, motor-vehicle and inheritance taxes. In addition, they receive an assigned equal share of federal revenue accruing from VAT, income tax and corporation tax and are responsible for carrying out the administration of federal matters. The *Länder* are, as a consequence, today, responsible for half of total government spending in West Germany and rely on the federal exchequer for only a quarter of their revenue needs. Federal-state disputes are policed by an independent 16-member Federal Constitutional Court. In practice, however, German federalism is largely consensual in character, based on the striking of pragmatic committee-room deals between senior federal and state politicians and civil servants in Bonn. For this reason, the term 'bureaucratic federalism' is frequently employed to describe the West German federal system.

India: pop: 785.00m (WR 2); area: 3.29m km^2 (WR 7).
Geographical, historical and cultural: the land mass makes it the second-largest state

Table 2—Federal States in the Contemporary World (contd.)

in Asia and historically the country was apportioned during the British period into separate provinces, with specified areas of legislative and fiscal autonomy, and princely states, each owing separate allegiance to the crown. Today there are 25 self-governing states, organised primarily on language lines. Each has its own elected assembly, council of ministers and chief minister. There is also a figurehead governor appointed by the federal President. The states have primary control over health, agriculture, education, police and local government. Overall, however, although relatively strong in comparative terms, particularly when non-Congress parties control state assemblies, Indian federalism remains weighted towards the federal government, which has sole control of income tax, the states relying on land and sale taxes and federal grants for their revenue. The government at the centre also has the power to impose direct 'President's Rule' in any state during a period of turmoil. A substantially independent 18-member Supreme Court adjudges federal-state constitutional conflicts.

Malaysia: pop: 15.82m (WR 49); area: 0.33m km^2 (WR 60).
Historical and cultural: the state is a federation of eleven separate states and two British colonies which were brought together into a federation between 1963–65. Each state has its own constitution, elected assembly, led by a chief minister and cabinet, and head of state. The states, however, have only limited original powers in the spheres of land and natural resource management and are reliant upon the federal government for almost all of their funds. Federal-state constitutional disputes are ruled upon by a traditionally independent Supreme Court. This has, however, been subject to mounting central political pressure, exerted by the Prime Minister and monarch, during recent years.

Mexico: pop: 81.70m (WR 11); area: 1.97m km^2 (WR 14).
Geographical and partly imitative: the size of the country made a federal system sensible in geographical terms and also the United States constitution was seen as an attractive model to copy. The 31 states have their own elected assemblies, governors and constitutions. Most powers reside with the governor who is pre-selected by the dominant Institutional Revolutionary Party's (PRI) inner council. For this reason, Mexico remains, in practical terms, a significantly centralised state. For similar reasons, the Supreme Court is subject to effective PRI control.

Nigeria: pop: 105.45m (WR 9); area: 0.924m km^2 (WR 31).
Geographical, historical and cultural: the recognition of tribal and religious differences, particularly between the north and south-east, which culminated in civil war between 1967–70, has been made in a federal system. Prior to independence, Nigeria was divided, in accordance with the 1946 'Richards Constitution', into three semi-autonomous regions. These became four in 1963, twelve in 1967 and 19 in 1979. At present, each state is under the control of a military governor appointed by the central Armed Forces Ruling Council.

Pakistan: pop: 101.90m (WR 10); area: 0.80m km^2 (WR 35).
Historical and cultural: the absorption of twelve princely states into independent Pakistan in 1948 was achieved by recognising their earlier history and creating a federal structure of four provinces. These provinces exhibit strong cultural and ethnic distinctions and rivalries. The provinces are administered by centrally appointed governors and local governments drawn from elected provincial assemblies.

St Kitts-Nevis: pop: 0.04m (WR 163); area: 0.0002m km^2 (WR 163).
Geographical and historical: the state is a unique union of two islands which are the residue of what was to have been a wider West Indies federation. Nevis Island, with its own elected assembly, Prime Minister and cabinet, retains the option to secede.

Soviet Union: pop: 280.00m (WR 3); area: 22.40m km^2 (WR 1).
Historical, geographical and cultural: the federal system, which was established in 1922, allows the national minorities to be recognised while maintaining the unity of

Table 2—Federal States in the Contemporary World (contd.)

---

the state through the party machine. For this reason it is officially described (Article 70) as a 'unitary, federal, multinational state'. There are 15 Union Republics, each of which has its own assembly and council of ministers. The Union Republics have, in theory, a free hand in the welfare and social spheres, as well as the right of secession. The former is overridden, however, by the centrally planned nature of the Soviet economy and the principle of democratic centralism. The latter is, in practice, made impossible by the terms of Article 75 of the constitution. The Union Republics, as well as the 20 Autonomous Republics and eight Autonomous Regions which also exist, are thus principally of value in enabling slight adjustments to be made to centrally devised policies to suit local circumstances and of preserving local languages and cultural practices.

Switzerland: pop: 6.47m (WR 80); area: 0.04m km^2 (WR 121).
Historical and cultural: the state is a weak federation of 26 cantons (including six half-cantons), or political units, dating back to the late thirteenth century. The cantons also reflect the cultural diversity of a country divided among German-, French-, Italian- and Romansch-speaking communities and between Catholic majority and Protestant majority areas. Each canton has its own constitution, legislative assembly and government, with substantial powers in socio-economic spheres such as education, environmental issues, tourism, transport, and police affairs. Cantons also have protected sources of finance and the ability, through the successful use of referenda, effectively to veto federal policies.

United Arab Emirates: pop: 1.33m (WR 127); area: 0.08m km^2 (WR 110).
Historical: this is a loose federation of seven sheikhdoms which were under British protection between 1892 and 1971. Each of the sheikhs is an hereditary and absolute ruler in his own emirate.

United States: pop: 241.00m (WR 4); area: 9.37m km^2 (WR 4).
Historical and geographical: the federal system resulted from the voluntary coming together of the original 13 British colonies after the War of Independence. The state developed by expanding its federal membership and the structure also usefully recognises the geographical and cultural diversity of the country. Each of the 50 states that presently exist has its own constitution, assembly, elected governor and Supreme Court. The federal government has responsibilty for defence and foreign affairs and the authority to co-ordinate 'inter-state concerns'. A liberal interpretation of what the latter phrase might constitute has resulted in a steady expansion in federal government interests. State governments remain influential bodies, framing much of their own civil and criminal law; being substantially involved in health, educational and welfare affairs; and raising more than three-quarters of their funds from state property, sales and, in some cases, local income taxes. Federal-state constitutional disputes are adjudged by the independent nine-member Supreme Court.

Venezuela: pop: 17.80m (WR 43); area: 0.91m km^2 (WR 32).
Historical, cultural and imitative: the federal system recognises the historical and cultural differences in the country but also reflects admiration for the US model, the country having been called the United States of Venezuela until 1953. It is divided into 20 states, each with its own elected assembly and executive governor. Since, however, the governor is appointed by the federal President and the states are heavily dependent upon the centre for revenue resources, the federal system remains weak in practice. The adjudicatory Supreme Court is heavily susceptible to political influence.

Yugoslavia: pop: 23.20m (WR 32); area: 0.26m km^2 (WR 72).
Historical and cultural: the federal structure recognises the historical independence of the different national minorities and religious groupings which exist in this heterogeneous nation. Six Republics and two Autonomous Regions have thus been formed, each with its own elected assembly, council of ministers and collective presidency. The republics have exclusive jurisdiction in the social welfare, health and

Table 2—Federal States in the Contemporary World (contd.)

educational spheres and also considerable authority over local economic affairs. As a result of heightened inter-regional tensions and party rivalries, the Republics and Autonomous Regions have been able to force the steadily increased devolution of federal powers during recent years, moving the Yugoslavian political system, in a number of respects, towards that of a confederation. There is a Constitutional Court to adjudge federal-state disputes.

As Table 2 suggests, federalism is stronger in some countries than others, the most vigorous being Australia, Canada, Switzerland and the United States, with India and West Germany following closely behind. The weakest example is probably the Comoros, where most legislative power is retained by the federal assembly. The Mexican, Soviet Union and Venezuelan federal systems are also weak in practice as a result of the *de facto* control exerted over state/regional associates by the federal party leadership and machine.

2.8 The distribution of power

Whatever safeguards may be written into a constitution, political realities will ultimately determine the distribution of power between the centre and the localities and the most significant reality is, invariably, a financial one.

In Australia, for example, the states are dependent on the federal government for about 60 per cent of their revenue and even in the United States, where the clearest distinction between central and local power is made, most states rely on indirect sales taxes which are much less buoyant and stable than the direct income tax which forms the bulk of federal government revenue.

At the other extreme, in a unitary state such as the United Kingdom local authorities are entirely the creatures of parliament, which is controlled by the party in power, and dependent on central government not only for the bulk of their income but for their very existence. The abolition, in 1986, of a whole tier of local government, the metropolitan county councils, including the Greater London Council, is evidence of the disproportionate distribution of power in the United Kingdom.

2.9 The role of the judiciary

Most constitutions speak, directly or indirectly, about the supremacy of law. This is generally seen as the guarantee of personal liberty and the chief protection against the overweening power of the state. Clearly the law of the land is the law enacted and whether or not the laws which are passed are fair is a matter which the political system, as a dynamic entity, must determine.

However, once a law has been enacted it is the role of the judiciary to ensure that it is fairly enforced and in practice this means more than just adjudicating in disputes between individuals and groups or between them and the state. It also involves interpreting the law. Since it is virtually impossible to construct a law which is completely unequivocal the task of judicial interpretation is a continual process and of considerable importance. To have an independent and unbiased judiciary is, therefore, vital if personal liberty is to be protected.

Judges are generally guaranteed their independence in a constitution by a provision which ensures their continuance in office during 'good behaviour'. Although independence and security of tenure usually apply to judges in the higher courts, in lower courts this is not always true. In many states in the United States, for example, members of the state judiciary are elected and may be dismissed by the people who elected them: a notable recent example being the California voters' sacking of Chief Justice Rose Bird in November 1986 for alleged 'liberalism' in her conduct of affairs. This makes judicial office holders responsive to public opinion, but is not always the best prescription for justice. In most one-party states, as well as in many Latin American countries, it is the party which chooses the judges for election by the assembly, another process clearly open to abuse.

In the United Kingdom the judiciary are appointed by the government of the day and although the Lord Chancellor, as the head of the judiciary, provides advice, to ensure the quality of the appointees and in theory at least to avoid political bias, it should not be forgotten that he is himself a politician and a leading member of the government. In the United States, Supreme Court judges are appointed by the President, subject to Senate approval, which in recent years has been by no means automatic, so appointment is, inevitably, subject to some political influence. Nor is it possible to say that any judge, however qualified and experienced, can be completely free from the bias which stems from his own social background and political inclinations.

A constitution can therefore go some way towards ensuring an independent judiciary but it can never guarantee complete impartiality. In practice most constitutions go little further than setting out the structure of the judicial system, with a few adding something a little more specific. The constitution of the Republic of Algeria states: 'Judges obey only the law. They defend the socialist revolution', and in Cameroon and Gabon the President is given the task of ensuring the independence of the judiciary.

An important role of judges is, of course, to protect the constitution itself and, even in a state such as the United Kingdom which has no codified constitution, they are required and expected to uphold the rule of law. In federal states, as has been noted, the judiciary's task of upholding the constitution is particularly significant in that they have to interpret as well as enforce, so as to preserve the intended balance between the centre and the localities. In quasi-federal Spain there is a Constitutional Court with this specific task, as there is in Italy and, though the body is somewhat less influential, in France also. The similar apical judicial bodies which exist in fully federal states are set out in Table 2.

2.10 Religion and the state

Some states have adopted a particular belief as the national religion and enshrined this in their constitutions. Table 3 sets out the current established or state religions.

Table 3

STATE OR ESTABLISHED RELIGIONS

ISLAM (25) Afghanistan, Algeria, Bahrain, Bangladesh, The Comoros, Egypt, Iran, Iraq, Jordan, Kuwait, Malaysia, The Maldives, Mauritania, Mauritius, Morocco, Oman, Pakistan, Qatar, Saudi Arabia, Somalia, Sudan, Tunisia, United Arab Emirates, North Yemen, South Yemen.

ROMAN CATHOLICISM (11) Argentina*, Colombia*, Costa Rica, Dominican Republic, Haiti, Malta, Panama*, Paraguay†, Peru†, Seychelles*, Venezuela*.

EVANGELICAL LUTHERAN CHURCH (4) Denmark, Iceland, Norway, Sweden.

BUDDHISM (3) Bhutan, Cambodia (Kampuchea), Thailand.

GREEK ORTHODOX CHURCH (1) Greece.

JUDAISM (1) Israel.

HINDUISM (1) Nepal.

CHURCH OF ENGLAND (1) United Kingdom (England).

PRESBYTERIANISM (1) United Kingdom (Scotland).

PANCASILA (1) ‡ Indonesia.

* Quasi-state religion.
† Roman Catholicism is the official religion, although the constitution guarantees religious freedom.
‡ A national secular-state ideology, stressing unity and social justice, which is a compulsory belief for all social organisations.

2.11 Unusual constitutional features

Some constitutions contain unusual or unique provisions, most of them being products of the country's history, geography or social structure.

The Mexican constitution, reflecting the country's history of exploitation by the wealthy and powerful, places restrictions on the activities of the Church, large landowners and foreign organisations. Following a record of unequal educational opportunities, the constitution also stresses the importance attached to state education. In similar vein, the constitution of Paraguay provides for agrarian reform in its Chapter 6.

The Soviet Union's constitution specifically enshrines (Articles 40–45) certain socio-economic rights. These include 'the right to work, the right to rest and leisure, the right to health protection, the right to maintenance in old age and sickness, the right to housing, the right to education and the right to enjoy cultural benefits'.

Because of the small size of the country, the constitution of Nauru permits the President, who combines the roles of head of state and head of government, to take on additional personal portfolios in a cabinet of only five or six.

To ensure a balance between the religious communities, the Lebanese constitution prescribes that if the President is a Christian the Prime Minister must be a Muslim, and vice versa.

The constitution of Liberia includes a provision for monitoring and ensuring the maintenance of a one-party state.

Different geographical bases are required of the President and Vice-President by the Tanzanian constitution; if one is from the mainland, the other must be from the island of Zanzibar.

Finally, the recently adopted Brazilian constitution, whose 245 articles and 70 clauses took 19 months to be scrutinised and approved by the federal Congress, contains the most detailed statement of specific social and economic rights currently in force in a non-communist regime. These include a prescribed 44 hours for the working week and stipulated rights to five days of paternity leave and extended maternity leave. In addition, the new constitution, in its economic chapter, restricts the future levying of real interest rates to a maximum level 12.5 per cent above inflation.

2.12 How important are constitutions?

Are constitutions merely statements of a grand design and, as such, removed from the realities of the political process? In the final analysis surely naked military power must prevail? The answers to these questions, based on recent experience, must be yes and no.

In liberal democratic countries with long-established codified constitutions, such as the United States, there can be no doubt about their supreme significance. The content and importance of the American constitution are made clear to every school child and the newest immigrants will cherish the freedoms it proclaims. Specific provisions are frequently quoted in contemporary life. Both Rear-Admiral John Poindexter and Lieutenant-Colonel Oliver North pleaded the fifth amendment, the right to remain silent in a criminal case, when required to testify at the 1986 'Irangate' hearings. Since the Watergate affair all Americans must be aware of the impeachment powers contained in Articles I–II of the constitution. It is sufficiently alive to have accumulated no less than 26 amendments, the last being as recently as 1971.

Even in a country such as the United Kingdom, with an uncodified constitution, constitutional controversies arise over such matters as the powers of the House of Lords, devolution, parliamentary sovereignty *vis-à-vis* the European Community, electoral reform and the possibility of introducing a Bill of Rights.

Admittedly, given the necessary political will and military might, any constitution can be suspended or annulled and at the present time there are about ten which fall into this category. Nevertheless, the aura of legitimacy which, accurately or not, a constitution brings is almost universally sought, even by clearly despotic regimes.

RECOMMENDED READING

Bahl, R., *Financing State and Local Government in the 1980s*, Oxford University Press, 1984.

Banting, K. and Simeon, R. (eds), *The Politics of Constitutional Change in Industrial Nations: Redesigning the State*, Macmillan, 1985.

Burgess, M. (ed), *Federalism and Federation in Western Europe*, Croom Helm, 1986.

Charlton, R., *Comparative Government*, Longman, 1986, Ch 4.
Duchacek, I., *Federalism: The Territorial Dimension of Politics*, Holt Rinehart Winston, 1970.
Duchacek, I., *Power Maps: The Comparative Politics of Constitutions*, ABC Clio, Santa Barbara, California, 1973.
Finer, S., *Five Constitutions*, Harvester Press, 1979.
Griffith, J. A. G., *The Politics of the Judiciary*, 3rd edn., Fontana, 1985.
Hague, R. and Harrop, M., *Comparative Government and Politics: An Introduction*, 2nd edn., Macmillan, 1987, Ch 9.
Hicks, U. K., *Federalism: Failure and Success, A Comparative Study*, Macmillan, 1978.
Hodder-Williams, R., *The Politics of the US Supreme Court*, Allen and Unwin, 1980.
House, P. W. and Steger, W. A., *Modern Federalism: An Analytic Approach*, Lexington Books, 1982.
Reagan, M. and Sanzone, J. G., *The New Federalism*, 2nd edn., Oxford University Press, 1981.
Roberts, G. K., *An Introduction to Comparative Politics*, Edward Arnold, 1986, Chs 3 and 10.
Sawyer, G., *Modern Federalism*, Pitman, 1976.
Simons, W. B. and White, S. (eds), *The Party Statutes of the Communist World*, Lancaster Nijhoff, 1984.
Smith, G., *Politics in Western Europe: A Comparative Analysis*, 4th edn., Gower Publishing, 1986, Chs 5 and 9.
Unger, A. L., *Constitutional Development in the USSR: A Guide to the Soviet Constitutions*, Methuen, 1981.

CHAPTER 3

THE IDEOLOGICAL BASES

3.1 The nature of ideology

We are now entering the treacherous world of ideologies where we are as likely to be misled as informed. Nevertheless, it is an area which must be explored if we are to make distinctions between political systems which get beneath the layers of institutions to the cultures and attitudes which have shaped them.

It is not particularly important to the ordinary citizen that there is a two-chamber assembly or that the head of state is a King or a President. Whether the economy is planned from the centre or left to market forces, or whether there is a choice of political parties to support or only one: these things are important.

Identifying the ideology on which a political system is based or influenced will help us penetrate the façade of institutions and slogans, but we must first clarify what we mean by ideology.

It is generally recognised that the political system of the Soviet Union had its theoretical beginning in the writings of Karl Marx (1818–83) and Friedrich Engels (1820–95), subsequently developed and adapted by Vladimir Ilyich Lenin (1870–1924), and that the current regime in Iran is motivated by the religion of Islam, through its Shia branch, but what about the system in the United Kingdom? Is it not too evolutionary and pragmatic to have any substantial theoretical or philosophical basis?

It depends on how we construe ideology. It is a much abused, and over-used, word. In recent years it has, more often than not, been associated with zealots and fanatics. The spread of international terrorism has built up a picture of ruthless groups imbued with a single-mindedness which rejects customary morality so as to advance the aims of some particular ideology. Too often ideology has come to mean blind faith and irrationality. This is too narrow an interpretation, and indeed a distortion, of the word.

The definition which will be used for our purposes is one which might be found in any good general dictionary. An ideology is a body of ideas which reflects the beliefs and values of a nation and its political system. Such a definition is wide enough to encompass a variety of political cultures, from the mature, rational attitudes to be found in many states of Western Europe to the more inspirational, and often emotive, ideas found in countries with less experienced political systems.

Ideologies can be individually or socially inspired. More often than not they are both. Politicians are essentially doers rather than thinkers, even though some of them would have the public believe they are both. They adopt and use philosophies as a platform for political action.

But why and how does a philosophy eventually become so much a part of the beliefs and values of a country that it can be said to be the ideology on which its political system is based? Initially, it usually results from a revolution of one kind or another and then proceeds through a process of what might be called evolutionary absorption.

For example, the '*ancien régime*' of seventeenth- and eighteenth-century France was ended abruptly by the revolution of 1789. Opposition to the profligacy and inequity of the absolute monarchy, allied to the democratic message of the 'Enlightenment' philosophers and writers such as Jean-Jacques Rousseau (1712–78), brought about the dramatic change. Then, over a much longer period, the forces which had initially impelled the revolution were modified and absorbed into the French psyche so as to become the ideology which now underlies its political system.

Other writers, such as John Stuart Mill (1806–73) in England, expanded and amended Rousseau's concept of liberal democracy into a more practical idea of representative democracy, while in other countries French and British experience was adapted to suit differing social and political needs. Thus, liberal democracy became the ideology of a wide family of nations.

The inequities of the Tsarist regime in Russia also ended abruptly in the revolution of 1917, with practical discontent again, allying itself with theoretical justification through the writings of Marx and Engels and the 'praxis' of Lenin. The communist theology of the Soviet Union was, over the years, adopted and modified by another, mixed family of nations.

We have identified two major and contrasting ideologies, liberal democracy and communism, but it would be a distortion of reality if we tried to fit all the 165 states we have under review into one or other of these two categories. Indeed, a purist might argue that each nation has its own unique ideology and any classification would be misleading. If this view were accepted then the very notion of comparative politics would be questionable and a study such as this would have to be abandoned. The idea of the whole world being divided into one of two ideological camps is clearly unacceptable, so a wider, but still manageable, classification must be found.

Accepting again the arbitrary nature of the choice, a sevenfold grouping is offered, in the belief that any classification is preferable to none at all. At the same time, some of the deficiencies in the process should be noted.

The first is that the ideology associated with particular countries is, inevitably, a 'broad brush' description of something more subtle and complicated than the simple 'label' would suggest. The second defect is that a static situation has been assumed. This may be acceptable as far as long-established states, with stable political systems, are concerned, but less so for newer states whose systems are still in a state of flux. Where such conditions are believed to exist an appropriate caveat will be added.

With the foregoing reservations, the following ideologies will be identified and used:

1 Liberal democracy
2 Emergent democracy
3 Communism
4 Nationalistic socialism
5 Authoritarian nationalism
6 Military authoritarianism
7 Absolutism

South Africa is one state whose political system cannot be fitted into any one of these seven categories with confidence. It contains elements of several of them but, since any interpretation would be based on racial origins, and particularly on skin pigmentation, it must fall into a unique category of racism, because this ideology overwhelms and supplants any other beliefs or attitudes which may exist.

3.2 Liberal democracy

Liberal democracy is a product of two concepts: the right to representative government and the right to enjoy individual freedom. The term 'liberal' is derived from the first concept and 'democracy' from the second. The tests for a political system claiming to be based on this philosophy would therefore seem to be the extent to which the government truly represents the mass of the people and the extent to which rights which individuals claim to have are protected.

In practice the essential features of a liberal democratic system can be identified as:

1 Representative institutions based on majority rule, through free elections and a choice of political parties.
2 Limitations on the power of government, implying a pluralistic society in which the state is not all-embracing and exists alongside other, sometimes competing, interests.
3 Accountablity of the government to the electorate.
4 Freedom of expression, assembly and the person, guaranteed by an independent judiciary.
5 A skilled and impartial permanent public service responsible to the government of the day and, through it, to the electorate.

Of the 165 states under examination 50 have been identified as having political systems founded on liberal democracy and they are listed in Table 4. They embrace more than 1.6 billion people, a figure which corresponds to a third of the world's total population. The oldest are to be found in Western Europe but by no means all or even a majority because, although its roots are European, it is an ideology which has been successfully exported to all parts of the world. There is however a tendency, which is apparent from the national income data provided in Table 4, for this type of political system to flourish best in high-income, 'First World', states. Thus, liberal democracies are found in 21 of the world's 'Top 30' countries in terms of per capita incomes, but in only six of the 'Bottom 50'.

In compiling this list of liberal democratic states, the following seven markers have been looked for:

1 Evidence of constitutional government.
2 Evidence of free elections for assemblies and executives.
3 The active presence of more than one political party.
4 Evidence of checks and balances among the three elements of government: executive, legislative and judicial.
5 Evidence of an independent judiciary.
6 Evidence of the protection of personal liberties through constitutional or other legal guarantees.
7 Evidence of stability in liberal democratic government.

Only those political systems displaying all these features have been included in Table 4. Others showing many of the identified attributes but failing the test of stability have, therefore, been placed in the second category of emergent democracies.

It should be noted, however, that included in Table 4 are two borderline cases: Mexico and Singapore. In both these states, effective opposition movements are particularly weak, being hampered by alleged pro-government ballot-rigging in the first and by increasing direct harassment in the second. Despite this, however, in comparative terms the degree of liberal freedom which is tolerated in these two countries remains tolerably high. Moreover, the longevity and stability of the PRI and PAP party regimes in place render alternative classification in the emergent democracy category inappropriate. A more accurate descriptive term for these two countries would, however, be 'restricted' or 'partial' liberal democracies.

Table 4

LIBERAL DEMOCRATIC SYSTEMS (50)

Region & Country	*Index of Democratisation* (1970–79)*	*Human Rights Rating (%)† (1986)*	*Per Capita National Income‡ ($ 1985)‡*
WESTERN EUROPE (16)			
Austria	30.8 (WR 9)	96	7,631 (WR 19)
Belgium	38.0 (WR 4)	96	7,408 (WR 21)
Denmark	40.3 (WR 1)	98	9,709 (WR 10)
Finland	19.4 (WR 19)	98	9,211 (WR 13)
France	33.4 (WR 6)	94	8,126 (WR 17)
West Germany	32.8 (WR 8)	97	8,950 (WR 16)
Iceland	N/A	N/A	9,118 (WR 15)
Ireland	24.2 (WR 16)	86	4,090 (WR 37)
Italy	38.4 (WR 3)	87	5,592 (WR 30)
Luxembourg	N/A	N/A	11,960 (WR 6)
Malta	N/A	N/A	2,800 (WR 45)
The Netherlands	39.8 (WR 2)	98	7,710 (WR 18)
Norway	32.9 (WR 7)	97	11,784 (WR 7)
Sweden	35.9 (WR 5)	98	10,315 (WR 9)
Switzerland	22.3 (WR 17)	95	13,720 (WR 5)
United Kingdom	30.0 (WR 11)	94	7,156 (WR 22)
NORTH AMERICA (2)			
Canada	24.4 (WR 15)	96	11,778 (WR 8)
United States	17.6 (WR 22)	90	14,565 (WR 2)
CENTRAL AMERICA AND THE CARIBBEAN (13)			
Antigua & Barbuda	N/A	N/A	1,850 (WR 56)
Bahamas	N/A	N/A	5,000 (WR 32)
Barbados	N/A	N/A	4,400 (WR 34)
Belize	N/A	N/A	990 (WR 82)
Costa Rica	18.6 (WR 20)	91	1,304 (WR 69)
Dominica	N/A	N/A	1,040 (WR 79)
Dominican Republic	8.2 (WR 31)	84	684 (WR 99)
Jamaica	13.0 (WR 27)	77	810 (WR 92)
Mexico	3.4 (WR 41)	62	1,990 (WR 54)
St Kitts & Nevis	N/A	N/A	1,300 (WR 70)
St Lucia	N/A	N/A	1,100 (WR 74)

Table 4—Liberal Democratic Systems (contd.)

Region & Country	*Index of Democratisation* (1970–79)*	*Human Rights Rating (%)† (1986)*	*Per Capita National Income‡ ($ 1985)‡*
St Vincent & the Grenadines	N/A	N/A	900 (WR 87)
Trinidad & Tobago	6.6 (WR 35)	79	5,556 (WR 31)
SOUTH AMERICA (1)			
Venezuela	22.2 (WR 18)	88	2,519 (WR 48)
MIDDLE EAST AND NORTH AFRICA (1)			
Israel	29.4 (WR 12)	74	4,346 (WR 35)
CENTRAL AND SOUTHERN AFRICA (3)			
Botswana	3.1 (WR 43)	78	850 (WR 91)
The Gambia	N/A	N/A	260 (WR 136)
Mauritius	N/A	N/A	970 (WR 83)
ASIA (5)			
India	16.1 (WR 24)	60	226 (WR 143)
Japan	26.5 (WR 14)	88	9,452 (WR 12)
Malaysia	10.1 (WR 30)	53	1,770 (WR 61)
Singapore	N/A	59	6,100 (WR 26)
Sri Lanka	16.6 (WR 23)	52	330 (WR 124)
OCEANIA (9)			
Australia	30.1 (WR 10)	94	9,196 (WR 14)
Kiribati	N/A	N/A	350 (WR 121)
Nauru	N/A	N/A	7,000 (WR 22)
New Zealand	27.7 (WR 13)	98	6,100 (WR 26)
Papua New Guinea	N/A	91	598 (WR 108)
Solomon Islands	N/A	N/A	500 (WR 113)
Tuvalu	N/A	N/A	350 (WR 122)
Vanuatu	N/A	N/A	600 (WR 107)
Western Samoa	N/A	N/A	620 (WR 105)

ABBREVIATION:

WR=World Ranking

*This index has been compiled by G.T. Kurian from data collected by Tatu Vanhanen on the basis of two empirical political variables: *(a)* a competition variable based on 'the share of the smaller parties and independents of the votes cast in parliamentary and/or presidential elections'; and *(b)* a participation variable based on the degree of voter participation in elections. 119 states were covered. (Source: G.T. Kurian, *New Book of World Rankings,* Macmillan, 1984, Table 43, pp. 65–6).

†Source: C. Humana, *World Human Rights Guide,* Pan Books, 1987.

‡Source: *The World in Figures,* Economist Publications, 1987, p. 13.

3.3 Emergent democracy

The states identified as emergent democracies bear many of the characteristics of liberal democracies except evidence of stability in their political systems, the majority having experienced at least one non-democratic coup or change of government at some time or other during the past two decades. Some have enjoyed stable liberal democratic government for extensive periods only to revert to militaristic or other autocratic rule. Others have emerged from a prolonged spell of autocracy in relatively recent years and it is still too early to judge how permanent the new regime will be.

The three most prominent examples of emergent democracies in Western Europe are Spain, Portugal and Greece. Here liberal democratic regimes have been in operation for more than a decade, with registered civil rights ratings now matching those of their fellow European Community member-states.

By contrast, the roots of democratic and civil freedoms have barely been planted in more recently emergent regimes such as Afghanistan, Bangladesh, Liberia, Nicaragua, Pakistan and Uganda. In these states, the armed forces remain influential background watchdog arbiters who might be tempted to reassert direct control in the near future if the democratisation process moves ahead in a direction which sharply conflicts with their own interests. At present, however, the existence of multi-party politics in these states, despite its fragile, nascent form, merits their tentative inclusion in this political category.

Despite these clear variations in degrees of 'democratisation', all the states categorised as emergent democracies might usefully be described as liberal democracies on trial and the 33 so identified are listed in Table 5. The dates of origin of the current regimes are also shown. The states included embrace in excess of 0.9 billion people, or 18 per cent of the world's population. It is significant that a substantial number (26) are situated in the developing 'middle income' regions of Southeast Asia, Central and South America and the Middle East/North Africa. In these areas, popular support for multi-party regimes has shown signs of strengthening in recent years.

Table 5

EMERGENT DEMOCRATIC SYSTEMS (33)*

Region & Country	*Date of Origin of Current Liberal Democratic Regime*	*Index of Democratisation (1970–79)*	*Human Rights Rating (%) (1986)*	*Per Capita National Income ($ 1985)*
WESTERN EUROPE (5)				
Cyprus	1975	N/A	N/A	3,186 (WR 41)
Greece	1974	10.3 (WR 28)	92	2,971 (WR 42)
Portugal	1976	4.6 (WR 37)	91	1,820 (WR 59)
Spain	1978	3.0 (WR 44)	84	3,880 (WR 38)
Turkey	1983	18.1 (WR 21)	41	960 (WR 84)
CENTRAL AMERICA AND THE CARIBBEAN (5)				
El Salvador	1983	8.1 (WR 32)	Poor	1,113 (WR 74)
Grenada	1983	N/A	N/A	780 (WR 93)
Guatemala	1985	6.7 (WR 34)	Poor	1,300 (WR 70)
Honduras	1985	0.4 (WR 67)	Poor	696 (WR 98)
Nicaragua	1987	2.6 (WR 45)	Poor	1,000 (WR 80)
SOUTH AMERICA (9)				
Argentina	1983	1.7 (WR 50)	88	2,000 (WR 53)
Bolivia	1982	0.0 (WR 82)	70	700 (WR 95)

Table 5—Emergent Democratic Systems (contd.)

Region & Country	*Date of Origin of Current Liberal Democratic Regime*	*Index of Democratisation (1970–79)*	*Human Rights Rating (%) (1986)*	*Per Capita National Income ($ 1985)*
Brazil	1985	0.0 (WR 83)	71	1,300 (WR 70)
Colombia	1978	10.1 (WR 29)	57	1,100 (WR 74)
Ecuador	1978	0.8 (WR 58)	83	1,472 (WR 67)
Guyana†	1966	15.3 (WR 25)	N/A	515 (WR 111)
Peru	1980	0.0 (WR 110)	62	669 (WR 102)
Suriname	1987	N/A	N/A	2,700 (WR 46)
Uruguay	1985	2.6 (WR 46)	91	1,520 (WR 65)
MIDDLE EAST AND NORTH AFRICA (4)				
Egypt§	1970	1.4 (WR 52)	59	960 (WR 84)
Lebanon	1980	5.0 (WR 36)	N/A	850 (WR 90)
Morocco**	1972	0.8 (WR 59)	52	530 (WR 109)
Tunisia	1967	0.0 (WR 116)	60	1,040 (WR 79)
CENTRAL AND SOUTHERN AFRICA (2)				
Liberia‡	1984	0.0 (WR 100)	39	350 (WR 121)
Uganda‡	1986	0.0 (WR 117)	Poor	150 (WR 150)
ASIA (6)				
Afghanistan‡	1987	0.0 (WR 78)	Bad	180 (WR 147)
Bangladesh‡	1986	1.9 (WR 48)	44	150 (WR 150)
South Korea	1987	0.8 (WR 61)	59	1,830 (WR 58)
Pakistan‡	1986	4.1 (WR 38)	40	330 (WR 124)
Taiwan§	1986	N/A	50	2,871 (WR 44)
Thailand	1983	0.9 (WR 57)	57	661 (WR 103)
OCEANIA (2)				
Fiji	1987	13.3 (WR 26)	N/A	1,500 (WR 66)
Philippines	1987	0.8 (WR 60)	86	524 (WR 110)

*For sources see Table 4.

†Ballot rigging in Guyana has, since 1980, begun to establish the elements of a quasi one-party regime, representing a retrogression from liberal-democracy, although opposition parties do continue to operate.

‡The military remain an overarching political force.

§A quasi-one-party system still effectively operates.

**The monarch remains the dominant political force.

3.4 Communism

As an ideology communism stems from the writings of Marx and Engels which were subsequently taken up by Vladimir Ilyich Lenin and his associates and adapted to meet the needs of early twentieth-century Russia. According to Marx, communism is an ideal which is eventually reached when all private property and class distinctions have been abolished and the state has become redundant and 'withered away'. In these terms, the nations which are commonly referred to as communist can hardly be said to be 'without states'. Indeed, they possess some of the most elaborate structures of state institutions in the world.

Nor were the origins of the Soviet Union, established now as the 'model' for all communist systems, congruent with the classic texts of Marx and Engels. According to these, anti-capitalist revolutions should have first taken place in Western Europe, the most developed region of the world, where the industrial proletariat (working class) were expected to rise up in revolt against mounting exploitation by the bourgeoisie (industrial/ business middle class). This would then have led on to an intermediate 'socialist' phase in which the state remained in place, serving as the instrument of the working classes in a 'revolutionary dictatorship', and in which inequalities continued to be tolerated, with each producer being remunerated in accordance with work done. Later, as affluence increased, a final, 'higher' phase of full communism would be achieved, no longer requiring the apparatus of government for its sustenance, in which all labour divisions would be ended and each worker would be able to receive 'according to his needs'.

In reality, however, revolution occurred first in underdeveloped Russia, in October 1917. This revolution was, moreover, far from a spontaneous uprising of industrial workers. Instead, it was a wartime 'coup', stimulated and led by Lenin, a member of the white-collar intelligentsia, with most of its 'revolutionary troops' drawn from peasant stock. Theoretical justification for this was provided by Lenin's theory of 'Imperialism: The Highest Stage of Capitalism', with the 'vanguard' position it ascribed to disciplined communist parties, fomenting revolution at the periphery so as to sever the links which bound together the global capitalist system and thus precipitating a final revolutionary cataclysm in the advanced West. This subsequent revolution failed to take place, however, leaving the Soviet Union to protect and 'build socialism' alone during the inter-war period. Only since the end of the Second World War have significant new communist regimes become established. As in the Soviet case, however, they are to be found in the backward 'Second and Third Worlds' of Eastern Europe and Asia, having been imposed either by military force or following guerrilla-based, anti-colonial liberation struggles.

Today, the followers of Marx and Lenin reluctantly agree that the ideal of communism has not yet been reached and that the intermediate condition of socialism remains a truer description of the contemporary Soviet system and those of its imitators. In none of these countries has the state 'withered away'. Instead, the Communist Party is firmly in charge, dominating state institutions, having assumed its prescribed role as the 'vanguard of the proletariat', so as to protect socialist society before the advent of true communism. Events in the Soviet Union and its satellite states since the accession of Mikhail Gorbachev to leadership of the Communist Party in 1985 suggest that the likelihood of achieving this theoretical ideal remains remote.

Nevertheless, although not 'communist' as such, it can be said, without too much distortion, that there are states, the Soviet Union being the most notable, which subscribe to the ideology of communism, in Marxist terms. The 16 'core' communist states are listed in Table 6. Together they embrace a third of the world's population. All have political systems initially modelled on that of the Soviet Union.

Subsequently there have been significant departures from the Soviet model in several countries in this category, notably China, Cuba and Yugoslavia, which under the dominant leadership of Mao Zedong (and since 1978 Deng Xiaoping), Fidel Castro and (until 1980) Marshal Tito, have pursued varying 'paths to socialism'. These states have, however, been included because the similarities outweigh the differences.

Four distinguishing features characterise such communist states:

1 Marxism-Leninism (in the case of China, Maoism-Dengism) has been adopted as the official ideology, source of legitimacy and vocabulary of political affairs.
2 The bulk of economic activity is under state ownership and subject to administrative (central) planning.
3 One party, the Communist Party, dominates the political scene and is tightly controlled from above in accordance with the Leninist precept of 'democratic centralism'.
4 The influence of the Communist Party, constitutionally ascribed a 'leading role' in the nation's affairs, is all-pervasive, controlling state-organs, trade unions, the media, the judiciary and industrial and agricultural enterprises through both supervision and direct membership.

Table 6

COMMUNIST SYSTEMS (16)*

Region & Country	*Date Regime Established*	*Index of Democratisation (1970–79)*	*Human Rights Rating (%) (1986)*	*Per Capita National Income ($ 1985)*
EASTERN EUROPE (9)				
Albania	1944	0.0 (WR 79)	Bad	860 (WR 89)
Bulgaria†‡	1946	0.1 (WR 74)	23	3,200 (WR 39)
Czechoslovakia†‡	1948	0.1 (WR 75)	36	6,000 (WR 27)
East Germany†‡	1949	0.1 (WR 76)	33	5,400 (WR 31)
Hungary†‡	1949	0.5 (WR 65)	55	1,722 (WR 62)
Poland†‡	1947	0.3 (WR 69)	41	1,900 (WR 55)
Romania†‡	1947	0.5 (WR 66)	20	2,687 (WR 47)
Soviet Union †‡	1917	0.1 (WR 77)	20	4,200 (WR 35)
Yugoslavia	1945	0.6 (WR 64)	50	1,850 (WR 56)
CENTRAL AMERICA AND THE CARIBBEAN (1)				
Cuba†	1959	0.0 (WR 90)	26	1,600 (WR 64)
ASIA (6)				
China	1949	0.0 (WR 89)	23	270 (WR 131)
Cambodia	1975	0.7 (WR 62)	Bad	50 (WR 165)
North Korea	1948	0.0 (WR 108)	17	900 (WR 87)
Laos	1975	N/A	Bad	100 (WR 162)
Mongolia†	1924	0.0 (WR 105)	N/A	950 (WR 86)
Vietnam†	1945 (North) 1976 (South)	0.0 (WR 118)	25	130 (WR 155)

*For sources of data in columns 3–5 see Table 4. †Current (1988) full members of Comecon.

‡Current (1988) members of the Warsaw Treaty Organisation (Warsaw Pact).

Other states which claim to apply Marxist-Leninist principles, but which in practice have substantially adapted and modified both the Soviet model and Marxist-Leninist theories to accommodate their own individual needs, have been placed in the next ideological category of nationalistic socialism. This embraces 12 nations: Angola, Benin, Cape Verde, The Congo, Ethiopia, Guinea-Bissau, Madagascar, Mozambique, Sao Tome and Principe, Somalia, South Yemen and Zimbabwe, two of which, Angola and Ethiopia, currently enjoy membership of several Comecon institutions.

One state, Ghana, which is also sometimes described as 'Marxist', has been assigned to the military authoritarian category, and four 'liberalising' quasi-Marxist regimes, Afghanistan, Guyana, Nicaragua and Suriname, to the category of emergent democracy.*

*This list of contemporary regimes which have been popularly ascribed as Marxist has been derived from B. Szajkowski (ed), *Marxist Governments: A World Survey*, 3 vols, Macmillan, 1981, and the recent 33-country title *Marxist Regimes Series* produced by Pinter Publishers.

3.5 Nationalistic socialism

Countries which have been placed in this category display many of the attributes of a communist state but in a less developed and structured form. A key feature is the existence of one political party of avowed socialist orientation, but whose role, in practice, has been more that of a promoter of nationalism and an opponent of imperialism than of a 'guardian of the proletariat' and radical transformer of the country's economic structure. Private farming and petty manufacturing have, for example, remained predominant in these states.

In many countries subscribing to nationalistic socialism the presence of a 'charismatic leader' has been a distinctive characteristic. Muammar al-Kadhafi of Libya, Samora Machel of Mozambique, Julius Nyerere of Tanzania, Kenneth Kaunda of Zambia and Robert Mugabe of Zimbabwe are obvious examples, each of the latter four having established his reputation as a guerrilla or political leader during his nation's independence struggle. In addition, a significant number of the states included in this category, Angola, Ethiopia, Iraq, Libya, Mozambique, Somalia, Syria and South Yemen being the most prominent examples, have been involved in recent years in military border disputes with their neighbours. This has served to enhance the nationalist standing and inclination of their leaderships.

The 21 states which have been identified as having nationalistic socialist regimes are set out in Table 7 below. They embrace 0.23 billion people, or just under 5 per cent of the world's total population. Almost three-quarters (15) of the total are to be found in Central and Southern Africa, a region where one-party regimes of a strongly left-of-centre slant constitute the predominant political type. In addition, it is notable that nationalistic socialist regimes are to be found in 13 of the world's 50 poorest states and in 8 of its 'Bottom 30'.

In terms of civil rights restrictions, the overall ratings recorded by two-thirds of the 21 nationalistic socialist regimes are disappointingly low. Six regimes, Algeria, Benin, Senegal, Tanzania, Zambia and Zimbabwe, despite the monism of their political structures, stand out, however, as significantly more 'liberal', exceeding the rating registered by several emergent democratic nations.

The most liberal of these regimes is Senegal, which continues to allow opposition parties, currently numbering 17, to register freely and contest elections. Such, however, is the long-standing *de facto* dominance of the ruling Senegalese Socialist Party, regularly being returned in disputed circumstances with in excess of 70 per cent of the national vote and 80 per cent of the country's legislative assembly seats, that it has been sensible to include this regime in the nationalistic socialist category in preference to that of an emergent democracy.

Table 7

NATIONALISTIC SOCIALIST SYSTEMS (21)*

Region & Country	*Date Regime Established*	*Index of Democratisation (1970–79)*	*Human Rights Rating (%) (1986)*	*Per Capita National Income ($ 1985)*
MIDDLE EAST AND NORTH AFRICA (5)				
Algeria	1976	0.0 (WR 80)	54	2,400 (WR 50)
Iraq	1968	0.0 (WR 94)	19	2,900 (WR 43)
Libya	1969	0.0 (WR 101)	23	6,000 (WR 28)
Syria	1971	0.2 (WR 72)	29	1,800 (WR 60)
South Yemen	1970	0.0 (WR 114)	Bad	430 (WR 116)
CENTRAL AND SOUTHERN AFRICA (15)				
Angola	1975	N/A	Poor	500 (WR 113)
Benin	1972	0.0 (WR 81)	59	260 (WR 136)
Cape Verde	1981	N/A	N/A	280 (WR 128)
The Congo	1964	0.9 (WR 56)	N/A	1,100 (WR 75)
Ethiopia	1984	0.0 (WR 91)	13	110 (WR 161)
Guinea-Bissau	1981	N/A	N/A	160 (WR 150)
Madagascar	1977	1.1 (WR 53)	Poor	210 (WR 146)
Mozambique	1975	N/A	25	120 (WR 157)
Sao Tome & Principe	1975	N/A	N/A	270 (WR 131)
Senegal	1966	1.0 (WR 55)	77	400 (WR 117)
Seychelles	1979	N/A	N/A	2,300 (WR 51)
Somalia	1979	0.0 (WR 113)	Poor	250 (WR 138)
Tanzania	1977	1.7 (WR 51)	47	220 (WR 144)
Zambia	1972	3.7 (WR 39)	51	272 (WR 130)
Zimbabwe	1988†	N/A	45	620 (WR 105)
ASIA (1)				
Burma	1962	0.0 (WR 84)	Poor	162 (WR 149)

*For sources see Table 4. †Year in which one-party state was officially declared.

3.6 Authoritarian nationalism

In its starkest form nationalism is a belief that people of the same racial stock are so distinctive that only they have the right to be regarded as members of a nation. This extreme kind of nationalism is so intolerant of other races and creeds that, at the best, they are disenfranchised and, at the worst, eliminated. Nazi Germany exhibited this attitude in its most brutal form and the present white-dominated regime in South Africa pursues its own version of the 'final solution' through the operation of the system of apartheid.

Fortunately, extreme examples of this kind are rare and most present-day exponents of nationalism use it as a device to claim the loyalty and obedience of members of the public. Even liberal democratic states have nationalistic tendencies, even though they may disguise the fact under the banner of patriotism. The national flag and the national anthem are manifestations of nationalism under the guise of patriotism and even sport has succumbed to its temptations.

A state which subscribes to the ideology of authoritarian nationalism displays the following three features:

1 Restrictions on the activities of all political parties, or a limitation to one which gives undivided and uncritical support to the state.
2 An authoritarian personal or collective executive.
3 Either the absence of an assembly to balance the power of the executive or the presence of an assembly which is essentially the servant of the executive.

For many states adherence to authoritarian nationalism will be a stage in the progression of independence from the rule of a colonial power to emergent democracy and, eventually, to a full, pluralistic democracy. Given a much longer time span, it is conceivable that all states will eventually abandon nationalistic tendencies and move towards regional, and even global, groupings. These developments are examined in Part III.

The 16 countries identified as proponents of authoritarian nationalism are listed in Table 8. Within this grouping, it must be stressed, however, that there exist considerable differences between both the policy outlooks and the degree of illiberalism of the regimes in power.

At one extreme, for example, stands the fundamentalist Islamic nationalist regime of the IRP in Iran, bent on a revolutionary transformation of both the polity and society and which has become infamous for its human rights violations, most notably its summary executions of dissident Kurdish and left-wing opponents.

Towards the other end of the scale is the PDCI regime of the Ivory Coast, headed by Houphouet-Boigny, which has pursued a pro-Western foreign policy and a free-enterprise orientated domestic policy programme and has a relatively 'liberal' human rights record. It remains intolerant, however, of direct political opposition and retains tight control over such institutions as the media, judiciary and trade union movement, in a classic one-party manner.

In the middle ground between these two regimes are ranged the majority of the residual authoritarian nationalist states, pursuing policy programmes which range from right-of-centre to left-of-centre in a non-transformatory manner. Cameroon, Malawi and Sierra Leone are, for example, three examples of broadly centrist regimes.

Despite these clear variations, two elements remain common to all 16 states:

1 The existence of one-party dominance.
2 Policy orientations which fall short of being fully socialist.

The second characteristic serves to distinguish these states from those included in the nationalistic socialist category above, thus making their inclusion in this group defensible.

The 16 states identified embrace 0.32 billion people, or just over 6 per cent of the global population. More than two-thirds, that is eleven, of the total are located in Central and Southern Africa, while a similar proportion and number, ten, are to be found in states which rank among the poorest 50 in the world. The single most important authoritarian nationalist regime in demographic terms, accounting for half the combined population total, is Indonesia. Here the Golkar Party, the most dominant of the three political parties which are permitted to operate, controls affairs in a relatively sophisticated manner, ruling conjointly with the military in accordance with its own unique Pancasila philosophy.

Table 8

AUTHORITARIAN NATIONALIST SYSTEMS (16)*

Region & Country	*Date Regime Established*	*Index of Democratisation (1970–79)*	*Human Rights Rating (%) (1986)*	*Per Capita National Income ($ 1985)*
MIDDLE EAST AND NORTH AFRICA (3)				
Djibouti	1981	N/A	N/A	730 (WR 94)
Iran	1979	0.3 (WR 68)	Bad	3,600 (WR 39)
North Yemen†	1974	0.0 (WR 119)	Bad	680 (WR 100)
CENTRAL AND SOUTHERN AFRICA (11)				
Cameroon	1966	0.0 (WR 86)	53	710 (WR 95)
Chad	1982	0.0 (WR 88)	N/A	90 (WR 164)
The Comoros	1979	N/A	N/A	270 (WR 131)
Gabon	1968	N/A	N/A	2,500 (WR 48)
Ivory Coast	1960	0.0 (WR 95)	Poor	510 (WR 112)
Kenya	1969	0.0 (WR 97)	48	270 (WR 131)
Malawi	1966	0.0 (WR 102)	Poor	140 (WR 153)
Mali	1974	0.0 (WR 103)	Poor	120 (WR 157)
Sierra Leone	1978	3.2 (WR 42)	64	250 (WR 138)
Togo	1973	0.0 (WR 115)	Poor	190 (WR 147)
Zaire	1972	0.2 (WR 72)	30	100 (WR 162)
ASIA (2)				
Indonesia‡	1966	3.5 (WR 40)	30	483 (WR 115)
Maldives†	1968	N/A	N/A	400 (WR 117)

*For sources of data see Table 4. †There are no political parties.

‡Three political parties are permitted to operate, but the government party, Golkar, is predominant.

3.7 Military authoritarianism

Military authoritarianism is a form of authoritarian nationalism whereby military leaders take it upon themselves to impose a government on the people, claiming invariably that it is for the public good. History is littered with examples of regimes when 'men of action' have felt it necessary to use their military strength to overthrow and replace civilian administrations. In some cases the transition is short-lived; in others military rule has become a permanent feature.

The characteristics of a state accepting authoritarian nationalism will be found also in this category with, of course, a military regime always in control. Sometimes a state based on military authoritarianism will try to disguise itself by using a civilian administration as a façade, fronting the military power behind. Panama in recent years has provided an example of this.

The 16 states subscribing to military authoritarianism are listed in Table 9. They embrace 0.20 billion people, or 4.1 per cent of the global total, with 75 per cent being located in Central and Southern Africa.

Table 9

MILITARY AUTHORITARIAN SYSTEMS (16)*

Region & Country	*Date Regime Established*	*Index of Democratisation (1970–79)*	*Human Rights Rating (%) (1986)*	*Per Capita National Income ($ 1985)*
CENTRAL AMERICA AND THE CARIBBEAN (2)				
Haiti	1986	0.0 (WR 93)	Poor	360 (WR 120)
Panama	†	0.0 (WR 109)	79	2,038 (WR 52)
SOUTH AMERICA (2)				
Chile	1973	1.9 (WR 49)	35	1,050 (WR 78)
Paraguay	1954	7.2 (WR 33)	48	1,405 (WR 68)
CENTRAL AND SOUTHERN AFRICA (12)				
Burkina Faso	1980	1.1 (WR 54)	Poor	120 (WR 157)
Burundi	1987	0.0 (WR 85)	Poor	215 (WR 145)
Central African Republic	1981	0.0 (WR 87)	Bad	240 (WR 141)
Equatorial Guinea	1979	N/A	N/A	140 (WR 153)
Ghana	1981	0.6 (WR 63)	46	370 (WR 119)
Guinea	1984	0.0 (WR 92)	Poor	280 (WR 128)
Lesotho	1986	0.0 (WR 99)	Poor	270 (WR 131)
Mauritania	1978	0.0 (WR 104)	N/A	350 (WR 121)
Niger	1974	0.0 (WR 107)	Poor	240 (WR 141)
Nigeria	1983	0.2 (WR 70)	53	660 (WR 103)
Rwanda	1973	0.0 (WR 111)	Poor	250 (WR 138)
Sudan	1989	0.2 (WR 71)	Poor	310 (WR 127)

*For sources of data see Table 4. †Behind-the-scenes control by the military.

3.8 Absolutism

Absolutism is an ideology which can be traced back to *The Leviathan* written by Thomas Hobbes (1588–1679) soon after the mid-seventeenth-century English Civil War (1642–52), in support of the English monarchy as the guarantor of stability and order. The ideology had even earlier roots in the medieval European doctrine of 'The Divine Right of Kings'. It argues that no limits whatsoever should be placed on the activities of a legitimate government, which will usually be in the form of an absolute monarch. Legitimacy is often claimed through the accident of birth, although it is convenient to forget that at some stage in history that legitimacy must have been acquired by force.

For a nation in an early stage of economic and social development, or one threatened by external forces, absolutism is an attractive ideology to accept, offering a guarantee of stability and order. For some countries it may represent only a stage in their development, to be superseded by a republican form of government or by a constitutional monarchy. For others it has become a permanent condition.

The characteristics of a state based on absolutism are:

1 The absence of any constitutional form of government, or a popular assembly or judiciary to counter executive power.
2 The denial of the right to form political parties or other forms of organised interests.

The twelve states adhering to absolutism are listed in Table 10. In Bhutan there are signs of emergent democracy and the monarchies in Jordan and

Tonga, although absolute in the final analysis, do have vestiges of constitutional checks and balances. One other state, Morocco, is also characterised by monarchical rule, but within a more fully developed and party-based constitutional structure. For this reason it has been assigned instead to the emergent democracy category.

The twelve absolutist regimes embrace a population of 40 million, corresponding to less than 1 per cent of the world total. Seven are located in the Middle East, in which region it constitutes the predominant political type. It should also be noted that seven of these absolutist states, including six in the Middle East, are, as a consequence of their mineral oil wealth, among the world's 'Top 25' nations in terms of per capita national income. On the other hand, two, Bhutan and Nepal, are to be found among the world's 'Bottom 10'.

Table 10

ABSOLUTIST SYSTEMS (12)*

Region & Country	*Index of Democratisation (1970–79)*	*Human Rights Rating (%) (1986)*	*Per Capita National Income ($ 1985)*
MIDDLE EAST AND NORTH AFRICA (7)			
Bahrain	N/A	N/A	7,500 (WR 20)
Jordan	0.0 (WR 96)	Poor	1,658 (WR 63)
Kuwait	0.0 (WR 98)	49	13,980 (WR 3)
Oman	N/A	N/A	6,700 (WR 24)
Qatar	N/A	N/A	9,600 (WR 11)
Saudi Arabia	0.0 (WR 112)	28	6,900 (WR 24)
United Arab Emirates	N/A	N/A	16,100 (WR 1)
CENTRAL AND SOUTHERN AFRICA (1)			
Swaziland	N/A	N/A	680 (WR 100)
ASIA (3)			
Bhutan	N/A	N/A	105 (WR 161)
Brunei	N/A	N/A	13,600 (WR 5)
Nepal	0.0 (WR 106)	Poor	137 (WR 155)
OCEANIA (1)			
Tonga	N/A	N/A	700 (WR 95)

*For sources of data see Table 4.

3.9 The future state of ideologies

We have already defined an ideology as a body of ideas which reflects the beliefs and values of a nation and its political system. We should not, however, see the practical implementation of an ideology as something immutable and 'set in stone'. A political system is both the product of and guardian of an economic system and, as a nation seeks to change the structure and working of its economy, so, inevitably, its political system will change with it.

Therefore, the pluralism which a market-orientated economy demands will, sooner or later, be reflected in a country's politics and, eventually, but over a longer time scale, the ideology will undergo change.

It can be argued that what we have called liberal democracy is so inextricably allied to market economics that the ultimate situation will be a world of liberal democracies. That view is probably a little too simplistic, for we should also remember that the capitalistic system, if uncontrolled, contains as many pitfalls and dangers as its alternative.

The mixed economy, where public and private enterprise co-exist, is most likely to be the model for future generations and political ideologies and systems which are best able to accommodate such an economy are the ones which will survive.

RECOMMENDED READING

Brown, A. (ed), *Political Culture and Communist States,* Macmillan, 1984.

Cammack, P., Pool, D. and Tordoff, W., *Third World Politics: A Comparative Introduction,* Macmillan, 1988, Ch. 2.

Charlton, R., *Comparative Government,* Longman, 1986, Chs. 1 and 8.

Clapham, C., *Third World Politics: An Introduction,* Croom Helm, 1985, Ch. 3.

Decalo, S., *Coups and Army Rule in Africa: Studies in Military Rule,* Yale University Press, 1976.

Deutsch, K.W., Dominguez, J.I. and Heclo, H., *Comparative Government: Politics of Industrialized and Developing Nations,* Houghton Mifflin, 1981.

Finer, S.E., *Comparative Government: An Introduction to the Study of Politics,* Penguin, 1970.

Finer, S.E., *The Man on Horseback: The Role of the Military in Politics,* 2nd enl. edn. rev., Pinter, 1988.

Furtak, R., *The Political Systems of the Socialist States: An Introduction to Marxist-Leninist Regimes,* Wheatsheaf, 1986.

Ghayasuddin, G. (ed), *The Impact of Nationalism on the Muslim World,* Open Press, 1986.

Hague, R. and Harrop, M., *Comparative Government and Politics,* 2nd edn., Macmillan, 1987, Ch 4.

Hiro, D., *Islamic Fundamentalism,* Paladin, 1988.

Lijphart, A., *Democracies: Patterns of Majoritarian and Consensual Government in Twenty-One Countries,* Yale University Press, 1984.

Nordlinger, E.A., *Soldiers in Politics: Military Coups and Governments,* Prentice-Hall, 1977.

Bingham Powell Jr, G., *Contemporary Democracies: Participation, Stability and Violence,* Harvard University Press, 1982.

Smith, G., *Politics in Western Europe: A Comparative Analysis,* 4th edn., Gower Publishing, 1986, Chs 1–3.

White, S., Garner, J. and Schopflin, G., *Communist Political Systems: An Introduction,* 2nd edn., Macmillan, 1987, Chs. 1 & 2.

Wiles, P. (ed), *The New Communist Third World: An Essay in Political Economy,* Croom Helm, 1982.

CHAPTER 4

EXECUTIVES

4.1 Political executives

It is usual to make a distinction between the political executive and the non-political, or permanent, executive. The latter is the salaried civil service which normally remains in office to work for whichever politicians happen to be in power. They in turn constitute the political executive and, as such, provide the leadership for both the political system and the state.

The modern political executive can be personal or collective and is found in a variety of forms including President, Prime Minister and party chairman or Secretary-General. Whatever the contemporary form and title, each is a direct descendant of the personal autocrat or absolute monarch, at one time universal.

States with more than one political party operating have been identified as liberal democracies or emergent democracies. With only a few exceptions, their executives are either Presidents or Prime Ministers. We shall refer to them respectively as presidential or parliamentary executives. In the exceptions a dual executive, usually of a President and a Prime Minister, operates.

One-party states have been subdivided into communist, nationalistic socialist, authoritarian nationalist and military authoritarian. In these cases the most common form of executive is, again, presidential, although in those we have identified as communist the executive assumes a distinctive form, partly collective and partly personal, as at the apex of power the state and party machines merge.

Finally, there are the few surviving absolutist states, where political parties have no role to play, and the executives are individuals exercising virtually unbridled power in very much the same way as the original precursors of what we now call democratic governments.

4.2 The parliamentary executive

This is the most common form of political executive in the world today, 43 states having adopted it, embracing almost 28 per cent of the global population. Twenty-seven of them are constitutional monarchies and 16 republics. It is sometimes referred to as the 'Westminster model' because it originated, and is found in its clearest form, in the United Kingdom. It is not coincidental that of the 43 nations with parliamentary political executives 26, including Britain, were formerly part of the British Empire and are now independent members of the Commonwealth. It is useful therefore to examine the United Kingdom system, even though the executives of other countries have been adapted from the original example to suit their particular needs. All parliamentary executives are found in multi-party liberal (37) or emergent democracies (6), with 16 of the total being in Western Europe, eleven in the Caribbean region and eight in Oceania. More than half, 56 per cent, are located in island states. The full list, showing geographical distributions, is given in Tables 11 and 12.

The parliamentary executive displays three essential features.

1 The role of head of state is separate from that of head of government and is distant from party politics, serving mainly as the patriotic and ceremonial focus of the nation. The head of state can be a President, as in West Germany or India, or a monarch, as in the Netherlands or the United Kingdom. In the majority of Commonwealth countries with parliamentary executives, the head of state is still the British monarch, represented by a resident Governor-General.

2 The executive is drawn from the assembly and directly responsible to it, and its security of tenure is dependent on the support of the assembly, or parliament. In other words, a 'no confidence' vote in parliament can bring down the government, resulting in a change of executive or a general election. It is in such circumstances that the non-political head of state may become temporarily involved in politics by either inviting the leader of a party in opposition to form a new government, or by dissolving parliament and initiating elections.

   A particular characteristic of the 'Westminster model' is that it is historically based on the concept of a two-party system. The House of Commons, for example, is physically constructed to accommodate two opposing parties, the government party sitting on benches to the right of the chairman of the House, or Speaker, and the opposition party to his left. Also, the Leader of the Opposition is acknowledged formally in legislation, provided with suitable office accommodation, and paid a salary out of public funds. This practice is followed in several Commonwealth states, most notably Australia and New Zealand, but is not an essential feature of a parliamentary executive. Indeed, the majority of European states, including West Germany, Austria, Belgium, Denmark, Ireland, Italy, the Netherlands and Norway, have a wide range of parties, and governments are frequently, and in some cases invariably, formed by coalitions of these parties. Conversely, in a number of Asian states with parliamentary executive systems, for example, Japan, Malaysia and Singapore, effective one-party electoral dominance has been the norm, although opposition parties do operate.

3 The leader of the party, or coalition of parties, commanding the support of parliament is called upon by the head of state, monarch or President, to become Prime Minister and form a government. The Prime Minister then chooses a cabinet, drawn from parliament, and they, with other non-cabinet ministers, form the government.

The fact that the parliamentary executive is drawn from and responsible to the assembly makes it, in theory at least, particularly accountable. In reality much depends upon the state of the parties in parliament. A British Prime Minister for example, enjoying a clear parliamentary majority, usually has greater executive power and discretion than a United States President, subject to the checks and balances of a constitution which gives significant power and authority to an independent Congress. In countries where coalition governments are the norm prime ministerial authority is invariably weaker, with power being diffused among ministers drawn from a variety of parties. Special arrangements have been devised in a number of such cases, however, to buttress the chief executive's authority. The most notable example is West Germany in which, under the terms of the Basic Law (constitution) of 1949, members of the assembly can only force the replacement of the Chancellor (Prime Minister) through a 'constructive vote of no confidence' by which a majority of members vote positively in favour of a proposed successor.

Table 11

STATES WITH PARLIAMENTARY EXECUTIVES (43)

State	*Date Parliamentary Executive Established**	*Area ('000 km²)*	*Pop (m) (c 1985)*
Antigua & Barbuda (CM, C)	1981	0.44	0.085
Australia (CM, C)	1901	7,686.85	15.763
Austria (R)	1920/45	83.85	7.546
Bahamas (CM, C)	1973	13.94	0.235
Barbados (CM, C)	1966	0.43	0.255
Belgium (CM)	1831/1971	30.51	9.868
Belize (CM, C)	1981	22.97	0.168
Canada (CM, C)	1867/1982	9,975.22	25.625
Denmark (CM)	1849/1953	43.08	5.087
Dominica (R, C)	1978	0.75	0.074
Fiji (R, C)	1970	18.33	0.715
West Germany (R)	1949	248.67	60.734
Greece (R)	1975	131.99	9.954
Grenada (CM, C)	1974	0.34	0.100
Iceland (R)	1944	102.85	0.244
India (R, C)	1949	3,287.59	785.000
Ireland (R)	1937	68.39	3.624
Israel (R)	1948†	20.70	4.208
Italy (R)	1948	301.28	57.226
Jamaica (CM, C)	1962	11.42	2.366
Japan (CM)	1946	371.86	121.402
Luxembourg (CM)	1868/1956	2.59	0.367
Malaysia (CM, C)	1957	332.37	15.820
Malta (R, C)	1974	0.32	0.355
Mauritius (CM, C)	1968/69	2.04	1.029
Netherlands (CM)	1814/1983	34.00	14.481
New Zealand (CM, C)	1853†	269.06	3.305
Norway (CM)	1814	323.90	4.165
Papua New Guinea (CM, C)	1975	462.84	3.395
St Kitts-Nevis (CM, C)	1983	0.27	0.040
St Lucia (CM, C)	1979	0.62	0.123
St Vincent & the Grenadines (CM, C)	1979	0.39	0.103
Singapore (R, C)	1965	0.62	2.584
Solomon Islands (CM, C)	1978	29.79	0.283
Spain (CM)	1978	504.88	39.074
Sweden (CM)	1809	449.70	8.357
Thailand (CM)	1978	514.00	52.438
Trinidad & Tobago (R, C)	1976	5.13	1.204
Turkey (R)	1982	779.45	51.819
Tuvalu (CM, C)	1978	0.03	0.009
United Kingdom (CM, C)	1689†	244.10	56.458
Vanuatu (R, C)	1980	14.76	0.136
Western Samoa (R, C)	1962	2.84	0.180
Total (27 CM, 16 R, 26 C)	—	26,395.16	1,366.004

CM=Constitutional Monarch; R=Republic; C=Commonwealth member.
*Date of constitution/amended constitution. †No formal written constitution.

Table 12

DISTRIBUTION OF PARLIAMENTARY EXECUTIVES

(a) By Region

(Commonwealth Members in Brackets)

Region	*Number*		*Region*	*Number*	
Asia	5	(3)	Middle East & North Africa	1	(—)
Central America & the Caribbean	11	(11)	North America	1	(1)
Central & Southern Africa	1	(1)	Oceania	8	(8)
			South America	0	(—)
Eastern Europe	0	(—)	Western Europe	16	(2)
			Total	43	(26)

(b) By State Population Size

Population (m) (c 1985)	*Number*	*Population (m) (c 1985)*	*Number*
Below 0.1	4	50–100	5
0.1–1	13	100–200	1
1–10	14	200–500	0
10–20	3	500–1,000	1
20–50	2		
		Total	43

(c) By State Areal Sizes

State Areal Size ('000 km²)	*Number*	*State Areal Size ('000 km²)*	*Number*
Below 1	10	500–1,000	3
1–10	4	1,000–5,000	1
10–100	12	5,000–10,000	2
100–500	11		
		Total	43

4.3 The limited presidential executive

The limited presidency is the second most common form of political executive in the world today, 35 states having adopted it, embracing 22 per cent of the global population. The United States provides the clearest example and, although there are practical differences between individual systems, the essentials as found in the United States are virtually the same. Like parliamentary executives, all limited presidential executives occur in multi-party liberal (9) or emergent democracies (25). The full list with geographical distributions is given in Tables 13 and 14. It is notable that over half the total are situated in North and South America.

It should be remembered, however, that democracy is a rather delicate plant and in some of the states classified as emergent democracies that plant is still at a tender age. The evidence of a multi-party system has been taken as the main criterion for describing political systems as democratic and in the five states asterisked, Afghanistan, Bangladesh, Liberia, Nicaragua and Taiwan, democracy in a genuine sense is, as yet, more in the realms of anticipation than realisation. In each of these states considerable obstacles have been placed in the way of the unfettered operation of opposition parties, while the military also remain influential arbiters in the political process. In one other state, Uganda, political conditions are at present in a state of flux, with constitutional arrangements remaining unsettled.

A general point which does however emerge from these tables is the predilection for this system of executive in the mainland countries of the Americas. Of the 21 states in this broad region, only five, Belize, Canada, Chile, Paraguay and Suriname, have differing executive systems. The two former British colonies, Belize and Canada, have parliamentary executives; the former Dutch colony of Suriname a dual executive; and the remaining two states of Chile and Paraguay military executives. For the remaining states of the region, which secured independence from the early nineteenth century onwards, the influence of United States political and constitutional conventions and republican ideals is clear. In addition, the limited presidential executive form of government has been a popular model which has been adopted in recent years by newly emergent or re-established democracies, the most prominent recently being Argentina, Brazil, the Philippines and South Korea.

There are are four key features present in a limited presidential executive.

1 The President is elected for a fixed term to perform the dual role of head of state and head of government. As head of state he occupies a mainly ceremonial position and is the focus of popular patriotism. As head of government, he leads the executive branch of government, and is usually head of the armed forces and the state civil service. Also as head of government he is in charge of foreign affairs and is the main initiator of legislation.
2 The President's tenure is secure unless he commits a grave unconstitutional act. The United States President, for example, cannot be removed by Congress except by impeachment.
3 He governs with an advisory cabinet of non-elected departmental secretaries, whom he chooses and appoints and who are fully responsible to him.
4 Presidential powers are limited by the need for the approval of the assembly for certain executive actions. Under the United States constitution, for example, Congress has sole legislative powers and the President's veto of an Act of Congress can be overridden by a two-thirds vote. Although the President is expected to provide national leadership, his ability to do so is constrained by his ability to carry Congress with him. The United States Senate, in particular, has strong counterbalancing powers whereby the President can only make key federal appointments, judicial and cabinet, with Senate approval. Foreign treaties require a two-thirds majority of the chamber before coming into effect.

It is this balanced relationship between the President of the United States and Congress, as well as the clear statement of their respective roles written into the constitution, which make the presidency, although powerful, a limited form of executive and these are features which are found in the other 34 states whose political executives fall into this category. The degrees of emphasis differ, however, as do the arrangements for the election of Presidents and the restrictions on their length and terms of office. This information is set out in detail in the individual country entries in Part II.

In general, it would be true to say that few states with limited presidential executives approach the high degree of dispersal of power that exists in the United States. As a consequence, the effective authority of most of the Presidents included in Table 13 significantly exceeds that of the US chief executive. In a number of emergent democracies, the most prominent examples being Egypt, Guyana and Mexico, true competition from opposition parties remains circumscribed, further enhancing presidential authority. There are also seven states, Afghanistan, Bangladesh, South Korea, Liberia, Nicaragua, Pakistan and Taiwan, where the military remain an influential force. In such cases, the presidential system can only be viewed as partially limited.

Table 13

STATES WITH LIMITED PRESIDENTIAL EXECUTIVES (35)

State	*Date Executive Established*	*Area ('000 km²)*	*Pop (m) (c 1985)*
Afghanistan*	1987	647.50	18.136
Argentina	1853/1983	2,780.00	31.200
Bangladesh*	1986	144.00	104.100
Bolivia	1826/1947	1,098.60	6.430
Botswana	1966	600.40	1.100
Brazil	1969/1985	8,512.00	143.300
Colombia	1886/1974	1,139.00	30.000
Costa Rica	1949	50.70	2.700
Cyprus	1960	9.25	0.666
Dominican Republic	1966	48.73	6.614
Ecuador	1945/1979	283.56	9.600
Egypt	1971	1,001.50	50.500
El Salvador	1983/1985	21.39	5.100
The Gambia	1970	11.30	0.800
Guatemala	1985	108.89	8.600
Guyana‡	1980	215.00	0.800
Honduras	1982/1985	112.09	4.600
Kiribati	1979	0.68	0.062
South Korea	1987	98.50	43.300
Liberia*	1984	111.40	2.300
Mexico	1917	1,972.55	81.700
Nauru§	1968	0.02	0.008
Nicaragua*	1987	130.00	3.300
Pakistan†	1985	803.90	101.900
Peru	1980	1,285.22	20.200
Philippines	1987	300.00	58.100
South Africa**	1961/1984	1,222.16	33.200
Suriname	1987	163.82	0.400
Switzerland††	1874	41.29	6.470

Table 13—States with Limited Presidential Executives (contd.)

State	*Date Executive Established*	*Area ('000 km²)*	*Pop (m) (c 1985)*
Taiwan*	1947	36.00	19.600
Tunisia	1959	164.15	7.260
Uganda	1969/INT	236.88	15.200
United States of America	1787	9,372.57	241.000
Uruguay	1966	186.93	3.000
Venezuela	1961	912.05	17.800
Total	—	33,822.03	1,079.046

*The military remain influential and opposition parties operate under severe restrictions.

†Has moved towards a dual, or parliamentary, executive since the death of President Zia.

‡Although presidential, operates like a parliamentary executive.

§No formal parties. **White-only democracy.

††The Swiss presidency is, in reality, collective or collegial, comprising all seven members of the Federal Council (Bundesrat), one of whom is selected annually to assume the formal title of president of the Swiss Confederation (Bundespräsident).

INT: in an interim state.

Table 14

DISTRIBUTION OF LIMITED PRESIDENTIAL EXECUTIVES

(a) By Region

Region	*Number*	*Region*	*Number*
Asia	5	Middle East & North Africa	2
Central America & the Caribbean	7	North America	1
Central & Southern Africa	5	Oceania	3
		South America	10
Eastern Europe	0	Western Europe	2
		Total	35

(b) By State Populations

Population (m) (c 1985)	*Number*	*Population (m) (c 1985)*	*Number*
Below 0.1	2	50–100	3
0.1–1	4	100–100	3
1–10	13	200–500	1
10–20	4	500–1,000	0
20–50	5		
		Total	35

Table 14—Distribution of Limited Presidential Executives (contd.)

(c) By State Areal Sizes

Areal Size ('000 km²)	*Number*	*Areal Size ('000 km²)*	*Number*
Below 1	2	500–1,000	4
1–10	1	1,000–5,000	7
10–100	7	5,000–10,000	2
100–500	12		
		Total	35

4.4 The dual executive

The dual executive is found in a minority of liberal and emergent democracies, the most notable example being France. Altogether there are six identifiable dual executives: in Finland, France, Lebanon, Morocco, Portugal and Sri Lanka. There are significant differences between them, however, and, although the French system is usually cited as the model, it should not be assumed that the others contain all, or even most, of its features. In Finland, France, Lebanon, Portugal and Sri Lanka the executive consists of a working partnership between the President and the Prime Minister while in Morocco the partnership is between the monarch and the Prime Minister. The full list, with geographical distributions, is given in Tables 15 and 16.

Although not really a 'model' of the other systems, a description of how the dual executive operates in France will be helpful to an understanding of the variations which are found in other countries.

The constitution for the French Fifth Republic was framed in the short time span of three months, during the summer of 1958, while the new administration of Charles de Gaulle was settling into office. Conscious of the recent history of instability in French governments, its authors tried to combine elements of the United States and British constitutions, while at the same time they sought to strengthen the executive and encourage greater party discipline and stability. To these ends, provision was made for a two-headed executive of a President, to be elected by an electoral college for a seven-year term, and a Prime Minister, chosen by the President but responsible to the National Assembly.

Under the terms of the constitution the President has considerable powers, including, as well as the appointment of the Prime Minister, control of the armed forces, the right to preside over cabinet and Defence Council meetings, the right to dissolve the Assembly once a year, and powers to negotiate treaties, countersign legislation approved by the Assembly, and appoint ambassadors.

Nevertheless, the constitution made provision (Articles 20 and 21) for the Prime Minister and Council of Ministers to wield ultimate power while the President was expected to remain aloof from day-to-day government and act as a mediator and conciliator who ensured that the different factions in whatever coalition was formed on the basis of Assembly support worked successfully together.

The respective roles of President and Prime Minister were altered when, in October 1962, President de Gaulle forced through, by referendum, a change in the constitution making the President directly elected by the people. This gave him a justifiable claim of popular support and he and his immediate successors used this to dominate policy-making so that the Prime Minister became, in effect, the political servant of the President, who governed in the style of the United States presidency, but without the congressional checks and balances which limit it.

As long as the French President was able to appoint a Prime Minister amenable to his directions and acceptable to the National Assembly the unbalanced twin executive worked. In 1986, however, following Assembly elections which swept to power the opposition conservative coalition, President Mitterrand was forced to appoint a Prime Minister, Jacques Chirac, whose political stance was well to the right of his. An experiment of 'cohabitation' thus began, in which the Prime Minister assumed the upper hand. This lasted, at times uneasily, until the presidential and Assembly elections of April-June 1988, which were won by President Mitterrand and his Socialist Party, restored the *status quo*. The period of 'cohabitation' did at least prove that the constitution was sufficiently flexible to allow a President and Prime Minister from different parts of the political spectrum to work together, if need be, for an interim period with reasonable success.

The dual executive in Lebanon closely resembles that of France but the relationship between the President and Prime Minister is as much conditioned by religious as political factors. With the object of maintaining religious harmony, the President has always been, by tradition, a Christian and the Prime Minister a Muslim. The President is elected for a six-year, non-renewable, term by the National Assembly. In 1988 the inability to agree on a new Christian President resulted in the creation of two rival governments, which threatened the unity of the country.

In Finland, the dual executive is also very similar to that of France, with the President, who is popularly elected for a renewable six-year term, having responsibility for foreign affairs, the dissolution of the Eduskunta (parliament), the formation and dismissal of governments and the appointment of senior civil servants. The President also has substantial veto powers over legislation passed by the Eduskunta and, more limited, decree powers. The multi-party, coalition nature of Finnish politics has served to enhance the effective role of the President, as has the sensitivity and importance of foreign relations with Finland's neighbour, the Soviet Union. This was particularly the case between 1956 and 1981 when Urho Kekkonen, of the Centre Party of Finland (KP), was President and used the office to ensure the continuance in power of centre-left parliamentary coalitions, and to promote a foreign policy of 'active neutrality', despite dwindling electoral support. In recent years, however, there have been proposals to reduce significantly presidential powers in the legislative and executive spheres.

The Portuguese variant of the dual executive has been evolving since the adoption of a new constitution in 1976. To effect a smooth transition to civilian government after a long period of dictatorship and military rule, the role of the President was cast as a 'watchdog' for the army, to ensure that its interests were not neglected by a civilian Prime Minister. The relationship between the two parts of the executive depended as much on personalities as constitutional rules. The revised constitution of 1982 reduced the powers of the presidency and four years later the first civilian for 60 years was elected to that office. Political power is now weighted towards the Prime Minister but he does not yet head a genuine parliamentary executive.

The Sri Lankan constitution of 1978 is based loosely on the French model and provides for a directly elected President and a Prime Minister, drawn from the assembly, who is appointed by the President and acts as his 'parliamentary manager'. The President has considerably more powers than the Prime Minister and can hold several portfolios himself. Sri Lanka thus represents a weak form of dual executive, compared with the French version, yet falls short of being a full presidential executive, as in the United States.

In Morocco the executive partnership is between the monarch and the Prime Minister but it is a very one-sided affair, with the King holding a near-monopoly of power. Although in legalistic terms Morocco is a constitutional monarchy the near-absolutism of the King has been given a formal legitimacy and the Prime Minister and cabinet function more as royal advisers than independent politicians.

The dual executives of these six states demonstrate the variety of ways in which a constitution can be adapted to suit the circumstances of a particular political environment at a particular time.

Table 15

STATES WITH DUAL EXECUTIVES (6)

	*Date Executive Established**	*Area ('000 km²)*	*Pop (m) (c 1985)*
Finland	1919	337.05	4.931
France	1958	547.03	55.400
Lebanon	1927/1947	10.40	2.700
Morocco†	1972	458.73	23.700
Portugal	1976/1982	92.08	16.600
Sri Lanka	1978	65.61	16.344
Total	–	1,510.90	119.675

*Date of constitution/amended constitution. †Not termed president.

Table 16

DISTRIBUTION OF DUAL EXECUTIVES
(a) By Region

Region	*Number*	*Region*	*Number*
Asia	1	Middle East & North Africa	2
Central America & the Caribbean	0	North America	0
Central & Southern Africa	0	Oceania	0
Eastern Europe	0	Western Europe	3
		Total	6

Table 16—Distribution of Dual Executives (contd.)

(b) By State Population Size

Population (m) (c 1985)	*Number*	*Population (m) (c 1985)*	*Number*
Below 0.1	0	50–100	1
0.1–1	0	100–200	0
1–10	2	200–500	0
10–20	2	500–1,000	0
20–50	1		
		Total	6

(c) By State Areal Sizes

State Areal Size ('000 km²)	*Number*	*State Areal Size ('000 km²)*	*Number*
Below 1	0	500–1,000	1
1–10	0	1,000–5,000	0
10–100	3	5,000–10,000	0
100–500	2		
		Total	6

4.5 The communist executive

The Soviet Union provides the 'classic' example of a communist political executive, with its interlocking web of party and state personnel and interests, culminating in a concentration of power at the apex of the political system. In a communist system it is the party which determines policy objectives and it is the state apparatus which implements them. Whereas in a liberal democratic country, such as the United States, the constitution determines the distribution and exercise of power, in a communist country, such as the Soviet Union, the constitution is subservient to the needs of the state, as interpreted by the party. In fact, constitutions are fairly frequently changed to meet party requirements.

The word 'soviet' means elected council and the Supreme Soviet, the national assembly, is constitutionally, but not in reality, the supreme body of state power. It consists of some 542 members, elected by the broader Congress of the USSR People's Deputies and, in turn, elects a Council of Ministers (COMs) from its membership, as the equivalent of a formal government. The Council has about 70 members, embracing the heads of around 50 specialist ministries, state committees and defence and security institutions, as well as the chairmen of the 15 Union Republic COMs, and meets in full session four times a year. Day-to-day decision-making responsibilities are devolved to its Presidium, or permanent committee, which, with 13 or so members, can, in some respects, be viewed as a partial equivalent to a state cabinet in a liberal democratic system.

The chairman of this Presidium is usually referred to as Prime Minister or Premier; however, the office is by no means fully the equivalent of a head of government in a Western parliamentary system. The nearest to a head of state in the Soviet system is the chairman of the Presidium of the Supreme Soviet, a 39-member body, which represents the assembly when it is not sitting.

The state machinery of the Presidium of the Council of Ministers and the Presidium of the Supreme Soviet are the external constitutional manifestations of political power but the real power lies within the Communist Party, which ensures its hold on policy-making through its membership of the state institutions and the policy of *nomenklatura*. This means that key posts throughout Soviet society and government are reserved for persons of 'sound' judgement who have been vetted and approved by the party's apparatus. Presently around 3 million positions fall into this category.

It is in the 251-member Central Committee of the Communist Party where true authority can first be perceived and it is in the Politburo, a 12–20-member cabinet body which is 'elected' by the Central Committee and meets weekly, and the twelve-member Secretariat, its administrative and policy-formulating wing, where ultimate power lies. Leading members of these bodies, at the apex of the party, also hold key positions, including the chairs, in the Presidiums of the Supreme Soviet and the Council of Ministers. It is also usual for the General Secretary of the party, who is the country's effective political leader, to take a major state position, such as chairman of the Presidium of the Supreme Soviet, as formal insignia of office. His real power derives, however, from his position as head of the party.

The other Eastern European states within the Soviet bloc have political systems broadly similar to that of the Soviet Union. The two principal exceptions are Yugoslavia and Romania. Since the death of Marshal Tito, Yugoslavia has had a unique, rotating, collective leadership and a significant degree of regional decentralisation. In Romania, there is a quasi-presidential system, tailored to the needs of the pre-eminent figure of Nicolae Ceausescu.

The Asian communist states, including China, and Castro's Cuba, where a personalised, plebiscitarian form of leadership prevails, also display a number of significant variations from the Soviet model. In all cases, however, control of the state, including its full range of economic institutions, through the party is the dominant, and clearly recognisable, characteristic. It is this, more than anything else, that distinguishes communist from other one-party states.

The distribution of states with communist, or, as they should more correctly be termed, socialist, executives and their date of establishent are set out in Tables 17 and 18. As only two, the Soviet Union and Mongolia, date back to pre-1945, it is evident that this political type is a relatively recent development. It is, in addition, with the notable exception of Cuba in the Caribbean, to be found concentrated geographically in only two regions, Asia and Eastern Europe. However, despite the relatively small number (16) of states falling into this category, they embrace, in total, a third of the world's population and account for two-fifths of its industrial production.

Table 17

STATES WITH COMMUNIST EXECUTIVES (16)

State	Date Established*	Area ('000 km²)	Pop (m) (c 1985)
Albania	1946/1950	28.75	3.046
Bulgaria	1946/1971	110.84	9.000
Cambodia	1975/1981	181.00	7.284
China	1949/1982	9,561.00	1,050.000
Cuba	1959/1976	114.52	10.200
Czechoslovakia	1948/1968	127.90	15.502
East Germany	1949/1968	108.18	16.700
Hungary	1949/1983	93.03	10.644
North Korea	1948/1972	121.25	20.500
Laos	1975†	236.80	4.117
Mongolia	1924/1960	1,565.00	1.900
Poland	1947/1985	312.68	37.500
Romania	1947/1974	237.50	22.800
Soviet Union	1917/1977	22,402.20	280.000
Vietnam	1945/76(80)	329.60	62.000
Yugoslavia	1945/1981	255.80	23.200
Total	—	35,786.05	1,574.393

*Date of establishment of communist regime/most recent state constitution.

†Lacks a formal constitution.

Table 18

DISTRIBUTION OF COMMUNIST EXECUTIVES

(a) By Region

Region	Number	Region	Number
Asia	6	Middle East & North Africa	0
Central America & the Caribbean	1	North America	0
Central & Southern Africa	0	Oceania	0
		South America	0
Eastern Europe	9	Western Europe	0
		Total	16

(b) By State Population Size

Population (m) (c 1985)	Number	Population (m) (c 1985)	Number
Below 0.1	0	50–100	1
0.1–1	0	100–200	0
1–10	5	200–500	1
10–20	4	500–1,000	0
20–50	4	1,000–1,500	1
		Total	16

Table18—Distribution of Communist Executives (contd.)

(c) By State Areal Sizes

State Areal Size ('000 km²)	*Number*	*State Areal Size ('000 km²)*	*Number*
Below 1	0	500–1,000	0
1–10	0	1,000–5,000	1
10–100	2	5,000–10,000	1
100–500	11	10,000–30,000	1
		Total	16

4.6 The unlimited presidential executive

The term unlimited is used to describe the executive presidency in one-party, non-communist states, but in politics nothing is really unlimited. Even the seemingly all-powerful military dictator can be, and is at times, overthrown. Nevertheless, the states which have been classified as nationalistic socialist and authoritarian nationalist have considerably fewer limitations on their political executives than those in their liberal and emergent democratic counterparts.

As in communist systems, the party is the ultimate source of power but, unlike communist states, a strong, and sometimes charismatic, leader often predominates and the objectives of the party, even in socialist states, are subordinated to national interests. Most of the countries with this type of executive have comparatively short histories of release from rule by a colonial power and have felt the need to assert their independence. Many also have tribal, ethnic or regional differences which require strong leadership if all social groups are to cohere into a single state. More than 90 per cent of countries with unlimited presidential executives are to be found in Africa and the adjoining Middle East.

Despite this regional concentration, these states display considerable variations in their political systems and it is something of a distortion to group them together in this way. Some have, for example, histories of instability and their current leaders have reached the top through a bloody or bloodless military coup. This has been the experience of the Congo, the Seychelles, Syria, Togo and South Yemen, for example. Some, such as Angola, Chad and Ethiopia, have been racked by recent wars and border insurgency. In contrast, other states, such as Djibouti, Gabon, the Ivory Coast and Senegal, have long records of political stability.

Nevertheless, their political executives have certain features in common, including a much greater authoritarianism than is found in liberal and emergent democratic states. This results mainly from the absence of competition and choice which a multi-party political system clearly provides. They have no opposition party 'waiting in the wings' to take over should the electorate express a wish for a change. Some unlimited executive states, the most prominent example being Senegal, do formally tolerate opposition groupings but elections are so heavily stacked in the governing party's favour, through its control of the media and state sector resources, and through resort to electoral chicanery, that there is little or no possibility of its being defeated.

The importance of the political leader in such states cannot be overstressed. Some have been in office for much longer periods than their counterparts in liberal democratic states could ever hope for. Some became or are becoming virtual legends. Ahmadou Ahidjo led Cameroon for 22 years, between 1960 and 1982. Albert-Bernard Bongo, who changed his name to Omar because of his faith, has ruled Gabon without interruption for a quarter of a century and Felix Houphouet-Boigny of the Ivory Coast, Hastings Banda of Malawi, Mobutu Seseseko of Zaire, and Kenneth Kaunda of Zambia, have similar records. President Suharto of Indonesia has been at the helm for more than 20 years, as have Moussa Traore of Mali, Gnassingbe Eyadema of Togo, and General Ne Win of Burma, until his 'retirement' in July 1988. They are closely followed by figures such as Muammar al-Kadhafi of Libya, and Mohammed Siad Barre of Somalia.

In Iran, on the other hand, the focus of leadership in recent years has tended to shift from one individual to another, as different factions have wrestled for power. Sometimes the religious leader, Ayatollah Khomeini, a revered, charismatic figure, seemed to have the strongest voice and at other times the pragmatic Speaker of the Assembly, Hojatoleslam Ali Akbar Rafsanjani, seemed more influential.

To people accustomed to life in liberal democratic political systems the concept of one-party government and strong personal leadership may seem repressive and undemocratic. It would be unwise, however, to make such a sweeping judgement. A country's political system is inevitably the product of its history, culture and resource-base and the majority of the states with unlimited presidential executives are still on a 'learning curve' in their political development. Indeed some systems are so volatile that there are fundamental changes currently taking place or likely to become evident in the foreseeable future. In other cases, particularly across black Africa, the system of one-party monopoly appears to be firmly embedded, drawing its sustenance from older tribal political traditions, with their inclusive decision-making processes, and from the argument that open democracy, with its costly campaigns and inter-party quarrels, is an indulgence that cannot yet be afforded.

Table 19 shows that there are two states, the Maldives and North Yemen, categorised as having unlimited presidential executives, which do not follow the usual pattern of being one-party systems. Indeed, political parties, as such, do not exist at all. However, since they operate within constitutional frameworks, it was thought more sensible to place them in this category rather than regard them as having absolute executives.

Table 19

STATES WITH UNLIMITED PRESIDENTIAL EXECUTIVES (37)

State	*Date of Start of One-Party System*	*Date Current President First Took Office*	*Area ('000 km²)*	*Pop (m) (c 1985)*
Algeria (S)	1976	1979	2,381.75	22.972
Angola (S)	1975	1979	1,246.70	8.200
Benin (S)	1975	1972	112.60	4.100
Burma (S)	1962	1988††	678.00	37.700
Cameroon	1966	1982	474.00	10.000

Table 19—States with Unlimited Presidential Executives (contd.)

State	*Date of Start of One-Party System*	*Date Current President First Took Office*	*Area ('000 km²)*	*Pop (m) (c 1985)*
Cape Verde (S)	1981	1975	4.03	0.312
Chad*	1983	1982	1,284.00	5.200
The Comoros	1979	1978	1.86	0.469
Congo (S)	1964	1979	342.00	1.800
Djibouti	1981	1977	23.39	0.300
Ethiopia (S)	1984	1977	1,221.90	43.900
Gabon	1968	1964	266.70	1.200
Guinea-Bissau (S)	1981	1980	36.13	0.900
Indonesia*	1967	1967	1,925.00	173.103
Iran*	1978	1989	1,648.00	46.600
Iraq* (S)	1979	1979	444.00	16.278
Ivory Coast	1960	1960	322.46	10.500
Kenya	1982	1978	583.00	21.000
Libya† (S)	1969	1969	1,759.54	3.900
Madagascar (S)	1977	1975	595.79	10.300
Malawi	1966	1964	118.48	7.300
Maldives‡	—	1978	0.30	0.180
Mali	1974	1968	1,240.00	7.908
Mozambique (S)	1975	1986	799.38	14.000
Sao Tome & Principe (S)	1982	1975	1.00	0.105
Senegal* (S)	1966	1980	197.00	6.900
Seychelles (S)	1979	1977	0.45	0.066
Sierra Leone	1978	1985	73.33	3.883
Somalia (S)	1979	1969	637.66	7.800
Syria* (S)	1973	1971	185.18	10.535
Tanzania§ (S)	1977	1985	945.09	22.400
Togo	1979	1967	56.79	3.023
North Yemen‡	—	1978	195.00	6.300
South Yemen (S)	1970	1986	336.57	2.300
Zaire	1978	1965	2,345.00	31.300
Zambia (S)	1972	1964	752.62	7.100
Zimbabwe** (S)	1987	1980	390.60	9.000
Total (S=21)	—		23,625.30	558.834

S=Avowedly socialist. *Legally pluralist but effectively one-party.
†Leader is not termed president. ‡No political parties operate.
§Party chairman, though not head of government or head of state is the 'power behind the throne'.
**Although presidential, operates like a parliamentary executive.
††Currently under emergency military leadership.

Table 20

DISTRIBUTION OF UNLIMITED PRESIDENTIAL EXECUTIVES

(a) By Region

Region	*Number*	*Region*	*Number*
Asia	3	Middle East & North Africa	8
Central America & the Caribbean	0	North America	0
Central & Southern Africa	26	Oceania	0
		South America	0
Eastern Europe	0	Western Europe	0
		Total	37

Table 20—Distribution of Unlimited Presidential Elections (contd.)

(b) By State Populations

Population (m) (c 1985)	*Number*	*Population (m) (c 1985)*	*Number*
Below 0.1	1	50–100	0
0.1–1	6	100–100	1
1–10	16	200–500	0
10–20	6	500–1,000	0
20–50	7		
		Total	37

(c) By State Areal Sizes

State Areal Sizes ('000 km^2)	*Number*	*State Areal Sizes ('000 km^2)*	*Number*
Below 1	2	500–1,000	7
1–10	3	1,000–5,000	9
10–100	4	5,000–10,000	0
100–500	12		
		Total	37

4.7 The military executive

Of the 16 states listed in Table 21 as having military executives four are in Central and South America and twelve in Central and Southern Africa. The American states are all long-established whereas the African are all post-Second World War creations. The majority, however, share a common feature, a long record of military conflicts and coups. For good or ill, in each case the army has established order, though often at the expense of the loss of civil liberties.

Some countries have seen the pendulum swing from civilian to military rule with bewildering frequency. Burkina Faso, for example, has experienced no fewer than six coups in 20 years. In Latin America and Central and Southern Africa as a whole, nearly three-quarters of the 65 states have endured at least one military coup since 1960.

Some have suffered long periods of genuinely despotic rule. Jean-Bedel Bokassa, of the Central African Republic, who was in power between 1965 and 1979, brought his nation almost to economic ruin through his personal excesses, which included an elaborate ceremony to crown him emperor. The Duvalier family ruled Haiti for many years like gang bosses with their own private armies. In Burundi, in Central Africa, military rule has been ruthlessly used to sustain tribal despotism, in particular the economic and political pre-eminence of the minority Tutsis.

In contrast, some military rulers have brought great political stability. General Alfredo Stroessner of Paraguay enjoyed absolute power, without any real challenge, for 35 years, from 1954 to 1989, by dealing swiftly and harshly with dissidents and astutely allowing potential rivals to share in the spoils of office.

The policies pursued by some military regimes, most especially those in South America, have been strongly reactionary and conservative, designed to protect the interests of narrow business élites and stifle popular social movements. Others, often drawing their leaders and in-service support from the middle officer ranks, have pursued radical economic and social policies. These reformist regimes, usually having been prompted to seize power because of the corrupt excesses of preceding civilian administrations, have also tended to follow puritanical governing styles. The most notable contemporary examples are the populist, if not necessarily popular, regimes of Flight-Lieutenant Jerry Rawlings in Ghana and Captains Thomas Sankara (1983–87) and Blaise Compaore (1987–) in Burkina Faso.

The identification of the 16 military states has been comparatively straightforward but inevitably a little arbitrary. In at least a further 25 states classified under other categories the military remain an influential background political force. These include ten countries identified as limited presidential executives: Afghanistan, Bangladesh, Egypt, Guatemala, South Korea, Liberia, Nicaragua, Pakistan, Taiwan and Uganda. Thailand, which has been classified as a parliamentary executive, is another example of a state with a military presence in the background, as well as Suriname, categorised as a limited presidential executive. Laos, Cambodia, North Korea, Poland and Vietnam, which have been listed as communist executives, also fall into this category, as do the unlimited presidential executives of Benin, Burma, Ethiopia, Indonesia, Iraq, Libya, Syria and North Yemen.

Of the countries listed in Table 21, five, Burkina Faso, Burundi, Equatorial Guinea, Lesotho and Rwanda, are one-party states. Three, Haiti, Panama and Paraguay, have more than one party. The remaining eight, Central African Republic, Chile, Ghana, Guinea, Mauritania, Niger, Nigeria and Sudan, have banned all political activity. In all 16, however, the chief identifying feature is that the military are, overtly or more discreetly, in effective control. In Haiti, Panama and Paraguay, for example, the military hide behind a civilian façade.

Nevertheless, just as no political leader has the gift of eternal life, so no political system can be expected to last for ever in whatever form it has reached, and there is evidence that at least some of the military executive systems are becoming a little more democratic. In the Central African Republic, Guinea, Haiti, Nigeria, Panama and Rwanda promises of a return to more liberal and constitutional regimes have been made. Time will reveal whether or not such promises are honoured.

Table 21

STATES WITH MILITARY EXECUTIVES (16)

State	*Date Established*	*Date of Recent Coup**	*Area ('000 km²)*	*Pop (m) (c 1985)*
Burkina Faso	1960	1987	274.20	7.100
Burundi	1962	1987	27.83	4.900
Central African Republic	1960	1981	625.00	2.744
Chile	1818	1973	756.95	12.300
Equatorial Guinea	1968	1979	28.10	0.360
Ghana	1957	1981	238.54	13.552
Guinea	1958	1984	245.86	5.750

Table 21—States with Military Executives (contd.)

State	*Date Established*	*Date of Recent Coup**	*Area ('000 km²)*	*Pop (m) (c 1985)*
Haiti	1804	1986	27.75	5.900
Lesotho	1966	1986	30.35	1.555
Mauritania	1960	1984	1,030.70	1.750
Niger	1960	1974	1,267.00	6.715
Nigeria	1960	1985	923.80	105.448
Panama	1903	1968	77.08	2.227
Paraguay	1811	1954	406.75	4.119
Rwanda	1962	1973	26.34	6.500
Sudan	1956	1989	2,505.80	22.070
Total			8,492.05	203.897

*Most recent successful coup. (There have been unsuccessful coups subsequent to the date shown in Equatorial Guinea—in 1981 and 1983—and Guinea—in 1985.)

Table 22

DISTRIBUTION OF MILITARY EXECUTIVES

(a) By Region

Region	*Number*	*Region*	*Number*
Asia	0	Middle East & North Africa	0
Central America & the Caribbean	2	North America	0
Central & Southern Africa	12	Oceania	0
		South America	2
Eastern Europe	0	Western Europe	0
		Total	16

(b) By State Population Size

Population (m) (c 1985)	*Number*	*Population (m) (c 1985)*	*Number*
Below 0.1	0	50–100	0
0.1–1	1	100–200	1
1–10	11	200–500	0
10–20	2	500–1,000	0
20–50	1		
		Total	16

(c) By State Areal Sizes

State Areal Sizes ('000 km²)	*Number*	*State Areal Sizes ('000 km²)*	*Number*
Below 1	0	500–1,000	3
1–10	0	1,000–5,000	3
10–100	6	5,000–10,000	0
100–500	4		
		Total	16

4.8 The absolute executive

All the states listed in Table 23 as having absolute executives are monarchies of one kind or another. Bahrain, Brunei, Jordan, Kuwait, Oman, Qatar and Saudi Arabia are all Arab monarchies, sultanates or emirates and the United Arab Emirates are a federation of no fewer than seven emirates. Bhutan, Nepal, Swaziland and Tonga are hereditary monarchies.

Another factor they all have in common is a history of association with Britain, through either a treaty of protection or trade, or both. In ten of them political parties do not operate at all. In Brunei there is a quasi-party of businessmen loyal to the Sultan, and in Swaziland one party subservient to the ruling regime.

Unlike the military states, the absolute executives have not been imposed following a coup. They have usually been part of the social and political lives of the respective communities for many years, surviving during the colonial period as largely autonomous entities, and the rule, though autocratic, has usually been paternalistic.

The Kingdom of Jordan shows clear evidence of constitutionality, with a written constitutional code and two-chamber assembly but true democracy has had a fluctuating existence, with political activity banned in 1963, restored in 1971 and then banned again in 1976. Today only informal 'associations' are allowed to function. Despite a constitutional appearance, ultimate power remains with the King.

The one universal, and most certain, characteristic is that of government by personal, or, in the case of Saudi Arabia, family decree, rather than by collective discussion and agreement, and it is this which attracts the description of absolute executive.

Table 23

STATES WITH ABSOLUTE EXECUTIVES (12)

State	*Date Established*	*Date of Accession of Present Monarch*	*Area ('000 km²)*	*Population (m) (c 1985)*
Bahrain (C)	1971†	1961	0.62	0.442
Bhutan	1947†	1972	46.60	1.446
Brunei (C)	1984	1968	5.80	0.240
Jordan (C)	1946	1952	98.00	3.515
Kuwait (C)	1961 †	1977	19.00	1.771
Nepal (C)	1923/47†	1972	141.40	17.422
Oman	1951†	1970	212.00	1.271
Qatar (C)	1971†	1972	11.44	0.305
Saudi Arabia	1926–32‡	1982	2,150.00	11.519
Swaziland (C)	1968	1986	17.40	0.692
Tonga (C)	1970	1965	0.75	0.105
United Arab Emirates (C)	1971†	1971	83.60	1.326
Total	—	—	2,786.61	40.054

C=written constitution; Jordan also has some constitutionality.
†Never formally under colonial control.
‡Date of unification (Saudi Arabia was never subject to European colonial rule).

Table 24

DISTRIBUTION OF ABSOLUTE EXECUTIVES

(a) By Region

Region	*Number*	*Region*	*Number*
Asia	3	Middle East & North Africa	7
Central America & the Caribbean	0	North America	0
Central & Southern Africa	1	Oceania	1
		South America	0
Eastern Europe	0	Western Europe	0
		Total	12

(b) By State Population Size

Population (m) (c 1985)	*Number*	*Population (m) (c 1985)*	*Number*
Below 0.1	0	50–100	0
0.1–1	5	100–100	0
1–10	5	200–500	0
10–20	2	500–1,000	0
20–50	0		
		Total	12

(c) By State Areal Sizes

State Areal Sizes ('000 km²)	*Number*	*State Areal Sizes ('000 km²)*	*Number*
Below 1	2	500–1,000	0
1–10	1	1,000–5,000	1
10–100	6	5,000–10,000	0
100–500	2		
		Total	12

Table 25

WORLD DISTRIBUTION OF EXECUTIVE SYSTEMS

(a) By Region

Region	*Parliamentary Executives*	*Limited Presidential Executives*	*Dual Executives*	*Unlimited Presidential Executives*	*Communist Executives*	*Military Executives*	*Absolute Executives*	*Total*
Asia	5	5	1	3	6	—	3	23
Central America and the Caribbean	11	7	—	—	1	2	—	21
Central and Southern Africa	1	5	—	26	—	12	1	45
Eastern Europe	—	—	—	—	9	—	—	9
Middle East and North Africa	1	2	2	8	—	—	7	20
North America	1	1	—	—	—	—	—	2
Oceania	8	3	—	—	—	—	1	12
South America	—	10	—	—	—	2	—	12
Western Europe	16	2	3	—	—	—	—	21
Total	43	35	6	37	16	16	12	165

Table 25—World Distribution of Executive Systems (contd.)

(b) By Population and Land Area

Executive Type	*Number of States*	*Area ('000 km²)*	*% of World Area*	*Pop (m) (c 1985)*	*% of World Pop*	*Population Density (per km²)*
Parliamentary executives	43	26,395	19.4	1,366	27.6	51.8
Limited presidential executives	35	33,822	24.9	1,079	21.8	31.9
Dual executives	6	1,511	1.1	120	2.4	79.4
Unlimited presidential executives	37	23,625	17.4	559	11.3	23.6
Absolute executives	12	2,787	2.1	40	0.8	14.3
Military executives	16	8,492	6.3	204	4.1	24.0
Communist executives	16	35,786	26.4	1,574	31.8	44.0
Semi-sovereign states	5	0.7	—	0.1	—	162.0
Colonies and dependent territories*	43	3,212	2.4	13	0.3	4.0
World Total	213	135,630	100.0	4,955	100.0	36.5

*The figures here exclude Corsica and Western Sahara (whose areas and populations are included, with France and Morocco respectively, under the dual executive heading); the South African Bantustans (whose totals are included under the limited presidential executive heading); Xizang (Tibet) (whose totals are included with China under the communist executive heading); and the uninhabited Antarctic Territories.

Table 25—World Distribution of Executive Systems (contd.)

(c) By State Population Size

State Population Size (m) (c 1985)	*Parliamentary Executives*	*Limited Presidential Executives*	*Dual Executives*	*Unlimited Presidential Executives*	*Communist Executives*	*Military Executives*	*Absolute Executives*	*Total*
Below 0.1	4	2	—	1	—	—	—	7
0.1–1	13	4	—	6	—	1	5	29
1–10	14	13	2	16	5	11	5	66
10–20	3	4	2	6	4	2	2	23
20–50	2	5	1	7	4	1	—	20
50–100	5	3	1	—	1	—	—	10
100–200	1	3	—	1	—	1	—	6
200–500	—	1	—	—	1	—	—	2
500–1,000	1	—	—	—	—	—	—	1
1,000–1,500	—	—	—	—	1	—	—	1
Total	43	35	6	37	16	16	12	165

(d) By State Areal Sizes

State Areal Size ('000 km²)	*Parliamentary Executives*	*Limited Presidential Executives*	*Dual Executives*	*Unlimited Presidential Executives*	*Communist Executives*	*Military Executives*	*Absolute Executives*	*Total*
Below 1	10	2	—	2	—	—	2	16
1–10	4	1	—	3	—	—	1	9
10–100	12	7	3	4	2	6	6	40
100–500	11	12	2	12	11	4	2	54
500–1,000	3	4	1	7	—	3	—	18
1,000–5,000	1	7	—	9	1	3	1	22
5,000–10,000	2	2	—	—	1	—	—	5
10,000–25,000	—	—	—	—	1	—	—	1
Total	43	35	6	37	16	16	12	165

RECOMMENDED READING

Baynham, R. (ed), *Military Power in Black Politics,* Croom Helm, 1986.
Blondel, J., *World Leaders: Heads of Government in the Postwar Period,* Sage Publications, 1980.
Blondel, J., *The Organization of Governments: A Comparative Analysis of Government Structures,* Sage Publications, 1982.
Blondel, J., *Government Ministers in the Contemporary World,* Sage Publications, 1985.
Carter, S. and McCauley, M. (eds), *Leadership and Succession in the Soviet Union, Eastern Europe and China,* Macmillan, 1986.
Cartwright, J., *Political Leadership in Africa,* St Martin's Press, 1983.
Charlton, R., *Comparative Government,* Longman, 1986, Ch. 2.
Clapham, C. and Philip, G. (eds), *The Political Dilemmas of Military Rule,* Croom Helm, 1985.
Hague, R. and Harrop, M., *Comparative Government and Politics: An Introduction,* 2nd edn, Macmillan, 1987, Ch. 11.
Hodgson, G., *All Things to All Men, the False Promise of the Modern American Presidency,* Penguin Books, 1984.
Jackson, R. H. and Rosberg, C. G., *Personal Rule in Black Africa: Prince, Autocrat, Prophet, Tyrant,* University of California Press, 1982.
Johnson, N., *State and Government in the Federal Republic of Germany: The Executive at Work,* 2nd edn., Pergamon Press, 1983.
Kellerman, B., *The Political Presidency: Practice of Leadership,* Oxford University Press, 1984.
King, A. (ed), *Both Ends of the Avenue: The Presidency, the Executive Branch and Congress in the 1980s,* American Enterprise Institute, 1983.
King, A. (ed), *The British Prime Minister,* 2nd edn., Macmillan, 1985.
Lowenhardt, J., *The Soviet Politburo,* Canongate, 1982.
McKay, D., *Politics and Power in the USA,* Penguin, 1987, Ch. 5.
O'Brien and Cammack, P. (eds), *Generals in Retreat: The Crisis of Military Rule in Latin America,* Manchester University Press, 1985.
Ridley, F. F. (ed), *Government and Administration in Western Europe,* Martin Robertson, 1979.
Rose, R. and Sulieman, E. (eds), *Presidents and Prime Ministers,* American Enterprise Institute, 1980.
Saich, T., *China: Politics and Government,* Macmillan, 1981.
Smith, G. B., *Soviet Politics: Continuity and Contradiction,* Macmillan, 1988, Ch. 5.
Weller, P., *First Among Equals: Prime Ministers in Westminster Systems,* Allen and Unwin, 1985.
Wright, V., *The Government and Politics of France,* 2nd edn., Hutchinson, 1983, Chs. 1–4 and 6.

CHAPTER 5

ASSEMBLIES

5.1 The nature of assemblies

Although in formal constitutional terms the three arms of government are described as the executive, the judiciary and the legislature, the term assembly has been deliberately preferred for the third arm because the role of the vast majority of legislatures in the world today is deliberative and policy-influencing, rather than law-making. Indeed the old term parliament, which is still used in some political systems, best identifies the chamber as a place for debate.

Assemblies do, of course, play a major role in the law-making process but they now mostly legitimise policies presented to them by the executive, rather than initiate them themselves. In doing so, they usually also have a modifying, revising function, based on the concept that assembly members are more likely to have an understanding of what is practicable and acceptable to the electorate than politicians in government who, inevitably, become insulated in their positions of power from the real world outside.

Popularly elected assemblies have always epitomised democracy and it is not surprising, therefore, that even the most autocratic rulers have sought to make their regimes 'respectable' by establishing a façade of democratisation through puppet assemblies. In South Africa three separate assemblies have been created to give a semblance of democracy but only one, restricted to the white population, has any real political meaning, and the majority of South Africans are completely unrepresented within the system.

The nineteenth century was the 'golden age' of assemblies, characterised by the parliament in London where individual members had a genuine role to play before they were to become overwhelmed by the tyranny of the party system and the burgeoning, and increasingly specialist, scope of legislative affairs. Since that time the balance of power has shifted inexorably towards the executive until we are left with but a few shining examples of assemblies which can, and do, wield real political power. The most notable one today is undoubtedly the United States Congress. It is closely followed by the Riksdag of Sweden, with the Camera dei Deputati and Senato in Italy and the Legislative Assembly in Costa Rica also being influential bodies. Legislative chambers elsewhere are mostly pale shadows of these.

Despite the relative decline in assembly importance, they still operate in the vast majority of states and are found within a wide range of ideologies and working alongside all types of political executive. Table 26 gives the basic facts about them, showing that at the present time only 18 of the 165 states under consideration do not have active assemblies and, of these 18, only five, Brunei, Oman, Qatar, Saudi Arabia and the United Arab Emirates, have never had an institution which could be described as a popular assembly and show no disposition to establish one. In each of the other 13 cases either an established assembly is in abeyance, invariably as a result of the establishment of a military regime, or the constitution is in a transitional state with the likelihood of elections being held in the foreseeable future.

The contemporary scene, therefore, reveals little diminution in the number of assemblies but a marked deterioration in their power and influence, particularly *vis-à-vis* the political executive. Undoubtedly, the major reason for this decline is the increase in party strength. The political systems with parliamentary executives, drawn from and responsible to their assemblies, have in many cases seen the virtual disappearance of the independent politician and the rise of strong, highly disciplined parties, demanding unfailing allegiance from their members and consistent support in the voting lobbies. The United Kingdom parliament, and particularly the House of Commons, provides clear evidence of this trend, which in Britain has been reinforced by the simple plurality electoral system. This method of voting, almost presupposing the existence of a two-party regime, meant that the arrival of a significant third party in 1981 guaranteed parliamentary domination by whichever party gained 40 per cent or more of the popular vote. In the UK elections of 1979, 1983 and 1987, for example, the Conservatives' share of the national vote was, respectively, 43.9 per cent, 42.4 per cent and 42.3 per cent. Similar trends have been noted in the case of the Australian House of Representatives. Here the alternative vote majoritarian system is in force.

In one-party states, assemblies have traditionally always been more subservient, providing a comforting democratic gloss of legitimacy to policy decisions taken behind the closed doors of party caucuses. In communist states, the sheer size of 'parliamentary' bodies such as the pre-1989 Supreme Soviet (1,500 members) in the Soviet Union, and the National People's Congress (c 3,000 members) in China, and the fact that they meet in plenary session for, at most, only 10–14 days a year has been one factor behind such impotence. The new Supreme Soviet of the Soviet Union is, however, a 'full-time' assembly. The most important reason for their relative powerlessness, however, has been the rigid control over agenda and placements exerted by the party leadership above, buttressed by the principle of 'democratic centralism'. Similar tight leadership control is exerted in non-communist, one-party states.

The political systems where assemblies still retain a degree of virility are those with limited presidential executives and those parliamentary executive states with voting systems which encourage a multiplicity of parties.

In a limited presidential executive state, the constitution places clear restraints on the powers of the executive and protects the assembly in its counterbalancing role. This is evident in its purest and most extreme form in the United States, where it is enhanced by the notorious weakness of party structures. It is also the case, though to lesser degrees, in Brazil, Colombia, Costa Rica, the Dominican Republic, the Philippines and Venezuela. These are all countries where efforts have been made to copy the 'US model'.

In parliamentary states with electoral systems which stimulate party multiplicity, coalition executives are the norm and accountabilty to the assembly becomes a reality. Several West European countries fall into this category, most notably Italy, which has had 50 governments since the Second World War. Others include Belgium, Denmark and the Netherlands.

In the region we have called Oceania, the political system of Papua New Guinea, where more than six minor political parties effectively function, is an even more notable example of assembly atomisation, with votes of no-confidence being frequently registered against incumbent administrations, as members shift fluidly in and out of coalition groups.

Table 26

ASSEMBLIES OF THE WORLD

	First Chamber			*Second Chamber*		
State	*Name*	*No*	*Term*	*Name*	*No*	*Term*
Afghanistan	Council of Reps (E)	234	5	Senate (E/A)	128	3-5
Albania	People's Assembly (E)	250	4	—		
Algeria	Nat People's Assembly (E)	261	5	—		
Angola	People's Assembly (E/A)	223	3	—		
Antigua	House of Reps (E)	17	5	Senate (A)	17	5
Argentina	Camara de Diputados (E)	254	4	Senado (E)	46	9
Australia	House of Reps (E)	148	3	Senate (E)	76	4
Austria	Nationalrat (E)	183	4	Bundesrat (E)	63	—
The Bahamas	House of Assembly (E)	49	5	Senate (A)	16	5
Bahrain	—				—	
Bangladesh	Jatiya Sangsad (E/A)	330	5	—		
Barbados	House of Assembly (E)	27	5	Senate (A)	21	5
Belgium	Chamber of Reps (E)	212	4	Senate (E/A)	182	4
Belize	House of Reps (E)	28	5	Senate (A)	8	5
Benin	Nat Revolutionary Ass (E)	196	5	—		
Bhutan	Tshongdu (E/A)	151	3	—		
Bolivia	Chamber of Deputies (E)	130	4	Senate (E)	27	4
Botswana	National Assembly (E/A)	40	5	—		
Brazil	Chamber of Deputies (E)	479	4	Senate (E)	69	8
Brunei	—				—	
Bulgaria	National Assembly (E)	400	5	—		
Burkina Faso	—				—	
Burma	People's Assembly (E)	489	4	—		
Burundi	National Assembly (E/A)	65	5	—		
Cambodia	National Assembly (E)	123	5	—		
Cameroon	National Assembly (E)	180	5	—		
Canada	House of Commons (E)	282	5	Senate (A)	104	—
Cape Verde	Nat People's Ass (E)	56	5	—		
Central African Republic	—				—	
Chad	—				—	
Chile	Chamber of Deputies (E)	120	4	Senate (E/A)	35	4
China	Nat People's Congress (E)	2,970	5	—		
Colombia	House of Reps (E)	199	4	Senate (E)	114	4
The Comoros	Federal Assembly (E)	42	5	—		
The Congo	People's Nat Assembly (E)	153	5	—		
Costa Rica	Legislative Assembly (E)	57	4	—		
Cuba	National Assembly of People's Power (E)	500	5	—		
Cyprus	House of Reps (E)	56	5	—		
Czechoslovakia	Chamber of the People (E)	200	5	Chamber of Nations (E)	150	5
Denmark	Folketing (E)	179	4	—		
Djibouti	Chamber of Deputies (E)	65	5	—		
Dominica	House of Assembly (E/A)	30	5	—		
Dominican Republic	Chamber of Deputies (E)	120	4	Senate (E)	27	4
Ecuador	Nat Chamber of Reps (E)	71	4	—		
Egypt	People's Assembly (E/A)	458	5	—		

Table 26—Assemblies of the World (contd.)

	First Chamber			*Second Chamber*		
State	*Name*	*No*	*Term*	*Name*	*No*	*Term*
El Salvador	National Assembly (E)	60	3	—		
Equatorial Guinea	House of Reps of the People (E)	41	5	—		
Ethiopia	National Assembly (E)	835	5	—		
Fiji	House of Reps (E)	52	5	Senate (A)	22	6
Finland	Eduskunta (E)	200	4	—		
France	National Assembly (E)	577	5	Senate (E)	321	9
Gabon	National Assembly (E/A)	120	5	—		
Gambia	House of Reps (E/A)	50	5	—		
East Germany	Volkskammer (E)	500	5	—		
West Germany	Bundestag (E)	519	4	Bundesrat	45	—
Ghana	—				—	
Greece	Parliament (E)	300	4	—		
Grenada	House of Reps (E)	15	4	Senate (A)	13	4
Guatemala	National Assembly (E)	100	5	—		
Guinea	—				—	
Guinea-Bissau	National People's Ass (E)	150	5	—		
Guyana	National Assembly (E)	65	5	—		
Haiti	—				—	
Honduras	National Assembly (E)	134	4	—		
Hungary	National Assembly (E)	387	5	—		
Iceland	Althing (E)	63	4	*		
India	House of the People (Lok Sabha) (E)	544	5	Council of States (Rajya Sabha) (E)	245	6
Indonesia	House of Rep (E/A)	460	5	—		
Iran	Majlis (Islamic Consultative Assembly) (E)	270	4			
Iraq	National Assembly (E)	250	4	—		
Ireland	Dail (E)	166	5	Seanad (E/A)	60	5
Israel	Knesset (E)	120	4	—		
Italy	Camera del Deputati (E)	630	5	Senato (E/A)	322	5
Ivory Coast	National Assembly (E)	175	5	—		
Jamaica	House of Reps (E)	60	5	Senate (A)	21	5
Japan	House of Reps (E)	512	4	House of Councillors (E)	252	6
Jordan	House of Deputies (E)	60	4	House of Notables (A)	30	8*
Kenya	National Assembly (E/A)	172	5	—		
Kiribati	Maneaba (E/A)	41	4	—		
North Korea	Supreme People's Ass (E)	655	4	—		
South Korea	National Assembly (E)	299	4	—		
Kuwait	—				—	
Laos	Supreme People's Ass (E)	79	5	—		
Lebanon	National Assembly (E)	99	4	—		
Lesotho	—				—	
Liberia	House of Reps (E)	64	6	Senate (E)	26	6
Libya	General People's Congress (E)	1,112	1	—		
Luxembourg	Chamber of Deputies (E)	64	5	—		
Madagascar	National People's Ass (E)	137	5	—		
Malawi	National Assembly (E/A)	c101	5	—		
Malaysia	House of Reps (E)	177	5	Senate (E/A)	58	6
Maldives	Majlis (E/A)	48	5	—		
Mali	National Assembly (E)	82	3	—		
Malta	House of Reps (E)	65	5	—		
Mauritania	—				—	
Mauritius	Legislative Assembly (E/A)	71	5	—		
Mexico	Chamber of Deputies (E)	500	3	Senate (E)	64	6
Mongolia	Ardyn Ih Hural (E)	370	5	—		
Morocco	Chamber of Reps (E)	306	6	—		
Mozambique	People's Assembly (E)	250	9	—		
Nauru	Parliament (E)	18	3	—		
Nepal	Rashtriya Panchayat (E/A)	140	5	—		
Netherlands	2nd Chamber (E)	150	4	1st Chamber (E)	75	6

Table 26—Assemblies of the World (contd.)

	First Chamber			*Second Chamber*		
State	*Name*	*No*	*Term*	*Name*	*No*	*Term*
New Zealand	House of Reps (E)	97	3	—		
Nicaragua	National Constituent Assembly (E)	96	6	—		
Niger	—				—	
Nigeria	—				—	
Norway	Storting (E)	157	4	*		
Oman	—				—	
Pakistan	National Assembly (E/A)	237	5	Senate (E)	87	6
Panama	Legislative Assembly (E)	67	5	—		
Papua New Guinea	National Parliament (E)	109	5	—		
Paraguay	Chamber of Deputies (E)	60	5	Senate (E)	30	5
Peru	Chamber of Deputies (E)	180	5	Senate (E)	60	5
Philippines	House of Reps (E/A)	250	3	Senate (E)	24	6
Poland	Sejm (E)	460	4	Senate (E)	100	4
Portugal	Assembly (E)	250	4	—		
Qatar	—				—	
Romania	Marea Adunare Nationala (E)	369	5	—		
Rwanda	National Development (E) Council	†	5	—		
St Kitts Nevis	National Assembly (E/A)	14	5	—		
St Lucia	House of Assembly (E)	17	5	Senate (A)	11	5
St Vincent and the Grenadines	House of Assembly (E/A)	19	5	—		
Sao Tome & Principe	National People's Assembly (E)	40	5	—		
Saudi Arabia	—				—	
Senegal	National Assembly (E)	120	5	—		
Seychelles	National Assembly (E/A)	25	5	—		
Sierra Leone	House of Reps (E/A)	104	5	—		
Singapore	Parliament (E)	81	5	—		
Solomon Islands	National Parliament (E)	38	4	—		
Somalia	People's Assembly (E/A)	177	5	—		
South Africa	House of Assembly (E/A)	178	5	—		
Soviet Union	People's Council of the Union (E)	271‡	5	Soviet of the Nationalities (E)	271‡	5
Spain	Congress of Deputies (E)	350	4	Senate (E)	257	4
Sri Lanka	National State Assembly (E)	225	6	—		
Sudan	Legislative Assembly (E)	264†	4	—		
Suriname	National Assembly (E)	51	5	—		
Swaziland	House of Assembly (E/A)	50	4	Senate (E/A)	20	4
Sweden	Riksdag (E)	349	3	—		
Switzerland	National Council (E)	200	4	Council of States (E)	46	4
Syria	Majlis al-Sha'ab (E)	195	4	—		
Taiwan	Legislative Yuan (E/A)	313	3	—		
Tanzania	National Assembly (E)	231	5	—		
Thailand	House of Reps (E)	357	4	Senate (A)	243	6
Togo	National Assembly (E)	77	5	—		
Tonga	Legislative Assembly (E/A)	29	3	—		
Trinidad and Tobago	House of Reps (E)	36	5	Senate (A)	31	5
Tunisia	National Assembly (E)	136	5	—		
Turkey	National Assembly (E)	450	5	—		
Tuvalu	Parliament (E)	12	4	—		
Uganda	National Assembly (E)	126	5	—		
United Arab Emirates	—				—	
United Kingdom	House of Commons (E)	650	5	House of Lords (A)	1,150+	—
United States	House of Reps (E)	435	2	Senate (E)	100	6
Uruguay	Federal Chamber of Deputies (E)	99	5	Senate (E)	30	5

Table 26—Assemblies of the World (contd.)

	First Chamber			*Second Chamber*		
State	*Name*	*No*	*Term*	*Name*	*No*	*Term*
Vanuatu	Parliament (E)	46	4	—		
Venezuela	Chamber of Deputies (E)	196	5	Senate (E/A)	44+	5
Vietnam	National Assembly (E)	496	5	—		
Western Samoa	Assembly (E)	47	3	—		
North Yemen	Shura Consultative Council (E/A)	159	2	—		
South Yemen	Supreme People's Council (E)	111	5	—		
Yugoslavia	Federal Chamber (Skupstina) (E)	220	4	Chamber of Republics & Provinces (E)	88	4
Zaire	National Legislative Council (E)	210	5	—		
Zambia	National Assembly (E/A)	135	5	—		
Zimbabwe	House of Assembly (E)	100	5	Senate (E/A)	40	5

KEY:
E/A—Elected/Appointed.
No—Number of members.
Term—Normal length of term in years.
*Formed from first chamber after election.
†Assembly not currently functioning.
‡Elected by and from the 2,250-member Congress of People's Deputies (CUPD).

5.2 Assembly functions

Whatever degree of virility or supineness they display, what are the functions of contemporary assemblies?

First, they have the obvious task of legitimising policies, in other words turning political decisions into law. Although, at its worst, this may mean little more than 'rubber stamping' the actions of the executive, it is a basic function of an assembly and the foundation of what states which claim to be democratic call the 'rule of law'.

Second, they are required to act as the people's representatives and, as such, carry their views to the executive. This is what representative democracy is supposed to be about, but if it is to be effective then the assembly must be able to influence the executive. This brings us back to the question of an assembly's virility.

Third, they are expected to be a 'talking shop': the national debating chamber. This is the role for which assemblies in liberal and emergent democracies are best equipped and which they generally best perform. In one-party states it is the party, through whatever closed institutions it devises, which predominantly fulfils this function. However, in one-party states which may be going through a transitional period, as is the case in several contemporary communist regimes, or are riven with internal factions, as for example in contemporary Iran, assembly debates can be surprisingly lively and relatively open.

Fourth, in liberal and emergent democracies, assemblies perform the vital 'reactive' role of supervising and scrutinising the actions of the political executive and bureaucracy, calling attention to abuses of authority and inefficiencies, and suggesting improvements to legislative packages presented to them.

5.3 Comparing assemblies

Table 26 provides a variety of data with which to compare assemblies in different states but if it is to be used effectively some criteria need to be established.

For example, is it important that some assembles are unicameral, with one chamber, and others, bicameral, with two? Why, in two-chamber assemblies, are the 'upper' chambers usually less powerful than the 'lower'? Is it important that membership of some chambers is on the basis of election and in others by appointment? Does the duration of the term of office of assembly members have any real significance?

Before these questions can be answered sensibly they must be qualified in some way.

The relationship between assemblies and political executives is arguably the most important basis of comparison because if democratic, rather than autocratic, government is to be achieved then there must be some limits on executive power and in most political systems the only representative body likely to be able to impose such limits is a popular assembly.

As the basis for objective comparisons, we shall, therefore, look at single- and two-chamber assemblies, and, where there are two, the relationships between them; the membership of assemblies and the criteria for membership; and the relationships between assemblies and executives.

5.4 One chamber or two?

First, the question of one or two chambers. There is a clear link between federalism and two-chamber assemblies. Of the 20 federal states listed in Table 2, 16, or 80 per cent, have two-chamber assemblies, compared with only 32 of the 145 unitary states, or just over 22 per cent. In the majority of cases the reason for the link will be obvious and this is illustrated in Table 27. In this Table the generic term second chamber or upper house has been used for convenience, but this can be slightly misleading. As we will see later, the so-called 'upper house' is often the weaker of the two and in the Netherlands what is listed in Table 27 as the 'second chamber' is in fact the 'first chamber' of the bicameral States-General.

It is interesting to observe that two states, Iceland and Norway, ostensibly have single-chamber assemblies but, after election, these divide into two. In Iceland the 63-member Althing becomes a lower house of 42 and an upper house of 21. Members may speak in either house but only vote in the one for which they have been chosen. Legislation must be passed by both houses and on some occasions, for example, when considering the budget and dealing with parliamentary questions, they both sit together as the Combined Althing. In Norway a quarter of the 157-member Storting becomes an upper house, the Lagting, and the remaining three-quarters the lower house, the Odelsting. Legislation must start in the Odelsting and then be passed by the Lagting. If there is a conflict of view between the two houses they can consider legislation jointly, as a combined Storting, and approve it by a two-thirds majority.

In making this first comparison between states with one- or two-chamber assemblies, Table 27 is relevant, indicating whether the state is unitary or federal, whether members are elected or appointed on a national or regional basis, and whether or not a representative or appointee is required to reside in the constituency he or she represents.

Of the 16 federal states 14, or 88 per cent, have second chambers which are regionally representative, whereas only five out of 32, or 16 per cent, unitary states have similar regionally representative bases. There are eight states where the representation is part-national and part-regional, and one federal and seven unitary states fall into this category.

This pattern illustrates one of the chief reasons for having a second chamber: to help resolve regional differences in countries which are geographically large and/or socially and culturally diverse. Regional interests which might object to a centralised government are to some extent pacified by the knowledge that they are formally represented at the centre by a 'local' politician.

Incidentally, it is interesting to note that, whereas the majority of states recognise regional aspirations through second chamber representation, two, Peru and Uruguay, seek to achieve this in a reverse way, by having national representation in the second chamber and regional representation in the first.

A minority of constitutions carry this regional representation a stage further by requiring politicians to reside in the region they represent. Argentina, Canada and the United States have adopted this rule.

The relationship between first and second chambers in terms of political power and authority is another interesting basis of comparison. It is not easy to make clear distinctions and, inevitably, a certain amount of subjectivity will creep in. Table 27 attempts this comparison, using criteria such as the ability to veto legislation, the respective controls of financial legislation and the extent to which a chamber has powers to interrogate the executive and curb its powers. On the basis of such criteria, it will be seen, in Table 27, that the majority of second chambers are weaker than, or enjoy parity with, first chambers and only one, the United States Senate, can, with certainty, be said to be stronger.

Table 27

SECOND CHAMBERS OR UPPER HOUSES

State	*Federal or Unitary*	*Relative Term (yrs)*	*Relative Powers*	*Basis of Representation*
Afghanistan	U	Varies	*	Mixed
Antigua	U	5/5	<	National
Argentina	F	9/4	<	Regional
Australia	F	4/3	<	Regional
Austria*	F	Varies	<	Regional
Bahamas	U	5/5	<	National
Barbados	U	5/5	<	National
Belgium	U	4/4	=	Mixed
Belize	U	5/5	<	National
Bolivia	U	4/4	=	Regional
Brazil	F	8/4	=	Regional
Canada	F	*	<	Regional
Chile	U	4/4	*	Regional
Colombia	U	4/4	=	National
Czechoslovakia*	F	5/5	=	Regional

Table 27—Second Chambers or Upper Houses (contd.)

State	*Federal or Unitary*	*Relative Term (yrs)*	*Relative Powers*	*Basis of Representation*
Dominican Republic	U	4/4	=	Regional
Fiji	U	6/5	<	Mixed
France	U	9/5	<	Mixed
West Germany*	F	*	<	Regional
Grenada	U	4/4	<	National
India*	F	6/5	<	Regional
Ireland	U	5/5	<	National
Italy	U	5/5	=	Regional
Jamaica	U	5/5	<	National
Japan*	U	6/4	<	National & Local
Jordan*	U	8/4	>	National
Liberia	U	6/6	=	National
Malaysia	F	6/5	<	Mixed
Mexico	F	6/3	=	Regional
Netherlands*	U	6/4	<	Regional
Pakistan	F	6/5	<	Regional
Paraguay	U	5/5	<	National
Peru	U	5/5	=	National
Philippines	U	6/3	*	National
Poland	U	4/4	<	National
St Lucia	U	5/5	<	National
Soviet Union*	F	5/5	=	Regional
Spain	U	4/4	<	Mixed
Swaziland	U	4/4	=	Mixed
Switzerland	F	4/4	=	National
Thailand	U	6/4	=	National
Trinidad & Tobago	U	5/5	<	National
United Kingdom*	U	*	<	National
United States	F	6/2	>	Regional
Uruguay	U	5/5	=	National
Venezuela	F	5/5	=	Regional
Yugoslavia*	F	4/4	=	Regional
Zimbabwe	U	5/5	<	Mixed

KEY:
Relative Term: compared with First Chamber or Lower House
Relative Powers: compared with First Chamber or Lower House;
=is equal;<is weaker;>is stronger; *see notes below
Basis of Representation: National/Regional/Mixed
Most second chambers are termed 'senates'; where another name applies this is noted below.

*NOTES

Afghanistan	In transitional state
Austria	Bundesrat
Canada	Senators appointed for life
Chile	In transitional state
Czechoslovakia	Chamber of Nations
West Germany	The Bundesrat's composition varies as state governments change, rather than being dependent on elections
India	Council of States
Japan	House of Councillors
Jordan	House of Notables
Netherlands	First chamber
Philippines	In transitional state
Soviet Union	Council of Nationalities
United Kingdom	House of Lords composed of hereditary and life members
Yugoslavia	Chamber of Republics

5.5 Membership of assemblies

Table 26 shows that in the vast majority of states membership of an assembly is on the basis of election. It would be surprising if it were otherwise since the main purpose of having an assembly is to ensure, or at least suggest, that the ordinary person has an opportunity to be represented by a politician who has been freely chosen. How this is done and whether or not it is done successfully will be examined in the next chapter.

There are a few first chambers or single chambers where a combination of election and appointment is used. In the vast majority of such cases the non-elected members are executive appointees, giving a President or monarch the opportunity of placing his own people. Occasionally appointments are made to try to ensure a particular distribution of membership. In Tanzania, for example, a complicated mixture of election and appointment makes provision for regional, female and party representation as well as presidential nominees. Similarly, in Bangladesh and Pakistan a set quota of National Assembly seats, 30 and 20 respectively, are reserved for women appointees. In India, two Lok Sabha seats are reserved for the Anglo-Indian community.

In the majority of one-party states assembly representatives, whether elected or appointed, are initially selected by the party. In communist systems there is an interweaving of party and state membership, with the party nominees, because of their greater experience and 'professionalism', dominating proceedings. The non-party deputies are selected as exemplary representatives of the full cross-section of society by sex, age, ethnic and occupational groups. They serve their constituents as mandated delegates on a part-time basis, being given only minor 'out of pocket' expenses for the five to ten days spent each year at the national assembly.

Of the 48 states with second chambers, members are wholly elected in 25, wholly appointed in 13 and part-elected and part-appointed in ten. In some of the small states, with a parliamentary executive fashioned on the 'Westminster model', the mixture of election and appointment is constructed so as to reflect the political balance in the first chamber. In Antigua, the Bahamas, Barbados, Belize, Grenada, St Lucia, and Trinidad & Tobago, for example, the Prime Minister and the official Leader of the Opposition are entitled to nominate members.

In states with political systems modelled on the United States, most notably those in Latin America, direct popular election of the second chamber predominates.

In Europe and South Asia, by contrast, members of the second chambers are predominantly elected indirectly, in the majority of cases by regional assemblies. Austria, Belgium, France, India, Ireland, West Germany, the Netherlands, Pakistan and Yugoslavia all provide examples of indirectly elected second chambers.

The most popular term of membership is five years. The complete analysis is given in Table 28.

Table 28

ASSEMBLY
TERMS OF MEMBERSHIP

Term	*First or single chamber*		*Second chamber*	
(years)	*Number*	*%*	*Number*	*%*
1	1	0.7	—	—
2	2	1	—	—
3	13	9	—	—
4	42	29	12	27
5	84	57	16	37
6	4	3	11	26
8	—	—	2	5
9	1	0.7	2	5
Total	147	100	43	100

The popularity of a five-year term is understandable. A newly elected government, with a policy package it wished to implement, would probably spend at least the first two years framing the necessary legislation and ensuring its passage through the legislative machine. If a proposal was thought to be beneficial in the long term but unpopular in a short time span then a reasonable period would be needed for the public to appreciate its benefits. That would be the government's view. On the other hand, immediately popular proposals might be innately flawed and these defects might only reveal themselves over time. A five-year term of office would give the electorate time to assess a government's performance before it submitted itself again for election. That would be the opposition's view.

Politicians in states with first chambers with limited lives of three years, such as Australia, have expressed reservations from time to time about the shortness of the term and some of the practical consequences. Short-term assemblies tend to make governments cautious in their policy proposals, fearing a loss of public support with insufficient time to prove that short-term unpopularity can be replaced by long-term satisfaction.

It should be remembered, however, that assemblies in states with parliamentary executives rarely run their full terms. They may end because the government loses assembly support or, as frequently happens, it or a coalition partner seeks a dissolution at what it considers to be the most propitious time to ensure electoral success.

In states with limited presidential executives assembly terms are invariably of a fixed duration. This is of potential value to opposition parties, removing the incumbent administration's control over the election timetable and thus subjecting all members equally to the whims of random external forces. It also serves, however, to institutionalise electioneering, sometimes to an unhealthy degree. This is most clearly seen in the case of the United States House of Representatives whose members, facing biennial elections, find themselves condemned to a non-stop cycle of campaigning and fund-raising. Fixed-term assemblies are also the norm in two Scandinavian countries with parliamentary executives, Norway and Sweden, and also in Switzerland.

Second chambers with terms of six years or more often stagger those of individual members, with half or a third submitting themselves for election at a time. This serves to 'keep fresh' the accountability of the assembly, but can create problems for a new administration assuming office following a sudden election swing in the lower chamber. The states falling into this staggered category are:

Nine-year term with a third retiring every three years:	Argentina and France
Eight-year term with a third and two-thirds retiring alternately every four years:	Brazil
Eight-year term with a half retiring every four years:	Jordan
Six-year term with a half retiring every three years:	Japan and Netherlands
Six-year term with a third retiring every two years:	United States, India and Pakistan

Finally, constitutions invariably specify qualifications for candidates in assembly elections, including a mimimum age. Most states with two-chamber assemblies stipulate a more mature entry age for members of the second chamber. In Venezuela, for example, the minimum ages are 21 years for the Chamber of Deputies and 30 years for the Senate. In Argentina and the United States they are 25 years for the Chamber of Deputies/House of Representatives and 30 years for the Senate. In Thailand and the Philippines the figures are 25 years for the House of Representatives and 35 years for the Senate. In Italy, the ages are 25 years for the Camera dei Deputati and 40 years for the Senato.

This requirement of greater maturity, frequently combined with a longer term of office than in the first chamber, tends to add to the authority of second chamber members, who have often already had sufficiently long political careers to qualify them for the description of 'elder statesmen'.

5.6 Assembly size

In Table 29 the size distribution of contemporary world assemblies, lower and upper chambers, is set out and in Table 30 general population per lower house member has been calculated for each state with an assembly.

Table 29

SIZE DISTRIBUTION OF CONTEMPORARY WORLD ASSEMBLIES

Membership Size	*Lower Chambers*	*Upper Chambers*	*Lower Chambers (%)*	*Upper Chambers (%)*
10 or Below	—	1	—	2
11–50	25	22	17	47
51–100	29	12	20	25
101–200	41	5	28	10
201–300	20	5	13	10

Table 29—Size Distribution of Contemporary World Assemblies (contd.)

Membership Size	*Lower Chambers*	*Upper Chambers*	*Lower Chambers (%)*	*Upper Chambers (%)*
301–400	10	2	7	4
401–500	11	—	8	—
501–750	7	—	5	—
751–1,000	1	—	1	—
1,001–3,000	2	1	1	2
Total	146*	48	100	100

*Not including Afghanistan.

Table 30

POPULATION PER LOWER HOUSE MEMBER

State	*Thousands of People per Lower House Member*	*State*	*Thousands of People per Lower House Member*
Nauru	0.44	The Gambia	16.00
Tuvalu	0.75	Cuba	20.40
Kiribati	1.51	South Yemen	20.72
Dominica	2.47	Benin	20.92
Sao Tome & Principe	2.63	Ireland	21.83
Seychelles	2.64	Bulgaria	22.50
St Kitts-Nevis	2.86	Sweden	23.94
Vanuatu	2.96	Finland	24.65
Libya	3.51	Norway	26.53
Tonga	3.62	Lebanon	27.27
Maldives	3.75	Botswana	27.50
Iceland	3.81	Hungary	27.50
Western Samoa	3.83	Denmark	28.42
Djibouti	4.62	Uruguay	30.30
Bahamas	4.80	Papua New Guinea	31.15
Antigua	5.00	North Korea	31.30
Mongolia	5.14	Singapore	31.90
St Vincent & Grenadines	5.42	Switzerland	32.35
Malta	5.46	Greece	33.18
Cape Verde	5.57	Panama	33.23
Luxembourg	5.73	East Germany	33.40
Belize	6.00	Trinidad & Tobago	33.44
Guinea-Bissau	6.00	New Zealand	34.07
Grenada	6.67	Honduras	34.33
St Lucia	7.24	Nicaragua	34.38
Solomon Islands	7.45	Israel	35.07
Suriname	7.84	Liberia	35.94
Equatorial Guinea	8.78	Angola	36.77
Barbados	9.44	Sierra Leone	37.34
Bhutan	9.58	Togo	39.26
Gabon	10.00	Jamaica	39.43
Comoros	11.17	North Yemen	39.62
Congo	11.76	Austria	41.23
Cyprus	11.89	Somalia	44.07
Albania	12.18	Belgium	46.55
Guyana	12.31	Costa Rica	47.37
Fiji	13.75	Bolivia	49.46
Swaziland	13.84	Laos	52.11
Mauritius	14.49	Ethiopia	52.57

Table 30—Population per Lower House Member (contd.)

State	Thousands of People per Lower House Member	State	Thousands of People per Lower House Member
Zambia	52.59	Mali	96.44
Tunisia	53.38	Netherlands	96.54
Syria	54.03	Tanzania	96.97
Dominican Rep	55.12	Chile	102.50
Cameroon	55.56	Yugoslavia	105.45
Mozambique	56.00	Australia	106.51
Senegal	57.50	Egypt	110.26
Jordan	58.58	Spain	111.64
Cambodia	59.21	Peru	112.22
Ivory Coast	60.00	Turkey	115.15
Romania	61.79	West Germany	117.02
Taiwan	62.62	Uganda	120.63
Iraq	65.11	Kenya	122.09
Portugal	66.40	Argentina	122.83
Paraguay	68.65	Nepal	124.44
Malawi	72.28	Vietnam	125.00
Sri Lanka	72.64	Ecuador	135.21
Madagascar	75.18	South Korea	144.82
Burundi	75.38	Thailand	146.89
Burma	77.10	Zaire	149.05
Morocco	77.45	Colombia	150.75
Czechoslovakia	77.50	Mexico	163.40
Poland	81.52	Iran	172.59
El Salvador	85.00	South Africa	186.52†
Guatemala	86.00	Philippines	232.40
United Kingdom	86.86	Japan	237.11
Sudan	87.01	Brazil	299.16
Algeria	87.36	Bangladesh	315.45
Malaysia	89.38	Indonesia	346.21
Zimbabwe	90.00	China	353.54
Venezuela	90.82	Soviet Union*	373.33
Italy	90.83	Pakistan	429.96
Canada	90.87	United States	554.02
France	96.01	India	1,443.01

*A population:member ratio has not been calculated for Afghanistan, whose political system remains in a transitional condition. At present the lower chamber of its National Assembly should have 234 members, but 48 of these seats have been left unfilled in the hope that moderate mujaheddin opposition leaders will be attracted in. If all the seats are eventually taken up the population:member ratio would stand at 77.5:1.

†This has been calculated by dividing the total population by a figure corresponding to the 178-members of the House of Assembly. In reality, however, South Africa's unique, racially discriminatory, political system has resulted in the establishent of three separate chambers for the white, coloured and Asian communities, while, at the same time, excluding blacks from the national political process entirely. To be truly accurate, separate deputy-population ratios have been calculated for each community. The resulting figures are: for the white community–33.57 (thousands of persons per member); for the coloured community–39.05; for the Asian community–22.13; for the black community—not applicable.

From Table 29, it emerges that almost two-thirds of the world's lower chambers have memberships of 200 or fewer, with the median size being around 150. In addition, it is apparent that upper houses of bicameral assemblies are almost uniformly smaller than their lower house counterparts, being on average half the size. As a consequence, 73 per cent of upper chambers have memberships of 100 or fewer, the median figure being 58.

From Table 30, it emerges, not surprisingly, that a state's population size is the principal determinant both of the membership size of its assembly and of the resultant population:member ratio. Thus, the larger in demographic terms the state, the larger on average the size of its assembly and, notwithstanding this, the higher its population:member ratio. For this reason, India, the second most populous country in the world, appears at the bottom of the Table 30 ratio listings, followed by the United States, the world's fourth most populous state. Conversely, tiny island states such as Nauru, Tuvalu and Kiribati are to be found clustering at the head of the listings, having small assemblies, with memberships substantially fewer than 50, yet despite this still registering unusually low population:member ratios.

There are two notable exceptions to this general, regular pattern.

First, communist or nationalistic socialist states usually have assemblies far larger than equivalent-sized liberal or emergent democracies, or one-party non-socialist states. As a natural corollary, their resulting population:member ratios are lower than might be expected. China, with its 2,970-member National People's Congress; Libya, with its 1,112-member General People's Congress; the Soviet Union, with its 2,250-member Congress of the USSR People's Deputies (CUPD); Ethiopia, with its 835-member National Assembly; and North Korea, with its 655-member Supreme People's Assembly are the most prominent examples. The rationale behind the election of these 'jumbo-assemblies' would, in theory, appear to be a desire to broaden the participation base. In practice however, as has been noted earlier, these assemblies meet in plenary session for less than two weeks a year. They delegate their authority to smaller 'inner assemblies', standing committees and general secretariats, which generally comprise between 40 and 140 members, a figure substantially below the membership average for the permanent assemblies in liberal or emergent democracies.

In four other countries, Afghanistan, Indonesia, Taiwan and North Yemen, large quasi-assemblies are found, with memberships in excess of 900, which have powers to amend their constitutions and, in the first three, to appoint the state Presidents. These are, however, only *ad hoc* bodies, meeting variously at two-, five-, six- or seven-year intervals, unless specially summoned. In the interim periods, they delegate effective authority to smaller, regular national assemblies below them. For this reason, they have not been treated as full assemblies in this chapter, being excluded from the listings in Table 26 and from the calculations made for Table 30 above.

The second, and more specific, anomaly which emerges when Tables 29 and 30 are studied, in conjunction with Table 26, is found in the United Kingdom. The United Kingdom has by far the largest lower house, 650 members, of all the world's liberal democracies and, for this reason, has a comparatively low population:member ratio for its total population size. Furthermore, it is the only country in the world having an upper chamber with a larger membership than its lower. This results from the anachronistic combination of hereditary succession and government appointment that is still used to fill the House of Lords, as well as the fact that in earlier years it was the pre-eminent chamber. Today the House of Lords comprises roughly 800 hereditary peers and 400 life peers, including the law lords and the 'lords spiritual', but in practice its active membership is less than 400. Indeed, 300 hereditary peers have never even visited the chamber to take the oath of membership.

5.7 Assembly-executive relationships

There are three possible bases on which to examine the assembly-executive relationship. First, the extent to which an assembly can initiate legislation. Second, the extent to which an assembly can influence policy-making. Third, the extent of an assembly's ability to criticise the executive, block its policies and even dismiss it.

The vast majority of contemporary assemblies are not significant initiators of legislation. They are, as has already been said, mainly amenders and approvers. For this reason they have frequently been categorised as 'reactive' chambers. There are, however, some notable exceptions which stand out as examples of 'active' legislatures. Non-adversarial Sweden, where assembly members are mainly grouped in constituency rather than party blocks, is one. So, to an even greater extent, is the United States.

In Sweden private members' proposals (*motioner*) are ten times as numerous in the Riksdag as government bills (*propositioner*), although the bulk of the former are amendments or party alternatives to government bills, designed to spark off new discussion and inquiries.

In the United States Congress thousands of bills and resolutions are introduced each year by Senators and Representatives, several hundred of which ultimately become law. Even here, however, the key legislative measures are those proposed in January by the President in his annual 'State of the Union' address to both chambers and which are subsequently adopted by party supporters within Congress under the promptings of the White House's liaison staff.

The ability of assemblies to influence policy-making is also slight, Sweden again being somewhat unusual in this respect. An assembly in a state with a parliamentary executive is, in theory, in a strong position to make policy since the executive is drawn from it and responsible to it. In practice, however, an assembly member who has joined the executive to a great extent loses his or her allegiance to the assembly and becomes, psychologically but not physically, separate from it. The obvious example is the distinction between a front-bench, government, member of the United Kingdom House of Commons and a back-bencher.

So we are left with the third basis on which to examine the assembly-executive relationship: the ability to criticise, block policies and, *in extremis*, to dismiss an executive.

Most assemblies in parliamentary executive systems have built-in mechanisms for regular questioning of ministers. The United Kingdom House of Commons has an hour set aside for this for four days per week, and on two of these days fifteen minutes for questions specifically addressed to the Prime Minister. Although probably the most popular event of the parliamentary week in Britain, as far as the media and public are concerned, there is little evidence that Question Time in the House of Commons is anything more than an opportunity for rival parties to score points against each other. In West Germany and Finland 'interpellation' seems more successful, the oral questioning of a minister often being accompanied by a snap vote.

Most assemblies in limited presidential and parliamentary executive systems have strong committee structures, partly to expedite the legislative process and partly to oversee the actions of the executive. The United States Congress undoubtedly has the strongest committees of any contemporary assembly in the world. The power and authority of these committees, well provisioned with research staff and armed with extensive rights to subpoena staff from the executive, have been dramatically highlighted in recent years through the wide publicity given to the Watergate and 'Irangate' hearings. The fact that sessions of the congressional committees can receive nationwide television coverage has increased public awareness and enhanced their influence.

By comparison, assembly committees in other states seem weak. In the United Kingdom, as the result of the composition of the House of Commons and the disciplined party system, standing committees which consider government legislation are government-dominated, introducing only minor amendments to bills presented. Even weaker are the investigative select committees which were introduced into the chamber in 1979 to 'shadow' the work of government departments. Although producing informative reports, their impact as parliamentary watchdogs has not been great. Their counterparts in Canada and France have been only marginally more successful.

Stronger committee systems operate in West Germany, Italy and Japan, all three having constitutions partly modelled on that of the United States. These committees are primarily concerned with legislation but, from time to time, *ad hoc* investigative committees have been influential. In Japan in 1976 an assembly committee vigorously investigated the Lockheed bribes scandal, its work eventually resulting in the arrest and trial of former Prime Minister Tanaka. More recently in West Germany, a committee successfully probed the 'Flick scandal' which was concerned with illegal party financing.

In one-party states, assemblies are inevitably subservient to the party, and hence the executive. However, in the Soviet Union, working with, rather than against, the party, the 34 or so specialised permanent standing commissions of the Supreme Soviet have, in recent years, grown in stature and become part of the policy-making machine. Similar bodies are also influential in the Polish Sejm and Hungary's National Assembly.

On balance, however, it must be said that, with some rare exceptions, contemporary assemblies have shown little sign of keeping up with, let alone overtaking, the increasing power and authority of executives of all types.

5.8 The representation of interests

The representation of interests is one activity that assemblies usually do well, especially in liberal democratic and emergent democratic states. This representation falls into three broad categories: constituency representation, party representation and specific group representation.

Constituency representation is a traditional function of all assemblies. In the United States Congress it has been developed to a high degree and is reinforced by the residential factor in both the House of Representatives and the Senate. Some Congressmen have devoted virtually their entire political careers to the economic advancement of the constituencies they represent, knowing that this is the surest route to re-election.

Similar, but less well-developed, examples can be found in assemblies in other parts of the world, including Kenya, the Philippines, South Korea, Yugoslavia, France and the United Kingdom. In the British House of Commons, for example, it is not unknown for a member to ignore a major policy line of his party in order to support his constituency. Some United Kingdom Labour Party MPs have in recent years been confronted with 'dilemmas of conscience' in trying to follow a non-nuclear power policy when their constituents have been dependent on nuclear generation for their livelihoods.

Party representation has been the fastest-growing activity in most assemblies in recent years. The last independent MP in the British House of Commons disappeared in the 1960s and there is now only a minority of assemblies that accommodate them. Kiribati, the Maldives, Nauru and Tuvalu seem to be the few contemporary states where assembly elections are contested by politicians standing as independents.

The representation of group interests is another growing activity of assembly members, particularly in liberal democratic countries. In the British House of Commons many Labour members are sponsored by trade unions and some Conservatives are paid by a variety of interests to present their points of view. In an effort to bring this activity into the open, the House of Commons has produced a Register of MPs' Interests and members are requested, but not compelled, to register their interests as well as declare them during the course of debates. In the United States, with the growing influence of Political Action Committees, which provide a quarter of the funds used in contesting congressional elections, the influence of single-issue ideological interest groups is substantially stronger.

RECOMMENDED READING

Arter, D., *The Nordic Parliaments: A Comparative Analysis*, Hurst, 1984.

Blondel, J. *et al* in: M. Curtis (ed), *Introduction to Comparative Government*, Harper & Row, 1985.

Blondel, J., *Comparative Legislatures*, Prentice-Hall, 1973.

Charlton, R., *Comparative Government*, Longman, 1985, Ch 3.

Goodwin, Jr, G., 'The New Congress', in: P. J. Davies and F. A. Waldstein (eds), *Political Issues in America Today*, Manchester University Press, 1987.

Hague, R. and Harrop, M., *Comparative Government and Politics: An Introduction*, 2nd edn., Macmillan, 1987, Ch 10.

Inter-Parliamentary Union, *Parliaments of the World: A Reference Companion*, Macmillan, 1976.

Judge, D., *The Politics of Parliamentary Reform*, Heinemann, 1983.

Kim, C. *et al*, *The Legislative Connection: The Politics of Representation in Kenya, Korea and Turkey*, Duke University Press, 1984.

Lees, J. and Shaw, M. (eds), *Committees in Legislatures: A Comparative Analysis*, Duke University Press, 1979.
Loewenberg, G. and Patterson, S. C., *Comparing Legislatures*, Little Brown, 1979.
Lovenduski, J. and Woodall, J., *Politics and Society in Eastern Europe*, Macmillan, 1987, Ch 9.
Mann, T. E. and Ornstein, N. J. (eds), *The New Congress*, American Enterprise Institute, 1981.
Mezey, M., *Comparative Legislatures*, Duke University Press, 1979.
Nelson, D. and White S. (eds), *Communist Legislatures in Comparative Perspective*, Macmillan, 1982.
Norton, P. (ed), *Parliament in the 1980s*, Basil Blackwell, 1985.
Paxton, P., *World Legislatures*, Macmillan, 1974.
Roberts, G. K., *An Introduction to Comparative Politics*, Edward Arnold, 1985, Ch 7.
Smith, G., *Politics in Western Europe: A Comparative Analysis*, 4th edn., Gower Publishing, 1986, Ch 7.
Sundquist, J. L., *The Decline and Resurgence of Congress*, The Brookings Institution, 1981.
Vanneman, P., *The Supreme Soviet: Politics and the Legislative Process in the Soviet Political System*, Duke University Press, 1977.
Waller, D. J., *The Government and Politics of the People's Republic of China*, 3rd edn., Hutchinson, 1981, Ch 3.
White, S., Gardner, J. and Schopflin, G., *Communist Political Systems: An Introduction*, 2nd edn., Macmillan, 1987, Ch. 3.

CHAPTER 6

ELECTIONS AND VOTERS

6.1 The importance of elections

The majority of contemporary states claim to be democratic and seek to prove their democratic credentials under the banner of representation. The right to vote is almost the only universal right in the world today. Of the 165 states we are examining only five, Brunei, Oman, Qatar, Saudi Arabia and the United Arab Emirates, do not have, and never have had, any institutions which can, even in the loosest sense, be described as popularly representative. A further 13 states have 'suspended' legislatures and thus no currently functioning electoral systems. Among the other 147 there are wide differences in kinds and degrees of representation.

The first, and obvious, difference is between multi-party and one-party political systems. It is reasonable to assume that an election in a multi-party state means a choice of policies as well as representatives, whereas in a one-party system a representative may be changed but the basic policy thrust, as derived from the party, remains the same.

Why then do one-party states bother to go through the charade of elections? First, most of them, indeed probably all of them, would claim that the elections were not a charade. They might well argue that the reality of choice is no greater in a multi-party system than in their own. They might, with some justification, select one of the world's oldest democracies, the United Kingdom, and point out that no government in the post-war period has been elected by a clear majority of the people voting. They might also compare turnouts of less than 80 per cent in general elections in the UK with turnouts well in excess of 90 per cent in most communist one-party states.

The politician in a liberal democratic state, while conceding these points, would probably argue that a choice between parties was nonetheless a substantially greater choice even though, through ignorance or apathy, some people failed to exercise it. He would say that the opportunity of voting for a complete change of policy, and even philosophy, was a vital element in a democratic political system and that without it genuine choice was limited.

Leaving aside such arguments, it is clear that in one-party states the voter knows that whatever decision he or she takes in the polling booth the party in power will not change, so the earlier question must be repeated: why are elections held?

The main reason is to demonstrate popular support for the regime. The important work of selecting the candidate has already been done, within the party machine. The election just legitimises the 'behind the scenes' decisions. In some one-party states the question asked is simply 'Yes or No?'. There is only one candidate and therefore choice is given only in a negative form. In other states a choice of candidate may be given. East

Germany, Hungary, Poland, Romania and Yugoslavia have offered candidate choice for some years and the practice has recently been adopted in the Soviet Union and China. In non-communist one-party states candidate choice is fairly common.

Although in one-party states the election would appear to make the candidate choice legitimate, the practice is invariably unnecessary on constitutional or practical grounds. The party decision, once taken, is inviolate. The size of the turnout in each constituency will, however, be of interest to party officials because it will indicate the degree of activity, or apathy, in different areas. It will enable them to gauge the work being done by individual candidates and provide public 'feedback' on sensitive issues, allowing them to take steps to improve local morale and efficiency and, if pressed, introduce measures to deal with grass-roots grievances. This is particularly relevant in communist states.

In non-communist one-party states elections may be important on more personal grounds. In some countries, where candidates are fighting each other within the one party, success will often depend on which politician, in the eyes of the voter, offers the best deal. In Kenya, for example, there is usually a large (40–50 per cent) turnover of parliamentary representatives as the record of one politician is judged unsatisfactory in terms of what he has 'delivered' by way of state money for some local development and so is replaced by another who appears to offer more. This is a variant of what is described in congressional elections in the United States as 'pork barrel' politics: the ability to 'bring home the bacon'.

In multi-party political systems elections are much more significant. Not only do they provide the non-politically active public, who invariably comprise more than 95 per cent of the population in most liberal-democratic societies, with an opportunity to participate in the political process. They actually determine who shall wield power. This is why in liberal and emergent democracies so much attention is paid to voting qualifications and voting methods.

6.2 Voting qualifications

The great majority of constitutions refer to voting on the basis of universal adult suffrage which, in simple terms, means the right of all adults to cast their vote. For some countries this is a comparatively recently acquired right and it is a right which still varies in detail from state to state.

The age of majority varies and, although 18 is the most common, being the rule in 108 states, there are some states, 21 in all, where it is as high as 21 and others, such as Guinea-Bissau and, in presidential elections in Iran, as low as 15. Moreover, in some Latin American states, Colombia being an example, the franchise is extended to married persons at an earlier age, 18, than to those who are single, 21. Under some constitutions literacy is also a necessary qualification, whereas in countries, such as India, Honduras and Madagascar, where the level of literacy is low, there is often provision for people to vote on the basis of symbols rather than names.

Women were the last group in most countries to acquire the right to vote. In New Zealand they were given the franchise as early as 1893, long before it was a fully independent state. In Jordan, by way of contrast, they did not acquire it until 1982.

South Africa remains the one country in the world where a significant proportion of the population are excluded from electoral participation on racial-ethnic grounds. Between 1909 and 1936, a portion of the black and coloured community of Cape Province did enjoy the right to vote. Thereafter, however, the introduction of a series of new laws served effectively to eliminate black suffrage. This was formally acknowledged in 1959, the official date of complete disenfranchisement for blacks. In 1984 voting rights were restored to coloureds, who comprise 11 per cent of the population, and Indians, who constitute another 3 per cent, for elections to their own assemblies. The black community, who comprise more than 68 per cent of the country's total population, still remain excluded from a political process which is effectively controlled by the 18 per cent white minority.

6.3 Voting systems

Elections are usually held to choose either executives or assemblies, or both. In multi-party states where the executive, usually the President, is separate from, and usually limited by, the assembly, the two elections are quite separate. They may take place at the same time but there are two distinct sets of choices. In parliamentary systems where the executive is drawn from and responsible to the assembly, the assembly determines which party will form the executive and thus only assembly elections are necessary. In one-party states the executive is usually chosen by the party and then 'legitimised' either by the assembly or through a separate election.

The election of executives is generally a fairly straightforward process but considerable ingenuity has been shown in some multi-party states in devising methods of electing assemblies to try to ensure as close a correlation as possible between the number of votes cast for a particular party and the number of seats that party wins.

6.3.1 Simple plurality (SP)

The most frequently used voting system is the simplest and easiest to understand, the simple plurality, or 'first-past-the-post', method. It is used for assembly elections in the world's two largest liberal democracies, the United States and India, as well as in the United Kingdom and most of the former British colonies which, after independence, retained a 'Westminster model' constitution.

This voting system does not make any pretence of trying to equate the number of seats won with the number of votes cast. Consequently, in countries with two major parties, such as the United Kingdom and New Zealand, third or fourth parties tend to win disproportionately fewer seats than votes, as Table 31 clearly shows. In countries where numerous minor parties, usually regionally or occupationally based, but only one significant national party, operate, the larger grouping is usually consistently able to hold power, despite capturing a relatively low share of the total vote. This has been apparent in India, where the Congress Party is the predominant force. In countries where there are strong localised ethnic concentrations, such as Northern Ireland and parts of Scotland and Wales, the SP system can be of potential advantage to smaller parties.

Table 31

PARTIES' SHARE OF HOUSE OF COMMONS IN UK GENERAL ELECTIONS: 1945-1987*

(a) By Votes

General Election Year	*Conservative Share (%)*	*Labour Share (%)*	*Lib/Alliance† Share (%)*	*Total Votes (m)*	*Voter Turnout (%)*
1945	40	48	9	24.1	73
1950	43	46	9	28.8	84
1951	48	49	2	28.6	82
1955	50	46	3	26.8	77
1959	49	44	6	27.9	79
1964	43	44	11	27.7	77
1966	42	48	8	27.3	76
1970	46	43	7	28.3	72
1974 Feb	38	37	19	31.3	78
1974 Oct	36	39	18	29.2	73
1979	44	37	14	31.2	76
1983	42	28	25	30.7	73
1987	42	31	23	32.6	75

(b) By Seats

General Election Year	*Conservative Share (%)*	*Labour Share (%)*	*Lib/Alliance† Share (%)*	*Total Seats (number)*	*Voter Turnout (%)*
1945	33	61	2	640	73
1950	48	50	1	625	84
1951	51	47	1	625	82
1955	55	44	1	630	77
1959	58	41	1	630	79
1964	48	50	1	630	77
1966	40	58	2	630	76
1970	52	46	1	630	72
1974 Feb	47	47	2	635	78
1974 Oct	44	50	2	635	73
1979	53	42	2	635	76
1983	61	32	4	650	73
1987	59	35	3	650	75

*Source: J. D. Derbyshire and I. D. Derbyshire, *Politics in Britain: From Callaghan to Thatcher*, W & R Chambers, 1988, Table 4, p. 6.

†The Alliance fought its first general election in 1983.

Currently, it is employed by 87 states for lower chamber assembly elections, 40 being either liberal or emergent democracies. The remainder are one-party or quasi-one-party states. In some of the latter, Cameroon being an example, 'slate-system' variants of SP operate. Here, the party which gains the majority of votes cast secures all the available assembly seats. In many communist states, the SP system is nominal, no opposition candidates being put up.

The alternatives to the SP system fall into two broad categories, the absolute majority (see 6.3.2–6.3.3) and the proportional systems (6.3.4–6.3.7). Within each of these two groups are variations, sometimes of detail and sometimes of substance.

6.3.2 The alternative vote (AV)

The alternative vote (AV) is not theoretically a form of proportional representation in that it cannot guarantee a close relationship between votes and seats and, indeed, can sometimes produce surprising results. It does however go some way towards making the voting system fairer and is relatively simple and easy to understand.

It uses single-member constituencies, the voter choosing a candidate by marking 1 against his name on the ballot paper. If he wants, he can also mark 2 against his second choice and so on, but this is not compulsory. First preference votes are then counted and if any one candidate collects more than 50 per cent of all the votes cast he is automatically elected. If this does not happen the candidate with the least number of first choice votes is eliminated and the second preferences of those who chose him as number 1 are distributed among the other candidates. This process continues until one candidate emerges with more than 50 per cent.

The main objection to AV is that it tends to help compromise candidates and its results can sometimes be quite unpredictable, with the successful candidate being someone whom very few people positively want. At present, only Australia employs this voting system. It was first introduced in 1919 and applies to its lower chamber, the House of Representatives. It has had little perceptible impact on the party system, which remains firmly set in a two- to three-party mould.

6.3.3 The second ballot (SB)

The second ballot is similar in some respects to AV. A simple majority election is held and if no one gets more than 50 per cent of the total vote, the candidate with the fewest votes is eliminated and a second election is held, usually within the next week to ten days. The rules concerning who can participate in the 'run-off' contest vary considerably. In France, where the system is used for National Assembly elections, candidates who have received support from at least 12.5 per cent of the registered electorate are entitled to compete in the following week's second ballot. The candidate who achieves a majority in this second contest is the one who is elected. For French presidential elections, only the top two candidates go forward to the 'run-off' ballot.

In terms of achieving better proportionality, the second ballot generally fares worse than AV and even SP. In addition, it is more costly to operate. The reason for its adoption by the framers of France's Fifth Republic constitution was their concern to encourage the emergence of more streamlined and disciplined party groupings, following the '*immobilisme*' of the Fourth Republic, whose assembly had contained representatives from more than a dozen competing parties, elected by the party list system of proportional representation.

Despite these roots, eleven countries currently use the SB system for their lower chamber elections. In addition to France, they are Czechoslovakia, Egypt, Hungary, Iran, the Ivory Coast, Kiribati, Poland, Romania, the Soviet Union and Vanuatu. In the Ivory Coast, the SB system is of a 'slate variety', in which the party which receives the majority of the national vote captures all the available National Assembly seats. SB is also used by several other states, including Cyprus, Ecuador and Peru, for presidential contests, and for governorship contests in some southern states of the United States.

In theory, many other communist states, in addition to those listed above, can be viewed as SB countries, their constitutions requiring assembly candidates to secure a full majority of the votes. In practice, however, because of a lack of effective competition, national level contests have always been settled by one ballot.

Compared with the SP system, both the SB and AV have had a tendency to promote tactical alliances between minor parties or major and minor parties, to improve their chances of success.

Majority voting systems are concerned principally with returning effective governments, usually of a single party, even though they do not always achieve this. In contrast, proportional electoral systems place their chief priority on the principle of representation, seeking to effect the return of assemblies which, in party, social, gender and ethnic composition, closely mirror the profile and wishes of the electorate. Four principal variants of proportional representation (PR) are currently to be found in operation.

6.3.4 The party list (PL)

List systems are, potentially, the most truly representative form of PR, being designed to return members reflecting the broadest possible spectrum of public opinion. To achieve this, unlike absolute majority systems, they are, of necessity, based on large multi-member constituencies of either a regional or, in the case of Israel, for example, a national character.

The first stage in the complicated operation of the PL system is the production of lists of candidates by each of the political parties fighting the election. Each list shows names in descending order of preference, as chosen by the party. In many cases, an elector merely votes for the party of his or her choice and seats are then allocated to each party according to the total proportion of votes received. Thus a party winning 30 per cent of the votes would be entitled to 30 per cent of the seats and enough names would be taken from the party's list to fill those seats.

Like AV, the party list system cannot always guarantee full proportional representation. In general, however, it has been calculated that it results in a correspondence between parties' shares of the national vote and assembly seats of 90–98 per cent. In contrast, the 'index of proportionality' for SP systems is, on average, ten points lower, at between 80–92 per cent, while that for Australia's AV stands at 87 per cent and for France's SB 79 per cent.

Some versions of the list system, such as the inflexible 'closed list', used in Israel and Spain, where the voter is given no choice of candidate and simply votes for the party, can make an election very impersonal. Others, however, allow voters to indicate a preference for an individual as well as a party. Varying examples of these are the 'flexible list' system, used in Belgium, and its variant in Italy, the 'open list' system of Finland, and the most liberal of all, the 'free list' system of Luxembourg and Switzerland.

List systems can be 'doctored' by stipulating a 'cut-off' point of percentage votes to be won below which very small parties get no representation at all. If this is not done then virtually any party, whatever its size, will have a chance of winning at least one seat and an assembly could be peppered with 'one off' representatives. The nature and size of the 'cut-off' threshold can vary considerably. In Denmark it is as low as 2 per cent of the vote, in Sweden 4 per cent and in West Germany 5 per cent.

Currently, 32 states employ list systems. Sixteen are in Western Europe. They are Austria, Belgium, Cyprus, Denmark, Finland, Greece, Iceland, Italy, Luxembourg, Netherlands, Norway, Portugal, Spain, Sweden, Switzerland and Turkey. The other 16 are Brazil, Colombia, Costa Rica, the Dominican Republic, Ecuador, Guyana, Honduras, Indonesia, Israel, the Lebanon, Nicaragua, Paraguay, Peru, Sri Lanka, Uruguay and Venezuela. Details of the salient features of these various systems are given in Table 32 below.

On the whole, list systems have tended to favour the development of multi-party coalition politics. In the Netherlands, for example, where the purest possible form of list system is to be found, no 'cut-off' limits being imposed, a dozen or so parties frequently secure representation in the 'Second Chamber', although the three principal parties, the Labour Party (PvdA), the Christian Democratic Appeal (CDA) and the People's Party for Freedom and Democracy (VVD), invariably capture around 80–85 per cent of the total vote and assembly seats. Included in the ranks of the minor parties are Calvinist and Evangelical religious groupings, as well as peace, communist and ecological organisations.

In Italy, Switzerland, Belgium, Finland, Denmark and Iceland, where almost similarly liberal 'cut-off' restrictions are in operation, in the 1987–88 lower chamber elections 14, 13, 11, 9, 8, and 7 parties respectively won seats.

The absence of a suitable cut-off point for elections to the Knesset in Israel has recently resulted in 'hung' assemblies, giving minor parties a disproportionately larger influence over the composition of the government than their voting strengths would normally merit.

In contrast, tighter 'cut-off' variants of the list system are used in some countries so as to favour the larger parties. The most prominent example is Turkey, where parties need 10 per cent of the national vote to secure entry to parliament and 25 or 33 per cent respectively of the vote in three- or four-member constituencies. In addition, bonus seats are given to the party achieving the most votes. This 'up-loaded' system is designed partly to exclude small religious extremist parties from the National Assembly but also as a means of discouraging coalition government. It had the consequence in the November 1987 general election of giving the incumbent Motherland Party (ANAP) 65 per cent of Grand National Assembly (GNA) seats with only a 36 per cent share of the popular vote. Turkey's two other major national parties, the opposition Social Democrats (SHP) and True Path (DYP) parties, captured 25 and 19 per cent of the national vote respectively and 22 and 13 per cent of GNA seats. In contrast, the remaining minor parties, despite receiving 20 per cent of the popular vote, secured no GNA representation at all.

In less democratic countries, even cruder forms of 'up-loading' are to be found. In Paraguay, for example, where congressional elections are fought on single national party lists, the party which receives most votes is automatically awarded two-thirds of the assembly seats. This can be termed a form of 'disproportionate representation'.

An important consequence of the operation of party list systems is the effect on female representation. A clear feature of its working in Western Europe has been to promote the return of substantially higher proportions of female members than has been the case in elections based on absolute majority systems, operating in similar socio-cultural conditions. Thus, at the present time, in the assemblies of the Scandinavian countries where a party list system is used, women comprise more than a quarter of their memberships. In Iceland an all-female political party, the Women's Alliance Movement, has held seats in the Althing since 1983. Elsewhere in continental Europe the proportionate figure for female assembly representation invariably exceeds 10 per cent. In comparison, in the SP legislatures of the United Kingdom, New Zealand and United States the figure stands at less than 5 per cent.

Another useful aspect of list systems is that there is no necessity for by-elections when members retire or depart. Candidates ranking next on the party's previous list are automatically drafted in to fill vacancies as they arise. There are some exceptions to this, however, Greece being one.

By-elections are also avoided in France, where the SB operates, since all candidates must fight with a running-mate (*suppléant*) who will take their place if they resign to assume ministerial office, retire or die in office.

6.3.5 The additional member (AM)

The additional member system makes use of party lists but also allows the elector to vote for a candidate, two votes being cast, one for the candidate and one for the party. Half the assembly is then elected on a simple plurality (SP) basis and the other half, using the party lists, is chosen so that the membership of the chamber accurately reflects the national vote. The party lists, therefore, are used to correct any unfairness in the SP system.

The main advantage of the additional member system is that it uses single-member constituencies and so keeps the link between the candidate and the elector. At the same time, however, a high level of 'proportionality', comparable with the 'best' list systems, is achieved.

AM is used principally in elections to West Germany's Bundestag. Here lists operate at the state (*Land*) level, but to qualify for assembly representation on the second list ballot (*Zweitstimme*) parties need to secure at least 5 per cent of the national vote.

Forms of AM also operate in Senegal, where the system was introduced in 1973 with the assistance of West German political consultants; in Guatemala, for a quarter of its Congress; and in South Korea, for a similar proportion of National Assembly seats. Mexico has only a partial AM system used for two-fifths of the 500 seats in the Chamber of Deputies, which are filled predominantly from minority parties' lists. The Upper Chamber of the Japanese Diet has also been elected by a variant of AM since 1982, with 40 per cent of its seats being filled by national level PR.

6.3.6 The single transferable vote (STV)

The single transferable vote (STV) is, in many respects, theoretically the best method of ensuring proportional representation. It uses multi-member constituencies which may be large but which can be small enough to elect three representatives. All the candidates are listed on the ballot form, usually in alphabetical order, and the elector states an order of preference, from 1, 2 downwards. All the votes cast are counted and the 'electoral quota' is calculated, in other words, the minimum number of votes needed to be elected.

The calculation would work as follows:

$$\frac{(\text{total number of votes})}{(\text{number of seats} + 1)} + 1 = \text{electoral quota (Droop formula)}$$

Thus, in a three-member constituency with a total of 120,000 votes cast, the quota would be:

$$\frac{(120{,}000)}{(3 + 1)} + 1 = 30{,}001$$

and any candidate with 30,001 or more first preference votes would automatically be elected.

For example, there might be 12 candidates for the three seats and only one who obtained more than the 30,000 quota, in fact 31,001, or 1,000 more than was needed. All the second preferences of voters who made the top candidate their first choice would be counted and their percentage distribution among the other candidates calculated. The 1,000 'surplus' votes would then be redistributed on this percentage basis. If this redistribution brought another candidate up to to the 30,001 quota he or she would be elected and the process would continue until all three seats were filled. If all the surplus second preference votes were used up and there were still seats to be filled then the bottom candidates would be progressively eliminated, with their second preferences redistributed among the other candidates on a proportionate basis.

STV requires multi-member constituencies but they are often smaller than those used in some varieties of the party list system. STV is also usually more 'personalised' than the list system, theoretically giving electors the power to choose between candidates of the same party. Despite this, high degrees of proportionality, ranging from 90 to 95 per cent, have been achieved.

Described as the 'Anglo-Saxon version of PR', STV is currently used in lower chamber elections by both Ireland and Malta. It is also used for elections to Australia's Senate and to the lower House of the Assembly in the state of Tasmania, as well as for Sri Lankan presidential elections and local government elections in Northern Ireland.

6.3.7 The limited vote (LV)

The final PR variant, the limited vote (LV), is currently used in two states, by Japan for lower chamber elections, and by Spain for its upper house contests. Under this system, multi-member constituencies are used, each returning between three to five members, but electors are allowed only one, non-transferable, vote. The three to five candidates winning most votes in each constituency are then subsequently returned on a simple plurality basis.

The use of multi-member constituencies means that minor parties, through restricting themselves to one candidature per constituency, can win seats on relatively low shares, about 15–30 per cent, depending on the size of the constituency, of the total vote. In this respect, the LV system, which is really only 'semi-proportional', differs significantly from the SP, with its single-member constituencies.

6.4 Election turnouts

The size of the election turnout provides some information about popular participation in the political process but it can also be misleading.

Turnouts in the United Kingdom parliamentary general elections of 1979, 1983 and 1987 were 76.2, 72.7 and 75.4 per cent respectively. These figures compare favourably with those for UK local government elections and for elections to the European Parliament, which were as low as 33 per cent in 1984 and 36 per cent in 1989 for the whole of country, and lower still for England alone. West German Bundestag election turnouts have varied between 84 and 91 per cent for the years 1976–87, showing a generally declining tendency. In France, National Assembly election turnouts have invariably ranged between 71 and 83 per cent during the last two decades, while presidential election figures have averaged 86–87 per cent. In the Scandinavian countries of Denmark, Finland, Norway and Sweden, parliamentary election turnouts of between 80 and 90 per cent are the norm.

In general, then, in the liberal democracies of Western Europe turnouts for elections to national assemblies currently cluster within a range band of 70–90 per cent. In all the countries for which turnout figures have been quoted voting is not compulsory. The state, however, shoulders the burden of responsibility for registering electors and compiling the electoral roll in advance of polling day.

In contrast, in the United States the burden of registration falls upon individual citizens, with parties being employed as a private back-up mobilising force. At the present, however, fewer than 70 per cent of the US population of voting age are registered, including only 40 per cent of Hispanics and 50 per cent of those in the lowest socio-economic category. For this reason, US national election turnouts are, by comparative standards, unusually low, standing at barely 50 to 53 per cent of the adult population, though 75 to 80 per cent of those registered, for the presidential elections between 1980 and 1988, and at only 37 per cent for the mid-term congressional and governorship elections of November 1986. Similar low turnout figures can be found in Switzerland, only 49 per cent of the electorate taking the trouble to vote in the October 1987 Nationalrat elections.

Low electoral participation is also, not surprisingly, a feature of many of the world's poorer liberal and emergent democracies. In India and Botswana, for example, turnouts have averaged 50–60 per cent for recent Lok Sabha and National Assembly elections. In Mexico, the figures have been around 50 per cent for presidential and Chamber of Deputies elections, and in Colombia and Thailand, below 40 per cent for elections to their assemblies.

There are, however, some notable exceptions. In Sri Lanka and the Bahamas, for example, parliamentary election turnouts have invariably exceeded 85 per cent; in Gambia, Honduras, Morocco and Vanuatu 80 per cent; in Costa Rica, Dominica and Suriname 75 per cent; in Barbados and Malaysia 70 per cent; and in Papua New Guinea, despite the remoteness of many polling stations, above 66 per cent. In Lebanon, the archaic requirement that electors must cast their ballot in their ancestral villages or towns serves to depress turnouts to a level of 50–55 per cent.

In communist states, turnouts for elections at all levels are invariably high, usually exceeding 95 per cent and sometimes getting as near to a 100 per cent response as is physically feasible. In the Albanian People's Assembly election of 1987, for example, there was, officially, only one spoiled ballot paper among the entire electorate of 1.83 million.

In the USSR's Supreme Soviet elections of 1984 a turnout of 99.99 per cent was registered, implying that fewer than 20,000, out of an electorate of more than 184 million, failed to vote. This does not, however, necessarily denote great popular enthusiam for the party or the electoral process. For such ritualised contests, the local party machine usually puts considerable effort into securing high turnouts, with up to a quarter of the adult population, party members, local state and work council representatives and 'reputable citizens', being brought into action as campaign workers. Special transport is laid on for the house-bound and ballot boxes are posted at every workplace and housing complex, as well as being carried out to those living in remote areas.

Faced with this huge mobilisation and publicity drive, the average citizen who is not a party member may well feel that for the small cost of casting a vote there may be some potential advantage in openly showing support for the official candidate. Only rarely, as was the case in Polish local elections of 1984, do citizens 'rebel' and stay at home. On this occasion, the official turnout slumped to 75 per cent, although government opponents suggested the true figure was closer to 60 per cent.

High electoral turnouts are also invariably the case in one-party nationalistic socialist and authoritarian nationalist regimes. In Indonesia, for example, turnouts are put at over 90 per cent and in Togo at 98 per cent. In Syria and the Ivory Coast, however, they have been as low as 45 and 30 per cent respectively.

Some countries make voting compulsory. This compulsion may be real, in the sense of running the risk of being fined for not voting, but in most cases the offenders are rarely, if ever, prosecuted. Some constitutions, including most in communist states, specify voting as a 'civic' or 'socialist' duty but stop short of compulsion. Whether or not the requirement is enforced, there is evidence that turnouts in countries which formally make voting compulsory are generally perceptibly higher than in those which do not. Turnouts of 95–98 per cent are, for example, the norm in Australia and Belgium. However, lower turnouts of 80 per cent, and sometimes substantially less, have been recorded in the Dominican Republic, Greece and Peru.

Table 32

WORLD ELECTION AND VOTING PATTERNS

	Executive Choice	Assembly Choice				Minimum Voting Age	Voting Compulsory	Date of 1st Female Franchise
		Lower Chamber		Upper Chamber				
Afghanistan	College	Direct	UAS SP	Direct	UAS SP	20	Yes	1964
Albania	Party	Direct	UAS SP	—	—	18	SD	1946
Algeria	Direct	Direct	UAS SP	—	—	18	—	1958
Angola	Party	Coll/App	UAS SP	—	—	18	—	1975
Antigua & Barbuda	Assembly	Direct	UAS SP	Appointed	—	18	—	1951
Argentina	College	Direct	UAS SP	College	—	18	Yes	1947
Australia	Assembly	Direct	UAS AV	Direct	UAS STV	18	Yes	1902
Austria	Assembly	Direct	UAS PLS	College	—	19	—	1919
Bahamas	Asembly	Direct	UAS SP	Appointed	—	18	—	1962
Bahrain	Absolute	—	—	—	—	—	—	—
Bangladesh	Direct	Direct	UAS SP	—	—	18	—	1956
Barbados	Assembly	Direct	UAS SP	Appointed	—	18	—	1951
Belgium	Assembly	Direct	UAS PLS	El/Coll	—	18	Yes	1948
Belize	Assembly	Direct	UAS SP	Appointed	—	18	—	1954
Benin	Assembly	Direct	UAS SP	—	—	18	—	1956
Bhutan	Absolute	E/A	UAS SP	—	—	—	—	—
Bolivia	Direct	Direct	UAS SP	Direct	UAS SP	21	Yes	1952
Botswana	Assembly	Direct	UAS SP	—	—	21	—	1966
Brazil	Direct	Direct	UAS PLS	Direct	UAS PLS	16	Yes	1932
Brunei	Absolute	—	—	—	—	—	—	—
Bulgaria	Party	Direct	UAS SP	—	—	18	SD	1947
Burkina Faso	Military	—	—	—	—	—	—	1956
Burma	Party	Direct	UAS SP	—	—	18	—	1935
Burundi	Direct	E/A	UAS SP	—	—	18	—	1961
Cambodia	Party	Direct	UAS SP	—	—	18	SD	1956
Cameroon	Direct	Direct	UAS SP	—	—	21	—	1956
Canada	Assembly	Direct	UAS SP	Appointed	—	18	—	1920
Cape Verde	Assembly	Direct	UAS SP	—	—	18	—	1975

Table 32—World Election and Voting Patterns (contd.)

	Executive Choice	*Assembly Choice* *Lower Chamber*		*Upper Chamber*		*Minimum Voting Age*	*Voting Compulsory*	*Date of 1st Female Franchise*
Central African Rep	Military	—	—	—	—	—	—	—
Chad	Military	—	—	—	—	—	—	1956
Chile	Military	Direct	UAS SP	E/A	UAS SP	18	—	1949
China	Party	College	UAS SP	—	—	18	SD	1947
Colombia	Direct	Direct	UAS PLS	Direct	UAS PLS	18	—	1957
Comoros	Direct	Direct	UAS SP	—	—	18	—	1978
Congo	Party	Direct	UAS SP	—	—	18	—	1956
Costa Rica	Direct	Direct	UAS PLS	—	—	18	Yes	1949
Cuba	Party	Direct	UAS SP	—	—	16	SD	1934
Cyprus	Direct/SB	Direct	UAS PLS	—	—	21	Yes	1959
Czechoslovakia	Party	Direct	UAS SB	Direct	UAS SB	18	SD	1919
Denmark	Assembly	Direct	UAS PLS	—	—	18	—	1915
Djibouti	Direct	Direct	UAS SP	—	—	18	—	1957
Dominica	Assembly	E/A	UAS SP	—	—	18	—	1967
Dominican Republic	Direct	Direct	UAS PLS	Direct	UAS SP	18	Yes	1942
Ecuador	Direct/SB	Direct	UAS PLS	—	—	18	Yes	1929
Egypt	Direct	E/A	UAS SB	—	—	18	Yes	1956
El Salvador	Direct	Direct	UAS SP	—	—	18	Yes	1950
Equatorial Guinea	Direct	Direct	UAS SP	—	—	18	—	1982
Ethiopia	Party	Direct	UAS SP	—	—	18	—	1955
Fiji	Assembly	Direct	UAS SP	Appointed	—	18	—	1970
Finland	El/Coll	Direct	UAS PLS	—	—	18	—	1906
France	Direct/SB	Direct	UAS SB	College	—	18	—	1944
Gabon	Direct	E/A	UAS SP	—	—	21	—	1956
Gambia	Direct	E/A	UAS SP	—	—	21	—	1961
East Germany	Party	Direct	UAS SP	—	—	18	SD	1919
West Germany	Assembly	Direct	UAS AMS	Appointed	—	18	—	1919
Ghana	Military	—	—	—	—	18	—	1955
Greece	Assembly	Direct	UAS PLS	—	—	18	Yes	1952
Grenada	Assembly	Direct	UAS SP	Appointed	—	18	—	1967

Table 32—World Election and Voting Patterns (contd.)

	Executive Choice	*Assembly Choice*				*Minimum Voting Age*	*Voting Compulsory*	*Date of 1st Female Franchise*
		Lower Chamber		*Upper Chamber*				
Guatemala	Direct	Direct	UAS AMS	—	—	18	Yes	1965
Guinea	Military	—	—	—	—	—	—	1956
Guinea-Bissau	Assembly	College	UAS SP	—	—	15	—	1973
Guyana	Party	El/Coll	UAS PLS	—	—	18	—	1966
Haiti	Direct	—	—	—	—	18	—	1950
Honduras	Direct	Direct	UAS PLS	—	—	18	Yes	1955
Hungary	Party	Direct	UAS SB	—	—	18	SD	1945
Iceland	Assembly	Direct	UAS PLS	—	—	18	—	1915
India	Assembly	E/A	UAS SP	College	—	18	—	1949
Indonesia	College	E/A	UAS PLS	—	—	18	—	1945
Iran	Direct	Direct	UAS SB	—	—	16	—	1963
Iraq	Party	Direct	UAS SP	—	—	18	—	1964
Ireland	Assembly	Direct	UAS STV	Coll/App	—	18	—	1922
Israel	Assembly	Direct	UAS PLS	—	—	18	—	1948
Italy	Assembly	Direct	UAS PLS	E/A	UAS PLS	18	CD	1945
Ivory Coast	Direct/SB	Direct	UAS SB	—	—	21	—	1956
Jamaica	Assembly	Direct	UAS SP	Appointed	—	18	—	1944
Japan	Assembly	Direct	UAS LV	Direct	UAS AMS	20	—	1945
Jordan	Heredit	Direct	UAS SP	Appointed	—	20	—	1982
Kenya	Direct	E/A	UAS SP	—	—	18	—	1963
Kiribati	Direct	E/A	UAS SB	—	—	18	—	1979
North Korea	Party	Direct	UAS SP	—	—	17	SD	1946
South Korea	Direct	Direct	UAS AMS	—	—	20	—	1946
Kuwait	Absolute	—	—	—	—	—	—	—
Laos	Party	Direct	UAS SP	—	—	18	—	1956
Lebanon	College	Direct	UAS PLS	—	—	21	—	1957
Lesotho	Heredit	—	—	—	—	—	—	1966
Liberia	Direct	Direct	UAS SP	Direct	UAS SP	18	—	1946
Libya	Party	College	UAS SP	—	—	18	—	1963
Luxembourg	Assembly	Direct	UAS PLS	—	—	18	Yes	1918

Table 32—World Election and Voting Patterns (contd.)

	Executive Choice	*Assembly Choice*				*Minimum Voting Age*	*Voting Compulsory*	*Date of 1st Female Franchise*
		Lower Chamber		*Upper Chamber*				
Madagascar	Direct	Direct	UAS SP	—	—	18	—	1956
Malawi	Direct	E/A	UAS SP	—	—	21	—	1964
Malaysia	Assembly	Direct	UAS SP	Coll/App	—	21	—	1957
Maldives	Direct	E/A	UAS SP	—	—	21	—	1964
Mali	Direct	Direct	UAS SP	—	—	18	—	1956
Malta	Assembly	Direct	UAS STV	—	—	18	—	1947
Mauritania	Military	—	—	—	—	—	—	1956
Mauritius	Assembly	E/A	UAS SP	—	—	18	—	1958
Mexico	Direct	Direct	UAS AMS	Direct	UAS SP	18	—	1953
Mongolia	Party	Direct	UAS SP	—	—	18	SD	1924
Morocco	Heredit	El/Coll	UAS SP	—	—	21	—	1959
Mozambique	Party	Direct	UAS SP	—	—	18	—	1975
Nauru	Assembly	Direct	UAS SP	—	—	20	Yes	1968
Nepal	Heredit	E/A	UAS SP	—	—	21	—	1951
Netherlands	Assembly	Direct	UAS PLS	College	—	18	—	1919
New Zealand	Assembly	Direct	UAS SP	—	—	18	—	1893
Nicaragua	Direct	Direct	UAS PLS	—	—	18	—	1955
Niger	Military	—	—	—	—	—	—	1956
Nigeria	Military	—	—	—	—	18	—	1954
Norway	Assembly	Direct	UAS PLS	—	—	18	—	1913
Oman	Absolute	—	—	—	—	—	—	—
Pakistan	Direct	E/A	UAS SP	College	—	18	—	1956
Panama	Direct	Direct	UAS SP	—	—	18	—	1946
Papua New Guinea	Assembly	Direct	UAS SP	—	—	18	—	1975
Paraguay	Military	Direct	UAS PLS	Direct	UAS PLS	18	Yes	1961
Peru	Direct/SB	Direct	UAS PLS	Direct	UAS PLS	18	Yes	1955
Philippines	Direct	E/A	UAS SP	Direct	UAS SP	16	Yes	1937
Poland	Party	Direct	UAS SB	Direct	UAS SB	18	SD	1918
Portugal	Direct	Direct	UAS PLS	—	—	18	—	1975
Qatar	Absolute	—	—	—	—	—	—	—

Table 32—World Election and Voting Patterns (contd.)

	Executive Choice	*Assembly Choice*				*Minimum Voting Age*	*Voting Compulsory*	*Date of 1st Female Franchise*
		Lower Chamber		*Upper Chamber*				
Romania	Party	Direct	UAS SB	—	—	18	SD	1948
Rwanda	Military	Direct	UAS SP	—	—	18	—	1962
St Christopher & Nevis	Assembly	E/A	UAS SP	—	—	18	—	1967
St Lucia	Assembly	Direct	UAS SP	Appointed	—	18	—	1967
St Vincent & Grenadines	Assembly	E/A	UAS SP	—	—	18	—	1967
Sao Tome & Principe	Party	College	UAS SP	—	—	18	—	1982
Saudi Arabia	Absolute	—	—	—	—	—	—	—
Senegal	Direct	Direct	UAS AMS	—	—	21	—	1956
Seychelles	Direct	E/A	UAS SP	—	—	17	—	1979
Sierra Leone	Party	E/A	UAS SP	—	—	21	—	1961
Singapore	Assembly	Direct	UAS SP	—	—	21	Yes	1965
Solomon Isles	Assembly	Direct	UAS SP	—	—	21	—	1978
Somalia	Party	E/A	UAS SP	—	—	18	—	1958
South Africa	Assembly	E/A	UAS SP	—	—	18	—	1930
Soviet Union	Party	Direct	UAS SB	Direct	UAS SB	18	SD	1917
Spain	Assembly	Direct	UAS PLS	Direct	UAS LV	21	—	1977
Sri Lanka	Direct	Direct	UAS PLS	—	—	18	—	1934
Sudan	Military	Direct	UAS SP	—	—	18	—	1965
Suriname	Assembly	Direct	UAS SP	—	—	18	—	1975
Swaziland	Heredit	Coll/App	—	Coll/App	—	18	—	1968
Sweden	Assembly	Direct	UAS PLS	—	—	18	—	1919
Switzerland	Assembly	Direct	UAS PLS	Direct	UAS SP	20	—	1971
Syria	Direct	Direct	UAS SP	—	—	18	—	1949
Taiwan	College	El/App	UAS SP	—	—	20	—	1947
Tanzania	Party	El/App	UAS SP	—	—	18	—	1961
Thailand	Assembly	Direct	UAS SP	Appointed	—	21	—	1932
Togo	Party	Direct	UAS SP	—	—	18	—	1956
Tonga	Heredit	E/A	UAS SP	—	—	21	—	1960
Trinidad & Tobago	Assembly	Direct	UAS SP	Appointed	—	18	—	1946
Tunisia	Direct	Direct	UAS SP	—	—	20	—	1959

Table 32—World Election and Voting Patterns (contd.)

	Executive Choice	Assembly Choice: Lower Chamber		Assembly Choice: Upper Chamber		Minimum Voting Age	Voting Compulsory	Date of 1st Female Franchise
Turkey	Assembly	Direct	UAS PLS	—	—	21	—	1934
Tuvalu	Assembly	Direct	UAS SP	—	—	18	—	1978
Uganda	Assembly	Direct	UAS SP	—	—	18	—	1962
United Arab Emirates	Absolute	—	—	—	—	—	—	—
United Kingdom	Assembly	Direct	UAS SP	Heredit/ Appointed	—	18	—	1928
United States	College	Direct	UAS SP	Direct	UAS SP	18	—	1920
Uruguay	Direct	Direct	UAS PLS	Direct	UAS PLS	18	CD	1932
Vanuatu	Assembly	Direct	UAS SB	—	—	18	—	1980
Venezuela	Direct	Direct	UAS PLS	Direct	UAS PLS	18	Yes	1947
Vietnam	Party	Direct	UAS SP	—	—	18	SD	1956
Western Samoa	Assembly	College	—	—	—	—	—	1962
North Yemen	College	Direct	UAS SP	—	—	18	—	1979
South Yemen	Party	Direct	UAS SP	—	—	18	—	1970
Yugoslavia	Party	College	UAS SP	College	UAS SP	18	SD	1946
Zaire	Party	Direct	UAS SP	—	—	18	—	1960
Zambia	Party	E/A	UAS SP	—	—	18	—	1964
Zimbabwe	Party	Direct	UAS SP	Coll/App	—	18	—	1980

KEY:

Direct	—Direct election by the electorate	El/Coll	—Part elected direct and part indirectly elected by college
College	—Indirect election by an electoral college	LV	—Limited Vote
Assembly	—Indirect election by the assembly	SP	—Simple plurality vote
Party	—Indirect de-facto election by the party	AV	—Alternative Vote
Absolute	—Absolute executive	SB	—Second Ballot
Military	—Military executive or sole nominee of the military	PLS	—Party List System
Heredit	—Hereditary	AMS	—Additional Member System
UAS	—Universal adult suffrage	STV	—Single Transferable Vote
E/A	—Part elected and part appointed	CD	—'Civic Duty' or 'Obligation'
Coll/App	—Part elected by college and part appointed	SD	—'Socialist Duty'

Table 33

WORLD ELECTION SYSTEMS
SUMMARY TABLE
DIRECT VOTING SYSTEMS FOR LOWER CHAMBERS

All States

Voting System	*Number of States*	*As % of Total States*
Simple Plurality	87	64
Party List PR	32	22
Second Ballot	11	8
Additional Member PR	5	3
Single Transferable Vote	2	1
Alternative Vote	1	1
Limited Vote	1	1
Total	139*	100

*The assemblies in eight other states are elected indirectly by other assemblies below them or by electoral colleges.

Liberal-Democratic and Emergent-Democratic States

Voting System	*Number of States*	*As % of Total States*
Simple Plurality	40	49
Party List PR	30	37
Second Ballot	4	5
Additional Member PR	4	5
Single Transferable Vote	2	2
Alternative Vote	1	1
Limited Vote	1	1
Total	82*	100

*The assembly of the remaining state, Western Samoa, is indirectly elected.

Minimum Voting Ages

Minimum Voting Age	*Number of States*	*As % of Total States*
15 Years	1	1
16 Years	4	3
17 Years	2	1
18 Years	108	74
19 Years	1	1
20 Years	8	5
21 Years	21	14
Total	145*	100

*In two states, Bhutan and Western Samoa, voting is restricted to extended family heads.

6.5 Election rigging: methods and extent

One hundred and forty-seven countries currently hold regular national assembly elections. However, the great majority of these polls are either uncompetitive, involving no candidate or party choice, or of a 'façade' character, involving outward shows of open debate and candidate pluralism but with outcomes that are ultimately rigged by the incumbent regime.

To be truly free and democratic, election contests need to satisfy seven basic criteria:

1. Voting rights: all adults, regardless of race or religion, should enjoy the right to vote.
2. Voting practices: the ballot should be cast freely and secretly, without intimidation or subsequent redress.
3. Election timetable: elections should be held regularly, within prescribed time-limits and in accordance with constitutional rules.
4. Candidature rules: all sections of the community should be free to put forward candidates, form political parties and campaign openly.
5. Campaign: the campaign period should be of sufficient length to enable all parties and candidates to get their messages across. There should be reasonable equity in media access and coverage. Voter bribery by candidates and parties should be disallowed and maximum limits placed on campaign spending.
6. Election supervision: the campaign and vote counting should be supervised by an impartial administration, with an independent body being available to adjudicate in electoral disputes.
7. Power transfer: all parties and candidates should accept the adjudged results, handing over power to the successful party(ies) within a prescribed timetable.

At present, these conditions are approached only by the 83 countries which we have designated in Chapter 3 as liberal democracies or emergent democracies. Communist and other one-party states fall short of the important pluralism condition 4 above, while authoritarian regimes, which allow semblances of candidature pluralism, invariably breach conditions 2, 5, and 6. Even many liberal and emergent democracies, totalling up to half, fall substantially short of meeting these conditions and can thus be viewed as holding only partially democratic elections.

This is true of the two liberal democratic states of Mexico and Singapore which hold what have been termed 'dominant-party elections'. In these contests, restrictions are placed on the free operation of opposition parties, media coverage is slanted in the ruling party's favour and state resources are employed both to bribe and intimidate voters.

In Mexico, the ruling Institutional Revolutionary Party (PRI), which has monopolised power at both federal and state levels for six decades since its inception in 1929, has succeeded in winning elections through building up an extensive rural and urban corporate client network. In return for pledging electoral support, the party has ensured a steady flow of contracts, pay rises and assured employment to its local political bosses (*caciques*). In recent years, however, as economic modernisation has progressively weakened the links binding together this traditionalist patronage-system, the PRI has been forced to resort to cruder ballot-rigging as a means of ensuring its continued electoral dominance. For example, in the 1986 Chihuahua governorship election, with the help of the government appointed Federal Election Commission, it set about falsifying the electoral rolls in areas of PRI strength and restricting polling station access elsewhere. The actual count was also rigged by impersonations and the crude stuffing of ballot boxes. In the July 1988 presidential and congressional elections, faced with a strong challenge by Cuauhtemoc Cardenas of the National Democratic Front (FDN), these practices continued. As counting got under way, the Electoral Commission's computer mysteriously broke down. It was a week later before official returns were published, giving the PRI's presidential candidate 50.7 per cent of the national vote. Condition 7 of a fully democratic electoral system had clearly been breached.

In Singapore, the dominant People's Action Party (PAP) has so far eschewed such crude methods of ballot-rigging. Instead, it has maintained its electoral dominance by infringing democratic election requirements 2 and 5. First, both prior to and during election campaigns, opposition candidates have been mercilessly hounded by the state, falling prey, for example, to trumped-up fraud and tax evasion charges. Second, and more generally, the electorate has been intimidated by fears that any votes cast against the government party might be traced, with adverse employment and financial consequences. By these means the PAP has invariably been able to secure well over 70 per cent of the popular vote in parliamentary elections. In elections in September 1988 the PAP's share of the national vote fell somewhat to 63 per cent; nevertheless, it succeeded in capturing all but one of the 82 available assembly seats.

For both Mexico and Singapore the striking feature of the past decade has been the marked and steady decline in dominant party support, even on the manipulated official returns. It remains an open question however whether official totals, particularly in Mexico where the psychological 50 per cent mark is being rapidly approached, will be permitted to fall much further in future contests. A peaceful change of regime, moreover, appears out of the question.

At least four other countries which have been classified in Chapter 3 as liberal democracies have only partially democratic elections. In three of these, Costa Rica, the Dominican Republic and Venezuela, election contests have been marred by civil violence which is such a prominent feature of this region. In the fourth, Western Samoa, vote buying, both with cash and goods, and impersonation have been past features of electoral contests. In the February 1982 elections the Human Rights Protection Party (HRPP), led by Prime Minister Va'ai Kolone, was removed from office by the Supreme Court on these grounds.

The remaining 44 liberal democracies listed in Table 4 substantially meet all seven of the above 'free-election' criteria. In addition, the majority of them have experienced electorally induced changes of government at some stage or other during the past two decades: a useful, though by no means essential, indicator of election fairness. These states can reasonably be said to hold democratic elections. Within the total, however, there exist gradations of openness in relation to condition 5: election campaign periods, media access and spending ceilings.

To these 44 liberal democracies which conduct substantially democratic elections can be added, from the evidence of recent polls, eight rapidly progressing emergent democracies: Argentina, Brazil, Cyprus, Fiji, Greece, Portugal, Spain and Turkey. South Korea and the Philippines could also tentatively be added to this list, although vote-buying and intimidation remained noticeable features of the recent 1987–88 presidential and assembly elections. In the remaining 23 emergent democracies election contests continue to be marred by combinations of vote-counting frauds, dominant party candidate list rigging and bribery, as well as voter intimidation by both government and opposition groups.

A recent prominent example of electoral fraud was the Bangladesh Jatiya Sangsad election of March 1988, which was boycotted by the opposition. It was reported that one villager, Shawkat Ali, from near Dhaka, complained, typically, 'I went to cast my vote, but found that someone else had already done it.'

Vote-buying has been a conspicuous feature of recent elections in Thailand. In the July 1988 assembly elections, despite the imposition of official spending limits of 350,000 baht (US$ 15,000) per candidate, well over 3 billion baht (US$ 120 million) were distributed to voters by the 3,606 candidates standing. In the poor north east 100 baht (US$ 4.5) packages were openly on offer for each vote pledged, plus 10,000 baht bounties for entire villages which successfully elected candidates. Altogether, it has been estimated that this election resulted in an increase of expenditure equivalent to 0.5 per cent of Thailand's GDP.

Physical violence and intimidation, both during the campaign and on election day, have been a recurrent feature of contests in South and Central America. For example, the left-wing Farabundo Marti National Liberation Front (FMLN) seriously disrupted the March 1988 assembly elections in El Salvador by guerrilla terrorist tactics, reducing turnout levels to barely 50–60 per cent. The Colombian local election contest in the same month was marred by even more serious intimidation, by both right- and left-wing 'hit-squads', with more than 150 candidates and several hundred campaign activists being brutally assassinated.

Of the 54 liberal and emergent democracies which on the broadest count can be viewed as holding substantially democratic elections 39 per cent are in Western Europe, 19 per cent in Oceania, another 19 per cent in the Caribbean and 9 per cent in Asia. Of the remaining 93 countries holding assembly elections, 16 are communist states. Here, election contests are subject to rigid 'democratic-centralist' control although moves towards a new type of 'socialist pluralism' are under way in Hungary, Poland and the Soviet Union. A further 24, the bulk of which are in Africa, are one-party socialist or nationalist states, in which non-party candidates are outlawed. This leaves 53 countries, 32 per cent of the world total, in which elections are at present of a 'façade' nature. In these states, despite outward semblances of candidature pluralism, the results are effectively rigged to the incumbent regime's advantage. Control of the media, the electoral commission and the vote-counting process are the principal means of achieving this, following the cynical maxim, 'He who counts, elects'.

Also of importance is the imposition of severe constraints, and frequently outright bans, by the ruling regime on the candidature and campaign activity of opposition members. All such features were prominent in the February 1988 presidential and assembly elections in Paraguay, which returned General Alfredo Stroessner and his ruling Colorado Party with a 90 per cent share of the vote, the remaining 10 per cent being apportioned between legalised opposition candidates. A turnout of 93 per cent was officially claimed, but the opposition-formed Committee for Free Elections estimated the true figure to be below 50 per cent in many areas. The stuffing of ballot boxes and the impersonation of dead electors were practices which were frequently alleged.

Not surprisingly, such loaded contests are often succeeded by frustrated eruptions of opposition, leading to street violence. In Senegal, where the prepared result for the February 1988 presidential election was announced almost as soon as voting stopped, riots erupted in the streets of Dakar and Thies, prompting the government to arrest opposition leaders and declare a state of emergency which lasted for two months. In the Philippines, in February 1986, stronger and better co-ordinated public opposition to flagrant ballot rigging succeeded in bringing down the regime of Ferdinand Marcos. Even the long-established Stroessner regime in Paraguay was ousted by the military within a year of the disputed election result.

RECOMMENDED READING

Bogdanor, V. and Butler, D. (eds), *Democracy and Elections: Electoral Systems and Their Consequences*, Cambridge University Press, 1983.

Bogdanor, V., *What is Proportional Representation?: A Guide to the Issues*, Martin Robertson, 1984.

Crewe, I. and Denver, D. (eds), *Electoral Change in Western Democracies: Campaign of 1983*, Croom Helm, 1985.

Dalton, R. L., Flanagan S. and Beck, P. A. (eds), *Electoral Change in Advanced Industrial Societies: Realignment or Dealignment*, Princeton University Press, 1984.

The Economist, *World Atlas of Elections*, Economist Publications, 1986.

Eisenstadt, S. N. and Lemarchand, R. (eds), *Political Clientelism, Patronage and Development*, Sage Publications, 1981.

Hague, R and Harrop, M., *Comparative Government and Politics: An Introduction*, 2nd edn., Macmillan, 1987, Ch. 6.

Harrop, M. and Miller, W., *Elections and Voters: A Comparative Introduction*, Macmillan, 1987.

Hermet, G., Rose, R. and Rouquie, A. (eds), *Elections Without Choice*, Macmillan, 1978.

Mackie, T. T. and Rose, R., *International Almanac of Electoral History*, Macmillan, 1982.

Roberts, G. K., *An Introduction to Comparative Government*, Edward Arnold, 1986, Ch. 4.

CHAPTER 7

POLITICAL PARTIES

7.1 The mobilisation of sectional interests

Everyone has an interest in something, even if it amounts to little more than pure self-interest or self-preservation. Millions of people are regular television watchers and if someone sought to deprive them of this pleasure it is certain that they would be up in arms immediately. Some people attach great value to personal privacy and will resist any intrusion, particularly by a public body. Others are more concerned about what they see as the rights of others. Often they feel a duty to protect the seemingly defenceless, especially in the animal kingdom.

Whereas interests are shared by thousands, or even millions, of people, only a relative few will take the trouble to mobilise them into a source of influence and power. These are the organisers of interests: the active members of interest groups.

An interest group is therefore an association of people who come together, or are brought together, to represent, promote and defend a particular interest or set of interests. There are numerous examples to choose from.

Some are chiefly promotional, seeking to bring attention to the needs of particular people, such as the unmarried mother or the disabled. Others are mainly defensive, such as the environmental groups, anxious to protect natural conditions and phenomena. All are representational in one way or another but some, such as the labour unions and professional organisations, are particularly strong in this respect.

A distinction can be made between groups which are concerned with limited, specific interests and those which aim to promote and defend a much wider cross-section. These wider interest groups are often referred to as cause groups. They fight for a particular cause, irrespective of whether or not the people they seek to help have direct contact with them, or even know of their existence. They are usually impelled by higher motives than self-interest and could well be called conscience groups.

Cause groups usually ignore national boundaries and can be found throughout the world. Greenpeace, Amnesty International, Oxfam, Christian Aid are all well-known examples.

7.2 Pressure groups

Sometimes interest groups are referred to as pressure groups as if the two terms are synonymous. This is not strictly the case.

A pressure group is a group representing an interest which seeks to achieve its aims by putting pressure on government. It will use a wide range of tactics to try to influence public opinion but it knows that ultimately the pressure must be on the government in whichever country it operates.

International cause groups will usually exert pressure on governments indirectly, knowing that they are unlikely to gain direct access to national seats of power. They make their case to the public at large, utilising the mass media, hoping that popular opinion in each country will apply the necessary pressure to produce action.

7.3 Monism, pluralism and corporatism

A monistic state may be said to be one in which interest group activity is frowned upon, discouraged or even banned. This contrasts with a pluralistic state where independently organised groups freely operate and act as intermediaries between the public and the government.

Communist regimes and most other one-party states are essentially monistic, mainly because they find it difficult to 'manage' an organisation which is outside the established political system. Because it is outside, its actions are unpredictable and unpredictability is seen as a threat to the settled order of things. A good example of this has been the protracted opposition of the Polish government to the labour union, Solidarity.

Churches in one-party states produce similar problems. The activities of religious organisations extend beyond national interests, as defined by the ruling regime, and, again, tend to produce unpredictable behaviour. There are, however, states where a religion has been absorbed into the political system so as to become not only acceptable but its main driving force. Iran provides a striking example of this kind of theocratic state.

Some secular one-party states have accepted that interest activity cannot be ignored but can be managed if absorbed into the political system. Thus the pressures which in a pluralistic system express themselves in a wide variety of outlets are channelled into the state machine. As the state institutions are invariably controlled by party activists, interests become easily controllable too.

In stark contrast, pressure groups flourish in pluralistic systems, even though the most liberally inclined governments may find them an inconvenience. The United States is an example of a country where interest groups are particularly virile. Over the years their activities have become increasingly evident and their methods more sophisticated so that members of Congress, state governments, and even the presidency, ignore them at their peril.

In some parts of the world the pluralistic state has become the corporate state in which a limited number of powerful interest groups, industrial, financial and labour, dominate the political scene, the government choosing, or being forced, to negotiate with them before making a major policy decision.

In Austria, for example, political decisions are often arrived at, with the government's blessing, following discussions between strong chambers of commerce and labour unions. Once agreement between these powerful bodies has been reached the government takes over the task of legitimising and implementing what has been agreed.

The so-called 'social contract' in the United Kingdom in the mid-1970s, between the Labour governments of Harold Wilson and James Callaghan and the Trades Union Congress, whereby the unions accepted a policy of wage restraint in return for the government's promise to follow an agreed social welfare programme, was another strong example of corporatism in a liberal democratic state.

It can be argued that pluralism extends and enhances democracy, because it encourages people who would not normally involve themselves in politics to contribute to the policy-making process. Corporatism, on the other hand, can be said to be anti-democratic in that it increases the power of those sections of the community who organise themselves in the pursuit of self-interest.

Furthermore, corporatism is often associated with the fascist regimes of the 1930s when, in Italy in particular, the government incorporated interest groups representing capital and labour into the state machinery.

The dividing line between thriving pluralism and corporatism is not always easy to discern and sometimes, as in the United Kingdom in the 1970s, an essentially pluralistic state may become temporarily corporatist and then, with a change of government, revert. There is evidence of corporatism in some Central and South American countries. Here not only powerful groups representing capital and labour wield enormous power and influence, but both the Church and the military are involved in major policy decisions. Indeed, those states where the military have seized executive power may be said to have taken corporatism to its ultimate limits.

In economically undeveloped areas of the world it is probably misleading to discuss interest group activity in the form of monism, pluralism or corporatism. Here, groups are considerably less well organised and less sophisticated and sometimes represent little more than an updating and extension of old tribal allegiances.

7.4 Pressure groups and political parties

A political party can best be described as an association of people who hold similar views about what should be a community's social and economic priorities and come together to establish these priorities by gaining control of the machinery of government. It is this wish to govern which distinguishes a party from an interest group but there are other important differences.

First, an interest group is concerned with a clearly defined range of interests whereas a political party is prepared to take on board a virtually unlimited number. Second, each interest group tends to play a distinctive and individualistic role while the agenda of one political party may be similar to that of another, the differences between them being based on alternative solutions to the same problems. The third difference has already been identified. An interest group aims to influence the government while a party is, or wants to be, the government.

Occasionally an interest group will step over the dividing line and become a party itself. Small political parties with narrowly defined aims, making them little removed from interest groups, have been organised in several countries. Some have been short-lived, some have survived for considerable periods with minimal memberships and funds and a few have achieved enough popular support to make them formidable political organisations.

In Denmark there is the Single Tax Party (Retsforbund) advocating the theories of the nineteenth-century US economist, Henry George (1839–97). Even on such a narrow base it has managed from time to time to win seats in the Folketing. The conservative, anti-bureaucracy Finnish Rural Party represents the interests of the lower middle class in Finland and, with a membership of about 25,000 has won assembly seats but not a position in government. In France the Ecology Political Movement (MEP) speaks for ecological and environmental interests and the National Restoration and New Royalist Action parties, although attracting little support, aim for the return of the monarchy. In West Germany the Five Per Cent Block was established in the mid-1970s, with a membership of barely 100, as a political movement to oppose the 5 per cent clause which denies parliamentary representation to parties failing to gain 5 per cent of the national vote. In contrast, the Green Party, with a large and growing membership, has emerged from among a number of ecology parties to become a significant political force. In the January 1987 election it captured 8.3 per cent of the national vote and 42 Bundestag seats.

Women's interests are being increasingly represented throughout the world by parties which have grown from non-political groups. In Belgium, for example, there is the Unified Feminist Party, in Iceland the Women's Alliance Movement and in West Germany the German Women's Movement. Parties based on specific religious aims are also found. In Israel the National Religious Party advocates the unity of people of the Jewish faith in Israel and throughout the world and the Netherlands Roman Catholic Party presses for adherence to Catholic principles on subjects such as abortion, euthanasia and sexuality.

Whereas interest groups in one form or another have existed since the beginnings of civilised life, political parties are relatively new, being products of the eighteenth century onwards. Their predecessors were cliques and factions, based usually on personal or family power. The modern party displays three essential features: a permanent structure and organisation; an authority to represent people, whether or not they are members of the party, based on open elections; and an intention to form a government or participate in government.

Table 34 lists the leading parties in the contemporary world and their political orientations. The number of active parties in each state, as shown, is something of an approximation in some cases because the emergence and disappearance of minor groupings is often a notable feature of some political systems.

Table 34

POLITICAL PARTIES OF THE WORLD

*See notes below

State	*Number of Parties*	*Leading Parties*	*Orientation*
Afghanistan	5*	Communist People's Democratic Party of Afghanistan (PDPA)	Marxist-Leninist
Albania	1	Party of Labour of Albania (PLA)	Marxist-Leninist
Algeria	1	National Liberation Front (FLN)	Socialist-Islamic
Angola	1	People's Movement for the Liberation of Angola—Workers' Party (MLPA-PT)	Marxist-Leninist

Table 34—Political Parties of the World (contd.)
*See notes below

State	*Number of Parties*	*Leading Parties*	*Orientation*
Antigua & Barbuda	6	Antigua Labour Party (ALP)	Moderate left of centre
		Progressive Labour Movement (PLM)	Moderate left of centre
Argentina	19	Radical Union Party (UCR)	Moderate centre
		Justice Party	Right wing
Australia	9	Australian Labor Party	Moderate left of centre
		Liberal Party of Australia	Centre right
		National Party of Australia (National Country Party in Western Australia)	Centre with emphasis on non-metropolitan needs
Austria	13	Socialist Party of Austria (SPO)	Moderate left of centre
		Austrian People's Party (OVP)	Progressive centre
		Freedom Party of Austria (FPO)	Moderate left of centre
Bahamas	5	Progressive Liberal Party (PLP)	Moderate centre nationalist
		Free National Movement (FNM)	Centre left
Bahrain	0		
Bangladesh	19	Jatiya Dal (National Party)	Islamic nationalist (military-backed)
		Bangladesh National Party (BNP)	Right of centre, Islamic
		Awami League (AL)	Moderate socialist (socialist)
Barbados	2	Barbados Labour Party (BLP)	Moderate left of centre
		Democratic Labour Party (DLP)	Left of centre
Belgium	20	Christian People's Party (CVP)	Christian centre-left Dutch-speaking
		Christian Social Party (PSC)	Christian centre-left French-speaking
		Socialist Party (SP)	Left of centre, Dutch-speaking
		Socialist Party (PS)	Left of centre, French-speaking
		Freedom and Progress Party (PVV)	Moderate centre, Dutch-speaking
		Liberal Reform Party (PRL)	Moderate centre, French-speaking
		People's Union's (VU)	Flemish nationalist
Belize	2	People's United Party (PUP)	Moderate left of centre
		United Democratic Party (UDP)	Right of centre
Benin	1	Party of the People's Revolution of Benin (BRBP)	Marxist-Leninist
Bhutan	0		
Bolivia	33	National Revolutionary Movement (MNR)	Nationalist centre
		Nationalist Democratic Action Party (ADN)	Nationalist right wing
		Movement of the Revolutionary Left (MIR)	Nationalist Marxist
Botswana	6	Botswana Democratic Party (BDP)	Nationalist moderate centre
		Botswana National Front (BNF)	Left of centre
		Botswana People's Party (BPP)	Nationalist

Table 34—Political Parties of the World (contd.)
*See notes below

State	*Number of Parties*	*Leading Parties*	*Orientation*
Brazil	6	Social Democratic Party (PDS)	Moderate left of centre
		Brazilian Democratic Movement Party (PMDB)	Centre left
		Democratic Labour Party (PDT)	Moderate left of centre
		Brazilian Labour Party (PTB)	Moderate left of centre
		Independent Labour Party (PT)	Moderate left of centre
Brunei	1	Brunei National United Party (BNUP)	Businessmen loyal to the Sultan
Bulgaria	2	Bulgarian Communist Party (BCP)	Marxist-Leninist
Burkina Faso	3*	Organisation for Popular Democracy—Workers' Movement (ODP-MT)	Nationalist communist
Burma	1*	National Unity Party (NUP)	Nationalist communist
Burundi	1	Union for National Progress (UPRONA)	African socialist
Cambodia	1	Kampuchean People's Revolutionary Party (KPRP)	Marxist-Leninist
Cameroon	1	Democratic Assembly of the Cameroon People (RDPC)	Nationalist centre left
Canada	17	Progressive Conservative Party	Centre right
		Liberal Party	Nationalist centre left
		New Democratic Party	Moderate left of centre
Cape Verde	1	African Party for the Independence of Cape Verde (PAICV)	African nationalist
Central African Republic	0*		
Chad	15*	National Union for Independence (UNIR)	Nationalist
Chile	0*		
China	9	Chinese Communist Party (CCP)	Marxist-Maoist-Dengist
Colombia	10*	Liberal Party (PL)	Centrist
		Conservative Party (PCC)	Right of centre
		Democratic Unity of the Left	Left-wing coalition
Comoros	1	Union for the Progress of the Comoros (Udzima)	Nationalist Islamic
Congo	1	Congolese Labour Party (PCT)	Marxist-Leninist
Costa Rica	20	National Liberation Party (PLN)	Left of centre
		Unity Party (PUSC)	Christian centrist
		People's United Coalition (PU)	Left-wing coalition
Cuba	1	Cuban Communist Party (PCC)	Marxist-Leninist
Cyprus	7	Democratic Rally (DISY)	Centre
		Democratic Party (DIKO)	Federalist centre left
		Progressive Party of the Working People (AKEL)	Communist
		Socialist Party of Cyprus (EDEK)	Socialist
Czechoslovakia	1	Communist Party of Czechoslovakia (CPCZ)	Marxist-Leninist
Denmark	15	Social Democratic Party	Moderate left of centre
		Conservative People's Party	Free enterprise centrist
		Liberal Party	Centre left
		Socialist People's Party	Socialist
		Radical-Liberal Party	Radical centrist
Djibouti	1	People's Progress Assembly (RPP)	Nationalist
Dominica	4	Dominica Freedom Party (DFP)	Centrist
		Dominica Labour Party (DLP)	Moderate left of centre

Table 34—Political Parties of the World (contd.)
*See notes below

State	*Number of Parties*	*Leading Parties*	*Orientation*
Dominican Republic	19	Dominican Revolutionary Party (PRD)	Moderate left of centre
		Revolutionary Social Christian Party (PRSC)	Independent socialist
		Dominican Liberation Party (PLD)	Nationalist
Ecuador	21	Democratic Left (ID)	Moderate socialist
		Social Christian Party (PSC)	Christian socialist
		Concentration of Popular Forces (CFP)	Left of centre
		Radical Alfarista Front (FRA)	Radical centrist
		Radical Liberal Party (PLR)	Radical liberal
Egypt	7	National Democratic Party (NDP)	Moderate left of centre
		New Wafd Party	Nationalist
		Socialist Labour Party	Right of centre
		Socialist Liberal Party	Free enterprise centrist
El Salvador	9	Christian Democratic Party (PDC)	Moderate left of centre
		Nationalist Republican Alliance (ARENA)	Right wing
		National Conciliation Party (PCN)	Right of centre
Equatorial Guinea	1	Democratic Party of Equatorial Guinea (PDGE)	Nationalist military
Ethiopia	1	Workers' Party of Ethiopia (WPE)	Marxist-Leninist
Fiji	5	Fiji Labour Party (FLP)	Left of centre
		National Federation Party (NFP)	Moderate left of centre
		Alliance Party (AP)	Moderate centrist
Finland	12	Social Democratic Party (SDP)	Moderate left of centre
		National Coalition Party (KOK)	Moderate right of centre
		Centre Party (KP)	Moderate centrist
		Finnish People's Democratic League (SKDL)	Left-wing coalition
		Swedish People's Party	Centre left
		Finnish Rural Party (SMP)	Moderate decentralist
France	39†	Rally for the Republic (RPR)	Right of centre
		Socialist Party (PS)	Left of centre
		Union for French Democracy (UDF)	Centre right
		Communist Party (PCF)	Marxist-Leninist
		Republican Party (RP)	Centre right
		National Front (FN)	Extreme right wing
		Centre of Social Democrats (CDS)	Centrist
		Left Radical Movement (MRG)	Left of centre
Gabon	1	Gabonese Democratic Party (PDG)	Nationalist
Gambia	3	People's Progressive Party (PPP)	Moderate centrist
		National Convention Party (NCP)	Left of centre
East Germany	5	Socialist Unity Party of Germany (SED)	Marxist-Leninist
West Germany	68	Social Democratic Party (SPD)	Left of centre
		Free Democratic Party (FDP)	Centrist
		Christian Democratic Union (CDU)	Centre right
		Christian Social Union (CSU)	Right of centre (Bavarian based)
		The Greens	Environmentalist
Ghana	0		
Greece	17	Pan-Hellenic Socialist Movement (PASOK)	Nationalist socialist
		New Democracy Party (ND)	Centre right
		Communist Party (KKE-Exterior)	Marxist-Leninist
		Communist Party (KKE-Interior)	Non-Soviet communist

Table 34—Political Parties of the World (contd.)
*See notes below

State	*Number of Parties*	*Leading Parties*	*Orientation*
Grenada	7	New National Party (NNP)	Centrist
		Grenada United Labour Party	Nationalist left of centre
Guatemala	9	Guatemalian Christian Democratic Party (PDCG)	Christian centre left
		Centre Party (UCN)	Centrist
		National Democratic Co-operation Party (PDCN)	Centre right
		Revolutionary Party (PR)	Radical
		Movement of National Liberation (MLN)	Extreme right wing
		Democratic Institutional Party (PID)	Moderate right of centre
Guinea	1	Democratic Party of Guinea (PDG)	Progressive socialist
Guinea Bissau	1	African Party for the Independence of Portuguese Guinea & Cape Verde (PAIGC)	Socialist
Guyana	7	People's National Congress (PNC)	National socialist
		People's Progressive Party (PPP)	Marxist-Leninist
Haiti	1*	National Progressive Party (PNP)	Right-wing military
Honduras	7	Liberal Party of Honduras (PLH)	Centre left
		National Party (PN)	Traditional right wing
Hungary	1*	Hungarian Socialist Workers' Party (HSWP)	Marxist-Leninist
Iceland	7	Independence Party	Right of centre
		Progressive Party	Radical socialist
		Social Democratic Party	Moderate left of centre
		People's Alliance	Socialist
		Citizens' Party	Centrist
		Women's Alliance	Women's & children's interests
India	34†	Indian National Congress (Indira)/Congress (I)	Broad based, secular, left of centre
		Janata Dal	Opposition umbrella coalition
		Jan Morcha	Centrist
		Janata (People's) Party	Socialist
		Bharatiya Janata Party (BJP)	Conservative Hindu
		Lok Dal (People's Movement)	Left of centre
		Communist Party of India	Marxist-Leninist (pro-Soviet)
		Communist Party of India (Marxist)-CPI (M)	Marxist-Leninist (independent)
		Telugu Desam (Land of Telugu)	Left of centre (Andhra Pradesh based)
		All-India Anna Dravidian Progress Movement (ADMK)	Left of centre decentralist (Tamil Nadu based)
Indonesia	3	Golkar	Right-wing military
		United Development Party (PPP)	Right-wing Islamic
		Indonesian Democratic Party (PDI)	Moderate non-Islamic
Iran	5*	Islamic Republican Party	Fundamentalist Islamic
Iraq	1*	Arab Baath Socialist Party	National socialist
Ireland	14	Fianna Fail	Moderate centre right
		Fine Gael	Moderate centrist left
		Progressive Democrats	Radical centre left
		Labour	Moderate left of centre

Table 34—Political Parties of the World (contd.)
*See notes below

State	*Number of Parties*	*Leading Parties*	*Orientation*
Israel	28	Israel Labour Party	Left of centre
		Consolidation Party (Likud)	Nationalist right of centre
Italy	14	Christian Democratic Party (DC)	Christian centrist
		Italian Communist Party (PCI)	Eurocommunist
		Italian Socialist Party (PSI)	Moderate socialist
		Italian Social Movement—National Right (MSI-DN)	Extreme right wing
		Italian Republican Party (PRI)	Left of centre
		Italian Social Democratic Party (PSDI)	Moderate left of centre
		Italian Liberal Party (PLI)	Right of centre
Ivory Coast	1	Democratic Party of the Ivory Coast (PDCI)	Free enterprise nationalist
Jamaica	6	Jamaica Labour Party (JLP)	Moderate centrist
		People's National Party (PNP)	Left of centre
Japan	20	Liberal-Democratic Party (LDP)	Right of centre
		Socialist Party of Japan (JSP)	Moderate socialist
		Clean Government Party (Komeito)	Left of centre
		Japan Communist Party (JCP)	Marxist-Leninist
		Democratic Socialist Party (DSP)	Left of centre
Jordan	0		
Kenya	1*	Kenya African National Union (KANU)	Nationalist centrist
Kiribati	2	National Party	Pro-government assembly grouping
		Christian Democratic Party	Anti-government assembly grouping
North Korea	1	Korean Workers' Party (KWP)	Nationalist communist
South Korea	11	Democratic Justice Party (DJP)	Right of centre
		Party for Peace and Democracy (PPD)	Left of centre
		Reunification Democratic Party (RDP)	Centre left
		New Democratic Republican Party (NDRP)	Right of centre
Kuwait	0		
Laos	1	Lao People's Revolutionary Party (LPRP)	Nationalist communist
Lebanon	19	Phalangist Party	Christian radical nationalist
		Progressive Socialist Party	Muslim moderate socialist
		National Liberal Party	Centre left
		Parliamentary Democratic Front	Sunni Muslim moderate centrist
		Lebanese Communist Party (PCL)	Nationalist communist
Lesotho	4	Basotho National Party (BNP)	Traditional nationalist
Liberia	5	National Democratic Party of Liberia (NDPL)	Nationalist military
Libya	1	Arab Socialist Union (ASU)	Radical left wing
Luxembourg	6	Christian Social Party (PCS)	Christian moderate left of centre
		Socialist Workers' Party (POSL)	Moderate socialist
		Democratic Party (PD)	Centre left
		Communist Party	

Table 34—Political Parties of the World (contd.)
*See notes below

State	*Number of Parties*	*Leading Parties*	*Orientation*
Madagascar	1*	National Front for the Defence of the Malagasy Socialist Revolution (FNDR)	Nationalist socialist
Malawi	1	Malawi Congress Party (MCP)	Right-wing multi-racial
Malaysia	36	New United Malays' National Organisation (UMNO Baru)	Malay nationalist unity
		Malaysian Chinese Association (MIC)	Right of centre (Chinese)
		Democratic Action Party (DAP)	Moderate left of centre (Chinese)
		Islamic Party of Malaysia (PAS)	Malay Islamic nationalist
Maldives	0		
Mali	1	Malian People's Democratic Union (UDPM)	Nationalist
Malta	4	Malta Labour Party (MLP)	Moderate left of centre
		Nationalist Party	Christian centrist
Mauritania	0		
Mauritius	14	Mauritius Labour Party (MLP)	Centre left
		Mauritius Socialist Movement (MSM)	Moderate socialist
		Mauritian Militant Movement (MMM)	Marxist
Mexico	13	Institutional Revolutionary Party (PRI)	Moderate left wing
		National Action Party (PAN)	Christian socialist
		Socialist Workers' Party (PST)	Trotskyist
		Mexican Unified Socialist Party (PSUM)	Nationalist socialist
		Mexican Democratic Party (PCM)	Democratic socialist
		Popular Socialist Party (PPS)	Marxist-Leninist
		Authentic Party of the Mexican Revolution (PARM)	Right wing
Mongolia	1	Mongolian People's Revolutionary Party (MPRP)	Marxist-Leninist
Morocco	11	Constitutional Union (UC)	Right wing
		National Rally of Independents (RNI)	Royalist
		Popular Movement (MP)	Moderate agrarian socialist
		Independence Party (Istiqlal)	Nationalist right of centre
		Socialist Union of Popular Forces (USFP)	Progressive socialist
		National Democratic Party (PND)	Nationalist moderate
Mozambique	1	National Front for the Liberation of Mozambique (Frelimo)	Marxist-Leninist
Nauru	2	Democratic Party of Nauru (DPN)	Assembly opposition grouping
Nepal	0		
Netherlands	19	Christian Democratic Appeal (CDA)	Christian right of centre
		Labour Party (PvdA)	Moderate left of centre
		People's Party for Freedom and Democracy (VVD)	Liberal centrist
		Democrats '66 (D'66)	Environmental centrist

Table 34—Political Parties of the World (contd.)
*See notes below

State	*Number of Parties*	*Leading Parties*	*Orientation*
Netherlands *(contd.)*		Political Party of Radical Democrats (PPR)	Moderate socialist and ecological
		Communist Party of the Netherlands (CPN)	International communist
		Pacifist Socialist Party (PSP)	Left-wing pacifist
		Political Reformed Party (SGP)	Calvinist
		Evangelical Political Federation (RPF)	Calvinist reformist
		Reformed Political Association (GPV)	Calvinist
New Zealand	11	New Zealand Labour Party	Moderate left of centre
		New Zealand National Party	Centre right
		New Zealand Democratic Party	Moderate radical
Nicaragua	12	Sandinista National Liberation Front (FSLN)	Marxist-Leninist
		Democratic Conservative Party (PCD)	Centrist
		Independent Liberal Party (PLI)	Moderate centre left
		Popular Social Christian Party (PPSC)	Christian socialist
Niger	0		
Nigeria	0		
Norway	14	Norwegian Labour Party (DNA)	Moderate left of centre
		Conservative Party	Progressive right of centre
		Christian People's Party (KrF)	Christian centre left
		Centre Party (SP)	Left of centre non-socialist
Oman	0		
Pakistan	18	Pakistan People's Party (PPP)	Left of centre
		Islamic Democratic Alliance (IDA)	Anti-Bhutto, right-wing Islamic coalition
		Pakistan Muslim League (PML)	Islamic right wing
		Mohajir Quami Movement (MQM)	Sind-based partition immigrants (*mohajir*) rights
		Jamiat-i-Ulema-i-Islam (JUI)	Islamic
		Awami National Party (ANP)	Socialist and federalist
Panama	11	Labour Party (PALA)	Right wing
		National Liberal Republican Movement (MOLIRENA)	Right of centre
		Authentic Panama Party (PPA)	Right wing
		Republican Party (PR)	Right wing
		Democratic Revolutionary Party (PRD)	Centre left
		Christian Democratic Party (PDC)	Christian moderate left of centre
Papua New Guinea	12	Pangu Pati (PP)	Nationalist
		National Party	Right of centre
		People's Democratic Movement (PDM)	Centrist
		Melanesian Alliance (MA)	Left of centre
Paraguay	9	National Republican Association-Colorado Party	Right of centre
		Radical Liberal Party (PLR)	Moderate right of centre
		Liberal Party (PL)	Right of centre

Table 34—Political Parties of the World (contd.)
*See notes below

State	Number of Parties	Leading Parties	Orientation
Peru	18	American Popular Revolutionary Alliance (APRA)	Moderate left wing
		United Left (IU)	Left wing
Philippines	25†	People's Power	Left of centre pro-Aquino coalition
		Convenors' Group	Liberal left
		PDP-Laban Party	Centrist
		Liberal Party	Centrist
		Union for United Action	Right-wing anti-Aquino coalition
		New Society Movement	Right-wing pro-Marcos
		Grand Alliance for Democracy (GAD)	Right-wing anti-Aquino
Poland	5*	Polish United Workers' Party (PZPR)	Marxist-Leninist
Portugal	19	Social Democratic Party (PSD)	Moderate left of centre
		Socialist Party (PS)	Progressive socialist
		Democratic Renewal Party (PRD)	Centre left
		Democratic Social Centre Party (CDS)	Moderate left of centre
Qatar	0		
Romania	1	Romanian Communist Party (RCP)	Marxist-Leninist
Rwanda	1	National Revolutionary Development Movement (MRND)	Socialist
St Kitts-Nevis	4	People's Action Movement (PAM)	Centre right
		Nevis Reformation Party (NRP)	Separationist
		Labour Party	Moderate left of centre
Saint Lucia	3	United Workers' Party (UWP)	Moderate left wing
		St Lucia Labour Party (SLP)	Moderate left wing
		Progressive Labour Party (PLP)	Moderate left wing
Saint Vincent and The Grenadines	9	New Democratic Party (NDP)	Moderate left of centre
		St Vincent Labour Party (SVLP)	Moderate left of centre
Sao Tome & Principe	1	Movement for the Liberation of Sao Tome and Principe (MLSTP)	Nationalist socialist
Saudi Arabia	0		
Senegal	16	Sengalese Socialist Party (PS)	Democratic socialist
Seychelles	1	Seychelles People's Progressive Front (SPPF)	Socialist
Sierra Leone	1	All People's Congress (APC)	Socialist
Singapore	21	People's Action Party (PAP)	Right of centre
		Workers' Party (WP)	Socialist
Solomon Islands	5	Solomon Islands United Party (SIUPA)	Right of centre
		National Front for Progress (NFP)	Right of centre
		People's Alliance Party (PAP)	Centre left
Somalia	1	Somali Revolutionary Socialist Party (SRSP)	Socialist
South Africa	13*	National Party (NP)	(Whites) Right centre racialist
		Democratic Party (DP)	(Whites) Moderate non-racial
		New Republic Party (POB)	Whites) Left of centre multi-racial

Table 34—Political Parties of the World (contd.)
*See notes below

State	*Number of Parties*	*Leading Parties*	*Orientation*
South Africa *(contd.)*		Conservative Party of South Africa	(Whites) Extreme right wing
		United Democratic Front (UDF)	Multi-racial Church orientated
		Afrikaner Resistance Movement (AWB)	Right wing
		Labour Party of South Africa	(Coloureds) Left of centre
		People's Congress Party	(Coloureds) Right of centre
		National People's Party	(Asians) Right of centre
		Solidarity Party	(Asians) Left of centre
Soviet Union	1	Communist Party of the Soviet Union (CPSU)	Marxist-Leninist
Spain	21	Spanish Socialist Workers' Party (PSOE)	Democratic socialist
		Popular Coalition (CP)	Moderate centre right
Sri Lanka	15	United National Party (UNP)	Centre right
		Sri Lanka Freedom Party (SLFP)	Nationalist socialist
Sudan	40*	New National Umma Party (NNUP)	Islamic nationalist
		Democratic Unionist Party (DUP)	Islamic nationalist
		National Islamic Front	
Suriname	15	National Democratic Party (NDP)	Military-backed centrist
		Front for Democracy and Development (FDD)*	Left of centre, multi-racial coalition
Swaziland	1	Imbokodvo National Movement (INM)	Traditional nationalist
Sweden	10	Social Democratic Labour Party (SAP)	Moderate left of centre
		Moderate Party	Right of centre
		Liberal Party	Centre left
		Centre Party	Moderate centrist
		Christian Democratic Party	Christian centrist
		Communist Left Party	European Marxist
Switzerland	22	Christian Democratic Party of Switzerland (PDC)	Christian moderate centrist
		Radical Democratic Party of Switzerland (FDP)	Radical centre left
		Swiss Social Democratic Party (SPS)	Moderate left of centre
		Swiss People's Party (SVP)	Centre left
		Swiss Liberal Party	Federalist centre left
		Green Party	Ecological
Syria	1*	National Progressive Front	Arab socialist (Baath Arab Socialist Party) Arab Socialist Party (ASP) Arab Socialist Union (ASU) Socialist Unionist Movement (SUM) Syrian Communist Party (SCP))
Taiwan	7	Nationalist Party of China (Kuomintang: KMT)	Nationalist (Chinese)
		Democratic Progress Party (DPP)	Centre left
		Party of Workers of Labour	Left of centre

Table 34—Political Parties of the World (contd.)
*See notes below

State	*Number of Parties*	*Leading Parties*	*Orientation*
Tanzania	1	Revolutionary Party of Tanzania (CCM)	African socialist
Thailand	18	Thai Nation Party	Right wing
		Social Action Party (SAP)	Moderate right of centre
		Democratic Party	Moderate right of centre
		Thai Citizens' Party	Far right monarchist
		Citizens' Party	Right wing
Togo	1	Assembly of the Togolese People	Nationalist socialist
Tonga	0		
Trinidad and Tobago	9	National Alliance for Reconstruction (NAR)	Moderate left-wing coalition
		People's National Movement (PNM)	Moderate nationalist
Tunisia	4	Constitutional Democratic Rally (RDC)	Nationalist socialist
Turkey	11	Motherland Party (ANAP)	Nationalist Islamic right of centre
		Social Democratic Populist Party (SDP)	Moderate left of centre
		True Path Party (TPP)	Centre right
Tuvalu	0		
Uganda	7	National Resistance Movement (NRM)	Centrist
		Democratic Party (DP)	Centre left
		Conservative Party (CP)	Centre right
		Uganda People's Congress (UPC)	Left of centre
		Uganda Freedom Movement (UFM)	Left of centre
United Arab Emirates	0		
United Kingdom	21*	Conservative and Unionist Party	Right of centre
		Labour Party	Moderate left of centre
		Social and Liberal Democrats (SLD)	Centre left
		Social Democratic Party (SDP)	Centre left
		Green Party	Environmentalist
		Scottish National Party (SNP)	Scottish nationalist
		Party of Wales (Plaid Cymru)	Welsh nationalist
		Official Unionist Party (OUP)	Northern Ireland Protestant right of centre
		Democratic Unionist Party (DUP)	Northern Ireland Protestant nationalist
		Social Democratic Labour Party (SDLP)	Northern Ireland Catholic centre left
		Sinn Fein	Northern Ireland Catholic nationalist
United States	20	Republican Party	Right of centre
		Democratic Party	Centre left
Uruguay	5*	Colorado Party (PC)	Progressive centre left
		National (Blanco) Party (PN)	Traditional right of centre
		Amplio Front	Moderate left wing
Vanuatu	10	Vanuaaku Party (VP)	Melanesian socialist
		Union of Moderate Parties (UMP)	Centre left (Francophone)
Venezuela	13	Democratic Action Party (AD)	Moderate left of centre
		Christian Social Party (COPEI)	Christian centre right
		Movement towards Socialism (MAS)	Left of centre
		Democratic Republican Union (URD)	Left of centre

Table 34—Political Parties of the World (contd.)
*See notes below

State	*Number of Parties*	*Leading Parties*	*Orientation*
Vietnam	1	Communist Party of Vietnam (CPV)	Marxist-Leninist
Western Samoa	3	Human Rights Protection Party (HRPP)	Centre right
		Christian Democratic Party (CDP)	Centre left
		Va'ai Kolone Group (VKG)	Centrist
North Yemen	0		
South Yemen	1	Yemen Socialist Party (YSP)	Marxist-Leninist
Yugoslavia	1	League of Communists of Yugoslavia (SKJ)	Marxist-Leninist
Zaire	1	Popular Movement of the Revolution (MPR)	African socialist
Zambia	1	United National Independence Party (UNIP)	African socialist
Zimbabwe	1*	Zimbabwe African National Union-Patriotic Front (ZANU-PF)	African socialist

*NOTES

Afghanistan, Burma, Chad, Chile, Haiti, Hungary, Poland, Sudan	The political systems in these countries are currently in a particularly fluid state.
Burkina Faso	Effectively one-party, controlled by the National Revolutionary Council.
Central African Republic	Political parties are currently banned but a number of passive opposition groups exist.
Colombia	The number of active parties is very variable.
Iran, Iraq, Kenya, Madagascar, Syria, Zimbabwe	These are all effectively, if not legally, one-party states.
South Africa	There are no legal political parties for blacks.
United Kingdom	The number of parties fighting general elections and by-elections fluctuates from year to year.
Uruguay	The two main parties, PC and PN, are both broad coalitions of a number of factions.

†In addition to those parties listed, there are three regional parties in France, 61 in India and 30 in the Philippines.

7.5 Parties in liberal and emergent democracies

It is possible to distinguish five different bases of party formation and support in the states we have defined as liberal or emergent democracies. They are: social class, economic status, religion, regional differences and philosophical leanings. All parties are based on at least one of these factors, some on most, or all.

The United Kingdom provides a clear example of class-based parties, although the divisions are not as stark in contemporary society as they were earlier in the century. The creation of the Labour Party, known originally as the Labour Representation Committee, in 1900, to represent the working classes, provided a striking contrast to the Conservative Party, which sought to protect and promote the interests of the middle and upper classes. Before the advent of the Labour Party Britain's two-party political system had been based on a division between the Conservatives, representing landed interests, and the Liberals, representing urban industrialists.

Class-based parties are not as marked in most other countries. The Labor Party of Australia and the New Zealand Labour Party, although similar in origin to their counterpart in the United Kingdom, reflect the greater social openness in those two countries.

Ironically, communist parties in liberal democratic states have tended to be homes for left-wing, middle-class intellectuals rather than for the proletariat and have seldom won sufficient popular support to control the levers of political power. This is increasingly true of the two most significant of such bodies in Western Europe, the Italian Communist Party (PCI) and French Communist Party (PCF).

Economic status has largely replaced, or is replacing, class as an indicator of social position in most liberal democracies. In Italy, for example, class divisions are not clearly defined and economic status is becoming a dominant feature of party support. In West Germany the post-war rise of a non-unionised working class and a new middle class provide further evidence of the importance of economic, rather than social, factors as a basis for party allegiance.

Religion still provides a widely occurring foundation for political parties in contemporary liberal and emergent democracies. Parties in Italy, Israel, the Netherlands, Austria, West Germany, France and other Western European states display this characteristic to varying degrees, having their roots in sides taken during earlier secular-clerical battles. In the United Kingdom economic disparities in Northern Ireland have been underlined by religious divisions.

Regional differences are, arguably, the most common foundation for party support. In the United States, for example, clearly distinguishable parties might well disappear if they were not supported on regional bases. In the Netherlands and Belgium regional variations, accentuated by linguistic differences, have multiplied the party groupings. In Belgium each of the four principal parties, Christian Democrat, Socialist, Liberal and Green, is currently divided into autonomous, and often antagonistic, Flemish and French wings.

Philosophy has not provided a reliable basis for mass party support in liberal democratic states in recent years. Indeed, surveys suggest that the great majority of contemporary electors not only care little for social and political theory but have no clear understanding of the philosophical stance of the parties for which they vote. The 'thinking elector' is certainly in a minority throughout the world and the chances of representation by a party which accurately mirrors the views of this kind of voter are very much determined by the vagaries of the electoral system, as we shall see later in this chapter. The new 'post-industrial' ecological parties, which have made notable progress in North-West European states, as a result of proportional representation, during the past decade, are examples of this process. They contrast significantly with the eclectic 'catch-all' nature of most major liberal democratic parties.

7.6 Parties in communist states

The all-pervading influence of the party provides the sharpest contrast between communist one-party and multi-party states. It is the ultimate source of power and permeates all aspects of the political system and the state institutions.

In contrast to parties in most western democracies, membership of the party in communist states is a privileged and élitist acquisition. Whereas parties in liberal democracies actively compete with each other to increase their memberships, communist parties are highly cautious and selective about the people who are eventually admitted into full membership. Aspirants are initially inducted into the party's 'youth' wing for 14–28-year-olds, known in the Soviet Union as Komsomol. Years later, when old enough for consideration for full party membership, they must be nominated by three full party members of at least five years' standing. Then, if accepted, they are required to serve a year's probation under the title of 'candidate member'.

Despite these hurdles to be surmounted, party membership, with its associated economic and social advantages, is highly sought after in communist states. For this reason, party membership as a proportion of the total population is invariably at a higher level in communist than liberal democratic states, as Table 35 shows.

Table 35

POLITICAL PARTY MEMBERSHIP AS A PROPORTION OF STATE POPULATIONS IN COMMUNIST AND LIBERAL DEMOCRATIC STATES

Communist States			*Liberal-Democratic States**		
State	*Ruling Party Membership (m)*	*% of Total Pop*	*State*	*Combined Party Membership (m)*	*% of Total Pop*
Romania	3.500	15.4	Sweden	1.600	19.2
N. Korea	3.000	14.6	Austria	1.300	17.2
E. Germany	2.300	13.8	Malta	0.060	17.0
Czechoslovakia	1.650	10.6	Israel	0.700	16.6
Bulgaria	0.932	10.4	Finland	0.700	14.3
Yugoslavia	2.200	9.5	Venezuela	2.200	12.7
Hungary	0.871	8.2	New Zealand	0.400	12.3
Soviet Union	19.038	6.8	Norway	0.500	12.0
Poland	2.126	5.7	Luxembourg	0.040	10.9
Cuba	0.524	5.1	Barbados	0.025	9.9
Albania	0.147	4.8	Italy	4.500	7.9
Mongolia	0.088	4.6	Belgium	0.700	7.1
China	44.000	4.2	Belize	0.010	6.0
Vietnam	1.750	2.8	Denmark	0.300	5.9
Laos	0.042	1.0	Switzerland	0.370	5.7
Cambodia	0.008	0.1	Ireland	0.150	4.2
			Japan	4.350	3.6
			West Germany	2.030	3.3
			United Kingdom	1.800	3.2
			France	1.700	3.1
			Netherlands	0.400	2.8
			Australia	0.420	2.7
			Sri Lanka	0.200	1.3

*This is a selective sample as accurate data are lacking for other liberal-democratic states.

Parties in communist states have clear ideological bases. Indeed, one of the main purposes, if not the main purpose, of the party is to preserve and project the ideology. This is done by the presence of party representatives throughout the political and social systems, including the media and work places.

This all-pervasiveness must be clearly recognised if the political systems of communist states are to be properly understood. Using the Soviet Union as the salient example, it can be seen that any position of reasonable seniority within the state must be 'confirmed' by the party; the more important the post the higher the echelon of approval. The most senior posts of all, amounting to nearly a third of a million, are closely controlled by the secretariat of the Central Committee of the party. From its earliest, Leninist, days the Communist Party of the Soviet Union set out to be an élite 'vanguard' organisation, comprising the country's 'best citizens', and, although the membership net has been cast more widely since the Second World War, more than quadrupling between 1945 and 1985, it has never deviated from that original aim. The stress on quality, rather than crude numbers or social background, has, in recent years, been a prominent theme for the new Gorbachev administration.

Other communist states, and some nationalistic socialist states, have similarly developed and promoted the party as the custodian of the nation's political future and the 'vanguard of the proletariat'. As Table 35 reveals, however, there exist significant variations in membership 'densities' between the 'mass parties' of Romania, North Korea, Bulgaria, Czechoslovakia and the GDR and the élitist cadres of Vietnam, Laos and Cambodia.

7.7 The party in non-communist, one-party states

Most contemporary non-communist, one-party states are found in what has become fashionable to describe as the Third World, even though this description can be a little ambiguous.

In these states the party, in addition to acting as a political recruitment, socialisation and resource distribution agency, usually performs two main functions: the promotion of nationalism and patriotism and the maintenance of a certain stable economic and social order. Support for nationalism invariably receives a high priority, the dominant parties usually being those which had spearheaded the independence movement, and the economic and social order is that which is determined by the ruling élite within the party.

Additionally, the non-communist single party often tends to support and sustain the strong, charismatic leader. Most of the black African states display this characteristic, although it should be noted that the dominance of a strong leader is not always confined to one-party states. The constitution of the French Fifth Republic was originally designed with Charles de Gaulle in mind and the party which supported him not only made his continuance in office its main aim but assumed his name as the popular description of the political movement. Other states, particularly in South America, have spawned strong, autocratic leaders within a highly factionalised, multi-party system.

Compared with parties in liberal and emergent democracies and communist states, those in non-communist one-party countries are, with notable exceptions in black Africa, such as Mozambique, Tanzania, Zambia and Zimbabwe, relatively weak organisations and very much the instruments of those nations' political leaders. Some countries, although in theory one-party states, might better be regarded as having no parties at all. The reason for the comparative docility of party politics in these states stems mainly from history and social organisation. Modern political parties are not a 'natural' development in most so-called Third World states and many years may elapse before the economic and social environments can sustain a 'sophisticated' multi-party system. Social organisation, sometimes based on tribal loyalties or strong regional differences, has also favoured allegiance to the strong, personal leader rather than the 'anonymous' party.

7.8 Parties in militaristic and absolutist states

In states controlled by the military or absolute rulers political parties either do not exist or, if they do, are puppets of the ruling élite and façades for what is little more than autocratic, personal government.

Absolutist states such as those in the Arab world have never experienced what might be described as popular political activity, with representative institutions. Most of the countries which are today under the sway of military rulers have, in contrast, previously enjoyed some form of democratic government so that their present condition may be a temporary aberration. There is evidence that military rulers find it difficult to sustain their leadership for protracted periods without creating a single party and building it into the framework of the state or reverting to a multi-party political system.

In Bangladesh, the Jana Dal (People's Party) was formed in 1983 by Lieutenant-General Hossain Mohammad Ershad to support his presidential candidature. Now known as the Jatiya (National) Front, the party has subsequently established itself as a civilian governing front for what still remains a military-dependent regime. Similarly in Indonesia, the Joint Secretariat of Functional Groups (Golkar Party), which had been created in 1964 as a loose alliance of anti-communist sectional interest groups, was transformed into a civilian ruling front for the military when, in 1968, it was brought under government control by General Suharto.

7.9 Political parties and electoral systems

Is there a direct connection between a country's electoral system and the structure and numbers of its political parties? Writers tend to be ambivalent, suggesting a 'chicken and egg' situation. Some argue that the kinds of parties in a particular country simply reflect its social and economic structure while others attribute much greater influence to the methods of voting available to electors. What is the evidence?

Of the 50 countries identified in Table 4 as liberal democracies 29 employ majoritarian voting systems of an alternative vote, simple plurality or second ballot type. The remaining 21 have some variety of proportional representation. An analysis of of the respective party systems reveals the pattern set out in Table 36 on page 128.

Table 36

VOTING AND PARTY SYSTEMS IN LIBERAL DEMOCRACIES

States with Majoritarian Voting Systems	States with Some Form of Proportional Representation	Party Systems
Antigua and Barbuda (SP)		Two-party
Australia (AV)		Two-party
	Austria (PL)	Multi-party*
Bahamas (SP)		Two-party
Barbados (SP)		Two-party
	Belgium (PL)	Multi-party
Belize (SP)		Two-party
Botswana (SP)		Two-party
Canada (SP)		Multi-party*
	Costa Rica (PL)	Two-party
	Denmark (PL)	Multi-party
Dominica (SP)		Two-party
	Dominican Republic (PL)	Multi-party*
	Finland (PL)	Multi-party
France (SB)		Multi-party*
Gambia (SP)		Two-party
	West Germany (AM)	Multi-party*
	Iceland (PL)	Multi-party
India (SP)		Dominant party†
	Ireland (STV)	Multi-party*
	Israel (PL)	Multi-party*
	Italy (PL)	Multi-party
Jamaica (SP)		Two-party
	Japan (LV)	Dominant party†
Kiribati (SB)		Two-party‡
	Luxembourg (PL)	Multi-party
Malaysia (SP)		Multi-party§
	Malta (STV)	Two-party
Mauritius (SP)		Multi-party*
	Mexico (AM)	Dominant party†
Nauru (SP)		Two-party‡
	Netherlands (PL)	Multi-party
New Zealand (SP)		Two-party
	Norway (PL)	Multi-party
Papua New Guinea (SP)		Multi-party
St Kitts-Nevis (SP)		Two-party
St Lucia (SP)		Two-party
St Vincent & the Grenadines (SP)		Two-party
Singapore (SP)		Dominant party†
Solomon Islands (SP)		Two-party
	Sri Lanka (PL)	Two-party
	Sweden (PL)	Multi-party
	Switzerland (PL)	Multi-party
Trinidad and Tobago (SP)		Two-party
Tuvalu (SP)		No parties
United Kingdom (SP)		Two-party
United States (SP)		Two-party
Vanuatu (SB)		Two-party
	Venezuela (PL)	Multi-party*
Western Samoa (Coll)		Two-party

ABBREVIATIONS:
AM—Additional Member
AV—Alternative Vote
Coll—College
LV—Limited Vote
PL—Party List
SB—Second Ballot
SP—Simple Plurality
STV—Single Transferable Vote

*Within these multi-party systems two major parties or alliances exist alongside one or two minor parties, which frequently hold the balance of power.

†One major party dominates in what is otherwise a multi-party system.

‡Formal party structures are weak, with candidates being elected substantially as independents. Within the assembly, however, a division between majority and minority members has emerged.

§Dominated by one party within a ruling multi-party coalition.

Of the 29 countries with majoritarian voting methods 21 have effectively a two-party system operating, two have a 'dominant party system', in which one party usually dominates electoral contests, and one has a system in which parties as such do not operate, candidates fighting assembly seats as independents. Only five majoritarian voting countries have political systems of a multi-party nature, with three or more parties regularly exchanging or sharing power. Conversely, of the 21 states employing some kind of proportional representation 16 have multi-party systems and only three have effectively two parties operating. In the remaining two countries 'dominant party systems' are in force. Although the evidence is not conclusive, a link between electoral systems and party systems seems more than a possibility.

The classic examples of two-party competition, in which minor parties are virtually non-existent, are to be found in the small island states of the Caribbean and Oceania. In these regions 18 (86%) of the 21 liberal democratic systems, excluding mainland Mexico, operate in this way. The smallness of their populations, which in the majority of cases average around 100,000–200,000, and of their assemblies, varying between 11 and 49 elected members, are important explanatory factors. The personalised style of politics and party formation in these regions has had the effect of creating polarisation, as have their simple plurality voting systems.

The textbook example of a two-party system is, however, the United Kingdom. Here the simple plurality voting system has played, arguably, a paramount role in fostering polarisation. The two major parties, Conservative and Labour, have shared power exclusively for more than 40 years because the electoral system has made it extremely difficult for third or fourth parties to secure enough parliamentary seats to break the monopoly. The advent of a strong challenge from 1981 onwards, first in the form of the Liberal-SDP Alliance and then the Democrats, on the centre-left of the political spectrum, has benefited the centre-right Conservatives, giving them clear majorities in three successive general elections.

Canada is only a partial exception to the rule of simple plurality voting producing a two-party system because, although the seats in the House of Commons have been shared in recent years by three parties, for most of the present century the Liberals and Progressive Conservatives have dominated Canadian politics. Similarly, in France and Mauritius, two other majoritarian electoral states which currently have multi-party systems, the assemblies are invariably dominated by two principal party groupings, with minor 'half-parties' holding a much smaller number of seats, though sometimes the balance of power. Only in one majoritarian state, Papua New Guinea, does a full-blown multi-party system operate.

The tendency for majoritarian voting systems to foster restricted party systems thus appears to be strong. In the cases of Canada, the United States and the United Kingdom the size, social complexity and regional differentiation of the countries are such that it seems almost certain that if proportional voting systems were in place a multiplicity of party groupings would emerge, although a core of three or four major parties would still be likely to predominate. In the case of France firm evidence exists from the Fourth Republic period and, briefly, from the National Assembly election of 1986, when party list systems were in operation, that the second ballot majoritarian method has served to restrict party development.

The evidence presented in Table 36 also shows, however, that proportional voting systems do not always result in a multiplicity of parties vying for, or sharing, power. The fact that small parties are not disadvantaged by the voting system will not necessarily guarantee them better access to government, as the experiences of Costa Rica and Malta reveal. Historical and social factors can sometimes result in domination by two parties, however open the political system might be. In many other states with proportional representation systems, although a multiplicity of parties may have assembly representation, it is usual for three or four major parties to hold a majority of seats.

7.10 Parties and the legal environment

The majority of one-party states have the party's monopoly enshrined within the constitution. In some ostensibly multi-party states legal controls will sometimes favour the dominant government party, making life for opposition groups difficult. Singapore and Paraguay provide evidence of this. In genuine multi-party states the legal environment can range from positive encouragement at one extreme to minimum restraints on fraudulent practices at the other.

Austria provides probably the clearest example of positive support for political parties, the Party Law stating: '. . . the existence and diversity of political parties is an essential component of the democratic order of the Republic of Austria.' Here the state gives generous financial support. Each party with at least five members in the National Council receives a lump sum and then additional finance is provided on the basis of the number of votes won in the previous federal election. Parties which did not win seats but obtained at least 1 per cent of the popular vote are not overlooked, receiving *pro rata* support according to votes obtained.

Similarly in West Germany, under the law of July 1967, parties are described as a 'constitutionally necessary element of a free democratic order', with state subsidies of DM 5 (US$3) per vote being provided to all political parties which secure 0.5 per cent or more of the popular poll.

Several other states give finance to help cover election expenses in varying degrees. They include Costa Rica, Denmark, Ecuador, Israel, Italy, Netherlands, Norway, Portugal, Spain, Sweden and Turkey, and the United States for presidential elections only. The amount of the grant usually depends on the size of the vote obtained at the last election but in Denmark on the size of the party. In many countries free time is made available to parties on the state radio and television networks. In the United Kingdom, although there are no state funds for elections, the official opposition party, once elected, is given finance, its leader and a limited number of its parliamentary managers receiving state salaries.

Many states require parties to register and sometimes the conditions of registration can be severe, making it difficult for small or new parties to obtain a foothold on the political slope. Argentina, Brazil, India (where strict regulations were introduced in 1985 to discourage inter-election changes of allegiance by deputies: 'floor-crossing'), Malaysia, Mexico, Philippines, Thailand and Venezuela are among the countries requiring evidence of popular support as a condition of registration. In Indonesia the number of parties permitted to operate has been restricted to three since 1975.

At the other extreme, there are states where control is at a very minimum. They include Belgium, where one party fought an election under the banner of 'Snow White and the Seven Dwarfs', Bolivia, whose elections are generally subject to widespread fraud, France, where restrictions are minimal, Honduras, New Zealand, Sri Lanka, Switzerland and the United Kingdom, where 'oddball parties' are allowed to contest elections provided they are prepared to sacrifice a deposit of £500 if their vote count falls below 5 per cent.

RECOMMENDED READING

Ball, A. and Millward, F., *Pressure Politics in Industrial Societies: A Comparative Introduction*, Macmillan,1986.

Bell, D.S. (ed), *Contemporary French Political Parties*, Croom Helm, 1982.

Cammack, P., Pool, D. and Tordoff, W., *Third World Politics: A Comparative Introduction*, Macmillan, 1988, Ch. 3.

Charlton, R., *Comparative Government*, Longman, 1986, Chs. 5 & 6.

Daalder, H and Mair, P. (eds), *Western European Party Systems*, Sage Publications, 1983.

Day, A.J. and Degenhardt, H.W. (eds), *Political Parties of the World: A Keesings Reference Publication*, Longman, 2nd edn., 1984.

Epstein, L., *Political Parties in the American Mold*, University of Wisconsin Press, 1986.

Hague, R. and Harrop, M., *Comparative Government and Politics: An Introduction*, Macmillan, 2nd edn., 1987, Chs. 7 & 8.

Hill, R.J. and Frank, P., *The Soviet Communist Party*, George Allen & Unwin, 2nd edn., 1983.

Lawson, K., *The Comparative Study of Political Parties*, St Martin's Press, 1976.

Merkl, P.H. (ed), *Western European Party Systems*, Free Press, 1980.

Roberts, G.K., *An Introduction to Comparative Politics*, Edward Arnold, 1986, Chs. 5 & 6.

Sartori, G., *Parties and Party Systems: A Framework for Analysis*, Cambridge University Press, 1976.

Solomon, S.G. (ed), *Pluralism in the Soviet Union*, Macmillan, 1983).
Stammen, T., *Political Parties in Europe*, John Martin Publishing, 1980
Thomas, A. and Paterson, W. (eds), *The Future of Social Democracy*, Oxford University Press, 1986.
Von Beyme, K., *Political Parties in Western Democracies*, Gower, 1985.
Ware, A. (ed), *Political Parties: Electoral Change and Structural Response*, Basil Blackwell, 1987.
Wattenberg, M.P., *The Decline of American Political Parties, 1952-1980*, Harvard University Press, 1984.
Wilson. G.K., *Interest Groups in the United States*, Clarendon Press, 1981.

PART II

POLITICAL SYSTEMS OF THE WORLD'S NATION-STATES

INTRODUCTION

Having considered the various ingredients of a political system and suggested bases for comparing one with another, it is now time to look at the circumstances of individual states as they are found in the world today. In the ensuing pages 165 independent nations will be examined and, as has already been intimated, for comparative purposes they will be grouped in nine regions: Western Europe, Eastern Europe, the Middle East and North Africa, Central and Southern Africa, North America, Central America and the Caribbean, South America, Asia and Oceania.

Much of the information in Tables 1 to 36 has been extracted and summarised for each country within a region and additional data have been included, so as to produce a social, economic and political profile for each state. Summaries of this information, showing how particular features of political systems are distributed globally, on a regional basis, are given in Tables 37 to 48 below.

Even though a sovereign nation comes into existence at a particular point in time, it is not created in a vacuum, or some sterile laboratory. It is essentially the product of history and so the political development of each country is also outlined, with particular emphasis on the period since the Second World War, or since independence was achieved if this was later.

Table 37

REGIONAL DISTRIBUTION OF STATES BY DATE OF THEIR FORMATION

	(Period of State Formation)								
Region	*Pre 17th C*	*17th & 18th Cs*	*19th C*	*1900–1920*	*1921–1945*	*1946–1965*	*1966–1975*	*Since 1975*	*State Total*
W Europe	5	3	4	3	3	3	—	—	21
E Europe	—	—	1	7	—	1	—	—	9
Middle East & N Africa	1	—	—	1	4	9	4	1	20
C & S Africa	1	—	1	1	—	29	11	2	45
C America & Caribbean	—	—	9	1	—	2	3	6	21
N America	—	1	1	—	—	—	—	—	2
S America	—	—	10	—	—	—	2	—	12
Asia	3	2	—	1	1	14	1	1	23
Oceania	—	—	1	1	—	2	4	4	12
Total	10	6	27	15	8	60	25	14	165

Table 38

REGIONAL DISTRIBUTION OF STATES BY THEIR TYPE

Region	*Lib Dem*	*Emgt Dem*	*Communist*	*Auth National*	*Nat Socialist*	*Mil Authorit*	*Absolutist*	*State Total*
W Europe	16	5	—	—	—	—	—	21
E Europe	—	—	9	—	—	—	—	9
Middle East & N Africa	1	4	—	3	5	—	7	20

Table 38—Regional Distribution of States by Their Type (contd.)

Region	*Lib Dem*	*Emgt Dem*	*Communist*	*Auth National*	*Nat Socialist*	*Mil Authorit*	*Absolutist*	*State Total*
C & S Africa	3	2	—	11	15	12	1	45*
C America & Caribbean	13	5	1	—	—	2	—	21
N America	2	—	—	—	—	—	—	2
S America	1	9	—	—	—	2	—	12
Asia	5	6	6	2	1	—	3	23
Oceania	9	2	—	—	—	—	1	12
Total	50	33	16	16	21	16	12	165

*This total includes South Africa—'Racist Democracy' state type—which is not shown in any of the columns here.

Table 39

REGIONAL DISTRIBUTION OF STATES BY EXECUTIVE TYPE

Region	*Parliament*	*Lim Pres*	*Dual Exec*	*Unlim Pres*	*Communist*	*Military*	*Absolute*	*State Total*
W Europe	16	2	3	—	—	—	—	21
E Europe	—	—	—	—	9	—	—	9
Middle East & N Africa	1	2	2	8	—	—	7	20
C & S Africa	1	5	—	26	—	12	1	45
C America & Caribbean	11	7	—	—	1	2	—	21
N America	1	1	—	—	—	—	—	2
S America	—	10	—	—	—	2	—	12
Asia	5	5	1	3	6	—	3	23
Oceania	8	3	—	—	—	—	1	12
Total	43	35	6	37	16	16	12	165

Table 40

REGIONAL DISTRIBUTION OF STATES BY POLITICAL STRUCTURE AND NUMBER OF ASSEMBLY CHAMBERS

	Political Structure		*Number of Assembly Chambers*			
Region	*Unitary*	*Federal*	*None*	*One*	*Two*	*State Total*
W Europe	18	3	—	11	10	21
E Europe	6	3	—	5	4	9
Middle East & N Africa	19	1	6	13	1	20
C & S Africa	43	2	9	33	3	45
C America & Caribbean	19	2	1	10	10	21
N America	—	2	—	—	2	2
S America	9	3	—	3	9	12
Asia	20	3	1	16	6	23
Oceania	11	1	—	9	3	12
Total	145	20	17	100	48	165

Table 41

REGIONAL DISTRIBUTION OF STATES BY PARTY AND VOTING SYSTEMS

	Party System					*Voting System*								
Region	*None*	*One*	*Two*	*Three*	*Multi*	*None*	*SP*	*SB*	*PL*	*AM*	*STV*	*AV*	*LV*	*State Total*
W Europe	—	—	3	—	18	—	1	1	16	1	2	—	—	21
E Europe	—	9	—	—	—	—	4	5	—	—	—	—	—	9
Middle East & N Africa	8	8	1	—	3	6	10	2	2	—	—	—	—	20
C & S Africa	5	33	2	—	5	9	34	1	—	1	—	—	—	45
C America & Caribbean	—	2	13	—	6	1	14	—	4	2	—	—	-	21
N America	—	—	1	—	1	—	2	—	—	—	—	—	—	2
S America	1	—	4	—	7	—	4	—	8	—	—	—	—	12
Asia	3	9	1	1	9	1	18	—	2	1	—	—	1	23
Oceania	2	—	4	1	5	—	9	2	—	—	—	1	—	12
Total	19	61	29	2	54	17	96	11	32	5	2	1	1	165

Table 42

SUMMARY OF SOCIAL AND ECONOMIC DATA FOR SOVEREIGN STATES BY REGIONS OF THE WORLD

Region	*Area km² (m)*	*As % of World Total*	*Population (m) (1985)*	*As % of World Total*	*Population Density per km²*	*In Relation to World Mean†*
W Europe	4.376	3.3	413.426	8.4	94	254
E Europe	23.550	17.8	418.392	8.5	18	49
Middle East & N Africa	11.204	8.5	217.702	4.4	19	51
C & S Africa	23.474	17.7	472.331	9.6	20	54
C America & the Caribbean	2.720	2.1	135.694	2.7	50	135
N America	19.348	14.6	266.625	5.4	14	38
S America	17.740	13.4	279.149	5.6	16	43
Asia	21.094	16.0	2,656.426	53.7	126	341
Oceania	8.786	6.6	82.061	1.7	9	24
*World Total**	132.292	100.0	4,941.806	100.0	37	100

*Excluding colonies, dependencies and semi-sovereign states.

†World mean=100

Table 43

REGIONAL DISTRIBUTION OF STATES BY AREAL SIZE

	(Size of State: km²)						
Region	*Below 1,000*	*1,000–10,000*	*10,001–100,000*	*100,001–500,000*	*500,001–1,000,000*	*Over 1,000,000*	*State Total*
W Europe	1	2	7	8	3	—	21
E Europe	—	—	2	6	—	1	9
Middle East & N Africa	1	—	7	7	—	5	20

Table 43—Regional Distribution of States by Areal Size

Region	Below 1,000	1,000–10,000	10,001–100,000	100,001–500,000	500,001–1,000,000	Over 1,000,000	State Total
	(Size of State: km²)						
C & S Africa	1	4	9	13	9	9	45
C America & Caribbean	7	1	8	4	—	1	21
N America	—	—	—	—	—	2	2
S America	—	—	—	5	2	5	12
Asia	2	1	4	8	4	4	23
Oceania	4	1	3	3	—	1	12
Total	16	9	40	54	18	28	165

Table 44

REGIONAL DISTRIBUTION OF STATES BY POPULATION SIZE

Region	Below 0.5m	0.5–1m	1–10m	10–20m	20–50m	50–100m	Over 100m	State Total
	(State Population Size in 1985)							
W Europe	3	1	9	2	1	5	—	21
E Europe	—	—	2	3	3	—	1	9
Middle East & N Africa	3	—	10	3	3	1	—	20
C & S Africa	5	3	24	6	6	—	1	45
C America & Caribbean	9	—	10	1	—	1	—	21
N America	—	—	—	—	1	—	1	2
S America	1	1	4	2	3	—	1	12
Asia	2	—	5	5	3	2	6	23
Oceania	7	1	2	1	—	1	—	12
Total	30	6	66	23	20	10	10	165

Table 45

REGIONAL DISTRIBUTION OF STATES BY POPULATION DENSITY

Region	10 and Below	11–50	51–100	101–250	251–500	Over 500	State Total
	(State Population Density: per km² in 1985)						
W Europe	1	3	5	9	2	1	21
E Europe	—	1	3	5	—	—	9
Middle East & N Africa	5	9	3	1	1	1	20
C & S Africa	11	18	8	6	1	1	45
C America & Caribbean	1	5	4	8	2	1	21
N America	1	1	—	—	—	—	2
S America	4	8	—	—	—	—	12
Asia	1	6	2	8	2	4	23
Oceania	4	2	2	2	2	—	12
Total	28	53	27	39	10	8	165

Table 46

REGIONAL DISTRIBUTION OF STATES BY LITERACY LEVELS

Region	30% and Below	(% of Population who are Literate) 31%–50%	51%–70%	71%–90%	Over 90%	State Total
W Europe	—	—	—	4	17	21
E Europe	—	—	—	2	7	9
Middle East & N Africa	6	8	5	—	1	20
C & S Africa	19	14	10	2	—	45
C America & Caribbean	—	2	4	6	9	21
N America	—	—	—	—	2	2
S America	—	—	2	6	4	12
Asia	5	3	3	10	2	23
Oceania	—	1	2	3	6	12
Total	30	28	26	33	48	165

Table 47

REGIONAL DISTRIBUTION OF STATES BY SHARES OF WORLD GDP AND INCOME TYPE

Region	*GDP ($m) (1985)*	*Share of World Total (%)*	*Average per Capita GDP ($) (1985)*	*State Distribution by Income Type* High	*Middle*	*Low*	*State Total*
W Europe	2,891,484	22.7	6,994	15	6	—	21
E Europe	1,647,525	12.9	3,938	2	6	1	9
Middle East & N Africa	567,245	4.5	2,606	8	6	6	20
C & S Africa	211,244	1.7	447	—	5	40	45
C America & Caribbean	250,019	2.0	1,843	1	15	5	21
N America	4,295,982	33.7	16,112	2	—	—	2
S America	427,725	3.4	1,532	—	9	3	12
Asia	2,241,865	17.6	844	3	3	17	23
Oceania	214,719	1.7	2,616	3	1	8	12
Total	12,747,808	100.0	2,580	34	51	80	165

Table 48

REGIONAL DISTRIBUTION OF STATES BY HUMAN RIGHTS RATINGS

Region	*N/A*	*Bad*	*Poor*	*(Human Rights % in 1986)* 30% and Below	*31%–50%*	*51%–70%*	*71%–90%*	*Over 90%*	*State Total*
W Europe	4	—	—	—	1	—	3	13	21
E Europe	—	1	—	3	4	1	—	—	9
Middle East & N Africa	6	3	1	4	1	4	1	—	20
C & S Africa	14	1	15	2	6	5	2	—	45

Table 48—Regional Distribution of States by Human Rights Ratings (contd.)

				(Human Rights % in 1986)					
Region	*N/A*	*Bad*	*Poor*	*30% and Below*	*31%–50%*	*51%–70%*	*71%–90%*	*Over 90%*	*State Total*
C America & Caribbean	9	—	5	1	—	1	4	1	21
N America	—	—	—	—	—	—	1	1	2
S America	2	—	—	—	2	3	4	1	12
Asia	4	3	2	4	3	6	1	—	23
Oceania	8	—	—	—	—	—	1	3	12
Total	47	8	23	14	17	20	17	19	165

General Note

In the references to income type in Table 47 and subsequently, the designation 'High Income' indicates a per capita national income in excess of US$5,000, 'Middle Income' between US$1,000 and 5,000 and 'Low Income' less than US$1,000; all figures are based on 1985 data.

Scale 1:25 000 000
0 200 400 600 800 Km
Arctic Circle
Arctic Ocean
ICELAND
NORWAY
SWEDEN
FINLAND
North Sea
SOVIET UNION
IRELAND
UNITED KINGDOM
DENMARK
Atlantic Ocean
NETHER-LANDS
EAST GERMANY
POLAND
BELGIUM
WEST GERMANY
LUX
CZECHOSLOVAKIA
FRANCE
SWITZER-LAND
AUSTRIA
HUNGARY
ROMANIA
PORTUGAL
ANDORRA
SPAIN
YUGOSLAVIA
Black Sea
ITALY
Corsica (Fr)
BULGARIA
Balearic Is (Sp)
Sardinia (It)
ALBANIA
TURKEY
Sicily
GREECE
MOROCCO
MALTA
CYPRUS
TUNISIA
Mediterranean Sea
ALGERIA
LIBYA
EGYPT

WESTERN EUROPE

Western Europe, as we have defined it, stretches from the Arctic Ocean in the north to the Mediterranean Sea in the south, and from the Atlantic Ocean in the west to the Black Sea in the east. For our purposes, it includes 21 nation-states, whose total populations amount to over 413 million, or about 147 million more than the total number of people inhabiting the whole of the North American continent. However, the land area occupied by these 21 countries is less than a quarter of that within the boundaries of the United States and Canada. We are, therefore, looking at a comparatively large region, fairly densely populated, but with this density greatest near the geographical centre and discernibly thinning out at the peripheries.

Climatically there are substantial variations, ranging from the tundra of northern Scandinavia to the warm temperate conditions enjoyed by those countries bordering the Mediterranean. Ethnically the differences are not as great and, with a few exceptions, most of the countries in this region have a common cultural heritage, a common Christian foundation and a shared history. There are distinct language differences, however, from country to country, the dominant tongues being English, French, German and the Latin languages of Italy, Spain and Portugal.

Paradoxically, although twelve of these 21 states are now members of the European Community and some of the remainder show signs of wishing to join, the history of Western Europe has been one of division and war rather than co-operation and unity. Most of the major states have been rivals at one time or another and most have clashed militarily. England has been at war with Spain and France. France has clashed with most of Europe and, most recently, Germany has attempted to subjugate the entire continent. A desire to prevent a recurrence of war in Europe was the genesis of the European Community and that wish has clearly been fulfilled, since the continent has enjoyed greater peace and stability since the Second World War than most other areas of the world.

The idea of dividing Europe rigidly into west and east is very much a post-war phenomenon, even though there were cultural and historical differences before then. It is another paradox that the war which most of Europe fought to preserve democracy resulted in dividing former allies and uniting former foes. The iron curtain which Winston Churchill said had come down over Europe is still there, making Germany, and particularly Berlin, a frontier between two profoundly different political cultures, as well as a potential battlefield where the military power of the West and the East might be tested. It is encouraging that the emergence of a new outlook in the Soviet Union may result in that curtain being at least partially lifted.

Economically, the 21 states of Western Europe now have much in common. All operate some form of mixed economy, based partly on market forces and state intervention, although within this mixture sharp policy differences are evident. Whereas there has been a tendency in recent years for a majority of governing regimes to have a left-of-centre, or centrist, orientation, a minority, the most notable among them being the United Kingdom, have shifted to the right. Fifteen have high-income economies and the other six, Cyprus, Greece, Malta, Portugal, Spain and Turkey, are middle-income states, with clear signs that most of them are rapidly moving into the upper echelon. Some nations, such as Sweden and Switzerland, are among the wealthiest in the world and none can now be classified as poor.

All 21 countries boast acceptably high literacy rates, most, are in fact, in the 90 per cent plus category, and their human rights ratings, with the notable exception of Turkey, are also high. Turkey is a comparatively recent recruit to the ranks of fully democratic states and its future behaviour in the field of individual liberties will be closely watched by its West European neighbours.

Some of the 21 states have significant regional problems within their national boundaries, based on linguistic, religious or cultural differences. The most notable examples are to be found in Belgium, Cyprus, Spain and the United Kingdom.

In Belgium differences between the Flemish-speaking north and the French-speaking south have resulted in a multiplicity of political parties, based on language distinctions as well as economic and social priorities. Successive governments have fought shy of seeking a federal solution, and, instead, have tried to satisfy competing groups by creating regional assemblies and a separate cultural council for the French-speaking minority. In reality, however, disagreements between the north and the south, and dissatisfaction with the peculiar position of Brussels, which is linguistically out of step with the rest of the country, owe more to economic than cultural disparities.

In Finland demands for greater recognition of the Swedish-speaking minority are growing progressively weaker. In Norway language differences are based more on dialects and these are being gradually assimilated into a common rural-urban approach. The passion generated by linguistic minorities on the Danish-German and Austrian-Italian borders has diminished markedly in recent years.

Switzerland provides a good example of how language and cultural variations can be successfully accommodated without disrupting social and political harmony. The fact that a federal approach was taken is less important than the willingness, over a long period of time, to show a tolerant respect for cultural and social differences. The strength of the Swiss economy, and the high living standards enjoyed by its citizens, have also helped to create these harmonious relationships.

In Cyprus cultural, religious and linguistic differences have resulted in the physical partitioning of the island but, with the election of a new President in Cyprus and the return to democratic government in Turkey, there are now genuine hopes for a settlement of the dispute.

While Spain was under a virtual military dictactorship the demands of Basque separatists could be kept in check by force but since the return to pluralist politics a different approach has been necessary. A substantial devolution of powers, short of full federalism, seems to have gone some way towards meeting regional aspirations.

What to do about Northern Ireland has been on the agenda of United Kingdom governments for more than half a century and a permanent answer has not yet been found. For the past two decades the approach has been to match violence with violence and an attempt to find a political solution, which would involve all sides in the argument, has so far been avoided. The nationalist movement in Wales has now lost much of its momentum but calls for Scottish devolution, or even separation, have been revived and are likely to become stronger in the ensuing years. This is because, unlike Wales, the sense of nationalism in Scotland is based more on economic and social factors than on cultural differences.

Putting aside regional disputes, politically the 21 nations now show great similarities. Sixteen have been classified as liberal democracies and the remaining five, Cyprus, Greece, Portugal, Spain and Turkey, have only attracted the description of emergent democracies because of non-democratic interruptions in their political development over the past four decades or so.

A close examination of Table 49 below reveals the extent of their political similarities. Three, Austria, West Germany and Switzerland, are federal states and the remaining 18 are unitary. Ten have two-chamber assemblies and eleven are content with one. Sixteen have parliamentary executives, two, Cyprus and Switzerland, have limited presidential executives and in three, France, Finland and Portugal, they are 'dual', with responsibility shared between a President and a Prime Minister.

Table 49

WESTERN EUROPE

Political Data

State	*Date of Formation*	*Political Structure*	*State Type*	*Executive*	*Assembly No of Chambers*	*Party System*	*Voting System*
Austria	1918	Federal	Lib Dem	Parliament	Two	Multi	PL
Belgium	1830	Unitary	Lib Dem	Parliament	Two	Multi	PL
Cyprus	1960	Unitary	Emgt Dem	Lim Pres	One	Multi	PL
Denmark	c940	Unitary	Lib Dem	Parliament	One	Multi	PL
Finland	1917	Unitary	Lib Dem	Dual	One	Multi	PL
France	741	Unitary	Lib Dem	Dual	Two	Multi	SB
West Germany	1949	Federal	Lib Dem	Parliament	Two	Multi	AM
Greece	1829	Unitary	Emgt Dem	Parliament	One	Multi	PL
Iceland	1944	Unitary	Lib Dem	Parliament	One	Multi	PL
Ireland	1937	Unitary	Lib Dem	Parliament	Two	Multi	STV
Italy	1861	Unitary	Lib Dem	Parliament	Two	Multi	PL
Luxembourg	1848	Unitary	Lib Dem	Parliament	One	Multi	PL
Malta	1964	Unitary	Lib Dem	Parliament	One	Two	STV
Netherlands	1648	Unitary	Lib Dem	Parliament	Two	Multi	PL
Norway	1905	Unitary	Lib Dem	Parliament	One	Multi	PL
Portugal	1128	Unitary	Emgt Dem	Dual	One	Multi	PL
Spain	1492	Unitary	Emgt Dem	Parliament	Two	Two	PL
Sweden	1523	Unitary	Lib Dem	Parliament	One	Multi	PL
Switzerland	1648	Federal	Lib Dem	Lim Pres	Two	Multi	PL
Turkey	1923	Unitary	Emgt Dem	Parliament	One	Multi	PL
United Kingdom	1707/ 1921	Unitary	Lib Dem	Parliament	Two	Two	SP

Social and Economic Data

State	*Area (km^2)*	*Population (m) (1985)*	*Population Density (per km^2)*	*Literacy Rate (%)*	*Income Type*	*Human Rights Rating (%)*
Austria	83,850	7.546	90	100	High	96
Belgium	30,510	9.868	323	100	High	96
Cyprus	9,250	0.666	72	91	Middle	N/A

Table 49—Western Europe (contd.)

	Social and Economic Data					
State	Area (km²)	Population (m) (1985)	Population Density (per km²)	Literacy Rate (%)	Income Type	Human Rights Rating (%)
Denmark	43,080	5.087	118	99	High	98
Finland	337,050	4.931	15	100	High	98
France	547,030	55.400	101	99	High	94
West Germany	248,670	60.734	244	100	High	97
Greece	131,990	9.954	75	90	Middle	92
Iceland	102,850	0.244	2	100	High	N/A
Ireland	68,390	3.624	53	100	High	86
Italy	301,280	57.226	190	94	High	87
Luxembourg	2,590	0.367	142	100	High	N/A
Malta	320	0.355	1,109	81	Middle	N/A
Netherlands	34,000	14.481	426	100	High	98
Norway	323,900	4.165	13	100	High	97
Portugal	92,080	16.600	180	79	Middle	91
Spain	504,880	39.074	77	93	Middle	84
Sweden	449,700	8.357	19	100	High	98
Switzerland	41,290	6.470	157	100	High	95
Turkey	779,450	51.819	66	74	Middle	41
United Kingdom	244,100	56.458	231	99	High	94
Total/Average	4,376,260	413.426	94	74-100	High	41-98

It is in the areas of party politics and electoral systems that a clear majority-minority situation arises. Eighteen of the 21 states have multi-party politics operating whereas three, Malta, Spain and the United Kingdom, have more polarised, two-party systems. Twenty, or over 95 per cent, of the countries in this region, have adopted proportional or majoritarian electoral systems, while only one, the United Kingdom, prefers the simple plurality system of voting.

It would be dangerous to draw too firm conclusions about the effects of voting systems on party structures from this small sample, particularly since Spain has, effectively, a two-party system operating within a proportional representation framework, but it can be said that multi-party politics and some form of PR seem to go hand in hand in most countries in Western Europe. It can also be said that the fact that many have had coalition governments for most of the post-war period does not seem to have in any way diminished the degree of democracy they have enjoyed, or their economic performances. Indeed, it can be cogently argued that the reverse is true.

In summary, although there are clear differences in approach to the political, economic and social challenges facing them, the 21 states of Western Europe have more shared values than disagreements. Above all else, most have mature political systems which have survived many changes in the environments in which they function and this maturity has created a keen sense of reality and tolerance in their dealings with the rest of the world. Probably the most encouraging sign is that the nations of Western Europe, whether or not they are Community members, are increasingly coming together, rather than drifting apart.

AUSTRIA

Republic of Austria
Republik Österreich

Capital: Vienna

Social and economic data
Area: 83,850 km^2
Population: 7.546m*
Pop density per km^2: 90*
Literacy rate: 100%*
GDP: $66,051m*; per capita GDP: $8,753
Economy type: high income
Labour force in agriculture: 9%

*1985

Ethnic composition
Ninety-eight per cent of the population are German, 0.7 per cent Croatian and 0.3 per cent Slovene.

Religions
About 85 per cent of the population are Roman Catholics, about 400,000 belong to other Christian religions and there are about 7,000 Jews.

Political features
State type: liberal democratic
Date of state formation: 1918
Political structure: federal
Executive: parliamentary
Assembly: two-chamber
Party structure: multi-party
Human rights rating: 96%

Local and regional government
Austria is a federal republic divided into nine provinces or states (*Länder*), each with its own assembly and government. The states, with their populations, are: Wien (1.5m), Niederösterreich (1.4m), Oberösterreich (1.3m), Steiermark (1.2m), Tirol (600,000), Kärnten (500,000), Salzburg (400,000), Voralberg (300,000) and Burgenland (270,000). The assemblies (*Landtag*) are very similar to the lower house of the federal assembly. Executive power is exercised by governors elected by the provincial assemblies.

Although, constitutionally, Austria is a federal state, there is a high degree of centralisation, with the federal government being responsible for education, the police, the postal service, the railways, social policies and taxation.

Head of state
President Kurt Waldheim, since 1986.

Head of government
Federal Chancellor Franz Vranitzky, since 1986.

Political leaders since 1970
1970-83 Bruno Kreiksky (SPO), 1983–86 Fred Sinowatz (SPO-FPO coalition), 1986– Franz Vranitzky (SPO-OVP coalition).

Political system
The 1920 constitution was amended in 1929, suspended during the Hitler years, and reinstated in 1945. It provides for a two-chamber federal assembly, consisting of a National Council (Nationalrat) and a Federal Council (Bundesrat). The National Council has 183 members elected by universal adult suffrage, through a party list system of proportional representation, for a four-year term. It is subject to dissolution during this period. The Federal Council has 63 members elected by the provincial assemblies for varying terms, depending upon the life of each individual assembly. Each province provides a chairman for the Federal Council for a six-month term of office. The federal President is the formal head of state and is elected by popular vote for a six-year term. The federal Chancellor is head of government and chosen by the President on the basis of support in the National Council. He governs with a cabinet of his own choosing.

Political parties
There are currently 13 active political parties, the most significant being the Socialist Party of Austria (SPO), the Austrian People's Party (OVP), the Freedom Party of Austria (FPO), the United Green Party of Austria (VGO) and the Green Alternative Party (ALV).

The SPO was founded in 1889 as the Social-Democratic Party. It advocates democratic socialism and the maintenance of Austria's neutrality. It has a membership of about 720,000.

The OVP was founded in 1945 as the Christian-Democratic Party. It describes itself as a 'progressive centre party' and has a membership of about 800,000.

The FPO dates from 1955, and afterwards took over from the League of Independents, which was wound up in 1956. It has a moderate, left-of-centre, orientation and advocates social reform, worker participation in management and greater European co-operation.

The VGO and ALV are ecological parties which have recently arrived on the political scene, both originating in 1982. The VGO is the more conservative of the two, the ALV being the result of a union, in 1987, between the Austrian Alternative List (ALO) and another Green party, the BIP. The VGO declined to take part in the merger.

Latest elections
In the 1986 presidential election Dr Kurt Waldheim defeated his SPO rival, Dr Kurt Seyrer, in the second ballot run-off, by 53.89 per cent of the popular vote to 46.11 per cent.

The results of the 1985 Nationalrat elections were:

	% Votes	*Seats*
SPO	43.12	80
OVP	41.30	77
FPO	9.73	18
VGO/ALV	4.82	8

The results of the 1987 Bundesrat elections were: OVP 33 seats, SPO 30 seats.

Political history

The first Austrian Republic was proclaimed in November 1918 after the break-up of the Dual Monarchy of Austria-Hungary. A constituent assembly, which had been formed, voted to make Austria an integral part of Germany but the peace treaties ruled out any Austria-German union. With the rise of Nazism in Germany in the 1930s there was considerable pressure on Austria, culminating, in 1938, in the Anschluss, or union, making Austria a province of Greater Germany until the end of the war in 1945.

Austria returned to its 1920 constitution in 1945, with a provisional government led by Dr Karl Renner. The Allies had divided the country into four zones, occupied by the USSR, the United States, Britain and France. The first post-war elections were held while the country was still occupied and resulted in an SPO-OVP coalition government. Austria's full independence was formally recognised in October 1955.

The first post-war non-coalition government was formed in 1966 when the OVP came to power with Josef Klaus as Chancellor. In 1970 the SPO formed a minority government under Dr Bruno Kreisky and increased its majority in the 1971 and 1975 general elections. In 1978 opposition to the government's proposals to install the first nuclear power plant nearly resulted in its defeat but it survived and, although the idea of a nuclear plant was abandoned, nuclear energy continued to be a controversial issue. In 1983 the SPO regime came to an end when it lost its overall majority and Kreisky resigned, refusing to join a coalition. The SPO decline was partly attributed to the emergence of new environmentalist groups, the VGO and the ALO. Dr Fred Sinowatz, the new chairman of the SPO, formed an SPO-FPO coalition government.

In April 1985 international controversy was aroused with the announcement that Dr Kurt Waldheim, former UN Secretary-General, was to be a presidential candidate. Despite allegations of his complicity in the Nazi regime, as a war-time officer in Yugoslavia, Waldheim was eventually elected President in January 1986. In June of that year Sinowatz resigned the chancellorship, for what he described as personal reasons, and was succeeded by Franz Vranitzky but the SPO-FPO coalition broke up when an extreme right-winger, Jorg Haider, became FPO leader.

In the November 1985 elections the SPO tally of National Council seats fell from 90 to 80, the OVP's from 81 to 77 while the FPO increased from 12 to 18. For the first time the Green lobby was represented, the VGO winning eight seats. Vranitzky offered his resignation but was persuaded by the President to try to form a 'grand coalition', between the SPO and the OVP, on the lines of Austria's first post-war government. Agreement was eventually reached and Vranitzky remained as Chancellor with the OVP leader, Dr Alois Mock, as Vice-Chancellor. Sinowatz denounced the coalition as a betrayal of socialist principles and resigned his chairmanship of the SPO.

In May 1988 it was disclosed that Austria might make a serious application to join the European Community. The reaction to this was mixed. Members of the European Free Trade Agreement (EFTA), of which Austria was a founder member, thought it might weaken their moves to work more closely with the EC, and some Community countries, including the United Kingdom, were not anxious to have another non-aligned member.

BELGIUM

Kingdom of Belgium
Royaume de Belgique
Koninkrijk België

Capital: Brussels

Social and economic data
Area: 30,510 km^2
Population: 9.868m*
Pop density per km^2: 323*
Literacy rate: 100%*
GDP: $81,037m*; per capita GDP: $8,212
Economy type: high income
Labour force in agriculture: 3%

*1985

Ethnic composition
The northern part of the country consists mainly of Flemings, of Teutonic stock, who speak Flemish, while in the south the majority of people are Walloons, of Latin stock, who speak French. Fifty-five per cent of the population are Flemings, 33 per cent Walloons and the rest of mixed stock.

Religions
About 88 per cent of the population are Roman Catholics. There are also about 35,000 Jews, and substantial minorities of a number of Protestant denominations, including the Lutheran Church, the Church of England, the United Belgian Prtotestant Church, the Belgian Evangelical Mission and the Union of Evangelical Baptist Churches.

Political features
State type: liberal democratic
Date of state formation: 1830
Political structure: unitary
Executive: parliamentary
Assembly: two-chamber
Party structure: multi-party
Human rights rating: 96%

Local and regional government
Since 1980 Flanders and Wallonia have had regional 'sub-governments', each with an elected regional assembly, with certain cultural and economic powers. There is also a separate Walloon Cultural Council.

For administrative purposes, the country is divided into nine provinces which are further subdivided into communes. Local government is conducted by a partnership of officials, appointed by the central government, and elected councillors, representing the views of the localities.

Head of state
King Baudouin, since 1951.

Head of government
Prime Minister Dr Wilfried Martens, since 1981.

Political leaders since 1970
1968–72 Gaston Eyskens (CVP coalitions), 1972–74 Edmond Leburton (PSB coalition), 1974–78 Leo Tindemans (CVP coalitions), 1978–79 Paul Vanden Boeynants (PSC coalitions), 1979–81 Wilfried Martens (CVP coalitions), 1981 Mark Eyskens (CVP coalition), 1981– Wilfried Martens (CVP coalitions).

Political system
The constitution dates from 1831 and was subsequently amended a number of times and then rewritten in 1971. The parliamentary system contains features found in both Britain and the United States. For example, the Prime Minister and cabinet are drawn from and are responsible to the assembly, which in turn, through a powerful committee system, exercises considerable control over the executive.

The assembly consists of two chambers, the Senate, with 182 members, and the Chamber of Representatives, with 212. One hundred and six members of the Senate are nationally elected, through a party list system of proportional representation, 50 are elected by Provincial Councillors, 25 are co-opted and, by right, the heir to the throne is also a member. The Senate has a life of four years. The Chamber of Representatives has 212 members elected by universal adult suffrage, through a party list system of proportional representation, also for a four-year term.

The Prime Minister is appointed by the King on the basis of assembly support. The King then appoints a cabinet on the advice of the Prime Minister.

Political parties
There are currently 20 active political parties, most of them reflecting the linguistic and social divisions within the country. The most significant parties are the Flemish-speaking Social Christian Party (CVP), the French-speaking Social Christian Party (PSC), the Flemish-speaking Socialist Party (SP), the French-speaking Socialist Party (PS), the Flemish-speaking Liberal Party (PVV), the French-speaking Liberal Reform Party (PRL), and the Flemish People's Party (VU).

The CVP was founded in 1945. It has a centre-left orientation. The PSC was formed at the same time and is the CVP's French-speaking equivalent. Collectively, they now have over 180,000 members.

The SP is the Flemish wing of the Socialist Party and was founded in 1885. The PS is the French-speaking wing, which broke away in 1979. Both wings have a left-of-centre orientation.

The PVV is the Flemish wing of the Liberal Party and was formed in 1961, to replace the former Liberal Party. The PRL is the French-speaking wing and dates from 1979. Before that it was known as the Walloon Freedom and Reform Party. Both wings have a moderate, centrist orientation.

The VU was founded in 1954 and advocates a federal structure for the country, to allow full scope for the promotion of a Flemish identity.

Latest elections

The results of the 1987 Chamber of Deputies elections were as follows:

	% Votes	*Seats*
CVP	19.5	43
PS	15.7	40
SP	14.9	32
PVV	11.5	25
PRL	9.4	23
PSC	8.0	19
VU	8.0	16
Other parties	13.0	14

Political history

What is now the modern Kingdom of Belgium has experienced many changes of rule under many different political regimes, from the Romans of pre-Christian times, to the French, then Spanish, then Austrians and then the French again. It formed part of the French Empire between 1794 and 1815, after which it was united with the Netherlands. Linguistic, religious and historical differences made the marriage an unhappy one and in 1830 the Belgians rebelled. The great powers intervened and Belgium was given international recognition as an independent kingdom, under Leopold of Saxe-Coburg. From that date the country developed rapidly to become a significant industrial and commercial force.

The experience of two world wars fought on its territory has made Belgium acutely aware of the dangers of the pursuit of purely national ends and since 1945 it has played a major part in international co-operation in Europe, being a founder member of the Benelux Economic Union, the Council of Europe and the European Community.

Its main internal political problems have stemmed from the division between French- and Flemish-speaking members of the population, aggravated by the polarisation between Flanders in the north, which is predominantly conservative, and French-speaking Wallonia in the south, which tends to be mainly socialist. About 55 per cent of the population are Flemish-speaking, 44 per cent French-speaking and the remainder speak German. It has been an hereditary monarchy since 1830 and King Leopold III, who had reigned since 1934, abdicated in 1951 in favour of his son, Baudouin.

Between 1971 and 1973, in an attempt to close the language and social divisions, amendments to the constitution were made. These involved the transfer of greater power to the regions, the inclusion of German-speaking members in the cabinet and linguistic parity in the government overall. Then, in 1974, separate regional councils and ministerial committees were established. In 1977 a coalition government, headed by Leo Tindemans (CVP), proposed the creation of a federal Belgium, based on Flanders, Wallonia and Brussels, but the proposals were not adopted and in 1978 Tindemans resigned. He was followed by another coalition government headed by Wilfried Martens. In 1980 the language conflict developed into open violence and it was eventually agreed that Flanders and Wallonia should have separate regional assemblies with powers to spend up to 10 per cent of the national budget on cultural facilities, public health, roads and urban projects. Brussels was to be governed by a three-member executive.

Such was the political instability that by 1980 Martens had formed no fewer than four coalition governments. In 1981 a new coalition, led by Mark Eyskens (CVP), lasted less than a year and Martens again returned to power. Between 1981 and 1982 economic difficulties resulted in a series of damaging public-sector strikes and in 1983 linguistic divisions again threatened the government.

Between 1983 and 1985 there was considerable debate about the siting of US cruise missiles in Belgium before parliament eventually agreed to their installation by a majority vote.

Martens formed yet another coalition government after the 1985 general election but this broke up in 1987 and the Prime Minister was asked by the King to continue until after further elections. These were held in December 1987 but failed to produce a conclusive result and, after a series of exploratory talks between political leaders, Martens formed a CVP-PS-SP-PSC-VU coalition in May 1988.

CYPRUS

Republic of Cyprus; and
Turkish Republic of Northern Cyprus
Kipriaki Dimokratia and
Kibris Cumhuriyeti

Capital: Nicosia

Social and economic data

Area: 9,250 km^2
Population: 0.666m*
Pop density per km^2: 72*
Literacy rate: 91%*
GDP: $2,335m*; per capita GDP: $3,506
Economy type: middle income
Labour force in agriculture: 17%

*1985

Ethnic composition

About 77 per cent of the population have Greek origins and are Greek-speaking, while about 18 per cent have Turkish roots and speak

Turkish. Most of the Turkish community live in the northern part of the island, within the self-styled Turkish Republic of Northern Cyprus.

Religions
There are about 444,000 members of the Greek Orthodox Church, mainly in the south, and about 105,000 Muslims, mainly in the north.

Political features
State type: emergent democratic
Date of state formation: 1960
Political structure: unitary
Executive: limited presidential
Assembly: one-chamber
Party structure: multi-party
Human rights rating: N/A

Local and regional government
For administrative purposes, the country is divided into six districts, ranging in population from just over 30,000 to over 230,000.

Head of state and head of government
Greek: President Georgios Vassilou, since 1988.
Turkish: Rauf Denktash, since 1976.

Political leaders since 1970
1960–75 Archbishop Makarios III (EOKA), 1975 Nicos Sampson (Military), 1975–77 Archbishop Makarios III (DIKO), 1977–88 Spyros Kyprianou (DIKO), 1988– Georgios Vassilou (Independent).

Political system
The 1960 constitution provided for power-sharing between Greek and Turkish Cypriots, on a basis of numerical parity, but in 1963 the Turks declined to participate and the following year set up a separate community in northern Cyprus, refusing to acknowledge the Greek government in the south. The Greek Cypriot government claims to be the government of all Cyprus and is generally accepted as such, except by the Turkish community. *De facto* there are, therefore, two republics, each with its own President, Council of Ministers, assembly and judicial system. The self-styled 'Turkish Republic of Northern Cyprus' even has its own representatives overseas.

Greek Cyprus has a President, elected for five years by universal adult suffrage, through a second ballot majoritarian voting system, and a single-chamber assembly, the House of Representatives, with 56 members, elected through a party list system and also for five years. Originally its membership was 50 (35 Greek and 15 Turkish) but now all 56 are Greek. The President appoints and heads a Council of Ministers.

Turkish Cyprus adopted a separate constitution, after a referendum in 1985, providing for a President, Council of Ministers and assembly similar to that in the southern part of the island. This separate government has received external recognition only from Turkey. In 1988 the newly elected president, Georgios Vassilou, pledged himself to construct a national government and to work speedily towards an end to the division of the island. Later that year talks between him and the Turkish Cypriot leader began, under United Nations auspices.

Political parties

Of seven political parties, the four most significant in the Greek sector are the Democratic Front (DIKO), the Progressive Party of the Working People (AKEL), the Democratic Rally (DISY) and the Socialist Party (EDEK).

DIKO was formed in 1976. It has a centre-left orientation and believes that the solution to Cyprus's problems lies in a federal strategy, achieved through the good offices of the United Nations.

AKEL was formed in 1941 as the successor to the Communist Party of Cyprus. Although its orientation is socialist, it is not formally aligned with the Soviet bloc. It supported the candidature of George Vassilou for the presidency in 1988, even though he himself stood as an independent.

DISY was formed in 1976. In 1977 it absorbed the Democratic National Party (DEK) into its ranks. It has a centrist orientation and supports the idea of Western nations taking an active part in bringing Cyprus's racial and religious troubles to an end.

EDEK was formed in 1969 as the Socialist Party of Cyprus. It supports the idea of a non-aligned, independent, unitary and demilitarised Cyprus, with a socialist social and economic structure.

Latest elections

In the 1985 House of Representatives elections the reults were as follows:

	% Votes	*Seats*
DISY	33.56	19
DIKO	27.65	16
AKEL	27.24	15
EDEK	11.27	6

In the 1988 presidential election the results were as follows:

1st Ballot:	Glafcos Clerides (DISY)	33.32%
	Georgios Vassilou (Ind)	30.11%
	Spyros Kyprianou (DIKO)	27.29%
2nd Ballot:	Georgios Vassilou	51.63%
	Glafcos Clerides	48.37%

Political history

Originally Greek, Cyprus was conquered by the Turks in 1571 and then by the British in 1878, and annexed in 1914. In 1955 a guerrilla war against British rule was started by Greek Cypriots seeking *Enosis*, or unification with Greece. The chief organisation in this campaign was the National Organisation of Cypriot Combatants (EOKA) and its political and military leaders were the Head of the Greek Orthodox Church in Cyprus, Archbishop Makarios III, and General George Grivas. Because of their activities Makarios and other Enosis leaders were deported by the British government in 1956.

After three years of intensive negotiations, Makarios was allowed to return to Cyprus and, with the granting of full independence in 1960, was elected President of the new Greek-Turkish state. As part of the independence agreement, Britain was allowed to retain its military and naval bases.

Relations between the Greek and Turkish political leaders deteriorated and in 1963 the Turks withdrew from power-sharing and fighting broke out between the two communities. The following year a UN peace-keeping force was established to keep the two sides apart. After a prolonged period of mutual hostility, relations improved to the extent that talks were resumed, with the Turks arguing for a federal state and the Greeks wanting a unitary one.

In 1971 General Grivas returned to the island and started a guerrilla campaign against the Makarios government, believing that it had failed the Greek community. Three years later Grivas died and Makarios carried out a purge of his supporters but in 1975 he himself was deposed by Greek officers of the National Guard and Nicos Sampson, who was a political extremist calling again for Enosis, was appointed President. Makarios fled to Britain.

At the request of the Turkish Cypriot leader, who feared the extremism of Sampson, Turkey sent troops to the island, taking control of the northern region and dividing Cyprus along what became known as the 'Attila Line', cutting off about a third of the total territory. Later in 1975 Sampson resigned, the military regime which had appointed him collapsed, and Makarios returned. The Turkish Cypriots had, however, by now established their own, *de facto*, independent government for what they called the 'Turkish Federated State of Cyprus' (TFSC), with Rauf Denktash as President.

In 1977 Makarios died and was succeeded by Spyros Kyprianou, who had been President of the House of Representatives. He saw the way forward through international mediation and in 1980 UN-sponsored peace talks between the Greek and Turkish communities were resumed. The Turkish Cypriots offered to hand back about 4 per cent of the territory they controlled and to re-settle 40,000 of the 200,000 refugees who had fled to the north, but this failed to satisfy the Greek Cypriots and stalemate was reached. The Turks wanted equal status for the two communities, equal representation in government and firm links with Turkey. The Greeks, on the other hand, favoured an alternating presidency, strong central government and representation in the assembly on a proportional basis. Between 1982 and 1985 several attempts by the Greek government in Athens and the United Nations to find a compromise solution failed and the Turkish Republic of Northern Cyprus (TRNC), with Denktash as President, was formally declared, but recognised only by Turkey.

In 1985 a summit meeting between Denktash and Kyprianou failed to reach agreement and the UN Secretary-General drew up proposals for a bi-zonal federal Cyprus, with a Greek President and a Turkish Vice-President but this was not found acceptable. Meanwhile, both Kyprianou and Denktash had been re-elected.

The dispute between the two communities seemed to be insoluble until the election of the independent candidate, Georgios Vassilou, to the presidency in 1988. Vassilou seemed likely to be better placed to find a solution because of his lack of involvement in party politics. He immediately set about creating a government of national unity and steps to bridge the Greek-Turkish divide.

DENMARK

Kingdom of Denmark
Kongeriget Danmark

Capital: Copenhagen

Social and economic data
Area: 43,080 km^2
Population: 5.087m*
Pop density per km^2: 118*
Literacy rate: 99%*
GDP: $57,818m*; per capita GDP: $11,366
Economy type: high income
Labour force in agriculture: 6%

*1985

Ethnic composition
The Danes are a branch of the Scandinavian race which embraces the whole peninsula, including Sweden, Norway and Finland as well as Denmark.

Religions
The Danish Lutheran Church is the established Church and about 91 per cent of the population are members of it.

Political features
State type: liberal democratic
Date of state formation: *c* AD 940
Political structure: unitary
Executive: parliamentary
Assembly: one-chamber
Party structure: multi-party
Human rights rating: 98%

Local and regional government
Denmark is divided into 14 counties, varying in population from about 47,000 to nearly 620,000, plus one city and one borough. All have elected councils. At a lower level are 277 districts, each with an elected council and mayor.

The Faroe Islands and Greenland enjoy home rule, with elected assemblies and executives. They also elect representatives to the national assembly, the Folketing.

Head of state
Queen Margarethe II, since 1972.

Head of government
Prime Minister Poul Schluter, since 1982.

Political leaders since 1970
1973–75 Poul Hartling (Liberal), 1975–82 Anker Jorgensen (Social Democrat-led coalition), 1982– Poul Schluter (Conservative coalition).

Political system
The 1849 constitution has been revised on several occasions, the last being in 1953. It provides for an hereditary monarch, with no personal political power, and a single-chamber assembly, the Folketing. The Prime Minister and cabinet are drawn from and collectively responsible to the Folketing, which has 179 members, elected by adult franchise, 175 of the members representing metropolitan Denmark, 2 the Faroe Islands and 2 Greenland. Voting is by a party list system of proportional representation and the Folketing has a life of four years, but may be dissolved within this period if the government is defeated on a vote of confidence. The government, however, need only resign on what it itself defines as a 'vital element' of policy.

Political parties
The proportional representation voting system favours the growth of political parties with distinctively different attitudes and policies. There are currently 15, the eight most significant being the Social Democrats (SD), the Conservative People's Party (KF), the Liberal Party (V), the Socialist People's Party (SF), the Radical Liberals (RV), the Centre Democrats (CD), the Progress Party (FP) and the Christian People's Party (KrF).

The SD was founded in 1871 on Marxist principles but now has a moderate, left-of-centre orientation. It has about 100,000 members, drawn mainly from blue-collar workers and public service employees.

The KF was formed in 1916 by a mixture of landowners, intellectuals and academics. It is a moderate, free-enterprise party which accepts the need for state intervention to preserve the nation's social and economic balance.

The Venstre or V party is the Liberal Party of Denmark and was established in 1870. It is a centre-left grouping which supports free trade, a well-funded welfare system but a minimum of state interference in other respects.

The SF was formed in 1959 by Aksel Larsen who had been the leader of the Danish Communist Party but was expelled because he refused to toe the Soviet line. As now constituted, it is a moderate, left-wing party which seeks to apply socialism in a distinctively Danish way.

The RV split from the Liberals in 1905 to pursue more radical policies. It is a strongly internationalist party which favours domestic policies of social reform, worker participation in industrial management, the control of monopolies and the strengthening of private enterprise.

The CD is a moderate, centrist party which was formed in 1973. It opposes extremes in politics and is a strong supporter of EC and NATO membership.

The FP began in 1972 as a strongly anti-bureacratic movement, promoting such radical ideas as the abolition of income tax, the disbanding of the civil service and a drastic reduction in legislation.

The KrF was founded in 1970 as an inter-denominational grouping which places emphasis on family values. It is a strong opponent of abortion and pornography.

Latest elections

The results of the 1988 Folketing elections were as follows:

	% Votes	*Seats*
SD	29.9	55
KF	19.3	35
SF	13.0	24
V	11.8	22
FP	9.0	16
RV	5.6	10
CD	4.7	9
KrF	2.0	4

Political history

Part of a united Scandinavian kingdom until the fifteenth century and then remaining linked with Norway until 1815, Denmark became an independent state in 1849. The constitution which was then adopted reaffirmed its status as a constitutional monarchy. Neutral in the First World War, Denmark tried to preserve its neutrality in 1939 by signing a pact with Hitler, but was invaded by the Germans in 1940 and occupied until liberated by British forces in 1945.

Although traditionally a neutralist country, Denmark joined NATO in 1949 and the European Free Trade Association (EFTA) in 1960, resigning to join the European Community in 1973. Iceland was part of the Danish kingdom until 1945 and the other parts of non-metropolitan Denmark, the Faroe Islands and Greenland, were given special recognition by a constitution which has been successfully adapted to meet changing circumstances. The last rewriting was in 1953 when, among other things, provision was made for a daughter to succeed to the throne in the absence of a male heir, and a system of voting by proportional representation was introduced.

Moderate left-wing policies have tended to dominate Danish politics, and the voting system, often resulting in minority or coalition governments, has, on the whole, encouraged this moderate approach. In 1985 Denmark's tradition of neutrality was exemplified by evidence of a growing non-nuclear movement.

In the 1987 general election the centre-right coalition, led by Poul Schluter, lost seven seats but Schluter decided to continue with a minority government, holding 70 of the 179 Folketing seats. A government defeat over Denmark's non-nuclear defence policy prompted him to call a snap general election in May 1988. This resulted in slight gains for his centre-right coalition but overall an inconclusive result. The Queen asked Schluter to form a new government which he did, in June 1988, on the basis of Conservative, Liberal and Radical Liberal support.

FINLAND

Republic of Finland
Suomen Tasavalta

Capital: Helsinki

Social and economic data
Area: 337,050 km^2
Population: 4.931m*
Pop density per km^2: 15*
Literacy rate: 100%*
GDP: $54,030m*; per capita GDP: $11,026
Economy type: high income
Labour force in agriculture: 11%

*1985

Ethnic composition
The great majority of Finns are descended from the inhabitants of Russia who were pushed northwards by Slav migrations.

Religions
Ninety per cent of the population are members of the Evangelical Lutheran Church.

Political features
State type: liberal democratic
Date of state formation: 1917
Political structure: unitary
Executive: dual
Assembly: one-chamber
Party structure: multi-party
Human rights rating: 98%

Local and regional government
The country is divided into 12 provinces (*lahni*), each administered by an appointed governor. One of the provinces, Ahvenanmaa, which comprises the Aland Islands, also has an elected assembly (*landsting*) and local powers of legislation.

Head of state
President Mauno Koivisto, since 1982.

Heads of government
President Mauno Koivisto, since 1982.
Prime Minister Harri Holkeri, since 1987.

Political Leaders Since 1970

1970 Teuve Aura (Cabinet of Experts), 1970–71 Ahti Karjalainen (KP-led coalition), 1971–72 Teuve Aura (Caretaker Cabinet), 1972 Rafael Paasio (SDP), 1972–75 Kalevi Sorsa (SDP-led coalition), 1975 Keijo Liinamaa (Caretaker Cabinet), 1975–77 Martti Miettunen (KP-led coalitions), 1977–79 Kalevi Sorsa (SDP-led coalition), 1979–82 Mauno Koivisto (SDP-led coalition), 1982–87 Kalevi Sorsa (SDP-led coalitions), 1987– Harri Holkeri (KOK-led coalition).

Political system

Finland is a republic which combines a parliamentary system with a strong presidency. The single-chamber assembly, the Eduskunta, has 200 members, elected by universal adult suffrage, through a party list system of proportional representation, for a four-year term. The President is elected for six years by popular vote, or, if there is not a clear majority, by a 301-member electoral college, chosen by popular vote in the same way as the assembly. The President appoints a Prime Minister and a cabinet, called a Council of State, all members of which are collectively responsible to the Eduskunta.

The relationship between the President and the Prime Minister and the Council of State is unusual, the nearest equivalent being in France. The President is entrusted with supreme executive power, and can ignore even a unanimous decision reached in the Council of State, but the Prime Minister is concerned with the day-to-day operation of the government so that to some extent they can, at times, both act as heads of government. Both the President and the Eduskunta can initiate legislation and he has a right of veto, but that veto can be overruled by a newly appointed assembly. Because of the system of proportional representation, there is a multiplicity of parties, and the Prime Minister invariably heads a coalition Council of State.

Political parties

There are twelve political parties, the six most significant being the Social Democratic Party (SDP), The National Coalition Party (KOK), The Centre Party (KP), the Finnish People's Democratic League (SKDL), the Swedish People's Party, the Finnish Rural Party (SMP).

The SDP was founded in 1899 as a product of the growing working-class movement. It has a moderate, left-of-centre orientation. The KOK was formed in 1918. It has a moderate, right-of-centre stance. The KP dates from 1906 and is a radical, centre party, promoting the interests of rural areas and favouring decentralised government. The SKDL was formed in 1944 by dissident Social Democrats, independent socialists and communists and represents, therefore, a left-wing coalition. The Swedish People's Party was founded in 1906 to represent the numerous Swedes who had become resident in Finland and established themselves as something of an élite group. The SMP dates from 1956 and seeks to defend the interests of small farmers, industrial workers and small businessmen.

Latest elections
In the 1987 Eduskunta elections the results were as follows:

	% Vote	*Seats*
SDP	24.14	56
KOK	23.13	53
KP	17.63	40
SKDL	9.37	16
Swedish People's Party	5.32	12
SMP	6.31	9
Other parties	14.10	14

In the 1988 presidential election Mauno Koivisto narrowly failed to be elected by popular vote but won in the electoral college election by securing 47.92 per cent of the votes, his nearest rival obtaining 20.15 per cent.

Political history
Finland was formerly an autonomous part of the Russian Empire and during the 1917 Russian revolution it proclaimed its independence. The new Soviet regime initially tried to regain control but acknowledged its independence in 1920. In 1939 the Soviet Union's request for military bases in Finland was rejected and the two countries were involved in the 'Winter War', which lasted for 15 weeks. Finland was defeated and forced to cede territory. In the hope of getting its lands back, Finland joined Nazi Germany in attacking the Soviet Union in 1941 but agreed a separate armistice in 1944. It was again forced to cede territory and in 1948 signed the Finno-Soviet Pact of Friendship, Co-operation and Mutual Assistance (the YYA Treaty). This was extended in 1955, 1970 and 1983.

Although the Treaty requires it to repel any attack on the USSR through Finnish territory by Germany or its allies, Finland has adopted and maintained a policy of strict neutrality. It signed a trade treaty with the EC in 1973 and a 15-year trade agreement with the USSR in 1977.

Finnish politics have been characterised by instability in governments, more than 60 having been formed since independence, including many minority coalitions. The presidency, on the other hand, has been very stable, with only two Presidents in over 30 years. The unusual device of a dual executive has, therefore, countered the instability and provided a consistency which might otherwise have been lacking. The Social Democratic and Centre parties have dominated Finland's coalition politics for many years but the 1987 general election resulted in the Social Democrats entering government with their arch-enemies, the Conservatives, and the Centre Party being forced into opposition.

FRANCE

French Republic
République Française

Capital: Paris

Social and economic data
Area: 547,030 km^2

Population: 55.400m*
Pop density per km^2: 101*
Literacy rate: 99%
GDP: $511,650m*; per capita GDP: $9,236
Economy type: high income
Labour force in agriculture: 7%

*1985

Ethnic composition
The population is overwhelmingly drawn from French ethnic stock, of Celtic and Latin origins, with a Basque minority residing in the south-west. There are, in addition, more than 4.5 million immigrants, constituting 8 per cent of the population. A third of them are drawn from North Africa and reside mainly in the Marseilles region and in major city areas. A further fifth originate from Portugal and a tenth each from Italy and Spain.

Religions
About 90 per cent of the population are Roman Catholics, although barely 15 per cent are regular church attenders; 5 per cent are Muslims; and 2 per cent are Protestants.

Political features
State type: liberal democratic
Date of state formation: AD 741
Political structure: unitary
Executive: dual
Assembly: two-chamber
Party structure: multi-party
Human rights rating: 94%

Local and regional government
There are 21 regional councils (*conseils régionaux*) concerned primarily with economic planning, which were originally set up in 1973 as indirectly elected advisory bodies and have since 1986 been directly elected. Below these are 96 department (large county) councils (*conseils généraux*) and more than 36,000 village and town councils. Corsica, which was designated a *collectivité territoriale* in 1982, has its own directly elected 61-seat legislative assembly, which has the authority to scrutinise National Assembly bills and to propose amendments applicable to the island. This is described in more detail in Part III.

Head of state
President François Mitterrand, since 1981.

Head of government
Prime Minister Michel Rocard, since 1988.

Political leaders since 1970
Presidents: 1969–74 Georges Pompidou (UDR), 1974–81 Valéry Giscard D'Estaing (RP/UDF), 1981– François Mitterrand (PS).*

*Shared power between 1986–88 in a 'dual administration' with Jacques Chirac (RPR).

Political system

Under the October 1958 Fifth Republic constitution, the nation's seventeenth since 1789, France has a two-chamber parliament (*parlement*) and a 'dual' or shared executive. The parliament comprises the National Assembly (Assemblée Nationale) and the Senate (Sénat). The 577 members of the National Assembly are elected for a five-year term, subject to dissolution during this period, from single-member constituencies on the basis of a two-ballot, 'run-off' absolute majority voting system. The 321 members of the Senate are indirectly elected, a third at a time, triennially, for nine-year terms by an electoral college composed of local National Assembly members, mayors, department council members and delegates from municipal councils. Twenty-two National Assembly and 13 Senate seats are elected by overseas departments and territories and twelve Senate seats by French nationals abroad.

For the March 1986 National Assembly elections, a party list system of proportional representation was employed, based on department level multi-member constituencies. Within months of this contest, however, the new Chirac administration restored the traditional two-ballot, 'run-off' system employed since 1958. Under this system, it is possible for candidates to be elected on the first ballot if they secure an absolute majority of the votes cast and at least one-quarter of the registered votes. Otherwise, a second poll is held a week later in which all the candidates who secured at least 12.5 per cent of the total first ballot 'primary' vote are entitled to participate and which is decided on a relative majority or simple plurality basis. In practice, left and right coalition party pacts are invariably entered into locally for this second ballot, with low polling first-ballot candidates agreeing to stand down, turning the follow-up ballot into a head-to-head duel between two contestants. Three-quarters of National Assembly seats are, in general, decided on the second ballot.

The National Assembly, whose work is conducted through six large, 61- and 121-member, functional standing committees, is the more dominant of the two chambers. It examines the annual budget first; from its ranks is drawn the Prime Minister; while, most importantly, its members are in a position to overthrow the government on a censure or confidence motion.

The Senate, whose membership as a consequence of its electoral base is skewed towards centrist- and independent-minded rural and small town representatives, acts as a partial, and sometimes salutary, check. It has the authority to veto temporarily legislation passed by the National Assembly and to force amendments in specially convened 'joint conciliation conferences'. Senate vetoes can, however, be overridden by a 'definitive vote' in the National Assembly.

In comparative terms, the most striking feature of the French parliament is its restricted powers *vis-à-vis* the political executive. Under the terms of Article 34 of the 1958 constitution, it may pass laws only in a 'restricted domain', including areas such as taxation, civic rights, electoral laws, nationalisation, and penal matters, and may lay down only general guidelines or 'principles' in the areas of education, labour law, national defence organisation, local government and social security. In other policy spheres, the government is empowered to legislate by executive decree. Even within areas inside its own domain, parliament may occasionally, for a specified period, delegate authority to the executive branch to rule by ordinances, countersigned by the President.

In addition, the French parliament is given, by Article 47, only 70 days to debate and vote on the annual budget. Once this period has elapsed, the government is permitted to impose the measure by ordinance. For other bills, the executive can employ 'guillotine' procedures, pledging its 'responsibility'. The bill then automatically proceeds if no opposition vote of censure is called and successfully passed within 24 hours. The executive can also insist on a single vote on the full text (*vote bloqué*) without accepting any floor amendments.

Finally, the parliamentary year has been restricted, under the terms of Article 28, to a maximum length of only 170 days, distributed in two sessions between October–December and April–June. Outside this period the government may rule by decree.

These restrictions on parliamentary authority were deliberately imposed by the framers of the 1958 constitution in an effort to strengthen the executive branch which had been notoriously weak during the assembly-dominated Third (1870–1940) and Fourth (1946–58) Republics. In this purpose they have succeeded, though in the process the balance has arguably been shifted too greatly in the executive's favour.

The authority of this powerful executive is shared between the two figures of President and Prime Minister. The President is directly elected for a seven-year term by universal adult suffrage, candidates being required to gain an absolute poll majority either in a first ballot open to a range of challengers or in a second 'run-off' contest held a fortnight later between the two top-placed candidates who wish to participate again.

Once elected, the President combines the formal posts of head of state and commander-in-chief of the armed forces and assumes, by virtue of Article 5, the role of umpire, or 'guardian', of the constitution. The formal powers of the President are extensive, embracing the right to select the Prime Minister; preside over meetings of the Council of Ministers, or cabinet; countersign government bills; negotiate foreign treaties; initiate referenda; and dissolve the National Assembly and call fresh elections, subject to the qualification that only one dissolution is permitted per year.

According to the terms of Articles 20 and 21 of the 1958 constitution, ultimate control over policy-making, at least in the domestic field, seemed to have been assigned to the Prime Minister and Council of Ministers. The constitutional amendment of October 1962, which provided for the direct election of the President, to replace the previous arrangement of indirect election by a 'college' of members of parliament and department and municipal councillors, radically changed the executive power balance, enhancing the President's authority, since he was the sole nationally elected figure in the Republic. As a consequence, between 1958 and 1986 the President was seen as the 'legitimate' leader of the incumbent governing coalition. He was served by an extensive and influential 'Elysée office' and was able to assert his dominance over the broad outlines of both domestic and external policy, the Prime Minister being assigned to the lowlier role of 'parliamentary manager', government organiser and detailed policy implementer.

In March 1986, when the opposition coalition managed to secure a National Assembly majority and force President Mitterrand to appoint their leader, Jacques Chirac, as Prime Minister, this power balance was temporarily re-ordered. The new Prime Minister proceeded, between 1986 and 1988, to establish himself, in the domestic sphere at least, as the dominant executive force, leaving to the President a narrower figurehead, or symbolic, role until fresh presidential and Assembly elections in 1988 brought to an end this party political executive split.

The cabinet ministers serving the President and Prime Minister are unusual in that they are drawn from both political and technocratic backgrounds and, as a consequence of the 'incompatibility' clause (Article 23) built into the 1958 constitution, are unable to hold parliamentary seats during their period in government. For this reason, National Assembly candidates are required to designate a running mate (*suppléant*) to assume their positions as deputies if they are appointed as government ministers or Constitutional Council members, or if they are elected to the Senate, or if they die. These *suppléants* are expected to stand down if a minister later resigns or is dismissed.

In some respects, the French ministerial cabinet is thus closer to the American 'specialist presidential' than the British parliamentary 'collective executive' model. French ministers do, however, participate in and lead Assembly debates in their relevant areas, appear before standing committees and are subject to written and oral questioning by Assembly members. Cabinet ministers also work closely with an unusually skilled and influential civil service, being served, themselves, by small, high-powered advisory 'cabinets'.

The 1958 constitution can be amended by parliament by means of a 60 per cent majority vote in both chambers. Alternatively, under the terms of Article 11, the President is allowed, theoretically at the request of the government or parliament, to call a national referendum on constitutional change, as well as in connection with treaty ratification. Since 1961, there have been seven such referenda. The most recent, which concerned new constitutional arrangements for New Caledonia, was held in November 1988, with a turnout of only 37 per cent: a figure barely half that obtained in the five referenda called by President de Gaulle between 1958 and 1969.

Functioning as a judicial 'watchdog', there is a nine-member Constitutional Council (CC), whose task is to ensure that decrees and legislation proposed by the government and parliament conform to the precepts of the constitution and that a correct 'balance' is maintained between the executive and the legislature. Its members, who serve non-renewable nine-year terms, are chosen, three at a time, at triennial intervals, a third by the President of the Republic, another third by the president of the Senate, and a final third by the president of the National Assembly.

The Conseil d'Etat (CE), staffed by senior civil servants, is an additional, and older, judicial review body, which gives non-binding advice on the constitutionality of bills introduced and serves as a final court of appeal in disputes between the citizen and the administration. Compared with the American Supreme Court or the West German Federal Constitutional Court, both the CC and CE are bodies of restricted authority. Since 1974, however, when it was made possible for groups of 60 senators or Assembly members to send bills direct to the Constitutional Council for binding constitutional vetting, its influence has increased significantly.

The French Republic also comprises four constituent 'overseas departments', French Guiana, Guadeloupe, Martinique and Réunion, each of which has its own elected general and regional council, two overseas 'collective territories', Mayotte and St Pierre & Miquelon, which are administered by appointed commissioners assisted by elected general councils, and four 'overseas territories', French Polynesia, the French Southern and Antarctic Territories, New Caledonia and the Wallis and Futuna Islands, which are governed by appointed High Commissioners working with elected territorial assemblies. These territories, whose political structures are described more fully in Part III, send members, as has already been noted, to the Republic's parliament.

Political parties

Contemporary French politics are dominated by three major and two minor political parties. On occasions, impelled by the country's pact-inducing two-ballot electoral process, these parties informally group themselves into two broader-based 'left' and 'right' coalitions, which are based around an ideological divide whose roots can be traced back to the French revolution.

The dominant force on the left, and the current ruling party, is the Socialist Party (PS: Parti Socialiste). The PS, though dating back ideologically to the Radical Republicans of the nineteenth century, was originally formed as a unified force in 1905 by Jean Jaurès. Later, at the December 1920 Tours congress, it split, the left-wing majority breaking away to form the French Communist Party (PCF: Parti Communiste Français), and leaving behind a moderate socialist rump under the banner Section Française de l'Internationale Ouvrière (SFIO) and led by Léon Blum.

The Socialists remained dwarfed by the PCF until the 1970s, but participated in a number of Third and Fourth Republic coalition governments and built up a solid local government base. The party's fortunes rapidly advanced from 1969, when the SFIO was radically remodelled. It adopted the designation PS, and absorbed several smaller left and centre-left groupings, while accepting a new electoral strategy based upon a tactical alliance with the PCF, the 'Union of the Left', which was established in 1972. The motive force behind these changes was François Mitterrand, a shrewd former wartime Resistance leader and post-war centre-left National Assembly member, who eventually brought the PS into power in 1981, establishing in the process, the party's clear ascendancy over the outmanoeuvred, fading PCF.

Currently, the PS, which formally is led by first secretary Pierre Mauroy, has a membership of 200,000 and a national support rating of around 35 per cent. Much of this support is drawn from blue- and white-collar workers, particularly those in the public sector. Currently 40 per cent of its National Assembly members are ex-teachers or lecturers. Regionally, it polls strongest in the industrialised Central-Nord and Paris outer suburbs, as well as in the poor, small-farmer areas of the south-east and south-west. The PS also enjoys the backing of the influential, 650,000 member, Confédération Française Démocratique du Travail (CFDT) labour union.

Within the party, there are a number of ideological and personality-based factions. These include groupings led by the defence minister Jean-Pierre Chevènement, the 'Socialism and Realism' organisation, and the former first secretary Lionel Jospin, on the left, and by former Prime Minister Fabius and current Prime Minister Rocard on the right. A dominant 'Mitterrandiste current' receives support from both Jospin and Fabius, thus bridging the divide. Each faction enjoys representation on the party's ruling Executive Committee and National Secretariat through an internal system of proportional representation.

Closely allied to the PS, and currently participating in the government coalition, is the Left Radical Movement (MRG: Mouvement des Radicaux de Gauche), a party which was founded in 1973 as a breakaway from the Radical Party and is currently led by the trade and artisan industries minister-delegate, François Doubin.

Further to the left is the PCF, a party which participated in a government coalition with the PS between 1981 and 1984. The PCF, although secure in the support of the powerful, one million-member, Confédération Générale du Travail (CGT) labour union and with firm local government bases in the 'red belt' inner suburbs around Paris, has been a declining electoral force since the mid 1970s, its share of the national vote having been halved to barely 10–11 per cent. The party's close ties with Moscow and its fossilised, Brezhnevite ideological outlook have been prime alienating factors. Led since 1972 by Georges Marchais, the PCF's current membership is 405,000. The party is organised on strict, hierarchical 'democratic-centralist' lines and controlled from above by a 15–20 member Politburo. In 1987–88, the PCF was weakened further by its expulsion of a small modernising, 'renovator', faction led by Pierre Juquin, who subsequently stood as an Independent Communist candidate in the April 1988 presidential election.

On the right of the political spectrum, French party politics have become unusually fractionalised during recent years, with the coalition which monopolised central power between 1958 and 1981 showing increasing signs of strain. The dominant party in the 'right coalition' is the Rally for the Republic (RPR: Rassemblement pour la République), which was formed in December 1976 by Jacques Chirac as a successor to the Union of Democrats for the Republic (UDR). The UDR, which was founded in 1968, was itself a successor to the Union for a New Republic (UNR), established by de Gaulle in 1958. Neo-Gaullist in general policy outlook, the RPR, though showing signs of mellowing, favours a nationalistic approach in foreign policy matters and, domestically, a firm law and order programme. In the economic sphere, however, the contemporary RPR espouses a 'new-conservative' freer market, and de-regulationary strategy which differs substantially from the state interventionist and protectionist programme favoured by its UNR and UDR precursors. The RPR claims a membership of 700,000 and currently is supported by around 20 per cent of the electorate. Middle-class business and small-shopkeeping groups, Catholic churchgoers, the elderly and the rural areas of northern, western and central France constitute core categories and bases of party support.

Challenging the RPR as the principal political force on the right is the Union for French Democracy (UDF: Union pour la Démocratie Française), an organisation which was formed by President Valéry Giscard d'Estaing, Prime Minister Raymond Barre and Jean Lecanuet in February 1978, to bring together the smaller parties of the centre-right into an effective electoral alliance. Today, the 300,000-member UDF still remains an umbrella coalition rather than a formal political party, embracing an extensive range of opinions. In general, however, the policy outlook of UDF members is more liberal in the domestic and social, and more internationalist in the external, policy spheres than the RPR.

Within the UDF, which is currently chaired by Giscard d'Estaing, there are four leader-orientated parties: the Republican Party (RP: Parti Républicain), which was founded, under the designation Independent Republicans, in 1962 by Giscard d'Estaing and is currently formally led by the free-market liberal, François Léotard; the Centre of Social Democrats (CDS: Centre des Démocrates Sociaux), formed in 1976 and now led by Pierre Mehaignerie; the Social Democratic Party (PSD: Parti Social-Démocrate), which was formed in 1973 and is led by Max Lejeune; and the Radical Republican and Radical Socialist Party (PRRRS: Parti Républicain Radical et Radical-Socialiste), led by André Rossinot, which dates back to 1901 and was a dominant force during the Third and Fourth Republics.

Since the June 1988 National Assembly elections, the UDF has fragmented, several members having left to join the new broadly based Rocard government. More seriously, in June 1988, the CDS established a new centrist group in the National Assembly, termed the Union of the Centre (UDC: Union du Centre), to which a number of UDF independents, including Raymond Barre, pledged their allegiance.

On the far right of the political spectrum, the National Front (FN: Front National), which was established in 1972 by the demagogic, former paratrooper Jean-Marie Le Pen, has risen to national prominence since the early 1980s through its promotion of a crude racist and extremist programme, founded on the twin planks of immigrant repatriation and the restoration of capital punishment. The FN has been excluded, with partial local exceptions, from electoral coalitions with the parties of the 'conventional right'. Despite this, it has managed to secure a steady 10 per cent share of the popular vote in national contests between 1984 and 1988, polling particularly strongly in the Marseilles region.

There are more than 30 other minor national and regional parties currently operating. These include the state interventionist 'orthodox Gaullist' Movement of Democrats, which was established in 1974, and is led by Michel Jobert; the far left Revolutionary Communist League (LCR), which was formed in 1973, and is led by Alain Krivine; the Workers' Struggle Party (LO), dating from 1968 and led by Arlette Laguiller; the leftist Unified Socialist Party (PSU), founded in 1960, and led by Jean-Claude Le Scornet; and the increasingly popular ecologist Greens (Les Verts), which was established in 1984, and is led by Guy Marimot and Antoine Waechter.

Latest elections

In the most recent presidential election, which was held in April-May 1988, François Mitterrand (PS) was re-elected on the second ballot, securing 54 per cent of the popular vote compared to Jacques Chirac's (RPR) 46 per cent. Turnout was 84 per cent. In the first round of voting, nine candidates participated, the leading five being: Mitterrand (PS), who had a 34 per cent vote share; Chirac (RPR), 20 per cent; Raymond Barre (UDF), 17 per cent; Jean-Marie Le Pen (FN), 14 per cent; and Andre Lajoinie (PCF), 7 per cent. First round turnout was 81 per cent.

In the ensuing June 1988 National Assembly elections, the PS captured 260, or 45 per cent, of the 577 seats, after securing 35 per cent of the first and 45 per cent of the second ballot vote. Allied MRG and 'various left' groups won 17 seats, or 3 per cent of the Assembly total, based on a 1 per cent vote share; the UDF 129 seats, or 22 per cent, the RP holding 58 of these seats, the CDS 49 and the PSD 3, on an 18 per cent share in the first and 21 per cent in the second ballot vote; the RPR 128 seats, or 22 per cent, on 19 per cent and 23 per cent vote shares; the PCF 27 seats, or 5 per cent, on 11 per cent and 3 per cent vote shares; the FN 1 seat, on 10 per cent and 1 per cent vote shares; and 'various right' groupings 15 seats, or 3 per cent, on a 3 per cent vote share. Electoral turnout was 66 per cent in the first round and 70 per cent in the second.

After the most recent Senate elections, which were held in September 1986, 77 of the 319 seats were held by the RPR Group, 70 by the Union of Centrist and Progressive Democrats Group, 64 by the Socialist Group, 54 by the Union of Republicans and Independents Group, 35 by the Democratic Left Group, 15 by the PCF Group and 4 by independents.

Political history

A united French state was first constituted in AD 741 by King Pepin, founder of the Frankish Carolingian dynasty, whose successor, Charlemagne, established a pan-European empire. Authority was thereafter decentralised until the founding of the Paris-centred Capetian dynasty (987–1328), whose branches, the Valois (1328–1589) and Bourbon (1589–1792), ruled France for eight centuries. Under the Bourbon King Louis XIV, who reigned from 1643 to 1715, a centralised absolutist state was established, served by a well-organised bureaucracy. This monarchical *ancien régime* was overthrown during the early stages of the French revolution (1789–99), with a republic being declared in 1792 and parliamentary democracy established.

Later, following a coup in 1799, this system gave way to the military dictatorship of Napoléon Bonaparte, who was proclaimed Emperor of the French in 1804, inaugurating the First Empire (1804–14). A new pan-European empire was temporarily carved out, before military defeats, between 1812 and 1814, forced Napoléon's abdication and the restoration, under Louis XVIII, Charles X and Louis-Philippe, of the Bourbon dynasty.

Attempts to increase the monarch's powers were checked by revolutions in 1830 and 1848, the latter resulting in the crown's overthrow and the establishment of the Second Republic in 1848. This was brought to an end in 1852 when the Republic's President, Louis Napoléon, the nephew of Napoléon Bonaparte, re-established an expansionary system of plebiscitary autocracy, designated the Second Empire. Following his defeat in the Franco-Prussian War (1870–71), Louis Napoléon was ousted and a liberal parliamentary democracy, based on universal manhood suffrage, the Third Republic (1870–1940), was established. This republic, riven by conflicts between the clerical and militarist right and the radical and socialist left, was characterised by government instability, with more than 100 different administrations during its life. Despite these strains and inner tensions, the Third Republic's political structure survived, remaining intact until the invasion, defeat and occupation by German forces during the early stages of the Second World War.

During this war, a collaborationist, puppet government, the Vichy regime, headed by the veteran military leader, Marshal Pétain, was established, with Nazi German backing, but was opposed by the underground *maquis* and UK-based Free French Resistance organisation, led by General Charles de Gaulle.

With Allied support, France was liberated in August 1944 and a 'united front' provisional government, headed by de Gaulle, and including communists, was installed, while a new constitution was being framed. This interim administration was successful in restoring a sense of national unity. It also introduced a far-reaching series of pragmatic social and economic reforms, including the nationalisation of strategic enterprises, the extension of the franchise to women and the creation of a comprehensive social security system.

In January 1946, a new constitution was adopted, proclaiming the establishment of a Fourth Republic and providing for a weak political executive and powerful parliament, the National Assembly, which was to be elected under a generous system of proportional representation. De Gaulle, who had favoured a strong presidentialist system, immediately resigned as interim President and set up, in 1947, a populist political movement of his own, the Rally for French People (RPF), which briefly rose to prominence, before fading and being disbanded in 1953.

With numerous small party groupings achieving Assembly representation, political activity in the new Fourth Republic was characterised by intense factional bargaining and renewed executive instability: 26 different governments held power between 1946 and 1958. In these circumstances, effective executive authority passed into the hands of the French civil service, which, by introducing a new system of 'indicative economic planning', engineered rapid economic reconstruction. Decolonisation in French Indo-China, in 1954, and Morocco and Tunisia, in 1956, and entry into the European Community (EC), in 1957, were also achieved.

The Fourth Republic eventually collapsed in 1958 as a result of a political and military crisis over Algerian independence, which threatened to lead to a French army revolt. De Gaulle was called back from retirement in May 1958 to head a government of national unity. He proceeded to oversee the framing of a constitution for the new Fifth Republic which considerably strengthened the executive, in the shape of a President and Prime Minister. De Gaulle, who became President in January 1959, restored domestic stability and presided over the decolonisation of Francophone Africa, including the grant of independence to Algeria in April 1962. Close economic links were maintained, however, with France's former colonies. He also initiated a new independent foreign policy, withdrawing France from the integrated military command structure of the North Atlantic Treaty Organisation (NATO) in 1966 and developing an autonomous nuclear deterrent force, the *force de frappe*.

The de Gaulle era was one of rapid economic growth, per capita GDP almost doubling between 1960 and 1970, and socio-economic change, involving large scale rural-urban migration and occupational transformation. Politically, however, it was a period characterised by a strong centralisation of power and tight media censorship. In March 1967, the public reacted against this paternalism by voting the 'right coalition' a reduced National Assembly majority. A year later, in May 1968, major student and workers' demonstrations, termed the 'May Events', in Paris, which spread to the provinces, paralysed the nation and briefly threatened the government's continued existence. De Gaulle responded by calling fresh National Assembly elections in June 1968 in which, fighting on a law and order platform, his Union of Democrats for the Republic (UDR) secured a landslide victory. Ten months later, however, in April 1969, de Gaulle was defeated in a referendum over proposals for Senate and local government reform. He resigned the presidency and retired from political affairs at the age of 79.

The man who had been de Gaulle's Prime Minister between 1962 and 1968, Georges Pompidou, was elected as the new President in June 1969 and continued to pursue Gaullist policies until his death in April 1974.

Pompidou's successor as President was Valéry Giscard d'Estaing, leader of the centre-right Independent Republicans. He attempted to set the country on a new, modernist course, introducing liberalising reforms in the social sphere and establishing a more co-operative and activist role within the European Community. His policies were undermined, however, by the internal wranglings of his ambitious 'right coalition' partner, Jacques Chirac, who served as Prime Minister between 1974 and 1976, before leaving to set up a new neo-Gaullist party, Rally for the Republic (RPR). The government was also operating in the context of deteriorating external economic conditions.

Nevertheless, France performed better than many of its European competitors between 1974 and 1981, with the President launching a major nuclear power programme to save on energy imports and appointing a new Prime Minister, in the person of the former Sorbonne monetarist professor, Raymond Barre, who followed a new liberal 'freer-market' economic strategy. However, with unemployment standing at 1.7 million on polling day, Giscard was defeated by the experienced Socialist Party (PS) leader, François Mitterrand, in the presidential election of May 1981.

Mitterrand's victory, which constituted the first presidential success for the 'left coalition' during the Fifth Republic, was immediately succeeded by a landslide victory for the PS and its Communist Party (PCF) and Left Radical Movement (MRG) allies in the elections to the National Assembly which were held in June 1981. The new government, which was headed by the socialist-traditionalist former mayor of Lille, Pierre Mauroy, as Prime Minister, and included in its ranks four PCF ministers, set about implementing a radical and ambitious policy of social reform and political decentralisation, with the aim of fundamentally transforming the character of French society. In the economic sphere, a programme of industrial and financial nationalisation and enhanced state investment and formal planning was instituted, while a series of reflationary budgets attempted to curb unemployment. In March 1983, however, financial constraints, during a period of deepening world recession, forced a switch towards a more conservative fiscal strategy of austerity, *le rigueur*. This U-turn in economic policy was completed in July 1984 when Mauroy was replaced as Prime Minister by the young social democratic technocrat, Laurent Fabius, a move which prompted the resignation from the government of the PCF's four cabinet ministers.

During 1985 and 1986, with a tightening of the fiscal screw, unemployment rose sharply to more than 2.5 million, and, as a consequence, racial tensions and workers' unrest increased in urban areas. The extreme right-wing National Front (FN), led by Jean-Marie Le Pen, campaigning for immigrant repatriation and a tougher penal policy, benefited from these conflicts, capturing 10 per cent of the popular vote in the National Assembly elections of March 1986 and, helped by the recent adoption of a new proportional representation system, 35 Assembly seats. In this election, the 'left coalition', now in tatters, lost its Assembly majority, compelling President Mitterrand to appoint the leader of the 'right coalition' and mayor of Paris, Jacques Chirac, as his new Prime Minister in what was to be a unique experiment in power sharing, or 'co-habitation'.

Chirac quickly succeeded in establishing himself as the dominant force in this 'shared executive' and proceeded to set about introducing a radical 'new-conservative' programme of denationalisation, deregulation and 'de-socialisation'. In this strategy, utilising 'guillotine' and decree powers to steam-roller measures through, he had initial success. However, during the autumn and winter months of 1986–87, Chirac's educational and economic reforms encountered serious opposition from students and workers, necessitating policy concessions which, combined with growing acrimony within the ranks of the 'right coalition', served fatally to undermine the Prime Minister's national standing.

As a consequence, Chirac was comfortably defeated by the incumbent Mitterrand in the presidential election of May 1988. However, in the new National Assembly elections, called a month later, the PS, despite disarray in the ranks of the 'right coalition', emerged as the largest single party but failed to secure a parliamentary majority.

Interpreting the result as a reflection of the public's desire for government from the 'centre', President Mitterrand appointed Michel Rocard, a popular, moderate social democrat, as Prime Minister at the head of a minority PS government, which included several prominent centre party representatives. The new Prime Minister pledged himself to implement a progressive programme, aimed at protecting the under-privileged and improving the quality of life, and called upon the opposition parties to work with the PS for 'tolerance, justice, progress and solidarity'.

Terming their strategy the 'opening to the centre', the longer-term aim of the President and Prime Minister appeared to be to encourage defections from the ranks of the centre-right Union for French Democracy (UDF) to a new left-of-centre, PS-led alliance. This would serve to strengthen the position of the 'conventional left' *vis-à-vis* the RPR-led 'conventional right', thus creating an effective, social democratic and conservative-based, two-party system and leaving the extremist PCF and FN isolated and marginalised on the political fringes.

WEST GERMANY

Federal Republic of Germany
Bundesrepublik Deutschland

Capital: Bonn

Social and economic data
Area: 248,670 km^2
Population: 60.734m*
Pop density per km^2: 244*
Literacy rate: 100%

GDP: $624,966m*; per capita GDP: $10,290
Economy type: high income
Labour force in agriculture: 5%

*1985

Ethnic composition
The population is overwhelmingly of Germanic stock but in the far north there is a notable Danish ethnic minority. Also, in 1985, 4.7 million foreigners, including 1.9 million officially recognised *Gastarbeiter* (guest workers), predominantly Turks and South Europeans, resided in the country, constituting 7.7 per cent of the total population.

Religions
Forty-five per cent of the population are Roman Catholics, the faith being strongest in the south, and 42 per cent Protestants: 22 per cent United Evangelical Church, 17 per cent Lutheran and 1 per cent Reformed Church.

Political features
State type: liberal democratic
Date of state formation: 1949
Political structure: federal
Executive: parliamentary
Assembly: two-chamber
Party structure: multi-party
Human rights rating: 97%

Local and regional government
Below the *Land* administrations, which are described in the Political system section, there are 26 elected town and district councils, empowered to levy and collect property taxes.

Head of state
Federal President Dr Richard von Weizsäcker, since 1984.

Head of government
Chancellor Dr Helmut Kohl, since 1982.

Political leaders since 1970
Chancellors: 1969–74 Willy Brandt (SPD), 1974–82 Helmut Schmidt (SPD), 1982– Dr Helmut Kohl (CDU).

Political system
With memories of the destructive 1933–45 Nazi autocracy fresh in their minds, the Allied military governors and German provincial leaders, in 1948–49, drafted West Germany's constitution with the clear goal of creating a stable, parliamentary form of government, diffusing authority

and safeguarding liberties. The document, termed the 'Basic Law', borrowed eclectically from British, American and neighbouring European constitutional models, while drawing specific lessons from Germany's own flawed constitutional history.

To prevent an excessive centralisation of power, a federal system of government was established, built around ten *Länder*, or states, as shown in Table 50 below, each with its own constitution and elected single-chamber, assembly (*Landtag* or *Bürgerschaft*), from which a government is drawn, headed by a minister-president. Bavaria is the exception, having two chambers. These *Länder* have original powers in the spheres of education, police, local government, culture and environmental protection and are responsible for the administration of federal legislation through their own civil services. They have substantial local taxation authority and are assigned shares of federal income tax and value added tax (VAT) revenues, being responsible for a half of total government spending in the Federal Republic.

Table 50

THE *LÄNDER* (STATES) OF THE FEDERAL REPUBLIC OF GERMANY

Land	*Area (km²)*	*Population (m) (1983)*	*Capital*	*Land* Government*	*Bundersrat Seats*
Baden-Württemberg	35,751	9.243	Stuttgart	CDU	5
Bavaria	70,553	10.970	Munich	CSU	5
Bremen	404	0.677	Bremen	SPD	3
Hamburg	755	1.610	Hamburg	SPD-FDP	3
Hesse	21,114	5.565	Wiesbaden	CDU-FDP	4
Lower Saxony	47,447	7.249	Hanover	CDU-FDP	5
North-Rhine-Westphalia	34,062	16.836	Düsseldorf	SPD	5
Rhineland-Palatinate	19,848	3.634	Mainz	CDU-FDP	4
Saarland	2,571	1.053	Saarbrücken	SPD	3
Schleswig-Holstein	15,721	2.617	Kiel	SPD	4
West Berlin	480	1.855	West Berlin	SPD-AL†	4

*In May 1989.
†Alternative Liste (Greens).

At the centre, the May 1949 constitution, established, through a deliberate system of checks and balances, a firmly rooted parliamentary democracy, built around a two-chamber legislature comprising a directly elected lower house, the Bundestag (Federal Diet or Assembly) of at least 518 members, currently 519, and an indirectly elected 45-member upper house, the Bundesrat (Federal Council).

Bundestag members are elected by universal adult suffrage for a four-year term through a complicated form of 'personalised proportional representation', termed the Additional Member system (AM). Under this system, electors are given two votes, one, the *Erststimme*, for a local, single-member, district constituency seat, the result being decided by a simple plurality, and the other vote, the *Zweitstimme*, for a *Land* (state) party list. Excluding those returned from West Berlin, half the assembly is filled by 'constituency members' and half by 'list members'. The *Zweitstimme* votes are decisive in determining proportionate party representation. They are totalled so as to establish percentage levels of party support at the state level and to work out proportionate seat allocations. To achieve such proportionality, list seats are added, where necessary, to those already gained by the parties locally from the *Erststimme* constituency contests. In this allotment process, 'balancing' *Zweitstimme* seats are drawn in rank order from the topmost names appearing on the relevant party's state list. To qualify for shares of these state list seats, political parties must however have won at least 5 per cent of the national vote or alternatively three district *Erststimme* seats. Occasionally, as a result of unusual, regionally concentrated, *Erststimme* support, a party may secure more district *Erststimme* seats than it appears 'entitled' to on a state-wide percentage basis. It is allowed to retain these 'excess' (*Überhangmandate*) seats, the size of the Bundestag being increased accordingly.

Members of the Bundesrat are not directly elected. Instead, individual *Land* governments send nominated party delegations, consisting of between three and five members, dependent upon population size. For this reason, the Bundesrat is never dissolved, its composition only changing as *Land* governments rise and fall. The delegations sent to Bonn, which comprise senior *Land* ministers, automatically led by the minister-president, are required to cast their votes *en bloc*.

The Bundestag is the more dominant of the two chambers in the federal assembly, electing from the ranks of the majority party or coalition a Chancellor (Prime Minister) and a 16–20 member cabinet to constitute the executive government of the Federal Republic. Once elected, a Chancellor can only be removed by Bundestag members through a 'constructive vote of no confidence', in which a majority of members vote positively in favour of an alternative executive leader. This constitutional device has been been employed successfully on only one occasion, in September 1982, and brought into office the present Chancellor.

The Chancellor, who is served by a large, 400-member, private office, is a potentially powerful leader. However, the coalition character of post-war West German politics, with the consequent apportionment of cabinet posts on a negotiated party basis, has meant that a number of leading ministers, for example foreign affairs minister Genscher, who has held his post since 1974, have established a significant degree of independence. More generally, West German cabinet ministers, who are not required to be Bundestag deputies, although most are, are frequently technocrats who specialise in their department's affairs, serving lengthy terms, in contrast to the generalist ministers of most other West European states.

Work in both the Bundestag and Bundesrat is effected through a vigorous system of all-party functional committees. The Bundestag takes the lead in this legislative process. However, although the Bundesrat has few initiating rights, it enjoys considerable veto powers. Thus, all legislation relating to *Länder* responsibilities must receive its approval: more than 60 per cent of Bundestag laws fall into this category. In addition, constitutional amendments, of which there have been 30 since 1949, require a two-thirds Bundesrat, and Bundestag, majority. Finally, on other matters, the Bundesrat is allowed to suggest amendments to Bundestag legislation, send disputed items to joint, 22-member, Bundestag-Bundesrat 'conciliation committees' and can temporarily block items of which it disapproves until a countervailing 50 or 66 per cent Bundestag vote is passed.

For the purpose of electing a Federal President (Bundespräsident) as head of state, members of the Bundestag join together, every five years, with an equal number of representatives elected by *Land* parliaments in a special Federal Convention (Bundesversammlung). The President is, however, primarily a titular and ceremonial figure, possessing few effective powers.

Adherence to the 1949 constitution is ensured by a special, independent Federal Constitutional Court, based at Karlsruhe, which is staffed by 16 judges. They are selected half by the Bundestag and half by the Bundesrat, following nominations by balanced all-party committees, and serve terms of up to twelve years. The Court functions as a guarantor of civil liberties and adjudicator in federal-*Land* disputes. Similar constitutional courts function at the *Land* level.

West Berlin, although classed in the 'Basic Law' as a *Land* of the Federal Republic, remains subject to the supreme authority of the three Allied Powers, the United States, France and Britain, in accordance with post-war agreements. Nevertheless, it has its own elected assembly (Abgeordnetenhaus) and government and sends 22 'honorary representatives', nominated by the state assembly to reflect proportionate party strength, to the federal Bundestag and four to the Bundesrat. These representatives, whose number has been included in the member totals given for the federal legislative chambers above, possess restricted voting rights.

Political parties

West German politics have been dominated since 1949 by two major parties, the Christian Democratic Union (CDU: Christlich Demokratische Union Deutschlands) and Social Democratic Party (SPD: Sozialdemokratische Partei Deutschlands), and one minor party, the Free Democratic Party (FDP: Freie Demokratische Partei). A fourth party, The Greens (Die Grünen), has emerged as a notable challenging force since the early 1980s, while the Bavarian-based Christian Social Union (CSU: Christlich Soziale Union) has worked in close, though sometimes uneasy, partnership with the CDU at the federal level.

With the exception of the November 1972 Bundestag election, the conservative CDU has consistently gained most support at national level, forming the principal party of government between 1949 and 1969 and since 1982. The party was originally established at the state level in the autumn of 1945 as a loose amalgamation of independent Catholic and Protestant zonal parties who had resisted National Socialism during the inter-war years and whose members shared a commitment to private enterprise, state welfare provision and an antipathy to communism. During the 1950s, the CDU's support base, which had traditionally been concentrated in the rural, Catholic *Länder* of southern and western Germany and in rural, Protestant Schleswig-Holstein and Lower Saxony, broadened as it absorbed further minor regional, centrist and conservative parties. Ideologically, it became identified with the 'social market economy' approach to economic management, which became a key element behind the post-war German 'economic miracle'. The success of this strategy drew to the party new blue-collar support, establishing it as a broadly based, 'catch-all', centre-right force. In its approach to external relations, the CDU gave firm and early support to membership of the European Community and the North Atlantic Treaty Organisation (NATO).

In 1986, the CDU, led by Chancellor Kohl, claimed a membership of 720,000. Its sister party in Bavaria, the CSU, which was established in 1946, has a membership of 190,000. The CSU is a noticeably more conservative body and was led between 1961 and 1988 by the forthright Dr Franz-Josef Strauss. It is currently headed by Theo Waigel.

The CDU, constituting as its name suggests a 'Union' of *Land* groupings, is notoriously decentralised in structure. Financially, it draws an unusually high proportion, almost 30 per cent, of its annual income in the form of donations, chiefly from business.

The dominant party on the left of the political spectrum is the SPD. Formed in 1875, during the Bismarckian era, it began as a Marxist body, drawing initial support from urban industrial workers. With a membership in excess of one million, it became the major political party in Germany during the liberal Weimar Republic (1918–33), forming governments between 1919 and 1920 and between 1928 and 1930. Following the defection of ultra-leftist groupings, its policy stance moderated but it was forced into exile during the Nazi era and subsequently electorally weakened by the country's partition in 1945.

During the 1950s the SPD, with a national support rating of only 30 per cent, found itself in perpetual opposition at the federal level, but held power at the state level in the industrialised *Länder* of Bremen, Hamburg, Hesse and North-Rhine-Westphalia. However, at its 1959 Bad Godesberg conference, a fundamental revision of policy strategy was effected, bringing to an end the party's earlier opposition to membership of the EC and NATO, disavowing its traditional Marxist connections, class orientation and anti-clericalism and proclaiming its acceptance of the country's post-war 'social market economy' strategy. The adoption of this moderate, new, left-of-centre Godesberg Programme of Principles, coupled with the party's innovative espousal of East-West détente (*Ostpolitik*), and the dynamic, new-generation leadership provided by Willy Brandt and Helmut Schmidt, proved successful in broadening significantly the SPD's support base. This enabled it, in alliance with the FDP, to become the party of federal government between 1969 and 1982.

Since 1982, as a result of mounting internal divisions over domestic and foreign policy which shifted its centre of gravity leftwards and encouraged the FDP to switch allegiance to the CDU, the SPD has been forced back into opposition at the federal level. The party remains, however, a significant force, having, in 1986, a membership of 920,000 and enjoying informal labour union support. Its organisational structure is the most effective in the Federal Republic, being unusually centralised, with control from above being effected by an elected 42-member National Executive Committee and inner nine-member Presidium, chaired by Hans-Jöchen Vogel. Its organisation is also among the most progressive following rules passed at the SPD congress of August 1988, with at least 40 per cent of the party's posts, and a similar proportion of its Bundestag seats, being required to be filled by women by 1998.

The FDP, a centrist, liberal grouping, although very small compared to the CDU and SPD in terms of national support, averaging 8 per cent of the national vote in elections since 1949, has functioned as a critical 'hinge party'. Helped by the AM electoral system, with the 'ticket-splitting' which this makes possible, the FDP has regularly been in a position to hold the balance of power in the Bundestag and has formed the junior partner in federal coalition governments in all but seven years, 1957–61 and 1966–69, since 1949. As a reward for its assembly support, the FDP has received 20 per cent of cabinet portfolios in these administrations, including such key ministries as foreign affairs, economic affairs and, until 1983, the interior. In addition, it has secured the election of two of its leaders, Dr Theodor Heuss, between 1949 and 1959, and Walter Scheel, between 1974 and 1979, to the prestigious post of Federal President.

The FDP, although its antecedents go back to previous Second Reich (1871–1918) and Weimar Republic centrist groupings, was originally formed by Heuss in December 1948, by absorbing smaller liberal parties. During the 1950s its support came chiefly from marginal farming communities, the self-employed and small-town conservatives. However, after Scheel became party chairman in 1968, it became more progressive in its outlook, winning new support from white-collar groups. Today, there is still tension between its conservative-liberal wing, of which its present leader, Count Otto Lambsdorff, is a prominent member, and which espouses a free market economic approach, and a more socially and environmentally conscious progressivist faction, with a strong regional base in Baden-Württemberg, in the south-west, and the northern city states of Hamburg and Bremen. In 1986 party membership stood at 70,000.

The Federal Republic's fourth significant party, the Greens, originated as a loose coalition of locally based environmental action groups which began operations during the later 1970s and had growing successes in a number of *Land* constituency contests. In January 1980 they were established as an umbrella organisation which embraced these groupings and began to develop a unique 'post-industrial' or 'new politics' policy programme, which included opposition to nuclear weapons and the NATO alliance, environmentalism, feminism and utopian eco-socialism. Having secured representation in a number of *Landtage* and *Bürgerschäfte* between 1980 and 1983, the Greens succeeded in surmounting the 5 per cent national support hurdle and captured seats in the Bundestag at both the 1983 and 1987 general elections.

Outside the assembly chambers, they played an even more prominent role at the head of a burgeoning 'peace movement' during the early and mid 1980s. By 1987 they claimed a national membership of 42,000. However, the party had become progressively divided into antagonistic radical (*Fundi*), moderate (*Realo*) and neutral (*Neutralo*) factions, fomenting a series of anarchic feuds. The party has a highly decentralised organisational structure which has exacerbated such infighting. More impressively, the Greens, since their inception, have pioneered and operated a unique collective form of national and parliamentary leadership, with personnel being regularly rotated and women assured of equal representation at all executive levels.

Numerous minor parties also operate both nationally and regionally in the Federal Republic. At the national level are the 47,000-member German Communist Party (DKP: Deutsche Kommunistische Partei), which was founded in 1968, and the far-right, 15,000-member German National Party (NPD: Nationaldemokratische Partei Deutschlands), which dates from

1964. The NDP rose briefly to prominence between 1966 and 1968 and recently performed well in city council elections in Frankfurt in March 1989. The right-wing nationalist Republicans (die Republikaner), a party formed in 1983 and led by the former Nazi Waffen-SS officer Franz Schönhuber, similarly polled strongly in state and local contests in West Berlin and Hesse in 1989.

Also at the *Land* level, is the South Schleswig Electoral Union (SSW: Südschleswigscher Wahlerverband), which was established in 1948 to represent the Danish-speaking minority of northern Schleswig-Holstein. Although it has secured barely 1 per cent of the state vote, it enjoys *Landtag* representation, the 5 per cent requirement for assembly membership having been specially waived.

Under the terms of Article 21 of the 'Basic Law', political parties have been assigned a special role, described as 'forming the political will of the people'. As a result, under the terms of the Party Law of 1967, which was amended in 1981, public financial support has been provided to assist their operations. Currently, parties which secure in excess of 0.5 per cent of the federal vote are given an official subsidy of DM5 per vote received. Similar, though lower, subsidies are paid by *Land* governments for state contests and by the central government for European Parliament elections. These subsidies constitute a third of annual party revenues.

In return for this support, the parties are subject to regulation concerning internal financial and electoral matters, and the Federal Constitutional Court reserves the right to ban groupings which are deemed to be anti-democratic, and thus unconstitutional. This sanction was employed in 1952 and 1956, when the quasi-fascist Socialist Reich Party and ultra-leftist Communist Party of Germany (KPD: Kommunistische Partei Deutschlands), a progenitor of the contemporary DKP, were outlawed. It was also used in 1989 to ban the neo-Nazi National Gathering (Nationale Sammlung) Party.

Latest elections

The results of the most recent Bundestag elections, which were held in January 1987, are shown below. The CDU, led by Chancellor Kohl, did not, as usual, contest Bavaria, and the CSU, led by Franz-Joseph Strauss, fought only Bavarian seats.

	% Votes	*% Seats*	*No of Seats**
CDU	34	35	174
CSU	10	10	49
SPD	37	37	186
FPD	9	9	46
Greens	8	8	42

The electoral turnout was 84 per cent.

*Excludes West Berlin's 22 'honorary representatives'.

Political history

The Federal Republic was formed in May 1949 out of the British, American and French occupation zones in the western portion of the German Empire which had been under Allied military control following Germany's surrender in May 1945. A policy of demilitarisation, decentralisation and democratisation was instituted by the Allied control powers and a new, intended to be provisional, constitution framed. This constitution included the goal of eventual German reunification. Between 1948 and 1949, West Berlin was subjected to blockade by the Soviet Union, but survived to form a constituent *Land* in the Federal Republic, following an airlift operation by the Allied powers.

Politics during the Federal Republic's first decade were dominated by the Christian Democratic Union (CDU), led by the popular Dr Konrad Adenauer, a former Lord Mayor of Cologne who had been imprisoned by the Nazis between 1934 and 1944 for opposition to the regime. Chancellor Adenauer and his economics minister, Dr Ludwig Erhard, established a successful new approach to economic management termed the 'social market economy' (*soziale Marktwirtschaft*), which involved the state's encouragement of free-market productive forces, combined with strategic interventions so as to reconcile interest-group differences, guide the market in a socially responsible direction, and secure adequate welfare provision.

This new 'liberal-corporatist' managerial approach, combined with the injection of Marshall Aid and the enterprise of the nation's labour force, more than 2 million of whom were refugees from the partitioned East, contributed towards a phase of rapid economic reconstruction and growth during the 1950s and 1960s, an era now termed the 'miracle years'. During this period, West Germany was also reintegrated into the international community. It regained its full sovereignty in 1954, entered the North Atlantic Treaty Organisation (NATO) in 1955, emerging as a loyal supporter of the United States, and, under Adenauer's committed lead, joined the new European Community (EC) in 1957. Close relations were also developed with France, enabling the Saarland to be returned amicably to Germany in January 1957.

In August 1961, East Germany's construction of a fortified wall around West Berlin, to prevent refugees from leaving the Democratic Republic (DDR), created a political crisis which vaulted West Berlin's mayor, Willy Brandt, to international prominence. Domestically, Brandt played a pivotal role in shifting the Social Democratic Party (SPD) away from its traditional Marxist affiliation towards a more moderate position, following the party's 1959 Bad Godesberg conference. Support for the SPD steadily increased after this policy switch and the party joined the CDU in a 'Grand Coalition' led by Dr Kurt Kiesinger (CDU), between 1966 and 1969, and then secured power itself, with the support of the Free Democratic Party (FDP), under the leadership of Brandt in 1969.

As Chancellor, Brandt, working closely with the SPD's defence expert Egon Bahr, introduced the new foreign policy of *Ostpolitik*, which sought reconciliation with Eastern Europe as a means of improving social contacts between the two Germanies. Treaties in 1970 normalised relations with the Soviet Union and Poland and recognised the Oder-Neisse border line, while in September 1972 a 'Basic Treaty' was effected with East Germany, which acknowledged the DDR's borders and separate existence, enabling both countries to join the United Nations in 1973.

Willy Brandt resigned as Chancellor in May 1974, following a revelation that his personal assistant, Günther Guillaume, had been an East German spy. Brandt's replacement as Chancellor, the former finance minister, Helmut Schmidt, adhered to *Ostpolitik* and emerged as a leading advocate of

European co-operation, while at home he introduced a series of important social reforms.

In the federal election of October 1976, the SPD-FDP coalition only narrowly defeated the CDU-CSU. Four years later, however, it secured a comfortable victory after the controversial Dr Franz-Josef Strauss had forced his way to the head of the CDU-CSU ticket. Soon after this election triumph, divisions emerged between the left wing of the SPD and the liberal-conservative wing of the FDP on defence policy, particularly over the proposed stationing by the end of 1983 of new short- and medium-range (Cruise and Pershing-II) American nuclear missiles in West Germany. There were also differences on economic strategy during a period of gathering world recession. Chancellor Schmidt fought to maintain a moderate, centrist course and to hold together his party's factions, but the FDP eventually withdrew from the federal coalition in September 1982 and joined forces with the CDU, led by Dr Helmut Kohl, to unseat the Chancellor in a 'constructive vote of no confidence'. Helmut Schmidt immediately retired from politics and the SPD, led by the efficient but colourless Hans-Jöchen Vogel, was heavily defeated in the Bundestag elections of March 1983.

In this contest, the SPD significantly lost votes on the left to the ascendant environmentalist Green Party which, capturing 5.6 per cent of the national vote, became the first new party since 1957 to gain representation in the Bundestag.

The new Kohl administration, with the FDP's Hans-Dietrich Genscher remaining as foreign affairs minister, adhered closely to the external policy of the previous chancellorship. At home, however, a freer, market economy approach was pursued. With unemployment rising to a level of 2.5 million in 1984, problems of social unrest emerged, while violent demonstrations greeted the stationing of American nuclear missiles on German soil during 1983–84. Internally, the Kohl administration was also rocked by scandals over illegal party funding by business donors, the 'Flick affair', which briefly touched the Chancellor himself. However, a strong recovery in the German economy from 1985 enabled the CDU-CSU-FDP coalition to secure re-election in the federal election of January 1987.

In this contest, both the minority parties, the FDP and the Greens, polled strongly. In contrast, the opposition SPD, led this time by Johannes Rau, the popular Schmidtite minister-president of North-Rhine-Westphalia, secured its lowest share of the national vote since 1961. This defeat opened serious divisions within the party over future tactical strategies, with a number of influential figures advocating an alliance with the Greens. By the autumn of 1988, however, with the fortunes of the Greens apparently in decline, as a result of internal conflicts and changing global strategic conditions, and with popular support for the SPD showing signs of returning, the party, now led once again by Hans-Jöchen Vogel, recommitted itself to a centre-left course. At the *Land* level, the SPD, helped by local factors, such as the 'Barschel scandal', concerning the running of a 'dirty tricks' campaign against the local SPD leader, Bjorn Engholm, secured a notable success, in May 1988, by gaining control of the *Landtag* in the traditionally strongly conservative Schleswig-Holstein, as public disenchantment with the Kohl government grew. Meanwhile, in Hamburg, a coalition was ominously formed between the local SPD and FDP to secure control of the *Bürgerschaft* government.

This suggested the possibility of the re-establishment of a SPD-FDP centre-left coalition at the federal level in the near future. However, conditions changed with the death, in October 1988, of the CSU's right-wing leader, Franz-Josef Strauss, whose policy utterances had done much to alienate the FDP from the ruling coalition. The election, as FDP chairman, five days later, of Count Otto Lambsdorff, a conservative-liberal in economic matters who had been forced to resign as federal economic affairs minister in June 1984 over the 'Flick affair', appeared to make the prospect of a SPD-FDP coalition even more remote, possibly sentencing the SPD to an extended term in the federal wilderness. Instead, in the spring of 1989, discussion began to mount of the prospect of the future formation of a mould-breaking SPD-Greens coalition at the federal level. This followed the marginalisation of the Greens' 'fundi' wing at the party's Duisburg conference in March 1989 and the formation, in the same month, of a SPD-Alternative Liste government in West Berlin. Nationally, opinion poll support for the SPD had risen to a figure of 41 per cent, well above its 1987 election level, while support for the CDU-CSU had plummetted to 38 per cent as a result of unpopular economic measures and the uncertain leadership of Chancellor Kohl.

GREECE

Hellenic Republic
Elliniki Dimokratia

Capital: Athens

Social and economic data
Area: 131,990 km^2
Population: 9.954m*
Pop density per km^2: 75*
Literacy rate: 90%
GDP: $32,781m*; per capita GDP: $3,293
Economy type: middle income
Labour force in agriculture: 27%

*1985

Ethnic composition
Over 97 per cent of the population are Greek. The main minorities are Turks, Slavs and Albanians.

Religions
The Eastern Orthodox Church is the established religion and it has about 9 million adherents, or most of the population. There are also about 47,000 Roman Catholics, 5,000 Protestants and 5,000 Jews.

Political features
State type: emergent democratic
Date of state formation: 1829
Political structure: unitary
Executive: parliamentary
Assembly: one-chamber
Party structure: two-party
Human rights rating: 92%

Local and regional government
Although the 1975 constitution prescribes that 'the administration of the State shall be organised on the basis of decentralisation', Greece has tended to be a highly centralised state. In 1983 measures were introduced to devolve more power to the ten regions into which the country is divided and the departments into which they, in turn, are subdivided.

Head of state
President Christos Sartzetakis, since 1985.

Head of government
Tzannis Tzannetakis, since 1989.

Political leaders since 1970
1967–74 George Papadopoulus (Military), 1974–80 Constantine Karamanlis (ND), 1981–89 Andreas Papandreou (PASOK), 1989– Tzannis Tzannetakis (ND-Communist coalition).

Political system
The 1975 constitution provides for a parliamentary system of government, with a President, who is head of state, a Prime Minister, who is head of government, and a single-chamber parliament. The President is elected by parliament for a five-year term. He appoints the Prime Minister on the basis of parliamentary support. Amendments to the constitution in 1986 transferred virtually all executive powers from the President to the Prime Minister. He and his cabinet are collectively responsible to parliament. This has 300 members, all elected by universal adult suffrage, through a party list system of proportional representation, for a four-year term. Bills passed by parliament must be ratified by the President, but his veto can be overridden by an absolute majority of the total number of members of parliament.

Political parties
There are 17 political parties, the two most significant being the Panhellenic Socialist Movement (PASOK), and the New Democracy Party (ND).

PASOK was formed in 1974 by the incorporation of the Democratic Defence and the Panhellenic Liberation Movement, two organisations committed to the removal of the military regime which had been dominating Greek politics. Although strongly nationalistic, it favours socialisation through international co-operation.

The ND was also formed in 1974. It is a broad-based, centre-right party, favouring social reform through a free enterprise system. It is a strong supporter of EC and NATO membership.

Latest elections
In the 1989 general election PASOK won 125 parliamentary seats, and ND 144, the Communist block winning 29.

Political history
Historically the birthplace of democracy, Greece became an independent, modern nation-state in 1829 and a constitutional monarchy in 1843. Relations with neighbouring Turkey were strained for much of the nineteenth century, resulting in an unsuccessful war in 1897 and a more successful one in 1912–13. The monarchy was removed between 1923 and 1925 and then restored by the army. Soon after the outbreak of the Second World War an attempted invasion by Italy was successfully resisted but a determined onslaught by Germany proved too powerful and occupation followed.

During the German occupation, between 1941 and 1944, a communist-dominated resistance movement armed and trained a guerrilla army and after the war the National Liberation Front, as it was called, attempted to create a socialist state. If the Greek royalist army had not been massively assisted by the United States, this undoubtedly would have happened. As it was, the monarchy, in the shape of King Paul, was re-established, and in 1964 he was succeeded by his son, Constantine.

Dissatisfaction with the performance of the government and conflicts between the King and his ministers resulted in a coup, in 1967, led by Colonel George Papadopoulos. The monarchy was replaced by a new regime, which, despite its democratic pretensions, was little more than a military dictatorship. All political activity was banned and opponents of the government forced out of public life. In 1973 Greece declared itself a republic and Papadopoulus became President.

A civilian cabinet was appointed but before the year was out another coup brought Lieutenant-General Phaidon Ghizikis to the presidency, with Adamantios Androutsopoulus as Prime Minister. The failure of the government to prevent the Turkish invasion of Cyprus led to its downfall and a former Prime Minister, Constantine Karamanlis, was recalled from exile to form a new Government of National Salvation. Karamanlis immediately ended martial law, press censorship and the ban on political parties and in the 1974 general election his New Democracy Party (ND) won a decisive majority in parliament. A referendum held the same year emphatically rejected the idea of a return of the monarchy and in 1975 a new constitution for a democratic 'Hellenic Republic' was adopted, with Constantine Tsatsos as the new President.

ND won the 1977 general election with a reduced majority and in 1980 Karamanlis resigned as Prime Minister and was elected President. The following year Greece became a full member of the European Community, having been an associate since 1962. Meanwhile, the ND found itself faced with a growing challenge from the Panhellenic Socialist Movement (PASOK) which won an absolute majority in parliament in the 1981 general election. Its leader, Andreas Papandreou, became Greece's first socialist Prime Minister.

PASOK had been elected on a radical socialist platform, which included withdrawal from the European Community, the removal of US military bases and a sweeping programme of domestic reform. Important social changes, such as lowering the voting age to 18, the legalisation of civil marriage and divorce, and an overhaul of the universities and the army, were carried out, but, instead of withdrawing from Europe, Papandreou was content to obtain a modification of the terms of entry, and, rather than close US bases, he signed a five-year agreement on defence and economic co-operation. In 1983 he also signed a ten-year economic co-operation agreement with the USSR.

Despite introducing tight austerity measures to deal with growing inflation, PASOK won a comfortable majority in the 1985 elections, gaining approval for another term of reforming, socialist government. In March 1986 the constitution was amended, limiting the powers of the President in relation to those of the Prime Minister.

In 1988 relations with Turkey showed a marked improvement. Papandreou met Prime Minister Ozal of Turkey for talks in Switzerland and later Ozal paid a visit to Athens, the first by a Turkish Prime Minister for over 35 years. Later in 1988 the personal life of Prime Minister Papandreou became difficult. It was announced that he and his wife were about to divorce and then that he himself had a heart condition which required surgery. This was successfully carried out in London in the autumn of that year. In 1989 Papandreou sought a renewal of his mandate but the general election result was inconclusive, resulting in a coalition government of the conservative ND and the Communists.

ICELAND

Republic of Iceland
Lyàveldió Fuland

Capital: Reykjavik

Social and economic data
Area: 102,850 km^2
Population: 0.244m*
Pop density per km^2: 2*
Literacy rate: 100%*
GDP: $2,635m*; per capita GDP: $11,146
Economy type: high income
Labour force in agriculture: 12%
*1985

Ethnic composition
Most of the population are descended from Norwegians and Celts.

Religions
The Evangelical Lutheran Church of Iceland is the national Church, to which about 93 per cent of the population are adherents, but there is complete religious freedom. There are also about 1,800 Roman Catholics.

Political features
State type: liberal democratic
Date of state formation: 1944
Political structure: unitary
Executive: parliamentary
Assembly: one-chamber
Party structure: multi-party
Human rights rating: N/A

Local and regional government
There are seven administrative districts, ranging in population from about 10,000 to about 140,000.

Head of state
President Vigdis Finnbogadottir, since 1970.

Head of government
Prime Minister Thorsteinn Palsson, since 1987.

Political leaders since 1970
1970–71 Johann Hafstein (IP-SDP coalition), 1971–74 Olafur Johannesson (PP-PA coalition), 1974–78 Geir Hallgrimsson (IP-PP coalition), 1978–79 Olafur Johannesson (PP-PA-SDP coalition), 1979–80 Benedikt Grondal (SDP), 1980–83 Gunnar Thoroddsen (IP-PA-PP coalition), 1983–87 Steingrimur Hermannsson (PP-IP coalition), 1987– Thorsteinn Palsson (IP-PP-SDP coalition).

Political system
The constitution dates from independence in 1944. It provides for a President, as head of state, who is elected for four years by universal adult suffrage, and an assembly, called the Althing. It has 63 members, also elected by universal adult suffrage, through a party list system of proportional representation, for a four-year term.

Once elected, the Althing divides into an upper house of 21 members and a lower house of 42. The 21 upper house members are chosen by the Althing itself and the residue of 42 automatically constitute the lower house. Members may speak in either house but only vote in the one for which they have been chosen. Legislation must pass through three stages in each house before being submitted to the President for ratification. On some occasions the Althing sits as a single house, called the Combined Althing.

The President appoints the Prime Minister and cabinet on the basis of parliamentary support and they are collectively responsible to the Althing.

Political parties
There are seven parties and the electoral system tends to encourage a spread of assembly representation and hence coalitions of parties. The main parties are the Independence Party (IP), the Progressive Party (PP), the People's Alliance (PA), the Social Democratic Party (SDP), the Citizens' Party and the Women's Alliance.

The IP was formed in 1929 by an amalgamation of the Conservative and Liberal parties. It has a right-of-centre orientation.

The PP dates from 1916 and is a radical socialist party.

The PA was founded in 1956 by a union of SDP dissidents and the Socialist Unity Party. It has a socialist orientation.

The SDP was formed in 1916 as the political arm of Iceland's labour movement. It has a moderate, left-of-centre orientation.

The Citizens' Party is a new party, dating from 1987. It has a centrist orientation, following a similar policy line to that of the IP, but with a greater emphasis on individualism.

The Women's Alliance is also a comparatively new party, having been formed in 1983. It is concerned with the promotion of women's and children's interests.

Latest elections

The results of the 1987 general election were as follows:

	% of Votes	*Seats*
IP	27.2	18
PP	18.9	13
SDP	15.2	10
PA	13.3	9
Citizens' Party	10.9	7
Women's Alliance	10.1	6
Other parties	4.4	1

Political history

Iceland became independent in 1944, when the Convention which linked it to Denmark was terminated. In 1949 it joined NATO and the Council of Europe and in 1953 the Nordic Council. Since independence it has always been governed by coalitions of the leading parties, sometimes right-wing and sometimes left-wing groupings, but mostly moderate.

Externally, most of Iceland's problems have been connected with the excessive exploitation of the fishing grounds around its coasts, while domestically governments have been faced with the recurring problem of inflation. In May 1985 the Althing unanimously declared the country a 'nuclear-free zone', banning the entry of all nuclear weapons. The 1987 elections ended control of the Althing by the coalition of the Independence and Progressive parties, giving more influence to the minor parties, including the Women's Alliance which doubled its seat tally.

IRELAND

Republic of Ireland
Eire

Capital: Dublin

Social and economic data

Area: 68,390 km^2
Population: 3.624m*

Pop density per km^2: 53*
Literacy rate: 100%*
GDP: $18,387m*; per capita GDP: $5,074
Economy type: high income
Labour force in agriculture: 14%

*1985

Ethnic composition
Most of the population have Celtic origins.

Religions
Almost all the population are Christians, about 95 per cent of them Roman Catholics.

Political features
State type: liberal democratic
Date of state formation: 1937
Political structure: unitary
Executive: parliamentary
Assembly: two-chamber
Party structure: multi-party
Human rights rating: 86%

Local and regional government
The country is divided into four provinces containing 26 counties. The counties and towns have elected councils.

Head of state
President Dr Patrick J. Hillery, since 1976.

Head of government
Charles Haughey, since 1987.

Political leaders since 1970
1966–73 Jack Lynch (Fianna Fail), 1973–77 Liam Cosgrave (Fine Gael-Labour coalition), 1977–79 Jack Lynch (Fianna Fail), 1979–81 Charles Haughey (Fianna Fail), 1981–82 Garret FitzGerald (Fine Gael-Labour coalition), 1982 Charles Haughey (Fianna Fail), 1982–87 Garret FitzGerald (Fine Gael-Labour coalition), 1987–89 Charles Haughey (Fianna Fail), 1989– Charles Haughey (Fianna Fail-Progressive Democrats coalition).

Political system
The 1937 constitution provides for a President, elected by universal adult suffrage for a seven-year term, and a two-chamber National Parliament, consisting of a Senate (Seanad Eireann) and a House of Representatives (Dail Eireann), serving a five-year term. The Senate has 60 members, 11 nominated by the Prime Minister and 49 elected by panels representative of most aspects of Irish life. The Dail consists of 166 members elected by universal adult suffrage, through the single transferable vote system of

proportional representation. The President appoints a Prime Minister who is nominated by the Dail. He chooses his cabinet and all are collectively responsible to the Dail, which is subject to dissolution by the President if the government loses its confidence within the five-year term.

Political parties

The system of proportional representation encourages the formation of several parties, of which there are 14, the four most significant being Fianna Fail, Fine Gael, the Labour Party and the Progressive Democrats.

The term Fianna Fail literally means Soldiers of Destiny. The party was formed in 1926 by the charismatic leader, Eamonn de Valera, and was originally a wing of Sinn Fein (The Workers' Party). It was always a party of radical republicanism, calling for the complete independence of Ireland. It now has a moderate, centre-right, orientation and favours the peaceful reunification of the island.

Fine Gael, means Irish Tribe, or United Ireland Party, and is descended from the Society of the Irish. It was originally founded in 1922 to support the first government established within the new Irish Free State, and was reformed in 1933. It has a moderate, centre-left orientation.

The Labour Party dates from 1912, when it was part of the Irish Trade Union Congress. In 1930 it was decided to separate the industrial and political functions of the movement and the Labour Party became a separate organisation. It has a moderate, left-of-centre orientation.

The Progressive Democrats Party was formed as recently as 1985 and represents a new departure in Irish politics, being more radical than the other, established parties. It seeks a peaceful solution to the problems in Northern Ireland, the encouragement of private enterprise, the abolition of the Seanad and a clear distinction between Church and state.

Latest elections

The results of the 1989 Dail elections were as follows:

	Seats
Fianna Fail	77
Fine Gael	55
Progressive Democrats	6
Labour Party	15
Other parties	13

Political history

Ireland was joined to Great Britain by the Act of Union of 1801 but by the 1880s there was a strong movement for home rule. This was conceded in 1914 but its implementation was delayed by the First World War, resulting in fierce riots in Dublin in 1916, the Easter Rebellion. Guerrilla activities continued after the war, through what was called the Irish Republican Army (IRA), which was formed by Michael Collins in 1919. In 1921 a treaty gave southern Ireland dominion status within the British Commonwealth, while six northern counties in the province of Ulster remained part of the United Kingdom, but with limited self-government.

The Irish Free State, as southern Ireland was formally called in 1922, was accepted by IRA leader, Michael Collins, but not by many of his colleagues, who transferred their allegiance to Eamonn De Valera, leader of the Fianna Fail party. He too eventually acknowledged the partition, in 1937, when a new constitution was proclaimed in Dublin, giving the country the name of Eire and establishing it as a sovereign state. The IRA continued its fight for an independent, unified Ireland through a campaign of violence, mainly in Northern Ireland but also on the British mainland and, to a lesser extent, in the Irish Republic. Eire remained part of the Commonwealth until 1949, when it left, declaring itself the Republic of Ireland, while Northern Ireland remained a constituent part of the United Kingdom.

Despite the sympathy of governments in Dublin for reunification, all have condemned the violence of the IRA and have dealt strongly with it within Ireland itself. In 1973 Ireland's traditional party, Fianna Fail, which had held office for more than 40 years, was defeated and Liam Cosgrave formed a coalition of the Fine Gael and Labour parties. In 1977 Fianna Fail returned to power, with Jack Lynch as Prime Minister. Meanwhile, the IRA violence intensified, with the murder in Ireland of Earl Mountbatten of Burma, in 1979, and the massacre of 18 British soldiers in Northern Ireland.

Lynch resigned later the same year and was succeeded by Charles Haughey, now leader of Fianna Fail. His aim was a united Ireland, with a large measure of independence for the six northern counties. He called an early general election, in 1981, but failed to win a majority, allowing Garret FitzGerald, leader of the Fine Gael Party, to form another coalition with Labour. The following year, however, he was defeated on his budget proposals and resigned. Charles Haughey returned to office, with a minority government, but he, too, was forced to resign later the same year, resulting in the return of FitzGerald.

Since then various ideas have been explored in an effort to resolve the Irish problem. In 1983 all the main Ireland and Northern Ireland political parties initiated the New Ireland Forum as a vehicle for discussion. Its report was rejected by Margaret Thatcher's government but discussions between London and Dublin were started and eventually resulted in the signing of the Anglo-Irish Agreement, in 1985, providing for regular consultation and exchange of information on political, legal, security and cross-border matters. The Agreement also said that no change in the status of Northern Ireland would be made without the consent of a majority of the people. The Agreement has been strongly criticised by the leaders of Ulster's two main Protestant Unionist parties, who, early in 1987, organised a petition to the British monarch to rescind the Agreement.

At the end of 1986 Garret FitzGerald's coalition came to the end of its life and a general election was called in February 1987. It was won by Fianna Fail and Charles Haughey returned to power. His relations with the British government proved to be more successful than many people had predicted and the Anglo-Irish Agreement, which had been signed by his predecessor, Garret FitzGerald, continued to be honoured by the new Fianna Fail administration. Meanwhile, the young former finance and justice minister, Alan Dukes, had succeeded FitzGerald as leader of Fine Gael. During 1988 Irish-UK relations deteriorated, mainly because of disagreements about extradition procedures. In 1989 Haughey, in an attempt to secure an overall majority in the Dail, called a general election. Again he failed and was forced to form a coalition with the Progressive Democrats.

ITALY

Republic of Italy
Republica Italiana

Capital: Rome

Social and economic data
Area: 301,280 km^2
Population: 57.226m*
Pop density per km^2: 190*
Literacy rate: 94%*
GDP: $358,744m*; per capita GDP: $6,269
Economy type: high income
Labour force in agriculture: 10%

*1985

Ethnic composition
The population is mostly Italian but there are minorities of German origin in the Dolomites and Slovenes around Trieste.

Religions
About 90 per cent of the population are Roman Catholics. This was the state religion between 1929 and 1984.

Political features
State type: liberal democratic
Date of state formation: 1861
Political structure: unitary
Executive: parliamentary
Assembly: two-chamber
Party structure: multi-party
Human rights rating: 87%

Local and regional government
The country is divided into 20 regions, five of which, Sicily, Sardinia, Trentino-Alto Adige, Friuli-Venezia Giulia and Valle d'Aosta, have a special status and enjoy a greater measure of autonomy, because of their geographical, cultural or linguistic differences. Each region has a popularly elected council.

Head of state
President Francesco Cossiga, since 1985.

Head of government
Prime Minister Giulio Andreotti, since 1989.

Political leaders since 1970

1970 Mariano Rumor (DC-led coalition), 1970–72 Emilio Colombo (DC-led coalition), 1972–73 Giulio Andreotti (DC-led coalition), 1973–74 Mariano Rumor (DC-led coalition), 1974–76 Aldo Moro (DC-led coalition), 1976 Aldo Moro (DC), 1976–79 Giulio Andreotti (DC), 1979–80 Francesco Cossiga (DC-led coalition), 1980–81 Arnaldo Forlani (DC-led coalition), 1981–83 Giovanni Spadolini (PRI-led coalition), 1983 Amitore Fanfani (DC-led coalition), 1983–87 Bettino Craxi (PSI-led coalition), 1987 Amitore Fanfani (DC-led coalition), 1987–88 Giovanni Goria (DC-led coalition), 1988–89 Ciriaco De Mita (DC-led coalition), 1989– Giulio Andreotti (DC-led coalition).

Political system

The 1948 constitution provides for a two-chamber assembly, consisting of a 315-member Senate and a 630-member Chamber of Deputies. Both are elected by universal adult suffrage, through a party list system of proportional representation, for a term of five years. The 315 elected members of the Senate are regionally representative and there are also seven life senators. The two chambers have equal powers.

The President is a constitutional head of state and is elected for a seven-year term by an electoral college consisting of both assembly chambers and 58 regional representatives. The President appoints the Prime Minister and cabinet, which is called the Council of Ministers, and they are all collectively responsible to the assembly.

In October 1988 the Chamber of Deputies voted to abolish the practice of secret voting in the chamber, except on civil rights issues or matters affecting non-Italian groups.

Political parties

The voting system encourages a multiplicity of political parties, of which there are currently 14. The most significant are the Christian Democratic Party (DC), the Italian Communist Party (PCI), the Italian Socialist Party (PSI), the Italian Social Movement-National Right (MSI-DN), the Italian Republican Party (PRI), the Italian Social Democratic Party (PSDI) and the Liberals (PLI). Coalitions between the parties have also been a feature of post-war Italian politics.

The DC was formed in 1943 as the successor to the pre-fascist Popular Party. It is a Christian, centrist party and strongly anti-communist.

The PCI is the largest communist party in Western Europe. It was founded in 1921 after a split within the Socialist Party. It has a pro-European, socialist orientation.

The PSI was established in 1892 as Italy's first mass party. Rifts within it have, over the years, resulted in the creation of several current groups, including the PCI and the PSDI. The present-day PSI has a moderate, socialist orientation.

The MSI-DN is a neo-fascist party which was founded in 1946. It now has a membership of about 400,000.

The PRI was formed in 1894 as a radical, populist party. In its present form it has a social democratic, left-of-centre orientation.

The PSDI dates from 1947, following a split in the PSI. It has a moderate, left-of-centre orientation, a little to the right of the PSI.

The PLI was founded in 1848 by Count Camilio di Cavour, who played such a key role in the unification of Italy. The PLI dominated the nation's politics in its early years. It now has a right-of-centre orientation.

Latest elections

The 1987 general election results were as follows:

	Senate	
	% Votes	*Seats*
DC	33.6	125
PCI	28.3	100
PSI	10.9	36
MSI-DN	6.5	17
Other parties	20.7	39

	Chamber of Deputies	
	% Votes	*Seats*
DC	34.3	234
PCI	26.6	177
PSI	14.3	94
MSI-DN	5.9	35
PRI	3.7	21
PSDI	3.0	17
PR	2.6	13
Other parties	9.6	26

Political history

Italy became a unified kingdom in 1870 and soon afterwards set about acquiring a colonial empire by a mixture of purchase and seizure. The fascist period, between 1922 and 1943, was notable for an extensive programme of public works but the liaison with Nazi Germany drew it into the Second World War and eventual defeat. In 1946, after a referendum, the monarchy was abolished and Italy became a republic, adopting a new constitution in 1948.

The post-war period has seen rapid changes of government and the striking of many deals between the political parties. Until 1963 the Christian Democrats were dominant but this was followed by a succession of coalition governments, most with Christian Democratic involvement. In 1976 the Communists became a significant force, winning more than a third of the votes for the Chamber of Deputies. With this show of support, they pressed for what they called the 'historic compromise', a broad-based government with representatives from the Christian Democratic, Socialist and Communist parties, which would, in effect, be an alliance between Communism and Roman Catholicism. This was rejected, however, by the Christian Democrats.

Apart from a brief period in 1977–78, the other parties successfully excluded the Communists from power-sharing, forcing them to become part of the opposition. In 1980 the Socialists returned to share power with the Christian Democrats and Republicans and they continued in a number of subsequent coalitions of mixed composition. Then in 1983 the leader of the Socialist Party, Bettino Craxi, became the first Socialist Prime Minister in the republic's history, leading a coalition of Christian Democrats,

Socialists, Republicans, Social Democrats and Liberals. Despite criticisms of Craxi's strong-willed style of leadership, the coalition parties could find no acceptable alternative so continued to give him support. The Craxi government saw an improvement in the state of the Italian economy, although the north-south divide in productivity and prosperity persisted, despite attempts to increase investment in the south and to improve its infrastructure.

In foreign affairs Italy has demonstrated its firm commitments to the European Community, NATO and the United Nations. In 1983, for example, it played an important part in the multi-national peace-keeping force in Beirut.

In August 1986 an agreement was reached that Prime Minister Craxi would hand over power to the DC leader, Ciriaco De Mita, in March 1987, allowing the coalition to stay in office until the general election in June 1988. However, when Craxi did resign the Socialists withdrew their support from the Christian Democrats, precipitating a constitutional crisis. Amintore Fanfani, of the Christian Democrats, headed a caretaker government for a time; then Giovanni Goria formed another unstable coalition, leaving Italian politics in a state of continuing uncertainty. Goria held office for eight months, twice threatening to resign, but was eventually persuaded to remain. In March 1988 he submitted his resignation on a nuclear power issue and it was accepted by the President. Ciriaco De Mita, leader of the Christian Democrats, then accepted the challenge and this decision was almost immediately followed by the killing of one of his closest aides, Roberto Ruffilli, by the Red Brigade, because of De Mita's proposals to reform the political system. In April 1988 De Mita was formally sworn in to lead a five-party coalition, including the Socialists led by Craxi. In February 1989 De Mita was replaced as DC leader by Arnaldo Forlani, but continued as Prime Minister. In May 1989, however, he resigned, complaining of a 'barrage of insults' from the Socialist members of his government. After much manoeuvring the veteran politician Giulio Andreotti was recalled to form yet another coalition.

LUXEMBOURG

Grand Duchy of Luxembourg
Grand-Duché de Luxembourg

Capital: Luxembourg

Social and economic data

Area: 2,590 km^2
Population: 0.367m*
Pop density per km^2: 142*
Literacy rate: 100%*
GDP: $4,163m*; per capita GDP: $11,343
Economy type: high income
Labour force in agriculture: 5%

*1985

Ethnic composition
Most of the people are descended from the Moselle Franks.

Religions
Ninety-five per cent of the population are Roman Catholics. There are also about 4,000 Evangelicals.

Political features
State type: liberal democratic
Date of state formation: 1848
Political structure: unitary
Executive: parliamentary
Assembly: one-chamber
Party structure: multi-party
Human rights rating: N/A

Local and regional government
The country is divided into three districts, which are further subdivided into twelve cantons. The cantons are administered by the central government and at a lower level are municipalities, with elected councils and appointed mayors.

Head of state
Grand Duke Jean, since 1964.

Head of government
Prime Minister Jacques Santer, since 1984.

Political leaders since 1970
1969–74 Pierre Werner (PCS-PD coalition), 1974–79 Gaston Thorn (POSL-PD coalition), 1979–84 Pierre Werner (PCS-PD coalition), 1984– Jacques Santer (PCS-POSL coalition).

Political system
Luxembourg is an hereditary and constitutional monarchy. The constitution dates from 1868 but has been revised in 1919 and 1956. It provides for a single-chamber assembly, the Chamber of Deputies, with 64 members, elected by universal adult suffrage through a party list system of proportional representation, for a five-year term. There is also an advisory body called the Council of State whose 21 members are appointed by the Grand Duke for life. Any decision of the Council of State can be overruled by the Chamber. The Grand Duke also appoints a Prime Minister and Council of Ministers who are collectively responsible to the Chamber.

Political parties
There are six political parties, the four most significant being the Christian Social Party (PCS), the Luxembourg Socialist Workers' Party (POSL), the Democratic Party (PD), and the Communist Party of Luxembourg.

The PCS was founded in 1914 as the Party of the Right. It took its present name in 1944. It has often been seen as the 'natural' party of government, having been a member of most coalitions. It stands for political stability and planned economic expansion, and is a strong European Community supporter. It has a moderate, left-of-centre orientation.

The POSL was formed in 1902 as the working-class party, with strong links with the union movement. It has a moderate socialist orientation.

The PD dates from 1945 and was partly based on the anti-German resistance movement. Its predecessor was the pre-war Liberal Party and PD members are now popularly described as the 'Liberals'. The party has a centre-left orientation.

The Communist Party was founded in 1921 by dissidents from the PCS. It was for a long time strongly pro-Soviet but has modified its stance in recent years and become more European.

Latest elections

The results in the 1984 general election were as follows:

	% Votes	*Seats*
PCS	34.8	25
POSL	33.6	21
PD	18.7	14
Communist Party	4.9	2
Other parties	8.0	2

Political history

Originally part of the Holy Roman Empire, Luxembourg became a Duchy in 1354. It was made a Grand Duchy in 1815 but, like Belgium, under Netherlands rule. Belgium secured its independence in 1839, taking part of Luxembourg with it. The Grand Duchy achieved full independence in 1848.

Although a small country, Luxembourg occupies an important pivotal position in Western Europe, being a founder member of many international organisations, including the European Coal and Steel Community (ECSC), the European Atomic Energy Community (EURATOM) and the European Community (EC) itself. It formed an economic union with Belgium and the Netherlands in 1948 (Benelux), which was the forerunner of wider European co-operation.

Grand Duchess Charlotte, who had been the country's ruler for 45 years, abdicated in 1964 and was succeeded by her son, Prince Jean. She died in 1985, aged 89.

The proportional representation voting system has resulted in a series of coalition governments. The Christian Social Party headed most coalitions between 1945 and 1974 when its dominance was challenged by the Socialists. It regained his pre-eminence in 1979 and is a leading member of the current administration.

MALTA

Republic of Malta
Repubblika Ta'Malta

Capital: Valetta

Social and economic data

Area: 320 km^2
Population: 0.355m*

Pop density per km^2: 1,109*
Literacy rate: 81%*
GDP: $1,005m*; per capita GDP: $2,830
Economy type: middle income
Labour force in agriculture: 5%

*1985

Ethnic composition
The population is essentially European, supposedly originating from Carthage. Both Maltese, which is a Semitic language, and English are spoken.

Religions
Roman Catholicism is the state religion and about 98 per cent of the population practise it.

Political features
State type: liberal democratic
Date of state formation: 1964
Political structure: unitary
Executive: parliamentary
Assembly: one-chamber
Party structure: two-party
Human rights rating: N/A

Local and regional government
There is no local government as such, the whole country being administered, as a single unit, from the capital, Valetta.

Head of state
President Paul Xuereb, since 1987.

Head of government
Prime Minister Dr Edward Fenechi Adami, since 1987.

Political leaders since 1970
1962–71 Borg Olivier (Nationalist Party), 1971–84 Dom Mintoff (MLP), 1984–87 Mifsud Bonnici (MLP), 1987– Edward Fenechi Adami (Nationalist Party).

Political system
The 1974 constitution provides for a single-chamber assembly, the House of Representatives, with 65 members elected by universal adult suffrage, through a system of proportional representation, using the single transferable vote, for a five-year term. The President is the formal head of state and is elected by the House, again for a five-year term. He appoints a Prime Minister and cabinet, drawn from and collectively responsible to the House, which is subject to dissolution within its five-year term.

The constitution was amended in 1987, providing for a change in assembly representation. Under the amendment any party which wins more than 50 per cent of the total vote in a general election will automatically be given a majority in the House of Representatives, regardless of the number of seats it actually wins.

Political parties

There are four political parties but two have dominated Malta's politics since independence. They are the Malta Labour Party (MLP) and the Nationalist Party.

The MLP was officially founded in 1921 and first came to power in 1955. It has a moderate, left-of-centre orientation and argues strongly for Malta's neutrality and non-alignment.

The origins of the Nationalist Party go back to 1880 but it became a recognisable party in the 1920s. It has a Christian, centrist orientation and believes in European co-operation.

Latest elections

In the 1987 general election the Nationalist Party won 31 seats with a 50.91 per cent share of the vote. The MLP won 34 seats with a 48.87 per cent vote. In accordance with the 1987 constitutional amendment, the Nationalist Party was given an additional four seats, to ensure that it had a majority of one.

Political history

Malta became a British Crown Colony in 1815 and subsequently a vital naval base. Its importance was recognised by the unique distinction of the award of the George Cross decoration by the British monarch in 1942. From 1945 onwards the island enjoyed growing self-government and in 1955 Dom Mintoff, leader of the Malta Labour Party (MLP), became Prime Minister.

A referendum held in 1956 approved a proposal by the MLP for integration with the United Kingdom but this was strongly opposed by the conservative Nationalist Party, led by Dr Giorgio Borg Olivier. Eventually, in 1958, the British proposals were rejected by Mintoff, who resigned, causing a constitutional crisis. By 1961 both parties were in favour of independence and, after Borg Olivier became Prime Minister in 1962, independence talks began. Malta became a fully independent state within the Commonwealth and under the British crown, having in 1964 signed a ten-year defence and economic aid treaty.

In 1971 Mintoff and the MLP were returned to power with a policy of international non-alignment. He declared the 1964 treaty invalid and began to negotiate a new arrangement for leasing the Maltese NATO base and obtaining the maximum economic benefit from it for his country. Eventually, in 1972, a seven-year agreement was signed and Malta became a republic in 1974.

In the 1976 general election the MLP was returned with a reduced majority. It also won a narrow majority in the House of Represenatives in 1981, even though the Nationalists had a bigger share of the popular vote. As a result, Nationalist MPs refused to take up their seats for over a year. Relations between the two parties were also damaged by allegations of pro-government bias in the broadcasting service. At the end of 1984 Mintoff announced his retirement and Dr Mifsud Bonnici succeeded him as MLP leader and Prime Minister.

In the 1987 general election the Nationalist Party won a narrow votes victory and, as a result of a constitutional change, a narrow assembly majority. Its leader, Dr Adami, became Prime Minister. Because of the difference in international outlooks between the two parties, Dr Adami's administration favours a foreign policy switch to a more European and pro-American stance.

NETHERLANDS

Kingdom of the Netherlands
Koninkrijk der Nederlanden

Capital: Amsterdam (Seat of government: The Hague)

Social and economic data
Area: 34,000 km^2
Population: 14.481m*
Pop density per km^2: 426*
Literacy rate: 100%*
GDP: $124,983m*; per capita GDP: $8,631
Economy type: high income
Labour force in agriculture: 5%

*1985

Ethnic composition
Most of the population are primarily of Germanic stock, with some Gallo-Celtic mixtures. There is also a sizeable minority of Indonesians and Surinamese, from the former colonies.

Religions
About 38 per cent of the population are Roman Catholics, about 30 per cent Protestants, distributed among eleven different denominations, and there are also other Christian and Jewish religious communities.

Political features
State type: liberal democratic
Date of state formation: 1648
Political structure: unitary
Executive: parliamentary
Assembly: two-chamber
Party structure: multi-party
Human rights rating: 98%

Local and regional government
The Netherlands has a well developed system of regional and local government. The country is divided into eleven provinces, each with an appointed Sovereign's Commissioner, who presides over a Provincial Council, elected in a similar fashion to the Second Chamber of the national

assembly, and a Provincial Executive. There are also about 770 municipalities, with elected councils and executives, presided over by appointed Burgomasters.

Head of state
Queen Beatrix Wilhelmina Armgard, since 1980.

Head of government
Prime Minister Rudolph (Ruud) Lubbers, since 1983.

Political leaders since 1970
1967–71 Petrus J. S. de Jong (VVD-led coalition), 1971–73 Barend Biesheuvel (ARP-led coalition), 1973–77 Joop den Uyl (PvdA-led coalition), 1977–83 Andries van Agt (CDA-led coalition), 1983– Rudolph Lubbers (CDA coalition).

Political system
The Netherlands is a constitutional and hereditary monarchy. Its first constitution dates back to 1814 and, after many revisions, a new version, preserving much of what had preceded it, came into force in February 1983. It provides for a two-chamber assembly, called the States-General, consisting of a First Chamber of 75 and a Second Chamber of 150. Members of the First Chamber are indirectly elected by representatives of eleven Provincial Councils, for a six-year term, half retiring every three years, and Second Chamber members are elected by universal adult suffrage, through a party list system of proportional representation, for a four-year term.

The Queen appoints a Prime Minister as head of government, and a cabinet, or Council of Ministers, chosen by the Prime Minister. Athough they are not permitted to be members of the assembly, they may attend its meetings and take part in debates and they are all collectively responsible to it.

Legislation is introduced in the Second Chamber but must be approved by both before it becomes law. The Second Chamber has the right to amend bills but the First Chamber can only approve or reject. There is also a Council of State, which is the government's oldest advisory body and acts like a collective elder statesman. Its members are intended to represent a broad cross-section of the country's life, and include former politicians, scholars, judges and businessmen, all appointed for life. The Queen is its formal President but its day-to-day operation is in the hands of an appointed Vice-President.

Political parties
The proportional representation system of elections to the Second Chamber encourages a multiplicity of political parties. Religion, as well as politics, often plays a large part in the formation of the various groups. There are currently 19 parties, the ten most significant being the Christian Democratic Appeal (CDA), the Labour Party (PvdA), the People's Party for Freedom and Democracy (VVD), the Democrats '66 (D'66), the Political Party of Radical Democrats (PPR), the Communist Party of the Netherlands (CPN), the Pacifist Socialist Party (PSP), the Political Reformed Party (SGP), the Evangelical Political Federation (RPF) and the Reformed Political Association (GPV).

The CDA was formed in 1980 by federating the Anti-Revolutionary Party (ARP), the Christian Historical Union (CHU) and the Catholic People's Party (CDA). It has a Christian, right-of-centre orientation.

The PvdA was created in 1946 by the union of the Socialist Democratic Workers' Party with other left-wing, progressive groups. It is now a moderate, left-of-centre party.

The VVD dates from 1948 and is largely the present-day equivalent of the pre-war Liberal State Party and the Liberal Democratic Party. It is a free-enterprise, centrist party which strongly supports state welfare policies and industrial democracy.

D'66, as its name implies, was founded in 1966 on a platform calling for constitutional reform. It is now a centrist party with a strong advocacy of environmental issues.

The PPR was started in 1968 by dissidents from a number of Christian parties. It now has an anti-nuclear and ecological stance.

The CPN was formed in 1918 as a breakaway group from the Social Democratic Workers' Party. It has an internationalist socialist orientation.

The PSP dates from 1957. It is a left-wing party, opposing membership of NATO and the use of nuclear weapons.

The SGP is a Calvinist party dating from 1918, when the Anti-Revolutionary Party split. It has a centrist orientation.

The RPF is another Calvinist party which was formed in 1975. It has a more radical stance than the SGP.

The GPV is a third Calvinist party, dating from 1948. It is largely supported by the more fundamentalist members of the Church.

Latest elections

The results of the 1987 assembly elections were as follows:

	1st Chamber Seats	*2nd Chamber Seats*
CDA	26	54
PvdA	26	52
VVD	12	27
D'66	5	9
SGP		3
PPR		2
Other parties	6	3

Political history

Holland, Belgium and Flanders, then known as the Low Countries, were ruled by the Dukes of Burgundy in the fifteenth century and then by Spain from the sixteenth. The Dutch rebelled against the tyranny of Philip of Spain, and particularly his attempts to stamp out Protestantism. They temporarily won their freedom, only to have it taken away again, until eventually, in 1648, the independence of the Dutch Republic was recognised. Between 1795 and 1813 the country was overrun by the French, and then the Congress of Vienna joined the north as the kingdom of United Netherlands, under William I, in 1814. The southern part broke away, in 1830, to form the separate kingdom of Belgium.

Until 1945 The Netherlands had always followed a path of strict neutrality but its occupation by the Germans between 1940 and 1945 persuaded it to adopt a policy of mutual co-operation with its neighbours. It became a member of the Western European Union (WEU), the North Atlantic Treaty Organisation (NATO), the Benelux Customs Union, the European Coal and Steel Community (ECSC), the European Atomic Energy Community (EURATOM) and the European Community (EC) itself. In 1980 Queen Juliana, who had reigned since 1948, abdicated in favour of her eldest daughter, Beatrix.

All governments since 1945 have been coalitions of one kind or another, differences between the parties being concerned mainly with economic policies. In 1981, however, there was a major debate about the siting of US cruise missiles on Dutch soil, their installation eventually being delayed until after the 1987 general election. This resulted in yet another coalition, with the CDA and the PvdA sharing 106 of the 150 seats in the Second Chamber. In May 1989 Prime Minister Ruud Lubbers resigned following opposition to his proposals for tighter pollution laws, which would bear heavily on motorists. A general election date of September 1989 was agreed by the monarch.

NORWAY

Kingdom of Norway
Kongeriget Norge

Capital: Oslo

Social and economic data

Area: 323,900 km^2
Population: 4.165m*
Pop density per km^2: 13*
Literacy rate: 100%*
GDP: $57,908m*; per capita GDP: $13,903
Economy type: high income
Labour force in agriculture: 7%

*1985

Ethnic composition

The majority of the population are of Nordic descent and there is a Lapp minority of about 20,000 in the far north of the country.

Religions

About 92 per cent of the population belong to the Church of Norway which is the established Evangelical Lutheran Church. There are also about 21,000 Roman Catholics.

Political features

State type: liberal democratic
Date of state formation: 1905
Political structure: unitary
Executive: parliamentary
Assembly: one-chamber
Party structure: multi-party
Human rights rating: 97%

Local and regional government
The country is divided into 19 counties, ranging in population from under 80,000 to nearly 450,000. The administrative head of each county is appointed by the central government and below the county level are municipalities. There are elected county and municipal councils.

Head of state
King Olav V, since 1957.

Head of government
Gro Harlem Brundtland, since 1986.

Political leaders since 1970
1965–71 Per Borten (SP coalition), 1971–72 Trygve Bratteli (DNA), 1972–73 Lars Korvald (CPP coalition), 1973–76 Trygve Bratteli (DNA), 1976–81 Odvar Nordli (DNA coalition), 1981 Gro Harlem Brundtland (DNA coalition), 1981–83 Kaare Willoch (Conservative Party), 1983–86 Kaare Willoch (Conservative coalition), 1986– Gro Harlem Brundtland (DNA coalition).

Political system
Norway is a constitutional hereditary monarchy and its constitution dates from 1814. The King is the formal head of state and the assembly consists of a single-chamber parliament, the Storting. The Storting has 157 members, elected for a four-year term by universal adult suffrage through a party list system of proportional representation. Once elected, it divides itself into two parts, a quarter of the members being chosen to form an upper house, the Lagting, and the remainder a lower house, the Odelsting.

All legislation must be first introduced in the Odelsting and then passed to the Lagting for approval, amendment or rejection. A bill must be passed by both houses before it can become law, unless it has been passed twice by the Odelsting and rejected twice by the Lagting. In this case it will be considered by the combined Storting who may then pass it by a two-thirds majority. Once a bill has had parliamentary approval it must receive the royal assent.

The King appoints a Prime Minister and State Council on the basis of support in the Storting, to which they are all responsible.

Political parties
There are currently 14 political parties, the four most significant being the Norwegian Labour Party (DNA), the Conservative Party (the 'Right'), the Christian People's Party (KrF) and the Centre Party (SP).

The DNA was founded in 1887 and now has about 170,000 members. It has a moderate, left-of-centre orientation.

The Conservative Party was founded in 1884 to oppose the Liberal Party, which at the time was pressing for the a transfer of more power from the monarchy to parliament. Its orientation is now progressive, right-of-centre.

The KrF was formed in 1933 by a group of religious, temperance, Liberal Party dissidents. Since that time it has grown and widened its appeal. It has a centre-left orientation.

The SP originally started in 1920 as the Agrarian League. It soon changed its name to the Farmers' Party and adopted its present title in 1959. It now has a left-of-centre, non-socialist orientation, with particular concern for rural interests.

Latest elections
The results of the 1985 general election were as follows:

	% Votes	*Storting Seats*
DNA	41.2	71
Conservative Party	30.1	50
KrF	8.3	16
SP	6.7	12
Other parties	13.8	8

Political history
Norway was linked to Sweden until 1905 when it chose its own monarch, Prince Charles of Denmark, who took the title of King Haakon VII. He ruled for 52 years until his death in 1957. He was succeeded by his son Olav V who is the reigning monarch.

The experience of German occupation between 1940 and 1945 persuaded the Norwegians to abandon their traditional neutral stance and join NATO in 1949, the Nordic Council in 1952, and the European Free Trade Area (EFTA) in 1960. Norway was accepted into membership of the European Community in 1972 but a referendum held that year rejected the proposal and the application was withdrawn.

The country has enjoyed a generally stable political history, with the proportional representaton system of voting often producing coalition governments. Its exploitation of the oil and gas resources of the North Sea have given it a per capita income higher than most of its European neighbours, including France, West Germany and the United Kingdom, and it has succeeded in maintaining good relations with the USSR without damaging its commitments in the West. In 1988 Prime Minister Gro Harlem Brundtland was awarded the Third World Foundation annual prize for her leadership in environmental and development issues.

PORTUGAL

Republic of Portugal
Republica Portuguesa

Capital: Lisbon

Social and economic data
Area: 92,080 km^2
Population: 16.600m*
Pop density per km^2: 180*
Literacy rate: 79%*
GDP: $20,685m*; per capita GDP: $1,246
Economy type: middle income
Labour force in agriculture: 22%

*1985

Ethnic composition
Carthage and Rome were early influences on the ethnic composition of Portugal which is one of the oldest European countries. Most of the present-day population are descended from the Caucasoid peoples who inhabited the whole of the Iberian peninsula in classical and pre-classical times. There are a number of minorities from Portugal's overseas possessions and former possessions.

Religions
About 90 per cent of the population are Roman Catholics but there is freedom of worship for all faiths.

Political features
State type: emergent democratic
Date of state formation: 1128
Political structure: unitary
Executive: dual
Assembly: one-chamber
Party structure: multi-party
Human rights rating: 91%

Local and regional government
There are two autonomous regions, in the Azores and Madeira, to which significant powers have been devolved. Each has a minister responsible for it in the mainland government and a chairman of a regional government, appointed by the minister. Local government on the mainland and in the autonomous regions is based on municipalities and parishes with elected councils.

Head of state
President Dr Mario Alberto Nobre Lopes Soares, since 1986.

Head of government
Prime Minister Professor Anibal Cavaco Silva, since 1985.

Political leaders since 1970
1968–74 Marcello Caetano (Military), 1974–75 Antonio Ribeiro de Spinola (Military), 1975–76 Francisco da Costa Gomes, 1976–78 Mario Lopez Soares (PS), 1978–79 Carlos Mota Pinto (PS-CDS coalition), 1979–80 Francisco Sa Carneiro (AD coalition), 1980–83 Francisco Pinto Balsemao (PSD coalition), 1983–85 Mario Lopez Soares (PSD coalition), 1985– Anibal Cavaco Silva (PSD).

Political system
The 1976 constitution, revised in 1982, provides for a President, elected by universal adult suffrage for a five-year term, and a single-chamber, 250-member Assembly, elected through a party list system of proportional representation, and serving a four-year term. The President is limited to two successive terms. Four of the Assembly members represent Portuguese overseas.

The President appoints a Prime Minister and his chosen Council of

Ministers, who are all responsible to the Assembly, which is subject to dissolution during its four-year term. There is also a Council of State, chaired by the President, which acts as a supreme national advisory body.

The relationship between the President and Prime Minister has been rather different from that of a constitutional head of state to a political head of government and, at times, has displayed aspects of the executive of the Fifth Republic of France. The President has often been an active politician, rather than a formal symbol, and this has sometimes led to clashes between the two. Presidents have also been drawn largely from the armed forces and have had to work with civilian Prime Ministers. The current President is not only the first civilian to hold the post since the 1920s, but also a former Prime Minister himself. He has pledged himself to create a more open and co-operative presidency than has sometimes operated in the past.

Political parties

There are currently 19 political parties, the four most significant being the Social Democratic Party (PSD), the Socialist Party (PS), the Democratic Renewal Party (PRD), and the Democratic Social Centre Party (CDS). An electoral alliance, the CDU, of left-wing and ecological parties, was formed specifically to fight the 1986 elections.

The PSD was quickly organised immediately after the coup of 1974 by former liberal members of the old National Assembly. It has a moderate, left-of-centre orientation.

Originally the PS was founded in 1875 as Portugal's first socialist party. In its present form it dates from 1973. It is an internationalist party which takes a progressive, socialist stance.

The PRD was formed in 1985. It has a centre-left orientation.

The CDS was formed in 1974 by officials of the Caetano government soon after it had been removed from office. It has a moderate, left-of-centre orientation.

Latest elections

In the 1986 presidential election Mario Soares was elected with 51.3 per cent of the vote. His rival, Diego Freitas Do Amaral, obtained 48.7 per cent.

In the 1986 Assembly elections the results were as follows:

	% Votes	*Seats*
PSD	50.22	148
PS	22.24	60
CDU	12.14	31
PRD	4.91	7
CDS	4.44	4

Political history

After being a monarchy for nearly 800 years, Portugal became a republic in 1910. The country remained economically backward and riddled with corruption until the start of the virtual dictatorship of Dr Antonio de Oliveira Salazar in 1928. Social conditions were greatly improved at the cost of a loss of personal liberties.

Salazar was succeeded as Prime Minister in 1968 by Dr Marcello Caetano who was unsuccessful at liberalising the political system or dealing with the costly wars in Portugal's colonies of Angola and Mozambique. Criticisms of his administration led to a military coup in April 1974 to 'save the nation from government'. A Junta of National Salvation was set up, headed by General Antonio Ribeiro de Spinola. He became President a month later, with a military colleague replacing the civilian Prime Minister. The new President promised liberal reforms, but, after disagreements within the Junta, Spinola resigned in September and was replaced by General Francisco da Costa Gomes. In 1975 there was a swing to the left among the military and President Gomes narrowly avoided a communist coup by collaborating with the leader of the moderate Socialist Party, Mario Soares.

In April 1976 a new constitution, designed to return the country gradually to civilian rule, was adopted, and the Supreme Revolutionary Council (SRC), which had been set up to head the new military regime, was renamed the Council of the Revolution and demoted to the role of a consultative body, under the chairmanship of the President. Then Portugal's first free Assembly elections in fifty years were held. The Socialist Party won 36 per cent of the vote and Soares formed a minority government. In June the army chief, General Antonio Ramalho Eanes, won the presidency, with the support of centre and left-of-centre parties. After surviving precariously for over two years, Soares resigned in July 1978.

A period of political instability followed, with five Prime Ministers in two and a half years until, in December 1980, President Eanes invited Dr Francisco Balsemao, a co-founder of the Social Democratic Party (PSD), to form a centre-party coalition. Dr Balsemao survived many challenges to his leadership, which included his temporary resignation following a vote of no confidence, and in August 1982, won a major victory when the Assembly approved his draft of a new constitution, which would reduce the powers of the President, abolish the Council of the Revolution and move the country to a fully civilian government. In December 1982, however, Balsemao resigned but was recalled, as a caretaker Prime Minister, until a successor as PSD leader could be agreed.

In the April 1983 general election the Socialist Party (PS) won 101 of the Assembly's 250 seats and, after lengthy negotiations, Soares entered a coalition with the PSD, whose leader was now former finance minister, Professor Anibal Cavaco Silva. In June 1985 the PS-PSD coalition broke up and a premature general election was called. The result was again inconclusive and the new PSD leader eventually managed to form a minority government. In the 1986 presidential election Mario Soares, the PS leader, won a surprising victory to become Portugal's first civilian President for sixty years. He promised a more open style of presidency which would work more co-operatively with the Prime Minister.

After a three-week political crisis, in which the left-wing opposition to Cavaco Silva's coalition forced a vote of confidence, President Soares dissolved the Assembly and called a general election, Cavaco Silva being asked to continue as caretaker Prime Minister. The result was an overwhelming victory for the PSD, strengthening Cavaco Silva's position at the expense of the PRD and communists.

It was announced in November 1988 that Portugal, with Spain, had joined the Western European Union (WEU), both having joined the EC two years earlier.

In June 1989 the constitution was amended to remove the ban on the privatisation of state industries.

SPAIN

Kingdom of Spain
Reino de España

Capital: Madrid

Social and economic data
Area: 504,880 km^2
Population: 39.074m*
Pop density per km^2: 77*
Literacy rate: 93%*
GDP: $171,000m*; per capita GDP: $4,376
Economy type: middle income
Labour force in agriculture: 15%

*1985

Ethnic composition
The present-day population can mostly trace their origins back to Moorish, Roman and Carthaginian ancestry.

Religions
The majority of people are Roman Catholics. There are also about 300,000 Muslims and about 12,000 Jews.

Political features
State type: emergent democratic
Date of state formation: 1492
Political structure: unitary
Executive: parliamentary
Assembly: two-chamber
Party structure: multi-party
Human rights rating: 84%

Local and regional government
The country is divided into 50 provinces and although not a federal state, Spain has developed a system of regional self-government, whereby each of the provinces has its own Council (Diputacion Provincial) and Civil Governor. The devolution process was extended in 1979 when 17 autonomous communities were approved, each with an assembly, elected through a party list system of proportional representation for a four-year term, and a president of government, elected by the assembly. The powers of the autonomous communities are specified in the constitution. The 17 communities are Andalucia, Aragon, Asturias, the Balearic Islands, the Basque country, the Canary Isles, Cantabria, Castilla y Leon, Castilla-La Mancha, Catalonia, Extremadura, Galicia, Madrid, Murcia, Navarra, La Rioja and Valencia.

Head of state
King Juan Carlos I, since 1975.

Head of government
Prime Minister Felipe Gonzalez Marquez, since 1982.

Political leaders since 1970
1939–1974 Francisco Franco y Bahamonde (National Movement), 1974–76 Carlos Arias Navarro (National Movement), 1976–81 Adolfo Suarez Gonzalez (CDS), 1981–82 Leopoldo Calvo Sotelo (CDS), 1982– Felipe Gonzales Marquez (PSOE).

Political system
The 1978 constitution creates a constitutional monarchy, with an hereditary King as formal head of state. He appoints a Prime Minister, called a President of Government, and a Council of Ministers, all of whom are responsible to the National Assembly (Las Cortes Generales). The Cortes consists of two chambers, the Congress of Deputies, with 350 members, and the Senate, with 208. Deputies are elected by universal adult suffrage through a party list system of proportional representation, and 208 of the senators are directly elected to represent the whole country and 49 to represent the regions. All serve a term of four years.

Political parties
Until 1975 only one political party was permitted, the Falange, later to be known as the National Movement, but now 21 national parties currently operate, the most significant being the Socialist Workers' Party (PSOE), the Popular Alliance (AP), the Christian Democrats (DC) and the Liberal Party (PL). The AP, DC and PL joined together, as the Popular Coalition (CP), to fight the 1986 election. There are also some 35 regionally based parties.

The PSOE can be traced back to 1879 and the Socialist Workers' Party, which merged with the Popular Socialist Party in 1978 and adopted its present name. It now has about 215,000 members and a democratic socialist orientation.

The AP was formed in 1976, shortly after General Franco's death. It has a centre-right orientation and about 150,000 members.

The DC was formed in 1982 as the Popular Democratic Party and changed its name in 1988. It is a centrist party with about 50,000 members.

The PL was formed, again following the liberalisation of political activity, in 1976. It merged with the Liberal Union and adopted its present name in 1985. It is a left-of-centre party with about 6,800 members.

Latest elections
The results of the 1986 general election were as follows:

	Senate	*Congress of Deputies*
PSOE	124	184
CP	63	105
Other parties	21	61

Political history
Prior to the declaration of a republic in 1931, Spain had been a kingdom since the 1570s. It was a major international power in the seventeenth and

eighteenth centuries but was weakened by political disunity in the nineteenth century. The creation of a republic did little to heal the regional rifts, particularly in Catalonia and the Basque area. At the same time, a political swing to the left by the republican government, coupled with criticisms and physical attacks on the Church, antagonised the military. In 1936 a group of army commanders in Spanish Morocco revolted and the Spanish Civil War began. Spain soon became a battleground for virtually every ideology in Europe, as well as a test bed for the weaponry of the rising Fascist and Nazi dictatorships. With their help the insurgents, led by Francisco Franco, won and in 1939 established a regime of strong, personal rule.

In 1947 Franco allowed the revival of an assembly with limited powers. He also announced that after his death the monarchy would be restored and named the grandson of the last monarch, Prince Juan Carlos de Borbon, as his successor. Franco died in 1975 and King Juan Carlos succeeded him as head of state. There followed a slow but steady progress to democratic government, with a new constitution being endorsed by referendum in December 1978. It confirmed Spain as a constitutional monarchy, allowed political parties to operate freely and guaranteed self-government to the provinces and regions. Adolfo Suarez, leader of the Democratic Centre Party (UCD), became the first Prime Minister under the new constitution.

As Spain adjusted itself to constitutional government after 36 years of military rule, it faced two main internal problems, the demands for independence by extremists in the northern, Basque region and the possibility of right-wing elements in the army seizing power and reverting to a Franco-style government. It therefore embarked upon policies which were aimed to satisfy the calls for regional recognition and to establish Spain firmly within the international community. They included a devolution of power to the regions, entry into NATO and later membership of the European Community.

By 1981, however, the government was showing signs of strain and Suarez suddenly resigned, to be succeeded by his deputy, Calvo Sotelo, who was immediately confronted with an attempted army coup in Madrid led by Lieutenant-Colonel Antonio Tejero. At the same time the military commander of Valencia, Lieutenant-General Milans del Bosch, declared a state of emergency there and sent tanks on to the streets. Both uprisings failed and the two officers were tried and imprisoned. Sotelo's decision to take Spain into NATO was widely criticised and, after defections from the party, he was forced to call a general election in October 1982.

The result was a sweeping victory for the Socialist Workers' Party (PSOE), led by Felipe Gonzalez. With the Basque separatist organisation, ETA, stepping up its campaign for independence by widespread terrorist activity, the government committed itself to strong anti-terrorist measures while, at the same time, promising a greater degree of devolution for the Basques. ETA's activities increased in intensity, however, spreading in 1985 to the Mediterranean holiday resorts and threatening Spain's lucrative tourist industry.

The PSOE had fought the election on a policy of taking Spain out of NATO and carrying out an extensive programme of nationalisation. Once in office, however, Gonzalez showed himself to be a supreme pragmatist. His nationalisation programme was much more selective than had been expected and he left the decision whether or not to remain in NATO to a referendum to be held in the spring of 1986. In January 1986 Spain became a full member of the European Community and in March the referendum showed popular support for remaining in NATO. The PSOE won a clear majority in the July general election of that year, despite being faced with an electoral alliance by some of the main opposition parties. Gonzalez was therefore returned for another term as Prime Minister. Tough policies to tackle the country's economic problems resulted in a wave of industrial strikes in 1987 and other expressions of dissatisfaction with the government. By 1988, however, there were clear signs that the government's prescriptions were working and the economy had become one of the fastest-growing in Europe. The PSOE had moved significantly to the right, however, and by April 1989 a truce with ETA had collapsed.

SWEDEN

Kingdom of Sweden
Konungariket Sverige

Capital: Stockholm

Social and economic data

Area: 449,700 km^2
Population: 8.357m*
Pop density per km^2: 19*
Literacy rate: 100%*
GDP: $100,247m*; per capita GDP: $11,996
Economy type: high income
Labour force in agriculture: 5%

*1985

Ethnic composition

The population consists almost entirely of Teutonic stock, with small minorities of Lapps, Finns and Germans.

Religions

The Evangelical Lutheran Church (Church of Sweden) is the established Church and about 92 per cent of the population belong to it. There are other Protestant denominations, about 120,000 Roman Catholics and about 16,000 Jews.

Political features

State type: liberal democratic
Date of state formation: 1523
Political structure: unitary
Executive: parliamentary
Assembly: one-chamber
Party structure: multi-party
Human rights rating: 98%

Local and regional government
There is a strongly devolved system of local government, with 24 counties and 279 municipalities, all with representative institutions. It is estimated that at least 40 per cent of public administration is conducted at a sub-national level.

Head of state
King Carl XVI Gustav, since 1973.

Head of government
Prime Minister Ingvar Carlsson, since 1986.

Political leaders since 1970
1969–75 Olof Palme (SAP), 1975–78 Thorbjorn Falldin (Centre Party coalition), 1978–79 Ola Ullsten (Liberal coalition), 1979–81 Thorbjorn Falldin (Centre-Moderate-Liberal coalition), 1981–82 Thorbjorn Falldin (Centre Party), 1982–86 Olof Palme (SAP), 1986– Ingvar Carlsson (SAP).

Political system
Sweden is a constitutional hereditary monarchy with the King as formal head of state and a popularly elected government. The constitution dates from 1809 and has been since been amended several times. It is based on four fundamental laws, the Instrument of Government Act, the Act of Succession, the Freedom of the Press Act and the Riksdag (Parliament) Act. It provides for a single-chamber assembly, the Riksdag of 349 members, elected by universal adult suffrage, through a party list system of proportional representation, for a three-year term. The Prime Minister is nominated by the Speaker of the Riksdag and then confirmed by a vote of the whole House. The Prime Minister chooses a cabinet and all are then responsible to the Riksdag. The King now has a purely formal role, the normal duties of a constitutional monarch, such as dissolving the Riksdag and deciding who should be asked to form an administration, being undertaken by the Speaker of the Riksdag.

Political parties
There are currently ten active political parties, the most significant being the Social Democratic Labour Party (SAP), the Moderate Party, the Liberal Party, the Centre Party, the Christian Democratic Party and the Left (Communist) Party.

The SAP was founded in 1889 and is Sweden's largest political party, with over one million members. It has a moderate, left-of-centre orientation.

The Moderate Party was formed in 1904 as the Conservative Party. It changed its name in 1969. It has a right-of-centre stance.

The Liberal Party dates from 1902 and used to be the main opposition to the Conservatives. It has a centre-left orientation.

The Centre Party was founded in 1910 as the Agrarian Party, mainly to represent farming interests. It changed its name in 1958 in an attempt to widen the basis of its support. As its name implies, it has a centrist orientation.

The Christian Democratic Party is a more recent development, having been formed in 1964 to promote Christian values in political life. It takes a Christian, centrist stance.

The Left Party (Communists) dates originally from 1917 when it was the Left Social Democratic Party of Sweden. In 1921 it was renamed the Communist Party and later, in 1967, it adopted its present name. It has a European, Marxist orientation.

Latest elections
The results of the 1988 Riksdag elections were as follows:

	Seats Won
Social Democrats (SAP)	156
Moderate Party	66
Liberal Party	44
Centre Party	42
Left Party (Communists)	21
Green Party	20

Political history
Sweden has been a constitutional monarchy since the beginning of the nineteenth century. It has a long tradition of neutrality, a record of great political stability, a highly developed social welfare system and a flair for innovative and open, popular government. For example, the ombudsman system, which provides the ordinary citizen with redress against the abuse of administrative power, is a Swedish invention and Sweden was one of the first countries in the world to adopt a system of open government.

Between 1951 and 1968 the Social Democratic Labour Party (SAP) was in power, sometimes alone and sometimes as the senior partner in a coalition. In 1968 the Social Democrats formed their first majority government since the mid-1940s and in 1969 the leadership of the party changed hands, Olof Palme becoming Prime Minister. In the general election two years later Palme lost his overall majority but continued at the head of a minority government. During the next six years he carried out two major reforms of the constitution, reducing the chambers in the assembly from two to one, in 1971, and, in 1975, removing the last vestiges of the monarch's constitutional powers.

The 1976 general election was fought on the issue of the level of taxation needed to fund the welfare system and Palme was defeated, Thorbjorn Falldin, leader of the Centre Party, forming a centre-right coalition government. The Falldin administration fell in 1978 on the issue of its wish to follow a non-nuclear energy policy and was replaced by a minority Liberal government, led by Ola Ullsten. Falldin returned in 1979, heading another coalition, and in a referendum held in the following year there was a narrow majority in favour of continuing with a limited nuclear energy programme. Falldin remained in power, with some cabinet reshuffling, until 1982, when the Social Democrats, with Olof Palme, returned with a minority government.

During the next few years Palme was faced with deterioriating relations with the USSR, arising from suspected violations of Swedish territorial waters. However, the situation had improved substantially by 1985. After the general election in that year, Palme was able to continue with Communist support and then, in February 1986, the world, as well as Sweden, was shocked by the news of his murder by an unknown assailant in the centre of Stockholm, as he and his wife were returning home on foot from a visit to a cinema.

The Deputy Prime Minister, Ingvar Carlsson, took over as Prime Minister and leader of the SAP, continuing the broad policy line of his predecessor. In the 1988 general election the SAP government of Carlsson was re-elected but with a slight fall in its seat count in the Riksdag. The Green Party vote rose dramatically.

SWITZERLAND

The Swiss Confederation
Schweizerische Eidgenossenschaft
Confédération Suisse
Confederazione Suizzera

Capital: Bern

Social and economic data

Area: 41,290 km^2
Population: 6.470m*
Pop density per km^2: 157*
Literacy rate: 100%*
GDP: $92,698m*; per capita GDP: $14,327
Economy type: high income
Labour force in agriculture: 6%

*1985

Ethnic composition

The great majority of people are of Alpine stock. There is also a strong Nordic element. German (65%), French (18%), Italian (12%) and Romansch (1%) are spoken.

Religions

About 47 per cent of the population are Roman Catholics and about 44 per cent Protestants.

Political features

State type: liberal democratic
Date of state formation: 1648
Political structure: federal
Executive: limited presidential
Assembly: two-chamber
Party structure: multi-party
Human rights rating: 95%

Local and regional government

Switzerland is a federation of 20 cantons and 6 half-cantons, a canton (derived from Old French) being the name for a political division. The federal government is allocated specific powers by the constitution and the residue is left with the cantons, each having its own constitution, assembly and government. At a level below the cantons are more than 3,000 communes, whose populations range from fewer than 20 to 350,000, in the case of Zürich. Direct democracy is encouraged through communal assemblies and referenda.

Head of state and head of government
President Jean-Pascal Delamuraz (1989).

Political leaders since 1970
The Federal President is appointed by the Federal Assembly to serve a one-year term, from January to December.

Political system
The constitution dates from 1874 and provides for a two-chamber Federal Assembly, consisting of a National Council and a Council of States. The National Council has 200 members, elected by universal adult suffrage, through a party list system of proportional representation, for a four-year term. The Council of States has 46 members, each canton electing two representatives and each half-canton one. Members of the Council of States are elected for three or four years, depending on the constitutions of the individual cantons. The federal government is in the hands of a Federal Council, consisting of seven members elected for a four-year term by the Assembly, and each heading a particular federal department. The Federal Assembly also appoints one member to act as federal head of state and head of government for a year, the term of office beginning on 1 January.

Political parties
There are currently 22 nationally based political parties, the most significant being the Radical Democratic Party of Switzerland (FDP), the Swiss Social Democratic Party (SPS), the Christian Democratic Party of Switzerland (PDC), the Swiss People's Party (SVP), the Swiss Liberal Party (PLS) and the Green Party.

The FDP led the movement which resulted in the creation of the Federative State and Constitution of 1848 and has been an important force in Swiss politics ever since. It has a radical, centre-left orientation.

The PDC was formed in 1912 as the Conservative People's Party. It changed its name in 1957. It is a Christian, moderate-centrist party.

The SPS was founded in 1888 as a Marxist party. Since then its outlook has been modified so that it now has a moderate, left-of-centre stance.

The SVP dates from 1919 when it began more as a broad-based interest group than a political party. At one time it had the name of the Farmers', Artisans' and Bourgeois Party. It now has a centre-left orientation.

The PLS began in the early nineteenth century as the Swiss Liberal-Democratic Union. It changed its name in 1977. It is a federalist, centre-left party.

The Green Party is a product of the growth of ecological interest groups and parties which has been evident throughout Europe during the past decade.

Latest elections
The results of the 1987 general election were as follows:

	National Council Seats	*Council of States Seats*
FDP	51	14
PDC	42	19
SPS	41	5
SVP	25	4
PLS	9	3
Greens	9	—
Other parties	24	—

Political history
Switzerland has for centuries been recognised as the leading neutral country of the world and, as such, has been the base for many international organisations and the host of many international peace conferences. Although it was once the home of the League of Nations, it has not, as yet, itself become a member of the United Nations. A referendum held in 1986 rejected the advice of the government and came out overwhelmingly against membership. Its domestic politics have been characterised by coalition governments and a stability which has enabled it to become one of the richest per capita countries in the world.

Switzerland has tended to be a male-oriented nation and women were not allowed to vote in federal elections until 1971. The first female cabinet minister was not appointed until 1984.

The 1987 general election resulted in the continuation of a four-party (FDP-PDC-SPS-SVP) coalition, but with the Green Party showing significant advances.

TURKEY

Republic of Turkey
Turkiye Cumhuriyeti

Capital: Ankara

Social and economic data
Area: 779,450 km^2
Population: 51.819m*
Pop density per km^2: 66*
Literacy rate: 74%*
GDP: $52,699m*; per capita GDP: $1,017
Economy type: middle income
Labour force in agriculture: 58%

*1985

Ethnic composition
Over 90 per cent of the population can be said to be Turks but only about 5 per cent can claim Turki or Western Mongoloid ancestry. Most people are descended from earlier conquerors of their country, such as the Greeks.

Religions
About 99 per cent of the people are Muslims, mainly of the Sunni sect. Islam was the state religion for a brief period, between 1924 and 1928.

Political features
State type: emergent democratic
Date of state formation: 1923
Political structure: unitary
Executive: parliamentary
Assembly: one-chamber
Party structure: multi-party
Human rights rating: 41%

Local and regional government
The country is divided into 67 provinces, ranging in population from under 150,000 to 4.75 million. The provinces are further subdivided into districts. The provinces have appointed governors and there are elected assemblies at all levels.

Head of state
President Kenan Evren, since 1982.

Head of government
Prime Minister Turgut Ozal, since 1983.

Political leaders since 1970
1965–71 Suleyman Demirel (JP), 1971–73 'non-party' leaders (Military), 1973–74 Bulent Ecevit (RPP-NSP coalition), 1974–75 Transitional coalition, 1975–78 Suleyman Demirel (JP coalition), 1978–79 Bulent Ecevit (RPP coalition), 1979–80 Suleyman Demirel (JP), 1980–83 Kenan Evren (Military), 1983– Turgut Ozal (ANAP).

Political system
After a military coup in 1980, a National Security Council (NSC) was installed with its President as head of state. Then, in 1982, a new constitution was adopted, and later amended in 1987. It provides for a single-chamber National Assembly of 450 members, elected by universal suffrage through a weighted party list system of proportional representation, for a five-year term. To discourage too great a fragmentation of membership, parties must obtain at least 10 per cent of the popular vote before they can win representation in the National Assembly. The President is elected by the Assembly for a seven-year term. He then appoints a Prime Minister to lead the government.

Political parties
Political activities were banned between 1980 and 1983 when new parties were allowed to form. There are now eleven active groups, the three main ones being the Motherland Party (ANAP), the Social Democratic Populist Party (SDPP) and the True Path Party (TPP).

ANAP was founded in 1983 by Turgut Ozal. It has a nationalist-Islamic, right-of-centre orientation.

The SDPP was formed in 1985 by a merger of the Populist and Social Democratic parties. It has a moderate, left-of-centre orientation.

The TPP dates from 1983 when it replaced the old Justice Party. It merged with the Citizen Party in 1986. It has a centre-right stance.

Latest elections

The results of the 1987 general election were as follows:

	% Votes	*National Assembly Seats*
ANAP	36.31	292
SDPP	24.74	99
TPP	19.14	59
Other parties	19.81	

There was a 91.28 per cent turnout. Because they failed to reach the 10 per cent threshold, none of the other parties was able to win assembly seats.

Political history

During the Middle Ages Turkey's power and influence were legendary and the Ottoman Empire spread into southern Russia, Hungary, Syria, Arabia, Egypt and Cyprus. Its power began to decline in the seventeenth century, as the armies of Russia and Austria pushed the Turks back towards the Bosporus. Britain and France, however, saw Turkey's value as a bulwark against Russia's imperialist ambitions and fought the Crimean War to defend its frontiers. Towards the end of the nineteenth century the Ottoman Empire began to disintegrate and Turkey was spoken of as 'the sick man of Europe'. The European powers were quick to take advantage of this weakness, France seizing Tunis, in 1881, and Britain Egypt, in 1882. The final humiliation came after the 1914–18 war when Turkey had allied itself with Germany and consequently shared in its defeat. The Treaty of Sèvres finally finished the Ottoman Empire and, after a period of unrest and confusion, the army, led by Kemal Ataturk, removed the Sultan in 1922 and proclaimed a republic in 1923.

Ataturk ruled the country with a firm, almost despotic, hand until his death in 1938. During this time he secularised and westernised his nation, emancipated women and turned Turkey into a modern industrial state, substituting national pride for the old Islamic loyalties. His experience served as an example for other leaders to follow, one of whom was Gamal Nasser of Egypt.

Ataturk was succeeded by Ismet Inonu, who continued his predecessor's work, but in a more pluralist fashion. During the Second World War Inonu allied himself with Britain and the United States, although he delayed entering the war until near its end, in 1945. He liberalised the political system and was then defeated in Turkey's first free elections, held in 1950, which were won by the Democratic Party (DP), led by Celal Bayar and Adnan Menderes. Bayar became President and Menderes Prime Minister.

In the post-1945 period Turkey felt itself threatened by the USSR and joined a number of collective defence organisations, including NATO in 1952 and the Baghdad Pact in 1955. This became the Central Treaty

Organisation (CENTO) in 1959 and was eventually dissolved in 1979. Turkey strengthened Western links and by 1987 was making overtures about possible membership or association with the European Community.

In 1960 the government was overthrown in a military coup and President Bayar was later imprisoned and Menderes executed. A new constitution was adopted in 1961 and civilian rule restored even though the leader of the coup, General Cemal Gursel became President. There followed a series of civilian governments, led mainly by Ismet Inonu, now very much an elder statesman, until 1965, when the Justice Party (JP), led by Suleyman Demirel, came to power.

Following strikes and student unrest, the army forced Demirel to resign in 1971 and for the next two years the country came under military rule again. A civilian government was restored in 1973 in the shape of a coalition led by Bulent Ecevit. The following year Turkey sent troops to Cyprus to protect the Turkish-Cypriot community, resulting in the effective partition of the island. Ecevit's government fell when he refused to annex north Cyprus and in 1975 Suleyman Demirel returned at the head of a right-wing coalition.

Elections held in 1977 were inconclusive and Demirel precariously held on to power until 1978 when Ecevit returned, leading another coalition. He was faced with a deteriorating economy and outbreaks of sectional violence and by 1979 had lost his working majority and resigned. Demirel returned in November but the violence continued and in September 1980 the army stepped in and set up a National Security Council (NSC), with Bulent Ulusu as Prime Minister. Martial law was imposed, political activity suspended and a harsh regime established.

Law and order were eventually restored but at a high cost in the loss of civil liberties. Strong international pressure was put on Turkey to return to a more democratic system of government and work was begun on the draft of a new constitution. In May 1983 political parties were allowed to operate again. The old parties reformed under new names and in November three of them fought the Assembly elections, the conservative Motherland Party (ANAP), the Nationalist Democracy Party (MDP) and the Populist Party (SDHP). ANAP won a narrow but clear majority and its leader, Turgut Ozal, became Prime Minister.

Turkey continued to be criticised for the harshness of its penal system and its violation of human rights. Its future role in the world, and particularly any association with the European Community, will certainly depend upon its willingness and ability to create a more democratic and humane system of government. Following a referendum in September 1987, the political ban on the opposition leaders Suleyman Demirel and Bulent Ecevit was removed and in a relatively free and open general election two months later Prime Minister Turgut Ozal and the ANAP retained their National Assembly majority. This reflected public acknowledgment of the steps taken by Ozal to reform and modernise the sluggish Turkish economy. Immediately after the election Bulent Ecevit announced his retirement from active politics. At the beginning of 1988 meetings took place between Turkish and Greek leaders, suggesting the start of a genuine rapprochement. A failure to produce a significant improvement in the economy resulted in public discontent, evidenced by huge defeats for ANAP in the March 1989 local elections.

UNITED KINGDOM

United Kingdom of Great Britain and Northern Ireland

Capital: London

Social and economic data
Area: 244,100 km^2
Population: 56.458m*
Pop density per km^2: 231*
Literacy rate: 99%*
GDP: $455,622m*; per capita GDP: $8,070
Economy type: high income
Labour force in agriculture: 2%

*1985

Ethnic composition
The people of the United Kingdom comprise 81.5 per cent English, 9.6 per cent Scots, 2.4 per cent Irish, 1.9 per cent Welsh and 2 per cent West Indians, Asians and Africans.

Religions
There are two established religions, the Church of England and the Church of Scotland. However, regular church attenders in both religions are in a minority. There are also substantial numbers of Roman Catholics, Jews, Muslims and Hindus, many of whom are devout adherents to their sects.

Political features
State type: liberal democratic
Date of state formation: 1707/1921*
Political structure: unitary
Executive: parliamentary
Assembly: two-chamber
Party structure: two-party
Human rights rating: 94%

*Great Britain 1707. United Kingdom 1921

Local and regional government
The United Kingdom consists of four countries, within a unitary system: England, with about 83 per cent of the total population, Scotland, with about 9 per cent, Wales, with about 5 per cent, and Northern Ireland, with about 3 per cent.

The government minister responsible for the internal affairs of England is the Home Secretary, who is based in London. Three 'territorial' cabinet ministers, the Secretaries of State for Scotland, for Wales and for Northern Ireland are responsible for internal affairs in their respective countries, and are based partly in London and partly in the respective capital cities of Edinburgh, Cardiff and Belfast.

From 1922 until 1972 Northern Ireland had its own elected parliament, but the violence and discord there persuaded the United Kingdom government in London to dissolve it in 1972 and to govern the Province directly through the Secretary of State.

Geographically within the British Isles, and enjoying the protection of the United Kingdom government, but politically not a part of the United Kingdom, are the Channel Islands of Jersey, Guernsey, Sark and their dependencies, and the Isle of Man. The Channel Islands have their own assembly and government and are not bound by legislation of the UK parliament. The Isle of Man enjoys a broadly similar independence.

For administrative purposes, England and Wales are divided into 47 counties, 369 districts and, within the districts, several thousand parishes. Greater London is divided into 28 boroughs, plus the City of London. Counties and districts and the London boroughs have elected councils and parishes have either elected councils or meetings.

Scotland is divided into nine regions, within which are 53 districts, and three islands areas. The regions, districts and islands all have elected councils.

Northern Ireland is divided into six counties within which are districts, with elected councils having rather narrower powers than those in England and Wales.

Head of state

Queen Elizabeth II, since 1952.

Head of government

Prime Minister Margaret Hilda Thatcher, since 1979.

Political leaders since 1970

1970–74 Edward George Heath (Conservative), 1974–76 James Harold Wilson (Labour), 1976–79 Leonard James Callaghan (Labour), 1979– Margaret Hilda Thatcher (Conservative).

Political system

The United Kingdom is a classic example of a constitutional monarchy based on a system of parliamentary government. There is no written constitution, the main features being contained in individual pieces of legislation and certain practices followed by successive governments which are regarded as constitutional conventions. Cabinet government, which is at the heart of the system, is founded on convention and the relationship between the monarch, as head of state, and the Prime Minister, as head of government, is similarly based. In theory this makes the unwritten constitution extremely flexible. In practice, however, it is as rigid as if it were written, and more rigid than many that have been formally set down. The features that provide this rigidity, as well as ensuring political stability, are the fact that parliament is sovereign, in that it is free to make and unmake any laws that it chooses, and the concept of the rule of law, which says that all governments are subject to the laws which parliament makes, as interpreted by the courts. The Queen is one part of the trinity of parliament, the other parts being the two legislative and debating chambers, the House of Lords and the House of Commons.

The House of Lords has three main kinds of members: those who are there by accident of birth, the hereditary peers; those who are there because of some office they hold; and those who are appointed to serve for life, the life peers. There are nearly 800 hereditary peers and they include five royal dukes, 26 non-royal dukes, 29 marquesses, 157 earls, 103 viscounts and 474 barons. Among those sitting because of the position they hold are two archbishops and 24 bishops of the Church of England and 9 senior judges, known as the law lords. The rest are the appointed life peers, who now include about 65 women.

The House of Commons has 650 members, elected by universal adult suffrage, by a simple plurality voting system, from single-member geographical constituencies, each constituency containing on average about 65,000 electors. Although the House of Lords is termed the Upper House, its powers in relation to those of the Commons have been steadily reduced so that now it has no control over financial legislation, and merely a delaying power of a year over other bills. Before an Act of Parliament becomes law it must pass through a five-stage process in each chamber, first reading, second reading, committee stage, report stage and third reading, and then receive the formal royal assent. Bills, other than financial ones, can be introduced in either House, but most begin in the Commons.

The monarch appoints the Prime Minister on the basis of support in the House of Commons and he or she in turn chooses and presides over a cabinet. The simple voting system favours two-party politics and both chambers of parliament are physically designed to accommodate two parties, the government sitting on one side of the presiding Speaker and the opposition on the other. No matter how many parties are represented in parliament only one, that with the second largest number of seats in the Commons, is recognised as the official opposition, and its leader is paid a salary out of public funds and provided with appropriate office facilities within the Palace of Westminister, as the Houses of Parliament are called.

Political parties

There are currently 21 active political parties but this number is subject to variation, particularly when elections are taking place. Parties are not required to register and the only restriction on their operations is the requirement for a parliamentary candidate to make a deposit of £500, which will be forfeited if less than 5 per cent of the total votes cast in the constituency are obtained. There are also restrictions on the amount that can be spent by candidates during an election campaign.

Despite the number of parties in existence, the simple plurality voting system, combined with a number of social, economic and demographic factors, has invariably resulted in two-party politics, the two major groups being the Conservative and Unionist Party and the Labour Party. There are two other national parties currently represented in the House of Commons: the Social and Liberal Democrats (SLD or Democrats) and the Social Democratic Party (SDP) although the SDP is not likely to persist as a national force. Contesting only Scottish constituences is the Scottish National Party (SNP), and only Welsh constituencies, the Welsh nationalist party, Plaid Cymru. There are also five Northern Ireland parties represented at Westminster: the Official Ulster Unionist Party (OUP), the Democratic Unionist Party (DUP), the Social Democratic Labour Party (SDLP), the Ulster People's Unionist Party (UPUP) and Sinn Fein.

The Conservative Party dates from the Tories of the seventeenth century who supported the Duke of York's claim to the English throne against the Whigs. They were regarded as 'conservators' because of their belief in traditional values and came to be called the Conservatives in the early 1830s. The title Unionist was added to indicate their support for the union of Ireland and England. In its present form, the party was established in 1870. It now has about 1.5 million members and has a right-of-centre orientation.

The Labour Party was founded in 1900 following a meeting of trade unionists and a number of socialist organisations. Prior to this there had been an Independent Labour Party and, later, a Labour Representation Committee. It now has about 300,000 individual members plus about 5.75 million affiliated members, through membership of trade unions or other affiliated bodies. The party has a moderate, left-of-centre orientation.

The SLD, or Democrats, were formed in 1988 by a merger of the Liberal Party and a majority of members of the SDP. The Liberals can trace their origins back to the Whigs of the seventeenth century, when they were the main opponents of the Tories. They changed their name to the Liberal Party in the 1850s. The SDP was formed in 1981 by four leading dissidents from the Labour Party. The SLD has a centre-left orientation.

The present SDP consists of the minority of members of the party formed in 1981 who chose not to merge with the Liberal Party

The SNP was formed in 1934 with the aim of securing the recognition of an independent Scotland, with its own elected assembly. The degree of independence currently sought is a matter of debate within the party.

Plaid Cymru was formed in 1925 with aims for Wales similar to those of the SNP for Scotland. The two parties have co-operated from time to time in pursuit of their common purposes.

The OUP was formed in 1905 and for a long time supported the policies of the Conservative Party. However, since the signing of the Anglo-Irish Agreement in 1985, differences have arisen between them. The OUP is the largest single party in Northern Ireland.

The DUP was formed in 1971 by dissident Ulster Unionists who adopted a less moderate and more right-wing stance than the OUP, and bitterly oppose the Anglo-Irish Agreement.

The SDLP was formed in 1970 and has strong links with the Labour Party, which has never contested seats in Northern Ireland. The party has a radical, left-of-centre orientation and supports the Anglo Irish Agreement.

The UPUP is a Protestant loyalist party, campaigning for the full devolution of power to Ulster.

Sinn Fein was formed in 1970 and is the political wing of the Irish Republican Army (IRA). The party's one representative in the UK parliament has never attended a session. It is strongly in favour of a united Ireland.

Latest elections

The results of the 1987 general election were as follows:

	% Share Vote	*House of Commons Seats*
Conservatives	42.3	376
Labour	30.8	229
Alliance*	22.6	22

*Alliance of Liberal Party and original SDP

	% Share Vote	House of Commons Seats
SNP	1.3	3
Plaid Cymru	0.4	3
Northern Ireland Parties†	2.2	17

†OUP—9 seats, DUP—3 seats, SDLP—3 seats, Sinn Fein—1 seat, UPUP—1 seat

Political history

England has been a monarchy since the tenth century, apart from the brief period of the Commonwealth, between 1649 and 1660, and Wales a united principality since the eleventh century. The two nations were united in 1535. Scotland has been a kingdom since the ninth century and joined England and Wales to form the state of Great Britain in 1707. Northern Ireland was originally joined to Great Britain, as part of the single nation of Ireland, in 1801. In 1921 Southern Ireland broke away to become the Irish Free State, and eventually the Republic of Ireland, while six of the nine northern counties of Ulster remained in the United Kingdom of Great Britain and Northern Ireland.

By exploration, commercial enterprise and force of arms, on land and sea, a great empire was created, particularly during the eighteenth and nineteenth centuries, which covered a quarter of the world's surface and included a quarter of its population. In 1945 the United Kingdom was still at the hub of this empire and, although two world wars had gravely weakened it, many of its citizens, and some of its politicians, still saw it as a world power. The reality of its position soon became apparent in 1945 when the newly elected Labour government, led by Clement Attlee, confronted the problems of rebuilding the damaged economy. This renewal was greatly helped, as in other West European countries, by support from the United States in the shape of the Marshall Plan.

The period of Labour government, from 1945 to 1951, saw the carrying through of an ambitious programme of public ownership and investment and the laying of the foundations of a national health service and welfare state which became the envy of the world. During the same period a civilised dismemberment of the British Empire, restyled the Commonwealth, was started. It was a process which was to continue through to the 1980s.

In 1951 the Conservative Party returned to power under Sir Winston Churchill and, although there were changes in emphasis in domestic and foreign policies, the essential features of the welfare state and the public sector were retained. Both administrations, Labour and Conservative, however, missed an opportunity to seize the leadership of Europe so that by the mid-1950s the framework for the European Community had been created, with the United Kingdom an onlooker rather than a participant. In 1955 Sir Winston Churchill, now in his eighty-first year, handed over to his heir apparent, the distinguished Foreign Secretary, Sir Anthony Eden.

In little more than a year he found himself confronted by what he perceived to be a threat as great as that from Germany in the 1930s, but now it was from the President of Egypt, Gamal Nasser, who had taken possession of the Suez Canal. Eden's perception of the threat posed by Nasser was not shared by everyone, not even within the Conservative Party. The invasion of Egypt, in conjunction with France and Israel, brought widespread criticism and was abandoned in the face of pressure from the United States and the United Nations. Eden resigned, on the grounds of ill health, and the Conservatives chose Harold Macmillan as their new leader and Prime Minister.

Macmillan skilfully and quickly repaired the damage caused within the party, and internationally, by his predecessor's ill judged adventure and, with a booming economy and rising living standards had, by the early 1960s, won himself the reputation of 'Super Mac'. Internationally, he acquired a reputation for wise statemanship, establishing a close working relationship with his United States contemporary, President Eisenhower and then the relatively youthful John F. Kennedy. He also did much to cement the unique voluntary partnership of nations which the Commonwealth had become. He was, nevertheless, sufficiently realistic to see that the United Kingdom's long-term economic and political future lay in Europe. The Conservatives won the 1959 general election with an increased majority and in 1961 the first serious, if belated, attempt was made to join the European Community, only to have it blocked by the French President, Charles de Gaulle.

Despite rising living standards, the UK's economic performance was not as successful as that of many of its competitors, particularly West Germany and Japan. There was a growing awareness that there was insufficient investment in industry, that the best young talent was going into the professions or financial institutions rather than manufacturing, and that training was poorly planned and inadequately funded. It was against this background that Macmillan unexpectedly resigned in 1963, on the grounds of ill health, and was succeeded by the Foreign Secretary, Lord Home, who immediately renounced his title to become Sir Alec Douglas-Home.

In the general election in the following year the Labour Party was returned with a slender majority and its leader, Harold Wilson, became Prime Minister. The election had been fought on the issue of the relative decline of the economy and the need to regenerate it. Wilson's immediate prescription was institutional change. He created a new Department of Economic Affairs (DEA), to challenge the short-term conservatism of the Treasury, and brought in a leading trade unionist, Frank Cousins, to head a new Ministry of Technology. In an early general election in 1966 Wilson increased his Commons majority appreciably but his promises of fundamental changes in economic planning, industrial investment and improved work practices were not fulfilled. The DEA was disbanded in 1969 and in the same year an ambitious plan for the reform of industrial relations was also dropped in the face of trade union opposition.

In 1970 the Conservatives returned to power under Edward Heath, who was as much committed to economic and industrial reform as his Labour predecessor. He, too, saw institutional change as one way of achieving the results he wanted and created two new central 'super-departments', Trade and Industry, and Environment, and a high-powered 'think tank' to advise the government on long-term strategy, the Central Policy Review Staff (CPRS). He chose to change the climate of industrial relations through legislation, introducing a long and complicated Industrial Relations Bill.

He also saw entry into the European Community as the 'cold shower of competition' which industry needed and membership was successfully negotiated in 1972. Heath's 'counter-revolution', as he saw it, was frustrated by economic events. Powerful trade unions thwarted his industrial relations reforms and the European 'cold shower' combined with the sharp rise in oil prices in 1973, forced a drastic U-turn in economic policy. Instead of 'lame ducks' being forced to seek their own salvations, he found it necessary to take ailing industrial companies, such as Rolls-Royce, into public ownership. The introduction of a statutory incomes' policy precipitated a national miners' strike in the winter of 1973–74 and Heath decided to challenge the unions by holding an early general election in 1974.

The result was a 'hung' parliament, with Labour winning the biggest number of seats but no single party having an overall majority. Heath tried briefly to form a coalition with the Liberals and, when this failed, resigned. Harold Wilson returned to the premiership, heading a minority government, but in another general election later the same year won enough additional seats to give him a working majority. He had taken over a damaged economy and a nation puzzled and divided by the events of the previous years. He turned to Labour's natural ally and founder, the trade union movement, for support and jointly they agreed a 'social contract'. The government pledged itself to redress the imbalance between management and unions which had resulted from the Heath industrial relations legislation and the unions promised to co-operate in a voluntary industrial and incomes policy. Wilson was at the same time faced with opposition from within his party, with a growing left-wing movement critical of what they saw as his too moderate policies and impatient for radical change. In March 1976 Wilson, apparently tired and disillusioned, decided to retire in mid-term, arguing that it was a move he had always planned.

He was succeeded by James Callaghan, his senior by some four years. Callaghan was now leading an increasingly divided party and a government with a dwindling parliamentary majority. Meanwhile, there had been changes in the other two parties, Edward Heath being unexpectedly ousted by the relatively inexperienced Margaret Thatcher, and the Liberal Party leader, Jeremy Thorpe, resigning after an unsavoury personal scandal and being succeeded by the young Scottish MP, David Steel. Callaghan and his strong cabinet team decided to continue along the path of solid, consensual economic recovery, built around the 'social contract' incomes policy and then, in 1976, their plans were upset by an unexpected financial crisis arising from a drop in confidence in the overseas exchange markets, a rapidly falling pound and a drain on the country's foreign reserves. After a soul-searching debate within the cabinet, it was decided to seek help from the International Monetary Fund (IMF) and submit to its stringent economic policies. Within weeks the crisis was over and within months the economy was showing clear signs of improvement. Whether or not the storm could have been weathered without IMF help was a matter debated for some time afterwards. Then in 1977, to shore up his slender parliamentary majority, Callaghan entered into an agreement with the new leader of the Liberal Party, David Steel, the 'Lib-Lab Pact'. This lasted for some eighteen months, resulting in Labour pursuing moderate, non-confrontational, policies in consultation with the Liberals, who in turn voted with the government. During this period the economy improved dramatically and by the summer of 1978 it seemed certain that Callaghan would call a general election with every chance of winning it. Without apparently consulting his cabinet colleagues, he decided to continue until at least the spring of 1979 but in the winter events turned destructively against him. The Lib-Lab Pact had effectively finished by the autumn and, soon afterwards, the social contract with the unions began to disintegrate. The government was faced with widespread and damaging strikes in the public sector, with essential services badly affected. Callaghan's pre-election period became the 'winter of discontent'. At the end of March 1979 he lost a vote of confidence in the House of Commons and was forced into a general election.

The Conservatives returned to power under the United Kingdom's first female Prime Minister, Margaret Thatcher. She had inherited a cabinet containing a majority of Heath men and it was nearly two years before she made any major changes. She had also inherited a number of inflationary public sector pay awards which were a residue of the winter of discontent. The honouring of these, plus a budget from the Chancellor, Sir Geoffrey Howe, which doubled the rate of value-added tax, resulted in a sharp rise in price levels and interest rates. As the Conservatives had come into power pledged to reduce inflation, this became the government's main if not sole economic target and, in pursuing it by mainly monetarist policies, the level of unemployment rose from 1.3 million to 2 million in the first year. Mrs Thatcher had had a narrow experience in government, being a cabinet minister in only one department, but it was in foreign affairs where she was least equipped. She relied strongly, therefore, on the Foreign Secretary, Lord Carrington and it was under his influence that the independence of Rhodesia was achieved bloodlessly in 1980.

Meanwhile, important changes were taking place in the other parties. Callaghan resigned the leadership of the Labour Party in 1980 and was replaced by the left-winger, Michael Foot, and early in 1981 three Labour shadow cabinet members, David Owen, Shirley Williams and William Rodgers, with the former deputy-leader Roy Jenkins, broke away to form a new centre-left group, the Social Democratic Party (SDP). The new party made an early and spectacular impression, winning a series of by-elections within months of its creation.

Meanwhile, unemployment continued to rise, passing the three million mark in January 1982 and the Conservatives, and their leader in particular, were receiving low ratings in the public opinion polls. A fortuitous and unforeseen event rescued them, the Argentine invasion of the Falkland Islands. Margaret Thatcher's determined decision to launch an invasion to recover them, in the face of apparently appalling odds, finally confirmed her as the resolute, 'conviction' politician she claimed to be. The general election of 1983 was fought with the euphoria of the Falklands victory still in the air and the Labour Party, under its new leader, divided and unconvincing. The Conservatives had a landslide victory, winning more Commons seats than any party since 1945, and yet with appreciably less than half the popular vote.

Mrs Thatcher was now able firmly to establish her position, making changes which meant that more than half her original cabinet had been replaced. The next three years were, however, marked by a sequence of potentially damaging events: rising unemployment; a dispute at the government's main intelligence-gathering station, GCHQ; a bitter and protracted miners' strike; increasing violence in Northern Ireland; an attempted assassination of leading members of the Conservative Party during their annual conference; riots in inner city areas; embarrassing prosecutions under the Official Secrets Act; and the resignations of two prominent cabinet ministers. Meanwhile, the violence in Northern Ireland continued and, in 1985, in an effort to secure some improvement, an agreement was signed with the Irish government, providing for greater co-operation in security matters, including the exchange of intelligence. The Anglo-Irish Agreement was strongly opposed by Unionist parties in the province. On the positive side, the inflation rate continued to fall and by the winter of 1986–87 the economy was buoyant enough to allow the Chancellor to allow a pre-election spending and credit boom.

Meanwhile, there had been leadership changes in two of the other parties. Michael Foot was replaced by his young Welsh protégé, Neil Kinnock, and Roy Jenkins was smoothly replaced by David Owen as SDP leader. Despite the unemployment figures and criticisms of Margaret Thatcher's increasingly authoritarian style of government, her standing, and that of her party, held up in the opinion polls, making the prospect of a general election in 1987 highly attractive. The Conservatives won the June election with virtually the same share of the popular vote as they had secured four years earlier, but with a slightly reduced parliamentary majority. Although the Labour Party had run what was generally considered to have been a very good campaign, its share of the popular vote showed only a marginal improvement and its seat tally only a modest gain. The Liberal-SDP Alliance experienced a poor election, its vote share dropping and its seat count remaining virtually static.

The main political parties reacted differently in the aftermath of the 1987 general election. Margaret Thatcher regarded the result as a vindication of her earlier policies and strengthened her control of the party and her government, at the same time pressing ahead with an expansive privatisation programme. Her stated aim was to obliterate all traces of socialism from the British political scene. The Labour Party, stung by the jibes of its opponents that it was 'unelectable', embarked upon a massive reassessment of its policies and structure. The Liberal leader, David Steel, disillusioned with the election result and tired of being the dog wagged by the tail of the SDP leader, David Owen, made an immediate call for a full merger of the two parties. This was eventually agreed, amid considerable acrimony and some confusion, and in 1988 the new party of the Social and Liberal Democrats (SLD), or the Democrats, as some of its members preferred to be called, was born, with a new leader, the youngish member for Yeovil, Paddy Ashdown. Not all of the SDP members chose to join the new grouping. Three MPs, led by Dr David Owen, and a few thousand followers, stayed together and retained the SDP label. With the opposition to Mrs Thatcher remaining so fragmented, observers began to speculate on whether the Conservative hegemony would ever be ended during the present century. However, in the early summer of 1989, the Labour Party published its 'policy review' which embraced multi-national, rather than unilateral, nuclear disarmament, and more market-orientated economic policies, suggesting that it could now be regarded as a realistic possible replacement for the Conservatives.

Arctic Circle
Scale 1:15 000 000
0
200
400
600 Km
NORWAY
SWEDEN
FINLAND
DENMARK
Baltic Sea
SOVIET UNION
EAST GERMANY
POLAND
WEST GERMANY
CZECHOSLOVAKIA
AUSTRIA
HUNGARY
ROMANIA
Black Sea
YUGOSLAVIA
BULGARIA
ITALY
Adriatic Sea
ALBANIA
GREECE
TURKEY

EASTERN EUROPE

The nine states of Eastern Europe form a politically homogeneous block, each, as Table 51 shows, having a communist political system. The first regime of this kind was established in 1917 in the Soviet Union (USSR) when, following the March and October revolutions, the Tsarist autocracy was toppled and a new socialist republic, under the 'guiding hand' of the Communist Party of the Soviet Union (CPSU), was created. The other communist political executives in Eastern Europe date from the end of the Second World War. In most cases, they were set up with Soviet support soon after their liberation from Nazi occupation, as the Red Army advanced westwards in 1944.

The actual method by which these communist systems were established and the degree of popular support which they initially enjoyed varied substantially from country to country.

In the cases of Poland, the newly created German Democratic Republic (DDR) and Romania, the new system was arbitrarily imposed by fiat.

In Bulgaria and Hungary, more subtle quasi-parliamentary means were pursued, with the Soviet-linked, indigenous communist parties (CPs) initially forming a 'Popular Front' coalition with moderate socialist and radical-centrist groupings. Then, between 1947 and 1949, by establishing control over the media, police and state electoral commissions, the CPs, despite enjoying less than 15 per cent of popular support, won majorities in the elected assemblies and proceeded to remodel the constitutions in a new one-party direction.

In Czechoslovakia the CP inherited a stronger, pre-war base and enjoyed broad popular support, so that it was able to secure the majority of the national vote in the free election of May 1946.

Finally, in Albania and Yugoslavia, the new communist regimes which assumed control in 1944–45 differed significantly from those to the north west, having been established without direct Red Army aid by local guerrilla resistance leaders, Enver Hoxha in Albania and Marshal Tito in Yugoslavia. Because of their 'Partisan' anti-Nazi activities, they initially enjoyed popular support.

By 1949, all the states of contemporary Eastern Europe had communist systems firmly in place, all of which have survived until today. They were initially structured, with the notable exception of Tito's Yugoslavia, in close conformity with the 'Stalinist model' then prevailing in the USSR. This involved tight, hierarchical party control over all aspects of political, social and cultural life; the promotion of leadership 'personality cults'; the terroristic use of secret police to suppress internal political opposition and dissent; and, in the economic sphere, agrarian collectivisation, bureaucratic central planning and concentration on heavy industrialisation.

However, with the maverick exception of Hoxha's Albania, which broke with the USSR in 1961 in opposition to Khrushchev's denunciation of the Stalin era, 'Stalinisation' was never fully completed in these East European satellites. Bulgaria came closest. Elsewhere, internal opposition, pressing for more liberal and inclusive political structures, periodically surfaced in the form of workers' revolts and intelligentsia campaigns, forcing prudent changes of course. In the cases of East Berlin in 1953, Hungary in 1956 and Prague in 1968, Soviet or Warsaw Pact troops had to be employed to restore CP control. In Poland, in December 1981, martial law was imposed by the country's own military forces as a means of suppressing a serious internal challenge to the incumbent Polish United Workers' Party regime.

In Eastern Europe the post-war era has thus been characterised, on the one hand, by broad stability and on the other by periodic challenges to the authority of the ruling CPs. The stability has been achieved by tight links with their dominant eastern neighbour, the USSR, through the economic, military and political structures of Comecon, the Warsaw Treaty Organisation and the Cominform. Only the Balkan states of Albania and Yugoslavia have remained aloof from these. The recurrent periods of opposition have forced policy adjustments and partial departures from the Soviet model in both the political and economic spheres. The socio-cultural heterogeneity of this region, coupled with a history of subjection to autocratic, external rule, economic backwardness and nascent democratisation during the inter-war decades, are crucial factors which help to explain these conflicting trends. They have resulted in the creation of a unique 'political culture'.

With the exception of the Muscovy (RSFSR) heartland of the contemporary Soviet Union, which formed the core for the successive Kiev-based (tenth to twelfth centuries), Moscow-based (1462–1709), and St Petersburg (Leningrad)-based (1709–1917), Russian empires, state creation came late to Eastern Europe. Although several of the present-day countries of Albania, Bulgaria, Czechoslovakia, Hungary, Poland, Romania and Yugoslavia had formed the cores of medieval kingdoms, notably Bulgaria, Poland and Serbia, none emerged as a substantially coherent nation-state until the late nineteenth and early twentieth centuries. The majority were formed only at the close of the First World War.

Before this, and because of their strategically important position between Asia and North-Western Europe, they found themselves at various times under the authority of either the Turkish, Austrian, German or Russian empires. As a consequence, the tract we have called Eastern Europe was exposed to a variety of influences, religious, legal, scriptural and institutional.

Although differing in detail, all the empires had a common autocratic-bureaucratic character. This served to rule out autonomous political evolution in a liberal-democratic direction. Similarly, it checked the growth of national cultural traditions, fostering instead localised, sub-regional identities. These were to be legacies which are still apparent today. They have generated, on the one hand, deferential and subservient attitudes to those in positions of authority and, on the other hand, regional divisions which have tended to undermine the cohesion of national movements, pro- or anti-government.

In the economic sphere, the centuries of control by alien empires resulted in Eastern Europe's relative underdevelopment compared with that of adjoining Western Europe. This arose partly from resource deficiencies, but, more significantly, from the retention of outmoded socio-economic structures, most notably serfdom, more than a century after they had been discarded in the West. Industrial development was consequently retarded and began only fitfully at the close of the nineteenth century, with the state playing a directing role and large capital-intensive factories becoming the norm. This tended to restrict the growth of urban working-class communities and a virile middle class. Only in East Germany and in parts of Czechoslovakia and West Poland did a more rounded development occur.

During the inter-war years, there were significant changes in the East European political and socio-economic scene as new states came into existence and tentative experiments were made with new liberal-democratic constitutional forms. The exception, of course, was the USSR where, under Stalin's lead, attention was focused on establishing 'socialism in one country', by a radical restructuring of the nation's economic and political system.

Elsewhere in the region, the 1919 Treaty of Versailles had established new parliamentary structures supported by broad franchises and generous proportional-representation electoral systems. Unfortunately, the new states were in many respects arbitrary territorial constructions, below the foundations of which lay the seeds of internal religious and ethnic conflicts. These differences worked themselves through into the political systems, resulting in a multiplicity of parties achieving assembly representation and creating chronic governmental instability.

Reacting against this, the conservative-nationalist parties who gained the upper hand over centrist-liberal groups during the mid- and later 1920s, proceeded, in all the East European states, with the notable exception of Czechoslovakia, to abrogate parliamentary forms of government and establish new monarchic or presidential autocracies of a quasi-fascist kind.

The resulting regimes, such as those of King Boris in Bulgaria, 1934–43; Admiral Horthy in Hungary, 1920–44; King Karol in Romania, 1930–40; King Zog in Albania, 1928–39; Ullmanis in Latvia, 1934–39; Voldemaras and Smetona in Lithuania, 1926–29 and 1929–40; Marshals Pilsudski and Smigly-Rydz in Poland, 1926–35 and 1935–39; and King Alexander and Regent Paul in Yugoslavia, 1929–34 and 1934–39, continued to hold power until the outbreak of the Second World War. During this period the socialist and communist parties, which had drawn 10–20 per cent of the national vote during the early 1920s, were proscribed and forced underground.

The inter-war years were, therefore, with the notable exception of economically advanced and socially differentiated Czechoslovakia, a period of abortive democratisation for the non-communist states of Eastern Europe. Nevertheless, despite its failure, the democratic experiment at the start of this period was to have a long-term impact on the 'political culture' of the region. It remains important today and has tended to undermine traditional attitudes of political subservience and shifted popular political expectations in a more pluralist direction than has been evident in the Soviet Union.

The nine states which make up Eastern Europe today, cover more than a sixth of the world's land area and embrace a twelfth of its population. They are dominated in areal, demographic, economic, as well as political and military terms, by the Soviet Union, a giant supra-national formation which is the largest state in the world, more than double the area of its nearest challengers, Canada and the United States, and, after China and India, the third most populous.

From the Pacific coast to the Polish border, the USSR extends east-west for 10,900 km, bestriding eleven international time-zones. From the Arctic tundra permafrost wastes to the arid deserts of Turkmenistan and Uzbekistan, it stretches a further 5,600 kilometres between north and south. Barely 10 per cent of the total area is however at present cultivated, making its areal population density particularly low.

Seven of the remaining states of Eastern Europe, Bulgaria, Czechoslovakia, East Germany, Hungary, Poland, Romania and Yugoslavia, are broadly similar in spatial and demographic size. With areas of between 93,000 and 313,000 km^2, populations of between 9 and 37 million and demographic densities of between 81 and 154 per km^2, they occupy the middle range of world states in terms of areal sizes, as Table 43 indicates, and the upper-middle in terms of population, as can be seen in Tables 44 and 45. The region's ninth state, isolated, mountain-enclosed Albania, is considerably smaller.

As Table 47 shows, the states of Eastern Europe currently account for an eighth of the world's GDP, with three-quarters of this total being contributed by the USSR. During the post-war period their economic performances have been creditable, GDP advancing at an average annual rate of 4.5 per cent between 1950 and 1979. As part of this growth process, the developing middle-income nations of the region underwent a fundamental structural transformation, with a major rural to urban-industrial shift occurring, and the proportion of the population engaged in agriculture falling from 45 per cent in 1960 to 25 per cent in 1985. Since the later 1970s, however, as the economies of the nations of Eastern Europe have 'matured', growth rates have slumped. Between 1980 and 1985 regional GDP advanced by only 2 per cent per annum, while in strife-torn and debt-encumbered Poland and Yugoslavia negative growth was recorded.

In terms of literacy levels, as Table 51 reveals, the states of Eastern Europe rank high. Other indices of social provision which are not displayed here, such as education and health for example, show the socialist states of Eastern Europe to be among the world's most advanced. Less favourable are their rankings in terms of human rights, as can be seen from Table 51. Five of the countries for which data are available, Bulgaria, Czechoslovakia, East Germany, Romania and the Soviet Union, are among the bottom quartile of world states surveyed, lying close to Chile, Libya and South Africa. Hungary, Yugoslavia and Poland, however, can be found alongside the 'emergent' or 'partial democracies' of Malaysia, Singapore and South Korea.

In comparative terms, the states of Eastern Europe are also notable for the high degree of their militarisation. Some 1–2 per cent of the region's population are directly engaged in military service, while between 2 per cent, in the case of Romania, and 10 per cent, in the case of the Soviet Union, of state GDP is devoted to the defence sector.

Over the centuries, the religious and ethnic heterogeneity of the peoples inhabiting the territories of Eastern Europe has bred intense intra- and inter-state rivalries, undermining the cohesion of national identities and engendering recurrent instability. These tensions remain clearly visible today, creating pressures which have forced significant modifications of established political structures in at least two states, Czechoslovakia and Yugoslavia, during the course of the last three decades.

One basic indicator of the socio-cultural heterogeneity of contemporary Eastern Europe is to be found in the religious affiliations of its peoples. Despite the professed atheism of the post-war communist regimes and periodic attempts to suppress worship, religious allegiances remain strong. Reliable figures on adherence are lacking but the best available data have been collected and presented in the individual state entries. Drawing upon these returns, two general points can be made concerning religious denominations and ethnic differences.

First, within the broad region of Eastern Europe four principal faiths are to be found, each with its own regional concentration of support. Roman Catholicism predominates in the three westerly states of Poland, Czechoslovakia and Hungary, all of which were at one time under Austrian imperial control. Protestantism is found in the west-central states of East Germany and Hungary. Eastern Orthodoxy, with its Serbian, Romanian and Russian branches, is practised in the eastern and southern Slav lands of Bulgaria, Romania, the USSR and Yugoslavia. Islam is the predominant religion in Albania and southern portions of Bulgaria, the USSR and Yugoslavia.

The most spiritually homogenous states in Eastern Europe are Poland, where 95 per cent of the population are baptised as Catholics, Czechoslovakia, where 70 per cent are Catholics, and the RSFSR Muscovy heartland of the Soviet Union. All these areas are also noted for their strong national traditions. The most spiritually heterogeneous state is Yugoslavia.

Second, the distribution of ethnic and national groups across Eastern Europe closely follows that of religious communities, adding a further dimension to community rivalries. The most culturally diverse state within the region, not surprisingly when account is taken of its size, is the Soviet Union, whose population of 280 million embraces more than 100 ethnic-language groups. Twenty-two of them are designated 'major ethnic groups', each having more than a million members. During recent years, ethnic tensions within the USSR have intensified, with calls for greater autonomy and even independence being made by nationalists in the Baltic and Caucasus republics.

Elsewhere in Eastern Europe, intra-state ethnic rivalries have been prominent in Czechoslovakia, between Czechs and Slovaks, and in the Transylvania region of Romania, between Magyar Hungarians and Romanians, during the post-war period, precipitating internal and inter-state political crises in 1968 and 1988.

The most serious and generalised ethnic conflicts have, however, occurred in Yugoslavia, a country which is fundamentally divided, in territorial, socio-economic and religious terms, among Serbs, Croats, Muslims, Slovenes, Albanians and Macedonians, and with the ruling Communist Party itself becoming factionalised along ethnic-regional lines.

Not surprisingly, strong basic similarities exist among the structures, operation and policies of the nine communist political regimes of Eastern Europe. Interesting divergences from the original 'Soviet model' are however also apparent. These have arisen for a variety of reasons. The most significant have been differences in the histories of 'communist imposition'; differences in levels of socio-economic development and ethnic structures; variations between internal worker and intelligentsia reform pressures; and, lastly, leadership and generational factors, based apparently on pure chance.

Today, a broad spectrum of differentiation is discernible, with, at one end, a reformist western wing, headed by 'non-aligned' Yugoslavia and adjoining Hungary, followed by Poland, Czechoslovakia and East Germany and the 'controlling power' of the Soviet Union. A combination of 'market socialist' policies and decentralised self-management has been apparent in Yugoslavia since the early 1950s. This approach has been less evident in the other states, political reform receiving, until lately, a far lower priority than economic restructuring.

It should also be noted that the reformist zeal of the states other than Yugoslavia has varied substantially over the years, with the lead being temporarily, and abortively, assumed by Hungary in 1956, Czechoslovakia between 1965 and 1968, and then again, more cautiously, but more effectively, by Hungary during the 1970s. Latterly, however, since the advent of the Gorbachev administration, the USSR, somewhat unusually, has emerged towards the head of the 'reform pack', pressing the reluctant DDR and Czechoslovakia to follow its example in both the political and economic spheres.

The remaining three south-eastern states, Albania, Bulgaria and Romania, have been the least innovatory, retaining political structures and adhering to policy prescriptions that are substantially Stalinist in character. Significantly, perhaps, these are the most socio-economically backward states in the region. They have been subject to a far more personalised type of rule than elsewhere, with quasi-presidential systems, founded around 'personality cults', being the norm. Leadership turnover rates have, in addition, been unusually low. Three party leaders, or fewer, since the end of the Second World War has been the norm in each of them.

Enver Hoxha, who ruled Albania with an iron rod for more than four decades, has been the most extreme example of personalised control. In contemporary Romania, a more familial form of rule has emerged which has been termed 'dynastic socialism'. Here the Ceausescu family, which has held the reins of power for more than two decades, has pursued an individualist governing style, combining clientism with a nationalistic populism, and effectively merging state and party institutions. In Bulgaria, a more cautious and collective leadership approach has been favoured by Todor Zhivkov, who has been party leader since 1954, and has based his approach on a bureaucratic, conservative Brezhnevite strategy of 'reformed Stalinism'.

The individual country entries which follow shed more light on the full variety of structural and policy departures from the 'Soviet model' that have been made by the 'satellite states' of Eastern Europe.

Table 51

EASTERN EUROPE

			Political Data				
State	*Date of Formation*	*Political Structure*	*State Type*	*Executive*	*Assembly No of Chambers*	*Party System*	*Voting System*
Albania	1912	Unitary	Communist	Communist	One	One	SP
Bulgaria	1908	Unitary	Communist	Communist	One	One	SP
Czechoslovakia	1918	Federal	Communist	Communist	Two	One	SB

Table 51—Eastern Europe (contd.)

			Political Data				
State	*Date of Formation*	*Political Structure*	*State Type*	*Executive*	*Assembly No of Chambers*	*Party System*	*Voting System*
East Germany	1949	Unitary	Communist	Communist	One	One	SP
Hungary	1918	Unitary	Communist	Communist	One	One	SB
Poland	1918	Unitary	Communist	Communist	Two	One	SB
Romania	1881	Unitary	Communist	Communist	One	One	SB
Soviet Union	1917-22	Federal	Communist	Communist	Two	One	SB
Yugoslavia	1918	Federal	Communist	Communist	Two	One	SP

		Social and Economic Data				
State	*Area (km²)*	*Population (m) (1985)*	*Population Density (per km²)*	*Literacy Rate (%)*	*Income Type*	*Human Rights Rating (%)*
Albania	28,750	3.046	106	75	Low	Bad
Bulgaria	110,840	9.000	81	95	Middle	23
Czechoslovakia	127,900	15.502	121	100	High	36
East Germany	108,180	16.700	154	100	High	33
Hungary	93,030	10.644	114	99	Middle	55
Poland	312,680	37.500	120	99	Middle	41
Romania	237,500	22.800	96	96	Middle	20
Soviet Union	22,274,900	280.000	12	100	Middle	20
Yugoslavia	255,800	23.200	91	90	Middle	50
Total/Average	23,549,580	418.392	18	75-100	Middle	20-55

ALBANIA

People's Socialist Republic of Albania
Republika Popullore Socialiste e Shqiperise

Capital: Tirana

Social and economic data
Area: 28,750 km²
Population: 3.046m*
Pop density per km²: 106*
Literacy rate: 75%
GDP: $2,900m*; per capita GDP: $952
Economy type: low income
Labour force in agriculture: 50%

*1985

Ethnic composition
The Albanians are a non-Slavic race.

Religions
Historically, 70 per cent of the population have been adherents to Islam, Sunni and Bektashi; 20 per cent, predominantly in the south, to the Eastern

Orthodox Church; and between 5 and 10 per cent, mainly in the north, to Roman Catholicism. In 1967 Albania officially declared itself an 'atheist state', outlawing all forms of religious worship and organisation.

Political features
State type: communist
Date of state formation: 1912
Political structure: unitary
Executive: communist
Assembly: one-chamber
Party structure: one-party
Human rights rating: bad

Local and regional government
There are 26 districts, each under a People's Council.

Head of state
President Ramiz Alia, since 1982.

Head of government
Prime Minister Adil Carcani, since 1982.

Political leaders since 1970*
1944–85 Enver Hoxha (PLA), 1985– Ramiz Alia (PLA).

*Communist Party leaders

Political system
The People's Republic's first constitution was adopted in March 1946 and amended in July 1950. It was based closely on the Soviet Union's 'Stalin Constitution' of 1936. A new, 112-article version was adopted in December 1976. This described the country as 'a state of the dictatorship of the proletariat' which was entering the stage of a 'comprehensive construction of the socialist society'.

The sole and supreme legislative organ in Albania is the People's Assembly (Kuvend Popullore), a 250-member body whose members are elected every four years by universal adult suffrage in broadly equal-sized single-member constituencies, by simple plurality voting. It convenes twice a year for 'rubber-stamping' sessions which last several days. It 'elects' a smaller, permanent 15-member Presidium, headed by a president who acts as *de facto* state President, to assume its functions in its absence. These include the ratification of international treaties.

In addition, the Assembly elects, from its members, a Council of Ministers (COM), headed by a chairman or Prime Minister, and composed of four deputy chairmen, 16 departmental ministers and two state commission chairmen. This body functions as Albania's day-to-day executive government, directing the work of the state ministries and People's Councils, which are triennially elected local administrative bodies. The COM is also responsible for framing the state budget and economic plan and the conduct of foreign policy. It has its own inner Presidium.

In reality, however, the controlling political force in Albania is the Communist Party (Party of Labour of Albania: PLA), which is assigned a 'leading role' by the 1976 constitution and is the sole permitted party. It operates in a 'democratic centralist' manner, with its Politburo functioning as the *de facto* national cabinet. In May 1988, the Politburo comprised 13 full members and five non-voting 'candidate' members, and was headed by First Secretary Ramiz Alia. Eight Politburo members also held positions in the Presidium of the People's Assembly and COM, including the top posts of Presidium chairman, Ramiz Alia, and COM chairman, Adil Carcani.

The PLA is the leading force in the Democratic Front of Albania (DFA) which puts up single lists of candidates in local and national government elections. The chairwoman of the DFA's ruling General Council is Nexhmije Hoxha, the widow of Enver Hoxha.

Political parties

The Party of Labour of Albania (PLA) was founded, with Yugoslav assistance, in November 1941 by a French-educated schoolteacher, Enver Hoxha, as a small 200-member underground body. It adopted its present name in 1948. It is organised on Leninist pyramidal lines with, at its base, 2,000 primary organisations, established in factories, offices and villages. A national Party Congress, which has supreme *de jure* authority, is convened every five years. This 'elects' a Central Committee, which had 85 full and 46 'candidate' members in 1988, and which assumes authority in its absence and 'elects' the Politburo and five-member Secretariat.

The PLA adheres to traditional Marxist-Leninist-Stalinist doctrines, viewing itself as the only Communist Party in the world which is constructing 'genuine' Marxism and which has avoided 'revisionism'. In 1962 party membership stood at 54,000, in 1976 at 101,500 and in 1986 it had 128,000 full and 15,300 'candidate' members. The full membership corresponds to 4.2 per cent of the total population, the lowest proportionate figure for a Communist Party in Eastern Europe. Thirty-eight per cent of the party members are blue-collar workers, 33 per cent white-collar and 29 per cent farmers. Thirty-seven per cent are women. The Union of Labour Youth of Albania and the Women's Union of Albania function as additional wings of the PLA.

Latest elections

The most recent People's Assembly election was held in February 1987, with the 250 members put foward by the DFA being elected unopposed. A 100 per cent elector turnout was recorded, with 1.83 million votes being cast in favour and only one vote declared invalid.

Political history

Albania successively formed part of the Byzantine and Ottoman Empires between the fifth century and 1347 and between 1468 and 1912. It achieved independence in November 1912, but was then occupied by Italy between 1914 and 1920. In 1925 a republic was proclaimed, with Prime Minister Ahmet Beg Zogu, a conservative Muslim landlord, as President. Three years later, he was enthroned as King Zog I and was to reign continuously as an absolute monarch until Albania was occupied once again by Italian forces in April 1939. The country remained backward and rural-based,

80 per cent of the population being dependent on agriculture in 1930, with a feudal Islamic landholding structure still surviving.

During the Second World War a communist-led National Liberation Front (NLF) was established, in 1941, with help from Yugoslav communists. Under the leadership of Enver Hoxha, the NLF emerged as the most successful resistance group in the country and in 1944 forced the withdrawal of German forces, who had entered Albania in the previous year. Liberation was thus achieved without Soviet Red Army assistance.

In November 1944 the NLF, now known as the Democratic Front, following the purge of non-communist elements, assumed power and called elections in December 1945, based on a single list of Communist Party-sponsored DFA candidates. The new Constituent Assembly proclaimed Albania a republic in January 1946, forcing the deposed King Zog to continue to live in exile. A Soviet-style communist constitution was adopted in March 1946, with the PLA now the sole legal political party.

At first the new regime was closely allied to Yugoslavia, its armed forces being controlled by Yugoslav advisers and the economic plans of both Balkan states being co-ordinated. Yugoslavia's expulsion from the Cominform in 1948, following an ideological rift between Stalin and Tito, provided an opportunity for this state of dependency to be severed. Instead, Albania developed close economic links with the Soviet Union between 1949 and 1955, entering Comecon in 1949 and the Warsaw Pact in 1955.

During the late 1950s and early 1960s Soviet-Albanian relations progressively deteriorated as the country's leader, Enver Hoxha, a committed Stalinist, refused to accept Khrushchev's 'revisionist' denunciations of the Stalin era and his overtures to Yugoslavia. Following attacks on the Soviet leadership by Hoxha, the USSR terminated its economic aid in June 1961 and broke off diplomatic relations in December 1961. Albania responded by ceasing co-operation within Comecon in 1962 and formally withdrawing in 1968 from the Warsaw Treaty Organisation, after the Soviet invasion of Czechoslovakia. Close ties were now developed instead with Mao Zedong's communist China.

Inside the country, a strict Stalinist economic and political system was imposed by Hoxha, involving rural collectivisation, industrial nationalisation, central planning, totalitarian one-party control, the frequent purging of cadres to prevent the emergence of an élitist governing stratum and the propagation of a 'cult of personality' centred upon Hoxha himself. A major drive against the Islamic and Christian religions was also launched, in 1967, involving the closure of more than 2,000 mosques and churches, in an effort to create the world's 'first atheist state' and expunge all remaining centrifugal tendencies.

Initially, between 1946 and 1954, Hoxha combined the key posts of PLA leader and state premier but in 1954 he was replaced in the second post by Mehmet Shehu, who remained as COM chairman until his death in December 1981. Shehu was officially reported to have committed suicide but non-official sources suggest he was 'liquidated' after having been involved in a leadership struggle against Hoxha. His replacement was his deputy, Adil Carcani.

The 'Hoxha experiment', with its stress on national self-reliance, the 1976 constitution forbidding the acceptance of foreign credits, and on the minimisation of urban-rural and blue- and white-collar income differentials, despite progress in the agricultural and energy spheres, left Albania with the lowest per capita income in Europe by the time of the leader's death in 1985. Internationally, the country became one of the most isolated in the world, diplomatic relations with communist China having been severed in 1978, following the post-Mao leadership's accommodation with the United States.

Ramiz Alia, the Moscow-trained President of the Presidium of the People's Assembly, was elected First Secretary of the PLA on Hoxha's death in April 1985. The new regime, although pledging to uphold the independent policy line of its predecessor, has begun to make policy adjustments in both the foreign and domestic spheres.

External contacts have broadened and the number of countries with which Albania has diplomatic relations has increased from 74 in 1978 to 111 in 1988, Canada, Greece, Spain, East and West Germany being the most recent additions. In February 1988 foreign minister Reis Malile attended the conference of Balkan states, the first attendance at a full meeting since the 1930s. This diplomatic 'thaw' has been accompanied by a growth in two-way external trade.

Internally, political reforms remain limited. There have recently, however, been signs of some greater openness in political reporting. In addition, in the economic sphere, new incentives, in the form of wage differentials for skilled tasks, are slowly being introduced. The continuing rapid rate of demographic growth, the country's population having almost doubled since 1960, will add pressure for more market-orientated reform, particularly in the agricultural sphere.

BULGARIA

People's Republic of Bulgaria
Narodna Republika Bulgaria

Capital: Sofia

Social and economic data
Area: 110,840 km^2
Population: 9.000m*
Pop density per km^2: 81*
Literacy rate: 95%
GDP: $31,000m*; per capita GDP: $3,444
Economy type: middle income
Labour force in agriculture: 17%

*1985

Ethnic composition
The Bulgarians are a southern Slavic race. Ten per cent of the population are ethnic Turks who have recently been subjected to government pressure to adopt Slavic names and to resettle elsewhere. In 1989 many fled to Turkey.

Religions
Eighty per cent of the religiously active population are adherents to the Bulgarian Orthodox faith and 14 per cent to Islam. There are, for example,

500 acting regional imams, or caliphs. In addition, there are 65,000 adherents to the Latin branch of Roman Catholicism and 10,000 to its Bulgarian, Byzantine-Slav rite, branch, as well as 20,000 followers of the Armenian Orthodox Church. Church and state are officially separate according to the 1971 constitution, with all citizens having freedom of religion and conscience as long as this right is not misused for 'political ends'.

Political features
State type: communist
Date of state formation: 1908
Political structure: unitary
Executive: communist
Assembly: one-chamber
Party structure: one-party*
Human rights rating: 23%

*Effectively

Local and regional government
There are nine regions (*oblasti*), each with an elected Regional People's Council, with districts and municipalities below.

Head of state
President Todor Zhivkov, since 1971.

Head of government
Prime Minister Georgi Atanasov, since 1986.

Political leaders since 1970*
1954– Todor Zhivkov (BKP).

*Communist Party leader

Political system
The country's first socialist constitution was framed and adopted in December 1947. Based largely on the Soviet Union's 1936 'Stalin Constitution', it described Bulgaria as a 'People's Democratic State' guided by its Communist Party. A new version was adopted by referendum in November 1971. This described the country as in a stage of transition from a dictatorship of the proletariat to an 'all-people's state'.

The supreme legislative and executive organ of state power is the 400-member National Assembly (Narodno Sobraniye). The Assembly is elected every five years by universal adult suffrage, through a simple plurality voting system, members being returned from equal-sized single-member constituencies. It meets in plenary session at least three times a year, but 'elects' a smaller, permanent 27-member State Council, headed by a President who acts as head of state, to assume its functions in its absence. This body has the authority to issue decrees.

The National Assembly also 'elects' a Council of Ministers (COM), headed by a chairman, or Prime Minister, with 14 additional ministers and commission chairmen. This constitutes the nation's executive government. It is responsible for the conduct of domestic and external policy and supervises the activities of ministries and People's Councils, the local government bodies which are elected every two and a half years. The COM is supervised, in turn, by the State Council, which has the authority to appoint and remove individual COM members upon the Prime Minister's recommendation.

The controlling force in Bulgaria is the Bulgarian Communist Party (BKP), led since 1954 by General Secretary Todor Zhivkov. It is prescribed a leading role in state affairs by Article 1 of the 1971 constitution. The party is organised on Leninist 'democratic centralist' lines, with its leading members dominating the organs of state power. In January 1988, for example, the BKP's Politburo consisted of eleven full and six non-voting 'candidate' members. Six of these occupied prominent positions in the State Council, including that of President, Todor Zhivkov. A further seven were members of the COM, these included the positions of chairman, Georgi Atanasov, deputy chairman, Grigor Stoichkov, foreign minister, Petur Mladenov, and defence minister, General Dobri Dzhurov. The BKP heads the broader Fatherland Front mass organisation which puts up single lists of candidates in all state elections and has a combined membership of 4.4 million.

Political parties

The Bulgarian Communist Party (BKP: Bulgarska Komunisticheska Partiya) was formed in 1919 by a radical faction which split away from the Bulgarian Social Democratic (Workers') Party, which had been established in 1891. It has been closely tied to the Russian communist movement since its earliest days. The party was banned within Bulgaria in 1923 and thus forced underground during much of the inter-war period.

It is organised pyramidally with, at its base, 'primary party units' in factories, farms, offices and other workplaces. A national Party Congress, which is convened every five years, serves as its supreme policy ratifying body. The Congress 'elects' a 195-member Central Committee (CC) to assume powers in its absence. This CC 'elects', in turn, the 17-member Politburo and nine-member Secretariat, headed by a General Secretary, which have *de facto* charge of policy making, personnel appointments and day-to-day party, and state, affairs.

Membership of the BKP has increased from 530,000 in 1962 to 932,000 in 1986. This represents 10.4 per cent of the total population. Forty-three per cent of the membership are described as blue-collar workers, 22 per cent as farmers and 31 per cent as white-collar workers. Twenty-eight per cent are female. Separate youth and women's organisations are also attached to the BKP.

A second political party, the Bulgarian Agrarian People's Union (BZNS), is also allowed to operate. This peasant organisation, which was founded as the Agrarian Party in 1899, has 120,000 members, a figure which has been permanently fixed. Eighty per cent of its members are collective farm peasants and agricultural workers. It is subservient to the BKP, putting up approved candidates under the Fatherland Front umbrella in state elections and being used to mobilise rural elements.

Latest elections

The most recent National Assembly elections were held in June 1986. Of the 400 candidates who were elected unopposed, 276 were members of the

BKP, 99 of the Bulgarian Agrarian Union, this number being its fixed 'quota', and 25 were non-party 'independents'.

In December 1987 a new electoral law was adopted making a choice of candidates mandatory in all future assembly elections, though all contestants would continue to require endorsement by the Fatherland Front.

Political history

Settled by the Slavs in the late sixth century, the area covered by contemporary Bulgaria was conquered in the seventh century by Turkish Bulgars who merged with the local population. They adopted Eastern Orthodox Christianity in the later eighth century and established powerful empires in the tenth and twelfth centuries. From 1396 Bulgaria formed part of the Ottoman Empire. National liberation revolts occurred during the later nineteenth century but full independence was not achieved until 1908.

During the First World War, Bulgaria allied itself with Germany, and, after its early defeat, lost Aegean coastal lands, which it controlled, to the Allied forces. The retreating troops mutinied and proclaimed a republic. The uprising was, however, suppressed with German military aid. After the war, support for the left-wing Social Democratic and Agrarian Parties increased and in 1919 an independent Agrarian government was formed under the leadership of A. Stamboliiski. It introduced a series of radical measures, including land reform, before being overthrown in a fascist coup, in June 1923, in which Stamboliiski was murdered. A further coup in 1934 established a monarchical-fascist dictatorship under the leadership of King Boris III. The country remained backward, with more than 70 per cent of the labour force employed in agriculture.

In 1941 Bulgaria again allied itself with Germany, joining in the occupation of Yugoslavia and declaring war on Britain and the United States. King Boris mysteriously died in 1943, following a visit to Hitler, and was succeeded by his young son Simeon II. The country was subjected to German occupation, and then invaded by the USSR, in September 1944.

The Soviet Union put into power a communist-inclined, anti-fascist alliance, the Fatherland Front, under the leadership of General Kimon Georgiyev. Within the Front, the Bulgarian Communist Party (BKP), led by Georgi Dimitrov, who had returned from exile, controlled the key interior and justice ministries and set about purging the bureaucracy and armed forces of opposition elements.

In September 1946, following a referendum, the monarchy was abolished and a new People's Republic proclaimed. In October 1946, elections were held to the Grand National Assembly (Sobranje) on a single Fatherland Front basis, with the Communists gaining 73 of the 414 seats. A new, Soviet-style constitution was then drafted and adopted in December 1947, establishing a single-party state.

The new regime, headed respectively by BKP First Secretaries Georgi Dimitrov and Vulko Chervenkov, the brother-in-law of Dimitrov, between 1945 and 1949 and between 1950 and 1954, proceeded to nationalise industrial and financial institutions and introduce co-operative farming, central planning and repressive police control in a Stalinist manner. Political opponents were summarily executed, including the Agrarian Party leader, Nikola Petkov.

The more moderate Todor Zhivkov succeeded Chervenkov as BKP leader in 1954. He pursued a determined industrialisation programme, creating significant growth in the engineering and electronics sectors during the 1960s. In May 1971 he introduced a new presidential constitution. This enabled him to relinquish the chairmanship of the COM, a post he had held since 1962, and become President of the newly formed State Council. Stanko Todorov became chairman of the COM, holding the post continuously until 1981, when he was replaced by Grisha Filipov.

Under Zhivkov, who enjoyed particularly close relations with the Soviet leader, Leonid Brezhnev, Bulgaria emerged as one of the Soviet Union's most loyal satellites. Only limited political and economic reforms were tolerated at home, industrial growth being based on the formation of large, integrated State Economic Organisations (SEOs). Externally, Bulgaria strictly adhered to Brezhnev's 'Moscow line' during international disputes and became a closely integrated member of Comecon and the Warsaw Treaty Organisation. During recent years, however, the country has faced mounting economic problems, caused primarily by the rising cost of energy imports from the Soviet Union.

Since 1985, as a result of pressure from the vigorous new Soviet leader, Mikhail Gorbachev, significant administrative and economic reforms, under the slogan *preustroistvo* (restructuring), have been introduced and a new generation of leaders promoted to power. The reform measures have involved greater decentralisation in the planning process, based on factory 'self-management'; greater openness in party affairs; the introduction of market efficiency principles ('the new economic mechanism') to eliminate weak enterprises; the streamlining of the state bureaucracy; and the launching of a series of campaigns against corruption and inefficiency.

Multi-candidate elections have been promised for future National Assembly contests and it has been proposed that the State Council and COM be replaced by a new 'national co-ordinating body'. At a Special Party Conference convened in January 1988, Zhivkov suggested that a limitation of two terms should be placed on senior party posts.

Todor Zhivkov has continued as state President and BKP General Secretary, being re-elected to both posts in April and June 1986 respectively. The dismissal, in July 1988, of three radical reformist Politburo and Secretariat members, Chudomir Aleksandrov, Stanko Todorov and Stoyan Mikhailov, suggested however that clear limits still existed on the degree of political 'liberalisation' that would be tolerated.

CZECHOSLOVAKIA

Socialist Republic of Czechoslovakia
Ceskoslovenska Socialisticka Republika (CSR)

Capital: Prague

Social and economic data
Area: 127,900 km^2
Population: 15.502m*

Pop density per km^2: 121*
Literacy rate: 100%
GDP: $100,000m*; per capita GDP: $6,451
Economy type: high income
Labour force in agriculture: 13%

*In 1985

Ethnic composition
The Czechs, who constitute 65 per cent of the population, and Slovaks, about 30 per cent, are a Western Slav race. A Hungarian-speaking minority resides in Slovakia in the south and a German minority in the north.

Religions
Historically, 70 per cent of the population have been adherents to the Roman Catholic faith, but the relationship between Church and state has been uneasy. Catholic identity is particularly strong in Slovakia. Ten per cent of the population are Protestants, 400,000 belonging to the Slovak Lutheran Church, 500,000 to the Czech Hussite Church, and 200,000 each to the Presbyterian Evangelical Church of Czech Brethren and the Reformed Church of Slovakia. A quarter of a million are adherents to the Eastern Orthodox Church.

Political features
State type: communist
Date of state formation: 1918
Political structure: federal
Executive: communist
Assembly: two-chamber
Party structure: one-party*
Human rights rating: 36%

*Effectively

Local and regional government
Below the two republics, the country is divided into 12 regions (*kraje*), two of which are the cities of Prague and Bratislava; 112 districts (*okresy*); and around 10,000 local units, governed by elected councils.

Head of state
President Dr Gustav Husak, since 1975.

Head of government
Prime Minister Ladislav Adamec, since 1988.

Political leaders since 1970*
1969–87 Gustav Husak (CPCZ), 1987– Milos Jakes (CPCZ)

*Communist Party leaders

Political system

Czechoslovakia adopted a Soviet-style constitution in May 1948, proclaiming the establishment of a 'people's democracy' in which the Communist Party of Czechoslovakia (CPCZ) was allotted a leading role. This was superseded by a new constitution adopted in June 1960, which described the country as a 'socialist state'. It was substantially amended in October 1968, when a federal system was established, based on two national republics, one for the Czechs and one for the Slovaks. They enjoy equal rights and each has its own constitution and assembly. Further, more minor, constitutional amendments were adopted in July 1971 and May 1975.

Since 1969, the supreme legislative body in the CSR has been the Federal Assembly (Federalni Shromazdeni), which is composed of two chambers of equal powers, the directly elected, 200-deputy Chamber of the People (Snemovna lidu) and the 150-deputy Chamber of Nations (Snemovna narodu). The first chamber is elected for a five-year term in single-member constituencies across the country in accordance with population. It has a 2:1 Czech majority, consisting of 134 deputies from the Czech Socialist Republic and 66 from the Slovak Socialist Republic. The second, upper, chamber is divided equally between members elected in 75 single-member constituencies in each of the two republics. Candidates require an absolute majority of the votes cast, there being provision, which it has never been necessary to employ, for run-off races within 15 days if this majority is not immediately obtained.

All candidates are nominated as part of a single list put forward by the National Front mass movement, which was established in 1945. The list is screened and approved beforehand by the CPCZ. Between 60 and 70 per cent of the list places are allocated to the CPCZ, the remainder to allied bloc-party and non-party candidates. In future contests, multiple candidacies will be permitted.

The Federal Assembly convenes twice a year, in the spring and autumn, for several days and has the formal authority to approve 'basic' legislation, initiate ordinary laws and decide on the medium-term economic plan and annual budget.

To prevent domination by either nationality, special procedural safeguards have been established. The most notable of these provides for Czech and Slovak deputies to vote separately when adopting the economic plan and budget, with majorities from both groups needed before they can be passed. If no common decision is reached, there is provision for the formation of a 'conference committee', consisting of ten members from each chamber, whose task it is to hammer out a compromise package. All legislation must be approved by both houses, constitutional amendments needing 60 per cent approval. Each chamber of the Federal Assembly also 'elects', from among its members, 20 to serve in a Presidium which assumes a number of the Assembly's functions when it is not sitting. The chairman and deputy chairman of this body must be drawn from different republics.

The Federal Assembly also 'elects', for a five-year term, the President of the CSR, who represents the federation in foreign relations; is commander-in-chief of the armed forces; and has authority to appoint and dismiss a Prime Minister and a government accountable to the Assembly. He also has the right to initiate Bills, chair cabinet meetings, but not vote, and dissolve the Federal Assembly. Candidates for the post of President need first to be nominated by the Central Committee of the CPCZ and then receive at least 60 per cent support from each of the Assembly's chambers. The President resides in Prague Castle and enjoys considerable prestige, partly as a reflection of the public respect for the office as it was built up by the country's founder and first President, Thomas G. Masaryk.

The federal government consists of a Prime Minister (Predseda Vlady), First Deputy Prime Minister, nine Deputy Prime Ministers, two of whom are Prime Ministers of the republics, and 18 departmental, or commission, ministers. The Prime Minister and Deputy Prime Ministers form an inner Presidium, decisions being taken on a simple majority basis. The federal government has exclusive authority within the federation in the spheres of defence, foreign affairs, transport, post and telecommunications and overseas trade. In other areas, power is shared with the national governments and parliaments (National Councils), which are elected by each of the Czech and Slovak republics. In practice, however, as a result of the system of 'democratic centralism', the centre dominates this form of 'co-operative federalism'.

The Czech National Council is composed of 200 members and the Slovak National Council of 150. Each body functions and is organised on a similar basis to the Federal Assembly, electing a permanent Presidium and government headed by a Prime Minister. The republics have special jurisdiction over such matters as culture, education, health and justice.

The dominant controlling force in the CSR is the Communist Party of Czechoslovakia (CPCZ), which has been led since 1987 by the General Secretary, Milos Jakes. The CPCZ works with the smaller Czechoslovak Socialist Party and the Czechoslovak People's Party, which are both based in the Czech National Republic, and with the Slovak Freedom Party and Slovak Revival Party, which are based in the Slovak National Republic. Collectively, they comprise the National Front of the Czechoslovak Socialist Republic (NFCSR), which, headed by the CPCZ, puts up agreed single lists of candidates in all state elections.

Through the 'nomenklatura' system, the establishment of supervisory 'shadow bodies' and the intermeshing of senior party and state office holders, the CPCZ maintains firm control over decision-making and policy implementation. In January 1988, for example, the Presidium (Politburo) of the Central Committee of the CPCZ was composed of eleven full and six, non-voting, 'candidate' members. Three of these held senior positions in the federal government, including the post of Prime Minister, Lubomir Strougal, while one was President of the Republic, Gustav Husak. In addition, two of them were Prime Ministers of the national republic governments.

Political parties

The ruling Communist Party of Czechoslovakia (Komunista Strana Ceskoslovenska: CPCZ) was founded in May 1921 by a left-wing breakaway faction from the Czechoslovak Social Democratic Party, which originated in 1897. The party, which had an initial membership of 350,000, was multi-ethnic in character. It was allowed to operate legally throughout the inter-war period, capturing more than 10 per cent of the vote, but did not share power in any of the cabinets of that period. Membership declined to less than 100,000 and the party was forced underground when Hitler invaded the country.

In 1945, however, the CPCZ received a massive influx of new members and captured 38 per cent of the vote in the free elections of 1946. It later endured major purges during the early 1950s and immediately after the 'Prague Spring' of 1968. As a result, party membership contracted from 1.68 million in 1962 to 1.17 million in 1971. In 1986 it rose again to 1.68 million, representing 10.8 per cent of the total population. Forty-two per cent of these members are blue-collar workers, 35 per cent white-collar and 5 per cent farmers; 30 per cent are women.

The CPCZ is organised hierarchically, with more than 45,000 'cells' established in factories, collective farms and other work places. These units, which meet monthly, have the tasks of training members, directing enterprises and supervising social activities. Above them are district, regional and republican party bodies. At the apex of the CPCZ structure is the Party Congress, which convenes for week-long sessions every five years. The most recent was in March 1986 when around 1,500 delegates attended. The Congress adopts policy resolutions and 'elects' a Central Committee (CC) to assume its authority when it is not sitting.

The CC, which in 1986 had 133 full and 62 'candidate' members, meets at least three times a year and 'elects' a Presidium (Politburo) and a twelve-member Secretariat, headed by a General Secretary. The Secretariat is in effective charge of day-to-day party and national affairs and controls appointments.

The four other legalised political parties which participate in the NFCSR are: the Czechoslovak People's Party, a Roman Catholic party founded in 1919; the Czechoslovak Socialist Party, an urban white-collar middle-class party formed in 1948 by elements from the Czechoslovak National Socialist Party which was itself originally established in 1897; the Slovak Freedom Party, dating from 1946; and the Slovak Reconstruction Party, which was founded in 1948. The Czech and Slovak parties are each usually assigned around 18 and four Federal Assembly seats respectively, and their membership sizes are limited by statute. Also in the National Front, whose chairman is Milos Jakes, are 17 mass organisations, or interest groups, which include the Czechoslovak Union of Women, the Czechoslovak Union of Journalists and the Socialist Union of Youth.

Latest elections

The most recent elections to the Federal Assembly were held in May 1986, with all the NFCSR-nominated candidates being elected unopposed. Voter turnout exceeded 99.95 per cent.

Political history

Czechoslovakia emerged as an independent state in 1918 following the dissolution of the Austro-Hungarian Empire at the close of the First World War. Despite the problems posed in integrating the diverse ethnic groups within the new nation, Czechoslovakia was the only East European state to retain a parliamentary democracy throughout the inter-war period. This took the form of a five-party coalition government, dominated by the Agrarian and National Socialist parties, under the leadership of the influential Slovak-born president, Thomas Masaryk. It was made possible by the relatively advanced state of the country's economic and social development. In 1930, for example, as few as a third of the population were involved in agricultural activities, while 40 per cent of males were employed in the industrial sector.

During the later 1930s, with the rise to power of Hitler in Germany, opposition to the government was fomented by German and Magyar-speaking irredentists. This provided the pretext for the Munich agreement of September 1938 among Britain, France, Germany and Italy under which Czechoslovakia was forced to surrender its Sudeten-German districts to Nazi Germany. Six months later, the German army invaded and annexed the remainder of the country. President Eduard Benes immediately resigned in opposition to these actions, setting up a government in exile in London.

During the Second World War, the Czech lands were subjected to direct German occupation, although Slovakia was granted 'independent' status in 1944 and Bohemia-Moravia was governed as a 'protectorate'. Liquidation campaigns were directed against the intelligentsia. The country was liberated in 1945 by Soviet and American troops, including a Soviet-trained native contingent under the direction of General Ludvik Svoboda. A government of national unity was immediately formed, with Benes as President, but with communists occupying prominent ministries, including the Interior, which included the police, and Information. Communists also dominated local administration. Two million Sudeten Germans were summarily expelled.

In elections to the 300-member Constituent National Assembly, in May 1946, the left, which included communists and social democrats, achieved a narrow majority, enabling the CPCZ leader, Klement Gottwald, to become Prime Minister. By 1948 the CPCZ was in full control, seizing power in a coup in February and, under the National Front banner, winning a single list ballot victory in May, following the framing of a new, Soviet-style constitution. Benes duly resigned as President, in June, and was succeeded by Gottwald.

Czechoslovakia's historic provinces were abolished in 1948, the country being divided, first into 19 and then, under the new constitution of July 1960, twelve regions. Earlier, in 1945, the nation's leading industries and financial institutions had been taken into state ownership and a programme of agricultural collectivisation launched.

During the 1950s, under Presidents Gottwald, Antonin Zapotocky and Antonin Novotny, a strict Stalinist regime was maintained, opposition members being purged. Policy adjustments began to be made, however, from the mid-1960s, as a result of mounting pressure from students and intellectuals, particularly among the Slovaks, and from deteriorating economic conditions.

In January 1968 the orthodox CPCZ leader, Antonin Novotny, was replaced by the reformist Slovak, Alexander Dubcek. In March the war hero, General Svoboda, became President and in April Oldrich Cernik was appointed Prime Minister. The new regime embarked on a major liberalisation programme (the 'Socialist Democratic Revolution'), promising the restoration of freedom of assembly, speech and movement; the imposition of restrictions on the secret police; decentralised economic reform; and the introduction of elements of democratised political pluralism. These proposed changes, despite assurances that Czechoslovakia would remain within the Warsaw Pact and that the the CPCZ would retain its leading political role, were viewed with suspicion by the Soviet Union and on 20–21 August 1968 600,000 Soviet, Bulgarian, East German, Hungarian and Polish troops invaded Czechoslovakia to restore the orthodox line and eradicate an experiment which had been termed 'socialism with a human face'.

Following the Soviet invasion, a major purge of liberals within the CPCZ was launched, party membership falling by a third, and Dr Gustav Husak, a Slovak Brezhnevite, replaced Dubcek as CPCZ leader, in April 1969, and Lubomir Strougal, a Czech, was appointed Prime Minister, in January 1970. However, General Svoboda remained as President until May 1975, successfully negotiating the phased withdrawal of Soviet troops. A new federal constitution was adopted in October 1968, satisfying the nationalist aspirations of the country's Slovak minority.

In 1973 an amnesty was extended to some of the 40,000 who had fled Czechoslovakia after the 1968 invasion, signalling a slackening of repression. However, in 1977, following the signature of a human rights manifesto, 'Charter 77', by more than 700 intellectuals and former party officials, in response to the 1975 Helsinki Agreements, a new crack-down commenced. The arrest of dissidents continued in May 1981 during the Polish 'Solidarity' crisis.

Under the leadership of Gustav Husak, Czechoslovakia emerged during the 1970s and early 1980s as a loyal ally of the Soviet Union. Minor economic reforms were introduced, but ideological orthodoxy and strict party control were maintained in the political sphere. In recent years, however, following the accession of the reformist Mikhail Gorbachev to the Soviet leadership, outside pressure has been growing for a restructuring of Czechoslovakia's economic and administrative system on more decentralised, market-orientated and politically pluralist lines. Husak was re-elected President in May 1985 and CPCZ General Secretary at the Seventeenth Party Congress, which was held in March 1986. He resigned from the latter post, however, at the CPCZ Central Committee meeting of December 1987, being replaced by the Czech-born economics expert, Milos Jakes.

Husak retained his position as President, but was replaced by Jakes as chairman of the National Front. Viewed as a pragmatic conservative and enjoying close personal contacts with Mikhail Gorbachev, Jakes pledged the party to pursue a programme of moderate economic and political reform on the Soviet Union's *perestroika* model. In October 1988, he instituted a thorough-going reconstitution of top-tier party and state bodies, with the long-serving, though reform-minded, Prime Minister, Lubomir Strougal, being replaced by the technocrat Ladislav Adamec, and the foreign and interior ministers also being dismissed. At the same time, Strougal was ousted from the CPCZ Presidium, to which five new members were added, increasing its size to 15.

These changes brought forward fresh cadres to grapple with the country's mounting economic problems. Many of these newcomers, however, are seen as reformers with conservative leanings. This, coupled with the tight rein kept on opposition dissident groupings, suggests that the Czech *perestroika* experiment will be more centralist and gradualist than that of the Soviet Union.

EAST GERMANY

German Democratic Republic
Deutsche Demokratische Republik (DDR)

Capital: East Berlin

Social and economic data

Area: 108,180 km^2
Population: 16.700m*
Pop density per km^2: 154*
Literacy rate: 100%
GDP: $100,00m*; per capita GDP: $5,988
Economy type: high income
Labour force in agriculture: 12%

*1985

Ethnic composition

The population is of predominantly Germanic stock, although a small Sorbian-speaking minority also exists.

Religions

Five million, or about 30 per cent of the population, belong to the Evangelical (Lutheran) Church. The Church is organised under the banner, the Federation of Evangelical Churches (BEKDDR), and enjoys significant autonomy. It has criticised a number of government policies, most notably the re-introduction of conscription in 1962, and plays a leading role in the peace and ecological movements. In recent years, there has been a growing Church-state rapprochement, the Church having been provided with state funds. Membership of the Evangelical Church is, however, on the decline. In 1950 70 per cent of the population were adherents. Seven per cent of the population, 1.2 million people, were members of the Roman Catholic Church in 1984.

Political features

State type: communist
Date of state formation: 1949
Political structure: unitary
Executive: communist
Assembly: one-chamber
Party structure: one-party*
Human rights rating: 33%

*Effectively

Local and regional government

The country was divided into five *Länder*, or states, Brandenburg, Mecklenburg, Saxony, Saxony-Anhalt and Thuringia, between 1945 to 1952. These were replaced by 14 regions (*Bezirke*), plus the city of East Berlin. Each region has an assembly (*Bezirkstag*) which is elected on the same day as the Volkskammer. Below the *Bezirke* are 219 urban and rural districts (*Stadtkreise* and *Landkreise*), with their own elected assemblies, and 7,620 communes.

Head of state
President Erich Honecker, since 1976.

Head of government
Prime Minister Willi Stoph, since 1976.

Political leaders since 1970*
1950–71 Walter Ulbricht (SED), 1971– Erich Honecker (SED).

*Communist Party leaders

Political system
East Germany's first constitution was adopted in October 1949 by the Provisional People's Chamber and amended in April 1968 and then again in October 1974. It comprises 106 Articles and describes the German Democratic Republic (DDR) as a 'socialist state of workers and peasants' in which the Communist Party (Socialist Unity Party of Germany: SED), is prescribed a leading role (Article 1).

The DDR's supreme legislative body is the People's Chamber (Volkskammer), whose 500 members, including 66 from East Berlin, are elected every five years by 'block-vote' universal adult suffrage in multi-member constituencies. The National Front, which was first established in 1950, presents SED-approved lists containing more candidates than positions available and voters are, theoretically, able to delete names. This requires, however, the use of screened booths. Propaganda and social pressures have discouraged all but fewer than 0.1 per cent of voters to make alterations to ballot forms, with the result that the approved top names on the list are regularly elected.

The Volkskammer debates and passes laws, committees being formed for this purpose, but meets in full session only four times a year, each session lasting from one to three days. To assume responsibilities on its behalf when it is not sitting, the Volkskammer chooses a 29-member Council of State (*Staatsrat*), which functions as a permanent collective organ. The Council's chairman serves as the effective head of state. Prior to the constitutional amendment of October 1974, the Council of State had the power to pass 'law decrees'. This no longer applies. It may merely pass 'resolutions', thus somewhat reducing its formal authority *vis-à-vis* the Volkskammer. In foreign affairs it is, however, an influential body, appointing the members of the National Defence Council.

Day-to-day executive government is conducted by the Council of Ministers (COM: Ministerrat), headed and selected by a chairman, or Prime Minister, drawn from the largest single party grouping within the Volkskammer. In January 1988, the COM consisted of a Presidium of twelve members, a chairman, three first deputy chairmen and eight deputy chairmen, or ministers, and 32 additional ministers and state secretaries. The twelve-member Presidium functions as an 'inner cabinet' and supervises the work of departments below as well as managing the domestic economy and conducting foreign relations.

The dominating controlling force in East Germany is the SED, headed since 1971 by the General Secretary, Erich Honecker. It provides the major grouping within the Volkskammer and is supported by four allied dependent parties, the Democratic Farmers' Party (DBD), the Christian Democratic Union (CDU), the Liberal Democratic Party (LDPD) and the National Democratic Party (NDPD). Together they form the National Front of the German Democratic Republic.

Organised on Leninist 'democratic centralist' lines, the SED's Politburo functions as the country's *de facto* cabinet, while its Secretariat controls entry into key state posts through the 'nomenklatura' system. In January 1988, the SED's Politburo consisted of 22 full and five non-voting 'candidate' members, of whom six had positions in the Council of State and seven in the COM. In addition, Willi Stoph held senior positions in both bodies, being chairman of the COM and a vice-chairman of the Council of State, while Erich Honecker was chairman of the latter body, 60 per cent of whose members must, by law, belong to the SED.

Political parties

The dominant Socialist Unity Party (SED) was formed in April 1946 by a merger of the existing Social Democratic Party (SPD) and Communist Party (KPD), which was originally established in 1918. It is organised hierarchically on the Soviet model, including, at its base, around 80,000 'primary party units' located in factories, collective farms and other workplaces, each with around 30 full members. Above these are town, county and district party units, which parallel and oversee the work of state bodies. The SED's theoretically supreme organ is the national Party Congress, which is 'elected' every five years. This body 'elects', in turn, a Central Committee (CC) of about 160 members which, meeting four times a year, acts on behalf of the Congress when it is not sitting.

The CC 'elects' a Politburo and Secretariat which are the real controlling bodies. The Politburo meets weekly and takes decisions by majority votes, in contrast with other political organs where unanimous voting is the practice. The Secretariat oversees more than 40 party departments, employing a central staff of around 1,000. It controls cadre selection. In 1987, the SED's membership stood at 2.3 million, equivalent to 13.8 per cent of the total population and representing an increase of 700,000 since 1962. Fifty-eight per cent of the membership are blue-collar workers, 31 per cent white-collar and 5 per cent farmers. Thirty per cent are women. In addition, the attached Free German Youth (FDJ) organisation comprises 2.3 million members, aged between 14 and 25.

The four officially recognised allied parties, which were originally members of the Anti-Fascist Democratic Bloc between 1945 and 1949, do not compete with the SED for seats in state bodies. Instead, they are assigned set quotas. Their function is to broaden support for the regime and integrate potentially hostile citizens and social groups. The Christian Democratic Union, which was established in 1945, currently has 140,000 members; the Democratic Farmers' Party, which dates from 1948, 115,000; the Liberal Democratic Party, founded in 1945, 105,000; and the National Democratic Party, established in 1948, 110,000. The last two bodies are orientated towards the urban middle classes.

Latest elections

In the most recent Volkskammer election of June 1986, National Front candidates received 99.94 per cent of the total vote. Seats are regularly apportioned within the assembly among the legal political parties and social organisations as follows

Party or Group	*No of seats*
SED	127
The 'bloc parties': CDU, DBD, LDPD and NDPD	52 each
The Free Confederation of German Trade Unions	68
The Free German Youth	40
The Democratic Women's League	35
The Culture League	22

Political history

The territory occupied today by the DDR formerly comprised key portions of three German Empires, the Second Reich, the Weimar Republic and the Third Reich, of the later nineteenth and early twentieth centuries. By the outbreak of the Second World War the area was highly industrialised, with fewer than a quarter of its population dependent on agricultural activities.

Following the surrender of Nazi Germany in May 1945, East Germany formed part of the Soviet zone of occupation, although Berlin was subject to joint allied control. The most popular political party was the Social Democratic Party (SPD). This was merged, under Soviet pressure, with the Communist Party (KPD) in April 1946 to form the communist-dominated SED. Other licensed parties joined the SED, in the Anti-Fascist Democratic Bloc, to fight assembly elections in the autumn of 1946.

Once elected, the assembly adopted a provisional constitution based on the Weimar model of 1919. This was replaced in October 1949 by a new, Soviet-style, version, which declared the founding of the German Democratic Republic. However, full sovereignty was not finally conceded by the Soviet Union until March 1954. Moreover, the DDR's sovereign status was initially recognised only by the communist powers. In 1973, however, following the adoption by the West German Federal Republic of a new policy of *Ostpolitik*, a Basic Treaty governing relations between East and West Germany was ratified by both states. The treaty fell short of full recognition by the Federal Republic, permanent missions being stationed in the respective nations rather than ambassadors. It led, however, to the admission of East Germany into the United Nations, in 1973, and to its full recognition by other Western states.

Domestically, the years immediately after 1945 saw the rapid establishment of a socialist regime on the Soviet Stalinist model, involving the creation of an effectively one-party political system, the nationalisation of industry and finance institutions, and the formation of agricultural collectives. Popular opposition to this 'Sovietisation' led, during a period of food shortages, to mass demonstrations and a general strike in June 1953, which had to be forcibly suppressed by Soviet troops. Party purges followed. Eight years later, in August 1961, the Berlin Wall was erected to stem the growing movement of refugees to the Federal Republic. During the 1960s, however, economic reforms, known as the 'New Economic System', gave a boost to the East German growth rate, significantly improving living conditions and easing social tensions.

During the 1970s, with the replacement of the Stalinist SED leader, Walter Ulbricht, by the more pragmatic Erich Honecker, a less rigid, and more moderate, political approach was pursued at home, while abroad, during this *détente* era, economic and diplomatic relations with the West were extended. Since 1985, with the coming to power of the innovative Gorbachev administration in the Soviet Union, Honecker has been under increasing pressure to introduce more liberalising economic and political changes. This pressure has so far been largely resisted, with East Germany suggesting, instead, that the USSR should emulate its 'model' of cautious reform, based in the economic sphere on partially autonomous, *Kombinate*, or integrated production units, while maintaining firm party control in the social and ideological spheres.

The present leadership is well entrenched, Honecker having held his position as SED leader for more than 15 years while Willi Stoph has, except for a break between 1973 and 1976, when he was chairman of the Council of State, served as premier since 1964. The SED's Politburo, eight of whose members are over the age of 70, and the Central Committee were re-elected, largely unchanged, at the Eleventh Party Congress held in April 1986. However, there have recently been protest calls by dissident groups seeking an 'opening out' of society.

The GDR has been a loyal and vital member of Comecon, since 1950, and of the Warsaw Pact, since 1955. During the early 1980s, Soviet medium-range nuclear missiles were based on its soil, but their removal has begun in accordance with the 1987 Soviet-US Intermediate Nuclear Forces (INF) Treaty. The country's external relations remain circumscribed, however, by changes in opinion in Moscow. In 1983–84, and again in 1985–86, for example, the planned inaugural official visit of Erich Honecker to West Germany was postponed as a result of Soviet pressure. It finally took place in September 1987, resulting in the creation of a new commission to develop closer inter-German economic and commercial relations.

HUNGARY

Hungarian People's Republic
Magyar Népköztársaság

Capital: Budapest

Social and economic data
Area: 93,030 km^2
Population: 10.644m*
Pop density per km^2: 114*
Literacy rate: 99%
GDP: $20,625m*; per capita GDP: $1,938
Economy type: middle income
Labour force in agriculture: 23%

*1985

Ethnic composition

The majority of the population are native Hungarians, or Magyars, of non-Slavic stock. There exist, in addition, minorities of about 170,000 Germans, 120,000 Slovaks, 50,000 Croats, and 20,000 Romanians.

Religions

About 60 per cent of the population, or 6.4 million people, are Roman Catholics. Until the 1960s, this Church was subject to state repression, Primate Cardinal Josef Mindszenty, being imprisoned and given a life sentence. Since then there has been a rapprochement and there are now 3,250 active churches operating. Twenty-five per cent of the population are Protestants, their principal denominations being the Presbyterian Reformed Church of Hungary, with 2 million members, and the Lutheran Church of Hungary, with 400,000.

Political features

State type: communist
Date of state formation: 1918
Political structure: unitary
Executive: communist
Assembly: one-chamber
Party structure: one-party
Human rights rating: 55%

Local and regional government

For local administration, the country is divided into 19 counties (*megyed*) and four urban areas with county status, subdivided into 22 districts and hundreds of communes, governed by committees elected every five years. Commune and city district councils are elected directly, with at least two candidates being nominated for every seat. Regional councils are elected indirectly by and from commune and district councils.

Head of state

President Professor Bruno Straub, since 1988.

Head of government

Prime Minister Miklos Nemeth, since 1988.

Political leaders since 1970*

1956–88 Janos Kadar (HSWP), 1988– Karoly Grosz (HSWP)†

*Communist Party leaders †Part of collective leadership

Political system

The country's first socialist constitution was adopted in August 1949. This document, similar in substance to the Soviet Union's 1936 'Stalin Constitution', described the state as a 'people's republic' in which the Communist Party was afforded a guiding role. It was amended in April 1972 and December 1983, with further changes currently being drafted.

Under this constitution, the sole and supreme legislative body in the state is the 387-member National Assembly (Orszaggyules). It consists of

35 members elected unopposed on a single national list. These are either representatives of national minority groups or political, trade union or Church personalities. The remaining 352 members are elected for five-year terms by universal adult suffrage in territorial single-member constituencies, each comprising roughly 30,000 inhabitants. Following the constitutional amendments introduced in December 1983, competition has been introduced into candidate selection, with at least two people now being required to contest the nomination for seats. To be elected, nominees must either secure an absolute majority of the votes cast on the first ballot or achieve a simple majority in a second round of voting held a fortnight later.

The National Assembly meets four times a year, for several days at a time, to pass laws, establish the state budget and economic plan and discuss and approve the government's programme. It elects, from among its members, a 21-member Presidential Council (Presidium) to operate on its behalf, in legislative matters, when it is not sitting. This Council serves as both a 'substitute parliament' and as a collective presidency, with its President acting as an effective, though largely ceremonial, head of state. The Council has the power to issue law decrees and to call referenda on 'questions of national significance'. Under new constitutional changes currently being discussed, it is planned however to abolish the Presidential Council in 1990.

The National Assembly also elects a 17-member Council of Ministers (COM), headed by a chairman, or Prime Minister, and composed of ministry and commission heads. It functions as the executive government, overseeing state departments and local government units, and having responsibility to frame and execute the economic plan.

The Hungarian state system is comparatively streamlined by normal communist standards, both the Presidential Council and COM being unusually small. Another notable feature is the relative liveliness and openness of National Assembly debates and the influential character of its labyrinth of standing committees, which work on draft bills between sessions. In recent years, as policy struggles have developed between party reformers and conservatives, the Assembly has become much less of a 'rubber-stamping' body. In 1988, for example, three proposed state budgets introduced by finance minister Miklos Villanyi were rejected by Assembly members, the final, accepted document being a budget plan drawn up by the Assembly's own planning and budget committee.

Despite these changes, state functionaries continue to remain subservient to the Communist Party (Hungarian Socialist Workers' Party: HSWP), which is the controlling political force in the country and the only permitted party. Led since 1988 by Karoly Grosz, the HSWP dominates the broader mass movement, the Patriotic People's Front (PPF), which was established in 1954, and which draws up lists of approved candidates for election contests. The HSWP maintains its control through the 'nomenklatura' system; the 'shadowing' of state agencies; and the practice of joint party and state office holding. In February 1988, for example, the HSWP's Political Committee (Politburo) comprised 13 full members. Three of these held posts in the Presidential Council, including that of President, Karoly Nemeth, and a further two in the COM, including the position of chairman, Karoly Grosz.

Political parties

The ruling Hungarian Socialist Workers' Party (HSWP) is an offspring of the Hungarian Communist Party (HCP) which was founded in November 1918 and, in alliance with the Hungarian Social Democratic Party (HSDP), which dates from 1890, briefly established a 133-day 'Soviet Republic' under the leadership of Bela Kun, between March and August, 1919. It was proscribed and forced underground by the succeeding Horthy dictatorship, many of its thousand or so members fleeing to Moscow. There, the party was purged and 'Stalinised'.

With Soviet military support, it moved into a dominant position in the country from 1945, forcing the left wing of the HSDP to merge and form a new United Workers' Party, in 1948. It was renamed the Hungarian Workers' Party (HWP) in 1949 and the HSWP in 1956, being substantially reconstituted, following the 'national rising' of that year.

It is organised pyramidally and functions on Leninist 'democratic centralist' lines. At the base there are 24,000 small, workplace 'primary party units', while at the top a Party Congress, comprising between 400 and 800 selected district delegates. The Congress meets every five years to adopt a policy programme and 'elect' a Central Committee (CC) to assume its responsibilities in its absence. At the most recent, the thirteenth, Congress, held in March 1985, a 105-member Central Committee was 'elected'. The CC, in turn, 'elects' a Political Committee (Politburo) and nine-member Secretariat, headed by a General Secretary, who is the party's leader, to direct the party and state machines.

In 1987 HSWP membership stood at 880,000, constituting 8.3 per cent of the total population. This represents a considerable advance on the 1962 figure of 500,000, but is below the immediate post-Second World War total of 1.5 million. Forty-three per cent of the present membership are blue-collar workers, 42 per cent white-collar and 6 per cent farmers. Twenty-eight per cent are women. Attached to the HSWP are the 930,000-member Communist Youth of Hungary and 160,000-member National Council of Hungarian Women organisations. Trade unions, peasant, Church and national minority movements are also linked to the HSWP via the PPF.

In 1989 the National Assembly approved legislation providing for the legalisation of independent associations, including political parties and labour unions. This measure, which was not expected to come fully into force until 1990, provided the basis for the creation of the first genuine multi-party system in the communist world. However, to secure registration, prospective parties will need to pledge acceptance of the 'socialist order'. Several unofficial opposition 'political associations' already exist. They include: the 10,000-member Hungarian Democratic Forum, a loose coalition of reformist Communists, Christian Socialists, and Christian Democrats which came together in September 1988; and the 1,800-member Alliance of Free Democrats, a body set up by dissident intellectuals in November 1988. Efforts are also now being made to revive the once important Smallholders' and Social Democratic parties.

Latest elections

In the most recent National Assembly elections held on 8 June 1985, 873 candidates were put forward for the 352 territorial constituencies. Seven hundred and ninety-five of these were nominated by the PPF and 78 were proposed from the floor of the nomination meetings. Forty-three of the floor nominees were eventually elected. In 78 constituencies more than two candidates contested the ballot. A second round of voting was held on 22 June in 45 constituencies where no absolute majority had been gained. This follow-up contest was decided by simple plurality voting. The turnout was 94 per cent for the first ballot and 83 per cent for the second. Overall, 244 'freshmen' members were elected, with PPF candidates securing 98.8 per cent of the total votes cast. Fifty-four, or 31 per cent, of the 172 incumbent deputies who stood for re-election were defeated.

Political history

Having previously been subjected to Roman and Germanic rule, a Magyar kingdom was first established by St Stephen, in AD 997, who converted the country's inhabitants to Christianity. From the early fourteenth century the nation again came under foreign control, with the south and centre falling to the Turks, from the sixteenth century. They were replaced in the later seventeenth century by the Austrian Habsburgs. Lajos Kossuth led a Hungarian renaissance during the mid nineteenth century, with an independent republic being proclaimed and serfdom abolished in 1848–49. This was quickly suppressed by joint Austrian and Russian forces and an Austro-Hungarian empire was re-established within which Hungary enjoyed substantial self-government.

Full independence was finally obtained in 1918, following the dismemberment of the Austro-Hungarian Empire at the close of the First World War. A brief 'Soviet Republic' experiment during 1919 was suppressed by Romanian and Czechoslovak troops and a conservative dictatorship was then established, under the leadership of the regent, Admiral Nikolaus Horthy de Nagybanya.

The new regime restricted the franchise to only 27 per cent of the population, paving the way for perpetual dominance by the right-wing Party of Unity, although during the later 1930s the fascist Arrow Cross party emerged as a serious challenger. Only limited advance was achieved in the economic sphere during these years, with still, in 1930, more than half the population remaining dependent upon agricultural activities. In these circumstances, the subsequent depression in the 1930s had a particularly adverse effect on the country.

On the outbreak of the Second World War, Admiral Horthy allied Hungary with Germany and the Axis powers, joining Hitler in the invasion of the Soviet Union in 1941. In March 1944, however, the country was overrun by Soviet forces and the Horthy regime toppled. A provisional five-party coalition government was formed in December 1944, headed by General Miklos. It included the communist agriculture minister, Imre Nagy, who set about distributing land to the peasants as a means of broadening the party's support base. In addition, the Communist Party (HCP) held a majority of seats in the temporary assembly and was given control of the police forces.

In free elections held in November 1945, the HCP secured 17 per cent of the total votes and 70 of the 409 seats. The Smallholders Party emerged as the most popular force, capturing a majority of seats, but the HCP, with Soviet support, succeeded in forcing the formation of a coalition with other leftist parties. It then proceeded to introduce a programme of nationalisation and central economic planning. In February 1946 a republic was inaugurated and from June 1948, when the HCP and HSDP merged to form the HWP, all other political parties were outlawed. This was followed, in August 1949, by the adoption of a new Soviet-style constitution.

Under HWP leader Matyas Rakosi, a strict Stalinist regime was imposed between 1946 and 1953, involving forced collectivisation and the launching of a wave of secret police terror. Liberalisation in the economic sphere began tentatively between 1953 and 1955, when Imre Nagy, supported by the Soviet premier, Georgi Malenkov, replaced Rakosi as Prime Minister. However, Nagy in turn was removed in April 1955, after the fall of Malenkov.

In 1956, in the wake of Nikita Khrushchev's denunciation of Stalin in his February 'secret speech', pressure for democratisation mounted. Rakosi stepped down as HWP leader, in July, and, following student and worker demonstrations in Budapest on 23 October, Nagy was recalled as Prime Minister and Janos Kadar was appointed General Secretary of the HWP. Nagy proceeded to lift restrictions on the formation of political parties, released the anti-communist primate, Cardinal Mindszenty, and announced plans for Hungary to withdraw from the Warsaw Pact and become a neutral power. These changes were, however, opposed by Kadar, who set up a rival government in East Hungary. He then returned to Budapest, with Soviet tanks, and overthrew the Nagy government, on 4 November. Two hundred thousand refugees fled to the West during the 1956 'Hungarian National Rising'.

In the immediate wake of this 'rebellion', the HWP was purged and reconstituted as the HSWP. Several years of repression followed. During the 1960s, however, Kadar proceeded to introduce pragmatic, liberalising reforms, including a decentralisation of economic planning, styled in 1968 the 'New Economic Mechanism'. This gave Hungary the reputation of being one of the freest and most market-orientated Eastern European states. It became a member of the International Monetary Fund (IMF) and the World Bank in 1982, and enjoyed a considerable improvement in living standards. Greater participation in local affairs was also encouraged as part of this 'self-governing' process. Externally, Hungary emerged as a loyal member of the Warsaw Pact and Comecon during the 1960s and 1970s.

Relations between the Hungarian leadership and the new reformist Gorbachev administration in Moscow have been warm and close, Gorbachev even adopting a number of Kadar's post-1968 economic initiatives. In recent years, however, the country's economic growth rate has slowed down considerably and the inflation rate and degree of external indebtedness have crept upwards, forcing further, more radical, 'restructuring' reforms. These have involved additional price deregulation; the establishment of a stock-market; the introduction of value-added tax (VAT) and personal income tax, in 1988; the establishment of enterprise councils with elected managers; and the introduction of a series of emergency austerity wage 'freezes'. An adverse side-product of this process has been a rise in the number of unemployed, to a figure of 50,000 in 1988.

As part of a 'stabilisation package' unveiled in 1987, there has also been considerable bureaucratic 'rationalisation' and an accelerated turnover of senior personnel. In June 1987 Pal Losonczi retired as President of the

Presidential Council, a post which he had held since 1967, and was replaced by Karoly Nemeth. Gyorgy Lazar, who had been Prime Minister since 1975, was replaced by the pragmatic Budapest party leader, Karoly Grosz.

These changes were followed, in May 1988, at a specially convened National Party Conference, by the replacement of the ageing Kadar as HSWP General Secretary by Grosz. Kadar was removed from the Politburo and given the symbolic, newly created, position of HSWP President, which he later gave up, in May 1989. Seven other Politburo colleagues, including Lazar and Nemeth, fell, together with 40 per cent of the Central Committee. Two radical reformers, Imre Pozsgay, the PPF Secretary-General until July 1988, and Rezso Nyers, a former HSDP member and the architect of the 1968 economic reforms, were brought into the new eleven-member Politburo as replacements and the non-communist scientist, Dr Bruno Straub, an 'independent' politician and chairman of the Environmental Council, was chosen as the new President of the Presidential Council.

This dramatic turnover appears set to usher in a batch of radical new reforms in the political sphere, with the stated aims of achieving a clearer separation between party and state and of introducing a new system of 'socialist pluralism', which would involve the admission of non-communist groupings into a more influential, decision-taking parliament. Outside momentum has been added to this process by the formation of 'reform clubs' by intellectuals and dissidents, under the 'Network of Free Initiatives' umbrella organisation, which was superseded in September 1988 by the new Hungarian Democratic Forum. Coupled with this, Hungary's first free trade union, the Democratic Trade Union of Scientific Workers (TDDSZ), was established, in May 1988, followed by the formation of the blue-collar Workers' Solidarity union, in February 1989.

Additional internal momentum to these changes has been provided by the HSWP Central Committee's election, in November 1988, in a genuinely contested ballot, of Miklos Nemeth, a trained economist, as the country's new Prime Minister, with Rezso Nyers working alongside him as minister of state in charge of economic affairs. Two months later, in January 1989, a Bill was presented to the National Assembly legalising the formation of rival political parties, with substantially free, multi-party national elections being envisaged for 1990. The new reformist leadership has also revised the HSWP's official verdict on the events of 1956, accepting that, initially at least, it was a 'popular uprising' rather than a 'counter-revolution'. It has also allowed the remains of the once disgraced Imre Nagy to be exhumed for a proper burial.

POLAND

People's Republic of Poland
Polska Rzeczpospolita Ludowa

Capital: Warsaw

Social and economic data
Area: 312,680 km^2
Population: 37.500m*

Pop density per km^2: 120*
Literacy rate: 99%
GDP: $78,000m*; per capita GDP: $2,080
Economy type: middle income
Labour force in agriculture: 28%

*1985

Ethnic composition
The Poles are a Western-Slav race.

Religions
Ninety-five per cent of the population are adherents to the Roman Catholic faith, 2 per cent, or 850,000, to the Polish Autocephalous Orthodox and 100,000 to Protestant denominations, mainly the Evangelical Augsburg Church.

The Roman Catholic Church is an influential autonomous institution with a buoyant membership. It is closely connected with the idea of Polish nationhood and has played an important role, particularly during the primacy of Cardinal Stefan Wyszynski, in the campaign for human rights. In recent years, under the leadership of Cardinal Jozef Glemp, the Church has acted as a neutral 'honest-broker' in helping to resolve state-dissident disputes. It has political representation in the parliament (Sejm) through the Pax and Znak groups, and publishes extensively.

Political Features
State type: communist
Date of state formation: 1918
Political structure: unitary
Executive: communist
Assembly: two-chamber
Party structure: one-party*
Human rights rating: 41%

*Effectively

Local and regional government
The country is divided into 49 provinces (*voivodships*) administered by People's Councils elected every four years. Candidates for these bodies can be nominated by a broad range of social organisations.

Head of state
President General Wojciech Jaruzelski, since 1985.

Head of government
Prime Minister Tadeusz Mazowiecki, since 1989.

Political leaders since 1970*
1970–80 Edward Gierek (PZPR), 1980–81 Stanislaw Kania (PZPR), 1981– General Wojciech Jaruzelski (PZPR).

*Communist Party leaders

Political system
Poland's first socialist constitution was adopted in July 1952. It was modelled closely on the Soviet Union's 1936 'Stalin Constitution' and designated the state a 'people's republic'. It was amended in February 1976, with the new description of 'socialist state' being adopted and the 'leading' role of the Communist Party (the Polish United Workers' Party: PZPR) being formally recognised and was recently amended again in 1989. Under this revised constitution, Poland has a two-chamber legislature, comprising a 460-member lower assembly, the Sejm (parliament), and a 100-member upper chamber, the Senate.

Prior to 1989, deputies were elected to the Sejm for four-year terms by universal adult suffrage, with 410 seats being allocated to multi-member district-list constituencies in which there was a choice between candidates put forward by the PZPR-dominated mass movement, the Patriotic Movement for National Rebirth (PRON), which was established in 1982. To be elected, candidates needed to secure an absolute majority of valid votes cast on the first ballot and electoral turnout had to exceed 50 per cent. Otherwise, a second ballot was held in which a simple plurality sufficed. The remaining 50 seats in the Sejm were filled from a national list of conspicuous figures.

Now, following the reforms of 1989, 55 per cent (253) of the Sejm's seats are reserved for contests between PRON candidates and 10 per cent (46) for a national list of dignitaries, with the two-ballot majority voting system again applying. The remaining 35 per cent (161) of Sejm seats have been left open to non-PZPR-sponsored opposition candidates fighting in freely democratic contests. The sole requirement for candidacy in these races is the gathering of 3,000 signatures on a petition.

The Sejm's tasks are to pass bills, adopt the state budget and economic plan and 'appoint' the executive, which is the 24-member Council of Ministers (COM), headed by a chairman, or Prime Minister. The COM has charge of day-to-day government administration, frames the state budget and economic plan, oversees the work of government departments and may issue ordinances. The Senate was created in 1989 to function as a partial check on the Sejm. Its members are elected in open, freely democratic, contests and the body has been granted the power of veto in a number of areas. Its veto can, however, be overridden by a two-thirds majority vote in the Sejm. In addition, the Senate participates with the Sejm in the election, for a six-year term, of an executive President, who is responsible for defence and foreign affairs and who has the authority to dissolve parliament and veto bills passed, call referendums and impose martial law. This new post of executive President, which is modelled, to some extent, on that in France, replaces the 17-member Council of State, headed by a President, which was formerly elected by the Sejm. It has been promised that when the first assembly-elected President has served his full term a new system of direct, popular election will be introduced and that the Sejm will also be fully opened to free competition.

During periods of regime crisis, the authority and autonomy of the Sejm and its members have tended to increase substantially and this has particularly been the case since 1980, when it won charge of the Supreme Board of Control, which oversees the work of central and local government organs. It promises to become even more assertive during the coming years. However, although the Sejm is a comparatively virile and influential institution by Eastern Bloc standards, political power in Poland still ultimately resides with the ruling PZPR, headed, since 1989 by First Secretary Dr Mieczyslaw Rakowski. The party leads and dominates the PRON mass organisation, which includes two minor parties. The principle of 'democratic centralism' and the systems of 'nomenklatura' and joint party and state office holding serve to ensure this dominance.

In April 1988, for example, the PZPR's Political Bureau (Politburo) consisted of 16 full and five non-voting 'alternate' members. Two of them were also members of the Council of State, Jaruzelski being its President. Four held the senior posts of chairman, Professor Zbigniew Messner, foreign minister, Professor Marian Orzechowski, defence minister, General Florian Siwicki, and internal affairs minister, Lieutenant-General Czeslaw Kiszczak. However, the new party statute, adopted at the Ninth Extraordinary PZPR Congress in July 1981, has placed limits on this practice, in an effort to secure a clearer separation between the party and the state. In addition, the autonomous position within the Polish state of the Roman Catholic Church, and the popular challenge presented by the growth of the 'Solidarity' free trade union movement, have served to circumscribe the PZPR's monopoly of power.

Political parties

The ruling Polish United Workers' Party (PZPR: Polska Zjednoczona Partia Rabotnicza) is heir to the Communist Workers' Party of Poland (KPRP) which was founded in 1918 by Marxist wings of the nationalist Polish Socialist Party (PPS) which dates back to 1892, and the internationalist Social Democracy of the Kingdom of Lithuania and Poland Party (SDKPiL), which was established as long ago as 1895.

The KPRP later changed its name to the Communist Party of Poland (KPP) in 1925, but was forced to operate underground when proscribed by the Pilsudski regime. Because of its close Soviet links, it enjoyed little domestic support, membership standing at barely 10,000, and it was dissolved by Stalin in 1938. Four years later the pro-Moscow Polish Workers' Party (PPR) was established as a successor body. It was divided into two wings, a Moscow-based Stalinist faction, led by Boleslaw Bierut, and a 'native', anti-German resistance wing led by party First Secretary, Wladyslaw Gomulka. Gomulka was ousted by Bierut as leader in 1948 and the party was soon afterwards merged with the PPS to form the PZPR.

The PZPR is organised pyramidally. At its base are small, 3- to 100-member, 'local party organisations' which operate at the work place and housing-complex level. Above these are district and provincial party committees and, at the apex, a national Party Congress, which is elected quinquennially. The Congress has the task of adopting a party programme and 'electing' a new Central Committee (CC) to assume its responsibilities when it is not in session. At the most recent, the tenth, PZPR Congress, held in June 1986, a CC of 230 members was elected, of whom 175 were newcomers. The CC, which meets three times a year, 'elects', in turn, a Politburo and ten-member Secretariat which have *de facto* control over both party and state affairs.

During recent years, under new party rules, a degree of democratisation and genuine competition has been introduced into elections for executive posts. Elections are now secret and more candidates must stand than the number of seats available. In addition, only one successive re-election is allowed for an executive party office.

Membership of the PZPR currently stands at 2.13 million. This corresponds to 5.7 per cent of the total population, a comparatively low proportion by communist standards. It represents a significant advance on the 1962 total of 1.27 million, but is well below the 1978 high of 3.04 million. However, the party has been substantially reconstituted since the 'troubles' of 1980–81. Forty-three per cent of the current members are blue-collar workers, about 30 per cent are white-collar and 9 per cent farmers. Twenty-four per cent are female. At the uppermost Politburo level the military are unusually important, serving or former army officers occupying four of the 16 full membership positions.

Two other, non-competitive, political parties are permitted to operate under the umbrella of the PRON. They are the United Peasants' Party (ZSL) and the Democratic Party (SD). The ZSL was established in 1948 as a successor to the earlier peasant nationalist movement, the Polish People's Party, and currently has a membership of 500,000. The SD, which was founded in 1939, draws its support, and 110,000 members, from the ranks of white-collar urban professionals, intellectuals and private craftsmen. Prior to 1989 the ZSL and SD were 'allocated' around 110 and 40 Sejm seats respectively, while the PZPR received 260 and the Christian associations and 'independents' 50.

Recently a fourth political party, the revived PPS, began to operate outside the PRON umbrella. It functioned in exile after its forced merger with the PPR in 1948 and was reactivated inside the country by Solidarity-linked dissidents in November 1987. It was, however, swiftly declared illegal by the authorities, and its leaders detained in police custody.

Following the political reforms of the spring of 1989, and the re-legalisation of Solidarnosc, it has been superseded by the 'citizens' committee' of Solidarnosc which has emerged as the most significant opposition political force in the country. A new, Church-supported, Christian Democratic Party has also been founded by Wladyslaw Sila-Nowicki.

Latest elections

The most recent Polish legislature elections were held in June 1989. Turnout was disappointingly low, at only 62 per cent, but the Solidarnosc opposition movement swept the board in the seats for which it was entitled to compete, capturing 161 Sejm and 99 Senate seats. Senior government figures, including Prime Minister Rakowski, who stood unopposed for the 35 national list seats, were humiliatingly defeated, their names being crossed off the ballot papers by more than 50 per cent of the voters. Indeed, no PZPR-approved candidate was clearly elected in the first round of voting, and all were forced to stand again in the run-off elections a fortnight later.

Political history

During the medieval period, particularly from the fourteenth century, Poland was an influential Central European power under its own Jagellion dynasty, which was in power between 1386 and 1572. When it was united with Lithuania in 1569, it became the largest country in Europe. Defeat in the mid-seventeenth century in a war against Russia, Sweden and Brandenburg brought about its decline and a century later the country was partitioned among Russia, ruling the east, Prussia, the west, and Austria, the south-centre, where a measure of autonomy was granted. There were uprisings in 1830 and 1863 against the repressive Russian regime, leaving behind a legacy of deep antipathy.

At the close of the First World War, in November 1918, a fully independent Polish republic was established. Marshal Joseph Pilsudski, the founder of the PPS, was elected the country's first President and, taking advantage of upheavals in the Soviet Union, he proceeded to launch an advance into Lithuania and the Ukraine which reached stalemate in 1921. Politically, the immediate post-independence years were characterised by instability, with 14 multi-party coalition governments holding power between 1918 and 1926. Marshal Pilsudski then seized complete power in a coup, in May 1926, and proceeded to govern in an increasingly autocratic manner until his death in 1935. The country remained backward, only pockets of industrialism existing at Lodz and in Upper Silesia, with, in 1930, 60 per cent of the total population remaining dependent upon agricultural activities.

A military regime, under the leadership of Smigly-Rydz, remained in power until the German invasion of September 1939. Western Poland was immediately incorporated into the Nazi Reich, while the remainder of the country, except for a brief Soviet occupation of East Poland between 1940 and 1941, was treated as a colony and endured tremendous suffering. A third of the educated élite were liquidated, while, in all, six million Poles lost their lives: half of them Jews, slaughtered in concentration camps. By the middle of 1944, parts of eastern Poland had been liberated by Soviet Red Army forces, allied with Polish troops commanded by General Rola-Zymierski, and a communist-dominated, multi-party coalition government was set up at Lublin. In March 1945 the remaining German forces were driven out of the country.

The Soviet Union immediately recognised the 'Lublin coalition' as the provisional government of all Poland, but this was challenged by the Polish government in exile, based in London and backed by the Western Allies. It was headed, as Prime Minister, by the peasant leader Mikolajcyk. Following the Yalta Conference, in February 1945, it was agreed to set up a joint government, but this was dominated by the 'Lublin coalition' and PPR, which secured effective control of the security police and armed forces. Their position was further strengthened when, at the manipulated Sejm elections of January 1947, the 'Lublin coalition's' list of candidates, the 'Democratic Bloc', secured 80 per cent of the votes and 88 per cent of the 444 seats. A month later, a 'People's Republic' was proclaimed, with the PPR predominant, and in October 1947 Mikolajcyk fled to the West.

The new regime was faced with immediate resettlement problems as a result of the drastic 240-kilometre westward shift of the borders of the Polish state engineered at the Potsdam Conference, in July 1945. Under the terms of this agreement, Poland's eastern frontier was set at the 1921 Curzon Line, 180,000 km^2 in the east being lost to the Soviet Union, while 100,000 km^2 of former German territories along the line of the Oder and Neisse rivers were added from the west.

A Soviet-style, one-party constitution was adopted in July 1952 and a harsh, Stalinist form of rule instituted by Boleslaw Bierut, the PZPR leader between 1948 and 1956. This involved rural collectivisation and the persecution of Catholic Church opponents, including the arrest, in 1953, of Cardinal Wyszynski. During this period, Poland also joined Comecon, in 1949, and the Warsaw Pact, in 1955, and remained under close Soviet supervision, with the USSR's Marshal Rokossovsky serving as minister for war between 1949 and 1956.

In June 1956 serious strikes and riots, resulting in 53 deaths, erupted in Poznan in opposition to Soviet 'exploitation' and food shortages. This prompted the reinstatement of the more pragmatic 'nativist', Wladyslaw Gomulka, as PZPR First Secretary and the introduction of a series of moderate reforms, involving, most importantly, the re-introduction of private farming, the release of Cardinal Wyszynski and toleration of Catholicism. Today 85 per cent of Poland's cropped area is privately tilled.

Sudden food price rises, in December 1970, caused a further outbreak of strikes and rioting in Gdansk, Gdynia and Szczecin. These demonstrations had to be forcibly suppressed. This led to Gomulka's replacement as PZPR leader by the Silesia party boss and leader of the party's 'technocratic faction', Edward Gierek, who proceeded to institute a new economic reform programme directed towards achieving a rapid rise in living standards and consumer goods production. The country became heavily indebted, however, to foreign creditors and further strikes and demonstrations took place at Radom and Ursus, in June 1976, on the announcement of a proposal to raise food prices.

Opposition to the Gierek regime, which was accused of gross corruption, mounted in 1979, following a visit paid to his homeland by the recently elected Pope John Paul II, the former Cardinal Wojtyla of Kracow. Strikes commenced in Warsaw in June 1980, following a poor harvest and meat price rises, and rapidly spread across the country. The government attempted initially to appease workers by entering into pay negotiations with unofficial strike committees, but at the Gdansk shipyards demands emerged for permission to form free, independent trade unions. The government conceded this request and recognised the right to strike, resulting in the formation, in August 1980, in Gdansk, of the Solidarnosc (Solidarity) union, under the leadership of the electrician, Lech Walesa.

In September 1980, the ailing Gierek was replaced as PZPR First Secretary by Stanislaw Kania, but the unrest continued as the 10 million-member Solidarnosc campaigned for a five-day working week and a rural Solidarnosc was established. Meanwhile, inside the PZPR, rank and file pressure began to grow for greater democratisation, and a quarter of the party's members actually joined Solidarnosc. With mounting food shortages and PZPR control slipping, Kania was replaced as PZPR leader by the joint Prime Minister and Defence Minister, General Wojciech Jaruzelski, in October 1981.

With Soviet military activities taking place on Poland's borders, martial law was imposed, on 13 December 1981. Trade union activity was banned, the leaders of Solidarnosc arrested, a night curfew imposed and a Military Council of National Salvation established, headed by Jaruzelski. Five months of severe repression ensued, resulting in 15 deaths and 10,000 arrests. The actions of the Polish government were condemned by the United States administration and economic sanctions were imposed.

In June 1982, curfew restrictions were eased, prompting further serious rioting in August. Three months later, Lech Walesa was released and in December 1982 martial law was suspended, and then formally lifted, in July 1983. Pope John Paul II visited Poland in June 1983 and called for conciliation. The authorities responded in July by dissolving the Military Council and granting an amnesty to political prisoners and activists. This amnesty was broadened in July 1984, with the release of 35,000 prisoners and detainees on the fortieth anniversary of the People's Republic, prompting the American government to relax its economic sanctions. The residual sanctions were later fully removed, in February 1987.

During the next three years, the Jaruzelski administration sought to engineer a slow return to normality through pragmatic reform, including the liberalisation of the electoral system. Conditions remained tense, however, and became strained after the murder of Father Jerzy Popieluszko, a pro-Solidarnosc priest, by members of the security force, in October 1984. Anti-government feelings were fanned by the continued ban of Solidarnosc and by a threat, which was eventually withdrawn, in February 1986, to try Lech Walesa for slandering state electoral officials when disputing the October 1985 Sejm turnout figures.

Economic conditions slowly improved, as farm output increased in response to raised procurement prices, but Poland's foreign debt problems remained huge. In September and December 1986, with the release of further prominent dissidents and the establishment of a new broadly based 56-member Consultative Council discussion forum attached to the Council of State, the Jaruzelski administration sought to regain the public's trust. This was followed in July 1987 by the Sejm's creation of the new post of ombudsman to 'increase the guarantee that state bodies function in accordance with the law'.

Further, more radical, economic and political reforms were framed in 1987 and presented to the public in a national referendum in November. They comprised, in the economic sphere, a three-year restructuring package, involving immediate price rises of between 40 and 200 per cent, and increased resort to market mechanisms and the private sector. In the political sphere the reforms included a further liberalisation of electoral processes, decision-making devolution and the creation of a second Sejm chamber, staffed by 'self-governing' local council representatives. However, the referendum was opposed by dissidents, including Solidarnosc's leaders, who called for a boycott. As a result, turnout reached barely 67 per cent. Of those who voted, 69 per cent favoured political reform and 66 per cent economic change. These approval ratings, when converted as proportions of the total electorate, fell about 4–6 per cent short of the required 50 per cent mandate which the government had sought in advance. As a consequence, the reform programme had to be diluted, damaging the standing of the Jaruzelski regime.

Further problems mounted for the government in the spring and summer of 1988 as a new wave of strikes and demonstrations was launched by workers under the Solidarnosc banner, demanding higher wages, to offset recent substantial price rises, and union recognition. The strikes, which paralysed the country's shipyards, steelworks, coal-mines and port facilities at Gdansk, Nowa Huta, Silesia and Szczecin, were finally called off in September by Lech Walesa, after pay increases and an agreement by the government to hold a Church-state-union round-table conference at which the question of legalising Solidarnosc would be discussed.

During the same month, Professor Zbigniew Messner, who had been Prime Minister since 1985, tendered his government's resignation, because of the collapse of its economic strategy. He was replaced by the reformist Dr Mieczyslaw Rakowski, and in December 1988 a fundamental re-shuffle of the PZPR's Politburo was effected, bringing into the body eight young reformist technocrats.

The PZPR-Solidarnosc round-table negotiations eventually took place in February 1989 and lasted for six weeks. At their end, in April 1989, an historic agreement was signed which provided for the re-legalisation of Solidarnosc, the ending of the state's media monopoly, the toleration of opposition political associations and a substantive package of social, economic and political reforms. The latter included the formal conferment of legal rights to the Catholic Church, enabling it to run its affairs free from state interference and to operate private Church schools and hospitals, and the substantial (80 per cent) indexation of wages to the inflation level. In addition, a new two-chamber political structure was established, involving fully open and democratic elections—the first in the communist world—to a newly created Senate and the partial opening of the Sejm to non-PZPR-approved candidates. The new post of executive President was also created at the head of, what was officially described as, a 'socialist parliamentary democracy'. With elections to the new parliament being set for June 1989, Solidarnosc swiftly set about establishing its own political wing, termed the 'citizens' committee', and began publishing a daily newspaper. Receiving pulpit support from the Catholic Church, it secured sweeping victories in the open seats contested, sufficient to deny the government a two-thirds Sejm majority with which to steamroller through controversial legislation.

The PZPR leadership, humiliated in the polls, with many of its candidates winning barely 10 per cent of the vote, appealed to Solidarnosc to join in a 'grand coalition' government. Such a government was formed in August 1989 with Solidarnosc holding the position of senior partner.

ROMANIA

Socialist Republic of Romania
Republica Socialista Romania

Capital: Bucharest

Social and economic data
Area: 237,500 km^2
Population: 22.800m*
Pop density per km^2: 96*
Literacy rate: 96%

GDP: $69,000m*; per capita GDP: $3,026
Economy type: middle income
Labour force in agriculture: 29%

*1985

Ethnic composition
The Romanians are a non-Slavic race. There exist within the country substantial Hungarian, German and Serbian minorities. The Hungarians amount to 1.7 million and are concentrated in Transylvania, in the north-west, a region which formed part of Hungary prior to 1918 and was traditionally more affluent than neighbouring parts of Romania. Recent plans by Nicolae Ceausescu to demolish 8,000 villages here and replace them with 500 new agro-industrial complexes, involving the dispersed resettlement of ethnic Hungarians, form part of a controversial forced assimilation, or 'Romanisation', policy. The proposal precipitated a diplomatic crisis between Hungary and Romania in the summer of 1988.

Religions
Eighty-five per cent of believers are adherents to the Romanian Orthodox Church, a body which is organised into patriarchates and kept under tight political control. Ten per cent are Roman Catholics, belonging to the Armenian, Latin and Romanian, or Byzantine rite sects. These bodies lack official legal status. Among Protestant Churches, which draw support from the German and Hungarian ethnic communities, the Reformed (Calvinist) Church currently has 600,000 adherents; the Evangelical Church of the Augsburg Confession 120,000; the Unitarian Church 80,000; and the Synodo-Presbyterian Evangelical Church 30,000. Islam has 40,000 followers, mostly among the Turkish-Tartar community.

Political features
State type: communist
Date of state formation: 1881
Political structure: unitary
Executive: communist
Assembly: one-chamber
Party structure: one-party
Human rights rating: 20%

Local and regional government
The country is divided into 40 administrative counties (*judete*), excluding the municipality of Bucharest, each with its own People's Council elected for a five-year term. Bodies below, including about 250 municipalities and 2,700 communes, are elected for two-and-a-half-year periods.

Head of state
President Nicolae Ceausescu, since 1974.

Head of government
Prime Minister Constantin Dascalescu, since 1982.

Political leaders since 1970*
1965– Nicolae Ceausescu (PCR).

*Communist Party leader

Political system
The first socialist constitutions adopted by the republic in April 1948 and September 1952 adhered closely to the Soviet Union's 1936 'Stalin Constitution' model. They established the Communist Party's 'leading role' in the state and society. The new constitution, which was adopted in August 1965, changed the country's description from a 'People's Republic' to a 'Socialist Republic' and established a more presidentialist executive system. This constitution was amended in March 1974, with the new office of President of the Republic being formally created.

Under the 1965 constitution, the supreme body of state power and sole legislative organ is the 369-member Grand National Assembly (GNA: Marea Adunare Nationala). The Assembly is elected every five years by universal adult suffrage. Candidates are drawn from a single list put forward by the Front of Socialist Unity and Democracy (FSUD), which was established in 1968, under the approval of the Romanian Communist Party (PCR), and stand in single-member constituencies. Since 1975 more than one candidate has been allowed to contest each seat. Candidates need to obtain an absolute majority of votes cast, with run-off ballots being held if this result is not initially achieved. So far, however, there has been no need for a second ballot.

The GNA meets for two working sessions for several days each year and 'elects' from among its members a smaller, subordinate, 20-member State Council to sit in permanent session and assume its functions in its absence. The GNA also 'elects' a Council of Ministers (COM), headed by a chairman, or Prime Minister. The current COM has 66 members who have responsibility for day-to-day executive administration.

Since 1974 the GNA has also 'elected' a President of the Republic for its duration. Nominees need to receive a two-thirds assembly majority. The President combines the duties of head of state, president of the State Council, supreme commander of the armed forces and president of the Defence Council and is the dominant figure in the Romanian polity. He is served by an extensive office staff and has the right to chair COM meetings and appoint and dismiss ministers. As a result, both the State Council, which does not constitute a collective head of state, and the chairman of the COM are far weaker in Romania than their opposite numbers elsewhere in Eastern Europe.

The controlling force and only permitted political party in Romania is the PCR, which leads the broader FSUD. Party and state are, by comparative communist standards, fused to an unusually high degree, in accordance with Ceausescu's concept of the 'socialisation of the state'.

First, special party bodies have been established to supervise state ministries and the observance of party guidelines. They are additional to the usual party executive committees. Two such bodies are the Supreme Council for Economic and Social Development and the Central Council of Workers' Control of Economic and Social Activity, both of which include trade union interest group representatives.

Second, the PCR's Central Committee has been accorded the right to propose members to the Council of State and the candidate for President, as well as to initiate legislation directly.

Third, the multiple holding of senior party and state posts is a pronounced feature of the 'Romanian system'. In April 1988, for example, the Political Executive Committee (Politburo) of the PCR consisted of 19 full and 24 non-voting 'alternate' members. Five of these were also members of the State Council and an additional 18 held seats on the COM.

Fourth, there is a regular rotation of senior party personnel, who are forced to alternate between positions in the central state and party apparatus.

The other distinctive feature of the Romanian political system is its unusually personalised nature, a 'ruling dynasty' having now been established. The dominant figure is Nicolae Ceausescu, who has been PCR General Secretary since 1965, and President of the Republic since 1974. Ceausescu is also chairman of the FSUD, while many members of his family, most notably his wife Elena and son Nicu, as well as more distant relatives, hold prominent posts in the party and state executives. Ceausescu, who has established a personality cult unmatched elsewhere in Eastern Europe, governs in an autocratic manner, blending nationalism with populism.

Political parties

The sole legal political party, the Romanian Communist Party (PCR), was established in May 1921 by a left-wing section of the Social Democratic Workers' Party (SDWP), which was itself originally founded in 1893. The party was proscribed by the Romanian government in 1924 and forced underground, during which period it developed close links with Moscow. It merged with the SDWP in October 1947 to form the Romanian Workers Party, changing its name to the PCR in July 1965.

The party is organised pyramidally, with small 'institution cells' at its base established in factories, collective farms and other workplaces. Other units operate at successive municipal and regional levels above. A national Party Congress, which functions as its supreme organ, is convened every five years. It debates and adopts policy programmes and 'elects' a Central Committee (CC), which currently comprises 265 full and 181 'alternate' members, to assume its functions in its absence.

The CC, in turn, 'elects' a Political Executive Committee (PEC) and ten-member Secretariat to run the party's day-to-day affairs. Real power lies with these bodies and, in particular, with the eight-member Permanent Bureau of the PEC, which is chaired by the party's General Secretary, who is elected by the Congress. The Bureau functions as an 'inner cabinet'.

Membership of the PCR stood at 3.69 million in 1987, a figure which corresponds to 16.2 per cent of the total population. This is the highest proportion for any East European communist state. Fifty-six per cent of the membership are blue-collar workers, 20 per cent white collar and 16 per cent farmers. Thirty-two per cent are female. Allied to the party is the Union of Communist Youth, which has four million members, aged between 14 and 30. PCR membership has increased phenomenally during the last three decades, standing at 900,000 and 2.0 million in 1962 and 1971 respectively.

Latest elections

In the most recent Grand National Assembly elections, held in March 1985, 594 FSUD nominated candidates contested the 369 available seats. Only 2.3 per cent of 'No' votes were polled in this election, and the turnout was officially recorded as 99.99 per cent.

Political history

Part of the Ottoman Empire since the fifteenth century, and then subject to Russian suzerainty, between 1859 and 1866, a Romanian nation-state was initially formed by Prince Alexandru Ioan Curza, between 1959 and 1966, by the union of the principalities of Moldavia and Wallachia. The Great Powers recognised Romania's full independence in 1881, under King Karol I. The country, having fought on the Allied side during the First World War, extended its boundaries in 1918, receiving Transylvania and Bukovina from the dismembered Austro-Hungarian Empire as well as, until 1940, Bessarabia from Russia. It thus emerged as the largest state in the Balkans.

During the inter-war period Romania remained economically backward, with 72 per cent of its population dependent upon agriculture. It enjoyed a brief experiment with representative institutions, until, in 1930, as a means of countering the growing popularity of the Fascist 'Iron Guard' mass movement, King Karol II abolished the democratic constitution of 1923 and established his own dictatorship.

Early in the Second World War, the country was forced to surrender Bessarabia, North Transylvania, and South Dobruja to the Soviet Union, Hungary and Bulgaria respectively, in accordance with the August-September 1940 Vienna Arbitration and Craiova Treaty. Additionally, as a result of German pressure, King Karol II abdicated, handing over power to General Ion Antonescu, who, ruling in the name of Karol's son King Michael, signed the Axis Pact, in November 1940, allying Romania with Germany. This was followed, in June 1941, by Romania's declaration of war on the Soviet Union.

In August 1944, with the Red Army on Romania's borders, King Michael supported a coalition of left and centre parties, including the Romanian Communist Party, to oust the Antonescu regime. Romania subsequently joined the war against Germany and in the Paris Peace Treaty, of February 1947, recovered Transylvania, but lost South Dobruja to Bulgaria and Bessarabia and North Bukovina to the Soviet Union.

The initial post-liberation government was a broadly based coalition, termed the National Democratic Front (NDF), under the leadership of General Santescu. Then, in March 1945, under Soviet pressure, a communist-dominated administration was set up, nominally headed by the radical peasants' Ploughmans' Front leader, Petru Groza. Parliamentary elections were held in November 1946, in which the NDF stood as the Bloc of Democratic Parties, polling 80 per cent of the votes. In the following year, all the non-communist parties were dissolved and King Michael I was forced to abdicate. This paved the way for the adoption of a one-party Soviet-style republican constitution, in April 1948.

A programme of industrial nationalisation and agricultural collectivisation was immediately launched by the new regime and there was a rapid purge of opposition leaders, so as to establish the PCR firmly in power. Soviet troops remained in the country, however, until 1958. The dominant political personality between 1945 and 1965 was PCR leader and head of state, Gheorghe Gheorghiu-Dej. He took Romania into the Comecon in 1949 and the Warsaw Treaty Organisation in 1955.

On his death in March 1965, power passed to Nicolae Ceausescu, who immediately oversaw the framing of a new constitution, in June 1965, which placed greater emphasis on national autonomy. Under Ceausescu, Romania has adopted a foreign policy line independent of the Soviet Union, condemning the 1968 invasion of Czechoslovakia and refusing to participate directly in Warsaw Pact manoeuvres or to allow Soviet troops to cross its borders. Additionally, Ceausescu has called for multilateral nuclear disarmament and the creation of a Balkan nuclear-weapons-free zone. He has also maintained warm relations with communist China. At home, the Ceausescu regime has sought broader participation in policy making, but a tight Stalinist rein has been kept on dissident activities.

In recent years, political affairs in Romania have been dominated by mounting economic difficulties, faltering industrial output and growing foreign indebtedness, and energy shortages. Widespread power cuts and the military occupation of leading power plants were endured in the winters of 1985 and 1986 and in November 1986 defence spending was reduced by 5 per cent, after the holding of a national referendum on the issue. Energy and food shortages worsened during 1987, resulting in widespread workers' strikes and demonstrations, the most serious occurring at Brasov. Hundreds of arrests were made. Nevertheless, Ceausescu has remained steadfast in his policies, ruling out any question of reforms on the 'Gorbachev model' in the Soviet Union. He was re-elected General Secretary of the PCR in November 1984 and state President in March 1985.

SOVIET UNION

Union of Soviet Socialist Republics (USSR)
Soyuz Sovyetskikh Sotsialisticheskikh Respublik

Capital: Moscow

Social and economic data
Area: 22,402,000 km^2
Population: 280.000m*
Pop density per km^2*: 13
Literacy rate: 100%
GDP: $1,200,000m*; per capita GDP: $4,286
Economy type: middle income
Labour force in agriculture: 25%

*1985

Ethnic composition
Just over 50 per cent, or 141 million, of the population of the USSR are of 'Great Russian' nationality, 15 per cent, or 42 million, are Ukrainians and 4 per cent, or 10 million, Byelorussian. All three categories are 'Eastern Slav' races. In addition, there are more than 100 non-Slav ethnic/national

groups. Twenty-one of these embrace more than a million members each, the most important of them being : Uzbeks, 15 million, Kazakhs, nine million, Tatars, seven million, Azerbaijanis, six million, Georgians, five million, Tadzhiks, Armenians and Moldavians, four million each, Lithuanians and Kirghizians, three million each, Germans, Jews and Latvians, two million each, and Poles and Estonians, one million each. With the exception of the Germans, Poles, Tatars and Jews, each of which groups has its own 'Autonomous Republic' and 'Autonomous Region' within the RSFSR, all of the national communities have been accorded their own Union Republic within the USSR. Table 52 below sets out the relative ethnic distributions within these Union Republics. This shows the clustering of titular communities as well as the extensive settlement of 'Great Russians' throughout the USSR, the outcome of a policy of deliberate urbanward out-migration. Only in Lithuania and the Trans-Caucasian region of Armenia, Azerbaijan and Georgia does the 'Great Russian' proportion fall below 10 per cent of the total population. Local community opposition to such 'Russification' has surfaced periodically during recent years, particularly in the economically advanced and politically liberal Baltic lands of Estonia, Latvia and Lithuania and in the rapidly demographically expanding Islamic Central Asian republics of Turkestan. One hundred and twelve recognised languages are spoken in the Soviet Union, Russian being the mother tongue for 58 per cent of the population.

Table 52

ETHNIC POPULATION DISTRIBUTIONS IN THE CONSTITUENT UNION REPUBLICS OF THE USSR

				Population Shares		
Union Republic	*Capital*	*Area ('000 km²)*	*Pop (m) (1985)*	*Titular Nation (%)*	*Ethnic Russian (%)*	*Date of Joining USSR*
Armenia	Yerevan	29.8	3.36	90	2	1936*
Azerbaijan	Baku	86.6	6.70	78	8	1936*
Byelorussia	Minsk	207.6	10.07	79	12	1922
Estonia	Tallinn	45.1	1.55	64	28	1940
Georgia	Tbilisi	69.7	5.27	69	7	1936*
Kazakhstan	Alma-Ata	2,717.3	16.16	36	40	1936†
Kirghizia	Frunze	198.5	4.02	48	25	1936†
Latvia	Riga	63.7	2.64	53	33	1940
Lithuania	Vilnius	65.2	3.62	80	9	1940
Moldavia	Kishinev	33.7	4.16	64	13	1940
Russian (RSFSR‡)	Moscow	17,075.4	144.95	83	83	1922
Tadzhikistan	Dushanbe	143.1	4.56	59	10	1929†
Turkestan	Ashkhabad	488.1	3.23	69	12	1924†
Ukraine	Kiev	603.7	51.50	73	21	1922
Uzbekistan	Tashkent	447.4	18.21	69	11	1924†
USSR	Moscow	22,274.9	280.00	—	50	1922

*Formerly part of the Trans-Caucasian Soviet Socialist Republic which joined the USSR in 1922.

†Formerly Autonomous Republics within the USSR.

‡Russian Soviet Federated Socialist Republic.

Religions

According to Article 52 of the 1977 constitution, citizens are guaranteed freedom of conscience and the right 'to profess or not to profess any religion'. In practice, however, only private worship at home or in an institution registered with and controlled by the state's Council for the Affairs of Religious Cults is tolerated. The Russian Orthodox is the most important Church, currently boasting 50 million adherents, constituting 18 per cent of the total population. It draws its support from the 'Great Russian', Ukrainian and Byelorussian 'Eastern Slav' communities, but its overall membership has halved since the 1917 revolution. There are currently 7,000 'working' churches and 6,500 clergy, compared to more than 54,000 churches and 51,000 clergy in 1917. The Georgian Orthodox Church has an additional five million members.

Islam, drawing its support from the Central Asian and east Trans-Caucasian regions, now rivals the Eastern Orthodox Churches, boasting an estimated 45–50 million adherents in 1987, equivalent to 16–18 per cent of the total population. The majority of these are Sunni Muslims, although a significant Shia Muslim community resides in Azerbaijan. There are 365 officially recognised mosques, but an estimated 1,800 unofficially function. In 1917 there were 26,000.

Roman Catholicism has 4 million adherents, concentrated in the Baltic region, particularly in Lithuania; the Armenian Apostolic Church a similar membership, distributed across the Trans-Caucasian region; Judaism, 2 million, scattered across the whole country, although fewer than 5 per cent of Jews are recorded as practising; the Lutheran Church, between 1 and 2 million, concentrated in the Baltic lands; and Buddhism 400,000, in the Mongolia border region. In the western Ukraine the Eastern-Rite Catholic Church, with an estimated 3 million members, operates underground, the Church having been outlawed in 1946 because of its links with Ukrainian nationalism.

Political features

State type: communist
Date of state formation: 1917
Political structure: federal
Executive: communist
Assembly: two-chamber
Party structure: one-party
Human rights rating: 20%

Local and regional government

Below the 15 Union Republics, 20 Autonomous Republics, eight Autonomous Regions and ten Autonomous Districts, the units of local government are provinces/regions (*oblasti*), 'rural territories' (*kraia*), city- and rural-districts (*raiony*), towns/boroughs (*gorodskie raiony*), and villages (*sela*), each administered by a local council (*soviet*), which is elected every two and a half years but which is dominated by an executive committee. There are currently 129 regions and territories, 3,852 urban and rural districts, 2,152 towns, 3,968 urban settlements and 42,176 rural soviets, with 2.3 million citizens serving on them. In the June 1987 local soviet elections, competitive multiple-candidacies were permitted in 5 per cent of the seats.

Head of state
President Mikhail Gorbachev, since 1988.

Head of government
Prime Minister Nikolai Ryzhkov, since 1985.

Political leaders since 1970*
1964–82 Leonid Brezhnev (CPSU), 1982–84 Yuri Andropov (CPSU), 1984–85 Konstantin Chernenko (CPSU), 1985– Mikhail Gorbachev (CPSU).

*Communist Party leaders

Political system
The Soviet Union's initial socialist constitution was adopted in 1918. An interim, revolutionary document, it placed all power in the hands of the 'soviets', abolished private land ownership and established the rudiments of a federal structure. A new constitution was framed in 1922, and ratified in 1924, soon after the close of the civil war. It clearly specified the respective, theoretical, powers of federal and constituent republic bodies. The third, 'Stalin Constitution', of 1936 enshrined the Communist Party (CPSU: Communist Party of the Soviet Union) as a 'vanguard' force, created the bicameral Supreme Soviet as a successor to the existing Congress of Soviets, and redefined the country as a 'socialist state of workers and peasants'. This document was modified in 1977, when a new, fourth, constitution was adopted which kept in force the existing institutional structure, but specified citizens' rights more clearly. It also gave formal recognition to the CPSU as 'the leading and guiding force in Soviet society' (Article 6).

Under the 1977 constitution, the Soviet Union is a federal state comprising 15 constituent Union Republics, as shown in Table 52 above. Each of these Union Republics enjoys, in theory, the right of secession and has its own constitution, with the exception of the RSFSR, a single chamber, as well as a 285 to 975-member assembly (Supreme Soviet) and a government (Council of Ministers) which is responsible for local administration. Within several Union Republics there are also 20 Autonomous Republics, eight Autonomous Regions and ten National Districts, in which special regard is paid to local culture, customs and languages.

The central, federal, government is solely responsible for defence, foreign policy, foreign trade, communications, heavy industries and monetary affairs. In other spheres the scope for initiative by Union and Autonomous Republic/Region governments is restricted by the centrally planned nature of the Soviet economy, by the principle of 'democratic centralism' and by the constant scrutiny of CPSU bodies. The Soviet federal system is thus weak in comparison with many others in the world today, overall authority being exercised by the centre.

Prior to the constitutional reforms of 1988–89, the highest organ of the Moscow-based central government has traditionally been the Supreme Soviet (Verchovnyi Soviet) of the USSR, a two-chamber assembly which consisted of the Soviet (People's Council) of the Union (Soviet Soyuza) and the Soviet of Nationalities (Soviet Nationalnotsey). The powers of the two chambers were equal and each had 750 members elected every five years by universal adult suffrage from a single, unopposed list of CPSU-approved candidates. Members of the Soviet of the Union were elected from single-member constituencies on the rough basis of one deputy for every 350,000 people. Seats in the Soviet of Nationalities were distributed regionally on the basis of 32 deputies from each Union Republic, eleven from each Autonomous Republic, five from each Autonomous Region and one from each of the ten National Districts within the RSFSR. The result of such allocation had been to enhance the proportionate representation of the Baltic, Trans-Caucasian and Central Asian regions *vis-à-vis* the RSFSR and the Ukraine. These two last named republics accounted for 73 per cent of the total number of members sent to the Soviet of the Union, but only 37 per cent of those sent to the Soviet of Nationalities.

Candidates needed to receive at least 50 per cent of the votes cast, with provision existing for follow-up ballots if this result was not immediately achieved. Once elected, members served on a part-time basis, being granted leave of absence from work to attend sittings and being paid special allowances. They were also expected to hold regular constituency 'surgeries', in which local grievances could be aired, and to arrange annual general meetings.

The Supreme Soviet met for brief sessions of three to four days twice a year, usually in June and December, to ratify policy programmes introduced by the government and to adopt the annual budget and economic plan. Voting was by a show of hands, with majorities being required from both houses for bills to be passed. In practice, there was never a dissenting vote.

Additionally, the Supreme Soviet had the task of scrutinising social and economic legislation in its draft stage and of monitoring the work of state bodies. To expedite its work, 34 functionally specialist standing committees, 17 in each chamber, were formed on which 1,210 members, or 81 per cent of the total, sat. These committees were convened three to four times a year and worked in conjunction with solicited, outside experts. They were important bodies in the legislative process, being able to propose improving amendments which were frequently adopted. Attached to them were smaller sub-committees which met more regularly to carry out preparatory investigations.

To take over its functions and responsibilities when it was not sitting, the Supreme Soviet 'elected', in joint session, a Presidium of 39 members, who included, as *ex officio* members, the chairmen of the Presidiums of each of the 15 Supreme Soviets of the Union Republics. The Presidium served as a collective presidency and standing committee of the Supreme Soviet, having the right to confer honorific titles; appoint the members of the Defence Council; form and abolish state ministries and commissions, and promote or demote their heads; and issue edicts (*ukazy*) and decrees (*postanovleniya*). It met in plenary session every two months and was headed by a chairman who served as titular head of state or President.

The Supreme Soviet also elected the Council of Ministers (COM), a body of around 120 members, headed by a chairman, or Prime Minister, which functioned as the executive government of the USSR, being responsible for day-to-day state administration. Included in the COM, as *ex officio* members, were the chairmen of each of the 15 Union Republic COMs. Additionally, 55 of the members were heads of all-union or union-republican ministries and 30 were heads of inter-departmental state committees or commissions. There were also 12 vice-chairmen. The COM met in full session once every three months.

A smaller permanent Presidium, composed of its chairman and vice-chairmen, had daily responsibilities, and functioned as a co-ordinating inner cabinet. It directed economic, social and cultural activities, including the drafting of the economic plan and state budget, and foreign affairs, and had the authority to issue ordinances and decrees within its spheres of responsibility. Individual ministers within the COM were professional specialists, the task of each being to oversee the performance of his department and of relevant state enterprises below. Each was served by a small advisory cabinet (*collegia*) composed of the chief deputy ministers of his department.

With the implementation, in 1989, of constitutional reforms framed in June 1988 at a special All-Union CPSU Conference, substantive changes have been made to the Soviet Union's legislative and executive structure.

The Supreme Soviet has been replaced by a new Congress of the USSR People's Deputies (CUPD), which comprises 2,250 members. Seven hundred and fifty are elected for five-year terms, as before, from roughly equal-sized territorial constituencies spread across the USSR, and 750 from national-territorial constituencies at the Union Republic, Autonomous Republic, Autonomous Region and National District levels. For these seats, genuine competition between candidates approved by selection committees has been introduced. The remaining 750 seats have been allocated among 32 officially recognised 'social organisations', with, for example, the CPSU and trade unions each being reserved 100 seats and the Communist Youth League 75 seats, while, for example, the Cinema Fans' Society and Philatelic Association have been accorded one seat each. An additional 'chamber' has thus been added to the old Supreme Soviet to create the new CUPD. However, the CUPD differs from the Supreme Soviet in that it acts as an 'overarching' constitutional assembly rather than an effective legislature. It convenes for several days each year to decide on major constitutional, political and socio-economic questions and elects, at its outset, a state President (chairman of the Supreme Soviet), Vice-President, Prime Minister and chairman of the Supreme Court. The new President has substantive executive power, with responsibility for guiding the drafting of legislation and socio-economic programmes and directing defence and foreign policy.

The CUPD also, in a particularly novel fashion, elects from its ranks, and by secret ballot, 542 members to serve in a new slimmed-down Supreme Soviet which, meeting in two spring and autumn sessions for eight months a year, serves as the country's effective legislature. Its members are elected in accordance with regional quotas, with a proportion being annually rotated. Like its predecessor, the new Supreme Soviet is a two-chamber body, consisting of a 271-member Soviet of Nationalities, whose task it is to concentrate on legislation which specifically affects the territorial subdivisions of the USSR, and a 271-member Soviet of the Union, which concentrates on socio-economic, civil rights, defence and international relations matters. The state President presides over the Supreme Soviet's

Presidium and there is a structure of standing commissions and committees.

The new CUPD and Supreme Soviet promise to be livelier and more influential bodies than their predecessor. In the opening televised debates of the CUPD in May 1989 there were vigorous exchanges and the procedural votes taken suggested that around a fifth of its members were radical and independent-minded 'progressive reformers'. However, few from this 'reform bloc' gained subsequent election to the new Supreme Soviet.

Described in the 1977 constitution as a 'parliamentarian republic', the constitutional changes of 1988–89 have served to move the Soviet polity somewhat closer to this position. However, the dominating force in the country is still the CPSU, which is prescribed a 'leading' role in state affairs and is the only permitted political party. The CPSU dominates through its vetting of the electoral process; through its establishment of a parallel and dominating labyrinth of party committees, which inspect the work of state bodies; and through the practice of joint party and state office holding. As a consequence of the operation of the system of 'democratic centralism', the real controlling force in the Soviet political system is thus the CPSU's supreme body, its Politburo, which functions as a national cabinet. In May 1988, it consisted of 13 full and seven non-voting 'candidate' members. Six of these also held positions within the Presidium of the Supreme Soviet, including the post of chairman, Andrei Gromyko, and a further seven within the COM, including its chairman, Nikolai Ryzhkov.

Political parties

The ruling Communist Party of the Soviet Union (CPSU: Kommunisticheskaya Partiya Sovietskovo Soyuza) was founded in 1903, following a split in the Russian Social Democratic Workers' Party (RSDWP), which was founded in 1898 by Georgii Plekhanov, between a majority (Bolshevik) wing led by Lenin, which saw the need, in Russian conditions, to organise the party as a tightly disciplined vanguard of professional revolutionaries ready to lead a sudden workers-peasant revolution, and a minority (Menshevik) wing led by Martov, which favoured a traditional mass organisation and viewed the attainment of socialism as still distant, and needing to be preceded by a bourgeois revolution. In 1912, Lenin's Bolsheviks formally set themselves up as a separate group and became the sole permitted party within the Soviet Union when they seized power from the Mensheviks in the revolution of October 1917. The party, which had a membership of 23,600 on the eve of the revolution, subsequently changed its name to the All-Russian Communist Party (Bolsheviks) in 1918, to the All-Union Communist Party (Bolsheviks) in 1925, and to the CPSU in 1952.

The party is organised pyramidally on Leninist 'democratic-centralist' lines. At its base, there are more than 440,000 Primary Party Units (PPUs), which are established at any workplace, such as a factory, collective farm, office or shop, where more than three party members are employed. A PPU which has more than 15 members elects a committee and bureau to oversee its affairs. Sixty per cent of the PPUs fall into this category. A PPU with fewer members, 34 per cent of the total being of this type, elects only a part-time secretary. One with more than 150 members, 6 per cent of the total being of this size, is served by a full-time salaried official. The PPU's task is to ensure that instructions from above are implemented and that the enterprise in which it is based is running properly and meeting targets. Monthly general meetings are held for this purpose.

Above the PPUs, are district, town and regional party units, which are, theoretically, elected from below, but which, as a result of the 'democratic centralist' process, are effectively appointed from above, with candidates for election being vetted and selected in advance by their superiors. The party committees (*raikoms* and *obkoms*) and permanent bureaux, headed by first secretaries, at these levels have the task of overseeing and directing the operation of state bodies at the same level. They are served by an extensive permanent party bureaucracy (*apparat*).

At the apex of the CPSU pyramid stands the All-Union Party Congress, a huge assembly with more than 5,000 members, which convenes every five years for a week-long session. This body is formally the supreme sovereign organ of the party. It has the task of adopting new party programmes and policy resolutions and of 'electing' a Central Committee (CC) to assume its authority once it closes. At the most recent, twenty-seventh, Party Congress, held in March 1986, a CC of 307 full and 170 non-voting 'candidate' members was elected, 40 per cent of whom were local, regional and national party secretaries and 41 per cent were newcomers.

The CC meets twice a year, in one-day sessions, just prior to the convening of the Supreme Soviet. It 'elects' a Politburo and twelve-member Secretariat, to take charge of day-to-day party affairs. The Politburo, which currently has twelve full and seven 'candidate' members, is by far the most important political body in the Soviet Union, including within its ranks key figures from both the party and state spheres. In the May 1988 Politburo, for example, was the chairman of the COM, chairman of the Presidium of the Supreme Soviet, the foreign and defence ministers, the head of the KGB security service, the chairman of Gosplan, the State Planning Committee, the chairman of the RSFSR's COM, as well as the heads of the CPSU of such important areas as Moscow, the Ukraine and Leningrad.

Sitting weekly, every Thursday, as an executive cabinet, the Politburo controls and determines the policy of the CPSU and sets out the medium- and long-term goals for the nation. Its members select from their ranks a General Secretary who presides over its discussions, chairs the Defence Council, is a member of the Presidium of the Supreme Soviet, and serves as the *de facto* leader of the Soviet Union.

The Secretariat serves the Politburo as an administrative and policy-making adjunct, being organised, traditionally, into more than 20 well-staffed, functionally specialist departments. The body has control over personnel selection, drawing up the 'nomenklatura' lists that are a key feature of the Soviet political system, and supervises and directs the work of the state bureaucracy, working in close liaison with state agencies.

Following the extraordinary CC Plenum of September 1988, the structuring of the apical party bodies has been significantly modified, as part of a streamlining process designed to curb pettifogging party interference into state affairs, and the number of administrative and policy-making departments under the control of the CC and Secretariat has been substantially reduced. In their stead, six broad Party Commissions have been established, each under the charge of a Politburo member: agriculture, Yegor Ligachev, economic and social policy, Nikolai Slyunkov, legal affairs, Viktor Chebrikov, ideology, Vadim Medvedev, international policy, Aleksandr Yakovlev, and party construction and cadres policy, Georgy Razumovsky.

Full membership of the CPSU stood, in 1987, at 18.57 million, constituting 6.6 per cent of the total population. This represents a significant advance on the 1953 total of 6 million, or 3.3 per cent, and 1971 figure of 14.46 million, or 5.9 per cent, but is below the 1982 high of 18.72 million, or 6.8 per cent. This must reflect the greater stress that has been placed on quality and commitment by the new Gorbachev leadership compared with the lax, later Brezhnev years. Forty-four per cent of party members are described as blue-collar workers, 43 per cent as white-collar professionals and intelligentsia and 12 per cent as collective farmers. Sixty per cent are 'Great Russians' and 28 per cent are female. There are, in addition, 700,000 'candidate' members, still on probation, while the party's 'youth' wing, Leninist Young Communist League of the Soviet Union (Komsomol) has 40 million members, aged between 14 and 28.

Latest elections

The most recent Congress of USSR People's Deputies elections were held in March 1989. Overall turnout was put, genuinely it appears, at the level of 89.8 per cent, compared with an alleged figure of 99.99 per cent for the previous 1984 Supreme Soviet elections. Turnout was lowest in Armenia, 71.9 per cent, and highest in Azerbaijan, 98.5 per cent. In the territorial and national-territorial constituencies, 2,895 candidates contested the 1,500 available seats. There was a choice between two or more candidates in 73 per cent of the constituencies and second ballot run-off races later had to be held in May 1989 for 274 seats where no clear winner emerged on the first ballot or where turnout had fallen to below 50 per cent of the registered electorate. Eight hundred and seventy-one candidates contested the 750 seats reserved for 'social organisations', with second ballot run-offs being required for 18 of these seats.

The election saw the humiliating defeat of a number of unpopular party apparatchiks, including the Leningrad party chief, Yury Solovev, and success in the Baltic republics for Popular Front nationalist candidates. In Moscow, the CPSU reformist 'dissident', Boris Yeltsin, was swept in with an 89 per cent share of the vote, defeating the official CPSU candidate, and the human rights campaigner, Dr Andrei Sakharov, was also elected to the CUPD as a representative of the Academy of Sciences. In the southern republics, however, traditional ballot-rigging by local party bosses continued.

Eighty-eight per cent of the deputies elected to the CUPD were members or candidate members of the CPSU and 60 different nationalities were represented. Nineteen per cent were described as manual workers and 11 per cent as collective farm workers. Seventeen per cent were women.

Political history

The 'Muscovy' (RSFSR) heartland of the contemporary Soviet Union was originally settled by nomadic Slavs, Turks and Bulgars between the third and seventh centuries before, in the ninth and tenth centuries, Viking chieftains established a Russian dynasty based around the town of Novgorod in the north-west. The centre of control moved to Kiev between the tenth and twelfth centuries, and this formed the capital of the first Russian Empire. Its peoples were converted to Eastern Orthodox Christianity, which had been introduced by Greek missionaries from Byzantium, or Constantinople.

Mongol-Tatar rule was subsequently imposed over the east and centre of the country, during the thirteenth and fourteenth centuries, with Byelorussia and the Ukraine ruled by Poland. It was not until the late fifteenth century that a new Russian Empire was established by Ivan III, and the capital located in what is now Moscow. The empire was considerably extended in scope by Ivan IV, who resumed control of the north-west, annexed Kazan and Astrakhan and began the colonisation of Siberia. Under the subsequent Tsars and Tsarinas, Peter I and Catherine II, the Baltic lands, the Crimea, West Ukraine and eastern Poland were added, and the capital was moved to St Petersburg, now named Leningrad, in the north-west. Under Tsar Alexander II (1855–81), the borders of the Russian Empire were further extended, being pushed east to the Pacific and south into Central Asia.

Although militarily a 'Great Power' by the later nineteenth century, the country remained economically and politically backward compared with its neighbours in Western Europe, from which it remained culturally isolated. Serfdom persisted until 1861 and it was in 1906, following the abortive revolution of 1905, that the country's first constitution and national representative assembly, the Duma, were established. However, this body was elected on a narrow franchise, with, in 1910, barely 2.4 per cent of the population enjoying the right to vote. It thus did little to temper the despotic character of the Tsarist regime.

At the start of the twentieth century a state-led crash industrialisation programme was belatedly launched, but towards the close of the First World War, when its armed forces were in retreat and the economy was in ruins, the Tsarist autocracy was finally overthrown in the revolution of March 1917 by a combination of disaffected soldiers, workers, peasants and RSDWP activists. Tsar Nicholas II abdicated and a republic was declared, headed first by Prince Lvov and then by the agrarian-populist Socialist Revolutionary Party leader, Aleksandr Kerensky.

This provisional government was soon itself overthrown, in the 'October Revolution' of 1917, by the Bolsheviks, led by the charismatic, white-collar intellectual, Vladimir Ilyich Lenin, who had recently returned from exile in Zürich, and the Ukrainian Jew who had played a directing role in the 1905 revolution, Leon Trotsky. This second 'revolution' was, in fact, a coup, rather than a popular uprising. This is demonstrated by the fact that the Bolsheviks polled only 25 per cent of the votes in the free elections held to the Constituent Assembly in November 1917, compared with the 63 per cent secured by other socialist parties. Lenin, however, ignored the result of this election, swiftly dissolved the Constituent Assembly, in January 1918, and established, instead, one-party control through an extensive system of Bolshevik-dominated soviets.

The initial four years of the new Bolshevik regime were consumed with repelling external attacks by the allied powers and Poland and fighting an internal civil war against a combination of pro-Tsarist, 'bourgeois democrat', socialist revolutionary and Menshevik 'White' forces. These problems were eventually overcome and, in December 1922, the USSR was formally established as a federation and a new constitution was adopted in 1923.

The problems of reconstruction meant that, in the economic sphere, a pragmatic, mixed enterprise, approach was initially pursued, between 1921 and 1927, under the title of the 'New Economic Policy' (NEP). Peasants were allowed to till their own land and small and medium-sized private industries operated, while the 'commanding heights' of the economy were brought under state control. This social democratic strategy was gradually abandoned, however, by Lenin's successor as party leader, Josef Stalin, the son of a poor Georgian cobbler-serf.

Seeking to transform the nation rapidly from an agrarian to a top-ranking industrial power and, in the process, re-arrange its socio-economic base fundamentally, in a socialist direction, he embarked from 1927 on a radical programme of forced collectivisation and heavy industrialisation, founded on a system of firm, party-controlled, central planning. The first Five Year Plan was introduced in 1928.

Stalin's programme of 'socialism in one country' was opposed by some of his leading party colleagues, including Trotsky, who favoured an internationalist policy of fomenting supportive revolutions abroad. Other opponents were Trotsky's 'leftist' supporter, Lev Kamenev, the moderate pro-NEP 'rightist', Nikolai Bukharin, the 'Old Bolshevik', Grigorii Zinoviev, and the Leningrad Party leader, Sergei Kirov. Stalin's response was a series of ruthless party purges and 'liquidations' which were launched during the 1920s and 1930s. As a result, party membership fell, from 3.5 million in 1933 to 1.9 million in 1938.

In the economic sphere, Stalin's ambitious transformatory programme had significant results, Soviet industry recording a growth rate of 16 per cent per annum between 1929 and 1940, its blue-collar work force quadrupling in size and the country's urban population doubling. However, the social and political costs were enormous. Millions of 'rich peasants' (*kulaks*) were executed or sent to labour camps in Siberia, agricultural produce was forcibly marketed, depressing rural per capita living standards, and the countryside was squeezed to provide investment income for industry. Both the party and state political structures were disfigured, democratic consultation giving way to personalised control, supported by the intrusive and terroristic use of the NKVD secret police, under the direction of Stalin's Georgian crony, Lavrenti Beria.

The Stalin regime, although unpopular with rural groups and with the intelligentsia, did, however, receive support from a number of sections of Soviet society. These included the new post-revolution generation of socialist educated 'worker-bureaucrats' who had benefited from the new opportunities for rapid advancement. Support also came from urban workers and the military, the groups which had been the prime beneficiaries of the 'forced industrialisation' strategy. In addition, during the Second World War, Stalin's role as a determined leader (*Vozhd*), successfully standing up to German Nazi aggression in a bitter struggle, termed the 'Great Patriotic War', in which 25 million Russians perished, brought him broad popular, nationalist support.

The Red Army's success in repelling Germany's forces in 1943 re-established the country as a 'Great Power' and at the close of the Second World War it was able to gain effective dominance over Eastern Europe, setting up a series of satellite socialist governments, as well as securing the direct annexation of Baltic and Polish territories in the north-west and a substantial area in Moldavia and the West Ukraine in the south-west, which had formerly been controlled by Romania. During the immediate post-war period these gains were consolidated, and indirect support was provided to anti-colonial movements in the Far East. The USSR therefore became established as a globally active 'Superpower' and this approach inaugurated a new East-West 'Cold War' era.

On Stalin's death in March 1953 a collective leadership, which included the CPSU's First (General) Secretary, Nikita Khrushchev, the Prime Minister, Georgi Malenkov, the Foreign Minister, Vyacheslav Molotov, as well as the First Deputy Prime Ministers, Nikolai Bulganin and Lazar Kaganovich, assumed power. They swiftly combined to remove police chief Beria, in December 1953, and proceeded to introduce a new legal code which regularised the political system. However, although agreed on the need to reform and 'humanise' the 'Stalin system', strong intra-leadership differences soon emerged over the exact emphasis and direction of new policy approaches. As a consequence, a fierce succession contest developed between 1953 and 1958.

Khrushchev emerged as the victor, succeeding in first ousting the 'anti-party' triumvirate of Malenkov, Molotov and Kaganovich, in June 1957, and then Bulganin, who had succeeded Malenkov as Prime Minister in 1955, in June 1958. Khrushchev was now able to combine the key posts of Prime Minister and CPSU First Secretary. Once installed in power, Khrushchev introduced a radical new party programme, at the twenty-second CPSU Congress of October 1961, which envisaged rapid agricultural, industrial and technological development, to enable the Soviet Union to move ahead of the United States in economic terms by 1980, and for the nation to attain full communism.

To achieve these goals, an ambitious 'virgin lands' cultivation campaign was launched in underdeveloped Kazakhstan, with the aim of swiftly boosting agricultural output. In addition, a programme of decentralised industrial management was unveiled, based on the formation of new regional economic councils (*sovnarkhozy*). Material incentives were also introduced in the rural sector.

In the political, social and diplomatic spheres, Khrushchev introduced radical new party rule changes, directed towards curbing the authority of entrenched officials (*apparatchiki*); sanctioned a cultural 'thaw'; and enunciated the new principle of 'peaceful co-existence' with the West, as a means of diverting resources away from the defence sector.

These reforms enjoyed initial success and following the explosion of its first hydrogen bomb in 1953 and the launching of a space satellite, the *Sputnik I*, in 1957, the Soviet Union appeared to be emerging for the first time as a serious technological rival to the United States. However, Khrushchev's liberalisation policy and his denunciation of the errors and crimes of the 'cult of personality' Stalin era, at the February 1956 twentieth Party Congress, had serious repercussions among the Soviet Union's East European satellites, encouraging a nationalist revolt in Hungary. A breach in relations with China also resulted and his administrative reforms were fiercely opposed by senior party and state bureaucrats.

After a series of poor harvests in overcropped Kazakhstan, workers' riots in Soviet cities and the Cuban missile crisis climbdown of 1962, opposition to Khrushchev began to coalesce, and at the Central Committee meeting of October 1964, the party leader was dismissed and forced into retirement.

A new and conservative collective leadership, centred around the figures of former state President Leonid Brezhnev, First Deputy Prime Minister Alexei Kosygin, Party Organisation Secretary Nikolai Podgorny and Party Ideology Secretary, Mikhail Suslov, assumed power. They immediately abandoned Khrushchev's *sovnarkhozy* and party reforms and re-imposed strict censorship in the cultural sphere. Priority was now given to the expansion and modernisation of the Soviet armed forces, including the creation of a naval force with a global capability. This, coupled with the Soviet invasion of Czechoslovakia, in 1968, to suppress a gathering reform movement, resulted in a renewal of the East-West 'Cold War', between 1964 and 1970.

During the later 1960s and early 1970s, Leonid Brezhnev, by inducting his supporters into the CPSU Politburo and Secretariat, slowly established himself as the dominant figure within the Soviet polity. He continued to govern, however, in a cautious and consensual manner, bringing into the Politburo, in April 1973, leaders from all the significant centres of power, including the KGB security police, in the person of Yuri Andropov, the army, Marshal Andrei Grechko, and the diplomatic service, Andrei Gromyko.

Working with Prime Minister Kosygin, Brezhnev introduced a series of minor economic reforms and gave new priority to agricultural and consumer goods production. In 1977 he oversaw the framing of a new constitution which established a settled new political system in which the limits for dissent were clearly set out and which described the state as in a stage of 'developed socialism' whose future development would rely increasingly on the technocratic use of scientific innovation.

Brezhnev, who became the new state 'President' in May 1977, emerged as an international statesman during the 1970s, frequently meeting Western leaders during what was a new era of *détente*. The landmarks of this period were the SALT-1 and SALT-2 Soviet-American arms limitation agreements of 1972 and 1979 and the Helsinki Accord of 1975, which brought Western recognition of the post-war division of Eastern Europe.

During this *détente* era there was a new cultural 'thaw' which resulted in the emergence of a vocal dissident movement, led by the nuclear physicist, Dr Andrei Sakharov. The political and military influence of the Soviet Union was also extended into Africa and the 'Horn' with the establishment of new communist-leaning governments in Angola, in 1975, Mozambique, in 1974, Ethiopia, in 1975, and South Yemen, in 1978.

The *détente* era was eventually ended, however, by the Soviet invasion of Afghanistan in December 1979 and the Polish crisis of 1980–81, ushering in a further 'cold war' era and a period of domestic repression. Sakharov, for example, was arrested and sent into internal exile in 1980.

During its final years, the Brezhnev administration, with its leader physically incapacitated by a series of strokes, and his rivals jockeying for position to succeed him, was characterised by policy sclerosis, mounting corruption and economic stagnation.

On his death, in November 1982, Yuri Andropov, a former KGB chief, was elected CPSU chairman by his Politburo colleagues. He proceeded, energetically, to introduce a series of substantive economic reforms, styled the 'enterprise management' initiative, which were aimed at streamlining and decentralising the planning system and inculcating greater labour discipline. Andropov also launched a major campaign directed against corrupt and complacent party and state bureaucrats. These measures had a perceptible impact on the Soviet economy during 1983.

The reform impetus waned, however, when Andropov died in February 1984 and was succeeded by the cautious and elderly Konstantin Chernenko, a man who had previously served as Brezhnev's political secretary and closest aide. Chernenko held power as a stop-gap leader for 13 months, his sole initiative being a renewed search for *détente* with the United States which was rejected by the hardline Reagan administration.

On Chernenko's death in March 1985, power was transferred to a new generation led by Mikhail Gorbachev, the protégé of Yuri Andropov and a former agriculture secretary, who, at the age of 54, was the CPSU's youngest leader since Stalin. Although elected on a divided Politburo vote, Gorbachev proceeded vigorously to take up the reins of reform, sharply criticising the preceding Brezhnev era. His reform prescription was three-pronged.

First, in the economic sphere, under the slogan of *perestroika*, or 'restructuring', Gorbachev began to press for a greater decentralisation of decision-taking. Farmers and factory managers were to be freed from pettifogging bureaucratic interference and there was to be an increased emphasis on material incentives, cost accounting and factory self-financing, or the *khozrachiot* system, in a 'market socialist' manner.

Second, working with CPSU Ideology Secretary Yegor Ligachev, who chaired the Secretariat, and Prime Minister Nikolai Ryzhkov, Gorbachev set about radically overhauling both the party and state bureaucracies, by replacing cautious Brezhnevite placemen with ambitious new technocrats. He also sought to make apparatchiks more accountable to their rank and file and set about creating new co-ordinating 'super-ministries'. To support these political changes, Gorbachev, under the slogan *glasnost*, or 'openness', encouraged criticism of bureaucratic inefficiencies and opened up a free discussion in the media of existing problems, reform options and previous party history. As part of this 'liberalising' process, the dissident leader, Dr Andrei Sakharov, was released from detention, in December 1986, and a commission was established to re-appraise post-1917 historical developments, including the Stalin era.

Third, Gorbachev embarked on a major '*détente* initiative' abroad in the hope of effecting an arms reduction agreement with the United States which would enable greater resources to be diverted to the civilian sector. Working with foreign minister Edvard Shevardnadze, he made skilful use of the international television media to put the Reagan administration on the defensive over the issues of space weapons and nuclear testing.

Following summit meetings held in Geneva, in November 1985, Reykjavik, in October 1986, and Washington, in December 1987, Gorbachev signed an INF (Intermediate Nuclear Forces) Treaty with the United States, designed to eliminate all medium-range nuclear missiles. As part of this *détente* process, the Soviet Union also agreed upon a phased withdrawal of its troops, numbering over 100,000, from Afghanistan, the process commencing in May 1988 and being completed in February 1989. In addition, in December 1988 Gorbachev announced a unilateral 500,000 reduction in the size of the country's armed forces within two years, including the withdrawal of 50,000 men and 5,000 tanks from Eastern Europe.

The new Soviet leader's political position was consolidated at the twenty-seventh CPSU Congress, held in March 1986, when a number of ailing Brezhnevites were ousted from the Politburo and Secretariat and 40 per cent of the party's CC was replaced. However, during 1987 and 1988, Gorbachev, who pressed for an acceleration in the reform process, including a comprehensive economic revitalisation plan, the 'New Economic Mechanism', began to encounter increasing domestic opposition. In particular, senior party colleagues, led by Yegor Ligachev, voiced their concern that the pace of change was becoming too rapid and that criticisms of past regimes, particularly the Stalin era, were too excessive. Above all, this conservative-reformist grouping argued for the maintenance of the CPSU's control over the lower levels of the state and economic apparatus and of its monopoly political status.

The grouping was opposed by a smaller, more radical faction, led by Moscow party boss Boris Yeltsin who recklessly criticised the timorous pace of reform and the 'blocking' activities of party apparatchiks at the CC meeting of November 1987. For this he was dismissed, signalling a victory for the 'Ligachev faction'.

As a means of adding momentum to the reform process, Gorbachev convened, in June 1988, a 4,991-delegate Special All-Union Party Conference, the first since 1941, at which radical new proposals were unveiled and adopted.

In the political sphere, they included, first, the introduction of inner-party democracy, based on secret multi-candidate balloting and the limitation of the tenure of all posts, including the Politburo, to a maximum of two consecutive five-year terms. Second, the enhancement of the authority of local soviets, now to be directly elected for five-year terms in multi-candidate contests, with party First Secretaries being invited to submit themselves for election as their presidents. Third was a restriction of the CPSU to an ideological and longer-term planning role and the freeing of state bodies from detailed control. Fourth, the creation, in 1989, of a third 750-member chamber of the Supreme Soviet, elected by various public bodies, including the CPSU, Komsomol and other mass organisations. This would form part of a new 2,250-deputy 'Congress of the USSR People's Deputies' (CUPD) which would elect a bicameral Supreme Soviet to operate as a permanently sitting legislative body, equipped with specialist commissions and headed by a French-style executive President.

In the economic sphere, the adopted resolutions included plans to re-introduce private leasehold agriculture, encourage private enterprise in the service and small-scale industry sectors and reform fundamentally the price system to reflect more accurately demand and supply conditions.

The resolutions adopted in June 1988 constituted potentially the most fundamental re-ordering of the Soviet polity and society since the 'Stalinist departure' of 1928. Gorbachev's aim was to introduce a new system of 'socialist democracy', based on encouraging greater political accountability and competition for office, albeit within CPSU-confined lines. However, the proposals remained controversial, being fiercely opposed locally by traditionalist apparatchiks and, at the centre, by the 'Ligachev faction'.

The eruption of serious nationalist challenges to the administration in Kazakhstan, the Baltic Republics, Armenia-Azerbaijan, Georgia and Uzbekistan, the Nagorny Karabakh dispute, and the continuing sluggish performance of the economy between 1987 and 1988 appeared to strengthen the position of these opposition forces and imperil the Gorbachev 'reform experiment'. However, at an extraordinary CC Plenum and Supreme Soviet session held in September-October 1988, Gorbachev struck back, ousting several 'old guard' members from the Politburo, moving to new posts his conservative opponents Yegor Ligachev and Viktor Chebrikov, the former KGB chief, and assuming for himself, from the retiring Andrei Gromyko, the position of head of state.

Gorbachev's position was further strengthened in March 1989 by the elections to the new CUPD, in which public opposition to conservative apparatchiks was clearly visible. A month later, in April 1989, a purge of 'old guard' members of the CPSU CC was successfully accomplished, with 110 senior figures, including former head of state Andrei Gromyko and former Prime Minister Nikolai Tikhonov, being persuaded to step down. They were replaced by 24 rising technocrats, with the overall size of the body being reduced to 251 full members. In the following month, May 1989, the CUPD convened for its inaugural session and elected Gorbachev, unopposed, to the newly created position of executive President.

Table 53

POST-WAR POLITICAL LEADERS OF THE SOVIET UNION

Head of the CPSU		*Prime Minister*	
Josef Stalin	1946–53	Josef Stalin	1946–53
Georgi Malenkov	1953–53	Georgi Malenkov	1953–55
Nikita Khrushchev	1953–64	Nikolai Bulganin	1955–58
Leonid Brezhnev	1964–82	Nikita Khrushchev	1958–64
Yuri Andropov	1982–84	Alexei Kosygin	1964–80
Konstantin Chernenko	1984–85	Nikolai Tikhonov	1980–85
Mikhail Gorbachev	1985–	Nikolai Ryzhkov	1985–

Head of State		*Head of State**	
Nikolai Shvernik	1946–53	Yuri Andropov	1983–84
Klimentiy Voroshilov	1953–60	Vasily Kuznetsov†	1984–84
Leonid Brezhnev	1960–64	Konstantin Chernenko	1984–85
Anastas Mikoyan	1964–65	Vasily Kuznetsov†	1985–85
Nikolai Podgorny	1965–77	Andrei Gromyko	1985–88
Leonid Brezhnev	1977–82	Mikhail Gorbachev	1988–
Vasily Kuznetsov†	1982–83		

*Chairman of the Presidium of the Supreme Soviet.
†Temporary acting head of state (Kuznetsov was First Deputy Chairman of the Presidium).

Table 54

THE CPSU POLITBURO IN OCTOBER 1988

Full Members	
General Viktor Chebrikov	Vladimir Shcherbitsky
Mikhail Gorbachev	Edvard Shevardnadze
Yegor Ligachev	Nikolai Slyunkov
Vadim Medvedev	Vitali Vorotnikov
Viktor Nikonov	Aleksandr Yakovlev
Nikolai Ryzhkov	Lev Zaikov

Candidate Members	
Aleksandra Biryukova	Yury Solovev
Anatoly Lukyanov	Nikolai Talyzin
Yury Maslyukov	Aleksandr Vlasov
Georgy Razumovsky	Dmitri Yazov

YUGOSLAVIA

Socialist Federal Republic of Yugoslavia
Socijalisticka Federativna Republika Jugoslavija

Capital: Belgrade

Social and economic data
Area: 255,800 km^2
Population: 23.200m*
Pop density per km^2: 91*
Literacy rate: 90%*
GDP: $46,000m*; per capita GDP: $1,983
Economy type: middle income
Labour force in agriculture: 29%

*1985

Ethnic composition
Yugoslavia consists of a patchwork of contending, regionally based, ethnic communities, with differing histories, religions, languages and social customs and at differing levels of prosperity and development.

Serbs comprise 36 per cent of the total population, Croats 20 per cent, Slovenes 8 per cent, Macedonians 6 per cent and Albanians 8 per cent. The four first groupings are of 'Southern Slav' stock. Their regional distribution is set out in Table 55, below. Albanians are concentrated in the poor south-east, Slovenes in the richer, and more politically liberal, extreme north-west, Croats in the adjoining north-west, Macedonians in the far south-east, Montenegrins in the central south and Serbs are more widely dispersed throughout the central area.

Muslims comprise about 9 per cent of the total population and, as such, constitute an important ethnic community in the central south. Hungarians, who amount to about 2 per cent, are found around Vojvodina, in the central north, and 'Yugoslavs', numbering about 5 per cent, in the centre.

Serbo-Croat is spoken by Croats, Montenegrins, Serbs and Bosnian-Muslims, with Macedonian and Slovenian constituting the other official languages.

Table 55

THE REGIONAL DISTRIBUTION OF YUGOSLAVIA'S ETHNIC COMMUNITIES

Republic/ Auton Prov	*Pop (m) (1985)*	*Albanians*	*Croats*	*Macedonians*	*Montenegrins*	*Muslims*	*Serbs*	*Slovenes*
			(As % of Republic and Autonomous Province populations)					
Bosnia-Herzegovina (R)	4.280	0.1	18.4	0.1	0.3	39.5	32.0	0.1
Croatia (R)	4.760	0.1	75.1	0.1	0.2	0.5	11.6	0.6
Macedonia (R)	1.920	19.8	0.2	67.0	0.2	2.1	2.3	0.0
Montenegro (R)	0.610	6.5	1.2	0.0	68.5	13.4	3.3	0.0
Serbia (R)*	5.890	1.3	0.6	0.5	1.4	2.7	85.4	0.1
Slovenia (R)	1.980	0.1	2.9	0.2	0.2	0.7	2.2	90.5
Kosovo (AP)	1.645	77.4	0.6	0.1	1.7	3.7	13.2	0.0
Vojvodina (AP)	2.115	0.2	5.4	0.9	2.1	0.2	54.4	0.2
Yugoslavia	23.200	7.7	19.7	6.0	2.6	8.9	36.3	7.8

*Excluding Kosovo and Vojvodina 'autonomous provinces'.

Religions

Forty-three per cent of the population, mainly in Serbia and Montenegro, are adherents to the Serbian Orthodox faith; 15 per cent, principally in the south-east and central south, follow Islamic beliefs; 32 per cent, largely in Croatia and Slovenia in the north-west, are Roman Catholics; and 1 per cent are Protestants. Church and state are separated under the constitution.

Political features

State type: communist
Date of state formation: 1918
Political structure: federal
Executive: communist
Assembly: two-chamber
Party structure: one-party
Human rights rating: 50%

Local and regional government

Within the six republics and two autonomous provinces, the country is divided into 527 communes. Each commune has its own three-chamber assembly consisting of about 100 members who are elected indirectly by local communities and 'basic organisations' below them.

Head of state

President Janez Drnovsek, since May 1989.

Head of government

Prime Minister Ante Markovic, since 1988.

Political leaders since 1970*

1944–80 Marshal Tito (SKJ), 1980 Doronjski (SKJ:Vojvodina), 1980–81 Lazar Mojsov (SKJ: Macedonia), 1981–82 Dusan Dragosavac (SKJ:Croatia), 1982–83 Mitja Ribicic (SKJ:Slovenia), 1983–84 Dragoslav Markovic (SKJ:Serbia), 1984–85 Ali Sukrija (SKJ:Kosovo), 1985–86 Vidoje Zarkovic (SKJ:Montenegro), 1986–87 Milanko Renovica (SKJ:Bosnia-Herzegovina), 1987–88 Bosko Krunic (SKJ: Vojvodina), 1988–89 Stipe Suvar (SKJ: Croatia)†, 1989– Milan Pancevski (SKJ: Macedonia).

*Communist Party leader
†There has been an annually rotating leadership since 1980

Political system

The country's first communist constitution was adopted in January 1946. It was modelled on the Soviet Union's 1936 'Stalin Constitution', describing its type of government as a 'people's democracy' and establishing a federation of six republics. In January 1953, following Yugoslavia's 'break' from the Soviet Union, a new revised constitution was adopted, establishing the executive post of President of the Republic, which was to be occupied by Marshal Tito, and introducing the principle of 'self-management'. A third, 'liberal', constitution, adopted in April 1963, changed the country's designation from 'Federative People's Republic' to 'Socialist Federal Republic' and established a complex five-chamber assembly. A fourth, substantially revised, 406-article constitution was adopted in February 1974. This, following amendments in 1967, 1968 and 1971, strengthened the federal structure, encouraging the devolution of power in a participatory manner through a system of workers' self-management and tiered decision-making processes, and introduced a complicated indirect electoral system. Eight amendments were promulgated in 1981, following Tito's death, formally regulating the system of collective, rotating leadership which had been operative since the early 1970s.

Under the 1974 constitution, as amended, Yugoslavia is a federal republic consisting of six 'socialist republics', Bosnia-Herzegovina, Croatia, Macedonia, Montenegro, Serbia and Slovenia, and two 'socialist autonomous provinces', Kosovo and Vojvodina, both of which lie within Serbia. Each republic and autonomous province has its own legislative assembly, divided into three chambers, the Chamber of Associated Labour, the Chamber of Communes and the Socio-Political Chamber. Members are indirectly elected for a four-year term by Commune Assemblies at a lower level. At the head of each assembly are an executive council and collective presidency.

The Federal Republic has a two-chamber Federal Assembly (Savezna Skupstina), consisting of the 220-member Federal Chamber (Savezno Vece) and 88-member Chamber of Republics and Provinces (Vece Republika i Prokrajina). Federal Assembly members are indirectly elected every four years in a tiered manner by Commune and Republican or Provincial Assemblies below. The process begins with each workplace or self-managing organisation initially choosing a delegate to serve on a higher level delegation. This in turn selects candidates to serve on bodies above. These delegates are ordinary workers who remain in their traditional employment throughout their terms of office. Terms can only be renewed once successively. The lowest level of delegations comprise 680,000 delegates, the Commune Assembly level, 50,000, and the Republican and Provincial Assembly level, 2,028.

The electoral process extends over four to five months. For Federal Chamber elections, each constituent republic is assigned 30 delegates and each autonomous province 20 and elections are held at the Commune Assembly level. For the Chamber of Republics and Provinces, the delegate quotas are twelve and eight respectively. Elections are also held at the Republic and Autonomous Province Assembly level.

The Federal Assembly convenes in plenary sessions several times a year and serves as a vigorous debating forum. The Federal Chamber has primary responsibility for 'laying down the fundamentals of internal and foreign policy' and ratifying international treaties, decisions being taken by majority vote. The Chamber of Republics and Provinces is responsible for formulating economic and social plans, as well as the federal budget, its members sitting and voting in regional, republic and autonomous province delegations.

The two federal chambers jointly elect, by secret ballot, the executive branch of government, which, since Tito's death in May 1980, has been a nine-member Collective State Presidency (CSP), consisting, *ex officio*, of the head of the Communist Party (League of Communists of Yugoslavia: SKJ), as well as a representative from each constituent republic and autonomous province. The Presidency's members serve for five-year terms, with titular leadership of the body rotating annually in a fixed sequence of republics and provinces. Following the constitutional amendments of 1981, no one may be elected more than twice in succession to the CSP.

Day-to-day administration is carried out by the 18-member Federal Executive Council, which is headed by a President, who functions as *de facto* Prime Minister. The Council includes two Vice-Presidents, three 'members without portfolio', drawn variously from the republics, and twelve federal departmental secretaries. Members are elected by the Federal Assembly for four-year terms which can be renewed once. The President's term is non-renewable and his successor must each time come from a different republic or autonomous province.

The Yugoslav federal system, in contrast to that of communist Czechoslovakia and the USSR, is a functioning reality, substantive power being held by the republics and autonomous provinces. The latter have exclusive jurisdiction in the fields of education, health, welfare, research, sport and mass communications, as well as in local socio-economic planning.

The federal government has responsibility for foreign, defence and financial and monetary affairs. Decisions which require the participation of the regions can be taken by the Assembly only after an unanimous vote by all delegations in the Chamber of Republics and Provinces, giving this body effective veto rights. Below the republics and automonous provinces, 'self-managing' communes and 'basic organisations' also have scope for separate initiatives.

Nevertheless, despite the decentralised and participatory character of the Yugoslav polity, ultimate, *de facto*, control is exercised by the SKJ, the sole permitted political party. Under the constitution of 1974, the SKJ is assigned a 'leading role', supervising political activity through the 14-million-strong Socialist Alliance of the Working People of Yugoslavia (SSRNJ) mass movement. This is a body which incorporates a variety of economic and social organisations, equivalent to interest groups, and has the task of screening the selection of assembly candidates. Restrictions placed on joint party and state office holding in recent years have, however, begun to undermine the SKJ's monopoly control.

Political parties

The ruling League of Communists of Yugoslavia (SKJ) was founded in April 1919 under the title the Socialist Workers' Party of Yugoslavia (SWPY) by a union of socialist organisations based in Serbia, Croatia, Slovenia and Bosnia. With a membership of 60,000, it changed its name to the Communist Party of Yugoslavia (CPY), in June 1920, and in the Yugoslav Constituent Assembly elections of that year emerged as the third largest grouping, capturing 200,000 votes and 59 seats.

A year later it was banned and forced underground, its membership dwindling to several hundred during the early 1930s. The Croatian-born Josip Broz (Tito) assumed the party's leadership in 1937, and began building up its membership. He later developed it into a popular 'Partisan', anti-Nazi, liberation force during the Second World War, so that it was eventually able to assume power in November 1943. The designation SKJ was adopted in 1952 to symbolise its alignment on a new, non Soviet-linked, socialist course.

The party is organised hierarchically on Leninist 'democratic centralist' lines. At its base there are more than 65,000 'basic organisations' established among local self-management units. Higher up, the SKJ has commune organisations electing, above that, republican and autonomous province congresses. The supreme authority is the National Congress which meets and is 'elected' every four years. This body, with about 2,000 members, adopts a party programme and 'elects' a Central Committee (CC) to assume its responsibilities in its absence.

At the most recent, thirteenth, SKJ National Congress, which was held in June 1986, a 165-member CC was 'elected'. One hundred and twenty-seven, or 77 per cent, of the members were newcomers. They had previously been proposed, 15–20 each, by SKJ republic, autonomous province and army congresses which had been held several months beforehand.

The CC meets three times a year and elects a Presidium (Politburo), currently with 23 members, to direct party and state affairs. The Presidium is a collective body, whose leadership rotates annually. It consists of three members from each republic and two from each autonomous province. These automatically include the party President of each republic and autonomous province, as well as the President of the party's army organisation. The Presidium, in turn, appoints a ten-member Secretariat to function as its administrative and policy-making support wing. Secretariat members serve four-year terms and the position of head Secretary rotates annually.

Membership of the SKJ in 1987 stood at 2.10 million, which figure corresponds to 9.1 per cent of the total population. This constitutes a considerable advance on the 1945 and 1962 totals of 140,000 and 1.04 million respectively, but is below the 1984 figure of 2.5 million.

Twenty-nine per cent of the membership are blue-collar workers, 41 per cent white-collar and 16 per cent farmers. Fifty per cent are Serbs and 20 per cent are women. Some 3.8 million, between the ages of 15 and 27, are also members of the party's 'youth' wing, the League of Socialist Youth of Yugoslavia (SSOJ). The distinctive feature of all SKJ organs is their strongly regionalised character, with antipathetic republican factions having emerged during recent decades. This has tended to undermine the party's 'democratic centralist' cohesion.

Latest elections

The most recent Skupstina elections were held in 1986, taking place in four, monthly, stages. Candidate choice was permitted, subject to SSRNJ screening.

Political history

Formerly under Roman rule, during the early medieval period the contemporary republics of Yugoslavia existed as substantially independent entities. The kingdom of Serbia was the most important, being the nucleus of an extensive Balkan empire during the fourteenth century. From the late fourteenth to the mid-fifteenth centuries much of eastern, southern and central Yugoslavia, Bosnia-Herzegovina, Macedonia and Serbia, was conquered by Turks and incorporated into the Ottoman Empire. Mountainous Montenegro was an exception and survived as a sovereign principality. During this period north-western Yugoslavia, consisting of the republics of Croatia and Slovenia, became part of the Austro-Hungarian Habsburg Empire. They were to enjoy, however, a greater measure of political autonomy than the Turk lands.

Uprisings against Turkish rule in the early nineteenth century won Serbia a similar degree of autonomy, before full independence was achieved in 1878. The new kingdom of Serbia proceeded to enlarge its territory, at the expense of Turkey and Bulgaria, during the Balkan Wars of 1912–13. However, it was not until December 1918, following the collapse of the Austro-Hungarian Empire, that Croatia and Slovenia were 'liberated' from foreign control. A new 'Kingdom of the Serbs, Croats and Slovenes' now came into existence, with the Serbian Peter Karageorgevic, Peter I, assuming its leadership, as a constitutional monarch, and working with an elected legislative assembly. Montenegro joined the union after its citizens had voted for the deposition of their own ruler, King Nicholas.

Peter I died in August 1921 and was succeeded by his son and regent, Alexander, who renamed the country Yugoslavia, or 'Nation of the Southern Slavs'. Faced with opposition from Croatian federalists at home and from the Italians abroad, in January 1929 he established a Serbian-dominated military dictatorship. The country remained backward during this period, with more than three-quarters of the population dependent on agricultural activities.

Alexander I was assassinated in October 1934 in Marseilles by a Macedonian with Croatian dissident links. His young son, Peter II, succeeded him and a regency under the boy's uncle, Paul, was set up and came under increasing influence from Nazi Germany and Italy. The regency was briefly overthrown in a coup by pro-Allied air force officers in March 1941, precipitating a successful invasion by German troops. Peter II fled to safety in England, while two guerrilla groups began resistance activities. One was the pro-royalist, Serbian-based Chetniks, or 'Army of the Fatherland', led by General Draza Mihailovic, and the other the communist Partisans, or 'National Liberation Army', led by Josip Broz, later to be known as Marshal Tito.

The communist partisans, comprising, towards the end of the war, 800,000 men, gained the upper hand in their struggle with the Axis forces and at liberated Jajce, in Bosnia, Tito established a provisional government, called the 'Executive Committee of National Liberation', in November 1943. Two years later, in November 1945, following the expulsion, with only limited Soviet assistance, of the remaining German forces, a new Yugoslav Federal People's Republic was proclaimed.

Following Constituent Assembly elections based on a single list of candidates for the communist-dominated People's Front, a new Soviet-style federal constitution was adopted, in January 1946, which established the dominance of the CPY and during the succeeding years remaining royalist opposition was expunged. Although at first closely linked with the USSR, Tito objected to Soviet 'hegemonism', broke with Stalin in 1948 and proceeded to introduce his own independent brand of communism. This was given shape in the Constitutional Law of January 1953, which established the framework of a more liberal and decentralised system, based on the concept of workers' self-management and supported the notion of private farming. As a result, today 85 per cent of Yugoslavia's cropped area is privately tilled. Having established himself as the clearly dominant force in the Yugoslav polity, Tito also assumed the newly created post of President of the Republic, in 1953. This was a position which he was to hold until his death in May 1980.

In foreign affairs, the country, which had been expelled from Cominform in June 1948 and which remained outside the Warsaw Treaty Organisation and Comecon, sought to establish for itself an intermediate position between East and West, playing a leading role in the creation of the non-aligned movement, in 1961.

Domestically, the nation endured continuing regional discontent, particularly in Croatia, where a violent separatist movement gained ground in the 1960s and early 1970s. To deal with these problems, Tito initially encouraged further decentralisation and devolution of power to the constituent republics in amendments to the constitution which were introduced between 1966 and 1968. In addition, a system of collective leadership and a regular rotation of office posts was introduced in July 1971, in an effort to prevent the emergence of regional cliques. Partial corrective recentralisation was, however, a feature of the February 1974 constitution.

On Tito's death in May 1980 the position of executive President, which he had been accorded for life under the terms of the 1974 constitution, was effectively abolished and a collective and rotating presidential leadership assumed power instead. However, this new collective leadership, lacking a dominant 'guiding hand' personality at its head, became subject to internal cleavages, resulting in fudged policy paralysis, and confused demarcation lines emerging between differing federal and republican executive bodies.

In these circumstances, there has been a recrudescence of regionalist conflict, with a serious popular movement emerging in 1981–82 among the

Albanians of Kosovo autonomous province who campaigned for full republican status. These demonstrations had to be suppressed by the armed forces. In Bosnia-Herzegovina and Croatia, unrest emerged among the Muslim and Catholic communities respectively during the mid-1980s. This regionalist discontent has been aggravated by a general decline in living standards since 1980, caused by a mounting level of foreign debt, whose servicing now absorbs 10 per cent of GDP, and a spiralling inflation rate, which reached 200 per cent in 1988.

In 1987–88, the federal government, under the leadership of Prime Minister Branko Mikulic, a Bosnian, introduced a radical 'market socialist' package, in an effort to restructure the economy. This involved the freeing of prices and wages from residual controls, the introduction of a federal value-added tax (VAT) and a new bankruptcy law. The private sector was extended further and foreign 'inward investment', in special free-trade zones, encouraged. There was also a general switch towards an 'indicative', rather than central, planning system. The short-term consequence of this programme has, however, been an austerity wage freeze, sparking off a wave of industrial strikes, a rise in the unemployment level to above one million, or 15 per cent of the work force, and an unprecedented parliamentary vote-of-confidence challenge to the Mikulic government.

In the political sphere, constitutional amendment proposals were put forward by the Federal Presidency in 1988, aimed at enhancing the federal government's authority and abolishing the right of veto enjoyed by republican and provincial assemblies. In addition, an emergency 'Extraordinary Party Conference' was convened in May 1988, in an effort to formulate fresh solutions to the economic and political crisis. At this meeting, the system of regional rotation employed for filling the top party post was temporarily abandoned, and the new leader, Stipe Suvar, elected in a competitive ballot. The party remained acutely divided, however, between regionally based liberal, Slovenian, and conservative, Serbian, wings on the questions of decentralisation and democratisation.

The most significant recent development has been the emergence of a potential new national 'strongman' (*vozhd*) in the form of the SKJ's Serbian party leader, Slobodan Milosevic. He is a populist hardliner who has lent his support to a grassroots campaign to terminate Kosovo and Vojvodina's autonomous province status and fully integrate the regions within Serbia. These aims were substantially secured in March 1989 when the Vojvodina and Kosovo assemblies, following Serbian pressure, endorsed earlier changes to the Serbian constitution which served to return control over their defence, state security, foreign relations, justice and planning to Serbia. These actions immediately triggered a wave of violent ethnic riots in Kosovo which claimed at least 29 lives. In addition, Milosevic has been seen to have been behind street protests in Titograd in October 1988 which forced the resignation of the entire state and party leadership of the Montenegro republic and its replacement with pro-Serbian cadres. His Serbian nationalist stance and conservative policy prescriptions are firmly opposed, however, by the north-western republics of Croatia and Slovenia.

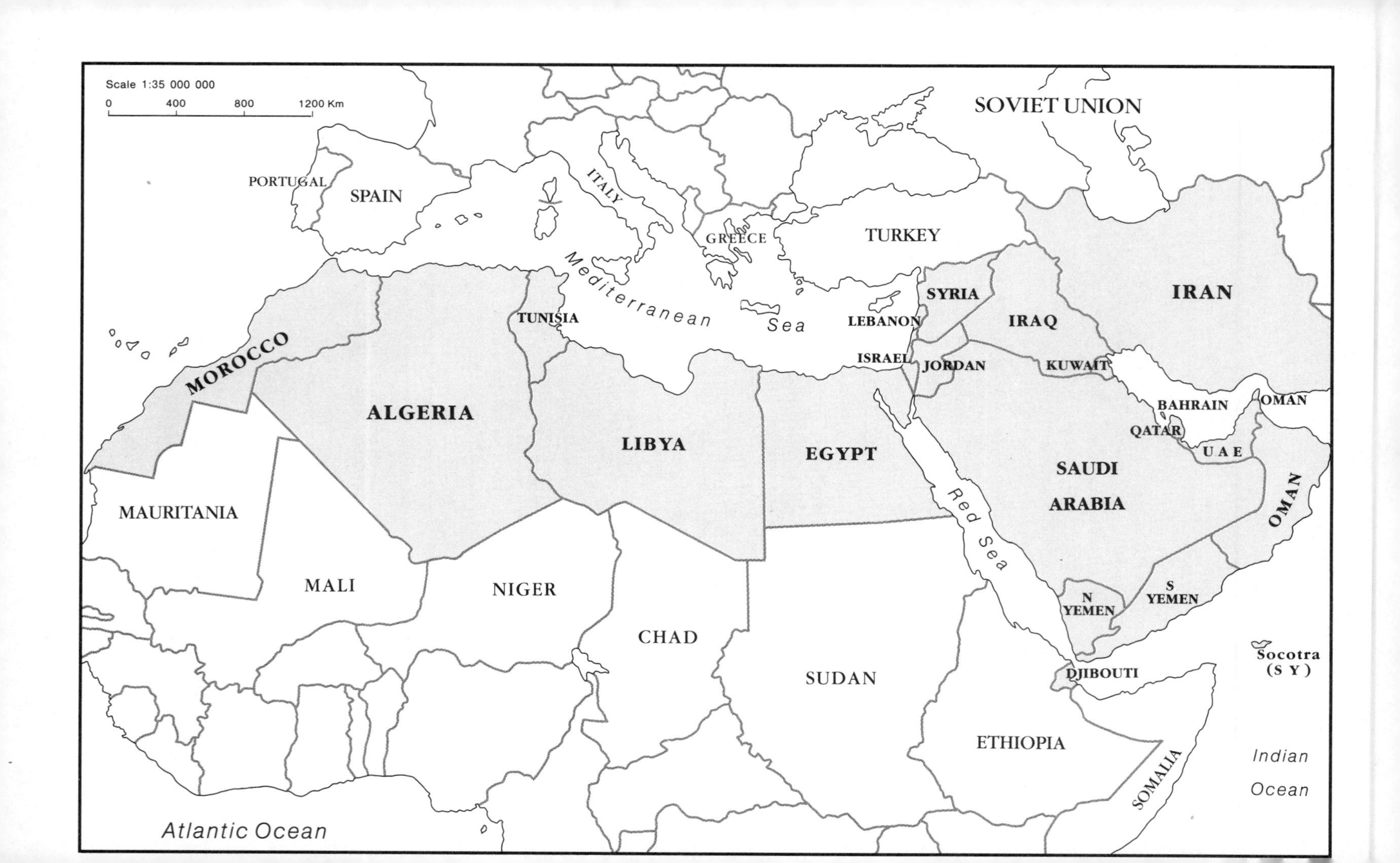
Scale 1:35 000 000
0
400
800
1200 Km
SOVIET UNION
PORTUGAL
SPAIN
ITALY
GREECE
TURKEY
Mediterranean
Sea
SYRIA
IRAN
TUNISIA
LEBANON
IRAQ
ISRAEL
JORDAN
KUWAIT
MOROCCO
ALGERIA
LIBYA
EGYPT
BAHRAIN
OMAN
QATAR
U A E
SAUDI
ARABIA
OMAN
Red Sea
MAURITANIA
MALI
NIGER
CHAD
N
YEMEN
S
YEMEN
Socotra
(S Y)
SUDAN
DJIBOUTI
ETHIOPIA
SOMALIA
Indian
Ocean
Atlantic Ocean

THE MIDDLE EAST AND NORTH AFRICA

This region extends from the Mediterranean Sea in the north to the Arabian Sea and the Tropic of Cancer in the south and from the Atlantic Ocean in the west to the borders of Afghanistan and Pakistan in the east. It is mostly desert country, with climatic conditions associated with this kind of terrain and is traditionally the home of the nomad, who was forced into that way of life in a search for vegetation. It is also, of course, with the notable exception of Israel, the land of the Arab. Indeed, the whole region is often referred to as the Arab World. The total population of the region is in excess of 217 million and is thinly dispersed over an area of more than eleven million square kilometres.

Islam is the dominant religion and is officially decreed as such in 15 of the 20 states. The kingdom of Saudi Arabia lies at the heart of this Islamic domain, housing the two cities most revered by Muslims, Mecca and Medina. In contrast, Israel is the home of Judaism, despite the presence of more than half a million Muslims. The other state in the region where a substantial number of its citizens do not follow Islamic codes is Lebanon, which has a Maronite Christian minority of nearly a million.

The Jewish question, of whether Israel can co-exist with its Arab neighbours, has been at the heart of politics in this part of the world for more than 70 years, and for much of that time it was associated with the British and French presence in the Middle East.

After the First World War, Britain, as one of the victors, was given control, by the League of Nations, of Iraq, Palestine and Transjordan while France, as the other major European victor, acquired responsibility for Lebanon and Syria. The two European powers colluded in extending their control of the region, Britain taking Egypt under its protection and then, by a series of treaties with the ruling monarchs, most of the states in the Persian Gulf. Only Saudi Arabia retained its independence, under the skilful guidance of King Ibn Saud. France, in turn, took control of Morocco, Algeria and Tunisia.

Meanwhile, Britain, while fulfilling its pledge to free the Arabs from Turkish rule, also promised, through the declaration by Foreign Secretary Arthur Balfour in 1917, to establish in Palestine a 'National Home for the Jewish people'. This resulted in an increase in Jewish immigration during the 1920s and 1930s, in the face of growing Arab opposition. Even though the Balfour Declaration had been made, Britain, largely out of self-interest, tended to side with the Arab states, but the holocaust in Nazi Germany created such worldwide sympathy for the Jewish cause that it became impossible for anyone to resist the demands for an independent state of Israel. The rest of the account of the relations between Jews and Arabs is given in the political histories of the countries involved. It has been partly recounted at this stage because the current political situation in the region cannot be properly understood if this aspect of its history is overlooked.

In economic terms the Middle East and North Africa constitute a relatively wealthy region, but that wealth is unevenly distributed. Bahrain, Israel, Kuwait, Libya, Oman, Qatar, Saudi Arabia and the United Arab Emirates all enjoy high per capita incomes, some comparable to, or better than, those of West European states. The average citizen of Bahrain, Kuwait, Qatar and the United Arab Emirates, for example, enjoys a higher living standard than his opposite number in the United Kingdom or Austria. At the other extreme, Egypt, Jordan, Lebanon, Morocco and North and South Yemen have low-income economies, with Algeria, Djibouti, Iran, Iraq, Syria and Tunisia all falling into the middle-income bracket. The wealth of most of the wealthiest countries has been derived from oil, while Israel has maintained its living standards through industry and enterprise, plus substantial subsidies from its friends in the Western world, notably in the USA.

The comparatively high literacy rates in some of the richest states are a reflection of the generous, if paternalistic, way in which their rulers have invested their wealth in education and social services. On the other hand, there are other countries in the region where more than three-quarters of the population are illiterate, and in a minority of states, as many as nine out of every ten inhabitants. It is difficult to obtain an accurate picture of the degree of civil liberties enjoyed in some countries, particularly the absolutist states. but, with some few exceptions, human rights ratings over the region are not good.

The political systems of the 20 states, as shown in Table 56, fairly accurately reflect their respective cultures and histories. Seven have absolutist regimes and these can be mostly traced back to Islamic traditions and a long acceptance of monarchical rule. Five have been classified as nationalistic socialist systems, most of which were created as a reaction to domination by a European power and the need to establish a national, independent identity. The same may be said of the three states with authoritarian nationalist regimes.

Five states can be said to have democratic systems, that of Israel being now well established but the other four of more recent origin. Egypt has had a pluralist political system since 1970, Tunisia since 1967 and Morocco since 1972, while Lebanon has struggled to maintain some semblance of democratic government since 1980, with internecine struggles always threatening to destroy it.

After the ceasefire in the Iran-Iraq war, there is a chance of peace returning to this troubled region but Israel, and its relations with the Arab world, remains the key to long-lasting stability. There have been positive moves from the Arab side, and particularly the Palestine Liberation Organisation, but the Israeli response has been cautious and sceptical. Much may now depend upon the efforts of a revitalised United Nations Organisation.

Table 56

MIDDLE EAST AND NORTH AFRICA

Political Data

State	*Date of Formation*	*Political Structure*	*State Type*	*Executive*	*Assembly No of Chambers*	*Party System*	*Voting System*
Algeria	1962	Unitary	Nat Soc	Unlim Pres	One	One	SP
Bahrain	1971	Unitary	Absolutist	Absolute	None	None	None
Djibouti	1977	Unitary	Auth Nat	Unlim Pres	One	One	SP
Egypt	1922	Unitary	Emgt Dem	Lim Pres	One	Two	SB

Table 56—Middle East and North Africa (contd.)

			Political Data				
State	*Date of Formation*	*Political Structure*	*State Type*	*Executive*	*Assembly No of Chambers*	*Party System*	*Voting System*
Iran	1499	Unitary	Auth Nat	Unlim Pres	One	One	SB
Iraq	1932	Unitary	Nat Soc	Unlim Pres	One	One	SP
Israel	1948	Unitary	Lib Dem	Parliament	One	Multi	PL
Jordan	1946	Unitary	Absolutist	Absolute	Two	None	None
Kuwait	1961	Unitary	Absolutist	Absolute	None	None	None
Lebanon	1944	Unitary	Emgt Dem	Dual	One	Multi	PL
Libya	1951	Unitary	Nat Soc	Unlim Pres	One	One	SP
Morocco	1956	Unitary	Emgt Dem	Dual	One	Multi	SP
Oman	1951	Unitary	Absolutist	Absolute	None	None	None
Qatar	1971	Unitary	Absolutist	Absolute	None	None	None
Saudi Arabia	1932	Unitary	Absolutist	Absolute	None	None	None
Syria	1946	Unitary	Nat Soc	Unlim Pres	One	One	SP
Tunisia	1956	Unitary	Emgt Dem	Lim Pres	One	One	SP
United Arab Emirates	1971	Federal	Absolutist	Absolute	None	None	None
North Yemen	1918	Unitary	Auth Nat	Unlim Pres	One	None	None
South Yemen	1967	Unitary	Nat Soc	Unlim Pres	One	One	SP

		Social and Economic Data				
State	*Area (km²)*	*Population (m) (1985)*	*Population Density (per km²)*	*Literacy Rate (%)*	*Income Type*	*Human Rights Rating (%)*
Algeria	2,381,750	22.972	10	45	Middle	54
Bahrain	620	0.442	713	70	High	N/A
Djibouti	23,390	0.300	13	12	Middle	N/A
Egypt	1,001,500	50.500	50	38	Low	59
Iran	1,648,000	46.600	28	37	Middle	Bad
Iraq	444,000	16.278	37	43	Middle	19
Israel	20,700	4.208	203	92	High	74
Jordan	98,000	3.515	36	6	Low	Poor
Kuwait	19,000	1.771	93	68	High	49
Lebanon	10,400	2.700	260	68	Low	N/A
Libya	1,759,540	3.900	2	39	High	23
Morocco	458,730	23.700	52	21	Low	52
Oman	212,000	1.271	6	38	High	N/A
Qatar	11,440	0.305	27	51	High	N/A
Saudi Arabia	2,150,000	11.519	5	25	High	28
Syria	185,180	10.535	57	40	Middle	29
Tunisia	164,150	7.260	44	47	Middle	60
United Arab Emirates	83,600	1.326	16	54	High	N/A
North Yemen	195,000	6.300	32	9	Low	Bad
South Yemen	336,570	2.300	7	27	Low	Bad
Total/Average	11,203,570	217.702	19	6-92	Middle	19-74

ALGERIA

Democratic and Popular Republic of Algeria
Al-Jumhuriya Al-Jazairiya

Capital: Algiers (al-Jazair)

Social and Economic Data
Area: 2,381,750 km^2
Population: 22.972m*
Pop density per km^2: 10*
Literacy rate: 45%
GDP: $55,000m*; per capita GDP: $2,394
Economic type: middle income
Labour force in agriculture: 30%

*1985

Ethnic composition
Ninety-nine per cent of the population are of Arab-Berber origins, the rest being of European extraction, mainly French.

Religions
Islam is the state religion and 99 per cent of the population are Sunni Muslims.

Political features
State type: nationalistic socialist
Date of state formation: 1962
Political structure: unitary
Executive: unlimited presidential
Assembly: one-chamber
Party structure: one-party
Human rights rating: 54%

Local and regional government
Revealing a combination of French and Arab influence, the country is divided into 31 departments (*wilaya*), ranging in population from 2 million to less than 65,000, which are further subdivided into communes (*daira*). Each department and commune has an elected assembly. These assemblies are under the direct supervision of the Minister of the Interior, who appoints administrative governors (*wali*).

Head of state and head of government
President Benjedid Chadli, since 1979.

Political leaders since 1970
1965–79 Houari Boumédienne (Military), 1979– Benjedid Chadli (FLN).

Political system
The current constitution was adopted in 1976 and amended in 1979. It created a socialist Islamic republic with the National Liberation Front

(FLN) as the only legally permitted political party. FLN nominates the President, who is then elected by popular vote for a five-year term. He, in turn, chooses the Prime Minister and a Council of Ministers and is the effective head of government as well as head of state. There is a single-chamber, National People's Assembly of 295 deputies, all nominees of FLN, elected for a five-year term, by a simple plurality voting system. In February 1989 a referendum on a new constitution, allowing for pluralist politics, resulted in overwhelming support for change.

Political parties

From a number of radical Muslim organisations which were started from the 1920s onwards, calling for the expulsion of France from Algeria, there developed a young socialist group who in 1954 formed the National Liberation Front (FLN), with a military wing, the National Army of Liberation (ALN). When full independence from France was obtained in 1962 the FLN became the only legal party. Some of the more radical figures in the independence movement had been imprisoned in France and one of them, Ahmed Ben Bella, returned to Algeria to take over the leadership of the party and become the country's first President. FLN now has a mass membership with a number of groups within it representing, for example, women and young people. Its orientation is socialist, nationalist and Islamic. The party's role in government was weakened after the military coup of 1965 but to some extent restored in 1978 when a civilian administration returned. If a new constitution is adopted, the FLN is expected to break up into separate socialist and liberal tendencies.

Latest elections

In the 1987 elections for the National People's Assembly voters were given the choice from three candidates, all FLN nominees, for each seat. The turnout was 87 per cent of the electorate.

Political history

Algeria was conquered by the French in the 1830s and soon became one of France's major colonies. French nationals were encouraged to settle there and become permanent residents, enjoying greater economic and political power than the local Muslim inhabitants. Unlike most of France's other overseas possessions, however, Algeria was regarded as an extension and part of mainland France. The disparity between the rights of the European minority and the Arab majority led to a bitter war for independence, led by FLN, in 1954. Under considerable international pressure, the French President, Charles de Gaulle, in 1959, accepted the principle of national self-determination for Algeria and full indpendence was eventually achieved in 1962. The following year a one-party republic was created with Ahmed Ben Bella as its first President.

In 1965 a military group, led by Colonel Houari Boumédienne, deposed Ben Bella, suspended the constitution and ruled through a Revolutionary Council. In 1976 a new constitution, confirming Algeria as an Islamic, socialist, one-party state, was approved. Boumédienne died in 1978 after a long illness and there was a smooth transfer of power to Benjedid Chadli, Secretary-General of FLN, who, in 1979, felt sufficiently confident of his position to release Ben Bella from the house arrest which had been imposed following the 1965 coup. In the same year FLN adopted a new structure, with a Central Committee nominating the party leader who would automatically become President. Under this revised system, Chadli was re-elected in 1983.

During Chadli's terms as President significant steps have been made in improving relations with France and the US and some progress in achieving greater co-operation with neighbouring states, particularly Tunisia. In 1981 Algeria enhanced its international reputation by acting as an intermediary in securing the release of the American hostages in Iran. In 1987 a proposal by Colonel Kadhafi for political union with Libya met with a cool response, Algeria preferring a 'treaty of friendship'. In May 1988 Algeria restored diplomatic relations with Morocco after a twelve-year break and was hoping for a similar restoration with Egypt.

Despite Algeria's considerable wealth of natural resources, including oil, gas and minerals, the economy has not grown sufficiently to match the population increase and President Chadli has been forced to introduce austerity measures which have proved unpopular with consumers. This unpopularity has been heightened by the feeling that Chadli was moving away from the socialist principles of his predecessor, Boumédienne, and favouring an élite few at the expense of the majority. Acts of violence erupted in 1988 to which the army acted promptly and harshly, killing many of the young protesters. President Chadli managed to moderate the uprisings by promising constitutional changes which would make the government more responsive to popular opinion. Despite this, there was evidence that electoral changes would favour the ruling FLN.

BAHRAIN

State of Bahrain

Capital: Manama

Social and economic data

Area: 620 km^2
Population: 0.442m*
Pop density per km^2: 712*
Literacy rate: 70%
GDP: $4,000m*; per capita GDP: $9,000
Economy type: high income
Labour force in agriculture: 3%

*1985

Ethnic composition

About 73 per cent of the population are Arabic and about 9 per cent Iranian. There are Pakistani and Indian minorities.

Religions

Islam is the state religion and of the 300,000 Muslims, about 60 per cent are Shia and 40 per cent Sunni. There are about 25,000 Christians.

Political features
State type: absolutist
Date of state formation: 1971
Political structure: unitary
Executive: absolute
Assembly: there has been no assembly since 1975
Party structure: there are no parties
Human rights rating: N/A

Local and regional government
There is no recognisable local government system.

Head of state and head of government
Emir, Sheik Isa bin-Sulman al-Khalifa, since 1961.

Political leaders since 1970
1961– Sheik Isa bin-Sulman al Khalifa (Emir).

Political system
The 1973 constitution provided for an elected National Assembly of 30 members but it was dissolved in 1975 after the Prime Minister said he could not work with it. Bahrain is now governed by the Emir, by decree, through a cabinet chosen by him and consisting mainly of his close relatives. Those who are not related are drawn from the wealthiest merchant families in the state.

Political parties
There are no recognisable political parties.

Latest elections
There have been no elections since the dissolution of the assembly.

Political history
Bahrain is a traditional Arab monarchy and became a British Protected State in the nineteenth century, with government shared between the ruling Sheikh and a British adviser. In 1928 Iran, then called Persia, claimed sovereignty but in 1970 accepted a UN report showing that the inhabitants of Bahrain preferred independence.

In 1968 Britain, as part of a policy of reducing its overseas commitments, announced its intention to withdraw its forces and Bahrain joined two other territories which were also under British protection, Qatar and the Trucial States, now called the United Arab Emirates, to form a Federation of Arab Emirates. In 1971 both Qatar and the Trucial States left the Federation and Bahrain became an independent nation, signing a new treaty of friendship with Britain.

In 1973 a constitution was introduced providing for an elected National Assembly but two years later the Prime Minister, Sheikh Khalifa, complained of obstruction by the Assembly which was then dissolved. Since then the Emir and his family have ruled with virtually absolute powers. Following the Iranian revolution of 1979, relations between the two countries became uncertain, with fears of Iranian attempts to disturb

Bahrain's stability. It became a focal point in the Gulf region, its international airport the centre of Gulf aviation and Bahrain the site of the new Gulf University. A causeway linking it to Saudi Arabia has also been constructed.

While the ending of the Iran-Iraq war has made the Gulf area less dangerous, the return to full peacetime economies by Iraq and Iran may reduce Bahrain's economic and political influence in the region.

DJIBOUTI

Republic of Djibouti
Jumhouriyya Djibouti

Capital: Djibouti

Social and economic data
Area: 23,390 km^2
Population: 0.300m*
Pop density per km^2: 13*
Literacy rate: 12%*
GDP: $340m*; per capita GDP: $1,133
Economy type: middle income
Labour force in agriculture: N/A

*1985

Ethnic composition
The population is divided roughly equally into two Hamitic groups, the Issas in the south and the Afars in the north and west. There are also minorities of Europeans, mostly French, Arabs, Sudanese and Indians.

Religions
Virtually the whole population are Muslims.

Political features
State type: authoritarian nationalist
Date of state formation: 1977
Political structure: unitary
Executive: unlimited presidential
Assembly: one-chamber
Party structure: one-party
Human rights rating: N/A

Local and regional government
For administrative purposes, the country is divided into five districts.

Head of state and head of government
President Hassan Gouled Aptidon, since 1977.

Political leaders since 1970
1977– Hassan Gouled Aptidon (RPP).

Political system
The 1981 constitution made Djibouti a one-party state, the only legal party being the People's Progress Assembly (RPP). The constitution also provides for a single-chamber assembly, the Chamber of Deputies, with 65 members elected by universal adult suffrage, through a simple plurality voting system, for a five-year term. The President, who is both head of state and head of government, is nominated by the party and then popularly elected for six years. He may not serve more than two terms.

Political parties
The People's Progress Party (RPP) was formed in 1979 to replace the African People's League for Independence. It was made the sole legal party in 1981. Its orientation is basically nationalist.

Latest elections
In the 1987 assembly elections voters were presented with a single list of RPP-nominated candidates. All were elected, unopposed.

Political history
Djibouti became a French colony in 1862, being part of French Somaliland, and in 1945 was declared an overseas territory. In 1967 it was renamed the French Territory of the Afars and the Issas. There were frequent calls for independence, sometimes resulting in violence, and this goal was eventually achieved in 1977. Hassan Gouled Aptidon, who had been active in the independence movement, was elected the first President.

In 1979 all existing political parties were combined to form the RPP and the government embarked on the task of bringing together the two main tribes, the Issas, who traditionally had strong links with Somalia, and the Afars, who had been linked with Ethiopia, through a policy of 'rapid detribalisation'.

In 1981 a new constitution was adopted, making RPP the only legal party and providing for the election of a President after nomination by RPP. President Gouled was subsequently elected. The following year a Chamber of Deputies was elected from a list of RPP nominees. Under Gouled, Djibouti has pursued a largely successful policy of amicable neutralism with its neighbours, concluding treaties of friendship with Ethiopia, Somalia, Kenya and the Sudan, and has tried to assist the peace process in East Africa. Although affected by the 1984–85 droughts, it managed to maintain stabilty with the help of famine relief aid from the EC. In 1987 Gouled was re-elected to serve his second, and final, term under the 1981 constitution. He received 98.71 per cent of the popular vote.

EGYPT

Arab Republic of Egypt
Jumhuriyat Misr al-Arabiya

Capital: Cairo

Social and economic data
Area: 1,001,500 km^2
Population: 50.500m*

Pop density per km^2: 50*
Literacy rate: 38%*
GDP: $50,000m*; per capita GDP: $990
Economy type: low income
Labour force in agriculture: 37%

*1985

Ethnic composition
Native Egyptians comprise over 93 per cent of the population, mainly of Hamitic stock.

Religions
Islam is the state religion and 90 per cent of the population are Muslims, nearly all Sunni.

Political features
State type: emergent democratic
Date of state formation: 1922
Political structure: unitary
Executive: limited presidential
Assembly: one-chamber
Party structure: multi-party
Human rights rating: 59%

Local and regional government
For administrative purposes, the country is divided into 25 governorates, ranging in population from about 10,000 to over 5 million. Each has an appointed governor and elected council.

Head of state and head of government
President Hosni Mubarak, since 1981.

Political leaders since 1970
1970–81 Anwar Sadat (ASU), 1981– Hosni Mubarak (NDP).

Political system
The 1971 constitution provides for a single-chamber People's Assembly of 458, ten nominated by the President and 448 elected. Four hundred of the candidates for election are chosen from lists prepared by the parties and the remaining 48 are independents. The second-ballot majoritarian system of voting is used. The Assembly serves a five-year term. The President is nominated by the Assembly and then elected by popular referendum for a six-year term. He is eligible for re-election. He appoints one or more Vice-Presidents and a Council of Ministers.

Political parties
There are seven political parties, the four most significant being the National Democratic Party (NDP), the Socialist Labour Party, the Socialist Liberal Party and the New Wafd Party.

The NDP was formed in 1978 as the official government party, absorbing the older Arab Socialist Party. It has a moderate, left-of-centre orientation.

The Socialist Labour Party was also founded in 1978 and is the official opposition party. It has its origins in the Egyptian Youth party and has a right-of-centre orientation.

The Socialist Liberal Party dates from 1978. It has a strongly free-enterprise outlook, favouring an 'open door' economic policy.

The New Wafd Party is Egypt's oldest political grouping, dating back to 1919. After being banned, it was reconstituted in 1978 as the New Wafd Party, then disbanded and re-formed in 1983. It is strongly nationalist.

Latest elections

In the 1987 elections for the People's Assembly the results were as follows:

	% Votes	*Seats*
NDP	69.3	345
Socialist Labour Coalition (Socialist Labour Party; Socialist Liberal Party; Muslim Brotherhood)	17.0	60
New Wafd Party	10.9	35
Others	2.8	8

Political history

Egypt has existed as a unified state for more than 50 centuries, during which time it has come under Persian, Roman and Byzantine rule. From the sixteenth century until 1882, when it was occupied by Britain, Egypt was part of the Turkish Ottoman Empire. In 1914 it was made a British protectorate and given nominal independence in 1922, under King Fuad I. He was succeeded in 1936 by King Farouk and Britain agreed to recognise Egypt's full independence, announcing a phased withdrawal of its forces, except from the Suez Canal, Alexandria and Port Said, where there were important naval bases. The departure of the British was delayed by the start of the Second World War, and the consequent campaign in Libya which ended in the defeat of the German and Italian forces which had threatened the security of the Canal Zone. British troops were eventually withdrawn in 1946, except for the Suez Canal garrison.

In the immediate post-war years a radical movement developed, calling for an end to the British presence and opposition to Farouk for his extravagant life style and his failure to prevent the growth of the new state of Israel. This led, in 1952, to a bloodless coup by a group of young army officers, led by Colonel Gamal Nasser, who overthrew Farouk and replaced him with a military junta. The 1923 constitution was suspended and all political parties were banned. The following year Egypt declared itself a republic, with General Mohammed Neguib, President and Prime Minister. In 1954 Nasser assumed the post of Prime Minister and an agreement was signed for the withdrawal of British troops from the Canal Zone by 1956. Then, following a dispute with Neguib, Nasser took over as head of state.

At home he embarked on a large scale programme of social reform and abroad became a major force for the creation of Arab unity. In 1956 a new constitution was adopted, strengthening the presidency, to which Nasser was elected, unopposed. Later that year, British forces were withdrawn, in accordance with the 1954 agreement. When the United States and Britain cancelled their offers of financial help to build the ambitious Aswan High Dam, Nasser responded by announcing the nationalisation of the Suez Canal. In a contrived operation, Britain, France and Israel invaded the Sinai Peninsula and two days later Egypt was attacked. Strong pressure from the United States brought a cease-fire and an Anglo-French withdrawal. The effect of the abortive Anglo-French operation was to push Egypt towards the USSR and enhance Nasser's reputation in the Arab world.

In 1958 Egypt and Syria merged to become the United Arab Republic (UAR), with Nasser as President, but three years later Syria withdrew, although Egypt retained the title of UAR until 1971. The 1960s saw several short-lived, but unsuccessful, attempts to federate Egypt, Syria and Iraq. Despite these failures Nasser enjoyed increasing prestige among his neighbours while at home, in 1962, he founded the Arab Socialist Union (ASU), as Egypt's only recognised political organisation.

In 1967 Egypt, as the acknowledged champion of the Arab world, led an attack on Israel which developed into the 'Six Day War'. It ended ignominiously, with Israel defeating all its opponents, including Egypt. One result of the conflict was the blocking of the Suez Canal which was not opened again to traffic until 1975. Following Egypt's defeat, Nasser offered his resignation but was persuaded to stay on. In 1969, at the age of 52, he suffered a fatal heart attack and was succeeded by the Vice-President, Colonel Anwar Sadat.

In 1971 a new constitution was approved and the title of Arab Republic of Egypt adopted. Sadat continued Nasser's policy of promoting Arab unity but proposals to create a federation of Egypt, Libya and Syria again failed. In 1973 an attempt was made to regain territory lost to Israel and after 18 days' fighting the US Secretary of State, Henry Kissinger, arranged a cease-fire, resulting in Israel's evacuation of parts of Sinai, with a UN buffer zone separating the rival armies. This US intervention strengthened the ties between the two countries while relations with the USSR cooled.

In 1977 Sadat, surprisingly, travelled to Israel, to address the Israeli parliament and make a dramatic plea for peace. Other Arab states were dismayed by this move and diplomatic relations with Syria, Libya, Algeria and the Yemen, as well as the Palestinian Liberation Organisation (PLO), were severed. Despite this opposition, Sadat pursued his peace initiative and, at the Camp David talks in the United States, he and the Israeli Prime Minister, Menachem Begin, signed two agreements. The first laid a framework for peace in the Middle East and the second a framework for a peace treaty between the two countries. In 1979 a treaty was signed and Israel began a phased withdrawal from the Sinai Peninsula. Egypt was, in consequence, expelled from the Arab League.

Soon after his accession to the presidency, Sadat began a programme of liberalising his regime, but met opposition from Muslim fundamentalists, and in 1981 was assassinated by a group of them. He was succeeded by Lieutenant-General Hosni Mubarak, who had been Vice-President since 1975. The line of succession from Nasser had thus been maintained and, just as Sadat had continued the policies of his predecessor, so did Mubarak. In the 1984 elections the National Democratic Party (NDP), which Sadat had formed in 1948, won an overwhelming victory in the Assembly, strengthening Mubarak's position.

Although the treaty with Israel remains intact, relations between the two countries have been strained, mainly because of Israel's activities against the Palestinians in Lebanon and the occupied territories. Egypt's relations with other Arab nations have, however, improved and in 1987 it was readmitted into membership of the Arab League. Domestically, Mubarak has had increasing problems with Muslim fundamentalists, making him increasingly dependent on the support of the army. In the April 1987 general election the NDP, although gaining re-election with a sizeable majority, lost significant support to the fundamentalist Muslim Brotherhood-Labour-Liberal alliance, which, campaigning under the slogan 'Islam is the Solution', and calling for the abrogation of the 1979 treaty with Israel, and for the full application of Islamic law, captured 17 per cent of the national vote and emerged as the main opposition grouping in the new Assembly. Mubarak was himself re-elected President, by referendum, in October 1987. By the end of 1988 full diplomatic relations with Algeria had been restored, leaving only Lebanon, Libya and Syria without formal links but by May 1989 relations with Libya had markedly improved.

IRAN

Islamic Republic of Iran
Jomhori-E-Islami-E-Iran

Capital: Tehran

Social and economic data
Area: 1,648,000 km^2
Population: 46.600m*
Pop density per km^2: 28*
Literacy rate: 37%*
GDP: $170,000*; per capita GDP: $3,648
Economy type: middle income
Labour force in agriculture: 37%

*1985

Ethnic composition
About 63 per cent of the population are of Persian origin, 18 per cent Turkic, 13 per cent other Iranian, 3 per cent Kurdish and 3 per cent Arabic.

Religions
Islam is the state religion and most of the population are Shia Muslims. There is a minority of Sunni Muslims, and about 300,000 Christians and 80,000 Jews.

Political features
State type: authoritarian nationalist
Date of state formation: 1499
Political structure: unitary
Executive: unlimited presidential
Assembly: one-chamber
Party structure: one-party
Human rights rating: bad

Local and regional government
Iran has a long tradition of strong local government and the country is divided into 23 provinces, 472 counties and 499 municipalities. The provinces are administered by governors-general the counties by governors and the municipalities by lieutenant-governors or *sherifs*.

Head of state and head of government
President Ali Akbar Hoshemi Rafsanjani, since 1989.

Political leaders since 1970
1953–79 Shah Mohammed Reza Pahlavi, 1979–80 Mehdi Bazargan (IRP), 1980–81 Abolhasan Bani-Sadr (IRP), 1981–89 Sayed Ali Khamenei (IRP), 1989– Ali Akbar Hoshemi Rafsanjani (IRP).

Political system
The constitution, which came into effect on the overthrow of the Shah in 1979, provides for a President elected by universal adult suffrage and a single-chamber legislature, called the Islamic Consultative Assembly (Majlis), of 270 members, elected by the majoritarian voting system of the second ballot. The President and the Assembly serve a term of four years.

All legislation passed by the Assembly must be sent to the Council for the Protection of the Constitution, consisting of six religious and six secular lawyers, to ensure that it complies with Islamic precepts. The President is the executive head of government but his authority, and that of the Assembly, were ultimately subject to the will of the religious leader. With the death of Ayatollah Khomeini the balance of power is likely to undergo substantial change.

Political parties
Although some 16 parties exist, Iran is fundamentally a one-party state, the Islamic Republican Party (IRP) having been founded in 1978 to bring about the Islamic revolution.

Latest elections
In the 1987 elections for the Majlis there was an overwhelming majority for the IRP on a 68 per cent turnout.

The 1989 presidential election was won by the former Speaker of the Assembly, Ali Akbar Hoshemi Rafsanjani.

Political history
Persia, as Iran was known before 1935, has been a sovereign state since the end of the fifteenth century. It adopted its first democratic constitution in 1906 after revolutionaries had rebelled against the despotism of the Shahs of the Qajar dynasty, who had ruled Persia since the eighteenth century. In the early part of the present century the country became the subject of British, Russian and Turkish exploitation until a coup, in 1925, by Colonel Reza Khan, a Cossack officer, deposed the Shah and resulted in his election as Shah, with the title Reza Shah Pahlavi. He soon embarked on a massive programme of modernisation to bring the country into the twentieth century. In 1941 he abdicated in favour of his son, Mohammed Reza Pahlavi.

During the Second World War, Iran, as it had become, was occupied by British, American and Russian troops until the spring of 1946. Anti-British and anti-American feeling grew and in 1951 the newly elected Prime Minister, Dr Mohammed Mussadeq, obtained legislative approval for the nationalisation of Iran's, largely foreign-owned, petroleum industry. With American connivance, Mussadeq was deposed in a 1953 coup and the dispute over nationalisation was settled the following year when oil drilling concessions were granted to a consortium of eight companies. The Shah assumed complete control of the government and between 1965 and 1977 Iran enjoyed a period of political stability and economic growth, based on oil revenue.

In 1975 the Shah had introduced a one-party system, based on the Iran National Resurgence Party (Rastakhis) but opposition to his regime was becoming increasingly evident. The most effective challenge came from the exiled religious leader, Ayatollah Khomeini, who carried on his campaign from France. He demanded a return to the principles of Islam and pressure on the Shah became so great that in 1979 he left the country, leaving the way open for Khomeini's return.

He proceeded to appoint a provisional government but power was placed essentially in the hands of the 15-member Islamic Revolutionary Council, controlled by Khomeini himself. Iran was declared an Islamic Republic and a new constitution, based on Islamic principles, was adopted. Relations with the United States were badly affected when a group of Iranian students seized 63 American hostages at the US embassy in Tehran, to give support to a demand for the return of the Shah to face trial. Even the death of the Shah, in Egypt in 1980, did little to resolve the crisis which was not ended until all the hostages were released, in January 1981. The hostage crisis had not only damaged US-Iranian relations but had dealt a mortal blow to President Jimmy Carter's hopes of winning the US presidency for a second term.

In its early years several rifts developed within the new Islamic government and although by 1982 some stability had been attained, disputes between different factions developed again in the years that followed. Externally, the war with Iraq which broke out in 1980 following a border dispute, continued, with considerable loss of life on both sides. By 1987 both sides in the war had increased the scale of their operations, each apparently believing that outright victory was possible. Then, in 1988, following strenuous efforts by the UN Secretary-General, the leaders of the two countries, somewhat surprisingly, agreed to a cease-fire and the start of talks about a permanent solution to the dispute.

The year 1988 saw not only the end of the war but the beginnings of a rapprochement between Iran and the Western powers. The burden of the fighting, and the enormous loss of life, had obviously affected the attitude of the ruling regime, allowing more moderate elements, such as the Speaker of the Assembly, to exercise greater influence. The restoration of diplomatic relations with Britain at the end of 1988 was reversed because of Islamic opposition to the publication of *The Satanic Verses* by the British author Salman Rushdie. Ayatollah Khomeini publicly ordered his assassination and Iran seemed to have reverted to its extremist, unpredictable character. This was underlined in April 1989 when Khomeini announced that he had dismissed his appointed successor as religious leader, Ayatollah Hossein

Ali Montazeri. Then in early June 1989 he died, leaving a vacuum and an inevitable power struggle for the succession, which was resolved in July 1989 by the election of a new President.

IRAQ

Republic of Iraq
Al Jumhouriya Al'Iraquia

Capital: Baghdad

Social and economic data

Area: 444,000 km^2
Population: 16.278m*
Pop density per km^2: 37*
Literacy rate: 43%*
GDP: $46,796m*; per capita GDP: $2,875
Economy type: middle income
Labour force in agriculture: 30%

*1985

Ethnic composition

About 79 per cent of the population are Arabs, 16 per cent Kurds, mainly in the north-east, 3 per cent Persians and 2 per cent Turks. The Kurds have, for a long time, pressed for greater autonomy which has been promised and then often replaced by harsh, repressive measures.

Religions

Islam is the state religion and about 95 per cent of the population are Muslims, half Shia and half Sunni. The Sunni are mainly in the north of the country and the Shia in the south.

Political features

State type: nationalistic socialist
Date of state formation: 1932
Political structure: unitary
Executive: unlimited presidential
Assembly: one-chamber
Party structure: one-party
Human rights rating: 19%

Local and regional government

The country is divided into 15 provinces, administered by appointed governors, and three governorates, which together comprise a partially autonomous Kurdish region.

Head of state and head of government

President Saddam Hussain, since 1979.

Political leaders since 1970
1968–79 Ahmed Hassan al-Bakr (Arab Socialist Baath Party), 1979– Saddam Hussain (Arab Socialist Baath Party).

Political system
The 1970 constitution, amended in 1973, 1974, 1980 and 1988, provides for a President who is head of state, head of government and chairman of a Revolutionary Command Council (RCC). Day-to-day administration is under the control of a Council of Ministers over which the President also presides. He is also Regional Secretary of the Arab Baath Socialist Party which, although not the only political party in Iraq, so dominates the country's institutions as to make it virtually a one-party state. In effect, therefore, Iraq is ruled by the Arab Baath Socialist Party through its Regional Secretary and other leading members. In February 1988 a constitutional change gave the National Assembly powers to summon before it any minister or official to explain his actions.

Political parties
Although there are, in theory, a number of parties, in reality there is only one which has real political power, the Arab Baath Socialist Party. It was originally founded in Damascus in 1947 and came to prominence in Iraq in 1968 and since then has dominated the country's politics. Its orientation is socialist and strongly nationalistic.

Latest elections
In the 1984 elections for the National Assembly the Arab Baath Socialist Party won 173 of the 250 seats, with 73 per cent of the vote.

Political history
Formerly part of the Turkish Ottoman Empire, Iraq was placed under British administration by the League of Nations in 1920. It was the start of a long, and generally amicable, relationship. In 1932 Iraq became a fully independent kingdom and the following year the reigning King, Faisal I, died, to be succeeded by his son, Ghazi. The leading figure behind the throne was the strongly pro-Western General Nuri-el-Said, who held the post of Prime Minister from 1930 until 1958. In 1939 King Ghazi was killed in a motor accident and Faisal II became King at the age of three, his uncle Prince Abdul Ilah acting as Regent until 1953 when the King assumed full powers.

In 1955 Iraq signed the Baghdad Pact, a regional collective security agreement, with the USSR seen as the main potential threat and in 1958 joined with Jordan to form an Arab Federation, with King Faisal as head of state. In July of that year, however, a revolution overthrew the monarchy and King Faisal, Prince Abdul Ilah and General Nuri were all killed. The constitution was suspended and Iraq was declared a republic, with Brigadier Abdul Karim Kassem as head of a left-wing, military regime. He withdrew from the Baghdad Pact in 1959 and, after tenuously holding on to power for five years, was killed in another coup, in 1963.

The leader of this coup was Colonel Salem Aref. He established a new government, ended martial law and within two years had introduced a civilian administration. He died, however, in an air crash in 1966. His brother, who succeeded him, was, in turn, ousted in 1968 and replaced by Major-General al-Bakr who concentrated power in the hands of a Revolutionary Command Council (RCC), taking for himself the posts of head of state, head of government and chairmanship of the RCC.

In 1979, Saddam Hussain, who for several years had been the real power behind the scenes, replaced al-Bakr as chairman of RCC and state President. In 1980 he introduced a 'National Charter', reaffirming a policy of non-alignment and a constitution which provided for an elected National Assembly. The first elections took place that year.

Externally, Iraq had, since 1970, enjoyed a fluctuating relationship with Syria, sometimes distant and sometimes close enough to contemplate a complete political and economic union. By 1980, however, the atmosphere was cool. Relations between Iraq and Iran had been tense for some years, with disagreement about the border between them, which runs down the Shatt-al-Arab waterway. The 1979 Iranian revolution made Iraq more suspicious of Iran's future intentions and in 1980 a full-scale war broke out.

Despite Iraq's potentially weaker military strength, Iran made little territorial progress and by 1986 it seemed as if a stalemate might have been reached. The fighting intensified however in late 1986 and early 1987, by which time hundreds of thousands of lives had been lost on both sides and incalculable damage to industry and property sustained. By 1988 Iraq was enjoying greater military success and regaining some of the territory lost in earlier years of the war. Then, somewhat unexpectedly, the Iranian government responded to an initiative by the UN Secretary-General and agreed to a cease-fire and talks about finding a permanent solution to the dispute between the two countries.

The cease-fire became effective and peace talks between the previously warring countries began, under UN auspices. The end of hostilities freed Iraq's well disciplined army to deal with the Kurdish rebels who, in their quest for greater autonomy, had taken advantage of the government's preoccupation with the Gulf War. Many Kurds were reported to have fled the country into neighbouring Turkey or Iran. One aftermath of the war was the revelation that Iraq had used chemical weapons to secure an advantage over its foes.

ISRAEL

State of Israel
Medinat Israel

Capital: Jerusalem (not recognised by the United Nations)

Social and economic data
Area: 20,700 km^2
Population: 4.208m*
Pop density per km^2: 203*
Literacy rate: 92%*
GDP: $22,024m*; per capita GDP: $5,234
Economy type: high income
Labour force in agriculture: 5%

*1985

Ethnic composition

About 83 per cent of the population are Jewish. Most of the others are Arabs.

Religions

Judaism is the state religion and about 85 per cent of the population profess to be adherents. There are also about 527,000 Muslims and about 94,000 Christians.

Political features

State type: liberal democratic
Date of state formation: 1948
Political structure: unitary
Executive: parliamentary
Assembly: one-chamber
Party structure: multi-party
Human rights rating: 74%

Local and regional government

The country is divided into six administrative districts, each controlled by a district commissioner. Within the districts there are 31 municipalities and 115 local councils. There are also 48 regional councils, containing representatives from 700 villages. Elections for regional and local councils coincide with those for the Knesset and also operate through a proportional representation voting system.

Head of state

President General Chaim Herzog, since 1983.

Head of government

Prime Minister Itzhak Shamir, since 1986.

Political leaders since 1970

1969–74 Golda Meir (Labour Party), 1974–77 Itzhak Rabin (Labour Alignment coalition), 1977–83 Menachem Begin (Likud coalition), 1983–84 Itzhak Shamir (Likud coalition), 1984–86 Shimon Peres (Labour-Likud National Unity coalition), 1986–88 Itzhak Shamir (Likud-Labour National Unity coalition), 1988– Itzhak Shamir (Likud-Labour Party coalition).

Political system

Israel does not have a written constitution. In 1950 the single-chamber assembly, the Knesset, voted to adopt a state constitution by evolution over an unspecifed period of time. As in the other few states without written constitutions, such as the United Kingdom and New Zealand, a number of laws have been passed which are considered to have particular constitutional significance and they could, at some time, be codified into a single written document.

Supreme authority rests with the Knesset, whose 120 members are elected by universal adult suffrage, through a party list system of proportional representation, for a four-year term. It is, however, subject to dissolution within that period. The President is a constitutional head of state and is elected by the Knesset for a five-year term. The Prime Minister and cabinet are mostly drawn from, and collectively responsible to, the Knesset, but occasionally a cabinet member may be chosen from outside.

Political parties

There are currently 28 political parties, several of the small ones being rather like religious pressure groups. The two most significant of the main parties are the Israel Labour Party and the Consolidation Party (Likud). The proportional representation voting system not only encourages the growth of small, specifically orientated, parties but also frequently results in broad-based coalition governments.

The Israel Labour Party was formed in 1968 by a merger of three existing Labour groups, Mapai, Rafi and Achdut Ha'avoda. Mapai was the Israel Workers' Party and started life in 1930 but its origins go back to the turn of the century in Europe, and particularly in Russia. In its present form, the Labour Party has a generally moderate, left-of-centre orientation.

Likud was founded in 1973 as an alliance of several right-of-centre groupings. Under its present leadership it has adopted a much harder line than the Labour Party towards its Arab neighbours and Israeli-Palestinian relations generally.

Latest elections

The result of the 1988 general election were as follows:

	Seats
Consolidation Party (Likud)	40
Labour Alignment	39
Other parties	41

Political history

The Zionist movement, calling for an independent community for Jews in their historic homeland of Palestine, started in the nineteenth century, and in 1917 Britain declared its support for the idea. In 1920 Palestine was placed under British administration by the League of Nations and the British government was immediately faced with the rival claims of Jews who wished to settle there and the indigenous Arabs who were opposed to them. In 1937 Britain proposed two separate communities, Arab and Jewish, an idea which was accepted by the Jews but not by the Arabs, and fighting broke out between the two races. In 1947 this plan for a partition was supported by the United Nations and when, in 1948, Britain ended its Palestinian mandate, Jewish leaders immediately proclaimed a new, independent State of Israel, with David Ben Gurion as Prime Minister.

Although it had no specific frontiers, the new state won wide recognition in the non-Arab world. Neighbouring Arab states reacted by sending forces into Palestine to crush the new nation but with no success. Indeed, when a cease-fire agreement had been reached, in 1949, Israel was left in control of more land than had originally been allocated under the UN partition plan. The non-Jewish-occupied remainder of Palestine, known as the West Bank, was incorporated into Jordan. The creation of this *de facto* state encouraged Jewish immigration on a large scale, about two million having arrived from all over the world by 1962. Meanwhile, hundreds of thousands of Arab residents had fled from Israel to neighbouring countries, such as Jordan and Lebanon. In 1964 a number of exiled Palestinian Arabs founded the Palestine Liberation Organisation (PLO), with the declared ultimate aim of overthrowing the state of Israel.

Throughout the 1960s there was considerable tension between Israel and Egypt, which, under President Nasser, had become an important leader in the Arab world. His nationalisation of the Suez Canal in 1956 provided an opportunity for Israel, in collusion with Britain and France, to attack Egypt and occupy the Gaza Strip, a part of Palestine which Egypt had controlled since 1949. The British-French-Israeli attack on Egypt was soon called off under US and UN pressure and Israel was forced to withdraw from the Strip, in 1957. Ten years later, the Six Day War, as it was called, between Egypt and Israel, eventually left the Israelis with large territorial gains, including the whole of Jerusalem, the West Bank area of Jordan, the Sinai Peninsula in Egypt, and the Golan Heights in Syria. These were all immediately incorporated into the state of Israel.

Ben Gurion resigned in 1963 and was succeeded by Levi Eshkol, leading a coalition government and then in 1968 three of the coalition parties combined to form the Israel Labour Party. In 1969 Golda Meir, the Labour Party leader, became Prime Minister, continuing in office until 1974. In the final months of her last administration another Arab-Israeli war broke out, coinciding with Yom Kippur, the holiest day of the Jewish year. Israel was attacked simultaneously by Egypt and Syria and after nearly three weeks of bitter fighting, resulting in heavy losses, cease-fire agreements were reached.

Golda Meir resigned in June 1974 and was succeeded by General Itzhak Rabin, heading a Labour-led coalition. In the 1977 elections the Consolidation (Likud) bloc, led by Menachem Begin, won an unexpected victory and Begin became Prime Minister. Within five months relations between Egypt and Israel underwent a dramatic change, mainly because of initiatives by President Sadat of Egypt, encouraged by the US administration of Jimmy Carter. Sadat made an unprecedented visit to Israel to address the Knesset and the following year the Egyptian and Israeli leaders met at Camp David, in the United States, to sign agreements for peace in the Middle East. A peace treaty was signed in Washington in March 1979 and the following year Egypt and Israel exchanged ambassadors, to the dismay of most of the Arab world.

Israel withdrew completely from Sinai by 1982 but continued to occupy the Golan Heights. In the same year a major crisis was created when Israel, without consulting Egypt, advanced through Lebanon and surrounded West Beirut, in pursuit of 6,000 PLO fighters who were trapped there. A complete split between Egypt and Israel was narrowly avoided by the efforts of the US special negotiator, Philip Habib, who secured the evacuation from Beirut to various Arab countries of about 15,000 PLO and Syrian fighters, in August 1982. Israel's alleged complicity in the massacre of hundreds of people in two Palestinian refugee camps increased Arab hostility.

Prolonged talks between Israel and Lebanon, between December 1982 and May 1983, resulted in an agreement, drawn up by US Secretary of State George Shultz, calling for the withdrawal of all foreign forces from Lebanon within three months. Syria refused to acknowledge the agreement and left some 30,000 troops, with about 7,000 PLO members, in the north-east, and Israel retaliated by refusing to withdraw its forces from the south. During this time Begin was faced with increasingly difficult domestic problems, including rapidly rising inflation. There was also growing opposition to his foreign policies. He had also become depressed by the death of his wife. In September 1983 he resigned and Itzhak Shamir formed a shaky coalition. Elections in July 1984 failed to produce a conclusive result, with the Labour Alignment, led by Shimon Peres, winning 44 Knesset seats and Likud, led by Shamir, 41. Neither leader was able to form a viable coalition, so eventually after weeks of negotiation it was agreed that a Government of National Unity would be formed, with Peres as Prime Minister for the first 25 months, and Shamir as his deputy, and then a reversal of the positions. Peres was, therefore, in charge of the government until October 1986, when Shamir took over.

Meanwhile, the problems in Lebanon continued. In March 1984, under pressure from Syria, President Gemayel of Lebanon rejected the 1983 treaty with Israel, but the Government of National Unity in Tel Aviv continued with its plans for the withdrawal of its forces, even though it might lead to outright civil war in southern Lebanon. Guerrilla groups of the Shia community of southern Lebanon took advantage of the situation by attacking and inflicting losses on the departing Israeli troops. Israel replied with ruthless attacks on Shia villages. Most of the withdrawal was completed by June 1985.

Several peace initiatives by King Hussein of Jordan failed, largely because of Israeli and US suspicions about the role and motives of the PLO, some of whose supporters were alleged to have been involved in hijack and other terrorist incidents in and around the Mediterranean area. There were, however, signs of improvements in 1985. Prime Minister Peres met King Hussein secretly in the south of France and later, in a speech to the United Nations, Peres said he would not rule out the possibility of an international conference on the Middle East, with wide representation. PLO leader Yasser Arafat also had talks with Hussein and later, in Cairo, publicly denounced the use of terrorism by the PLO outside territories occupied by Israel.

Domestically, the Government of National Unity was having some success with its economic policies, inflation falling in 1986 to manageable levels, but differences developed between Peres and Shamir over the concept of an international peace conference. Towards the end of 1987 international criticism of Prime Minister Shamir's handling of uprisings in the occupied territories grew and this widened the gulf between him and Peres. Despite Foreign Minister Peres' support for a conference proposed by US Secretary of State, George Schultz, Prime Minister Shamir resolutely opposed the idea. Meanwhile, the deaths of Palestinians continued. In April 1988 the military commander of the PLO, and Yasser Arafat's closest colleague, Abu Jihad, was assassinated at his home in Tunis, allegedly by the Israeli secret service. His death triggered off an increase in violence in the occupied territories.

King Hussein's unexpected announcement, in July 1988, that Jordan was shedding its responsibility for the West Bank and transferring it to the PLO seemed likely to have an impact on Israel's general election in November of that year. Prime Minister Shamir said he would abide by the Camp David

Agreement, and not try to annex the West Bank after Jordan's withdrawal, but would resist any attempt by the PLO to set up a Palestinian government there. Shimon Peres' reaction was more conciliatory.

The 1988 general election failed to produce a clear victory for either of the two main parties, Likud winning 40 seats and Labour 39, the balance of power resting with an assortment of small, mainly religious, groups. After months of discussion Labour agreed to join another coalition with Likud, under the leadership of Itzhak Shamir.

The public acceptance by the PLO of Israel's right to exist as a sovereign independent state put considerable pressure on Shamir to agree to take part in an international peace conference at which the PLO would be represented.

JORDAN

Hashemite Kingdom of Jordan
Al Mamlaka al Urduniya al Hashemijah

Capital: Amman

Social and economic data
Area: 98,000 km^2
Population: 3.515m*
Pop density per km^2: 36*
Literacy rate: 6%*
GDP: $1,658m*; per capita GDP: $472
Economy type: low income
Labour force in agriculture: 65%

*1985

Ethnic composition
The majority of the people are of Arab descent and there are minorities of Circassians, Armenians and Kurds.

Religions
Eighty per cent of the population are Sunni Muslims. The King can trace his unbroken ancestry back to the prophet Muhammad. There is also a Christian minority.

Political features
State type: absolutist
Date of state formation: 1946
Political structure: unitary
Executive: absolute
Assembly: two-chamber
Party structure: there are no parties
Human rights rating: poor

Local and regional government
The country is divided into eight governorates. Three of them are known collectively as the West Bank and responsibility for them was relinquished by Jordan in 1988.

Head of state and head of government
King Hussein Ibn Talal, since 1952.

Political leaders since 1970
1952– King Hussein Ibn Talal.

Political system
Jordan is not a typical constitutional monarchy on the Western model, since the King is effectively both head of state and head of government. The current constitution dates from 1952 but has been amended in 1974, 1976 and 1984. It provides for a two-chamber National Assembly of a Senate (House of Notables) of 30, appointed by the King for an eight-year term, and a House of Representatives (House of Deputies), of 142, elected by universal adult suffrage, through a simple plurality voting system, for a four-year term. The House is subject to dissolution within that period. The King governs with the help of a Council of Ministers whom he appoints and who are responsible to the Assembly. Despite the existence of an elected assembly, Jordan has more absolutist than democratic characteristics.

Political parties
Political parties were banned in 1963, partially restored in 1971, and then banned again in 1976.

Latest elections
The last full elections for the National Assembly were held in 1967. Since then the House has been dissolved, reconvened and increased in size. By-elections were held in 1984.

Political history
Palestine, which included the West Bank of present-day Jordan, and Transjordan, which is the present-day East Bank, were part of the Turkish Ottoman Empire until it was dissolved after the First World War. They were then both placed under British administration by the League of Nations. Transjordan acquired increasing control over its own affairs, separating from Palestine in 1923 and achieving complete independence when the British mandate expired in 1946. The mandate for Palestine ran out two years later, in 1948, whereupon Jewish leaders claimed it for a new state of Israel. Fighting broke out between Jews and Arabs until a cease-fire was agreed in 1949. By then Transjordan forces had occupied part of Palestine to add to what they called the new state of Jordan. The following year they annexed the West Bank.

In 1952 Hussein Ibn Talali came to the Jordanian throne at the age of 17 because of his father's mental illness. He has ruled his country ever since. In February 1958 Jordan and Iraq formed an Arab Federation which came to an end five months later when the Iraqi monarchy was overthrown. During his reign, King Hussein has survived many upheavals in his own country and neighbouring states, including attacks on his life, and has maintained his personal control of Jordan's affairs as well as playing an important role in Middle East affairs. His relations with his neighbours have fluctuated but on the whole his has been a moderating influence.

After the Israeli invasion of Lebanon, in 1982, Hussein found himself playing a key role in attempts to bring peace to that part of the world, establishing an acceptable working relationship with the Palestine Liberation Organisation (PLO) leader, Yasser Arafat. By 1984 the Arab world was clearly split into two camps, with the moderates represented by Jordan, Egypt and Arafat's PLO, and the militant radicals by Syria, Libya and the rebel wing of the PLO. In 1985 Hussein and Arafat put together a framework for a Middle East peace settlement. It would have involved bringing together all the interested parties, including the PLO, but Israel objected to the PLO representation. Further progress was hampered by the alleged complicity of the PLO in a number of terrorist operations in that year. Hussein tried to revive the search for peace by secretly meeting the Israeli Prime Minister, Shimon Peres, in France and persuading Yasser Arafat publicly to denounce violence by the PLO in territories not occupied by Israel.

In July 1988 Hussein dramatically announced that he would cease to regard the West Bank as part of Jordan and would no longer have responsibility for its administration. His main motive seemed to be to provoke the PLO into taking over Jordan's previous role and accelerating the movement towards the creation of a Palestinian state.

KUWAIT

State of Kuwait
Dowlat al Kuwait

Capital: Kuwait

Social and economic data

Area: 19,000 km^2
Population: 1.771m*
Pop density per km^2: 93*
Literacy rate: 68%*
GDP: $20,290m*; per capita GDP: $11,457
Economy type: high income
Labour force in agriculture: 2%

*1985

Ethnic composition

About 42 per cent of the population are Kuwaitis, 40 per cent non-Kuwaiti Arabs, 5 per cent Indians and Pakistanis and 4 per cent Iranians.

Religions

Islam is the state religion and most of the population are Muslims, about 70 per cent of them Sunni and 30 per cent Shia.

Political features
State type: absolutist
Date of state formation: 1961
Political structure: unitary
Executive: absolute
Assembly: the National Assembly was dissolved in 1986
Party structure: there are no parties
Human rights rating: 49%

Local and regional government
The country is divided, for administrative purposes, into four districts, each with an appointed governor.

Head of state and head of government
Sheikh Jaber al-Ahmad al-Sabah, since 1977.

Political leaders since 1970
1965–77 Sheikh Sabah al-Salem al Sabah, 1977– Sheikh Jaber al-Ahmad al-Sabah.

Political system
The 1962 constitution was partly suspended by the Emir in 1976 and reinstated in 1980. It vests executive power in the hands of the Emir, who governs through an appointed Prime Minister and Council of Ministers. The current Prime Minister is the Emir's cousin, the Crown Prince. There is a single-chamber National Assembly of 50 members, elected on a restricted suffrage for a four-year term, but in July 1986 it was dissolved, Sheik Jaber preferring to govern with an unelected consultative council. Despite some semblance of constitutional government, Kuwait is, in effect, a personal monarchy and an absolutist state.

Political parties
No parties are allowed.

Latest elections
Elections were held in 1985 for 28 of the 50 National Assembly seats.

Political history
Part of the Turkish Ottoman Empire from the sixteenth century, Kuwait made a treaty with Britain in 1899 enabling it to become a self-governing protectorate until it achieved full independence in 1961. Oil was first discovered in 1938 and its large-scale exploitation began after 1945, transforming Kuwait City from a small fishing port into a thriving commercial centre. The oil revenues have enabled ambitious public works and education programmes to be undertaken.

Sheikh Abdullah al-Salem al-Sabah took the title of Emir in 1961 when he assumed full executive powers. He died in 1965 and was succeeded by his brother, Sheikh Sabah al-Salem al-Sabah. He, in turn, died in 1977 and was succeeded by Crown Prince Jaber, who appointed Sheikh Saad al-Abdullah al-Salem al-Sabah as his heir apparent.

Kuwait has used its considerable wealth not only to improve its infrastructure and social services but also to secure its borders, making, for example, substantial donations to Iraq, which in the past had made territorial claims on it. It has also been a strong supporter of the Arab cause generally. Its position in the Gulf, and its association with Iraq, made Kuwait particularly vulnerable during the prolonged war between Iran and Iraq. The ending of the war may have the effect of reducing Kuwait's influence in the region, as Iraq is able to play a wider political role.

LEBANON

Republic of Lebanon
al-Jumhouria al-Lubnaniya

Capital: Beirut

Social and economic data
Area: 10,400 km^2
Population: 2.700m*
Pop density per km^2: 260*
Literacy rate: 68%*
GDP: $2,500m*; per capita GDP: $926
Economy type: low income
Labour force in agriculture: 17%

*1985

Ethnic composition
About 90 per cent of the population are Arabs. There are Armenian, Assyrian, Jewish, Turkish and Greek minorities.

Religions
There are about 1 million Christians (Maronite, Greek Orthodox, Roman Catholic and Protestant), 860,000 Shia and 620,000 Sunni Muslims, and 78,000 Druze.

Political features
State type: emergent democratic
Date of state formation: 1944
Political structure: unitary
Executive: dual
Assembly: one-chamber
Party structure: multi-party
Human rights rating: N/A

Local and regional government
The country is divided into five regional units, called *maofazats*, each administered by an appointed prefect.

Head of state
The presidency has been unfilled since September 1988 and a military government, headed by General Michel Aoun is in place.

Head of government
Prime Minister Selim El-Hoss, since 1986. He currently heads a rival government to that of General Aoun.

Political leaders since 1970
1970–76 Sulaiman Franjiya (Military-led coalition), 1976–82 Elias Sarkis (Lebanese Front), 1982 Bachir Gemayel (assassinated before he assumed office), 1982–88 Amin Gemayel (Phalangist Party), 1988– Michel Aoun (Military).

Political system
Under the 1926 constitution, which was amended in 1927, 1929, 1943 and 1947, legislative power is held by the National Assembly, whose 99 members are elected by universal adult suffrage, through a party list system of proportional representation, so as to give a fair reflection of all religious groups in the country. The Assembly serves a four-year term. The President is elected by the Assembly for a six-year term. He appoints a Prime Minister and cabinet who are collectively responsible to the Assembly. Power is shared between the President and Prime Minister, in a broadly similar pattern to that in France. In an attempt to preserve religious harmony, the constitution was amended so as to ensure that the President is always a Maronite Christian, while the Prime Minister is a Muslim. The President is, therefore, usually dependent on the Prime Minister for securing him Muslim support. From September 1988 the constitution has been in a state of semi-suspension, with the threat of the country's partition hanging over it.

Political parties
There are currently 19 political parties but membership of the National Assembly is more easily recognised in terms of religious groupings. The five most significant parties are the Phalangist Party, the Progressive Socialist Party (PSP), the National Liberal Party (NLP), the Parliamentary Democratic Front and the Lebanese Communist Party (PCL).

The Phalangist Party was established in 1936 by a group of young, right-wing nationalists who were impressed by the growth of fascism in Nazi Germany. Their main aim was to secure independence from France. In its present form the party has moved nearer to the centre and can best be described as having a nationalistic, Christian and radical orientation.

The PSP was founded in 1949 by Kamal Jumblat, the Druze leader. It is now led by his son, Walid. It has a moderate-socialist orientation.

The NLP dates from 1958 and was formed by Camille Chamoun at the end of his presidential term. It has a centre-left orientation.

The Parliamentary Democratic Front is a moderate, recently formed, Sunni Muslim grouping in the centre of the political spectrum.

The PCL was originally established in 1924 but did not become politically active until 1936. It is a nationalist communist party and was once closely allied with its Syrian counterpart, but this link seems now to have been broken.

Latest elections

Elections to the Assembly were last held in 1972 and its life has most recently been extended until 1990.

Following the 1972 elections, seats were distributed as follows:

Maronite Christians	30
Sunni Muslims	20
Shia Muslims	19
Greek Orthodox	11
Greek-Melkite Catholics	6
Druzes	4
Others	9

Political history

Originally part of the Turkish Ottoman Empire, Lebanon was administered by France, under a League of Nations mandate, from 1920 to 1941. Independence was declared in 1941, it became a republic in 1943 and achieved full autonomy in 1944. Historically, it has had strong links with Syria, but Lebanon has had a much richer mix of religions and cultures, including a large Christian community and Arabs of many sects. Christians and Muslims lived peacefully together for many years and this social stability enabled Lebanon, until the mid-1970s, to become a major commercial and financial centre.

The thriving business district of Beirut was largely destroyed in 1975–76 and Lebanon's role as an international trader has been greatly reduced. After the establishment of the state of Israel in 1948, Lebanon was a natural haven for thousands of Palestinian refugees and the Palestine Liberation Organisation (PLO) was founded in Beirut in 1964, moving its headquarters to Tunis in 1982. The presence of PLO forces in Lebanon has been the main reason for Israel's invasion and much of the subsequent civil strife. This internal fighting has been largely between left-wing Muslims and conservative Christian groups, mainly members of the Phalangist Party. There have also been differences between traditional Muslims, with pro-Iranian attitudes, such as the Shia, and the deviationist Muslims, such as the Druze, backed by Syria. In 1975 the fighting had developed into a full-scale civil war.

A cease-fire was agreed in 1976 but fighting broke out again in 1978, when Israeli forces invaded south Lebanon in search of PLO guerrillas. The United Nations secured Israel's agreement to a withdrawal and set up an international peace-keeping force but to little avail. In 1979 Major Saad Haddad, a right-wing Lebanese army officer, with Israeli encouragement, declared an area of about 2,000 square kilometres in southern Lebanon an 'independent free Lebanon' and the following year Christian Phalangist soldiers took over an area north of Beirut. Throughout this turmoil the Lebanese government found itself virtually impotent. In 1982 the presidency was won by Bachir Gemayel, the youngest son of the founder of the Phalangist Party, but, before he could assume office, he was assassinated and his brother, Amin, took his place.

Following exhaustive talks between Lebanon and Israel, under United States auspices, an agreement was signed in May 1983, declaring an end to hostilities and calling for the withdrawal of all foreign forces from the country within three months. Syria refused to recognise the agreement and left about 40,000 troops, with about 7,000 PLO fighters, in northern Lebanon. Israel responded by refusing to take its forces from the south. Meanwhile, a full-scale war blew up between the Christian Phalangists and the Muslim Druze soldiers in the Chouf mountains, resulting in the defeat of the Christians and the creation of another mini-state, controlled by the Druze. The multi-national force was drawn gradually, but unwillingly, into the conflict until it was eventually withdrawn in the spring of 1984.

Attempts were made in 1985 and 1986 to bring the civil war to an end but rifts within both the Muslim and Christian groups prevented it. Meanwhile Lebanon, and particularly Beirut, has seen its infrastructure and earlier commercial prosperity virtually destroyed as it continues to be a battlefield for the rival factions, particularly the Iranian-backed Shia Hezbollah ('Children of God') and the Syrian-backed Shia Amal. In May 1988 President Assad of Syria, after several previous abortive attempts, sent his troops into southern Beirut, with the agreement of Lebanon and Iran, to attempt to restore order and secure the release of the hostages still believed to be held there. This initiative has not yet proved to be entirely effective.

The end of Amin Gemayel's presidency in 1988 threatened to add a fresh dimension to Lebanon's troubles. Attempts to agree a suitable Maronite Christian successor in August of that year initially failed and the presidential election was postponed. When his term came to an end, in September, President Gemayel felt it necessary to establish at least a caretaker administration and appointed General Michel Aoun to head a military government. This decision was opposed by Prime Minister, Selim El-Hoss, who set up his own rival administration, operating from his office in Beirut. The threat of the partitioning of the country, a fate which politicians had so strenuously sought to avoid since independence, thereafter seemed a possibility. After renewed fighting between the forces of General Aoun and Syrian-backed Muslims, in May 1989 the Arab League succeeded in arranging a truce, but its durability is in great doubt.

LIBYA

Socialist People's Libyan Arab State of the Masses
Al-Jamahiriyah Al-Arabiya
Al-Libya Al-Shabiya
Al-Ishtirakiya

Capital: Tripoli

Social and economic data
Area: 1,759,540 km^2
Population: 3.900m*
Pop density per km^2: 2*
Literacy rate: 39%*
GDP: $26,000m*; per capita GDP: $6,666
Economy type: high income
Labour force in agriculture: 11%

*1985

Ethnic composition
The great majority of people are of Berber and Arab origin, with a small number of Tebou and Touareg nomads and semi-nomads, mainly in the south.

Religions
Most of the population are Sunni Muslims but Islam is not the state religion. There are also about 38,000 Roman Catholics.

Political features
State type: nationalistic socialist
Date of state formation: 1951
Political structure: unitary
Executive: unlimited presidential
Assembly: one-chamber
Party structure: one-party
Human rights rating: 23%

Local and regional government
For administrative purposes, the country is divided into ten provinces. Below this level are municipalities. A feature of Libya's approach to government is the spread of people's committees, to encourage popular involvement, at all levels.

Head of state and head of government
Revolutionary Leader Colonel Muammar al-Kadhafi, since 1969.

Political leaders since 1970
1969– Muammar al-Kadhafi (ASU).

Political system
The 1977 constitution created an Islamic socialist state and the machinery of government is designed to allow the greatest possible popular involvement, through a large Congress and smaller secretariats and committees. There is a General People's Congress (GPC), of 1,112 members, which elects a Secretary-General who was intended to be the head of state. In 1979, however, Colonel Kadhafi, although still head of state, gave up the Secretary-General post. The GPC is serviced by a General Secretariat, which is the nearest equivalent to an assembly in the Libyan system. The executive organ of the state is the General People's Committee, which replaces the structure of ministries which operated before the 1969 revolution.

Political parties
The Arab Socialist Union (ASU) is the only political party and, despite the elaborately democratic structure that has been created, ultimate political power rests with the party and the revolutionary leader, Colonel Kadhafi.

The ASU was formed by Colonel Kadhafi in 1971 as a mass party equivalent of the Arab Socialist Union of Egypt. Since its establishment he has tried to increase popular involvement almost to the extent of making its active membership too diffused. It has a radical, left-wing orientation, accurately reflecting the predisposition of its leader.

Latest elections

It is difficult to identify elections in the conventional sense. Voting is often by a show of hands or a division into Yes and No camps. The thirteenth ordinary session of the General People's Congress (GPC), with its 1,000-plus membership, took place in March 1988.

Political history

Formerly an Italian colony, Libya was occupied and then governed by Britain from 1942 until it achieved independence, as the United Kingdom of Libya, in 1951, Muhammad Idris-as-Sanusi becoming King Idris. The country enjoyed internal and external stability until a bloodless revolution, in 1969, led by young nationalist officers, deposed the King and proclaimed a Libyan Arab Republic. Power was placed in the hands of a Revolution Command Council (RCC), with Colonel Muammar al-Kadhafi as chairman and the Arab Socialist Union (ASU) as the only legally permitted political party.

Kadhafi was soon active in the Arab world, proposing a number of schemes for unity, none of which was permanently adopted. It 1972 it was for a federation of Libya, Syria and Egypt and then, later in the same year, a merger between Libya and Egypt. In 1980 the proposal was for a union with just Syria and in 1981 with Chad. Domestically, he tried to run the country on a socialist-Islamic basis, with people's committees pledged to socialism and the teachings of the Holy Koran. A constitution adopted in 1977 made him Secretary-General of the General Secretariat of a large General People's Congress (GPC), with over 1,000 members, but in 1979 he resigned the post so that he could devote more time to 'preserving the revolution'.

His attempts to establish himself as a leader of the Arab world have brought him into conflict with the Western powers, and particularly the United States. He became in the eyes of US President Reagan a threat to world peace similar to Fidel Castro of Cuba. In particular, the US administration objected to Libya's presence in Chad and its attempts to unseat the French- and US-sponsored government of President Habré. The United States has linked Kadhafi to terrorist activities throughout the world, despite his denials of complicity, and the killing of a US serviceman in a bomb attack in Berlin in April 1986 prompted a raid by US aircraft, some of them based in Britain, on Kadhafi's personal headquarters.

Within the Arab world Kadhafi is seen as something of a maverick. In the spring of 1988, encouraged by a marked improvement in the state of the Libyan economy, he embarked on a dramatic programme of liberalisation, freeing political prisoners and encouraging private businesses to operate. In consequence he enjoyed a sharp increase in national popularity.

In May 1988 the Libyan leader made a surprisingly conciliatory offer to meet President Habré of Chad, recognise its independence formally and give material help for the reconstruction of the country. In October of the same year diplomatic relations between the two countries were fully restored.

In September 1988 Kadhafi, again surprisingly, won praise from Amnesty International by his announcement of the ending of a formal army and its replacement by a 'people's army', the Jamahariya Guard. At the same time he declared an end to frontiers and prisons.

Early in 1989 the United States government accused Libya of building a chemical weapons factory. Soon afterwards, but in a supposedly unrelated incident, two Libyan fighter planes were shot down by aircraft operating with the US navy off the North African coast.

MOROCCO

Kingdom of Morocco
Al-Mamlaka al-Maghrebia

Capital: Rabat

Social and economic data
Area: 458,730 km^2
Population: 23.700m*
Pop density per km^2: 52*
Literacy rate: 21%*
GDP: $11,700m*; per capita GDP: $494
Economy type: low income
Labour force in agriculture: 39%

*1985

Ethnic composition
Most of the population are indigenous Berbers. Pure Berbers are, however, gradually becoming less numereous than Arab-Berbers, although the distinction now has little social or political significance. There is a sizeable Jewish minority.

Religions
Islam is the state religion and about 99 per cent of the population are Muslims. There are also about 60,000 Christians, mostly Roman Catholics, and about 30,000 Jews.

Political features
State type: emergent democratic
Date of state formation: 1956
Political structure: unitary
Executive: dual
Assembly: one-chamber
Party structure: multi-party
Human rights rating: 52%

Local and regional government
The country is divided into seven provinces and 41 prefectures. The four provinces of Spanish Sahara are also administered by Morocco. The provinces and prefectures have appointed governors and prefects and there are indirectly elected councils.

Head of state
King Hassan II, since 1961.

Head of government
Prime Minister Mohamed Karim Lamrani, since 1984.

Political leaders since 1970
1961– King Hassan II.

Political system
Morocco is not a normal constitutional monarchy in that the King, in addition to being the formal head of state, also presides over his appointed cabinet and has powers, under the 1972 constitution, to dismiss the Prime Minister and other cabinet ministers, as well as to dissolve the assembly. The executive thus displays aspects of the French model but with the balance of power tilted towards the monarch.

The assembly consists of a Chamber of Representatives of 306 members, serving a six-year term. Two hundred and six are directly elected by universal adult suffrage, through a simple plurality voting system, and the remainder are chosen by an electoral college of local councillors and employers' and employees' representatives.

Political parties
There are currently eleven political parties, the six most significant being the Constitutional Union (UC), the National Rally of Independents (RNI), the Popular Movement (MP), Istiqlal, the Socialist Union of Popular Forces (USFP) and the National Democratic Party (PND).

The UC was formed in 1982 and has a right-wing orientation.

The RNI was founded in 1978 by an independent group of pro-government politicians. It has an essentially royalist orientation.

The MP dates was created in 1957 and legalised in 1959. It draws much of its support from the rural communities and has a moderate, socialist orientation.

Istiqlal was formed in 1943 as the independence party. It has a nationalistic, right-of-centre orientation.

USFP started in 1959 as part of the National Union of Popular Forces (UNFP). Dissidents broke away in 1974 to found USFP. It has a progressive socialist orientation.

PND was founded in 1981 as a result of a split within the RNI. It has a moderate, nationalistic stance.

Latest elections
The results of the 1984 general election were as follows:

	Seats by Direct Election	*Seats by Indirect Election*	*Total*
UC	56	27	83
RNI	39	22	61
MP	31	16	47
Istiqlal	24	17	41
USFP	35	1	36
PND	15	9	24
Other parties	6	8	14

Political history

After hundreds of years of being part of a series of vast Muslim empires, Morocco came under European influence in the sixteenth century, in the shape of the Portuguese. It was then the turn of the Spanish and French in the nineteenth century. In 1912 it was split into Spanish and French protectorates and then became fully independent as the Sultanate of Morocco in 1956, with Mohammed V, who had been reigning since 1927, as head of state. The two former protectorates were soon joined by Tangier, which until then had been designated an international zone. The Sultan was restyled King Mohammed of Morocco in 1957 and died three years later, in 1960.

He was succeeded by the Crown Prince, who became King Hassan II. During his reign Hassan has appointed numerous Prime Ministers and, despite several attempts to depose or kill him, has retained his personal position. Between 1960 and 1972 a number of constitutions were formulated in an attempt to find a successful marriage between personal royal rule and demands for a more democratic form of government. The most recent is the 1972 constitution and this has lasted to the present day.

Most of Hassan's reign has been dominated by Morocco's claims to what was Spanish Sahara, an area to the south-west of Morocco, considered to be historically Moroccan. Under pressure from Hassan, Spain agreed, in 1975, to cede the region to Morocco and Mauritania, leaving the eventual division to them. The local inhabitants, who had not been consulted, reacted violently through an independence movement, the Polisario Front, which won the support of Algeria. Within a year of Spain's departure, Morocco and Mauritania found themselves involved in a guerrilla war. Algeria's support for Polisario, which included permitting the establishment of a government in exile, in Algiers, the Sahrawi Arab Democratic Republic (SADR), prompted Hassan, in 1976, to sever diplomatic relations. In 1979 Mauritania agreed a peace treaty with the Polisario forces, whereupon King Hassan immediately annexed that part of Western Sahara which Mauritania had vacated. Polisario reacted by raising the scale of its operations. In 1983 a summit meeting of the Organisation of African Unity (OAU) proposed an immediate cease-fire, direct negotiations between Morocco and Polisario and the holding of a referendum in Western Sahara on the issue of self-determination.

Morocco agreed in principle to the proposals but refused to deal directly with Polisario. Although the war was costly, it allowed Hassan to capitalise on the patriotic fervour it generated among Moroccans. Then, in 1984, he surprised the world by signing an agreement with Colonel Kadhafi of Libya, who, until then, had been helping Polisario. At the same time, Morocco was becoming increasingly isolated, with more countries recognising SADR, which had embarked upon a new military and diplomatic offensive. The isolation showed signs of ending with the announcement in May 1987 that better relations with Algeria had been achieved. In November 1987 Polisario guerrillas agreed to a cease-fire in Western Sahara and South Morocco and in May 1988 Morocco and Algeria announced that they were resuming full diplomatic relations. Although a peace plan with the Polisario Front had been agreed, fighting still continued, throwing doubt upon the effectiveness of the plan. Early in 1989 it was announced that diplomatic relations with Syria had been restored.

OMAN

Sultanate of Oman

Capital: Muscat

Social and economic data
Area: 212,000 km^2
Population: 1.271m*
Pop density per km^2: 6*
Literacy rate: 38%*
GDP: $10,350m*; per capita GDP: $8,143
Economy type: high income
Labour force in agriculture: 61%

*1985

Ethnic composition
The great majority of the population are Arabs but there are also substantial Iranian, Baluchi, Indo-Pakistan and East African minorities.

Religions
Islam is the state religion and about 75 per cent of the population are Ibadi Muslims and the rest Sunni Muslims.

Political features
State type: absolutist
Date of state formation: 1951
Political structure: unitary
Executive: absolute
Assembly: there is no assembly
Party structure: there are no political parties
Human rights rating: N/A

Local and regional government
The country is divided into 41 provinces, or *wilayats*, each under the control of a provincial governor, or *wali*, appointed by the Sultan.

Head of state and head of government
Sultan Qaboos bin Said, since 1970.

Political leaders since 1970
1970– Sultan Qaboos bin Said.

Political system
Oman has no written constitution and the Sultan has absolute power, ruling by decree. There is no democratic assembly as such but he takes advice from an appointed cabinet. There is a purely advisory Consultative Assembly of 55 nominated members.

Political parties
There are no political parties.

Latest elections
No free elections are held.

Political history
As Muscat and Oman, the country had a very close relationship with Britain, being under its protection since the nineteenth century. When its complete independence was recognised in 1951, as the Sultanate of Oman, the two countries signed a Treaty of Friendship. Said bin Taimur, who had been Sultan since 1932, was overthrown by his son, Qaboos bin Said, in a bloodless coup in 1970. He embarked on a much more liberal and expansionist policy than that of his conservative father. Oman benefits from its natural wealth but conflicts in neighbouring countries, such as the Yemens, Iran, Iraq and Afghanistan, have not only emphasised the country's strategic importance but put its own security at risk. The Sultan has tried to follow a path of non-alignment, maintaining close ties with the United States and other NATO countries but also keeping good relations with the USSR.

QATAR

State of Qatar
Dawlat Qatar

Capital: Doha

Social and economic data
Area: 11,440 km^2
Population: 0.305m*
Pop density per km^2: 27*
Literacy rate: 51%*
GDP: $3,300m*; per capita GDP: $10,819
Economy type: high income
Labour force in agriculture: N/A
*1985

Ethnic composition
Only about 25 per cent of the population are indigenous Qataris, 40 per cent being Arabs, 18 per cent Pakistanis, 18 per cent Indians and 10 per cent Iranians.

Religions
Islam is the state religion. Most people are Sunni Muslims of the strict Wahhabi persuasion.

Political features
State type: absolutist
Date of state formation: 1971
Political structure: unitary
Executive: absolute
Assembly: there is no assembly
Party structure: there are no political parties
Human rights rating: N/A

Local and regional government
Local government is the overall responsibility of the Minister of Municipal Affairs. Each of the largest towns has a partly elected and partly appointed municipal council.

Head of state and head of government
Sheikh Khalifa bin Hamad al-Thani, since 1972.

Political leaders since 1970
1949–72 Sheikh Ahmad al-Thani, 1972– Shiekh Khalifa bin Hamad al-Thani.

Political system
A provisional constitution adopted in 1970 confirmed Qatar as an absolute monarchy, with the Emir holding all executive and legislative powers. He appoints a Council of Ministers and leads them in the role of Prime Minister. An Advisory Council was established in 1972, with limited powers to question ministers.

Political parties
There are no political parties in the state.

Latest elections
There is no constitutional machinery for elections.

Political history
Formerly part of the Turkish Ottoman Empire, Qatar was evacuated by the Turks in 1914 and the British government gave formal recognition, in 1916, to Sheikh Abdullah al-Thani as its ruler, guaranteeing protection in return for an influence over the country's external affairs.

In 1968 Britain announced its intention of withdrawing its forces from the Persian Gulf area by 1981 and Qatar decided to try to form an association with other Gulf states but the terms could not be agreed and on 1 September 1971 the country became fully independent. A new Treaty of Friendship with Britain was signed to replace the former arrangements.

In the meantime the ruler, Sheikh Ahmad, had announced a provisional constitution which would provide for a partially elected consultative assembly, while retaining ultimate power in the Emir's hands. However, in 1972, while Sheikh Ahmad was out of the country, his cousin, the Crown Prince, Sheikh Khalifa, who held the post of Prime Minister, led a bloodless coup and declared himself Emir. He embarked upon an ambitious programme of social and economic reform, curbing the extravagances of the royal family. An Advisory Council was appointed, in accordance with the 1970 constitution, and its membership was expanded in 1975. Qatar has good relations with most of its neighbours and is regarded as one of the more stable and moderate Arab states.

SAUDI ARABIA

Kingdom of Saudi Arabia
Al-Mamaka al-'Arabiya as-Sa'udiya

Capital: Riyadh

Social and economic data
Area: 2,150,000 km^2
Population: 11.519m*
Pop density per km^2: 5*
Literacy rate: 25%*
GDP: $83,000m*; per capita GDP: $7,205
Economy type: high income
Labour force in agriculture: 40%

*1985

Ethnic composition
About 90 per cent of the population are Arabs and 10 per cent Afro-Asians.

Religions
Islam is the state religion. The majority of the population are Sunni Muslims and the rest Shia. Saudi Arabia is the centre of Islam, containing the two holiest places, Mecca and Medina.

Political features
State type: absolutist
Date of state formation: 1932
Political structure: unitary
Executive: absolute
Assembly: there is no assembly
Party structure: there are no political parties
Human rights rating: 28%

Local and regional government
The country is divided into 14 provinces which are subdivided into districts and sub-districts. Each province is administered by a governor-general, each district by a governor and each sub-district by a headman. There are provincial councils whose members are elected by tribal chiefs.

Head of state and head of government
King Fahd Ibn Abdul Aziz, since 1982.

Political leaders since 1970
1964–75 King Faisal, 1975–82 King Khalid, 1982– King Fahd.

Political system
Saudi Arabia is an absolute monarchy with no written constitution, no assembly and no political parties. The King rules, in accordance with the ancient law of Islam, by decree. He appoints and heads a Council of Ministers whose decisions are the result of a majority vote, but always subject to the ultimate sanction of the King.

Political parties
There are no parties.

Latest elections
There is no provision for free elections.

Political history

Originally part of the Turkish Ottoman Empire, modern Saudi Arabia is almost entirely the creation of King Ibn Saud who, after the dissolution of the Ottoman Empire in 1918, fought rival Arab rulers until, in 1926, he had established himself as the undisputed King of the Hejaz and Sultan of Najd, which, six years later, became the united Kingdom of Saudi Arabia. Oil was discovered in the 1930s and commercially exploited from the 1940s and became the basis of the country's great prosperity.

Ibn Saud died in 1953 and was succeeded by his eldest son, Saud. During King Saud's reign relations between Saudi Arabia and Egypt became strained and criticisms of the King within the royal family grew to such an extent that in November 1964 he was forced to abdicate in favour of his brother, Crown Prince Faisal. Under King Faisal, Saudi Arabia became an influential leader among Arab oil producers.

In 1975 Faisal was assassinated by one of his nephews and his half-brother, Khalid, who had been made Crown Prince, succeeded him. Khalid was in failing health and found it increasingly necessary to rely on his other brother, Crown Prince Fahd, to perform the duties of government, so that he became, in effect, the country's ruler. Saudi Arabia had by now become the most influential country in the Arab world, giving financial support to Iraq in its war with Iran and drawing up proposals for a permanent settlement of the Arab-Israeli dispute.

King Khalid died suddenly of a heart attack in 1982 and was succeeded by Fahd, his half-brother Abdullah becoming Crown Prince. As the Iraq-Iran war continued the geographical position of Saudi Arabia made its task of avoiding direct involvement increasingly difficult. The cease-fire was therefore welcomed with relief by the country's ruler.

SYRIA

Syrian Arab Republic
Al-Jumhuriyah al-Arabiyah as-Suriyah

Capital: Damascus

Social and economic data

Area: 185,180 km^2
Population: 10.535m*
Pop density per km^2: 57*
Literacy rate: 40%*
GDP: $19,400m*; per capita GDP: $1,841
Economy type: middle income
Labour force in agriculture: 30%

*1985

Ethnic composition

More than 90 per cent of the population are Arabs but there are enormous differences between them in language and regional affiliations and, to a lesser extent, religion. There are also differences between the settled and nomadic people.

Religions

The majority of people are Sunni Muslims but Islam is not the state religion. The constitution merely says 'Islam shall be the religion of the head of state'.

Political features

State type: nationalistic socialist
Date of state formation: 1946
Political structure: unitary
Executive: unlimited presidential
Assembly: one-chamber
Party structure: one-party
Human rights rating: 29%

Local and regional government

The country is divided into 13 provinces which are further subdivided into administrative districts, localities and villages. There are elected provincial assemblies and district and village councils.

Head of state and head of government

President Hafez al-Assad, since 1971.

Political leaders since 1970

1970– Hafez al-Assad (Baath Arab Socialist Party).

Political system

The 1973 constitution provides for a President elected by universal adult suffrage, through a simple plurality voting system, for a seven-year term. He is head of state, head of government, Secretary-General of the Baath Arab Socialist Party and President of the National Progressive Front, the umbrella organisation for five socialist parties which dominate the country's politics. Syria is, therefore, in reality, if not in a strictly legal sense, a one-party state. There is a single-chamber assembly, the Majlis al-Sha'ab, also elected by universal adult suffrage, by simple plurality voting. The President governs with the help of a Prime Minister and Council of Ministers whom he appoints.

Political parties

There are some six political groupings but, since 1972, five of them have operated as a single party under the name of the National Progressive Front. The sixth group is the Communist Action Party which sees itself as independent of the other parties.

Syria has a long history of left-wing politics and the National Progressive Front includes the Communist Party of Syria, a pro-Soviet party established in 1924, the Arab Socialist Party, the Arab Socialist Unionist Party, the Syrian Arab Socialist Union Party and the Baath Arab Socialist Party, which is the hub of the organisation. It dates from 1947 and is the result of a merger of the Arab Revival Movement and the Arab Baath Party, both of which were founded in 1940. The National Progressive Front has a pro-Arab, socialist orientation.

Latest elections

The results of the 1986 elections for the Majlis Al-Sha'ab were as follows:

	Seats
Baath Arab Socialist Party	129
Arab Socialist Unionist Party	8
Syrian Arab Socialist Union Party	9
Arab Socialist Party	5
Communist Party of Syria	9
Independents	35

Political history

Syria was part of the Turkish Empire until 1918 and came under French control, in 1920, as a result of a secret treaty, the Sykes-Picot Agreement, concluded by two British and French diplomats, Sir Mark Sykes and Georges Picot. They agreed the partitioning of the Turkish Empire, identifying the respective spheres of influence of Britain and France in the Middle East and North Africa. As part of the deal, France was given a free hand in Syria.

The Syrians resented the French occupation and there were several revolts in the 1920s and 1930s. As the Second World War loomed, the government in Paris changed its policy, against the wishes of the French army in Syria, and promised independence. This was proclaimed in 1944 but, because of the reluctance of French officers to relinquish power, full independence did not come until 1946. There followed a period of military dictatorship and a series of coups. In 1958 Syria merged with Egypt, to become the United Arab Republic (UAR), but in 1961, following another army coup, it seceded and an independent Syrian Arab Republic was established.

In 1963 a government was formed mainly from members of the Arab Socialist Renaissance (Baath) Party but three years later it was removed in another coup by the army. In 1970 the moderate wing of the Baath Party, led by Lieutenant-General Hafiz al-Assad, seized power in yet another bloodless coup and in the following year Assad was elected President. Soon afterwards he formed the five main political parties into one broad group, under his leadership, as the National Progressive Front.

Since then President Assad has remained in office without any serious challenges to his leadership. In 1983 he was reported to have suffered a heart attack but recovered in an apparently weakened condition. This event aroused speculation about his possible successor but no specific name emerged.

Externally, Syria has, under President Assad, played a leading role in Middle East affairs. In the Six-Day War of 1967 it lost territory to Israel and after the Yom Kippur War of 1973 Israel formally annexed the Golan Heights, which had previously been part of Syria. During 1976 Assad progressively intervened in the civil war in Lebanon, eventually committing some 50,000 troops to the operations. Relations between Syria and Egypt cooled after President Sadat's Israel peace initiative in 1977 and the subsequent Camp David agreement. Assad has consistently opposed US-sponsored peace moves in Lebanon, arguing that they infringed Lebanese sovereignty. He has also questioned Yasser Arafat's leadership of the PLO and supported opposition to him. In 1984 President Assad and the Lebanese President Amin Gemayel approved plans for a government of national unity in Lebanon, which would give equal representation to Muslims and Christians, and secured the reluctant agreement of Nabih Berri, of the Shia Amal Militia, and Walid Jumblatt, leader of the Druze. Fighting continued, however, and Assad's ability to control events came under scrutiny. His claim to leadership of the Arab world was also questioned as Egypt's position was gradually restored.

His authority was, however, made evident in 1985 when he secured the release of 39 US hostages from an aircraft hijacked by the extremist Shia group Hezbollah (Party of God). It is certain, therefore, that any long-term peace in the Middle East will, to a great extent, be dependent on the role Syria is willing to play.

Syria's activities in the Lebanon have achieved variable results. In February 1987 President Assad sent a sizeable force into Beirut to restore order at the request of the Lebanese Muslim Prime Minister but against the wishes of the Christian President. It did not have long-lasting results. In June 1987 moves were underway to improve relations with the United States and secure the release of Western prisoners. This action was only a qualified success. In May 1988, after prolonged secret negotiations with Iran, Syrian troops were sent into the southern suburbs of Beirut in another attempt to halt the fighting between the Iranian-backed Hezbollah and the Syrian-supported Amal and to release the hostages. Again, success was only partial.

The ending of the Iraq-Iran war in 1988 brought fears of possible Iraqi reprisals against Syria because of its backing of Iran during the war. In the meantime, peace in the Middle East remained a fragile commodity, with Syria still in an important, pivotal position.

TUNISIA

Republic of Tunisia
Al-Djoumouria Attunusia

Capital: Tunis

Social and economic data

Area: 164,150 km^2
Population: 7.260m*
Pop density per km^2: 44*
Literacy rate: 47%*
GDP: $8,219m*; per capita GDP: $1,132
Economy type: middle income
Labour force in agriculture: 30%

*1985

Ethnic composition

About 10 per cent of the population are pure Arabs, the remainder being of Berber-Arab stock. There are small Jewish and French communities.

Religions
Islam is the state religion and about 99 per cent of the people are Muslims. There are also Jewish and Christian minorities.

Political features
State type: emergent democratic
Date of state formation: 1956
Political structure: unitary
Executive: limited presidential
Assembly: one-chamber
Party structure: one-party
Human rights rating: 60%

Local and regional government
The country is divided into 18 governorates which are further subdivided into delegations and sectors, all administered by appointed officials. Municipalities are more democratically governed by elected councils.

Head of state and head of government
President Zine el Abidine Ben Ali, since 1987.

Political leaders since 1970
1956–87 Habib Bourguiba (PSD), 1987– Zine el Abidine Ben Ali (PSD).

Political system
A new constitution was adopted in 1959, providing for a President, who is both head of state and head of government, elected by universal adult suffrage, through a simple plurality voting system, for a five-year term and eligible for re-election. In 1975 Habib Bourguiba was made President for Life but in 1988 his successor announced a number of important constitutional changes. They include the abolition of the post of Life President; a limitation on the presidency to a maximum of three five-year terms; the maximum age for presidential candidates to be 70; and the minimum age for assembly candidates to be reduced from 28 to 25. There is a single-chamber National Assembly of 141 members, elected in the same way and for the same term as the President. The President governs through an appointed Council of Ministers.

In 1963 Tunisia became a one-party state, the party being the Socialist Destourien Party (PSD), led by the President, but since 1981 additional parties have been officially recognised. The PSD, now called the Constitutional Democratic Rally (RDC), still dominates the political scene, however, but President Ben Ali has warned his followers to prepare themselves for operating in a more pluralistic system.

Political parties
There are now four active political parties and the number is likely to grow, but the party which Habib Bourguiba made the sole legal party in 1963, the Socialist Destourien Party (PSD), in its revised form, continues to be the dominant political force.

The PSD was formed in 1934 as a splinter group from the old Destour (Constitution) Party. In 1988, under the direction of Bourguiba's successor, Ben Ali, it changed its name to the Constitutional Democratic Rally (RDC). It has a moderate, nationalistic-socialist orientation.

Latest elections

In the 1989 National Assembly elections the RDC won all 141 seats, the opposition parties claiming that the elections were fraudulent.

Political history

After being subjected to rule by Phoenicians, Carthaginians, Romans, Byzantines, Arabs, Spaniards and Turks, Tunisia came under French control in 1883. After the First World War an independence movement began to grow and in 1934 the Socialist Destourien Party (PSD) was founded by Habib Bourguiba to lead the campaign. Tunisia was granted internal self-government in 1955 and full independence in 1956, with Bourguiba as Prime Minister. A year later the monarchy was abolished and Tunisia became a republic, with Bourguiba as President.

A new constitution was adopted in 1959 and the first National Assembly elected. Between 1963 and 1981 PSD was the only legally recognised party but since that date others have been allowed to operate. President Bourguiba followed a distinctive line in foreign policy, establishing close links with the Western powers, including the United States, but joining other Arab states in condemning the US inspired Egypt-Israeli treaty. He also allowed the Palestine Liberation Organisation (PLO) to use Tunis for its headquarters. This led to an Israeli attack in 1985 which strained relations with the United States. Relations with Libya also deteriorated to such an extent that diplomatic links were severed in 1985.

Bourguiba ruled his country firmly and paternalistically and his long period in Tunisian politics made him a national legend, evidenced by the elaborate mausoleum which has been built in anticipation of his eventual departure. In November 1987, however, his younger colleagues became impatient and staged an internal coup, forcing him to retire at the age of 84. The former Prime Minister, Zine el Abidine Ben Ali, replaced him as President and chairman of the ruling Socialist-Destourien Party and Hedi Baccouche was appointed Prime Minister.

Since taking up supreme office Ben Ali has moved quickly to establish his own distinctive policy line and style. His new government has shown itself to be more tolerant of opposition than Bourguiba's and in December 1987 over 2,000 political prisoners were granted an amnesty. They included 608 members of the fundamentalist Islamic Tendency Movement (MTI). As a further indication of greater liberalisation, the unpopular State Security Court, established during Bourguiba's regime, has been disbanded. In 1988 Ben Ali changed the PSD's name to the Constitutional Democratic Rally (RDC) and tightened his personal control of it by appointing two-thirds of the membership of its Central Committee. The new spirit in Tunisia has also been recognised overseas, Colonel Kadhafi of Libya restoring full diplomatic relations and making overtures again about a possible union between the two countries. Despite competition from opposition parties, the RDC won all National Assembly seats in the April 1989 elections.

UNITED ARAB EMIRATES

Federation of the Emirates of Abu Dhabi, Ajman, Dubai, Fujairah, Sharjah, Umm Al Quaiwain, Ras Al-Khaimah

Capital: Abu Dhabi

Social and economic data
Area: 83,600 km^2
Population: 1.326m*
Pop density per km^2: 16*
Literacy rate: 54%*
GDP: $25,633m*; per capita GDP: $19,331
Economy type: high income
Labour force in agriculture: 5%

*1985

Ethnic composition
The Emirates have a very mixed population. About 75 per cent are Iranians, Indians or Pakistanis and only about 25 per cent Arabs.

Religions
Islam is the state religion and almost universally followed.

Political features
State type: absolutist
Date of state formation: 1971
Political structure: federal
Executive: absolute
Assembly: there is no assembly
Party structure: there are no political parties
Human rights rating: N/A

Local and regional government
The country is a federation of seven self-governing emirates, each with its own, absolute ruler.

Head of state and head of government
President Sheikh Zayed Bin Sultan Al-Nahayan, since 1971.

Supreme Council of Rulers
Abu Dhabi—Sheikh Zayed Bin Sultan Al-Nahayan, since 1966.
Ajman—Sheikh Humaid Bin Rashid Al-Nuami, since 1981.
Dubai—Sheikh Rashid Bin Said Al-Maktoum, since 1958.
Fujairah—Sheikh Hamad Bin Muhammad Al-Sharqi, since 1974.
Ras al-Khaimah—Sheikh Saqr Bin Muhammad Al-Quasimi, since 1948.
Sharjah—Sheikh Sultan Bin Muhammad Al-Quasimi, since 1972.
Umm al-Qaiwain—Sheikh Rashid Bin Ahmad Al-Mu'alla, since 1981.

Political leaders since 1970
1971– Sheikh Zayed Bin Sultan Al-Nahayan.

Political system

A provisional constitution for the United Arab Emirates was put into effect in December 1971. It provided for the union of seven sheikhdoms, formerly known as the Trucial States, in a federal structure. These provisional arrangements have subsequently been extended, until a permanent constitution is produced.

In accordance with the provisional constitution, the highest authority is the Supreme Council of Rulers which includes the Sheikhs of all the emirates. The Council elects two of its members to be President and Vice-President of the federal state. The President then appoints a Prime Minister and Council of Ministers. There is a federal National Council of forty members appointed by the emirates for a two-year term and this operates as a consultative assembly. Each of the rulers is an hereditary Emir and an absolute monarch in his own country.

Political parties

There are no political parties.

Latest elections

There are no popularly elected bodies.

Political history

The British government signed treaties with the Sultans and Sheikhs of seven emirates on the southern shores of the Persian Gulf and the Gulf of Oman during the nineteenth century and, from 1892, became responsible for their defence. Collectively, they were called the Trucial States. In 1952, on British advice, they set up a Trucial Council, consisting of all seven rulers, with a view to eventually establishing a federation.

In the 1960s they became very wealthy through the exploitation of oil deposits and, believing that they were now strong enough to stand alone, and as part of a policy of disengagement from overseas commitments, in 1968 the British government announced that it was withdrawing its forces within three years.

The seven Trucial States, with Bahrain and Qatar, formed a Federation of Arab Emirates, which was intended to become a federal state, but in 1971 Bahrain and Qatar decided to secede and become independent nations. Six of the Trucial States then agreed to combine to form the United Arab Emirates which came into being in December 1971. The remaining sheikhdom, Ras al-Khaimah, joined in February 1972. Sheikh Zayed, the ruler of Abu Dhabi, became the first President.

Since the Federation came into being it has encountered some problems of integration and in 1976 Sheikh Zayed, disappointed with the slow progress towards centralisation, announced that he would not accept another five-year term as President. He was persuaded to continue, however, with assurances that the federal government would be given more control over such activities as defence and internal security. In recent years the United Arab Emirates have played an increasingly important role in Middle East affairs and in 1985 established diplomatic and economic links with the USSR and the People's Republic of China.

In 1986 the provisional federal constitution was renewed for another five years and Sheikh Zayed unanimously re-elected President. The following year diplomatic relations with Egypt were resumed and Sheikh Zayed paid an official visit to Cairo during which he signed a trade treaty between the two countries.

NORTH YEMEN

Yemen Arab Republic
Al Jamhuriya al Arabiya al Yamuniya

Capital: Sanaa

Social and economic data
Area: 195,000 km^2
Population: 6.300m*
Pop density per km^2: 32*
Literacy rate: 9%*
GDP: $3,600m*; per capita GDP: $571
Economy type: low income
Labour force in agriculture: 65%

*1985

Ethnic composition
Until the departure of Yemenite Jews for Israel in 1948, they were the predominant ethnic group in the country. Now most of the population are Arabs.

Religions
Most of the people are Muslims, divided roughly equally between the Sunni and Shia orders. Islam is the state religion.

Political features
State type: authoritarian nationalist
Date of state formation: 1918
Political structure: unitary
Executive: unlimited presidential
Assembly: one-chamber
Party structure: there are no political parties
Human rights rating: bad

Local and regional government
The country is divided into ten provinces and then further subdivided into districts and villages. There are appointed governors at the higher levels and traditional village headmen.

Head of state and head of government
President Colonel Ali Abdullah Saleh, since 1978.

Political leaders since 1970
1967–74 Abdur Rahman al-Iriani (Republican), 1974–77 Ibrahim al-Hamadi (Military), 1977–78 Ahmed ibn Hussein al-Ghashmi (Military), 1978– Ali Abdullah Saleh (Republican).

Political system

The system of government is based on a provisional constitution published in June 1974 by the Military Command Council, which seized power some six days before. In February 1978 the Command Council appointed a 99-member Constituent People's Assembly to draw up proposals for a permanent constitution and in April the Command Council was dissolved. In 1987 the Constituent People's Assembly was replaced by a 159-member Consultative Council (Majlis al Shura), 128 members popularly elected and 31 appointed by the President. The President of the republic is both head of state and head of government and is elected for a five-year term by the Consultative Council. He governs with an appointed Prime Minister and Council of Ministers. All elections are conducted by the simple plurality voting system.

Political parties

There are no political parties as such.

Latest elections

In 1988 Ali Abdullah Saleh was elected President for a third term by the Consultative Council. There were 152 votes in favour, two abstentions and five absentees.

In the first general election for the Consultative Council in 1988 there were 1,200 candidates for the 128 elected seats. They were won by members of the Muslim Brotherhood, an Islamic political organisation, or by close relatives or friends of tribal leaders.

Political history

The Yemen Arab Republic, or North Yemen, was under Turkish rule from 1517 to 1918, when it secured its independence. The Imam Yahya became King and remained monarch until he was assassinated in 1948. His son, Imam Ahmad, succeeded him and ruled in what can best be described as a sadistic fashion, keeping the country isolated and backward, until he was deposed in a military coup in 1962.

The kingdom of Yemen was renamed the Yemen Arab Republic (YAR), provoking a civil war between royalist forces, assisted by Saudi Arabia, and republicans, helped by Egypt. By 1967 the republicans, under Marshal Abdullah al-Sallal, had won. Later that year Sallal was deposed while on a foreign visit and a Republican Council took over.

Meanwhile, Britain had withdrawn from South Yemen and, with the installation of a repressive regime there, hundreds of thousands of South Yemenis fled to the YAR, many of them forming guerrilla groups with the aim of overthrowing the communist regime in South Yemen. This resulted in a war between the two Yemens from 1971 until 1972, when, under the auspices of the Arab League, a cease-fire was arranged. Both sides agreed to a union of the two countries but the agreement was never implemented.

In 1974 the pro-Saudi Colonel Ibrahim al-Hamadi seized power and by 1975 there were rumours of a possible attempt to restore the monarchy. In 1977 Hamadi was assassinated and another member of the Military Command Council, which Hamadi had set up in 1974, Colonel Ahmed ibn Hussein al-Ghashmi, took over. In 1978 a gradual move towards a more constitutional form of government was started, with the creation of an appointed Constituent People's Assembly, the dissolution of the Military Command Council and the installation of Ghashmi as President. In 1978, however, he was killed when a bomb exploded in a suitcase carried by an envoy from South Yemen.

Colonel Ali Abdullah Saleh became President and another war broke out between the two Yemens. A cease-fire was again arranged by the Arab League and, for the second time, the two countries agreed to unite. This time, however, more progress was made and there have been regular meetings of a Joint Council and, in March 1984, a joint committee on foreign policy sat for the first time in Aden. In 1983 President Saleh submitted his resignation to the Assembly as his term of office neared its end. His resignation was refused and he was re-elected for a further five years.

In 1988 President Saleh was re-elected for a third term and, at the same time, North Yemen's first general election for the new 159-member Consultative Council took place.

SOUTH YEMEN

People's Democratic Republic of Yemen
Jumhurijah al-Yemen al Dimuqratiyah al Sha'abijah

Capital: Aden

Social and economic data

Area: 336,570 km^2
Population: 2.300m*
Pop density per km^2: 7*
Literacy rate: 27%*
GDP: $1,106m*; per capita GDP: $481
Economy type: low income
Labour force in agriculture: 36%

*1985

Ethnic composition

The indigenous people are nearly all Arabs, distributed among over 1,000 tribes.

Religions

Islam is the state religion and most of the population are Muslims.

Political features

State type: nationalistic socialist
Date of state formation: 1967
Political structure: unitary
Executive: unlimited presidential
Assembly: one-chamber
Party structure: one-party
Human rights rating: bad

Local and regional government

The country is divided into six governorates which are subdivided into 28 provinces. They are administered by appointed governors and provincial administrators.

Head of state and head of government

President Haydar Abu Bakr Al-Attas, since 1986.

Political leaders since 1970

1969–78 Salim Rubai Ali (NF), 1978–80 Abd al-Fattah Ismail (UPO-NF-YSP), 1980–86 Ali Nasser Muhammad (YSP), 1986– Abu Bakr al-Attas (YSP).

Political system

The 1970 constitution provides for a one-party state, based on the Yemen Socialist Party (YSP), a single-chamber assembly, the Supreme People's Council (SPC), and a President who is both head of state and head of government. The SPC has 111 members, elected on a simple plurality vote, 71 representing the YSP and 40 independents. It appoints a Presidium whose chairman is the President. He combines this post with that of Secretary-General of the party. He governs through a Council of Ministers which is also appointed by the SPC. The YSP, is, therefore, the ultimate source of political power through the SPC and the Political Bureau.

Political parties

The only legally permitted party is the Yemen Socialist Party (YSP). Its forerunner was the National Liberation Front (NLF), which fought for independence in the 1960s. In 1970 it became the Marxist National Front (NF) and in 1975 merged with two smaller parties to form the United Political Organisation-National Front (UPO-NF). In 1978 the YSP was declared to be a Marxist-Leninist 'vanguard' party, based on 'scientific socialism'.

Latest elections

In the 1986 election for the Supreme People's Council 71 of the members elected were YSP nominees and 40 were classified as independents.

Political history

The fishing port of Aden, which is now the capital of South Yemen, was first occupied by Britain in 1839. It subsequently became an important trading post and coaling station for British naval and merchant shipping. The town and its immediate surroundings were taken over as a British colony and protectorate, administered from Bombay.

As part of the process of Britain's disengagement from overseas commitments, the People's Republic of Southern Yemen was founded in 1967 by bringing together Aden and South Arabia. Before Britain withdrew, however, two rival factions fought for power, the Marxist National Liberation Front (NLF) and the Front for the Liberation of Occupied South Yemen (FLOSY). The NLF eventually won and assumed power as the National Front (NF).

On the anniversary of three years of independence, on 1 November 1970, the country was renamed the People's Democratic Republic of Yemen (PDRY) and in the following year a Provisional Supreme People's Council (SPC) was set up as the nation's parliament. The accession of the left-wing NF government caused hundreds of thousands of people to flee north to the Yemen Arab Republic (YAR), where a more moderate regime was in power. This resulted in clashes between the PDRY government and mercenaries operating from within YAR and the outbreak of war between the two countries.

The Arab League eventually arranged a cease-fire and the two nations signed an agreement to merge, but the agreement was never honoured. Relations between the two Yemens again worsened in 1978 when the President of YAR was killed by a bomb carried by a PDRY envoy. In the aftermath of the killing the PDRY President, Rubayi Ali, was deposed and executed. Two days later the three political parties in South Yemen agreed to merge to form a 'Marxist-Leninist vanguard party', the Yemen Socialist Party (YSP), and Abdul Fattah Ismail became its Secretary-General. In December Ismail was appointed head of state but four months later resigned, on the grounds of ill health. He subsequently went into exile in the USSR. He was succeeded by Ali Nasser Muhammad.

The PDRY's neighbours became concerned in 1979 when a 20-year Treaty of Friendship and Co-operation was signed, which allowed the USSR to station troops in the country, and three years later an aid agreement between the two countries was also concluded. A similar agreement with Kuwait did something to reduce anxieties. However, tension between the two Yemens increased after the death of the YAR President and war broke out once more. The Arab League again intervened to arrange a cease-fire and for the second time the two countries agreed to unite. This time, however, definite progress was made so that by 1983 a joint Yemen Council was meeting at six-monthly intervals.

In 1985 Ali Nasser Muhammad was re-elected Secretary-General of the YSP and its Political Bureau for another five years. He soon began taking steps to remove his opponents, his personal guard shooting and killing three Bureau members. This act of violence led to a short civil war and the eventual dismissal of Ali Nasser from all his posts in the party and the government. A new administration was formed, with Haydar Abu Bakr al-Attas as President, chairman of the Presidium of the Supreme People's Council and Secretary-General of the YPS Political Bureau. The new government immediately committed itself to continuing the process of eventual union with YAR and in November 1987 the presidents of the two Yemens met for talks.

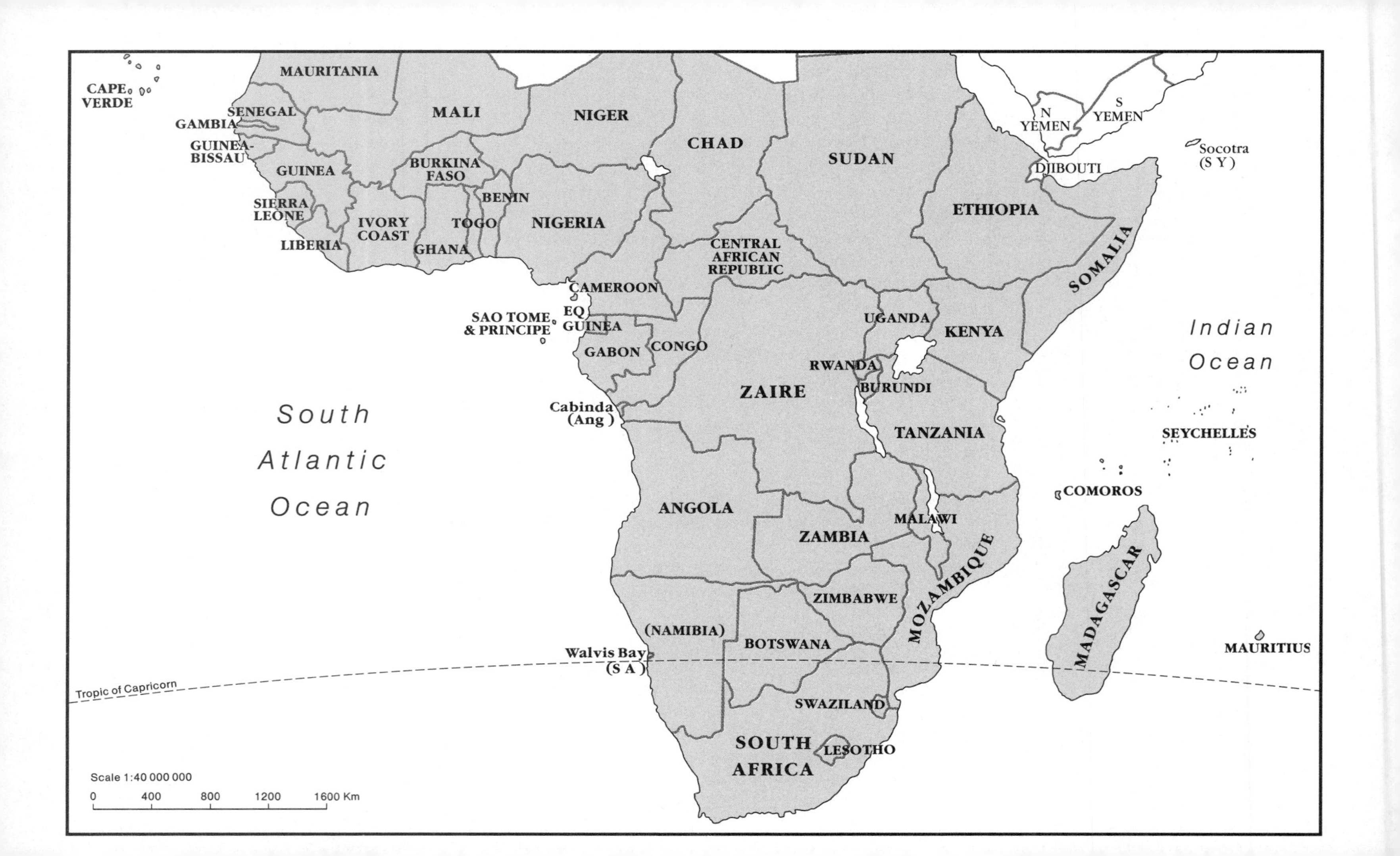
CAPE VERDE
MAURITANIA
SENEGAL
GAMBIA
GUINEA-BISSAU
GUINEA
SIERRA LEONE
LIBERIA
IVORY COAST
MALI
BURKINA FASO
GHANA
TOGO
BENIN
NIGER
NIGERIA
CHAD
SUDAN
N YEMEN
S YEMEN
Socotra (S Y)
DJIBOUTI
ETHIOPIA
SOMALIA
CENTRAL AFRICAN REPUBLIC
CAMEROON
SAO TOME & PRINCIPE
EQ GUINEA
GABON
CONGO
UGANDA
KENYA
RWANDA
BURUNDI
ZAIRE
Cabinda (Ang)
TANZANIA
Indian Ocean
SEYCHELLES
COMOROS
South Atlantic Ocean
ANGOLA
ZAMBIA
MALAWI
MOZAMBIQUE
MADAGASCAR
ZIMBABWE
(NAMIBIA)
BOTSWANA
Walvis Bay (S A)
MAURITIUS
Tropic of Capricorn
SWAZILAND
SOUTH AFRICA
LESOTHO
Scale 1:40 000 000
0
400
800
1200
1600 Km

CENTRAL AND SOUTHERN AFRICA

The region we have defined as Central and Southern Africa covers, as Table 43 shows, an area of more than 23 million square kilometres, over five times as large as Western Europe, and comparable in size to Eastern Europe or Asia. It has a comparatively low population density, however: less than a quarter of that of Western Europe and less than a sixth of that of Asia. Lying mostly between the Tropic of Cancer and the Tropic of Capricorn it enjoys a mainly tropical or sub-tropical climate, although marked variations can be found between the Atlantic and Indian Ocean coasts and between the mountainous and low-lying areas. The great majority of the inhabitants of the region are indigenous, black Africans. Even in white-dominated South Africa only about 30 per cent of the population are not of black ethnic stock.

As Table 37 reveals, 42 of the 45 states in Central and Southern Africa, or over 93 per cent, are of post-1945 origin. Before that time virtually the entire region was controlled by one or other of the major West European powers, yet the 'scramble for Africa', as it has been described, began comparatively late in the nineteenth century, the big 'share out' taking place between 1870 and 1914. Table 57, below, gives the distribution of 43 of the current 45 states among the European colonial powers during this period. This distribution does not necessarily indicate the European power which was the first to exploit a particular country, but the settlement finally agreed after much bargaining by the major powers during the late nineteenth and early twentieth centuries.

Ethiopia and Liberia were the exceptions to the rule. Ethiopia has managed to retain its independence, apart from an Italian occupation of the northern province of Eritrea between 1882 and 1923, since the eleventh century. Liberia was created by the American Colonisation Society, as a home for liberated American slaves, and formally recognised as the Free and Independent Republic of Liberia by Britain and France in 1847.

Table 57

EUROPEAN CONTROL OF CENTRAL AND SOUTHERN AFRICA: 1870–1914

UNITED KINGDOM	Botswana
	Gambia
	Ghana
	Kenya
	Lesotho
	Malawi
	Mauritius
	Nigeria
	Seychelles
	Sierra Leone
	Somalia (part)
	South Africa
	Sudan
	Swaziland
	Uganda
	Zambia
	Zimbabwe

Table 57—European Control of Central and Southern Africa: 1870–1914 (contd.)

FRANCE	Benin
	Burkina Faso
	Central African Republic
	Chad
	Comoros
	Congo
	Gabon
	Guinea
	Ivory Coast
	Madagascar
	Mali
	Mauritania
	Niger
	Senegal
	Somalia (part)
PORTUGAL	Angola
	Cape Verde
	Guinea-Bissau
	Mozambique
	Sao Tome and Principe
GERMANY	Burundi
	Cameroon
	Rwanda
	Tanzania
	Togo
SPAIN	Equatorial Guinea
BELGIUM	Zaire
ITALY	Somalia (part)

Historically and culturally the most arresting aspect of Central and Southern Africa is its tribal nature. This has resulted in a great variety in its political systems and considerable social and political disunity. Although most of the European powers, initially at any rate, attempted to export their own, tried and tested, systems of democratic government, as civilising and unifying devices, after independence most were significantly changed and adapted to suit local conditions, or were replaced with something much more authoritarian.

For example, in the 16 countries which were under British control during the first half of this century, only three, Botswana, Gambia and Mauritius have pluralistic, democratic systems. The rest are either one-party states or under military rule. Similarly, of the 15 states which were part of the French colonial empire only Chad has, in a very tenuous fashion, tried to fashion a form of representative democracy. An examination of the rest of the political systems in the region reveals a similar picture. As Tables 39 and 42 show, only 15 per cent of the Central and Southern African states have multi-party political systems. This figure compares with 25 per cent for the Middle East and North Africa, 48 per cent for Asia, 83 per cent for South America, 86 per cent for Central America and the Caribbean, 92 per cent for Oceania and 100 per cent for Western Europe and North America.

There are some good and valid reasons for this marked contrast and it would be unwise to compare political systems in this region with those in other parts of the world in any censorious fashion. The need to cohere tribal loyalties into a sense of national identity and pride has clearly been a major imperative. A useful and comparatively recent example of this has been the merging of the two main political parties in Zimbabwe, which has meant, among other things, an agreement to subordinate tribal differences to the common good. Examples of what can happen if tribal feelings are allowed to run completely free are to be found in the civil war in the Congo, in the early 1960s, and the more recent killings of the Hutus by the Tutsis in Burundi.

It should also be remembered that the cultural histories of the people of Central and Southern Africa are very different from those of many of their counterparts in other parts of the world. Tribal decision-making was conducted on the basis of discussion, leading to a consensus enunciated by the chief, and the proliferation of one-party systems is, to a great extent, a modern manifestation of this approach.

Furthermore, the comparative sophistication of Western-style political systems is not necessarily appropriate for communities where levels of literacy are still comparatively low. For example, Table 58 shows literacy levels of less than 50 per cent for 73 per cent of the states in Central and Southern Africa, compared with under 35 per cent of the states in Asia and under 10 per cent in Central America and the Caribbean. Only the Middle East and North African region shows lower levels of literacy. Within this overall picture there are, however, considerable variations, ranging from under 10 per cent in Angola, Burkina Faso, Guinea, Mali, and Somalia, to over 50 per cent in Ethiopia, Lesotho, Madagascar, Mauritius, Sao Tome and Principe, Seychelles, South Africa, Swaziland, Uganda, Zaire, Zambia and Zimbabwe. The high literacy level, of 85 per cent, in Mauritius has contributed to the establishment, and maintenance, of a sophisticated, multi-party political system.

Again, it would be unwise to be too critical. We should remember that a political system should be the servant, and not the master, of the country in which it is found, and who can say, with complete confidence, that, ignoring economic disparities, a citizen of Tanzania is less free, politically, than a citizen in, say, Northern Ireland?

Table 58

CENTRAL AND SOUTHERN AFRICA

			Political Data				
State	*Date of Formation*	*Political Structure*	*State Type*	*Executive*	*Assembly No of Chambers*	*Party System*	*Voting System*
Angola	1975	Unitary	Nat Soc	Unlim Pres	One	One	SP
Benin	1960	Unitary	Nat Soc	Unlim Pres	One	One	SP
Botswana	1966	Unitary	Lib Dem	Lim Pres	One	Two	SP
Burkina Faso	1960	Unitary	Mil Auth	Military	None	One	None
Burundi	1962	Unitary	Mil Auth	Military	One	One	SP
Cameroon	1960	Unitary	Auth Nat	Unlim Pres	One	One	SP
Cape Verde	1975	Unitary	Nat Soc	Unlim Pres	One	One	SP
Cen Afr Rep	1960	Unitary	Mil Auth	Military	None	None	None
Chad	1960	Unitary	Auth Nat	Unlim Pres	None	Multi	None
Comoros	1975	Federal	Auth Nat	Unlim Pres	One	One	SP
Congo	1960	Unitary	Nat Soc	Unlim Pres	One	One	SP
Equat Guinea	1968	Unitary	Mil Auth	Military	One	One	SP

Table 58—Central and Southern Africa (contd.)

			Political Data				
State	*Date of Formation*	*Political Structure*	*State Type*	*Executive*	*Assembly No of Chambers*	*Party System*	*Voting System*
Ethiopia	11thC	Unitary	Nat Soc	Unlim Pres	One	One	SP
Gabon	1960	Unitary	Auth Nat	Unlim Pres	One	One	SP
Gambia	1965	Unitary	Lib Dem	Lim Pres	One	Two	SP
Ghana	1957	Unitary	Mil Auth	Military	None	None	None
Guinea	1958	Unitary	Mil Auth	Military	None	One	None
Guinea-Bissau	1974	Unitary	Nat Soc	Unlim Pres	One	One	SP
Ivory Coast	1960	Unitary	Auth Nat	Unlim Pres	One	One	SB
Kenya	1963	Unitary	Auth Nat	Unlim Pres	One	One	SP
Lesotho	1966	Unitary	Mil Auth	Military	None	One	None
Liberia	1847	Unitary	Emgt Dem	Lim Pres	Two	One	SP
Madagascar	1960	Unitary	Nat Soc	Unlim Pres	One	One	SP
Malawi	1964	Unitary	Auth Nat	Unlim Pres	One	One	SP
Mali	1960	Unitary	Auth Nat	Unlim Pres	One	One	SP
Mauritania	1960	Unitary	Mil Auth	Military	None	None	None
Mauritius	1968	Unitary	Lib Dem	Parliament	One	Multi	SP
Mozambique	1975	Unitary	Nat Soc	Unlim Pres	One	One	SP
Niger	1960	Unitary	Mil Auth	Military	None	None	None
Nigeria	1960	Federal	Mil Auth	Military	None	None	None
Rwanda	1962	Unitary	Mil Auth	Military	One	One	SP
Sao Tome and P	1975	Unitary	Nat Soc	Unlim Pres	One	One	SP
Senegal	1960	Unitary	Nat Soc	Unlim Pres	One	One	AM
Seychelles	1976	Unitary	Nat Soc	Unlim Pres	One	One	SP
Sierra Leone	1961	Unitary	Auth Nat	Unlim Pres	One	One	SP
Somalia	1960	Unitary	Nat Soc	Unlim Pres	One	One	SP
South Africa	1910	Unitary	Racist Dem	Lim Pres	One	Multi	SP
Sudan	1956	Unitary	Mil Auth	Military	One	Multi	SP
Swaziland	1968	Unitary	Absolutist	Absolute	Two	One	SP
Tanzania	1961	Unitary	Nat Soc	Unlim Pres	One	One	SP
Togo	1960	Unitary	Auth Nat	Unlim Pres	One	One	SP
Uganda	1962	Unitary	Emgt Dem	Lim Pres	One	Multi	SP
Zaire	1960	Unitary	Auth Nat	Unlim Pres	One	One	SP
Zambia	1964	Unitary	Nat Soc	Unlim Pres	One	One	SP
Zimbabwe	1980	Unitary	Nat Soc	Unlim Pres	Two	One	PL

		Social and Economic Data				
State	*Area (km²)*	*Population (m) (1985)*	*Population Density (per km²)*	*Literacy Rate (%)*	*Income Type*	*Human Rights Rating (%)*
Angola	1,246,700	8.200	7	28	Low	Poor
Benin	112.600	4.100	36	17	Low	59
Botswana	600,400	1.100	2	41	Low	78
Burkina Faso	274,200	7.100	33	9	Low	Poor
Burundi	27,830	4.900	176	34	Low	Poor
Cameroon	474,000	10.000	21	41	Low	53
Cape Verde	4,030	0.312	77	37	Low	N/A
Cen Afr Rep	625,000	2.744	4	27	Low	Bad
Chad	1,284,000	5.200	4	12	Low	N/A
Comoros	1,860	0.469	252	48	Low	N/A
Congo	342,000	1.800	5	16	Middle	N/A
Equat Guinea	28,100	0.360	13	37	Low	N/A
Ethiopia	1,221,900	43.900	36	62	Low	13
Gabon	266,700	1.200	4	12	Middle	N/A
Gambia	11,300	0.800	71	20	Low	N/A
Ghana	238,540	13.552	57	30	Low	46

Table 58—Central and Southern Africa (contd.)

		Social and Economic Data				
State	*Area (km²)*	*Population (m) (1985)*	*Population Density (per km²)*	*Literacy Rate (%)*	*Income Type*	*Human Rights Rating (%)*
Guinea	245,860	5.750	23	9	Low	Poor
Guinea-Bissau	36,130	0.900	25	20	Low	N/A
Ivory Coast	322,460	10.500	33	35	Low	Poor
Kenya	583,000	21.000	36	47	Low	48
Lesotho	30,350	1.555	51	59	Low	Poor
Liberia	111,400	2.300	202	20	Low	39
Madagascar	595,790	10.300	17	53	Low	Poor
Malawi	118,480	7.300	62	31	Low	Poor
Mali	1,240,000	7.908	6	9	Low	Poor
Mauritania	1,030,700	1.750	2	17	Low	N/A
Mauritius	2,040	1.029	504	85	Low	N/A
Mozambique	799,380	14.000	18	27	Low	25
Niger	1,267,000	6.715	5	10	Low	Poor
Nigeria	923,800	105.448	114	34	Low	53
Rwanda	26,340	6.500	247	38	Low	Poor
Sao Tome and P	1,000	0.105	105	57	Low	N/A
Senegal	197,000	6.900	35	22	Low	77
Seychelles	450	0.066	147	58	Middle	N/A
Sierra Leone	73,330	3.883	53	24	Low	64
Somalia	637,660	7.800	12	6	Low	Poor
South Africa	1,222,160	33.200	27	80	Middle	N/A
Sudan	2,505,800	22.970	9	31	Low	Poor
Swaziland	17,400	0.692	40	55	Low	N/A
Tanzania	945,090	22.400	24	46	Low	47
Togo	56,790	3.023	53	31	Low	Poor
Uganda	236,880	15.200	64	52	Low	Poor
Zaire	2,345,000	31.300	13	55	Low	36
Zambia	752,620	7.100	9	69	Low	51
Zimbabwe	390,600	9.000	23	69	Low	45
Total/Average	23,473,670	472.331	20	6-85	Low	13-78

The distribution of religions throughout the region tends to reflect patterns of colonisation based sometimes on trade and sometimes on missionary fervour. For example, the countries where Islam is the main religion, which include Comoros, Gambia, Guinea, Mali, Mauritania, Niger, Senegal, Somalia, Sudan and Tanzania, are found near the early Arab coastal or northern trading routes, which pre-date European exploitation. On the other hand the countries where Christians are in the majority, such as Burundi, Cape Verde, Equatorial Guinea, Gabon, Lesotho, Sao Tome and Principe, Seychelles, Swaziland, Uganda and Zambia came under the influence of European missionaries.

Just as Israel is the anomaly in the Middle East and North Africa, so South Africa is the anomalous state in this region. Not only does a white minority dominate and exploit a black majority, but it has one of the highest per capita incomes of any country in Central and Southern Africa, exceeded only by Gabon and Seychelles. Whereas in these two countries the income is fairly evenly distributed, in South Africa it is concentrated mainly within the white community.

The social and political disunity in the region, arising from tribal differences, which has already been referred to, goes some way towards explaining how some 6 million whites can operate a highly discriminatory political regime in the face of opposition from nearly 80 times as many blacks. The other factors in the explanation are economic and military but the main reason must be the inability of bodies such as the Organisation of African Unity (OAU) to agree a workable policy to dismantle the system of apartheid. In the absence of this the only prospect for a multi-racial political system in South Africa would appear to lie in either an uprising of the majority in that country, with all the inevitable, consequential bloodshed, or firm and concerted action by politicians in the developed world.

ANGOLA

People's Republic of Angola
Republica Popular de Angola

Capital: Luanda

Social and economic data
Area: 1,246,700 km^2
Population: 8.200m*
Pop density per km^2: 7*
Literacy rate: 28%*
GDP: $4,843m*; per capita GDP: $590
Economy type: low income
Labour force in agriculture: 55%

*1985

Ethnic composition
There are eight main tribal groups, the Bakonga, the Mbunda, the Ovimbundu, the Lunda-Tchokwe, the Nganguela, the Nyaneka-Humbe, the Hiriro and the Ambo, and about 100 sub-groups. There was a major exodus of Europeans in the early 1970s and there are now about 30,000 left, mainly Portuguese. The official language is still Portuguese.

Religions
Most of the population adhere to traditional beliefs but Roman Catholicism also attracts a considerable following.

Political features
State type: nationalistic socialist
Date of state formation: 1975
Political structure: unitary
Executive: unlimited presidential
Assembly: single-chamber
Party structure: one-party
Human rights rating: poor

Local and regional government
The country is divided into 18 provinces, each governed by a Provincial Commissioner who is an *ex officio* member of the central government.

Head of state and head of government
President José Eduardo dos Santos, since 1979.

Political leaders since 1970
1975–79 Agostinho Neto (MPLA), 1979– José Eduardo dos Santos (MPLA-PT).

Political system
With independence, the 1975 constitution, which was amended in 1976 and 1980, created a one-party 'People's Republic', with ultimate political power held by the People's Movement for the Liberation of Angola-Workers' Party (MPLA-PT). The President is elected by the Congress of MLPA-PT. He chooses and chairs the Council of Ministers and is commander-in-chief of the armed forces. There is a 223-member People's Assembly, 20 of whom are nominated by MLPA-PT and the rest elected by electoral colleges of all 'loyal' citizens, through a simple plurality voting system.

Political parties
The People's Movement for the Liberation of Angloa (MPLA) was formed in 1965 as a 'liberation movement' with the specific aim of securing the country's independence from Portugal. The early leaders were a group of Portuguese-speaking intellectuals of mixed Portuguese-African parentage, the most prominent being Agostinho Neto. MPLA waged a guerrilla war against the Portuguese and when independence was obtained in 1975 it became the party of government, with Neto as the country's first president. In 1977 it was reconstructed to become a Marxist-Leninist 'vanguard' party, adopting the title the People's Movement for the Liberation of Angola-Workers' Party (MPLA-PT). It is the only legally permitted party in Angola and currently has some 31,000 members.

Latest elections
Elections for the People's Assembly were to have been held in 1983 but were postponed because of the continuing guerrilla war.

Political history
Angola had been colonised by Portugal as early as the seventeenth century and became an overseas province in 1951. A strong independence movement began in the 1950s, with guerrilla warfare organised by the MPLA, which was based in the Congo. Two other nationalist movements, were formed, the National Front for the Liberation of Angola (FNLA) and the National Union for the Total Independence of Angola (UNITA) and the struggle for independence developed, in 1961, into a civil war. MPLA attracted support from socialist and communist states, UNITA was helped by the Western powers and FNLA was backed by the 'non-left' power groups of southern Africa.

After the granting of full independence in 1975 there was a return to a confused state of civil war, with MPLA and UNITA the main contestants and foreign mercenaries and South African forces helping FNLA. By 1975 MPLA, led by Dr Agostinho Neto and with the help of mainly Cuban forces, was in control of most of the country and the People's Republic of Angola was established, with Luanda as its capital and Neto as its first president. It soon won international recognition. In the meantime, FNLA and UNITA had proclaimed their own People's Democratic Republic of Angola, based in Nova Lisboa, renamed Huambo, in the west-central area of the country.

President Neto died in 1979 and was succeeded by José Eduardo dos Santos, who maintained the policy of retaining strong links with the Soviet bloc. UNITA guerrillas, supported by South Africa, continued their guerrilla operations and in 1980 and 1981 South African forces made direct raids into Angola to attack bases of the South West Africa People's Organisation (SWAPO), who were fighting for the independence of Namibia, whose claims Angola supported.

By 1982 there were international diplomatic moves to end the hostilities and secure Namibia's right to govern itself but both South Africa and the United States called for the withdrawal of Cuban troops from Angola before the departure of South African units from Namibia. In 1983 South Africa proposed a complete withdrawal of its forces if it could be assured that the areas it vacated would not be filled by Cuban or SWAPO units. In the following year the Angolan government accepted the South African proposals and a settlement was concluded, known as the Lusaka Agreement, whereby a Joint Monitoring Commission (JMC) was set up to oversee the South African withdrawal. In 1985 South Africa announced that its withdrawal had been completed and JMC was wound up. Relations between the two countries deteriorated however when, in 1986, new South African raids into Angola occurred. UNITA also continued to receive South African support.

By 1988 there was clear evidence that South Africa would welcome an opportunity of withdrawing from the conflict and secret talks between its country's representatives and those of Angola and Cuba were held in London under US auspices. However, the continued South African occupation of Namibia, contrary to UN Resolution 435, remained the main stumbling block to a lasting settlement. At the end of 1988, however, a peace agreement was signed and steps towards Namibian independence started. At about the same time the Portuguese government announced its willingness to assist in the rebuilding of Angola's economy.

BENIN

People's Republic of Benin
République Populaire du Bénin

Capital: Porto Novo

Social and economic data
Area: 112,600 km^2
Population: 4.100m*
Pop density per km^2: 36*
Literacy rate: 17%*
GDP: $1,100m*; per capita GDP: $268
Economy type: low income
Labour force in agriculture: 44%

*1985

Ethnic composition

Ninety-nine per cent of the population are indigenous Africans and are distributed among 42 tribes, the largest being the Fon, the Adja, the Yoruba and the Bariba. There is a small European, mainly French, community.

Religions

Sixty-five per cent of the population follow traditional animist beliefs, about 13 per cent are Muslims, 12 per cent Roman Catholics and 3 per cent Protestants. Religion and spiritual cults have been discouraged since 1975.

Political features

State type: nationalistic socialist
Date of state formation: 1960
Political structure: unitary
Executive: unlimited presidential
Assembly: one-chamber
Party structure: one-party
Human rights rating: 59%

Local and regional government

The country is divided into six provinces, which are further subdivided into 84 districts. The intermixing of the state and party machines is reflected at regional and local levels, as well as nationally, each province being administered by a prefect and a party official, assisted by a Provincial Revolutionary Council, a Regional Planning and Development Committee and a conference of regional heads of department. A significant amount of general and financial policy-making has been devolved in this way.

Head of state and head of government

President General Mathieu Kerekou, since 1972.

Political leaders since 1970

1970–72 Hubert Maga (Civilian-Military Triumvirate), 1972 Justin Ahomadegbe (Civilian-Military Triumvirate), 1972–75 Mathieu Kerekou (Military), 1975–1977 Mathieu Kerekou (PRPB-Military), 1977– Mathieu Kerekou (PRPB).

Political system

The constitution is based on a Fundamental Law (*Loi Fondamentale*) of 1977 which established a National Revolutionary Assembly, of 196 members, representing socio-professional classes, rather than geographical constituencies, elected for a five-year term by universal adult suffrage, through a simple plurality voting system. The Assembly, in turn, elects the President, as head of state, to serve a similar five-year term. Since 1975, when the nation's name was changed from Dahomey to Benin, it has been a one-party state, committed to the path of 'scientific socialism'. The party is the Party of the People's Revolution of Benin (PRPB) and, as well as being President, General Kerekou chairs its Central Committee. It is within the PRPB that ultimate political power lies.

Political parties
The Party of the People's Revolution of Benin (PRPB) is the only legally permitted party. It was formed in 1975 as the political vehicle for General Kerekou. It has a Marxist-Leninist orientation.

Latest elections
In the 1984 elections for the National Revolutionary Assembly all candidates were PRPB nominees.

Political history
Benin used to consist of a number of small, generally warring, principalities, the most powerful being the Kingdom of Dahomey, which was established in the seventeenth century. The area was conquered by the French in 1892 and became the French Protectorate of Dahomey. It was made part of French West Africa in 1904, and in 1958 became a self-governing dominion within the French Community. In 1960 it became a fully independent state.

For the next twelve years it went through a period of acute political instability, with swings from civilian to military rule and with disputes among the inhabitants of the northern, central and southern regions. In 1972 the Deputy Chief of the army, Mathieu Kerekou, established a military regime pledged to give fair representation to each region, his initial instrument of government being an appointed National Council of the Revolution (CNR). In 1974 Kerekou announced that the country would follow a path of 'scientific socialism', based on Marxist-Leninist principles, and the following year the nation's name was changed from Dahomey to Benin.

In 1977 the CNR was dissolved and a civilian government formed, a Fundamental Law establishing a National Revolutionary Assembly which, in 1980, elected Kerekou as President and head of state. He was re-elected in 1984. After some initial economic and social difficulties, the Kerekou government showed signs of growing stability and relations with France, Benin's biggest trading partner, improved considerably. In 1983 President Mitterrand paid the first visit of a French head of state to Benin. In 1987 Kerekou resigned from the army, further to demonstrate the movement towards genuine democracy, at the same time announcing a more liberal economic policy.

BOTSWANA

Republic of Botswana

Capital: Gaborone

Social and economic data
Area: 600,400 km^2
Population: 1.100m*
Pop density per km^2: 2*
Literacy rate: 41%*

GDP: $1,100m*; per capita GDP: $1000
Economy type: low income
Labour force in agriculture: 77%

*1985

Ethnic composition
About 94 per cent of the population are Tswana, 5 per cent are Bushmen and 1 per cent are European.

Religions
The majority of the population follow traditional animist beliefs and about 30 per cent are Christians.

Political features
State type: liberal democratic
Date of state formation: 1966
Political structure: unitary
Executive: limited presidential
Assembly: one-chamber
Party structure: two-party
Human rights rating: 78%

Local and regional government
The country is divided into nine districts, ranging in population from under 20,000 to over 300,000, and six independent townships. Each has an elected council and is mainly reponsible for primary education, licensing and collecting taxes in its own locality.

Head of state and head of government
President Dr Quett Ketamile Joni Masire, since 1980.

Political leaders since 1970
1966–80 Sir Seretse Khama (BDP), 1980– Dr Quett Ketamile Joni Masire (BDP).

Political system
The 1966 constitution contains features which blend the British system of parliamentary accountability with the distinctive tribal nature of the country. It provides for a National Assembly of 40 members, 34 elected by universal adult suffrage, four elected by the Assembly itself, all through a simple plurality voting procedure, plus the Speaker and the Attorney-General. It has a life of five years. The President is elected by the Assembly for its duration and is an *ex officio* member of it. There is also a House of Chiefs of 15, consisting of the Chiefs of the country's eight principal tribes, plus four members elected by the Chiefs themselves and three elected by the House in general. The President is answerable to the Assembly. He may delay a bill for up to six months and then either sign it or dissolve the Assembly, putting both it and himself up for election. The House of Chiefs is consulted by the President and the Assembly in matters affecting them. The President chooses and appoints a cabinet which is answerable to the Assembly.

Political parties

The main political parties are the Botswana Democratic Party (BDP) and the Botswana National Front (BNF). There are four other smaller parties or political groupings. The BDP was formed in 1962 and has a moderate, centrist orientation. The BNF was formed in 1967 and its support comes mainly from the urban working class. Its stance is moderate, left-of-centre.

Latest elections

In the 1984 National Assembly elections BDP won 29 of the 34 seats with a 68 per cent share of the vote, the BNF winning four seats with a 20.4 per cent vote.

Political history

With South Africa to the south and east, Zimbabwe to the north-east and Namibia to the west and north, Botswana occupies a delicate position geographically and politically. It was originally Bechuanaland and, at the request of local rulers who feared an invasion by Boer farmers, became a British protectorate in 1885. When the British parliament passed the Union of South Africa Act in 1910, making South Africa independent, it made provision for the possibility of Bechuanaland eventually becoming part of South Africa, but stipulated that this would not happen without the consent of the local inhabitants. Successive South African governments requested the transfer but the Chiefs always resisted it, preferring full independence to a South African takeover.

In 1960 a new constitution was agreed, providing for a Legislative Council but still under the control of a British High Commissioner. In 1963 High Commission rule was ended and in the Legislative Council elections the newly formed Bechuanaland Democratic Party (BDP) won a majority of seats. Its leader, Seretse Khama, had been deposed as chief of the Bangangwato Tribe in 1950, following his marriage to an Englishwoman two years before. He was in exile in England and returned to lead his party as Prime Minister. In 1966 the country, renamed Botswana, became an independent state within the Commonwealth and Sir Seretse Khama, as he had now become, was the new nation's first President.

He continued to be re-elected until his death in 1980 when he was succeeded by the Vice-President, Dr Quett Masire. Dr Masire was re-elected in 1984. Since independence Botswana has earned a reputation for political and economic stability and has successfully followed a path of non-alignment. From time to time it has been provoked by South Africa, which has accused it of providing bases for the African National Congress (ANC). This has always been denied by both Botswana and the ANC itself. South Africa has persistently pressed Botswana to sign a non-aggression pact, similar to the Nkomati Accord, agreed between South Africa and Mozambique, but it has always refused. In 1985 South African forces raided the capital, Gaborone, allegedly in search of ANC guerrillas, killing twelve people. Botswana demanded compensation. In 1987 the governments of Botswana and Mozambique agreed to set up a permanent joint commission to improve political, economic and cultural relations between the two countries.

BURKINA FASO

People's Republic of Burkina Faso
'Land of Upright Men'

Capital: Ouagadougou

Social and economic data
Area: 274,200 km^2
Population: 7.100m*
Pop density per km^2: 33*
Literacy rate: 9%*
GDP: $870m*; per capita GDP: $123
Economy type: low income
Labour force in agriculture: 79%

*1985

Ethnic composition
There are over 50 tribes in the country. They include the nomadic Mossi, 48 per cent of the population, the Gourma, 5 per cent, and the Fulani, 10 per cent. The settled tribes include, in the north, the Lobi-Dagari, 7 per cent, and the Mande, 7 per cent; in the south-east, the Bobo, 7 per cent; and in the south-west the Senoufo, 6 per cent, and the Gourounsi, 5 per cent.

Religions
Fifty-seven per cent of the population follow traditional, animist religions, about 30 per cent are Muslims and there are about 1 million Christians, the vast majority being Roman Catholics.

Political features
State type: military authoritarian
Date of state formation: 1960
Political structure: unitary
Executive: military
Assembly: suspended in 1977
Party structure: one-party
Human rights rating: poor

Local and regional government
For administrative purposes, the country is divided into 25 provinces, ranging in population from about 88,000 to nearly 800,000, and they in turn are subdivided into 44 *cercles*, or districts, within which are the villages.

Head of state and head of government
President Blaise Compaore, since 1987.

Political leaders since 1970
1966–1980 Sangoule Lamizana (Military), 1980–82 Zerbo (Military), 1982–83 Jean-Baptiste Ouedraogo (Military), 1983–87 Thomas Sankara (Military), 1987– Blaise Compaore (Military).

Political system
Since achieving independence in 1960, the country has experienced only a brief period of civilian rule. The original constitution was suspended and then a military coup, in 1980, suspended a later, 1977, version. After two further coups, in 1982 and 1983, power was taken by a National Revolutionary Council, comprising the only permitted political factions, the Patriotic League for Development (LIPAD), the Union of the Communist Struggle (ULC) and the Communist Officers' Regrouping (ROC), led by Thomas Sankara. The 57-member National Assembly was dissolved and the President now rules through an appointed Council of Ministers.

Political parties
The National Revolutionary Council comprises the three left-wing groupings of LIPAD, ULC and ROC. LIPAD was formed in 1973 as a Marxist, pro-Soviet party. ULC dates from 1978 and ROC from 1983. As all three are under the control of the military regime. Burkina Faso is, effectively, a one-party state.

Latest elections
There have been no free elections since 1978.

Political history
Formerly known as Upper Volta, Burkina Faso was a province of French West Africa. In 1958 it became a self-governing republic and two years later achieved full independence, with Maurice Yameogo as its first President. A military coup in 1966 removed Yameogo and installed Colonel Sangoule Lamizana as President and Prime Minister. He suspended the constitution, dissolved the National Assembly, put a ban on political activities and set up a Supreme Council of the Armed Forces as the instrument of government. In 1969 the ban on political activities was lifted and in the following year a referendum approved a new constitution, based on civilian rule, which was to come into effect after a four-year transitional period of combined military and civilian government.

However, after disagreements between the military and civilian members of the government, General Lamizana announced, in 1974, a return to rule by the army and the dissolution of the National Assembly. Three years later political activities were again permitted and another referendum approved a constitution which would create a civilian government. In the 1978 elections the Volta Democratic Union (UDV) won a majority in the National Asembly and Laminaza was elected President, but a deteriorating economy led to a wave of strikes and Laminaza was overthrown in a bloodless coup in 1980.

Colonel Zerbo, who had led the coup, formed a Government of National Recovery, suspended the constitution again and dissolved the National Assembly. In 1982 Zerbo was, in turn, ousted by junior officers and Major Jean-Baptiste Ouedraogo emerged as leader of a new military regime, with Captain Thomas Sankara as Prime Minister. In 1983 Sankara led another coup and seized supreme power. Opposition politicians were put under arrest and a National Revolutionary Council (CNR) set up. In 1984 Sankara announced that the country would be known as Burkina Faso ('land of upright men'), symbolising a break with its colonial past. The government strengthened ties with neighbouring Ghana and established links with Benin and Libya. In October 1987 President Sankara was killed, allegedly accidentally, in a coup led by a close colleague, Captain Blaise Compaore, who then succeeded him.

BURUNDI

Republic of Burundi

Capital: Bujumbura

Social and economic data
Area: 27,830
Population: 4.900m*
Pop density per km^2: 176*
Literacy rate: 34%*
GDP: $1,078m*; per capita GDP: $220
Economy type: low income
Labour force in agriculture: 93%

*1985

Ethnic composition
There are two main tribes in the country: the Hutu, comprising about 85 per cent of the population, and the Tutsi, about 14 per cent. A virtual tribal apartheid has been operated for many years by the Tutsi-controlled government and massive killings of Hutus were reported in 1988. There is a small Pygmy minority, comprising about 1 per cent of the population, and a few Europeans and Asians.

Religions
About 60 per cent of the population, mostly Hutus, are Roman Catholic, most of the other inhabitants following traditional beliefs, mainly in a God *imana*. There are also about 160,000 Pentacostalists and 60,000 Anglicans.

Political features
State type: military authoritarian
Date of state formation: 1962
Political structure: unitary
Executive: military
Assembly: one-chamber
Party structure: one-party
Human rights rating: poor

Local and regional government
For administrative purposes, the country is divided into eight provinces, which are further subdivided into 18 *arrondissements* and 78 communes.

Head of state and head of government
President Pierre Buyoya, since 1987.

Political leaders since 1970
1966–1976 Michel Micombero (UPRONA), 1976–1987 Jean-Baptiste Bagaza (Military), 1987– Pierre Buyoya (Military).

Political system
Under its 1981 constitution, Burundi is a one-party state, the party being the Union for National Progress (UPRONA), at whose head is the President. He is elected by universal adult suffrage for a five-year term. A National Assembly of 65 members has the same period of tenure. Fifty-two members of Assembly are elected on the basis of adult suffrage, through a simple plurality voting system, and 13 are appointed by the President. After the 1987 coup the Assembly was dissolved. Ultimate political power lies with UPRONA.

Political parties
The Union for National Progress (UPRONA) is the only legally permitted party. It was founded in 1958, while Urundi, as the country was then called, was a monarchy, and given its monopoly position, by royal decree, in 1966. It is a socialist party with a strong nationalist orientation.

Latest elections
In the 1982 National Assembly elections there were 104 candidates for the 52 elected seats. All were UPRONA nominees.

Political history
What is now called Burundi was a Tutsi kingdom known as Urundi which became part of the empire of German East Africa in 1899. During the First World War it was occupied by Belgian forces and later, as part of Ruanda-Urundi, was administered by Belgium as a League of Nations, and later United Nations, trust territory.

As a prelude to full independence, elections in 1961 were supervised by the UN, and won by UPRONA, which had been formed by Louis, one of the sons of the reigning King, Mwambutsa IV. Louis became Prime Minister but was assassinated after only two weeks in office and succeeded by his brother-in-law, André Muhirwa.

In 1962 Urundi separated from Ruanda, and, as Burundi, was given internal self-government and then full independence. In 1966 King Mwambutsa IV, after a 50-year reign, was deposed by another son, Charles, with the assistance of the army, and the constitution was suspended. Later in the year Charles, now Ntare V, was himself deposed by his Prime Minister, Captain Michel Micombero, who declared Burundi a republic. Micombero was a member of the Tutsi tribe whose main rivals were the numerically superior Hutus. In 1972 the deposed Ntare V was killed, allegedly by Hutus, and this provided an excuse for the Tutsis to carry out a series of large-scale massacres of Hutus, many of whom fled the country. In 1973 amendments to the constitution made Micombero President and Prime Minister and in the following year UPRONA was declared the only legal political party, with the President as its Secretary-General.

In 1976 Micombero was himself deposed in an army coup led by Colonel Jean-Baptiste Bagaza, who was appointed President by a Supreme Revolutionary Council. He was assisted by the Prime Minister. The following year the Prime Minister announced a return to civilian rule and a five-year plan to eliminate corruption and secure social justice. In 1978 the post of Prime Minister was abolished and in 1981 a new constitution, providing for a National Assembly, was adopted after a referendum. In the 1984 election Bagaza, as the only presidential candidate, secured over 99 per cent of the votes cast.

In September 1987 another coup, led by Major Pierre Buyoya, ousted Bagaza and a Military Council for National Redemption was established. Despite Buyoya's promises to improve the human rights situation in Burundi, discrimination against the Hutus continues to be practised by the Tutsi minority and widespread killings were reported in 1988, many of them, allegedly by Tutsi soldiers. In October 1988 the appointment of the first Hutu Prime Minister provided a hint of a rapprochement between the two tribes.

CAMEROON

Republic of Cameroon
République du Cameroun

Capital: Yaounde

Social and economic data
Area: 474,000 km^2
Population: 10.000m*
Pop density per km^2: 21*
Literacy rate: 41%*
GDP: $7,800m*; per capita GDP: $780
Economy type: low income
Labour force in agriculture: 79%

*1985

Ethnic composition
The main ethnic groups include the Cameroon Highlanders, 31 per cent, the Equatorial Bantu, 19 per cent, the Kirdi, 11 per cent, the Fulani, 10 per cent, the Northwestern Bantu, 8 per cent, and the Eastern Nigritic, 7 per cent.

Religions
About 40 per cent of the population are Christians, mostly Roman Catholics, about 39 per cent have traditional, animist beliefs and about 21 per cent are Muslims.

Political features
State type: authoritarian nationalist
Date of state formation: 1960
Political structure: unitary
Executive: unlimited presidential
Assembly: one-chamber
Party structure: one-party
Human rights rating: 53%

Local and regional government

The country is divided into ten provinces, ranging in population from under 400,000 to over 1.5 million. These are further subdivided into departments. A hierarchy of officials, responsible for regional and local administration, report to the President's representatives.

Head of state and head of government

President Paul Biya, from 1982.

Political leaders since 1970

1960–82 Ahmadou Ahidjo (UNC), 1982– Paul Biya (RPDC).

Political system

Cameroon was a federal state until 1972 when a new constitution, revised in 1975, made it unitary. The constitution provides for a President elected for a five-year term and a single-chamber National Assembly of 120 elected for a similar term. All elections are conducted through the simple plurality voting system. The President can lengthen or shorten the life of the Assembly. He chooses his own cabinet and may submit himself for re-election. He is also president of the RDPC, where ultimate political power lies.

Political parties

The only permitted political party is the Democratic Assembly of the Cameroon People (RDPC). It was formed in 1966, under the name of the Cameroon National Union (UNC), by a merger of the governing party of each state of the original federation and the four opposition parties. The name was changed to RDPC in 1985. Its orientation is nationalist and left-of-centre.

Latest elections

In the 1988 National Assembly elections voters were given the opportunity of choosing between two lists of candidates, all RPDC nominees. In the 1988 presidential election Paul Biya received 98.75 per cent of the vote.

Political history

Although subject to slave trading by the Belgians, Cameroon avoided colonial rule until 1884 when it became a German protectorate. After the First World War the League of Nations gave France a mandate to govern about 80 per cent of the area, mainly in the east and south, with Britain administering the remaining 20 per cent. In 1946 both became United Nations trust territories.

In 1957 French Cameroons became a state within the French Community and three years later fully independent as the Republic of Cameroon. A 1961 plebiscite resulted in the northern part of British Cameroons deciding to merge with neighbouring Nigeria, which had recently obtained its independence, and the southern part joining the Republic of Cameroon. Together they became the Federal Republic of Cameroon, with French and English as the official languages. The former French zone was called East Cameroon and the former British part West Cameroon.

Ahmadou Ahidjo, who had been elected the first President of the original republic in 1960, became President of the new federal republic and was re-elected in 1965. In 1966 it became a one-party state, when the two government parties and most of the opposition parties merged into the Cameroon National Union (UNC). Extreme left-wing opposition to the single party was finally crushed in 1971. In 1972 a new constitution abolished the federal system and in 1973 a new National Assembly was elected.

In 1982 Ahidjo resigned, nominating Paul Biya as his successor. Soon after taking office in 1983 Biya began to remove supporters of his predecessor and Ahidjo accused him of trying to create a police state, resigning from the presidency of UNC. Biya was, nevertheless, re-elected in 1984 while Ahidjo went into exile in France. Biya strengthened his personal control by abolishing the post of Prime Minister and reshuffling his cabinet. He also announced that the nation's name would be changed from the United Republic of Cameroon to the Republic of Cameroon. An attempt to overthrow him by supporters of the exiled Ahidjo was defeated and many of the people involved were executed. In 1985 UNC changed its name to RPDC and Biya tightened his control still further by more cabinet changes. In 1988 he was re-elected for the second time.

CAPE VERDE

Republic of Cape Verde
Republica de Cabo Verde

Capital: Praia

Social and economic data

Area: 4,033 km^2
Population: 0.312m*
Pop density per km^2: 77*
Literacy rate: 37%*
GDP: $100m*; per capita GDP: $320
Economy type: low income
Labour force in agriculture: 54%

*1985

Ethnic composition

About 60 per cent of the population are mixed descendants of Portuguese settlers and African slaves and are called *Mestiços* or Creoles. The rest are mainly African. The European population is very small.

Religions

About 98 per cent of the total population are Roman Catholics.

Political features
State type: nationalistic socialist
Date of state formation: 1975
Political structure: unitary
Executive: unlimited presidential
Assembly: single-chamber
Party structure: one-party
Human rights rating: N/A

Local and regional government
Cape Verde is divided into two districts (*distritos*), each of which is subdivided into seven councils (*concelhos*). The island of Santo Antao comprises three councils and the island of Sao Tiago four councils.

Head of state and head of government
President Aristedes Pereira, since 1975.

Political leaders since 1970
1975– Aristedes Pereira (PAICV).

Political system
The current constitution dates from 1980 and provides for a National People's Assembly of 83, elected by universal adult suffrage, through a simple plurality voting system, for a term of five years. All candidates for Assembly seats are nominees of the sole legal political party. The President, who is both head of state and head of government, is elected by the Assembly for the same length of term. The constitution had also provided for an eventual union with Guinea-Bissau but this was deleted in 1981.

Political parties
The only legal party was originally formed, before independence from Portugal in 1975, as the African Party for the Independence of Portuguese Guinea and Cape Verde (PAIGC), in anticipation of the eventual union of the two countries, but when this was abandoned it became the African Party for the Independence of Cape Verde (PAICV). The President is its Secretary-General. Its orientation is African-nationalist.

Latest elections
In the 1985 National Assembly elections there was a single list of 83 PAICV-nominated candidates. The turnout was 94.5 per cent.

Political history
The Cape Verde islands were colonised by the Portuguese in the fifteenth century and from the 1950s onwards a liberation movement developed. The mainland territory to which the Cape Verde archipelago was linked, Guinea, now Guinea-Bissau, was granted independence in 1974, and a process began for the eventual union of Cape Verde and Guinea-Bissau.

In 1975 Cape Verde secured its own independence from Portugal and a provisional government was set up, composed of Portuguese settlers and locally born members of the PAIGC. In the same year the first National People's Assembly was elected and Aristides Pereira, Secretary-General of PAIGC, became President of the new state.

A constitution was adopted in 1980 making provision for the coming together of Cape Verde and Guinea-Bissau but by 1981 it had become clear that there was not enough support for the union so the idea was dropped and PAIGC became PAICV. Relations with Guinea-Bissau, which had cooled, gradually improved and under the guidance of Pereira, who was re-elected in 1981 and 1986, Cape Verde has followed a careful policy of non-alignment and achieved considerable respect within the region.

CENTRAL AFRICAN REPUBLIC

République Centrafricaine

Capital: Bangui

Social and economic data
Area: 625,000 km^2
Population: 2.744m*
Pop density per km^2: 4*
Literacy rate: 27%
GDP: $670m*; per capita GDP: $244
Economy type: low income
Labour force in agriculture: 85%

*1985

Ethnic composition
There are over 80 ethnic groups but 68 per cent of the population fall into one of three: the Banda, 30 per cent, the Baya-Mandjia, 29 per cent, and the Mbaka, 7 per cent. There are clearly defined ethnic zones: the forest region, inhabited by Bantu groups, the Mbaka, Lissongo and Mbimu, and the Pygmies, Babinga; the river banks, populated by the Sango, Yakoma, Baniri and Buraka; and the savannah region, where the Banda, Zande, Sara, Ndle and Bizao live. Europeans number less than 7,000, the majority being French.

Religions
Figures for adherents to particular religions are not very reliable but it is estimated that the majority of the population hold traditional, animist beliefs; about a third are Christians, mainly Roman Catholics; and about 5 per cent are Muslims.

Political features
State type: military authoritarian
Date of state formation: 1960
Political structure: unitary
Executive: military
Assembly: none sitting
Party structure: none active
Human rights rating: bad

Local and regional government
On the basis of French experience, the country is divided into 15 prefectures, further subdivided into 47 subprefectures.

Head of state and head of government
President General André Kolingba, since 1981.

Political leaders since 1970
1965–79 Jean-Bedel Bokassa (Military), 1979–81 David Dacko (Military), 1981– André Kolingba (Military).

Political system
The original constitution, adopted following independence in 1960, was annulled in 1972 and then a new version, which came into force in 1981, was suspended in a military coup within months of its adoption and legislative powers, which were to be held by an elected National Assembly, were placed in the hands of a Military Committee for National Recovery (CMRN). Four years later CMRN was dissolved and a new 22-member Council of Ministers, containing both military and civilians, was established. A new constitution was approved by referendum in 1986. It provides for a President to be popularly elected for a six-year term and a two-chamber Congress consisting of a National Assembly of 52 members, elected by universal adult suffrage, through a simple plurality voting system, and an Economic and Regional Council, half elected by the Assembly and half appointed by the President. The Assembly has a five-year term and meets at the summons of the President.

Despite the outward manifestations of democratic government, the government of the Central African Republic still displays many of the characteristics of a militarily controlled state.

Political parties
All political activity was banned after the 1981 coup but opposition groups, although passive, still exist. The major ones are the Patriotic Front Ubangi Workers' Party (FPO-PT), the Central African Movement for National Liberation (MCLN) and the Movement for the Liberation of the Central African People (MLPC). Collectively, they comprise the Central African Revolutionary Party (PRC). In 1987 the Central African Democratic Assembly (RDC) was founded as the only legal party. It acts as the political organ of the militarily controlled governing regime.

Latest elections
In the 1987 National Assembly elections there were 142 candidates for the 52 seats. All were RDC nominees.

Political history
The territory of Ubangi-Shari was given self-government within what was then French Equatorial Africa in 1958 and two years later achieved full independence. The leading political figure was Barthelemy Boganda who had founded the Movement for the Social Evolution of Black Africa (MESAN) and had been a leading figure in the campaign for independence. He became the country's first Prime Minister. A year before full independence he was killed in an air crash and succeeded by his nephew, David Dacko, who became President in the independent nation in 1960. In 1962 he established a one-party state, with MESAN as the only legal

political organisation. Dacko was overthrown in a military coup in December 1965 and the commander-in-chief of the army, Colonel Jean-Bedel Bokassa, assumed power.

Bokassa progressively increased his personal control of the political system and, in 1972, annulled the constitution and made himself Life President. Two years later he awarded himself the title of Marshal of the Republic. In 1976 ex-President Dacko was persuaded to return as Bokassa's personal adviser and later that year the republic was restyled the Central African Empire (CAE). In 1977 Bokassa was crowned Emperor at a lavish ceremony his country could ill afford. His rule became increasingly dictatorial and idiosyncratic, leading to revolts by students and, in April 1979, by school children, who objected to the compulsory wearing of school uniforms, manufactured by a company owned by the Bokassa family. Many of the children were imprisoned and it is estimated that at least 100 were killed, with the Emperor, allegedly, being personally involved.

In September 1979, while Bokassa was in Libya, Dacko ousted him in a bloodless coup, backed by France. The country became a republic again, with Dacko as President. He initially retained a number of Bokassa's former ministers but, following student unrest, they were dropped and in February 1981 a new constitution was adopted, with an elected National Assembly. Dacko was elected President for a six-year term in March but opposition to him grew and in September 1981 he was deposed in another bloodless coup, led by the armed forces chief-of-staff, General André Kolingba. The constitution was suspended, as well as all political activity, and a military government installed. Undercover opposition to the Kolingba regime continued, with some French support, but relations with France improved following an unofficial visit by President Mitterrand in October 1982.

By 1984 there was some evidence of an eventual return to constitutional government. The leaders of the banned political parties were granted an amnesty and at the end of the year the French president paid a state visit. In January 1985 proposals for a new constitution were announced and in September civilians were introduced for the first time into Kolingba's administration.

In 1986 former President and Emperor Bokassa returned from exile and was tried for murder, illegal detentions and embezzlement of state funds. Although he was found guilty and sentenced to death, President Kolingba announced in March 1988 that, on the recommendation of the country's senior judges, he had decided to commute the death sentence.

Athough the excesses of the Bokassa regime are now a thing of the past, the Central African Republic is still under authoritarian, military rule. The adoption of a new constitution and the revival of an elected assembly fail to provide sufficient proof of a complete return to democratic government.

CHAD

Republic of Chad
République du Tchad

Capital: N'djamena

Social and economic data
Area: 1,284,000 km^2

Population: 5.200m*
Pop density per km^2: 4*
Literacy rate: 12%
GDP: $490m*; per capita GDP: $94
Economy type: low income
Labour force in agriculture: 80%

*1985

Ethnic composition
Northern Chad is populated mainly by Arabs and the south by Pagan, or Kirdi, groups. There is no single, dominant group in any region, the largest being the Sara, who comprise about a quarter of the total population. Europeans, mainly French, constitute a very small minority.

Religions
About 52 per cent of the population are Muslims, about 43 per cent follow traditional, African religions and about 5 per cent, mainly the Sara, are Christians.

Political features
State type: authoritarian nationalist
Date of state formation: 1960
Political structure: unitary
Executive: unlimited presidential
Assembly: none sitting
Party structure: multi-party
Human rights rating: N/A

Local and regional government
Following French experience, the country is divided into 14 prefectures within which are 54 subprefectures, 27 administrative posts and nine municipalities.

Head of state and head of government
President Hissène Habré, since 1982.

Political leaders since 1970
1960–75, François Tombalbaye (PPT), 1975–79, Felix Malloum (Military), 1979–82, Goukouni Oueddi (Military), 1982– Hissène Habré (UNIR).

Political system
A provisional constitution of 1982, following a civil war, provides for a President and Council of Ministers, appointed and led by the President. Executive and legislative power is exercised by the Council.

Political parties
In 1984 a new party regrouping, the National Union for Independence (UNIR), was formed in an attempt to consolidate the President's position, but a number of opposition groups also exist. There are currently 15 active groupings but most tend to be more like factions than parties.

Latest elections

There have been no elections since the military coup of 1975.

Political history

Chad, then called Kanem, was settled by Arabs from the seventh century onwards. From 1913 it was a province of French Equatorial Africa and then became an autonomous state within the French Community, in 1958, with François Tombalbaye as its Prime Minister. Full independence was achieved in 1960 and Tombalbaye was elected President. His party, the Sara-dominated Chadian Progressive Party (PPT), held 57 of the 85 National Assembly seats. He was soon faced with unrest, mainly because of disagreements between the nomadic Arabs of the north, who saw Libya as a natural ally, and and the Sara Christians of the south, who felt more in sympathy with neighbouring Nigeria.

A conflict began less on the basis of party divisions and more on the basis of loosely organised private armies, each loyal to a particular leader. By 1975 at least three groups claimed to be the true revolutionaries. In the north the Chadian National Liberation Front (Frolinat) led a revolt, the two leading figures in it being Goukouni Oueddi and Hissène Habré.

Meanwhile Tombalbaye's largely inept attempts at 'Chadisation', forcing the adoption of Sara beliefs and practices, aroused opposition within government ranks and in 1975 he was killed in a coup led by the former army chief of staff, Felix Malloum, whom Tombalbaye had removed two years earlier. Malloum made himself President of a Supreme Military Council but despite his appeals for national unity, Frolinat continued to oppose him, with support from Libya, which was thought to be interested in a small strip of land in the north, believed to contain uranium deposits.

By 1978 Frolinat, now led by General Goukouni, had expanded its territorial control but was halted with the aid of French troops. Malloum tried to reach a political settlement by making the other former Frolinat leader, Hissène Habré, Prime Minister but disagreements between the two men soon developed. In 1979 fighting broke out again between government and Frolinat forces and Malloum was forced to flee the country.

Conferences of rival groups convened in Nigeria eventually resulted in the formation of a provisional government (GUNT), with Goukouni as President. He remained in power, mainly through Libyan support, but proposals for a merger with Libya proved so unpopular that Goukouni rejected them and Libya withdrew most of its forces. The Organisation for African Unity (OAU) set up a peace-keeping force, composed of Nigerian, Senegalese and Zairean troops but this failed to prevent civil war breaking out between the armies of Goukouni and Habré.

By April 1981 Habré's Armed Forces of the North (FAN)) were in control of half the country, forcing Goukouni to flee, eventually setting up a 'government in exile'. In 1983 a majority of OAU members agreed to recognise Habré's regime as the legitimate government but Goukouni, with Libyan support, fought on. After bombing raids by Libya, Habré appealed to France for help and 3,000 troops were sent as military instructors, but with orders to retaliate should they come under attack. Following a Franco-African summit, in August 1983, a cease-fire was agreed in December, the latitude line 16 degrees north eventually becoming the dividing line between the opposing forces. The Libyan President, Colonel

Kadhafi, proposed a simultaneous withdrawal of French and Libyan troops and this was eventually accepted. By December all French troops had been withdrawn but there was scepticism about Libya's compliance with the agreement. Meanwhile Habré had dissolved the military arm of Frolinat and formed a new political party, the National Union for Independence (UNIR) but opposition to his regime grew.

In 1987 Goukouni was reported to be at odds with the Libyan leader, Colonel Kadhafi and under house arrest in Tripoli, but despite these rumours the Libyans intensified their military operations in northern Chad, producing an equal response from the Habré government, and renewed, if reluctant, support by France. It was announced in September 1987 that France, Chad and Libya had agreed to observe a cease-fire proposed by the Organisation of African Unity and in the same year Goukouni publicly backed Habré as the legitimate head of state. In May 1988 Colonel Kadhafi made a surprisingly generous offer to meet President Habré and resolve outstanding differences and in October of the same year full diplomatic relations between the two countries were restored. In December 1988 a 'reconciliation accord' between the National Chadian Front (FNT), which had succeeded GUNT, and the government was signed.

COMOROS

Federal Islamic Republic of Comoros
Républiqne Federale Islamique des Comores

Capital: Moroni

Social and economic data

Area: 1,860 km^2
Population: 0.469m*
Pop density per km^2: 252*
Literacy rate: 48%*
GDP: $110m*; per capita GDP: $234
Economy type: low income
Labour force in agriculture: 62%

*1985

Ethnic composition

The islands have a population of mainly mixed origins, Africans, Arabs and Malaysians predominating. The principal ethnic group is known as the Antalaotra.

Religions

The majority of people are Muslims and Islam is the state religion. There are about 2,000 Roman Catholics.

Political features
State type: authoritarian nationalist
Date of state formation: 1975
Political structure: federal
Executive: unlimited presidential
Assembly: one-chamber
Party structure: one-party
Human rights rating: N/A

Local and regional government
The Comoros consists of three main islands, Grande Comore, with a population of 189,000, Anjouan, with 148,000, and Moheli, with 19,000. Although each of the islands has a certain amount of autonomy, with its own governor and Council, it all constitutes a very limited form of federalism. The President appoints the governors and the federal government has responsibility for the islands' resources.

Head of state and head of government
President Ahmed Abdallah Abderemane, since 1978.

Political leaders since 1970
1975–76 Admed Abdallah Abderemane (Udzima), 1976–78 Ali Soilih (Front National Uni), 1978– Ahmed Abdallah Abderemane (Udzima).

Political system
The 1978 constitution provides for a President, who is both head of state and head of government. He appoints and presides over a Council of Ministers. The President is elected by universal adult suffrage, through a simple plurality voting system, for a six-year term. There is a single-chamber Federal Assembly of 42 members, elected in a similar fashion for a five-year term.

Political parties
Since 1979 Comoros has been a one-party state although unofficial opposition groups still exist, but mostly based in France. The party is the Comoran Union for Progress (Udzima). Its orientation is nationalist and Islamic.

Latest elections
In the 1987 elections for the Federal Assembly candidates in opposition to the government party were allowed to stand but, although they collectively obtained 35.5 per cent of the vote in 20 contested constituencies, Udzima won all the seats.

Political history
The Comoros islands of Grande Comoro, Anjouan, Moheli and Mayotte became a French colony in 1912 and were attached to Madagascar in 1914. They separated from Madagascar and their status changed to that of a separate French Overseas Territory in 1947. Internal self-government was obtained in 1961 but full independence was not achieved until 1975 because of Mayotte's reluctance to sever its links with France. Although the

Comoros were admitted into UN membership in 1975, with Ahmed Abdallah Abderemane as the first President, the island of Mayotte did not favour wholehearted independence and insisted on maintaining a link with France. In August 1975 a coup, led by Ali Soilih, deposed Abdallah and abolished the Assembly, resulting in a deterioration in relations with France. Ali Soilih was elected President and took on increased powers under a new constitution. In the following year Mayotte voted overwhelmingly to remain with France as a dependency.

In 1978 Soilih was killed by French mercenaries, supposedly working for Abdallah. A federal Islamic republic was proclaimed, a new constitution adopted and Abdallah was elected President. With these changes, diplomatic relations with France were restored. In 1979 the Comoros became a one-party state and the powers of the federal government were increased. In the same year a plot by British mercenaries to overthrow Abdallah was foiled. In 1984 he was re-elected President and in the following year the constitution was amended, abolishing the post of Prime Minister and making Abdallah head of government as well as head of state.

CONGO

People's Republic of the Congo
République Populaire du Congo

Capital: Brazzaville

Social and economic data
Area: 342,000 km^2
Population: 1.800m*
Pop density per km^2: 5*
Literacy rate: 16%*
GDP: $2,200m*; per capita GDP: $1,222
Economy type: middle income
Labour force in agriculture: 31%

*1985

Ethnic composition
The vast majority of Congolese are Bantus and comprise 15 main ethnic groups and 75 tribes. The Kongo, or Bakongo as they are sometimes called, account for about 45 per cent of the population, then come the Teke, or Bateke, about 20 per cent, and then the Mboshi, or Boubangui, about 16 per cent.

Religions
About half the population follow traditional, animist beliefs and the rest are mostly Christians. There are also about 40,000 Muslims.

Political features
State type: nationalistic socialist
Date of state formation: 1960
Political structure: unitary
Executive: unlimited presidential
Assembly: one-chamber
Party structure: one-party
Human rights rating: N/A

Local and regional government
The country is divided into nine provinces, each with its popularly elected regional council and executive committee. They act under the direction of commissars appointed by the central committee of the governing party, the PCT.

Head of state and head of government
President Colonel Denis Sassau-Nguesso, since 1979.

Political leaders since 1970
1968–77 Marien Ngouabi (PCT), 1977–79 Yhombi-Opango (Military), 1979– Denis Sassau-Nguesso (PCT).

Political system
The Congo is a one-party state based on the Congolese Labour Party (PCT). The President of the Central Committee of PCT is automatically elected state President for a five-year term. He chairs the Council of Ministers. The single-chamber legislature is the People's National Assembly and consists of 153 members who are elected by universal adult suffrage, through a simple plurality voting procedure, from a list prepared by the PCT.

Political parties
The PCT was formed in 1969 to replace the National Revolutionary Movement (MNR). It is a Marxist-Leninist party, committed to the path of what it calls 'scientific socialism'.

Latest elections
In the 1984 National Assembly elections there was a single list of PCT-nominated candidates and all were elected.

Political history
After years of exploitation by Portuguese slave traders, the Congo became a colony within French Equatorial Africa in 1910. It was declared an autonomous republic within the French Community in 1958 and Abbé Youlou, a Roman Catholic priest, who involved himself in politics and was suspended by the Church, was elected Prime Minister and then President when full independence was achieved in 1960. Two years later plans were announced for the creation of a one-party state but in 1963, following industrial unrest, Youlou was forced to resign.

A new constitution was approved and Alphonse Mossamba-Debat, a former finance minister, became President, adopting a policy of what he described as 'scientific socialism'. He declared the National Revolutionary Movement (MNR) to be the only permitted political party. In 1968 a military coup, led by Captain Marien Ngouabi, overthrew Mossamba-Debat and the National Assembly was replaced by a National Council of the Revolution. Ngouabi proclaimed a Marxist state but kept close economic links with France.

In 1970 the nation became the People's Republic of the Congo, with the PCT as the sole legal party and three years later a new constitution provided for an Assembly chosen from a single party list. In 1977 Ngouabi was assassinated and eventually replaced by Colonel Joachim Yhombi-Opango. Two years later Yhombi-Opango, having discovered a plot to overthrow him, handed over the government to the Central Committee of PCT and eventually Denis Sassou-Nguessou became President.

Sassou-Nguessou has steadily moved his country out of the Soviet sphere of influence and strengthened links with France, the United States and China. In 1982 the new regime received formal recognition by France when President Mitterrand paid an official visit. In 1984 Sassou-Nguessou was elected for another five-year term. Since taking office he has increased his control of the nation by combining the posts of head of state, head of government and president of the Central Committee of PCT.

EQUATORIAL GUINEA

Republic of Equatorial Guinea
Republica de Guinea Ecuatorial

Capital: Malabo

Social and economic data
Area: 28,100 km^2
Population: 0.360m*
Pop density per km^2: 13*
Literacy rate: 37%*
GDP: $60m*; per capita GDP: $166
Economy type: low income
Labour force in agriculture: 72%

*1985

Ethnic composition
Between 80 per cent and 90 per cent of the population are of the Fang ethnic group, of Bantu origin. Most of the other groups have been pushed to the coast by the Fang expansion.

Religions
About 96 per cent of the population are Roman Catholics. The rest follow traditional beliefs.

Political features
State type: military authoritarian
Date of state formation: 1968
Political structure: unitary
Executive: military
Assembly: one-chamber
Party structure: one-party
Human rights rating: N/A

Local and regional government
For administrative purposes, the country is divided into seven provinces.

Head of state and head of government
President Teodoro Obiang Nguema Mbasogo, since 1979.

Political leaders since 1970
1968–79 Francisco Macias Nguema (Military), 1979– Teodoro Obiang Nguema Mbasogo (Military).

Political system
The 1973 constitution was suspended in a military coup of 1979 after which a Supreme Military Council ruled by decree. In 1982 a new constitution was approved by referendum, providing for a President and a House of Representatives of the People, elected by universal adult suffrage, through a simple plurality voting system, for a five-year term. The House of Representatives sat for the first time in 1983, its 41 members all being nominated by the President and elected unopposed. The President governs with the Supreme Military Council and a transition to civil, constitutional government has been promised.

Political parties
All political parties, apart from the Democratic Party of Equatorial Guinea (PDGE), have been banned until the restoration of democracy. PDGE was formed in 1987 as the government party.

Latest elections
In the 1988 assembly elections all the PDGE nominees were elected unopposed.

Political history
After 190 years of Spanish rule, Equatorial Guinea became fully independent in 1968 with Francisco Macias Nguema as the nation's first President, heading a coalition government. He soon assumed dictatorial powers, however, and in 1970 outlawed all existing political parties, replacing them with one, the United National Party (PUN). Two years later he declared himself President for life and established a tight control of the press and radio. Between 1976 and 1977 there were many arrests and executions. He also established close relations with the Soviet bloc.

In 1979 he was overthrown in a coup led by his nephew, Colonel Teodoro Obiang Nguema Mbasogo, with at least the tacit approval of Spain. Macias was later tried and executed. Obiang expelled the many Soviet technicians and advisers and renewed economic and political ties with Spain. He banned PUN and other political parties and ruled through a Supreme Military Council. In 1982 a new constitution was adopted, promising an eventual return to civilian rule. There were unsuccessful coups against Obiang in 1981 and 1983.

ETHIOPIA

People's Democratic Republic of Ethiopia
Amharic Hebretesebawit Ityopia

Capital: Addis Ababa

Social and economic data
Area: 1,221,900 km^2
Population: 43.900m*
Pop density per km^2: 36*
Literacy rate: 62%*
GDP: $5,100m*; per capita GDP: $116
Economy type: low income
Labour force in agriculture: 77%

*1985

Ethnic composition
The country contains over 70 different ethnic groups, the two main ones being the Galla, mainly in the east and south of the central plateau, who comprise about 40 per cent of the population, and the Amhara and Tigrais, largely in the central plateau itself, who constitute about 35 per cent.

Religions
About 45 per cent of the population are Muslims and 40 per cent members of the Ethiopian Orthodox Church (Tewahida). There are also significant numbers of Christians.

Political features
State type: nationalistic socialist
Date of state formation: eleventh century
Political structure: unitary
Executive: unlimited presidential
Assembly: one-chamber
Party structure: one-party
Human rights rating: 13%

Local and regional government
Between 1952 and 1962 Ethiopia was a federation and now is a unitary state. For administrative purposes, the country is divided into 24 regions, ranging in population from just under 1 million to over 8 million. There are also five autonomous regions. The 1987 constitution provides for elected regional assemblies.

Head of state and head of government
President Mengistu Haile Mariam, since 1977.

Political leaders since 1970
1916–74 Haile Selassie (Emperor), 1974–77 Terefi Benti (Military), 1977– Mengistu Haile Mariam (WPE).

Political system
A traditional monarchy until 1974, Ethiopia was, until 1987, ruled by a Provisional Military Administrative Council (PMAC), chaired by the head of state. He also presided over a Council of Ministers. The parliament was suspended when the Emperor was deposed in 1974 and Ethiopia proclaimed itself a socialist state. In September 1987 a new constitution for the People's Democratic Republic of Ethiopia (PDRE) was adopted and an 835-seat National Assembly established, its members being nominated by WPE or other organisations, such as trade unions or the army, and then popularly elected, through a simple plurality voting system. The only legally permitted party, the Workers' Party of Ethiopia (WPE), is the country's ruling political force, through the President who is also its Secretary-General.

Political parties
The only legal political party is the Marxist-Leninist Workers' Party of Ethiopia (WPE), which was established in 1984. It has a membership of about 50,000.

Latest elections
In the 1987 presidential election Mengistu Haile Mariam was elected as the sole candidate.

In the 1987 assembly elections 835 members were elected from a list approved by the WPE.

Political history
After a long period of subordination to Egypt, Ethiopia became independent in the eleventh century as the Kingdom of Abyssinia. In the present century, one man, Haile Selassie, came to dominate the country for more than fifty years. He became Regent in 1916, King in 1928 and Emperor in 1930. He was deposed by the armed forces in 1974, following famine, high inflation, growing unemployment and demands for a more democratic form of government. His palace and estates were nationalised, parliament was dissolved and the constitution suspended. He died in 1975, at the age of 83, in a small apartment in his former palace in Addis Ababa.

General Teferi Benti, who had led the uprising and had been made head of state, was killed in 1977 by fellow officers and Colonel Mengistu Haile Mariam replaced him. Throughout the period of Haile Selassie's reign, and that of his predecessor, Emperor Menelik, there had always been attempts to secede by various regions which had been annexed. The 1975 revolution encouraged these secessionist movements to increase their efforts and the military government had to fight to hold on to Eritrea and the south-east region of Ogaden, where Somalian troops were assisting local guerrillas. The USSR, which had adopted Ethiopia as a new ally, threatened to cut off aid to Somalia and Cuban troops assisted Mengistu in ending the fighting there. The struggle for independence by Eritrea, and another province adjoining it, Tigre, continued. In the midst of this confusion there was acute famine in the northern provinces, including Eritrea, after the failure of the rains for three successive seasons. In addition to a massive emergency food aid programme from many Western nations, the Ethiopian government tried to alleviate the problem by resettling people from the northern area to the more fertile south. By 1986 more than half a million had been resettled. Meanwhile, the military regime had re-established normal relations with most of its neighbours.

In September 1987 civilian rule was formally reintroduced under a new constitution, with Mengistu elected as the country's first President. He was the only candidate and retained his emergency powers. Opposition groups continued to be at war with the government dominated by WPE. In 1988, following discussions with representatives of the International Monetary Fund (IMF) about the possibility of loan facilities, President Mengistu agreed to relax his strict, socialist economic policies to make private investment in Ethiopia more attractive. A coup attempt by army officers in May 1989 was foiled and resulted in a purge of the army high command.

GABON

The Gabonese Republic
République Gabonaise

Capital: Libreville

Social and economic data
Area: 266,700
Population: 1.200m*
Pop density per km^2: 4*
Literacy rate: 12%*
GDP: $3,600m*; per capita GDP: $3,000
Economy type: middle income
Labour force in agriculture: 74%

*1985

Ethnic composition
There are 40 Bantu tribes in four main groupings: the Fang, the Eshira, the Mbede and the Okande. There are also Pygmies and about 10 per cent of the population are European, mostly French.

Religions
About 60 per cent of the population are Christians, mainly Roman Catholics, and the rest mostly follow traditional, animist beliefs.

Political features
State type: authoritarian nationalist
Date of state formation: 1960
Political structure: unitary
Executive: unlimited presidential
Assembly: one-chamber
Party structure: one-party
Human rights rating: N/A

Local and regional government
For administrative purposes, the country is divided into nine provinces, ranging in population from about 50,000 to nearly 200,000. These are, in turn, subdivided into 37 departments. The provinces are administered by governors and the departments by prefects, all appointed by the President.

Head of state and head of government
President Omar Bongo, since 1967.

Political leaders since 1970
1967– Omar Bongo (PDG).

Political system
The 1961 constitution, revised in 1967, 1975, 1981 and 1986, provides for a President elected by universal adult suffrage for a seven-year term. He appoints and presides over a Council of Ministers. There is a single-chamber National Assembly, of 120 members, 111 elected, by simple plurality voting, and nine appointed by the President. They serve a five-year term. Gabon became a one-party state in 1968. Although the President appoints a Prime Minister, the former is head of government as well as head of state.

Political parties
The only legally permitted party is the Gabonese Democratic Party (PDG). It was formed in 1968 by Omar Bongo, who dissolved the former ruling party, the Gabonese Democratic Bloc (BDG) and created a one-party state. The party has a strongly nationalist orientation and is a political vehicle for the President, who is its Secretary-General.

Latest elections
In the 1985 general election all the elective assembly seats were won by PDG nominees.

Political history
Gabon was a province of French Equatorial Africa from 1889 until it achieved full independence in 1960. There were then two main political parties, the Gabonese Democratic Bloc (BDG), led by Leon M'ba, and the Gabonese Democratic and Social Union (UDSG), led by Jean-Hilaire Aubame. Although the two parties were evenly matched in popular support, M'ba became President on independence and Aubame Foreign Minister. In 1967 the BDG wanted the two parties to merge but this was resisted by the UDSG, whereupon M'ba called a general election. Before the elections took place M'ba was deposed in a military coup led by

supporters of Aubame but, with the help of France, M'ba was restored to office. Aubame was later found guilty of treason and imprisoned. The UDSG was outlawed and most of its members joined the BDG.

In 1967 M'ba, although in failing health, was re-elected. He died later the same year and was succeeded by Albert-Bernard Bongo. In the following year he dissolved the BDG and established the Gabonese Democratic Party (PDG) as the only legal political party. Bongo was re-elected in 1973 and, announcing his conversion to Islam, changed his first name to Omar. In 1979 Bongo stood as the sole presidential candidate and was re-elected for a further seven years.

Gabon, with its great reserves of uranium, manganese and iron, is the richest per capita country in black Africa and both M'ba and his protégé, Bongo, have successfully exploited these resources, gaining control of the iron-ore ventures, originally half-owned by the Bethlehem Steel Corporation of the United States, and concluding economic and technical agreements with China as well as maintaining close ties with France. Although he has operated an authoritarian regime, the country's prosperity has diluted any serious opposition to President Bongo. He was re-elected for a further term in November 1986.

GAMBIA

Republic of the Gambia

Capital: Banjul

Social and economic data
Area: 11,300 km^2
Population: 0.800m*
Pop density per km^2: 71*
Literacy rate: 20%*
GDP: $210m*; per capita GDP: $262
Economy type: low income
Labour force in agriculture: 77%

*1985

Ethnic composition
There is a wide mix of ethnic groups, the largest being the Mandingo, comprising about 40 per cent of the population. The other main groups are the Fula, the Wolof, the Jola and the Serahuli.

Religions
Eighty-five per cent of the population are Muslims. The rest are mainly Christians or animists, following the beliefs of the Jola tribe.

Political features
State type: liberal democratic
Date of state formation: 1965
Political structure: unitary
Executive: limited presidential

Assembly: one-chamber
Party structure: two-party
Human rights rating: N/A

Local and regional government
There is considerable variety in the forms of local government in Gambia. In the capital city there is an elected council and some areas have part-elected and part-appointed councils. In others authority rests with the tribal chiefs.

Head of state and head of government
President Sir Dawda Karaba Jawara, since 1970.

Political leaders since 1970
1970– Dawda Karaba Jawara (PPP).

Political system
Gambia is an independent republic within the Commonwealth. The constitution dates from independence in 1970 and provides for a single-chamber assembly, the House of Representatives, consisting of 49 members, 35 directly elected by universal adult suffrage, through a simple plurality voting system, five elected by the Chiefs, eight non-voting, nominated members and the Attorney-General, *ex officio*. It serves a five-year term. The President is elected by direct universal suffrage, again for a five-year term. He appoints a Vice-President, who is also leader of the House of Representatives, and a cabinet.

Political parties
There are four political parties, the two most significant being the Progressive People's Party (PPP) and the National Convention Party (NCP).

The PPP was formed in 1959 and in 1965 merged with the Democratic Congress Alliance and then, in 1968, with the Gambia Congress Party. In its various forms, it has been the dominant party since the granting of independence and there were calls at one time to make Gambia a one-party state but they were resisted by the President, who is also the party's Secretary-General. It has a moderate-centrist orientation and is a strong supporter of the Commonwealth.

The NCP dates from 1975. It is a left-of-centre party, advocating fairer shares of the nation's wealth.

Latest elections
In the 1987 presidential election Sir Dawda Jawara (PPP) was re-elected with 58.71 per cent of the popular vote. The NCP candidate, Sherif Mustapha Dibba, won 27.29 per cent.

In the 1987 elections for the House of Representatives the PPP won 31 seats, with 56.61 per cent of the vote and the NCP won five seats, with 27.60 per cent.

Political history
Originally united with Sierra Leone, Gambia became a British Crown Colony in 1843 and an independent colony within the British Empire in

1888. Political parties were formed in the 1950s, internal self-government granted in 1963, and full independence within the Commonwealth achieved in 1965, with Dawda K. Jawara as Prime Minister.

It declared itself a republic in 1970, Jawara becoming President, thus replacing the British monarch as head of state. He was re-elected in 1972, 1977, 1982 and 1987. In 1981 an attempted coup against him was thwarted with the help of Senegalese troops and this strengthened the ties between the two countries to such an extent that plans were announced for their merger into a confederation of Senegambia. The process has not yet been completed and there are signs that Senegal has doubts about the wisdom of its full implementation. In economic terms The Gambia would seem to have more to gain.

GHANA

Republic of Ghana

Capital: Accra

Social and economic data
Area: 238,540 km^2
Population: 13.500m*
Pop density per km^2: 57*
Literacy rate: 30%*
GDP: $5,500m*; per capita GDP: $407
Economy type: low income
Labour force in agriculture: 48%

*1985

Ethnic composition
There are over 75 ethnic groups in the country. The most significant are the Akan, in the south and west, comprising about 44 per cent of the population, then come the Mole-Dagbani, in the north, the Ewe, in the south, the Ga, in the region of the capital city, and the Fanti, in the coastal area.

Religions
About 48 per cent of the population are Christians, about 38 per cent follow traditional beliefs and about 12 per cent are Muslims.

Political features
State type: military authoritarian
Date of state formation: 1957
Political structure: unitary
Executive: military
Assembly: there is no assembly, the constitution having been suspended
Party structure: there are no parties operating
Human rights rating: 46%

Local and regional government
The country is divided into nine regions, ranging in population from just over 1 million to just over 2 million. They are subdivided into 58 districts, which, in turn, are further subdivided into 267 sub-districts. Tribal chiefs still wield considerable authority in some areas, however.

Head of state and head of government
Flight-Lieutenant Jerry Rawlings, since 1981.

Political leaders since 1970
1969–72 Akwasi Afrifa (Military-PP), 1972–78 Ignatius Acheampong (Military), 1978–79 Frederick Akuffo (Military), 1979–81 Hilla Limann (PNP), 1981– Jerry Rawlings (Military).

Political system
The 1979 constitution was suspended in 1981 when Flight-Lieutenant Jerry Rawlings seized power and set up a Provisional National Defence Council (PNDC), with himself as chairman. Parliament and the Council of State were abolished and the government now rules by decree. All political parties were banned but a number of opposition groups still operate from outside the country.

Political parties
All parties were banned when the constitution was suspended in 1981.

Latest elections
There have been no free elections since 1979.

Political history
Ghana was formed by a merger of a British colony, The Gold Coast, with a British-administered UN Trust Territory which was part of Togoland. It achieved full independence in 1957, with Dr Kwame Nkrumah, who had been Prime Minister of The Gold Coast, as President. He embarked on a policy of what he called 'African socialism' and established an authoritarian regime. In 1964 he declared it a one-party state, with the Convention People's Party (CPP), which he led, as the only legal political organisation. He then dropped his original stance of international non-alignment and forged links with the USSR and other communist countries.

His autocratic methods created many enemies and in 1966 he was deposed, while on a visit to China, and the leader of the coup, General Joseph Ankrah, established a National Liberation Council. It released many political prisoners and carried out a purge of CPP supporters. In 1969 Ankrah was replaced by General Akwasi Afrifa, who announced plans for a return to civilian government. A new constitution established an elected National Assembly and a non-executive presidency. The Progress Party (PP) won a big majority in the Assembly and its leader, Kofi Busia, was appointed Prime Minister. The following year Edward Akufo-Addo became the civilian President.

However, the state of the economy worsened and, disenchanted with the civilian administration, the army seized power again in 1972. The constitution was suspended and all political institutions replaced by a

National Redemption Council (NRC), under Colonel Ignatius Acheampong. In 1976 he, too, promised a return to civilian rule but critics doubted his sincerity and in 1978 he was replaced by his deputy, Frederick Akuffo, in a bloodless coup. Like his predecessors, he also announced a speedy return to civilian government but before elections could be held he, in turn, was deposed by junior officers led by Flight-Lieutenant Jerry Rawlings. Their argument for doing so was that previous governments had been corrupt and had mismanaged the economy.

In 1979 Rawlings fulfilled his promise and civilian rule was restored again, but two years later he led another coup, again complaining about the incompetence of the government. He established a Provisional National Defence Council (PNDC), with himself as chairman, again suspending the constitution, dissolving parliament and banning political parties. Although Rawlings' policies were initially supported, particularly by workers and students, his failure to revive the economy has caused discontent and his regime has been threatened on a number of occasions by popular demonstrations and attempted coups.

GUINEA

Republic of Guinea
République de Guinée

Capital: Conakry

Social and economic data
Area: 245,860 km^2
Population: 5.750m*
Pop density per km^2: 23*
Literacy rate: 9%*
GDP: $1,800m*; per capita GDP: $313
Economy type: low income
Labour force in agriculture: 78%

*1985

Ethnic composition
There are some 24 tribal ethnic groups, the main ones being the Malinke, the Peul and the Soussou. Since independence the government has tried to unify the country by breaking down traditional ethnic barriers.

Religions
About 95 per cent of the population are Muslims and 5 per cent Christians.

Political features
State type: military authoritarian
Date of state formation: 1958
Political structure: unitary
Executive: military
Assembly: there is no assembly, the constitution having been suspended
Party structure: no parties operate
Human rights rating: poor

Local and regional government
The country is divided into eight provinces, each administered by an appointed governor. There are also elected provincial councils.

Head of state and head of government
Brigadier-General Lamsana Conte, since 1984.

Political leaders since 1970
1958–1984 Sekou Touré (PDG), 1984– Lamsana Conte (Military).

Political system
The 1982 constitution, which provided for an elected National Assembly, was suspended in 1984, following a military coup. A Military Committee for National Recovery (CMRN) assumed power. The President combines the roles of head of state and head of government and leads an appointed Council of Ministers. The country's sole political party, the Democratic Party of Guinea (PDG) was dissolved after the coup and opposition groups now operate from abroad.

Political parties
No parties have operated since the suspension of the constitution in 1984.

Latest elections
There have been no elections since 1980.

Political history
Guinea was formerly French Guinea, and part of French West Africa. It became fully independent in 1958, after a referendum had rejected a proposal to remain a self-governing colony within the French Community. The first President was Sekou Touré, who made the Democratic Party of Guinea (PDG) the only legal political organisation and embarked upon a policy of socialist revolution. There were unsuccessful attempts to overthrow him in 1961, 1965, 1967 and 1970 and, suspicious of conspiracies by foreign powers, he put his country for a time into virtual diplomatic isolation. By 1975, however, relations with most of his neighbours had returned to normal.

Touré initially trod a path of rigid Marxism, ruthlessly crushing opposition to his policies, but gradually moved towards a mixed economy, private enterprise becoming legal in 1979. His domestic regime was, nevertheless, authoritarian and harsh. Externally, he positively sought closer relations with the Western powers, particularly France and the United States. He was re-elected unopposed in 1980 but in 1984 died while undergoing heart surgery in the United States.

Before the normal machinery for electing his successor could be put into operation, the army staged a bloodless coup, suspending the constitution and setting up a Military Committee for National Recovery, with Colonel Lansana Conte at its head. He pledged to restore democracy and respect human rights, releasing hundreds of political prisoners and lifting restrictions on the press. Conte then made strenuous efforts to restore his country's international standing through a series of overseas visits. He was successful enough to persuade some 200,000 Guineans who had fled the country during the Touré regime to return. Nevertheless, he continued to head an unelected military regime. In 1985 an attempt to overthrow him while he was out of the country was foiled by loyal troops.

GUINEA-BISSAU

Republic of Guinea-Bissau
Republica da Guine-Bissau

Capital: Bissau

Social and economic data
Area: 36,130 km^2
Population: 0.900m*
Pop density per km^2: 25*
Literacy rate: 20%*
GDP: $150m*; per capita GDP: $167
Economy type: low income
Labour force in agriculture: 72%

*1985

Ethnic composition
The majority of the population originate from Africa and comprise five main ethnic groups, the Balante, in the central region, the Fulani, in the north, the Malinke, in the north-central area, and the Mandyako and the Pepel near the coast.

Religions
About 65 per cent of the population follow traditional, animist beliefs, about 30 per cent are Muslims and about 5 per cent Christians, mainly Roman Catholics.

Political features
State type: nationalistic socialist
Date of state formation: 1974
Political structure: unitary
Executive: unlimited presidential
Assembly: one-chamber
Party structure: one-party
Human rights rating: N/A

Local and regional government
The country is divided into eight regions and one autonomous section, based on the capital, Bissau. All have elected councils.

Head of state and head of government
President Joao Bernardo Vieira, since 1980.

Political leaders since 1970
1974–80 Luiz Cabral (PAIGC), 1980– Joao Bernardo Vieira (PAIGC).

Political system

Guinea-Bissau is a one-party state, the 1984 constitution describing the African Party for the Independence of Portuguese Guinea and Cape Verde (PAIGC) as 'the leading force in society and in the nation'. Although Cape Verde chose not to be united with Guinea-Bissau, preferring independence, the title of the original party which served the two countries has been retained. The constitution also provides for a National People's Assembly of 150 members. All are nominees of PAIGC and are selected from members of regional councils, which have been directly elected through a simple plurality voting system. The Assembly elects the President, who combines the roles of head of state and head of government. Policy is determined by PAIGC and it is there that ultimate political power lies, the President being its Secretary-General.

Political parties

PAIGC is the only legally permitted party. It was formed in 1956 and was originally the ruling party for both Guinea-Bissau and Cape Verde. When Cape Verde withdrew from the union, in 1980, the party name and initials were retained. It has a nationalistic-socialist orientation.

Latest elections

In the 1984 elections for the National People's Assembly all 150 members were PAIGC nominees, selected from members of eight elected regional councils.

Political history

Guinea-Bissau, as part of the Portuguese empire, was governed jointly with Cape Verde until 1879, when it became a separate colony, with the name Portuguese Guinea. Agitation for independence intensified after the Second World War and this resulted in the formation, in 1956, of the African Party for the Independence of Portuguese Guinea and Cape Verde (PAIGC). In the face of Portugal's refusal to grant independence, fighting broke out and by 1972 PAIGC claimed to be in control of two-thirds of the country. The following year the 'liberated areas' were declared independent and in 1973 a National People's Assembly was set up and Luiz Cabral appointed President of a State Council. Some 40,000 Portuguese troops were used to try to put down the uprising, suffering heavy losses. However, before a clear outcome was reached, a sudden coup in mainland Portugal proved a sufficient distraction to bring the fighting to an end and PAIGC negotiated independence with the new government in Lisbon. In 1974 Portugal formally acknowledged Guinea-Bissau as a sovereign nation.

PAIGC set about laying the foundations for a socialist state which, was intended to include Cape Verde, but in November 1980, four days before approval of the constitution, the inhabitants of Cape Verde, feeling that Guinea-Bissau was being given preferential treatment in the constitutional arrangements, decided to withdraw. Cabral was deposed in a coup and Joao Vieira became chairman of a Council of Revolution. At its 1981 Congress, PAIGC decided to retain its name, despite Cape Verde's withdrawal, and its position was confirmed as the only legal party, with Vieira as its Secretary-General. Normal relations between Guinea-Bissau and Cape Verde, which had been severed following the coup, were restored in 1982. In 1984 a new constitution was adopted, making Vieira head of government as well as head of state.

IVORY COAST

Republic of the Ivory Coast
République de la Côte d'Ivoire

Capital: Abidjan (Yamoussouko: capital designate)

Social and economic data
Area: 322,460 km^2
Population: 10.500m*
Pop density per km^2: 33*
Literacy rate: 35%*
GDP: $5,800m*; per capita GDP: $552
Economy type: middle income
Labour force in agriculture: 77%

*1985

Ethnic composition
There is no single, dominant ethnic group and the main tribes include the Agni, Baoule, Krou, Senoufou and Mandingo. There are also about 2 million Africans who have settled from neighbouring countries, particularly Burkina Faso. Europeans number about 70,000.

Religions
About 65 per cent of the population follow traditional, animist beliefs, about 23 per cent are Muslims and 12 per cent Christians, mainly Roman Catholics.

Political features
State type: authoritarian nationalist
Date of state formation: 1960
Political structure: unitary
Executive: unlimited presidential
Assembly: one-chamber
Party structure: one-party
Human rights rating: poor

Local and regional government
The country is divided into 49 departments, each with its own elected council.

Head of state and head of government
President Felix Houphouet-Boigny, since 1960.

Political leaders since 1970
1960– Felix Houphouet-Boigny (PDCI).

Political system
The constitution dates from independence in 1960 and was amended in 1971, 1975, 1980 and 1985. It provides for a President, who is head of state and head of government, elected by universal adult suffrage, through the

majoritarian voting system of the second ballot, for a five-year term, and a single-chamber National Assembly of 175 members, elected in the same way and also serving a five-year term. The President chooses and heads a Council of Ministers.

Political parties

Although a multi-party system is legally permitted no opposition group has been officially recognised since independence other than the Democratic Party of the Ivory Coast (PDCI). Houphouet-Boigny founded it as a branch of the African Democratic Rally (RDA) in the 1940s. It has a nationalistic, free-enterprise orientation.

Latest elections

In the 1985 elections for the National Assembly 546 candidates contested the 175 seats. All were PDCI nominees.

Political history

Formerly a province of French West Africa, the Ivory Coast was given self-government within the French Community in 1958 and then full independence in 1960, when a new constitution was adopted. Felix Houphouet-Boigny, leader of the Democratic Party of the Ivory Coast (PDCI), has been the country's only President. He has maintained close links with France since independence and this support, combined with a good economic growth rate, has given his country a high degree of political stability. He is very much a pragmatist in politics and has been criticised by some other African leaders for maintaining links with South Africa. He has countered the criticism by arguing that a dialogue between blacks and whites is essential. As a strong believer in independence for black African states, he has denounced Soviet and other forms of intervention in African affairs. He has also travelled extensively to improve relations with the Western powers.

KENYA

Republic of Kenya
Jamhuri ya Kenya

Capital: Nairobi

Social and economic data

Area: 583,000 km^2
Population: 21.000m*
Pop density per km^2: 36*
Literacy rate: 47%*
GDP: $5,772m*; per capita GDP: $275
Economy type: low income
Labour force in agriculture: 75%

*1985

Ethnic composition
The main ethnic groups are the Kikuyu, about 21 per cent, the Luhya, 14 per cent, the Luo, 13 per cent, the Kalejin, 11 per cent, the Kamba, 11 per cent, the Kisii, 6 per cent, and the Meru, 5 per cent.

Religions
The adherence to religions varies from tribe to tribe and area to area. About 25 per cent of the population are Christians, there are Muslims near the coast and around Nairobi, and many follow traditional animist beliefs.

Political features
State type: authoritarian nationalist
Date of state formation: 1963
Political structure: unitary
Executive: unlimited presidential
Assembly: one-chamber
Party structure: one-party
Human rights rating: 48%

Local and regional government
Regional and local governments display features from the days of British colonial rule. The country is divided into eight provinces which are further subdivided into 40 districts. The provinces are administered by provincial commissioners and the districts by district commissioners. Below the commissioner level there are municipal councils, town councils, county councils, urban councils and area councils.

Head of state and head of government
President Daniel Arap Moi, since 1978.

Political leaders since 1970
1964–78 Jomo Kenyatta (KANU), 1978– Daniel Arap Moi (KANU).

Political system
Kenya became a republic, within the Commonwealth, in 1964 and the constitution dates from the granting of internal self-government in 1963. It was amended in 1964, 1969 and 1982. It provides for a President, elected by universal adult suffrage for a five-year term, and a single-chamber National Assembly, serving a similar term. The Assembly has 172 members, 158 elected by universal adult suffrage, through a simple plurality voting system, twelve nominated by the President and the Attorney-General and Speaker as *ex officio* members. From 1969 to 1982 Kenya was a one-party state in fact and since then it has become one in law. In theory non-party candidates for the Assembly can offer themselves but in practice they are rarely chosen. Parliamentary elections have usually been tinged with bribery, which is now accepted as a political fact of life.

Political parties
The only legitimate party is the Kenya African National Union (KANU), whose leader is the President. The predecessor to KANU was the Kenya

African Union (KAU), which was formed in 1944, mainly by members of the Kikuyu tribe, as part of a campaign for achieving independence. Jomo Kenyatta became its leader in 1947 and then KAU was proscribed in 1952, following the Mau Mau violence and Kenyatta's imprisonment. On his release, in 1961, he set about merging KAU with its rival, the Kenya African Democratic Union (KADU), which had been formed to oppose the dominance of the Kikuyus. KANU was subsequently formed, with Kenyatta as its leader. Its orientation is now nationalistic and centrist, and very much a political vehicle for the President.

Latest elections
In the 1988 presidential election Moi was elected for a third successive term as an unopposed candidate.

For the 1988 assembly elections the practice of 'public queuing' was introduced, whereby candidates who recorded 70 per cent or more support from people standing in line were automatically elected. Only KANU members were allowed to stand as candidates.

Political history
Kenya was a British colony until 1964 when it achieved full independence within the Commonwealth. During the two decades before independence the country came close to civil war, as pro-nationalist groups carried out a campaign of violence. The Kenya African Union (KAU) was founded in 1944 and in 1947 Jomo Kenyatta, a member of Kenya's largest tribe, the Kikuyu, became its president. Three years later a secret society of young Kikuyu militants was formed, called Mau Mau, which had the same aims as KAU but sought to achieve them by violent means. Although Kenyatta disassociated himself from Mau Mau, he was not trusted by the British authorities and imprisoned in 1953.

The terrorist campaign had largely finished by 1956 and the state of emergency which had been imposed was lifted and Kenyatta released. The country was granted internal self-government in 1963 and Kenyatta, who had become leader of the Kenya African National Union (KANU), became Prime Minister, and then President after full independence in 1964. He continued as President until his death in 1978, during which time his country achieved considerable stability and he became a widely respected world leader.

He was succeeded by the Vice-President, Daniel Arap Moi, who built on the achievements of his predecessor, launching an impressive four-year development plan. An attempted coup by junior air force officers in 1982 was foiled and resulted, for a while, in political detentions and press censorship. The air force and Nairobi University were also temporarily dissolved. In the same year the National Assembly declared Kenya a one-party state. President Moi was re-elected in 1983 and 1988 and his position seems secure. He has had some success in tackling corruption and inefficiency in the public services and, externally, has re-established better relations with most of his East African neighbours, although territorial disputes with Uganda still occasionally erupt. Although he had shown signs of increasing authoritarianism in his style of government, in June 1989 he unexpectedly announced the release of all known political prisoners.

LESOTHO

Kingdom of Lesotho

Capital: Maseru

Social and economic data
Area: 30,350 km^2
Population: 1.555m*
Pop density per km^2: 51*
Literacy rate: 59%*
GDP: $270m*: per capita GDP: $174
Economy type: low income
Labour force in agriculture: 81%

*1985

Ethnic composition
Almost the entire population are Bantus, of Southern Sotho, or Basotho, stock.

Religions
About 80 per cent of the people are Christians, in the order of Anglicans, Lesotho Evangelicals and Roman Catholics.

Political features
State type: military authoritarian
Date of state formation: 1966
Political structure: unitary
Executive: military
Assembly: one-chamber
Party structure: one-party
Human rights rating: poor

Local and regional government
For administrative purposes, the country is divided into ten districts. Each district has an appointed co-ordinator and an elected council.

Head of state
King Moshoeshoe II, since 1966.

Head of government
Chairman of the Military Council, Major-General Justin Lekhanya, since 1986.

Political leaders since 1970
1970–86 Chief Leabua Jonathan (BNP), 1986– Justin Lekhanya (Military).

Political system
Lesotho is an independent monarchy within the Commonwealth. The constitution, which dates from independence in 1966, was suspended, reinstated and then suspended again and all executive and legislative powers are currently vested in the hereditary King, assisted by a

six-member Military Council and a Council of Ministers. The constitution provides for a single-chamber elected National Assembly of 99 members but there have been no free elections since 1973.

Political parties

In theory there are four political parties but, prior to the military takeover, there was effectively only one, the Basotho National Party (BNP). It was formed in 1958 by Chief Leabua Jonathan and soon became his personal political machine. It has a traditionalist, nationalist orientation.

Latest elections

The elections which should have been held in 1985 were cancelled by the King because no candidates were put forward in opposition to the BNP, all of whose nominees were deemed to have been returned unopposed.

Political history

Lesotho was formerly called Basutoland and, as such, a British dependency and then a colony. It was given internal self-government in 1965 with the Paramount Chief, Moshoeshoe II, as King. It achieved full independence, as Lesotho, in 1966. The Basotho National Party (BNP), a conservative group favouring limited co-operation with South Africa, remained in power from independence until 1986. Its leader, Chief Leabua Jonathan, became Prime Minister in 1966 and after 1970, when the powers of the King were severely curtailed, the country was effectively under the Prime Minister's control.

Since 1975 an organisation called the Lesotho Liberation Army (LLA) has carried out a number of attacks on BNP members, with the support, it has been alleged, of the South African government. The South Africans have denied complicity but, at the same time, have pointed out that Lesotho allows the banned South African nationalist movement the African National Congress (ANC), to use it as a base. Economically, Lesotho is dependent on South Africa but has openly rejected the policy of apartheid. In retaliation, South Africa has tightened its border controls, causing food shortages. Allegations have been made that the South African government has encouraged BNP dissenters to form a new party, the Basotho Democratic Alliance (BDA) and plotted with the BDA to overthrow the Lesotho government. Lesotho has also been under pressure from South Africa to sign a non-aggression pact, similar to the Nkomati Accord between South Africa and Mozambique, but Jonathan's government consistently refused to do so.

In January 1986 South Africa imposed a border blockade, cutting off food and fuel supplies to Lesotho, and a few weeks later the government of Chief Jonathan was ousted and replaced in a coup led by General Justin Lekhanya. He announced that all executive and legislative powers would be placed in the hands of the King, ruling through a Military Council, chaired by General Lekhanya, and a Council of Ministers. A week after the coup about 60 ANC members were deported to Zambia and on the same day the South African blockade was lifted. Although South Africa has denied playing any part in the coup, it is clear that this new government will be more acceptable to South Africa's political leaders than the old. It was announced, in April 1987, that Chief Jonathan had died in hospital in Pretoria, South Africa.

LIBERIA

Republic of Liberia

Capital: Monrovia

Social and economic data
Area: 111,400 km^2
Population: 2.300m*
Pop density per km^2: 202*
Literacy rate: 20%*
GDP: $811m*; per capita GDP: $353
Economy type: low income
Labour force in agriculture: 67%

*1985

Ethnic composition
Ninety-five per cent of the population are members of indigenous tribes, which include the Kpelle, the Bassa, the Gio, the Kru, the Grebo, the Mano, the Krahn, the Gola, the Gbandi, the Loma, the Kissi, the Vai and the Bella. The other 5 per cent are descended from slaves repatriated from the United States.

Religions
Liberia is officially a Christian state but all religions are tolerated. The main Christian Churches are Lutheran, Anglican, Roman Catholic, Baptist and United Methodist. There are also about 670,000 Muslims.

Political features
State type: emergent democratic
Date of state formation: 1847
Political structure: unitary
Executive: limited presidential
Assembly: two-chamber
Party structure: one-party
Human rights rating: 39%

Local and regional government
The country is divided into nine counties, each administered by an appointed superintendent. In addition, there are six territories and the capital district of Monrovia.

Head of state and head of government
President General Samuel Kenyon Doe, since 1980.

Political leaders since 1970
1944–71 William Tubman (TWP), 1971–80 William Tolbert (TWP), 1980– Samuel Kenyon Doe (NDPL).

Political system
From 1980 to 1984 Liberia was under the military rule of a People's Redemption Council (PRC). In 1984 the PRC was dissolved and its

functions taken over by an Interim National Assembly of 58 members, 22 of them former members of the PRC and 36 civilians appointed by the President, pending a new constitution which was later approved by referendum. This provides for a two-chamber National Assembly, consisting of a Senate with 26 members and a House of Representatives of 64, elected by universal adult suffrage, through a simple plurality voting system, for a six-year term. The President is elected in the same way for a similar term.

Political parties

All political parties were banned in 1980 but since 1984 they have been allowed to operate, provided they register with a Special Electoral Commission (SECOM). Five have now registered but, for the moment at least, Lesotho is still a one-party state, dominated by the National Democratic Party of Liberia (NDPL). However, the creation of opposition groups does suggest a future pluralist political system and, because of this, it has been categorised as an emergent democracy.

The NDPL was formed in 1984 by Samuel Doe, as a modern equivalent of the True Whig Party (TWP), which had been the leading force in Liberia's politics since the early years of the state's creation.

Latest elections

In the 1985 presidential election Samuel Doe won with 50.9 per cent of the vote. In the 1985 Assembly elections the NDPL won 22 of the 26 Senate seats and 51 of the 64 House seats, in the face of allegations of electoral frauds.

Political history

Liberia was founded in 1847, as an independent republic, by liberated black slaves from the southern United States. William Tubman was President from 1944 until his death in 1971 and was succeeded by the Vice-President, William R. Tolbert, who was re-elected in 1975.

In 1980 Tolbert was assassinated in a military coup led by Master Sergeant Samuel Doe, who suspended the constitution, banned all political parties and ruled through an appointed People's Redemption Council (PRC). He proceeded to stamp out corruption in the public service, encountering considerable opposition and making enemies who were later to threaten his position.

A new draft constitution, providing for an elected two-chamber National Assembly and an elected President, was approved by the PRC in 1983 and by national referendum in the following year. Political parties were allowed to function again, provided they registered with a new body, the Special Electoral Commission (SECOM). In August 1984 Doe founded the National Democratic Party of Liberia (NDPL) and announced that he proposed to stand for the presidency.

By early 1985 eleven political parties had been formed but they complained about the difficulties of the registration process and only five eventually registered in time for the elections. In the Assembly elections Doe's party won clear majorities in both chambers of the Assembly, although there were complaints of election frauds. Doe himself was elected

President by popular vote. In November 1985 there was an unsuccessful attempt to unseat him. Doe alleged complicity by neighbouring Sierra Leone and dealt harshly with the coup leaders.

MADAGASCAR

Democratic Republic of Madgascar
Repoblika Demokratika n'i Madagaskar

Capital: Antananarivo

Social and economic data
Area: 595,790 km^2
Population: 10.300m*
Pop density per km^2: 17*
Literacy rate: 53%*
GDP: $2,300m*; per capita GDP: $223
Economy type: low income
Labour force in agriculture: 80%

*1985

Ethnic composition
There are 18 main Malagasy tribes of Malaysian-Polynesian origin. There are also minorities of French, Chinese, Indians, Pakistanis and Comorans. Despite a common ethnic heritage, the inhabitants of the highlands, mainly the Merinas, have frequently found themselves in conflict with the coastal tribes, known as the *côtiers*.

Religions
About 57 per cent of the population follow traditional, animist beliefs and about 40 per cent are Christians, about half of them Roman Catholics. There is also a Muslim minority.

Political features
State type: nationalistic socialist
Date of state formation: 1960
Political structure: unitary
Executive: unlimited presidential
Assembly: one-chamber
Party structure: one-party
Human rights rating: poor

Local and regional government
The country is divided into six provinces, with a three-tiered sub-structure, based on traditional village assemblies, or *fokonolona*.

Head of state and head of government
Didier Ratsiraka, since 1975.

Political leaders since 1970
1960–72 Philibert Tsiranana (PSD), 1972–75 Gabriel Ramanantsoa (Military), 1975– Didier Ratsiraka (FNDR).

Political system
The 1975 constitution made radical changes in the structure of government and renamed the state the Democratic Republic of Madagascar. The constitution provides for a single-chamber National People's Assembly of 137 members, elected by universal adult suffrage, through a simple plurality voting system, for a five-year term, and a President elected in the same way for a seven-year term. The President appoints and is chairman of a Supreme Revolutionary Council (SRC), which acts as 'the guardian of the Malagay Socialist Revolution'. A third of the appointed members are nominated by the Assembly and the others are the President's personal choice. The President is also the Secretary-General of the political organisation which embraces all the various party factions, the National Front for the Defence of the Malagasy Socialist Revolution (FNDR). Political power therefore ultimately lies with the President and the party he leads. For day-to-day administration, the President appoints a Prime Minister and Council of Ministers.

Political parties
The only permitted political movement is the National Front for the Defence of the Malagasy Socialist Revolution (FNDR).

FNDR was formed in 1976 around the Advance Guard of the Malagasy Revolution (AREMA) which Didier Ratsiraka established as the nucleus of a single national party, as provided for in the constitution. Within FNDR are six other groups, three of them left-wing and three left-of-centre.

Latest elections
In the 1989 general election AREMA won 120 of the 137 Assembly seats, the remainder being shared between the other six groups within FNDR.

In March 1989 Ratsiraka was re-elected for a third seven-year term with 62.62 per cent of the vote. There was an 81 per cent turnout.

Political history
Formerly a French colony, Madagascar became an autonomous state within the French community in 1958 and achieved full independence, as a republic, in 1960. The country's history since independence has been greatly influenced by the competing interests of Madagascar's two main ethnic groups, the coastal tribes, known as the *côtiers*, and the highland people, represented by the Merina.

The first President of the republic was Philibert Tsiranana, leader of the Social Democratic Party (PSD), which identified itself with the *côtiers*. In 1972 the army, representing the Merina, took control of the government and pursued a more nationalistic line than Tsiranana. This caused resentment among the *côtiers* and, with rising unemployment, led to a government crisis in 1975 which resulted in the imposition of martial law under a National Military Directorate and the banning of all political parties.

Later that year a new, socialist constitution was approved and Lieutenant-Commander Didier Ratsiraka, a *côtier*, was elected President of the Democratic Republic of Madagascar. Political parties were allowed to operate again and in 1976 the Front-Line Revolutionary Organisation (AREMA) was formed by Ratsiraka, as the nucleus of a single party for the state. By 1977 all political activity was concentrated in the National Front for the Defence of the Malagasy Socialist Revolution (FNDR) and all the candidates for the National People's Assembly were FNDR nominees. In 1977 the National Movement for the Independence of Madagascar (MONIMA), a radical socialist party, withdrew from the FNDR and was declared illegal. MONIMA's leader, Monja Jaona, unsuccessfully challenged Ratsiraka for the presidency and, although his party did well in the capital, AREMA won 117 of the 137 Assembly seats in the 1983 elections. Despite this victory, social and political discontent continued, particularly among the Merinas, who openly demonstrated their opposition to government policies. Nevertheless, Ratsiraka was re-elected, and AREMA marginally increased its Assembly seat total in the 1989 elections.

MALAWI

Republic of Malawi

Capital: Lilongwe

Social and economic data

Area: 118,480 km^2
Population: 7.300m*
Pop density per km^2: 62*
Literacy rate: 31%*
GDP: $1,081m*; per capita GDP: $148
Economy type: low income
Labour force in agriculture: 81%

*1985

Ethnic composition

Almost all the people are indigenous Africans but divided ethnically into numerous tribes, the main ones being the Chewa, the Nyanja, the Tumbuka, the Yao, the Lomwe, the Sena, the Tonga and the Ngoni. There are also Asian and European minorities.

Religions

About 50 per cent of the population are Christians. The remainder are mostly Muslims or Hindus or follow traditional, animist beliefs.

Political features

State type: authoritarian nationalist
Date of state formation: 1964
Political structure: unitary
Executive: unlimited presidential
Assembly: one-chamber
Party structure: one-party
Human rights rating: poor

Local and regional government
For administrative purposes, the country is divided into three regions, which are further subdivided into 24 districts. Regions are the responsibility of cabinet ministers and districts are administered by appointed commissioners. At a lower level there are chiefs' and sub-chiefs' areas.

Head of state and head of government
Life President Dr Hastings Kamusu Banda, since 1966.

Political leaders since 1970
1966- Hastings Kamusu Banda (MCP).

Political system
The 1966 constitution dates from the year Malawi became a republic. It provides for a President, elected for a five-year term, but was amended in 1971 so as to make Hastings Banda President for Life. Malawi is a one-party state and all adults are required to be members of the national party. There is a single-chamber National Assembly, with 112 members elected by universal adult suffrage, through a simple plurality voting system. The President has power, under the constitution, to appoint an unlimited number of additional members. In 1987 the number of appointees was six. He also appoints a cabinet, members of which are directly responsible to him. Hastings Banda has thus developed a system of personal, paternalistic rule which has not been seriously challenged in more than 20 years of office.

Political parties
The Malawi Congress Party (MCP) is the only party legally allowed to operate. It was founded in 1959 by Hastings Banda to lead the fight for independence. It has now become very much his personal political machine. Its orientation can best be described as right-wing, multi-racial.

There are at least three opposition political groups which operate from outside Malawi.

Latest elections
In the 1987 assembly elections only 69 of the 112 seats were contested. All candidates were MCP nominees.

Political history
Malawi was formerly the British protectorate of Nyasaland and, between 1953 and 1964, part of the Federation of Rhodesia and Nyasaland, which comprised what are now Zimbabwe, Zambia and Malawi. Dr Hastings Banda, through the Malawi Congress Party (MCP), led a campaign for independence and in 1963 the Federation was dissolved. Nyasaland became independent, as Malawi, in 1964 and two years later a republic and a one-party state, with Dr Banda as its first President.

He has governed his country in a very personal way, brooking no opposition, and his foreign policies have, at times, been rather idiosyncratic. He astonished his black African colleagues in 1967 by officially recognising the Republic of South Africa and, in 1971, became the first African head of state to visit that country. In 1976, however, he also recognised the socialist government in Angola. Banda keeps a tight control over his government colleagues and, as yet, no successor has been appointed or obviously emerged.

In 1977 he embarked upon a policy of what can best be described as cautious liberalism, releasing some political detainees and allowing greater press freedom. His external policies are based on a mixture of national self-interest and practical reality and have allowed Malawi to live in reasonable harmony with its neighbours, regardless of their political complexions.

MALI

Republic of Mali
République du Mali

Capital: Bamako

Social and economic data
Area: 1,240,000 km^2
Population: 7.908m*
Pop density per km^2: 6*
Literacy rate: 9%*
GDP: $1,070m*; per capita GDP: $135
Economy type: low income
Labour force in agriculture: 85%

*1985

Ethnic composition
About half the population belong to the Mande group of tribes, which include the Bambara, the Malinke and the Sarakole. Other significant tribes are the Fulani, the Minianka, the Senutu, the Songhai and the Tuareg.

Religions
About 65 per cent of the population are Muslims, about 2 per cent are Christians and the rest mostly follow traditional, animist beliefs.

Political features
State type: authoritarian nationalist
Date of state formation: 1960
Political structure: unitary
Executive: unlimited presidential
Assembly: one-chamber
Party structure: one-party
Human rights rating: poor

Local and regional government
The country is divided into six regions and 42 counties, or *cercles*, which are further subdivided into 279 *arrondissements*. All are administered by officials of the national government.

Head of state and head of government
President General Moussa Traore, since 1968.

Political leaders since 1970
1968– Moussa Traore (UDPM).

Political system
The 1974 constitution was amended in 1981 and 1985. It provides for a one-party state, with a President elected by universal adult suffrage, through a simple plurality voting system, and a National Assembly of 82 members, similarly elected, from a list prepared by the party. The President serves for six years and may be re-elected an unlimited number of times. The Assembly has a three-year term.

Political parties
The only legally permitted party is the Malian People's Democratic Union (UDPM). It has a women's wing (UNFM) and a youth wing (UNJM). It was founded in 1976, in accordance with the 1974 constitution, as the government party. Although it is a socialist party and organised on Marxist-Leninist lines, its predominant orientation is nationalistic.

Latest elections
All the candidates for the 1988 Assembly elections were on a single list of nominees of UDPM local branch committees and all were elected. The turnout was 87.83 per cent.

Political history
Because of its comparatively isolated position, Mali escaped European contact until France established a colony in the nineteenth century. It then was called French Sudan and formed part of French West Africa. In 1959, with Senegal, it formed the Federation of Mali. Senegal soon left and Mali became a fully independent republic in 1960, with Modibo Keita as its first President.

Keita imposed an authoritarian socialist regime but the failure of his economic policies led to his removal in an army coup in 1968. The constitution was suspended and all political activity banned, the government being placed in the hands of a Military Committee for National Liberation (CMLN) with Lieutentant Moussa Traore as its President and head of state. The following year he became Prime Minister as well.

He promised a return to civilian rule and in 1974 a new constitution was adopted, formally making Mali a one-party state. A new national party, the Malian People's Democratic Union (UDPM), was announced in 1976. Despite opposition from students to a one-party state and objections by the army to civilian rule, Traore successfully made the transition so that by 1979 Mali had a constitutional form of government, but with ultimate power lying in the party and the military establishment.

In 1983 an agreement was signed between Mali and Guinea for eventual economic and political integration but this aim has not yet been fulfilled. In 1985 a border dispute with Burkina Faso resulted in a brief, five-day conflict which was settled by the International Court of Justice. This apart, Mali has enjoyed generally amicable relationships with its neighbours.

MAURITANIA

Islamic Republic of Mauritania
République Islamique de Mauritanie

Capital: Nouakchott

Social and economic data
Area: 1,030,700 km^2
Population: 1.750m*
Pop density per km^2: 2*
Literacy rate: 17%*
GDP: $710m*; per capita GDP: $406
Economy type: low income
Labour force in agriculture: 80%

*1985

Ethnic composition
Over 80 per cent of the population are of Moorish, or Moorish-black origin. About 18 per cent are blacks and there is a small European minority.

Religions
Islam is the state religion and almost the entire population are Muslims of the Malekite rite.

Political features
State type: military authoritarian
Date of state formation: 1960
Political structure: unitary
Executive: military
Assembly: there has been no assembly since the suspension of the constitution in 1978
Party structure: there are no political parties
Human rights rating: N/A

Local and regional government
The country is divided into twelve regions plus the capital district of Nouakchott. Each region has its own governor and within it are departments, administered by prefects, and within the departments, *arrondissements*. There are appointed regional assemblies.

Head of state and head of government
President Colonel Maawiya Ould Sid'Ahmed Taya, since 1984.

Political leaders since 1970
1960–78 Moktar Ould Daddah (PPM), 1978–79 Moustapha Ould Mohamed Salek (Military), 1979 Ahmed Ould Bouceif (Military), 1979–84 Mohamed Khouni Ould Haidalla (Military), 1984– Maawiya Ould Sid'Ahmed Taya (Military).

Political system

The 1961 constitution was suspended in 1978 after a coup and replaced by a charter which gave executive and legislative power to a Military Committee for National Recovery (CMRN). Its name was changed in 1979 to the Military Committee for National Salvation (CMSN). The chairman of the CMSN is also President of the Republic, Prime Minister and Minister of Defence. A new constitution was proposed in 1980 but abandoned in 1981.

Political parties

The only political party, the Mauritanian People's Party (PPM) was banned in 1978 and some of its exiled supporters now operate from Paris, through the Alliance for a Democratic Mauritania (AMI), or from Dakar, in Senegal, through the Organisation of Nationalist Mauritanians.

Latest elections

There have been no national elections since the dissolution of the National Assembly in 1978.

Political history

French influence was first apparent in Mauritania in the seventeenth century and, after a period of partial colonisation, it became a full colony, and part of French West Africa, in 1920. It was given internal self-government, within the French Community, in 1958 and full independence in 1960. Moktar Ould Daddah, leader of the Mauritanian People's Party (PPM), was elected President in 1961.

In 1975 Spain ceded the western part of Sahara to Mauritania and Morocco, leaving it to them to decide how to share it. Without consulting the Saharan people, Mauritania occupied the southern area, leaving the rest to Morocco. A resistance movement developed against this occupation, called the Popular Front for Liberation, or the Polisario Front, with the support of Algeria, and both Mauritania and Morocco found themselves engaged in a guerrilla war, forcing the two countries, who had formerly been rivals, into a mutual defence pact. Mauritania's economy was gravely weakened by the conflict and in 1978 President Daddah was deposed in a bloodless coup led by Colonel Mohamed Khouni Ould Haidalla.

Meanwhile, efforts were still being made to agree a peace with the Polisario and this was eventually achieved in August 1978. This allowed diplomatic relations with Algeria to be restored. Diplomatic relations with Morocco were broken in 1981 and attitudes worsened in 1984 when Mauritania formally recognised the Polisario regime in Western Sahara. Normal relations were restored in 1985.

Meanwhile, in December 1984, while Colonel Haidalla was attending a Franco-African summit meeting in Burundi, Colonel Maawwiya Ould Sid'Ahmed Taya, a former Prime Minister, led a bloodless coup to overthrow him. In April 1989 riots involving Mauritanians in Senegal, over disputed border grazing rights, caused a violent reaction in Mauritania, putting normal relations between the two countries at risk.

MAURITIUS

State of Mauritius

Capital: Port Louis

Social and economic data
Area: 2,040 km^2
Population: 1.029m*
Pop density per km^2: 504*
Literacy rate: 85%
GDP: $1,059m*; per capita GDP: $1,029
Economy type: middle income
Labour force in agriculture: 26%

*In 1985

Ethnic composition
There are five principal ethnic groups within the islands, French, African Negroes, Indians, Chinese and Mulattos, or Creoles. Indo-Mauritians predominate, constituting 67 per cent of the population, followed by Creoles 29 per cent, Sino-Mauritians 3.5 per cent and Europeans 0.5 per cent. The communities have sharply differing values and occupations so that inter-ethnic rivalries are intense. English is the official language but Creole is spoken by more than 50 per cent of the population, Hindi by 22 per cent and Bhojpuri by 19 per cent.

Religions
Fifty-one per cent of the population are Hindus, 17 per cent Muslims, 31 per cent Christians, mostly Roman Catholics, and less than 1 per cent are Buddhists. Roman Catholicism is the oldest religion and on Rodrigues island, where 90 per cent of the population are Europeans or Creoles, almost all are adherents to it.

Political features
State type: liberal democratic
Date of state formation: 1968
Political structure: unitary
Executive: parliamentary
Assembly: one-chamber
Party structure: multi-party
Human rights rating: N/A

Local and regional government
The island of Mauritius is divided into nine districts, while Rodrigues island has one of its two representative on the Legislative Assembly acting as 'Minister for Rodrigues'. Locally, there are elected urban and village councils.

Head of state
Queen Elizabeth II, represented by Sir Veerasamy Ringadoo since 1986.

Head of government
Aneerood Jugnauth, since 1982.

Political leaders since 1970
1968–82 Dr Seewoosagur Ramgoolam (MLP) and 1982– Aneerood Jugnauth (MSM).

Political system
Mauritius is an independent state within the Commonwealth, with a Governor-General, who is a native Mauritian, as head of state, representing the British monarch. Its constitution, which dates from independence in 1968, was amended in 1969. It provides for a single chamber Legislative Assembly of 71 members. Sixty-two are elected by universal adult suffrage, through a simple plurality voting system, in multi-member constituencies, for a five-year term. The island of Mauritius has 20 three-member constituencies and Rodrigues island one two-member constituency. There are a further eight 'additional members', selected by the Governor-General, in consultation with the judiciary, from among the 'runners up' at the general election. This is done in an effort to ensure a balance in representation between the islands' different ethnic groups. The Speaker is the last, 71st, Assembly member.

There is a parliamentary-type executive, with a Prime Minister appointed by the Governor-General from the Legislative Assembly on the basis of Assembly support. The Governor-General also appoints a cabinet, on the advice of the Prime Minister, and all are collectively responsible to the Assembly.

Political parties
The are 14 active political parties, the four most significant being the Mauritius Socialist Movement (MSM), the Mauritius Labour Party (MLP), the Mauritius Social Democratic Party (PMSD) and the Mauritius Militant Movement (MMM).

The MSM was formed in 1983 as a successor to the Mauritius Socialist Party, which itself was an outgrowth from the Mauritius Militant Movement. It has a moderate socialist orientation, and is pledged to make Mauritius a republic within the Commonwealth.

The MLP describes itself as 'democratic socialist' in outlook, but is really a centrist body, orientated towards Hindu Indians. It was originally formed in 1936 to campaign for the rights of cane-field workers and proceeded to dominate Mauritian politics up to 1982.

The PMSD is also an old-established party, but of a more conservative hue. Drawing its support from Franco-Mauritian landowners and the Creole middle classes, it is pro-Western, anti-communist and determinedly Francophile in its policy outlook.

The principal opposition party, the Mauritius Militant Movement (MMM: Mouvement Militant Mauricien), was formed in 1970 as a workers' party, enjoying strong backing from the trade-union movement and boasting broad cross-community membership. It is officially Marxist in policy outlook, seeking to nationalise the sugar, transport and insurance industries, establish a republic and introduce 'self-managing socialism'.

Latest elections

In the 1987 general election the results were as follows:

	Seats
MSM	26
MLP	9
PMSD	4
MMM and associated minor parties	21
Other parties	2

An alliance of the MSM, PMSD and MLP won 39 of the 62 elective seats, with 48.8 per cent of the popular vote, while the MMM, which had campaigned with the Movement of Democratic Workers and Socialist Workers' Front minor parties, captured 21 seats and 48.1 per cent of the total vote. Five of the eight 'additional seats' were allocated to the MSM-PMSD-MLP alliance and three to the MMM.

Political history

The state of Mauritius is in the Indian Ocean east of Madagascar and consists of the island of Mauritius and the dependencies of Rodrigues island, Agalega island and the Cargados Carajos, or St Brandon islands.

Mauritius island, then uninhabited, was discovered by the Dutch in 1598 and named after Prince Maurice of Nassau. It was colonised during the seventeenth century, but abandoned in 1710. The French re-occupied it, with Rodrigues, in 1715 and established sugar-cane plantations to be worked by imported African slaves. During the Napoleonic War of 1803–15 the island group was captured by Britain and then formally ceded to it by France in 1814. From then until 1903 it was administered with the Seychelles as a single colony. As a separate colony, Mauritius developed rapidly to become a major sugar-cane producer. With the abolition of slavery in 1834, a switch from imported African workers to indentured labour from India took place. Although originally brought in on short-term contracts, many Indian immigrants chose to stay, establishing the ethnic pattern which exists today.

Following several decades of campaigning for self-rule, spearheaded by the Mauritius Labour Party (MLP), the islands were granted internal self-government in July 1957 and full independence, within the Commonwealth, in March 1968. The MLP's leader, Dr Seewoosagur Ramgoolam, who had been Chief Minister since September 1961, became the country's first Prime Minister.

During the 1960s Mauritius enjoyed rapid economic growth on the basis of a strong market for sugar. This made possible a substantial rise in social spending and the successful implementation of an urgently needed population control programme. However, in the early 1970s, as export markets declined and economic conditions generally deteriorated, opposition to the Ramgoolam government grew, led by the newly formed left-wing Mauritius Militant Movement (MMM), headed by Paul Berenger. It played a leading role in organising a wave of strikes in 1971, the government responding by imposing a state of emergency and postponing the Legislative Assembly elections which were due in August 1972.

The governing MLP and Mauritius Social Democratic Party (PMSD) coalition eventually broke up in December 1973, but Ramgoolam stayed in power by establishing a new alliance with the Muslim Committee of Action (CAM). In the December 1976 general election the MMM emerged as the largest single party, but Ramgoolam succeeded in forming a new governing coalition of the MLP, CAM and PMSD.

Against a background of rising unemployment and industrial unrest, the ruling coalition was eventually defeated in the election of June 1982, the MMM, in alliance with the Mauritius Socialist Party (PSM), winning all 60 seats on Mauritius island. The PSM's leader, Aneerood Jugnauth, became the new Prime Minister, promising to pursue radical policies, based on non-alignment in foreign affairs, the extension of state control of the economy and a proposal to make Mauritius a republic within the Commonwealth. Within a year, however, sharp differences emerged within the coalition, including Jugnauth's objection to a MMM campaign to make Creole the national language. He dissolved the coalition in March 1983 and formed a new PSM minority administration.

Lacking a working majority, Jugnauth had to call for fresh elections in August 1983. These resulted in the MSM forming an electoral alliance with the MLP and PMSD and Jugnauth becoming Prime Minister again, on the understanding that the MLP's leader, Sir Seewoosagur Ramgoolam, as he now was, would be made President if Mauritius became a republic. When the government failed to secure legislative approval for this constitutional change, Ramgoolam was appointed Governor-General on the retirement of the existing holder of the post, in December 1983. He died two years later and was replaced as Governor-General by Sir Veerasamy Ringadoo, a former finance minister.

The new MSM, MLP, PMSD coalition was weakened in February 1984, when the MLP withdrew, but it remained in office with the support of eleven dissident MLP members. Then, in December 1985, its reputation was tarnished when an attempt was made to 'cover up' a Mauritius-Netherlands drugs smuggling scandal involving MSM and PMSD members. Despite these difficulties, improvements in the economy enabled a new alliance of the three parties to secure another majority in the 1987 general election.

Mauritius has no standing army and has pursued a moderately non-aligned foreign policy during recent years. It has, however, had minor territorial disputes with Britain and France.

MOZAMBIQUE

People's Republic of Mozambique
Republica Popular de Moçambique

Capital: Maputo

Social and economic data
Area: 799,380 km^2
Population: 14.000m*
Pop density per km^2: 18*
Literacy rate: 27%*
GDP: $2,000m*; per capita GDP: $143
Economy type: low income
Labour force in agriculture: 84%
*1985

Ethnic composition

The majority of people belong to local tribal groups, the largest being the Makua-Lomue, comprising about 38 per cent of the population. The other significantly large group, of about 24 per cent, is the Tsonga.

Religions

Most people follow traditional beliefs. There are about 2 million Muslims, 2 million Christians and a smaller number of Hindus.

Political features

State type: nationalistic socialist
Date of state formation: 1975
Political structure: unitary
Executive: unlimited presidential
Assembly: one-chamber
Party structure: one-party
Human rights rating: 25%

Local and regional government

The country is divided into ten provinces, within which are districts, cities and localities. Each province has an appointed governor and there is provision for elected assemblies at each level but few seem to have been formed. The government party, Frelimo, is active at both provincial and local levels.

Head of state and head of government

Joaquim Chissano, since 1986.

Political leaders since 1970

1975–86 Samora Machel (Frelimo), 1986–Joaquim Chissano (Frelimo).

Political system

The constitution dates from independence in 1975 and was revised in 1978. It provides for a one-party, socialist state, based on the National Front for the Liberation of Mozambique (Frelimo). The President heads its Political Bureau and Central Committee Secretariat. There is a 250-member People's Assembly, comprising 130 members of the Central Committee of Frelimo plus 120 other people drawn from the central and provincial governments, the armed forces and citizens' representatives. The Assembly is convened by the President and normally meets twice a year, but can be extraordinarily summoned. When it is not sitting its functions are performed by an inner group of 15 members, called the Permanent Commission. This, too, is convened and presided over by the President.

Political parties

The National Front for the Liberation of Mozambique (Frelimo) is the only legally permitted party. It was formed in 1962 by a merger of three nationalist parties, the Mozambique National Democratic Union (UDENAMO), the Mozambique African Nationalist Union (MANU) and the African Union of Independent Mozambique (UNAMI). Frelimo was reconstituted in 1977 as a 'Marxist-Leninist vanguard party', but moderated its stance in July 1989 to attract wider support.

Latest elections

In the 1986 assembly elections Frelimo put forward 299 candidates for the 250 seats, giving a limited electoral choice.

Political history

Mozambique became a Portuguese colony in 1505 and was subsequently exploited for its gold and ivory, as well as being a source of slaves for export. Guerrilla groups had actively opposed Portuguese rule from the early 1960s, the various left-wing factions combining to form Frelimo. As the government in Lisbon came under increasing strain, Frelimo's leader, Samora Machel, demanded nothing short of complete independence and, in 1974, internal self-government was granted, with Joaquim Chissano, a member of Frelimo's Central Committee, as Prime Minister. A year later full independence was achieved and Machel became the country's first President.

He was immediately faced with the problem of hundreds of thousands of Portuguese settlers departing, leaving no trained replacements in key economic positions. Two activities had been the mainstay of the Mozambique economy, transit traffic from South Africa and Rhodesia and the export of labour to South African mines. Although Machel declared his support for the African National Congress (ANC) in South Africa, and the Patriotic Front in Rhodesia, he knew that he still had to co-exist and trade with his two white-governed neighbours. He put heavy pressure on the Patriotic Front for a settlement of the guerrilla war and this eventually bore fruit in the Lancaster House Agreement of 1979 and the eventual electoral victory of Robert Mugabe, a reliable friend of Mozambique.

From 1980 onwards the country was faced with the twin problems of widespread drought, which affected most of southern Africa, and attacks by dissidents, under the banner of the Mozambique National Resistance (Renamo), also known as the MNR, who were covertly, but strongly, backed by South Africa. These attacks were concentrated on Mozambique's vital and vulnerable transport system. Machel, showing considerable diplomatic skill, had, by 1983, repaired relations with the United States, undertaken a successful European tour, and established himself as a respected African leader. His sense of realism was shown in his relations with South Africa. In March 1984 he signed the Nkomati Accord, under which South Africa agreed to deny facilities to the MNR and Mozambique, in return, agreed not to provide bases for the banned ANC. Machel took steps to honour his side of the bargain but was doubtful about South Africa's good faith. On 19 October 1986 he died in an air crash near the South African border on a return flight from Zambia. Despite the suspicious circumstances of his death, a subsequent inquiry pronounced it an accident.

The following month Frelimo's Central Committee elected the foreign minister, and former Prime Minister, Joaquim Chissano, as his successor. In his acceptance speech, Chissano pledged himself to carry on with the policies of his predecessor. Chissano has strengthened the ties Machel had already forged with Zimbabwe and Britain and in February 1987 he took the unprecedented step of informally requesting permission to attend the Commonwealth Heads of Government summit in Vancouver in October. This has been seen by some observers as a prelude to a request for

Commonwealth membership, but the Commonwealth Secretary-General, Sonny Ramphal, has described such speculation as misleading. Mozambique's economic problems were aggravated in the early months on 1987 by food shortages, following another year of drought.

Despite the Nkomati Accord, South Africa continued to train and arm the MNR to the extent that people in rural areas found it too dangerous to remain in their villages or cultivate their land. Thousands fled to neighbouring Malawi. Mozambique's reply to the South African-backed MNR was to mount a Front Line States' regional army with a combination of Zimbabwean, Tanzanian and Mozambique troops. In May 1988 it was announced that Mozambique and South Africa had agreed to revive a joint security commission which had originally been set up under the Nkomati Accord but which had broken up because of Mozambique's suspicions about South Africa's honouring of the Accord. In September 1988 President Botha of South Africa paid a visit to Mozambique, as part of a strategy of trying to improve relations with black Africa. The meeting between him and Chissano was reported to be 'brisk and businesslike'. In December 1988 the Tanzanian government announced the withdrawal of its troops from Mozambique, initiating a relaxation of tension and guerrilla activity in the country.

NIGER

Republic of Niger
République du Niger

Capital: Niamey

Social and economic data
Area: 1,267,000 km^2
Population: 6.715m*
Pop density per km^2: 5*
Literacy rate: 10%*
GDP: $1,700m*; per capita GDP: $253
Economy type: low income
Labour force in agriculture: 85%

*1985

Ethnic composition
Three tribes make up over 75 per cent of the population. They are the Hausa, mainly in the central and southern areas, the Djerma-Songhai, in the south-west, and the Beriberi-Manga, in the east. There is also a significant number of the Fulani tribe, mainly nomadic.

Religions
About 85 per cent of the population are Muslims. Most of the rest follow traditional beliefs.

Political features
State type: military authoritarian
Date of state formation: 1960
Political structure: unitary
Executive: military
Assembly: there has been no assembly since the suspension of the constitution in 1974
Party structure: there are no political parties
Human rights rating: poor

Local and regional government
The country is divided into seven departments, each headed by a prefect, assisted by a regional advisory council. Within the departments are 32 *arrondissements* and 150 communes.

Head of state and head of government
President Ali Seybou, since 1987.

Political leaders since 1970
1970–74 Hamani Diori (PPN), 1974–87 Seyni Kountche (Military), 1987– Ali Seybou (Military).

Political system
The 1960 constitution was suspended following a military coup in 1974 and Niger is now ruled by a Supreme Military Council of army officers and a Council of Ministers appointed by the President, who is head of state as well as head of government and also combines the portfolios of Interior and National Defence. In a move towards greater democracy, a National Development Council, of 150 elected members, was reconstituted in 1983 and given the task of drawing up a National Charter.

Political parties
Since 1974 all political parties have been banned. Prior to that date the government party was the Niger Progressive Party (NPP). It moved from being the majority party to suppressing all opposition and this policy contributed to the eventual military takeover.

Latest elections
There have been no open elections since the military coup in 1974.

Political history
Formerly part of French West Africa, Niger achieved full independence in 1960. Hamani Diori was elected President and re-elected in 1965 and 1970. Maintaining very close and cordial relations with France, Diori seemed to have established one of the most stable regimes in Africa, and the discovery of uranium deposits promised a sound economic future. However, his practice of suppressing opposition to his party, the NPP, coupled with a severe drought between 1968 and 1974, resulted in widespread civil disorder and, in April 1974, he was ousted in a coup led by army chief of staff, Lieutentant-Colonel Seyni Kountche.

Kountche suspended the constitution and established a military government with himself as President. He immediately set about trying to restore the economy and negotiating a more equal relationship with France. This was eventually done through a co-operation agreement signed in 1977. Still threatened by possible droughts, and consequential unrest, Kountche tried to widen his popular support by liberalising his regime and releasing political prisoners, including former President Diori. More civilians were introduced into the government with the eventual prospect of a return to constitutional rule. In November 1987 Kountche died while undergoing surgery in a Paris hospital and was succeeded by the army chief of staff, Colonel Ali Seybou.

NIGERIA

Federal Republic of Nigeria

Capital: Abuja

Social and economic data

Area: 923,800 km^2
Population: 105.448m*
Pop density per km^2: 114*
Literacy rate: 34%*
GDP: $66,000m*; per capita GDP: $626
Economy type: low income
Labour force in agriculture: 50%

*1985

Ethnic composition

There are more than 250 tribal groups in the country, the main ones being the Hausa and Fulani in the north, the Yoruba in the south, and the Ibos in the east. The non-African population is relatively small and numbers no more than about 30,000.

Religions

About half the population are Muslims, about 30 per cent Christians and the remainder mostly follow traditional beliefs.

Political features

State type: military authoritarian
Date of state formation: 1960
Political structure: federal
Executive: military
Assembly: there is no assembly at present
Party structure: there are no parties at present
Human rights rating: 53%

Local and regional government

The country is divided into 19 states plus a Federal Capital Territory. Each of the 19 states has a military governor, appointed by the AFRC, who, in turn, appoints and leads a State Executive Council. There is also a co-ordinating federal body called the National Council of States, which includes the President and all the state governors. Although the governors have some local autonomy, there is still tight central control. Some states have lower tiers of authority, at the governors' discretion.

Head of state and head of government
President Major General Ibrahim Babangida, since 1985.

Political leaders since 1970
1966–1975 Yakubu Gowon (Military), 1975–79 Olusegun Obasanjo (Military), 1979–83 Shehu Shagari (NPN-NPP coalition), 1985– Ibrahim Babangida (Military).

Political system
Nigeria is a federal republic of 19 states. The present constitution is based on one of 1979 which was amended following a military coup in December 1983. Another coup in 1985 made further changes. The President is head of state, commander-in-chief of the armed forces and chairman of a 28-member Armed Forces Ruling Council (AFRC), composed of senior officers of the army and police force. The AFRC appoints a National Council of Ministers which is also headed by the President. A new draft constitution was published in 1988 but agreement on its ratification was not reached.

Political parties
All political parties are now banned but, prior to the coup, six organisations had been registered with the Federal Electoral Commission in readiness for the 1983 elections. Four of these groups had agreed to merge into a single party, the Progressive Parties' Alliance (PPA). The other two are the National Party of Nigeria (NPN) and the Nigerian Advance Party (NAP).

The creation of PPA was agreed in principle in 1982 and the merger was to take place after the 1983 elections. The merging groups would have been the Greater Nigeria People's Party (GNPP), the Nigerian People's Party (NPP), the People's Redemption Party (PRP) and the United Party of Nigeria (UPN). The eventual orientation of the merged party would probably have been left-of-centre.

The NPN was formed in 1978 as a coalition of most of the major groups and political figures who were active prior to the military coup of 1966. Its orientation is pragmatic, right-of-centre.

The NAP was founded in 1978 but did not register until 1982. It is a centrist party which aims to appeal particularly to the younger voters.

Latest elections
There have been no elections since 1979 when the NPN won 168 seats in the 449-member House of Representatives and formed a coalition government with the NPP.

Political history
The British founded a colony at Lagos in 1861 and gradually extended it by absorbing surrounding areas until by 1914 it had become Britain's largest African colony. It achieved full independence, as a constitutional monarchy within the Commonwealth, in 1960 and became a republic in 1963. The

republic was based on a federal structure so as to accommodate the regional differences and the many tribes.

The ethnic differences, including the fact that groups of tribes were in different parts of the vast country, always contained the ingredients for a potential conflict. The discovery of oil in the south-east in 1958 made it very much richer than the north and this exaggerated the differences.

Nigeria's first President was Dr Nnamdi Azikiwe, who had been a banker, then established an influential newspaper group and played a leading part in the nationalist movement, pressing for independence. He came from the Ibo tribe. His chief rival was Tafawa Balewa, who was Prime Minister from 1957 until he was assassinated in a military coup in 1966. The coup had been led by mainly Ibo junior officers, from the eastern region. The offices of President and Prime Minister were suspended and it was announced that the state's federal structure would be abandoned.

Before this took place, the new military government was overturned in a counter-coup by a mostly Christian faction from the north, led by Colonel Yakubu Gowon. He re-established the federal system and appointed a military governor for each region. Soon afterwards thousands of Ibos in the north were slaughtered. In 1967 a conflict developed between Gowon and the military governor of the eastern region, Colonel Chukwuemeka Odumegwu-Ojukwu, about the distribution of oil revenues, which resulted in Ojukwu's declaration of an independent Ibo state of Biafra. Gowon, after failing to pacify the Ibos, ordered federal troops into the eastern region and a civil war began. It lasted until January 1970, when Biafra surrendered to the federal forces. It had been a bitter conflict and the economy was gravely weakened.

In 1975, while he was out of the country, Gowon was replaced in a bloodless coup led by Brigadier Murtala Mohammad, who became head of state, but he was killed within a month, in a coup led by General Olusegun Obasanjo, who announced a gradual return to civilian rule. In fulfilment of that undertaking, in 1979 the leader of the National Party of Nigeria (NPN), Shehu Shagari, became President.

In December 1983, following a deterioration in the economy caused by falling oil prices, Shagari's civilian government was deposed in another bloodless coup, this time led by Major-General Muhammadu Buhari, who established a military administration with himself as head of state. In 1985 there was another peaceful coup which replaced Buhari with a new military government, led by Major-General Ibrahim Babangida, the army chief of staff.

At the end of 1985 another attempted coup by rival officers was thwarted. Babangida promised a return to a democratic civilian government in 1989 but in 1987 announced that the transition would not now take place until 1992. This decision has dismayed many politicians who fear that they will be too old to seek office by that date. A draft constitution was debated in the assembly throughout 1988 but agreement on its final form was not reached. In March 1989 President Babangida announced that he would soon lift the ban on political activity and urged all tribes and sections to work together. In the following month it was announced that the government would operate from the nation's new capital, Abuja, in central Nigeria.

RWANDA

Republic of Rwanda
Republika y'u Rwanda

Capital: Kigali

Social and economic data
Area: 26,340 km^2
Population: 6.500m*
Pop density per km^2: 247*
Literacy rate: 38%*
GDP: $1,600m*; per capita GDP: $246
Economy type: low income
Labour force in agriculture: 93%

*1985

Ethnic composition
About 84 per cent of the population are members of the Hutu tribe, most of the others being Tutsis. There are also Twa and Pygmy minorities.

Religions
About 50 per cent of the population follow traditional beliefs and there are about 2.75 million Roman Catholics and about 120,000 Anglicans.

Political features
State type: military authoritarian
Date of state formation: 1962
Political structure: unitary
Executive: military
Assembly: one-chamber
Party structure: one-party
Human rights rating: poor

Local and regional government
The country is divided into ten prefectures which are further subdivided into 143 communes, or municipalities. The communes are administered by appointed governors and have elected councils.

Head of state and head of government
President Major-General Juvenal Habyarimana, since 1973.

Political leaders since 1970
1962–73 Gregoire Kayibanda (Democratic Republican Movement-Parmehutu), 1973– Juvenal Habyarimana (Military).

Political system
The 1978 constitution provides for a President and a single-chamber assembly, the National Development Council, all elected by universal adult suffrage, through a simple plurality voting system, for a five-year term. All candidates for election to the assembly are nominees of the ruling party, MRND. The President appoints and leads a Council of Ministers.

Political parties
Rwanda is a one-party state, the sole legal party being the National Revolutionary Development Movement (MRND). It was formed in 1975 two years after General Habyarimana's successful coup. It has a nationalistic, socialist orientation.

Latest elections
In the 1988 National Development Council elections 70 deputies were elected from a list of 140 MRND nominees. In the 1988 presidential election General Habyarimana was the sole candidate.

Political history
In the sixteenth century the Tutsi tribe moved into the country and took over from the indigenous Hutus, establishing a kingdom. Then, at the end of the nineteenth century German colonisers arrived and forced the Tutsi king to allow the country to become a German protectorate. It was linked to the neighbouring state of Burundi within the empire of German East Africa until after the First World War, when it came under Belgian administration as a League of Nations, then United Nations, Trust Territory.

In 1961 the monarchy was abolished and Ruanda, as it was then called, became a republic. It achieved full independence in 1962 as Rwanda, with Gregoire Kayibanda as its first President. Fighting broke out in 1963 between the two main tribes, the Hutu and the Tutsi, resulting in the loss of, it is estimated, some 20,000 lives, before an uneasy peace was agreed in 1965. Kayibanda was re-elected President in 1969 but by the end of 1972 the tribal warfare had restarted and in July 1973 the head of the National Guard, Major-General Juvenal Habyarimana, led a bloodless coup, ousting Kayibanda and establishing a military government.

Meetings of the assembly were suspended and all political activity banned until a new ruling party was formed. It was the National Revolutionary Development Movement (MRND) and was the only legally permitted political organisation. A referendum held at the end of 1978 approved a new constitution designed to fulfil Habyarimana's promise in 1973 to return to normal constitutional government within five years. Despite this, Rwanda is still effectively a militarily controlled state.

SAO TOME E PRINCIPE

Democratic Republic of Sao Tome and Principe

Capital: Sao Tome

Social and economic data
Area: 1,000 km^2
Population: 0.105m*
Pop density per km^2: 105*
Literacy rate: 57%*
GDP: $30m*; per capita GDP: $286
Economy type: low income
Labour force in agriculture: 54%
*1985

Ethnic composition
The population is predominantly African.

Religions
About 90 per cent of the people are Christians, mostly Roman Catholics.

Political features
State type: nationalistic socialist
Date of state formation: 1975
Political structure: unitary
Executive: unlimited presidential
Assembly: one-chamber
Party structure: one-party
Human rights rating: N/A

Local and regional government
For administrative purposes, the country is divided into seven counties. Six of them are on Sao Tome island and one on Principe.

Head of state and head of government
President Dr Manuel Pinto da Costa, since 1975.

Political leaders since 1970
1975– Manuel Pinto da Costa (MLSTP).

Political system
Sao Tome and Principe is a one-party state, with small opposition groups operating from outside the country, mainly in Lisbon. The 1982 constitution describes the MLSTP as the leading political force in the nation and the National People's Assembly as the supreme organ of the state. It has 40 members, all MLSTP nominees, who until 1987 were elected by People's District Assemblies for a five-year term. The President is also nominated by the MLSTP and was elected for a similar term by the Assembly. Now all are elected by direct universal suffrage, through a simple plurality voting system.

The 1987 changes allow independent candidates to offer themselves for election, but with the proviso that the MLSTP will continue to nominate a single presidential candidate. The central committee of the MLSTP also announced in 1987 that greater democratisation would be progressively introduced. The first step might be the re-establishment of the separate post of Prime Minister, which was absorbed into the presidency in 1979.

Political parties
The only legal party is the Movement for the Liberation of Sao Tome and Principe (MLSTP). It was founded in 1972 by Pinto da Costa from an earlier nationalistic group. It has a nationalist and socialist orientation.

Latest elections
In the 1985 Assembly elections all 40 members elected were MLSTP nominees.

Political history
The two islands of Sao Tome and Principe were first colonised by the Portuguese in the late fifteenth century. They became important trading posts for ships on their way to the East Indies, supplying sugar and later cocoa and coffee. They were declared an overseas province of Portugal in 1951 and were given internal self-government in 1973. An independence movement, the Movement for the Liberation of Sao Tome and Principe (MLSTP), led by Dr Manuel Pinto da Costa, took advantage of a military coup in Portugal, in 1974, and persuaded the new government in Lisbon to recognise it formally as the sole representative of the people of the islands. Full independence followed, in July 1975.

Dr Pinto da Costa became the first President and in December a National People's Assembly was elected. During the first few years of his presidency there were several unsuccessful attempts to depose him and, with a worsening economy, Pinto da Costa began to reassess his country's international links which had made it over-dependent on the Eastern bloc and, in consequence, isolated from the West.

In 1984 he formally proclaimed that in future Sao Tome and Principe would be a non-aligned state and the number of Angolan, Cuban and Soviet advisers was sharply reduced. Gradually, the country has turned more towards nearby African states such as Gabon, Cameroon and Equatorial Guinea, as well as maintaining its links with Lisbon. In March 1988 there was another unsuccessful coup to unseat Pinto da Costa by dissidents from outside the country.

In 1987 there were signs of a movement towards a more democratic political system but any process so far has been minimal and largely superficial.

SENEGAL

Republic of Senegal
République du Sénégal

Capital: Dakar

Social and economic data
Area: 197,000 km^2
Population: 6.900m*
Pop density per km^2: 35*
Literacy rate: 22%*
GDP: $2,700m*; per capita GDP: $391
Economy type: low income
Labour force in agriculture: 72%

*1985

Ethnic composition
Senegal has a great ethnic diversity. The Wolof group are the most numerous tribes, comprising about 36 per cent of the population. The Fulani comprise about 21 per cent, the Serer 19 per cent, the Diola 7 per cent and the Mandingo 6 per cent. Within each main group are many individual tribes.

Religions
Ninety per cent of the population are Muslims, 5 per cent Christians and 5 per cent follow traditional beliefs.

Political features
State type: nationalistic socialist
Date of state formation: 1960
Political structure: unitary
Executive: unlimited presidential
Assembly: one-chamber
Party structure: one-party
Human rights rating: 77%

Local and regional government
The country is divided into ten regions, each with an appointed governor and elected assembly. There is a further subdivision into departments, *arrondissements* and villages. Departments are administered by prefects, *arrondissements* by sub-prefects and villages by chiefs.

Head of state and head of government
President Abdou Diouf, since 1981.

Political leaders since 1970
1960–80 Léopold Sedar Senghor (UPS-PS), 1981– Abdou Diouf (PS).

Political system
The constitution dates from 1963 and has since been amended. It provides for a single-chamber, 120-member National Assembly, and a President who is head of state and head of government. The Assembly and President are elected at the same time by universal adult suffrage, through the additional member majoritarian system of voting, to serve a five-year term. The President appoints and leads a Council of Ministers.

Political parties
Between 1966 and 1974 Senegal became a one-party state but now opposition is allowed, although the party led by the President, the Senegalese Socialist Party (PS), dominates the political scene. The main opposition comes from the Senegalese Democratic Party (PDS), but there is now a total of 16 registered parties.

The PS began in 1949 as the Senegalese Progressive Union (UPS). In 1976 it was reconstituted in its present form. It is a democratic socialist party. The PDS was recognised in 1976 as the liberal democratic party.

Latest elections
In the 1988 presidential election Abdou Diouf was re-elected with 73.2 per cent of the vote, while his PDS rival won 25.8 per cent

In the 1988 National Assembly elections the results were as follows:

	% Votes	*Seats*
PS	71.34	103
PDS	24.74	17

Political history
After 300 years as a French colony, Senegal became an independent republic in September 1960, with Léopold Sedar Senghor, leader of the Senegalese Progressive Union (UPS), as its first President. In 1962 Senghor took over the post of Prime Minister and four years later, in 1966, made the UPS the only legal party. In 1970 he relinquished the office of Prime Minister to a young protégé, Abdou Diouf, who, in 1976, was to be named his successor. In 1973 Senghor was re-elected and began to honour his promise to allow the return to multi-party politics. In December 1976 the UPS was reconstituted to become the Senegalese Socialist Party (PS) and two opposition parties were legally registered. In the 1978 elections the PS won over 80 per cent of the Assembly seats and Senghor was decisively re-elected. He retired at the end of 1980 and was succeeded by Diouf who immediately sought national unity by declaring an amnesty for political offenders and permitting more parties to register.

In 1980 Senegal sent troops to Gambia to protect it against a suspected Libyan invasion, and it intervened again in 1981 to thwart an attempted coup. As the two countries came closer together, agreement was reached on an eventual merger and the, as yet loose, confederation of Senegambia came into being in February 1982. Senegal has always maintained close links with France, allowing it to retain military bases.

In the 1983 elections Diouf and his party were again clear winners and later that year he further tightened his control of his party and the government, abolishing the post of Prime Minister. As Diouf secured his position, there were signs of open opposition, sometimes violent, but he and the PS remained firmly in power and were decisively re-elected in 1988. The opening up of the party system, ironically, strengthened, rather than weakened, the one-party state. In April 1989 violent clashes over border grazing rights, in both Senegal and Mauritania, threatened to harm relations between the two countries, but a subsequent meeting between the two Presidents helped to restore them.

SEYCHELLES

Republic of the Seychelles

Capital: Victoria

Social and economic data
Area: 450 km^2
Population: 0.066m*
Pop density per km^2: 147*
Literacy rate: 58%*
GDP: $170m*; per capita GDP: $2,575
Economy type: middle income
Labour force in agriculture: 10%
*1985

Ethnic composition
The majority of the population are Creoles, of mixed African-European parentage. There is a small European minority, mostly French and British.

Religions
About 90 per cent of the people are Roman Catholics and Roman Catholicism is a quasi-state religion. About 8 per cent are Anglicans.

Political features
State type: nationalistic socialist
Date of state formation: 1976
Political structure: unitary
Executive: unlimited presidential
Assembly: one-chamber
Party structure: one-party
Human rights rating: N/A

Local and regional government
There is no local government as such, administration coming almost entirely from the centre.

Head of state and head of government
President France-Albert René, since 1977.

Political leaders since 1970
1970–77 James Mancham (SDP), 1977– France-Albert René (SPUP).

Political system
Seychelles is a republic within the Commonwealth. The constitution, which came into force at independence in 1976, was temporarily suspended, following a coup, and then reinstated in 1977. A new one was later adopted in 1979. It made Seychelles a one-party state. The constitution also provides for a President, who is both head of state and head of government, and a single-chamber National Assembly. Both serve five-year terms. The President and 23 of the 25 Assembly members are elected by universal adult suffrage, through a simple plurality voting system. The other two members are presidential appointees.

Political parties
The only legally permitted party is the Seychelles People's Progresssive Front (SPPF). It was founded in the 1960s as the Seychelles People's United Party (SPUP) and in 1978 adopted its present name. It has a nationalistic socialist stance.

Latest elections
In the 1987 assembly elections there was a 66 per cent turnout and 36 candidates for the 23 elected seats. 10 members were elected unopposed. All candidates were SPPF nominees. In the 1989 presidential election René was re-elected for a third term.

Political history
Seychelles is a group of 115 islands, scattered over an area of more than a million square kilometres. They were colonised by the French in 1768, captured by the British in 1794, and formally ceded by France in 1814 to became a British crown colony in 1903.

In the 1960s several political parties were formed, campaigning for independence, the most significant being the Seychelles Democratic Party (SDP), led by James Mancham, and the Seychelles People's United Party (SPUP), led by France-Albert René. At a constitutional conference in London in 1970 René demanded complete independence while Mancham favoured integration with the United Kingdom. Agreement was not reached and so a further conference was held in 1975 when internal self-government was agreed.

The two parties then formed a coalition government, with Mancham as Prime Minister. Eventually, full independence was achieved, in June 1976. Seychelles became a republic within the Commonwealth, with Mancham as President and René as Prime Minister. The following year René staged an armed coup, while Mancham was attending a Commonwealth conference in London, and declared himself President.

After a brief suspension of the constitution, a new one was adopted, creating a one-party state, with the SPUP being renamed the Seychelles People's Progressive Front (SPPF). René, as the only candidate, was formally elected President in 1979 and then re-elected in 1984 and 1989. There have been several unsuccessful attempts to overthrow him, the most serious being in 1981 when 44 mercenaries, mainly South Africans, joined rebels on the main island of Mahe. Another reported plot in 1987 resulted in the dismissal of three senior army officers.

René has followed a policy of non-alignment and has forbidden the use of port facilities to vessels carrying nuclear weapons. He has, however, maintained close links with Tanzania, which has provided defence support.

SIERRA LEONE

Republic of Sierra Leone

Capital: Freetown

Social and economic data

Area: 73,330 km^2
Population: 3.883m*
Pop density per km^2: 53*
Literacy rate: 24%*
GDP: $1,100m*; per capita GDP: $283
Economy type: low income
Labour force in agriculture: 62%

*1985

Ethnic composition

There are some 18 tribal groups in the country, three of which comprise nearly 70 per cent of the population. They are the Mende, the Tenne and the Limbe.

Religions

Most people follow traditional, animist beliefs. There are Muslim and Christian minorities.

Political features
State type: authoritarian nationalist
Date of state formation: 1961
Political structure: unitary
Executive: unlimited presidential
Assembly: one-chamber
Party structure: one-party
Human rights rating: 64%

Local and regional government
The country is divided into three provinces, Northern, Southern and Eastern, plus the Western area, which includes Freetown. Each province has a cabinet minister responsible for it. The provinces are divided into districts, within which are 148 chiefdoms, each controlled by a tribal chief.

Head of state and head of government
President Major-General Joseph Saidu Momoh, since 1985.

Political leaders since 1970
1968–85 Siaka Stevens (APC), 1985– Joseph Saidu Momoh (APC).

Political system
The 1978 constitution made Sierra Leone a one-party state. It also provided for a President, who is both head of state and head of government, and a single-chamber assembly, the House of Representatives. The House has 127 members, 105 elected for five years by universal adult suffrage, through a simple plurality voting system, twelve Paramount Chiefs, as *ex officio* members, one for each district, and ten additional members appointed by the President. The President is endorsed by the party as the sole candidate and then popularly elected for a seven-year term. He appoints a cabinet and two Vice-Presidents.

Political parties
The only permitted party is the All People's Congress (APC), which was founded by Sierra Leone's first President, Siaka Stevens, in 1960. It has a moderate-socialist orientation.

Latest elections
In the 1986 general election there were 335 candidates for the 105 elected seats in the House of Representatives. All were APC nominees.

Political history
In the 1780s the area which is now Sierra Leone was bought by English philanthropists to provide a settlement for freed slaves and in 1808 it became a British colony. It achieved full independence, as a constitutional monarchy, within the Commonwealth, in 1961, with Sir Milton Margai, leader of the Sierra Leone People's Party (SLPP), as Prime Minister.

He died in 1964 and was succeeded by his half-brother, Dr Albert Margai. The 1967 general election was won by the All-People's Congress (APC), led by Dr Siaka Stevens, but the result was disputed by the army which assumed control and set up a National Reformation Council, forcing the Governor-

General to leave the country temporarily. In the following year another army revolt brought back Stevens as Prime Minister and in 1971, after the 1961 constitution had been changed to make Sierra Leone a republic, he became President.

He was re-elected in 1976 and the APC, having won the 1977 general election by a big margin, began to demand the creation of a one-party state. A new constitution, making APC the sole legal party, was approved by referendum in 1978 and Stevens was sworn in as President for another seven-year term.

As the date for the next presidential election drew near, Stevens, who was now 80, annnounced that he would not stand for re-election and an APC conference in August 1985 endorsed the commander of the army, Major-General Joseph Momoh, as the sole candidate for party leader and President. He was formally elected in October. Momoh appointed a civilian cabinet and immediately disassociated himself from the policies of his predecessor, who had been criticised for failing to prevent corruption within his administration. The new President also pledged himself to improve the state of the economy by increasing productivity and reducing inflation.

SOMALIA

Somali Democratic Republic
Jamhuriyadda Dimugradiga Somaliya

Capital: Mogadishu

Social and economic data
Area: 637,660 km^2
Population: 7.800m*
Pop density per km^2: 12*
Literacy rate: 6%*
GDP: $1,258m*; per capita GDP: $160
Economy type: low income
Labour force in agriculture: 78%

*1985

Ethnic composition
Somalia is one of the most ethnically homogeneous countries in Africa. Ninety-eight per cent of the population are indigenous Somalis, including about 84 per cent of Hamitic stock and 14 per cent Bantu. About 70% of people are nomadic.

Religions
Islam is the state religion, most people being Sunni Muslims. There is also a Roman Catholic minority.

Political features
State type: nationalistic socialist
Date of state formation: 1960
Political structure: unitary

Executive: unlimited presidential
Assembly: one-chamber
Party structure: one-party
Human rights rating: poor

Local and regional government
The country is divided into 16 regions which are further subdivided into 78 districts. The regions are administered by commissioners and there are appointed district councils and elected village councils.

Head of state and head of government
President Major-General Mohamed Siad Barre, since 1969.

Political leaders since 1970
1969– Mohamed Siad Barre (SRSP).

Political system
The constitution dates from September 1979 and defines Somalia as a socialist, one-party state, with ultimate political power in the hands of the Somali Revolutionary Socialist Party (SRSP). The President is chosen by the party as head of state and head of government and derives his authority from his positions as Secretary-General of the SRSP and President of its Politburo.

As in most socialist states, there are two systems operating alongside each other, the party and the state system, with the President bestriding both. In the party system policy is formulated by the SRSP's 51-member central committee, operating through 13 bureaux, and sanctioned by the Politburo. On the state side there is a Council of Ministers, appointed by the President, to implement, on a day-to-day basis, the policies agreed by the central committee and the Politburo. Also on the state side, there is a People's Assembly of 177 members, six being presidential nominees and 171 elected by universal adult suffrage, through a simple plurality voting system, for a five-year term, from a single list of candidates approved by the party. The Assembly provides a democratic gloss to the total structure.

Political parties
The only legally permitted party is the Somali Revolutionary Socialist Party (SRSP). There are some unofficial opposition groups which operate outside the country, from Ethiopia and London. The SRSP was formed in 1976 by President Barre to legitimise his military regime with a declared aim of creating 'scientific socialism'.

Latest elections
In the 1984 Assembly elections members were chosen from a single list of 171 SRSP candidates. The turnout was claimed to be 99.86 per cent

Political history
European interest in this part of Africa was stimulated by the opening of the Suez Canal in 1869. Britain and Italy established colonies and Somalia became a fully independent republic in 1960 through the merger of British and Italian Somaliland.

Since achieving independence Somalia has been involved in disputes with its neighbours because of its insistence on the right of all Somalis to self-determination, wherever they have settled. This has applied particularly to those living in the Ogaden district of Ethiopia and in north-east Kenya. A dispute over the border with Kenya resulted in a break in diplomatic relations with the United Kingdom for five years, between 1963 and 1968. A dispute with Ethiopia led to an eight-month war, in 1978, in which Somalia was defeated by Ethiopian troops assisted by Soviet and Cuban weapons and advisers. There was a rapprochement with Kenya in 1984 and, in 1986, the first meeting for ten years between the Somalian and Ethiopian leaders.

The first President of independent Somalia was Aden Abdullah Osman and he was succeeded, in 1967, by Dr Abdirashid Ali Shermarke, of the Somali Youth League (SYL), which had become the dominant political party. In October 1969 President Shermarke was assassinated, providing an opportunity for the army to seize power, under the leadership of the commander-in-chief, Major-General Mohamed Siad Barre. He suspended the 1960 constitution, dissolved the National Assembly and banned all political parties. He then formed a military government, the Supreme Revolutionary Council (SRC), to rule by decree, and the following year declared Somalia a socialist state.

In 1976 the SRC transferred power to a newly created Somali Revolutionary Socialist Party (SRSP) and in 1979 a new constitution for a socialist, one-party state was adopted. Over the next few years Barre consolidated his position by increasing the influence of his own tribe and reducing that of its northern rival, despite some violent opposition. He was re-elected in January 1987. Some five months later an attempted coup against him failed. However, opposition to his regime grew in the north, led by the Ethiopian-backed Somali National Movement (SNM), operating across the Ethiopian border. Early in 1989 there were signs that Barre was seeking a political, rather than military, solution to the conflict. Later in the year opposition to the government was reflected in widespread outbreaks of ethnic and religious violence.

SOUTH AFRICA

Republic of South Africa
Republiek van Suid-Afrika

Capital: Pretoria (Judicial Capital: Bloemfontein. Legislative Capital: Cape Town)

Social and economic data
Area: 1,222,160 km^2
Population: 33.200m*
Pop density per km^2: 27*
Literacy rate: 80%*
GDP: $53,157m*; per capita GDP: $1,601
Economy type: middle income
Labour force in agriculture: 15%

*1985

Ethnic composition
Seventy per cent of the population are black Africans, 18 per cent whites, of European stock, 9 per cent coloureds, of mixed African-European parentage, and 3 per cent Asians.

Religions
Most whites and coloureds and about 60 per cent of the Africans are Christians. There are over 2 million Roman Catholics, about 2 million Anglicans and about one 1.5 million members of the Dutch Reformed Church. About 60 per cent of the Asians are Hindus and 20 per cent Muslims. There are also about 120,000 Jews.

Political features
State type: racialist nationalist
Date of state formation: 1910
Political structure: unitary
Executive: limited presidential
Assembly: one-chamber
Party structure: restricted multi-party
Human rights rating: 22%

Local and regional government
Although it is not a federal state, South Africa has a strongly devolved system of government based on four provinces: the Orange Free State, with about 7.5 million people, Cape Province, with about 5 million, Natal, with about 2 million and the Transvaal, with about 1.8 million. Each province has an appointed administrator and a white elected council. The organs of the central government are regionally dispersed, the administrative capital being at Pretoria, in the Transvaal, the seat of the judiciary in Bloemfontein, in the Orange Free State, and the national assembly at Cape Town, in Cape Province.

In accordance with the policy of *apartheid*, there are, for the black majority, four 'independent' Homelands: Transkei, Ciskei, Bophuthatswana and Venda. The Homelands are supposed to enjoy a high degree of political independence but, as their economies are virtually wholly dependent on the white-dominated government of South Africa, and as they exist within a national framework of racial discrimination, this independence is highly spurious. Only the South African government recognises the Homelands. They have no international status. There are also six 'non-independent' black, national states: Gazankulu, Lebowa, QwaQwa, KwaZulu, KaNgwane and KwaNdebele. Thus, although the South African economy is dependent on the black African workforce, they are kept apart from the white minority, socially and politically. In statistical terms, South Africa, with a per capita income of more than $1,000 can be classified as a 'middle income' country, but the wealth is so unequally distributed that the white minority falls into the 'high income' bracket while the black majority equates with the 'low income' group of states.

Namibia, which was formerly South West Africa, and adjoins South Africa, was a German colony in the nineteenth century and then a League of Nations mandated territory, and later a United Nations Trust Territory. The South African government, however, refused to recognise the UN's authority and governed the country as if it were a fifth province, to the degree of extending the apartheid laws to it. The future of Namibia became a key issue in the talks among South Africa, Angola and Cuba about the withdrawal of South African and Cuban forces from Angola. Following the successful conclusion of the talks, it was agreed that Namibia should achieve independent status. This should formally take effect during 1989. A more detailed account of the Homelands and Namibia is given in Part III.

Head of state and head of government

Acting State President F. W. de Klerk, since 1989.

Political leaders since 1970

1966–78 B.J. Vorster—Prime Minister (National Party), 1978–84 Pieter W. Botha—Prime Minister (National Party), 1984–89 Pieter W. Botha—President (National Party), 1989– F. W. de Klerk—Acting President (National Party).

Political system

Since 1948 South Africa has operated a system of *apartheid*, or segregation on the basis of race, and this is reflected in its system of government. When it left the Commonwealth and became a republic, in 1960, the constitution it adopted provided for an assembly and government composed entirely of Europeans, termed whites in the context of apartheid. A new constitution was adopted in 1984 which was claimed to be more democratic in that it allowed conditional participation in government for non-whites, in the form of coloureds, or persons of mixed European and African descent, and Asians. Black Africans are still completely unrepresented at national level.

The essentials of the 1984 constitution are a state President, who combines the roles of head of state and head of government, and a three-chamber parliament, consisting of the House of Assembly, for whites, the House of Representatives, for coloureds, and the House of Delegates, for Asians.

The House of Assembly has 178 members, 166 elected by universal adult, white suffrage, through a simple plurality voting system, four nominated by the state President on the basis of one for each province and eight elected by the 166 who are themselves directly elected.

The House of Representatives has 85 members, 80 elected by universal adult, coloured suffrage, through a simple plurality system, two nominated by the state President and three elected by the 80 directly elected members.

The House of Delegates has 45 members, 40 elected by universal adult Asian suffrage, through a simple plurality system, two nominated by the state President, and three elected by the 40 directly elected members.

Each House is responsible for what are called its 'own affairs', in other words matters affecting only whites, coloureds or Asians, as the case may be. General legislation, applying to all races, including black Africans, has to be approved by all three Houses and the state President. Members of all three Houses serve a five-year term.

The state President is elected by an electoral college of 88 members of Parliament, 50 from the House of Assembly, 25 from the House of Representatives and 13 from the House of Delegates. His term of office is the duration of parliament. He appoints and presides over a cabinet which is dominated by whites. In his 1986 cabinet of 21, including himself, there were 19 whites, one coloured and one Asian. He is advised by an appointed President's Council of 60 members, 20 from the House of Assembly, ten from the House of Representatives, five from the House of Deputies and 25 chosen by the state President himself. There are also three Ministers' Councils which advise him, one for the whole country, one for the coloured community and one for the Asians.

It is an elaborate structure but, whatever permutations of representation are made, the whites are always in a dominant position and the black majority are effectively disenfranchised.

Political parties

There are currently eleven legally acceptable political parties, all representing white, coloured or Asian citizens. The one party claiming multi-racial membership, with the aim of creating a multi-racial society, the African National Congress (ANC), was banned in 1960.

The main white parties are the National Party (NP), the Conservative Party of South Africa (CPSA), and the Democratic Party (DP). The National Democratic Movement (NDM) was formed in 1987 by the coming together of leading members of the Progressive Federal Party (PFP), and the Independents, led by the former South African ambassador to the UK, Dr Denis Worrall. Then in April 1989, a full merger took place, creating the DP. There are extra-parliamentary groupings such as the anti-apartheid United Democratic Front (UDF), supported by the Churches, and the right-wing Afrikaner Resistance Movement (AWB), calling for an exclusively Afrikaner state.

The NP was founded in 1912 and has been the ruling party ever since. It has a right-of-centre, racialist orientation. The PFP was created in 1977 by the coming together of some liberals and the Progressive Reform Party (PRP). In its new form, as the DP, it is the most liberal of the white parties, advocating the ending of racial discrimination. The CPSA was formed in 1982 by an NP defector, Dr Andries Treurnicht. It is an extreme right-wing, racialist, neo-fascist party.

The main coloureds parties are the Labour Party of South Africa, a left-of-centre grouping led by Revd Allan Hendrickse, and the People's Congress Party, which has a right-of-centre orientation.

The main Asian parties are the National People's Party, a right-of-centre group, and the Solidarity Party, which is left-of-centre.

The ANC was formed in 1912 and banned in 1960. In 1985 it opened its membership to all races. Nelson Mandela is its Life President and Oliver Tambo its President. The ANC now operates outside South Africa.

Latest elections

The results of the 1984 House of Representatives (coloureds) elections were as follows:

	% Votes	*Seats*
Labour	74.72	76
People's Congress Party	11.77	1
Others	13.51	3

The results of the 1984 House of Delegates (Asians) elections were as follows:

	% Votes	Seats
Solidarity Party	36.58	17
National People's Party	36.45	18
Progressive Independents	1.61	1
Independents	25.36	4

The results of the 1987 House of Assembly (whites) elections were as follows:

	% Votes	Seats
NP	52.7	123
CPSA	26.83	22
Others	20.47	21

Political history

South Africa was first settled by Europeans in the seventeenth century. The Dutch were the first, followed by the French and then the British. The descendants of the Dutch and French Huguenots were the farmers, or Boers, who established their first republic in Natal, in 1839. The British, meanwhile, had annexed the Cape and were moving in the same direction as the Boers. By the middle of the nineteenth century the British controlled the Cape and had acquired Natal through helping the Boers defend themselves against the Zulus. The Boers then trekked northwards and westwards and created republics in the Transvaal and Orange Free State, which were later recognised by the British. The discovery of diamonds and gold led to rivalry between the British and the Boers, and this, together with Boer resentment of the British policy of imperialism and the fear of their culture being destroyed, resulted in a series of wars between 1880 and 1902. After fortunes had wildly fluctuated, peace was agreed with the signing of the Treaty of Vereeniging in 1902.

The eventual outcome was the passing by the British parliament, in 1909, of the South Africa Act, which established a new British dominion called the Union of South Africa, consisting of the former colonies of the Orange River, Transvaal, the Cape and Natal. The Act guaranteed equal status for people of British or Boer descent. The Union came into being in 1910, with Louis Botha, the Boer leader, as the first Prime Minister of the new state. He was succeeded by his protégé, Jan Christian Smuts, in 1919.

Smuts headed the South Africa Party, preaching toleration and conciliation, and, had it remained in power, it might eventually have led the country to a truly multi-racial social and political system. However, the National Party, which had been established in 1912 as an opposition movement, was much less liberal in outlook and composition and was to become more illiberal as time went on, particularly under its post-Second World War leader, Daniel Malan.

The National Party (NP) came to power in 1948 and has governed South Africa ever since. Under Daniel Malan it introduced the policy of apartheid, or race segregation, attempting to justify it on the grounds of separate, but equal, development. The effects of apartheid, however, have been to deny all but the white minority a genuine voice in the nation's affairs. In the 1950s the African National Congress (ANC) led a campaign of civil disobedience until it, and other similar movements, were, in 1960, declared illegal. In 1964 its leader, Nelson Mandela, was given life imprisonment for alleged sabotage. He was to become a central symbol of black opposition to the white regime.

Malan was succeeded, in 1958, by Hendrik Verwoerd, who refused to change his policies, despite criticisms from within the Commonwealth, and then, following a decision to assume republican status, in 1961, South Africa withdrew from membership. Verwoerd remained in office until his assassination in 1966 and his successor, B. J. Vorster, continued to follow the same line. 'Pass laws', restricting the movement of blacks within the country, had been introduced, causing international outrage, and, as part of the apartheid policy, ten Homelands (Bantustans) were established to contain particular ethnic groups. By the 1980s many of the white regime's opponents had been imprisoned without trial and it was estimated that more than three million people had been forcibly resettled in black townships between 1960 and 1980. Complaints of police brutality brought international condemnation which grew to an outcry when news was given of the death in detention of the black community leader, Steve Biko, in September 1977.

Despite this, the NP continued to increase its majority at each election, with the white opposition parties failing to make any significant impact. In 1978 Vorster resigned and was succeeded by Pieter W. Botha who seemed determined to resist the pressures from his party's extreme right-wing hardliners and give more scope to its liberal members. He embarked upon a policy of constitutional reform which would involve coloureds and Asians, but not blacks, in the governmental process. The inevitable clash occurred and in March 1982 Dr Andries Treurnicht, leader of the hardline (*verkrampte*) wing, and 15 other extremists, were expelled from the NP. They later formed a new party, the Conservative Party of South Africa (CPSA).

Although there were considerable doubts about Botha's proposals within the coloured and Asian communities, as well as among the whites, he went ahead and, in November 1983, they were approved by 66 per cent of the voters in an all-white referendum. The new constitution came into effect in September 1984. In 1985 a number of apartheid laws were amended or repealed, including the ban on sexual relations or marriage between people of different races and the ban on mixed racial membership of political parties, but the underlying inequalities in the system remained and the dissatisfaction of the black community grew. Serious rioting broke out in the black townships, with Soweto, near Johannesburg, becoming a focal point, and, despite the efforts of black moderates, such as the Anglican Bishop of Johannesburg, Desmond Tutu, to encourage peaceful resistance, violence grew.

The ANC was being led in exile by Nelson Mandela's colleague, Oliver Tambo, who was receiving increasing moral support in meetings with politicians throughout the world, while in South Africa itself the white government was reluctant to face the consequences of taking action against Mandela's wife, Winnie, who, during her husband's continuing imprisonment, was not afraid to condemn the system publicly.

Calls for economic sanctions against South Africa grew during 1985 and 1986. At the Heads of Commonwealth conference, in Nassau, in October 1985, it was decided to appoint an Eminent Persons' Group (EPG), comprising leading Commonwealth statesmen, to investigate the likelihood of the South African government dismantling apartheid and thus avoiding the need to impose full sanctions. The EPG reported to a specially convened Commonwealth Heads' meeting in July 1986 that there were no signs of genuine liberalisation in South Africa. Reluctantly, the British Prime Minister, Margaret Thatcher, agreed to limited measures. Some leading Commonwealth countries, noticeably Australia and Canada, took additional independent action. The US Congress eventually forced President Reagan to move in the same direction but the decisions by individual major international companies to close down their South African operations seemed likely, in the long term, to have the greatest effect.

In the face of this international criticism, state President Botha announced that he would call elections in 1987 to seek a renewal of his mandate. The results were gains for the National and Conservative parties. In February 1988 new restrictions were announced on the activities of religious, trade-union and other organisations which pressed for greater liberalisation. The new curbs seemed to be a political move to placate the right wing of the government party. Growing support for the Conservative Party was evidenced by wins in Assembly by-elections in March 1988.

State President Botha's reaction, in April 1988, was to propose more 'constitutional reform', which would give blacks more control over their own affairs. The proposals were criticised by both whites and blacks. By South African standards Botha's plans were revolutionary and involved: a national forum to oversee constitutional change; black elected regional councils; a new post of Prime Minister to relieve the state President of the day-to-day running of the country; the downgrading of the President's Council to a part-time body; and the broadening of the electoral college which elects the State President to include blacks. Ultimately, however,the whites would retain the main levers of power. It was announced in May 1988 that a group of white South African politicians opposed to apartheid, including two members of the House of Assembly, had had secret discussions with representatives of the ANC in West Germany.

In January 1989 state President Botha suffered a stroke and early in February announced that he was giving up the NP leadership but would remain President until the end of his current term and would not seek re-election. In an unusually speedy election the party leadership passed to F. W. de Klerk by a very narrow majority in a third ballot. In June 1989 de Klerk, announced a five-year plan for 'constitutional reform'. It was widely criticised by his opponents as a continuation of apartheid in a disguised form.

SUDAN

Republic of Sudan
Jamhuryat Es-Sudan

Capital: Khartoum

Social and economic data
Area: 2,505,800 km^2
Population: 22.970m*

Pop density per km^2: 9*
Literacy rate: 31%*
GDP: $7,400m*; per capita GDP: $322
Economy type: low income
Labour force in agriculture: 75%

*1985

Ethnic composition
There are over 50 ethnic groups and nearly 600 sub-groups in the country, but the population is broadly distributed between Arabs, in the north, and black Africans, in the south. The Arabs are numerically greater and dominate national affairs.

Religions
People of the north are mostly Muslims and Islam is the state religion. In the south they are mostly Christians or followers of traditional animist beliefs. Overall, about 70 per cent of the population are Sunni Muslims, about 20 per cent follow traditional beliefs and 5 per cent are Christians.

Political features
State type: military authoritarian
Date of state formation: 1956
Political structure: unitary
Executive: limited presidential
Assembly: one-chamber
Party structure: multi-party (in suspension)
Human rights rating: poor

Local and regional government
The country is divided into six regions, each administered by an appointed governor. Khartoum has its own Commissioner-General.

Head of state and head of government
President Omar Hasan Ahmed el-Bashir, since 1989.

Political leaders since 1970
1969–71 Gaafar Mohammed Nimeri (Military), 1971–85 Gaafar Mohammed Nimeri (SSU), 1985–86 Swar al-Dahab (Military), 1986–89 Sadiq Al-Mahdi (NNUP-DUP coalition), 1989–Omar Hasan Ahmed el-Bashir (Military).

Political system
The 1973 constitution was suspended following a military coup in April 1985 and the country placed under a 15-member Transitional Military Council (TMC), as the supreme legislative body, and a 15-member non-party cabinet. A new, transitional constitution was approved by the TMC and cabinet in October 1985, providing for a 264-member Legislative Assembly, to be elected in April 1986, with a Supreme Council, under a President, and a Council of Ministers, led by a Prime Minister. The Assembly was to be charged with the task of producing a new constitution

and, after a further transitional period, of declaring itself a parliament, subject to election every four years, but in July 1989 a military coup put these developments into question, and a National Salvation Revolutionary Council was established.

Political parties

More than 40 parties emerged to contest the 1986 general election, the three most significant being the New National Umma Party (NNUP), an Islamic nationalist grouping, the Democratic Unionist Party (DUP), with a similar, but more moderate, orientation, and the National Islamic Front, another Islamic party. Since the military coup in 1989 their future is in doubt.

Latest elections

In the 1986 general election the NNUP won 99 Assembly seats, the DUP 63 and the National Islamic Front 51.

Political history

In the early nineteenth century Egypt tried to gain control of the Sudan but was thwarted by the resistance of the many, fragmented tribes. In the 1880s, however, a fanatical religious leader, Abdullah al Taashi, succeeded where Egypt could not. He launched a rebellion against Egypt, and its protector, Britain, leading to the fall of Khartoum. It was eventually recovered by a combined British-Egyptian force, led by Lord Kitchener, and an Anglo-Egyptian condominium was established which lasted until Sudan achieved independence, as a republic, in 1956.

Two years later a coup ousted the civil administration and a military government was set up under a Supreme Council of the Armed Forces. In 1964 it, too, was overthrown and civilian rule reinstated, but, five years later, the army returned in a coup led by Colonel Gaafar Mohammed Nimeri. All political bodies were abolished, a Revolutionary Command Council (RCC) set up and the country's name changed to the Democratic Republic of the Sudan. Close links were soon established with Egypt and in 1970 an agreement in principle was reached for eventual union. In 1972 this should have become, with the addition of Syria, the Federation of Arab Republics, but internal opposition blocked both developments.

In 1971 a new constitution was adopted, Nimeri confirmed as President and the Sudanese Socialist Union (SSU) declared to be the only legally permitted party. Nimeri came to power in a left-wing revolution but soon turned to the West, and particularly the United States, for support. The most serious problem initially confronting him was the near-civil war between the Muslim north and the non-Muslim south, which had started as long ago as 1955. He tackled it by agreeing, at a conference in Addis Ababa in 1972, to the three southern provinces being given a considerable degree of autonomy, including the establishment of a High Executive Council (HEC) to cater specifically for their distinctive needs. Towards the end of 1973 elections took place for a Regional People's Assembly for southern Sudan and some months later a National People's Assembly, for the whole country, was established.

By 1974 Nimeri had broadened his political base but his position still relied on army support. Three years later, as he felt his position to be more secure, he embarked on a policy of reconciliation, bringing some of his former opponents into his administration and then, in 1980, creating a high degree of devolution by reorganising the country into six regions, each with its own assembly and limited executive autonomy. The National People's Assembly was dissolved, as powers had been devolved to the regional assemblies, and the southern HEC was also disbanded. There was still dissatisfaction, however, about a proposed redivision of the southern region.

In 1983 Nimeri was re-elected for a third term but his regional problems persisted and he was forced to send more troops from the north to the south. In trying to pacify the south he alienated the north and then caused considerable resentment among the non-Muslim southerners by announcing the imposition of strict Islamic laws to replace the existing penal code. By 1984 he was faced with widespread unrest, demonstrated by strikes in the north, in protest against his economic policies, and disillusionment in the south. The situation there had deteriorated so much that a separatist movement had emerged, the Sudan People's Liberation Movement (SPLM), whose troops had taken control of large areas in the region of the Upper Nile.

In March 1985 a general strike was provoked by a sharp devaluation of the Sudanese pound and an increase in bread prices but the underlying discontent was more deep-seated. While he was on a visit to the United States he was deposed in a bloodless coup, led by General Swar al-Dahab, a supporter of Nimeri who had been forced to take over because of the threat of an army mutiny. Swar al-Dahab set up a Transitional Military Council (TMC) and announced that he would hand over power to a civilian administration within a year. At the end of the year the country's name was changed to 'the Republic of Sudan'.

The SPLM's initial response to the 1985 coup was encouraging. It declared a cease-fire and then presented Swar al-Dahab with a series of demands. He tried to conciliate by suggesting the cancellation of the redivision of the southern region and the reinstatement of the HEC there but these concessions were not enough and fighting broke out again. This continued throughout 1985 but, although the SPLM refused officially to recognise the TMC, secret, informal discussions were taking place between representatives of both sides.

A provisional constitution was adopted in October 1985 and elections held for a Legislative Assembly in April 1986. The election was fought by more than 40 parties but no one emerged with a clear majority. A coalition government was formed, with Ahmed Ali El-Mirghani of the DUP as head of state, and Oxford-educated Sadiq Al-Mahdi, of the NNUP, as Prime Minister, heading a coalition Council of Ministers. The Assembly was charged with producing the draft of a permanent constitution. In another move towards reconciliation with the south, John Garang, the SPLM leader, was offered a seat on the Council of Ministers but declined it.

By 1987 the south had become even more unstable and was now in the throes of a civil war between the army and the SPLM. The situation there was aggravated by drought, famine and an unprecedented influx of refugees from neighbouring states, such as Ethiopia and Chad, which had been experiencing their own internal conflicts.

In April 1988 Dr Al-Mahdi announced the second break-up of his coalition and the formation of a new government of national unity. He was re-elected Prime Minister for another term and in May 1988 a new coalition was formed, which included members of the NNUP, DUP and NIF. In December 1988 a peace accord with the SPLM was signed, causing splits in the ruling coalition. Fighting continued however until the SPLM leader, Colonel Garang, unilaterally declared a one month's truce. In July 1989 Dr Al-Mahdi was removed in a coup led by Brigadier-General Omar Hasan Ahmed el-Bashir, who suspended all political activities and established a National Salvation Revolutionary Council and declared a unilateral cease-fire in the civil war.

SWAZILAND

Kingdom of Swaziland

Capital: Mbabane

Social and economic data
Area: 17,400 km^2
Population: 0.692m*
Pop density per km^2: 40*
Literacy rate: 55%*
GDP: $460m*; per capita GDP: $665
Economy type: low income
Labour force in agriculture: 68%

*1985

Ethnic composition
About 90 per cent of the population are indigenous Africans and are distributed among the Swazi, Zulu, Tonga and Shangaan tribes. There are European and Afro-European, called Eurafrican, minorities numbering about 22,000.

Religions
About 60 per cent of the people are Christians and about 40 per cent follow traditional beliefs.

Political features
State type: absolutist
Date of state formation: 1968
Political structure: unitary
Executive: absolute
Assembly: two-chamber
Party structure: one-party
Human rights rating: N/A

Local and regional government
The country is divided into four regions, with regional councils consisting of representatives of the 40 chieftancies into which the nation is further subdivided.

Head of state and head of government
King Mswati III, since 1986.

Political leaders since 1970
1968–82 King Sobhuza II, 1982–83 Queen Dzeliwe, 1983–86 Queen Ntombi, 1986– King Mswati III.

Political system
Swaziland is a monarchy within the Commonwealth. The 1978 constitution represents an attempt to combine the traditional pattern of government with the need for a more modern system of consultation and administration. It makes the King the head of state and the effective head of government, with a Prime Minister and cabinet whom he chooses himself. There is a two-chamber assembly, the Libandla, consisting of a 20-member Senate and a 50-member House of Assembly. Ten senators are appointed by the King and ten elected by and from an 80-member electoral college. The electoral college is made up of two representatives from each of the country's 40 chieftancies (*Tinkhundla*). Forty of the House of Assembly deputies are also elected by the electoral college, with the remaining ten appointed by the King.

Political parties
Political activity by groups other than the Imbokodvo National Movement (INM) was banned in 1973 and this ban was formalised in the 1978 constitution. There are at least three opposition groups which operate outside Swaziland. The King has a supreme advisory body, the Liqoqo, all of whose eleven members are appointed by him. The INM was formed in 1964 and has a traditional, nationalist orientation. It serves as a political instrument for the monarchy.

Latest elections
In October 1983 arrangements were started for elections to the House of Assembly and Senate. It was announced that they would be conducted 'according to our customs and traditions and not according to party political systems which are alien to our people'. The first stage was the election of the 80-member electoral college by the tribal assemblies. Once elected, the college would elect 40 of its own members to the House, and the monarch would then appoint a further ten. Another ten members of the electoral college would be chosen for the Senate, plus a further ten nominated by the King.

Political history
Swaziland was jointly ruled by the United Kingdom and the Transvaal republic, established by the Boers, from 1890 until the end of the South African war of 1899–1902. It then became a British protectorate and, in 1907, a High Commission Territory. The United Kingdom Act of Parliament which established the Union of South Africa, in 1910, made provision for the possible inclusion of Swaziland, with other High Commission Territories, within the Union, but the British government said that this would never be done without the agreement of the people of the Territories. In the knowledge of this constitutional provision, the South African government repeatedly asked for Swaziland to be placed under its jurisdiction but this was resisted by the British government and by the people of Swaziland themselves. The requests ended when, in 1967,

Swaziland was granted internal self-government and then achieved full independence, within the Commonwealth, in 1968.

The 1963 constitution, which the British government introduced before full independence, provided for a parliamentary system of government with King Sobhuza II as head of state. In 1973, with the agreement of the assembly, the King suspended the constitution and assumed absolute powers. Then in 1978 a new constitution was announced, providing for a two-chamber assembly, whose members would be partly appointed by the King and partly elected by an electoral college representing the 40 chieftancies.

King Sobhuza died in 1982 and, in accordance with Swazi tradition, the role of head of state passed to the Queen Mother, Dzeliwe, until the King's heir, Prince Makhosetive, reached the age of 21, in 1989. In August 1983, however, Queen Dzeliwe was ousted by another of King Sobhuza's wives, Ntombi, who was formally invested as Queen Regent in October. A power struggle developed within the royal family and in November 1984 it was announced that the Crown Prince would succeed to the throne in April 1986, three years before he would attain his majority. In April 1986 he was formally invested as King Mswati III.

Swaziland has tried to maintain good relations with South Africa as well as with other African states but this has often been difficult, particularly as the banned African National Congress (ANC) has tried to use it as a base.

TANZANIA

United Republic of Tanzania

Capital: Dodoma

Social and economic data
Area: 945,090 km^2
Population: 22.400m*
Pop density per km^2: 24*
Literacy rate: 46%*
GDP: $4,900m*; per capita GDP: $219
Economy type: low income
Labour force in agriculture: 79%

*1985

Ethnic composition
Ninety-nine per cent of the population are Africans, and are ethnically classified as Bantus, but they are distributed among over 130 tribes. The main tribes are the Bantu, the Nilotic, the Nilo-Hamitic, the Khoisan and the Iraqwi.

Religions
About 60 per cent of the people on the mainland are Muslims and about 97 per cent on the island of Zanzibar. The rest of the population are mainly Christians, in the Anglican, Greek Orthodox, Lutheran or Roman Catholic Churches.

Political features
State type: nationalistic socialist
Date of state formation: 1961
Political structure: unitary
Executive: unlimited presidential
Assembly: one-chamber
Party structure: one-party
Human rights rating: 47%

Local and regional government
Zanzibar has its own constitution, providing for a President, elected by universal adult suffrage, through a simple plurality voting system, for a five-year term, and a 45-55 member House of Representatives, similarly elected. The national constitution stipulates that if the President comes from the mainland the first Vice-President must come from Zanzibar. The present President of Tanzania was formerly President of Zanzibar and so his first Vice-President comes from the mainland.

The country is divided into 20 mainland regions and two island divisions, of Zanzibar and Pemba, administered by appointed regional or divisional commissioners. On the mainland the regions are further subdivided into districts, and on Zanzibar the divisions are subdivided into areas. There are part-elected and part-appointed representative councils.

Head of state and head of government
President Ali Hassan Mwinyi, since 1985.

Political leaders since 1970
1964–85 Julius Nyerere (CCM), 1985– Ali Hassan Mwinyi (CCM).

Political system
The 1977 constitution made Tanzania a one-party state, the party being the Revolutionary Party of Tanzania (CCM). It provides for a President who is chosen by the party to serve a maximum of two five-year terms. There is a single-chamber National Assembly of up to 231 members. One hundred and one are elected by universal adult suffrage, through a simple plurality voting system, for the mainland, up to 55 similarly elected for the islands of Zanzibar and Pemba, five elected by the Zanzibar House of Representatives, 15 allocated specifically for women, 15 representing party organisations, 15 nominated by the President, and 25 *ex officio* regional commissioners.

The President appoints two Vice-Presidents from members of the National Assembly and the second Vice-President is termed Prime Minister. The President also appoints and presides over a cabinet. Until the retirement of Julius Nyerere in 1985, the offices of state President and chairman of CCM were held by the same person. Now, although Nyerere has given up the presidency, he is still party chairman and thus an important 'power behind the throne'.

Political parties
The only legal party is the Revolutionary Party of Tanzania (CCM). It was founded in 1977 by an amalgamation of the Tanganyika African National

Union (TANU), covering the mainland, and the Afro-Shirazi Party, covering the islands of Zanzibar and Pemba. The CCM's constitution pledges it 'to establish a socialist democratic state by self-help'. The party has an African-socialist orientation.

Latest elections

In the 1985 National Assembly elections there were 328 CCM-nominated candidates for 169 seats.

Political history

What is now Tanzania had strong links with Arab, Indian and Persian traders long before Europeans arrived and there is still evidence of those links in the country's religions and customs. The Germans were the first Europeans to establish themselves on the mainland, and Tanganyika, as it was called, became part of German East Africa. Meanwhile, the British had declared Zanzibar a protectorate. Tanganyika was taken away from Germany after the First World War and Britain was given a mandate to govern it. After the Second World War a movement for independence developed and, in 1961, Tanganyika was given internal self-government and later the same year full independence, within the Commonwealth. Tanzania was founded by the merger of Tanganyika and Zanzibar in 1964.

Julius Nyerere became the country's first Prime Minister but gave up the post some six weeks after independence to devote himself to the development of the Tanganyika African National Union (TANU). However, in December 1962, when Tanganyika became a republic, he returned to become the nation's first President. Zanzibar became an independent sultanate in 1963 and, following an uprising, a republic within weeks. The Act of Union with the mainland was signed in April 1964 and Nyerere became President of the new United Republic of Tanzania. Despite the union, the island of Zanzibar has retained its own constitution.

Nyerere dominated the nation's politics for the next 20 years, being re-elected in 1965, 1970, 1975 and 1980, and became one of Africa's most respected politicians. Known throughout Tanzania as Mwalimu (teacher), he established himself as a genuine Christian socialist who attempted to put into practice a philosophy which he fervently believed would secure his country's future. He committed himself in the Arusha Declaration of 1967, the name coming from the northern Tanzanian town where he made his historic statement, to building a socialist state for the millions of poor peasants, through a series of village co-operatives (*ujamas*). In the final years of his presidency economic pressures, domestic and international, forced him to compromise his ideals and accept a more capitalistic society than he would have wished, but his achievements have been many: the best public health service on the African continent, according to UN officials; a universal primary school system; and an adult literacy rate of 85 per cent, compared with 10 per cent in Senegal or 47 per cent in Kenya.

Relations between Tanzania and its neighbours have been variable. The East African Community (EAC), of Tanzania, Kenya and Uganda, which was formed in 1967, broke up in 1977 and links with Kenya became uneasy, particularly as Kenya had embarked on a more capitalistic economic policy than Tanzania. In 1979 Nyerere sent troops into Uganda to support the Uganda National Liberation Front in its bid to overthrow President Idi

Amin. This enhanced Nyerere's reputation but damaged his country's economy. Tanzania was also a strong supporter of the liberation movements in Mozambique and Rhodesia.

In March 1984 Nyerere announced his impending retirement and it was widely expected that he would be succeeded by the Prime Minister, Edward Sokoine, but the latter was killed in a road accident in the same year. The President of Zanzibar, Ali Hassan Mwinyi, was adopted as the sole presidential candidate by the CCM Congress in December 1985. In October 1987 Nyerere was renominated for another term as CCM leader.

TOGO

Republic of Togo
République Togolaise

Capital: Lomé

Social and economic data
Area: 56,790 km^2
Population: 3.023m*
Pop density per km^2: 53*
Literacy rate: 31%*
GDP: $690m*; per capita GDP: $228
Economy type: low income
Labour force in agriculture: 66%

*1985

Ethnic composition
Most of the people in the north are of Sudanese Hamitic origin while those in the south are mostly Negroid. They are distributed among some 37 different tribes. There are also European, Syrian and Lebanese minorities.

Religions
About 50 per cent of the population follow traditional, animist beliefs, about 35 per cent are Christians and about 15 per cent Muslims.

Political features
State type: authoritarian nationalist
Date of state formation: 1960
Political structure: unitary
Executive: unlimited presidential
Assembly: one-chamber
Party structure: one-party
Human rights rating: poor

Local and regional government
The country is divided into four regions, administered by appointed Inspectors, who are advised by elected councils.

Head of state and head of government
President General Gnassingbe Eyadema, since 1967.

Political leaders since 1970
1967– Gnassingbe Eyadema (RPT).

Political system
The 1979 constitution created a one-party state, based on the Assembly of the Togolese People (RPT). The President is elected by universal adult suffrage for a seven-year term and is eligible for re-election. He is both head of state and head of government and appoints and presides over a Council of Ministers. He is also President of RPT. There is a single-chamber National Assembly, of 77 members, elected by universal adult suffrage, by simple plurality voting, from a list of RPT nominees, and serving for five years.

Political parties
The only legal party is the Assembly of the Togolese Pepole (RPT). It was founded in 1969 and all people in work, except those on very low wages, are expected to pay subscriptions to it. It has a nationalist, socialist orientation.

There is an illegal opposition party, the Togolese Movement for Democracy, which is based in Paris.

Latest elections
In the 1985 National Assembly elections there was a list of 211 RPT-nominated candidates for the 77 seats.

Political history
Originally part of the Kingdom of Togoland, Togo was a German protectorate from 1894 to 1914, when the country was invaded by French and British forces. In 1922 it became a League of Nations mandated territory and responsibility for it was split between France and Britain. The French part was administered separately, as French Togo, while the British part, called British Togoland, was included within the British Gold Coast. In 1957 the inhabitants of British Togoland chose to remain part of the Gold Coast, which was later to become Ghana, while French Togoland voted to become an autonomous republic within the French Union.

The new Togolese republic was given internal self-government, in 1956, and full independence, in 1960, and Sylvanus Olympio, leader of the United Togolese (UT) party, became the first President in an unopposed election in April 1961. In 1963 Olympio was overthrown and killed in a military coup and his brother-in-law, Nicolas Grunitzky, who had gone into exile, was recalled to become Provisional President. A referendum approved a new constitution and Grunitzky's presidency was confirmed. In 1967 he, in turn, was deposed in a bloodless military coup, led by Lieutenant-General Etienne Gnassingbe Eyadema. The constitution was suspended and Eyadema assumed the presidency and banned all political activity. Two years later he founded a new party, the Assembly of the Togolese People (RPT) and declared it the only legal political organisation.

Between 1967 and 1977 there were several unsuccessful attempts to overthrow him but by 1979 Eyadema felt sufficiently secure to propose a new constitution and embark upon a policy of gradual democratisation. In October 1986 another weak attempt to overthrow him by mercenaries based in Ghana or Burkina Faso was easily thwarted with French help.

UGANDA

Republic of Uganda

Capital: Kampala

Social and economic data
Area: 236,880 km^2
Population: 15.200m*
Pop density per km^2: 64*
Literacy rate: 52%*
GDP: $2,200m*; per capita GDP: $145
Economy type: low income
Labour force in agriculture: 78%

*1985

Ethnic composition
There are about 40 different tribes concentrated into four main groups : the Bantu, who are the most numerous, the Eastern Nilotic, the Western Nilotic and the Central Sudanic. There are also Rwandan, Sudanese, Zairean and Kenyan minorities.

Religions
Approximately 60 per cent of the population are Christians, half of them Roman Catholics and half Protestants, about 5 per cent are Muslims and the remainder mostly follow traditional beliefs.

Political features
State type: emergent democratic
Date of state formation: 1962
Political structure: unitary
Executive: limited presidential
Assembly: one-chamber
Party structure: multi-party
Human rights rating: poor

Local and regional government
The country is divided into ten provinces which are further subdivided into 34 districts. The provinces are administered by governors, appointed by the President, and they, in turn, appoint commissioners to administer the districts. There is no representative local government as such.

Head of state and head of government
President Yoweri Museveni, since 1986.

Political leaders since 1970
1966–71 Milton Obote (UPC), 1971–79 Idi Amin Dada (Military), 1979 Yusof Lule (UNLF), 1979–80 Godfrey Binaisa (UNLF), 1980–85 Milton Obote (UPC), 1985–86 Basilio Okello (Military), 1986– Yoweri Museveni (NRA-NRM broad coalition).

Political system

The 1969 constitution was revived in 1981. It provides for a single-chamber National Assembly of 126 members and a President who is both head of state and head of government. The President and the Assembly are elected by universal adult suffrage, through a simple plurality voting system, for a five-year term.

In 1985 a military coup suspended the constitution and dissolved the National Assembly. A power-sharing agreement between the head of a Military Council, General Tito Okello, and Yoweri Museveni, leader of the National Resistance Army (NRA), which had been formed to overthrow the regime of Milton Obote, was concluded in December 1985 and this led to the dissolution of the Military Council and the establishment of a National Resistance Council (NRC), to act as a legislative body prior to the holding of elections for a National Assembly in 1989.

Political parties

There are currently seven active political parties, five of which are represented in the present coalition government. They are the National Resistance Movement (NRM), the Democratic Party (DP), the Conservative Party (CP), the Uganda People's Congress (UPC) and the Uganda Freedom Movement (UFM).

The NRM is the political wing of Yoweri Museveni's National Resistance Army (NRA). It was originally established in 1980 to oppose the regime of Milton Obote. The DP was founded in 1953 and banned in 1969 when a one-party state was established. It has a centre-left orientation. The CP dates from 1979. It has a centre-right orientation. The UPC was formed in 1960 and was made the only legal party, by Milton Obote, between 1979 and 1981. It has a left-of-centre orientation. The UFM has a left-of-centre stance.

Latest elections

The National Assembly was dissolved in 1985 and elections for a new body are scheduled for 1989. In the last elections, in 1980, the UPC won 74 seats, the DP 51 and the Uganda Patriotic Movement (UPM) one.

Political history

The British East Africa Company concluded treaties with local rulers to develop Uganda in the 1890s. In 1894 it became a British protectorate, the country being divided into five regions, four of them governed directly by Britain, with the assistance of native chiefs, and one, Buganda, ruled by its traditional prince, the Kabaka, under the British crown. In the 1950s internal self-government was given, with four provinces controlled by local ministers and Buganda by the Kabaka.

Uganda achieved full independence, within the Commonwealth, in 1962, with Dr Milton Obote, leader of the Uganda People's Congress (UPC), as Prime Minister. Buganda and the other four regions continued to enjoy a fair degree of self-government so that in 1963, when republican status was assumed, it was on a federal basis and King Mutesa II, the former Kabaka of Buganda, became President of the whole country, with Obote as his Prime Minister.

Obote wanted to establish a one-party state, to which the King objected so, having failed to win the argument by persuasion, he mounted a coup in 1966 and deposed King Mutesa. Obote took over as head of state as well as head of government, making himself Executive President.

One of his first acts was to end the federal status. After an attempt to assassinate him in 1969, Obote banned all opposition and established what was effectively a one-party state. In 1971 he was overthrown in an army coup led by Major-General Idi Amin Dada, who suspended the constitution and all political activity and took legislative and executive powers into his own hands. Obote fled the country and took refuge in neighbouring Tanzania.

Amin proceeded to wage what he called an 'economic war' against foreign domination, resulting in mass expulsions of Asians, many of whom settled in Britain. Then in 1976 he claimed that large tracts of Kenya historically belonged to Uganda and also accused Kenya of co-operating with the Israeli government in a raid on Entebbe airport to free Jewish hostages held in a hi-jacked aircraft. Relations with Kenya became strained and diplomatic links with Britain were severed. During the next two years the Amin regime carried out a widespread campaign against any likely opposition, resulting in thousands of deaths and imprisonments.

In 1978, when he annexed the Kagera area of Tanzania, near the Uganda border, the Tanzanian President, Julius Nyerere, sent troops to support the Uganda National Liberation Army (UNLA), which had been formed to fight Amin. Within five months Tanzanian troops had entered the Uganda capital, Kampala, forcing Amin to flee, at first to Libya, then to Saudi Arabia and Zaire.

A provisional government, comprising a cross-section of exiled groups, was set up, with Dr Yusuf Lule as President. Two months later Lule was replaced by Godfrey Binaisa who, in turn, was overthrown by the army. A Military Commission made arrangements for national elections which were won by the UPC and Milton Obote came back to power. Obote's government was soon under pressure from a range of exiled groups operating outside the country and guerrilla forces inside and he was kept in office only because of the presence of Tanzanian troops. When they were withdrawn in June 1982 a major offensive was launched against the Obote government by the National Resistance Movement (NRM), led by Dr Lule and Yoweri Museveni, and its military wing, the National Resistance Army (NRA). By 1985 Obote was unable to control the army, which had been involved in indiscriminate killings, and was ousted, in July, in a coup led by Brigadier Basilio Okello. Obote fled to Kenya and then Zambia, where he was given political aslyum.

Okello had little more success in controlling the army and, after a short-lived agreement of power-sharing with the NRA, in January 1986 he left the country and fled to Sudan. Yoweri Museveni was sworn in as President and immediately announced a policy of national reconciliation, promising a return to normal parliamentary government within three to five years. He formed a cabinet in which most of Uganda's political parties were represented.

ZAIRE

Republic of Zaire
République du Zaïre

Capital: Kinshasa

Social and economic data
Area: 2,345,000 km^2
Population: 31.300m*
Pop density per km^2: 13*
Literacy rate: 55%*
GDP: $2,600m*; per capita GDP: $83
Economy type: low income
Labour force in agriculture: 72%

*1985

Ethnic composition
Almost the whole population are of African descent and are distributed among over 200 tribes, the most numerous of which are the Kongo, the Luba, the Lunda, the Mongo and the Zande.

Religions
About half the people follow traditional, animist beliefs and the other half are Christians, mainly Roman Catholics.

Political features
State type: authoritarian nationalist
Date of state formation: 1960
Political structure: unitary
Executive: unlimited presidential
Assembly: one-chamber
Party structure: one-party
Human rights rating: 36%

Local and regional government
The country is divided into eight regions, below which are sub-regions. Administration is by appointed commissioners.

Head of state and head of government
President Marshal Mobutu Sese Seko Kuku Ngbendu Wa Za Banga, since 1965.

Political leaders since 1970
1965– Mobutu Sese Seko Kuku Ngbendu Wa Za Banga (MPR).

Political system
Zaire is a one-party state, based on the Popular Movement of the Revolution (MPR). The 1978 constitution provides for a President who is head of state and head of government as well as the leader of the MPR. As party leader he is automatically elected President for a seven-year term,

which may be renewed only once. There is a single-chamber assembly, the National Legislative Council, whose 210 members are elected by universal adult suffrage, through a simple plurality voting system, for a five-year term. The President appoints and presides over a National Executive Council. Ultimate power lies with the MPR, whose highest policy-making body is a 80-member Central Committee, which elects a 14-member Political Bureau.

Political parties

The Popular Movement of the Revolution (MPR) was formed in 1967 as Zaire's only political party. and immediately fused into the state machinery, party officials being, at the same time, government officials. The party has an African, socialist orientation. There are a number of opposition groups in exile.

Latest elections

In the 1987 elections for the National Legislative Council there were 1,075 candidates for the 210 seats. All were MPR nominees.

Political history

In the 1870s King Léopold II of Belgium claimed what is now Zaire as a personal colony, the Belgian Free State, and this claim received international recognition in 1895. It ceased to be a personal possession and was renamed the Belgian Congo in 1907. In the post-Second World War period an independence movement gathered momentum and the Belgian government quickly acceded to the movement's demands, granting the country full independence in June 1960, as the Republic of the Congo. Many thought the Belgium government's decision too precipitate in that it produced a number of immediate problems which could have been anticipated, and perhaps avoided.

The new state was intended to have a unitary structure and be governed centrally from Léopoldville by President Joseph Kasavubu and Prime Minister Patrice Lumumba, but Moise Tshombe, a wealthy businessman, argued for a federal solution and, becoming dissatisfied with the government's response to his requests, established his own political party and declared the rich mining province of Katanga, where he was based, an independent state, under his leadership.

Fighting broke out, which was not properly quelled by Belgian troops, and the United Nations Security Council agreed to send a force to restore order and protect lives. Meanwhile, there were disagreements between President Kasavubu and Prime Minister Lumumba on how the crisis should be tackled and this division between them prompted the Congolese army commander, Colonel Joseph-Désiré Mobutu, to step in and take over the reins of government temporarily. Lumumba was imprisoned and later released and five months later power was handed back to Kasavubu.

Soon afterwards it was announced that Lumumba had been murdered and the white mercenaries employed by Tshombe were thought to be responsible. The outcry which followed this announcement resulted in a new government being formed, with Cyrille Adoula as Prime Minister. During the fighting between Tshombe's mercenaries and UN forces the UN Secretary-General, Dag Hammarskjöld, flew to Katanga province to mediate and was killed in an air crash on the Congolese-Northern Rhodesian border. The attempted secession of Katanga was finally stopped in 1963 when Tshombe went into exile, taking many of his followers with him to form the Congolese National Liberation Front (FNLC). In July 1964 Tshombe returned from exile and President Kasavubu appointed him interim Prime Minister until elections for a new government could be held.

In August the country embarked upon what was hoped to be a new era of stability, as the Democratic Republic of the Congo, but a power struggle between Kasavubu and Tshombe soon developed and again the army, led by Mobutu, intervened. He established what he called a 'second republic', in November 1965. Two years later a new constitution was adopted and in 1970 Mobutu was elected President.

The following year the country was renamed the Republic of Zaire and in 1972 the Popular Movement of the Revolution (MPR), which had been founded in 1967, was declared the only legal political party. In the same year the President adopted the name of Mobutu Sese Seko.

In 1977 Mobutu was re-elected for another term and the following year a new constitution was adopted. Under it the presidency is limited to a maximum of two seven-year terms. Mobutu will, therefore, unless the constitution is changed again, have to stand down by, at the latest, 1998. During his presidencies so far he has carried out a large number of political and constitutional reforms and, although he has dealt harshly with opponents, has gradually improved the structure of public administration and brought stability to what had once seemed an ungovernable country.

However, the harshness of some of his policies has brought international criticism and in 1983, specifically in response to a damning report by Amnesty International, he offered an amnesty to all political exiles. Despite some demonstrations of opposition, Marshal Mobutu, as he now was, was re-elected, yet again, in 1984. Any groups showing outright opposition to his regime are, however, still in exile. Towards the end of 1988 a potentially dangerous, but not fully explained, rift with Belgium seemed imminent but was eventually avoided.

ZAMBIA

Republic of Zambia

Capital: Lusaka

Social and Economic Data

Area: 752,620 km^2
Population: 7.100m*
Pop density per km^2: 9*
Literacy rate: 69%*
GDP: $2,333m*; per capita GDP: $329
Economy type: low income
Labour force in agriculture: 64%

*1985

Ethnic composition
Over 95 per cent of the population are indigenous Africans, belonging to more than 70 different tribes, the most numerous being the Bantu-Botatwe and the Bemba.

Religions
About 70 per cent of people are Christians, about half of them Roman Catholics and half Protestants. There are also substantial Muslim and Hindu minorities.

Political features
State type: nationalistic socialist
Date of state formation: 1964
Political structure: unitary
Executive: unlimited presidential
Assembly: one-chamber
Party structure: one-party
Human rights rating: 51%

Local and regional government
The country is divided into eight provinces, each with a responsible minister of state, working through civil servants. Below this level local administration reflects some of the features of the pre-1970s English local government system.

Head of state and head of government
President Dr Kenneth David Kaunda, since 1964.

Political leaders since 1970
1964– Kenneth David Kaunda (UNIP).

Political system
Zambia is an independent republic within the Commonwealth. It was proclaimed a one-party state in 1972 and this was incorporated into a new constitution which was adopted in 1973. The party is the United National Independence Party (UNIP), and its President is the state President, Kenneth Kaunda. The constitution provides for the election of the President by universal adult suffrage for a five-year term. There is no limit to the number of times he may be re-elected. There is a single-chamber National Assembly of 135 members, 125 elected by universal adult suffrage, through a simple plurality voting system, and ten nominated by the President. The Assembly has a life of five years. The President governs with an appointed cabinet and is advised by a House of Chiefs, consisting of chiefs from the country's eight provinces. Ultimate power lies with UNIP, whose Central Committee is chaired by the President.

Political parties
The United National Independence Party (UNIP) was formed in 1959 as a breakaway group from the African National Congresss (ANC), which called itself the Zambian African National Congress (ZANC). It changed to its present name in 1964 and became the only legally permitted party in 1972. It has an African-socialist orientation.

Latest elections

In the 1988 National Assembly elections 610 candidates, all UNIP nominees, contested the 125 elective seats.

In October 1988 President Kaunda was re-elected, unopposed, with 95.5 per cent of the vote, for a sixth term.

Political history

As Northern Rhodesia, Zambia was administered by the British South Africa Company between 1889 and 1924, when it became a British protectorate. In 1953 it became part of a federation which included Southern Rhodesia, now Zimbabwe, and Nyasaland, now Malawi, but the mainly black Northern Rhodesians objected to the white dominance of Southern Rhodesia and started an independence movement. The Federation of Rhodesia and Nyasaland was dissolved in 1963 and Northern Rhodesia was granted internal self-government. Within months it became the independent republic of Zambia, within the Commonwealth, with Dr Kenneth Kaunda, leader of the United Independence Party (UNIP), as its first President.

Between 1964 and 1972, when it was declared a one-party state, Zambia was troubled with frequent outbreaks of violence because of disputes within the governing party and conflicts between the country's numerous tribes. After 1972 there was greater internal stability.

Externally, Zambia was economically dependent on neighbouring white-ruled Rhodesia and relations between the two countries deteriorated because of the operation of liberation groups on the borders between them. The border was closed in 1973 and in 1976 Kaunda declared his support for the Patriotic Front, led by Robert Mugabe and Joshua Nkomo, which was fighting the Rhodesian white regime. Zambia's economic problems continued and in 1980 there was an unsuccesful coup against the President, allegedly promoted by South Africa.

Despite his imposition of strict economic policies, Kaunda was convincingly re-elected in 1983 and 1988. During his presidencies he has played an important role in African politics and in 1985 was appointed to succeed President Nyerere of Tanzania as chairman of the black African 'front line states'. In 1987 Kaunda was elected to the chairmanship of the Organisation of African Unity (OAU).

ZIMBABWE

Republic of Zimbabwe

Capital: Harare

Social and economic data

Area: 390,600 km^2
Population: 9.000m*
Pop density per km^2: 23*
Literacy rate: 69%*

GDP: $5,300m*; per capita GDP: $589
Economy type: low income
Labour force in agriculture: 58%

*1985

Ethnic composition
There are four distinct ethnic groups in the country: indigenous Africans, who account for about 95 per cent of the population, Europeans, mainly British, about 3.5 per cent, and Afro-Europeans and Asians, who each comprise about 0.5 per cent.

Religions
About 80 per cent of the people follow traditional, animist beliefs and about 20 per cent are Christians.

Political features
State type: nationalistic socialist
Date of state formation: 1980
Political structure: unitary
Executive: unlimited presidential
Assembly: two-chamber
Party structure: one-party
Human rights rating: 45%

Local and regional government
The country is divided into eight provinces, administered by the central government. There are local authorities in cities and towns, with elected mayors and councils.

Head of state and head of government
Executive President Robert Gabriel Mugabe, since 1987.

Political leaders since 1970
1980– Robert Gabriel Mugabe (ZANU-PF).

Political system
Zimbabwe is an independent republic within the Commonwealth. Its constitution dates from independence in 1980 and originally contained many features of the British parliamentary system. However seven amendments have made significant changes so that what originally approximated to a parliamentary executive is now a presidential one, and what was formerly a multi-party system has become, in effect, a one-party one.

In its amended form, the constitution provides for a President who is both head of state and head of government, with the title Executive President. The current President was elected by a simple plurality of members of the assembly but future elections will be by universal adult suffrage, and the holder of the office will serve a five-year term. The President chooses and appoints a Vice-President and cabinet. He has power to veto a bill passed by the assembly but this veto can be overruled by a two-thirds assembly vote. In several respects the Zimbabwean presidency contains features of the limited executive of the United States, but the absence of effective opposition parties in the assembly must put it into the unlimited presidential category.

The assembly consists of two chambers, a 40-member Senate and a 100-member House of Assembly. In recognition of the rights of the white minority, the constitution in its original form provided for two sets of constituencies for parliamentary elections, a 'common roll', which included all voters, and a 'white roll' for white voters. This distinction was, however, abolished, in 1987, by the sixth constitutional amendment.

Membership of the Senate is on a mixed basis of election, appointment and *ex officio* status. Twenty-four are elected by an electoral college, which is itself elected by universal adult suffrage; five are elected by another electoral college consisting of Mashonaland Chiefs; five are Mashonaland Chiefs who are *ex officio* members; and six are appointed by the President. The 100 members of the House of Assembly are elected by universal adult suffrage, through a party list system of proportional representation. Both chambers serve a five-year term and are subject to dissolution within that period.

Political parties

The two main political parties, the Zimbabwe African National Union-Patriotic Front (ZANU-PF) and the Zimbabwe African People's Union (ZAPU) merged in 1987, to become ZANU-PF. Although ZANU-PF is not officially declared as the only legal party and other groups continue to function, they have little electoral impact so that Zimbabwe is, effectively, a one-party state.

ZANU-PF began in 1963 as the Zimbabwe African Union (ZANU), led by Robert Mugabe, breaking away from the Zimbabwe African National Union (ZAPU), founded by Joshua Nkomo two years earlier. During the years of opposition to the white-dominated regime the two groups operated together as the Patriotic Front (PF) and between 1974 and 1979 both were banned. The two leaders returned to take a leading part in the independence negotiations, in 1979–80, and the parties merged in 1987. The new, combined party has an African socialist orientation.

In May 1989 the Zimbabwe Unity Movement (ZUM) was formed by former ZANU Secretary-General, Edgar Tekere, in an attempt to prevent a one-party state functioning.

Latest elections

In 1987 Robert Mugabe was elected Executive President for a six-year term by the assembly.

In the 1985 House of Assembly elections ZANU-PF won 63 seats, ZAPU 15 and the other parties one. One seat was vacant, because of the death of one of the candidates, but was subsequently won by ZANU-PF.

Political history

Cecil Rhodes, through the British South Africa Company, began the exploitation of the rich mineral resources of the region north of South Africa in the 1880s, the area north and south of the Zambezi river becoming known as Rhodesia. When the British South Africa Company's charter expired in 1923 the southern section, or Southern Rhodesia, became a self-governing British colony and 30 years later, in 1953, it joined Northern Rhodesia and Nyasaland to form a multi-racial federation. The federation's economy was to be built on labour from Nyasaland, mineral resources from Northern Rhodesia and expertise from Southern Rhodesia. Within ten years, however, the federation was dissolved, and Northern Rhodesia and Nyasaland went their separate, and independent, ways as the new states of Zambia and Malawi.

The degree of self-government to be enjoyed by Southern Rhodesia after disengagement from the federation was limited by the British government's insistence on retaining the power to veto any legislation which discriminated against black Africans. This was accepted by some, but not all, white Rhodesians. Among those who objected to it were the members of the Rhodesian Front Party (RF), a grouping of white politicians committed to maintaining racial segregation. Their leader, Winston Field, became the country's first Prime Minister.

Meanwhile, African nationalists were campaigning for full racial democracy and the African National Congress, which had been formed in 1934, was, in 1957, reconvened under the leadership of Joshua Nkomo. It was banned in 1959 and Nkomo went into exile to become leader of the National Democratic Party (NDP), which had been formed by some Congress members. When the NDP was also banned, in 1961, Nkomo created the Zimbabwe African People's Union (ZAPU) and this, too, was declared unlawful, in 1962. In 1963 a spilt developed within ZAPU, one group, led by the Revd Ndabaningi Sithole forming the Zimbabwe African National Union (ZANU), with Robert Mugabe as its Secretary-General.

In April 1964 Field resigned and was replaced by Ian Smith, who rejected terms for independence proposed by Britain, which would require clear progress towards majority rule. Four months later ZANU and ZAPU were banned, and Nkomo and Mugabe imprisoned. In November 1965, after further British attempts to negotiate a formula for independence, Smith annulled the 1961 constitution and unilaterally announced Rhodesia's independence. Britain broke off diplomatic and trading links and the United Nations initiated economic sanctions, which were by-passed by many multi-national companies. The British Prime Minister, Harold Wilson, had talks with Smith in 1966 and 1968 but they were abortive on both occasions. In 1969 Rhodesia declared itself a republic and adopted a new constitution, with white majority representation in a two-chamber assembly.

ZAPU and ZANU had begun a guerrilla war against the Smith regime, which at times was supported by armed South African police. In 1971 the draft of another agreement for independence was produced which the British government said must be acceptable to the Rhodesian people 'as a whole'. A commission was sent from Britain in 1972 to test public opinion and it reported back that the proposals were unacceptable. Informal discussions continued and in 1975 a conference was convened in Geneva, attended by deputations from the British government, the Smith regime and the African nationalists, represented by Bishop Abel Muzorewa, President of the African National Council, which had been formed in 1971 to oppose the earlier independence arrangements, and Robert Mugabe and Joshua Nkomo, who had been released from detention and had formed a joint Patriotic Front. An independence date of 31 March 1978 was agreed, but not the composition of an interim government. Smith prevaricated and at the beginning of 1979 produced a new 'majority rule' constitution, which contained an in-built protection for the white minority, but which he had managed to get Muzorewa to accept. In June 1979 Bishop Muzorewa was pronounced Prime Minister of what was to be called Zimbabwe Rhodesia.

The new constitution was denounced by Mugabe and Nkomo as another attempt by Smith to perpetuate the white domination, and they continued to lead the Zimbabwe African National Liberation Army from bases in neighbouring Mozambique. In August of that year the new British Prime Minister, Margaret Thatcher, attended her first Commonwealth Heads of Government conference in Lusaka. She was not expected to be sympathetic to the exiled black nationalists but, under the influence of the Foreign Secretary, Lord Carrington, and the conference host, President Kaunda of Zambia, agreed to a constitutional conference in London, at which all shades of political opinion in Rhodesia would be represented. The conference, in September 1979, at Lancaster House, resulted in what became known as the Lancaster House Agreement and paved the way for full independence. A member of the British cabinet, Lord Soames, was sent to Rhodesia as Governor-General, with full powers to arrange a timetable for independence.

Economic and trade sanctions were immediately lifted and a small Commonwealth Monitoring Force supervised the disarming of thousands of guerrilla fighters who brought their weapons and ammunition from all parts of the country. A new constitution was adopted and elections were held, under independent supervision, in February 1980. They resulted in a decisive win for Robert Mugabe's ZANU-PF party. The new state of Zimbabwe became fully independent in April 1980, with the Revd Canaan Banana as President and Robert Mugabe as Prime Minister.

During the next few years a rift developed between Mugabe and Nkomo and between ZANU-PF and ZAPU supporters. Nkomo was accused of trying to undermine Mugabe's administration and was demoted and then dismissed from the cabinet. Fearing for his safety, he left the country, spending some months in Britain. ZAPU was also opposed to the proposal by ZANU-PF, in 1984, for the eventual creation of a one-party state.

Mugabe's party increased its majority in the 1985 elections and relations between the two leaders eventually improved so that by 1986 discussions about a complete merger were underway, a joint rally being held in March 1986. The parties merged in 1987 and in the same year, as President Banana retired, Mugabe combined the roles of head of state and head of government and assumed the title of Executive President. Nkomo, now becoming something of an elder statesman, was given a senior cabinet post, with the title of Vice-President.

Arctic Ocean
ALASKA (USA)
GREENLAND
Arctic Circle
CANADA
UNITED STATES OF AMERICA
Atlantic Ocean
Tropic of Cancer
MEXICO
CUBA
Pacific Ocean
PUERTO RICO (USA)
Caribbean Sea
Scale 1:35 000 000
0
400
800
1200 Km

NORTH AMERICA

The northern half of the continent of America encompasses a vast region of over 19 million square kilometres, nearly five times the size of Western Europe, or almost 15 per cent of the world's surface. Despite this areal size, its inhabitants constitute only about 5 per cent of the world population and it contains only two nation-states, Canada and the United States of America.

Geographically and climatically, it is a region of great contrasts and extremes. Parts of northern Canada and Alaska are well within the Arctic Circle while southern Florida is only a few degrees north of the Tropic of Cancer. The two countries share an enormous coastline, which includes the Arctic, Atlantic and Pacific oceans, within which are the Bering Sea, the Beaufort Sea, Hudson Bay and the Gulf of Mexico.

Although the overall population density of the region is low, there are areas of considerable concentration, for example, 25 United States cities have populations of 500,000 or more, seven of them in excess of 1 million and New York itself contains more than 7 million people. Canada, with a much smaller population than its neighbour, does not display equivalent concentrations, but its two largest cities, Toronto and Vancouver, have populations of nearly 3 million and more than 1 million respectively.

North America is a markedly 'high income' region, in fact the two countries which occupy it enjoy, between them, a third of the world's annually created wealth. It follows naturally from this that Canadian and United States citizens experience very high living standards compared with most other people in the world.

Although the region was originally peopled by Indians and Eskimos, the majority of today's inhabitants trace their histories back to European beginnings. Both Canada and the United States were once British colonies, Canada remaining a dependency, in one form or another, for over 280 years, while some of the states on the US eastern seaboard experienced colonial rule for about 200 years before, violently, winning their independence. Britain, however, was not the only European power to place its imprint on the region. France and Spain also vied for control, usually to secure a commercial advantage. Reminders of this early European exploitation are found in the French-speaking parts of Canada, in the southern states of the United States, particularly Louisiana, and in the Spanish-speaking communities of states such as California and New Mexico.

This colonial experience has affected the political cultures and structures of the two countries, but in different ways. Canada has retained its allegiance to the crown and has adhered to parliamentary institutions, even to the extent of calling one chamber of its assembly the House of Commons. The United States, on the other hand, has less kind memories of the past and has resolutely sought to ensure that individual political and social liberties can never again be usurped by an autocratic executive. Both countries rank high in human rights ratings but these have been achieved through different political routes.

Both, however, have federal structures of government, a fact that reflects the size of each country and its ethnic and cultural diversity. Within these federal systems can be seen the strong sense of independence still felt by individual provinces and states, each jealous of its right to retain a unique identity within the overall, national picture. Both countries can be proud of a long history of political stability. For example, neither has been troubled by a serious threat to its established democratic system for more than 100 years.

Relations between the two states sharing this half-continent have generally been civilised and correct, rather than warm. Canada has always been conscious of being close to 'big brother' and has been suspicious of moves to 'Americanise' the Canadian way of life, culturally as well as economically. Realistically, however, Canadian political leaders have recognised the existence of common needs and goals and have been happy to join the United States in mutually beneficial endeavours, such as the North Atlantic Treaty Organisation (NATO). At the same time, they have recognised that, as a 'superpower', the United States' interests are far wider than Canada's could ever be, or than Canadians would want them to be. In recent years this recognition of the need to share the region in a constructive way has resurfaced in the shape of the free trade agreement reached between the Canadian Prime Minister and the United States President.

Table 59

NORTH AMERICA

Political Data

State	*Date of Formation*	*Political Structure*	*State Type*	*Executive*	*Assembly No of Chambers*	*Party System*	*Voting System*
Canada	1867/1948	Federal	Lib Dem	Parliament	Two	Multi	SP
United States	1776	Federal	Lib Dem	Lim Pres	Two	Two	SP

Social and Economic Data

State	*Area (km^2)*	*Population (m) (1985)*	*Population Density (per km^2)*	*Literacy Rate (%)*	*Income Type*	*Human Rights Rating (%)*
Canada	9,975,220	25.625	3	96	High	96
United States	9,372,570	241.000	26	99	High	90
Total/Average	19,347,790	266.625	14	96-99	High	90-96

CANADA

Dominion of Canada

Capital: Ottawa

Social and economic data

Area: 9,975,220 km^2
Population: 25.625m*
Pop density per km^2: 3*

Literacy rate: 96%*
GDP: $348,982m*; per capita GDP: $13,619
Economy type: high income
Labour force in agriculture: 5%

*1985

Ethnic composition
About 45 per cent of the population are of British origin, 29 per cent French, 23 per cent of other European stock and about 1.5 per cent are indigenous Indians or Eskimos. The official languages are English and French.

Religions
There are about 11.2 million Roman Catholics, 900,000 Anglicans, 316,000 members of the Greek Orthodox Church and 150,000 members of the Ukrainian Greek Orthodox Church.

Political features
State type: liberal democratic
Date of state formation: 1867/1948
Political structure: federal
Executive: parliamentary
Assembly: two-chamber
Party structure: multi-party
Human rights rating: 96%

Local and regional government
Canada is a federation of ten provinces, Alberta, British Columbia, Manitoba, New Brunswick, Newfoundland, Nova Scotia, Ontario, Prince Edward Island, Quebec and Saskatchewan, and two territories, Northwest Territories and Yukon. The provinces range in territorial size from Prince Edward Island, with 5,660 square kilometres to Quebec, with 3,246,389 square kilometres. Their populations vary from 123,000 for Prince Edward Island to 8,625,000 for Ontario. The size and populations of the territories are equally diverse. Yukon is the smaller, with 22,000 people within 531,844 square kilometres, compared with Northwest Territories, with 47,000 people spread over an area of 3,246,389 square kilometres.

Each province has a single-chamber assembly, popularly elected for a five-year term, and a premier who is appointed by the Lieutenant-Governor on the basis of support in the provincial assembly.

The respective powers of the federal and provincial governments are set out in the constitution, the former being essentially concerned with matters affecting the whole nation, and the latter purely provincial affairs. In 1987 the constitution was amended to devolve more power to the provinces, through what became known as the Meech Lake Accord. It does not, however, have universal support among the provincial legislatures nor the political parties.

Head of state
Queen Elizabeth II, represented by Governor-General Jeanne Sauve, since 1984.

Head of government
Prime Minister Brian Mulroney, since 1984.

Political leaders since 1970
1968–79 Pierre Trudeau (Liberal), 1979–80 Joe Clark (Progressive Conservative), 1980–84 Pierre Trudeau (Liberal), 1984– Brian Mulroney (Progressive Conservative).

Political system
The constitution is based on five Acts of the British parliament, the Quebec Act, 1774, the Constitutional Act, 1791, the Act of Union, 1840, the British North America Act, 1867 and the Canada Act, 1982. The British North America Act stated that the constitution should be similar in principle to that in Britain and the Canada Act gave Canada power to amend its constitution and added a Charter of Rights and Freedoms, to recognise the nation's multi-cultural background. Paradoxically, although Britain had always avoided adopting a written constitution for itself, it took powers to prescribe for another sovereign state. The Canada Act therefore represented the formal ending of these powers and the guarantee of Canada's complete independence. Canada has, nevertheless, voluntarily retained the British monarch as a symbolic head of state and maintained its membership of the Commonwealth.

The federal parliament consists of two chambers, the Senate and the House of Commons. The 104 members of the Senate are appointed for life, or until the age of 75, by the Governor-General. They must be resident in the province they represent and, as persons of standing, are the equivalent of life peers in the British House of Lords. The House of Commons has 295 members elected by universal suffrage, through a simple plurality voting system. The federal Prime Minister is chosen by the Governor-General from the party which can command support in the House of Commons and, as in the British system, is accountable, with the cabinet, to it. Parliament has a maximum life of five years but may be dissolved within that period. Again as in Britain, legislation must be passed by both chambers and then signed by the Governor-General.

Political parties
Of 17 political parties, the most significant are the Progressive Conservative Party, the Liberal Party, and the New Democratic Party.

The Progressive Conservative Party was founded in 1854. In its earliest days it was staunchly pro-British, pro-Empire and anti-American. It is now more internationalist and in closer harmony with its United States neighbour. It advocates individualism and free enterprise.

The Liberal Party of Canada developed in the late nineteenth century as the Canadian counterpart of the Liberal Party in Britain. It strongly supports the autonomy of Canada, the maintenance of universal welfare policies and freedom of trade, particularly within the continent of North America.

The New Democratic Party dates from 1961. Before then it was known as the Co-operative Commonwealth Federation, which had itself grown out of the United Farmers Party and the Socialist Party of Canada. It has a moderate, left-of-centre orientation and is a social democratic member of the Socialist International.

Latest elections

In the 1988 House of Commons general election the results were as follows:

	Seats	*% Votes*
Progressive Conservatives	170	43
Liberals	82	26
New Democratic Party	43	20

Political history

Canada was discovered in 1497 by John Cabot, who thought he had found the route to China. In 1534 Jacques Cartier landed and claimed the country for France and in 1583 Sir Humphrey Gilbert visited Newfoundland and claimed it for England. During the next two centuries both countries expanded their trading activities and colonisation schemes, the rivalry inevitably leading to war. The former French colonists resented the British victory over France, in 1759, and, in an effort to pacify them, in 1791, the country was divided into English-speaking Upper and French-speaking Lower Canada. The two parts were united in 1841 and in 1867 the self-governing dominion of Canada, within the British Empire, was founded.

From 1896 to 1911 the Liberal Party was in power, under a French-Canadian, Wilfred Laurier. His government fell because of dissatisfaction with his attempts to strengthen trade links with the United States and he was succeeded by Robert Borden, heading a Conservative administration. He successfully organised Canada for war in 1914 and was the first Dominion Prime Minister to attend an Imperial War Cabinet meeting. In 1921 the Liberals returned to office,under Mackenzie King, and they were to dominate Canadian politics for the next three decades, with King until 1948, and then with Louis St Laurent until 1957.

The Progressive Conservatives returned to power in 1957, after 36 years in the wilderness. The Liberals, under Lester Pearson, returned to office in 1963 and Pearson remained Prime Minister until he was succeeded by the former law professor, Pierre Trudeau, in 1968. Trudeau maintained Canada's defensive alliance with the United States but sought to widen its influence on the world stage. At home he was faced with the problem of dealing with the separatist movement in Quebec and set about creating what he called the 'just society'. Although a French-Canadian himself, Trudeau was totally opposed to the idea of separatism for any part of the country. His success in achieving his objectives may be judged by his ability to win two elections in a row, in 1972 and 1974.

Then, in 1979, with no party having an overall majority in the Commons, the Progressive Conservatives, led by Joe Clark, formed a government. Later that year Trudeau announced his retirement from politics but when, in 1980, Clark was defeated on his government's budget proposals, Trudeau reconsidered his decision and, with the dissolution of parliament, won the general election with a large majority. Trudeau's third administration was concerned with the question of 'patriation', or the extent to which the parliament in Westminster had power to determine the constitution of Canada. Eventually the position was resolved with the passing of the Canada Act 1982, which was the last piece of legislation of the United Kingdom parliament to have force in Canada.

In 1983 Clark was replaced as leader of the Progressive Conservatives by Brian Mulroney, a businessman with no previous political experience, and in 1984 Trudeau retired to be replaced as Liberal leader and Prime Minister by John Turner, a former Minister of Finance. Within nine days of taking office, Turner called a general election and the Progressive Conservatives, under Mulroney, won the largest majority in Canadian history. Soon after forming his administration, Mulroney began an international realignment, placing less emphasis on links Trudeau had established with Asia, Africa and Latin America, and more on co-operation with Europe and a closer 'special relationship' with the United States. One aspect of this closer co-operation was discussion about the possibility of greater freedom of trade between the two countries, culminating in a free-trade agreement which was signed in 1988.

Although, less urgent than it was in the 1970s, the relationship between the federal government and the provinces is still a live political issue. In April 1987 Prime Minister Mulroney reached agreement with the ten provincial premiers, the 'Meech Lake Accord'. This would give all the provinces considerable powers in appointments to the Senate and Supreme Court, a veto over many possible constitutional amendments and financial compensation to any province which opted out of any new national shared-cost programme in favour of its own programme. The Accord was strongly criticised by former Prime Minister Trudeau as likely to destroy the equilibrium between Ottawa and the provinces which he had created and which Mulroney had inherited. The 1988 general election was fought mainly on the issue of the free-trade agreement negotiated with the United States, the Conservatives winning with a clear, but reduced, majority. In May 1989 John Turner announced his resignation as Liberal Party leader.

UNITED STATES OF AMERICA (USA)

Capital: Washington DC

Social and economic data

Area: 9,372,570 km^2
Population: 241.000m*
Pop density per km^2: 26*
Literacy rate: 99%
GDP: $3,947,000m*; per capita GDP: $16,378
Economy type: high income
Labour force in agriculture: 3%

*1985

Ethnic composition

Seventy-nine per cent of the population are of European origin, including 30 per cent who trace their descent from British and Irish stock, 8 per cent from German, 5 per cent from Italian and 3 per cent each from Scandinavian and Polish. Twelve per cent are black, 7 per cent Hispanic and 2 per cent Asian. Six per cent of the current population are officially registered as foreign-born.

Religions
There is a wide spread of religious denominations covering: Protestants (including Baptists, Methodists, Lutherans, Seventh Day Adventists, Presbyterians and Anglicans), 79 million (33%); Roman Catholics, 52 million (22%); Jews, 5.9 million (2.4%); Eastern, including Greek, Orthodox, 4.3 million (1.8%); Mormons, 3.9 million (1.6%); and Muslims, 2 million (0.8%). The rest of the population profess no religion or are to be found in small, distinctive sects or creeds.

Political features
State type: liberal democracy
Date of state formation: 1776
Political structure: federal
Executive: limited presidential
Assembly: two-chamber
Party structure: two-party
Human rights rating: 90%

Local and regional government
Below the state level, there are 3,100 counties, over 18,000 municipalities and almost 17,000 townships, with wards and precincts below. Office-holders are elected to fill political and administrative and judicial posts at all these levels.

Head of state and head of government
George H. W. Bush, since 1989.

Political leaders since 1970
1969–74 Richard M. Nixon (R), 1974–76 Gerald R. Ford (R), 1977–80 Jimmy E. Carter (D), 1981–88 Ronald W. Reagan (R), 1989– George H. W. Bush (R).

Political system
The United States is a federal republic comprising 50 states and the District of Columbia. Under its 1787 constitution, which became effective in March 1789 and has since been subject to 26 amendments, the constituent states are reserved considerable powers of self-government. The federal, or central, government concentrated originally on defence, foreign affairs and the co-ordination of 'interstate' concerns, leaving legislation in other spheres to the states, each with its own constitution, elected assembly (bicameral in all states except Nebraska), governor, Supreme Court and local taxation powers. Since Roosevelt's 1930s 'New Deal', however, the federal government has increasingly impinged upon state affairs and become the principal revenue-raising and spending agency.

The US federal government is characterised by a deliberate separation of the executive from the legislative and judicial functions. At the head of the executive branch of government is a President, elected every four years at a fixed date, in November, in a national contest by universal adult suffrage. Votes are counted at the state level on a first-past-the-post, winner-takes-all, basis, with each state being assigned a slate of seats, equivalent to the sum of its congressional representatives, in a national 538-member electoral college. This college later, in mid-December, formally elects the President. The victor is thus the candidate who secures the highest number of electoral college votes, not necessarily the highest number of popular votes across the country. Once elected, the President, who must be at least 35 years of age, serves as head of state, commander-in-chief of the armed forces and head of the civil service. He is restricted, under the provisions of Amendment 22, which was adopted in 1951, to a maximum of two terms and, once elected, cannot be removed except through impeachment by Congress.

The President works with a personally selected cabinet team, subject to the Senate's approval, whose members are debarred from serving in the legislature. For this reason, the cabinet is composed of specialists, who concentrate on the work of their own departments and who are frequently drawn from business or academic, rather than party political, backgrounds. To co-ordinate policy-making and draw up strategic plans, the President is served by an ever-growing White House office of personal political aides and trouble-shooting assistants. This team is headed by a chief of staff, and includes the National Security Council (NSC), the Domestic Council, the Office of Management and Budget (OMB) and the Council of Economic Advisers (CEA), as functionalist support units.

The second branch of government, Congress, the federal legislature, consists of two almost equally powerful chambers, the 100-member Senate and the 435-member House of Representatives. Senators, who must be at least 30 years of age, serve fixed six-year terms, two being elected from each state, in a state-wide race, regardless of size or population. A third are elected at a time, biennially, with no restrictions being placed on re-election.

Representatives, who must be at least 25 years of age, are elected from single-member constituencies of roughly equal demographic size, of 400,000 to 650,000, to serve for fixed two-year terms, again with no restrictions on re-election.

Congress has sole powers of legislation and operates through a system of specialised standing, select and investigative committees, which are composed of members drawn from parties in accordance with their relative strength in each chamber. They have the authority to call forth an array of witnesses from the executive branch and outside. These powerful committees, whose work is televised, are chaired by senior members of the party controlling the chamber and are liberally staffed by advisory assistants.

The Senate is perhaps the more powerful chamber of Congress, its approval being required for key federal appointments and for the ratification of foreign treaties. In addition, it is the Senate which hears cases of impeachment brought against federal officials.

The House of Representatives is of greatest importance in the fiscal sphere, all spending bills being required, under the terms of Section 7 of Article 1 of the constitution, to originate in this chamber. This makes the House's budget and finance committees particularly important.

The President needs to work with Congress to persuade it to adopt his policy programme, addressing it in January for an annual 'State of the Union' speech and sending periodic 'messages' and 'recommendations'. His success depends on his party support in Congress, his bargaining skills and the current level of his public standing. To become law, legislation, which is initially proposed by individual Senators and Representatives and worked upon in committee, requires the approval of both chambers of Congress. If differences arise, a special 'Joint Congressional Committee', composed of senior members drawn from both chambers, is convened to produce a compromise agreement. The President retains, however, the option of imposing vetoes which can only be overridden by two-thirds majorities in both Congressional houses.

Constitutional amendments require two-thirds majorities from both chambers of Congress and subsequent ratification by at least three-quarters, or 38, of the nation's 50 state legislatures, within a seven-year time span. Alternatively, it is possible for a constitutional amendment to be initiated by two-thirds of state legislatures, calling for the convening of a special National Constitutional Convention. Measures adopted at this convocation then require the subsequent approval by constitutional conventions in 38 states to become law.

The third branch of government, the judiciary, headed by the Supreme Court, interprets the written US constitution to ensure that a correct balance is maintained between federal and state institutions, and the executive and legislature, and that the civil rights enshrined in Amendments 1-10, 'The Bill of Rights', adopted in 1791, are upheld.

The Supreme Court consists of nine judges appointed by the President, subject to the Senate's approval, who serve life terms and are removable only through impeachment. Currently headed by Chief Justice William H. Rehnquist, it is an unusually influential and potentially 'activist' body, enjoying the power effectively to veto legislation and overturn executive actions which it rules to be unconstitutional.

The United States is, in addition, responsible for the administration of a number of Pacific Island territories, including American Samoa and the US Virgin Islands, which are governed by local legislatures and a governor. They are described more fully in Chapter 8. Each of these territories, as well as the 'self-governing territories' of Puerto Rico and Guam, sends a non-voting delegate to the US House of Representatives.

Political parties

Two broad 'catch-all' party coalitions, divided regionally and ideologically, dominate American politics, the Democrats and the Republicans. The first-past-the-post electoral system, the presidentialist nature of American politics, and the ability of the existing parties to embrace broad ranges of opinion have been key factors in fostering this party polarisation and working against the emergence of additional third or fourth parties.

The Democratic Party (D) was originally founded in 1792 by Thomas Jefferson, one of the drafters of the Declaration of Independence, of 1776, to defend the rights of individual states against the centralising moves of the Federalists. First, under the designation Democratic Republicans and then, from 1828, Democratic Party, it held power almost continuously between 1800 and 1860. During the American Civil War, or 1861 to 1865, it became identified with the defeated, rural Confederacy States of the South, a region which became a stronghold for the party, electing senators and representatives of a conservative and illiberal hue.

In the north-eastern seaboard states, a substantially different, in terms of ideological outlook, Democratic Party emerged during the years between 1865 and 1920. It sought out and won over the majority of the new immigrant minority communities, the Irish, Poles, Italians, Catholics and Jews, who flooded into the industrialising coastal cities during this period.

During the 1930s Great Depression, this new urban power base was strengthened when, under the leadership of Franklin D. Roosevelt, the party pressed ahead with a 'New Deal' programme of social reform and state interventionism. This attracted to the Democrats a broad coalition of support, establishing the party, which had been overshadowed by the Republicans between 1861 and 1932, as the new majority party at both the local and congressional level. This is shown in Table 60, below.

Table 60

PARTY CONTROL OF THE PRESIDENCY AND CONGRESS SINCE 1859

The Presidency		*Senate*		*House of Representatives*	
Democrat	1857–1860	Democrats	1859–1860	Republicans	1859–1874
Republican	1861–1865	Republicans	1861–1878	Democrats	1875–1880
Democrat	1865–1868	Democrats	1879–1880	Republicans	1881–1882
Republican	1869–1884	Republicans	1881–1892	Democrats	1883–1888
Democrat	1885–1888	Democrats	1893–1894	Republicans	1889–1890
Republican	1889–1892	Republicans	1895–1912	Democrats	1891–1894
Democrat	1893–1896	Democrats	1913–1918	Republicans	1895–1910
Republican	1897–1912	Republicans	1919–1932	Democrats	1911–1916
Democrat	1913–1920	Democrats	1933–1946	Republicans	1917–1932
Republican	1921–1932	Republicans	1947–1948	Democrats	1933–1946
Democrat	1933–1952	Democrats	1949–1952	Republicans	1947–1948
Republican	1953–1960	Republicans	1953–1954	Democrats	1949–1952
Democrat	1961–1968	Democrats	1955–1980	Republicans	1953–1954
Republican	1969–1976	Republicans	1981–1986	Democrats	1955–
Democrat	1977–1980	Democrats	1987–		
Republican	1981–				

Between 1933 and 1968 the Democratic Party secured the presidency for its candidate during 28 of the 36 years and control of both chambers of Congress during all but four of these years. The party's north-eastern wing, founded on a network of strong, worker-orientated, urban organisational 'machines', was dominant during these years, espousing a philosophy of liberalism which favoured an extended role for the federal government. During the 1960s, however, as this north-eastern wing pressed for civil rights reform, de-segregation, equal opportunity and voting rights for the black community, the party's southern conservative, 'Dixiecrat', wing became increasingly alienated.

In presidential elections, southern electors began to vote regularly for Republican nominees, and, within Congress, 'historical Democrat' Dixiecrats voted against the Democrat Presidents Kennedy and Johnson on social issues. Intra-party divisions widened during the later 1960s, as northern liberal opposition to the Vietnam War mounted, setting in train a drive to democratise the party's organisational structure and selection procedures, with the use of primary, or delegate election, contests open to all voters identifying themselves as party supporters. Election procedures replaced the caucus, or closed-door party meeting, and state convention, or open-door party meeting, systems.

The Democratic Party today is composed of at least five significant wings or tendencies. The first is a still sizeable, though now reduced, southern conservative faction, sometimes referred to as the party's 'congressional wing'. The second is a larger, dominant grouping of northern, 'New Deal' liberals, known as the 'presidential wing'. The third group are the radical, prairie-populist liberals of the mid-western, agricultural-industrial states, most notably Minnesota. The fourth, smaller, faction are the Trumanite 'Defense Democrats'. The fifth, and increasingly important, party faction, which is strongest outside Congress at the city government level, is the ultra-liberal 'Rainbow Coalition' movement.

The southern, 'congressional wing' comprises around 14 senators and 40 to 50 representatives and is organised in the Conservative Democratic Forum (CDF). This forms a 'swing' grouping within Congress, often aligning with Republican congressmen in votes on economic, social and defence issues. Southern conservatives and moderate liberals also work together in the Democratic Leadership Council (DLC), an organisation which was founded in 1985, and incorporates state governors.

The northern, 'presidential wing' is interventionist in both the economic and social spheres, and moderate on defence. It adheres to many of the tenets of the Americans for Democratic Action (ADA) organisation, which was established in 1947. Its leading representatives include Massachusetts Senator Edward Kennedy and New York governor Mario Cuomo.

The roots of the mid-western populists can be traced back to the People's Party, founded during the 1890s, and the Progressive Party, which operated during the inter-war years, to represent the interests of small farmers against those of big business.

The Trumanite 'Defense Democrats' are currently represented by New York senator Daniel Patrick Moynihan. While liberal in the economic and social sphere, they favour the pursuit of a firm anti-communist foreign policy.

The 'Rainbow Coalition' is a movement embracing black, hispanic, feminist, student, homosexual and anti-nuclear minority groupings, and is led by the charismatic civil rights leader, the Revd Jesse Jackson.

All of these minority communities support the Democratic Party by overwhelming margins in elections. Catholics, Jews, unionised workers and families on lower incomes constitute other important and, more general, Democrat support blocks.

The Republican Party (R), also popularly known as the Grand Old Party (GOP), was formed in Michigan in 1854 by a coalition opposed to slavery. It secured the election of its candidate, Abraham Lincoln, to the presidency, in 1860, and became identified with the wealthy and industrialising, victorious North, during the Civil War. The party also won the support of people in the rural and small town areas of the Mid-West. These included the long-settled Protestant majority community, and the new frontier states of the Pacific coast. All this support was put together in an electoral coalition which dominated at the federal level until the early 1930s.

The Republicans were outflanked by Roosevelt during the 1930s and 1940s, but under the leadership of Eisenhower, during the 1950s, came to accept the popular social and economic reforms of the 'New Deal' era and its aftermath, and, in the process, extended their support base. In ideological outlook, however, they continued to be positioned to the right of the Democrats in both the economic and social spheres. In terms of voter identification also they lagged behind their centre-left rivals, registering a national identification level of 35 per cent compared to 45 per cent by the Democrats.

During recent decades, the Republicans have dominated at the presidential level, having won five of the six electoral contests held since November 1964. They enjoy a firm regional support base in the centre and west of the country and poll strongly among the white Protestant community and those on higher incomes. The party has also begun to make inroads, at the state and local level, into the traditionally Democrat-dominated South.

Ideologically, until the election of Richard Nixon as President in 1968, the GOP was dominated by a big-business-orientated, and relatively liberal, north-eastern 'Wall Street' wing, one of whose most prominent members was the influential former New York governor, and Vice-President, Nelson A. Rockefeller. This northern liberal grouping has, however, contracted significantly since the 1970s, and is now reduced to a minority rump.

Instead, the Republicans have become dominated by a western and mid-western, small-town majority grouping, described as a 'Main Street' wing, and epitomised by the figures of Barry Goldwater and Ronald Reagan. This wing adheres to a conservative and individualist 'small government' philosophy. The Conservative Caucus, which is an organisation established in 1974, and run by Howard Phillips, and the Heritage Foundation, established by Paul Weyrich, serve as lobbyists and think-tanks for this faction.

To the right of the new party mainstream stands an increasingly vocal Christian, fundamentalist, activist grouping, led by the Revd Pat Robertson.

Each of the major parties has only a rudimentary national organisation, with no official membership, and, although party politicians in Congress group together for committee assignment purposes, they seldom vote *en bloc*.

A four-day National Convention is convened every four years, during the summer immediately preceding a presidential contest, to elect a presidential candidate and adopt a party 'platform', which is a non-binding manifesto. Delegates to these large, 2,200- to 4,200-member, bodies are elected through state-level primaries, caucuses or conventions, and are pledged to vote for particular candidates.

Between Conventions, party business is carried on by a National Committee, elected by state parties. The Committee's primary functions are to set the rules for the presidential primaries and National Conventions and co-ordinate fund-raising activities. The Republican National Committee is the better organised, having made considerable progress in the use of modern direct-mail fund-raising and leafleting services since the early 1970s and thus established itself as an important source of finance for Senate, as well as presidential, campaigns.

Despite this progress, party organisation remains concentrated at the state level. Here the true, localised 'party systems' of American politics are to be found. In comparison with West European political parties, however, state parties are informally organised, the choice of party candidates being unusually open because of the primary system of selection and because aspirants for office are heavily reliant on generating their own finance. They do this by drawing on donations from interest groups via Political Action Committees (PACs) to contest expensive, media-dominated elections. This pattern has fed through to Congress, where the legislative process is unusually atomised and individualistic.

Numerous minor parties also operate in the United States. None has, however, made any impact at either the state or federal level. For example, the most notable of the minor parties, the ultra-individualist and free-market Libertarian Party, which was established in 1971, has secured less than 1 per cent of the vote in presidential contests. It did, however, win a seat in the Alaska state legislature in 1978 and 1984. Of greater importance have been the independent presidential challenges by breakaway members from the major parties. For example, George Wallace, a renegade southern Democrat, secured 13 per cent of the national vote and 46 electoral college seats in November 1968 and John Anderson, a liberal Republican, 7 per cent of the popular vote, though no electoral college seats, in November 1984.

Latest elections

In the most recent presidential election, held on 8 November 1988, George H. W. Bush (R), secured a comfortable victory, capturing 54 per cent of the popular vote and 426 electoral college seats. Michael Dukakis (D) secured a 46 per cent share of the national vote and 112 electoral college seats, emerging the victor in the north-western states of Oregon and Washington, the mid-western, farm-belt states of Iowa, Minnesota and Wisconsin, and the north-eastern states of Massachusetts, New York, Rhode Island and West Virginia, as well as in Hawaii and the District of Columbia. Only 50 per cent of the voting-age population participated in the election. This turnout was a post-war low.

As usual, the November presidential election was preceded by a prolonged 'primary campaign' among an assortment of candidates seeking the party's nomination, by securing a majority of delegate votes at the July-August National Conventions. Officially, this nomination race began on 8 February 1988, with caucuses at Iowa, followed by the New Hampshire primary, of 16 February, a large 'Super Tuesday' of co-ordinated, mainly southern, caucuses and primaries, held on 8 March, and finished with the North Dakota primary on 14 June. In reality, unofficial campaigning for the party's presidential nomination began as early as August 1986, when the Republicans held a precinct delegate caucus in Michigan state, in which prospective presidential contenders participated.

Eight figures competed for the Democrat nomination. However, after 'Super Tuesday', the contest narrowed down to a three-cornered battle between Michael Dukakis, Revd Jesse Jackson and the Tennessee Senator, Albert Gore Jr. The decisive primary battle was at New York, on 19 April, in which the well-financed Dukakis established his dominance. Jackson, however, continued to mount a challenge all the way to the party's July Convention.

Six politicians contested the Republican nomination. However, despite initial success at Iowa for Kansas Senator Robert Dole and Revd Pat Robertson, Vice-President George Bush, supported by a professional and liberally financed campaign team, rebounded in New Hampshire and, helped by an expensive 'media blitz', effectively sealed the race with sweeping victories in the southern states, on 'Super Tuesday'.

In the concurrent congressional and gubernatorial, or state governorship, contests, of November 1988, the Democrats retained their control of both chambers of Capitol Hill. They captured 56 seats in the Senate to the Republicans' 44, a net gain of one, and 262 House of Representatives seats to the Republicans' 173, a net gain of four. The Democrats also won 28 state governorships to the Republicans' 22, a net gain of two.

Political history

The land-area covered by the contemporary United States of America (USA) was first settled by 'Indian' groups who migrated from Asia across the Bering land bridge over 25,000 years ago. Today, a million of their descendants survive, more than half living on reservations. European exploration of the continent commenced with the Norse in the ninth century. Later, during the sixteenth century, Florida and Mexico were colonised by the Spanish, and, during the seventeenth century, portions of the east coast, in New England and Pennsylvania, were occupied by the British, the Great Lakes and Louisiana by the French, New Jersey by the Dutch, and Delaware by the Swedes. The Swedish and Dutch settlements were subsequently acquired by the British, who controlled the territory between New England and the Carolinas. Following the Anglo-French Seven Years War, between 1756 and 1763, Canada, Florida and East Louisiana were also brought under British sovereignty by the terms of the Treaty of Paris, 1763.

In 1775, the 13 English-speaking colonies of Connecticut, Delaware, Georgia, Maryland, Massachusetts, New Hampshire, New Jersey, New York, North Carolina, Pennsylvania, Rhode Island, South Carolina and Virginia revolted against British colonial tax impositions, proclaiming their independence in July 1776. A provisional constitution, the Articles of Confederation, was adopted in 1777. Led by George Washington and with French aid, the confederated states succeeded in defeating the armies of George III in the War of American Independence, 1775–83.

A new constitution was drawn up for the independent, federal republic, in 1787, at the Philadelphia Convention, and came into force in 1789. A 'Bill of Rights' was added in 1791. This constitution provided for a directly elected House of Representatives, but, until the ratification of the 17th Amendment in 1913, only an indirectly elected Senate, whose members were chosen by state legislators. The President was selected by an electoral college, with Washington, of the Federalist Party, being the first to occupy the position.

Initially, the United States extended west only to the Mississippi river and north to the Great Lakes. Louisiana, which was purchased from France, was added in 1803 and Florida, which was acquired from Spain, in 1819. Further former Spanish states, including California and Texas, joined the Union between 1821 and 1853, following a war with Mexico, between 1846 and 1848.

In 1861 Civil War broke out between the cotton-growing southern, Confederate states of Alabama, Arkansas, Florida, Georgia, Louisiana, Mississippi, North Carolina, South Carolina, Tennessee, Texas and

Virginia and the more industrialised, and urbanised, north-eastern Federal states, over the issue of 'states' rights' and the maintenance of slavery in the South. More than 600,000 died in the conflict, the North triumphing after the surrender of General Robert E. Lee to General Ulysses S. Grant, at Appomattox, in April 1865.

Northern troops subsequently occupied the South, between 1865 and 1877, during a 'Reconstruction Period', and constitutional Amendments 13-15, which abolished slavery and guaranteed blacks civil rights, were adopted. Five days after the South's surrender, however, the North's Republican President, Abraham Lincoln, who had been re-elected for a second term in November 1864, was assassinated by John Wilkes Booth.

During the half-century following the Civil War, the north-eastern seaboard states underwent rapid industrialisation, more than 30 million overseas, predominantly European, immigrants being attracted to its cities. With the spread of railways, the agricultural frontier extended westwards towards the Rockies and Pacific, while the new territories of Alaska, which was purchased from Russia in 1867, and Hawaii, which was acquired in 1898, were added. Externally, the US adhered to an isolationist policy, not entering the First World War of 1914–18, until 1917.

After the war, the franchise was extended to women in 1920 by Amendment 19, and economic growth continued until the Wall Street stock market crash of October 1929. Thereafter, the country was plunged into a severe industrial and agricultural depression, bringing mass unemployment. Franklin D. Roosevelt, the Democrat former governor of New York, who was elected President in November 1932, responded to this crisis by abandoning the *laissez-faire* policies of his Republican predecessor, Herbert C. Hoover, and launching, under the slogan 'New Deal', a radical programme of state intervention. 'Soft loans' were provided to agriculturists and local authorities, employment-generating public-works projects launched, farm prices raised and old-age and unemployment insurance schemes introduced. These measures helped to alleviate the depression, although it was not until the Second World War that full employment was re-established.

Politically, this 'New Deal' programme drew to the Democratic Party new blocks of support, establishing it as the new, dominant, national party. Because of this, Roosevelt was re-elected President in 1936, 1940 and 1944, thus becoming the country's longest-serving leader.

The United States, after initially adhering to its isolationist stance, entered the Second World War, in December 1941, following Japan's attack on Pearl Harbor, in Hawaii. Its navy subsequently defeated the Japanese fleet at the Battle of Midway, in June 1942, and its army divisions helped turn the tide against Germany in Europe, between 1943 and 1945. However, it was not until August 1945, and the dropping of atom bombs on Hiroshima and Nagasaki, that Japan formally ceased hostilities and surrendered.

Having established itself as a global 'superpower', through its decisive actions between 1941 and 1945, the United States remained internationalist during the post-war era. Under the presidency of the Democrat, Harry S. Truman, who served between 1945 and 1952, a 'doctrine' of intervention in support of endangered 'free peoples', and of containing the spread of communism, was devised by Secretary of State (foreign minister) Dean

Acheson. This led to America's safeguarding of Nationalist Taiwan in 1949 and its participation, under United Nations' (UN) auspices, in the Korean War of 1950–53.

The United States, in addition, took the lead in creating new global and regional organisations, designed to maintain the peace: the United Nations (UN), in 1945, the Organisation of American States (OAS), in 1948, the North Atlantic Treaty Organisation (NATO), in 1949, the South East Asia Treaty Organisation (SEATO), in 1954. It also launched the Marshall Plan, between 1947 and 1952, to strengthen the economies of its European allies.

Domestically, President Truman sought to introduce liberal reforms, with the aim of extending civil and welfare rights, under the slogan a 'Fair Deal'. These measures were blocked, however, by a combination of southern Democrats and Republicans, in Congress.

Truman's foreign policy was criticised as being 'soft on communism' between 1950 and 1952, as a wave of anti-Soviet hysteria, spearheaded by the work of Senator Joseph McCarthy, swept the nation. This rightward shift in the public mood provided the basis for Republican victories in the congressional and presidential elections of November 1952. The popular military commander General Dwight ('Ike') Eisenhower became President and was re-elected by an increased margin in November 1956.

Working with Secretary of State John Foster Dulles, Eisenhower adhered to the Truman-Acheson doctrine of 'containment', while at home he pursued a policy of 'progressive conservatism', designed to encourage business enterprise.

The Eisenhower era was one of growth, prosperity and social change, involving the migration of southern blacks to the northern industrial cities and a rapid expansion in the educational sector. In the southern states racial tensions emerged, as a new black rights movement developed under the leadership of Dr Martin Luther King. Responding to these new demands and developments, the youthful Massachusetts Democrat, John F. Kennedy, on the promise of a 'New Frontier' programme of social reform, gained victory in the presidential election of November 1960. However, the new President, having emerged as a firm opponent of communism abroad, as evidenced by the Bay of Pigs Affair, of 1961, and the Cuban Missile Crisis, of 1962, and having proposed a sweeping domestic Civil Rights Bill, was assassinated, in November 1963. It was left to his deputy and successor, the Texan, Lyndon B. Johnson, to oversee the passage of what the latter termed the 'Great Society' reforms.

These measures, which included the Equal Opportunities, Voting Rights, Housing and Medicare Acts, guaranteed blacks new civil rights, including the effective right to vote in southern states, and significantly extended the reach of the federal government. They were buttressed by the judicial rulings of the Supreme Court chaired by Chief Justice Earl Warren, who occupied the post between 1953 and 1969.

Abroad, however, President Johnson became embroiled in the Vietnam War, 1964–75, which, with casualty numbers mounting, polarised American public opinion and created deep divisions within the Democratic Party.

Johnson decided not to run for re-election in November 1968 and the Democrat candidate, former Vice-President Hubert Humphrey, was defeated by the experienced Republican, Richard M. Nixon. Nixon, a staunch conservative, encountered worsening student and racial conflicts at home but enjoyed greater success abroad. Working with National Security Adviser, Henry Kissinger, he began a gradual disengagement from Vietnam and launched an imaginative new policy of *détente* which brought about improvements in relations with the Soviet Union, a Strategic Arms Limitation Treaty (SALT 1) being signed in 1972, and with communist China.

Faced by a divided opposition, led by the radical George McGovern, Nixon gained re-election, by an overwhelming margin, in November 1972. During the campaign, however, Nixon's staff illegally broke into the Democratic Party's headquarters, in the Watergate building, in Washington DC. The resulting 'cover-up' created a damaging scandal which, with a congressional impeachment impending, forced the resignation of the President, in August 1974.

Watergate shocked the American public, eroding confidence in the presidency, Republicans and the Washington establishment. The upright, liberal Republican, Gerald R. Ford, who had been Vice-President only since December 1973, succeeded Nixon as President. Maintaining the services of Kissinger, Ford adhered to his predecessor's policy of *détente*. He faced, however, a resurgent and hostile, Democrat-dominated, Congress which introduced legislation curbing the powers of the presidency, by means of the War Powers Resolution 1973, which prohibits the President from keeping US forces in hostile situations for more than 90 days without congressional authorisation, and forcing isolationism abroad. The new President also had to deal with an economic recession and fuel shortages. These had resulted from the 1973 Arab-Israeli War and the emergence of the Organisation of the Petroleum Exporting Countries (OPEC), who proceeded to force up world oil prices.

Ford contested the presidential election of November 1976, but was defeated by the 'born-again' southern, Christian, and anti-Washington outsider, James ('Jimmy') E. Carter, who promised a new era of open and honest government.

Carter, the former governor of Georgia, was a fiscal conservative, but a social liberal, who sought to extend welfare provision through greater administrative efficiency. In addition, he pledged to end the fuel crisis by enforced conservation. This he substantially achieved through the Energy Acts of 1978 and 1980.

Overseas, President Carter pursued a 'new foreign policy' which emphasised human rights in America's foreign relations. In the Middle East, Carter came close to a peace settlement in 1978–79, effecting the Camp David Agreements of September 1978 between Egypt and Israel, followed by a peace treaty, in March 1979. Also, in January 1979 America's diplomatic relations with communist China were fully normalised.

The Carter presidency was brought down, however, by a twin set of foreign policy crises in 1979–80: the fall of the Shah of Iran in January 1979 and the consequent Iranian Revolution, and the Soviet invasion of Afghanistan in December 1979. The President's vacillating leadership style, defence economies and moralistic foreign policy were blamed for weakening America's influence abroad. As a consequence, there was a resurgence in anti-communist feeling and mounting support for a new policy of re-armament and selective interventionism.

Carter responded to this new mood by enunciating the hawkish Carter

Doctrine, of 1980. This asserted that the United States had a vital interest in the Gulf region, which it would defend by force. He also supported a major new arms development programme. The President's popularity plunged, however, during 1980, as, mainly because of a new round of OPEC-induced oil price rises, economic recession gripped the country. During the same period American embassy staff were held hostage by Shia Muslim fundamentalists in Tehran.

The radical Republican, Ronald W. Reagan, benefited from Carter's difficulties and was swept to victory in the November 1980 presidential election, the Democrats also losing control of the Senate for the first time in 26 years.

The new President, like his predecessor, was an 'outsider politician', who, from being a former screen actor and governor of California, had risen to prominence as an effective, television-skilled campaigner. Reagan, drawing support from the 'Moral Majority' movement and 'New Right', believed in a return to traditional religious and family values and propounded a supply-side economic strategy, founded on reduced taxation, deregulation and political decentralisation, to get 'government off people's backs'.

In his approach to foreign affairs, Reagan rejected *détente* and spoke of the Soviet Union as an 'evil empire', which needed to be checked by a military build-up. He launched the space-based Strategic Defense Initiative (SDI) in 1983, and spoke of a readiness to employ force when necessary.

The early years of the Reagan presidency witnessed substantial reductions in taxation and sweeping cutbacks in federal welfare programmes. This created serious hardship, as economic recession gripped the nation between 1981 and 1983. The official unemployment rate rose from a level of 7.8 per cent in May 1980 to a post-war high of 10.8 per cent in November 1982. Abroad, the President's new foreign policy led to a sharp deterioration in Soviet-American relations, ushering in a new 'cold war' era during the Polish 'Solidarity' crisis of 1981.

By the autumn of 1983, however, the US economy began a strong, neo-Keynesian recovery, the unemployment level falling to 7 per cent in June 1984, and, helped by the successful invasion of Grenada by US marines, in October 1983, to foil an alleged Marxist coup, President Reagan recovered his popularity and was swept to a landslide victory on a wave of optimistic patriotism, in the presidential election of November 1984. He defeated the Democrat ticket of Walter Mondale and Geraldine Ferraro by a record margin.

During 1985 and 1986 public support for President Reagan was maintained, as a radical, tax-cutting bill was successfully pushed through Congress. In 1986, however, clouds began to emerge on the economic horizon as a huge budget and trade deficit developed, while overseas the President faced mounting public opposition to his policies in Central America. He also encountered a formidable, new, superpower adversary, in the form of the new Soviet leader, Mikhail Gorbachev. Gorbachev pressed for arms reductions during superpower summits held at Geneva, in November 1985, and Reykjavik, in October 1986.

The Reagan presidency was rocked, in November 1986, by the Republican party's loss of control of the Senate, following mid-term elections, and the disclosure of a damaging 'Iran-Contragate' scandal, concerning American arms sales to Iran in return for the release of hostages held in Beirut, and the 'laundering' of profits to help the Nicaraguan Contra, anti-communist, guerrillas. This scandal dented public confidence in the administration and forced the resignation or dismissal of key cabinet members, including National Security Adviser Admiral John Poindexter, in November 1986, and chief of staff, Donald Regan, in February 1987.

Having re-asserted presidential authority between 1981 and 1986, the ailing President Reagan began to forfeit power to a resurgent Congress during 1987. However, under the skilled leadership of his new chief of staff, Howard Baker, the President began to recover his standing in the national polls through emerging as a 'born-again' convert to *détente*. This was evidenced by his signing, in Washington, in December 1987, an historic agreement with the Soviet Union to scrap intermediate range nuclear forces.

Reagan's popularity transferred itself to Vice President George H. W. Bush, who, having selected the young, two-term Indiana senator, Dan Quayle, as his running-mate, comfortably defeated the Democrat ticket of Massachusetts governor, Michael S. Dukakis, and Texas Senator, Lloyd M. Bentsen, thus becoming the first sitting Vice-President since Martin van Buren (D), in 1836, to secure the presidency through the ballot box.

The new President assumed power at a time when unemployment had fallen to only 5.3 per cent, inflation was steady at a low annual level of 4 per cent and industrial output was growing vigorously, by more than 5 per cent. The country was faced, however, by grave fiscal problems, with pressure mounting, fuelled by the Wall Street share crash of October 1987, to reduce the huge budget and balance of payments deficits. The former stood at $155 billion per annum, and the latter at $145 billion per annum. Both had continued to grow since 1983, turning the US into a debtor nation for the first time in its history.

Bush promised, on his inauguration as President in January 1989, to work to 'make kinder the face of the nation and gentler the face of the world' and, despite his campaign rhetoric, seemed set to steer a more moderate and consensual course, both domestically and overseas, than his predecessor. He sought to secure the passage through Congress of a bipartisan budget package, involving significant defence economies, and responded to the Soviet Union's continuing disarmament initiative by unveiling, in May 1989, a proposal for substantial conventional forces' reductions. However, the start of Bush's presidency was marred by the Senate's rejection, by 53 votes to 47, of his nominee for the post of Defence Secretary, the former Texas Senator John Tower, as a result of criticisms of his private lifestyle and close links with defence contracting companies. This was the first time in 30 years that the Senate had refused to confirm a cabinet nominee and the first ever occasion for a newly elected President.

UNITED STATES
OF AMERICA
North
Atlantic
Ocean
Tropic of Cancer
BAHAMAS
MEXICO
CUBA
HAITI
DOMINICAN
REPUBLIC
PUERTO
RICO
ST KITTS
-NEVIS
BARBUDA
ANTIGUA
DOMINICA
ST LUCIA
BARB-
ADOS
ST VINCENT
GRENADA
TOBAGO
TRINIDAD
JAMAICA
Caribbean Sea
BELIZE
GUATEMALA
HONDURAS
EL
SALVADOR
NICARAGUA
COSTA
RICA
PANAMA
Pacific
Ocean
VENEZUELA
COLUMBIA
Scale: 1:30 000 000
0
250
500
750
1000 Km

CENTRAL AMERICA AND THE CARIBBEAN

The region we have called Central America and the Caribbean contains 21 sovereign states. Eight are on the American mainland and 13 are islands, or island groups, within that part of the Atlantic Ocean usually referred to as the Caribbean Sea, or simply the Caribbean.

This is the smallest of the nine regions in areal size and the second smallest in population. It extends over 2.720 million square kilometres, or 2.1 per cent of the world's land area, compared with figures of 14.6 per cent for North America, and 13.4 per cent for South America. The total population is 136 million, or 2.7 per cent of the world's total, compared with 5.4 per cent in North America and 5.6 per cent in South America. The region includes a substantial number of small states, nine having populations of less than half a million, and seven with less than 150,000. All of these small countries form part of island groupings in the Caribbean Sea.

In political terms it is a strongly pluralistic region, 18 of the 21 states being liberal or emergent democracies. The remaining three, Cuba, Haiti and Panama, have communist or military-dominated regimes. The historical backgrounds of all the countries have had a marked impact on their present political systems.

The eleven former British colonies, which are now independent members of the Commonwealth, all display the key characteristics of the 'Westminster model', including a two-party system, a parliamentary executive, a simple plurality voting system, and even an officially recognised opposition to the party in power.

In contrast, most of the countries which were formerly under Spanish rule have adopted political systems more in line with that of the United States, with executive presidents, whose powers are balanced and limited by elected assemblies.

Of the three nations which do not conform to either of these two patterns, Haiti and Panama have a façade of democratic government, behind which lies military power, and Cuba has a distinctive, populist, communist system, dominated by its charismatic leader, Fidel Castro.

Another interesting difference between the former British and former Spanish colonies is that the Commonwealth group are all post-1945 creations, six of them having been fully independent states only since 1975, whereas the 'Spanish empire' countries are mostly nineteenth-century creations, the youngest, Panama, having achieved full sovereignty as long ago as 1903.

In many ways the region is one of striking contrasts, with few signs of unity. For example, it is easier to fly from Jamaica to the Dominican Republic via Miami, in other words a round trip of some 1,600 km, than to attempt to travel by the direct route of less than 800 km. Frontier formalities also restrict international movement, with strict passport and customs controls operating even between Commonwealth countries.

The one feature all the Central American and Carribbean states have in common is the fact that they live in the shadow of the northern colossus, the United States. In other words, they are in America's 'back yard'. US interest in the region stems from the Monroe Doctrine of 1823, when the then

Secretary of State (US foreign minister) warned off European powers from interfering in what he saw as his country's domestic affairs.

The Spanish-American War of 1898, fought mainly over Cuba, reaffirmed the dominance of the United States and this strategic paternalism was rekindled as recently as 1983, when US forces, without consulting Britain, the British crown or the Commonwealth Secretariat, were given orders to invade Grenada.

In trade and culture, United States influence has grown dramatically in the post-Second World War years. For example, 72 per cent of the Dominican Republic's exports are to the United States, and 61 per cent of those of Trinidad and Tobago. Exports from the United States to countries in the region are similarly high. Over 60 per cent of tourists to Caribbean countries come from the United States, compared with less than 10 per cent from Europe, or from Commonwealth countries, such as Canada.

Economically, it is not a rich region by European standards, but, on the other hand, only five of the 21 states, Dominican Republic, Grenada, Haiti, Honduras and Jamaica, fall into the 'low income' category, and some of them only marginally so, while the Bahamians enjoy a 'high income' status.

Despite the current evidence of disunity, there are encouraging signs that the countries of the Caribbean wish, and intend, to function in a more cohesive fashion. The Caribbean Community and Common Market (CARICOM) was founded in 1973, in Trinidad, as a successor to the Caribbean Free Trade Association. Its declared purpose is to further the integration process which the Association began and its members include Antigua and Barbuda, Bahamas, Barbados, Belize, Dominica, Grenada, Guyana, Jamaica, St Christopher and Nevis, St Lucia, St Vincent and the Grenadines, and Trinidad and Tobago, as well as Montserrat, which is still a British possession. On the mainland, some of the Central American states have developed closer ties with their hispanic neighbours in the south.

It makes good sense for the Caribbean countries, with their small populations and vulnerable economies and frontiers, to work more closely together, but the proximity of the United States cannot be ignored. The Organisation of American States (OAS), which includes 19 of the Central American and Caribbean countries, as well as ten of the eleven South American states, has its headquarters in Washington DC and is very much an instrument of United States foreign policy.

Table 61

CENTRAL AMERICA AND THE CARIBBEAN

			Political Data				
State	*Date of Formation*	*Political Structure*	*State type*	*Executive*	*Assembly No of Chambers*	*Party System*	*Voting System*
Antigua	1981	Unitary	Lib Dem	Parliament	Two	Two	SP
Bahamas	1973	Unitary	Lib Dem	Parliament	Two	Two	SP
Barbados	1966	Unitary	Lib Dem	Parliament	Two	Two	SP
Belize	1981	Unitary	Lib Dem	Parliament	Two	Two	SP
Costa Rica	1821	Unitary	Lib Dem	Lim Pres	One	Two	PL
Cuba	1899	Unitary	Communist	Communist	One	One	SP
Dominica	1978	Unitary	Lib Dem	Parliament	One	Two	SP

Table 61—Central America and the Caribbean (contd.)

			Political Data				
State	*Date of Formation*	*Political Structure*	*State type*	*Executive*	*Assembly No of Chambers*	*Party System*	*Voting System*
Dominican Rep	1844	Unitary	Lib Dem	Lim Pres	Two	Multi	PL
El Salvador	1838	Unitary	Emgt Dem	Lim Pres	One	Multi	SP
Grenada	1974	Unitary	Emgt Dem	Parliament	Two	Two	SP
Guatemala	1839	Unitary	Emgt Dem	Lim Pres	One	Multi	AM
Haiti	1804	Unitary	Mil Auth	Military	None	One	None
Honduras	1838	Unitary	Emgt Dem	Lim Pres	One	Two	PL
Jamaica	1962	Unitary	Lib Dem	Parliament	Two	Two	SP
Mexico	1821	Federal	Lib Dem	Lim Pres	Two	Multi	AM
Nicaragua	1838	Unitary	Emgt Dem	Lim Pres	One	Multi	PL
Panama	1903	Unitary	Mil Auth	Military	One	Multi	SP
St Kitts-Nevis	1983	Federal	Lib Dem	Parliament	One	Two	SP
St Lucia	1979	Unitary	Lib Dem	Parliament	Two	Two	SP
St Vincent	1979	Unitary	Lib Dem	Parliament	One	Two	SP
Trinidad	1962	Unitary	Lib Dem	Parliament	Two	Two	SP

			Social and Economic Data			
State	*Area (km²)*	*Population (m) (1985)*	*Population Density (per km²)*	*Literacy Rate (%)*	*Income Type*	*Human Rights Rating (%)*
Antigua	440	0.085	193	88	Middle	N/A
Bahamas	13,940	0.235	17	89	High	N/A
Barbados	430	0.255	593	99	Middle	N/A
Belize	22,970	0.168	7	91	Middle	N/A
Costa Rica	50,700	2.700	53	88	Middle	91
Cuba	114,520	10.200	98	98	Middle	26
Dominica	750	0.074	99	94	Middle	N/A
Dominican Rep	48,730	6.614	135	69	Low	84
El Salvador	21,390	5.100	238	67	Middle	Poor
Grenada	340	0.100	294	98	Low	N/A
Guatemala	108,890	8.600	79	46	Middle	Poor
Haiti	27,750	5.900	213	35	Low	Poor
Honduras	112,090	4.600	41	57	Low	Poor
Jamaica	11,420	2.366	207	96	Low	77
Mexico	1,972,550	81.700	41	83	Middle	62
Nicaragua	130,000	3.300	25	57	Middle	Poor
Panama	77,080	2.227	29	86	Middle	79
St Kitts-Nevis	270	0.040	148	98	Middle	N/A
St Lucia	620	0.123	198	82	Middle	N/A
St Vincent	390	0.103	264	96	Middle	N/A
Trinidad	5,130	1.204	234	95	Middle	79
Total/Average	2,720,400	135.694	50	35-99	Middle	26-91

ANTIGUA AND BARBUDA

State of Antigua and Barbuda

Capital: St John's

Social and economic data
Area: 440 km^2
Population: 0.085m*
Pop density per km^2: 193*
Literacy rate: 88%*
GDP: $170m*; per capita GDP: $2,000
Economy type: middle income
Labour force in agriculture: N/A
*1985

Ethnic composition
The population is almost entirely of black African descent.

Religion
Christianity is the dominant religion, the majority of the population, about 60,000, being Anglicans.

Political features
State type: liberal democratic
Date of state formation: 1981
Political structure: unitary
Executive: parliamentary
Assembly: two-chamber
Party structure: two-party
Human rights rating: N/A

Local and regional government
The two islands of Antigua and Barbuda, which are about 50 km apart, are divided into seven parishes for administrative purposes.

Head of state
Queen Elizabeth II, represented by the Governor-General, Sir William E. Jacobs, since 1981.

Head of government
Prime Minister Vere C. Bird, since 1981.

Political leaders since 1970
1981– Vere C. Bird (ALP).

Political system
Antigua and Barbuda constitute an independent, sovereign nation within the Commonwealth, retaining Britain's monarch as head of state. The constitution dates from independence, in 1981. The Governor-General represents Queen Elizabeth and is appointed on the advice of the Antiguan Prime Minister in office at the time of the appointment.

The executive is parliamentary and operates in a similar fashion to that in the United Kingdom, the Prime Minister being chosen, normally after a general election, by the Governor-General as the person most likely to have the support of the assembly. Once appointed, the Prime Minister chooses the cabinet and all are responsible to the assembly. The leader of the party with the second largest number of seats in the House of Representatives is automatically the official Leader of the Opposition.

The assembly, or parliament, consists of two chambers, the 17-member Senate and the 17-member House of Representatives. Senators are appointed for a five-year term by the Governor-General, eleven on the advice of the Prime Minister, four on the advice of the Leader of the Opposition, one at his own discretion and one on the advice of the Barbuda Council, representing the island of Barbuda. Members of the House of Representatives are elected by universal adult suffrage, through a simple plurality voting system, for a similar term.

Political parties

There are six active political parties, the two most significant being the Antigua Labour Party (ALP), and the Progressive Labour Movement (PLM). The ALP was formed in 1968 and has a moderate, left-of-centre orientation. The PLM was founded in 1970 and has a similar orientation but is slightly less conservative in its political approach. Despite the existence of other political groups, there is effectively a two-party system, the ALP having been the more dominant force for most of the post-independence period.

In 1986 two of the smaller, centrist parties, the United People's Movement (UPM), founded in 1982, and the National Democratic Party (NDP), which had been established only the year before, merged to become the United National Democratic Party (UNDP).

Latest elections

In the 1989 general election Vere Bird and the ALP won another sweeping victory.

Political history

Antigua was visited by Christopher Columbus in 1493 and colonised by the British in the seventeenth century. The neighbouring island of Barbuda was annexed in 1860. Between 1860 and 1959 it was administered by Britain within a federal system known as the Leeward Islands and in 1967 given the status of associated state and full internal independence, with Britain retaining responsibility for defence and foreign affairs. What had been the Legislative Council became the House of Representatives, the post of Administrator was restyled governor and the Chief Minister became premier.

The ALP had held power since 1946 and in the first general election as an associated state, in 1971, its main opposition, the PLM, won a decisive victory, its leader George Walter replacing Vere Bird, leader of the ALP, as premier. The PLM fought the next election, in 1976, on a call for early independence whereas the ALP urged caution until a firm economic foundation had been laid. The electorate preferred the more gradualist approach and the ALP won.

Two years later, in 1978, the government declared itself satisfied that the country was now ready for full independence but opposition from the inhabitants of the island of Barbuda delayed the start of constitutional talks. The territory eventually became independent, as the State of Antigua and Barbuda, on 1 November 1981.

Since independence the ALP government has followed a foreign policy of non-alignment, but has retained close links with the United States, which it actively assisted in the invasion of Grenada in 1983.

THE BAHAMAS

The Commonwealth of the Bahamas

Capital: Nassau

Social and economic data
Area: 13,940 km^2
Population: 0.235m*
Pop density per km^2: 17*
Literacy rate: 89%*
GDP: $1,500m*; per capita GDP: $6,382
Economy type: high income
Labour force in agriculture: 5%

*1985

Ethnic composition
About 85 per cent of the population are black, of African origin, and 15 per cent of European ancestry, mostly British, American and Canadian.

Religions
Most people are Christian. There are about 50,000 Baptists, 40,000 Roman Catholics, 38,000 Anglicans, 12,000 Methodists and 10,000 Seventh Day Adventists.

Political features
State type: liberal democratic
Date of state formation: 1973
Political structure: unitary
Executive: parliamentary
Assembly: two-chamber
Party structure: two-party
Human rights rating: N/A

Local and regional government
Local administration is based on 18 natural island groupings. The islands of New Providence, where the national capital is located, and Grand Bahama have elected councils. The other 16 have district commissioners appointed by the central government.

Head of state
Queen Elizabeth II, represented by Governor-General Sir Gerald Cash, since 1979.

Head of government
Prime Minister Sir Lynden Oscar Pindling, since 1967.

Political leaders since 1970
1967– Sir Lynden Oscar Pindling (PLP).

Political system
Bahamas is an independent sovereign nation within the Commonwealth, accepting Britain's monarch as head of state and an appointed, resident Governor-General as her representative. The constitution, which came into effect at independence in 1973, provides for a two-chamber assembly consisting of a Senate and House of Assembly. The Governor-General appoints a Prime Minister and cabinet drawn from and responsible to the assembly. The leader of the second-largest party in the House of Assembly is the official Leader of the Opposition.

The Senate has 16 members appointed by the Governor-General, nine on the advice of the Prime Minister, four on the advice of the Leader of the Opposition, and three after consultation with the Prime Minister. The House of Assembly has 49 members, elected by universal adult suffrage through a simple plurality voting system. The assembly has a maximum life of five years and is subject to dissolution within that period.

Political parties
There are five active political parties but a two-party system operates through two major groupings, the Progressive Liberal Party (PLP) and the Free National Movement (FNM).

The PLP is a centrist party and was founded in 1953. It has been in power since independence, in 1973. The FNM was formed in 1972 by a coming together of the United Bahamian Party (UBP) and PLP dissidents. Its orientation is centre-left and it is the official opposition party.

Latest elections
In the 1987 general election the PLP House of Assembly's seat holding fell from 32 to 31, while the FNM's rose from 11 to 16. Two independents were also elected.

Political history
Bahamas became a British colony in 1783 and was given internal self-government in 1964. The first elections for a National Assembly on a full adult voting register were held in 1967. The PLP, drawing its support mainly from voters of African origin, won the same number of seats as the European-dominated UBP and Lynden Pindling, the PLP leader, by drawing support from outside his own party, became Prime Minister. In the 1968 elections the PLP scored a resounding victory and this success was repeated in 1972, enabling Pindling to lead his country into full independence, within the Commonwealth, in 1973.

With the opposition parties in some disarray, he increased his majority in 1977 but by 1982 the FNM had regrouped and were more convincing opponents. Despite this, coupled with allegations of government complicity in drug trafficking, the PLP was again successful and Pindling's leadership was unanimously endorsed at a party convention in 1984. The 1987 general election, fought again against a background of alleged drug trafficking, was again won by the PLP, but with a reduced majority.

BARBADOS

Capital: Bridgetown

Social and economic data
Area: 430 km^2
Population: 0.255m*
Pop density per km^2: 593*
Literacy rate: 99%*
GDP: 1,230m*; per capita GDP: $4,823
Economy type: middle income
Labour force in agriculture: 8%

*1985

Ethnic composition
About 80 per cent of the population are of African descent, about 16 per cent of mixed race and about 4 per cent of European origin, mostly British. English is the official language.

Religions
There are about 150,000 Anglicans, about 24,000 Roman Catholics and significant numbers of other Christian faiths.

Political features
State type: liberal democratic
Date of state formation: 1966
Political structure: unitary
Executive: parliamentary
Assembly: two-chamber
Party structure: two-party
Human rights rating: N/A

Local and regional government
Elected local government bodies were abolished in 1969 and replaced by eleven parishes, each administered by central government.

Head of state
Queen Elizabeth II, represented by Governor-General Sir Hugh Springer, since 1984.

Head of government
Prime Minister Erskine Lloyd Sandiford, since 1987.

Political leaders since 1970
1966–76 Errol Barrow (DLP), 1976–85 'Tom' Adams (BLP), 1985–86 Bernard St John (BLP), 1986–87 Errol Barrow (DLP), 1987– Erskine Lloyd Sandiford (DLP).

Political system
The country is a constitutional monarchy, with a resident Governor-General representing the United Kingdom monarch. The constitution

dates from independence in 1966 and provides for a system of parliamentary government on the British model, with a Prime Minister and cabinet drawn from and responsible to the assembly.

This consists of two chambers, the Senate and the House of Assembly. The Senate has 21 members appointed by the Governor-General, twelve on the advice of the Prime Minister, two on the advice of the Leader of the Opposition and the rest on the basis of wider consultations. The House of Assembly has 27 members elected by universal adult suffrage, through a simple plurality voting system. The assembly has a maximum life of five years and is subject to dissolution within this period.

The Governor-General appoints the Prime Minister on the basis of likely support in the House of Assembly. He also appoints the leader of the party with the second largest number of seats in the House as the official Leader of the Opposition.

Political parties

There are two active political parties, the Barbados Labour Party (BLP) and the Democratic Labour Party (DLP). The BLP was founded in 1938 and has a moderate, left-of-centre orientation. The DLP was formed in 1955, mainly from BLP dissidents, and has a roughly similar political stance.

Latest elections

In the 1986 general election the DLP increased its House of Assembly seat holding from ten to 24, defeating the BLP, whose share of the seats fell dramatically from 17 to three.

Political history

Barbados became a British colony in 1627 and remained so until it achieved full independence, within the Commonwealth, in November 1966. Moves towards a more independent political system began in the 1950s, universal adult suffrage being introduced in 1951, and the BLP winning the first general election. Ministerial government was established in 1954 and the BLP leader, Sir Grantley Adams, became the first Prime Minister. In 1955 the DLP was formed by party activists disenchanted with the BLP. Six years later full internal self-government was achieved and in the general election in December 1961 the DLP was victorious under its leader, Errol Barrow. When Barbados attained full independence in 1966 Barrow became the new nation's first Prime Minister.

The DLP was re-elected in 1971 but in the 1976 general election the BLP, led now by Sir Grantley Adams' son 'Tom', ended Barrow's 15 years of power. Both parties were committed to maintaining a free-enterprise system and alignment with the USA although the DLP government established diplomatic relations with Cuba in 1972 and the BLP administration supported the US invasion of Grenada in 1983. In 1981 the BLP was re-elected but Adams died suddenly in 1985 and was succeeded by his deputy, Bernard St John, a former BLP leader. In the 1986 general election the DLP, led by Barrow, was returned to power, winning 24 of the 27 seats in the House of Assembly. Errol Barrow died in 1987 and was succeeded by Erskine Lloyd Sandiford.

BELIZE

Capital: Belmopan

Social and economic data
Area: 22,970 km^2
Population: 0.168m*
Pop density per km^2: 7*
Literacy rate: 91%*
GDP: $192m*; per capita GDP $1143
Economy type: middle income
Labour force in agriculture: N/A

*1985

Ethnic composition
There is a wide mix of races, comprising Creoles, Mestizos, Caribs, East Indians and Europeans, including Spanish, British and Canadian Mennonites.

Religions
Christianity is the chief religion, about 64 per cent of the population being Anglicans and Methodists. There are also about 100,000 Roman Catholics.

Political features
State type: liberal democratic
Date of state formation: 1981
Political structure: unitary
Executive: parliamentary
Assembly: two-chamber
Party structure: two-party
Human rights rating: N/A

Local and regional government
For administrative purposes, the country is divided into six districts, ranging in population from under 12,000 to over 50,000. Local elections are usually contested as strongly as national elections.

Head of state
Queen Elizabeth II, represented by Governor-General Dame Elmira Minita Gordon, since 1981.

Head of government
Prime Minister Manuel Esquivel, since 1984.

Political leaders since 1970
1965–1984 George Price (PUP), 1984– Manuel Esquivel (UDP).

Political system
Belize is a constitutional monarchy, with a resident Governor-General representing the United Kingdom monarch. The constitution dates from independence in September 1981 and provides for parliamentary

government on the British model, with a Prime Minister and cabinet drawn from the assembly and responsible to it.

The two-chamber National Assembly consists of the Senate and the House of Representatives. The Senate has eight members appointed by the Governor-General for a five-year term, five on the advice of the Prime Minister, two on the advice of the Leader of the Opposition and one after wider consultations. The House of Representatives has 28 members elected by universal adult suffrage, through a simple plurality voting system. The Governor-General appoints the Prime Minister on the basis of majority support in the House of Representatives and the leader of the party with the next largest number of seats as the official Leader of the Opposition.

Political parties

The two active political parties are the People's United Party (PUP) and the United Democratic Party (UDP).

The PUP was founded in 1950 by a small group, believing strongly in the need for national independence and social justice, who called themselves the People's Committee. The group soon split up but one of the founders, George Price, remained to create the PUP. Its orientation is left-of-centre.

The UDP was formed in 1973 by the merger of three groups, the People's Development Movement, the Liberal Party and the National Independence Party. It is moderately conservative and is held together more by its opposition to the PUP than by a coherent ideology.

Latest elections

In the 1984 general election the UDP won 21 seats in the House of Representatives and the PUP seven.

Political history

Colonised as early as the seventeenth century, British Honduras, as it was then called, was not recognised as a British colony until 1862. A 1954 constitution provided for partial internal self-government, with Britain retaining responsibility for defence, external affairs and internal security. The first general election under the the new constitution was won by the PUP, led by George Price. PUP won all the subsequent elections until 1984. In 1964 full internal self-government was granted and Price became Prime Minister, working with a two-chamber assembly. In 1970 the nation's capital was moved from Belize City to the new town of Belmopan and in 1973 the whole country became known as Belize.

The frontier with Guatemala had long been a source of dispute and in 1975 British troops were sent to defend it. Two years later negotiations with Guatemala began but no final conclusion was reached. In 1980 the United Nations called for full independence for Belize but a constitutional conference, which was called in 1981, broke up because of a dispute over Guatemala's demand for territory rather than just access to the Caribbean. Eventually, in September 1981, full independence was achieved and George Price became the first Prime Minister of the new nation. Britain agreed to leave troops to protect the frontier and to assist in the training of Belizean forces.

In 1984 PUP's 30 years of uninterrupted rule ended and the new Prime Minister was the UDP leader, Manuel Esquivel. Britain reaffirmed its undertaking to protect Belize's frontier and, despite renewed talks with Guatemala in 1985, no permanent solution to the dispute between the two countries has yet been found.

COSTA RICA

Republic of Costa Rica
Republica de Costa Rica

Capital: San José

Social and economic data
Area: 50,700 km^2
Population: 2.700m*
Pop density per km^2: 53*
Literacy rate: 88%*
GDP: $3,814m*; per capita GDP: $1,412
Economy type: middle income
Labour force in agriculture: 27%

*1985

Ethnic composition
About 97 per cent of the population are of European descent, mostly Spanish, and about 2 per cent are of African origin.

Religions
Roman Catholicism is the official religion and about 90 per cent of the population practise that faith, although all beliefs are tolerated.

Political features
State type: liberal democratic
Date of state formation: 1821
Political structure: unitary
Executive: limited presidential
Assembly: one-chamber
Party structure: two-party
Human rights rating: 91%

Local and regional government
The country is divided into seven provinces, ranging in population from about 150,000 to nearly 900,000. Each province is administered by a governor who is appointed by the President. The provinces are subdivided into cantons and the cantons into districts. There is an elected council for each major city in a canton.

Head of state and head of government
President Oscar Arias Sanchez, since 1986.

Political leaders since 1970
1970–74 José Figueres Ferrer (PLN), 1974–78 Daniel Oduber Quiros (PLN), 1978–82 Rodrigo Carazo (PUO), 1982–86 Luis Alberto Monge Alvarez (PLN), 1986– Oscar Arias Sanchez (PLN).

Political system

The 1949 constitution provides for a President popularly elected for a four-year term, assisted by two Vice-Presidents similarly elected. The President selects and appoints his own cabinet.

There is a single-chamber Assembly, consisting of 57 members, elected through a party list system of proportional representation, for a four-year term. Voting is compulsory.

Political parties

Out of some 20 political parties, two have dominated the political scene for many years. They are the National Liberation Party (PLN) and what is now called the Christian Socialist Unity Party (PUSC).

The PLN began to form in 1948 and was officially founded in 1951. It is a left-of-centre, social democratic party with about 370,000 members and is affiliated to the Socialist International.

In its present form, the PUSC is a development from the Unity Party which was formed in 1978 as a coalition of four parties to oppose the PLN. It became the United Coalition (CU) and then, with other similarly orientated centrist groupings, the PUSC, in 1984.

Latest elections

In the 1986 presidential election Oscar Arias Sanchez (PLN) won 52.3 per cent of the vote and Rafael Angel Calderon Fournier (PUSC) 45.8 per cent

In the 1986 Assembly elections PLN won 29 seats, PUSC 25 and other parties two.

Political history

Costa Rica was first colonised by Spain in the sixteenth century and became an independent nation in 1821. Apart from a period of military dictatorship between 1870 and 1882, and a brief civil war in 1948 because of a disputed presidential election, it has been one of the most democratically governed states in Latin America.

Present-day Costa Rica dates from the civil war of 1948 when the army, under José Figueres, restored order and adopted a new constitution. Figueres abolished the army, relying on the Civil Guard for the country's future defence, and then surrendered power to a civilian government. He soon returned, however, to become President the following year. He co-founded the PLN, nationalised the banks and introduced a comprehensive social security system. He was re-elected in 1953.

There followed 16 years of mostly conservative rule, when some of the PLN policies were reversed. Then, in 1974, Daniel Oduber won the presidency for the PLN. He returned to socialist policies, extending the welfare state and establishing friendly relations with communist states. Communist and left-wing political parties were legalised.

In 1978 Rodrigo Carazo, leader of the conservative Unity Coalition (CU) became President. His presidency was marked by a disastrous collapse of the economy and allegations of involvement in illegal arms trafficking between Cuba and El Salvador.

The conservative administration was ended in 1982 when Luis Alberto Monge, a former trade union official and co-founder, with Figueres, of PLN, won a convincing victory in the presidential election. To reverse the damage done by the Carazo government, Monge introduced a 100-days emergency economic programme. He also maintained a policy of strict neutrality.

His government came under increasing pressure from the United States to abandon its neutral stance and condemn the left-wing Sandinista regime in Nicaragua. It was also urged to re-establish a national army. The pressures were resisted and in 1983 Monge reaffirmed his country's neutrality. However, relations with Nicaragua deteriorated after border clashes between Sandinista forces and the Costa Rica civil guard, so that, in 1985, Monge reluctantly agreed to create an anti-guerrilla guard, trained by the United States.

This increased doubts about Costa Rica's declared policy of neutrality but in 1986 Oscar Arias Sanchez won the presidential election on a neutralist platform, defeating the pro-US candidate, Rafael Angel Calderon. Arias worked vigorously for peace in the area, in 1987 proposing a Central American Peace Agreement which was signed by the leaders of Nicaragua, El Salvador, Guatemala and Honduras. It failed to halt the fighting in Nicaragua but contributed to the start of direct talks between the Nicaraguan government and the Contra rebels in the following year.

CUBA

Republic of Cuba
Republica de Cuba

Capital: Havana

Social and economic data
Area: 114,520 km^2
Population: 10.200m*
Pop density per km^2: 98*
Literacy rate: 98%*
GDP: $20,000m*; per capita GDP: $1,960
Economy type: middle income
Labour force in agriculture: 22%

*1985

Ethnic composition
The majority of the population are of mixed Spanish and African or Spanish and Indian origin. About a third are European and a tenth African.

Religions
All religions are permitted and there is no established Church but the majority of people are Roman Catholics.

Political features
State type: communist
Date of state formation: 1899
Political structure: unitary

Executive: communist
Assembly: one-chamber
Party structure: one-party
Human rights rating: 26%

Local and regional government
The country is divided into 14 provinces varying in population from just under 60,000 to nearly 2 million. Within the provinces are 169 municipalities, each with an elected assembly, which, in turn, elects an executive committee.

Head of state and head of government
Dr Fidel Castro Ruz, since 1976.

Political leaders since 1970
1959– Fidel Castro Ruz (PCC).

Political system
The 1976 constitution created a socialist state with the National Assembly of People's Power as its supreme organ. It consists of 510 deputies elected by universal adult suffrage, through a simple plurality voting system, for a five-year term. The National Assembly elects 31 of its members to form the Council of State. It also elects the head of state who is President of the Council, head of government, and First Secretary and chairman of the Political Bureau of the only authorised party, the Communist Party of Cuba (PCC). Fidel Castro thus occupies all the key positions within the state and the party, where ultimate political power lies.

Political parties
The origins of the PCC date back to 1925 when a socialist party was formed by a group of left-wing activists. In 1943 it became known as the People's Socialist Party (PSP). When Castro seized power in 1959 some of the old guard of the PSP found his methods and ideological leanings too anarchic for their comfort and were reluctant to give him their full support. Meanwhile Castro was leading his own movement and in 1961 the misgivings within the PSP were sufficiently allayed to allow it to merge, in 1961, with Castro's movement and other socialist groups, into the Integrated Revolutionary Organisation (ORI). Two years later this became the United Party of the Socialist Revolution (PURS) and finally, in 1965, the Communist Party of Cuba (PCC).

It is a Marxist-Leninist party organised on Soviet lines, with a 148-member Central Committee, a Political Bureau, Secretariat and five Commissions. Its membership is about 450,000.

Latest elections
Elections for the third five-year term of the National Assembly took place in December 1986. Five hundred and ten deputies, all PCC nominees, were elected.

Political history
After being under Spanish rule from the sixteenth century, Cuba was ceded to the United States in 1898, at the end of the Spanish-American War. It

became independent in 1902 but the United States retained its naval bases and a right to intervene in internal affairs until 1934. In 1933 an army sergeant, Fulgencio Batista, seized and held on to power until 1944, when he retired. In 1952, however, he seized power again in a bloodless coup and began another period of rule which many of his fellow countrymen found oppressive.

In the following year a young lawyer and son of a sugar planter, Dr Fidel Castro, tried to overthrow him but was defeated. He went into exile to prepare for another coup, returning in 1956 but was again unsuccessful. He fled to the hills with Argentine-born Dr Ernesto ('Che') Guevara and ten other fighters, to form a guerrilla force to fight the Batista regime.

In 1959 Castro's forces were finally successful and Batista was deposed, to great popular acclaim. The 1940 constitution was immediately suspended and replaced by a 'Fundamental Law', with all power vested in a Council of Ministers led by Castro as Prime Minister and his brother, Raul, as his deputy. Che Guevara, who had assisted in the overthrow of Batista, was reputedly made Castro's 'number three'.

The following year all US businesses in Cuba were appropriated without compensation, provoking the United States into breaking off diplomatic relations. In 1961 the US went further, sponsoring a full-scale, but abortive, invasion, the 'Bay of Pigs' episode. In December of the same year Castro announced that Cuba was now a communist state and would follow a Marxist-Leninist programme of economic development.

In 1962 Cuba was expelled from the Organisation of American States (OAS), which had originally been formed as a regional agency of the United Nations, but had become increasingly dominated by the United States. The Kennedy administration in Washington then initiated a full political and economic blockade. Castro's response was to tighten his relations with the USSR which, in the same year, supplied missiles, with atomic warheads, for installation on Cuban soil. A tense crisis was averted when, at the American President's insistence, they were dismantled. In 1965 Che Guevara left Cuba, ostensibly to fight causes in other parts of the world.

Between 1965 and 1972, with help from the USSR, Cuba made substantial economic and social progress and in 1972 became a full member of the Council for Mutual Economic Assistance (CMEA or Comecon), a Moscow-based organisation linking communist states. In 1976 a referendum approved a new socialist constitution and Fidel Castro and his brother were elected President and Vice-President. The following five years saw Cuba playing an increasingly evident role in world affairs, particularly in Africa, usually to the disquiet of the United States.

In 1981, after being re-elected for another term, Castro offered to discuss foreign policy with the US administration but the offer was not accepted. Castro's support for Argentina, against Britain, during the 1982 Falklands conflict, cooled relations with the United States but improved them with other Latin American countries. The US invasion of Grenada in 1983 cooled diplomatic relations again.

In recent years, and particularly since the Soviet Union's abandonment of the Brezhnev policy of supporting third-world revolutions, Cuba has adopted a more conciliatory posture in its international relations, including those with the United States. At the end of 1988, for example, it signed a peace treaty with South Africa for the withdrawal of Cuban forces from

Angola. As a further indication of Cuba's return to the fold of international politics, in September 1988 it established formal relations with the European Community.

DOMINICA

Commonwealth of Dominica

Capital: Roseau

Social and economic data
Area: 750 km^2
Population: 0.074m*
Pop density per km^2: 99*
Literacy rate: 94%*
GDP: $90m*; per capita GDP: $1,216
Economy type: middle income
Labour force in agriculture: 31%

*1985

Ethnic composition
Most of the inhabitants are descended from African slaves who were brought to the island as plantation labourers in the seventeenth and eighteenth centuries. A small number of the original people of Dominica, the Arawaks, remain.

Religions
The vast majority of the population are Christians, about 80 per cent of them Roman Catholics.

Political features
State type: liberal democratic
Date of state formation: 1978
Political structure: unitary
Executive: parliamentary
Assembly: one-chamber
Party structure: two-party
Human rights rating: N/A

Local and regional government
For administrative purposes Dominica is divided into ten parishes.

Head of state
President Sir Clarence Seignoret, since 1983.

Head of government
Prime Minister Mary Eugenia Charles, since 1980.

Political leaders since 1970
1978–80 Patrick John (DLP), 1980– Mary Eugenia Charles (DFP).

Political system

Dominica is an independent republic within the Commonwealth. The constitution dates from independence, in 1978, and is broadly modelled on the parliamentary system of the United Kingdom. It provides for a single-chamber, 30-member, House of Assembly. Twenty-one are representatives, elected by universal adult suffrage, through a simple plurality voting system, and nine are senators appointed by the President, who is head of state. Five of the senators are appointed on the advice of the Prime Minister, who is head of government, and four on the advice of the official Leader of the Opposition, who is the leader of the party with the second largest number of Assembly seats. The Assembly has a life of five years.

The President is elected by the Assembly for a five-year term and appoints the Prime Minister on the basis of support in the Assembly. The Prime Minister chooses the cabinet and all are collectively responsible to the Assembly.

Political parties

There are four political parties, the two main ones being the Dominica Freedom Party (DFP) and the Labour Party of Dominica (LPD).

The DFP was founded in 1970 as a centre party, drawing its leaders from the wealthier sections of the community but also receiving support from the poorer, rural sector.

The LPD was founded in 1985 as an alliance of three parties, the Dominica Labour Party (DLP), the Dominica Liberation Movement (DLM) and the United Dominica Labour Party (UDLP). The DLP dates from 1961, when it was formed to represent the labour movement. The alliance has a left-of-centre orientation.

Latest elections

In the 1985 general election the DFP won 15 of the 21 elected Assembly seats and the LPD five. The remaining seat was won by a UDLP dissident.

Political history

A British colonial possession since the eighteenth century, Dominica was part of the Leeward Islands federation until 1939. In 1940 it was transferred to the Windward Islands and remained attached to that group until 1960, when it was given a separate, semi-independent, status, with a Chief Minister and Legislative Council. In 1961 the leader of the Dominica Labour Party (DLP), Edward leBlanc, became Chief Minister and, after 13 years in office, retired, to be succeeded by Patrick John. The DLP held office until full independence was achieved in 1978 and its leader, John, became the first Prime Minister under a new constitution.

Opposition to John's increasingly authoritarian style of government soon developed and in the 1980 elections the DFP won a convincing victory on a free-enterprise policy programme. Its leader, Eugenia Charles, became the Caribbean's first woman Prime Minister, John losing his seat in the Assembly. In 1981 John was thought to be implicated in a plot to overthrow Charles' government and a state of emergency was imposed. The following year he was tried and acquitted. He was retried in 1985, found guilty and given a twelve-year prison sentence.

A regrouping of left-of-centre parties resulted in the Labour Party of

Dominica (LPD) becoming the main opposition to the DFP, but in the 1985 elections it was unable to prevent Eugenia Charles being re-elected. Under her leadership, Dominica has developed strong links with France and the United States and in 1983 contributed a small contingent to the US-backed invasion of Grenada.

DOMINICAN REPUBLIC

Republica Dominicana

Capital: Santo Domingo

Social and economic data
Area: 48,730 km^2
Population: 6.614m*
Pop density per km^2: 135*
Literacy rate: 69%*
GDP: $4,654m*; per capita GDP: $704
Economy type: low income
Labour force in agriculture: 22%

*1985

Ethnic composition
About 73 per cent of the population are mulattoes, of mixed European and African parentage, about 16 per cent European and 11 per cent African.

Religions
Roman Catholicism is the established religion and about 90 per cent of the population are adherents, although there is complete freedom for other beliefs.

Political features
State type: liberal democratic
Date of state formation: 1844
Political structure: unitary
Executive: limited presidential
Assembly: two-chamber
Party structure: multi-party
Human rights rating: 84%

Local and regional government
The country is divided into 27 provinces, ranging in population from under 40,000 to 1.5 million. Each province has a governor, appointed by the President. The provinces are subdivided into municipalities, each with a mayor and an elected council.

Head of state and head of government
President Joaquin Balaguer, since 1986.

Political leaders since 1970
1970–78 Joaquin Balaguer (PRSC), 1978–82 Silvestre Antonio Guzman (PRD), 1982–86 Jorge Blanco (PRD), 1986– Joaquin Balaguer (PRSC).

Political system
Although not a federal state, the Dominican Republic has a highly devolved system of regional and local government. The 1966 constitution provides for a President, popularly elected for a four-year term, and a two-chamber Congress, of Senate and Chamber of Deputies, elected for a similar term. Elections to the Senate are by a simple plurality voting system and to the Chamber by means of a party list system of proportional representation. The Senate has 30 members and the Chamber of Deputies 120. The President is head of government as well as head of state and chooses his own cabinet.

Political parties
There is a wide range of political parties, 19 in all, the three most significant being the Dominican Revolutionary Party (PRD), the Christian Social Reform Party (PRSC) and the Dominican Liberation Party (PLD).

The PRD was founded in Havana in 1939 by a group of anti-government exiles. It became active in the Dominican Republic after the death of the dictator, Rafael Trujillo. It is a moderate, left-of-centre party and now has about 400,000 members.

The PRSC was formed in 1961, after Trujillo's assassination, by the merger of several Christian, socialist and other democratic groups. It has an independent, socialist orientation.

The PLD was formed in 1973 by Juan Bosch, who had originally founded the PRD and then abandoned it. It has a strongly nationalist orientation.

Latest elections
In the 1986 presidential election the PRSC candidate, Joaquin Balaguer, won 857,942 votes, the PRD candidate, Jacobo Majluta Azar, 814,716 and the PLD candidate, Juan Bosch Gavino, 379,269.

In the 1986 National Congress elections the results were as follows:

	Senate Seats	*Chamber Seats*
PRSC	21	56
PRD	7	48
PLD	2	16

Political history
The Dominican Republic was established in 1844. Before that time it had been in French, Spanish and Haitian hands. It was later temporarily occupied by United States military forces, between 1916 and 1924. In 1930 the elected democratic government of Horacio Vazquez was overthrown in a military coup and General Rafael Trujillo began a long personal dictatorship until he was assassinated in 1961.

In the following year the country's first free elections were won by Dr Juan Bosch, founder and leader of the left-wing party PRD. Bosch, himself, had been in exile for more than thirty years. Within a year he too was overthrown by the military who set up their own three-man ruling junta. An attempt to re-establish Bosch in 1965 was defeated, with the help of US troops, and in 1966 Joaquin Balaguer, a protégé of Trujillo, and leader of the PRSC, won the presidency. A new, more democratically orientated, constitution was adopted and, Balaguer, despite his links with Trujillo, proved to be a popular leader, being re-elected in 1970 and 1974.

The 1978 election was won by the PRD candidate, Silvestre Antonio Guzman, and the PRD was again successful in the 1982 election when Jorge Blanco, the party's left-wing nominee, became President-designate. However the sitting President, Guzman, committed suicide before he had finished his full term, after allegations of fraud by his family. An interim President was, therefore, chosen before the start of Blanco's term in August.

Despite his left-wing credentials, Blanco steered a restrained course in foreign policy, maintaining good relations with the United States and avoiding too close an association with Cuba. The state of the economy began to worsen, however, and in 1985 the Blanco administration was forced to adopt harsh austerity measures in return for IMF help. The PRD became increasingly unpopular and it was not suprising when the PRSC, under Joaquin Balaguer, returned to power in 1986.

EL SALVADOR

Republic of El Salvador
Republica de El Salvador

Capital: San Salvador

Social and economic data

Area: 21,390 km^2
Population: 5.100m*
Pop density per km^2: 238*
Literacy rate: 67%*
GDP: $5,742m*; per capita GDP: $1,125
Economy type: middle income
Labour force in agriculture: 40%

*1985

Ethnic composition

El Salvador has a largely homogeneous population. About 92 per cent of the people are Mestizos, 6 per cent Indians and 2 per cent of European origin.

Religions

Roman Catholicism is the dominant religion, about 80 per cent of the population following that faith. There are also about 200,000 Protestants.

Political features

State type: emergent democratic
Date of state formation: 1830
Political structure: unitary
Executive: limited presidential
Assembly: one-chamber
Party structure: multi-party
Human rights rating: poor

Local and regional government
The country is divided into 14 departments, ranging in population from about 140,000 to nearly 700,000. Each department is administered by a centrally appointed official. Within the departments there are municipalities, with elected mayors.

Head of state and head of government
President Alfredo Cristiani, since 1989.

Political leaders since 1970
1967–72 Fidel Sanchez Hernandez (PCN-Military), 1972–77 Arturo Armando Molina (PCN-Military), 1977–79 Carlos Humberto Romeros Mena (PCN-Military), 1979–80 Military Junta, 1980–82 José Napoleon Duarte (PDC-Military), 1982–84 Alvaro Magana Borja (Independent-Military), 1984–89 José Napoleon Duarte (PDC), 1989– Alfredo Cristiani.

Political system
The 1983 constitution, amended in 1985, provides for a single-chamber National Assembly of 60, elected by universal adult suffrage, through a simple plurality voting system, for a three-year term. The Assembly chooses a President who is then popularly elected for a five-year term. The President is assisted by a Vice-President, chosen by the Assembly, and a Council of Ministers whom he appoints.

Political parties
Of the nine officially recognised political parties, the most significant are the Christian Democrats (PDC), the National Republican Alliance (ARENA), and the National Conciliation Party (PCN).

The PDC was formed in 1960 and now has about 150,000 members. It is strongly anti-imperialist and favours Latin American integration. ARENA was founded in 1981. It has an extreme right-wing orientation. PCN is another right-wing grouping which fought the 1985 elections on a joint platform with ARENA. It dates from 1961.

Latest elections
In the 1988 Assembly elections ARENA won 30 seats, PDC 23 and PCN seven. In an election in 1989 to find a successor to José Napoleon Duarte, the ARENA candidate, Dr Alfredo Cristiani, defeated the PDC candidate with 53.8 per cent of the vote.

Political history
El Salvador became a Spanish colony in 1523 and achieved independence in 1829. Since then there has been a history of frequent coups and political violence. In the 1930s a peasant uprising was put down with, reputedly, some 30,000 lives lost and there were three more military takeovers in 1944, 1948 and 1960.

Following another coup, in 1961, the conservative Party of National Conciliation (PCN) was established, winning all the seats in the National Assembly. PCN stayed in power, with reports of widespread violations of human rights, until challenged, in 1979, by a socialist guerrilla movement, the Farabundo Marti Liberation Front (FMLN). A civilian-military junta deposed the President and promised to introduce a democratic system of government with free elections. Elections were postponed, however, as the violence continued. In 1980 the Archbishop of San Salvador, Oscar Romero, who was a well-known champion of human rights, was shot dead in his cathedral. The murder of three American nuns and a social worker prompted US President Carter to suspend economic and military aid.

In December 1980 José Duarte, leader of a left-of-centre coalition, was sworn in as President. The Reagan administration gave him its backing, as an anti-communist, and encouraged him to call elections in 1982. The left-wing parties refused to enter the contest which was held amid great violence, at least 40 people being killed on election day. It was eventually won by the extreme right-wing ARENA party.

As the FMLN continued its activities, some 1,600 Salvadorean troops trained in the United States and US Military advisers were said to be actively involved in the conflict. It was estimated that about 35,000 people were killed between 1979 and 1982.

A new constitution eventually came into effect at the end of 1983 but guerrilla activity continued. Duarte won the 1984 presidential election and in 1985 the Christian Democrats (PDC) had a convincing victory in the Assembly. In September of that year the President's daughter was abducted by guerrillas, forcing him to negotiate with them, in the face of criticism from the opposition parties and the military. The guerrilla war continued, Duarte again attempting, in 1986, to reach a negotiated settlement with the rebels.

It was announced, in June 1988, that President Duarte had had tests in Washington which confirmed that he had terminal cancer. Despite this condition, and consequential absences for treatment, the President has remained in office until June 1989 when he was succeeded by an ARENA colleague, Dr Alfredo Cristiani.

GRENADA

Capital: St George's

Social and economic data
Area: 340 km^2
Population: 0.100m*
Pop density per km^2: 294*
Literacy rate: 98%*
GDP: $96m*; per capita GDP: $960
Economy type: low income
Labour force in agriculture: 25%

*1985

Ethnic composition
The majority of the population are of black African descent.

Religions
The great majority of people are Roman Catholics.

Political features
State type: emergent democracy
Date of state formation: 1974
Political structure: unitary
Executive: parliamentary
Assembly: two-chamber
Party structure: two-party
Human rights rating: N/A

Local and regional government
The country is divided into six parishes, each administered by an appointed district commissioner. The capital of St George's is administered by the central government.

Head of state
Queen Elizabeth II, represented by Governor-General Sir Paul Scoon, since 1978.

Head of government
Prime Minister Herbert A. Blaize, since 1984.

Political leaders since 1970
1974–79 Eric Gairy (GULP), 1979–1983 Maurice Bishop (NJM), 1983–84 Hudson Austin (Military), 1984– Herbert Blaize (GNP).

Political system
The constitution, which dates from full independence in 1974, has created a system modelled on that of the United Kingdom, with a resident Governor-General, representing the British monarch, as the formal head of state and a Prime Minister and cabinet drawn from and collectively responsible to parliament.

Parliament consists of two chambers, a 15-member House of Representatives, elected by universal adult suffrage, through a simple plurality voting system, and a Senate of 13, appointed by the Governor-General, seven on the advice of the Prime Minister, three on the advice of the Leader of the Opposition and three after wider consultation. The official opposition is the party with the second largest number of seats in the House. The normal parliamentary term is five years.

Political parties
There are seven political parties but, effectively, a two-party system operates. The two main parties are the New National Party (NNP) and the Grenada United Labour Party (GULP).

NNP was formed in 1984 by the merger of the Grenada Democratic Movement, the Grenada National Party and the National Democratic Party. It has a centrist orientation.

GULP dates from 1950 and is Grenada's oldest party. Its orientation is nationalist, left-of-centre.

Latest elections
In the 1984 general election NNP won 14 of the 15 House of Representatives seats, with 58.64 per cent of the vote, and GULP won one, with a vote count of 35.88 per cent.

Political history

Grenada was visited by Columbus in the fifteenth century but not colonised until about 200 years later. French settlers came from Martinique and ousted the local Caribs. Then, after being ceded to Britain, retaken by France and ceded to Britain again, it became a British colony in 1887. In 1958 it joined the Federation of the West Indies, until its dissolution in 1962, and then was granted internal self-government in 1967. It achieved full independence within the Commonwealth in 1974.

The early political life of the nation was dominated by two figures, Eric Gairy, a trade union leader who founded the Grenada United Labour Party (GULP) in 1950, and Herbert Blaize, of the Grenada National Party (GNP). On independence, in 1974, Gairy was elected Prime Minister. He was knighted in 1977 but his rule was regarded as increasingly autocratic and corrupt and in 1979 he was replaced, in a bloodless coup, by the leader of the left-wing party, the New Jewel Movement (NJM), Maurice Bishop.

Bishop suspended the 1974 constitution, established a People's Revolutionary Government (PRG) and announced the formation of a People's Consultative Assembly to draft a new constitution. He promised a non-aligned foreign policy but became increasingly convinced that the United States was involved in a plot to destabilise his administration. This was strenuously denied. Relations with Britain and the United States deteriorated while Grenada's links with Cuba and the USSR grew stronger. In 1983 Bishop tried to improve relations with the United States and announced the appointment of a commission to draft a new constitution. This conciliatory attitude was opposed by the more left-wing members of his regime, resulting in a military coup, during which Bishop and three of his colleagues were executed.

A Revolutionary Military Council (RMC), led by General Hudson Austin, took control. In response to the outcry caused by the executions, Austin promised a return to civilian rule as soon as possible but on 25 October about 1,900 US troops, accompanied by 300 from Jamaica and Barbados, invaded the island. It was not clear whether the invasion was in response to a request from the Governor-General or on the initiative of the Organisation of Eastern Caribbean States (OECS). In any event, concerned that Grenada might become a Cuban base, the United States readily agreed to take part. Neither Britain nor other members of the Commonwealth appear to have been consulted. The RMC forces were defeated and Austin and his colleagues arrested.

In November the Governor-General appointed a non-political interim council and then the 1974 constitution was reinstated. Several political parties which had gone into hiding re-emerged, including Sir Eric Gairy's GULP and Herbert Blaize's GNP. After considerable manoeuvring, an informal coalition of centre and left-of-centre parties resulted in the formation of the New National Party (NNP), led by Blaize. In the 1984 general election NNP won 14 of the 15 seats in the House of Representatives and Blaize became Prime Minister. The United States withdrew most of its forces by the end of 1983 and the remainder by July 1985. The merger of the three parties into the NNP proved to be not entirely satisfactory and doubts about Blaize's leadership were expressed, causing him to carry out a major cabinet reshuffle in February 1987. Early in 1989

Blaize relinquished the NNP leadership, and was succeeded by Keith Mitchell. He continued to lead the government, however, as Prime Minister.

GUATEMALA

Republic of Guatemala
Republica de Guatemala

Capital: Guatemala City

Social and economic data
Area: 108,890 km^2
Population: 8.600m*
Pop density per km^2: 79*
Literacy rate: 46%*
GDP: $11,130m*; per capita GDP: $1,294
Economy type: middle income
Labour force in agriculture: 54%

*1985

Ethnic composition
The population consists mainly of two ethnic groups, Indians and Ladinos. The word Ladino is used to describe all non-Indians, including Europeans, black Africans and mestizos. The Indians are descendants of the highland Mayas.

Religions
The great majority of the people are Christians, mostly Roman Catholics.

Political features
State type: emergent democratic
Date of state formation: 1839
Political structure: unitary
Executive: limited presidential
Assembly: one-chamber
Party structure: multi-party
Human rights rating: poor

Local and regional government
The country is divided into 22 departments, including Guatemala City, ranging in population from about 100,000 to 1.75 million, each administered by a governor appointed by the President.

Head of state and head of government
President Mario Vinicio Cerezo Arevalo, since 1986.

Political leaders since 1970
1970–74 Carlos Arana Osorio (MLN-Military), 1974–78 Kjell Laugerud Garcia (MLN-Military), 1978–82 Fernando Romeo Lucas Garcia (MLN-

Military), 1982–83 Efrain Rios Montt (Military), 1983–86 Oscar Humberto Mejia Victores (Military), 1986– Mario Vinicio Cerezo Arevalo (PDCG).

Political system

The 1985 constitution provides for a single-chamber National Assembly of 100 members, 75 elected directly by universal adult suffrage, by a simple plurality voting system, and the remaining 25 on the basis of a majoritarian method of the additional member system. They serve a five-year term. The President is also directly elected for a similar term. He appoints a cabinet and is assisted by a Vice-President. He is not eligible for re-election.

Political parties

There are nine political parties, the most significant being the Guatemalan Christian Democratic Party (PDCG), the Centre Party (UCN), the National Democratic Co-operation Party (PDCN), the Revolutionary Party (PR), the Movement of National Liberation (MLN) and the Democratic Institutional Party (PID).

The PDCG was founded in 1968. It is a Christian, centre-left party. The UCN dates from 1984 and is a centre party. The PDCN was formed in 1985 and has a centre-right orientation. The PR was originally founded in 1944 and reformed in 1957. It has a radical orientation. The MLN is an extreme right-wing party which dates from 1960. The PID is a moderate, conservative party which was formed in 1965.

Latest elections

In the 1985 presidential election the PDCG candidate, Mario Vinicio Cerezo Arevalo, won in a second round of voting, securing 68 per cent of the votes cast, the UCN candidate, Jorge Carpiuo Nicolle, winning the remaining 32 per cent.

In the 1985 elections for the National Congress the PDCG won an absolute majority over all other parties, with 51 of the 100 seats.

Political history

Guatemala obtained its independence successively from Spain, then Mexico and, in 1827, from the Federation of Central American States. It was then ruled by a succession of dictators until the presidency of Juan José Arevalo, in 1944, and his successor, Colonel Jacobo Arbenz. Their socialist administrations both followed programmes of reform, which included land appropriations but Arbenz's nationalisation of the plantations of the United Fruit Company, in 1954, so alarmed the United States government that it sponsored a revolution, led by Colonel Carlos Castillo Armas, who then assumed the presidency.

He was assassinated in 1963 and the army continued to rule until 1966. There was a brief return to constitutional government until the military returned, in 1970. The next ten years saw a spate of political violence, in which it was estimated that more than 50,000 people died. In the 1982 presidential election the government candidate won but his opponents complained that the election had been rigged and, before he could take office, there was a coup by a group of young, right-wing officers, who installed General Rios Montt as head of a three-man junta. He soon dissolved the junta, assumed the presidency, and embarked upon a policy of fighting corruption and ending violence. The anti-government guerrilla movement was, however, growing, and was countered by repressive measures by Montt, so that by the beginning of 1983 opposition to him was widespread. After several unsuccessful attempts to remove him, a coup, led by General Mejia Victores, was successful.

Mejia Victores declared an amnesty for the guerrillas, the ending of press censorship and the preparation of a new constitution. This was adopted in 1985 and in the elections which followed the Guatemalan Christian Democratic Party (PDCG) won a majority in the Congress as well as the presidency, Vinicio Cerezo becoming its first civilian President for 20 years. Despite Cerezo's attempts to increase democracy, Guatemala remains an extremely violent country, with numerous 'disappearances' of anti-government activists. In May 1989 an attempted coup against Cerezo was defeated by the army.

HAITI

Republic of Haiti
République d'Haiti

Capital: Port-au-Prince

Social and economic data
Area: 27,750 km^2
Population: 5.900m*
Pop density per km^2: 213*
Literacy rate: 35%*
GDP: $1,970m*; per capita GDP: $334
Economy type: low income
Labour force in agriculture: 57%

*1985

Ethnic composition
About 95 per cent of the population are of black African descent, the remainder being mulattos or Europeans.

Religions
About 80 per cent of the population follow Roman Catholicism, which is the official religion. Voodoo is also a folk religion.

Political features
State type: military authoritarian
Date of state formation: 1804
Political structure: unitary
Executive: military
Assembly: because the constitution is in a transitional state there is no elected assembly
Party structure: one-party
Human rights rating: poor

Local and regional government
The country is divided into nine departments, which are further subdivided into *arrondissements* and then communes. Departments are administered by appointed prefects and each commune has an elected mayor.

Head of state and head of government
Prosper Avril, since 1988.

Political leaders since 1970
1964–71 François Duvalier (National Unity Party), 1971–86 Jean-Claude Duvalier (PNP), 1986–88 Henri Namphey (Military), 1988– Prosper Avril (Military).

Political system
The constitution of 1950 was revised in 1957, 1964, 1971, 1983 and 1985 and then replaced with a new version in 1987. Between 1957 and 1986 the Duvalier family, father and then son, ruled Haiti with absolute power, maintaining their positions with the help of a private army. Although the constitution provided for an elected National Assembly, it had become a façade for the Duvaliers' own dictatorships.

The leader of the 1986 coup established a Governing Council, with himself as head but the future of democratic government in Haiti was again under test. Although a new constitution was introduced in 1987, providing for the sharing of executive power among a President, Prime Minister and two Houses of Congress, together with an independent judiciary, the congressional elections held in November 1987 and January 1988 were viewed by outside observers as largely fraudulent and the military seen as retaining considerable power behind the façade of the civilian government.

The civilian government which was restored at the beginning of 1988 was overthrown later in the year by the military, again casting doubt over Haiti's democratic future, despite the new regime's promises to establish 'an irreversible democracy'.

The 1987 constitution provides for a two-chamber assembly consisting of a Senate of 27 members and a Chamber of Deputies of 77 members, elected by universal adult suffrage through a simple plurality voting system, for a five-year term. There is also provision for a 'dual executive', with power being shared between a President, popularly elected for a five-year term, and a Prime Minister, appointed by the President on the basis of assembly support. The Prime Minister chooses a cabinet in consultation with the President.

Political parties
In the 1985 amendment to the constitution political parties were legalised, provided they conformed to strict guidelines, but only one registered, the National Progressive Party (PNP), which supported Duvalier policies. The National Progressive Democrats of Haiti were a group formed in the 1970s by Leslie Manigat, while exiled in Venezuela. Manigat returned to Haiti after the fall of the Duvalier regime and was elected President in 1988 but soon deposed by the army. Whether his party, or others, will play a role in Haiti's future is still a matter for speculation.

Latest elections
The presidential elections in 1987 and 1988 resulted in Leslie Manigat being elected with 50.2 per cent of the popular vote but the results were widely thought to be fraudulent.

The opposition parties claimed that assembly elections held concurrently with the 1988 presidential election were also fraudulent. The government claimed that the turnout was 35 per cent while the opposition alleged the true figure was 5 per cent.

Political history
Haiti became an independent state, after an uprising against French colonial rule, in 1804. There was constant friction between the African-descended Haitians and the mulattos, and between 1915 and 1924 the country's political instability brought a period of United States intervention and rule. In the 1940s and 1950s there was a series of coups, the last being in 1956, which resulted in Dr François Duvalier, a country physician, being elected President. After an encouraging start, the Duvalier administration degenerated into a personal dictatorship, maintained by a private army. In 1964 Duvalier, 'Papa Doc', cemented his position by amending the constitution to make himself Life President, with the power to nominate his son as his successor. On his death in 1971 Jean-Claude Duvalier therefore came to the presidency at the age of 19 and soon acquired the name of 'Baby Doc'. Although the young Duvalier repeatedly promised a return to democratic politics and his rule was judged to be less despotic than that of his father, there was little real change.

In 1985 Duvalier announced a further reform of the constitution, including the legalisation of political parties and the eventual appointment of a Prime Minister, but these were not enough to prevent his overthrow in 1986. The task of establishing democratic government fell to the new regime led by Lieutenant-General Henri Namphey. In 1987 a new constitution was adopted, providing for democratic government and an independent judiciary. However congressional elections in November 1987 had to be re-run in January 1988 because of widespread fraud and the conduct of the subsequent elections was deemed by outside observers to be little better. Leslie Manigat was elected President but was ousted in a military coup, led by General Prosper Avril, eight months later. Despite Avril's earlier support for the Duvalier regime, he installed a largely civilian government and said he wanted to be known as the man who 'saved Haiti from anarchy and dictatorship'. An attempted coup against Avril, in April 1989, was defeated within a week.

HONDURAS

Republic of Honduras
Republica de Honduras

Capital: Tegucigalpa

Social and economic data
Area: 112,090 km^2
Population: 4.600m*

Pop density per km^2: 41*
Literacy rate: 57%*
GDP: $3,362m*; per capita GDP: $731
Economy type: low income
Labour force in agriculture: 57%

*1985

Ethnic composition
About 90 per cent of the population are of mixed Indian and Spanish descent and known as ladinos, or mestizos.

There are also Salvadoran, Guatemalan, American and European minorities.

Religions
Most of the population are Roman Catholics, but other religions are tolerated.

Political features
State type: emergent democratic
Date of state formation: 1838
Political structure: unitary
Executive: limited presidential
Assembly: one-chamber
Party structure: two-party
Human rights rating: poor

Local and regional government
The country is divided into 18 departments which are further subdivided into municipalities. The muncipalities have councils elected at the same time and in the same way as the National Assembly.

Head of state and head of government
José Simeon Azeona del Hoyo, since 1986.

Political leaders since 1970
1965–71 Oswaldo Lopez Arellano (PLH), 1971–72 Ramon Ernesto Cruz Ucles (PN), 1972–74 Oswaldo Lopez Arellano (PLH), 1974–78 Juan Melgar Castro (Military), 1978–80 Policarpo Paz Garcia (Military), 1980–84 Roberto Suazo Cordova (PLH), 1984–86 Walter Lopez Reyes (Military), 1986– José Simeon Azeona del Hoyo (PLH).

Political system
The 1982 constitution, which underwent a major revision in 1985, provides for the election of a President, who is both head of state and head of government, by universal adult suffrage for a four-year term. A single-chamber National Assembly of 134 members is elected, through a party list system of proportional representation, for a similar term. The President may not serve two terms in succession.

Political parties
There are seven political parties some of which unite at times to form broad alliances for electoral purposes. The two most significant are the Liberal Party of Honduras (PLH) and the National Party (PN).

The PLH appeared in its present form in 1980 but its origins go back to the 1890s. It has a number of internal factions which sometimes oppose the leadership. It has a centre-left orientation.

The PN was formed in 1902, and underwent a major reorganisation in 1916. It is a traditional right-wing party and, like the PLH, it too has its own internal factions.

Latest elections

In the 1985 presidential election there were nine candidates. It was won by the PLH, with 51 per cent of the votes, the PN obtaining 45 per cent. The leading PLH candidate was therefore elected, under the terms of the constitution, even though the leading PN candidate personally secured the most votes.

In the 1985 National Assembly elections PLH won 67 of the 134 seats and PN 63.

Political history

After being a Spanish possession from the sixteenth century, Honduras achieved full independence in 1838. From 1939 to 1949 it was under the dictatorship of the leader of the National Party (PN). Then the government constantly changed hands in a series of military coups, until the return of civilian rule in 1980. The army, however, retained control of security and was able to veto cabinet appointments. Although the 1981 general election was won by the PLH and its leader, Dr Roberto Suazo, became President, real power was still in the hands of General Gustavo Alvarez, the commander-in-chief of the army, who, in 1982, managed to secure an amendment to the constitution which reduced government control over the armed forces. General Alvarez was virtually in charge of foreign policy, working closely with the United States and agreeing, in 1983, to the establishment of naval and air bases in Honduras. The American CIA was also active in providing assistance to Nicaraguan counter-revolutionaries based in Honduras.

In 1984 Alvarez was ousted by a group of junior officers and Honduras's close relationship with the United States came under review. In the same year divisions arose within the PLH over selection procedures for the party's presidential candidates and two years later the electoral law was changed. In the elections of that year Suazo was not eligible to stand for the presidency and the main PLH candidate was José Azeona. Although the PN nominee won most votes, the revised constitution made Azeona the eventual winner.

JAMAICA

Capital: Kingston

Social and economic data

Area: 11,420 km^2
Population: 2.366m*
Pop density per km^2: 207*
Literacy rate: 96%*

GDP: $2,200m*; per capita GDP: $930
Economy type: middle income
Labour force in agriculture: 27%

*1985

Ethnic composition
Nearly 80 per cent of the population are of pure African descent and about 15 per cent of mixed African-European origins. There are also Chinese, Indian and European minorities.

Religions
The great majority of people are Christians, the largest number being Anglicans. There is also a large Rastafarian community.

Political features
State type: liberal democratic
Date of state formation: 1962
Political structure: unitary
Executive: parliamentary
Assembly: one-chamber
Party structure: two-party
Human rights rating: 77%

Local and regional government
For administrative purposes, the country is divided into 14 parishes, each with an elected council.

Head of state
Queen Elizabeth II, represented by Governor-General Sir Florizel Augustus Glasspole, since 1973.

Head of government
Prime Minister Michael Manley, since 1989.

Political leaders since 1970
1967–72 Hugh Shearer (JLP), 1972–80 Michael Manley (PNP), 1980–89 Edward P. G. Seaga (JLP), 1989– Michael Manley (PNP).

Political system
The constitution came into force on independence in 1962. It follows closely the unwritten British model, with a resident constitutional head of state, in the shape of the Governor-General, representing the monarch. He appoints a Prime Minister and cabinet, collectively responsible to the assembly. This consists of two chambers, an appointed, 21-member Senate and a 60-member elected House of Representatives. Thirteen of the senators are appointed on the advice of the Prime Minister and eight on the advice of the leader of the opposition. Members of the House are elected by universal adult suffrage, through a simple plurality voting system, for a five-year term. It is subject to dissolution within that period.

Political parties

There are six political parties. The two which have been the main adversaries in the political contest since independence, are the Jamaica Labour Party (JLP) and the People's National Party (PNP).

The JLP was founded by Sir Alexander Bustamante in 1943, as the political wing of the Bustama Industrial Trade Union. It has a moderate, centrist orientation, and supports free enterprise in a mixed economy and co-operation with the United States.

The PNP was formed in 1938 by Norman Manley. It has a left-of-centre orientation and believes in the pursuit of socialist principles within a self-sufficient, national framework, although recently there has been some moderation of that stance.

Latest elections

In the 1989 House of Representative elections the results were as follows:

	% Vote	*Seats*
PNP	55.8	45
JLP	44.1	15
Independents	0.1	—

Political history

Jamaica was a British colony from 1655 until it was granted internal self-government in 1959 and then full independence within the Commonwealth in 1962. The two leading political figures in the early days of independence were Sir Alexander Bustamante and Norman Manley. Bustamante's JLP won the 1962 election and was again successful in 1967 under Bustamante's successor, Hugh Shearer. Then the PNP, under Norman Manley's son Michael, came into office in 1972.

Michael Manley was a strong advocate of social reform and economic independence from the developed world. Despite high unemployment, his party was returned to power in 1976 with an increased majority but by 1980 the economic position had worsened and, rejecting the conditions attached to an IMF loan, Manley sought support for his policies of economic self-reliance.

The 1980 general election campaign was extremely violent, despite calls by Manley and the leader of the JLP, Edward Seaga, for moderation. The outcome was a surprisingly decisive victory for the JLP. It won 51 of the 60 seats in the House of Representatives. Seaga thus received a mandate for a renewal of links with the United States and an emphasis on free enterprise. He severed diplomatic links with Cuba in 1981.

In 1983 Seaga called an early, snap election, with the opposition claiming they had been given insufficient time to nominate their candidates. On this occasion the JLP won all 60 seats. There were violent demonstrations when the new parliament was inaugurated and the PNP said it would continue its opposition outside the parliamentary arena.

In the 1989 general election Michael Manley's PNP won a landslide victory, after which Manley hastened to assure the nation and the world that he intended to pursue moderate economic policies and to establish good relations with the United States.

MEXICO

United States of Mexico
Estados Unidos Mexicanos

Capital: Mexico City

Social and economic data
Area: 1,972,550 km^2
Population: 81.700m*
Pop density per km^2: 41*
Literacy rate: 83%*
GDP: $177,456m*; per capita GDP: $2,172
Economy type: middle income
Labour force in agriculture: 26%

*1985

Ethnic composition
About 60 per cent of the population are mestizos, of Spanish-American and American-Indian parentage, about 30 per cent are Indians, and the rest are mainly of European origin.

Religions
About 96 per cent of the population are Roman Catholics. There is also a Protestant minority. Roman Catholicism was the established religion until 1857 and it is still under a measure of state control.

Political features
State type: liberal democratic
Date of state formation: 1821
Political structure: federal
Executive: limited presidential
Assembly: two-chamber
Party structure: multi-party
Human rights rating: 62%

Local and regional government
Mexico is a federal republic of 31 states and a federal district, based on Mexico City. It displays several of the features of the United States federal system, with each state having its own governor and single-chamber assembly, elected for six-year and three-year terms respectively. In broad terms, the powers of the federal government are set out in the federal constitution and the residue remains with the states. Within the states there are over 2,000 municipalities, each with an elected council.

Head of state and head of government
President Carlos Salinas de Gortari, since 1988.

Political leaders since 1970
1970–76 Luis Echeverria Alvarez (PRI), 1976–82 José Lopez Portillo (PRI), 1982–88 Miguel de la Madrid Hurtado (PRI), 1988– Carlos Salinas de Gortari.

Political system

The constitution dates from 1917, following the 1910 revolution which proclaimed a drastic change in land ownership, new labour legislation and a reduction in the powers of the Roman Catholic Church. Since then it has been amended several times but its essential provisions remain. It provides for an executive President, who is both head of state and head of government, and a two-chamber National Congress of Senate and Chamber of Deputies, broadly based on the United States model.

The President is directly elected for a six-year term and he chooses his own cabinet. The Senate has 64 members, each state and the Federal District being represented by two senators. The Chamber has 400 members, 300 representing single-member constituencies and 100 elected on a majoritarian, additional-member system of voting, intended to give due weight to the minority parties. All members of Congress are elected by universal adult suffrage.

Political parties

Under the constitution, as amended in 1977, political parties have to be registered and meet certain criteria if they wish to operate. There are currently 13 parties, the most significant being the Institutional Revolutionary Party (PRI), the National Action Party (PAN), the Socialist Workers' Party (PST), the Mexican Unified Socialist Party (PSUM), the Mexican Democratic Party (PDM), the Popular Socialist Party (PPS) and the Authentic Party of the Mexican Revolution (PARM).

The PRI was formed in 1929 as the natural succesor to the parties of the revolutionary period of Mexico's history and then called the National Revolutionary Party. It was redesignated as the Mexican Revolutionary Party in 1938. It is a broad-based party which has been a dominant force in Mexican politics for many years. It has a moderate, left-wing orientation.

PAN was formed in 1939. It now has about 500,000 members and its orientation is moderate, Christian socialist.

PST dates from 1985 and is a left-wing, Trotskyist party.

PSUM was formed in 1981 and is an umbrella organisation for five left-wing groupings. Its orientation is nationalistic and socialist.

PDM was founded in 1971 and has a left-of-centre, democratic socialist orientation.

PPS dates from 1948 and is a left-wing, Marxist-Leninist party.

PARM was founded in 1954 with the object of keeping alive the ideology of the Mexican constitution of 1917.

For the 1988 congressional elections five of the parties in opposition to the PRI, led by PARM, formed the National Democratic Front (FDM).

Latest elections

In the 1988 presidential election the PRI candidate, Carlos Salinas de Gortari, won with 50.36 per cent of the vote, amid claims of election frauds. The electoral college subsequently reviewed the results and declared the election of Salinas to be valid.

In the 1988 Chamber of Deputies elections the PRI won 176 seats, PAN 32 and FDM 20.

Political history

Mexico became a Spanish colonial possession in the sixteenth century but years of economic exploitation and harsh repression created a vigorous movement for independence. This was eventually achieved in 1821. Mexico's early history as an independent nation was marked by civil and foreign wars. In 1917 it adopted a new constitution, designed to establish a permanent form of democratic government. With some amendments, that constitution has lasted until the present day.

The broadly based Institutional Revolutionary Party (PRI) has dominated Mexican politics since the 1920s, pursuing largely moderate, left-of-centre policies. Its popularity has been damaged in recent years by the country's poor economic performance and rising international debts. However, despite criticisms from vested interest groups, such as the trade unions and the Church, the PRI scored a clear win over all other parties in the 1985 elections, with no serious challenger in evidence. Soon afterwards the government's problems were exacerbated by a massive earthquake in Mexico City, which caused thousands of deaths and made hundreds of thousands of people homeless.

Mexico has been strongly influenced by its proximity to the United States. Its constitution, for example, reflects many aspects of that of its more powerful neighbour. At times, however, the Mexican government has been strongly critical of US policy in Central America and, as a member, with Colombia, Panama and Venezuela, of the Contadora Group, has argued strongly for the withdrawal of all foreign advisers from the region.

The economic situation worsened so much in the 1980s that the Mexican government, after prolonged negotiations, felt obliged, in 1986, to sign an agreement with the International Monetary Fund (IMF) which would provide loans to keep the country solvent for at least the next few years.

In the 1988 presidential election the PRI candidate, Carlos Salinas, won by a small margin amid claims of election frauds. The PRI also retained its majority in the 1988 assembly elections.

NICARAGUA

Republic of Nicaragua
Republica de Nicaragua

Capital: Managua

Social and economic data
Area: 130,000 km^2
Population: 3.300m*
Pop density per km^2: 25*
Literacy rate: 57%*
GDP: $3,800m*; per capita GDP: $1,152
Economy type: middle income
Labour force in agriculture: 45%

*1985

Ethnic composition
Over 70 per cent of the population are of mixed Indian, Spanish and African blood. About 9 per cent are pure Africans and 5 per cent pure Indians.

Religions
All religions are tolerated. There are about 2 million Roman Catholics and a strong following of the Protestant Moravian Church, particularly along the Atlantic coast.

Political features
State type: emergent democratic
Date of state formation: 1838
Political structure: unitary
Executive: limited presidential
Assembly: one-chamber
Party structure: multi-party
Human rights rating: poor

Local and regional government
The country is divided into 16 departments, ranging in population from about 30,000 to over 800,000. Below the department level are municipalities, with elected councils, but limited powers.

Head of state and head of government
President Daniel Ortega Saavedra, since 1985.

Political leaders since 1970
1967–79 Anastasio Somoza Debayle (Military), 1979–85 Junta (FSLN), 1985– Daniel Ortega Saavedra (FSLN).

Political system
The 1974 constitution was suspended after a coup in 1979 which established a revolutionary junta. It immediately issued a 'Statute of Rights and Guarantees' and appointed a Council of State as an interim measure prior to an elected National Assembly and, eventually, the new constitution came into effect on 10 January 1987. The 96-member National Constituent Assembly is elected, by universal adult suffrage, through a party list system of proportional representation, for a six-year term. The President, popularly elected, also serves for six years, with the assistance of a Vice-President and an appointed cabinet.

Political parties
There are now 15 political parties operating, the four most significant being the Sandinista National Liberation Front (FSLN), the Democratic Conservative Party (PCD), the Independent Liberal Party (PLI) and the Popular Social Christian Party (PPSC).

The FSLN was founded in 1960 to pursue a guerrilla struggle against the ruling Somoza regime. Since 1979 it has been the principal government party. It is a Marxist-Leninist grouping.

The PCD was formed in 1979 originally as an anti-Somoza splinter group. It is a centre party.

The PLI is another anti-Somoza grouping which dates from 1944. It has a moderate, centre-left orientation.

The PPSC was formed in 1976 by members of the Social Christian Party (PSCN). It is a moderate, Christian socialist party.

Latest elections

In the 1984 presidential election the FSLN candidate, Daniel Ortega, was elected with 66.9 per cent of the popular vote, his nearest rival, the PCD candidate, Clemente Guido, winning 14.0 per cent.

In the 1984 assembly elections the seats won were as follows:

FSLN	61
PCD	14
PLI	9
PPSC	6
Other parties	6

Political history

Nicaragua achieved full independence from Spanish rule in 1838. In 1912, at the Nicaraguan government's request, the United States established military bases in the country but their presence was opposed by a guerrilla group, led by Augusto Cesar Sandino. The United States withdrew its forces in 1933 but not before it had established and trained a National Guard, commanded by a trusted nominee, General Anastasio Somoza.

Sandino was assassinated in 1934, reputedly on Somoza's orders, but some of his followers continued their guerrilla activity on a small scale. The Somoza family began a near-dictatorial rule which was to last for over 40 years. During this time they developed wide business interests and amassed a huge personal fortune. General Anastasio Somoza was elected President in 1936 and stayed in office until his assassination in 1956 when he was succeeded by his son, Luis. In 1962 the left-wing Sandinista National Liberation Front (FSLN), named after the former guerrilla leader, was formed with the object of overthrowing the Somozas by revolution. This was not to happen, however for some 17 years. Luis Somoza was followed by his brother, Anastasio, who was to head an even more notorious regime. In 1979, after considerable violence and loss of life, Somoza was ousted and fled the country.

The FSLN established a provisional Junta of National Reconstruction led by Daniel Ortega, published a Statute, guaranteeing civil rights, and appointed a Council of State, prior to an elected National Assembly and, later, a new constitution.

Nicaragua's relations with the United States deteriorated rapidly with the election of Ronald Reagan. He froze the package of economic assistance arranged by his predecessor, Jimmy Carter, alleging that the Sandinista government was supporting attempts to overthrow the administration in El Salvador. In March 1982 the Nicaraguan government declared a state of emergency in the wake of attacks on bridges and petroleum installations. The Reagan administration embarked on a policy of destabilising the Sandinista government by actively supporting the counter-revolutionary forces (the 'Contras') and by covert CIA operations to undermine the economy. In February 1985 President Reagan denounced Ortega's regime, saying that his objective was to 'remove it in the sense of its present structure'.

A Central American Peace Agreement, instigated by President Oscar Arias of Costa Rica, was signed in Guatemala by leaders of Nicaragua, El Salvador, Guatemala, Honduras and Costa Rica in August 1987 but it failed to halt the fighting. In January 1988, however, President Ortega instituted direct talks with the rebels and the US Congress refused to vote additional military aid to them. In October 1988 President Reagan announced that he would be seeking no more aid for the Contras.

In February 1989 the Presidents of Guatemala, El Salvador, Honduras and Costa Rica agreed to disarm the Sandinista rebels and Ortega agreed to hold new elections in February 1990 and to restore civil rights to everyone. In July 1989 US President Bush sent a clear message to the Contra rebels to concentrate their efforts on political, rather than violent, opposition.

PANAMA

Republic of Panama
Republica de Panama

Capital: Panama City

Social and economic data

Area: 77,080 km^2
Population: 2.227m*
Pop density per km^2: 29*
Literacy rate: 86%*
GDP: $4,881m*; per capita GDP: $2,192
Economy type: middle income
Labour force in agriculture: N/A

*1985

Ethnic composition

About 70 per cent of the population are mestizos, of Spanish-American and American-Indian parentage, and are called Panamenos. About 14 per cent are West Indian, 10 per cent white American or European and 6 per cent Indian.

Religions

Most of the population are Roman Catholics and Roman Catholicism is a quasi-state religion. There are also Protestant and Jewish minorities.

Political features

State type: military authoritarian
Date of state formation: 1903
Political structure: unitary
Executive: military
Assembly: one-chamber
Party structure: multi-party
Human rights rating: 79%

Local and regional government

The country is divided into nine provinces and three autonomous Indian reservations. Each province has a governor, appointed by the President.

The provinces are further subdivided into districts, each with its own mayor.

Head of state and head of government
President Manuel Solis Palma, since 1988.

Political leaders since 1970
1968–78 Omar Torrijos Herrera (Military), 1978–82 Aristedes Royo Sanchez (Effective Military), 1982–84 Ricardo de la Espriella (Effective Military), 1984–85 Ardito Barletta (Effective Military), 1985–88 Eric Arturo Delvalle (Effective Military), 1988– Manuel Solis Palma (Effective Military).

Political system
The constitution underwent a major revision in 1983, when a new, single-chamber Legislative Assembly of 67 members, elected by universal adult suffrage, through a simple plurality voting system, for a five-year term, was created. The President is elected in the same way for a similar period of office. He is assisted by two elected Vice-Presidents and an appointed cabinet.

Despite the trappings of democratic government, the military have been the ruling force, sometimes overtly, but often behind the scenes, for more than 20 years, formerly under the control of General Torrijos and latterly General Noriega.

Political parties
There are currently eleven political organisations, the most significant being represented in the Assembly by two coalitions, National Democratic Union (UNADE) and the Democratic Opposition Alliance (ADO).

The leading parties in UNADE are the Democratic Revolutionary Party (PRD), the Labour Party (PALA) and the Republican Party (PR). The PRD was founded in 1979 by supporters of General Torrijos and the army, headed by General Antonio Noriega, is now the force behind it. Both the PALA and the PR are 1980s groups. UNADE has a strong, right-wing orientation.

The three main groups within ADO are the National Liberal Republican Movement (MOLIRENA), the Authentic Panama Party (PPA) and the Christian Democratic Party (PDC). MOLIRENA first registered in 1981. The PPA was formed in 1938 as an anti-communist party. The PDC was formed in 1960 and grew out of a student movement. The ADO has a generally moderate, centre-left orientation.

Latest elections
In the 1984 presidential election the PRD candidate, Nicolas Ardito Barletta, was elected, with 300,748 votes. His nearest rival, the PPA candidate Arnulfo Arias Madrid, obtained 299,035 votes. In 1985 Barletta resigned and was succeeded by Arturo Delvalle and in 1988 the Assembly replaced him with Solis Palma.

The May 1989 Assembly elections were described by observers as totally fraudulent and subsequently declared invalid by General Noriega.

Political history

Panama, with the help of the United States, achieved full independence in 1903. The US support was a form of enlightened self-interest because, at the same time, it bought the rights to build the Panama Canal, which was eventually opened in 1914. Under the original 1903 treaty the United States was given control of a ten-mile-wide strip of territory, known as the Canal Zone, in perpetuity. At the same time, Panama was guaranteed US protection and an annuity. In 1939 Panama's protectorate status was ended by mutual agreement, and in 1974 the two countries agreed to negotiate an eventual complete transfer of the canal to Panama, despite opposition from the US Congress.

In 1977 two treaties were signed by Panama's President, Omar Torrijos Herrera and the US President, Jimmy Carter. One transferred the canal and the other guaranteed its subsequent neutrality. A referendum in Panama approved the change but the US Senate demanded amendments to the effect that, after the transfer only Panamanian forces would be stationed in the zone, and that the United States would have the right to use force to keep the canal open if it became obstructed. On this revised basis, the two treaties were finally approved.

The 1980s saw a deterioration in the state of Panama's economy, with opposition to the austerity measures which the government introduced to try to halt the decline. In the 1984 elections, after a very close result, Dr Nicolas Ardito Barletta, the Democratic Revolutionary Party (PRD) candidate was declared the winner, but in 1985 he resigned, amid speculation that he had been forced to by the Commander of the National Guard, General Noriega. Relations between Panama and the United States deteriorated with the departure of President Barletta, the Reagan administration announcing a cut in its financial aid. Barletta was succeeded by Eric Arturo Delvalle, who immediately set about seeking a national consensus on economic policy. US criticism continued, Noriega being accused of drug trafficking. In February 1988 President Delvalle attempted to dismiss Noriega as head of the armed forces and was immediately voted out of office by the National Assembly and replaced by the former education minister, Manuel Solis Palma. Delvalle's downfall was seen as further evidence of Noriega's power and influence. US support for the former President was also seen as a reason for his demise. The US government's immediate reaction was to increase its forces in the canal zone, as a show of military strength, and to put economic pressure on Panama by freezing its assets in the United States.

With mounting unrest in the country, a group of Panamanian officers, led by police chief Leonidas Macias, attempted a coup but this was quickly foiled by troops loyal to Noriega. With the failed coup, the US administration then attempted to negotiate the general's departure by offering to drop federal charges against him for drug trafficking. The attempted deal, however, had the effect of discrediting the Reagan administration and strengthening support for Noriega.

In May 1989 elections for the Legislative Assembly were clearly fraudulent and eventually declared invalid. The United States put pressure on Noriega to resign and strengthened its Canal Zone garrison. These moves seemed to strengthen, rather than weaken, Noriega's position.

ST CHRISTOPHER (ST KITTS) AND NEVIS

Capital: Basseterre

Social and economic data
Area: 270 km^2
Population: 0.040m*
Pop density per km^2: 148*
Literacy rate: 98%*
GDP: $65m*; per capita GDP: $1,625
Economy type: middle income
Labour force in agriculture: N/A

*1985

Ethnic composition
The population is almost entirely of African descent.

Religions
The majority of people are members of the Anglican Church.

Political features
State type: liberal democratic
Date of state formation: 1983
Political structure: federal
Executive: parliamentary
Assembly: one-chamber
Party structure: two-party
Human rights rating: N/A

Local and regional government
Despite the smallness of the land area and population, a limited federal system operates. Nevis island has its own Assembly, of five elected and three nominated members, a Prime Minister and cabinet and a Deputy Governor-General representing the monarch.

The two islands are divided into parishes, for administrative purposes, St Kitts having nine and Nevis five.

Head of state
Queen Elizabeth II, represented by Governor-General Sir Clement Arrindell, since 1983.

Head of government
Prime Minister Dr Kennedy Alphonse Simmonds, since 1980.

Political leaders since 1970
1967–78 Robert Bradshaw (Labour), 1978–79 Paul Southwell (Labour), 1979–80 Lee L. Moore (Labour), 1980– Kennedy Alphonse Simmonds (PAM-NRP coalition).

Political system
The islands of St Christopher, often called St Kitts, and Nevis are a Federation constituting an independent state within the Commonwealth.

Although the total population is only about 40,000 it has, in effect, a federal constitution which dates from independence in 1983 and provides for a parliamentary system for the two islands, on the lines of that of the United Kingdom. The Governor-General is the formal head of state, representing the monarch.

There is a single-chamber National Assembly of 14 members, eleven elected by universal adult suffrage, through a simple plurality voting system, and three appointed by the Governor-General, two on the advice of the Prime Minister and one on the advice of the Leader of the Opposition. The Governor-General also appoints the Prime Minister and cabinet who are drawn from and responsible to the Assembly. As in the United Kingdom, the leader of the second largest party in the Assembly is the official Leader of the Opposition.

Political parties

There are currently four political parties, the three most significant being the People's Action Movement (PAM), the Nevis Reformation Party (NRP) and the Labour Party.

The PAM was formed in 1965 in opposition to the Labour Party. It has a centre-right orientation.

The NRP was created in 1970 as the focus of a movement to secure the separation of Nevis from St Kitts.

The Labour Party is the country's oldest political organisation, dating back to the Workers' League of 1932. It is a moderate, left-of-centre party.

Latest elections

In the 1989 general election PAM won six, NRP two and the Labour Party two National Assembly seats. The other was won by a Nevis breakaway grouping.

Political history

St Christopher was the first British colony in the West Indies, dating back to 1623, and Nevis was settled very soon afterwards. Anguilla was joined to the two islands in 1816 and after the First World War a campaign began for their independence. The Labour Party was formed in 1932 as the vanguard of the independence movement. St Christopher-Nevis-Anguilla joined the West Indies Federation and remained in membership until its dissolution in 1962. There was an abortive attempt to form a smaller East Caribbean Federation and then the three islands became Associated States, with internal self-government, within the Commonwealth, in 1967.

Robert Bradshaw, leader of the Labour Party, became the first Prime Minister and was re-elected in 1971 and 1975. In 1970 the NRP was formed, calling for separation for Nevis, and the following year Anguilla, disagreeing with the government in St Christopher, chose to return to being a British dependency. Bradshaw died in 1978 and was succeeded by his deputy, Paul Southwell but he, too, died the following year to be replaced by Lee L. Moore.

The 1980 general election produced a 'hung' Assembly and, although Labour won more than 50 per cent of the popular vote, a PAM-NRP coalition government was formed, with the PAM leader, Dr Kennedy A. Simmonds, as Prime Minister. Full independence was scheduled for 1983 and the Labour Party argued there there should be a general election before then but this was rejected by the government, in the face of sometimes violent opposition.

On 1 September 1983 St Christopher and Nevis became a fully independent federal state, within the Commonwealth, with an opportunity for Nevis to secede, under certain conditions, being written into the constitution. In the 1984 general election the PAM-NRP coalition was decisively returned to office, and in 1989 the Kennedy Simmonds government was re-elected for a third consecutive term.

ST LUCIA

Capital: Castries

Social and economic data
Area: 620 km^2
Population: 0.123m*
Pop density per km^2: 198*
Literacy rate: 82%*
GDP: $160m*; per capita GDP: $1,301
Economy type: middle income
Labour force in agriculture: N/A

*1985

Ethnic composition
The great majority of the population are of African descent.

Religions
Eighty-two per cent of people are Roman Catholics. The rest belong mainly to the Anglican or other Protestant Churches.

Political features
State type: liberal democratic
Date of state formation: 1979
Political structure: unitary
Executive: parliamentary
Assembly: two-chamber
Party structure: two-party
Human rights rating: N/A

Local and regional government
The country is divided into 16 parishes, each representing a town or village. They have partly elected and partly appointed councils.

Head of state
Queen Elizabeth II, represented by Governor-General Sir Vincent Floissac, since 1987.

Head of government
Prime Minister John G. M. Compton, since 1975.

Political leaders since 1970

1964–79 John Compton (UWP), 1979–81 Allan Louisy (SLP), 1981–82 Winston Cenac (SLP), 1982– John Compton (UWP).

Political system

The constitution dates from independence in 1979. It provides for a constitutional monarchy with a parliamentary system based broadly on that of the United Kingdom. There is a two-chamber parliament, comprising a Senate, of eleven appointed members, and a House of Assembly, of 17 members, elected from single-member constituencies by universal adult suffrage, through a simple plurality system of voting. Members of the Senate are appointed by the Governor-General, six on the advice of the Prime Minister, three on the advice of the Leader of the Opposition, and two after wider consultation. Parliament has a life of five years but is subject to dissolution within that period. The Governor-General appoints a Prime Minister and cabinet on the basis of House of Assembly support. They are all drawn from and responsible to it. The leader of the party with the second highest number of seats in the House is the official Leader of the Opposition.

Political parties

There are three active political parties, the United Workers' Party (UWP), the St Lucia Labour Party (SLP) and the Progressive Labour Party (PLP).

The UWP was founded in 1964, the SLP developed from the Workers' Union in the late 1940s and the PLP was formed in 1981 by SLP dissidents. All three parties have a moderate, left-of-centre orientation.

Latest elections

The results of the 1987 general election were as follows:

	% Votes	*House of Assembly Seats*
UWP	53.18	9
SLP	40.80	8

Political history

St Lucia was a British colony within the Windward Islands federal system until 1960. The federal system was ended and, in 1967, it acquired internal self-government as a West Indies Associated State. The leader of the United Workers' Party (UWP), John Compton, became Prime Minister with the St Lucia Labour Party (SLP) forming the opposition. In 1975 the Associated States agreed to seek independence separately and, in February 1979, after prolonged negotiations, St Lucia achieved full independence within the Commonwealth, with Compton as Prime Minister.

Later that year the SLP returned to power under its leader, Allan Louisy, but a split developed within the party and in 1981 Louisy was forced to resign, being replaced by the Attorney-General, Winston Cenac. Soon afterwards George Odlum, who had been Louisy's deputy, left, with two other SLP members, to form a new party, the Progressive Labour Party (PLP). For the next year the Cenac government had to fight off calls for a change of government which culminated in a general strike. Cenac eventually resigned and in the general election held in May 1982 the UWP won a decisive victory enabling John Compton to return as Prime Minister. In new elections, in April 1987, however, Compton's UWP was only narrowly returned by a 9:8 majority over the SLP.

ST VINCENT AND THE GRENADINES

Capital: Kingstown

Social and economic data
Area: 390 km^2
Population: 0.103m*
Pop density per km^2: 264*
Literacy rate: 96%*
GDP: $103m*; per capita GDP: $1,000
Economy type: middle income
Labour force in agriculture: 50%

*1985

Ethnic composition
Most of the original, indigenous Caribs have disappeared and the population is now largely of African origin.

Religions
The great majority of people are Christian: Anglicans, Methodists or Roman Catholics, in that order of size.

Political features
State type: liberal democratic
Date of state formation: 1979
Political structure: unitary
Executive: parliamentary
Assembly: one-chamber
Party structure: two-party
Human rights rating: N/A

Local and regional government
For administrative purposes, the country is divided into five parishes with 13 divisions within them.

Head of state
Queen Elizabeth II, represented by Governor-General Sir Joseph Lambert Eustace, since 1985.

Head of government
Prime Minister James Mitchell, since 1984.

Political leaders since 1970
1967–72 Milton Cato (SVLP), 1972–74 James Mitchell (PPP), 1974–79 Milton Cato (SVLP-PPP coalition), 1979–84 Milton Cato (SVLP), 1984– James Mitchell (NDP).

Political system
The constitution dates from independence in 1979. It provides for a constitutional monarchy with a parliamentary system of government based in several respects on that in the United Kingdom, a resident Governor-General representing the monarch. There is a single-chamber House of Assembly, with 19 members, of whom 13 are elected by universal adult suffrage, through a simple plurality voting system, four appointed by the Governor-General on the advice of the Prime Minister and two on the advice of the Leader of the Opposition. The Assembly has a life of five years but is subject to dissolution within that time. The Governor-General appoints a Prime Minister and cabinet who are drawn from and responsible to the Assembly. The leader of the party with the second largest number of seats in the Assembly is the official Leader of the Opposition.

Political parties
There are nine political parties, the two most significant being the New Democratic Party (NDP) and the St Vincent Labour Party (SVLP).

The NDP was formed in 1975 by James Mitchell, a former SVLP member and Prime Minister. The SVLP dates from 1955. Both parties have a moderate, left-of-centre orientation.

Latest elections
In the 1989 general election the NDP won all 13 Assembly seats in a landslide victory and James Mitchell continued as Prime Minister.

Political history
Formerly a British colony and collectively known as St Vincent, the islands were part of the West Indies Federation until it was dissolved in 1962. They then acquired internal self-government in 1969 as an Associated State, within the Commonwealth. They achieved full independence, still within the Commonwealth, as St Vincent and the Grenadines, in October 1979.

Until the 1980s two political parties dominated politics in the islands, the St Vincent Labour Party (SVLP) and the People's Political Party (PPP). Milton Cato, SVLP leader, was Prime Minister at independence but his leadership was challenged in 1981 when a decline in the economy and his attempts to introduce new industrial relations legislation resulted in a general strike. Cato survived mainly because of divisions in the opposition parties and in 1984, hoping to take advantage of these divisions, he called an early general election. The New Democratic Party (NDP), which had been formed by an SVLP defector and former Prime Minister, James Mitchell, won a surprising victory, which was confirmed in 1989 when the NDP won all 13 elective seats.

TRINIDAD AND TOBAGO

Republic of Trinidad and Tobago

Capital: Port of Spain

Social and economic data
Area: 5,130 km^2
Population: 1.204m*
Pop density per km^2: 234*
Literacy rate: 95%*
GDP: $7,404m*; per capita GDP: $6,150
Economy type: middle income
Labour force in agriculture: 9%

*1985

Ethnic composition
There are two main ethnic groups, one comprising Africans, who were originally brought in as slaves, and the other East Indians, who came to the country as workers from India. There are also minorities of Europeans, Afro-Europeans and Chinese. The original Carib population has largely disappeared.

Religions
About 34 per cent of the people are Roman Catholics, about 25 per cent Hindus, about 15 per cent Anglicans and about 6 per cent Muslims.

Political features
State type: liberal democratic
Date of state formation: 1962
Political structure: unitary
Executive: parliamentary
Assembly: two-chamber
Party structure: two-party
Human rights rating: 79%

Local and regional government
The country is divided into four self-governing cities, six counties and the semi-autonomous island of Tobago. The local government system displays some of the features of the pre-1970s English system, with elected councillors and aldermen, politically responsible for the provision of local services.

Head of state
President Noor Hassanali, since 1987.

Head of government
Prime Minister Arthur Napoleon (Ray) Robinson, since 1986.

Political leaders since 1970
1967–81 Eric Williams (PNM), 1981–86 George Chambers (PNM), 1986– Arthur Robinson (NAR).

Political system

Trinidad and Tobago is an independent republic within the Commonwealth. The 1976 constitution provides for a President, who is a constitutional head of state, and a two-chamber assembly, consisting of a Senate of 31 members and a House of Representatives of 36. The President appoints the Prime Minister and cabinet who are collectively responsible to the House of Representatives. The leader of the party with the second largest number of seats in the House is the official Leader of the Opposition. The President also appoints the 31 senators, 16 on the advice of the Prime Minister, six on the advice of the Leader of the Opposition, and nine after wider consultation. The 36 members of the House of Representatives are elected by universal adult suffrage, through a simple plurality voting system. The assembly has a life of five years.

Tobago island was given its own House of Assembly in 1980. It has 15 members, twelve popularly elected and three chosen by the majority party.

Political parties

There are currently nine active political parties but two have dominated the country's politics since independence. They are the National Alliance for Reconstruction (NAR) and the People's National Movement (PNM).

The NAR was formed in 1984 as a coalition of moderate, left-wing parties. It became a united and distinct party in 1986. It has a nationalistic, left-of-centre orientation.

The PNM was founded in 1956 by Eric Williams, a well-known Caribbean historian. It had its origins in the Teachers' Economic and Cultural Association. The PNM has a nationalistic, moderate centrist stance.

Latest elections

The results of the 1986 general election were as follows:

	% Votes	*House of Representatives Seats*
NAR	66	33
PNM	32	3

Political history

Trinidad was colonised by Spain in the sixteenth century and ceded to Britain, under the Treaty of Amiens, in 1802. Tobago had been colonised by Dutch, English and French settlers and became a British colony, in the Windward islands group, in 1814. The two islands became a joint British crown colony in 1899 and, after the Second World War, movement towards self-government, and eventual independence, began.

The country's first political party, the People's National Movement (PNM), was formed by Dr Eric Williams, a renowned historian, in 1956, and when the colony was granted internal self-government in 1959 he became the first Chief Minister. Between 1958 and 1961 it was a member of the Federation of the West Indies but withdrew and achieved full independence, within the Commonwealth, in 1967, Dr Williams becoming the first Prime Minister.

A new constitution was adopted in 1976 which made it a republic. The former Governor-General, Ellis Clarke, became the first President and Dr

Williams continued as Prime Minister. He died in March 1981 without having nominated a successor and the President appointed George Chambers for an interim period until the PNM formally adopted him as leader, in May 1981. In the general election of that year the PNM marginally increased its majority, while the leader of a moderate left-wing party grouping, the Trinidad and Tobago National Alliance, Arthur Robinson, was Leader of the Opposition.

In the next few years the National Alliance was reorganised into a more credible party, as the National Alliance for Reconstruction (NAR), and in the 1986 general election it swept the PNM from power and Arthur Robinson became Prime Minister. By 1988 the fall in world oil prices had had an adverse effect on the country's economy, resulting in strains within the NAR and the government.

North Atlantic Ocean
PANAMA
VENEZUELA
GUYANA
SURINAME
FRENCH GUIANA
COLOMBIA
Equator
ECUADOR
PERU
BRAZIL
BOLIVIA
PARAGUAY
Tropic of Capricorn
URUGUAY
CHILE
ARGENTINA
South Atlantic Ocean
Pacific Ocean
Scale 1:40 000 000
0
400
800
1200
1600 Km

SOUTH AMERICA

The region of South America extends from the Mexican border in the north to Cape Horn in the south, and is bounded to the east by the Atlantic Ocean and to the west by the Pacific. The total land area is nearly 18 million square kilometres, more than four times greater than Western Europe, and only slightly smaller than the North American half-continent comprising the United States and Canada. Its total population is greater than that of the United States and Canada combined but, like them, it has a relatively low population density.

The fact that it is frequently referred to as Latin America, or Spanish America, reveals its colonial origins. Most of the present modern states were settled by Spanish explorers in the heyday of Spain's imperial supremacy, and most achieved independence during the nineteenth century. The major exception is Brazil, whose origins are Portuguese, rather than Spanish.

Of the twelve states in the region, ten are liberal, or emergent, democracies, the remaining two, Chile and Paraguay, being under military control, although Chile is now showing signs of developing a pluralist political system. The South American military men have, however, always tended to be near, or below, the surface of political activity in most states, so that the region is now enjoying perhaps its strongest period of democratic government.

Whereas the Caribbean states virtually universally adopted the Westminster style of political system, those of South America have been modelled more on that of the United States. All of them, apart from the two with military-dominated governments, have favoured a limited presidential executive.

Although democratic systems now predominate, the human rights records of some countries in the region are still not good and there is always a danger that representative institutions will be overthrown in some unpredictable coup. Parts of South America are rife with drug trafficking and this has impacted strongly, in some states, on political processes, making apparently fair elections fraudulent.

Spanish influence, or Spanishness (*hispanidad*) as it is often called, waned significantly during the years of the Franco regime but, with the return of the monarchy and the revival of pluralist politics in their 'home country', South Americans are showing a great resurgence of interest in Spain and are forging, or reforging, links with it. During 1988, for example, no fewer than six of the South American Presidents paid official visits to Madrid, and the Spanish Prime Minister and foreign minister are frequent travellers westwards, across the Atlantic.

Now that Spain is a member of the European Community (EC), links with its former South American colonies promise to give it more weight in discussions with other Community members than its previous, solitary, position might have credited. For the South American states there is an attraction, even in the case of Brazil, in Spain becoming an important power in the region again, particularly as United States influence has been showing signs of a decline. How the administration in Washington would react to such a challenge to its leadership is difficult to judge.

As Spain relinquished most of its South American colonies during the nineteenth century, France began to fill the cultural gap and Britain the economic one. In the present century, of course, the United States has been the rising influence. However, US interference in Latin American domestic affairs, particularly during the Reagan administration, has often had a boomerang effect and not realised its original purpose. It has merely succeeded in irritating, or antagonising, the proudly independent South American states.

Despite their long histories of political independence, and despite the wealth of natural resources in many areas, the economies of the twelve South American countries do not have a particularly good record. Only Argentina, Suriname and Venezuela have per capita national incomes approaching that of Spain. The rest fall into the 'middle income' or 'low income' categories. The international indebtedness of most of them continues to grow, but the future is not entirely bleak.

Political changes in Europe will, increasingly, have their impact on South America. The resurgence of Spain has already been noted but it is also interesting to speculate about the new attitudes in the Soviet Union, where its leaders look with much less favour on Castro's Cuba, in the neighbouring region of Central America and the Caribbean, than did their predecessors. Many observers of the political and economic scene see the 1980s as an era of lost opportunities, during which the countries in the region might have raised their levels of investment and living standards, but failed to do so. Some, optimistically, see hope in the future if South America embarks on its own kind of *perestroika*, guided by the more affluent nations of the West.

Table 62

SOUTH AMERICA

			Political Data				
State	*Date of Formation*	*Political Structure*	*State Type*	*Executive*	*Assembly No of Chambers*	*Party System*	*Voting System*
Argentina	1816	Federal	Emgt Dem	Lim Pres	Two	Two	SP
Bolivia	1825	Unitary	Emgt Dem	Lim Pres	Two	Multi	SP
Brazil	1822	Federal	Emgt Dem	Lim Pres	Two	Multi	PL
Chile	1818	Unitary	Mil Auth	Military	Two	None	SP
Colombia	1830	Unitary	Emgt Dem	Lim Pres	Two	Multi	PL
Ecuador	1830	Unitary	Emgt Dem	Lim Pres	One	Multi	PL
Guyana	1966	Unitary	Emgt Dem	Lim Pres	One	Two	PL
Paraguay	1811	Unitary	Mil Auth	Military	Two	Multi	PL
Peru	1824	Unitary	Emgt Dem	Lim Pres	Two	Two	PL
Suriname	1975	Unitary	Emgt Dem	Lim Pres	One	Two	SP
Uruguay	1825	Unitary	Emgt Dem	Lim Pres	Two	Multi	PL
Venezuela	1830	Federal	Lib Dem	Lim Pres	Two	Multi	PL

Table 62—South America (contd.)

	Social and Economic Data					
State	*Area (km²)*	*Population (m) (1985)*	*Population Density (per km²)*	*Literacy Rate (%)*	*Income Type*	*Human Rights Rating (%)*
Argentina	2,780,000	31.200	11	94	Middle	88
Bolivia	1,098,600	6.430	6	63	Low	70
Brazil	8,512,000	143.300	17	75	Middle	71
Chile	756,950	12.300	16	94	Middle	35
Colombia	1,139,000	30.000	26	85	Middle	57
Ecuador	283,560	9.600	34	80	Middle	83
Guyana	215,000	0.800	4	92	Low	N/A
Paraguay	406,750	4.119	10	88	Middle	48
Peru	1,285,220	20.200	16	82	Low	62
Suriname	163,820	0.400	2	65	Middle	N/A
Uruguay	186,930	3.000	16	94	Middle	91
Venezuela	912,050	17.800	20	85	Middle	88
Total/Average	17,739,880	279.149	16	63-94	Middle	35-91

ARGENTINA

Republic of Argentina
Republica Argentina

Capital: Buenos Aires

Social and economic data
Area: 2,780,000 km²
Population: 31.200m*
Pop density per km²: 11*
GDP: $870,000m*; per capita GDP: $2,243
Economy type: middle income
Labour force in agriculture: 15%

*1985

Ethnic composition
About 85 per cent of the population are of European descent, mainly Spanish, and 15 per cent are mestizos, offspring of Spanish-American and American-Indian parents.

Religions
About 90 per cent of the people adhere to the Roman Catholic faith, which is a quasi-state religion. The constitution, for example, requires the President to be a Roman Catholic.

Political features
State type: emergent democratic
Date of state formation: 1816
Political structure: federal
Executive: limited presidential
Assembly: two-chamber
Party structure: two-party
Human rights rating: 88%

Local and regional government

Argentina is a federal state comprising the Federal District, 22 provinces and the National Territory of Tierra del Fuego. Each province has its own elected governor and assembly, responsible for all matters which have not been specifically entrusted to the federal government. Each governor serves a four-year term and is either directly elected by popular vote or through an electoral college. Two-thirds of the provincial assemblies have single chambers and the other third have two. In most provinces the governor appoints the city mayors but the mayor of the capital city, Buenos Aires, is appointed by the President.

Head of state and head of government

President Carlos Saul Menem, since 1989.

Political leaders since 1970

1966–1973 (Military), 1973 Hector Campora (Justice-Peronist Party), 1973–74 Juan Peron (Peronist), 1974–76 Isabel Peron (Peronist), 1976–78 Jorge Videla (Military), 1978–81 Roberto Viola (Military), 1981–82 Leopoldo Galtieri (Military), 1983–83 Reynaldo Bignone (Military), 1983–89 Raul Alfonsin (UCR), 1989– Carlos Saul Menem (Justice Party).

Political system

The constitution dates from 1853 and, after a long history of successive military governments, was reinstated in 1983. It provides for a federal system of government with a President elected by an electoral college for a six-year term, and a two-chamber assembly consisting of a Senate and a Chamber of Deputies.

The Senate has 46 members chosen by provincial assemblies for a nine-year term, with one third of the seats being renewed every three years. The Chamber of Deputies has 254 directly elected members, through a simple plurality voting system, for a four-year term, one half being renewed every two years. The powers of the assembly include regulating foreign trade, fixing import and export duties, levying taxes for defence, safety and the common welfare and generally regulating the economy. It also approves or rejects treaties and authorises the President to declare war or make peace.

The President, as well as exercising supreme executive functions, is also commander-in-chief of the armed forces. He operates with a cabinet of his own choosing.

Political parties

The ban on political activity, which was imposed in 1976, was lifted in 1980 and there are now several active parties, the two most significant being the Radical Union Party (UCR) and the Justice Party. The UCR was formed in 1890 and now has about 1,400,000 members. It has a moderate-centrist orientation. The Justice Party represents the present day Peronist movement and was founded in 1945. It is on the political right and operates through two wings. Its total membership is about 3 million.

Latest elections

In the 1989 presidential election the Justice Party candidate, Carlos Saul Menem, defeated the UCR nominee, Eduardo Angeloz.

The results of the 1989 elections for the Chamber of Deputies were:

	% Votes	*Seats*
Justice Party	44.6	66
UCR	28.9	41
Other parties	26.5	20

Political history

After achieving independence from Spain in 1816, Argentina experienced a series of internal conflicts, peace only being achieved through strong, often dictatorial, governments. The first relatively free and democratic elections took place in 1916 and were won by the UCR, which had been formed 26 years earlier. In 1930 the first of what were to be a series of military coups ousted the civilian government. Two years later there was a return to civilian rule but a second military coup, in 1945, saw the arrival of Lieutenant-General Juan Domingo Peron, who, with his widely popular wife, Eva Duarte Peron (Evita), created the Peronista Party, favouring policies of extreme nationalism and social improvements. Peron admired Franco's Spanish brand of fascism and set about expanding and strengthening the urban working class, at the expense of the agricultural community. He relied heavily on the military for support.

Evita Peron died in 1952 and, with her death, her husband's popularity faded. Three years later he was forced to resign and a civilian government was restored. Peron went into exile in Spain from where he continued to oversee his party's affairs. Another coup in 1966 brought back military rule and then, in 1973, the success of the Justice (Peronist) Party brought Dr Hector Campora to the presidency, essentially to pave the way for Peron's return. Campora resigned after three months and was replaced by Peron, this time with a new wife, his third, Maria E. Martinez de Peron, 'Isabelita', as Vice-President. A year later Peron died and his widow took over.

Isabelita did not enjoy the same degree of popularity as Evita had done nor was her government successful in managing the economy. It was not surprising, therefore, that two years after her succession she was ousted in yet another military coup, led by Lieutenant-General Jorge Videla. The constitution was amended, political and trade union activity banned and a policy of harsh repression of left-wing elements was pursued, during which it is estimated that between 6,000 and 15,000 people 'disappeared'. Although he had been confirmed in office until 1981, in 1978 General Videla announced his retirement and was succeeded by General Roberto Viola, who promised a speedy return to democratic government. Three years later Viola died of a sudden heart attack and was replaced by the commander-in-chief of the army, General Leopoldo Galtieri.

During the next two years the state of the economy worsened and Galtieri, following the examples of many political leaders, sought to divert attention from internal problems by creating an external diversion. In April 1982 he ordered the invasion of the Islas Malvinas, or Falkland Islands, over which Britain's claims to sovereignty had long been disputed. After a short, undeclared, war, during which 750 Argentinians lost their lives, the islands were reoccupied by British forces and, with the defeat, Galtieri's stock fell and he was forced to resign in a bloodless coup. He and other members of the military junta he led were later declared by a military commission of inquiry to be responsible for the Falklands failure and were given prison sentences.

General Reynaldo Bignone took over the government and announced that the 1853 constitution would be revived and democratic elections held. The ban on political and trade union activity was lifted and in presidential and assembly elections in October 1983 the UCR, led by Dr Raul Alfonsin, secured the presidency and a narrow victory in the Chamber of Deputies. The new President announced a radical reform of the armed forces, leading to the retirement of more than half of the senior officers, and the setting up of a National Commission on the Disappearance of Persons (CONADEP), to investigate the events of the 'dirty war', between 1976 and 1983, when the thousands of 'disappearances' had taken place. A report by CONADEP, in 1984, gave details of the deaths of more than 8,000 people and named 1,300 army officers who had been involved in the campaign of repression.

The Alfonsin administration was, however, soon faced with economic problems, forcing it to seek help from the International Monetary Fund (IMF) and the adoption of an austerity programme, described by Alfonsin as an 'economy of war'. The government's popularity fell and a swing to the right in the September 1987 assembly elections gave the smaller parties in the Chamber of Deputies the balance of power and forced Alfonsin to reconstitute his cabinet. UCR remained the largest single block in the Chamber, with 117 seats against the Peronists' 105.

Externally, Alfonsin set about improving Argentina's international reputation by undertaking a six-nation tour in 1986. The re-establishment of normal relations with the United Kingdom continued to elude him, however, since Margaret Thatcher showed no obvious signs of wanting a rapprochement.

Alfonsin was limited by the constitution to one term as President and in elections for his successor in May 1989 the Justice candidate Carlos Saul Menem was victorious. With increasingly violent opposition to his economic austerity programme, there was considerable pressure on Alfonsin to hand over to his successor before the end of his allotted term in December 1989, and he conceded to this pressure in July. Although Menem had spoken belligerently about regaining the Falklands during the election campaign, soon after his assumption of the presidency there were signs of a possible rapprochement between Argentina and Britain.

BOLIVIA

Republic of Bolivia
Republica de Bolivia

Capital: Sucre (Legal capital and seat of the Judiciary) La Paz (Seat of Government)

Social and economic data
Area: 1,098,600 km^2
Population: 6.430m*
Pop density per km^2: 6*
Literacy rate: 63%*
GDP: $4,799m*; per capita GDP: $746
Economy type: low income
Labour force in agriculture: 44%
*1985

Ethnic composition
The population comprises 30 per cent Quechua Indian, 25 per cent Ayamara Indian, 25–30 per cent of mixed race and 5–15 per cent of European descent.

Religions
The great majority of people, over 5 million, follow the Roman Catholic faith, although religious freedom is guaranteed for everyone.

Political features
State type: emergent democratic
Date of state formation: 1825
Political structure: federal
Executive: limited presidential
Assembly: two-chamber
Party structure: multi-party
Human rights rating: 70%

Local and regional government
Bolivia is divided into nine departments, ranging in population from under 43,000 to nearly 2 million. Each department is governed by a prefect, appointed by the President.

Head of state and head of government
President Jaime Paz Zamora, since 1989.

Political leaders since 1970
1970–71 Torres Gonzales (Military), 1971–80 Hugo Banzer Suarez (Military), 1980–81 Luis Garcia (Military), 1981–82 Torrelio Villa (Military), 1982 Guido Vildoso (Military), 1982–85 Siles Zuazo (MNR), 1985–89 Victor Paz Estenssoro (MNR), 1989– Jaime Paz Zamora (MIR).

Political system
Bolivia became an independent republic in 1825 after nearly 300 years of Spanish rule. It adopted its first constitution in 1826 and since then a number of variations have been produced, the present one being based on that of 1947. After years of abrogation, it was revived, after a *coup d'état*, in 1964. It provides for a two-chamber Congress consisting of a 27-member Senate and a 130-member Chamber of Deputies, both elected for four years by universal adult suffrage, through a variation of the party list system of voting. Electors vote for a presidential candidate, and then presidential votes are distributed proportionately among Congressional candidates taken from party lists. The President serves for a four-year term and combines the roles of head of state and head of government. He chooses and appoints his own cabinet. If no candidate obtains a clear majority in the presidential election, the President is chosen by Congress.

Political parties
There is a large number of political parties, the three most significant being the National Revolutionary Movement (MNR), the Nationalist Democratic Action Party (ADN) and the Movement of the Revolutionary Left (MIR).

The MNR was founded in 1942 by Victor Paz Estenssoro. Its orientation is centre-right. The ADN is an extreme right-wing grouping which was formed in 1979. Another significant left-of-centre grouping is the Movement of the Revolutionary Left (MIR).

Latest elections

In the 1989 presidential election no candidate won a clear majority, General Hugo Banzer Suarez (ADN), being marginally ahead. The final decision was therefore left to Congress in August 1989.

As a result of the 1989 presidential election, MNR was allocated 49 seats, ADN 46 and the other parties 62 between them.

Political history

Bolivia became a Spanish colony in 1538 and took its name from Simon Bolivar, the legendary figure who liberated it in 1825. Since then it has had a very chequered political history, experiencing more than 60 revolutions, 70 Presidents and eleven constitutions. Distracted by its internal problems, Bolivia lost large tracts of land to its three neighbours, Chile in 1884, Brazil in 1903 and Paraguay in 1938.

In 1951 Dr Victor Paz Estenssoro, who had founded the MNR in 1942, returned from exile in Argentina, to fight the presidential election. He failed to get an absolute majority and the sitting President transferred power to an army junta. However, a popular uprising, supported by the MNR and a section of the army, demanded the return of Paz, who assumed the presidency in the following year and immediately embarked on a programme of social reform.

Paz lost the 1956 election to an MNR colleague, who was to become a bitter rival, Siles Zuazo, but was returned to power in 1960. In 1964, following strikes and civil disorder, a coup, led by the Vice-President, General Rene Barrientos, overthrew the Paz government and a military junta was installed. Two years later Barrientos fought and won the presidency. He met great opposition from left-wing groups and in 1967 a guerrilla uprising, led by Dr Ernesto ('Che') Guevara was put down only with US help. In 1969 President Barrientos was killed in an air crash and replaced by the Vice-President. He, in turn, was replaced by General Alfredo Ovando, who, after a military power struggle, was ousted by General Juan Torres, who too was to be removed, in 1971, by a fellow officer, Colonel Hugo Banzer.

Banzer announced a return to constitutional government but another attempted coup in 1974 prompted him to postpone elections, ban all trade union and political activity and proclaim that there would be military government until at least 1980. Succumbing to mounting pressure for a return to a more democratic form of government, Banzer agreed to elections in 1978. There were allegations of widespread electoral fraud, prompting, in the same year, two more military coups. Elections were eventually held in 1979 and the two ex-presidents Dr Siles and Dr Paz, who had been rivals before in 1956, received virtually identical votes. An interim administration was installed, pending fresh elections. An election in 1980 proved equally inconclusive and was followed by the 189th military coup in Bolivia's 154 years of independence.

General Luis Garcia was installed as President but forced to resign in the following year after allegations of involvement in drug trafficking. He was replaced by General Celso Torrelio who promised to fight corruption and return the country to democratic government within three years. In 1982 a mainly civilian cabinet was appointed but rumours of an impending coup resulted in Torrelio's resignation. A military junta, led by the hard-liner General Guido Vildoso, was installed. Because of the worsening economic situation, the junta decided to ask Congress to elect a president and Dr Siles, who had won most votes in the close elections of 1979 and 1980, was chosen to head a coalition cabinet. Economic aid from the USA and Europe, which had been cut off in 1980, resumed but the economy continued to deteriorate. There was widespread opposition to the government's austerity measures and additional turmoil in June when the President was temporarily abducted by a group of right-wing army officers, supported, it was believed, by drug dealers. In an attempt to secure national unity, President Siles even embarked on a five-day hunger strike.

A general strike and another abortive army coup followed, in 1985, prompting President Siles to resign. Again, the election was inconclusive, with no candidate winning an absolute majority. The veteran MNR leader, Dr Paz, at the age of 77, was chosen by Congress as the new president. Despite strict austerity measures, including a wage freeze, Bolivia's economy has worsened, with inflation continuing to rise and the currency weakening. In the 1989 presidential election there was no conclusive result, the eventual new president, Jaime Paz Zamora (MIR), being determined by Congress in August 1989.

BRAZIL

Federative Republic of Brazil
Republica Federativa do Brasil

Capital: Brasilia

Social and economic data
Area: 8,512,000 km^2
Population: 143.300m*
Pop density per km^2: 17*
Literacy rate: 75%*
GDP: $210,000m*; per capita GDP: $ 1,465
Economy type: middle income
Labour force in agriculture: 30%

*1985

Ethnic composition
There is a wide range of ethnic groups including about 55 per cent of European origin, mainly Portuguese, Italian and German, about 38 per cent of mixed parentage, about 6 per cent of black African origin, as well as American Indians and Japanese.

Religions
Nearly 90 per cent of the population are Roman Catholic, the rest being Protestant or Spiritualist.

Political features
State type: emergent democratic
Date of state formation: 1822
Political structure: federal
Executive: limited presidential*
Assembly: two-chamber
Party structure: multi-party
Human rights rating: 71%

*To become parliamentary

Local and regional government
Brazil is divided into five geographical regions, central-west, north-east, north, south-east and south. The regions are subdivided into 23 states, three territories and a federal district (Brasilia). The populations of the states range from about 300,000 to over 25 million, the federal district has a population of nearly 1.2 million, and the populations of the territories vary from just over 1,000 to nearly 80,000. Each state has a constitution modelled on that of the federal constitution, with an elected, single-chamber assembly and governor. The governor of the federal district is appointed by and directly responsible to the President.

The powers and duties of the federal government are set out in the constitution and include responsibility for external affairs, defence and nationwide services, such as communications, education, agriculture and maritime and labour law. The residue of powers and duties is left with the states.

Below state level there are municipalities with elected councils and mayors.

Head of state and head of government
President José Sarney Costa, since 1985.

Political leaders since 1970
1969–74 Emilio Garrastazu Medici (Military), 1974–78 Ernesto Geisel (Military), 1978–85 Baptista de Figueiredo (Military), 1985 Tancredo Neves (AD), 1985– José Sarney Costa (PDS).

Political system
The constitution of 1969 was revised in 1977, 1978 and 1985. It provided for a federal system, based broadly on the US model, with a two-chamber National Congress consisting of a Senate of 69 members, and a Chamber of Deputies of variable size according to population. Senators are elected, on the basis of one per state, for an eight-year term. Deputies are elected for a four-year term. The number of deputies is determined by the population of each state and each territory is represented by one deputy. Elections to both chambers are by universal adult suffrage, through a party list system of voting. The 1969 constitution also provided for a President to be elected by universal adult suffrage for a five-year term, not subject to renewal, governing through a cabinet of his own choosing.

After strong campaigning by the PMBD, which was at first unsuccessful, in October 1988 a new constitution was approved, the seventh since Brazil became a fully independent state. It transfers considerable power from the President to Congress, making the executive closer to being a parliamentary rather than a limited presidential one. The new constitution also abolishes an important source of presidential power, the National Security Council, but President Sarney has managed to retain an equivalent body, styled the Advisory Secretariat on National Defence.

Other novel features include the extension of the franchise to 16-year olds and an unusual legal device, the *habeas data*, which gives people the right of access to personal files held by the National Intelligence Agency.

Political parties

Historically, Brazilian political parties were built on the power of landowners who were also the local political bosses. As the country experienced its succession of military and civilian rulers, in the period after 1945, so the parties adapted to the changing political scene, regularly regrouping. In 1965 all political parties were banned except for two which were given official recognition, one as the government party and one as the opposition. The practice of operating controlled parties was ended in 1979 and for a period other parties were permitted to function under strictly regulated conditions. In 1985 all restrictions were removed and the free formation of parties was allowed.

Among six now operating, the three most significant are the Social Democratic Party (PDS), the Brazilian Democratic Movement Party (PMDB) and the Liberal Front Party (PFL).

The PDS was formed in 1980 as a pro-government party to replace ARENA, which had been artificially created to support the military between 1965 and 1979. It has had a generally moderate, left-of-centre stance.

The PMDB was formed in 1980 as a direct descendant of an older party, the Brazilian Democratic Movement (MBD) which, between 1965 and 1979, was the official opposition party. In its new form it retained most of the moderate elements of the old MBD and in 1982 merged with the Popular Party (PP). Its orientation is centre-left.

In 1984 some PDS members joined with others from the PMDB to fight the 1985 presidential election and formed the PFL.

Latest elections

The 1986 general election resulted in clear majorities for the PMDB in both the Senate and Chamber of Deputies.

	Senate Seats	*Chamber of Deputies Seats*
PMDB	44	259
PFL	16	115
PDS	5	36
Other parties	4	77

Political history

Brazil became a Portuguese colony from 1500 and in 1808 the King of Portugal, in the face of a French invasion of his country, moved the capital from Lisbon to Rio de Janeiro. He returned to Lisbon in 1821 leaving his son, Crown Prince Pedro, as Regent. In 1822 Pedro declared Brazil an independent kingdom and assumed the title Emperor Pedro I. He was succeeded by his son, Pedro II, who persuaded large numbers of Portuguese to emigrate, resulting in a rapid development of the centre of Brazil, largely on the basis of slavery. In 1888 slavery was abolished, in 1889 a republic established and in 1891 a constitution for a federal state adopted.

The 1920s saw great social unrest and the world economic crisis of 1930 produced a major revolt which brought Dr Getulio Vargas to the presidency. He continued in office, in the role of a benevolent dictator, until ousted by the army in 1945. General Eurico Dutra was elected President and a new constitution adopted. In 1950 Vargas returned to power but in 1954 committed suicide. He was succeeded by Dr Juscelino Kubitschek. Six years later the capital was moved from Rio de Janeiro to Brasilia.

In 1961 Dr Janio Quadros won the presidency but resigned after seven months, to be succeeded by the Vice-President, Joao Goulart, who was suspected by the army of having left-wing leanings. They forced an amendment to the constitution, restricting presidential powers and creating the office of Prime Minister. However, a referendum in 1963 brought back a fully presidential system, with Goulart choosing his own cabinet.

Dissatisfaction with the civilian administration resulted in a bloodless coup, in 1964, which brought the army, in the person of General Castelo Branco, to power. He immediately banned all political parties, then gave recognition to two artificially created groups on which he felt he could rely, the pro-government National Renewal Alliance (ARENA) and an opposition party, the PMBD.

In 1967 Branco named Marshal da Costa e Silva as his successor and a new constitution was adopted. In 1969, however, da Costa resigned because of ill health and a new military junta took over. In 1974 General Ernesto Geisel was chosen President, under the terms of the constitution, by an electoral college and he continued in office until succeeded by General Baptista de Figueiredo in 1978. The following year legislation was passed to allow a return to a multi-party operation, but under strictly controlled conditions. President Figueiredo continued in office until 1985, the last few years of his presidency witnessing a deterioration in the state of the economy. This resulted in a series of strikes and mass rallies calling for the return of full democratic government.

In 1985 restrictions on political activity were removed and Tancredo Neves became the first civilian President for 21 years, amid a nationwide wave of optimism. He died within months of assuming office and was succeeded by the Vice-President, José Sarney. The new President, who was distrusted because of his involvement with the former military regime, announced that he would keep the cabinet chosen by Neves and continue with his policies.

In the same year the constitution was again amended, this time to provide for the election of the President by direct universal suffrage. However, with their new-found freedom, the parties in Congress voted, in 1987, to adopt a new constitution, creating a parliamentary executive with a largely formal President, elected for a four, instead of a five-year term. This was adopted in October 1988, despite attempts by President Sarney to amend or delay it.

CHILE

Republic of Chile
Republica de Chile

Capital: Santiago

Social and economic data
Area: 756,950 km^2
Population: 12.300m*
Pop density per km^2: 16*
Literacy rate: 94%*
GDP: $15994m*; per capita GDP: $1300
Economy type: middle income
Labour force in agriculture: 15%

Ethnic composition
The population is fairly homogeneous, consisting of about 65 per cent mestizos (offspring of Spanish-American and American-Indian parents) and 30 per cent European, the remainder being mainly Indian. Class is a more divisive factor than race.

Religions
Roman Catholicism was the established religion until 1925 and it remains the dominant faith, being practised by about 90 per cent of the population. Among the religious minorities are about 30,000 Jews.

Political features
State type: military authoritarian
Date of state formation: 1818
Political structure: unitary
Executive: military
Assembly: two-chamber
Party structure: no parties currently operate
Human rights rating: 35%

Local and regional government
The country is divided into twelve regions which are further subdivided into 51 provinces.

Head of state and head of government
President General Augusto Pinochet, since 1973.

Political leaders since 1970
1970–73 Salvador Allende (Unidad Popular), 1973– Augusto Pinochet (Military).

Political system
Since a coup in 1973 Chile has been ruled by a military junta. A new constitution was announced in 1981, to take full effect in 1989. It provides for the election of a President, selected as the sole nominee of the four

armed forces commanders-in-chief, for an eight-year, non-renewable, term and a two-chamber assembly of a Senate and Chamber of Deputies. The Senate will have 26 elected and nine appointed members and the Chamber of Deputies 120 elected members, all serving a four-year term. This, however, has still to come into effect and until that time Chile is under military rule.

Political parties

All Marxist and 'totalitarian' groups are banned and no political activity will be permitted until the end of the 'period of transition to democratic government' in 1989.

Latest elections

There have been no elections since the coup in 1973, but in 1988 there was a national plebiscite intended to ratify Pinochet as President, as the sole nominee, for a further-eight year term. A majority 'Yes' vote would be regarded as a ratification and a majority 'No' vote would require an open election for the presidency at the expiration of the present term. In the event, there was a clear 'No' vote of 54.6 per cent.

Political history

The first European to sight Chile was Magellan, in 1520, and it became part of the Spanish Empire 21 years later. It won its independence from Spain in 1818 and soon became a dominant power in western Latin America. Through most of the present century, however, there have been struggles between left- and right-wing political factions.

Between 1964 and 1970 the Christian Democrats, under Eduardo Frei, were in power, followed by a left-wing coalition, led by Dr Salvador Allende, who was the world's first democratically elected Marxist head of state. He promised to create social justice by constitutional means and embarked upon an extensive nationalisation programme, which included the US-owned copper mines. Allende was seen by the CIA in Washington as a pro-Cuban communist and opposition to him within Chile was encouraged. The culmination of this movement to overthrow him was an attack on the presidential palace, in 1973, by the army, led by General Augusto Pinochet. The government was ousted and Allende killed, the new regime claiming he committed suicide. Pinochet became President and any opponents were imprisoned, after torture, or just made to 'disappear'.

In 1976 Pinochet established what he called an 'authoritarian democracy', all political parties being banned, despite UN condemnation, and in 1978 he secured an endorsement of his policies through a referendum. In 1980 a new constitution was announced, as a 'transition to democracy' by 1989, but reports of imprisonments and tortures continued to be received by the world outside.

Despite an expansion of the economy and the introduction of a capital works programme to improve the country's infrastructure and public services, opposition to the Pinochet regime grew, with widespread demands for a return to democratic government. The opposition was marked, in 1984, by a campaign of anti-government bombing, aimed mainly at electricity installations, resulting in a 90-day state of emergency, followed by a 90-day state of siege. In 1985, as opposition grew in the Catholic Church and the army as well as among the general public, another state of emergency was declared, but the bombings and killings continued.

In 1986 Pinochet, at the age of 71, announced that he was considering serving another eight-year term. This news prompted opposition groups to agree to work together to oppose him in the 1988 plebiscite to ratify him as the sole nominee for the presidency. The result of the plebiscite, answering the question whether or not Pinochet should continue for another term, was a 'No' vote of 54.6 per cent and a 'Yes' vote of 43.04 per cent. The general said he would honour the result but declined to step down before the end of his current term of office. After considerable discussion with opposition groups, in June 1989 Pinochet agreed to constitutional changes which would permit fully pluralist politics, the amendments to be put forward for approval in a national plebiscite.

COLOMBIA

Republic of Colombia
Republica de Colombia

Capital: Bogota

Social and economic data

Area: 1,139,000 km^2
Population: 30.000m*
Pop density per km^2: 26*
Literacy rate: 85%*
GDP: $34,000m*; per capita GDP: $1,133
Economy type: middle income
Labour force in agriculture: 28%

*1985

Ethnic composition

Although the main ethnic groups are of mixed Spanish, Indian and African blood, Colombia is one of the most Spanish of all South American countries and Spanish customs and values predominate.

Religions

About 95 per cent of the population are Roman Catholics and Roman Catholicism is sufficiently strong to be regarded as the quasi-state religion.

Political features

State type: emergent democratic
Date of state formation: 1830
Political structure: unitary
Executive: limited presidential
Assembly: two-chamber
Party structure: two-party
Human rights rating: 57%

Local and regional government

Although it does not have a federal system of government, the country is divided into 23 departments, four *intendencias* and five administrative territories enjoying considerable autonomy. The departments range in population from under 70,000 to 3.7 million, the *intendencias* from 16,000 to 30,000 and the territories from 3,000 to 13,000. Below these levels are municipalities. Each department has a governor appointed by the President and there are regional, elected assemblies.

Head of state and head of government

President Virgilio Barco Vargas, since 1986.

Political leaders since 1970

1970–74 Misael Pastrana Borrero (Conservative), 1974–78 Alfonso Lopez Michelsen (Liberal), 1978–82 Julio Cesar Turbay Ayala (Liberal), 1982–86 Belisario Betancur Cuartas (Conservative), 1986– Virgilio Barco Vargas (Liberal).

Political system

The 1886 constitution has been amended many times, the most recent changes being in 1957, 1968, 1970 and 1974. It provides for a strong President, who is both head of state and head of government, balanced by a two-chamber Congress consisting of a Senate and a House of Representatives. The Senate has 114 members and the House 199. All are elected by universal adult suffrage, through a party list system of voting, for a four-year term. The President appoints his own cabinet. The country has a long history of democratic government but has been classified as an emergent democracy because there have been post-Second World War periods of extreme violence. An unusual feature was introduced through an amendment to the constitution, in 1968. It requires that the 'minority' party must have 'adequate' representation in government. This became known as the 'National Front' accord but it was not adhered to by the newly elected administration in 1986.

Political parties

There are some ten political parties but the two most significant are the Liberal Party and the Conservative Party. They have dominated the political scene during most of the present century. Although there are strong democratic traditions, politics in Colombia have long been stained by violence between the the two ruling parties and from left-wing opposition groups and the drug barons, largely based in Colombia's second city, Medellin.

The Liberal Party was founded in 1815. It is divided into two factions, the official group and the independent group, who call themselves New Liberalism. The party has a centrist orientation.

The Conservative Party was formed in 1849. It too has a history of internal factionalism but this is not as clearly defined as in the Liberal Party. Its political stance is right-of-centre.

Latest elections

In the 1986 presidential election Virgilio Barco, the Liberal candidate, won with 4.1 million votes compared with the 2.5 million of his main rival, the Conservative candidate, Alvaro Gomez.

In the 1986 Congressional elections the results were as follows:

	Senate Seats	*House of Representatives Seats*
Liberals	58	98
Conservatives	43	80
Other parties	13	21

Political history

Colombia became a Spanish colony in the sixteenth century and obtained its independence in 1819, as part of a union with Ecuador, Panama and Venezuela. In 1903 it became entirely independent. Since then two main political parties, Conservatives and Liberals, have dominated Colombian politics. Between 1860 and 1884 the Liberals were in power, between 1884 and 1930 the Conservatives, the Liberals again between 1930 and 1946 and then the Conservatives between 1946 and 1953. In 1948 the left-wing mayor of the capital city, Bogota, was assassinated and there followed a decade of near-civil war, 'La Violencia', during which it is thought that well over a quarter of a million people died. The legacy of this war was the continuation of left-wing guerrilla activity through to the 1980s.

In 1957, in an effort to halt the violence, the Conservatives and Liberals agreed to form a National Front, with the presidency alternating between them. In 1970, the National Front was challenged by the National Popular Alliance (ANAPO), with a special appeal to the working classes, but the Conservative-Liberal co-operation continued and when in 1978 the Liberals won majorities in both chambers of Congress and the presidency they kept the National Front accord. In 1982 the Liberals retained their majorities in Congress but Dr Belisario Betancur won the presidency for the Conservatives. He sought a truce with the left-wing guerrillas by granting them an amnesty and freeing political prisoners. He also embarked upon a radical programme of public works expenditure. His plans suffered a major blow in 1984 when his Minister of Justice, who had been using harsh measures to curb drug dealing, was assassinated. Betancur's reaction was to strengthen his anti-drug campaign.

In the May 1986 elections the presidency changed hands again, going to Liberal Virgilio Barco Vargas by a record margin. Three months after assuming office, President Barco announced that he was going to end the tradition of the National Front accord, which had been written into the constitution, that the opposition party was always given an opportunity to participate in government if it wished to. Meanwhile, the country's long history of violence continued.

ECUADOR

Republic of Ecuador
Republica del Ecuador

Capital: Quito

Social and economic data

Area: 283,560 km^2
Population: 9.600m*

Pop density per km^2: 34*
Literacy rate: 80%*
GDP: $16,502m*; per capita GDP: $1,718
Economy type: middle income
Labour force in agriculture: 34%

*1985

Ethnic composition
The population is about 55 per cent mestizo, 25 per cent Indian, 10 per cent Spanish and 10 per cent African.

Religions
About 90 per cent of the people are Roman Catholics. There are also other Christian and Jewish minorities.

Political features
State type: emergent democratic
Date of state formation: 1830
Political structure: unitary
Executive: limited presidential
Assembly: one-chamber
Party structure: multi-party
Human rights rating: 83%

Local and regional government
Ecuador is not a fully federal state, but has a devolved system of 20 provinces, each administered by an appointed governor. The provinces range in population from under 2,000 to over 2 million. Below the provincial level are municipalities and parishes.

Head of state and head of government
President Rodrigo Borja Cevallos, since 1988.

Political leaders since 1970
1968–72 José Velasco (PLR), 1972–76 Guillermo Rodriguez Lara (Military), 1976–79 Alfredo Poveda Burbano (Military), 1979–81 Jaime Roldos Aguilera (CFP), 1981–85 Osvaldo Hurtado Larrea (CFP) 1985–88 Febres Cordero (DP), 1988– Rodrigo Borja Cevallos (Progressive Democratic Front).

Political system
The 1979 constitution provides for a President, elected by universal adult suffrage for a four-year term, and a single-chamber National Congress, the Chamber of Representatives, with 71 members. They too are popularly elected and serve a four-year term. The President is not eligible for re-election. Voting in presidential elections is by the majoritarian system of second ballot and for the Congress by the party list system of proportional representation.

Political parties

There are no fewer than 21 political parties, six of which, in 1986, formed a left-wing coalition, the Progressive Democratic Front. The six parties in the coalition are the Democratic Left (ID), the Democratic Party (PD), the Democratic Popular Movement (MPD), the Socialist Party (PSE), People, Change and Democracy (PCD) and the Left Broad Front (FADI). The main parties outside the coalition are the Concentration of Popular Forces (CFP), the Social Christian Party (PSC), the Radical Alfarista Front (FRA), the Popular Democracy/Christian Democratic Union (DP), the Radical Liberal Party (PLR), and the Conservative Party (PC).

The ID was formed in 1970 as a result of a split in the Liberal Party. It has a moderate socialist orientation. The PD is a social democratic party formed in 1977 by a former Liberal leader. The MPD is a Marxist-Leninist, pro-China party. The PSE is another left-wing grouping. The PCD was formed in 1980 by dissidents from the CFP and is a centre-left party. The FADI is an expanded group, including Communist Party members, who originally came together to fight the 1978 presidential election.

The PSC is a right-wing party formed in 1951. The CFP is a conservative party which was established in 1949. The FRA was founded in 1972 by dissidents from the Liberal Party. The DP dates from 1978 and is a progressive conservative faction. The PLR carries on the traditions of the old Liberal Party, which was originally founded in 1895. The PC is Ecuador's oldest party having been established in 1855 with a right-wing orientation.

Latest elections

In the 1988 elections for the National Congress seats were won as follows:

ID	27
DP	7
PSC	6
CFP	6
PRE	4
Others	21

In the 1988 presidential election Rodrigo Borja Cevallos, the Progressive Democratic Front candidate, won, with 48 per cent of the votes in the second ballot, over his rival, Abdala Bucaram Ortiz, who had 40 per cent.

Political history

Under Spanish rule from the sixteenth century, Ecuador became part of Gran Colombia in 1822 and then a fully independent state in 1830. From independence onwards the political pendulum has swung from the Conservatives to the Liberals, from civilian to military rule, and from democratic to dictatorial government. By 1948 some stability was evident and eight years of Liberal government ensued.

In 1956 Dr Camilo Ponce became the first Conservative President for 60 years. Four years later a Liberal, Dr José Maria Velasco, who had been President in 1933–35, 1944–47 and 1952–56, was re-elected. He was deposed in a 1961 coup by the Vice-President, who in the following year was himself dismissed and replaced by a military junta. In 1968 Velasco returned from exile and took up the presidency again. Another coup in 1972 put the military back in power until, in 1978, when it seemed as if Ecuador had returned permanently to its pre-1948 political pattern, a new, democratic constitution was adopted.

The 1978 constitution has survived, even though a deteriorating economy has resulted in strikes, demonstrations and, in 1982, a state of emergency. In the 1984 elections no party or coalition of parties won a clear majority in the National Congress, and Febres Cordero won the presidency for the PSC, on a promise of 'bread, roofs and jobs'. With no immediate support in Congress, his policies seemed likely to be blocked but in 1985 he won a majority there when five opposition members decided to change allegiance and support him. In the 1986 congressional elections the Progressive Democratic Front won most seats but not a clear majority over the other parties. At the end of his term of office, Febres Cordero was succeeded by one of the leaders of the left-wing Progressive Democratic Front coalition, Rodrigo Borja.

GUYANA

Co-operative Republic of Guyana

Capital: Georgetown

Social and economic data

Area: 215,000 km^2
Population: 0.800m*
Pop density per km^2: 4*
Literacy rate: 92%*
GDP: $462m*; per capita GDP: $577
Economy type: low income
Labour force in agriculture: 20%

*1985

Ethnic composition

About 51 per cent of the population are descended from settlers from the sub-continent of India, and about 43 per cent are Afro-Indian. There are also small American-Indian, Chinese and European minorities.

Religions

There are about 430,000 Hindus, 125,000 Anglicans, 120,000 Muslims and 94,000 Roman Catholics.

Political features
State type: emergent democratic
Date of state formation: 1966
Political structure: unitary
Executive: limited presidential
Assembly: one-chamber
Party structure: two-party
Human rights rating: N/A

Local and regional government
The country is divided into ten regions, each with an elected Regional Democratic Council, which is represented on the National Assembly by one member. Day-to-day administration is by an appointed commissioner.

Head of state and head of government
President Desmond Hoyte, since 1985.

Political leaders since 1970
1970–85 Forbes Burnham (PNC), 1985– Desmond Hoyte (PNC).

Political system
Guyana is a sovereign republic within the Commonwealth. The 1980 constitution provides for a single-chamber National Assembly of 65 members, 53 elected by universal adult suffrage, through a party list system of proportional representation, and twelve elected by the regions. They serve a five-year term. The President is the nominee of the party winning most votes in the National Assembly elections and he serves for the life of the Assembly. He appoints a cabinet which is collectively responsible to the Assembly. The political system therefore represents an adaptation of a parliamentary to a limited presidential executive.

Political parties
Although there are seven parties and a proportional representation system of voting is used, a two-party system operates, with the main parties being the People's National Congress (PNC) and the People's Progressive Party (PPP).

The PNC was formed in 1955 by dissidents from the PPP. Its supporters are mainly Indian descendants. It has a nationalistic-socialist orientation.

The PPP dates from 1950. It is a Marxist-Leninist mass party and draws its support mainly from Afro-Indians.

Latest elections
In the 1985 National Assembly elections PNC won 42 of the 53 directly elected seats, with 78.55 per cent of the popular vote. PPP won eight seats, with a vote of 15.77 per cent.

Political history
Guyana was originally a Dutch colony which was seized by Britain in 1814. It became a colony of the British Empire, as British Guiana, and achieved full independence, within the Commonwealth, in 1966.

The move from colonial to republican status was gradual and not entirely smooth. In 1953 a constitution, providing for free elections to an assembly, was introduced and the left-wing People's Progressive Party (PPP), led by Dr Cheddi Jagan, won the popular vote. Within months, however, the United Kingdom government suspended the constitution and put in its own interim administration, claiming that the PPP threatened to become a communist dictatorship.

In 1957 a breakaway group from the PPP founded a new party, the People's National Congress (PNC), which was socialist, rather than Marxist-Leninist. A revised constitution was introduced at the end of 1956 and fresh elections held in 1957. The PPP won again, Jagan becoming Chief Minister. Internal self-government was granted in 1961 and, with PPP again the successful party, Jagan became Prime Minister.

A system of proportional representation, based on party lists, was introduced in 1963 and in the 1964 elections, under the new voting procedures, PPP, although winning most votes, did not have an overall majority so a PPP-PNC coalition was formed, with the PNC leader, Forbes Burnham, as Prime Minister. This coalition took the country through to full independence in 1966.

PNC won the 1968 election and in 1970 legislation was passed to make Guyana a republic within the Commonwealth. PNC was again successful in 1973 but the PPP, dissatisfied with the results, decided to boycott the Assembly. Then, in 1976, it partly relented, offering the government its 'critical support'. Discussions began about framing a new constitution and in 1980, after a referendum, a new version was adopted. It turned a parliamentary executive into a limited presidential one, making the President both head of state and head of government.

The 1981 elections, which were declared fraudulent by the opposition parties, made Burnham the new executive President. The following years of his administration were marked by a deteriorating economy, which necessitated austerity measures, and cool relations with the Western powers, particularly the United States, whose invasion of Grenada he condemned. He died in August 1985 and was succeeded by Prime Minister Desmond Hoyte, who was expected to follow a similar policy line to that of his predecessor.

PARAGUAY

Republic of Paraguay
Republica del Paraguay

Capital: Asuncion

Social and economic data
Area: 406,750 km^2
Population: 4.119m*
Pop density per km^2: 10*
Literacy rate: 88%*
GDP: $5,808m*; per capita GDP: $1,416
Economy type: middle income
Labour force in agriculture: 43%

*1985

Ethnic composition
Paraguay is unusual in that, instead of the Spanish colonisers assimilating the indigenous population, the reverse has happened, so that now less than 5 per cent of the population can be said to be clearly Spanish or Indian. The overwhelming majority are, therefore, mestizos.

Religions
Roman Catholicism is the established religion and 90 per cent of the population practise it, but religious freedom for all is guaranteed in the constitution. There are also Anglican and Baptist minorities.

Political features
State type: military authoritarian
Date of state formation: 1811
Political structure: unitary
Executive: military
Assembly: two-chamber
Party structure: multi-party
Human rights rating: 48%

Local and regional government
The country is divided into 19 departments, each administered by a governor appointed by the President. The departments are further subdivided into municipalities, each with a small elected board. The largest municipalities have appointed mayors.

Head of state and head of government
General Andres Rodriguez, since 1989.

Political leaders since 1970
1954–1989 Alfredo Stroessner Mattiauda (Military), 1989– Andres Rodriguez (Military).

Political system
The 1967 constitution provides for a President, who is both head of state and head of government, popularly elected for a five-year term, and a two-chamber assembly, the National Congress, consisting of a Senate and Chamber of Deputies. Both chambers are elected by universal adult suffrage, through a modified party list system of proportional representation, and serve five-year terms.

The Senate has 30 members and the Chamber 60 and and the party winning the largest number of votes in the Congressional elections is allocated two-thirds of the seats in each chamber. The President appoints and leads his own cabinet, which is called the Council of Ministers. Congress can be dissolved within its five-year term.

Despite all the evidence of democratic government, Paraguay has, in effect, been under military rule since 1940, successive presidents cleverly suppressing opposition partly by using their powers of patronage and partly through the use of the army.

Political parties

A law passed in 1981 prescribes that a political party must have a minimum of 10,000 members, and must contest at least a third of the constituencies before it can operate. For many years there was a 'model' two-party system of Conservatives versus Liberals but now there are nine parties suitably registered, the three most significant being the National Republican Association, also known as the Colorado Party, the Liberal Party (PL) and the Radical Liberal Party (PLR).

The Colorado Party was founded in 1887 and was in power continuously until 1904 and returned to power from 1946 to the present day. It is officially regarded as the government party and all civil servants are obliged to be members of it. It now contains two factions, the militants and the traditionalists. Its overall orientation is right-of-centre.

The PL is what is left of the old Liberal Party which was originally formed in 1887. In 1962 it split into two, the other part being the PLR. The PL has a right-of-centre orientation while the PLR's stance is a little more moderate.

Latest elections

General Andres Rodriguez won the 1989 presidential election with 70 per cent of the popular vote.

In the 1989 congressional elections the Colorado Party won in excess of 70 per cent of the votes and two-thirds of the Senate and Chamber of Deputies seats.

Political history

Paraguay was first colonised by Spain in 1537 and it soon became a major settlement, the Jesuits arriving to convert the Indians in 1609. It achieved full independence in 1811. As a landlocked country, Paraguay sought access to the sea and this involved it in a violent and damaging war with Brazil, Argentina and Uruguay between 1865 and 1870. The two main political parties, Conservative and Liberal, were both founded in the late 1880s. There then followed a period of political instability until the Liberal leader, Edvard Schaerer, came to the presidency, in 1912, and formed an administration which gained foreign confidence and attracted foreign investment. This relative stability continued, even though many of the presidencies were shortlived, until another war erupted, with Bolivia, between 1932 and 1935. Paraguay was the victor but, again, the cost was great on both sides.

Since 1940 Paraguay has been mostly under the control of military governments led by strong, autocratic leaders. General Morinigo was President from 1940 to 1947 and General Alfredo Stroessner from 1954 to 1989. He was re-elected in 1958, 1963, 1968, 1973, 1978, 1983 and 1988. During the US presidency of Jimmy Carter the Stroessner regime came under strong criticism for its violation of human rights and this resulted in some tempering of the General's ruthless rule. Criticism by the Reagan administration was less noticeable. Stroessner maintained his supremacy by ensuring that the armed forces and business community shared in the spoils of office and by preventing any opposition groups from coalescing into a credible challenge.

From 1984 onwards there was increased speculation about the eventual succession to the presidency. There was a division of opinion within his own party, the militant faction favouring Stroessner seeking an eighth term, with his son, Gustavo, then succeeding him, while the traditionalists believing that he should retire in 1988. The General, however, decided to stay on and, in February 1988, was re-elected for yet another term. Early in 1989, however, he was overthrown and forced into exile, by General Andres Rodriguez, who replaced him. He promised early elections which he and the Colorado Party won.

PERU

Republic of Peru
Republica del Peru

Capital: Lima

Social and economic data
Area: 1,285,220 km^2
Population: 20.200m*
Pop density per km^2: 16*
Literacy rate: 82%*
GDP: $14,401m*; per capita GDP: $713
Economy type: low income
Labour force in agriculture: 38%

*1985

Ethnic composition
About 45 per cent of the population are American Indians, about 37 per cent mestizos, 15 per cent Europeans and 3 per cent Africans.

Religions
Roman Catholicism is the official religion and about 90 per cent of the people practise it, but all beliefs are tolerated.

Political features
State type: emergent democratic
Date of state formation: 1824
Political structure: unitary
Executive: limited presidential
Assembly: two-chamber
Party structure: two-party
Human rights rating: 62%

Local and regional government
The country is divided into the constitutional province of Callao and 24 departments. Each department is administered by an appointed prefect. Within the departments are provinces and districts administered by sub-prefects and governors respectively. There is no really representative local government.

Head of state and head of government
President Alan Garcia Perez, since 1985.

Political leaders since 1970
1968–75 Juan Velasco Alvarado (Military), 1975–78 Francisco Morales Bermudez (Military), 1978–80 Haya de la Torre (APRA), 1980–85 Fernando Belaunde Terry (AP), 1985– Alan Garcia Perez (APRA).

Political system
The 1980 constitution provides for a President, who is both head of state and head of government, elected by universal adult suffrage, by the majoritarian second ballot system, for a five year-term. He governs with an appointed Council of Ministers.

There is a two-chamber assembly, called the National Congress, comprising a 60-member Senate and a 180-member Chamber of Deputies, elected by universal adult suffrage, through a party list system of proportional representation for five years. Senators are elected on a national basis but members of the Chamber are elected so as to ensure that 40 of them are chosen by constituencies in the province of Lima and the remaining 140 by constituencies in the province of Callao and the rest of the country.

Political parties
There are currently 18 political parties but two groups have dominated Peruvian politics in recent years, the American Popular Revolutionary Alliance (APRA), and an alliance of six left-wing parties called the Unified Left (IU).

APRA was founded in 1924 in Mexico by Victor Raul Haya de la Torre, who had been exiled from Peru by the military regime. It was originally formed to fight imperialism throughout South America but Peru was the only country in which it became established. Haya de la Torre returned in 1930 and APRA became the first popular party to challenge the Peruvian establishment and its rivalry with the military leadership has been a constant feature since the 1930s. It has a moderate, left-wing orientation.

IU was formed in 1980 as an alliance of ten left-wing groups combining formed to fight the next elections.

Latest elections
In the 1985 general election the results were as follows:

	Senate Seats	*Chamber of Deputies Seats*
APRA	32	107
IU	15	48
Other parties	13	25

Political history
Spain had had a firm grip on Peru since the 1530s and the people had to fight long and hard to obtain their independence. They were eventually victorious in 1824.

The country was ruled by right-wing dictatorships from the mid-1920s until 1945 when free elections returned. Although APRA was the largest party in Congress it was constantly thwarted by smaller conservative groups, anxious to protect their business interests. In 1948 a group of army officers, led by General Manuel Odria, ousted the elected government, banned APRA and installed a military junta. Odria became President in 1950 and remained in power until 1956. In the meantime APRA had become a more moderate party and the ban on it had been lifted.

In 1963 military rule ended and Fernando Belaunde, the joint candidate of the Popular Action (AP) and Christian Democrat (PDC) parties, won the presidency, while APRA took the largest share of the Chamber of Deputies' seats. Following economic problems and industrial unrest, Belaunde was deposed in a bloodless coup in 1968 and the army returned to power with an all-military Council of Ministers, led by General Velasco. Another bloodless coup in 1975 brought in General Morales Bermudez who judged that the time for a return to constitutional government had come.

Elections for the presidency and both chambers of Congress took place in May 1980 and Fernando Belaunde was re-elected. He embarked upon a programme of agrarian and industrial reform but at the end of his presidency, in 1985, the country was in a state of economic and social crisis. Peru's fragile democracy somehow survived and Belaunde became the first civilian President to hand over power to another, constitutionally elected, civilian. His successor was the young Social Democrat, Alan Garcia Perez.

In his first presidential address Garcia promised to end internal terrorism and halt the decline in the economy. He declared his support for the Sandinista government in Nicaragua and criticised US policy throughout Latin America. He then embarked on a programme of cleansing the army and police of the 'old guard'. By February 1986 about 1,400 had elected to retire. After trying to expand the economy, while controlling inflation with price and exchange controls, he announced his intention of nationalising the banks and insurance companies. Considerable opposition from the business community caused a decision to be postponed. By the middle of 1988 the economy had still not revived and Garcia came under widespread pressure to seek help from the IMF.

SURINAME

Republic of Suriname

Capital: Paramaribo

Social and economic data
Area: 163,820 km^2
Population: 0.400m*
Pop density per km^2: 2*
Literacy rate: 65%*
GDP: $1,100m*; per capita GDP: $2,750
Economy type: middle income
Labour force in agriculture: 18%

*1985

Ethnic composition
There is a very wide ethnic composition, including Creoles, East Indians, Indonesians, Africans, Amerindians, Europeans and Chinese.

Religions
About 45 per cent of the population are Christians, 28 per cent Hindus and 20 per cent Muslims.

Political features
State type: emergent democratic
Date of state formation: 1975
Political structure: unitary
Executive: limited presidential
Assembly: one-chamber
Party structure: two-party
Human rights rating: N/A

Local and regional government
The country is divided into nine administrative districts, each controlled by a district commissioner. There is little or no representative local government.

Head of state and head of government
President Rameswak Shankar, since 1988.

Political leaders since 1970
1969–73 Jules Sedney (VHP), 1973–80 Henck Arron (NPS), 1980–82 Henk Chin A Sen (PNR), 1982–88 Desi Bouterse (Military-NDP), 1988– Rameswak Shankar (FDD).

Political system
The constitution was suspended in 1980 and in 1982 an interim President took office as head of state, with ultimate power held by the army, through its commander-in-chief who was also chairman of the Supreme Council, the country's controlling group. A nominated 31-member National Assembly was established in January 1985, consisting of 14 military, eleven trade union and six business nominees, and given 27 months in which to prepare a new constitution. This was approved in September 1987.

The new constitution provides for a National Assembly of 51, elected by universal adult suffrage, through a simple plurality voting system, for a five-year term. Once elected, the assembly then elects a President, who is both head of state and head of government, to serve a similar term.

Political parties
There are currently 15 political parties, the two main groupings being the Front for Democracy and Development (FDD) and the National Democratic Party (NDP).

The FDD is a coalition of three parties, the Party for National Unity and Solidarity (KTPI), the Suriname National Party (NPS) and the Progressive

Reform Party (VHP). It was formed in 1987 to fight the election. The KTPI dates from 1947 and draws its support mainly from the Indonesian population. The NPS began in 1946 and has largely Creole support. The VHP is a predominantly Indian party. The FDD has a left-of-centre orientation.

The NDP was formed in 1987 by Desi Bouterse, mainly to legitimise his regime. It is based on Standvaste, a mass movement which resulted from the coup of 1982.

Latest elections

In the 1987 National Assembly elections the FDD won 40 of the 51 seats, with 85 per cent of the popular vote. The Assembly then elected Rameswak Shankar as President.

Political history

Britain was the first European power to establish a settlement in Suriname, in 1651. In 1667 the Dutch took over, only to be removed by the British in 1799. The colony was finally restored to the Netherlands in 1819. As Dutch Guiana, it became, in 1954, an equal member of the Kingdom of the Netherlands, with internal self-government. Full independence was achieved in 1975, with Dr Johan Ferrier as President and Henck Arron, leader of the mainly Creole Suriname National Party (NPS), as Prime Minister.

In 1980 Arron's government was overthrown in an army coup but President Ferrier refused to recognise the military regime and appointed Dr Henk Chin A Sen, of the Nationalist Republican Party, to head a civilian administration. Five months later the army staged another coup and President Ferrier was replaced by Dr Chin A Sen. The new President announced details of a draft constitution which would reduce the role of the military, whereupon the army, led by Lieutenant-Colonel Desi Bouterse, dismissed Dr Chin A Sen and set up a Revolutionary People's Front.

There followed months of confusion in which a state of siege and then martial law were imposed. Between February 1980 and January 1983 there were no fewer than six attempted coups by different army groups. Because of the chaotic conditions, aid from the Netherlands and the United States was stopped and Bouterse was forced to look elsewhere for assistance, making agreements with Libya and Cuba. The partnership between the army, the trade unions and business, which had operated since 1981, eventually broke up in 1985 and Bouterse turned to the traditional parties which had operated prior to the 1980 coup.

The ban on political activity was lifted in anticipation of the adoption of a new constitution based on civilian rule. Leaders of the Creole, Indian and Indonesian parties were invited to take seats on a Supreme Council, with Wym Udenhout, a former colleague of Bouterse, as interim Prime Minister. In September 1987 a new constitution was approved and elections to the National Assembly were held in November. The combined opposition parties, which had formed an alliance under the umbrella name Front for Democracy and Development (FDD), won an overwhelming victory, and then elected Rameswak Shankar as the new President.

URUGUAY

Oriental Republic of Uruguay
Republica Oriental del Uruguay

Capital: Montevideo

Social and economic data
Area: 186,930 km^2
Population: 3.000m*
Pop density per km^2: 16*
Literacy rate: 94%*
GDP: $5,055m*; per capita GDP: $1,685
Economy type: middle income
Labour force in agriculture: 14%

*1985

Ethnic composition
The great majority of people are of European descent, about 54 per cent Spanish and about 22 per cent Italian. There are minorities from other European countries.

Religions
All religions are tolerated but most of the population are Roman Catholics.

Political features
State type: emergent democratic
Date of state formation: 1825
Political structure: unitary
Executive: limited presidential
Assembly: two-chamber
Party structure: multi-party
Human rights rating: 91%

Local and regional government
The country is divided into 19 departments, ranging in population from less than 24,000 to nearly 1.3 million. Each department is administered by an appointed *Intendente*. Cities have elected councils and mayors.

Head of state and head of government
President Dr Julio Maria Sanguinetti Cairolo , since 1985.

Political leaders since 1970
1967–72 Jorge Pacheo Areco (PN), 1972–76 Juan Maria Bordaberry Aroceno (PC), 1976–85 Aparacio Mendez Manfredini (Military), 1985– Julio Maria Sanguinetti Cairoto (PC coalition).

Political system
The 1966 constitution provides for a President, who is head of state and head of government, elected by universal adult suffrage for a five-year term, and a two-chamber assembly, consisting of a Senate and a Federal Chamber

of Deputies. The Senate has up to 30 members and the Chamber of Deputies 99, all elected by universal adult suffrage through a modified party list system of proportional representation, which ensures that there are at least two deputies representing each of the republic's 19 departments. Both chambers serve a five-year term. The President is assisted by a Vice-President and presides over a Council of Ministers. Constitutional government was suspended between 1973 and 1985 being replaced by a military dictatorship, but returned in 1985, operating under the 1966 constitution.

Political parties

There are currently five active political groupings, the three most significant being the Colorado Party (PC), the National (Blanco) Party (PN) and the Amplio Front (FA).

The PC was formed in 1836, following a successful revolt against the oppressive government of Fructuoso Rivera. It took the name of Colorado, or red, from the colour of the head bands of the revolutionaries who fought in the civil war. It now has a progressive, centre-left orientation.

PN supporters had white head bands, hence the name Blanco. It, too, began in 1836 in similar circumstances to the birth of the PC, but on the opposite side in the civil war. The PN has a traditionalist, right-of-centre orientation.

The FA was formed in 1971 and has always been a coalition of parties, with a fluctuating membership. In 1985, for example, it totalled 13 groups. It has a moderate, left-wing stance.

Latest elections

In the 1984 presidential election Julio Maria Sanguinetti (PC) was elected with 38.6 per cent of the popular vote. Alberto Saenz de Zumaran (PN) secured 32.9 per cent.

The results of the 1984 assembly elections were as follows:

	Senate Seats	*Chamber of Deputies Seats*
PC	13	41
PN	11	35
FA	6	21
Other parties	—	2

Political history

Uruguay was under Portuguese rule in the seventeenth century and under Spanish control for the next hundred years. It achieved full independence in 1825. The period that followed saw a series of local disturbances, leading to a civil war in 1836. After that the country enjoyed relative peace so that Uruguay gained a reputation for being not only the smallest, but the most politically stable of all South American republics.

Between 1951 and 1966 there was a collective leadership called 'collegiate government' and then a new constitution was adopted and the Blanco candidate, Jorge Pacheco Areco, was elected as a single President. His presidency was marked by high inflation, labour unrest and growing guerrilla activity by left-wing sugar workers, the Tupamaros.

In 1972 Pacheco was replaced by the Colorado candidate, Juan Maria Bordaberry Arocena. Within a year the Tupamaros had been crushed and all other left-wing groups banned. Bordaberry now headed a repressive regime, under which the normal democratic institutions had been destroyed. When, in 1976, he refused any movement towards constitutional government, he was deposed by the army and Dr Aparicio Mendez Manfredini was made President.

Despite promises to return to democratic government, the severe repression continued and political opponents were imprisoned. In 1981 the deteriorating economy made the army anxious to return to constitutional government and a retired general, Gregorio Alvarez Armellino was appointed to serve as President for an interim period until full constitutional government was restored. Discussions between the army and the main political parties failed to reach agreement on the form of constitution to be adopted and civil unrest, in the shape of strikes and demonstrations, grew. By 1984 anti-government activity had reached a crisis point and eventually all the main political leaders signed an agreement for a Programme of National Accord.

The 1966 constitution, with some modifications, was restored and in 1985 a general election was held. The Colorado Party won a narrow majority and its leader, Dr Julio Maria Sanguinetti, became President. The army stepped down and by 1986 President Sanguinetti was presiding over a government of National Accord in which all the main parties were represented. There are now signs that Uruguay is returning to the form of government which, historically, had made it a model democracy.

VENEZUELA

Republic of Venezuela
Republica de Venezuela

Capital: Caracas

Social and economic data
Area: 912,050 km^2
Population: 17.800m
Pop density per km^2: 20*
Literacy rate: 85%*
GDP: $49,604m*; per capita GDP: $2,786
Economy type: middle income
Labour force in agriculture: 15%

*1985

Ethnic composition
About 67 per cent of the population are mestizos, 21 per cent Europeans, 10 per cent Africans and 2 per cent Indians.

Religions
Roman Catholicism is the state religion and the great majority of people practise it. There is, however, complete freedom of worship for all denominations.

Political features
State type: liberal democratic
Date of state formation: 1830
Political structure: federal
Executive: limited presidential
Assembly: two-chamber
Party structure: multi-party
Human rights rating: 88%

Local and regional government
Venezuela is a federal nation of 20 states, two territories and one federal district, based on the capital, Caracas. It is, however, a comparatively weak federal system because each state is heavily dependent on the federal government for finance. State governments are headed by governors appointed by the President and have elected assemblies. For administrative purposes, they are further subdivided into electorates and then municipalities.

Head of state and head of government
President Carlos Andres Perez, since 1988.

Political leaders since 1970
1969–74 Rafael Caldera Rodriguez (COPEI), 1974–79 Carlos Andres Rodriquez (AD), 1979–84 Luis Herrera (COPEI), 1984–88 Jaime Lusinchi (AD),1988– Carlos Andres Perez (AD).

Political system
The 1961 constitution contains features similar to those of the United States and provides for a President, who is head of state and head of government and a two-chamber National Congress, consisting of a Senate and Chamber of Deputies. The President is elected by universal adult suffrage for a five-year term and may not serve two consecutive terms. The Senate has 44 members elected by universal adult suffrage, on the basis of two representatives for each state and two for the Federal District, plus all living ex-Presidents, *ex officio*. The Chamber has 196 deputies, elected by universal adult suffrage, through a party list system of proportional representation. Both chambers serve five-year terms. The President appoints and presides over a Council of Ministers.

Political parties
There are currently 13 active political parties, the most significant being the Democratic Action Party (AD), the Christian Social Party (COPEI) and the Movement towards Socialism (MAS).

The AD was formed in 1936 as the National Democratic Party and adopted its present name in 1941. Its membership now totals nearly 1.5 million. It has a moderate, left-of-centre orientation.

COPEI was founded in 1946 by the leader of the Catholic Student Movement. It now has a membership of about 400,000 and adopts a Christian, centre-right stance.

The MAS dates from 1971 and was formed by members of the Communist Party who broke away after the Soviet invasion of Czechoslovakia. It has a left-of-centre orientation.

Latest elections

In the 1988 presidential election Carlos Andres Perez (AD) defeated the COPEI candidate, Eduardo Fernandez (52.91% to 40.42%).

In the 1988 assembly elections the results were as follows:

	Senate Seats	*Chamber of Deputies Seats*
AD	23	97
COPEI	22	67
MAS	3	18
Other parties	1	19

Political history

Venezuela was first colonised by Spain in the sixteenth century and from then until independence was achieved, in 1830, there were repeated rebellions against Spanish rule. In the nineteenth century the independence movement was led by Simon Bolivar, who established the state of Gran Colombia, which included what are now Colombia, Ecuador and Venezuela, driving out the Spanish royalist forces. Venezuela became an independent republic when Gran Colombia was dissolved.

From 1909 to 1935 the country suffered under the harsh dictatorship of General Juan Gomez, who developed Venezuela's rich oil resources, making it the world's largest exporter of petroleum, but passing little of the wealth to the ordinary inhabitants. The first free elections were held in 1947 but were soon followed by another period of repression, this time under General Jimenez. Venezuela had to wait until 1959 before the democratically elected government of Romulo Betancourt came to power.

A new constitution was adopted in 1961 and three years later Betancourt became the first President to complete his full term of office. He was succeeded in 1964 by Dr Raul Leoni and then, in 1969, Dr Rafael Caldera Rodriguez was elected as Venezuela's first Christian Social President. He did much to bring economic and political stability, although underground abductions and assassinations still occurred. In 1974 Carlos Andres Rodriguez, of the Democratic Action Party (AD), came to the presidency and the movement towards greater stability continued. In 1979 Dr Luis Herrera, leader of the Christian Social Party (COPEI), was elected, but without a working majority in Congress, so he was dependent on the other parties for legislative support.

Against a background of growing economic problems, the 1983 general election was contested by 20 parties and 13 presidential candidates. It was a bitterly fought campaign and resulted in the election of Dr Jaime Lusinchi (AD) as President and a win for the AD in Congress. President Lusinchi's austere economic policies were unpopular and throughout 1985 he worked hard to try to conclude a social pact among the government, trade unions and business. He also reached an agreement with the government's creditor bankers for a rescheduling of Venezuela's large public debt. Lusinchi's AD rival Carlos Andres Perez won the 1988 presidential nomination and the presidency itself. He embarked upon a strict austerity programme in return for the IMF loans, resulting in protest riots in Caracas in the spring of 1989.

SOVIET UNION
MONGOLIA
CHINA
N KOREA
S. KOREA
JAPAN
Tropic of Cancer
Pacific Ocean
IRAN
AFGHANISTAN
PAKISTAN
U.A.E.
OMAN
NEPAL
BHUTAN
BANGLA-DESH
INDIA
BURMA
LAOS
THAILAND
VIETNAM
CAMBODIA
TAIWAN
PHILIPPINES
Equator
Socotra (S Y)
SOMALIA
SRI LANKA
MALDIVES
BRUNEI
MALAYSIA
SINGA-PORE
INDONESIA
PAPUA NEW GUINEA
Indian Ocean
AUSTRALIA
Scale 1:60 000 000
0 500 1000 1500 2000 Km

ASIA

The region of Asia, covering a sixth of the world's surface, is the third largest global block in areal terms, ranking behind Eastern Europe and Central and Southern Africa. In demographic terms, it is by far the largest, incorporating more than half the world's population and six of its ten most populous nations. Within the region there are 23 states. Sixteen are continental in situation, occupying the south-eastern, sub-Turkestan and sub-Siberian portion of the vast Euro-Asian land mass. The remaining seven are either offshore archipelagos or islands.

The region constitutes the world's most thickly peopled block, boasting an average population density three and a half times the world norm. It is also the world's second poorest in terms of per capita GDP, with a regional income barely a third of the global average. Indeed, 12 of the region's 23 countries occupy the bottom quartile of world states in terms of national incomes per capita, with Cambodia standing at the very base. A further five are located in the third quartile, while only three, mineral-rich Brunei, the city-state entrepôt of Singapore and industrialised Japan, are to be found in the first quartile of 'high income' nations.

The explanation for this poverty is the continued dominance of rural activities, the agricultural sector still providing employment for more than half the national labour force in 13 of the region's states, including eight of its ten most populous. Prior to the Second World War, only one state, Japan, was substantially industrialised. Since the war it has grown to become the world's economic power house, claiming a 10 per cent share of global GDP. Within the Asian region, its dominance is even more marked and accounts for 59 per cent of the region's GDP, but only 5 per cent of its population. Japan also provides more than $21 billion in investment capital. China and India, in contrast, while accounting for 69 per cent of Asia's population can claim barely a 22 per cent share of its GDP.

During recent decades, four other Asian countries, South Korea, Singapore, Taiwan and Thailand, have begun to industrialise rapidly, in an export-led manner, gaining the acronym NICs or 'newly industrialising countries'. Two other states, Indonesia and Malaysia, have attempted to follow. The demographic giant, China, now shows signs of an economic awakening, making the Pacific part of the Asian region currently the world's most dynamic area.

The successful growth of these NICs has resulted from a unique blend of free-market economics and selective state support. The industriousness, docility and high educational levels of the work forces in these countries, combined with the inbred sense of frugality of the general population, have also provided ideal conditions. These national traits are underpinned by ancient Confucian value systems, which have helped to sustain paternalistic, authoritarian political systems. Recently, however, as affluence has spread, there have been growing signs of internal pressure for greater political pluralism.

Further to the west, in the Indian Ocean region, industrial growth has been less impressive. Here, popular literacy and educational levels have traditionally been lower, literacy rates of below 30 per cent being recorded for contemporary Afghanistan, Bangladesh, Bhutan, Nepal and Pakistan. Islamic and Hindu cultural traditions have also proved to be less conducive than Confucianism to the growth process. Since the 1970s, however, with the spread of new 'green revolution' seeds and production technology, peasant-based agricultural advances have been seen in a number of the states, most notably in the Punjab regions of India and Pakistan. These have enabled the rapidly expanding populations of these countries, currently increasing at an annual rate of between 2 per cent and 3 per cent, to be fed without a fall in general living standards.

The Asian region is, historically and culturally, one of the richest in the world. It has served as the cradle for such ancient and impressive civilisations as the Harappan or Indus Valley, from *c*2500 to *c*1600 BC, the Xia, from *c*2220 to 1700 BC, the Shang, from *c*1500 to *c*1066 BC, the Zhou, from 1122 to 249 BC, the Mauryan, from 321 to 184 BC, the Han, from 206 BC to AD 220, the Gupta, from *c*300 to AD 500, the Tang, from AD 618 to 907, the Khmer, from the sixth to the fifteenth centuries, and the Ming, from 1368 to 1644. For this reason, an unusually high number, amounting to five, or 22 per cent, of the region's contemporary states date their founding to periods prior to the nineteenth century. This figure is based on territorial affinity. At least five other countries, India, Cambodia, the Koreas and Vietnam, which were the sites of ancient or medieval kingdoms of national proportions, might also be included in this category if a looser definition was to be used.

The two dominant civilisations in the region have been the Indian and Chinese, each having originated distinctive religious and moral-philosophical systems which were later diffused throughout Asia by their followers.

The five most important religions or moral systems which are indigenous to the Asian region and have retained their importance are Hinduism, Buddhism, Confucianism, Daoism and Shintoism. The first two originated in India, the second two in China, and the fifth in Japan. Their distribution across the region is clearly defined today. Hinduism, which is a non-proselytising faith, is predominant only in India and Nepal, although it is a minority religion in neighbouring Bangladesh, Bhutan and Sri Lanka. Shintoism, which is a unique, national religion, is similarly restricted to Japan. In contrast, Buddhism, although it originated in India around 500 BC, and gained popularity during the Mauryan era, has been widely diffused across Asia. Today, it constitutes the dominant faith in Bhutan, Burma, Cambodia, Laos, Mongolia and Sri Lanka. Mixed with Confucianism and Daoism, it also predominates in China, North Korea, South Korea, Singapore, Thailand and Vietnam and is an important minority faith in Brunei and Malaysia.

To these indigenous religions there were added, from early medieval times, the outside faiths of Islam and Christianity. Islam was spread by land to Afghanistan and Pakistan in West Asia, and by sea, further east, to Bangladesh, Brunei, Indonesia, Malaysia and the Maldives. Christianity, however, made only a tangential impact on the region. Today, therefore, even in its areas of highest support, such as South Korea, where 28 per cent of the population are Christians, Indonesia, 8 per cent, and Malaysia, 7 per cent, it remains a minority religion. In contrast, Islam, which was a proselytising faith in a number of important medieval and early modern kingdoms and is a state religion in 25 contemporary nations, has had a marked regional impact. Not only is it today the predominant religion in the seven countries noted above, but more than two-thirds of the world's Muslim population now reside within the Asian region. Indonesia, with 145 million, Pakistan, 93 million, Bangladesh, 91 million, and India, 75 million, possess the four largest national Islamic communities in the world.

With the exception of the Muslim incursions during the medieval period noted above, Asia, although open to trading contacts, remained substantially free from external territorial conquest and colonisation until the later sixteenth century, when the Dutch established settlements in some coastal areas of Indonesia. This served to reinforce the cultural distinctiveness of the region. Thereafter, however, particularly following the British conquest of the Indian sub-continent, European influence spread rapidly.

The height of the colonisation process was attained in the late nineteenth and early twentieth centuries, when three zones of imperial control were established: a 'British zone' in the west, a more tightly controlled 'French zone' in the central region, and a smaller, though intensively colonised, 'Japanese zone' to the east.

The British zone extended from Pakistan to Malaysia and was characterised by a substantial measure of 'indirect rule'. The French zone was mainly in Indo-China, and that of the Japanese in Formosa, now Taiwan, and Korea, and then it was later extended, though only briefly, between 1942 and 1945, to incorporate much of East Asia.

Compared with the equivalent process in Africa, the European colonisation of Asia began at an early date but also ended sooner. The Japanese colonial empire was dismembered in 1945, much of the British between 1947 and 1957, and the French in 1954. The strength of indigenous nationalist resistance was an important factor behind this early decolonisation. It was also important in explaining the failure of the European powers to impose direct control over China and Japan. Five other, more peripheral countries, Afghanistan, Bhutan, Mongolia, Nepal and Thailand, also escaped direct colonisation.

Despite its relative brevity, the experience of colonial rule has left a perceptible, though varied, political imprint on the states of the Asian region. Additional, and in many respects more important, political conditioning factors have been economic structures and conditions, and ethnic patterns and rivalries.

The influence of economic factors is most clearly seen in the four states of China, Cambodia, Laos and Vietnam. In these countries rural overpopulation and distress provided the material conditions, which made possible, and successful, the peasant revolutions of the later 1940s, the 1950s and the 1960s, particularly as they were linked to anti-colonial nationalism and communist ideology.

Ethnic rivalries have also been potent political forces, with many of the states experiencing conflict on their frontiers, where ethnic, often tribal, minority communities predominate, all deeply opposed to the imposition of cultural and political hegemony by the majority community. In Burma, Indonesia and Thailand, such minority versus majority hostility has sustained persistent peasant guerrilla insurgencies in border zones. In India, similar secessionist movements abound in the north-eastern hill zone, while in the economically successful, Sikh-dominated, Punjab and in culturally resilient Tibet different autonomy movements are found. More generalised, regionally-based, ethnic rivalries are also prevalent in contemporary Afghanistan and Pakistan, while in Malaysia and Sri Lanka tensions between the indigenous majority and immigrant minority communities have heightened during recent years.

As a result of these ethnic rivalries, as well as the continuing or simmering state conflicts in Afghanistan, Cambodia, Laos, the Koreas and Vietnam, contemporary levels of military mobilisation and defence expenditure are relatively high in the Asia. Thirteen of the countries in the region appear among the upper half of world states in ratios of soldiers per 1,000 inhabitants, with four, North Korea, Singapore, Taiwan and Mongolia, in the top ten. Consequently, defence spending as a proportion of GDP is high in all four countries, as well as in Vietnam, where it exceeds 33 per cent, and China, where it is above 10 per cent.

The range of political and executive types of the states in the region is unusually broad, all categories, with the exception of the military authoritarian, being represented. This reflects, at least in part, Asia's diversity in historical experiences and varieties of economies and religions. Eleven, or almost half, of the countries fall into the categories of either liberal or emergent democracies, while a further six have communist systems. The liberal democracies are predominantly parliamentary in character and are to be found among either the high or middle income states, or among parts of what was once British India, where citizens had been accustomed to democratic structures for at least a century. It is perhaps significant that the emergent democracies are to be found among either NICs or the other remaining parts of British India. By contrast, all the six communist states are low income countries, three of them, Cambodia, Laos and Vietnam, ranking among the four poorest states in the region. Bhutan is the exception in the emergent democracy category.

In terms of party systems, the Asian region is split evenly between countries with one- or multi-party systems. However, in several states which are apparently pluralist, *de facto* one-party dominance exists. In terms of voting systems, the simple plurality type predominates. Finally, only three of the region's states, India, Pakistan and Malaysia, have federal structures. This number is surprisingly small, the absence of federalism being especially notable in the cases of Afghanistan, China and Indonesia.

Table 63

ASIA

Political Data							
State	*Date of Formation*	*Political Structure*	*State type*	*Executive*	*Assembly No of Chambers*	*Party System*	*Voting System*
Afghanistan	1747	Unitary	Emgt Dem	Lim Pres	Two	One*	SP
Bangladesh	1971	Unitary	Emgt Dem	Lim Pres	One	Multi	SP
Bhutan	1907	Unitary	Absolutist	Absolute	One	None	SP
Brunei	1984	Unitary	Absolutist	Absolute	None	One	None
Burma	1948	Unitary	Nat Soc	Unlim Pres	One	One	SP
Cambodia	1953	Unitary	Communist	Communist	One	One	SP
China	2ndC BC	Unitary	Communist	Communist	One	One	SP
India	1947	Federal	Lib Dem	Parliament	Two	Multi†	SP
Indonesia	1949	Unitary	Auth Nat	Unlim Pres	One	Three†	PL
Japan	5thC	Unitary	Lib Dem	Parliament	Two	Multi†	LV

Table 63—Asia (contd.)

			Political Data				
					Assembly		
	Date of	*Political*			*No of*	*Party*	*Voting*
State	*Formation*	*Structure*	*State type*	*Executive*	*Chambers*	*System*	*System*
North Korea	1948	Unitary	Communist	Communist	One	One	SP
South Korea	1948	Unitary	Emgt Dem	Lim Pres	One	Multi	AM
Laos	1954	Unitary	Communist	Communist	One	One	SP
Malaysia	1957	Federal	Lib Dem	Parliament	Two	Multi	SP
Maldives	1965	Unitary	Auth Nat	Unlim Pres	One	None	SP
Mongolia	1921/46	Unitary	Communist	Communist	One	One	SP
Nepal	1768	Unitary	Absolutist	Absolute	One	None	SP
Pakistan	1947	Federal	Emgt Dem	Lim Pres‡	Two	Multi	SP
Singapore	1965	Unitary	Lib Dem	Parliament	One	Multi†	SP
Sri Lanka	1948	Unitary	Lib Dem	Dual	One	Two	PL
Taiwan	1949	Unitary	Emgt Dem	Lim Pres	One	Multi*	SP
Thailand	1350	Unitary	Emgt Dem	Parliament	Two	Multi	SP
Vietnam	1954/76	Unitary	Communist	Communist	One	One	SP

*Multi-party system in the process of emerging.

†Though dominated by one paramount party.

‡Evolving towards a parliamentary executive.

		Social and Economic Data				
			Population			
		Population	*Density*	*Literacy*		*Human Rights*
	Area	*(m)*	*(per*	*Rate*	*Income*	*Rating*
State	*(km²)*	*(1985)*	*km²)*	*(%)*	*Type*	*(%)*
Afghanistan	647,500	18.136	28	18	Low	Bad
Bangladesh	144,000	104.100	723	29	Low	44
Bhutan	46,600	1.446	31	18	Low	N/A
Brunei	5,800	0.240	41	78	High	N/A
Burma	678,000	37.700	56	71	Low	Poor
Cambodia	181,000	7.284	40	48	Low	Bad
China	9,561,000	1050.000	110	65	Low	23
India	3,287,590	785.000	239	41	Low	60
Indonesia	1,925,000	173.013	90	67	Low	30
Japan	371,860	121.402	326	100	High	88
North Korea	121,250	20.500	169	90	Low	17
South Korea	98,500	43.300	440	93	Middle	59
Laos	236,800	4.117	17	44	Low	Bad
Malaysia	332,370	15.820	48	70	Middle	53
Maldives	300	0.180	600	90	Low	N/A
Mongolia	1,565,000	1.900	1	90	Low	N/A
Nepal	141,400	17.422	123	21	Low	Poor
Pakistan	803,900	101.900	127	26	Low	40
Singapore	616	2.584	4,195	83	High	59
Sri Lanka	65,610	16.344	249	86	Low	52
Taiwan	36,000	19.600	544	89	Middle	50
Thailand	514,000	52.438	102	88	Low	57
Vietnam	329,600	62.000	188	84	Low	25
Total/Average	21,093,696	2656.426	126	18–100	Low	17–88

AFGHANISTAN

Republic of Afghanistan
De Afghanistan Jamhuriat

Capital: Kabul

Social and economic data
Area: 647,500 km^2
Population: 18.136m*
Pop density per km^2: 28*
Literacy rate: 18%
GDP: $3,600m*; per capita GDP: $199
Economy type: low income
Labour force in agriculture: 58%

*1985 (incl. exiled refugees)

Ethnic composition
Pathans, or Pushtuns, comprise the largest ethnic group, 60 per cent of the total population. Concentrated in the north are the Tajiks, 30 per cent, and the Uzbeks, 5 per cent. Currently, more than 5 million Afghan people reside as refugees in border areas of adjoining Iran and Pakistan. Pushtu and Dari, or Persian, constitute the official languages.

Religions
Eighty per cent of the population are adherents to Islam of the Sunni sect and 19 per cent are Shia.

Political features
State type: emergent democracy*
Date of state formation: 1747
Political structure: unitary
Executive: limited presidential*
Assembly: two-chamber
Party structure: one-party†
Human rights rating: bad

*Though currently in a state of suspension.
†Multi-party system is in the process of emerging.

Local and regional government
The country is divided into 30 provinces *(wilayat)*, each of which is administered by a centrally appointed governor. There are plans for the future establishment of elected local committees and councils at the provincial level, as well as in cities, districts, sub-districts and villages.

Head of state
President Dr Najibullah Ahmadzai, since 1986.

Head of government
Prime Minister Sultan Ali Keshtmand, since 1989.

Political leaders since 1970

1933–73 King Zahir Shah, 1973–78 General Daud Khan, 1978–79 Nur Mohammad Taraki (PDPA: Khalq)*, 1979–79 Hafizullah Amin (PDPA: Khalq)*, 1979–86 Babrak Karmal (PDPA: Parcham)*, 1986– Dr Najibullah Ahmadzai (PDPA: Parcham).*

*Communist Party leaders

Political system

Following the coup of April 1978, the constitution of 1977 was abolished and legislative and executive authority was assumed by a 57-member Revolutionary Council, which was controlled, in turn, by a smaller Presidium, composed of leaders from the communist People's Democratic Party of Afghanistan (PDPA). In April 1985, a Grand National Assembly (Loya Jirga) of indirectly elected tribal elders was convened to approve a temporary constitution. This enshrined the right to practise Islam and envisaged the future direct election of a National Assembly, which would function as the 'highest organ of state power'. In the interim, all effective powers were deemed to reside with the, now 165-member, Revolutionary Council and its permanent Presidium, while day-to-day administration was left to a Council of Ministers, headed by a chairman, or Prime Minister. The members of the Council of Ministers were appointed by the Revolutionary Council.

This transitional state of affairs was brought to an end in November 1987 when the reconvened Loya Jirga formally adopted a new permanent constitution which had been drafted by a 74-member commission. Under the terms of this constitution, the country is formally defined as a non-aligned, Islamic republic in which the formation of a multiplicity of political parties is to be permitted subject to certain restrictions, which are described below. State protection of private ownership and the inheritance of property are also explicitly recognised.

The new political system established under the terms of the November 1987 constitution is presidential and yet eclectic, seeking to combine diverse elements from communist, liberal democratic and traditional Afghan polities.

At the apex of the new political hierarchy stands the Loya Jirga, a vast body which comprises the members of the National Assembly, the Council of Ministers, the Supreme Court and the Council of the Constitution. It also includes representatives from the provinces, the executive board of the National Front of Afghanistan and at least 50 'outstanding political, scientific, social and religious figures'. Described as 'the highest manifestation of the political will of the people', the Loya Jirga is an *ad hoc* entity, which has the task of amending and interpreting the constitution, declaring war, adopting fundamental decisions 'concerning the nation's destiny', and electing, by majority vote, the President of the Republic.

The President is the most powerful figure in the country. Restricted to a maximum of two seven-year terms, he concurrently holds the post of Supreme Commander of the Armed Forces, appoints the Prime Minister and is empowered to approve the laws and resolutions of the National Assembly (Meli Shura).

The Meli Shura is the nation's legislature and has replaced the former Revolutionary Council. It is a two-chamber body, consisting of a

234-member lower house, the Council of Representatives (Wolosi Jirga), whose members are elected for a five-year term, to represent constituencies of equal population size, and a 128-member upper house, the Senate (Sena), or Council of Elders (Meshrano Jirga). Two-thirds of the members of the upper house are elected from the provinces to serve three- and five-year terms and one third are appointed by the President, from among the ranks of 'learned, scholarly and reliable persons and national personalities'. The National Assembly convenes twice a year, in late February and August, for three-month sessions.

From its ranks a 25 to 30-member Council of Ministers, headed by a chairman, or Prime Minister, is drawn, to function in cabinet fashion as the 'highest executive and administrative organ of state power'. This new 'limited presidential' system came into force after the April 1988 National Assembly elections. It has, however, been suspended following the Soviet troop withdrawal in February 1989, with a new emergency regime being temporarily established. Certain articles of the 1987 constitution, including the right of assembly, have been set aside; seven independent members of the Council of Ministers have been replaced by senior PDPA figures; and a new 20-member Supreme Council for the Defence of the Homeland (SCDH), headed by President Najibullah, has been established to direct political and military activities.

Political parties

In the wake of the April 1978 communist coup, Afghanistan became a one-party state, dominated and controlled by the People's Democratic Party of Afghanistan (PDPA: Jamiyat-e Demokrati Khalq-e Afghanistan). Organised on Leninist 'democratic centralist' lines, the PDPA was governed from above by a 15 to 20-member Politburo and operated more broadly under the guise of the National Fatherland Front. Party monism was ended in July and November 1987 by the passage of new constitutional laws which permitted the formation of additional political parties, 'provided that their rules, aims and activities were not contrary to the articles of the constitution or the laws of the country'.

By mid-1988 five political parties were operating. Three of them, the PDPA, the Toilers' Revolutionary Organisation of Afghanistan and the Toilers' Revolutionary Society of Afghanistan, are 'democratic left' in orientation. The other two are the Peasants' Justice Party of Afghanistan and the People's Islamic Party of Afghanistan.

The PDPA, which heads the new National Front of Afghanistan broad-front umbrella organisation, is the dominant force. It was founded, illegally, in 1965 by Nur Mohammad Taraki. Two years later, because of disputes over strategy, it split into two wings, the rural-based, Pushtu-speaking Khalq (Masses or People's) group, led by Taraki, and the urban-based, Dari-speaking Parcham (Banner or Flag) group, led by Babrak Karmal. After the overthrow of the monarchy, in 1973, factional differences widened when the Parcham group accepted Soviet Union orders to co-operate with the new Daud Khan regime, as part of a more moderate coalition strategy, while the Khalq wing rejected them, preferring a policy of radical class struggle. Unity, under Khalq leadership, was restored in July 1977, but rivalries swiftly re-emerged and intensified in 1979 following the ousting of Taraki as party leader and President of the Republic.

Since the Soviet Union's installation of Babrak Karmal as PDPA leader, and head of state, in December 1979, the Parcham group has dominated the PDPA, though intra-factional rivalries, Karmal versus Najibullah supporters, have recently emerged. Membership of the PDPA currently stands at 186,000, a figure which constitutes barely 1 per cent of the total population. The majority of members are drawn from urban areas.

Opposed to the present Najibullah regime are *mujaheddin* insurgent groupings, which have their headquarters in Pakistan. The most important are the fundamentalist, anti-Western Hesb-i Islami, whose two factions are led by the 'hard-line' Gulbuddin Hekmatyar and Maulavi Younis Khalis respectively; the more restrained fundamentalist Jamiat-i Islami, led by Professor Burhanuddin Rabbani; the Movement for Islamic Revolution of Afghanistan, led by Muhammad Nabi Muhammadi and Nasrullah Mansur; the traditionalist National Islamic Liberation Front, led by Pir Sayyed Ahmed Gailani; and the moderate National Liberation Front, led by Professor Imam Sibghatullah Mojaddedi. Unity among the groupings is notoriously strained, although a loose, seven-party, mujaheddin alliance, led in 1988 successively by Gulbuddin Hekmatyar, Barhanuddin Rabani, and Ahmed Shah Massoud, has been in operation since May 1985. In February 1989, this alliance announced that it had agreed on the composition of its own 'alternative government', with Professor Sibghatullah Mojaddedi being selected for the post of President, and the Wahabi Fundamentalist, Abdul Rasul Sayyaf, leader of Itihad-i-Islami, as Prime Minister.

Latest elections

Elections to the National Assembly were held in April 1988 and were contested by candidates put forward under the umbrella of the National Front of Afghanistan, which included within its ranks representatives from all five functioning political parties noted above, as well as from the armed forces, peasants' co-operatives, Council of Afghan Women and Central Council of Nomads. Only 184 Council of Representatives seats were actually contested, the remainder being reserved so as to tempt moderate mujaheddin elements to join the political process at a later date. Fifty-one Senate seats were subject to election, with a further 45 Senators being appointed by the President. 1.55 million voters were said to have participated, the majority of members returned being non-PDPA members.

Political history

Under the leadership of Ahmed Shah Durrani, Afghanistan became an independent emirate in 1747 and, although defeated by Britain in the 'Afghan wars', of 1838–42, 1878–80 and 1919, and subjected to a partial loss of autonomy, it was never formally placed under colonial control. After the third Anglo-Afghan War, in 1919, Afghanistan was re-established in 1926 as a fully independent, neutral monarchy.

During the 1950s, Lieutenant General Sardar Mohammad Daud Khan, the cousin of King Mohammed Zahir Shah, who had ruled between 1933 and 1973, became Prime Minister and introduced a major programme of social and economic modernisation, drawing economic aid from the Soviet Union. Opposition to the authoritarian nature of Daud's rule, however, forced his resignation, in 1963, and a new constitution was adopted. Under it the King became a constitutional monarch but political parties were outlawed.

Following a serious famine in 1972, the monarchy was overthrown in a military coup, on 17 July 1973, and King Zahir Shah fled to exile in Rome. A republic was declared, with General Daud Khan back at the head of the government. He received Soviet backing for this coup, but once in power tried to shift towards a more moderate policy programme, building up broader national support among minority tribes, and reducing Afghanistan's dependence on Russia. He began to develop close ties with the non-aligned, Middle East oil states, where large numbers of Afghans were then employed.

A new, presidential, constitution was adopted in 1977, but the government was undermined by fundamentalist Muslim insurgents, financed by Libya, Iran and Pakistan. In April 1978, President Daud was assassinated in a military coup, known, from its date, as the 'Saur Revolution', and Nur Mohammad Taraki, the imprisoned leader of the radical Khalq faction of the banned communist People's Democratic Party of Afghanistan (PDPA), took charge, as President of a Revolutionary Council. A new one-party constitution was adopted, a Treaty of Friendship and Mutual Defence signed with the Soviet Union, in 1978, and major social and land reforms were introduced.

These radical policy intitiatives, which were designed to mobilise the landless poor and weaken support for traditional social and economic structures and leaders, were opposed, however, by conservative Muslims. Thousands of refugees fled to Iran and Pakistan and there was a major uprising in the Herat region. The internal situation deteriorated rapidly and, following an intra-PDPA power struggle, Taraki was ousted and murdered, in September 1979. He was replaced, as President of the Revolutionary Council, by the Prime Minister and foreign minister, Hafizullah Amin.

Internal unrest continued, however, and the Soviet Union was persuaded to organise a further coup, in December 1979. Hafizullah Amin was executed and Babrak Karmal, the exiled leader of the, more gradualist, Parcham faction of the PDPA, installed in power, with the backing of 40,000 Soviet troops who invaded the country the day after Christmas.

The 'Soviet invasion' of December 1979 was condemned by many United Nations' members and resulted in the American Carter administration implementing a programme of economic and diplomatic sanctions against the Soviet Union, bringing about a serious deterioration in East-West relations. Despite these Western actions, however, Soviet forces remained in Afghanistan, with Red Army troop numbers increasing to more than 120,000 in 1985, as Muslim guerrilla resistance, by the mujaheddin, or 'holy warriors', continued. The guerrillas were now being aided indirectly by the United States, China and Pakistan. A war of attrition developed, with the Soviets launching regular land and air offensives, but failing to gain full control of many rural areas.

Faced with mounting troop casualties, which already exceeded 9,000, and a debilitating drain on economic resources, the new Soviet administration of Mikhail Gorbachev, in 1986, began to take steps to seek a compromise settlement. In May 1986 Babrak Karmal was replaced as PDPA leader by the Pushtun former KHAD secret police chief, Dr Najibullah Ahmadzai, and a number of non-communist politicians were introduced into the new government. Greater toleration of the practices of

Islam was also seen and in October 1986 8,000 Soviet troops were withdrawn, as an initial goodwill gesture. This withdrawal was followed, in January 1987, by an announcement from the Afghan government that there would be a unilateral six-month cease-fire, to allow discussions to take place about the formation of a possible 'coalition government of national unity', which would remain friendly towards the Soviet Union.

However, the Afghan guerrillas, who were divided along tribal and ideological lines into seven groupings, rejected this initiative, determined to effect a full Soviet withdrawal and a replacement of the communist government.

Additional unilateral extensions of the cease-fire by the Afghanistan government were made in July and November 1987, with in the latter month the ratification of a new multi-party constitution, to further the 'national reconciliation' initiative. In Geneva progress was also made in United Nations-sponsored talks between Afghan and Pakistan representatives about resolving the 'Afghan crisis'. This was followed in February 1988 by an announcement from the Soviet leader, Mikhail Gorbachev, of a phased nine-month plan for Soviet troop withdrawals, beginning in May 1988 and ending in February 1989.

This pull-out started, as planned, in May 1988, being preceded, in April, by the signing in Geneva of an agreement between the Afghan and Pakistan governments which provided for non-interference in each other's internal affairs and the voluntary return of refugees. The United States and Soviet Union were to guarantee the accord. This agreement promised to bring to an end a decade of direct Soviet interference in the internal affairs of Afghanistan, an involvement which had served to ignite a bitter civil war, resulting, according to official Soviet sources, in the loss of 15,000 Red Army troops and 70,000 Afghan security forces personnel, as well as, according to Western estimates, the lives of more than 1 million Afghans and the uprooting, as refugees, of a further 5 million.

After the Soviet troop withdrawal took place, in February 1989, a 'state of emergency' was imposed by the Najibullah regime, with a new Supreme Council for the Defence of the Homeland (SCDH) being established and Prime Minister Dr Mohammad Hasan Sharq being replaced by his predecessor, Sultan Ali Keshtmand, a Shia Muslim. The civil war intensified, with the mujaheddin claiming control over 85 per cent of the Afghan countryside. The PDPA regime, however, retained control over the principal urban centres and continued to press for a compromise political solution.

BANGLADESH

People's Republic of Bangladesh
Gana Projatantri Bangladesh

Capital: Dhaka

Social and economic data
Area: 144,000 km^2
Population: 104.100m*

Pop density per km^2: 723*
Literacy rate: 29%
GDP: $16,080m*; per capita GDP: $154
Economy type: low income
Labour force in agriculture: 58%

*1985

Ethnic composition
Ninety-eight per cent of the population are of Bengali ethnic stock, 400,000 are Bihari and around 1 million belong to 'tribal' communities. Bengali is the official language, with English also being widely spoken.

Religions
Eighty-seven per cent of the population are Muslims, adhering predominantly to the Sunni sect, though influenced by local Hindu practices, and 12 per cent are Hindus. Following a 1977 amendment to the 1972 constitution, Islam was made a 'guiding principle' of the political system. In 1988, with the passage of the Constitution Eighth Amendment Bill, it was declared the official state religion.

Political features
State type: emergent democracy
Date of state formation: 1971
Political structure: unitary
Executive: limited presidential
Assembly: one-chamber
Party structure: multi-party
Human rights rating: 44%

Local and regional government
The country is divided into 21 regions and 64 districts, with elected local councils. Below these, as part of a decentralisation programme, 493 sub-districts *(upazillas)* were created in 1983, each containing an average of 260,000 people. The *upazillas* are staffed by centrally appointed civil servants, working with local chairmen, who hold office for five-year terms. They are allotted annual development funds and their chief function is to increase local participation in the implementation of state projects. Below the *upazillas*, at the base of the local government hierarchy, there are more than 4,400 rural councils *(parishads)*, each serving a population of roughly 20,000. These councils are popularly elected in a fiercely contested manner, more than 150 people losing their lives during the most recent, February 1988, contests.

Head of state and head of government
President Lieutenant General Hossain Mohammad Ershad, since 1983.

Political leaders since 1970
1971–75 Sheikh Mujibur Rahman (Awami League), 1975–75 Khandakar Mushtaq Ahmed (Awami League), 1975–76 Abu Sadat Mohammad Sayem

(Independent), 1976–81 Major-General Ziaur Rahman (Military/Bangladesh Nationalist Party), 1981–82 Abdus Sattar (Bangladesh National Party), 1982– Lieutenant General Hossain Mohammad Ershad (Military/Jatiya Front).

Political system

Bangladesh's political system remains in a transitional state. The constitution of 1972 was suspended in March 1982, following a military coup by Lieutenant General Hossain Mohammad Ershad, who proceeded to govern, first as Chief Martial Law Administrator and then, from December 1983, as President, with the support of an appointed Council of Ministers. A movement back towards civilian rule began between December 1983 and May 1985, with the holding of local elections, and in 1986 the constitution was gradually revived and martial law lifted, in November.

At the apex of the current political system stands a powerful executive President, who is popularly elected for a renewable five-year term by universal adult suffrage, and who serves as head of state, head of the armed forces and head of government. He appoints cabinet ministers, judicial officers and a Vice-President.

There is a single-chamber assembly, or parliament (Jatiya Sangsad), which is composed of 300 members, directly elected for five-year terms from single-member constituencies and 30 female members elected by the assembly itself. From this body, cabinet members are drawn. In March 1988, President Ershad's cabinet (Council of Ministers) contained 25 full ministers and ten ministers of state, with the President also holding the defence and the establishment and reorganisation department portfolios.

Political parties

The present ruling party is President Ershad's National Party (JD: Jatiya Dal). It was originally formed as a civilian political vehicle for Ershad in November 1983, under the designation Jana Dal (People's Party). In September 1985 it was succeeded by the Jatiya Front, a five-party alliance, comprising the Jana Dal, the United People's Party, the Gonotrantrik Dal, the Bangladesh Muslim League and breakaway members from the Bangladesh Nationalist Party. In January 1986, these parties joined together to form a single pro-government organisation, the JD. The party is nationalist in outlook and committed to Islamic ideals.

The principal parliamentary opposition party is the Awami League (AL), led by Sheikha Hasina Wazed, the daughter of Sheikh Mujibur Rahman. The AL heads an eight-party alliance. It was originally formed in 1949 and currently claims a membership of around one million, boasting the best national organisational structure of any political party in Bangladesh. It is pro-Soviet and pro-Indian in international outlook and campaigns for a secular, moderately socialist, mixed-economy state, based on parliamentary democracy.

The AL's opposition rival is the Bangladesh National Party (BNP: Bangladesh Jatiyatabadi Dal), led by Begum Khalida Ziaur, the widow of Major-General Ziaur Rahman. The BNP heads a seven-party alliance. It was formed in 1978 by a merger of parties, including the Nationalist Democratic Party, which supported Major-General Ziaur Rahman. The party is a right-of-centre grouping which has traditionally been anti-Indian and pro-Islamic in policy outlook. It favours the establishment of a democratic presidential system of government.

At least 16 other minor parties are currently active, the three most important being: the Islamic fundamentalist, Jamat-i-Islami, which was established in 1941, and is led by Abbas Ali Khan; the pro-Soviet, Bangladesh Communist Party, which was formed in 1948, and is led by Saifuddin Ahmed Maniq; and the pro-Beijing, National Awami Party-Bhashani, which dates from 1957 and whose leader is Abdus Subhani. There are also five Marxist-Leninist parties which are currently allied in an electoral pact under the popular designation, the 'Combined Parties of the Left'.

Latest elections

In the most recent Jatiya Sangsad elections, which were held in March 1988, the ruling Jatiya Dal (JD) won 251 of the 300 elective seats; the Combined Opposition Alliance, a collection of 76 minor opposition parties, who were viewed as loyal to the regime, 18 seats; the pro-Islamic Freedom Party (FP), two seats; the left-wing Jatiya Samajtantrik Dal, two seats; and Independents, 27 seats.

The main opposition parties, the Awami League (AL), the Bangladesh Nationalist Party (BNP), the Jamat-i-Islami and the 'Combined Parties of the Left' boycotted the poll, which was the subject of substantial ballot rigging. Turnout was officially put at 50 per cent. However, the opposition leader, Sheikha Hasina Wazed, claimed that, in reality, it was below 1 per cent. Between 5 and 13 people died from election-related violence.

The most recent presidential election was held in October 1986. Again, the AL and BNP boycotted the poll, enabling Lieutenant General Ershad to achieve an overwhelming victory over eleven opponents. He captured 21.8 million votes, or 84 per cent of the total. His closest challengers were Maulana M.H. Huzur, with 1.5 million votes, and Colonel Syed Faruk Rahman, organiser of the 1975 assassination of Sheikh Mujibur Rahman, 1.2 million votes. Ballot rigging was more limited and discreet in this contest.

Political history

Contemporary Bangladesh, a vast, low-lying, deltaic plain where the great Ganges, Brahmaputra and Meghna rivers unite to flow into the Bay of Bengal, formerly consisted of the jute-growing East Bengal province and Sylhet district of Assam in British India. Being predominantly Muslim, it was formed into the eastern province of Pakistan when India was partitioned in August 1947. It differed substantially in culture, language and geography from the western provinces of Pakistan, 1,610 kilometres away and, with a larger population, resented the political and military dominance exerted by West Pakistan during the 1950s and 1960s.

An independence movement developed after 1954, under the leadership of the Awami League (AL), headed by Sheikh Mujibur Rahman. This gained strength because of the indifference shown by West Pakistan in 1970, when severe cyclones caused the deaths of half a million people in floods in East Pakistan.

In the first general elections held in Pakistan in December 1970 the AL gained an overwhelming victory in the East and an overall majority in the all-Pakistan National Assembly. Talks on re-drafting the constitution broke down, leading to East Pakistan's declaration of secession and the establishment of a Bangladesh ('Bengal Nation') government in exile, in Calcutta, in April 1971.

Civil war ensued, resulting in the flight of 10 million East Pakistani refugees to India. There was an administrative breakdown in East Pakistan and an outbreak of famine and cholera. On 16 December 1971 the West Pakistani troops in East Pakistan surrendered to the Bangladesh forces, who had been briefly helped by Indian troops. A republic of Bangladesh was proclaimed and it had gained broad international recognition by 1972.

Sheikh Mujibur Rahman became the nation's first Prime Minister, under a secular, parliamentary constitution, which was adopted in November 1972. He proceeded to introduce a socialist economic programme of nationalisation, but became increasingly intolerant of opposition. He established an emergency, one-party, presidential system of government, in January 1975.

On 15 August 1975 Sheikh Mujibur Rahman, and his wife and close relatives, were assassinated in a military coup. Power was held for three months by Khandakar Mushtaq Ahmed of the Awami League, before a further military coup in November 1975 established, as President and Chief Martial Law Administrator, the non-political chief justice, Abu Sadat Mohammad Sayem.

Two years later, in November 1976, the army chief of staff, Major-General Ziaur Rahman, became Chief Martial Law Administrator, before assuming the presidency, in April 1977. He adopted an Islamic constitution, which was approved in a May 1977 national referendum. In June 1978 he achieved victory by a 4:1 majority in a direct presidential election and released political prisoners and relaxed press censorship in readiness for parliamentary elections in February 1979.

Major-General Ziaur's newly formed Bangladeshi Nationalist Party (BNP) won a parliamentary majority and, with a civilian government installed, martial law and the state of emergency were lifted, between April and November 1979. The new administration was rapidly undermined, however, by charges of corruption and by a guerrilla secessionist movement among Chittagong hill tribesmen in 1980. On 30 May 1981 Ziaur was assassinated during an attempted coup, forcing Vice-President Justice Abdus Sattar to assume power as an interim leader.

With internal disorder increasing, the civilian administration of Sattar was overthrown, on 24 March 1982, in a coup led by army chief of staff Lieutenant-General Hossain Mohammad Ershad. Martial law was re-imposed and political activities banned. Under Ershad, because of the adoption of more market-orientated policies and the introduction of a major 'food for work' rural programme, economic conditions improved. Agitation for a return to democratic government gained strength, however, from September 1983, when a broad opposition party coalition, the Movement for the Restoration of Democracy (MRD), was formed.

Ershad promised to hold presidential and parliamentary elections in 1984, but these were cancelled after an opposition threat of a boycott and campaign of civil disobedience if martial law was not first lifted. In January 1986 the ban on political activities was removed and parliamentary elections were held in May 1986. The AL agreed to participate, but the BNP, together with many other opposition parties, boycotted the poll.

After an election campaign marked by violence, widespread abstentions and claims of ballot rigging, and the re-running of 37 constituency contests, Ershad and his Jatiya Dal (JD) party gained a two-thirds majority, giving him the constitutional right to pass a law granting retrospective immunity for any otherwise illegal acts.

In October 1986 Ershad, who had formally stepped down as army chief of staff in August and had been elected chairman of the JD a month later, was re-elected President in a direct election and in November 1986 martial law was lifted and the 1972 constitution restored. Both the AL and BNP had boycotted the presidential contest.

During 1987, opposition groups stepped up their campaign against the Ershad government, calling for the President's resignation and the holding of new free elections. A wave of violent strikes and demonstrations was launched by trade unions and students. The administration's attempt to pass a law which would enable army representatives to participate in district councils heightened the political temperature during the summer and autumn months, just at a time when the country was devastated by the worst floods for 40 years, which claimed at least 1,500 lives.

With the economy rapidly deteriorating and faced by a threat of a general strike, President Ershad proclaimed a state of emergency, on 27 November 1987, and banned all anti-government protests for 120 days. Political activity and civil rights were suspended and the opposition leaders Sheikha Hasina Wazed (AL) and Begum Khalida Zia (BNP) were placed under temporary house arrest. General urban curfews were also imposed. A month later, with the threat of the mass resignation of the AL's 73 members, parliament was dissolved and new elections were called for March 1988.

The elections were again boycotted by the AL and BNP and, again, there was evidence of flagrant ballot rigging. In these conditions, the JD gained a sweeping victory, with only a minority of the electorate voting. The President put together a new cabinet, with Moudud Ahmed as Prime Minister, lifted the state of emergency, in April 1988, and intimated that in the forthcoming parliamentary session a bill would be introduced to establish Islam as the state religion. This eighth amendment was duly passed by the Jatiya Sangsad, in June 1988.

Extra-parliamentary opposition to the Ershad regime remained strong, however, and to compound the government's difficulties, the country received its heaviest monsoon downpour for 70 years, in September 1988. The resulting floods left 30 million homeless. Thousands of lives were lost and more than a decade's infrastructural investment in roads, railways, bridges, dikes and drainage channels was destroyed.

In foreign affairs, Bangladesh has remained a member of the Commonwealth since 1972 and, although heavily dependent on foreign economic aid, has pursued a broad policy of non-alignment. Its relations with India have deteriorated since 1975, as a result of disputes over the sharing of Ganges water. The annual influx of 200,000 Bangladeshi refugees to Assam and West Bengal has prompted India to threaten to construct a barbed-wire frontier fence.

BHUTAN

Kingdom of Bhutan
Druk Yul

Capital: Thimphu

Social and economic data

Area: 46,600 km^2
Population: 1.446m*
Pop density per km^2: 31*
Literacy rate: 18%
GDP: $160m*; per capita GDP: $111
Economy type: low income
Labour force in agriculture: 93%

*1985

Ethnic composition

Fifty-four per cent of the population are of Bhotia ethnic stock, residing principally in the east and north; 32 per cent are descendants of Tibetan immigrants; while a substantial Nepali minority lives in the south, being prohibited from moving into the Bhotia-dominated north. Dzongkha, which is very similar to Tibetan, is the official language.

Religions

The principal, and state, religion is Mahayana Buddhism or Lamaism, which was introduced during the eighth century AD. Seventy per cent of the population adhere to it. Twenty-five per cent are Hindus, particularly in the southern districts. The country's 5,000 Buddhist monks play an influential role in national and local political affairs, with their head, the Je Khempo, occupying a prominent position in the Royal Advisory Council.

Political features

State type: absolutist
Date of state formation: 1907
Political structure: unitary
Executive: absolute
Assembly: one-chamber
Party structure: no parties
Human rights rating: N/A

Local and regional government

The country is divided into 18 districts *(Dzongkhags)*, each headed by an administrative and law and order officer *(Dzongda)*, and a judicial officer *(Thrimpon)*, both appointed by the Royal Civil Service Commission, which was established in 1982. Seven districts are further subidivided into sub-districts *(dungkhags)*, with 'village blocks' *(gewog)* below. Village level elections are held every three years, with each family being granted one vote.

Head of state and head of government

King Jigme Singye Wangchuk, since 1972.

Political leaders since 1970
1952–72 King Jigme Dorji Wangchuk, 1972– King Jigme Singye Wangchuk.

Political system
Bhutan is governed by an hereditary executive monarch and lacks a formal constitution. Since 1953, the King, who is called Druk Gyalpo, or 'precious ruler', has worked with an elected legislature, the National Assembly (Tshogdu) and, since 1965, with a partially elected Royal Advisory Council (RAC: Lodoi Tsokde), with which he shares power. Written rules govern the methods of electing members of the Royal Advisory Council and Tshogdu and define their duties and powers, thus giving the political system elements of a constitutional monarchy.

The National Assembly meets twice a year, in the spring and autumn, for sessions of ten to 14 days, to enact laws and serve as a debating forum. It currently comprises 151 members, 106 of whom are popularly elected by public consensus in villages, ten of whom represent regional monastic bodies and the remaining 35 are officials, ministers and members of the RAC. Every three years, the Tshogdu is required to pass a vote of confidence in the King by a two-thirds majority. Theoretically, the National Assembly also enjoys the power to remove the monarch and replace him with another member of the Royal Family. Also, its Bills cannot be vetoed by the King.

The Royal Advisory Council, as its name suggests, has the primary function of providing political advice to the monarch. It also supervises all administrative matters, serving essentially as the *de facto* standing committee of the Tshogdu. It consists of ten members. Two of them are nominees of the King, one of whom acts as chairman, two are Buddhist monks and six are 'people's representatives'. These representatives are endorsed by village assemblies, Dzongdas and the National Assembly. Members serve for renewable five-year terms. Today the RAC is the originator of most legislation.

Executive administration is the responsibility of an eight-member Council of Ministers (COM: Lhengye Shungtsog), headed by the King. It includes prominent additional members of the Royal Family. Like the RAC, this body is responsible to the Tshogdu. In practice, however, the King remains the dominant political force.

Political parties
There are no political parties within Bhutan. However, a Nepali opposition party, the Bhutan Congress Party, operates in exile in Assam and West Bengal, in India.

Latest elections
No detailed data on legislature elections are available.

Political history
Formerly ruled by Tibet during the sixteenth century and China from 1720, Bhutan was invaded by Britain, in 1865, and a trade agreement signed, under which an annual subsidy was paid to Bhutan in 'return for its good behaviour'. The country was thus never formally subjected to direct colonial rule. In December 1907 Bhutan's first hereditary monarch was installed and three years later, under the Anglo-Bhutanese (Punakha)

Treaty, foreign relations were placed under the control of the British government of India.

Soon after India achieved independence in 1947, an Indo-Bhutan Treaty of Perpetual Peace and Friendship was signed, in August 1949, under which Bhutan agreed to seek Indian advice on foreign relations but not necessarily to accept it. Although no formal defence treaty was signed, India has made it clear that it would regard an attack on Bhutan as an act of agression against itself.

In 1952 King Jigme Dorji Wangchuk was installed and in the following year a National Assembly (Tshogdu) established. In 1959, after the annexation of Tibet by communist China, Bhutan gave asylum to some 4,000 Tibetan refugees, but in June 1979, concerned with their alleged subversive activities, the Tshogdu gave the refugees until the end of the year to take up Bhutanese citizenship or return to Tibet. Most took up citizenship and the rest were accepted by India.

During the reign of King Jigme Dorji Wangchuk, between 1952 and 1972, a series of progressive social, economic and political reforms was gradually introduced, in an effort to modernise what remained a backward, traditionalist nation. These reforms included the abolition of slavery, in 1958, and the caste system; the emancipation of women; the establishment of a secular school system; and the introduction of an extensive programme of land reform and long-term economic planning. In the political sphere, as part of a democratisation process, the King appointed his first cabinet, in May 1968, and in the same year, renounced his right of veto and gave the Tshogdu the authority to select and remove the monarch.

The King died in July 1972 and was succeeded by his young, Western-educated, son, Jigme Singye Wangchuk. The new King, while maintaining close links with India, which had provided much of the finance for the country's post-1961, five-year economic plans, proceeded to pursue a somewhat more independent and outward-looking course in its external relations than had his father. Bhutan joined the non-aligned movement in 1973, entered into border negotiations with China and became a founder member of the South Asian Association for Regional Co-operation (SAARC). In May 1985 it increased its political involvement in the region by hosting the first meeting of SAARC foreign ministers.

BRUNEI

The Islamic Sultanate of Brunei
Brunei Darussalam

Capital: Bandar Seri Begawan

Social and economic data
Area: 5,800 km^2
Population: 0.240m*
Pop density per km^2: 41*
Literacy rate: 78%
GDP: $3,422m*; per capita GDP: $14,258
Economy type: high income
Labour force in agriculture: 5%

*1985

Ethnic composition

Sixty-eight per cent of the population are indigenous Malays, predominating in government service and agriculture, and 18 per cent are Chinese, predominating in the commercial sphere. Malay is the principal language.

Religions

Sixty-six per cent of the population, mainly the ethnic Malays, adhere to Islam, of the Sunni sect. Ten per cent of the people, chiefly Eurasians, are Christians and 14 per cent, largely ethnic Chinese, are Buddhists. Islam is the official state religion, and the Sultan is its national head.

Political features

State type: absolutist
Date of state formation: 1984
Political structure: unitary
Executive: absolute
Assembly: none
Party structure: one-party
Human rights rating: N/A

Local and regional government

The state is divided into four administrative districts, Brunei-Muara, Tutong, Belait and Temburong, each of which is governed by a District Officer (Malay) responsible to the Prime Minister (Sultan) and home affairs minister. There are also four municipalities.

Head of state and head of government

Sultan Sir Muda Hassanal Bolkiah Mu'izzaddin Waddaulah, since 1968.

Political leaders since 1970

1968– Sultan Sir Muda Hassanal Bolkiah Mu'izzaddin Waddaulah.

Political system

The September 1959 constitution gives supreme executive authority to the Sultan, advised by four constitutional councils: the Religious Council, the Privy Council, the Council of Cabinet Ministers and the Council of Succession. The Council of Cabinet Ministers (CCM) is the most important and, in 1988, had 11 members. The Sultan heads it, acting as both Prime Minister and minister of defence. Since 1962 he has ruled by decree. The most important of his advisers is the home minister, Pehin Dato Haji Isa, who functions, in many respects, as a chief minister *(mentri besar)*.

Political parties

Two political parties were formed in 1985–86: the Brunei National Democratic Party (BNDP: Partai Kebang-Saan Demokratik Brunei), an Islamic and liberal nationalist grouping with 1,500 members and led by Haji Abdul Latif Chuchu; and the Brunei National United Party (BNUP: Partai Perpaduan Kebang-Saan Brunei), a multi-ethnic splinter group, formed by ex-BNDP members and led by Awang Hatta Haji Zainal Abiddin.

In February 1988 the BNDP was dissolved, leaving only the BNUP. It is a party which is viewed as loyal to the government, but which favours the establishment of an elected prime ministerial system.

The opposition Brunei People's Party (BPP: Parti Ra'ayat Brunei) operates in exile. The party was formed in 1959 and won all elective seats to the Legislative Council in 1962, before staging a revolt against the government. As a result, it was banned, in December 1962.

Latest elections

There have been no elections since March 1965. Prior to this, a tiered system of indirect elections from district councils to a 21-member Legislative Council, ten of whom were elected, operated.

Political history

Brunei was an independent Islamic monarchy from the fifteenth century, ruling North Borneo, a region which includes contemporary Sabah and Sarawak states which today form part of Malaysia, between the sixteenth and nineteenth centuries. However, during the mid nineteenth century its authority waned, and it lost control of Sarawak in 1841, before eventually becoming a British protectorate in 1888. Under an agreement of 1906, a British Resident was appointed as adviser to the Sultan, turning the country into a British dependency.

During the Second World War, Brunei was occupied by the Japanese, from December 1941, but reverted to its former status after Japan's capitulation in September 1945. In 1950, Sir Muda Omar Ali Saiffuddin Saadul Khairi Waddien, popularly known as Sir Omar, became after the death of his father the new, twenty-eighth, Sultan.

His authority was increased in September 1959 when a written constitution was promulgated making Britain responsible for the country's defence and external affairs, but returning substantial control over internal affairs to the Sultan.

In December 1962 a proposal that Brunei should join the Federation of Malaysia, which was established in 1963, was opposed by a widespread revolution, organised by the Brunei People's Party (BPP), linked with the North Borneo Liberation Army. The revolt, after more than a week of fighting, was put down with the help of British forces from Singapore. A state of emergency was imposed, the BPP was banned and the Sultan began to rule by decree. In 1963 the idea of joining the Federation was abandoned.

In October 1967 the Sultan, Sir Omar, refusing to accede to British demands for more representative government, abdicated in favour of his son, Hassanal Bolkiah. He remained, however, as chief adviser. Four years later, in November 1971, Brunei was given full internal self-government. In December 1975 a UN General Assembly resolution called for the withdrawal of Britain and on 1 January 1984 full independence was achieved.

The Sultan became Prime Minister, minister of finance and minister of home affairs, presiding over a cabinet of six, three of whom were close blood relatives. Britain agreed to maintain a small force of Gurkha troops, paid for by the Sultan, to protect the oil and gas fields, which had been developed during the post-war period. These had made Brunei the wealthiest nation, per capita, in Asia and provided finance for social and welfare spending.

The 1975 UN resolution had also called for political liberalisation, including the return of political exiles and the holding of a general election. Progress in this direction has, however, been slow. In May 1985 the royal family cautiously allowed the formation of a political party, the Brunei National Democratic Party (BNDP), dominated by loyal businessmen. However, ethnic Chinese and government employees, who constitute 40 per cent of the work force, were forbidden to join. A second grouping, the Brunei National United Party (BNUP), which this time included ethnic Chinese, was tolerated in February 1986.

Since the death of Sir Omar in September 1986 the pace of political and economic modernisation has accelerated. In particular, in the new government, which was formed in October 1986, key portfolios were assigned to non-royal aristocrats and commoners. However, severe restrictions are still imposed on the operation of 'radical' opposition groupings. In addition, a conservative, nationalist socio-economic policy has been pursued in recent years, in which preferential treatment has been given to native Malays (*bumiputras*, or 'sons of the soil'), in the commercial sphere, at the expense of traditional Chinese, many of whom have emigrated since 1984. Also, an Islamic state is in the process of being constructed.

In its external relations since independence, Brunei has maintained close links with Western nations, particularly the United States and Britain, but has also joined ASEAN, and has begun to cultivate warm relations with neighbouring Singapore and Malaysia. In the economic sphere, there have been attempts at diversification, away from over-dependence on oil, the aim being to establish Brunei as a new centre for international finance and banking. Much of the interior of the country still remains, however, underdeveloped, 70 per cent of it covered by dense tropical jungle.

BURMA

Union of Myanma (UOM)

Capital: Rangoon (Yangon)

Social and economic data

Area: 678,000 km^2
Population: 37.700m*
Pop density per km^2: 56*
Literacy rate: 71%
GDP: $6,710m*; per capita GDP: $178
Economy type: low income
Labour force in agriculture: 50%

*1985

Ethnic composition

Burmans, who predominate in the fertile central river valley and southern coastal and delta regions, constitute the ethnic majority, comprising 72 per cent of the total population. Out of more than 100 minority communities, the most important are the Karen, 7 per cent of the population, the Shan, 6 per cent, Indians, 6 per cent, Chinese, 3 per cent, Kachin, 2 per cent, and Chin, 2 per cent. The indigenous minority communities, who predominate in mountainous border regions, show considerable hostility towards the culturally and politically dominant Burmans, undermining national unity. The official language is Burmese.

Religions
Eighty-five per cent of the population are Theravada Buddhists, 5 per cent animists, 4 per cent Christians, 4 per cent Muslims and 2 per cent Hindus. Animism and Christianity are concentrated among the ethnic minority communities.

Political features
State type: nationalistic socialist
Date of state formation: 1948
Political structure: unitary
Executive: unlimited presidential
Assembly: one-chamber
Party structure: one-party*
Human rights rating: poor

*Multi-party system is in the process of emerging

Local and regional government
The country is divided into 14 administrative divisions, including seven states. Below them there are townships, wards and village-tracts, each with an elected People's Council controlled by an inner Executive Committee.

Head of state and head of government
General Saw Maung, since 1988.

Political leaders since 1970*
1962–88 General U Ne Win (BSPP), 1988–88 Brigadier General Sein Lwin (BSPP), 1988–88 Dr Maung Maung (BSPP), 1988– General Saw Maung (Military).

* Ruling party leaders

Political system
Under the constitution of January 1974, which was temporarily suspended in September 1988, Burma is a unitary republic. The highest organ of state power is the 489-member People's Assembly (Pyithu Hluttaw), a single-chamber legislature which is elected by universal adult suffrage every four years and convenes twice a year for short sessions. The People's Assembly elects, from among its members, the nation's co-ordinating executive, the 29-member State Council, which includes a representative from each of Burma's 14 states and divisions and is headed by a chairman who acts as President. The State Council also has authority, delegated by the People's Assembly, to interpret and promulgate legislation. To undertake day-to-day administration, the State Council elects a 16- to 20-member Council of Ministers, headed by a Prime Minister, as well as three judicial bodies: the Council of People's Justices, the Council of People's Attorneys and the Council of People's Inspectors.

Political parties

Since 1962 the controlling force in the UOM has been the ruling Burma Socialist Programme Party (BSPP or Lanzin Party), which is closely intertwined with the military. With the passage of the Law to Protect National Solidarity, in March 1964, Burma legally became a one-party state. Recently, however, following the popular unrest of 1988, opposition parties have begun to form, re-establishing a *de jure* multi-party system.

The BSPP was established in July 1962 as a 'political arm' by the new military regime of General U Ne Win which had recently seized power. The party is organised on quasi-communist lines, with a hierarchy of ward, village and district branches at its lower levels and a controlling 280-member Central Committee and 17-member Central Executive Committee (CEC), 'elected' by a more-than-1,000-member quadrennial Congress, at its apex. It has been assigned a 'leading role' in state affairs, with members of its CEC monopolising senior executive posts. In 1985 membership of the BSPP was put at 2.3 million, a figure which constitutes 6.1 per cent of the total population. The BSPP's standing and dominance have been undermined, however, by the events of 1988, when major leadership changes were forced on it. In September 1988 a new name, the National Unity Party (NUP), was adopted.

Since September 1988, with the re-legalisation of a multi-party system, opposition parties have rapidly been formed. The most important new party is the 500,000-member National League for Democracy (NLD), a broad grouping which is the successor to the Democracy and Peace (Interim) League (DPIL). The DPIL had been illegally established in August 1988 by the former Prime Minister U Nu, former President U Mahn Win Maung, the influential former Chief of Staff and Defence Minister, General Thura Tin U, and Aung San Suu Kyi, the United Kingdom-based daughter of the assassinated national hero Aung San. Two other opposition political parties were registered in September 1988, the Democracy Party, led by U Thu Wai, and the National Democratic Party, led by Thakin Lwin.

Party formation accelerated from October 1988, so that by March 1989 it was reported that 223 registered political groupings had been recognised by the ruling military government.

Outside the formal party system, armed ethnic minority insurgent groups have been engaged in guerrilla warfare in border regions, against the incumbent BSPP, and preceding regimes, since independence. The outlawed, 10,000 member, Burmese Communist Party (BCP: White Flag Party) is the most serious insurgent force. Formed in 1946, when the Communist Party, which was established in 1939, split into White and Red Flag factions, it remains an unreconstructed Stalinist body which enjoyed military backing from China until recent years. It has established *de facto* control over parts of northern Burma.

Anti-communist groups operate in Karen, in the south-east, Kachin, in the north-east, Shan, in the east, Arakan, in the south-west, Chin, in the west, and Palaung, Mon, Wa, Lahu and Pa-O. They have been organised since 1975 within the 35,000-guerrilla-strong National Democratic Front (NDF). The NDF's goal is to re-establish a federal state based on national self-determination.

Latest elections

The most recent elections to the People's Assembly were held in November 1985, when all the candidates put forward were members of the BSPP.

Political history

As early as AD 850, a Burmese state was established, with its capital inland at Pagan. The country was overrun by the Mongols during the later thirteenth century, but a new Toungoo dynasty was uneasily established in 1486. The nation was re-united by Alaungpaya in 1752, and the port of Rangoon selected as the new capital. Later, however, during the nineteenth century, with the imperialist intrusion of Britain, this state was gradually dismembered. Following the Anglo-Burmese War of 1824–26, the Arakan coastal strip between Chittagong and Cape Negrais was ceded to British India. Then, in 1852, after defeat in the second Burmese War, Lower Burma, including Rangoon, was annexed by the British. Finally, in 1886, after Thibaw, the last Burmese King, had precipitated a third Burmese War, Upper Burma was conceded.

Britain immediately re-united these annexed portions to form the 'province of Burma', which was governed as part of British India, until constituted as a crown colony, with a degree of internal self-government, in 1937. It developed into a major rice, teak, and later oil, exporter, drawing into its coastal urban-commercial centres thousands of immigrant workers from India and China.

During the Second World War Burma was invaded and occupied by Japan, between 1942 and 1945, encouraging the flight of many of the more recent Indian émigrés. The Japanese proceeded to install a government of anti-British nationalists, headed by Ba Maw, and granted the country nominal independence. However, the nationalists, led by Aung San and U Nu, both of whom had earlier been imprisoned by the British for their pro-independence activities, later turned against their 'patrons', founding the Anti-Fascist People's Freedom League (AFPFL), which collaborated with the British in their drive against the Japanese occupiers.

The country was liberated by Allied forces, in 1945, and achieved full independence outside the British Commonwealth, under the designation the 'Union of Burma', on 4 January 1948. A parliamentary democracy was established in which the socialist AFPFL, led by Prime Minister U Nu, held power and states were specially created for the Shan, Karen, Kachin, Chin and Kayah minority peoples, who enjoyed a substantial measure of autonomy as part of a 'limited federal' system. The new republic was weakened, however, by a mounting internal insurgency movement, involving communist guerrillas, Karen tribesmen and other dissatisfied ethnic group separatists.

In 1958 a split within the AFPFL precipitated a political crisis which persuaded U Nu to 'invite' General U Ne Win, the army chief of staff, to form an emergency, caretaker government. This administration, which lasted for two years, was the prelude to a full-scale military coup in March 1962 and the abolition of the parliamentary system. Ne Win, claimed that parliamentary government had proved unworkable in Burma and assumed power as head of a Revolutionary Council composed of fellow military officers. He abrogated the 1948 constitution and established a strong, centralised one-party state.

Following a referendum in December 1973, a new presidential-style, unitary constitution was adopted, in 1974, and the Revolutionary Council was dissolved. The existing military leaders resigned their titles to become civilian rulers, through the vehicle of a specially constituted Burma Socialist Programme Party (BSPP).

Ne Win was elected President and re-elected again in 1978, before stepping down to be replaced by another former army chief of staff, U San Yu, in November 1981. The new post-1962 military-BSPP government adopted an external policy of neutralist isolationism. Domestically, it pursued an unique, self-reliant, Buddhist-influenced and state-dominated socio-economic strategy, termed the 'Burmese Way towards Socialism'. It was founded on strict price control in the agricultural sector, where farming was allowed to remain in private hands, and state enterprises in the commercial-industrial sector. This programme, coupled with the continuing internal insurgency, had a debilitating effect on the country's economy, turning Burma into one of the poorest countries, in terms of per capita GDP, in the Asia-Pacific region. This fact was recognised in December 1987 by the United Nations' grant of 'less developed country' (LDC) status.

Public dissatisfaction with the deteriorating economic situation first became evident in 1974 and 1976 and assumed the form of food shortage riots and student demonstrations. A decade later, in September 1987, new student demonstrations erupted in Rangoon after the introduction of precautionary demonetisation measures, soon after the domestic trading of rice, which was now in short supply, had been freed from existing restraints. Further, more widespread and better organised, anti-government student and workers' riots followed, in March and June 1988. These were sternly repressed by the armed forces and riot police, at the cost of several hundred lives.

Concerned about the mounting political and economic chaos, an extraordinary BSPP Congress was convened in July 1988 to review the situation. At this meeting, Ne Win, San Yu and Maung Maung Kha resigned from their respective positions as party leader, state President and Prime Minister respectively, and were replaced by Brigadier-General Sein Lwin, who became both President and BSPP chairman, and Thura U Tun Tin, who assumed the position of Prime Minister. A series of liberalising economic reforms was also ratified.

This failed, however, to calm the situation. Instead, in late July and early August 1988, unrest escalated, with more than 100,000 people taking part in demonstrations demanding the removal as President of the reviled Sein Lwin, a 'hard-liner' with a long history of dissident repression, and the installation of a new, democratically elected government. Strikes and demonstrations spread to northern urban centres and attracted the support of Buddhist monks and mutinous navy and air force personnel.

With government control of the country rapidly disintegrating, monks and demonstrators began to take charge of several city administrations. Following the killing of 3,000 unarmed demonstrators by riot police, on 12 August 1988, and after only 17 days in office, Sein Lwin resigned as BSPP leader and President. A week later, he was replaced in both posts by a civilian, the Western-educated former Attorney-General, Dr Maung Maung. Despite the apparent 'reformist' credentials of the new national leader, strikes and demonstrations continued, mainly because of the new President's close links with Ne Win, who continued to remain a decisive 'behind-the-scenes' figure.

Caving in to popular pressure, at a new, hastily convened, emergency BSPP Congress on 10 September 1988, the leadership finally approved the holding of a free multi-party general election 'within three months'. A week later, however, with internal disorder continuing, the armed forces, led by former Defence Minister General Saw Maung, assumed power, in an effort to stabilise the situation. All state institutions were declared abolished and power transferred to a 19-member military State Committee for the Establishment of Law and Order (SCELO), headed by Saw Maung. A night curfew was imposed and all gatherings of more than four people outlawed.

The new military regime, after initially killing hundreds of demonstrators in Rangoon, did succeed in calming the internal situation. Also, by introducing a new law legalising the formation of political parties, they prepared the ground for the holding of multi-party elections. These were promised by Saw Maung, 'as soon as possible'. Divisions within the ranks of the opposition made it uncertain, however, whether such planned elections would succeed in resolving the internal crisis.

CAMBODIA (KAMPUCHEA)

The State of Cambodia (SOC)

Capital: Phnom Penh

Social and economic data
Area: 181,000 km^2
Population: 7.284m*
Pop density per km^2: 40
Literacy rate: 48%
GDP: $400m*; per capita GDP: $55
Economy type: low income
Labour force in agriculture: 72%

*1985

Ethnic composition
Khmers constitute between 90 and 93 per cent of the population, Vietnamese 4 per cent and Chinese 3 per cent. The official language is Khmer, but French is also widely spoken.

Religions
The traditional religion is Theravada Buddhism, adhered to by 90 per cent of the population. Since 1975, however, the number of Buddhist priests (*bonzes*) has contracted from 20,000 to 6,000. Prior to the communist takeover in 1975, 1.4 per cent of the population, predominantly the Malayo-Polynesian-speaking Cham, also followed Islam and there were 14,000 Roman Catholics. In 1989 it was announced that Buddhism had, once more, been made the state religion.

Political features
State type: communist
Date of state formation: 1953
Political structure: unitary
Executive: communist
Assembly: one-chamber
Party structure: one-party
Human rights rating: bad

Local and regional government
The country is divided into 18 provinces (*khet*), 122 districts (*srok*), 1,325 sub-districts (*khum*) and 9,386 villages (*phum*), in addition to two muncipalities (*krung*), Phnom Penh and Kompong Som, which are themselves subdivided into wards (*sangkat*) and groups (*krom*). They are administered by Local People's Committees, which are directly elected triennially at the *khum* level and below, with candidate choice, and are indirectly elected quinquennially, by lower committee members, at the *srok* and *khet* levels. Committees are dominated by members of the ruling Kampuchean People's Revolutionary Party (KPRP) and are subject to tight 'democratic centralist' control from bodies above.

Head of state
President Heng Samrin, since 1979.

Head of government
Prime Minister Hun Sen, since 1985.

Political leaders since 1970
1970–75 Lieutenant-General Lon Nol, 1975–76 Prince Sihanouk, 1976–79 Pol Pot (Khmer Rouge), 1979–81 Pen Sovann (CPK)*, 1981– Heng Samrin (KPRP).*

*Communist Party leader

Political system
Cambodia's constitution was adopted in June 1981, superseding the earlier constitutions of May 1947, April 1972 and January 1976. Comprising 93 articles, it describes the republic as an 'independent sovereign state, gradually advancing towards socialism', with its national economy subject to the direction of the state, but divided into four sectors: 'the state-run, the collective, the private and the family-run economy'.

The sole and supreme legislative organ is the National Assembly. This body originally comprised 117 members, elected for five-year terms by universal adult suffrage, on the basis of candidate lists presented in multi-member constituencies. In 1987 a further six members were added. The National Assembly formally has the task of ratifying bills presented to it and adopting the state budget and economic plan. It also has authority to revise the constitution, by a two-thirds vote. It meets, however, only twice a year for brief, three- to five-day sessions, and 'elects', from its ranks, a smaller, permanent seven-member Council of State, to act on its behalf.

The Council has authority to promulgate laws and ratify international treaties and its President serves as the official head of state. He is also chairman of the National Defence Council and supreme commander of the armed forces.

Day-to-day government is in the hands of a 53-member Council of Ministers (COM), which is 'elected' by the National Assembly, but, in reality, is nominated by the Council of State. The COM is headed by a chairman, who functions as *de facto* Prime Minister, working with six vice-chairmen, three of whom are also ministers, in an 'inner cabinet'. There are, in addition, 15 other department ministers and 27 vice-ministers in the COM.

The dominating force, and sole permitted party, in Cambodia is the Communist Party (KPRP: Kampuchean People's Revolutionary Party), led by General Secretary Heng Samrin. It is supported by a mass organisation, the Kampuchean United Front for National Construction and Defence (KUFNCD). Party members dominate state institutions. For example, in March 1988, the KPRP's governing Politburo contained ten full and two non-voting 'candidate' members. Two of these also occupied the key positions of President, party leader Heng Samrin, and Vice-President, the influential Say Phouthang, in the Council of State. Six others were prominent members of the COM, Hun Sen being both its chairman and foreign minister; Ney Pena, interior minister; Koy Buntha, defence minister; and three, Say Phouthang, Chea Soth and Bou Thang, vice-chairmen.

Political parties

The ruling Kampuchean People's Revolutionary Party (KPRP: Pak Pracheachon Pativoat Kampuchea) was formed in January 1979 by 66 exiled Cambodian communists, at an *ad hoc* congress called under Vietnamese auspices to 're-organise the party'. Half of them were ex-Khmer Viet Minh and a half ex-Khmer Rouge. The KPRP's roots go back to 1951 when a Cambodian (Kampuchean) wing broke away from the existing Communist Party of Indo-China, which had been established in 1930 by Ho Chi Minh, to form the Khmer (Cambodian) People's Revolutionary Party. This soon divided into two factions: a pro-Vietnamese grouping, the Khmer Vietminh, which favoured collaboration with the Cambodian head of state, Prince Norodom Sihanouk; and an anti-Sihanouk grouping, led by the Paris-trained Marxist, Pol Pot (Saloth Sar).

The second faction became dominant in 1960 and proceeded to rename the party the Communist Party of Kampuchea (CPK) and pursue a new pro-Chinese and anti-Soviet course. Organising itself among the peasantry, Pol Pot's CPK, popularly known as the Khmer Rouge, engaged in a guerrilla struggle against first the Sihanouk and then the Lon Nol, governments during the later 1960s and early 1970s. As a result, it emerged as the governing force in Cambodia between 1975 and 1979. Its ruthless policies, however, alienated some people in the party's ranks, resulting in the defection of a number of leading figures, including Heng Samrin and Hun Sen, who formed the new pro-Vietnamese and pro-Soviet KPRP. The designation KPRP was officially adopted in 1981, superseding the title CPK.

The KPRP is organised hierarchically on 'democratic centralist' lines, but currently has a restricted number of local party units. There are provincial, municipal and, where there are enough members, district party organisations, while 'core groups' (*krom snoul*) have been established in state and army bodies. The supreme, and legitimising, party organ is the national Congress, which has the task of approving the party programme and 'electing' a Central Committee (CC) to assume its functions in its absence. Since the party's 1979 reformation, two national Congresses have been held, in May 1981 and October 1985. The 1981 Congress was officially termed the party's 'Fourth', the previous ones having been attributed to 1951, 1960 and 1979. 250 delegates, drawn from the KPRP's 22 divisions, attended the 1985 Congress. It 'elected' an expanded CC comprising 31 full and 14 non-voting 'alternate' members which, in turn, 'elected' a controlling Politburo, headed by the General Secretary, and five-member administrative Secretariat.

Membership of the KPRP is currently estimated to be between 7,500 and 10,000, constituting barely 0.1 per cent of the total population. This is by far the lowest in the communist world. One of the reasons for this low membership was the liquidation of many communist cadres during the Pol Pot era. The other has been the insistence on commitment and ideological purity by the KPRP leadership. The present figure constitutes, however, a significant advance on its 1979 total of barely 300.

Although it is a one-party state, three significant opposition groupings exist, in exile, outside Cambodia. They are pragmatically united in the 'Coalition Government of Democratic Kampuchea' (CGDK). They are: the Party of Democratic Kampuchea (Khmer Rouge), the Khmer People's National Liberation Front (KPNLF), and the Sihanoukist National Army (ANS). The first is the successor to Pol Pot's CPK, which was dissolved in 1981. The new group is led by Khieu Samphan, although Pol Pot remains an influential background figure. The KPNLF was formed in France in 1979 as a republican, anti-communist and élite-orientated party by the former Prime Minister, Son Sann. The ANS is effectively headed by the former King Norodom Sihanouk, with his son Prince Norodom Ranariddh in nominal charge, and enjoys considerable peasant support.

Latest elections

The last full-scale National Assembly elections were held in May 1981 when 148 KPRP-approved candidates contested the 117 available seats. Eighty-one of those elected were party members.

The Assembly, which, under the terms of the 1981 constitution was shortly due for re-election, had its life prolonged a further five years, by government fiat, in February 1986. However, supplementary elections were held in six provinces in June 1987, thus increasing the Assembly's size to 123 members.

Political history

Cambodia originally constituted part of the Kingdom of Fou-Nan, before being conquered by the Khmers during the sixth century. It became the heartland for the sophisticated and extensive Khmer Empire between the sixth and fifteenth centuries, whose capital was established at Angkor in north-west Cambodia. The region subsequently came within the jurisdiction of neighbouring Siam (Thailand) and Champa (Vietnam), but still retained a measure of independence. In 1863 it became a French protectorate but its traditional political and social structures were left largely intact.

From 1887 it formed part of the French Indo-China Union, but during the Second World War it was occupied by Japan. France regained control of what was then known as the Kingdom of Cambodia, and promulgated a constitution which established a modern parliamentary system. However, in the face of a rural-based guerrilla independence movement that was growing in strength, the country was granted semi-autonomy within the French Union, in November 1949, and full independence, in November 1953.

Prince Norodom Sihanouk, who had been elected King in 1941, abdicated in favour of his parents, in March 1955, and became Prime Minister, as leader of the Popular Socialist Community mass movement, which swept to power, winning all available seats, in the parliamentary elections of 1955, 1958, 1962 and 1966. In June 1960, following the death of his father, Sihanouk was elected head of state.

During the Vietnam War (1954-75), Sihanouk, although critical of the United States' military involvement in Indo-China, sought to maintain Cambodia's neutrality from the surrounding struggle. This became increasingly difficult during the later 1960s. Domestically the Sihanouk regime had to face a mounting communist insurgency, led by the Khmer Rouge.

With the economy deteriorating, Sihanouk was overthrown, in March 1970, while absent abroad, in a bloodless right-wing coup, led by the pro-American Prime Minister, Lieutenant-General, later Marshal, Lon Nol. The latter continued to serve as Prime Minister, between 1971 and 1972, before becoming President of what was termed, from October 1970, the new Khmer Republic. The political system had been reconstituted on presidential executive lines, following the promulgation, in April 1972, of a constitution modelled on that of France's Fifth (Gaullist) Republic. Lon Nol's regime was opposed, however, by the exiled Prince Sihanouk, now head of the Beijing-based, Royal Government of National Union of Cambodia (GRUNC), and by the communist Khmer Rouge, backed by North Vietnam and China. The two joined together to form the National United Front of Cambodia (FUNC).

A bitter civil war developed and, despite receiving substantial military aid from the United States during its early stages, the Lon Nol government lost control of rural, and then urban, areas and was toppled in April 1975. The country was renamed Kampuchea and Prince Sihanouk appointed head of state.

The Khmer Rouge proceeded ruthlessly to introduce an extreme Maoist communist programme, involving the abolition of money and markets, the forced removal of urban groups into the countryside and agricultural collectivisation, at a breakneck speed. This resulted in the death of numbers, variously estimated at 1–3 million people, from famine, disease and maltreatment. 'Reactionary' political opponents were also summarily executed. A new constitution was promulgated in January 1976, which renamed the state 'Democratic Kampuchea', removed Prince Sihanouk from power, appointed Khieu Samphan, the former Deputy Prime Minister, as President and placed the CPK, led by its notorious guerrilla leader, Pol Pot, in effective political control.

The new Khmer Rouge regime severed all Western contacts and developed close links with China. As a consequence, it fell out with its former sponsors, Vietnam and the Soviet Union, prompting Vietnam to launch raids into the country during 1977–78, culminating in a full-scale invasion, in December 1978. The Vietnamese successfully overthrew Pol Pot, who enjoyed little popular support, in January 1979, and put into power a pro-Vietnamese puppet government, led by Heng Samrin, a commander of the Khmer Rouge fourth division until 1978. He was now head of the Kampuchean National United Front for National Salvation (KNUFNS), which had been newly constituted in December 1978, and was later renamed KUFNCD, in 1981. It was an amalgam of anti-Pol Pot Cambodian communists. A new People's Republic of Kampuchea (PRK) was proclaimed.

Initially, Heng Samrin ruled as President of an emergency People's Revolutionary Council, sharing effective power with the CPK (later KPRP) General Secretary, Pen Sovann, an ex-Khmer Viet Minh who had lived in Vietnam between 1954 and 1979. In December 1981, however, Sovann, who was viewed by Vietnam as too gradualist in his approach, pro-Soviet in his outlook and autocratic in his governing style, was stripped of all his party and state posts and Samrin became the new KPRP leader and controlling personality. During the same year a constitution was framed and National Assembly elected, in an effort to legitimise the regime.

During its first year in power the Samrin government was faced with fierce guerrilla resistance by Pol Pot forces, based in jungle hideouts in the west of the country, near the border with Thailand, resulting in the flight of more than 300,000 Cambodian refugees to Thailand, where they now live in border camps. This resistance movement broadened in June 1982, with the formation, in Kuala Lumpur, in Malaysia, of a broad anti-Vietnamese coalition and Democratic Kampuchea government-in-exile. This comprised Prince Sihanouk, then living in North Korea, as President, Khieu Samphan, the political leader of the Khmer Rouge, as Vice-President and Son Sann, an ex-premier and contemporary leader of the non-communist KPNLF, as Prime Minister. The coalition received sympathetic support from the countries of ASEAN, Indonesia, Malaysia, the Philippines, Singapore and Thailand, as well as from China, and was officially recognised by both the United States and UN as the legitimate government of the country. Militarily, however, the coalition was weak. Its 60,000 troops, 60 per cent of whom were Khmer Rouge, were outnumbered by the 170,000 Vietnamese supporting the Heng Samrin government, and its base camps were repeatedly overrun during the annual December-April dry season offensives. The cumulative cost to Vietnam was more than 30,000 of its soldiers' lives.

The Heng Samrin administration at first pursued a relatively liberal policy programme, dismantling the Khmer Rouge-established commune structure and adopting a relaxed attitude towards the Buddhist religion, in an effort to secure popular support. Soon, however, these policies were reversed, communes were re-established and a 'Vietnamisation' of the country was launched, with more than 500,000 Vietnamese emigrating to south-eastern Cambodia. Since 1985, however, following the installation as Prime Minister of Hun Sen, and under pressure from the reformist new Gorbachev administration in the Soviet Union, a more flexible and pragmatic, mixed-economy, policy approach has been in evidence, while indigenous Khmers now dominate the regime and a Khmer cultural revival is underway.

Hopes of a political settlement to the 'Cambodian issue' also began to improve from 1985, helped by the retirement of the reviled Pol Pot as Khmer Rouge military leader, in August 1985, and by the beginning of a phased withdrawal of Vietnamese troops. The reconciliation process moved a step further, in December 1987 and January 1988, when Hun Sen and Prince Norodom Sihanouk met for a series of talks near Paris. These events were followed, in June 1988, by the withdrawal of 50,000, or half, of the remaining Vietnamese troops within Cambodia, including the high command. This was coupled with the promise to pull out the remainder by October 1989, and by the holding of informal all-party, PRK and CGDK, 'cocktail' talks in Bogor, in Indonesia, a month later. At these talks, Hun Sen put forward a peace plan which envisaged the creation of a broad, new, National Reconciliation Council, headed by Prince Sihanouk, to organise and oversee the holding of free, all-party national elections after the Vietnamese withdrawal. The CGDK opposition, however, called for the immediate dismantling of the PRK, as a precondition to any settlement, and for the formation of an interim coalition provisional government before the 1989 deadline. In further talks, held in Jakarta in the spring of 1989, additional substantive concessions were proffered by the Heng Samrin regime, including a package of constitutional changes which promised to liberalise the economy, render Buddhism the new state religion and alter the country's official designation from the PRK to the ideologically neutral 'State of Cambodia' (SOC). In return, Prince Sihanouk intimated that he might be willing to serve as head of state in an interim administration in tandem with Hun Sen. However, as October 1989 approached, both sides began to voice concern about whether the military strength of the SOC and the ANS/KPNLF would be sufficient to prevent a recrudescence of a new Khmer Rouge regime.

CHINA

People's Republic of China (PRC)
Zhonghua Renmin Gonghe Guo

Capital: Beijing (Peking)

Social and economic data
Area: 9,561,000 km^2*
Population: 1050.000m†
Pop density per km^2: 110†
Literacy rate: 65%
GDP: $310,000m†; per capita GDP: $295
Economy type: low income
Labour force in agriculture: 72%

*Two-thirds mountain or desert, with only 15 per cent of the country's area being arable.

†1985

Ethnic composition
Ninety-four per cent of the population are Han Chinese, the remainder being Zhuang, Uygur, Hui (Muslims), Yi, Tibetan, Miao, Manchu, Mongol, Buyi or Korean. There are numerous lesser nationalities, in 55 groups, numbering 67 million. The national minorities mainly reside in border regions. The principal language is Northern Chinese (Mandarin).

Religions
Confucianism, Buddhism and Daoism (Taoism) are the principal traditional religions, with Muslim, 15 million, and Christian, 6 million, minorities. The Christians are mainly Roman Catholics and live on the coast.

Political features
State type: communist
Date of state formation: 2ndC BC (1949*)
Political structure: unitary
Executive: communist
Assembly: one-chamber
Party structure: one-party
Human rights rating: 23%

*Present boundaries and communist regime.

Local and regional government
Below the 29 provinces *(sheng),* there are municipalities and autonomous regions. Within these are 286 municipalities, 552 rural districts, under city administration, and 2,080 rural counties *(xian).* People's Congresses and People's Governments operate at the township and county levels. Multiple, CCP-approved, candidacies were the norm in recent elections. Members are elected directly for three-year terms at the county level and below, and indirectly, by council members, for five-year terms to congresses above.

Head of state
President Yang Shangkun, since 1988.

Head of government
Prime Minister Li Peng, since 1987.

Political leaders since 1970*
1949–76 Mao Zedong (CCP),* 1976–81 Hua Guofeng (CCP),* 1981–87 Hu Yaobang (CCP),* 1987–89 Zhao Ziyang (CCP),* (1978– Deng Xiaoping (CCP)†, 1989–Jiang Zemin (CCP)*

*Communist Party leaders

†Effective national leader

Political system
Under its current constitution, the fourth since 1949, which was adopted in December 1982, superseding earlier 1954, 1975 and 1978 documents, China despite its size is a unitary state. The nation is divided, for administrative purposes, into 21 provinces, five autonomous regions, including Tibet

(Xizang), and three municipalities, Beijing, Shanghai and Tianjin. Each enjoys policy-making discretion in a number of defined areas, exercised by elected Local People's Congresses and governments.

Ultimate authority resides, however, in a single-chamber assembly, the National People's Congress (NPC: Quanghuo Renmin Diabiao Dahui). The NPC is composed of 2,970 members, indirectly elected every five years through a tiered system of Local People's Congresses. At their lower levels, members of Local People's Congresses are directly elected through universal adult suffrage in constituency contests which involve a measure of competition.

The NPC, which is described in the 1982 constitution as the 'highest organ of state power', meets in full session once a year, for two weeks, electing a permanent, 135-member Standing Committee to assume its functions between sittings. This Standing Committee is dominated by an inner body comprising a chairman and 19 vice-chairmen.

Meeting in session at least once every fortnight, the Standing Committee directs the work of the NPC's six functional Specialised Committees: finance and economic affairs; nationalities; education, science, culture and public health; foreign affairs; legal affairs; and overseas Chinese. It also drafts bills and resolutions. It operates as a 'substitute parliament', interpreting the constitution and current laws, issuing decrees, overseeing the work of lower level governments and appointing and dismissing ministers and officials.

In addition, for a five-year term, the NPC elects a state President and Vice-President, a state Central Military Commission, to supervise the work of the army, and leading members of the judiciary. The functions of the state President, who must be at least 45 years of age and who is restricted to two terms in office, are primarily ceremonial.

Executive administration is carried out by a 45-member State Council or national cabinet, which is headed by a Prime Minister and which includes three vice-premiers, 31 Departmental Ministers, eight State Commission chiefs, and the Auditor-General, Secretary-General and Governor of the Bank of China. The State Council is 'appointed' by and accountable to the NPC and its Standing Committee. It has the task of directing and overseeing the work of government departments, commissions and local bodies, enacting administrative regulations, drawing up and implementing the economic plan and annual budget, and submitting drafts to the NPC's Standing Committee. A 13-member inner cabinet, consisting of the Prime Minister, vice-premier and nine State Councillors, meets regularly to decide on day-to-day matters. Membership of this body is limited to two, five-year, terms.

The directing force in the PRC is, however, the Chinese Communist Party (CCP), headed by its General Secretary, Jiang Zemin, and controlled by its governing Politburo, with its inner Standing Committee. In May 1988 this Politburo comprised 17 full members and one, non-voting, 'alternate' member. One of these, Yang Shangkun, held the position of State President, while another, Li Peng, was Prime Minister. Another five members held senior positions within the State Council, including all three vice-premierships and the posts of state planning commission chairman, Yao Yilin, and defence minister, Qin Jiwei. An additional member, Wan Li, was chairman of the NPC's influential Standing Committee.

During recent years there has been both increased democratisation and decentralisation in the governmental process, the members of the new NPC's Standing Committee, for example, being elected in a purportedly competitive manner, in March 1988. Votes registered against candidates were recorded for the first time, and NPC deputies were allowed to play a more prominent and independent role in policy discussions. Additionally, an effort has been made to demarcate party and state spheres of responsibility more clearly, with the day-to-day interference of local party committees over state decision-taking being substantially reduced.

Also, as part of a revivified, broad-front, policy-formulating process, the Chinese People's Political Consultative Conference (CPPCC) has been reactivated, since 1978. The CPPCC is a broadly based, appointed body which originally operated between 1949 and 1954. It includes intellectuals, overseas Chinese and 'democratic party' representatives. It now convenes concurrently with the NPC so as to provide an additional advisory voice. The CPPCC has been chaired since March 1988 by the former state President, Li Xiannian.

Despite these substantive structural changes, ultimate power in the Chinese polity continues to reside at the uppermost level of the factionalised CCP. The party machine continues to vet nominations in state election contests and control state appointments, according to the 'nomenklatura' principle.

Political parties

The ruling Chinese Communist Party (CCP: Zhongguo Gongchan Dang) was founded in July 1921 at the French concession of Shanghai by a group of intellectuals, led by Chen Duxiu, who was its leader between 1921 and 1927, and Li Lisan, leader from 1927 to 1930. They had been strongly influenced by the 1917 Russian Revolution and by the theoretical writings of Marx, Engels and Lenin. Soon afterwards, in June 1922, a separate overseas branch, the Young Communist Party (YCP), was formed in Paris by a group of Chinese students, including Zhou Enlai and Deng Xiaoping, who had been sent abroad on a 'work and study' scheme.

The Shanghai-based CCP worked closely with the Moscow-based Communist International (Comintern), seeking to foment urban worker revolutions in the country's seaboard cities during the early 1920s. These proved, however, to be unsuccessful. The party, following Comintern orders, also allied itself closely, during the mid-1920s, with the larger and more popular Nationalist Party (KMT: Kuomintang), led successively by Dr Sun Yat-sen and General Chiang Kai-shek. They were duped, however, by the anti-communist Chiang, in April 1927, when the CCP's Shanghai cell was brutally purged, and its few surviving members forced underground.

Following the failure of the urban revolution approach, the party's rural wing, led by the charismatic self-taught Marxist, Mao Zedong, gained the ascendancy. Mao, who had been a founder member of the CCP in Shanghai, in 1921, began to construct a unique third-world brand of communism, based on an alliance with the peasantry and the use of anti-government guerrilla tactics. He established a rural soviet, or 'workers' republic', in Jiangxi province during the late 1920s and early 1930s and assumed leadership of the 300,000-member CCP, with the support of Zhou Enlai's pragmatic 'Paris wing', at the Zunyi conference of May 1935. All this happened in the midst of the 'Long March' of 1934–36.

The Maoist brand of rural-based revolution was further refined during the party's period at Yanan, from 1936, and eventually proved successful in overcoming Chiang Kai-shek's KMT forces, in 1948–49.

In the new PRC, politics after 1949 were to be characterised by periodic struggles between the different personality- and policy-based factions that had been apparent within the CCP since the later 1920s. At the head of the party's 'orthodox', pro-Soviet, faction stood Liu Shaoqi, gaining the ascendancy during the early 1950s and between 1962 and 1965, and pursuing an urban-industrial orientated and incentives-based development strategy. In stark opposition, stood Mao Zedong, predominant between 1957 and 1961 and between 1966 and 1973. He sought to establish a unique, 'Sinified' model of socialism, based on parallel progress in both the rural and urban spheres, the maintenance of close and regular contact between party members and the general population, which he called the 'mass line', and on ideological, as well as economic, transformation.

Finally, and in some respects intermediate between the 'right' and 'left' factions, stood the eclectic Paris 'work-study' wing, led initially by the adroit Zhou Enlai, and subsequently by the more innovative and risk-taking Deng Xiaoping. This wing, apart from a break between 1976 and 1978, has generally dominated policy-making in the PRC since 1973, seeking to build a new 'socialism with Chinese characteristics', in which market mechanisms are given a prominent role.

The present CCP is organised, parallel to the state government hierarchy, on pyramidal lines, based on a hierarchy of elected congresses and committees which function from the village and factory, or 'basic', level upwards and follow orders from above, in accordance with the tenets of Leninist 'democratic centralism'. A quinquennial, 1,959-member National Party Congress elects a 285-member Central Committee.

This Committee, 175 of whose members have full voting powers, meets at least once a year and 'elects' a smaller 18-member Politburo and five-member Secretariat. Seventeen of the Politburo and four of the Secretariat are full members. The two bodies exercise ultimate day-to-day control over the party and frame longer-term state and party policy goals.

The Politburo convenes weekly and is the single most significant political body in China. It is dominated by an inner Standing Committee which, in July 1989, comprised five members, Jiang Zemin, the CCP's General Secretary, Qiao Shi, Li Peng, Li Ruihuan, Song Ping and Yao Yilin. Following rule changes, which were adopted at the thirteenth National Party Congress in October-November 1987, the Standing Committee has formally been given power to nominate the members of the Secretariat. More generally, in recent years competitive inner-party democracy and discussion have been encouraged, particularly at the lower levels.

Other senior CCP bodies include the Military Affairs Commission (MAC), currently headed by Deng Xiaoping, which maintains party control over the armed forces, and the Central Advisory Commission (CAC), headed by Chen Yun, which was established in 1982 as an advisory forum to which elderly party, state and military figures could be honourably 'retired'.

In 1987 membership of the CCP stood at 46 million, a figure which corresponded to 4.4 per cent of the total population. This constituted an advance of 57 per cent on the 1973 total of 28 million and of 170 per cent on the 1961 figure of 17 million. Throughout this period, however, there have been recurrent purges of both 'ultra-Maoist' and 'ultra-rightist' elements.

Over the past few years the stress of the Deng administration has been on the recruitment of well qualified and educated technocrats, able to manage effectively at the local level, as more and more governmental responsibilities are decentralised. However, despite this recruitment bias, fewer than 5 per cent of party members can currently boast a higher education, while more than 50 per cent are illiterate or have been educated only to primary school level.

Closely linked to the CCP is the Young Communist League (YCL), a youth wing for citizens aged between 15 and 25. This has a membership of 48.5 million. Eight minor 'democratic parties' are now allowed to operate. They include: the China Association for Promoting Democracy, which was established in 1945, the China Democratic League, dating from 1941, the China Democratic National Construction Association, which was formed in 1945, the China Zhi Gong Dang, founded in 1925, the Chinese Peasants' and Workers' Democratic Party, which was established in 1947, the Kuomintang Revolutionary Committee, dating from 1948, the Jiu San (3rd September) Society, which originated in 1946, and the Taiwan Democratic Self-Government League, which dates from 1947. Orientated primarily towards bourgeois and intelligentsia groups, these bodies work in alliance with the CCP and are accorded representation in the NPC and on its Standing Committee.

Latest elections

The most recent NPC elections were held in January-March 1988, taking the form, as usual, of indirect elections by provincial, municipal and autonomous region-level People's Congresses and People's Liberation Army units. For the first time, there was an element of competition in some constituencies, with more candidates standing than the number of seats available.

Of the 2,970 who were elected, 863, or 29 per cent, were re-elected members from the previous NPC, while 2,107 or 71 per cent, were newcomers. One thousand, nine hundred and eighty-six or 67 per cent, of the successful candidates were CCP members, 634, or 21 per cent, were women and 445, or 15 per cent, were drawn from ethnic minority communities.

Political history

Chinese civilisation is believed to date from the Xia dynasty era, 2200–1700 BC, during which period a relatively sophisticated bronze-age state, utilising irrigation and the written word, was established, in the Shaanxi-Henan region of central China. During the Zhou (Chou) dynasty, 1122–249 BC, the great philosophers Confucius and Lao Zi lived. Lao Zi was the founder of Taoism and formulated a distinctive, new cultural-ethical system. Later, during the Qin, 221–207 BC, and Han, 206 BC–AD 220, dynasties, the country's warring states were finally unified and brought under central direction.

A Confucian-educated 'mandarin' bureaucracy was placed in charge of state affairs, with its members, from the Tang dynasty, AD 618–907, onwards, being recruited through a competitive and open system of public examinations. This scholar gentry élite, in conjunction with a 'divine' Emperor and powerful regional potentates, provided a stable political framework within which impressive technical and economic advances were achieved. Thus, during the Song, 960–1279, Ming, 1368–1644, and, early Manchu Qing, 1644–1911, dynasties, China became established at the forefront of world civilisation.

During the early Qing era, Chinese sovereignty was extended over the three north-eastern provinces of Heilongjiang, Jilin and Liaoning, commonly designated together as Manchuria, as well as the western provinces of Xinjiang, Xizang (Tibet), Qinghai and Nei Mongol (Inner Mongolia). This represented the apogee of the Imperial system. Thereafter, during the later Qing period, mounting economic difficulties, resulting from overpopulation, technological stagnation and the growing seaboard intrusion of the expansionary European powers and Japan, began to dissever the fragile bonds which had held together the Manchu polity.

In the wake of China's ignominious defeat at the hands of Japan in 1895 and the territorial concessions which were thereafter granted to foreign powers, popular nationalist sentiment grew, culminating in the anti-foreigner Boxer Rebellion of 1900. A decade later, in 1911–12, regional gentry and Western-trained New Model Army leaders combined to overthrow the infant Manchu Emperor Pu-Yi, in a 'Republican Revolution'.

A parliamentary regime, headed by the Western-educated, Cantonese 'Christian socialist', Dr Sun Yat-Sen, was, at first, established. This was replaced, in 1912, by the presidentialist rule of the northern-based military commander, Yuan Shikai. However, following Yuan's death in 1916, the new republican political system began to be torn apart, and power was increasingly devolved to regional military commanders. Eventually, internal civil war broke out between militarists and Dr Sun's Republicans (KMT: Nationalist Party), with the newly formed Chinese Communist Party (CCP), joining the fray in tactical alliance with the KMT. There began a destructive decade, which became known as the 'warlord period', 1916–26.

In northern and central China order was restored in 1928 by the Japanese-trained KMT leader, General Chiang Kai-shek, who had moved decisively both against his erstwhile CCP allies, in the Shanghai putsch of April 1927, and against the war lords of central and northern China, in the 'northern expedition' of 1926–28.

Chiang Kai-shek proceeded to establish a rightist, quasi-fascist, regime, founded on a close alliance with landlord, business and industrialist élite groups, the propagation of populist nationalism, the building up of a modern, substantial, German-trained army and new infrastructural, predominantly railway, investment. The nationalist regime faced, however, internal guerrilla opposition from the remnant forces of the CCP, now led by the Hunanese 'middle peasant', Mao Zedong (Mao Tse-tung). Mao's forces moved north along a 6,000-mile zig-zag course from Jiangxi province to isolated Shaanxi, in the 'Long March' of 1934–36, to establish a firm rural base at Yanan.

In addition, Chiang's regime faced the external threat of Japan, which forcibly annexed Manchuria (Dongbei) in September 1931, before attacking Beijing and invading northern China in 1937. To meet this challenge, a KMT-CCP truce was eventually declared and an anti-Japanese pact signed. However, the Chinese forces were rapidly overwhelmed by the Japanese, the KMT being forced into refuge in the remote western province of Sichuan, while the CCP retired to rural fastnesses in the north and centre of the country, from where they harassed the urban-based Japanese in classic guerrilla fashion.

During the war years the CCP established themselves as popular 'freedom-fighters' against a brutal Japanese regime, building up substantial support by their just treatment of the local population and the implementation of populist land reform programmes in the areas ('soviets') under their charge. By the early 1940s much of the hinterland of north-central China was effectively controlled by the CCP. This left the communists in a strong position when the Japanese finally withdrew, in August 1945.

A civil war between Chiang Kai-shek's US-backed KMT forces and the CCP's Red Army (PLA: People's Liberation Army) ensued between 1946 and 1949. Using mobile tactics, the PLA, led by Zhu De (Chu Teh), emerged triumphant, cutting Chiang's supply lines before decisively defeating his 550,000-strong army at the battle of Huai-Hai, in December 1948. Chiang Kai-shek and his nationalist supporters thereafter retreated to the island province of Taiwan, establishing a KMT regime which they claim still to be the legitimate government of all China. In reality, however, *de facto* power on the mainland passed to the communists, where a new People's Republic of China (PRC) was proclaimed by Mao Zedong, in Beijing on 1 October 1949.

The early years of the new CCP regime were, following more than a decade of constant warfare, consumed with the task of economic and political reconstruction. A centralised Soviet-style constitution was adopted, in September 1954; leading 'commanding-height' industries were nationalised; a system of quinquennial central planning instituted, from 1953; a programme of moderate, anti-gentry land reform introduced; and a major party recruitment drive was launched. This increased CCP membership from 4.5 million to 10.8 million between 1949 and 1956.

The general tone of the early 'post-liberation' years was one of consensual, 'united-front' co-operation, with small scale private enterprise being tolerated and the co-operation of white-collar intelligentsia and technocrat groups sought. Less tolerance was, however, shown towards the traditionally pro-KMT landed élite. In addition to being dispossessed of their holdings, members of this group were, between 1949 and 1953, publicly tried and forced to repent for past misdeeds. Two to four million of those who refused were publicly executed.

During its first decade in power, the CCP administration maintained close links with the Soviet Union, which provided the country with substantial economic and technical aid. A compelling factor behind this close relationship was the active hostility which the infant CCP regime faced from the United States. Thus, during the Korean War of 1950–53, the PLA clashed with American forces, fighting under the United Nations' flag, to defend the neighbouring North Korean communist regime. As a result, in 1954, the United States effected a Mutual Security Treaty with the Taiwan-based KMT, recognising it as the legitimate government of China.

Reflecting these close Soviet ties, the CCP leadership, in its first five-year plan of 1953–57, embarked on a heavy industrialisation, and material incentives-based, development strategy, which was substantially modelled on the USSR's Stalinist prototype. Concern grew, however, with the widening of social, regional and sectoral income and growth differentials which resulted from the implementation of this plan. In 1958, under the charismatic leadership of state President and CCP chairman, Mao Zedong, China suddenly shifted course, instituting a radical new policy programme, which Mao called the 'Great Leap Forward'.

Founded on the slogan, 'walking on two legs', this new programme sought to achieve rapid and simultaneous growth in both food and manufacturing output, by the collectivisation of land and the formation of large new, self-sufficient, agricultural and industrial communes. As well as functioning as co-operative production units, these communes were designed to act as residential units for political and ideological indoctrination, the aim being to remould attitudes and create a new breed of 'complete communists'. This new generation would serve as the progenitors of a new, classless and egalitarian 'true communist' society.

In practice, despite its lofty goals, the 'Great Leap' experiment proved to be over-ambitious and impossible to co-ordinate. It was, moreover, strongly opposed by ordinary peasants who were used to more individualistic forms of farming and living. Many cultivators resisted the collectivisation drive or co-operated only half-heartedly. As a consequence, with floods and famine ravaging the country, the distribution system falling into chaos and supply bottlenecks developing, more than 20 million died between 1959 and 1962. Output, both in the agricultural and industrial sectors, following an initial surge, dipped sharply during these years.

The 'Great Leap' departure also had serious repercussions for China's external relations, serving as the last straw which prompted the Soviet Union's increasingly estranged new Khrushchev leadership to break off formal relations. The Soviet Union had been subject to mounting criticisms from Mao for its 'hegemonistic' and 'revisionist' policy approach and the severing of diplomatic ties was accompanied by the withdrawal of technical advisers, in August 1960.

The failure of the 'Great Leap' experiment served to reduce the influence of Mao between 1962 and 1965. Instead, a successful 'recovery programme' was instituted, under the leadership of the CCP first vice-chairman, and new state President, the Moscow-trained Liu Shaoqi. This involved the re-introduction of private farming plots and markets, a reduction in the size of communes and a restoration of income differentials and material incentives. Mao soon struck back, however, against what he termed a return to the 'capitalist road', and against the recrudescence of a new, bureaucratic governing élite, by launching the 'Great Proletarian Cultural Revolution' (GPCR), between 1966 and 1969.

The GPCR was a broad-front 'rectification campaign' directed against 'rightist' elements in the CCP, with the aim of re-establishing the supremacy of ideology (Maoism) over economics, or 'putting politics in command', of re-emphasising egalitarian communist virtues and of bringing to the fore a new, and more radical, leadership generation. During the campaign, Mao, supported by the PLA chief, Lin Biao, and the Shanghai-based 'Gang of Four', encouraged student (Red Guard) demonstrations against incumbent party and government leaders. The 'Gang of

Four' was a grouping comprising Mao's wife, Jiang Qing, the radical intellectuals, Zhang Chunqiao and Yao Wenyuan, and the former millworker, Wang Hongwen. The chief targets were Liu Shaoqi, who was dismissed in October 1968 and died in prison in 1969, Deng Xiaoping, head of the CCP Secretariat, and Peng Zhen, mayor of Beijing. Each of them was forced out of office and publicly disgraced. The campaign grew anarchic, however, during 1967, necessitating direct intervention by the PLA and the dispersal of the Red Guards into the countryside to 'learn from the peasants'.

Traditional government institutions fell into abeyance during the Cultural Revolution and new 'Three-Part Revolutionary Committees', comprising Maoist party officials, trade unionists and PLA commanders, took over the administration. By 1970, however, Mao, concerned with the mounting public disorder, sided with the long-serving, and pragmatic, Prime Minister, Zhou Enlai (Chou En-lai), leader of the centrist faction within the CPC, and gradually set about restoring order and reconstructing a balanced party-state system. A number of 'ultra-leftists' were ousted during August 1970 and in September 1971 the PLA commander and Defence Minister, Lin Biao, died en route to Outer Mongolia, after a failed coup attempt.

During 1972–73 a rehabilitation of purged cadres, including Deng Xiaoping and finance minister Li Xiannian, commenced, while overseas a new policy of *détente* towards the United States was launched. This reconstruction movement was climaxed by the summoning of the National People's Congress (NPC) for the first time in eleven years, in January 1975, to ratify a new state constitution and approve a new, long-term economic strategy, termed the 'Four Modernisations'. This strategy, involving agriculture, industry, defence and science and technology, aimed at bringing China on a par with the West by the year 2000.

The reconstruction process was temporarily halted in 1976 when, following the deaths of Zhou Enlai and Mao Zedong, in January and September respectively, a violent succession struggle between the leftist 'Gang of Four', led by Jiang Qing, and moderate 'rightists', grouped around vice-premier Deng Xiaoping, was unleashed. Deng was forced into hiding by the 'Gang'. However, it was Mao's 'centre-left' protégé, Hua Guofeng, who was appointed CCP chairman, in September 1976, having already been selected as Prime Minister in January 1976.

Hua, in a pre-emptive move, proceeded to arrest the 'Gang', in October 1976, on charges of treason, and held power as a stop-gap leader between 1976 and 1978, implementing Zhou Enlai's 'Four Modernisations' programme. His authority was progressively challenged, however, by Deng Xiaoping, who was restored to office in March 1977, following wall-poster campaigns in Beijing. By December 1978, after further popular campaigns, Deng, who enjoyed substantial support among the state bureaucracy and military hierarchy, had gained effective control of the government, establishing a majority in the Politburo.

State and judicial bodies began to meet regularly again, the late Liu Shaoqi was rehabilitated as a party hero and major economic reforms were introduced. These involved the dismantling of the commune system and the introduction of direct farm incentives under a new 'responsibility system', as well as the encouragement of foreign investment in coastal enclaves ('Special Economic Zones').

By June 1981, Deng's paramountcy was assured by the installation of his protégés Hu Yaobang, as CCP chairman, later General Secretary, and Zhao Ziyang as Prime Minister, in June 1981 and September 1980 respectively. The 'Gang of Four' were sentenced to life imprisonment, Yao Wenyuan receiving 20 years, in January 1981, following a dramatic 'show trial'. A year later, in September 1982, Hua Guofeng was ousted from the Politburo, together with a number of senior colleagues, and in December 1982 a definitive new state constitution was adopted by the NPC.

This restored the post of state President, which had been abolished in January 1975, to which office Li Xiannian was elected. The military were placed under firmer party control and a new code of civil rights was introduced.

The new 'Deng administration' took the form of a collective leadership, with Hu Yaobang assuming control of party affairs, Zhao Ziyang overseeing state administration and Deng Xiaoping, a CCP vice-chairman and chairman of the State Central Military Committee (SCMC) and the CCP's Military Affairs Commission (MAC), the 'power behind the throne', concentrating on the formulation of the longer-term strategy, and maintaining a close eye on the PLA.

The triumvirate proceeded to pursue a three-pronged policy programme. The first aim was to streamline the party and state bureaucracies and promote to power new, younger and better educated technocrats. Second, they sought to curb the influence of the PLA through the retirement of senior commanders and a reduction in manpower numbers from 4.2 million to 3 million. The triumvirate's third priority was for economic modernisation, based on the extension of market incentives, 'market socialism', and local autonomy, and through the introduction of a new 'open door' policy to encourage foreign trade and investment.

By 1986 the policies had succeeded in effecting the replacement of half the CCP's provincial-level officers. The new economic reforms met with immediate success in the rural sector, agricultural output more than doubling between 1978–85. They had adverse side-effects, however, widening regional and social income differentials and fuelling a wave of 'mass consumerism', thus creating serious balance of payments and inflationary problems. These problems were exacerbated in 1984 when price reform in the urban industrial sector began to be implemented. In the political sphere, the new, pro-Western 'open-door' strategy and liberalisation programme served to generate, predominantly from the intelligentsia, demands for fuller internal democratisation. These calls culminated in a wave of major student demonstrations which swept across the country in December 1986. As a consequence of his failure to act promptly to check the disturbances, party chief Hu Yaobang was forced to resign, in January 1987.

The departure of Hu, Deng Xiaoping's closest associate, appeared to imperil the future of the post-1978 Dengist reform *(gai-ge)* programme, as more conservative forces, grouped around the senior figures of the Shanghai-born Politburo member Chen Yun and NPC Standing Committee Chairman, Peng Zhen, sought to halt the pace of change and re-establish firm central party control. As part of this strategy, a campaign against what was termed 'bourgeois liberalisation', or Western ideas, was launched by the CCP's conservative wing, during the spring of 1987. The more traditional Maoist virtues of frugality and self-reliance were stressed. However, the Dengist 'reform wing' of the CCP held its corner, Zhao Ziyang being temporarily elevated to the positions of both party General Secretary and Prime Minister.

At the CCP's thirteenth National Congress, held in October 1987, a 'work report' presented by Zhao which described the PRC as still in the 'initial stages of socialism', and thus requiring pragmatic resort to capitalist methods, was accepted. This document stressed the need for continuing reform, including price reform, though at a somewhat more cautious pace; an extension of the 'open door' strategy; and an enhanced separation between the party and state machines. At the Congress, and during its immediate aftermath, personnel changes were also effected which served to shift the balance on the CCP's Central Committee (CC) and Politburo significantly towards the 'reform faction'. A clutch of young new technocrats and successful mayors were inducted into the Politburo, replacing 'old guard' opposition figures, including Chen Yun and Peng Zhen. Deng Xiaoping also retired from both the Politburo and CC, but retained his position as head of the MAC.

However, in November 1987, shortly after the Congress, Li Peng, the Moscow-trained adopted son of Zhou Enlai, replaced Zhao Ziyang as acting Prime Minister and was formally confirmed in the position when the seventh NPC met for its inaugural session in March 1988. Viewed as a conservative, centralist, reformer, this move suggested that the Dengist reform wing had not triumphed completely and that factional and strategy differences still remained at senior party levels. As 1988 progressed, economic problems emanating from the price deregulation strategy mounted, with supply bottlenecks developing, as a consumer buying spree gained pace, particularly in the booming coastal provinces. The inflation rate rocketed to between 20 and 30 per cent. This forced a sharp application of the brakes on economic reform, following an emergency CC session held in September 1988, and the introduction of an austerity budget by Li Peng in March 1989.

A month later, following the death of the revered Hu Yaobang, students in Beijing took to the streets in pro-democracy demonstrations. These disturbances spread to provincial cities and gained in strength during May 1989, at the time of the visit to Beijing of the Soviet leader, Mikhail Gorbachev. The government effectively ceded control of the capital for a week to the students, buttressed by workers, as an intense CCP power struggle developed between conservatives, led by the unpopular Li Peng, and 'liberals', aligned to Zhao Ziyang. Li Peng, supported by Deng Xiaoping, gained the immediate upper hand and martial law was proclaimed and troops despatched to subdue the students. The PLA's officers refused, however, to use force against the demonstrators, creating a stalemate situation. However, at the beginning of June 1989, with the protest movement beginning to lose momentum, 27th Army troops, loyal to President Yang Shangkun, were sent into Tiananmen Square, in the centre of Beijing, to reclaim the capital, brutally shooting dead more than 2,000 unarmed protesters. This action put the hard-line Li-Deng-Yang triumvirate in immediate control of the Chinese polity.

A month later Zhao Ziyang was ousted as party leader and replaced by Shanghai party chief Jiang Zemin. A crackdown of dissidents was launched.

In foreign affairs, China's 1960 rift with Khrushchev's Soviet Union over policy differences became irrevocable in 1962 when Russia sided with India during a brief Sino-Indian border war. Relations with the Soviet Union deteriorated further in 1969 after border clashes in the disputed Ussuri river region. China pursued instead a non-aligned, 'Three Worlds', strategy, projecting itself as the spokesman for third-world nations, although it achieved a nuclear capability by 1964.

During the early 1970s, concerned with Soviet expansionism, a rapprochement with the United States was effected, bringing China's entry into the United Nations, at Taiwan's expense, in 1971 and culminating in the establishment of full Sino-American diplomatic relations, in January 1979. Relations with the West remained warm during the 1980s, under the Deng administration, with economic contacts broadening and solutions to the Hong Kong and Macao sovereignty questions being agreed with Britain and Portugal, on the basis of a pragmatic, 'one nation: two systems' formula.

In recent years, since the coming to power of the reformist Gorbachev leadership in the Soviet Union, Sino-Soviet relations have begun to thaw. Helped by progress over the divisive regional problems of Afghanistan and Cambodia (Kampuchea) and by border demarcation agreements, a heads of government-party summit between the two countries eventually took place in May 1989.

China's broader international relations have received a sharp setback as a result of the government's barbaric actions in June 1989. The international credit accumulated by the Deng regime has been forfeited, with its whole modernisation strategy now in peril.

INDIA

Republic of India
Bharat Janarajya

Capital: New Delhi

Social and economic data
Area: 3,287,590 km^2
Population: 785.000m*
Pop density per km^2: 239*
Literacy rate: 41%
GDP: $186,000m*; per capita GDP: $237
Economy type: low income
Labour force in agriculture: 63%

*1985

Ethnic composition
Seventy-two per cent of the population are of Indo-Aryan ethnic stock, 25 per cent, predominantly in the south, Dravidian and 3 per cent Mongoloid. The official language is Hindi, spoken by 31 per cent of the population,

concentrated in northern and central India, with English used as an associate official language. There are also 15 recognised regional languages and more than 1,400 local dialects.

Religions
Eighty-three per cent of the population are Hindus, 11 per cent Muslims, predominantly of the Sunni sect, 2 per cent Christians and 2 per cent Sikhs.

Political features
State type: liberal democracy
Date of state formation: 1947
Political structure: federal
Executive: parliamentary
Assembly: two-chamber
Party structure: multi-party
Human rights rating: 60%

Local and regional government
The country is divided into 25 substantially self-governing states and seven Union Territories, governed by centrally appointed administrators. Below them are divisions, districts, municipalities, development blocks and villages. Districts are administered by appointed 'district collectors', while corporations and councils *(panchayats)* operate at the urban and sub-district rural level, although elections have been infrequent. However, following a constitutional amendment proposed in 1989, the local *panchayat* tier will become increasingly important in the future.

Head of state
President Ramaswamy Iyer Venkataraman, since 1987.

Head of government
Prime Minister Rajiv Gandhi, since 1984.

Political leaders since 1970*
1966–77 Indira Gandhi (Congress), 1977–79 Morarji Desai (Janata), 1979–80 Chaudhury Charan Singh (Lok Dal), 1980–84 Indira Gandhi (Congress (I)), 1984– Rajiv Gandhi (Congress (I)).

*Prime Ministers

Political system
India is a federal republic whose January 1950 constitution, with 397 articles and nine schedules, making it one of the longest in the world, contains elements from both the American and British systems of government. It comprises 25 self-governing states, as shown in Table 64, each of which is administered by a figurehead governor appointed by the federal President, for a five-year term, on the advice of the Prime Minister.

Each state has a Legislative Assembly, or Vidhan Sabha, of between 30 and 425 members, popularly elected for a five-year term. Five of the larger states, Bihar, Jammu and Kashmir, Karnataka, Maharashtra, and Uttar Pradesh (UP), have a second, smaller, legislative chamber, called a Legislative Council or Vidhan Parishad. A Council of Ministers, headed by a Chief Minister, drawn from the Legislative Assembly, and responsible to it, is appointed on the basis of Assembly support.

The states have primary control over education, health, police and local government, and work in consultation with the centre in the economic sphere. In times of crisis, central rule, or 'President's rule', can be temporarily imposed.

There are, in addition, seven Union Territories: the Andaman and Nicobar Islands, Chandigarh, Dadra and Nagar Haveli, Daman and Diu, Delhi, Lakshadweep, and Pondicherry, which are governed by a Lieutenant-Governor or Administrator appointed by the federal President.

The federal government has sole responsibility in the fields of defence and foreign affairs and plays a key role in economic affairs. This, combined with its monopoly control over such 'growth taxes' as income tax, corporation tax and customs and excise, while the states rely on land and sales taxes and federal grants for their revenue, has served to weight the Indian federal system in the centre's favour compared, for example, with the US federal model.

Table 64

THE STATES OF INDIA

States	*Area (km^2)*	*Population (m) (1981)*	*Capital*	*Ruling Party* (March 1989)*
Andhra Pradesh	276,814	53.404	Hyderabad	Telugu Desam
Arunachal Pradesh	83,578	0.628	Itanagar	Congress (I)
Assam	78,523	19.903	Dispur	Asom Gana Parishad
Bihar	173,876	69.823	Patna	Congress (I)
Goa	3,496	0.992	Panjim	Congress (I)
Gujarat	195,984	33.961	Gandhinagar	Congress (I)
Haryana	44,222	12.851	Chandigarh	Lok Dal (B)
Himachal Pradesh	55,673	4.238	Simla	Congress (I)
Jammu & Kashmir	101,283	5.982	Srinagar	JKNCP & Congress (I)
Karnataka	191,773	37.043	Bangalore	Janata
Kerala	38,864	25.403	Trivandrum	CPI (M)
Madhya Pradesh	442,841	52.132	Bhopal	Congress (I)
Maharashtra	307,762	62.694	Bombay	Congress (I)
Manipur	22,356	1.434	Imphal	Congress (I)
Meghalaya	22,489	1.328	Shillong	Congress (I)
Mizoram	21,087	0.488	Aizawl	Mizo National Front and Congress (I)
Nagaland	16,527	0.773	Kohima	Congress (I)
Orissa	155,782	26.272	Bhubaneswar	Congress (I)
Punjab	50,362	16.669	Chandigarh	President's Rule
Rajasthan	342,214	34.013	Jaipur	Congress (I)
Sikkim	7,299	0.316	Gangtok	Sikkim Samgram Parishad
Tamil Nadu	130,069	48.297	Madras	DMK
Tripura	10,477	2.060	Agartala	Congress (I) & Tripura Upajati Juba Samity
Uttar Pradesh	294,413	110.858	Lucknow	Congress (I)
West Bengal	87,853	54.486	Calcutta	CPI (M)

*The party which provided the Chief Minister in March 1989.

The titular, executive head of the federal or 'Union' government is the President, who is elected for a five-year term by a large electoral college composed of members from both the federal and the state assemblies. Real executive power is, however, wielded by a Prime Minister and a 20- to 25-member cabinet, termed the Council of Ministers, drawn from the majority party or coalition within the federal parliament.

The Prime Minister is served by his own influential advisers and often reserves for himself, or herself, a number of important ministerial portfolios. For example, in March 1988, Prime Minister Rajiv Gandhi was also minister of external affairs, science and technology, atomic energy and space.

The federal assembly is a two-chamber body, comprising a dominant, 544-member, lower house, the House of the People (Lok Sabha), which has final authority over financial matters and 542 of whose members are directly elected for a five-year term from single member constituencies, by universal adult suffrage. Since 1989 the minimum voting age has been 18.

There is also a 245-member upper house, the Council of States (Rajya Sabha), 237 of whose members are indirectly elected, a third at a time for six-year terms, by state assemblies, on a regional quota basis. The remaining two seats in the Lok Sabha are reserved for Anglo-Indians, nominated by the President, while eight representatives of the Rajya Sabha are also reserved for presidential nominees.

To become law, bills require the approval of both chambers of the assembly, before formally receiving presidential assent. Ordinary amendments to the constitution require the approval of a two-thirds majority of the members of each house present and voting, and a simple majority of the total membership, to be followed by the President's assent. However, amendments which affect the distribution of powers between the centre and states, the representation of states in parliament and the workings of the adjudicatory Supreme Court and High Courts require ratification by at least half the state legislatures as well, to become law. Since 1950, 63 amendments have been adopted.

Political parties

The dominant national political party, which has held power for all but three years, from 1977 to 1979, since independence, has been the Congress Party. Under British rule it functioned as a 'catch-all' umbrella organisation for the nationalist movement, being originally formed by A. O. Hume in 1885, under the designation Indian National Congress, as a moderate, port-city based, intelligentsia pressure group. The movement's support base broadened and its policy outlook grew more radical during the inter-war years, under the charismatic leadership of Mahatma Gandhi and the Western-educated, Kashmiri Brahmin socialist, Jawaharlal Nehru. After splits, in 1969, 1978, 1981 1987, the main body of the party is today termed the All-India Congress Committee ((I)–for Indira) or, in short, Congress (I) and is led by Rajiv Gandhi.

The contemporary Congress (I) remains a broad, secular based, cross-caste and cross-religion, coalition, which advocates a moderate socialist policy approach and non-alignment in foreign affairs. It is liberally financed by the major Indian industrial conglomerates.

Its support base is strongest in the 'Hindi belt' of northern and central

India and in adjoining western India, from which regions it has drawn its leaders, and weakest in the Dravidian south. The party is a mass organisation, claiming a membership of over 10 million, but is controlled from above by a small 20-member 'High Command', the Congress Working Committee.

The principal national level opposition parties are the Janata (People's) Party, the Bharatiya Janata Party (Indian People's Party or BJP), the Lok Dal-B (People's Party), the Indian National Congress (Socialist or S), the Communist Party of India (CPI), the Communist Party of India-Marxist (CPI-M) and Jan Morcha (People's Front).

The Janata Party has 2 million members and was established in 1977. It is a left-of-centre body, led by the troika of Ajit Singh, the son of the late Jat leader, Charan Singh, Chandra Shekhar and former Karnataka chief minister, Ramakrishna Hegde. It includes the remnants of the Rashtriya Sanjay Manch (National Sanjay Organisation), a centrist body set up by Maneka Gandhi, the widow of Sanjay Gandhi, in 1983.

The BJP was founded in 1980 and is an urban, middle-class orientated, conservative Hindu grouping led by L. K. Advani and Atal Behari Vajpayee.

The People's Party dates from 1984 and is a middle peasant caste orientated party, led by Hemvati Nandan Bahuguna and Devi Lal.

The Indian National Congress (Socialist or S) is a neutralist, left-of-centre, 1981 breakaway from Congress (I) and is led by Sarat Chandra Sinha.

The CPI is a 480,000-member pro-Moscow party, which was formed in 1925, and is led by C. Rajeshwar Rao and Indrajit Gupta.

The CPI-M dates from 1964. It has 440,000 members, was formerly pro-Beijing, and is orientated towards the landless rural labourer. It is led by West Bengal Chief Minister, Jyoti Basu.

The People's Front is a left-of-centre party, led by the former finance and defence minister, Vishwanath Pratap Singh. It was founded in 1987.

In addition to these national organisations, there are numerous pro-federalist regional-level parties, the most important of which are: the All-India Anna Dravida Munnetra Kazhagam (ADMK), the Telugu Desam (Telugu Nation), the Jammu and Kashmir National Conference Party (JKNCP), the Shiromani Akali Dal (Akali Religious Party) and the Asom Gana Parishad (Assam People's Council or AGP).

The ADMK was established in 1972, in Tamil Nadu, and is currently split between factions led by V.N. Janaki Ramachandran and Jayalalitha Jayaram, who are, respectively, the widow and the former mistress of the film star, Marudud Gopalan Ramachandran, who died in January 1988.

The Telugu Desam was established in 1982, in Andhra Pradesh, and now has 1.2 million members. It is led by another former film star, N. T. Rama Rao.

The JKNCP dates from 1931 and is led by Dr Farook Abdullah.

The Akali Religious Party was formed in 1920, in Punjab. It has 1 million members, but is currently split. It is led by Simranjit Singh Mann.

The AGP was formed in 1985 and is led by Prafulla Kumar Mahanta.

Each of these groups held control of their respective state assemblies in 1988.

India's opposition parties have been notoriously fractious, faction-ridden bodies, subject to frequent splits and subsequent reformations in new guises. Personality and policy differences have tended to frustrate the formation of an united opposition to the Congress Party, with the notable exception of the success of 1977. Recently, however, an attempt has been made to re-establish unity under the leadership of the respected and popular V. P. Singh. As part of this process, four important national centrist and centre-left parties, the Janata, Lok Dal (B), Congress (S) and Jan Morcha, agreed to merge, in October 1988, under the designation Janata Dal (JD or People's Party). A National Front 'co-ordination' committee was established to link and make election pacts with 'friendly' regionalist parties, including the Telugu Desam, AGP and Dravida Munnetra Kazhagam (DMK), which is led by Dr K. Karunanidhi. V. P. Singh was formally elected President of the new JD, which has stressed power decentralisation, founded on Hegde's Karnataka model, and anti-corruption as key elements in its initial policy pronouncements. The right-wing BJP and the two communist parties have, initially, been excluded from this opposition 'broad-front'.

Latest elections

In the most recent Lok Sabha election, held in December 1984, although polling was postponed until January 1985 in five constituencies, and until September and December 1985, respectively, in strife-torn Punjab and Assam, the Congress (I) secured 400, or 75 per cent, of the 531 contested seats on a 49 per cent share of the national vote. The opposition BJP captured two seats on an 8 per cent share of the vote; the Janata Party, 13 seats with 7 per cent of the vote; the Lok Dal, three seats with 6 per cent of the vote; the CPI(M), 22 seats with 6 per cent of the vote; the Telugu Desam, 30 seats with 4 per cent of the vote; the ADMK, eleven seats with 2 per cent of the vote; and the CPI, six seats with 3 per cent of the vote. These figures highlight the impact of regionalised support concentrations on the seats:votes ratios under the first-past-the-post electoral system.

In the Rajya Sabha, following the elections of February 1988, Congress (I) held 57 per cent of the 245 seats.

Political history

The Indian sub-continent, with the exception of the Dravidian south, was first unified by the Mauryan regime (321–184 BC), whose emperor, Asoka, was converted to Buddhism. Later, north-central India was re-united by the Gupta dynasty (*c* AD 300–500), during which period Brahminical Hinduism re-established its dominance. Arab traders and invaders began to spread the Islamic faith in western and north-western regions from the seventh century, the process deepening with the establishment, over much of northern, central and western India, of the Delhi Sultanate (1206–1525) and Mughal Empire (1525–1780s) by Muslim conquerors from Central Asia. The south, however, which was the site of the Hindu Vijayanagar kingdom during the fourteenth and fifteenth centuries and was, later, only partially conquered by the Mughals, remained only tangentially exposed to Muslim influences.

Under British rule, which was established in stages between 1757 and 1856 and was to last until 1947, the sub-continent began, helped by the spread of railways and the creation of an extensive English-speaking bureaucracy, to be unified effectively for the first time. Nevertheless, during this period of the Raj, or British rule, almost half the land area, mainly the interior, remained free from direct British government. Instead, it was left to the control of 562 semi-independent, though loyal, 'Princely States'.

During the later nineteenth century, Indian national consciousness began to emerge among the intelligentsia, and was reflected in the creation, in 1885, of the Indian National Congress (INC), which campaigned for greater autonomy and eventual independence. The new nationalist movement grew more extensive and radical during the inter-war years, as economic pressures mounted. The progressive self-government concessions made by the government of India, including the 'dyarchy reforms' of 1919–21, which handed over much of provincial administrative responsibilities to elected assemblies, helping to inculcate a generalised respect for regular electoral processes, failed to satisfy the 'freedom fighters', Mahatma Gandhi and Jawaharlal Nehru. They led a series of civil disobedience campaigns for which activity they were repeatedly imprisoned.

The Indian sub-continent was eventually granted independence in August 1947 and, as a result of a split in the nationalist movement between the secular INC and the communalist Muslim League, led by Muhammad Ali Jinnah, the country was partitioned along religious lines, with initial bloody consequences. The result was a predominantly Hindu India and a Muslim-dominated Pakistan. Pakistan was, itself, divided into two, widely separated, western (Sind-Punjab-NW Frontier) and eastern (East Bengal) sectors, with the Indian land mass in between.

For more than two years after August 1947, India temporarily remained under the supervision of a Governor-General appointed by the British monarch, while a new constitution was framed and approved. This was achieved by January 1950, involving, in the process, the integration of former princely states and the restructuring of the old British provinces into new states, with boundaries based on linguistic lines. When the process was completed a fully independent, federal republic was proclaimed.

During its early years, the new republic faced problems in the resettlement of millions of Hindu refugees who had fled from Pakistan at the time of partition, losing, in the process, a similar number of Muslims who had moved out in the opposite direction. This resulted in a number of border skirmishes with its new neighbour over Kashmir.

Domestically, under the leadership of Prime Minister Nehru, limited land reforms and a new socialist economic programme were introduced. The programme, which involved protectionism, an emphasis on heavy industries and state planning, was initially successful. Meanwhile, the sovereignty of French- and Portuguese-held territories within India, including Chandernagore, Pondicherry and Goa, was recovered between 1950 and 1961. Resort to force was necessary in the case of Goa.

In its external relations, India remained within the Commonwealth and played a leading role in the formation of the non-aligned movement in 1961. It also, however, became involved in border clashes with communist China, in October 1962.

In May 1964, Prime Minister Nehru died and was briefly succeeded as national leader by his close associate, the Benares-born 'minister without portfolio', Lal Bahadur Shastri. The country became entangled in a second border conflict with Pakistan over Kashmir between August and September 1965 before Shastri died, in January 1966.

His successor as INC leader and Prime Minister was Indira Gandhi, the daughter of Jawaharlal Nehru. She adhered to the broad outlines of her father's policy programme, but also developed closer links with the Soviet Union, with whom India signed a 15-year economic and military assistance agreement in 1973.

In December 1971, Indian troops invaded East Pakistan in support of the local separatist government. After a twelve-day war, they succeeded in defeating Pakistan's forces and oversaw the creation of the new independent, and pro-Indian, state of Bangladesh. This military success, despite contemporary economic difficulties, boosted the national standing of Prime Minister Gandhi. However, her personalised style of control had begun to foment divisions within the ruling INC, precipitating an initial split, in November 1969, in which the Gujarat-born Morarji Desai, a former Deputy Prime Minister and 1966 party leadership challenger, together with a number of fellow senior colleagues, left to form a new Congress (O) (O for Organisation).

Criticism of the Prime Minister's autocratic methods mounted in June 1975 when, having been found guilty of electoral malpractice during the March 1971 general election by the High Court, in her Allahabad constituency, and been banned from holding elective office for six years, she imposed a draconian 'State of Emergency', involving the temporary outlawing of opposition parties and the imposition of tight censorship controls. Almost 1,000 of Mrs Gandhi's political opponents were imprisoned, under the provisions of the Maintenance of Internal Security Act. Despite her later being cleared of malpractice by the Supreme Court, in November 1975, the 'Emergency' continued for two years, during which time a harsh and unpopular compulsory birth control programme, by sterilisation, was introduced under the supervision of Sanjay Gandhi, Indira's youngest son.

The 'State of Emergency' was eventually lifted in March 1977 to allow parliamentary elections to take place. In this contest, the opposition parties, who had united under the umbrella of the newly formed Janata Party, were swept to power with a landslide victory. The new party's leader, Morarji Desai, defeated Indira Gandhi in her home constituency.

The new Janata government, the first non-INC administration since independence, headed by Prime Minister Desai, swiftly introduced constitutional amendments to reverse those pushed through by Indira Gandhi in 1976, thus restoring the 'democratic balance'. The Desai coalition was gradually undermined, however, by mounting economic difficulties and internal factional strife. This culminated, in July 1979, in the defection of many Janata members to a new secular party, the Lok Dal, under the leadership of the former health minister, Raj Narain, and home minister, Charan Singh. Desai was eventually toppled as Prime Minister in July 1979 and a coalition, under the leadership of Charan Singh, assumed power. A month later, however, after only 24 days in office, the Charan Singh government was defeated.

In the Lok Sabha elections, which followed in January 1980, Indira Gandhi's renamed and revamped Congress (I), promising a firmer and more decisive approach to government after the drift of the Janata years and faced with opposition disarray, was returned to power, gaining a landslide majority.

The new administration proceeded to record success in the economic sphere, helped by the spread of the 'green revolution' in the agricultural sector, which resulted in high yields of wheat and rice. It was beset, however, by mounting problems of inter-caste violence and regionalist unrest, centred in Gujarat, where there was caste strife, Muslim-dominated Kashmir, Southern India and Assam, where violence was aimed at Bangladeshi immigrants. This resulted in Congress (I)'s loss of control of a string of state assemblies.

The most serious unrest occurred in the prosperous Punjab. Here initial moderate Sikh demands for greater religious recognition and a resolution of water and land disputes with neighbouring states, escalated into more extreme calls for the creation of a separate state of 'Khalistan'. In June 1984, Indira Gandhi, concerned with the mounting level of disorder in the province, sent Indian troops into the Golden Temple at Amritsar to dislodge the young Sikh extremist leader, Sant Jarnail Singh Bhindranwale, and his armed followers. This 'storming' operation, which caused widespread damage to a revered holy shrine, as well as resulting in the death of Bhindranwale and hundreds of his 'disciples', provoked a Sikh backlash which served to radicalise and spread militancy through the community. Across India, regiments of Sikh troop immediately mutinied and, four months later, in October 1984 the Prime Minister was assassinated by her Sikh bodyguards in the garden of her residence in New Delhi. This, in turn, provoked savage Hindu retaliation in Delhi, in November 1984, involving the massacre of 2,000 Sikhs by vigilantes, before the new Prime Minister, Rajiv Gandhi, Indira's eldest son, was able to restore order.

In the new general election, which followed, in December 1984, Congress (I), benefiting from a wave of public sympathy, succeeded in securing a record victory, with its highest share, 49 per cent, of the national vote since independence. The new Prime Minister, Rajiv Gandhi, a former airline pilot who had only reluctantly been persuaded into politics in 1980, following the death of his younger brother, was a popular leader. He was viewed as an upright, managerial 'non-politician', unsullied by the corruptions of the political game. He proceeded to project himself as a forward-looking and healing leader, pledging, under the slogan 'bringing India into the twenty-first century', to modernise and inject greater market efficiency into the Indian economy and to resolve the Punjab, Assam, Kashmir and north-eastern hill states regional disputes.

Early deregulationary economic reforms, assaults on bureaucratic 'red tape', support for the launching of Indian space satellites and the spread of computer technology promised to give substance to these visions, while an early move was made to resolve the Punjab dispute and even greater progress made in Assam, Kashmir and the hill areas, including Mizoram. Here 25 years of rebellion were ended and it became a new state of the Indian Union.

By 1987, however, Rajiv Gandhi's national standing had been seriously diminished. In the economic sphere, the reformist zeal of 1985–86 had lost its impetus and prospects seemed poor, with the country in the grip of its worst drought of the century. In the external sphere, the Indian army, which had been sent to northern Sri Lanka to 'police' the July 1987 Jayawardene Peace Accord, had become bogged down in a civil war. Internally,

Sikh-Hindu ethnic violence remained a serious problem in Punjab, with communalist Hindu chauvinism gaining in strength in adjoining regions. Politically, Congress (I) support had slumped, the party enduring reverses in state polls, as well as the defection of a number of elder party members who were opposed to the centralisation of power within the hands of a tight-knit 'Doon clique' of young Gandhi associates. There were also public disputes between President Giani Zail Singh and the Prime Minister.

Most serious of all, however, the reputation that had initially been assigned to Rajiv Gandhi as the 'Mr Clean' of Indian politics had been seriously sullied by the uncovering by finance minister V.P. Singh of the 'Bofors scandal', involving financial 'kick-backs' received by, it was alleged, government-connected Indian 'front organisations', for facilitating a major arms contract with the Swedish munitions firm.

Although Rajiv Gandhi was cleared of any personal impropriety in this affair, the 'Bofors scandal' served to undermine popular confidence in his administration, while at the same time vaulting on to the national stage V. P. Singh as a zealous crusader against corruption. Singh, along with other prominent 'dissident' members, was dismissed from the Congress (I) in July 1987 and proceeded to form a new 'political forum', the Jan Morcha, in October. Following his election to the Lok Sabha, in a by-election held in his native Allahabad in June 1988, Singh became the focus for an opposition unity drive, culminating in the formation of the new National Front and Janata Dal, in October 1988. The emergence of an opposition leader of national standing and cross-caste appeal, to challenge the appeal of the 'Gandhi dynasty' constituted a serious threat to the prospects of Congress (I) securing electoral victory in the Lok Sabha elections due in 1989.

However, foreign policy success secured from decisive Indian military intervention in the Maldives in November 1988, coupled with improving economic conditions, following a bumper harvest in 1988, served to revive Congress (I) spirits in preparation for this poll.

INDONESIA

Republic of Indonesia
Republik Indonesia

Capital: Jakarta

Social and economic data
Area: 1,925,000 km^2
Population: 173.103m*
Pop density per km^2: 90*
Literacy rate: 67%
GDP: $84,468m*; per capita GDP: $488
Economy type: low income
Labour force in agriculture: 53%

*1985

Ethnic composition
The country is heterogenous in social composition, consisting of more than 300 ethnic groups, the majority of which are of Malay stock. The most important Malay communities are the Javanese, who comprise a third of the population, followed by the Sundanese, 7 per cent, and Madurese, 3 per cent. The Chinese, 2 per cent, constitute the largest non-Malay community, with substantial numbers of Indians, Melanesians, Micronesians and Arabs, invariably regionally based, also to be found. The official national language is Bahasa Indonesia, a form of Trade Malay, but 25 local languages, predominantly Javanese, and 250 local dialects, are also spoken.

Religions
Eighty-four per cent of the population are Muslims; 8 per cent Christians, the majority of them Roman Catholics. The Batak of Sumatra, the Minahasan of Sulawesi, the Ibans of Kalimantan and the Moluccans constitute the most important Christian communities. Two per cent of the population are Hindus, residing mainly in Bali, and 5 per cent adhere to tribal religions. The country has the largest Muslim community, some 145 million, in the world. The majority of Muslims are, however, nominal, following an amalgam of animistic, Muslim and Hindu beliefs and rituals. Aceh province in west Sumatra, where Islamic *sharia* law is acknowledged, is an exception. The official state 'religion' is the secular ideology of Pancasila, based on five general principles: a belief in one supreme God; a just and civilised humanity; the unity of Indonesia; democracy, led by the wisdom of deliberations *(musyawarah)* among representatives; and social justice for the whole of the people of Indonesia.

Political features
State type: authoritarian nationalist
Date of state formation: 1949
Political structure: unitary
Executive: unlimited presidential
Assembly: one-chamber
Party structure: multi-party*
Human rights rating: 30%

*With one party predominating

Local and regional government
The country is divided into 27 provinces *(propinsi)*, each headed by a centrally appointed governor, two-thirds of whom are drawn from the military. Within the provinces are 246 districts or regencies *(kabupaten)*, administered by regents *(bupats)*; 54 municipalities *(kota madya)*, under the charge of mayors *(walis)*; and 3,349 sub-districts *(kecamatan)*, headed by a *tjamat*. The three provinces of Aceh, Yogyakarta and Jakarta Raja have been designated 'special territories'. There is a three-tier system of elected provincial, regency and village assemblies at local and regional levels.

Head of state and head of government
President T. N. J. Suharto, since 1967.

Political leaders since 1970
1966– T. N. J. Suharto (Golkar).

Political system

Under the constitution of August 1945, which was amended in 1950 and 1969, the supreme political body in Indonesia is, in theory, the 1,000-member People's Consultative Assembly (MPR: Majelis Permusyawaratan Rakyat). This consists of 500 members of the House of Representatives and 500 selected representatives from 147 regional assemblies and 353 functional and political groups, including about 200 from the armed forces. It meets at least once every five years to elect an executive President and Vice-President and to determine the constitution and the 'broad lines of the policy of the State and Government'. All decisions, in accordance with the tradition of *musyawarah*, are taken unanimously.

The House of Representatives (DPR: Dewan Perwakilan Rakyat) functions as a single-chamber legislature and comprises 400 directly elected members and 100 presidential appointees, three-quarters of whom represent the armed forces. It meets at least once a year and elections are held every five years.

All statutes require the House's approval. Individual DPR members may submit draft bills. To become law, however, they need to be ratified by the President, who enjoys veto rights. As in the MPR, legislation is adopted by consensus, rather than voting, the chamber acting as a legitimator of presidential initiatives.

At the head of the executive, and the most powerful political figure in the country, is the President. He is elected by the MPR for a renewable five-year term. He works with an appointed cabinet, exercises, as has already been noted, the right of veto over House of Representatives' bills and appoints governors for each of Indonesia's 27 provinces. In March 1988 his cabinet had 38 members, the majority of whom were specialist technocrats, and a third were serving or retired military commanders. Each of these cabinet ministers is responsible only to the President.

The President is assisted by several advisory agencies, including the Supreme Advisory Council (DPA: Dewan Pertimbangan Agung), National Development Council and the National Security and Political Stabilisation Board. During periods of emergency, he has additional authority to enact ordinances which have the force of law, for up to a year, without parliamentary ratification.

Political parties

The dominant and governing, political party in Indonesia is Golkar (Joint Secretariat of Functional Groups: Sekretariat Bersama Golongan Karya), led by President Suharto. The party was formed in 1964 by a group of senior army officers as a means of establishing a loose alliance of sectional interests, farmers, fishermen, professionals, factory workers, young people, the older generation and women, so as to counter the growing influence of the Indonesian Communist Party which enjoyed national support of around 15 per cent during the 1950s, before being banned in 1966.

Golkar was brought under government control, in 1968, and transformed into the civilian arm of President Suharto's military regime. The party has an extensive national organisation, but is tightly controlled from above by an élite, 45-member Central Committee, comprising senior state officials and army officers, all close to the President. It has been described as 'not so much a political party as . . . the political arm of the bureaucracy', and is designed to restrict to a minimum the number of assembly seats obtained by other, genuine, political parties. Golkar currently claims a membership of 25 million and a retired Javanese general, Wahono, was elected its chairman, in October 1988.

There are two permitted 'opposition parties': the Indonesian Democratic Party (PDI: Partai Demokrasi Indonesia), and the United Development Party (PPP: Partai Persatuan Pembangunan).

The PDI was formed in 1973 through the enforced merger of five non-Islamic nationalist and Christian parties. It is currently led by Suryadi, and is heir to the radical and once influential, Sukarno-linked, Indonesian Nationalist Party (PNI). However, today it is viewed as being thoroughly penetrated by state intelligence officers, and its leader effectively appointed by the government.

The PPP was also formed in 1973, by the merger of four Islamic parties, including the Nahdlatul Ulama and Indonesian Muslims' Party. It is led by Dr Jailano Naro, is Islamic in outlook and enjoys strong support in Aceh province and in east and central Java. However, its four constituent elements remain poorly fused. On non-Muslim issues, the PPP's members generally support government initiatives.

To be officially registered, political parties must subscribe to the state philosophy of Pancasila and have a membership which covers more than a quarter of Indonesia. This has prevented the formation of narrowly regional-based groupings. Since 1975, only Golkar, the PDI and the PPP have been permitted to function. Also, the two non-Golkar parties are debarred from organising below the district level. To compensate for these restrictions, the state provides parties with finance to cover administrative, campaign and leadership expenses.

Latest elections

In the most recent DPR elections, which were held in April 1987, Golkar captured 299, or 75 per cent, of the 400 available seats on a 73 per cent share of the national vote. The Muslim-backed PPP won 61 seats, or 15 per cent of the total, and 16 per cent of the vote, while the PDI garnered 40 seats, or 10 per cent, on an 11 per cent vote share. Turnout was put at 91 per cent, with voting, as usual, taking place in multi-member provincial constituencies, based on a simple party list proportional representation system.

The election was viewed as relatively fair, except in East Timor, where a 100 per cent plus turnout was recorded. It was also reasonably peaceful. Only eight people died during the campaign, compared with 60 in 1982. However, the campaign speeches of the two 'opposition parties' were subjected to prior government vetting and it was apparent that many votes were cast on a 'patronage basis'.

In the concurrent regional assembly elections, Golkar gained control of all the country's 27 provinces for the first time.

Political history

Indonesia constitutes the largest archipelago nation in the world, comprising 13,667 mountainous and volcanic islands, 6,000 of which are inhabited. They are separated east-west by 5,271 kilometres and north-south by 2,210 kilometres. The islands were settled by immigrants from south China between 3000 and 500 BC, displacing the original Melanesian population. During the early centuries of the Christian era, they came under the influence of Hindu and Buddhist priests and traders, who spread their culture and religion and later, from AD 700 onwards, established substantial Hindu empires. Islam was introduced during the thirteenth century by Gujarati and Persian traders and had become the archipelago's chief religion by the fifteenth century. Portuguese traders followed, in the early sixteenth century, and established lucrative spice-trading posts.

The Portugese commercial monopoly over the 'spice islands' was successfully challenged by the Dutch, in 1595, and the archipelago, now designated the Netherlands Indies, was placed, between 1602 and 1798, under the supreme control of the Dutch East India Company. Initially, during the seventeenth century, the Dutch had concentrated purely on commerce, establishing new trading centres, while leaving internal administration to indigenous Indonesian kingdoms. During the nineteenth century, however, direct Dutch rule was imposed. The islands were proclaimed a Dutch colony in 1816 and a sugar-based plantation economy was established on Java. In 1922, the Netherlands Indies were designated an integral part of the Netherlands kingdom.

During the 1920s and 1930s the rural economy faced mounting difficulties including, in 1926, a communist-inspired revolt. A nationalist movement developed, under the leadership of the pro-communist Indonesian Nationalist Party (PNI), which was established in 1926, and headed by the charismatic Achmed Sukarno. This was suppressed by the Dutch administration, the PNI's leaders being imprisoned and exiled between 1929 and 1932, but, in March 1942, following the occupation of the islands by Japanese forces, the party was installed in power as an anti-Western puppet government.

When Japan surrendered to the Allies, in August 1945, President Sukarno proclaimed Indonesia's independence from Holland. The Dutch challenged this by launching military expeditions, between 1946 and 1949, before eventually agreeing to transfer sovereignty in December 1949. At the same time, a 'special union' was established between the two countries. This union was abrogated by Indonesia in February 1956.

The new republic was planned as a federation of 16 constituent regions, but was made unitary in August 1950. This naturally resulted in the dominance of Java, provoking revolts in Sumatra and the predominantly Christian South Moluccas. The paramount political figure in the new republic was President Sukarno, who, believing in the concept of 'guided democracy', ruled in an authoritarian manner and pursued an ambitious, expansionist and nationalist foreign policy. He succeeded in effecting the transfer of Netherlands New Guinea (Irian Jaya) to Indonesia, in May 1963, but failed, after a confrontation with Malaysia, in the cases of Sabah and Sarawak in North Borneo.

In September 1965, amid deteriorating economic conditions, caused by extravagant government overspending and corruption, a coup was attempted against Sukarno by groups connected with the 2.5 million-strong Indonesian Communist Party (PKI). This was firmly put down, with tens of thousands of PKI supporters losing their lives, by army chief of staff General Suharto. He then proceeded to assume power as emergency ruler, in March 1966.

General Suharto ended Indonesia's hostility towards Malaysia over Sabah and Sarawak, in August 1966, and formally replaced Sukarno as President in February 1967. He then proceeded to institute what was termed a 'New Order'. This involved: the concentration of political power in the hands of a coterie of army and security force (Kopkamtib) officers and, mainly American-educated, technocrat planners; the propagation of a new secular state philosophy of Pancasila, stressing unity and social justice; the pursuit of a liberal, free-enterprise and 'open door' economic policy; the fierce suppression of communist political activity; and the tight control of ordinary party political activity. All opposition groups were fused, by diktat, into two, 'neutered' units in 1973.

Aided by income from rising oil exports, significant industrial and agricultural growth was achieved during the 1970s, self-sufficiency in rice production being attained, for example, by the early 1980s. Per capita GDP rose by 4.8 per cent per annum in real terms between 1965 and 1985. In addition, Indonesia's territorial borders were extended by the forcible annexation of the predominantly Catholic, former Portugese, colony of East Timor, in 1975–76.

Suharto's authoritarian methods, however, promoted opposition from many quarters. The opposition came from left-wing organisations, radical Muslims and tribal separatist groups in the outlying islands of Irian Jaya and East Timor. In Irian Jaya there was the Free Papua Movement (OPM) and in East Timor, the Fretilin and UDI independence fronts.

Following the suppression of an OPM-organised rebellion in Irian Jaya, the Suharto government instituted, in 1986, a 'trans-migration programme', based on the resettlement there, and on other sparsely peopled 'outer islands', of a projected 65 million Javanese, by the year 2006. This scheme, which began in 1987, encountered strong opposition from indigenous Melanesians, prompting more than 10,000 refugees to emigrate to adjoining Papua New Guinea. In East Timor, meanwhile, it was reported that more than 100,000 Timorese, a sixth of the population, died from famine, disease and continuing internal warfare during the decade immediately following the province's annexation. The UN refused to recognise Indonesian sovereignty over East Timor, which continued to be imposed through military force, although travel restrictions were partially eased from 1988.

During the early 1980s economic problems developed as world oil prices fell, oil providing 70 per cent of Indonesia's foreign exchange earnings. The annual GDP growth rate dropped to 3.5 per cent between 1980 and 1985, while the country's population continued to expand at a compound rate of 3.3 per cent. Despite these difficulties, national support for Golkar rose nine points over its 1982 level to 73 per cent in the general election of April 1987. A year later, in March 1988, Suharto was unanimously re-elected, as the sole candidate, for a fifth five-year term.

In its external relations, Indonesia has for a long time pursued a non-aligned foreign policy, hosting the Bandung Conference of Third World nations in 1955. It has also been a prominent member of ASEAN since its inception in 1967. Under General Suharto, however, the country's relations, political and economic, with the West have notably improved.

JAPAN

Nippon

Capital: Tokyo

Social and economic data
Area: 371,860 km^2
Population: 121.402m*
Pop density per km^2: 326*
Literacy rate: 100%
GDP: $1,325,430m*; per capita GDP: $10,918
Economy type: high income
Labour force in agriculture: 9%

*1985

Ethnic composition
More than 99 per cent of the population are of Japanese ethnic stock.

Religions
Almost 85 per cent of the population nominally adhere to Shintoism, an indigenous religion embracing the worship of ancestors and nature, or the Buddhist faith. One per cent are Christians.

Political features
State type: liberal democracy
Date of state formation: fifth century
Political structure: unitary
Executive: parliamentary
Assembly: two-chamber
Party structure: multi-party*
Human rights rating: 88%

*But dominated by one paramount party

Local and regional government
The country is divided into nine regions, which are further subdivided into 47 prefectures, each of which is administered by an elected governor and has an elected assembly. Below, there are elected city, town and village chief executives and assemblies. Local bodies are substantially dependent, however, on the central government for funding and policy direction.

Head of state
Emperor Akihito, since 1989.

Head of government
Prime Minister Tokshiki Kaifu, since 1989.

Political leaders since 1970*
1964–72 Eisaku Sato (LDP), 1972–74 Kakuei Tanaka (LDP), 1974–76 Takeo Miki (LDP), 1976–78 Takeo Fukuda (LDP), 1978–80 Masayoshi Ohira (LDP), 1980–82 Zenko Suzuki (LDP), 1982–87 Yasuhiro Nakasone

(LDP), 1987–89 Noboru Takeshita (LDP), 1989 Sosuke Uno (LDP), 1989– Tokshiki Kaifu (LDP).

* Prime Ministers

Political system

Japan's 99-article, November 1946, constitution was framed by the occupying allied forces, with the intention of creating a consensual, parliamentary form of government and avoiding an over-concentration of executive authority. The head of the state is the Emperor, whose functions are purely ceremonial, being described as 'the symbol of the State and of the unity of the people'. Real power is concentrated in the elected assembly and is exercised by a Prime Minister and cabinet.

The Japanese assembly, the Diet (Kokkai), is a two-chamber body composed of a 252-member upper house, the House of Councillors (Sangiin), and a 512-member lower house, the House of Representatives (Shugiin). The former has 152 representatives elected from 47 prefectural constituencies on the basis of the 'limited vote' system and 100 elected nationally by proportional representation. Under the 'limited vote' system electors cast a single vote, the candidates with the highest number of votes in each single- or multi-member constituency being returned in rank order. Electors are given an additional, separate, vote for the extra 100 members. To be included in this national ballot, parties must submit a list of at least ten candidates, at least five of whom are existing Diet members, or they must have won at least 4 per cent of the vote at the previous election. Each Councillor serves a six-year term, half the chamber being elected every three years.

Members of the House of Representatives are elected for a four-year term, subject to dissolution, in large, three- to five-member constituencies, again on the basis of the 'limited vote'. The ballot is restricted to those of 20 years and over.

The House of Representatives is the dominant, and more important, of the two chambers. It is able to override vetoes on bills imposed by the House of Councillors if a two-thirds majority of those present is obtained. It also has paramountcy on financial questions. In practice, inter-house disputes, when they arise, are resolved by the convening of a special Joint Conference Committee. In both chambers, legislative business is effected through a system of Standing and Special Committees, with stress placed on achieving a consensus. Also, the opposition is allowed to chair a number of important committees. The legislature convenes at least once a year for a session which must last at least 150 days, but is usually far longer.

To amend the constitution, a two-thirds majority vote of all members of each chamber of the Diet is required, followed by a majority affirmation by the electors in a special referendum. Despite support for changes among elements within the ruling Liberal Democratic Party (LDP), the 'blocking' strength of the opposition parties has meant that no amendments to the 1946 'American Constitution' have so far been made.

Executive administration is entrusted to a Prime Minister chosen by the majority grouping within the Diet. He selects a cabinet, of about 20 to 25 members, and all are collectively responsible to the assembly, which can unseat the government by a successful 'no-confidence' motion. Cabinet members oversee the work of both government ministries and agencies and must, according to the rules of the constitution, be civilians. The majority, including the Prime Minister, must also be members of the Diet. The cabinet functions in a consensual, collective manner, with individual ministers working closely with their respective departmental senior bureaucrats, who, in reality, are the crucial policy-framing figures.

The post of Prime Minister, with its important patronage powers, has regularly been assigned, since the mid-1950s, to the president of the LDP. The frequent changes in personnel occupying the post are thus the result of a desire by party faction leaders to rotate and, thus secure temporary occupancy of, this 'plum' position, rather than of substantive 'political' factors. In addition, cabinet posts have also been liberally shared and rotated among senior faction members, ministers rarely serving more than two years in a post.

Japan possesses a 15-justice Supreme Court, whose members are appointed by the cabinet, with the exception of the High Judge, who is appointed by the Emperor, on the nomination of the cabinet. Once appointed, judges serve until the legal retirement age, but are subject to approval in decennial popular referenda. The Supreme Court enjoys administrative control over lower courts and the power of judicial review. It is able to determine the constitutionality of any law. In practice, however, as a result of the Japanese preference for settling disputes by negotiation and mediation, its use of these powers has been unusually limited.

Political parties

The dominant political party in Japan, is the Liberal Democratic Party (LDP: Jiyu-Minshuto). It has monopolised power for more than three decades, but failed to win House of Representatives majorities in 1976, 1979 and 1983.

Although tracing its origins back to the first parties established in the 1870s, the LDP was constituted in its present form in November 1955, when two conservative parties, the Liberals, led by Taketora Ogata, and the Japan Democratic Party, led by Prime Minister Ichiro Hatoyama, united. Traditionally, the party has enjoyed strong support in rural areas, these constituencies being currently substantially over-represented in the Diet, in voter: deputy terms, *vis-à-vis* the growing urban districts. It also enjoys liberal finance from the business community, both small and large, and has developed, during its years in government, close links with the bureaucracy. About a quarter of LDP Diet members are former civil servants, often of senior rank.

Although viewed as 'conservative' in its ideological outlook, the LDP is, in reality, more of a 'catch-all' organisation, embracing a broad and shifting variety of domestic and foreign affairs policy ideas which are applied in a pragmatic and corporatist manner. Its uniting principles, however, are a belief in the efficacy of private enterprise, support for the development of a welfare state and a continuation of Japan's alliance with the United States.

Membership of the LDP was put at 3.6 million in 1985, corresponding to 3 per cent of the total population. However, the party lacks an effective grass-roots constituency organisation in the West European sense and is notably divided into factions based on personalities, rather than ideology. In 1988 there were eight important factions of this kind.

The most sizeable, containing 121 LDP Diet members, was led by Prime Minister and party president Noboru Takeshita. It had only recently been formed as a breakaway from the older 'Tanaka faction', in July 1987. Fourteen other former members of the 'Tanaka faction' were said to be aligned in a new grouping, led by Susumu Nikaido. The LDP's second largest faction, with 89 members, was headed by LDP Secretary-General Shintaro Abe. It had formerly been known as the 'Fukuda faction'. Two, equal third, with 87 members apiece, were led by former Prime Minister Nakasone and former finance minister and party Vice-President Kiichi Miyazawa. They succeeded the older 'Suzuki faction'. Three other, smaller, factions were the Komoto, with 30 members, Sonoda and Hori.

These groupings, which involve the development of personalised patron-client ties between senior leaders and younger aspirants, operate as a means of promoting the ministerial interests of the former, while advancing the careers of the latter, through step by step progression up the political ladder. Based on the Japanese emphasis on the neo-Confucian principles of duty and obligation and traditional respect for family and personal ties (currently a third of the LDP's Diet members are related to another member by blood or marriage), the existence of factions has served to institutionalise competition within the party.

At the local level, factional groupings bargain for acceptance of their members as party candidates in multi-member constituencies. However, the ultimate goal of a faction is to secure for its leader the coveted post of LDP president. This is assigned biennially by a majority vote of the party's Diet members. Since 1955 this post has gone with that of Prime Minister.

More than 10,000 political parties are registered as functioning in Japan. Only four parties other than the LDP are, however, significant forces. The second-ranking party in the country and leading opposition body is the 55,000-member Japan Socialist Party (JSP: Nippon Shakaito). The JSP traces its roots back to the Socialist Party, which was established in 1925, but was allowed to play only a tangential role in inter-war politics. The JSP itself was set up in November 1946 and temporarily held power between May 1947 and March 1948. The party subsquently split, in 1951–52, over its response to the US-Japanese Peace Treaty, but re-united in 1955. It favours a democratic socialist economic strategy and the establishment of a non-aggressive mutual security system, embracing Japan, China, the US and the USSR. Strongest in urban areas and among unionised workers, it is closely linked to the General Council of Trade Unions of Japan (Sohyo), with a membership of over 4 million. Support for the party has, however, slumped since the 1960s, when its share of the national vote stood at 27–29 per cent. The JSP is currently led by Takako Doi, the country's first female party leader.

Further to the left stands the Japanese Communist Party (JCP: Nippon Kyosanto), which was founded in 1922, though subsequently banned until 1945, its leaders being imprisoned or exiled. Support for the JCP has increased since the early 1970s, following its assertion of independence from both the Chinese and Soviet communist ideological camps, its renouncing of a call for violent revolution and its focusing on economic and social improvement. The JCP is a mass party, with 440,000 members in 1985. It is organised on hierarchical, 'democratic centralist' lines and controlled by a Presidium (Politburo) chaired by Hiromu Murakami.

Occupying the centre-left ground is the 'humanitarian socialist' Komeito (Clean Government Party), which was formed in November 1964 as the political wing of the 8 million-member Buddhist sect, the Value Creation Society Soka Gakkai, which was itself established in 1930. It is led by Kashiro Ishida and claims a current membership of 180,000. The party has campaigned for greater honesty in politics and improving the lot of the poor. It draws much of its support from workers, especially female, in small and medium-sized urban industries. The party's religious affiliation has, however, tended to hamper its development.

Also on the centre left, is the Democratic Socialist Party (DSP: Minshato), which was formed in January 1960 by a right-wing faction which broke away from the JSP, in opposition to its alleged Marxist tendencies. The DSP favours the operation of a mixed economy, with greater welfare provision and selective nationalisation. Led by Ryosaku Sasaki, it currently has a membership of 72,000.

The Social Democratic Federation (SDF: Shaminren), formed in 1977 as a minor breakaway from the JSP and currently led by Hideo Den, is also a minor political force of some note. Another was the New Liberal Club (NLC: Shin Jyu Kurabu), which was established in June 1976, when, disillusioned by the 'Tanaka affair', Yohei Kono, and five younger members of the Diet, declared their independence from the LDP. In August 1986, however, following a poor showing in the July election, the NLC was disbanded and its members rejoined the parent LDP.

Latest elections

The most recent Diet elections were held in July 1986 and for the second half of the House of Councillors, July 1989. The results were as follows:

	House of Representatives		
	% Votes	*No of Seats*	*% Seats*
LDP	49	304	59
JSP	17	86	17
Komeito	9	57	11
JCP	9	27	5
DSP	6	26	5
NLC	2	6	1
SDF	1	4	1
Independents	6	2	0.4

	House of Councillors	
	Seat won in July 1989	*% Seats*
LDP	36	29
JSP	46	36
Komeito	10	8
JCP	5	4
DSP	3	2
Independents	10	8
Others	16	13

Political history

Originally inhabited by Ainu people, Japan was invaded and settled from an early date by Manchu-Koreans and Malayans. In the fifth century AD the country was unified by the Yamato state, and, in the sixth century, Buddhism was introduced from Korea and Confucian culture from China. During the seventh century a centralised monarchy on Chinese lines was established, but by the twelfth century power had devolved to regional potentates, subservient to a paramount general, termed the *shogun*. After a period of decentralisation, the Tokugawa family re-unified the country during the later sixteenth century, establishing a new capital at Edo, now Tokyo, in central Honshu and creating a bureaucratised and demilitarised quasi-feudal system. From this date, despite self-imposed isolation from the outside world, considerable economic progress was made.

Military pressure from the Western powers, particularly the United States, forced an end to this isolation in the mid-nineteenth century and, fearing colonial invasion, reformist elements within the *samurai*, or military caste, bureaucracy united with south-western regional lords *(daimyo)* to overthrow the Tokugawa Shogunate and restore executive power to the young emperor Meiji Tenno, in 1867. His family, based at Kyoto, had previously been Tokugawa puppets. To buttress imperial authority, shintoism was established as the state religion, and the Emperor defined as the 'Divine Ruler'. During the next two decades after this 'Meiji Restoration', the feudal system was abolished, *samurai* and *daimyo* lords were pensioned off, the land system reformed and a new constitutional system, with an elected assembly and Westernised legal code established.

The radical reforms of the early Meiji era constituted a 'revolution from above', carried out by a small clique of nationalistic members of the former Tokugawa bureaucracy, termed the 'Genro', who were to remain the real power-wielders, rather than the Emperor, until the strengthening of party government during the inter-war years. Impelled by a concern to 'catch-up' with the West, they oversaw the rapid development of new industries and the build-up of a modern new army and navy. In conflicts in 1894–5 and 1904–5 respectively, China and Russia were defeated, and new colonies were secured, in the form of Formosa, now Taiwan, South Manchuria, Korea and South Sakhalin. Rapid economic advance was achieved during the First World War and during the 1920s, the 'Taisho era', and there was movement towards democracy and party government, after the electorate had been substantially enlarged by the Reform Acts of 1919 and 1925. The 1925 Act established universal male suffrage for those of 25 years and over.

During the later 1920s, however, with economic conditions deteriorating, army leaders and ultra-nationalists gained the upper hand, launching the nation on an ultimately destructive phase of imperialist expansion. This began with the occupation of Manchuria in 1931, was followed by the invasion of China in 1937 and then war with the United States and Britain, after Japan's pre-emptive attack on the US Pearl Harbor naval base in Hawaii, in December 1941. Initially, during the early stages of the war, Japan successfully took control of much of the Asia-Oceania region, between Burma and the Philippines. By 1944, however, it was in retreat and, on 15 August 1945, following the United States' dropping of atomic bombs on Hiroshima and Nagasaki, Emperor Hirohito was compelled to tender the nation's unconditional surrender. An allied control commission assumed charge and Japan was placed under military occupation by allied, chiefly United States, troops, commanded by General Douglas MacArthur. In April 1952 the US-Japanese Peace Treaty came into force and full sovereignty was regained.

As a consequence of Japan's military defeat, Korea was made independent, Manchuria and Formosa were returned to China and the small, former German, Pacific islands, that had been mandated to Japan after the First World War, were now placed by the United Nations under American trusteeship. Japan was subsequently to regain the islands of Ryukyu, in 1972, and Bonin and Volcano, in 1968, from the United States. However, despite frequent appeals, the Northern Territories, which include the islands of the Shikotan and Habomai Group, and the southernmost Kurils, which include Kunashiri and Etorofu, are still controlled by the Soviet Union and have not been returned.

During the immediate post-war phase of allied rule, between August 1945 and April 1952, a sweeping 'democratisation campaign' was launched, involving radical land, social and educational reform and the framing of a new 'Peace Constitution', in 1946. Under it, Emperor Hirohito was persuaded to renounce his claims to divinity and become a figurehead constitutional monarch, while the nation, through Article 9, committed itself to a pacific foreign policy. During the 1950s Japan concentrated on economic reconstruction, retreating towards neutralism in foreign affairs, under the protection of the American umbrella provided by the September 1951 Security Pact.

Post-war Japanese politics were dominated by the new Liberal Democratic Party (LDP), which was formed in 1955 by the merger of existing conservative parties. It was to provide the country with a regular succession of Prime Ministers. Real decision-making authority, however, became focused on a broader, consensual, corporatist grouping of politicians, senior civil servants and directors of the major *zaibatsu* finance and industrial houses. Through a paternalist, guided approach to economic development, which was epitomised by the operations of the influential Ministry for International Trade and Industry (MITI), and by the inspired targeting of, and investment in, promising new transport, consumer-durable and electronics growth industries, the Japanese economy expanded dramatically during the 1950s and 1960s, with GDP regularly advancing at an annual rate of 10 per cent. During these years, Japan was also rehabilitated within the international community, entering the United Nations in 1958, re-establishing diplomatic relations with Western nations and, following the lead taken by America's Nixon presidency, with communist China, in 1972.

In 1960 and 1968–69, Japan's hitherto tranquil internal politics were rocked by violent demonstrations against alleged American domination, involving the anarchic 'Red Army' terrorist organisation. These were followed, in December 1974, by the resignation of Prime Minister Kakuei Tanaka, in the wake of a bribery scandal, involving the American Lockheed Corporation. This culminated in Tanaka's arrest and resignation from the LDP, in July 1976, and his later conviction and sentence to four years' imprisonment, in October 1983. This scandal seriously tarnished the image of the LDP and led to the loss of its majority in the House of Representatives in the general election of December 1976. It also resulted in the formation of the New Liberal Club, as a breakaway grouping. The LDP remained in power, however, as the largest single party within the Diet.

During the 1970s and early 1980s, Japanese economic growth continued, though at a reduced annual rate of 4.5 per cent, the country making a major impact on the markets of the United States and Europe, as an exporter of electrical goods, machinery, motor vehicles and new high-technology items. By 1985 Japan had become the world's largest exporter of manufactured goods, surpassing the United States and West Germany. The growth in Japan's trade surplus, and, in particular, the concentration of the country's export activity in a few sensitive sectors, served to create resentment overseas, however, as economic recession began to grip Europe and the United States between 1979 and 1982. This led to calls for Japan to open up its internal market to foreign exporters and to assume a greater share of the defence burden for the Asia-Pacific region. Prime Ministers Miki, Fukuda, Ohira and Suzuki firmly resisted these pressures, and the Japanese government, in 1976, imposed a rigid 1 per cent of GNP limit on the level of defence spending permissible.

However, under Prime Minister Yasuhiro Nakasone, who assumed power in November 1982, a review of policy was instituted. Nakasone favoured a strengthening of Japan's defence capability, a re-evaluation of attitudes towards the country's past and the introduction of a more liberal, open-market economic strategy at home. These proposed policy departures proved controversial and could only partially be implemented. However, the forthright Nakasone emerged as a popular national figure and, after becoming, in November 1984, the first Prime Minister since Eisaku Sato to be re-elected as LDP leader for more than one term, succeeded in securing a landslide victory in the July 1986 general election. In this contest, the LDP, after having experienced its worst-ever reverse in the previous national poll of December 1983, achieved its highest level of popular support since 1963 and a record number of House of Councillors' seats.

Soon after the July 1986 election the rules of the LDP were altered so as to allow party presidents a one-year extension beyond the normal limit of two two-year terms each, thus effectively extending Nakasone's tenure as Prime Minister until November 1987. During his final year in office, Nakasone introduced a sweeping tax reform bill, aimed at restoring 'justice and flexibility' to an archaic system, but was forced, because of Diet opposition, to make major compromises, including the withdrawal of plans to introduce a 5 per cent value-added tax (VAT). Despite this political 'defeat', Nakasone remained sufficiently influential within the LDP, and popular outside, effectively to select his successor as party and national leader. He nominated LDP Secretary-General, Noboru Takeshita, after a factional deadlock within the party.

The new Prime Minister pledged a continuation of his predecessor's domestic and foreign policies, including improving and extending the country's diplomatic relations, re-introducing a tax reform bill and making a determined effort to reduce its record $86,690 million balance of payments surplus. Takeshita had notable personal success in the area of tax reform, a bill being passed by the House of Representatives in 1988 which lowered income tax and introduced a national sales tax at 3 per cent. This measure proved, however, to be electorally unpopular. More seriously, the new government's popular standing was undermined by the eruption, in

July 1988, of the 'Recruit-Cosmos scandal'. This involved 'insider' share dealing, indirectly and directly, by more than 40 senior LDP and opposition party figures, including Takeshita, Nakasone and finance minister Kiichi Miyazawa. The latter resigned in December 1988, to be followed by justice minister Takashi Hasegawa and Deputy Prime Minister Ken Harada in January 1989. Finally, in April 1989, with the government's and LDP's popularity ratings standing at the unprecedentedly low levels of 4 and 25 per cent respectively, Takeshita announced that he would resign as soon as the annual budget was passed and a successor found. His replacement, in June 1989, was the former foreign minister, Sosuke Uno.

After barely 53 days in office, Uno, who was dogged by a geisha sex scandal and whose party endured loss of control over the upper house in the elections of July 1989, announced his intention to step down, in turn, as soon as a successor could be found. This marked an inauspicious start to the new Heisei ('achievement of universal peace') era, which had been proclaimed following the death, in January 1989, of Hirohito (Showa) and the accession to the Imperial throne of his son Akihito. In August 1989 his eventual successor was Tokshiki Kaifu.

NORTH KOREA

Democratic People's Republic of North Korea (DPRK)
Chosun Minchu-chui Inmin Konghwa-guk

Capital: Pyongyang

Social and economic data
Area: 121,250 km^2
Population: 20.500m*
Pop density per km^2: 169*
Literacy rate: 90%
GDP: $20,000m*; per capita GDP: $976
Economy type: low income
Labour force in agriculture: 38%

*1985

Ethnic composition
With the exception of a Chinese minority of 50,000, the population is fully Korean.

Religions
Buddhism and Confucianism are the traditional religions. Today, however, they enjoy little support, their practice having been actively discouraged by the communist regime.

Political features
State type: communist
Date of state formation: 1948
Political structure: unitary

Executive type: communist
Assembly: one-chamber
Party structure: one-party (E)
Human rights rating: 17%

(E)=Effective

Local and regional government
The country is divided into nine provinces and two cities, below which there are urban districts, regular cities and more than 150 counties. Each political unit has a Local People's Assembly, elected every four years at the provincial level and every two years below, which convenes once a year and 'elects' a Local People's Committee to serve as its permanent executive organ.

Head of state
President Kim Il Sung, since 1972.

Head of government
Prime Minister Yon Hyong Muk, since 1988.

Political leaders since 1970*
1948– Kim Il Sung (KWP)*.

*Communist Party leader

Political system
North Korea's original socialist constitution was adopted in September 1948, being based closely on the 1936 USSR's 'Stalin Constitution' model. It was superseded in December 1972 by the current 149-article version, which describes the People's Republic as a 'socialist state' in the stage of the 'dictatorship of the proletariat'. Significant, specifically Korean, departures from the earlier Soviet model are included in the document, most notably the stress that is placed on national self-reliance, called *Chuche Sasang*, or *Juche*, the use of mass mobilisation tactics (*Chongsalli*), and all-pervasive party control (*te an*). In addition, the document also specifically embraces, in Article 5, the goal of national re-unification, by 'peaceful means'.

Under the 1972 constitution, the sole and supreme organ of state power is the Supreme People's Assembly (SPA), or Choe Ko In Min Hoe Ui, a one-chamber body which comprises 655 members elected for four-year terms in single-member constituencies from a list of candidates put forward by the Democratic Front for the Reunification of the Fatherland (DFRF), which dates from 1946. The SPA convenes twice a year for short sessions, lasting several days, in the spring and autumn and 'elects' a 15-member Standing Committee to act for it when it is not sitting. It also elects a 15-member Central People's Committee (CPC), which the constitution describes as the 'supreme leadership organ of state power'. This is headed by the President of the Republic.

The CPC determines domestic and foreign policy, can issue decrees, and oversees the work of People's Committees below. It also supervises the day-to-day central executive, in the shape of the State Administrative Council (SAC), a 46-member body comprising 17 Departmental Ministers,

14 State Commission chairmen and nine vice-premiers. The SAC is headed by the Prime Minister, who is elected by the SPA. Members of the SAC are appointed and dismissed by the CPC.

It is, however, the President of the Republic, Kim Il Sung, who is the leading figure in the DPRK's presidentialist political system. Elected for renewable four-year terms by the SPA, he is commander-in-chief of the armed forces and chairman of the National Defence Commission. In addition, he is empowered to issue edicts, preside over SAC meetings and 'guide' the work of the CPC.

The controlling force, and sole permitted political party, in the DPRK is the Communist Party (KWP: Korean Workers' Party), which has been headed since its inception in 1945 by General Secretary Kim Il Sung. The party leads the broader DFRF mass organisation, which includes the minor Korean Social Democratic Party and the Chondoist Chongu Party, and puts forward single lists of candidates in elections. Its leading members also hold senior state posts, with, for example, in March 1988, eight of its 15 full Politburo members occupying seats in the CPC, including the positions of President and Vice-Presidents. The Prime Minister, Li Gun Mo, foreign minister, Kim Young Nam, and armed forces minister, Vice-Marshal O Jin U, were also full Politburo members.

The overriding and distinctive feature of the DPRK political system is, however, the dominance of the KWP's charismatic leader and state President, Kim Il Sung. Depicted, in a Confucian manner, as the nation's 'fatherly leader' and 'Sun of Mankind', Kim Il Sung has established the most pervasive personality cult witnessed in the contemporary communist world. With the promotion of his son, Kim Jong Il, to the position of 'designated heir', he has set about constructing a unique 'socialist dynasty'.

Political parties

The ruling Korean Workers' Party (KWP: Chosun No-Dong Dang) was established in October 1945 with the title Korean Communist Party (KCP), in the North Korean zone occupied by Soviet forces. It was a coalition of communist-leaning groups who had variously been based in the USSR, China (the 'Yanan faction'), and Manchuria and Korea, where they operated underground as anti-Japanese resistance fighters, prior to the Second World War. In August 1946 the party adopted the designation North Korean Workers' Party (NKWP), when its Chinese-trained wing, termed the New People's Party, merged with the KCP. In June 1949 it assumed its present name when the NKWP merged with the banned South Korean Workers' Party, led by Pak Hon-yong.

The party's leader, the peasant-born Kim Il Sung, who had originally founded the Manchuria-based Korean People's Revolutionary Army in 1932, enjoyed strong initial Soviet support. By the mid-1950s, following a series of purges of opposing factions, he had established an unchallenged control over the party machine and, thereafter, proceeded to develop a unique, personalised and Maoist- and Korean-nationalist-influenced policy approach, officially termed 'Kim Il Sungism', which diverged significantly from post-Stalin Soviet communism. Founded on 'mass-line' mobilising methods and based on constant propagandising, tight secret-police control and blanket censorship, it has successfully moulded the most highly regimented and controlled society in the contemporary world.

The KWP is organised hierarchically on 'democratic centralist' lines, with small, 3- to 100-member, workplace 'cells' established at its base, district and county committees higher up, all leading to a more-than-2,000-member national Party Congress. The Party Congress, which is formally the supreme party organ, convenes, in theory, quinquennially, although only three Congresses were, in fact, called between 1961 and 1980. It 'elects' a Central Committee (CC) of about 250 members to assume authority when it is not in session. The CC meets several times a year in full session and, in turn, 'elects' a Politburo, which currently has 15 full and 18 non-voting 'alternate' members, and a Secretariat, headed by the General Secretary, to control party, and state, affairs. The Politburo is dominated by an 'inner cabinet', or Presidium. This comprised, in March 1988, three members: Kim Il Sung, his son Kim Jong Il and Vice-Marshal O Jin U.

Membership of the KWP in 1987 totalled 3 million, which constitutes 14.6 per cent of the total population, and is one of the highest ratios in the communist world. The present figure represents a 50 per cent advance on the 1976 total.

Two loyal and subservient non-communist parties are permitted to function under the umbrella of the DFRF and enjoy SPA representation: the Korean Social Democratic Party and the Chondoist Chongu Party. The Korean Social Democratic Party was established in 1945 and was known, until 1981, as the Korean Democratic Party. The Chondoist Chongu Party was formed in 1946 and its members adhere to a syncretic Daoist-Buddhist-Confucian religious faith.

Latest elections

The most recent Supreme People's Assembly 'contest' was held in November 1986, with all 655 DFRF candidates being elected unopposed. Turnout was put at 99.99 per cent. Thirty-five per cent of the candidates elected were described as blue-collar workers, 10 per cent as co-operative farm workers and 50 per cent as white-collar professionals. Twenty per cent were female.

Political history

Korea was, according to legend, founded as a state in 2333 BC by the Tangun dynasty. More recent archaeological evidence suggests that the country was invaded and colonised by nomadic tribes from Manchuria and Siberia during the third millennium BC. The descendants of these conquerors established three regional kingdoms, the Koguryo, Shilla and Paekche at around the time of Christ. Of these, the economically and culturally advanced Buddhist Shilla kingdom, with its capital at Kyongju, was subsequently to emerge dominant, absorbing the others and unifying the peninsula, between AD 668 and 1000. This Shilla dynasty was succeeded by, first, the Koryu and, then the Chosun, or Yi, Dynasty (1392–1910). During the Yi period, Korea lost its full autonomy, becoming a vassal of China and being subjected to periodic invasions by Mongol and Japanese forces. The country was now also exposed to Confucianism, this philosophy displacing Buddhism as the dominant intellectual force. During the later nineteenth century, expansionary Japan began to challenge China as the paramount power in the Korean region, before formally annexing the peninsula in

1910, turning it into a colony, administered by a Governor-General, based at Seoul, now in South Korea.

Under the Japanese, Korea rapidly developed, new heavy industries being established in the coal-rich north and commercialised agriculture being promoted in the south. Japanese rule was, however, bitterly opposed, since the gains from economic growth were largely monopolised by immigrant Japanese nationals, and Korean workers were forcibly conscripted as low-paid factory and mine labour. In addition, the new rulers' determined attempt to eradicate Korean culture and enforce the adoption of the Japanese language and customs was deeply resented. Both communist and right-wing nationalist, exiled, resistance movements thus began to emerge during the inter-war period.

Following Japan's surrender in August 1945, at the close of the Second World War, Korea was divided at the 38th parallel into two military occupation zones, with Soviet forces in the North and American in the South. In the northern zone the Soviets installed, in February 1946, a 'North Korean Provisional People's Committee', manned predominantly by Moscow-trained Korean Communists, including Kim Il Sung. This held power, introducing a radical programme of land reform and nationalisation, until the election of a Supreme People's Assembly in 1947. This was based on a 'unity list' of communist-approved candidates. A year later, following the founding of the pro-American 'Republic of Korea', south of the 38th parallel, by the conservative nationalist leader Dr Syngman Rhee, North Korea was formally declared a a 'Democratic People's Republic', in September 1948, under the leadership of the KWP. Soviet Red Army troops initially remained in the country, but finally withdrew, in December 1948.

The two new Korean republics each claimed full jurisdiction over the entire peninsula and, on 25 June 1950, North Korea, seeking immediate unification by force, launched a large-scale invasion of the South, rapidly reaching Seoul. Thus began the three-year long Korean War, which, following the intervention of the United States, on the side of the South, and China, on the side of the North, ended in stalemate, but claimed the lives of 2 million.

The 38th parallel border line between North and South was re-established by the armistice agreement of July 1953 and a United Nations (UN) force patrolled a 4,000-metre-wide de-militarised buffer zone (DMZ) which had been created. North Korea, however, never fully accepted this agreement and remained committed to re-unification during the succeeding decades. As a result, despite the establishment in 1972 of a North-South co-ordinating committee to promote peaceful unification, relations with the South have remained tense and hostile. Border incidents have been frequent and in October 1983 four South Korean cabinet ministers were assassinated in Rangoon, in Burma, following a bombing incident organised by two North Korean army officers. In addition, a maze of North Korean-dug, secret, tank-sized tunnels under the DMZ were uncovered by the UN border command in October 1978.

Domestically, the post-1948 period has seen economic development in a planned socialist manner in the DPRK. During the 1950s, factories and financial institutions were nationalised and agriculture collectivised, with overall priority being given to heavy industries and rural mechanisation in investment programmes. The growth rate of the North Korean economy has, however, lagged considerably behind that of its more populous southern neighbour, which began to move ahead of the traditionally richer North, in terms of per capita GDP, during the 1960s. Today, South Koreans are more than twice as affluent as 'Northerners'. The maintenance of substantial armed forces, exceeding 800,000 and consuming more than 20 per cent of GDP, has been a factor in checking North Korea's growth. So has the autarchic, self-reliant policy stance of the KWP leadership, although there has been some relaxation, in a more market-orientated and 'open-door' direction, in recent years.

In its external relations, North Korea has adopted a determinedly neutral stance in the Sino-Soviet dispute, signing a friendship and mutual assistance treaty with China in July 1961, while at the same time continuing to draw substantial economic and military aid from the Soviet Union, with whom links have become closer during recent years. Overall stress, however, has been placed on nationalistic self-reliance, the country remaining largely isolated from external contacts.

Politics in North Korea have, in recent years, been dominated by the 'succession question', with Kim Il Sung seeking to establish his son, Kim Jong Il, as sole heir designate. Kim Jong Il has accompanied Kim Il Sung on diplomatic and factory tours, been designated 'Armed Forces Supreme Commander' and 'Dear Leader', begun to preside over key party and state government meetings, and his portrait has been placed on public display across the country. Elements within the Workers' Party and armed forces, in particular, appear, however, to oppose Kim's succession aims.

SOUTH KOREA

Republic of Korea (ROK)
Daehan Minguk

Capital: Seoul

Social and economic data

Area: 98,500 km^2
Population: 43.300m*
Pop density per km^2: 440*
Literacy rate: 93%
GDP: $86,182m*; per capita GDP: $1,990
Economy type: middle income
Labour force in agriculture: 24%

*1985

Ethnic composition

With the exception of a Nationalist Chinese minority of 50,000, the population is almost entirely of Korean ethnic stock.

Religions

Mahayana Buddhism, which claims 15 million adherents, or 35 per cent of the total population, is the principal religion, followed by Christianity, 12 million, Confucianism, 10 million, Won Buddhism, 1 million, and Chundo

Kyo, 1 million. Christianity was first introduced during the later sixteenth century and has, in recent years, been at the forefront of the human rights struggle. Of its adherents about 82 per cent are Protestants and 18 per cent Roman Catholics. Chundo Kyo is a syncretic religion, combining Shaman, Buddhist and Christian doctrines, which was developed by nationalists during the later nineteenth century. Freedom of worship and conscience is guaranteed under the constitution.

Political features
State type: emergent democracy
Date of state formation: 1948
Political structure: unitary
Executive: limited presidential
Assembly: one-chamber
Party structure: multi-party
Human rights rating: 59%

Local and regional government
The country comprises nine provinces and four special cities with provincial status: Seoul, Pusan, Taegu and Inchon. Below them, counties, towns and villages are the administrative units.

Head of state
President Roh Tae-Woo, since 1988.

Head of government
Prime Minister Kang Young-hoon, since 1988.

Political leaders since 1970
1962–79 Major General Park Chung-Hee (DRP), 1979–80 Choi Kyu-Hah (DRP), 1980–88 General Chun Doo-Hwan (DJP), 1988– Roh Tae-Woo (DJP).

Political system
The current, Sixth Republic, constitution, promulgated in October 1987, supersedes the earlier constitutions of 1980 (Fifth Republic), 1972 (Fourth Republic) and 1948 (First–Third Republics). By previous standards, it is a liberal document, guaranteeing the preservation of a 'plural party system'; the fair management of election contests, by a nine-member Central Election Management Committee (CEMC); the citizen's right of *habeas corpus* and freedom of speech, press, assembly and association; and establishing a nine-member Constitutional Court (CC) to police its maintenance. Included within the constitution is the aspiration of the 'peaceful unification of the Korean peninsula'.

Legislative power rests with the 299-member single-chamber National Assembly (Kuk Hoe), 224 of whose members are elected for fixed four-year terms, on a first-past-the-post basis, in single-member constituencies. The remaining 75 seats are filled by a form of proportional representation designed to favour the leading party; 38 seats are allocated to the party gaining most votes by direct election, with the remaining 37 allotted to other parties in proportion to the number of seats won directly.

The National Assembly convenes annually for a regular session of up to 100 days and also meets in 'extraordinary sessions', at the request of the President or three-quarters of its members. It has the authority to impeach the President; to recommend to him the removal of the Prime Minister or any other minister; to propose changes to the constitution, a two-thirds majority being required, followed by public approval in a referendum; and to appoint a third of the members of the CEMC and CC. Approval from the National Assembly is also required for the President's appointment of holders of senior judicial office.

Executive authority lies with the President, who is directly elected for a single, non-renewable five-year term. He governs with the assistance of an appointed cabinet, called the State Council, of between 15 and 30 members. Currently there are 22, headed by a Prime Minister. Serving members of the armed forces are debarred from cabinet office. The President is also empowered to appoint a third of the members of the CEMC and CC, as well as the Chief Justice and justices of the Supreme Court, subject to the National Assembly's assent.

Additionally, the President may take issues directly to the public through the use of referenda. He may issue vetoes, which can be overridden by the National Assembly, and assume broad powers, during times of emergency, subject to Assembly agreement. He cannot, however, dissolve the National Assembly.

The political structure established by the 1987 constitution is a mixture of the American and French presidential models, with significant checks built in so as to strengthen the National Assembly *vis-à-vis* the President. In this respect it differs from the preceding 1972 and 1980 constitutions, and this promises to engender instability during periods when party control over the executive and assembly is split, as is partly the case at present.

Political parties

The Democratic Justice Party (DJP) is the dominant political force in the ROK today. It was formed in January 1981, as a 'government party', by the country's newly installed leader, General Chun Doo-Hwan. The party is strongly supported and generously financed by the business community, whose interests it promotes in a corporatist manner. It is also backed by the armed forces. In addition to these important bases, it has succeeded in developing a mass membership of more than one million, mainly in the north and east-centre of the country, and particularly in rural areas. The DJP's political forerunner can be viewed, in many respects, as the Democratic Republican Party (DRP), which was established in February 1963 as a governing party to lend civilian legitimacy to the military regime of Major-General Park Chung-Hee.

The two principal opposition parties are the Party for Peace and Democracy (PPD), led by the Roman Catholic, Kim Dae-Jung, and the Reunification Democratic Party (RDP), led by the Presbyterian, Kim Young-Sam. The parties were formed in November and May 1987 respectively, as leader-orientated successor groupings to the earlier New Korea Democratic Party (NKDP), which had been established in January 1985. The NKDP was itself a successor to the New Democratic Party (NDP), which dated back to February 1967, and was the ideological heir to the Democratic Party. The PPD is the more radical in outlook of the two parties and draws its support from lower social strata than the centrist, middle-class, RDP. Support for both parties is highly regionalised.

The third significant opposition force is the New Democratic Republican Party (NDRP), a right-of-centre grouping which was founded by the former Prime Minister and DRP founder, Kim Jong-Pil, in October 1987. The party currently holds the balance of power in the National Assembly.

In addition, the NKDP continues to function as a minor party, as do the Social Democratic Party (SDP), Korea National Party (KNP), Democratic Korea Party (DKP) and the Civil Rights Party (CRP).

Latest elections

The results of the most recent National Assembly elections, held in April 1988, were as follows:

	% Votes	*Seats*
DJP	34	125
RDP	24	59
PPD	19	70
NDRP	16	35
Other parties	7	10

Turnout was 75.8 per cent and party support was highly regionalised. The PPD won 31 of the 32 available seats in the underdeveloped south-western region of Cholla, in the environs of Kwangju; the RDP secured 14 of the 15 seats in the south-eastern region of Kyongsang, in the environs of Pusan, Kim Young-Sam's home town; the NDRP captured 13 of the seats in Kim Jong-Pil's native South Chungchong province; and the DJP polled strongly in North Kyongsang, Roh Tae-Woo's home area.

In the preceding presidential election of December 1987, the DJP's candidate, Roh Tae-Woo, secured 36 per cent of the popular vote; Kim Young-Sam of the RDP, 27 per cent; Kim Dae-Jung of the PPD, 26 per cent; Kim Jong-Pil of the NDRP, 8 per cent; and 'others', 2 per cent. Turnout was 89.2 per cent.

Political history

The Republic of Korea was formed from the zone south of the 38th parallel of latitude, which had been occupied by American troops after the Japanese surrender in August 1945. The American military government remained in charge of the country until, following national elections, in May 1948, an independent republic was declared three months later. Dr Syngman Rhee, the royal-born, and American-educated, leader of the rightist Liberal Party, who had been previously exiled, became the nation's first President, under a constitution which was based partially on the United States model.

During its first two years the republic had to deal with a series of problems. They included a massive influx of more than 2 million refugees who had fled from the communist regime in the North and the return of people from forced labour in Japan and Manchuria. It then experienced invasion and bitter warfare during the 1950–53 Korean War.

President Syngman Rhee, whose autocratic and nationalistic regime, known as the 'First Republic', had been accused of corruption and nepotism, resigned in April 1960, following student-led disorder. A new, parliamentary-style, constitution, giving greater powers to the assembly, was adopted and the opposition Democratic Party (DP) leader, Chang Myon, was appointed Prime Minister. This parliamentary regime (Second Republic) was characterised, however, by chronic political instability, precipitating a military coup, led by Major-General Park Chung-Hee, in May 1961. The National Assembly was dissolved, martial law imposed, and a military junta, the 'Supreme Council for National Reconstruction', initially put into office. During this period, the Korean Central Intelligence Agency (KCIA) was also established, under the direction of Colonel Kim Jong-Pil, a relative of Park, and a government-sponsored party, the Democratic Republican Party (DRP), was created.

This paved the way for a return to 'civilian' rule, under a restored presidential system, with Park Chung-Hee, the DRP's nominee, being elected President in December 1963. He had narrowly defeated the opposition New Democratic Party (NDP) candidate, Yun Po-Sun.

President Park proceeded to embark on a major programme of export-led industrial development, founded on a series of five-year plans, and the extension of 'soft loan' financial support to integrated conglomerates (*chaebol*), in a determinedly corporatist manner. Benefiting from the nation's plentiful supply of well-educated, industrious and low-paid workers, this programme proved to be a remarkable success, with more than 9 per cent and 20 per cent per annum rates of GDP and industrial growth being attained during the 1960s and 1970s respectively. As a result, South Korea emerged as a major exporter of consumer goods, including textiles, footwear and electronics, and industrial products, such as steel, ships and petrochemicals. This 'economic miracle' fundamentally transformed the socio-economic base of what had been a predominantly agrarian economy. A huge urban-industrial sector was now developing through a process of migration from the countryside.

This buoyant economy, with incomes rising for middle and upper-middle urban groups, provided a material basis for the Third Republic regime, enabling Park, aided, the opposition claimed, by ballot-rigging and vote-buying, narrowly to defeat the NDP nominees, Yun Po-Sun and Kim Dae-Jung, in the presidential contests of 1967 and 1971.

Despite the economic growth achieved, opposition to the authoritarian and repressive character of the Park regime, and to the country's growing links with despised Japan, began to mount during the 1970s. In response, martial law was imposed in October 1972 and a new 'Yushin' ('revitalising') constitution, strengthening the President's powers, was adopted. This was done by a national referendum, in November 1972, which established a Fourth Republic.

Elections to the newly created presidential electoral college, the National Conference for Unification (NCU), and the now 'neutered' National Assembly, then followed, in December 1972. With more bribery and rigging, the DRP won a sweeping majority. The 2,359-member NCU duly ratified Park as President, for a new six-year term.

Two years later, in May 1975, a severe clamp-down on political dissent was launched, with the enactment of 'Emergency Measure Number Nine' (EMNN), making it a crime to criticise the yushin system and thus, in practice, the incumbent regime. Thousands of political opponents were jailed or placed under house-arrest, including Second Republic President,

Yun Po-Sun, and NDP leader, Kim Dae-Jung. The latter was kidnapped by KCIA forces while in a Tokyo hotel.

For the NCU elections of May 1978, which were followed by Park's re-election as President in July, there was a temporary political 'thaw'. However, with economic conditions briefly deteriorating, as the ROK experienced its first year of negative growth since the war, and with the inflation rate surpassing 30 per cent, worker and student protests erupted during 1979. These disturbances escalated, following the expulsion of NDP leader Kim Young-Sam from the National Assembly for alleged 'subversive activities'. Then, in October 1979, President Park was assassinated by Kim Jae-Gyu, the head of the KCIA, in a coup attempt.

Martial law was briefly imposed, before an interim government was set up, under the leadership of the former Prime Minister, Choi Kyu-Hah. This introduced a number of liberalising reforms, including the release of opposition leader Kim Dae-Jung, in February 1980, and the rescindment of EMNN. However, with anti-government demonstrations gaining strength, a new clamp-down on dissidents was launched in May 1980, involving the arrest of 30 political leaders, including Kim Dae-Jung, the re-imposition of martial law and the closure of the National Assembly. Riots immediately erupted in Kim's home city of Kwangju. They were forcibly suppressed by paratroopers with, according to official sources, the loss of 189 lives. Outside observers put the true figure at more than 2,000.

In August 1980, Choi Kyu-Hah resigned as President, to be replaced by the leader of the army and former military intelligence chief, the American-trained Major-General Chun Doo-Hwan. After a referendum, a new constitution was adopted, in October 1980. It abolished the NCU and restricted the presidency to a single, non-renewable, seven-year term. Martial law was lifted in January 1981 and, after Chun Doo-Hwan was elected President by a new 5,278-member electoral college, in February 1981, a new Fifth Republic was proclaimed. National Assembly elections followed, in which Chun's newly formed Democratic Justice Party (DJP), secured a substantial majority.

Under President Chun, the pace of economic growth accelerated once more. However, internal and external criticism of the suppression of civil liberties continued. A measure of cautious liberalisation was to be seen prior to the February 1985 National Assembly elections, involving the release of many political prisoners and the return from exile in the United States, where he had been since 1982, of Kim Dae-Jung. In these elections the New Korea Democratic Party (NKDP), which had recently been formed as a vehicle for the opposition leaders, Kim Young-Sam and Kim Dae-Jung, secured 30 per cent of the direct votes so that, when the new Assembly convened, 102 of its 276 members adopted the party's whip. The DJP held 148 seats, too few to force through fundamental constitutional changes.

Buoyed by their strengthened parliamentary position, the opposition forces proceeded to launch, outside the Assembly, during 1986 and 1987, a major new campaign for democratic constitutional reform, as the February 1988 date for President Chun's step down from power approached. The NKDP campaigned for a new system of government, based on direct presidential elections. The DJP countered with a proposal for a new prime ministerial system.

The scale of student unrest escalated in April and June 1987, now drawing support from ordinary workers and the middle classes. Two events triggered off this new spate of dissidence. The first was President Chun's announcement that the reform process would be suspended until after the Olympic Games had been held in Seoul, in September 1988. The second was the nomination of Roh Tae-Woo, a former Korean Military Academy colleague of Chun's, as the DJP presidential candidate for forthcoming indirect elections.

Roh Tae-Woo unexpectedly responded to the growing popular movement against the incumbent regime by submitting a pragmatic, and relatively liberal, eight-point plan of political, constitutional and electoral reform to President Chun. Its key elements included the formation of a new consensual, non-party, interim cabinet; the establishment of a bi-partisan committee to draft a new constitution; the liberalisation of labour and censorship laws; and the release from detention, and the restoration of the full political rights, of prominent opposition figures. The 'Roh plan' was accepted and in October 1987, following a national referendum, a new constitution was duly adopted. This provided for a directly elected presidency, serving a non-renewable five-year term.

In the presidential contest, which was held in December 1987, Roh Tae-Woo, the DJP's nomineee, although securing only 36 per cent of the popular vote, emerged victorious, as a result of the candidacy of both Kim Young-Sam and Kim Dae-Jung, respective leaders of the recently formed Reunification Democratic Party (RDP) and Party for Peace and Democracy (PPD), which served to split the opposition's vote. Electoral fraud on the part of the governing party was alleged, but was substantially unproved.

Roh Tae-Woo formally assumed the presidency in February 1988, replacing Chun Doo-Hwan, in what became a new Sixth Republic. In the new National Assembly elections which followed, however, in April 1988, the opposition regrouped and succeeded in preventing the DJP from securing a majority in the new 299-member chamber for the first time since the party's creation. This promised to create serious difficulties for Roh and the new Prime Minister, Kang Young-hoon, in the years ahead. In the shorter term, however, political conflict calmed during the summer of 1988, as the nation hosted the Olympic Games.

Nevertheless, student unrest continued periodically to erupt, with calls for re-unification of the peninsula growing in strength. In addition, public criticism of the preceding Chun regime mounted, fuelled by the televised investigative work of National Assembly committees which uncovered corruption among the former President's close friends and relatives. This forced a contrite Chun to make an apology on national television, in November 1988, for his administration's misdeeds, agreeing at the same time to hand over to the state his financial assets and retire, after an interval of meditation at a hill-top Buddhist monastery, to a small, secluded rural retreat in the Kosong area.

Externally, the constant threat of invasion from the North has been a key factor in South Korean politics since 1953, helping to justify stern rule. The country has been forced to devote significant resources to modernising its armed forces, which number 630,000 and annually consume 6 per cent of GDP, even though they have been supported by more than 40,000 American troops. Both political and economic relations with the United States have remained close since 'liberation' and the US currently provides a market for

40 per cent of the ROK's exports. Anti-American sentiment is, however, strong among opposition groups.

Close political and economic links have also been developed with Japan. In recent years, however, as part of what has been termed a re-unification-directed 'Northern policy', attempts have also been made to improve diplomatic relations with the communist powers of China and the Soviet Union.

LAOS

People's Democratic Republic of Laos
Saathiaranagroat Prachhathippatay Prachhachhon Lao

Capital: Vientiane

Social and economic data
Area: 236,800 km^2
Population: 4.117m*
Pop density per km^2: 17*
Literacy rate: 44%
GDP: $430m*; per capita GDP: $104
Economy type: low income
Labour force in agriculture: 74%

*1985

Ethnic composition
Sixty per cent of the population are Laotian, predominantly Lao Lum, 35 per cent hill tribes and 5 per cent Vietnamese and Chinese. Lao is the principal language, spoken by two-thirds of the population, with French also widely used. The non-Lao tribal ethnic groups, particularly the Meo, have forcibly opposed the new regime's challenges to their traditional way of life.

Religions
An estimated 58 per cent of the population adhere to traditional Theravada Buddhism, although a secular state was officially established in 1975. Thirty-five per cent of the people follow tribal, predominantly animist, religions; while, prior to the communist takeover, Roman Catholicism claimed 35,000 adherents.

Political features
State type: communist
Date of state formation: 1954
Political structure: unitary
Executive: communist
Assembly: one-chamber
Party structure: one-party
Human rights rating: bad

Local and regional government

The country is divided into 16 provinces (*khoueng*), administered by People's Revolutionary Committees, which are headed by a governor and controlled by the ruling Lao People's Revolutionary Party (LPRP). In the northern highlands, where non-Lao ethnic groups predominate, a greater measure of self-government is enjoyed. Below the provinces, the units of administration are districts (*muong*), cantons (*tasseng*) and villages (*ban*). At the sub-provincial level there are People's Councils and Committees which, in theory, are subject to triennial election.

Head of state

President Phoumi Vongvichit, since 1986.

Head of government

Prime Minister Kaysone Phomvihane, since 1975.

Political leaders since 1970

1962–75 Prince Souvanna Phouma, 1975– Kaysone Phomvihane (LPRP).*

*Communist Party leader

Political system

At the moment Laos has no formal constitution, although a draft document was completed in 1986 and has been the subject of government discussion. All power resides with the ruling Lao People's Revolutionary Party (LPRP). The state has been described as having entered the Marxist phase of the 'dictatorship of the proletariat', with socialism now in the process of being 'built' through a transformation of the 'relations of production', or the socio-economic organisation, and by ideological conversion.

Currently the Supreme People's Assembly (SPA) serves as the effective legislature. It originally comprised 45 members who were appointed by the National Congress of People's Representatives (NCPR)—a 264-member assembly elected by local bodies—in December 1975. It now, after the elections of March 1989, comprises 79 deputies returned for five-year terms and meets twice a year to ratify government policies formally. Meetings of the SPA are chaired by the President, who serves as the ceremonial head of state.

Executive authority is exercised by the Council of Ministers (COM), a body which is headed by a chairman, or Prime Minister, and which comprises an 'inner cabinet' of 23 vice-chairmen, department ministers and state committee chairmen, as well as more than sixty vice-ministers. The COM, which, like the SPA, was also initially appointed by the NCPR in 1975, has, since 1989, been 'nominated' by the SPA. It has the task of framing the economic plan and budget and overseeing the day-to-day work of state ministries, committees and local bodies.

The controlling force and sole permitted political party in Laos is the LPRP. Its senior members monopolise key state positions, with state and party fused to an unusually high degree. In March 1988, for example, the LPRP's ruling Politburo comprised eleven full and two non-voting 'alternate' members. Three of these held senior positions in the SPA, including the post of President, Phoumi Vongvichit. A further seven held key portfolios within the COM's 'inner cabinet', such as the chairman and party leader, Kaysone Phomvihane, the first vice-chairman, Nouhak Phounsavanh, defence minister, General Khamtai Siphandon, foreign minister, General Phoune Sipraseuth, interior minister, General Sisavat Keobounphanh, and state planning committee chairman, Saly Vongkhamsao.

Political parties

The ruling Lao People's Revolutionary Party (LPRP: Phak Pasason Pativat Lao) originated as the Lao Independence Front, which was founded in 1951 by Prince Souphanouvong, a member of the royal family, as a breakaway wing from the Communist Party of Indo-China, which was founded in 1930 by Ho Chi Minh. The movement became known as the Pathet Lao (Lao People's Front) in 1954 and was taken over by North Vietnamese-backed Kaysone Phomvihane in 1955, although Prince Souphanouvong remained its figurehead leader in negotiations with the incumbent government. Under the designation People's Party of Laos, it played a leading role in the Laotian Patriotic Front during the 1960s, functioning as a guerrilla wing, before adopting its present name in 1972.

The LPRP is organised hierarchically, with a stepped series of local, or branch, district and provincial committees, leading up to an 'elected' national Congress. In the past, the Congress has met irregularly, only two being called between 1955 and 1972. Since 1982, it has been convened at regular five-yearly intervals. The most recent session, the fourth, was in November 1986, and was attended by 303 delegates. The Congress ratifies the party programme and 'elects' a Central Committee (CC) to act when it is not sitting. The CC is presently composed of 51 full and nine 'alternate' members. They have an average age of 52 and include five women.

The CC, in turn, 'elects' a smaller Politburo and nine-member Secretariat, headed by a General Secretary. The Politburo, in accordance with the precepts of 'democratic centralism', dominates both party and state machines. Four of its current members are military figures.

In 1986, membership of the LPRP stood at 44,000, a figure which constitutes barely 1 per cent of the total population. This is one of the lowest party:citizens ratios in the communist world, although membership has more than doubled since the late 1970s. Rigorous entry rules are imposed, with the aim of maintaining the LPRP as a disciplined and committed 'vanguard' force. The party dominates the broader Lao Front for National Reconstruction (LFNR), which was established in 1979 as the successor to the Laotian Patriotic Front mass organisation. The LFNR includes within its ranks representatives of economic and social 'interest groups' and is designed to mobilise non-party support for government policy.

Latest elections

The first SPA election since the communist takeover in 1975 was held in March 1989. It involved an element of choice between LFNR-approved candidates, with 121 men and women contesting the 79 seats available. Turnout was described as 'high'. Seventy per cent of the elected deputies were members of the LPRP and seven were female.

Political history

Laos was first occupied by Chinese immigrants during the fourth and fifth centuries AD and adopted Buddhism during the seventh century. Between the eleventh and thirteenth centuries it constituted part of the culturally advanced Khmer Empire and became subject to immigration by Lao from Thailand. Not until the fourteenth century, when the region was united by the legendary King Fa Ngum, was an independent Laos kingdom established.

Initially visited by Europeans in the seventeenth century, Laos became a French protectorate between 1893 and 1945, and consisted of the three principalities of Luang Prabang, Vientiane and Champassac. After a brief occupation by the Japanese during the Second World War, the French re-established control in 1946, despite opposition from the Chinese-supported Lao Issara (Free Laos) nationalist movement. The country was granted semi-autonomy in 1949, when, under the constitutional monarchy of the King of Luang Prabang, Sisavang Vong, it became an Associated State of the French Union. In December 1954, following the Geneva Agreements, Laos secured full independence.

A sporadic civil war subsequently broke out between two factions of former supporters of the Lao Issara. The first was a moderate, royalist-neutralist, group, led by Prince Souvanna Phouma, who served as Prime Minister on several occasions. It had supported the 1949 French compromise and was the recognised government for the bulk of the country. The second was a more extreme, communist resistance group, the Pathet Lao (Land of the Lao), led by ex-Prince Souphanouvong, the half-brother of Prince Souvanna, and Kaysone Phomvihane. This was supported by China and the Vietminh, who were in control of much of north-eastern Laos.

Following the Vientiane Agreement of 1957, a coalition government was temporarily established. This soon collapsed, however, after the May 1958 National Assembly elections had produced an inconclusive result. In 1960 a third, right-wing, force emerged when General Phoumi Nosavan, backed by the royal army, overthrew Prime Minister Souvanna Phouma and set up a pro-Western government, headed by Prince Boun Oum. A new Geneva Agreement was signed in 1962, establishing a tripartite, broad-spectrum, government, under the leadership of Prince Souvanna Phouma.

Fighting continued, however, between the Pathet Lao, assisted by North Vietnam, and the neutralists and the right wing, assisted by the United States. The fighting was exacerbated by the neighbouring Vietnam War, until the Vientiane Agreement of 1973 established a cease-fire line, dividing the country north-west to south-east. The communists were given two-thirds of the country, including the Plain of Jars and the Bolovens Plateau, but the Souvanna Phouma government was made responsible for two-thirds of the population.

All foreign forces, North Vietnamese, Thai and American, were to be withdrawn, and both sides received equal representation in Souvanna Phouma's provisional government of 1974. In 1975, however, the communist Pathet Lao, now renamed the Lao People's Front, following success in Assembly elections, seized full power. King Savang Vatthana, who had succeeded his father in October 1959, abdicated in November and Laos became a 'People's Democratic Republic' under the presidency of

Prince Souphanouvong. Prince Souvanna Phouma remained as an 'adviser' to the government, but the real controlling force was now the LPRP leader and Prime Minister, Kaysone Phomvihane.

The new administration, which inherited a poor, war-ravaged economy, initially attempted rapidly to re-organise the country along socialist lines, nationalising businesses and industries and collectivising agriculture. However, faced with mounting food shortages and the flight of more than 250,000 refugees to Thailand, it began to modify this approach in 1979. The private sector was now allowed to continue to operate in a number of spheres and production incentives were introduced, with the stress now being placed on a gradual, step-by-step 'transition to socialism'.

In 1981, the country's first five-year plan came into force. However, in 1985-86, under pressure from the new Gorbachev leadership in the Soviet Union, which supplies the country with considerable economic aid, further 'liberalisation' reforms were introduced in the economic sphere, including the adoption of a new 'socialist business accounting system', which freed managers to set prices and wages and required enterprises to make a profit. In the rural sector, more than half the cropped area remains privately farmed.

Politically, the country has remained subject to firm LPRP control since 1975, no formal constitution having been promulgated. There have recently, however, been indications of moves towards a 'normalisation' of the political process. Local elections were held in 1988, and national elections followed in March 1989. Only limited leadership change has been seen since 1975. Kaysone Phomvihane, a mellowing radical, is still at the helm, as Prime Minister and LPRP General Secretary. In November 1986, however, Prince Souphanouvong stepped down as state President, after suffering a stroke. His replacement, Phoumi Vongvichit, is a fellow moderate.

Diplomatically, Laos has been closely tied to the Soviet Union and Vietnam, which, since 1975, has had 50,000 troops stationed in the country, as many as the whole domestic army. However, two-fifths of them are now set to be withdrawn. Relations with neighbouring Thailand, which Laos accuses of having 'expansionist' designs, have been strained, border disputes intermittently breaking out in disputed regions. In addition, Laos has accused both Thailand and China of providing assistance to rebel groups which operate in border tracts in the south and north. Recently, however, for economic reasons, there have been attempts to improve relations with both countries.

MALAYSIA

Federation of Malaysia (FOM)

Capital: Kuala Lumpur

Social and economic data
Area: 332,370 km^2
Population: 15.820m*
Pop density per km^2: 48*

Literacy rate: 70%
GDP: $31,231m*; per capita GDP: $1,974
Economy type: middle income
Labour force in agriculture: 38%

*1985

Ethnic composition
Forty-eight per cent of the population are Malay (80 per cent of them in rural areas), 34 per cent Chinese (80 per cent of whom are in towns), and 9 per cent Indian. The official language is Bahasa Malaysia (Malay), but Chinese, Tamil and English are also spoken. The primacy of ethnic Malays has been built into the constitution, with the offices of head of state and Prime Minister being open only to this community. The distribution of Malays across the country is, however, uneven. In East Malaysia, ethnic Malays comprise less than a third of the population, Ibans and Kadazans predominating in Sarawak and Sabah, respectively.

Religions
Fifty-three per cent of the population are Muslim, 19 per cent Buddhist, 7 per cent Christian (nearly a third of them in East Malaysia), 12 per cent follow the Chinese Confucian and Daoist faiths, while many of the indigenous tribes of Sabah and Sarawak are animist. Islam is the official state religion, with the Paramount Ruler serving as the Federation's religious head and rulers in each state as the local heads of Islam.

Political features
State type: liberal democracy
Date of state formation: 1957
Political structure: federal
Executive: parliamentary
Assembly: two-chamber
Party structure: multi-party
Human rights rating: 53%

Local and regional government
Below the state and federal territory level, the country is divided into 130 administrative districts, headed by a district officer, who is a civil servant. Below these are *mukims*, administered by *penghulus*. Sabah and Sarawak differ from West Malaysia, being divided into residencies and divisions.

Head of state
Paramount Ruler Rajah Azlan Muhibuddin Shah (Sultan of Perak), since 1989.

Head of government
Prime Minister Datuk Seri Dr Mahathir bin Mohamad, since 1981.

Political leaders since 1970*
1970–76 Tun Abdul Razak (UMNO), 1976–81 Datuk Hussein bin Onn (UMNO), 1981– Datuk Seri Dr Mahathir bin Mohamad (UMNO).

*Prime Ministers

Political system

Malaysia is a federation of 13 states: Johore, Kedah, Kelantan, Malacca, Negri Sembilan, Pahang, Penang, Perak, Perlis, Sabah, Sarawak, Selangor and Trengganu, plus the capital city, Kuala Lumpur, and the island of Labuan, which are separate Federal Territories. Each state has its own written constitution, head of state and elected 14- to 48-seat Legislative Assembly, led by a chief minister and cabinet, and with powers to legislate on matters outside the federal parliament's sphere.

The federation is headed, under the constitution of 1957, by a constitutional monarch, the Paramount Ruler (Yang di-Pertuan Agong). He is elected, by secret ballot, for five-year terms by, and from among, the hereditary rulers of nine of the states, Malacca, Penang, Sabah and Sarawak being the exceptions. For this purpose, a special Conference of Rulers (Majlis Raja Raja) is convened. The Paramount Ruler's powers are similar to those of the British monarch, including discretion in the appointment of the Prime Minister (Perdana Mentri) and in granting a dissolution of parliament. In normal circumstances, however, the monarch acts on the advice of the elected Prime Minister and cabinet, who wield effective executive power. The monarch has no ultimate power of veto.

The Federal Legislature, or parliament, is a two-chamber body composed of a 68-member upper house, called the Senate (Dewan Negara) and a 177-member House of Representatives (Dewan Rakyat). The Senate comprises 42 members appointed by the monarch and two elected by each of the thirteen State Legislative Assemblies. All serve a six-year term. The members of the House of Representatives are elected for five-year terms from single-member constituencies by universal adult suffrage. One hundred and thirty-two represent Peninsular Malaysia, including seven from Kuala Lumpur, 24 Sarawak and 21 Sabah, including one from Labuan island. The House of Representatives is the dominant chamber, the Senate having only delaying powers over bills originating in, and approved by, the lower chamber: one month over money bills and one year over other bills.

The majority party or coalition in the House of Representatives provides the Prime Minister, who selects an executive council of ministers (Juma'ah Mentri), or cabinet, from within parliament, as the government of the day. The cabinet is collectively responsible to parliament. In March 1988 it had 23 members and the Prime Minister held the additional portfolios of home affairs and justice.

To amend the constitution, a two-thirds vote in the federal parliament is required.

Malaysia's federal system is substantially weighted towards the centre, the federal parliament enjoying sole authority to legislate in the fields of external affairs, defence and internal security, justice, except for Islamic law, industry, commerce, finance, education, transportation and communication. In all other cases, federal legislation takes precedence over state law whenever a conflict arises. In addition, the states enjoy few significant sources of revenue.

It is in the spheres of land and natural resource management and local administration that state authority is greatest. Exceptions are the two East Malaysia (Borneo) states of Sabah and Sarawak. They enjoy a greater measure of autonomy, having been granted special safeguards in matters of land law, local government, finance, official religion and official language.

Political parties

The principal political party in the Federation is the United Malays National Organisation (UMNO), which, headed by Prime Minister, Dr Mahathir bin Mohamad, is orientated towards native Malays and dominates a multi-party National Front (NF: Barisan Nasional) coalition, which contests national and state elections. The UMNO was originally formed in May 1946 to 'fight for independence and safeguard the interests of the indigenous people'. Since independence, the party has set as its aim the 'safeguarding of Malay interests', the promotion of national unity and the pursuit of a 'neutral foreign policy'.

Dissension grew within UMNO during 1987-88, culminating in a High Court ruling, in February 1988, which, as a result of irregularities in the party's internal elections of April 1987, declared the UMNO to be an 'unlawful' body. It therefore had to be disbanded, and a New UMNO (UMNO Baru) was immediately founded by Dr Mahathir. By June 1988 this grouping had a membership of 200,000, compared with the old UNMO's 1.4 million. Dissident UMNO members, led by former Prime Minister, Tunku Abdul Rahman, and former trade and industry minister, Tunku Tan Sri Razaleigh Hamzah, have been forced outside and in May 1989 formed an alternative party, Semangat '46 (Spirit of 1946).

Twelve other parties are currently also members of the ruling National Front coalition, the majority being communally or regionally based. The most important is the Chinese-orientated Malaysian Chinese Association (MCA), a conservative grouping, formed in 1949, which currently claims a membership of 500,000 and is led by Dr Ling Liong Sik. Another Chinese-orientated party within the NF is the 140,000-strong Gerakan Party (PGRM: Malaysian People's Movement Party), a socialist grouping, formed in 1968, and currently led by Dr Lim Keng Yaik. Orientated towards the Indian community is the 340,000 member Malaysian Indian Congress (MIC), which was established in 1946, and is led by Datuk S. Samy Vellu.

Also within the ruling coalition are: the Kadazan-supported Sabah United Party (PBS), the Hizbul Muslim, the Parti Bansa Dayak Sarawak (PBDS), the United Bumiputra Party (PPBBS), the People's Progressive Party (PPP), the Malaysian Islamic Council Front (FMIC), the Sarawak National Party (SNP), the Sarawak United People's Party (SUPP) and the United Sabah National Organisation (USNO). The PBS dates from 1985 and is led by the Roman Catholic, Datuk Joseph Pairin Kitangan, currently Chief Minister of Sabah state. The Hizbul Muslim was established in 1986 as a breakaway group from the PBS. The PBDS was founded in 1983, the FMIC in 1977, the SNP in 1961, and the SUPP in 1959.

The principal opposition party in the Federation is the predominantly Chinese, 12,000-member Democratic Action Party (DAP), led by Lim Kit Siang. Formed in 1966, the DAP advocates the establishment of a multi-racial society based on the principles of democratic socialism. Also important is the Islamic-radical, 250,000-member Pan-Malayan Islamic Party (PAS: Parti Islam Se Malaysia), which was formed in 1951 and advocates the establishment of a fully Islamic society. Smaller, regional parties operate at the state level.

Latest elections

In the most recent House of Representatives' elections, which were held in

August 1986, the National Front secured 57 per cent of the popular vote and 148 (84 per cent) of the 177 available seats. Within this broad coalition, the UMNO captured 83 seats, the MCA 17, the PBS ten, the PPBBS eight, the MIC six, the PGRM, PBDS and USNO five each, the SNP and SUPP four each and the Hizbul Muslim one. The opposition DAP received 21 per cent of the vote and captured 24 seats, or 14 per cent of the total, while the PAS secured 16 per cent of the national vote, but only one seat. Fourteen of the National Front's seats were won in uncontested elections.

In the state elections of August 1986, the National Front retained control of all the assemblies in Peninsular Malaysia, as well as Sarawak. Only one assembly, Sabah, was taken by the PBS, a party which has recently been brought into the National Front's federal coalition, and is not formally controlled by it. In all, the NF holds 327, or 77 per cent, of the country's 425 state assembly seats.

Political history

The history of the country is better understood on the basis of a knowledge of its geographical location. The Federation of Malaysia is divided into two broad regions: in the west, Peninsular Malaysia, comprising eleven states and 83 per cent of the total population, and Eastern Malaysia, which includes the states of Sabah and Sarawak, in the north and east of the island of Borneo. The southern and central portion of the island forms part of Indonesia. The small, independent coastal Sultanate of Brunei is encircled by Eastern Malaysia and the two broad regions of Malaysia are separated by 640 kilometres of the South China Sea.

The regions of present-day Malaysia formed part of the Buddhist Sri Vijaya Empire between the ninth and fourteenth centuries, an empire which was eventually overthrown by a Javanese Hindu Kingdom. Islam was subsequently introduced and a substantial empire built up, prior to the Portuguese conquest of Malacca in 1511. Thereafter the area came, successively, under Dutch (1641–1795), British (1795–1817) and again Dutch (1818–24) control.

From the mid 1820s, British sovereignty was progressively established over the Malaysia region, and a tin and rubber export-based economy was developed, particularly in the west. Chinese and Indian Tamil labourers were imported to work in the mines and on the plantations. Despite the British presence, local state chiefs were allowed to retain considerable political autonomy. Initially, in 1826, only the states of Singapore, Penang and Malacca were formally incorporated into the British Colony of the Straits Settlements. But in 1874 British protection was extended to Perak, Selangor, Pahang and Negri Sembilan. In 1895 they collectively formed the Federated Malay States. Johore came under British protection in 1885. Then, between 1910 and 1930, protection treaties were entered into with Kedah, Perlis, Kelantan and Trengganu, which, together with Johore, were known as the Unfederated Malay States. Finally, after the Second World War, and following the extension of British control over Sarawak, in 1948, the protectorates in Borneo and the Malay Peninsula were unified to form, in February 1948, the Federation of Malaysia Crown Colony.

Following several years of communist insurrection, the Federation was granted independence, within the Commmonwealth, in August 1957. Six years later, in September 1963, Britain relinquished sovereignty over its crown colonies of Sabah and Sarawak, and a new 14-state Federation was formed. North Borneo had been a British territory since 1881 and administered by the North Borneo Company until 1946. Sarawak was a British territory which had been ruled by the Brooke family since 1841. This new Federation initially included the internally self-governing state of Singapore. However, in August 1965, Singapore, alleging discrimination against its Chinese community, seceded from the Federation.

During its early years, between 1963 and 1966, the existence of the Federation was contested by guerrillas supported by the Sukarno government of Indonesia, while, in 1968, the Philippines disputed the sovereignty of East Malaysia. Tunku Abdul Rahman was the country's first Prime Minister, between 1963 and 1969, governing in a successful, consensual and multi-racial manner at the head of the Alliance Party, which had been established in 1952. Then, in August 1969, serious anti-Chinese race riots erupted in Kuala Lumpur, forcing the formation of an emergency administration. These riots followed a fall in support for the ruling United Malays National Organisation (UMNO) in the federal elections and were indicative of a deeper Malay resentment of the economic success and wealth of the Chinese business community.

The disturbances prompted the resignation of Tunku Abdul Rahman, in September 1970, and the creation, by his successor as Prime Minister, Tun Abdul Razak, of a broader ten-party, later 13, National Front governing coalition, to succeed the Alliance Party. The coalition included in its ranks previous opposition parties. In addition, a major 'New Economic Policy' was launched in 1971, with the aim of raising the share of businesses owned by ethnic Malays (Bumiputras) from a level of 4 per cent to 30 per cent by 1990. It was also planned to extend the use of pro-Malay 'affirmative action' quota systems for university entrance and company employment. At the same time, greater stress was placed on rural development, in an effort to achieve a better 'economic balance'.

During the 1970s, Malaysia enjoyed healthy rates of economic growth, of more than 7 per cent, but the problem of communist guerrilla actions near the Thailand border re-emerged after 1975. Relations with the Chinese community also deteriorated in the later 1970s as a result of the federal government's initial refusal to accept 'boat people' refugees, fleeing from Vietnam. Even more serious was the revival of a fundamentalist Islamic movement in the western and northern provinces.

Dr Mahathir bin Mohamad became the new leader of the UMNO and Prime Minister in July 1981 and proceeded to pursue a more narrowly Islamic and pro-Malay strategy than his predecessors. In addition, he embarked on an ambitious new industrialisation programme, seeking to 'Look East' and emulate Japan. He secured re-election in April 1982 and August 1986, but, between these dates, began to encounter growing opposition from his Malaysian Chinese Association (MCA) coalition partners. He was also faced with Christian-Muslim ethnic conflict in Sabah and a sudden slowdown in economic growth in 1985, as a result of the fall in world tin, rubber and palm oil commodity prices. Internal UMNO opposition to Dr Mahathir also began to surface in 1987, when, in April, trade and industry minister, Tunku Razaleigh Hamzah, unsuccessfully, but only by a small margin, challenged him for the party's presidency. Two months later, Razaleigh and his closest supporters were dismissed from their cabinet posts.

During the autumn of 1987, racial tensions worsened, Chinese language education and religion emerging as divisive issues. Fearing a renewed outbreak of riots, Prime Minister Mahathir, in October-November, ordered the arrest and detention without trial of 106 politicians, including the DAP leader and deputy leader Lim Kit Siang and Karpal Singh. Among the people arrested were journalists, lawyers and pressure group leaders. The action was taken under the provisions of the Internal Security Act (ISA). Press censorship regulations were also tightened, and several journals were forced to cease publication. These moves served to heighten intra-party opposition to Mahathir, to the extent that the party's moderate wing, led by Razaleigh and supported by former Prime Minister, Tunku Abdul Rahman, charged the Prime Minister with increasing authoritarianism. Eleven dissident members from this wing filed a legal suit, claiming that the party's leadership election of the previous year had been improperly conducted. Their claims were upheld by the High Court, in February 1988, which ruled that delegations taking part in the elections had not been legally registered and that, as a result, the UMNO was 'an unlawful society', and the 1987 elections were null and void.

This created a serious constitutional crisis, putting in doubt the legal status of the incumbent government. However, with the support of the head of state, Tunku Mahmood Iskander, and with subsequent favourable judicial rulings, Prime Minister Mahathir weathered the storm. Initially, the Razaleigh-Rahman wing of the UMNO attempted to register a new successor party, 'UMNO Malaysia', but the application was rejected by the Registrar of Societies. Dr Mahathir responded by applying to form a 'New UMNO' (UMNO Baru), which excluded dissident members of the old UMNO. This application was accepted by the Registrar.

Despite surviving the immediate political crisis of February 1988, Dr Mahathir's public standing had been seriously weakened. His New UMNO party subsequently suffered a heavy defeat in a by-election engineered by the resignation of a pro-Razaleigh UMNO deputy, in August 1988, and further controversy was created by the passage of a constitutional amendment, in March 1988, limiting the power of the judiciary to interpret laws. The dismissal, in July 1988, by the head of state, acting on the Prime Minister's advice, of the Lord President of the Supreme Court for 'anti-government bias', after ruling in favour of an appeal by members seeking to reconstitute the old UMNO, was another unpopular move. These actions represented a fundamental attack on the independence of the judiciary, seriously undermining Malaysian democracy.

In foreign affairs, Malaysia joined ASEAN in 1967 and originally, during the Tunku Abdul Rahman era, adopted a pro-Western, anti-communist posture. Since the 1970s, however, its relations with the communist powers have improved, while closer links have also been developed with Islamic nations. The country has advocated the creation of a zone of 'peace, freedom and neutrality' in South East Asia, under guarantees of the superpowers.

In the economic sphere, the government has, since the mid-1960s, pursued a system of indicative economic planning, based on the framing of five-year plans. In addition, in 1985, a ten-year Industrial Master Plan (IMP) was introduced, with the aim of fostering long-term development of the manufacturing sector. Joint venture projects have also been entered into with Japanese automobile manufacturing companies, while special tax and export incentives have been offered by the state's Malaysian Industrial Development Authority, in an effort to attract greater inward investment. These moves, involving a slackening of restrictions on foreign ownership, have meant that the 1971 goal of achieving 30 per cent ethnic Malay equity ownership by 1989 has, of necessity, been revised. In 1986 the Malay share stood at 18 per cent.

MALDIVES

Republic of Maldives
Divehi Jumhuriya

Capital: Malé

Social and economic data
Area: 300 km^2
Population: 180,000*
Pop density per km^2: 600*
Literacy rate: 90%
GDP: $84m*; per capita GDP: $467
Economy type: low income
Labour force in agriculture: 8%

*1985

Ethnic composition
The indigenous population comprises four 'ethnic strains': Dravidian, in the northern islands; Arab, in the middle islands; Sinhalese, in the southern islands; and black African, or Ravare. Divehi is the syncretic national language. There is also an Indian linguistic and religious immigrant minority.

Religions
The majority of the population are Sunni Muslims. Islam is the state religion and Sharia law is enforced.

Political features
State type: authoritarian nationalist
Date of state formation: 1965
Political structure: unitary
Executive: unlimited presidential
Assembly: one-chamber
Party structure: no parties
Human rights rating: N/A

Local and regional government
The country is divided into 20 administrative districts, comprising the capital, which is subject to direct central administration, and the 19 atolls, each of which is governed by an atoll chief (*verin*), appointed by the

President. The chief is assisted by an elected committee. Each island is subject to the jurisdiction of a headman (*kateeb*), also appointed by the President.

Head of state and head of government
President Maumoon Abdul Gayoom, since 1978.

Political leaders since 1970
1968–78 Ibrahim Nasir, 1978– Maumoon Abdul Gayoom.

Political system
The current constitution was adopted in November 1968 and is an amended version of an earlier 1964 document which was drawn up by the celebrated British constitutional lawyer, Sir Ivor Jennings. It provides for a single-chamber Citizens' Council (Majlis) of 48 members, and an executive President, nominated by the Majlis and then elected by referendum. They all serve a five-year term. Forty of the Majlis' members are elected by universal adult suffrage, two each being returned by the National Capital Island and the 19 constituent atolls, and eight are appointed by the President. The Majlis meets three times a year, acting principally as a debating forum. The President appoints and leads a cabinet, whose members are individually responsible to the Majlis. In March 1988 the cabinet had twelve members and President Gayoom held two of its key portfolios, defence and national security. There has also been, since July 1985, a 15-member, President-appointed, Special Consultative Council, which advises on economic matters. Women are precluded from holding political office.

Political parties
There are no political parties in the Maldives, candidates standing for election on the basis of their 'personal influence' and clan loyalties.

Latest elections
In the most recent presidential election, held in September 1988, Maumoon Abdul Gayoom was re-elected unopposed for a third term, securing a record 96.4 per cent of the popular vote. Majlis elections are held individually, with representatives elected in the middle of a term continuing to hold office through the following session until their five-year term is completed.

Political history
The Maldives comprise 1,196 small coral islands, 203 of which are inhabited, grouped in 19 atolls, situated in the North Indian Ocean, 650 kilometres south-west of Sri Lanka and barely a metre above a rising sea level. The original population, which was Dravidian, was displaced during the ninth century by seafaring Arabs, who introduced Muslim practices. During the sixteenth century, the islands came under Portuguese rule, before becoming a dependency of Ceylon, now Sri Lanka, from the mid seventeenth century, when Sinhalese and Indian colonies were established. Under the designation 'Maldive Islands', though still remaining a dependency of Ceylon, they were placed under British protection in 1887 and enjoyed a measure of internal self-government under a hereditary Sultan.

Between January 1953 and February 1954 a republic was briefly established, before the Sultanate, now subject to election, was restored, with Ibrahim Nasir serving as Prime Minister. In July 1965, with anti-British sentiment rising and reflected in a secessionist rebellion in Suvadivan in 1959–60, the islands were granted full independence outside the Commonwealth, under the new designation 'Maldives'. Three years later, after a referendum, the Sultan was deposed and a republic was again established, with the then Prime Minister, Ibrahim Nasir, elected President. He governed with the aid of a Prime Minister, Ahmed Zaki, until March 1975, when this post was abolished, after an attempt by Zaki to secure a Majlis no-confidence vote against the President. A fully presidential system was then adopted.

Between 1956 and 1975 Britain had a Royal Air Force staging post on the southern island of Gan and its closure meant a substantial loss of income. The President, nevertheless, refused an offer from the USSR, in October 1977, to lease the former base, saying that he did not want it used for military purposes again, nor leased to a superpower.

In 1978 President Nasir announced that he would not stand for re-election for a third term and the Majlis nominated Maumoon Abdul Gayoom, a member of Nasir's cabinet, as his successor. He was then elected unopposed in a popular presidential 'referendum', in July 1978, winning 90 per cent of the votes cast. Nasir, meanwhile, left the country for Singapore but was called back to answer charges of embezzling government funds. He denied the charges and attempts to extradite him were unsuccessful. Despite rumours of a plot by groups connected with Nasir to overthrow him, Gayoom was re-elected for a further five years in September 1983, securing 95.6 per cent of the popular vote.

During his period in charge, the country, despite a rapid population growth of over 3 per cent per annum, has enjoyed substantial economic progress. This has primarily been the result of the promotion of the tourist industry, which generates 20 per cent of current GDP. A further 25 per cent is generated by the fishing industry, in which 45 per cent of the labour force is engaged. The President has also concentrated on the development of poor rural regions and social provision, such as education and health services.

In foreign affairs, while adhering to his predecessor's general policy of non-aligment and close links with the Arab nations of the Middle East, Gayoom brought the Maldives back into the Commonwealth as a full member, in June 1985. The country is also a founder member of the South Asian Association for Regional Co-operation (SAARC).

President Gayoom was re-elected in September 1988, but was challenged in November 1988 by an abortive coup led by Abdullah Luthufi, an exiled businessman from the southern atoll of Adu, which had demanded secession during the 1970s. He had recruited a force of around 200 Tamil mercenaries in Sri Lanka. After fierce fighting, which claimed 19 lives, the rebels, who appeared to enjoy the backing of former President Nasir, captured the presidential palace and forced Gayoom into hiding. However, order was restored after the intervention, at Gayoom's request, of 1,600 paratroops sent by India, in fulfilment of its role as a member of SAARC. Luthufi and his co-conspirator, Sagar Nasir, were captured and sent for trial and Gayoom re-installed as President.

MONGOLIA

Mongolian People's Republic
Bugd Nayramdakh Mongol ard Uls

Capital: Ulan Bator

Social and economic data
Area: 1,565,000 km^2
Population: 1.900m*
Pop density per km^2: 1*
Literacy rate: 90%
GDP: $1,900m*; per capita GDP: $1,000
Economy type: low income
Labour force in agriculture: 36%

*1985

Ethnic composition
Ninety per cent of the population are Mongols, 4 per cent Kazakh, 2 per cent Chinese and 2 per cent Russians.

Religions
Tibetan Buddhism (Lamaism) has been the traditional religion for the Mongol community, but only one active monastery currently functions. The Kazakhs of western Mongolia are Sunni Muslims by descent, but there are no mosques currently in use.

Political features
State type: communist
Date of state formation: 1921/1946
Political structure: unitary
Executive: communist
Assembly: one-chamber
Party structure: one-party
Human rights rating: N/A

Local and regional government
The country is divided into 18 regions (*aymags*), three municipalities and over 350 rural districts (*somons*), served by elected local assemblies (People's Deputies Hurals) which are elected for three-year terms but are, in reality, controlled by local party secretaries.

Head of state
President Jambyn Batmunkh, since 1984.

Head of government
Prime Minister Dumaagiyn Sodnom, since 1984.

Political leaders since 1970*
1958–84 Yumjaagiyn Tsedenbal (MPRP), 1984– Jambyn Batmunkh (MPRP).

*Communist Party leaders

Political system

Mongolia's most recent constitution was adopted in July 1960, superseding that of November 1924. It describes the state as a 'People's Republic' and assigns a 'guiding and directing' role to the ruling Marxist-Leninist Mongolian People's Revolution Party (MPRP), the sole permitted political party.

Under the 1960 constitution, the country has a single supreme legislative assembly, the 370-deputy People's Great Assembly (PGA: Ardyn Ih Hural), whose members are elected by universal adult suffrage for five-year terms from single-member constituencies. Candidates stand on a single, unopposed list drawn up by the MPRP, but which usually contains around 35 representatives of an aligned 'non-party bloc'. The PGA convenes in full session once a year, for a week. It has the formal authority to establish the 'basic principles and measures' of domestic and foreign policy, including the budget and economic plan, and has a substructure of permanent commissions. In reality, however, the PGA serves as a rubber-stamping body for decisions taken in advance by the MPRP's leadership. It 'elects' a permanent nine-member policy-making Presidium, whose chairman functions as state President, to take over its responsibilities between sittings. In addition, the Assembly appoints a 30-member Council of Ministers (COM), headed by a chairman (Prime Minister), to carry out day-to-day administration, and a state Procurator, who heads the judicial system.

Overall control of the whole state system is exercised by the MPRP, as a result of the system of 'democratic centralism' and joint party and state office holding. Evidence of the latter is provided by the fact that, in June 1988, of the seven full and two 'candidate', non-voting, members of the MPRP's executive Political Bureau (Politburo), two were also members of the Presidium of the PGA, and included its chairman, Jambyn Batmunkh. A further four were key members of the COM, including the chairman, Dumaagiyn Sodnom.

Political parties

The ruling Marxist-Leninist Mongolian People's Revolution Party (MPRP) originated as a broad front of radical nationalist forces, inspired by the 1917 Russian Bolshevik revolution, who were opposed to China's attempts to restore its sovereignty over Mongolia in 1919. In 1921 those with communist leanings met in the USSR to form the Mongolian People's Party, which was renamed the MPRP in 1924, constituting the nucleus of the country's new 'Provisional People's Government'. The MPRP was divided between a radical left wing and a conservative, moderate right wing during the 1920s and 1930s and subject to repeated factional conflicts, until party strongman, Marshal Horloogiyn Choybalsan, established his dominance between 1939 and 1952. Under Choybalsan, the regular party machinery fell into disuse, only two congresses meeting, as power became personalised. Under his successors, however, a regularised structure was re-established.

The party is organised hierarchically on conventional Leninist lines, with small factory, state farm and livestock co-operative 'branch organisations', or 'cells', established at its base. Higher up there are district, city and regional units and, at the top, a national Party Congress. This consists of about 750 members and is convened every five years. It adopts a party programme and 'elects' a Central Committee (CC) to assume its authority until the next convention. At the most recent, the nineteenth, MPRP Congress, held in May 1986, 86 full and 65 non-voting 'candidate' members were elected to the CC.

The CC holds plenary meetings three to four times a year, 'electing' a Political Bureau, headed by a General Secretary, who is the party leader, and five-member Secretariat to direct party, and state, affairs on a permanent basis.

Membership of the MPRP currently stands at 89,588, constituting 4.7 per cent of the population, one of the lowest proportions in the communist world. Membership has, however, grown significantly in recent years, having stood at only 67,000 in 1977. Fifty per cent are white-collar workers, 30 per cent urban, blue-collar workers, and 20 per cent farmers or members of livestock co-operatives (*arats*). Also attached to the MPRP is the 260,000-member Mongolian Revolutionary Youth League, the party's 'youth' wing.

Latest elections

The most recent People's Great Assembly elections were held in June 1986, with a single list of MPRP-sponsored candidates being elected unopposed. Voter turnout was officially put at 99.99 per cent.

Political history

The area, dominated by nomadic tribes, was united by Genghis Khan during the early thirteenth century, and formed the nucleus of a vast Mongol Empire which stretched across Asia, reaching its zenith under Genghis' grandson, Kublai Khan. It was then conquered by China during the seventeenth century, being known as the Chinese province of 'Outer Mongolia' between 1689 and 1911. Following the Chinese 'republican revolution' of 1911, Mongolian nationalists proclaimed the country's independence and, receiving the support of Tsarist Russia, succeeded in gaining semi-autonomy, under the leadership of a traditionalist Buddhist monarchy, in the shape of a 're-incarnated' lama. Chinese sovereignty was asserted again in 1915 and, taking advantage of the turmoil in Russia, formal control was reintroduced in 1919. The new Soviet government came, however, to the support of Mongolian nationalists, helping them to overthrow Chinese rule for the last time in July 1921. A November 1921 treaty with the Russian Soviet Federal Socialist Republic guaranteed its autonomy, but constitutionally, Mongolia continued to remain subject to China's formal sovereignty until January 1946, after an October 1945 plebiscite had unanimously favoured full independence.

Initially, the newly independent state was subject to joint control by the monarchy and an MPRP-dominated 'People's Government'. However, on the death of King Javdzandamba Hutagt VIII in June 1924, the monarchy was abolished and a 'People's Republic' proclaimed. In November 1924 a Soviet-style constitution was adopted and a programme of 'de-feudalisation' launched. This involved the expropriation of the previously dominant nobility, the collectivisation of agriculture, predominantly herding, and the destruction of Lama Buddhism. An armed uprising by anti-government forces, in 1932, was forcibly suppressed, with Soviet assistance.

The dominant figure in the new state, following purges between 1936 and 1939, became the former independence fighter, Marshal Horloogiyn Choybalsan, who combined the offices of MPRP leader and Prime Minister and ruled in a strict Stalinist manner, with minimal consultation. On his death, in January 1952, the two posts were divided respectively between Dashiyn Damba and Yumjaagiyn Tsedenbal, a Soviet-educated economist, until, in November 1958, Tsedenbal once again combined the positions and emerged as the dominant figure, but governing in a more cautious and consensual manner than his predecessor. A new constitution was adopted in July 1960, in recognition of the 'higher stage' of socialist development which had been attained.

Throughout the inter-war period Mongolia has remained closely dependent on the Soviet Union militarily, economically and politically. Its MPRP leaders were all trained in Moscow and, today, 95 per cent of its foreign trade is with the USSR and Eastern Europe. This close interdependence received formal recognition in 1962, when Mongolia joined CMEA (Comecon), and in January 1966, when a 20-year friendship, co-operation and mutual assistance pact with the USSR was signed. This served further to sour relations with neighbouring communist China which, at this time, was in ideological dispute with the Soviet Union. As a consequence, border incidents between Mongolia and China became frequent during the early 1970s.

Internally, Mongolia remained substantially isolated from the outside world during the 1970s, but experienced considerable economic change as new urban industries developed and settled agriculture spread. Politically, MPRP leader Yumjaagiyn Tsedenbal remained the dominant figure, assuming the post of head of state in May 1972, on the death of the long-serving Jamsrangiyn Sambuu, who had been head of state since 1954. Jambyn Batmunkh took over Tsedenbal's post of Prime Minister. Tsedenbal finally retired, on the grounds of ill health, in August 1984, and was replaced as party leader and head of state by Jambyn Batmunkh. Dumaagiyn Sodnom, Batmunkh's deputy, became the new Prime Minister.

Mongolia's political leadership has been notoriously conservative and loyal to the 'Moscow line'. In recent years, however, following the accession to power in the Soviet Union of Mikhail Gorbachev, the country has been encouraged to be more innovative and to broaden its outside contacts. As a consequence, a number of changes have been in evidence. A large-scale re-organisation of government ministries was launched between 1986 and 1988, as a means of streamlining decision-taking and enhancing efficiency. In the diplomatic sphere, the level of cultural exchanges with China has significantly increased during recent years, and ambassadorial relations with the United States were established, in January 1987. Also, in May 1987, reductions of more than 20 per cent were made in the number of Soviet troops stationed within the country. This brought their number down to 50,000 with a further 75 per cent reduction being promised in 1989. Finally, there have been indications of the adoption of a more tolerant attitude towards traditional social customs and religion. The study and use of the Mongolian script has increased and this has encouraged a revival in Mongolian nationalism.

NEPAL

Kingdom of Nepal
Sri Nepala Sarkar

Capital: Kathmandu

Social and economic data
Area: 141,400 km^2
Population: 17.422m*
Pop density per km^2: 123*
Literacy rate: 21%
GDP: $2,390m*; per capita GDP: $137
Economy type: low income
Labour force in agriculture: 91%

*1985

Ethnic composition
Eighty per cent of the population are of Indo-Nepalese ethnic stock, which includes the Paharis, the Newars and the Tharus. The remaining 20 per cent are of Tibeto-Nepalese descent and are concentrated in the north and east and are mainly subsistence farmers. There is a caste system on the Indian model. Nepali is the official language and is spoken by 58 per cent of the population. Maithir and Bhojpuri are also important, with English used as the main second language.

Religions
Ninety per cent of the population are Hindus, 5 per cent Buddhists and 3 per cent Muslims. Hindu is the official state religion and the King is regarded as the incarnation of the Hindu god Vishnu.

Political features
State type: absolutist
Date of state formation: 1768
Political structure: unitary
Executive: absolute
Assembly: one-chamber
Party structure: no parties
Human rights rating: poor

Local and regional government
The country is divided into 14 zones for local administration, each of which is headed by an appointed Commissioner. Below, there are 75 districts, administered by a district officer. There are 3,524 villages (*gaon*) and 14 towns (*nagar*). Councils (*sabahs*) are elected at the village, town, district and zonal levels, in an indirect, tiered manner.

Head of state
King Birendra Bir Bikram Shah Dev, since 1972.

Head of government
Prime Minister Marich Man Singh Shrestha, since 1986.

Political leaders since 1970
1955–72 King Mahendra Bir Bikram Shah, 1972– King Birendra Bir Bikram Shah Dev.

Political system
Under the constitution of December 1962, which was amended in 1967, 1976 and, most recently, in December 1980, Nepal is ruled by a constitutional monarch. The King works with a one-chamber National Assembly (Rashtriya Panchayat), 112 of whose members are directly elected every five years and 28 of whom are nominated by the monarch. The Panchayat debates and passes bills and elects a Prime Minister. Its decisions can, however, be vetoed by the King. Executive power is exercised by the King and by a cabinet, called the Council of Ministers (COM), whose members are selected by the King following consultation with the Prime Minister, who heads the Council. In April 1988 the COM had 20 members and the Prime Minister held the additional portfolios of defence minister and royal palace affairs minister. There is also a State Council (Raj Sabha), whose function it is to decide upon the succession and give advice to the King during periods of emergency. It has 70 members and an inner standing committee of 7–15 members.

Political parties
Political parties have been banned since January 1961 but four opposition parties function unofficially. They are: the Communist Party of Nepal (CPN), which was established in 1949, and is led by the Maoist, Mana Mohan Adhikari; the Nepali Congress Party (NCP), which dates from 1947, and has been led, since 1972, by Ganesh Man Singh; the United Liberation Torchbearers (ULT: Samyukta Mukti Bahini), which was founded in 1985; and the Democratic Front (DF: Janawadi Morcha), which was established in 1985, and is led by the exiled former Assembly member, Ram Raja Prasad Singh. The last two of these organisations were implicated in the terrorist campaigns which swept the country during 1985.

Both the CPN and NCP support the replacement of the non-party, *panchayat* system and the restoration of democratic rights. Within the government majority coalition, there are personality-based factions.

Latest elections
In the local elections of March-April 1987, NCP candidates, standing as independents, won 15 per cent of the popular vote and candidates from the pro-Moscow Marxist-Leninist faction of the CPN, 20 per cent. This compared with the 65 per cent support received by pro-government candidates.

In the most recent National Assembly elections, held in May 1986, all 1,475 candidates nominally stood as independents, in multi-member constituencies. Results were decided on a simple plurality basis. Forty members retained their seats and there were 72 new entrants, of whom 16 were viewed as members of the Marxist-Leninist faction of the CPN. Despite attempts by the NCP and pro-Beijing wing of the CPN, neither of which group put up candidates, to organise a poll boycott, turnout reached 64 per cent. This compared with only 52.2 per cent in May 1981.

Political history

Nepal is a mountainous independent kingdom lying between India and China. Only 14 per cent of the land is cultivated, the remainder being under forest, river bed or snow. A third of the population live in the southern lowland 'terai' and two-thirds in the central hilly region, predominantly in the Vale of Kathmandu. It was formerly an assortment of small principalities, and was unified by the Gurkha King, Prithivi Narayan Shah, in 1768. In 1792 a commercial treaty was signed with Britain and in 1816, after the year-long, Anglo-Nepali 'Gurkha War', a British Resident was allowed to reside at Kathmandu and the kingdom became a British dependent 'buffer-state'.

During the remainder of the nineteenth century, Nepal remained an isolated, traditionalist outpost on the border of British India, its main value being the supply of Gurkha troops to the British Indian army. This created a 'remittance economy'. From 1846, effective executive power was wielded by the Rana family, who controlled the office of Prime Minister, making the monarch a titular figurehead.

In 1923 Britain formally recognised Nepal as a fully independent state. The country was, however, still bound by treaty obligations to the United Kingdom until 1947, the year of India's independence. In 1951, the controlling Rana oligarchy was overthrown in a 'palace revolution', supported by the Nepali Congress Party (NCP), and the monarchy, in the person of King Tribhuvan Bir Bikram Shah, was restored to power. In 1959, King Mahendra Bir Bikram Shah, who had succeeded him in 1955, promulgated the nation's first constitution, creating a two-chamber assembly, with a popularly elected lower house. Following elections, the NCP's pro-Indian socialist leader, Bisweswor Prasad Koriala, became Prime Minister but soon clashed with the King over policies. King Mahendra dissolved the assembly, in December 1960, and put a ban on political parties the following month.

In December 1962 he introduced a new constitution providing for a tiered, non-party system of village councils (*panchayats*), an indirectly elected National Assembly and a Prime Minister appointed by the monarch.

King Mahendra died in January 1972 and was succeeded by his son Birendra Bir Bikram Shah Dev, who, faced with mounting agitation for political reform led by B. P. Koriala, held a referendum on the constitution in May 1980. A majority, of 54.8 per cent, voted for a royal-backed, 'suitably reformed', *panchayat* system, in preference to a multi-party alternative. As a result, the constitution was amended, in December 1980, to provide for direct, though still non-party, elections to the National Assembly. The first elections, which were held in May 1981, led to the defeat of a third of the pro-government candidates and returned a more independent-minded National Assembly. In July 1983 the new body proceeded to unseat Prime Minister Surya Bahadur Thapa, through a 'no confidence' motion, despite his enjoyment of royal support, and put into office Lokendra Bahadur Chand.

Opposition to the banning of political parties increased in 1985, resulting in terrorist bombings in June. As a consequence, a stringent anti-terrorist law was approved by the National Assembly, in August 1985, and more than 1,000 dissidents were arrested. In May 1986, new elections to the National

Assembly returned an increased number of members opposed to the non-party, *panchayat* system, and led to the replacement of Prime Minister Chand by Marich Man Singh Shrestha, who had previously been chairman of the Assembly. In an effort to improve the image of the *panchayat* system, the government instituted a stringent anti-corruption drive during 1987. At the same time, however, strict curbs were placed on opposition activity, more than 100 supporters of the banned NCP, including its president, being arrested in the early months of 1988. Tight censorship controls were also imposed.

In its external relations since 1947, Nepal has traditionally been closely tied to India, entering into a mutual assistance pact soon after the latter's independence. In recent years, however, Nepal has pursued a more neutral, non-aligned course, seeking to create a 'zone of peace' in southern Asia and to maintain cordial relations with both its neighbours, India and China. In particular, commercial links with China have increased recently. This has been resented by India, who imposed a partial blockade of the country in 1989, as a result of a dispute over the renegotiation of expired transit and trade treaties.

Economically and socially, Nepal remains a backward country, rates of literacy continuing to be low, and per capita living standards depressed by over-rapid population expansion, currently 2.7 per cent per annum, and adverse agricultural conditions. Almost a sixth of current GDP is derived from overseas development aid.

PAKISTAN

Islamic Republic of Pakistan
Islami Jamhuria-e-Pakistan

Capital: Islamabad

Social and economic data
Area: 803,900 km^2
Population: 101.900m*
Pop density per km^2: 127*
Literacy rate: 26%
GDP: $31,300m*; per capita GDP: $307
Economy type: low income
Labour force in agriculture: 51%

*1985

Ethnic composition
Pakistan possesses four principal, regionally based and antagonistic ethnic communities: Punjabis in the Punjab, Sindhis in Sind, Baluchis in Baluchistan and fiercely independent, Pathans (Pushtans) in the North West Frontier province. Urdu and English are the official languages. However, 64 per cent of the population speak Punjabi, 12 per cent Sindhi, 9 per cent Baluchi, 8 per cent Pushtu, and only 7 per cent speak Urdu and 2 per cent English.

Religions
Almost 97 per cent of the population are Muslims, divided 85 per cent–15 per cent between Sunnis and Shias. Hindus form 1.6 per cent and Christians 1.3 per cent, 600,000 of them Catholics, 400,000 Church of Pakistan and 300,000 United Presbyterian Church of Pakistan. Islam is the state religion.

Political features
State type: emergent democracy
Date of state formation: 1947
Political structure: federal
Executive: limited presidential*
Assembly: two-chamber
Party structure: multi-party
Human rights rating: 40%

*In transition to parliamentary

Local and regional government
Below the provinces, the highest level of local administration is the division, followed by the district and then the *tahsil* and *taluka*. Commissioners and deputy commissioners operate at the divisional and district levels, alongside elected councils.

Head of state
President Ghulam Ishaq Khan, since 1988.

Head of government
Prime Minister Benazir Bhutto, since 1988.

Political leaders since 1970
1969–71 General Agha Muhammad Yahya Khan (Military), 1971–78 Zulfiqar Ali Bhutto (PPP), 1978–88 General Mohammad Zia ul-Haq (Military), 1988–88 Ghulam Ishaq Khan (Independent), 1988– Benazir Bhutto (PPP).

Political system
The political system of Pakistan is in a transitional state. In July 1977, following a military coup by General Zia ul-Haq, the constitution of 1973 was placed in abeyance, political parties banned and elected assemblies dissolved. Power passed into the hands of a four-man military council headed by General Zia, who had the title of Chief Military Law Administrator. Chief justices were put in charge at the state level.

Since 1981, however, much of the 1973 constitution has been restored, as part of a gradual return to democratic civilian government, culminating, in November 1988, in the election of Benazir Bhutto as Prime Minister.

Pakistan is today a federal republic, comprising four provinces: Sind, with a population of 23 million, Punjab, 57 million, North West Frontier Province, 13 million, and Baluchistan, 5 million. The provinces are administered by centrally appointed governors and local governments drawn from elected Provincial Assemblies and headed by Chief Ministers. There are also tribal areas, with a total population of 2.7 million, which are administered directly by the federal government. Responsibility for education, labour, health, industry, social welfare, agriculture and roads legislation is entrusted to the provinces.

Primary power resides, however, with the central government, which is headed by an executive President, who is elected for a renewable, five-year term at a joint sitting of the members of the federal assembly and four provincial assemblies. He must be a Muslim. The presidency was originally a titular post, but following the constitutional amendments of March 1985, the office holder was given powers to dissolve the National Assembly, and appoint and dismiss the Prime Minister, the cabinet and provincial governors. He, therefore, emerged as the dominant political figure. However, following the death, in August 1988, of General Zia, the primacy of this office has been put in question.

The federal legislature (Majlis i-Shura) consists of two chambers, a lower house, called the National Assembly, and an upper chamber, the Senate. The National Assembly has 207 members, directly elected for five-year terms by universal adult suffrage, plus 20 women, chosen by the Assembly, and ten separately elected minority group members. They represent Christian, Hindu, Parsi and other minority interests. The Senate has 87 members, elected, a third at a time, for six-year terms by provincial assemblies and tribal areas, in accordance with a quota system. The country's four provincial assemblies each elect 19 Senators, the tribal areas, eight, and the Federal Capital Territory, three. The federal legislature convenes twice a year, for not less than 130 working days, in sessions which are not more than 120 days apart.

The National Assembly is the more powerful of the two chambers, having sole jurisdiction over financial affairs. The Senate has mainly an advisory role, with the right to send back to the National Assembly, once only, bills of which it disapproves. Joint National Assembly and Senate sittings are convened to iron out differences, by majority vote, on a small number of bills. To become law, bills must be passed by both chambers and must also be approved by the President, who has the power of veto. The presidential veto may, however, be overridden by a simple majority of both chambers.

Day-to-day government is in the hands of a Prime Minister, drawn from the National Assembly, and a cabinet, appointed by the President. In March 1989 the cabinet contained 20 ministers with the Prime Minister holding the additional portfolios of defence and finance, while Benazir Bhutto's mother, Begum Nusrat Bhutto, was Deputy Prime Minister.

Political parties

Political parties have been permitted to operate since December 1985, but under tight registration restrictions, which involve a pledge of loyalty to the 'sovereignty, security and ideology of the state' and the submission of their manifestos and accounts to the government.

Until November 1988, the governing party was the Pagaro Group of the Pakistan Muslim League (PML), named after the Sind-based religious leader, the Pir of Pagaro. It had supported General Zia. The PML was originally founded in 1906 as the All-India Muslim League, but its strongest roots had traditionally been in the North Indian province of Uttar Pradesh. Following the death of the PML's leader, Muhammed Ali Jinnah, in 1948, and the assassination, three years later, of its influential Prime Minister,

Liaquat Ali Khan, the party suffered a relative decline. In 1979 it split into two factions, the pro-government Pagaro Group and the anti-Zia Chatta Group. This second faction joined the opposition Movement for the Restoration of Democracy (MRD), in 1981. The PML is a conservative party, traditionally viewed as the mouthpiece of large landlords and local 'clan chiefs'. The former Prime Minister, Mohammad Khan Junejo, who failed to secure election to the National Assembly in November 1988, leads a moderate wing of the party. A more conservative faction is led by the former North West Frontier Province governor, Fida Mohammed Khan, and by the ambitious West Punjab chief minister, Nawaz Sharif.

For the November 1988 National Assembly elections, the PML joined with eight other conservative and Muslim parties to form the Islamic Democratic Alliance (IDA: Islami Jamhori Ittehad).

The numerous opposition parties, about 18 parties operating in 1988, were loosely, and uneasily, grouped together in the MRD prior to the national elections of November 1988. The most important single party within this grouping was the Pakistan People's Party (PPP), led jointly by Benazir Bhutto and her mother, Begum Nusrat Bhutto. The PPP was formed in 1967, by Zulfiqar Ali Bhutto, a member of a wealthy Sind land-owning family, to campaign for democracy, moderate Islamic socialism, a non-aligned foreign policy and the creation of a federal state. It drew the bulk of its support from student, industrial worker and peasant ranks and from the provinces of Sind, especially its rural areas, and Punjab.

Disquiet among a number of PPP members about Benazir Bhutto's allegedly autocratic leadership style and overly moderate, middle-class-orientated, policies, embracing, for example, the 'privatisation' of selected state industries and the abandonment of the call for land reform, led, in August 1986, to the formation of a small breakaway, group, called the National People's Party (NPP). This disaffected group was led by the former Chief Minister of Sind, Ghulam Mustafa Jatoi. He subsequently became titular head of the IDA in 1988, but failed to gain election to the National Assembly in November.

As these elections approached, the MRD was dissolved while the PPP attracted to itself a number of opportunist conservative landlord converts, from Sind province especially. The expanded PPP emerged as the leading Assembly party after the election and Benazir Bhutto became Prime Minister.

The fundamentalist, Islamic Assembly (JIP: Jamaat-e-Islami Pakistan) which was established in 1941, seeks the establishment of a Sunni Islamic state and is an important political force on the right wing.

The pro-Soviet Awami National Party (ANP), which was founded in 1986 by an amalgamation of socialist groups, is a notable left-wing force, with a strong local base in the North West Frontier Province.

The Solidarity Party (TIP: Tehrik-i-Istiqlal) dating from 1968, is a moderate, liberal-democratic opposition body, led by former Air Marshal Mohammed Asghar Khan. It was a founder member of the MRD, but broke away in 1986 when it officially registered itself under the Political Parties (Amendment) Act.

The Mohajir National Movement (MQM: Mohajir Qaumi Mahaz), which was formed in 1986, is a Sind-based party, led by Altaf Hussain and orientated towards the middle-class, Urdu-speaking mohajir community, who migrated to the province from India at the time of partition. Since then they have opposed recent ethnic-quota employment restrictions. Though narrowly based, the MQM has been a rising political force during recent years, scoring heavily in Karachi and Hyderabad in the local elections of November 1987 and National Assembly elections of November 1988. In this contest it captured eleven of Karachi's 13 seats, benefiting from mounting ethnic tension and violence in contemporary Sind.

Party loyalties are weak and fickle in Pakistan and are based predominantly on patronage and regional ties. The major parties are themselves internally divided between provincial and personality-based factions.

Latest elections

In the most recent National Assembly elections, which were held in November 1988, the Pakistan People's Party (PPP) won 93 of the 207 elective seats, the Islamic Democratic Alliance (IDA) 54, the Mohajir Qaumi Mahaz (MQM) 13, the Jamiat-i-Ulema-i-Islam eight, the Awami National Party and Pakistan Awami Ittehad three apiece, the Baluch National Party two and the National People's Party and Pakistan Democratic Party one each. A further 27 seats were captured by independents, while in two cases polling was deferred as a result of the death of candidates.

One thousand three hundred and seventy candidates from 30 parties contested the election and the campaign was remarkably peaceful and restrained, only four deaths being recorded. Voting was generally fair, although a late Supreme Court ruling requiring voters to produce valid identity cards did serve effectively to debar many poor and illiterate, potential PPP supporters. Turnout fell to only 40 per cent, compared with 55 per cent in the free elections of 1977. Party voting was very much regionally based, the IDA, with army support, dominating in Punjab, but capturing no seats in Sind. Only the PPP, although Sind-skewed, obtained a significant national spread of support. The other prominent feature of the election was the voters' rejection of many 'old guard' and traditional élite candidates.

In the provincial elections, which were held three days after the National Assembly contests, the PPP won control of only one province, Sind, while the IDA maintained its control of Punjab.

Political history

The Indus Valley region of contemporary Pakistan supported an advanced, city-based ancient civilisation, the Harappan, between 2500 and 1600 BC. The north of the region was later invaded by Aryans from the west, about 2000–1500 BC, and thereafter by successive waves of conquering peoples from Central Asia and beyond, including Muslims from the tenth century AD. These invaders continued on into the North Indian plains, establishing a series of empires with regional capitals in both India and Pakistan. The Mughals, from 1527, constituted the last of these 'conquest empires', prior to the establishment of British sovereignty over the Indian subcontinent. Formal British control was extended over the Punjab and Sind, following wars against local regimes, notably the Sikh 'successor state' in the Punjab, during the 1840s, and over Baluchistan and the North West Frontier

Province in 1896. Subsequent British rule in Pakistan was notable for its substantial investment in major canal irrigation projects in the West Punjab and northern Indus Valley, establishing this tract as a major wheat and cotton exporting area and drawing in settlers from the east. Because of a perceived threat from Russia to the North West Frontier there was a concentration there of military installations and personnel.

Following the development of a cross-community nationalist movement in the Indian subcontinent, from the mid 1880s, a separate All-India Muslim League was established in 1906 to campaign specifically for Muslim interests. This body was initially dominated by Muslims from north India, before, in 1916, Muhammad Ali Jinnah, a Muslim lawyer educated in Karachi and England, became the League's president. During the inter-war period the League veered between campaigning for independence from British rule within a national federation and seeking to establish a separate Muslim state.

In 1933, Choudhary Rahmat Ali invented the name 'Pakistan', or, in Urdu, 'Pure Nation', for a fully independent Muslim territory which would embrace the four provinces of Sind, Baluchistan, Punjab and the North West Frontier. Four years later, he called for the inclusion of the Muslim majority areas of Bengal within such a state. Fearing domination by the Hindu majority within India, Jinnah finally adopted these ideas in 1940, resulting, in August 1947, in the partitioning of the Indian subcontinent into Hindu and Muslim majority spheres, in accordance with boundaries hastily established by the Radcliffe Commission. More than 7 million Muslims moved into Pakistan from India, while a similar number of Hindus and Sikhs moved in the opposite direction in the days and months preceding and following partition. Terrible violence resulted wherever the two refugee courses passed each other.

Independent Pakistan was formally constituted as a Dominion within the British Commonwealth, with the British monarch as head of state. It comprised the five former, and frequently antagonistic, British Indian states of Baluchistan, East Bengal, North West Frontier, Sind and West Punjab. It was more broadly divided between an eastern and western section, separated by 1,610 kilometres of Indian territory, and differing substantially in culture, language and geography. The only thing that united the two sections was religion. The charismatic and respected Jinnah became the country's first Governor-General and president of the new Constituent Assembly, but, already gravely ill at the time of independence, he died in September 1948. Khwajah Nazimuddin, Ghulam Mohammad and Iskander Mirza followed in the post of Governor-General, before a republic was declared, in March 1956, and an 'Islamic' constitution adopted. This constitution was abrogated in October 1958 and military rule imposed, following a coup by General Mohammad Ayub Khan.

The country enjoyed rapid economic growth during the 1960s but mounting regional tension between demographically dominant East Pakistan and West Pakistan, where political and military power was concentrated. Following serious strikes and riots in March 1969, General Ayub Khan stepped down to be replaced by commander-in-chief, General Agha Muhammad Yahya Khan. Pakistan's first elections with universal adult suffrage were subsequently held, in December 1970, the intention being to elect an assembly which would then frame a new constitution.

They resulted in Sheikh Mujibur Rahman's Awami League, which proposed autonomy, gaining a majority of seats in East Pakistan and the Pakistan People's Party (PPP) in the West. East Pakistan declared its independence from the West in March 1971, precipitating a civil war which resulted, following Indian military intervention on East Pakistan's side in December 1971, in the emergence of the independent republic of Bangladesh.

As a consequence of this defeat, General Yahya Khan resigned and passed power in West Pakistan to the PPP's populist leader, Zulfiqar Ali Bhutto. He proceeded to introduce a new federal parliamentary constitution, in April 1973, and a socialist economic programme of land reform and nationalisation. From the mid 1970s, however, the Sind-based Bhutto faced growing regional opposition, particularly from Baluchistan and from Pathans campaigning for an independent Pakhtoonistan. He was also confronted with deteriorating economic conditions.

Bhutto won a majority in the March 1977 Assembly elections, but was accused of ballot-rigging by the Pakistan National Alliance (PNA) opposition. Riots ensued and, following four months of unrest, the Punjabi Muslim army chief of staff, General Mohammad Zia ul-Haq, seized power in a bloodless coup in July 1977. Martial law was imposed and Bhutto imprisoned for alleged murder. He was hanged in April 1979.

Between 1979 and 1981 Zia imposed severe restrictions on political activity. Economic growth revived, however, helped by a new pro-business strategy, by remittance inflows from workers in the Middle East and by American aid, following the December 1979 Soviet invasion of Afghanistan. This led, additionally, to the influx of more than 3 million refugees, 75 per cent of them being housed in the North West Frontier Province and 20 per cent in Baluchistan.

At home, the General introduced a broad Islamisation programme, aimed at deepening his support base and appeasing Islamic fundamentalists. This was opposed, however, by middle-class professionals and by the country's Shia minority. In March 1981, nine banned opposition parties, including the PPP, formed the Movement for the Restoration of Democracy (MRD) alliance, campaigning for a return to parliamentary government. The military government responded by arresting several hundred opposition politicians. A renewed democracy campaign was launched in the autumn of 1983, resulting in considerable anti-government violence in Sind province.

From 1982, however, General Zia slowly began enlarging the civilian element in his government and, in December 1984, held a referendum on the Islamisation process. He obtained a majority for his proposals but the participation level was low. Nevertheless, the result was taken as legitimising his continuance as President for a further five-year term.

In February 1985 direct elections were held to the National and Provincial Assemblies, but on a non-party basis. The opposition, as in December 1984, boycotted the poll, and the resultant turnout was only 53 per cent. A new civilian cabinet was, nevertheless, formed and an amended constitution adopted. In December 1985, martial law and the ban on political parties were lifted, military courts were abolished and military administrators stepped down in favour of civilians. Opposition campaigns for democratisation continued, however, with Benazir Bhutto, the Oxford-

and Harvard-educated daughter of Zulfiqar Ali Bhutto, returning from self-exile in London, in April 1986, to launch a major autumn campaign for immediate 'open elections'. Riots erupted in Lahore, Karachi and rural Sind, the tensions being exacerbated by clashes between rival local and immigrant communities. These led to the temporary arrest of the PPP's leaders and the despatch of troops to Sind.

In May 1987, concerned with a downturn in the economy, the slow pace of implementation of the Islamisation programme, continuing law and order problems and with the growing independence of Prime Minister Mohammad Khan Junejo, President Zia summarily dismissed the Junejo government, dissolved the National Assembly and provincial legislatures and promised fresh elections within 90 days, as required by the constitution. Zia proceeded, in June-July 1988, to put together a new 18-member interim government, but without a Prime Minister. He also issued a presidential ordinance which decreed that the Sharia, the Islamic legal code, would immediately become the country's supreme law. He then outlined plans for the introduction of a formal presidential system and set 16 November as the date for new National Assembly elections.

Barely a month later, however, on 17 August 1988, the President was killed in a mysterious military air crash near Bahawalpur, 160 kilometres west of the Indian border, in east-central Pakistan. The crash was viewed by many as sabotage, with dissident elements within the Pakistan armed forces, or underground Afghan secret service agents, being variously blamed.

General Zia's death placed the country's political system in confusion, with no obvious successor apparent, within the government or the military forces. Pakistan's senior army commanders had been killed with Zia in the air crash. The elderly Senate chairman, Ghulam Ishaq Khan, took over as interim President, pledging to oversee the holding of the forthcoming national elections.

These were held, as scheduled, in November, and were preceded by intense party jockeying, involving the break-up of the MRD and the formation of a new nine-party conservative Muslim, anti-Bhutto and anti-PPP, Islamic Democratic Alliance (IDA), by elements from the Muslim League and incumbent Zia loyalists. The PPP, advocating a moderate, centrist policy programme and declaring its intention to seek a 'fresh start' and avoid retribution for past actions against its members, succeeded in emerging as the dominant force in the contest. Benazir Bhutto was duly sworn in as Prime Minister, in December 1988.

The new government faced many problems, including a deteriorating economy, exacerbated by a population growth of more than 3 per cent per annum, and the difficulties of adjusting to changing circumstances in bordering Afghanistan. More specifically, its majority, which was based partially on a coalition with the Karachi-based Mohajir National Movement, remained fragile, while opposition remained strong in the IDA-controlled Punjab, among conservative Muslim religious leaders (mullahs), and among the military. These circumstances promised to constrain the policy choices of the new administration, which pledged itself to continue to follow a free market economic programme, maintain support for the Afghan mujaheddin and leave untouched the country's substantial military budget. The decision of the PPP not to oppose Ghulam Ishaq Khan's continued tenure of the post of President reflected this pragmatic approach and he was overwhelmingly re-elected as President by the electoral college in December 1988.

In foreign affairs, Pakistan has experienced strained relations with India throughout the post-independence period, being involved in border wars over Kashmir in 1965 and East Pakistan in 1971. The country left the Commonwealth in 1972, following the acceptance of the new state of Bangladesh, and has been allied with China since the 1950s, mainly because of their shared hostility to India. In recent years it has developed close relations with the United States, while, at the same time, joining the non-aligned movement, in 1979, and improving its ties with the Islamic states of the Middle East and Africa. The new Bhutto administration has begun to improve relations with India and, in July 1989, applied to rejoin the Commonwealth.

SINGAPORE

Republic of Singapore

Capital: Singapore City

Social and economic data

Area: 616 km^2
Population: 2.584m*
Pop density per km^2: 4,195*
Literacy rate: 83%
GDP: $17,476m*; per capita GDP: $6,763
Economy type: high income
Labour force in agriculture: 1%

*1985

Ethnic composition

Seventy-seven per cent of the population are Chinese, predominantly Hokkien, Teochew and Cantonese, 15 per cent Malay and 7 per cent Indian. The national language is Malay, but Chinese (Mandarin), Tamil and English, the language of administration, are also official languages.

Religions

The majority of Chinese are Buddhists or Daoists; Malays and Pakistanis are Muslims; Indians, Hindus; and Europeans and Eurasians, Christians. The country is, however, a secular state, with religion, unlike neighbouring Malaysia and Indonesia, not a significant aspect of national life.

Political features

State type: liberal democracy*
Date of state formation: 1965†
Political structure: unitary
Executive: parliamentary
Assembly: one-chamber
Party structure: multi-party*
Human rights rating: 59%

*Though dominated, in practice, by one party
†As a fully independent state

Local and regional government

For administrative purposes, Singapore Island is divided into five districts: Singapore City, Katong, Serangoon, Bukit Panjang and Jurong. There is no elected tier of local government but 20- to 50-member Citizens' Consultative Committees have been established in each electoral district, staffed by nominees of the local Member of Parliament and subject to the approval of the Prime Minister's Office. The task of these committees is both to serve as a medium through which the government can 'educate' the local people on government policies and to act as a feedback channel, through which popular needs and grievances are made known. They are also employed for the administration of a number of public works programmes and to mediate in local ethnic disputes.

Head of state

President Wee Kim Wee, since 1985.

Head of government

Prime Minister Lee Kuan Yew, since 1959.

Political leaders since 1970

1959– Lee Kuan Yew (PAP).

Political system

Because of its small size, Singapore has a single-tier system of government. The constitution of December 1965, an amended version of an earlier, June 1959, constitution, has provided for a single-chamber parliament, whose 81 members are elected for five-year terms by universal adult suffrage from single-member constituencies through a simple plurality voting system. Parliament debates and votes on legislation and elects, for a four-year term, a President, who is a ceremonial head of state. All parliamentary bills, with the exception of defence, public security and the budget, are subject to the prior scrutiny of a 21-member Presidential Council, which was established in 1967, and is chaired by a Chief Justice. Its task is to ensure that proposed legislation does not discriminate against any ethnic or religious community.

Executive power is held by a Prime Minister and 13-member cabinet drawn from the majority party within parliament. The Prime Minister is served by an influential Prime Minister's Office, which contains an anti-pollution unit, a corrupt practices investigation bureau, an election department and a city district secretariat, which liaises with local citizens' consultative committees. First and Second Deputy Prime Ministers assist the Prime Minister in his responsibilities.

In practice, the bulk of decisions in Singapore are taken behind the scenes through consultation between the Prime Minister's Office and an élite of around 300 well-educated and loyal technocrats who staff senior posts in the state bureaucracy and in statutory boards and public corporations. They are renowned for their honesty and efficiency. For this reason, the country has been termed an 'administrative state', power being exercised in a paternalistic, though authoritarian, manner.

Although nominally a pluralist 'liberal democracy', the ruling People's Action Party (PAP), led by Prime Minister Lee Kuan Yew, tends to dominate the political scene. Since independence, it has tightly controlled all aspects of public and political life, including the mass media, labour unions, defence and police establishments and educational and social welfare systems.

Political parties

The People's Action Party (PAP) was originally formed in November 1954 by a small group of lawyers, trade unionists, journalists and intellectuals, under the direction of Lee Kuan Yew, a Cambridge-educated barrister, in response to a mounting, communist Chinese-supported, non-violent campaign for 'immediate independence for a free and non-communist Malaya'. The PAP initially won only three seats from the 30 available, in the Legislative Assembly elections of 1955. In the following election, in 1959, however, it established itself as the majority party, a position which it has held ever since. In its policy stance, the PAP has veered rightwards since its inception, originally describing itself as a 'democratic socialist' body. Today it adheres to a conservative, free-market economic programme and is strongly anti-communist in outlook. Efficiency, uninterrupted economic growth and the creation of a 'multi-ethnic, multilingual, secular society', imbued with the national values of austerity, discipline and unity, are the party's, and hence the country's, guiding goals. The PAP has also, however, placed strong emphasis on social welfare, having invested generously in education, public housing and health and social provision. It has branches in each of the country's electoral constituencies and a membership of around 30,000. It is, however, tightly controlled from above by a 20-member Central Executive Committee, headed by Secretary-General Lee.

There are currently 20 registered opposition parties, the majority, however, being 'paper entities', having no real organisational base. The five most important parties are the Workers' Party (WP), the Singapore Democratic Party (SDP), the Singapore United Front (SUF), the United People's Front (UPF), and the Socialist Front (Barisan Sosialis).

The WP was originally established in 1957 as a socialist grouping which favoured greater labour union and civil freedom. It fell into abeyance during the later 1960s before being revived in 1971 by the Sri Lankan-born lawyer, Joshua Benjamin Jeyaretnam, who assumed its leadership and later won a parliamentary by-election in the low-income district of Ansom, in October 1981. He retained this seat at the general election of December 1984. Jeyaretnam was, however, subsequently harassed by the government and forced out of parliament, in November 1986.

The SDP was formed in 1980 and led by the London-trained barrister, Chaim Se Tong. He also succeeded in capturing a parliamentary seat in the general election of December 1984.

The SUF was formed in 1973. It has a liberal democratic policy outlook. The UPF dates from 1975, and the Socialist Front from 1961, when it began as a left-wing breakaway faction from the PAP. These three parties are of some electoral importance, each capturing between 2 and 9 per cent of the popular vote in national elections.

All opposition parties operate in difficult circumstances, their leading members having been subjected to a mixture of crude and subtle harassment by state institutions since the early 1970s. Several have been bankrupted in libel, defamation and tax fraud suits, bankrupts being debarred from political activities by law.

Latest elections

In the most recent parliamentary elections, which were held in September 1988, the PAP won 62 per cent of the national vote and 80 of the 81 available seats. The opposition, splintered into more than 20 parties, despite obtaining 38 per cent of the vote, a 1 per cent advance on their December 1984 figure, captured one seat fewer than before.

Political history

Singapore Island was leased as a trading post in 1819 from the Sultan of Johore by the British East India Company, on the advice of Sir Stamford Raffles, at a time when it was a swampy jungle. Seven years later, in 1826, Singapore, Malacca and Penang were incorporated as the Straits Settlements, remaining under the charge of the Company. The territory, retaining the designation Straits Settlements, passed to the British crown in 1858 and formed a crown colony between 1867 and 1942. It had a burgeoning deep-water port complex to which Chinese coolies and Indian clerks were drawn.

During the Second World War, the island was a vital British military base. It had been designed to be invulnerable to naval attack, but was invaded by land and occupied by the Japanese, between February 1942 and September 1945. Singapore returned to British administration after Japan's surrender, becoming a separate crown colony in 1946 and fully self-governing, with Lee Kuan Yew as Prime Minister, between 1959 and 1963. It joined the Federation of Malaysia in September 1963, but, following Malay-Chinese race riots in 1964, seceded in August 1965, claiming discrimination against its Chinese citizens.

A new independent republic of Singapore was thus formed in September 1965, remaining in the Commonwealth and maintaining close commercial and defence ties with neighbouring Malaysia.

The new republic's internal political affairs were dominated by Prime Minister Lee Kuan Yew's People's Action Party (PAP), which gained a monopoly of all parliamentary seats in the elections between 1968 and 1980. Under Lee's stewardship, Singapore developed rapidly as a commercial and financial entrepôt and as a centre for new export industries, GDP growing at an average annual per capita rate of more than 8 per cent during the 1960s and 1970s. As a consequence, by the early 1980s it enjoyed the highest per capita standard of living in Asia outside Japan and the Sultanate of Brunei and had developed an extensive social welfare system. These advances were achieved by a combination of private enterprise, in the trading and financial spheres, and careful state planning and infrastructural support, in the industrial. It was also the result of a willingness on the part of the country's population to accept authoritarian state direction, including the effective control of trade unions, in a benevolent, Confucian manner.

During the early 1980s, however, as the country endured a brief halt in its growth course, opposition to the Lee regime began to surface, and then grow. In the December 1984 parliamentary elections, the PAP's share of the popular vote fell from 76 per cent to 63 per cent and two opposition parties, the Workers' Party (WP) and Singapore Democratic Party, won national seats for the first time.

This partial reverse encouraged Prime Minister Lee to take a progressively firmer line against the expression of dissent by both the media and political activists. As part of this process, in November 1986, J. B. Jeyaretnam, leader of the WP and a member of parliament, was sentenced to one month's imprisonment and fined S$5,000 for perjury in connection with bankruptcy proceedings. This fine was a sufficient sum, under the terms of the constitution, to deprive him of his parliamentary seat and debar him from standing for election for five years.

Despite these actions, and helped by a once-again booming economy, the PAP held its vote share steady at 62 per cent in the September 1988 general election, capturing all but one of the available parliamentary seats. After the election speculation mounted that Lee Kuan Yew, who had in 1984 suggested that he would retire at the age of 65, in 1988, would shortly step down as Prime Minister. If he did so it was expected that he would move up to the position of President, amending the constitution so as to make this post a directly elected executive office. In this position he would enjoy veto powers and serve a six-year term.

His officially designated successor is the Deputy Prime Minister and defence minister, Goh Chok Tong. However, Lee's son, the Cambridge-educated, former Brigadier-General, Lee Hsien Loong, who is currently the trade and industry minister, has also been cited as a possible political heir.

In its external relations, Singapore closely allied itself with the United States between 1965 and 1974. Since the mid 1970s, however, it has pursued a neutralist foreign policy, improving its contacts with communist China and playing an active role as a member of ASEAN. In general, however, diplomatic relations in Singapore are viewed as an extension of trade relations, the overriding goal being to promote exports and attract inward investment and technology flows.

SRI LANKA

Democratic Socialist Republic of Sri Lanka
Prajathanthrika Samajawadi Janarajaya Sri Lanka

Capital: Colombo

Social and economic data
Area: 65,610 km^2
Population: 16.344m*
Pop density per km^2: 249*
Literacy rate: 86%
GDP: $5,883m*; per capita GDP: $360
Economy type: low income
Labour force in agriculture: 37%

*1985

Ethnic composition

Seventy-four per cent of the population are Sinhalese, 18 per cent Tamil and 7 per cent Moors or Muslims, who are concentrated especially in the east. The Tamil community, which remains poorly integrated, is divided between the long-settled 'Sri Lankan Tamils', 10 per cent of the population, who reside in northern and eastern coastal areas, and the more recent immigrant 'Indian Tamils', 8 per cent, who were settled in the Kandyan highlands as tea plantation workers during the nineteenth and twentieth centuries and whose descendants have been disenfranchised since 1948. Sinhala is the official language.

Religions

Seventy per cent of the population, predominantly Sinhalese, are Buddhist, of the Theravada sect, 15 per cent, mainly Tamils, are Hindu, 8 per cent are Christian, chiefly Roman Catholic, and 7 per cent adhere to Islam.

Political features

State type: liberal democracy
Date of state formation: 1948
Political structure: unitary
Executive: dual
Assembly: one-chamber
Party structure: two-party
Human rights rating: 52%

Local and regional government

The country is divided into nine provinces and 24 administrative districts, each headed by a governor, working with an elected Development Council. Following constitutional amendments adopted in 1987–88, a network of eight upper-tier provincial councils and 68 lower-tier district councils (*pradeshiya sabhas*) is in the process of being established. For this purpose, the northern and eastern provinces will be merged into one unit.

Head of state

President Ranasinghe Premadasa, since 1989.

Head of government

Prime Minister Dingiri Banda Wijetunge, since 1989.

Political leaders since 1970

1970–77 Sirimavo Bandaranaike (SLFP), 1977–88 Junius Richard Jayewardene (UNP), 1989– Ranasinghe Premadasa (UNP).

Political system

Under the constitution of September 1978, Sri Lanka has a presidential form of government based loosely on the French 'dual-executive' model. The head of state and chief executive is the President who is directly elected by universal adult suffrage for a six-year term. A two-term limit applies and voting is by the single transferable vote (stv) system. The victor is required to secure at least 50 per cent of the national poll and electors are asked to list both first and, transferable, second preferences. The President appoints and dismisses cabinet ministers, including the Prime Minister, who functions as the President's 'parliamentary manager'. The President can hold selected portfolios of his own. He can also dissolve parliament 'at will' and may submit to national referendum matters of national importance. Junius Richard Jayewardene, who was President between 1978 and 1988, was particularly influential and, during his last years of office, held six departmental portfolios, including defence, civil security, plan implementation and higher education. His successor, Ranasinghe Premadasa, holds the defence, policy planning and implementation, and 'Buddha Sasana' portfolios.

Parliament, known as the National State Assembly, is a single-chamber body, which has supreme legislative authority and meets once a year for a session of up to four months. Currently it comprises 225 members who are directly elected by a 'modified' system of proportional representation for six-year terms. The country is divided into 22 multi-member constituencies, from which 198 deputies are returned, with the remaining 27 being elected on the basis of the total national vote of each party. A 12.5 per cent of the vote cut-off level applies for representation. A two-thirds parliamentary majority is required to alter the constitution.

Political parties

Sri Lanka has traditionally been a classic two-party state, power alternating between the United National Party (UNP: Eksath Jathika Pakshaya) and the Sri Lanka Freedom Party (SLFP: Sri Lanka Nidahas Pakshaya).

The UNP, whose political roots go back to the inter-war Ceylon National Congress (CNP), was founded in 1946 by the pro-Western liberal-conservative, Don Stephen Senanayake, and, after independence, was the country's first governing party, between 1948 and 1956. Its neglect of the poor, and of Sinhala-Buddhist sensitivities, led to electoral defeat in 1956, persuading the party to adopt a new, democratic socialist, policy programme in 1958. Following an even heavier reversal in 1970, the UNP was remodelled as a mass party by Junius Richard Jayewardene, who was related by marriage to both of the wealthy and influential upper-caste Senanayake and Bandaranaike families. The goal of *dharmishta*, or a just and righteous society, was espoused and greater stress placed on rural development, although private enterprise and foreign investment were also encouraged. This strategy enabled the UNP to broaden its support base from its original dependence on the urban and privileged to a much wider electorate.

The SLFP was founded in 1951 by the Oxford-educated barrister, Solomon W. R. Bandaranaike, previously a prominent member of both the CNP and the UNP government. He sought to construct a non-Marxist left-of-centre alternative to the ruling party. In 1956 Bandaranaike and the SLFP secured power, after heading a Sinhala-Buddhist orientated united front, directed against the UNP. However, conservative elements defected from the party in 1959, leading to a swing to the left in the policies which were adopted when it was in power, between 1960 and 1964 and between 1970 and 1977. During its long period in opposition after 1977, the SLFP machine has been weakened, power now being centralised within the ranks of the influential Bandaranaike family. The party's policy stance has also shifted towards the centre.

At least 13 other minor political parties currently operate in Sri Lanka. The most important, although officially banned since August 1983 as a result of its separatist stance, is the Tamil United Liberation Front (TULF: Tamil Vimukthi Peramuna), which, led, until his assassination in July 1989, by Appapillai Amirthalingam, and with its headquarters in Jaffna, is orientated towards the Tamil community and seeks to establish a separate, autonomous Tamil region in the north and east to be known as Eelam. Also banned in 1983 was the Marxist and Sinhalese extremist People's Liberation Front (JVP: Janatha Vimukthi Peramuna), currently led by Rohana Wijeweera. Another significant party is the Sri Lanka Muslim Congress, led by Mohammed Ashraff, which was founded as an eastern regional grouping in 1980, before becoming a national party in 1986.

Latest elections

The most recent presidential election was held in December 1988. As a result of the disruptive action of the JVP during the four-week campaign, which resulted in the loss of almost 500 lives, voter turnout fell to only 55 per cent, with a number of polling stations, in the more remote areas, either unable to open or forced to close early. Elsewhere, the presence of troops enabled voting to proceed. The UNP candidate, Prime Minister Ranasinghe Premadasa, emerged the victor, securing 50.4 per cent of the national vote on the 'first count', and defeating the SLFP's Sirimavo Bandaranaike, who obtained 44.9 per cent, and Ossie Abeygunasekera, 4.6 per cent. This last candidate represented the leftish Sri Lanka People's Party, which had been formed in 1984 as a breakaway from the SLFP.

However, the result was disputed by Bandaranaike, who claimed that it had been distorted by intimidation and violence, with many of the worst affected polling stations having been in traditionally pro-SLFP areas. She subsequently filed a petition of challenge before the Supreme Court.

In the parliamentary elections which followed in February 1989, the first such polls since July 1977, the JVP and Tamil extremists again resorted to terrorist violence. During a seven-week campaign, between 700 and 1,000 people were killed, including 14 parliamentary candidates, with 38 citizens being murdered on polling day itself. However, despite these activities, the electoral turnout was respectably high, standing at 64 per cent. 1,396 candidates from 19 parties contested the 225 available seats, and the UNP secured a narrow assembly majority, capturing 125 seats, based on a 51 per cent share of the national vote. The SLFP secured 67 seats and 32 per cent of the vote; the TULF 10 seats; the more extreme Tamil Eelavar Democratic Front, a northern- and eastern-based independent group closely associated with the Tamil Tiger guerrillas, 14 seats; and the SLMC, United Socialist Alliance (established in 1988 by supporters of the 1987 Indo-Sri Lankan peace accord) and the left-of-centre Mahajana Eksath Peramuna (People's United Front) three seats apiece.

Political history

The island of Sri Lanka which was known as Ceylon until 1972, was conquered by Sinhalese invaders from India about 550 BC and became a centre for Buddhism from the third century BC. Arab and Portuguese spice traders later introduced Islam and Christianity respectively. Coastal areas, but not the central kingdom of Kandy, became subject to foreign control from 1505 onwards, including Portugal (1505–1658), Holland (1658–1796) and Britain (1796–1802). Finally, in 1802, Ceylon became a British crown colony.

Under British rule, 'Sri Lankan Tamils', who had been settled in the northern and eastern regions for centuries, took up English education and progressed rapidly in administrative careers. In addition, new 'Indian Tamils' immigrated to work on the tea and rubber plantations which had been developed in the central highlands region around Kandy. Conflicts between the Sinhalese majority and Tamil minority began to surface during the 1920s, as nationalist politics developed. In 1931, universal adult suffrage was introduced for an elected assembly and executive council, in which power was shared with the British, before independence was achieved in February 1948.

Between 1948 and 1972, Sri Lanka remained within the British Commonwealth as a Dominion, with a two-chamber parliamentary system on the Westminster model. This comprised a directly elected House of Representatives, an indirectly elected Senate, and a titular Governor-General, who was the representative of the monarch. The liberal-conservative United National Party (UNP), led consecutively by Don Stephen Senanayake and Dudley Senanayake, initially held power. In 1956, however, the radical socialist, and more narrowly Sinhalese nationalist, Sri Lanka Freedom Party (SLFP), led by Solomon Bandaranaike, gained an electoral victory, at the head of the People's United Front (MEP: Mahajana Eksath Peramuna) coalition.

Once in power, it established Sinhalese, rather than English, as the official language to be used for entrance to universities and the civil service. This precipitated Tamil riots in 1958, while the dissatisfaction of the more extremist Sinhalese culminated in the Prime Minister's assassination, by a Buddhist monk, in September 1959. Solomon Bandaranaike's widow, Sirimavo, took over as Prime Minister and proceeded to hold office until 1977, except for UNP interruptions between March and June, 1960, and between 1965 and 1970. She was the world's first female Prime Minister and implemented a radical economic programme of nationalisation and land reform; a pro-Sinhalese educational and employment policy; and an independent non-aligned defence policy. In 1972, a new republican constitution was adopted in which the Senate upper chamber was abolished and the new national name Sri Lanka, which is Sinhalese for 'Resplendent Island', assumed.

During the 1970s, economic conditions deteriorated, spawning a serious wave of strikes in 1976, while Tamils complained bitterly of discrimination. For example, from 1956 onwards the Tamils' share of government posts fell dramatically. All this bred a separatist movement which demanded the creation of an independent Tamil state (Eelam) in the north and east. The Tamil United Liberation Front (TULF) coalition was formed in 1976 to campaign for this goal and emerged as the second-largest party in parliament in the elections of July 1977. These were fought under the old simple plurality voting system and brought a landslide victory for the United National Party, led by Junius Richard Jayewardene.

The new Jayewardene government proceeded to remodel the constitution on French presidential lines, in 1978. It discarded simple plurality voting, and introduced a new, free-enterprise, economic programme, which, initially, proved to be successful. The government's position was strengthened by the decision of a presidential commission, in October 1980, to deprive Sirimavo Bandaranaike of her civil rights for six years, as a result of alleged abuses of power during her period in office. The administration faced mounting unrest, however, in the north and east among Tamil separatist guerrillas, the Liberation Tigers of Tamil Eelam (LTTE), forcing the frequent imposition of a state of emergency.

Initially the UNP profited from a polarisation of Sinhalese and Tamil opinion, and Jayewardene was re-elected President in October 1982. Two months later a popular referendum showed 55 per cent in favour of prolonging the life of the UNP-dominated National State Assembly by six years. The referendum turnout was 77 per cent. However, in 1983, the level of terrorist organised violence escalated, more than 900 people, mainly Tamils in the Jaffna area, being killed. This adversely affected foreign exchange earnings from the tourist industry and discouraged inward investment. Legislation was introduced to outlaw separatist organisations, including the TULF, in August 1982. All-party talks aimed at solving the Tamil dispute took place, under Indian mediation, in 1984, 1985 and 1986, but broke down as a result of differences over the degrees of autonomy to be conceded. Meanwhile, by 1987 more than 300,000 Tamils, faced with a Sinhalese backlash, had fled from Sri Lanka to India and elsewhere.

By 1987 the LTTE had established almost *de facto* control of the northern Jaffna region, and the economy was in a debilitated condition. Unemployment stood at 27 per cent, inflation at 15 per cent and the annual GDP growth rate at 1.5 per cent, compared with 6 per cent between 1977 and 1983. In July of that year a Peace Accord, aimed at solving the 'Tamil issue', was signed by President Jayewardene and the Indian Prime Minister, Rajiv Gandhi. The plan's provisions included elevating Tamil and English to the status, alongside Sinhala, of official languages; the creation of eight new elected provincial councils, with the Tamil-dominated northern and eastern provinces being merged, subject to a referendum in the area; the repatriation of 130,000 Tamil refugees from South India; the disarming of Tamil militants, in return for a general amnesty; and the outlawing of LTTE training on, and supply from, the Indian mainland. Implementation of the Peace Accord in the Jaffna area was to be overseen by a 7,000-strong Indian Peace Keeping Force (IPKF).

This caused a storm of opposition from Sinhalese extremists, viewing the entry of Indian troops as an 'imperialist' invasion. More moderate Sinhalese elements, including the SLFP and several senior UNP government ministers, including Prime Minister Ranasinghe Premadasa, strongly criticised the Accord as a 'sell-out' to Tamil interests and protest riots erupted in the Colombo region. An assassination attempt was made on the life of President Jayewardene by the resurfaced, Sinhala-chauvinist People's Liberation Front (JVP), in August 1987.

Implementation of the Peace Accord in the Jaffna area by the IPKF met with initial success, but in October 1987 the surrender of arms by the LTTE ceased. The IPKF, which brought in 50,000 reinforcements, succeeded in gaining control of Jaffna city, but the LTTE militants, led by the elusive Velupillai Prabhakaran, escaped and established new guerrilla bases in rural areas to the east, inflicting casualty losses of between 600 and 700 on the IPKF. Meanwhile, in the south of the country, JVP terrorist attacks on UNP officials continued, claiming more than 500 lives.

Nevertheless, in April 1988, despite continuing inter-ethnic violence, elections were held for four of the newly created provincial councils, the UP capturing 57 per cent of the elective seats and control of all the councils. The United Socialist Alliance (USA), a loose grouping of small opposition parties who supported the July 1987 Peace Accord, secured 41 per cent of the seats. The SLVP boycotted the polls. These were followed, in November 1988, by provincial elections in the northern and eastern provinces. The LTTE were unsuccessful in their attempts to force a boycott of an election in which the Tamil, radical, Eeelam People's Revolutionary Front (EPRLF) and Eelam National Democratic Liberation Front (ENDLF) successfully participated, voter attendance being remarkably high.

A month later the presidential election followed. With President Jayewardene unable, under the provisions of the constitution, to seek a further term, Prime Minister Premadasa stood as the UNP candidate and was opposed by Sirimavo Bandaranaike, heading a seven-party alliance, which included the Sri Lanka Muslim Congress (SLMC). Opposition to the July 1987 Peace Accord was her principal rallying call. Initially she publicly pledged to abrogate the agreement and demand the withdrawal of the IPKF 'within 24 hours of being elected' but later moderated her stance. Prime Minister Premadasa, in contrast, called only for a 'renegotiation' of the Accord and a phased withdrawal of Indian troops, something that was already underway.

The election campaign was marred by disruptive JVP-induced violence and intimidation, which claimed between ten and 20 lives a day and prevented polling in a number of areas. Despite opposition claims of voting 'distortion', Premadasa emerged the victor. A member of the lowly Dhobi, laundrymen's, caste, he became Sri Lanka's first national leader since independence not to be drawn from the influential Goyigama élite. A crucial factor behind Premadasa's electoral victory had been the popular support generated by the programme of poverty alleviation and housing improvement that he had implemented during his ten years as Prime Minister. This programme he pledged to continue as President.

The 'state of emergency' imposed in May 1983 was briefly lifted in January 1989 as campaigning moved underway for National State Assembly elections. Despite the continuation of terrorist disruptive tactics, these elections were successfully held on schedule in February 1989, with the UNP securing a narrow parliamentary majority. The former finance minister, Dingiri Banda Wijetunge, was appointed Prime Minister a month later, retaining his departmental portfolio.

Both Wijetunge and President Premadasa pledged to work for national reconciliation, and, as part of this process, began formal round-table negotiations with LTTE leaders during May 1989.

Sri Lanka remains a member of the Commonwealth and non-aligned movement and joined the South Asian Association for Regional Co-operation (SAARC) in 1985. Its relations with India, which deteriorated during the early 1980s, as a result of the latter's alleged support for Tamil guerrillas, improved after the accession of Rajiv Gandhi as Indian Prime Minister, in 1984. They deteriorated once more in 1989, as a result of India's refusal to withdraw the IPKF.

TAIWAN

Republic of China (ROC)
Chung Hua Min Kuo

Capital: Taipei

Social and economic data
Area: 36,000 km^2
Population: 19.600m*
Pop density per km^2: 544*
Literacy rate: 89%
GDP: $59,149m*; per capita GDP: $3,017
Economy type: middle income
Labour force in agriculture: 28%

*1985

Ethnic composition
Ninety-eight per cent of the population are Han Chinese and 2 per cent aboriginal by descent. Eighty-five per cent are Taiwan-born and 15 per cent 'mainlanders'. The official language is Northern Chinese (Mandarin).

Religions
The predominant religion, with 3 million adherents, or 15 per cent of the total population, is Buddhism of the Mahayana and Theravada schools. There are also 2 million, or 10 per cent, adherents to Daoism, 300,000, or 2 per cent, Roman Catholics, 200,000, or 1 per cent, members of the Presbyterian Church in Taiwan, which was established in 1865, and 60,000 followers of Islam. The philosophy of Confucianism also has a wide following.

Political features
State type: emergent democracy
Date of state formation: 1949
Political structure: unitary
Executive: limited presidential
Assembly: one-chamber
Party structure: multi-party*
Human rights rating: 50%

*With restrictions

Local and regional government
The country has two special municipalities, Taipei and Kaohsiung, which are governed by centrally appointed KMT mayors of Taiwanese descent, although there have recently been proposals to replace them with directly elected mayors. In addition, there are five municipalities, Taichung, Keelung, Tainan, Chiai and Hsinchu, and 16 counties (*hsien*), each of which has its own elected local governing body. The task of deciding on the provincial budget and administrative policies and of overseeing the work of

appointed provincial governors has been delegated to a 77-member elected Provincial Assembly, 74 of whom are Taiwanese-born members of the KMT. This body works in conjunction with the central government.

Head of state

President Lee Teng-hui, since 1988.

Head of government

Prime Minister Lee Huan, since 1989.

Political leaders since 1970

1949–75 Chiang Kai-shek (KMT), 1975–88 Chiang Ching-kuo (KMT), 1988– Lee Teng-hui (KMT).

Political system

Taiwan operates under a constitution adopted in January 1947 by the Republic of China (ROC). It provides for a multi-layered, five-power system of government, combining both presidential and parliamentary executive features. At the apex of the political system is a powerful executive President, who is elected for a six-year term by a National Assembly (Kuo-Min Ta-Hui). The President serves as head of state and commander-in-chief of the armed forces and has the authority to promulgate laws.

The National Assembly, which convenes only once every six years, in addition to electing the President and Vice-President, has the power to amend the constitution. Its members were originally elected, in 1947, from constituencies in mainland China. These fell under communist Chinese control in 1949, making new elections impossible. The original elected members have thus retained their seats during the ensuing decades, being termed 'life members', while fresh elections have been held only for seats vacated by deceased members. The newcomers, who are termed 'supplementary' members, represent Taiwan-based, 'limited-term' seats and are subject to re-election every six years. Between 75 and 85 of such seats are normally contested. Originally, in 1947, the National Assembly had 3,330 members, of whom just under half moved to Taiwan in 1949. Natural attrition had, by 1988, reduced the number to around 920, of whom 106 comprised 'supplementary' members, representing 'government-controlled, Taiwan-situated, constituencies'. Twenty-five of the National Assembly's present members are in their nineties, 276 in their eighties and 459 in their seventies.

The President of the ROC works with an appointed, 20- to 25-member, cabinet, termed the Executive Yuan, which is headed by a Prime Minister and is responsible for policy formulation and executive administration. It is responsible to a single-chamber assembly, the Legislative Yuan (Li-Fa Yuan). The Legislative Yuan currently comprises 313 members, some of them presidential appointees, representing overseas Chinese and interest groups, but the majority, or about two-thirds of the total, are 'life members', representing former mainland seats. In 1947 the assembly comprised 933 members, of whom 525 fled from the mainland. It has since rapidly contracted, with the deaths of members. In an effort to rejuvenate the body, 70 'supplementary' seats have, on average, been subject to fresh elections at three-yearly intervals since 1972. However, despite these 'supplementary' elections, the Legislative Yuan, like the National Assembly, has become an ageing body, with, in 1988, 14 of its members nonagenarians and 105 octogenarians. The Legislative Yuan holds two sessions a year, of around eight months in duration, and is empowered to hear administrative reports presented by the Executive Yuan and amend government policy.

Three other bodies, the Control Yuan, the Judicial Yuan and the Examination Yuan also exist. They have, respectively, the tasks of investigating the work of the executive, interpreting the constitution and overseeing entrance examinations to public offices. All political bodies are dominated by members of the ruling Nationalist Party of China (Kuomintang), whose Central Standing Committee functions as the real controlling force in the ROC, performing a 'leading role' similar to communist parties in socialist states.

Political parties

The ruling Nationalist Party of China (KMT: Chung-kuo Kuo-min-tang or Kuomintang) was founded in November 1894 as the 'Hsing Chung Hui' by Dr Sun Yat-sen, who played a prominent role in the overthrow of China's Manchu regime in the 'Republican Revolution' of 1911. The party assumed the name Kuomintang (Guomindang in the mainland's *pinyin* transliteration) in October 1919 and was led by the Japanese-trained General Chiang Kai-shek, from 1925. Under Chiang's leadership the party, which had been moderately socialist in stance under Dr Sun, veered to the right and established close links with businessmen, gentry landlords and industrialists. It terminated the tactical, anti-warlord, alliance which it had maintained with the Chinese Communist Party (CPC) since the early 1920s, in a violent putsch in Shanghai in April 1927, and Chiang proceeded to establish control over much of China. In October 1928 he set up a new National Government. This Nationalist regime evolved in an authoritarian, quasi-fascist manner, acquiring a large, German-trained army, in an effort to expunge Mao Zedong's CPC guerrilla threat. In 1937, however, when the Japanese invaded China, the Nationalists were forced into hiding in the western province of Sichuan. Weakened by this enforced retreat, they proved ill-equipped to take on the strengthened CPC when a civil war for control of China began in 1946, after Japan's departure from the country.

The contemporary Taiwan-based KMT declares as its aim the implementation of the 'three principles of the people'. The first is the liberation of the Chinese mainland from communist control and the establishment of a 'democratic, prosperous and peaceful China', founded on a free-market economy, but with an equitable distribution of wealth. The second, the rejuvenation of the national culture. The third is to 'remain in the camp of democracy'.

Since 1924, the party has been organised on 'democratic centralist' lines similar to those of the Soviet Union's Communist Party. The KMT's supreme organ is the 1,209-delegate National Congress which meets for a week every five years, the most recent meeting being in July 1988, to ratify leadership decisions and 'elect' a Central Committee to undertake its work when it is not sitting. This Central Committee has 180 full members and 90 alternate, non-voting, members. The party is dominated by a 31-member

Central Standing Committee (CSC), headed by a chairman, assisted by a General Secretary, which controls appointments. Membership of the KMT was estimated at 2.4 million in 1988, constituting 12 per cent of the total population. Substantial numbers are Taiwanese, with political and professional advancement depending greatly on party membership.

The principal opposition party in Taiwan is the Democratic Progress Party (DPP), which was formed, illegally, in September 1986, to campaign for the lifting of martial law and to contest the December 1986 assembly elections. The DPP is the heir to an earlier, informal, non-party 'Tangwai' opposition grouping which had operated since the 1970s. Its leader, the American-educated and Taiwanese-born Yao Chia-wen, is currently on parole after having been imprisoned for seven years on charges of sedition at a human rights rally at Kaohsiung, in December 1979. The party advocates the establishment of direct trade, tourist and postal links with the Chinese mainland and 'self-determination' for Taiwan. In early 1988 it had a membership of around 10,000. In the December 1986 Legislative Yuan elections, the DPP won more than 20 per cent of the national vote. Since then, however, it has been weakened by internal, moderate versus radical, factional rivalries and by the formation of breakaway groups. The most notable of these is the Kungtang, or Workers of Labour Party, led by the Kaohsiung-based former DPP member, Wang Yi-hsiung. This splinter party adheres to a potentially popular, moderate, non-violent programme of social improvement.

Other recently formed opposition parties include the Democratic Liberal Party (DLP) and the China Freedom Party (CFP). The DLP was established in September 1987, and is led by Hung Chao-nan. It seeks to 'promote political democracy and economic liberty for the people of Taiwan'. The CFP was formed in 1987 and campaigns for the holding of free elections and the liberalisation of relations with the mainland. Two other parties date back to the pre-1949 period and still hold a number of seats in the National Assembly and Legislative Yuan, which they secured in the 1947 elections, and so are effectively tied to the KMT in a 'common front'. They are the Young China Party (YCP), which was formed in 1923, and is a small pro-KMT, and pro-unification, anti-communist grouping, and the China Democratic Socialist Party (CDSP) which dates from 1932.

Latest elections

The most recent National Assembly and Legislative Yuan elections were held in December 1986, with 84 of the former and 73 of the latter seats being contested. The KMT captured 68 and 59 seats respectively, based on a 69 per cent vote share; the newly formed DPP secured eleven Assembly and twelve Yuan seats, based on a 22 per cent vote share; independents captured four and two seats respectively; while the CDSP secured one National Assembly seat.

The most recent presidential election was held in March 1984, when Chiang Ching-kuo was re-elected for a second six-year term. On his death, in January 1988, Vice-President Lee Teng-hui, in accordance with constitutional provisions, automatically took over, as Vice-President Dr Yen Chia-kan had done between 1975 and 1978, to serve out the remaining 36 months of Chiang's term of office.

Political history

Taiwan, which lies 145 kilometres off the Chinese mainland, was originally peopled by aborigines of Malayan descent. It was later settled by Chinese from the sixth century AD onwards, first slowly and then, from the fourteenth century, at a rapid pace. The bulk of these immigrants were drawn from the adjacent mainland provinces of Guangdong and Fujian. Known as Formosa, or 'The Beautiful', the island was briefly occupied, and controlled by, first, the Spanish and Dutch (1624–61) and, then, a Chinese Ming General, Cheng Ch'engkung, during the mid and later seventeenth century, before being annexed by China's imperial rulers, the Manchus, in 1683. This encouraged further immigration from the mainland, so that by 1800 a permanent Chinese ethnic majority had been established. Taiwan was subsequently ceded to Japan in 1895, under the terms of the Treaty of Shimonoseki, which concluded the 1895 Sino-Japanese war, and was only regained, by the Nationalist (Kuomintang) regime, after Japan's surrender to the Allies, in August 1945.

In December 1949, Taiwan became the refuge for the right-wing Nationalist forces of Generalissimo Chiang Kai-shek, President of the Chinese Republic since 1928, which had been compelled to evacuate the mainland after their defeat at the hands of the communist troops of Mao Zedong. Chiang and his million or so Nationalist followers, although constituting a minority of only 15 per cent, proceeded, violently, to put down a Taiwanese rebellion in February 1947, and then dominated the island, maintaining an army of 600,000, in the hope of reconquering the mainland over which they still claimed sovereignty. They continued to be recognised as the legitimate government of China, under the designation 'Republic of China' (ROC), by the United States. The ROC leaders themselves viewed Taiwan as just one of their country's constituent 35 provinces. They also occupied China's United Nations General Assembly and Security Council seats until October 1971. Then, following a rapprochement between communist China and the USA, they were finally expelled and their seats taken over by the People's Republic (PRC).

During the Korean War (1950–53), Taiwan was protected by American naval forces, the country signing a mutual defence treaty with the United States in December 1954. Benefiting from this security, Taiwan enjoyed a period of rapid economic growth during the 1950s and 1960s, and emerged as an export-orientated, consumer-goods producer, acquiring the description of a newly industrialising country (NIC). In the process, Taiwan's socio-economic base was fundamentally moved away from its former dependence on agriculture towards the industrial and service sectors. Thus, while in 1950 60 per cent of the island's population had been engaged in agricultural activities and only 18 per cent in industrial, by 1986 the relative shares were 28 per cent and 42 per cent. This transformation was wrought, first, during the 1950s, by the institution of a radical, anti-gentry, 'land-to-the-tiller', land reform programme, which dramatically boosted agricultural output. Second, the change in the rural sector was accompanied by the launching of a determined state-guided programme of import substitution and export-led industrialisation. This was based on a succession of four-year economic plans, beginning in 1953, and substantial infrastructure and human resources investment. Low wages, a disciplined workforce and an expanding American market for the country's wares provided the means and stimulus for this transformation and, in response, the economy proceeded to expand at a 'miracle' rate of more than 8 per cent per annum throughout the 1950s, 1960s and 1970s. First producing textile goods, then electrical 'consumer durables' and then heavy machinery and petrochemicals, Taiwan now is very much involved in high-technology computer production. The country's per capita income, which had been below that of 'low income' mainland China in 1949, spectacularly leapfrogged into the higher ranges of the world's 'middle income' countries. Today it is the second wealthiest nation, of substantial size, after Japan, in Asia.

During these 'miracle' years, political change failed to match economic. Political power was monopolised by the Kuomintang (KMT) and armed forces, led by President Chiang Kai-shek, martial law being imposed and opposition activity outlawed. Constrained by its unification goals, an ossified political system was set up, no elections being held for assembly seats which had originally been secured in mainland constituency elections in 1947. During the 1970s, however, the Taiwanese government was forced to adjust to rapid external changes as the United States' administrations, under Richard Nixon (1969–74), Gerald Ford (1974–76) and Jimmy Carter (1977–80), adopted a new policy of *détente* towards communist China. This process gathered momentum after the death of Mao Zedong, in September 1976. It culminated in January 1979 in the full normalisation of Sino-American relations, the severing of American-Taiwanese diplomatic contacts and the annulment of America's 1954 Mutual Security Pact. Other Western nations followed suit during the 1970s and early 1980s, leaving, by 1988, only 22 countries with formal diplomatic links.

These far-reaching developments in the diplomatic sphere, coupled with changes within the ageing KMT, and the death of Chiang Kai-shek in April 1975, prompted a gradual review of Taiwanese policies, domestic and external. This re-appraisal was set in train by the KMT's pragmatic new leader, Chiang Ching-kuo. He was the son of Chiang Kai-shek and had been Prime Minister from 1972 to 1978, KMT chairman from 1975 to 1988, and state President from 1978 to 1988.

The outcome of the review was the adoption of a new programme of gradual democratisation and 'Taiwanisation'. Thus, in December 1972, elections were held for 53 'vacated seats' within the National Assembly and 52 in the Legislative Yuan. There was also an increasingly rapid induction of native Taiwanese into the ruling KMT. Elections for further National Assembly and Legislative Yuan 'supplementary' seats were held in 1975, 1980 and 1983. In these 'contests' the KMT won overwhelming victories over the independent 'Tangwai', 'outside the party', candidates. Then, in the December 1986 elections for 84 National Assembly and 73 Legislative Yuan seats, the participation of an opposition party was tolerated. This was the Democratic Progress Party (DPP), which had recently been illegally established by 135 dissident politicians, led by Chiang Peng-chien. The DPP captured 22 per cent of the popular vote and the KMT 69 per cent. Finally, in July 1987, martial law was lifted and replaced by a new national security law. Under the terms of this, and related laws, the operation of political parties other than the KMT was at last permitted, but subject to regulation and in conformity with constitutional precepts, most notably the forswearing of support for communism and Taiwanese independence.

Civilians were freed from the jurisdiction of military courts, press restrictions lifted, and demonstrations legalised. There was a resultant wave of protest marches by farmers, environmentalists and regime opponents in 1988.

The process of political liberalisation accelerated markedly during 1986 and 1987 as President Chiang Ching-kuo, afflicted by ailing health, sought both to pave the way for a stable succession and secure himself a favourable place in history. Chiang eventually died, in January 1988, and was succeeded, as both state President and KMT chairman, by Lee Teng-hui, the former mayor of Taipei, and the country's Vice-President since March 1984. Unusually, he was both Taiwanese-born and a devout Christian. The new President was one of a number of 'modernisers' who had been promoted by Chiang Ching-kuo, and formed a 'technocrat' faction within the KMT. Included in this group were KMT General Secretary Lee Huan, and head of the joint chiefs of staff, Hau Pei-tsun.

President Lee immediately set about accelerating the pace of political reform, as well as instituting a programme of economic liberalisation. In February 1988, the KMT's governing CSC approved a plan for drastically restructuring the country's legislature. Its key points were the phasing out, by 1992, through 'voluntary retirement' on substantial pensions, of between 150 and 200 'life term', mainland constituency members and the replacing of them with new members representing Taiwanese constituencies. Five months later, at the KMT's Thirteenth National Congress, held between 7 and 13 July, President Lee succeeded in packing the party's new Central Committee with 80 per cent of his own candidates and in removing ten 'old guard' conservative members from the CSC. Several days later, a major cabinet re-shuffle in the Executive Yuan was effected, five ministers being replaced, including those in charge of finance and economic affairs. A new clutch of Western-educated, Taiwan-born technocrats were moved in. These changes appeared to strengthen significantly the reformist wing within both the party and state machines. However, ranged against the 'Lee-Lee' modernising faction, there still existed a significant number of conservatives at both senior party and state levels. They included Prime Minister Yu Kuo-hwa, foreign minister Ding Mou-shih, and the late Chiang Kai-shek's nonagenarian widow, Soong May-ling.

In its external relations, the KMT government, despite decreasing international support for its cause since the early 1970s, has remained firm in its claims to legitimate sovereignty over mainland China. The United States, under the terms of the March 1979 Taiwan Relations Act, has continued to supply the country with military weapons, for 'defensive purposes', but in steadily diminishing quantities. Meanwhile, since the early 1980s, the new post-Mao leadership in mainland China has launched a succession of initiatives geared towards achieving re-unification in a federalist manner. Under these proposals Taiwan would officially become part of China, while retaining considerable autonomy as a 'special administrative region'. As such, it would maintain its own armed forces as well as a capitalist economic system. The model for this scheme, termed 'one country-two systems', has been the formula which has been accepted by Britain and Portugal for the transfer of sovereignty in their dependencies of Hong Kong and Macao, during the late 1990s.

However, between 1981 and 1987, the Taipei government met these PRC initiatives with its traditional response, the 'three noes': no contact, no negotiation and no compromise with the mainland regime. During the closing months of the Chiang Ching-kuo administration, however, a significant relaxation of this stance became apparent and human contacts between the two states were allowed to increase. This approach has been continued by President Lee. The fundamental problem for the KMT regime remains, however, that its personal goal of re-unification lacks support from the country's native Taiwanese majority who, it seems, would prefer 'self-determination' and the creation of an independent Taiwan.

THAILAND

Kingdom of Thailand
Prathet Thai

Capital: Bangkok

Social and economic data
Area: 514,000 km^2
Population: 52.438m*
Pop density per km^2: 102*
Literacy rate: 88%
GDP: $38,570m*; per capita GDP: $735
Economy type: low income
Labour force in agriculture: 66%

*1985

Ethnic composition
Seventy-five per cent of the population are of Thai ethnic stock and 14 per cent are Chinese, 33 per cent of them in Bangkok. Thai Malays constitute the next largest minority, followed by hill tribes. A substantial Cambodian (Khmer) refugee community also resides in the country in border camps. The official language is Thai, or Siamese, with English being used as a universal second language.

Religions
Ninety-five per cent of the population are Buddhists, 4 per cent are Muslims, predominantly ethnic Malays based in the south, while 0.5 per cent, or 0.28 million, are Christians, three-quarters of whom are Catholics. Theravada Buddhism is the state religion.

Political features
State type: emergent democracy
Date of state formation: 1350
Political structure: unitary
Executive: parliamentary*
Assembly: two-chamber
Party structure: multi-party
Human rights rating: 57%

*With special features: see Political system, below

Local and regional government

The country is divided into 70 provinces (*changwats*), headed by centrally appointed governors (*phuwaratchakan changwats*). Each province, in turn, is subdivided into 5–10 districts, each administered by a district officer (*nai amphoe*). Some 44,000 villages (*muban*) below are governed by elected chiefs (*phuyaiban*) who are removable by the district officer. The governor and provincial officials are advised by appointed provincial assemblies (*sapha changwats*). The Bangkok-Thonburi conurbation, in which 10 per cent of the nation's population lives, constitutes a separate municipality, governed by an elected mayor and municipal council.

Head of state

King Bhumibol Adulyadej, since 1946.

Head of government

Prime Minister Major General Chatichai Choonhavan, since 1988.

Political leaders since 1970

1963–73 General Thanom Kittikachorn (Military), 1973–75 Dr Sanya Dharmasakti Thammasak (Independent), 1975–75 Seni Pramoj (Democratic Party), 1975–76 Kukrit Pramoj (Social Action Party), 1976 Seni Pramroj (Democratic Party), 1976–77 Thanin Kraivichien (Independent), 1977–80 General Kriangsak Chomanan (Military), 1980–88 General Prem Tinsulanonda (Independent), 1988– Major General Chatichai Choonhavan (Thai Nation Party).

Political system

Under the constitution of December 1978, which superseded earlier documents of 1932, 1946, 1947, 1949, 1952, 1959, 1968, 1971, 1974, 1976 and 1977, Thailand is ruled by an hereditary constitutional monarch, working with an appointed and elected two-chamber National Assembly. The monarch, who remains a respected and revered figure and retains significant political power, acts as both head of state and head of the armed forces. He appoints a Prime Minister, on the advice of the National Assembly, selecting the person best able to secure majority support. The King is advised by an appointed twelve-member Privy Council and has the authority to dissolve the National Assembly and call new elections. In addition, acting on the advice of the Prime Minister, he may veto bills, with a two-thirds National Assembly majority being required for this act to be overturned.

The upper house of the National Assembly, the Senate (Wuthisapha), comprises 268 members who are appointed for a six-year term by the King on the recommendation of the Prime Minister. Senators must not be members of any political party and must be at least 35 years of age. In practice, the vast majority, 80 per cent in 1988, have been drawn from the armed forces and the police, giving these institutions an effective 'blocking position' in the Thai political system.

The lower house, the House of Representatives (Saphaphutan), comprises 357 members who are elected from single-member constituencies by universal adult suffrage for four-year terms. The chamber is subject to dissolution within this period. Representatives must be members of a political party and at least 25 years old.

The National Assembly debates and approves bills, joint meetings of the Senate and the House being required for the passage of money bills, important legislation and no-confidence motions. Overall, however, the legislature has restricted powers *vis-à-vis* the executive.

The Prime Minister (Kayoke Rathamontri) is appointed by the King, and a selected 25- to 30-member cabinet, called the Council of Ministers, constitutes the country's political executive. It is responsible for both policy formulation and day-to-day administration. Cabinet ministers may speak at National Assembly meetings, but, as in the French system of government, may not vote and do not need to be popularly elected. In addition, the Prime Minister and cabinet ministers may not be serving military officers or government employees. The Prime Minister also heads the National Economic Development Board, the National Security Council and the National Research Council and is served by a special policy-formulating advisory board, comprising academics and specialists. He enjoys extensive emergency powers, making him the most influential figure in the Thai political system. The strength of his influence is closely followed, however, by that of the army leadership. The Prime Minister is invariably a retired member of the military himself and it is in that area that effective political power ultimately lies. The current commander-in-chief, General Chaovalit Yongchaiyut, is a particularly influential figure.

Political parties

Almost 20 political parties currently function. The most important four, which have formed the hub of the ruling coalition since the early 1980s, are the Democratic Party (Prachatipat), the Thai Nation (Chart Thai), the Social Action Party (Kij Sangkhom) and the Citizens' Party (Rassadorn).

The Democratic Party was established in 1946 and is a moderate, conservative, pro-monarchist grouping, led by Bhichai Rattakul. It is the country's oldest legal political party and enjoys strong support in southern provinces. The Thai Nation was formed in 1974. It is a right-wing, pro-business party, dominated by the military, and led by Prime Minister Chatichai Choonhavan. It has a firm popular base in central and north-eastern provinces. The Social Action Party, also dates from 1974 and is a moderate, conservative grouping, led by Siddhi Savetsila. The Citizens' Party was formed in 1986 and is led by General Tienchai Sirisamphan. It is also conservative in its outlook.

Other members of the current coalition are the United Democratic Party (Saha Pracha Tippatai), which is a business-backed group, led by Colonel Phol Rerngprasertvit, and was formed in 1986, and the Muan Chon (Mass) Party, led by Police Captain Chalerm Yubamrung.

Other important parties are the United Thai Party (Ruam Thai), established in 1986 and led by the former agriculture minister, Narong Wongwan; the Thai Citizens' Party (Prachakorn Thai), a far-right, Bangkok-based monarchist body led by Samak Sundaravej, and dating from 1979; the Community Action Party (Kij Prachakorn), a liberal democratic body led by Boonchu Rojanastien, and founded in 1986; the Righteous Force (Palang Dharma), an austere anti-corruption, Buddhist party led by the popular Governor of Bangkok, Major-General Chamlong Srimuang, and established as recently as 1988; the anti-Prem Thai People's Party (Puangchon Chao Thai), led by Major-General Ravi Wanpen; and the

Prachachon (People) Party, led by Khunying Sasima Siwikon. This last named group was formed in 1988 by dissident members of the Democratic Party, the 'January 10 Group'. The country's oldest political party, the Communist Party of Thailand (CPT), which dates from 1925, is currently illegal.

Thailand's political parties are loosely constructed, patronage-linked coalitions. Once elected, party members are substantially independent, each enjoying his own firm local base. Changes of party affiliation, in response to inducements, are frequent. Only the Democratic Party, which has more than 80 branches, and the Social Action Party, have local party organisations.

Latest elections

In the most recent House of Representatives elections, which were held in July 1988, the results were as follows:

	Seats	*% Votes*
Thai Nation	87	24
Social Action Party	54	15
Democratic Party	48	13
United Thai Party	35	10
Thai Citizens' Party	31	9
Rassadorn	21	6
Prachachon	19	5
Thai People's Party	17	5
Righteous Force	14	4
United Democratic Party	5	1
Other parties	26	7

Three thousand, six hundred and six candidates from 16 parties contested the election. During the campaign 3 million baht, or about $120 million, was spent on vote-buying and numerous small, state-funded, local projects were, as usual, promised by aspirants in a 'pork-barrel' fashion. It was estimated by the Siam Commercial Bank that the money distributed by candidates would boost national spending power and GDP by 0.5 per cent.

Political history

Thailand supported a Bronze Age civilisation as early as 4000 BC. Control over the country was later contested territorially by Malay, Khmer, Tai and Mon tribes, before a unified Thai nation, termed Siam, was eventually founded in 1350. In 1826 and 1855 treaties of friendship and trade established Britain as the paramount power in the region and opened Siam to foreign commerce. The country was never formally colonised, however, being established instead as a neutral and independent buffer kingdom between British Burma and French Indochina, by the Anglo-French diplomatic agreements of 1896 and 1904.

After the First World War, a movement for national renaissance developed, which culminated, in 1932, in a coup against the absolute ruler, King Prajadhipok, and the establishment of a constitutional monarchy and an elected, representative system of government. Political parties developed in the new parliament and the name of Muang Thai, 'Land of the

Free', was adopted in 1939. During the Second World War Thailand was occupied by the Japanese between 1941 and 1945. The Thai government collaborated, although a guerrilla resistance movement also operated. A period of instability followed the Japanese withdrawal and King Ananda Mahidol was assassinated, in 1946, before the army seized power in a coup in 1947, led by Field Marshal Pibul Songgram.

The army retained control during the next two decades, ruling through a military junta whose leadership was periodically changed by a series of bloodless coups. Field Marshal Pibul Songgram dominated between 1947 and 1957, Field Marshal Sarit Thanarat between 1957 and 1963 and General Thanom Kittikachorn between 1963 and 1973. The monarch, in the person of King Bhumibol Adulyadej, operated as a figurehead ruler and experiments with elected assemblies were undertaken between 1957 and 1958, and 1968 and 1971. During this era of junta rule, Thailand allied itself with the United States and encountered serious communist guerrilla insurgency along its borders with Laos, Cambodia and Malaysia.

Despite achievements in the economic sphere, the junta was overthrown, after violent student riots in October 1973. A democratic constitution was adopted in October 1974, establishing a constitutional monarchy and a National Assembly, to which free elections were held in 1975 and 1976. A series of coalition governments followed, but they lacked stability and, following further student demonstrations, the military assumed power again in 1976–77, annulling the 1974 constitution. Initially, the Army Supreme Commander General Kriangsak Chomanan held power between 1977 and 1980 and promulgated a new constitution in December 1978. This strengthened the position of the military and established a mixed civilian-military form of of government, under the monarch's direction. However, General Kriangsak was forced to give way to General Prem Tinsulanonda, in March 1980. He formally relinquished his army office and headed a series of civilian coalition governments which were formed after the parliamentary elections of April 1983 and July 1986.

Coups, led by junior military officers, were attempted in April 1981 and September 1985, the latter involving General Kriangsak. They were easily crushed, however, by Prime Minister Prem, who governed in a cautious apolitical manner, retaining the confidence of the army leadership, state bureaucracy, business community and monarchy. Under Prem's stewardship, the country achieved a rapid rate of economic growth, of more than 9 per cent per annum, and began the process of establishing Thailand as an export-orientated newly industrialising country (NIC). During the spring of 1988, following the introduction of legislation, allegedly at the United States government's behest, to tighten up copyright regulations, divisions began to widen within the ruling four-party coalition. This prompted Prem, who was also concerned that a personal impropriety might be publicised in a forthcoming 'no-confidence' motion, to call, in April, for a dissolution of parliament. This request was acceded to by King Adulyadej.

Following the subsequent general election, in July 1988, a new five-party ruling coalition, consisting of the Thai Nation, Democratic, Social Action, Rassadorn and United Democratic parties, was constructed, which, once again, asked Prem to come into parliament and assume its leadership. Prem, however, surprisingly declined this offer on 'personal grounds'.

Instead, power passed to the former Deputy Prime Minister, Chatichai Choonhavan, leader of the Chart Thai Party. He was expected to pursue a similar policy course to that followed by Prem. The Muan Chon Party entered the ruling coalition as its sixth member.

Thailand's external relations during the past two decades have been dominated by the continuing civil war in neighbouring Cambodia and Laos, which has resulted in the flight of more than 500,000 refugees to Thailand since 1975 and provided justification for continued quasi-military rule and the maintenance of martial law. In addition, this border danger has encouraged a tightening of Thailand's relations with its ASEAN allies, who have, during recent years, jointly supported the Cambodian guerrilla movement and have sought a thawing in relations with communist China.

VIETNAM

Socialist Republic of Vietnam (SRV)
Cong Hoa Xa Hoi Chu Nghia Viet Nam

Capital: Hanoi

Social and economic data
Area: 329,600 km^2
Population: 62.000m*
Pop density per km^2: 188*
Literacy rate: 84%
GDP: $9,000m*†; per capita GDP: $145
Economy type: low income
Labour force in agriculture: 62%

*1985
†A third of GDP comprises economic and military aid provided by the Soviet Union

Ethnic composition
Eighty-eight per cent of the population are Viet, also known as Kinh, and are imbued with a strong sense of national identity; 2 per cent are Chinese, or Hoa, being predominantly based in South Vietnam and engaged in commercial activities; 2 per cent are Khmer; the remaining 8 per cent belong to more than 50 minority nationalities, the most important of which are the Hmong, Meo, Muong, Nung, Tay, Thai and Tho, who live mainly along the border with China, in the North, and are tribal groups. Vietnamese (Quoc-Ngu) is the main language.

Religions
The principal religion is Buddhism, of the Mahayana, 'Greater Wheel', variety, in the North and the Theravada, 'Lesser Wheel', sect in the South, with the cult of ancestor worship in clan temples being a conspicuous element in it. Confucianism and Daoism are also important related religions. Cadaoism, a manufactured, eclectic religion, which was developed in the 1920s, claims 2 million adherents, predominantly in the Mekong delta, while Hoa Hoa, a Buddhist-orientated, anti-communist sect,

founded in 1939, used to have 1.5 million members, chiefly in the western Mekong delta, in South Vietnam. Roman Catholicism claims 2 million followers and Protestant denominations 180,000. Under the constitution of 1980 complete freedom of worship has been guaranteed. In practice, however, restrictions are periodically enforced, involving the 're-education' of anti-regime Buddhist and Christian groups.

Political features
State type: communist
Date of state formation: 1954/1976
Political structure: unitary
Executive: communist
Assembly: one-chamber
Party structure: one-party*
Human rights rating: 25%

*Effectively

Local and regional government
The country is divided into 36 provinces, three municipalities, Hanoi, Haiphong and Ho Chi Minh City, and one special zone, Vung Tau-Con Dao, all directly under the control of the central authority. There are also 443 districts and town wards and 9,504 rural communes and street blocks. People's Councils operate and are elected at four-yearly intervals, in multi-candidate contests, in the case of the provinces, and every two years at other levels. The People's Councils elect People's Committees as their executive organs, each unit being responsible and accountable to the body immediately above, in accordance with the precept of 'democratic centralism'. Their work is supervised by the Communist Party committee at the same level.

Head of state
President Vo Chi Cong, since 1987.

Head of government
Prime Minister Do Muoi, since 1988.

Political leaders since 1970
1965–75 Lieutenant General Nguyen Van Thieu,* 1969–75 Le Duan (Lao Dong),† 1975–86 Le Duan (CPV),‡ 1986–86 Truong Chinh (CPV),‡ 1986– Nguyen Van Linh (CPV).‡

*South Vietnam leader
†North Vietnam (DRV) leader
‡Communist Party leaders

Political system
Vietnam, excluding the American client regime in the South, has had three constitutions since the Second World War. The first, which was adopted in November 1946, was a moderate, non-socialist 'united front' document, drawing significantly from both the United States and French systems, and providing for 'the transformation of the country on a democratic basis'. Its

replacement, which was adopted in December 1959, was unashamedly socialist, giving pride of place to central planning and collectivisation and describing the state as 'a people's democracy, advancing step by step to socialism'. The third, and most recent, constitution was adopted in December 1980 and is a 147-article document. Applying to the merged territories of both the North and South, it describes the country as in a 'period of transition to socialism on the national scale', with the 'socialisation of production' yet to fully be attained in the South. It borrows much from the Soviet Union's 1977 'Brezhnev constitution', explicitly prescribing, in Article 4, a 'leading' and 'vanguard' role to the ruling Communist Party of Vietnam (CPV).

Under the current constitution of 1980, the highest state authority and sole legislative chamber is the National Assembly (Quoc Hoi), a body which is composed of 496 members directly elected every five years by universal adult suffrage in 93 multi-member constituencies. Electors choose from a list of candidates selected by the Fatherland Front and its affiliated organisation, with an element of choice being theoretically available, there being more candidates than seats. To be elected a candidate must secure 50 per cent of the vote, a second contest being held if this not achieved. In practice, however, those placed towards the top of the list are uniformly elected, no run-off races being necessary.

The National Assembly formally has the authority to decide on 'fundamental questions' of domestic and foreign policy and has the task of adopting the economic plan and state budget. It meets, however, only twice a year in short, week-long, sessions and devolves its functions to a smaller, permanent, 15-member Council of State, which it 'elects' and which functions as both a 'substitute parliament' and collective presidency. The chairman, or President, of this body acts as the formal head of state, representing the country in domestic and foreign affairs. In addition, he presides over the National Defence Council and is often also commander in chief of the armed forces.

Day-to-day government is carried out by the Council of Ministers (COM), a 38-member body, headed by a chairman, or Prime Minister. It is 'elected' by and responsible to the National Assembly and, in its absence, the Council of State. Twenty-five of the COM's members are departmental ministers, five are chairmen of state commissions and there are five vice-chairmen, two of whom hold ministerial portfolios. It has overall jurisdiction over the management of the SRV's domestic and external affairs; frames the budget, economic plan and state laws and decrees; and supervises the work of both the central bureaucracy and local government bodies.

The dominating force in Vietnam, and sole permitted party, is the CPV, which has been headed since 1986 by General Secretary Nguyen Van Linh. The party controls the Vietnam Fatherland Front mass organisation, which puts up candidates in state election contests. Leading members of the CPV also occupy key positions in the state hierarchy. In May 1988, for example, the CPV's governing Politburo comprised twelve full and one non-voting 'alternate' member. One of these was chairman of the Council of State, Vo Chi Cong, while a further five held key positions in the COM, including those of chairman, Vo Van Kiet, interior minister, Major-General Mai Chi Tho, foreign minister, Nguyen Co Thach, and defence minister, General Le Duc Anh.

Political parties

The ruling Communist Party of Vietnam (CPV: Dang Cong san Viet-Nam) was founded in February 1930 through the union, under Comintern instructions, of three small existing communist groups, the most important of which was the Vietnamese Revolutionary Youth League, which was established in 1925. Initally designated the Indochinese Communist Party (ICP), it was led by the Paris- and Moscow-trained Ho Chi Minh and had an initial membership of 211, backed by 2,000 active collaborators, predominantly drawn from the ranks of the intelligentsia. In June 1941 the party, which now had a formal membership of 2,000 and was supported by 40,000 followers, adopted a new strategy of guerrilla resistance, against Japanese occupation, following the example set by Mao Zedong in China. A 'united front' organisation, the Viet Minh, was established for this purpose. By such means the party was swept to power in September 1945, although a further nine years of warfare ensued until its control, in the North, was recognised. In the meantime, following the separation of the Laotian and Cambodian sections, the party adopted a new name, the Lao Dong (Workers') Party, in February 1951, and became purely Vietnam-based. In December 1976, following the successful unification of North and South, the present designation of CPV was adopted.

The CPV is organised hierarchically on 'democratic centralist' lines. At the base there are local party cells (*chi bo*), which are established in factories, co-operatives, villages, wards and army units, and which have 3–10 members each. Above, there are party organisations, committees 'elected' by congresses, at the district, provincial and municipal levels, with, at the apex, a national Party Congress, convened quinquennially. The Party Congress is, theoretically, the supreme authority within the CPV. It meets for a week and has the task of approving the party programme and 'electing' a Central Committee (CC) to assume its powers in its absence. The most recent, the sixth, Party Congress, which was held in December 1986, the previous Congresses having been in 1935, 1951, 1960, 1976 and 1982, 'elected' a CC comprising 124 full and 40 non-voting, 'alternate' members. The CC, which meets twice a year, in turn, 'elects' a Politburo, headed by a General Secretary, and a 13-member Secretariat. These function as the real controlling bodies in the party, and state, structures, with a system of consensual, though factionalised, collective leadership operating. This leadership is of a gerontocratic nature, reflecting the continuing influence of Confucian political notions.

Membership of the CPV currently stands at 1.8 million, or 2.9 per cent of the total population, which is a low proportion by comparative communist state standards. Membership surged from a figure of barely 5,000 in 1945 to 760,000 in 1951, before falling during the 1950s, as stricter entry criteria were applied. Thereafter, the total climbed relatively slowly to 1.1 million in 1970 and 1.5 million in 1976. Reliable data on the party's social composition are lacking. However, in general, it appears that the bulk are drawn from peasant and white-collar backgrounds, the proportion who are described as 'blue-collar workers' constituting less than 10 per cent of the total.

Two other parties, the trader- and intelligentsia-orientated Democratic Party (Dang Dan Chu) and Socialist Party (Dang Xa Hoi), which were formed in 1944 and 1946, were allowed to operate as non-competing organisations, before eventually folding in October 1988. They participated in the Vietnam Fatherland Front, a CPV-dominated mass organisation, which was established in North Vietnam in 1955 as a mobilising body and successor to the League for National Union of Vietnam (Lien Viet), which itself had, in 1946, grown out of the Viet Minh. In January 1977 the Fatherland Front absorbed the South Vietnam-based National Liberation Front and the Alliance of National Democratic and Peace Forces.

Latest elections

The most recent National Assembly elections were held in April 1987, with 829 Vietnam Fatherland Front-approved candidates, who were selected at CPV-organised public meetings, contesting the 496 available seats. Twenty-one per cent of those successfully elected were described as 'collective peasants' by background, 18 per cent as 'workers', 25 per cent as 'intellectuals', 20 per cent as 'cadres', 10 per cent as 'soldiers', 4 per cent as 'handicraft and co-operative workers' and 2 per cent as 'democratic notables and religious groups'. Eighteen per cent were female and 14 per cent were from ethnic minorities. Turnout was reported as 98 per cent.

Political history

The Vietnamese are descended from Mongoloid nomads who settled in the Red River delta region in the north more than 2,000 years ago. The region came under Chinese control from the late second century BC, directly between 111 BC and AD 938, and indirectly thereafter. In south Vietnam, the Mekong delta region, however, an independent Indianised kingdom (the Fu-nan) held sway between the first and sixth centuries AD. From the mid-tenth century Vietnam enjoyed substantial independence, in the fifteenth century a united, north and south, kingdom being established. This disintegrated during the seventeenth and eighteenth centuries, and several small regionally based independent kingdoms took its place, but it was temporarily re-established in the early nineteenth century by Emperor Nguyen Anh.

The country, which had been exposed to European, initially Portuguese, commercial influence since the sixteenth century, was conquered by France between 1858 and 1884 and divided into the protectorates of Tonkin (North Vietnam) and Annam (South-central Vietnam) which, together with Laos and Cambodia, which embraced Cochin China, the southernmost tip of Vietnam, formed the French Indochinese Union. The Vietnamese protectorates were unified administratively in 1887, with a single governor-generalship being created, thus improving physical north-south links.

During the colonial period, a French expatriate-run plantation economy, based mainly on rubber and rice, was established in South Vietnam, drawing in press-ganged, migrant labourers from the densely populated and heavily taxed north and centre. This dislocated existing social patterns and bred an impoverished and embittered peasantry. During the Second World War, the country was occupied by Japan between 1940 and 1945, although a pro-Vichy French administration remained in place until March 1945. Then the Emperor of Annam, Bao Dai, was appointed as a figurehead ruler. In opposition to this regime, the Viet Minh (Independence) League was formed by the Indochinese Communist Party (ICP) leader, Ho Chi

Minh. It proceeded to wage a determined rural-based guerrilla war, which, during a period of severe economic difficulties, won considerable popular backing. The Viet Minh established a chain of rural enclaves, or 'base areas', within the Japanese-occupied territory, steadily gaining in strength. Finally, in August–September 1945, with famine stalking the country, and claiming the lives of 2 million, and with the Japanese forces in disarray, it successfully mobilised the population in a revolutionary uprising which swept away the Bao Dai puppet regime and established a new Democratic Republic of Vietnam (DRV), with Ho Chi Minh as President, and a communist-dominated government in control.

France refused to recognise the new republic and, re-establishing control in the Saigon area, attempted to re-conquer the country in the Indo-China War of 1946–54. The French set up a non-communist state in the South in 1949, but, after their defeat at Dien Bien Phu, in May 1954, agreed, in the Geneva Accords of July 1954, to a cease-fire and the partitioning of the country along the 17th parallel of latitude. Ho Chi Minh was recognised as state President and Communist Party chairman in the communist-controlled DRV in the North, which had its capital at Hanoi, while Ngo Dinh Diem, the former premier to Bao Dai, headed the pro-Western and anti-communist regime in the South, which was termed the Republic of Vietnam (ROV), and had its capital at Saigon.

The Diem regime, and its repressive military successors, were opposed by former members of the Viet Minh, who became known as the Viet Cong, and then, from December 1960, the National Liberation Front. The two sides became engaged in guerrilla warfare, the National Liberation Front being supplied with military aid by North Vietnam and China, and the Diem regime by the United States. After the Tonkin Gulf incident, in August 1964, when North Vietnamese torpedo boats allegedly attacked two American destroyers, the United States became directly involved militarily in what was to be called the Vietnam War. Meanwhile, Diem had been overthrown, in November 1963, in a coup led by Lieutenant-General Nguyen Van Thieu who, from June 1965, emerged as the nation's new 'strongman'.

Between 1964 and 1968 the scale of America's military involvement escalated. Major bombing campaigns were waged in the North and US troop strength was built up to a peak of 545,000. From 1969, however, as a result of mounting casualties and domestic opposition, including, and most importantly, opposition from Congress, the United States began to withdraw its forces gradually and to sue for peace. A cease-fire agreement was signed in Paris in January 1973, but was breached by the North Vietnamese, who proceeded to move southwards, surrounding and capturing Saigon, which they renamed Ho Chi Minh City, in April 1975.

A new Socialist Republic of Vietnam was proclaimed, in July 1976, and a programme to integrate the more affluent, capitalist South launched. Land reform and collectivisation had already been carried out in the North, as had the introduction of a central planning system and the launching of a heavy industrialisation drive.

The new republic was to encounter considerable problems. The economy was in ruins, more than 2 million people having been killed and 4 million maimed during the struggles of the preceding two decades. Fifty-seven per cent of the population had been made homeless, and 70 per cent of the country's industrial capacity had been destroyed by American bombing. Also, the new communist administration faced opposition from the intelligentsia, many of whom were now imprisoned, and from rural groups, who refused to co-operate in the drive to collectivise southern agriculture.

In December 1978 Vietnam was at war again, toppling the pro-Chinese Khmer Rouge government in Cambodia led by the brutal Pol Pot, which it alleged was showing expansionary ambitions, and installing a puppet administration led by Heng Samrin. A year later, following accusations of the maltreatment of ethnic Chinese living in Vietnam, China mounted a brief, but largely unsuccessful, punitive invasion of North Vietnam, between 17 February and 16 March 1979. These actions, coupled with the contemporary campaigns against private businesses in the South, induced the flight of an estimated 700,000 Chinese and middle-class Vietnamese from the country in 1978–79. Many of them left by sea, and became known, internationally, as the 'boat people'.

In addition, economic and diplomatic relations were severed with China, its former close ally, and Vietnam moved more closely into the Soviet orbit. It was admitted into the CMEA (Comecon) in June 1978 and signed a Treaty of Friendship and Co-operation in November 1978.

Between 1976 and 1985, despite the receipt of substantial economic aid from the Eastern Bloc, planned growth targets were not attained. This forced policy adjustments, involving the extension of material incentives and the decentralisation of decision-taking, in 1979 and 1985. In July 1986 the death was announced of Le Duan, the CPV's, and thus the country's, effective leader since September 1969, when Ho Chi Minh died. Then, at the December 1986, sixth CPV Congress, several of the prominent, septuagenarian and octogenarian, 'old guard' leaders retired. They included Prime Minister Pham Van Dong, President Truong Chinh and senior Politburo member Le Duc Tho.

These significant departures were followed by important policy changes under the direction of the party's pragmatic new leader, Nguyen Van Linh. They were termed 'renovation' , or *doi moi,* and included permitting the private marketing of agricultural produce and the establishment of private businesses; a partial dismantling of agricultural co-operatives; and the encouragement of foreign 'inward investment' in joint ventures. The measures were to have most success in the more entrepreneurial, and export-orientated, south. Liberalisation was also extended to the political sphere during 1987–88, when more than 10,000 political prisoners, including former high-ranking members of the pre-1976 ROV government, were released from 're-education'. In the diplomatic sphere plans were announced, after some Soviet prodding, for the full withdrawal of the country's 140,000 troops from Cambodia, by October 1989. The process was begun in June 1988 with a partial withdrawal.

However, the election, by the National Assembly, of the traditionalist northerner, Do Muoi, as Prime Minister, in June 1988, in preference, by a 60 per cent to 40 per cent margin, to the reformist southerner, Vo Van Kiet, suggested that conservative forces, who were grouped around the state President, Vo Chi Cong, remained significant.

In terms of population, Vietnam is today the third largest communist power in the world. In addition, it exerts *de facto* control, in a semi-colonial fashion, over both neighbouring Laos, which is bound to it by a 20-year

Treaty of Friendship and Co-operation, signed in July 1977, and Cambodia. These countries have combined populations of 11.4 million. As a result of these external commitments, however, and the continuing border threat posed by China, more than a third of the annual state expenditure has had to be directed to the defence sector. Vietnam's armed forces currently total 1.2 million and this resource transfer has held back the pace of economic development. Self-sufficiency in food was attained in 1983, but since 1985 population growth, which currently stands at the high figure of 2.1 per cent per annum, has outstripped food supply, leading, in 1988, to runaway inflation, at an annual rate of more than 1,000 per cent. All this led to a balance of payments crisis, severe famine and mounting urban unemployment, before a recovery began in 1989.

Pacific Ocean
PHILIPPINES
Mariana Islands
Marshall Islands
Guam Is
Caroline Islands
KIRIBATI
Equator
NAURU
PAPUA NEW GUINEA
INDONESIA
SOLOMON ISLANDS
TUVALU
W SAMOA
VANUATU
FIJI
New Caledonia
TONGA
Tropic of Capricorn
AUSTRALIA
NEW ZEALAND
Tasmania
Pacific Ocean
Scale 1:60 000 000
0
500
1000
1500
2000 Km

OCEANIA

The region we have called Oceania occupies a total land area of nearly nine million square kilometres, but, as its name implies, the total land-sea coverage is considerably greater and extends from 47 degrees South, at the foot of New Zealand, to 21 degrees North, at the top of the Philippines. The southern part enjoys a cool, temperate climate while the central and northern areas are sub-tropical or tropical. Above all, it is a region of water and islands. Some of the islands are small and uninhabited, others are large, and the biggest of all, Australia, is twice the size of India and large enough to be regarded as a continent. The number of islands defies comprehension; in the Philippines alone, for example, there are more than 7,000.

Within the region are twelve sovereign states, the largest in areal size being Australia and the largest in population, the Philippines. Oceania is very much a region of contrasts. For example Australia has a population density of three people per square kilometre, while tiny Nauru's is 381. Many countries are still undeveloped, or only partly developed, while others have well established secondary and tertiary industries and sophisticated infrastructures. Eight of the twelve nations within Oceania have low per capita GDPs, whereas those of Australia, Nauru and New Zealand are high.

Until comparatively recently much of the region was one of the most isolated, and inaccessible, parts of the world. The nearest neighbour to Nauru, for example, is Kiribati, over 300 kilometres away. Before the Second World War the journey from Europe to Australia was, for most people, a matter of weeks, rather than days. Today it can be accomplished, by scheduled airlines, in hours. The same can be said of most other parts of the region. The earlier isolation is now being removed, not just for a wealthy minority, but for an increasing number of people of comparatively modest incomes. All this has meant not only that Europeans and Americans are wanting, and getting, to know more about the region but that the inhabitants of Oceania are becoming less inward-looking themselves.

Despite many other differences, most of the twelve states in the region share certain common political features. They generally display high levels of representative government. Nine are established liberal democracies, two we have defined as emergent democracies and only one, Tonga, does not have a pluralist political system. Eight have parliamentary executives, on the British model, and three have limited presidential executives, on the lines of that in the United States. Tonga, with its virtually unique system of hereditary, paternalistic monarchs, is, again, the exception to the rule. Even their voting methods show a high degree of uniformity, nine of the twelve employing the simple plurality system and only three adopting a majoritarian one.

This comparative uniformity in political processes can be largely explained by the historical backgrounds of the twelve nations. Eleven of them were, at one time or another, under British control and ten of them are still active members of the Commonwealth. The one, 'non-British', exception, the Philippines, was a United States possession for nearly 50 years, until it achieved full independence in 1946. The links between the

United Kingdom and the other Commonwealth countries in the region, and those between the Philippines and the United States, are still strong, but not nearly as strong as they were in earlier decades. Britain's membership of the European Community has done much to force countries such as Australia and New Zealand to realign their attitudes and establish closer links with their neighbours and with the dominant economic force lying on the region's periphery, Japan.

The United States, in the nineteenth century and the early part of the present century, attracted the description of the 'New World'. Today that epithet could more appropriately be applied to parts of Oceania, and particularly Australia and New Zealand. Australia is no longer regarded as a cultural backwater, but rather a leader in the arts of literature, drama, music and film-making. Although much of its interior will probably remain undeveloped for many years to come, the potential for development is undoubtedly there. Many of the smaller Oceanic countries will be handicapped by geographical factors but, as they work together more in joint endeavours, they too have the capacities to improve their circumstances.

A final point should be made. Oceania, in the form we have defined it, is a somewhat artificial entity and its proximity to the fast growing economies in parts of neighbouring Asia should not be forgotten. If we include Japan, China, Taiwan, the Koreas, Thailand, Malaysia and Hong Kong in our calculations, then we are looking at a highly dynamic, and potentially very important, part of the world.

Table 65

OCEANIA

Political Data

State	*Date of Formation*	*Political Structure*	*State Type*	*Executive*	*Assembly No of Chambers*	*Party System*	*Voting System*
Australia	1901	Federal	Lib Dem	Parliament	Two	Two	AV
Fiji	1970	Unitary	Emgt Dem	Parliament	Two	Multi	SP
Kiribati	1979	Unitary	Lib Dem	Lim Pres	One	Two	SB
Nauru	1968	Unitary	Lib Dem	Lim Pres	One	Two	SP
New Zealand	1853/1947	Unitary	Lib Dem	Parliament	One	Two	SP
Papua NG	1975	Unitary	Lib Dem	Parliament	One	Multi	SP
Philippines	1946	Unitary	Emgt Dem	Lim Pres	Two	Multi	SP
Solomon Islands	1978	Unitary	Lib Dem	Parliament	One	Multi	SP
Tonga	1970	Unitary	Absolutist	Absolute	One	None	SP
Tuvalu	1978	Unitary	Lib Dem	Parliament	One	None	SP
Vanuatu	1980	Unitary	Lib Dem	Parliament	One	Multi	SB
Western Samoa	1962	Unitary	Lib Dem	Parliament	One	Three	SP

Social and Economic Data

State	*Area (km²)*	*Population (m) (1985)*	*Population Density (per km²)*	*Literacy Rate (%)*	*Income Type*	*Human Rights Rating (%)*
Australia	7,686,850	15.763	3	99	High	94
Fiji	18,330	0.715	39	79	Middle	N/A
Kiribati	680	0.062	91	90	Low	N/A

Table 65—Oceania (contd.)

		Social and Economic Data				
State	*Area (km²)*	*Population (m) (1985)*	*Population Density (per km²)*	*Literacy Rate (%)*	*Income Type*	*Human Rights Rating (%)*
Nauru	21	0.008	381	99	High	N/A
New Zealand	269,060	3.300	12	100	High	98
Papua NG	462,840	3.395	7	32	Low	91
Philippines	300,000	58.100	194	83	Low	86
Solomon Islands	29,790	0.283	9	54	Low	N/A
Tonga	751	0.105	140	99	Low	N/A
Tuvalu	26	0.009	330	95	Low	N/A
Vanuatu	14,760	0.136	9	53	Low	N/A
Western Samoa	2,840	0.180	63	98	Low	N/A
Total/Average	8,785,948	82.061	9	32–100	Middle	86–98

AUSTRALIA

Commonwealth of Australia

Capital: Canberra

Social and economic data
Area: 7,686,850 km^2
Population: 15.763m*
Pop density per km^2: 2*
Literacy rate: 99%*
GDP: $155,578m*; per capita GDP: $9,870
Economy type: high income
Labour force in agriculture: 6%

*1985

Ethnic composition
About 99 per cent of the population are of European descent, British, Maltese, Italian, Greek, Dutch and Polish, in that order. The remaining 1 per cent are Aborigines or Asian.

Religions
About 30 per cent of the population are practising Anglicans and 25 per cent Roman Catholics.

Political features
State type: liberal democratic
Date of state formation: 1901
Political structure: federal
Executive: parliamentary
Assembly: two-chamber
Party structure: two-party
Human rights rating: 94%

Local and regional government

Australia is a federal nation, consisting of the six states of New South Wales (801,428 km^2 and 5.6m population), Victoria (227,600 km^2 and 4.2m population), Queensland (1,727,200 km^2 and 2.7m population), Western Australia (2,525,500 km^2 and 1.5m population), South Australia (984,000 km^2 and 1.4m population) and Tasmania (67,800 km^2 and 450,000 population), and the two territories of Northern Territory (1,346,200 km^2 and 158,000 population) and Australian Capital Territory (2,400 km^2 and 263,000 population).

The states are modern-day equivalents of the nineteenth-century colonies which were federated to become a single nation. State identification therefore remains a strong feature of Australian life. This aspect is accentuated by the size of the country and the distribution of the population. Most communities are in coastal areas, and particularly on the east and south coasts, and around the major cities of Sydney, Melbourne, Brisbane, Perth, Adelaide and the capital, Canberra.

The federal system is modelled on that of the USA, with each state having its own governor, representing the Queen, and its own executive, legislative and judicial system, but the detailed arrangements for each state vary.

New South Wales has a two-chamber assembly consisting of a Legislative Council, of 45 members, directly elected for the duration of three federal parliaments, with a third retiring every four years, and a Legislative Assembly of 99 members, directly elected for a four-year term.

Victoria has a similar arrangement, with 44 members in the Legislative Council, elected for six years, half retiring every three years, and a Legislative Assembly of 88, elected for four years.

The Queensland assembly has a single chamber of 82 members directly elected for a three-year term.

South Australia has a two-chamber assembly consisting of a Legislative Council of 22 members, elected by proportional representation for a six-year term, half retiring every three years, and a House of Assembly of 47 members, directly elected for three years.

Western Australia also has a Legislative Council and a Legislative Assembly. The Council has 34 members elected for six years, a half retiring every three years, and the Assembly has 57 members elected for three years.

Tasmania has a two-chamber arrangement, with 19 members in the Legislative Council elected for six years, retiring in rotation, and 35 members in the House of Assembly, elected for four years.

The Northern Territory has a single-chamber assembly, the Legislative Assembly, with 25 members elected for a four-year term, and the Australian Capital Territory, in Canberra, has an elected House of Assembly of 18 members, with essentially an advisory function on matters affecting the Territory itself.

Head of state

Queen Elizabeth II, represented by Governor-General, William (Bill) Hayden, since 1989.

Head of government

Prime Minister Robert J. L. Hawke, since 1983.

Political leaders since 1970

1968–71 John Gorton (Liberal), 1971–72 William McMahon (Liberal-Country Party coalition), 1972–75 Gough Whitlam (ALP), 1975–83 Malcolm Fraser (Liberal-Country Party coalition), 1983– Bob Hawke (ALP).

Political system

Australia is an independent, sovereign nation within the Commonwealth, retaining the monarch as head of state, and a Governor-General as her representative. The constitution was adopted in 1900 and came into effect on 1 January 1901. As in the United Kingdom, there is a parliamentary executive, in the shape of the Prime Minister and cabinet, drawn from the federal assembly and answerable to it.

The federal assembly consists of two chambers, an elected Senate of 76, twelve for each of the six states, two for the Australian Capital Territory and two for the Northern Territory; and a House of Representatives of 148, elected by universal adult suffrage. Senators serve for six years and members of the House for three. Voting is compulsory and the majoritarian system of the alternative vote is used for elections to both chambers.

In March 1986 the United Kingdom parliament removed the last relics of British legislative control over Australia.

Political Parties

There are some ten political parties, the most significant being the Australian Labor Party (ALP), the Liberal Party of Australia, and the National Party of Australia. Although now all national organisations, there are still clear local divergences and parts of the country where each party is particularly strong or weak.

The ALP was founded in 1891 and is Australia's oldest party. It is moderately left-of-centre, supporting the democratic socialisation of industry, production, distribution and exchange.

The Liberal Party of Australia dates from 1944, although its origins go back towards the beginning of this century when free-traders and protectionists fused togther and were later joined by breakaway groups from the ALP. In its modern form it is largely the achievement of the notable Australian politician, Sir Robert Menzies. It advocates free enterprise, social justice, and individual initiative and liberty.

The National Party of Australia was formed in 1916 as the Country Party to represent the interests of farmers. Its orientation is centrist, with an emphasis on the needs of people outside the metropolitan areas.

Latest elections

The 1987 general election produced the following assembly results, the previous seat holdings being shown in brackets:

	Senate	*House*
Labour	32 (34)	86 (82)
Liberals	27 (28)	43 (45)
National Party	8 (5)	19 (21)
Australian Democrats	5 (7)	— —
Independents	4 (2)	— —

Political history

Although Australia was visited by Europeans as early as the seventeenth century, the main immigration came towards the end of the eighteenth century when Captain James Cook claimed New South Wales as a British colony. Exploration of the interior began in the next century when there was rapid expansion, aided by gold discoveries. With this growth other colonies were developed. A depression in the 1890s prompted the growth of trade unionism and the foundation of the Australian Labor Party. By the end of the century the movement towards a federation and self-government had developed sufficiently for the establishment of the Commonwealth of Australia, in 1901, with Canberra to be created as the federal capital.

Since 1945 Australia has strengthened its ties with India and other South East Asian countries and this realignment was accelerated following Britain's entry into the European Community in 1973. The links with its original founder are now more emotional and historic than economic or political.

Politically, the immediate post-war years were dominated by the Liberal Party which, under Robert Menzies, held power for 17 years. He retired in 1966 and was succeeded by Harold Holt. Holt died in a swimming accident the following year and in 1968 John Gorton took over the premiership. In 1971 he lost a vote of confidence in the House and resigned, to be succeeded by William McMahon, heading a Liberal-Country Party coalition.

Then, at the end of 1972, the Liberal hegemony was broken and the Australian Labor Party, led by Gough Whitlam, took office. A general election in 1974 gave the Labor Party a fresh mandate to govern although its majority in the House was reduced and it had lost control of the Senate. In 1975 the Senate blocked the government's financial legislation and, with Whitlam unwilling to resign, the Governor-General took the unprecedented step of dismissing him and his cabinet and inviting Malcolm Fraser to form a Liberal-Country Party coalition caretaker administration. The wisdom of the action of the Governor-General, Sir John Kerr, was widely questioned and eventually, in 1977, he himself resigned.

In the 1977 general election the coalition was returned with a reduced majority and this became even smaller in 1980. In the 1983 general election the coalition was eventually defeated and the Australian Labor Party, under Bob Hawke, again took office. Hawke immediately honoured an election pledge and called together leaders of employers and unions to agree a prices and incomes policy and to deal with the problem of growing unemployment. He called a general election in December 1984, 15 months earlier than necessary, and was returned with a reduced majority.

Since taking office, Hawke has developed a distinctive foreign policy for Australia, placing even greater emphasis than his predecessors on links with South East Asia and, in 1986, boldly imposing trading sanctions against South Africa as a means of influencing the dismantling of the system of apartheid.

In the 1987 general election Labor marginally increased its majority in the House but did not have an overall majority in the Senate, where the balance is held by the Australian Democrats. In state elections in 1988 there was a marked shift towards the Liberal Party. In the same year it was suprisingly announced that Bill Hayden, the Foreign Minister in Bob Hawke's administration, was to be Australia's next Governor-General, in

February 1989. He announced that he would not accept the customary knighthood. In August 1988 a free trade agreement with New Zealand was signed, providing for the creation of a single market within two years.

FIJI

Capital: Suva (on Viti Levu)

Social and economic data
Area: 18,330
Population: 715,000*
Pop density per km^2: 39*
Literacy rate: 79%*
GDP: $1,150*; per capita GDP: $1,608
Economy type: middle income
Labour force in agriculture: 45%

*1985

Ethnic composition
Fiji is one of the few countries in the world where the native population is in a minority. Fijians, who are ethnically a mixture of Melanesians and Polynesians, comprise only 43 per cent of the population, while about 51 per cent are Asians who were brought to the country from India as indentured labourers during the period of British colonial rule.

Religions
Most ethnic Fijians are Christians, mainly Protestant, while the Asian majority are Hindus, Muslims or Sikhs.

Political features
State type: emergent democratic
Date of state formation: 1970
Political structure: unitary
Executive: parliamentary
Assembly: two-chamber
Party structure: multi-party
Human rights rating: N/A

Local and regional government
For administrative purposes, the country consists of four divisions.

Head of state
President Ratu Sir Penaja Ganilau, since 1987.

Head of government
Prime Minister Ratu Sir Kamisese Kapaiwai Tuimacilai Mara, since 1987.

Political leaders since 1970
1970–87 Kamisese Kapaiwai Tuimacilai Mara (AP), 1987 Sitiveni Rabuka (Military), 1987– Kamisese Kapaiwai Tuimacilai Mara (AP).

Political system

Fiji was a constitutional monarchy within the Commonwealth, with the British monarch as the formal head of state, until a military coup in 1987 established a republic. The system of government retains much of its British origins, with a two-chamber parliament, comprising a Senate and a House of Representatives, and a parliamentary executive, consisting of a Prime Minister and cabinet, drawn from and responsible to the House of Representatives.

The Senate has 22 appointed members, eight on the advice of the Great Council of Fijian Chiefs, seven on the advice of the Prime Minister, six on the advice of the Leader of the Opposition and one on the advice of the Council of Rotuma Island, which is a dependency of Fiji. It has a life of six years.

The House of Representatives has 52 members, elected for five years through a simple plurality, cross-voting, system which ensures that all races in the country, Fijian, Indian and others, are represented.

Political parties

There are five political parties, the main three being the Alliance Party (AP), the National Federation Party (NFP) and the Fijian Labour Party (FLP).

The AP was founded in 1965, drawing support mainly from indigenous Fijians, and soon became the governing party. It has a moderate, centrist orientation.

The NFP was formed in 1960 by the merging of the multi-racial, but chiefly Indian, Federation Party and the National Democratic Party. Its orientation is moderate, left of centre.

The FLP dates from 1985. It is a left-of-centre party, drawing most of its support from the Indian community.

Latest elections

In the 1987 general election a coalition of the FLP and NFP won 28 seats and the AP 24.

Political history

A British possession since 1874, Fiji achieved full independence, within the Commonwealth, in 1970. Before independence there had been racial tensions between Indians, descended from workers who had been brought to Fiji in the late nineteenth century, and Fijians, so the constitution incorporated an electoral device which would help to ensure racial balance in the House of Representatives. The leader of the AP, Ratu Sir Kamisese Mara, became Prime Minister at the time of independence and held office until there was a brief military coup in 1987.

The AP has traditionally been supported by ethnic Fijians and the NFP by Indians. The main divisions between the two have centred on land ownership, with the Fijians owning more than 80 per cent of the land and defending their traditional rights, and the Indians claiming greater security of land tenure. The Fijian Labour Party was formed in 1985 and in the April 1987 general election gained power in association with the NFP. This provoked an unsuccessful coup the following month, led by Lieutenant-Colonel Sitiveni Rabuka. In September 1987 a second coup succeeded and

Rabuka announced that he had abrogated the constitution and assumed the role of head of state. After some indecision and confusion Fiji was declared a republic, the British monarch ceasing to be head of state and the country automatically leaving the Commonwealth.

In December 1987 a civilian government was restored, with Mara resuming as Prime Minister, and Rabuka retaining control of the security forces as minister for home affairs. The former Governor-General, Sir Penaja Ganilau, resumed his role as head of state, now in the position of Fiji's first President.

KIRIBATI

Republic of Kiribati

Capital: Bairiki (on Tarawa Atoll)

Social and economic data
Area: 680 km^2
Population: 62,000*
Pop density per km^2: 91*
Literacy rate: 90%
GDP: $25m*; per capita GDP: $403
Economy type: low income
Labour force in agriculture: N/A

*1985

Ethnic composition
The population is predominantly Micronesian, with a Polynesian minority also to be found, as well as a few Europeans and Chinese. I-Kiribati (Gilbertese) is the local language, with English being used for official business.

Religions
The islands adhere both to the Protestant and Roman Catholic faiths in almost equal proportions. Traditional beliefs and practices also survive.

Political features
State type: liberal democracy
Date of state formation: 1979
Political structure: unitary
Executive: limited presidential
Assembly: one-chamber
Party structure: two-party*
Human rights rating: N/A

*See Party section below.

Local and regional government
The islands are divided into seven administrative districts, Banaba, Northern Gilbert Islands, Central Gilbert Islands, Southern Gilbert

Islands, South-Eastern Gilbert Islands, Line Islands and the Phoenix Group, a district officer in charge of each. In addition, elected councils function on each inhabited island, enjoying considerable autonomy.

Head of state and head of government
President Ieremia T. Tabai, since 1979.

Political leaders since 1970
1974–78 Naboua Ratieta (Ind), 1978– Ieremia T. Tabai (Ind).

Political system
Kiribati is an independent republic within the Commonwealth, with a constitution which dates from independence in June 1979. It provides for a President, known as the Beretitenti, and a single-chamber assembly, the Maneaba ni Maungatabu. The President combines the roles of head of state and head of government, and is elected by universal adult suffrage for a four-year term. After each general election, the Maneaba nominates from among its members three or four candidates for President, who then stand in a national contest.

The Maneaba itself comprises 39 popularly elected members, one nominated representative of the inhabitants of the island of Banaba, and, if he is not an elected member, an attorney-general, who serves in an *ex officio* capacity. All members serve a four-year term, and the assembly is subject to dissolution during that period.

The President governs with the help of a Vice-President (Kauoman-ni-Beretitenti) and a cabinet composed of up to eight additional ministers, chosen from, and responsible to, the Maneaba. At present, the President holds the portfolio of foreign minister. A Council of State, composed of the Speaker of the Maneaba, the Chief Justice and the chairman of the Public Service Commission, carries out the functions of the President and Maneaba during the period between dissolution and the holding of fresh elections.

Political parties
Traditionally, all candidates for the Maneaba have fought as independents. In 1985, however, an opposition party, the Christian Democratic Party, was formed by Maneaba members opposed to the policy strategy of President Tabai. Its present leader is Teburoro Tito. The pro-government grouping in the assembly is generally known as the National Party, although it does not constitute a formal political party.

Latest elections
The most recent Maneaba elections were held on 12 and 19 March 1987. As usual, contests were fought in multi-member constituencies, with a second ballot in constituencies where no candidate obtained the requisite 50 per cent of the votes cast. In this election, two cabinet ministers and 14 other Maneaba members were defeated. Turnout was around 70 per cent.

The presidential election was held on 12 May 1987 and was contested by three candidates: Ieremia Tabai, who secured 50.1 per cent of the 21,547 votes cast; Tebururo Tito, 42.7 per cent; and Teatao Teannaki, 7.2 per cent.

Political history

Kiribati comprises three groups of 33 low-lying coral atolls plus Banaba, a raised volcanic atoll in the west. The whole group is situated in the south-west Pacific Ocean and scattered over an area of 3 million square kilometres. In the centre, lying on the equator, are the 16 Gilbert Islands; to the east are the eight uninhabited Phoenix Islands; and to the north lie eight of the eleven Line Islands, the remaining three being uninhabited dependencies of the United States. Thirty-three per cent of the population live on Tarawa Atoll, principally at the port and town of Bairiki, in the Gilbert group.

Kiribati was visited by the Spanish in 1606, before being officially 'discovered' by the British navy during the late eighteenth century. Designated the Gilbert Islands, in 1892 they were joined with the Ellice Islands, now called Tuvalu, to the south, to form a British protectorate. They became a formal colony in 1916, under the designation Gilbert and Ellice Islands Colony (GEIC). A resident commissioner was based at Tarawa Atoll, although supreme authority rested with the Western Pacific High Commission (WPHC), which had its headquarters in Fiji. The colony was extended to embrace Ocean Island, Christmas Island or Kiritmati, three of the Line Islands and the eight Phoenix Islands, then uninhabited, between 1916 and 1937.

The GEIC was invaded and occupied by the Japanese, in 1942, during the Second World War, but, following fierce fighting on Tarawa Atoll, they were removed by United States naval forces, in 1943, and British control was restored. During the 1960s, as a means of preparing the islands for self-government, a succession of legislative and executive bodies was established, culminating in the creation of a House of Assembly, in May 1974. This comprised 28 elected members and three official members. Naboua Ratieta was elected from among these members as the GEIC's first Chief Minister, and chose a four- to six-member ministerial cabinet.

In October 1975, following a referendum, the Polynesian-peopled Ellice Islands, fearing domination in an independent GEIC from the Micronesian Gilbert Islands majority, broke away to form the separate territory of Tuvalu. This reduced the size of the Gilbert Islands' House of Assembly by eight elected members. During the mid-1970s, a separatist movement also developed among the people of Ocean Island, or Banaba, an atoll which was rich in phosphate resources, producing more than 80 per cent of the country's export earnings and 50 per cent of government tax revenue. Opencast phosphate mining was in the hands of the British Phosphate Commission, who exported the produce to Australia and New Zealand as fertiliser. The mining had, however, adversely affected Banaba's environment, necessitating the resettlement of the local population on Rabi Island, 2,600 kilometres away in the Fiji group. Banaba's leaders, the Rabi Council of Leaders, pressed for large-scale compensation for this damage and opposed the distribution of revenue derived from phosphate mining over the whole Gilbert Islands territory. They, therefore, campaigned for the constitutional separation of the island. They eventually accepted a British government *ex gratia* compensation offer in April 1981, but, during recent years, have continued to campaign for separation.

The Gilbert Islands were granted internal self-government in January 1977 and the number of elective members in the House of Assembly was increased to 36. After the general election of February 1978, the opposition leader, Ieremia Tabai, was chosen as the new Chief Minister. In July 1979, the islands were finally granted full independence as a republic within the Commonwealth under the designation Kiribati. The House of Assembly was also now renamed the Maneaba ni Maungatabu and Chief Minister Tabai became the country's first President. He was re-elected after parliamentary and presidential elections in March and May 1982. Within seven months of the elections, however, as a result of the Maneaba's rejection of proposals to raise civil servants' salaries, the assembly had to be dissolved and fresh parliamentary and presidential elections were held, in January and February 1983. President Tabai was again returned to office.

During 1985 opposition to the Tabai government began to mount when a controversial fishing agreement was negotiated with a Soviet state-owned company, Sovrybflot. The move prompted the formation of the country's first political party, the Christian Democratic Party, by the opposition leader Dr Harry Tong and 15 members of the Maneaba. The one-year fishing agreement, which expired in October 1986, was not, however, renewed, the Soviet company claiming that the fees charged by the government had been too high. Following this, Tabai was elected for a fourth term as President, in May 1987.

Despite the 1985–86 Soviet fishing incident, Kiribati has generally pursued a moderate, pro-Western foreign policy. In September 1979, a treaty of friendship was signed with the United States, under which the US relinquished its claims to the Line and Phoenix Islands, including Canton and Enderbury. This was followed, in October 1986, by the signing of a five-year agreement by the South Pacific Forum, of which body Kiribati is an influential member, to grant American tuna boats the right to fish within the 'exclusive economic zones' of the Forum's member states. A significant factor behind this pro-Western policy approach has been Kiribati's heavy dependency on foreign development aid, particularly since the closure of the Banaba phosphate works.

NAURU

Republic of Nauru

Capital: Yaren

Social and economic data
Area: 21 km^2
Population: 8,000*
Pop density per km^2: 381*
Literacy rate: 99%
GDP: $70m*; per capita GDP: $8,750
Economy type: high income
Labour force in agriculture: N/A

*1985

Ethnic composition

Fifty-eight per cent of the population are indigenous Naurians of mixed Polynesian, Micronesian and Melanesian descent; 26 per cent are Tuvaluans/Kiribatians; 8 per cent are Chinese; and 8 per cent are a mixture of Australians and New Zealanders. Naurian is the national language, with English also being widely understood.

Religions

Fifty-eight per cent of the population are Protestants, 24 per cent Roman Catholics and 8 per cent, the Chinese community, Confucians and Daoists.

Political features

State type: liberal democracy
Date of state formation: 1968
Political structure: unitary
Executive: limited presidential*
Assembly: one-chamber
Party structure: two-party†
Human rights rating: N/A

*But with parliamentary features
†See Party section

Local and regional government

The country is divided into 14 districts, which are grouped, for electoral purposes, into eight divisions. Elected local councils function at the district level.

Head of state and head of government

President Hammer DeRoburt, since 1987.

Political leaders since 1970

1968–76 Hammer DeRoburt (Ind), 1976–78 Bernard Dowiyogo (NP), 1978–78 Hammer DeRoburt (Ind), 1978–78 Lagumot Harris (NP), 1978–86 Hammer DeRoburt (Ind), 1986–86 Kennan Adeang (Ind), 1986–86 Hammer DeRoburt (Ind), 1986–86 Kennan Adeang (Ind), 1987– Hammer DeRoburt (Ind).

Political system

The constitution dates from independence in January 1968. It provides for a single-chamber parliament of 18 members, elected by universal adult suffrage for a three-year term, and a President who is both head of state and head of government. Voting in parliamentary elections is compulsory for those over 20 years of age. The President and cabinet are elected by parliament, from among its members, and are responsible to it. Although the President has broad powers, parliament is, nevertheless, empowered to pass bills without his formal assent. The small size of the country allows for a very intimate style of government, with the President combining several portfolios, internal affairs, external affairs, island development and industry, and public service, in a cabinet of only five.

Political parties

Traditionally, members of parliament have been elected as independents, but have grouped themselves into majority and minority pro- and anti-government factions. In February 1987, however, a formal political party, the Democratic Party of Nauru (DPN), was formed by the opposition leader Kennan Adeang. It is a loose grouping, currently supported by eight parliamentary members. The party declares its principal aim to be the curtailment of presidential powers and the promotion of democracy. Non-DPN members in parliament form an even looser pro-DeRoburt majority grouping, principally held together by personal ties. A number of its members, including health minister, Reuben Kun, and justice minister, Bernard Dowiyogo, are former members of the Nauru Party (NP). This was formed by Lagumot Harris and Bernard Dowiyogo in December 1976, but no longer functions.

Latest elections

The most recent parliamentary elections were held in January 1987. All members were elected as independents, although subsequently ten emerged as supporters of President DeRoburt and eight of the opposition leader, Kennan Adeang.

Political history

Nauru is a small isolated island, composed of phosphatic rock, in the west-central Pacific Ocean, lying 42 kilometres south of the equator and 4,000 kilometres north-east of Sydney, Australia. The population lives in small, scattered, coastal settlements. There is no urban centre as such.

The island was discovered in 1798 by the British whaler, Captain John Fearn, and was called 'Pleasant Island'. Between the 1830s and 1880s, it became a haven for white, runaway, convicts and deserters, before being placed under German rule, in 1888, when the western Pacific was partitioned into British and German 'zones of influence'. The Germans discovered and intensively exploited the island's high-grade phosphate reserves. After Germany's defeat in the First World War, however, Nauru was placed under a joint British, Australian and New Zealand mandate by the League of Nations, and was then administered on the other trustees' behalf by Australia.

During the Second World War, Nauru was invaded and occupied by the Japanese, between 1942 and 1945, and was devastated. Two-thirds of the population were deported to Truk Atoll, 1,600 kilometres to the north-west, and all the mining facilities were destroyed. It was re-occupied by Australian forces in 1945 and the Naurians were repatriated from Truk. After the war, Nauru was designated a UN Trust Territory, subject to the continuing administration of the former mandatory powers. As part of a process of preparation for self-government, and in response to local community pressure, a local governing council was established in 1951 and an elected assembly in January 1966. Two years later, in January 1968, full independence was achieved. Nauru became a republic and was designated a 'special member' of the Commonwealth, which meant that, because of its small size, it did not have direct representation at meetings of heads of government.

Hammer DeRoburt, who had held the position of Head Chief of Nauru since 1956, was elected the country's first President, in May 1968, and was re-elected in May 1971 and December 1973. Criticisms of his personal style of government led to his replacement, in December 1976, by Bernard Dowiyogo, leader of the Nauru Party grouping. However, mounting assembly opposition to Dowiyogo by DeRoburt supporters forced his resignation in April 1978 and the recall of DeRoburt. President DeRoburt was duly re-elected in December 1978, December 1980 and in May and December 1983. Parliamentary opposition to the government's annual budget forced DeRoburt's resignation in September 1986 and his replacement as President by the opposition leader, Kennan Adeang. Within a fortnight, however, following a successful 'no-confidence' motion, Adeang was ousted. DeRoburt returned as President, but briefly lost power again to Adeang following the general election of December 1986. Fresh elections in January 1987 gave DeRoburt an effective majority and prompted the defeated Adeang to form the Democratic Party of Nauru, as a formal opposition grouping.

Nauru achieved economic independence in 1970 when the company called the British Phosphate Commissioners, which had been in charge of the phosphate industry during the period of Australian rule, was nationalised and renamed the Nauru Phosphate Corporation. However, with the island's phosphate reserves set to run out in 1995, recent attempts have been made to re-invest the substantial profits, which have hitherto enabled the people to enjoy a high standard of living and welfare provision. The aim is to establish new shipping and civil airline services, as part of a diversification programme.

In its external relations, Nauru has sought to pursue an independent course, remaining outside the United Nations, although links with Australia, Britain and New Zealand remain close. It is a member of the South Pacific Forum and, recently, in December 1987, announced its intention to establish diplomatic relations with the Soviet Union. Relations with the country's former trustee powers have, however, been damaged in recent years by disputes over compensation for the removal of the bulk of the country's phosphate-rich soil during the colonial period, an action which has served to leave Nauru agriculturally barren.

NEW ZEALAND

Capital: Wellington

Social and economic data

Area: 269,060 km^2
Population: 3.3m*
Pop density per km^2: 12*
Literacy rate: 100%*
GDP: $22,400m*; per capita GDP: $6,787
Economy type: high income
Labour force in agriculture: 11%

*1985

Ethnic composition
About 87 per cent of the population are of European origin, mostly British, about 9 per cent Maoris and about 2 per cent Pacific Islanders.

Religions
There are about 895,000 Anglicans, 495,000 Roman Catholics, 170,000 of other Christian denominations and 30,000 Maoris.

Political features
State type: liberal democratic
Date of state formation: 1853/1947
Political structure: unitary
Executive: parliamentary
Assembly: one-chamber
Party structure: two-party
Human rights rating: 98%

Local and regional government
For planning and civil defence purposes, the country is divided into 22 regions. For other administrative purposes there are counties, boroughs and urban and rural districts, based broadly on the British system of local government. Each unit has an elected council.

Head of state
Queen Elizabeth II, represented by Governor-General Sir Paul Alfred Reeves, since 1985.

Head of government
Prime Minister Geoffrey Palmer, since 1989.

Political leaders since 1970
1969–72 Keith Holyoake (National), 1972–74 Norman Kirk (Labour), 1974–75 Wallace Rowling (Labour), 1975–84 Robert Muldoon (National), 1984–89 David Lange (Labour), 1989– Geoffrey Palmer (Labour).

Political system
As a constitutional monarchy, New Zealand's system of government displays many features found in that of the United Kingdom, including the absence of a written constitution. As in Britain, the constitution is the progressive product of legislation, much of it passed by the parliament in London. The Governor-General represents the British monarch as formal head of state and appoints the Prime Minister and a cabinet chosen by him, all of whom are drawn from and collectively responsible to the single-chamber assembly, the House of Representatives. This has 97 members, including four Maoris, elected by universal adult suffrage from single-member constituencies, by a simple plurality voting system. It has a maximum life of three years and is subject to dissolution within that period.

Political parties
There are currently twelve active political parties, but only two have dominated the political scene for most of the time since New Zealand has

been an independent state. They are the Labour Party and the New Zealand National Party.

The Labour Party was formed in 1916. It has a moderate, left-of-centre orientation and advocates democratic socialist policies.

The New Zealand National Party was founded in 1936 as an anti-Labour party, during the period of economic depression. It has a centre-right, free-enterprise orientation.

Latest elections

In the 1987 general election Labour won 58 seats, and the National Party 39, subsequently, after an appeal, 1 Labour seat was transferred to the National Party.

Political history

New Zealand was a dependency of the colony of New South Wales, Australia, until 1841, when it became a separate British colony. It was made a Dominion in the British Empire in 1907 and then granted full independence by the Statute of Westminster of 1931. Independence was formally accepted by the New Zealand parliament in 1947.

New Zealand has been in the forefront of democratic government, being, for example, the first country in the world to give women the right to vote, in 1893. It also has a record of great political stability, with the centrist New Zealand National Party holding office from the 1930s until it was eventually replaced by a Labour Party administration, led by Norman Kirk, in 1972. During this period of stablity, New Zealand built up a social security system which became the envy of the world.

The economy was thriving at the time Kirk took office but there were clouds on the horizon, including the danger of growing inflation. This was aggravated by the 1973–74 energy crisis which resulted in a balance of payments deficit. Meanwhile, the Labour government was following a more independent foreign policy line, to some extent influenced by Britain's decision to join the European Community, with its possible effects on New Zealand's future exports. It began a phased withdrawal from some of the country's military commitments in South-East Asia and established diplomatic relations with China. Norman Kirk died in August 1974 and was succeeded by the Finance Minister, Wallace Rowling.

The state of the economy worsened and in the 1975 general election the National Party, led by Robert Muldoon, was returned to power with a clear working majority. However, the economy failed to revive and in the 1978 general election Muldoon's majority was greatly reduced. In 1984 he introduced controversial labour legislation which was widely opposed by the trade unions. To renew his mandate, he called an early election and was swept out of office by the Labour Party, now led by David Lange.

The Labour Party had fought the election on a non-nuclear defence policy, which Lange immediately put into effect, forbidding any vessels carrying nuclear weapons, or powered by nuclear energy, from entering New Zealand's ports. This put a great strain on relations with the United States. In 1985 the trawler *Rainbow Warrior,* the flagship of the environmentalist pressure group, Greenpeace, which was monitoring nuclear tests in French Polynesia, was mined, with loss of life, by French secret-service agents in Auckland harbour. The French Prime Minister eventually admitted responsibility and New Zealand subsequently demanded compensation.

In 1984 Sir Robert Muldoon, as he now was, was defeated in elections for the leadership of the National Party by James McLay but he, in turn, was replaced in 1986 by James Bolger. The National Party now supports the government in a bipartisan anti-nuclear policy. In August 1987 Lange was re-elected with a majority of 17 and in September, because of its non-nuclear defence policy, New Zealand officially became a 'friendly', rather than an 'allied', country in US eyes. In 1988 a free-trade agreement with Australia was signed. The 'free enterprise' economic policies of the Lange administration created tensions within the Labour Party, resulting in the creation of a small breakaway party, the New Labour Party (NLP) in 1989.

PAPUA NEW GUINEA

The Independent State of Papua New Guinea

Capital: Port Moresby

Social and economic data
Area: 462,840 km^2
Population: 3.395m*
Pop density per km^2: 7*
Literacy rate: 32%
GDP: $2,292m*; per capita GDP: $675
Economy type: low income
Labour force in agriculture: 71%

*1985

Ethnic composition
The population is mainly Melanesian, particularly in the coastal areas. Further inland, on New Guinea and on the larger islands, Papuans predominate. On the outer archipelagoes and islands mixed Micronesian-Melanesians are to be found. A small Chinese minority, numbering 3,000, also exists. The official language is pidgin English, but about 750 indigenous languages are spoken locally among what is an intensely regionalised population.

Religions
More than half the population are nominally Christians, 60 per cent of them Roman Catholics and 40 per cent members of the Evangelical Lutheran Church. The rest mainly follow traditional magico-ritual, pantheistic beliefs and practices.

Political features
State type: liberal democracy
Date of state formation: 1975
Political structure: unitary
Executive: parliamentary
Assembly: one-chamber
Party structure: multi-party
Human rights rating: 91%

Local and regional government
The country is divided into 19 provinces, plus a National Capital District. As part of a decentralisation programme launched in 1978, provincial assemblies and governments have been established in the provinces and enjoy a substantial measure of autonomy. Within the provinces there is a range of district, town and village councils.

Head of state
Queen Elizabeth II, represented by Governor-General Sir Kingsford Dibela, since 1983.

Head of government
Prime Minister Rabbie Namaliu, since 1988.

Political leaders since 1970
1972–80 Michael Somare (PP), 1980–82 Sir Julius Chan (PPP), 1982–85 Michael Somare (PP), 1985–88 Paias Wingti (PDM), 1988– Rabbie Namaliu (PP).

Political system
Papua New Guinea is a constitutional monarchy, within the Commonwealth, with the crown represented, as formal head of state, by a resident Governor-General. The constitution dates from independence in September 1975 and provides for a parliamentary system of government, broadly based on the Westminster model. There is a single-chamber assembly, the National Parliament, which consists of 109 members elected by universal adult suffrage for a five-year term, through a simple plurality voting system. Eighty-nine members represent 'open', or local, single-member constituencies, 20 provincial constituencies, and there is provision in the constitution, though, as yet unfulfilled, for a further three members to be nominated and appointed on a two-thirds majority vote of Parliament. Each elector has two votes, one of which is cast for the local and one for the provincial seat. The National Parliament is subject to dissolution within its term.

The Governor-General formally appoints a Prime Minister and National Executive Council (NEC), or cabinet, whose 28 members, the maximum number permitted under the constitution, are drawn from, and responsible to, the National Parliament. The government needs parliament's approval for its legislative proposals and may be removed by a vote of 'no-confidence', without fresh elections necessarily being required. Under the terms of a recently adopted convention, a no-confidence vote may not be called until at least six months after a government's formation.

The Governor-General, who must be a 'mature' and 'respected' citizen of Papua New Guinea, is appointed by the monarch on the recommendation of the Prime Minister. He serves a six-year term and is eligible for re-appointment once only, requiring a two-thirds parliamentary majority to secure a second term. His principal role, as a result of the shifting, coalition character of politics in faction-ridden Papua New Guinea, is as 'government-maker'. To amend the constitution, a two-thirds majority of the National Assembly members is required twice in succession, within a period of six weeks.

Political parties

Political parties in Papua New Guinea are weak organisations, dominated by personalities, patronage and regional differences. They lack the formal policy-making and membership structures of the West European kind. Their assembly members are frequently persuaded to 'cross the floor' and join temporarily other groupings in the National Parliament. Ideological differences between them are limited.

Of the twelve parties which currently function, the most important six, in terms of parliamentary representation, are: the Papua New Guinea Party (PP: Pangu Pati), the People's Democratic Movement (PDM),the National Party (NP), the Melanesian Alliance (MA), the People's Action Party (PAP) and the People's Progress Party (PPP).

The PP is the country's oldest and most influential party, having been founded in June 1967 to campaign for internal self-government and eventual independence and for the adoption of pidgin as the official language. It has a strong urban base in north New Guinea and the coast, and is the best organised party in the country, with more than 75 local branches. Its former leader, Michael Somare, governed the country for eight of the first ten years after independence. However, the formation of the PDM in 1985, by 15 of its former parliamentary representatives, including Paias Wingti, undermined the PP, siphoning away crucial support. Despite this, under the leadership of Rabbie Namaliu, it succeeded in returning to power as the governing party in July 1988.

The NP is a highlands-based party. It was formed in May 1978, under the designation the People's United Front (PUF), by Iambakey Okuk, a former member of the once influential United Party (UP). The UP was formed in 1969 initially to oppose independence and has fought since for maintaining close links with Australia. The NP is a generally conservative grouping and, following the death of Sir Iambakey Okuk, in November 1986, has been led by Michael Mel.

The MA had its origins in a secessionist movement which, in September 1975, declared the eastern, copper-producing island of Bougainville the 'Independent Republic of the North Solomons'. A year later, this movement, after securing the grant of greater autonomy for the region, accepted the island's position within Papua New Guinea. It subsequently transformed itself into a political party, originally called the Bougainville Pressure Group, and contested seats in the 1977 general election. It later adopted the designation Alliance for Progress and Regional Development (APRD), but is commonly known as the MA. Led since its inception by Father John Momis, currently the provincial affairs minister, the party is regarded as a left-of-centre socialist body, demanding 'liberation from foreign domination' and favouring greater local participation in economic decision-taking. The MA draws the bulk of its support from Bougainville dock and copper industry workers, and white-collar professionals.

The PAP was formed to fight the 1987 election. It is led by the retired Brigadier-General Ted Diro, formerly an influential figure within the NP and leader of its 'Independents' Group' faction.

The PPP is a much older party, dating back to 1970. A conservative, non-highlands-based grouping, it has long been led by Sir Julius Chan. The party enjoys strong support in the islands north of New Guinea: New Ireland, New Britain and the North Solomons.

Latest elections

In the most recent National Parliament elections, held between 13 June and 4 July 1987, the results were as folows:

	% Votes	*Seats*
PP	14.7	26
PDM	10.8	17
NP	5.1	12
MA	5.6	7
PAP	3.2	6
PPP	6.1	5
Marobe Independent Group (MIG)	2.2	4
League for National Advancement (LNA)	4.9	3
Papua Party	1.3	3
UP	3.2	1
'Independents'	42.9	22

Many of the 'independents' were expected later to align with one of the established parties. Elections in three constituencies were postponed because of the deaths of candidates.

As usual, because of the remoteness and ruggedness of much of the country, the election process extended over three weeks. In addition, illiterate voters were allowed to cast 'whispering votes', quietly intimating their choices in the ear of the presiding election officer who then proceeded to mark the ballot-paper accordingly. Turnout exceeded 65 per cent and more than 1,500 candidates contested the 109 seats. Indeed, in one constituency, Kerowagi, 45 candidates' names were put forward. As a consequence, successful candidates were returned on low vote shares, sometimes below 10 per cent. More than half of the incumbents who sought re-election were defeated.

Political history

Papua New Guinea is an extensive island grouping in the south-west Pacific Ocean, 160 kilometres north-east of Australia. It comprises the eastern half of the large island of New Guinea; the volcanic Bismarck (Mussau, New Britain, New Hanover and New Ireland) and Louisiade archipelagoes; the Trobriand and D'Entrecasteaux Islands; and an assortment of smaller groups. The country shares a 777-kilometre-long border with Indonesia (Irian Jaya) to the west and is skirted by the Solomon Islands in the east.

New Guinea had been inhabited by indigenous Melanesians for more than 9,000 years before it was first visited by a European, the Portuguese navigator, Jorge de Menezes, in 1526. Dutch merchants later made regular trips to the island during the seventeenth century, before the Dutch East India Company established control over the western portion of the island, incorporating it into the Netherlands East Indies in 1828. More than half a century later, in 1885, under the terms of the Anglo-Dutch Agreement of 1885, Britain took possession of the southern portion of New Guinea and adjacent islands, while Germany assumed control of the north-east, which included New Britain, New Ireland and Bougainville.

In 1901 Britain transferred its rights to Australia, who proceeded to rename the territories Papua, in 1906. Then, in 1914, during the First World War, Australia invaded and established control over German New Guinea. From the merged territories, Papua New Guinea was formed. It was designated, first, a Mandate Territory by the League of Nations between 1921 and 1946 and, then, from 1947, a Trust Territory by the United Nations, and placed under Australian guardianship. The two territories were administered jointly by Australia, but formally retained their separate status.

During the Second World War, parts of Papua New Guinea were invaded and occupied by the Japanese, between 1942 and 1945. The territory was reunited, however, after the war and Australia, under the terms of its UN agreement, began to prepare it for self-government. In November 1951, a Legislative Council was established and then, in June 1964, an elected House of Assembly. The state was formally named Papua New Guinea in July 1971 and secured internal self-government in December 1973. Finally, in September 1975, full independence, within the Commonwealth, was achieved, with the House of Assembly re-designated the National Parliament.

The first Prime Minister after independence was Michael Somare, leader of the nationalist Pangu Pati (PP). He had been Chief Minister in the interim government since 1972. Despite allegations of governmental inefficiency and discrimination against the highland provinces, Somare remained in office until 1980. At first, he headed a PP and People's Progress Party (PPP) coalition and then, from October 1978, a PP and United Party (UP) alliance. However, Somare, following a corruption scandal, was eventually defeated on a confidence vote in the National Assembly in March 1980 and a new government was formed by the PPP leader and former Deputy Prime Minister, Sir Julius Chan.

In the general election of June 1982 the PP won 47 National Parliament seats, compared with 39 in 1977, and the UP ten, compared with 38, enabling Somare to return to power, the following August, leading a coalition with the UP and nine independents. In March 1985, however, the Deputy Prime Minister, Paias Wingti, resigned from the PP and, forming a tactical alliance with PPP leader Chan, proceeded to challenge Somare for the premiership. Somare quickly responded by forming a new coalition with the National Party (NP) and Melanesian Alliance (MA) and successfully fought off, by 68 votes to 19, a 'no-confidence' challenge in parliament. Fourteen dissident members, who had been expelled from the PP by Somare, immediately set up a new opposition party, the People's Democratic Movement (PDM), under the leadership of Wingti.

Later, in August 1985, Iambakey Okey's NP departed from the government coalition. This, coupled with mounting opposition to Somare's tax-raising budget strategy, fatally weakened the government and in November 1985 Somare was eventually defeated, by 58 votes to 51, in a 'no-confidence' motion. Wingti took over as Prime Minister, at the head of a five-party coalition, comprising the PDM, PPP, NP, UP and MA, with Chan as Deputy Prime Minister, and set about instituting a new programme of public spending economies as a means of tackling the economic crisis. At the general election of June–July 1987 Wingti's PDM secured 18 seats, losing two, and formed the core of a new coalition government which incorporated the People's Action Party (PAP), whose leader, Ted Diro, was brought into the cabinet as 'minister without portfolio'. In November 1987, however, following charges of misappropriation of election funds, Diro was forced to resign.

Faced with a 'no-confidence' motion in April 1988, Wingti, requiring the PAP's support, brought Diro back into the NEC. This controversial move created a constitutional crisis, precipitating shifts in coalition alliances. Three months later, in July 1988, Wingti was defeated, by 58 votes to 50, on a 'no-confidence' motion. He was replaced as Prime Minister by the former foreign minister, Rabbie Namaliu, who had been elected the leader of the PP, in succession to Michael Somare in May 1988. Namaliu established a new six-party coalition government which comprised the PP, MA, PAP, Papua Party, NP and the League for National Advancement (LNA), with Michael Somare serving as foreign minister.

In its external relations, despite continuing border demarcation disputes, Papua New Guinea has maintained close diplomatic ties with Australia since independence, receiving, in return, substantial economic aid. The country, as a result of its relative size, has also been able to establish itself as the leader of the group of small island states in the South Pacific which have achieved independence during recent decades. It is a founder member of the South Pacific Forum and, together with Vanuatu and the Solomon Islands, a leader of the 'Spearhead Group', which was set up in March 1988 with the aim of preserving Melanesian cultural traditions and securing independence for the French Overseas Territory of New Caledonia. Relations with Papua New Guinea's western neighbour, Indonesia, have traditionally been strained as a result of the latter's maltreatment of Melanesians in Irian Jaya, the western part of New Guinea. In 1963 Indonesia foiled an independence bid by Irian Jaya and, in more recent years, has been involved in fighting guerrillas of the Free Papua Movement (OPM) and with importing Javanese settlers into the territory, the so-called 'trans-migration programme'. These actions have prompted the flight of more than 10,000 Melanesian refugees into Papua New Guinea. Despite these tensions, a Treaty of Mutual Respect, Friendship and Co-operation was signed by the two countries in October 1986, providing for the settlement of disputes by peaceful means.

During the early 1980s, Papua New Guinea experienced mounting economic difficulties as a result of both rapid population growth, of 2.6 per cent per annum, and falling world prices for its copra, coffee and cocoa exports. The country became heavily dependent on foreign development aid and its debt servicing ratio rose sharply. However, since the recent discovery of substantial gold and oil reserves, the country's economic prospects appear to be more promising.

THE PHILIPPINES

Republic of the Philippines
Republika ng Pilipinas

Capital: Manila

Social and economic data
Area: 300,000 km^2
Population: 58.100m*
Pop density per km^2: 194*
Literacy rate: 83%
GDP: $32,781m*; per capita GDP: $564
Economy type: low income
Labour force in agriculture: 47%

*1985

Ethnic composition
The Philippines is a pluralistic society, comprising more than 50 ethnic communities. However, a sense of national unity imbues these communities, with 95 per cent of the population designated 'Filipinos', an Indo-Polynesian ethnic grouping. The official language is Pilipino, based on Tagalog, with 72 local dialects and languages also being spoken.

Religions
Eighty-five per cent of the population adhere to the Roman Catholic faith, 4 per cent to Islam, 4 per cent to the Aglipayan, or Independent Philippine Christian, Church and 3 per cent to the Protestant Church.

Political features
State type: emergent democracy
Date of state formation: 1946
Political structure: unitary
Executive: limited presidential
Assembly: two-chamber
Party structure: multi-party
Human rights rating: 86%

Local and regional government
The country is divided into twelve regions, 75 provinces, headed by governors, 1,550 cities and muncipalities, governed by mayors, and 41,818 neighbourhoods. Local government is by citizens' assemblies *(barangays)*, with autonomy granted to any region if it is endorsed by referendum. Since January 1988 governors and mayors have been popularly elected, as have advisory councils. An active decentralisation programme is underway.

Head of state and head of government
President Corazon C. Aquino, since 1986.

Political leaders since 1970
1965–86 Ferdinand Marcos (Nationalist Party/New Society Movement), 1986– Corazon C. Aquino (People's Power Movement).

Political system
The present constitution, which, following approval by a national referendum, became effective in February 1987, replaced the earlier one of 1973, which had been amended in 1984. It provides for an US-style limited

presidential system, in which the executive works in tandem with an influential two-chamber legislature, termed Congress.

The upper chamber of Congress, the Senate, comprises 24 members who are directly elected by universal adult suffrage, initially for a special five-year term, but thereafter for a six-year term. Senators must be at least 35 years of age and may serve no more than two consecutive terms. They are elected in national level contests, with the top 24 candidates being returned.

The lower chamber, the House of Representatives, comprises a maximum of 250 members, 200 of whom are directly elected at the district level, with the remaining 50 appointed by the President from 'lists of nominees proposed by indigenous, but non-religious, minority groups, such as the urban poor, peasantry, women and youth'. However, by January 1988 only four nominated members had been appointed. Representatives must be at least 25 years of age and are restricted to a maximum of three consecutive three-year terms.

As in the United States, the Congress is a powerful legislative institution, enjoying substantial autonomy *vis-à-vis* the executive. Bills originate within Congress, the approval of both chambers being required for their passage. Joint 'conference sessions' are convened to iron out differences when they arise. The Senate has special authority over foreign affairs, two-thirds approval from it being required for the ratification of all international treaties and agreements.

Executive authority resides with the President, who serves as head of state, chief executive of the republic and commander-in-chief of the armed forces. The President, together with a Vice-President, who automatically assumes the presidency for the remainder of the unexpired term in the case of the President's death or resignation, is popularly elected in a direct national contest for a non-renewable six-year term. The office holder must be at least 40 years of age, a native-born, literate citizen and have resided in the country for at least ten years prior to the election. The President appoints an executive cabinet of around 25–35 members, to take charge of departmental administration. He, or she, also appoints ambassadors, military officers and government department chiefs. These appointments are subject, however, to the approval, by majority vote, of the Commission on Appointments (COA), a 25-member body consisting of twelve Senators and twelve Representatives, elected from the political parties represented in each chamber on the basis of proportional representation. The COA is chaired, *ex officio*, by the president of the Senate.

The President and his or her cabinet cannot directly introduce legislation into Congress. They are expected, however, to set the 'policy agenda' and ensure that suitable legislation is introduced by their party supporters within Congress. All bills that have been approved by Congress must also be signed by the President before they can become law. The President can veto such measures, but this veto can be overridden by a two-thirds majority in Congress. Finally, in an emergency, the President may proclaim martial law or suspend the writ of *habeas corpus* for a period of up to 60 days. However, these actions may be revoked by Congress by majority vote.

The 1987 constitution is a determinedly liberal and democratic document, building in substantial checks and balances between the legislative and executive branches of government, in an effort to prevent the recrudescence of authoritarian executive rule that was the feature of the 1972–86 period. A substantially independent judiciary, headed by a 15-member Supreme Court, whose members are appointed for four-year terms by the President, with the approval of the COA, and four Constitutional Commissions, for Appointments, Audit, Civil Service, and Elections, also operate as a means of checking abuses of privileges. In addition, the 1987 constitution includes a special 'Bill of Rights' which guarantees civil liberties, including 'freedom of speech, of the press and of petition to the Government'; access to official information; the right to form trade unions and to 'assemble in public gatherings'; the right of *habeas corpus;* and the prohibition of 'the intimidation, detention, torture or secret confinement of apprehended persons'.

Proposals to amend the constitution may initially be made either by a vote of three-quarters of the members of Congress; or by a Constitutional Convention, convened by a vote of two-thirds of the members of Congress; or through a public petition signed by at least 12 per cent of the country's registered voters. Proposed amendments are then submitted to the people in a national plebiscite and, to become valid, must secure a majority of the votes cast.

Political parties

Political parties were banned between 1972 and 1978, but permitted in the 1984 elections, since when, inspired by the events of 1986–87, a new 'party system', based on two broad government and opposition groupings, has begun to develop. In general, however, political parties in the Philippines, compared with those of Western Europe, are weak affairs, and based primarily on personalities and local patronage ties. Internally they are highly factionalised and formal organisational structures remain inchoate. Instead, fluid, opportunistic and ephemeral tactical alliances are effected between 'vote controlling' bosses at the local level.

The dominant governing coalition grouping is People's Power (Lakas ng Bayan), an umbrella movement for pro-Aquino parties. It was formed in 1987 to contest the congressional elections. It is a successor to the United Nationalist Democratic Organisation (UNIDO), which was formed in 1982, under the leadership of Salvador Laurel, the present Vice-President, as a coalition of anti-Marcos interests. One of the two principal forces within People's Power is the PDP-Laban Party, a grouping which was formed in February 1983 through the merger of the Pilipino Democratic Party, established in 1982 by ex-members of the Mindanao Alliance, and the Laban (Lakas ng Bayan–People's Power Movement), formed in 1978 by Benigno Aquino. The PDP-Laban, which is currently led by José Cojuangco Jr, the brother of President Aquino, is centrist in outlook and claims a membership of 110,000. The other influential member of the People's Power coalition is the Liberal Party, a centrist, liberal party, originally formed in 1946, and currently led by Jovito Salonga, who also holds the influential positions of president of the Senate and chairman of the COA. Since 1988, the Liberal Party has begun to establish itself as the dominant partner in the ruling coalition, having attracted defectors from both the PDP-Laban and from UNIDO. In so doing it has doubled its congressional strength. The party's leader, Salonga, has also become increasingly critical of government strategies. During the January 1988 local elections, candidates were put up against the PDP-Laban, indicating increasing independence on the former's part. Two smaller, pro-Aquino groupings, the Lakas ng Bansa (People's Struggle), established in 1987, and led by Paul Aquino, and Bandila, formed in 1984, also fought the 1987 congressional elections under the People's Power umbrella. So did a fifth, and larger, party, the rural and industrial workers' Labor Party of the Philippines, established in 1982 and led by Maniloto Paran.

Opposed to the People's Power coalition is the Grand Alliance for Democracy (GAD), which was formed in 1987, under the leadership of the former Marcos defence minister, Juan Ponce Enrile, to contest the 1987 national elections. It is an anti-communist and anti-Aquino grouping which supports the retention of US military bases in the Philippines. Within the GAD are the Mindanao Alliance, the Nationalist Party and the Social Democratic Party (SDP). The Mindanao Alliance was established in 1978 and is led by Homobono Adaza. It campaigns for the safeguarding of civil rights and the economic development of Mindanao Island. The Nationalist Party was founded in 1907, and is a right-wing grouping, now led by Salvador Laurel. It used to compete with the Liberal Party for power in a two-party manner between 1946 and 1972. The SDP dates from 1981 and is led by Andrea Corominan.

Also opposed to the government are the right-wing, pro-Marcos New Society Movement (Kilusan Bagong Lipunan) and the, officially banned, communist National Democratic Front. The New Society Movement was established in 1978 and is led by Vicente Mellora. The National Democratic Front is an umbrella alliance of 13 left-wing groups, the two most important of which are the Communist Party of the Philippines (PKP: Partido Kommunista ng Pilipinas) and the New People's Army (NPA). The PKP was established in 1930 and is a 30,000-member Maoist body, led by José Maria Sison, who was imprisoned between 1977 and 1986. The NPA is the PKP's 25,000-member guerrilla wing. It was founded in 1969 and is led by Romulo Kintanar, who was arrested by government forces in March 1988 but subsequently escaped from confinement. The NPA currently exercises *de facto* control over a sixth of the country's villages.

Latest elections

The most recent congressional elections, the country's first free elections since 1971, were held in May 1987. In the Senate contests, the pro-Aquino People's Power coalition won 22 seats, the remaining two being secured by Juan Enrile and Joseph Estrada of the GAD. Estrada, a popular film star, subsequently switched allegiance and joined the Liberal Party, in October 1987. In the House of Representatives elections, People's Power won 180 of the 200 elected seats, the remainder being shared between GAD and other opposition groupings.

Eighty-nine candidates contested the Senate seats and 1,900 the House. Voter turnout was put at 83 per cent. The elections were viewed as being substantially fair, although intimidation, predominantly by pro-Marcos factions, and isolated instances of vote buying and ballot box stuffing, by pro-Aquino groups, remained evident. On polling day, 34 people were killed in election-related violence. However, this death toll was well below the 158 killings recorded in the 1986 presidential campaign and the 124, including 41 candidates, during the January 1988 local election campaign. These figures all compare favourably with the 1971 local elections' death toll of 905.

Political history

The Philippines consist of an archipelago of more than 7,100 islands and islets, of which around 700 are inhabited, extending 1,851 km between the south-east and the north-west. Eleven islands, Luzon, Mindanao, Samar, Negros, Palawan, Panay, Mindoro, Leyte, Cebu, Bohol, and Masbate, account for 93 per cent of the land area and population, the two most important, Luzon and Mindanao, contributing two-thirds. More than half the country's total area is forested.

The islands of the Philippines were subject to successive waves of Malay, Indonesian and Chinese settlement, before being 'discovered' by Ferdinand Magellan, and subsequently conquered by Spanish forces, in 1565. Roman Catholicism was introduced during the reign of Philip II, after whom the islands were named, replacing the Muslim religion which had been spread by Arab traders and missionaries. Under Spanish rule, a sugar, tobacco, rubber and coffee based plantation economy was established, with rigid socio-economic stratification developing between the darker skinned, Malay-origin, peasantry (*indios*) and the fairer skinned, estate-owning 'mixed blood' (*mestizo*) élite, of Spanish and Chinese origin. A series of armed nationalist revolts broke out during the nineteenth century and continued after the islands were ceded by Spain to the United States, in December 1898, after the war the two countries fought over Cuba. This resulted in the concession of increasing degrees of internal self-government to the Philippines, in 1916 and 1935.

During the Second World War, the Philippines were occupied by the Japanese, between 1942 and 1945, before becoming a fully independent republic in July 1946. A succession of Presidents drawn from the islands' wealthy estate-owning élite followed between 1946 and 1948: Manual Roxas (1946–48), Elpidio Quirino (1948–53), Ramon Magsaysay (1953–57), Carlos Garcia (1957–61) and Diosdado Macapagal (1961–65). They did little to improve the lot of the ordinary peasant. A partial exception, between 1953 and 1957 was the honest, humble-born Ramon Magsaysay. During Magsaysay's presidency, the Philippines enjoyed a period of extended economic growth which temporarily established the country as the richest per capita, after Japan, in Asia. The internal menace posed by the communist Hukbalahap guerrillas, an insurgency grouping which had originally been formed to fight the Japanese but which had continued its operations after independence, was suppressed through a skilful combination of force and incentives. However, following Magsaysay's death in an air crash in 1957, the country rapidly retrogressed under the corrupt and lacklustre stewardships of Garcia and Macapagal.

In the presidential election of November 1965, Diosdado Macapagal, leader of the Liberal Party, was eventually defeated by Ferdinand Marcos, the dynamic young leader of the Nationalist Party. Marcos, promising a new start, initiated a programme of rapid economic development, based on import-substituting industrialisation and infrastructural investment. He was re-elected in 1969, but during his second term encountered growing opposition from new communist insurgents, the New People's Army

(NPA), in Luzon, in the north, and from Muslim separatists, the Moro National Liberation Front (MNLF), in Mindanao province, in the south. In September 1972, 14 months before his second, and constitutionally his last, term had been completed, and with the economy deteriorating rapidly and the communist insurgency growing in strength, Marcos declared martial law, suspended the constitution and began to rule by decree. The birth of a 'New Society' was proclaimed.

The following year, President Marcos announced a return to democratic government. A new constitution, providing for a single-chamber National Assembly (Batasang Pambansa), a constitutional President and an executive Prime Minister, elected by the Assembly, was formally promulgated. However, Marcos proposed that, for the time being, he should remain in office and continue to rule by decree. Referenda in July 1973, February 1975 and October 1976 approved these actions, allowing him to retain power. Criticisms of Marcos' authoritarian and corrupt leadership were, however, growing and in November 1977 the main opposition leader, Benigno Aquino, was sentenced to death, for alleged subversion, by a military tribunal.

In April 1978 martial law was relaxed and elections for an interim National Assembly held, resulting in an overwhelming victory for Marcos and his supporters' party, the New Society Movement, a party which had been specially formed for the election by former Nationalist Party members. Soon afterwards Aquino, who was a sick man, was temporarily released from prison to travel to the United States for medical attention. In January 1981, martial law was lifted completely and hundreds of political prisoners released. Marcos then won approval, by referendum, for a partial return to democratic government, with himself as President for a new six-year term, working with a Prime Minister and Executive Council. Political and economic conditions deteriorated, however, as the NPA guerrilla insurgency escalated. With GDP growth now negative, unemployment climbed to over 30 per cent and, following the sudden rise in the international oil price between 1979 and 1982, national indebtedness and debt-servicing problems increased sharply.

In August 1983, the opposition leader Benigno Aquino returned from the United States and was immediately shot dead on his arrival at Manila airport. A commission of inquiry reported eleven months later that Aquino had been killed by the military guard escorting him as part of a broader conspiracy. This act had momentous repercussions for the Marcos regime, serving to unite a previously disunited opposition. National Assembly elections were held in May 1984, amid violence and widespread claims of corruption, and although they resulted in success for the government party, which captured 68 per cent of the 183 elective seats, they also registered significant gains for the opposition. Then, early in 1986, the main anti-Marcos movement, the United Nationalist Democratic Organisation (UNIDO), chose Aquino's widow, Corazon, despite her political inexperience, to contest new elections for the presidency which Marcos had been persuaded to hold, as a means of maintaining American economic and diplomatic support.

The presidential campaign of December 1985–February 1986 proved violent, resulting in more than 150 deaths, and widespread electoral fraud was witnessed by international observers. On 16 February 1986, following polling a week earlier, the National Assembly declared Marcos the winner by 54 per cent to 46 per cent. This result, however, was immediately disputed by an independent electoral watchdog, the National Citizens' Movement for Free Elections (Namfrel). Corazon Aquino began a non-violent protest, termed 'People's Power', which gathered massive popular support, particularly from the Roman Catholic Church. President Marcos also came under strong international pressure, particularly from his former ally, the United States, to stand down. On 22 February 1986 the army, led by the chief of staff Lieutenant-General Fidel Ramos, and defence minister Juan Enrile, declared its support for Corazon Aquino and on 25 February Marcos, given guarantees of safe passage, left for exile in Hawaii.

On assuming the presidency, Corazon Aquino immediately dissolved the pro-Marcos National Assembly and announced plans for the framing of a new 'freedom constitution'. She proceeded to govern in a conciliatory fashion, working with an emergency coalition cabinet team, comprising a broad cross-section of radical, liberal and conservative opposition politicians and senior military figures. Five hundred political prisoners were freed and an amnesty granted to the NPA's communist guerrillas, in an effort to bring an end to the 17-year-old insurgency. She also introduced a major rural employment economic programme. The new administration was faced, however, during the summer and autumn months of 1986, with a series of attempted coups by pro-Marcos supporters, as well as internal opposition from defence secretary Enrile, resulting in his dismissal, in November 1986.

In February 1987, a new constitution was overwhelmingly approved by 76 per cent of the voters in a national plebiscite. This gave Aquino a mandate to rule as President until 30 June 1992 and paved the way for elections to the new two-chamber Congress in May 1987.

The congressional elections resulted in a huge majority for the supporters of President Aquino. In August 1987, however, the government was rocked by another attempted military coup, the most serious thus far, led by Colonel Gregorio Honasan, an army officer linked closely with Enrile, in which 53 people were killed in intense fighting in Manila and Cebu. Facing accusations of 'policy drift', President Aquino responded by making a major cabinet reshuffle, in September 1987. This involved the replacement of Vice-President Laurel as foreign affairs secretary by Senator Raul Manglapus, and the sacking of finance secretary Jaime Ongpin and the President's 'leftist' executive secretary Joker Arroyo. These changes signalled a shift to the right for the Aquino administration, which proceeded to approve a series of tough measures to deal with the NPA insurgency and a more conservative economic and social programme. Included in the latter was an important, though diluted, Land Reform Act, which was passed by Congress in June 1988, and which included favourable compensation terms for substantial estate holders.

President Aquino's policy shift disappointed her more radical 'People's Power' supporters but was viewed as necessary for the maintenance of internal order and as a means of preventing further coup attempts by the disaffected military. As part of this new pragmatic approach, and as a means of securing vital backing from the Philippines' long-time ally, the United States, President Aquino intimated that, subject to public approval in a national plebiscite, an agreement might be made to allow US forces to continue to use the important Subic Bay naval and Clark Field air bases, after the two countries' eight-year agreement, signed in June 1983, expired in 1991.

President Aquino has suggested that she will retire in 1992 and not seek office again as the country's first elected President under the new post-Marcos constititution. The American-trained General Fidel Ramos, a Protestant, who became defence secretary in January 1988, and who proved crucial in suppressing the anti-Aquino military coups of 1986–87, is viewed as a strong potential contender for this post. A likely rival is Vice-President Laurel who, now estranged from Aquino, formed a new right-of-centre opposition force, the Union for National Action (UNA), in August 1988 and became President of the revived Nationalist Party in May 1989.

SOLOMON ISLANDS

Capital: Honiara

Social and economic data

Area: 29,790 km^2
Population: 283,000*
Pop density per km^2: 9*
Literacy rate: 54%
GDP: $150m*; per capita GDP: $530
Economy type: low income
Labour force in agriculture: 32%

*1985

Ethnic composition

Ninety-three per cent of the population are Melanesian, 4 per cent Polynesian, 1.5 per cent Micronesian, 0.7 per cent European and 0.2 per cent Chinese. The official language is English, although many local languages are also spoken.

Religions

Ninety-five per cent of the population are Christians: 34 per cent adhering to the Church of Melanesia (Anglican), 19 per cent to the Roman Catholic Church, 17 per cent to the South Seas Evangelical Church, 11 per cent to the United Church and 10 per cent to the Seventh-day Adventist Church. Traditional, ancestor worship also prevails.

Political features

State type: liberal democracy
Date of state formation: 1978
Political structure: unitary
Executive: parliamentary
Assembly: one-chamber
Party structure: multi-party
Human rights rating: N/A

Local and regional government

The country is divided into four districts, within which there are eight elected local government councils. Seven of them have provincial assemblies, Western, Guidalcanal, Central, Malaita, Santa Isabel, Eastern and San Cristobal, and one, Honiara, has a town council.

Head of state

Queen Elizabeth II, represented by Governor-General Sir Baddeley Devesi, since 1978.

Head of government

Prime Minister Solomon Mamaloni, since 1989.

Political leaders since 1970

1974–76 Solomon Mamaloni (PPP), 1976–81 Peter Kenilorea (SIUPA), 1981–84 Solomon Mamaloni (PAP), 1984–86 Sir Peter Kenilorea (SIUPA), 1986–89 Ezekiel Alebua (SIUPA), 1989– Solomon Mamaloni (PAP).

Political system

The most recent constitution dates from independence in July 1978. This established the state as a constitutional monarchy within the Commonwealth, in which a resident Governor-General represents the crown as head of state. The Governor-General, who must be a Solomon Islands' citizen, is appointed for a renewable five-year term on the recommendation of the assembly. This is called the National Parliament and is a single-chamber body of 38 members elected by universal adult suffrage, on a simple plurality basis in single-member constituencies. The parliamentary system adheres closely to the Westminster model, with the Governor-General appointing a Prime Minister and cabinet, on the Prime Minister's recommendation, drawn from and collectively responsible to the assembly, which is subject to dissolution within its four-year term. In March 1989, the cabinet comprised 15 members, including representatives of the People's Alliance Party (PAP) and Solomon's Ano Sagufenua (SAS) as well as independents. Following the publication, in March 1988, of a report by a specially commissioned constitutional review committee, which recommended the establishment of a new federal republic, the country's future political structure has become the subject of lively internal debate.

Political parties

The two principal political parties are the opposition Solomon Islands United Party (SIUPA), led by Sir Peter Kenilorea, and the governing People's Alliance Party (PAP), led by Solomon Mamaloni. The SIUPA, an outgrowth of the Civil Servants Association, was formed in 1973 and initially participated in a coalition government with the PPP between 1975 and 1976, before emerging as the dominant force in 1976. A faction, the Nationalist Front for Progress (NFP), led by Andrew Nori, then the home affairs minister, split from the SIUPA in October 1985, establishing itself as an 'open forum' for those wishing to discuss land disputes. The PAP, which was the governing party, though in coalitions, between 1974–76 and 1981–84, is viewed as a more centre-left force than the conservative, pro-British SIUPA. It was formed in 1973 under the designation People's

Progressive Party (PPP), before uniting with the Rural Alliance Party, which was established in 1977, to form the PAP, in 1979. The PAP favours greater decentralisation of power and the strengthening of regional Melanesian alliances.

The two dominant political parties are both loose, personality-based regional alliances, rather than disciplined and ideologically-united units. Two other significant minor parties operate: the Solomons Ano Sagufenua (SAS), formed in 1984 and led by Alan Qurusu; and the Solomon Islands Liberal Party (SILP), led by Bartholomew Ulufa'alu, which was formed in 1976 as the National Democratic Party (NADEPA), functioning as the political wing of the trade union movement, before adopting its present name in 1986.

Latest elections

In the most recent elections, held in February 1989, the PAP captured 14 seats, the SIUPA six, the SILP four, the NFP three, the SAS two and independents nine. Voter turnout was around 60 per cent.

Political history

The Solomon Islands are an archipelago of several hundred small islands, situated in the south Pacific Ocean, scattered between Papua New Guinea in the north-west and Vanuatu in the south-east. The six principal islands are Choiseul, Guadalcanal, Malaita, New Georgia, San Cristobal and Santa Isobal. The bulk of the population reside in dispersed settlements along the coasts and are involved in subsistence agriculture or work on copra and palm oil plantations.

The islands, which at the time were inhabited by Melanesians, were 'discovered' by the Spanish navigator, Alvaro de Mendana, in 1568, but were not visited again by Europeans until the later eighteenth century. The Northern Solomon Islands became a German protectorate in 1885 and the Southern Solomon Islands a British protectorate in 1893. Five years later, Germany ceded its possessions to Britain and, in 1900, a unified British Solomon Islands Protectorate (BSIP) was formed. This was placed under the jurisdiction of the Western Pacific High Commission (WPHC), whose headquarters was in Fiji. A resident commissioner was placed in charge of day-to-day administration. During the Second World War, the islands were invaded by Japan, in 1942, but recaptured by the United States a year later.

After the war, the islands remained under British control, the WPHC moving its headquarters to Honiara. Elected island councils began to be established and, under a constitution adopted in October 1960, legislative and executive councils were established. These were amalgamated into a single elected Governing Council, based on a ministerial system, under the terms of the March 1970 constitution, as amended in 1973. In April 1974, following the adoption of a new constitution, the islands became substantially self-governing, a 24-member Legislative Assembly being established, from whose members a Chief Minister, who enjoyed the right of appointing a cabinet, or Council of Ministers, was selected. Solomon Mamaloni, leader of the newly formed People's Progressive Party (PPP), was chosen as the country's first Chief Minister, in August 1974.

The BSIP was renamed the Solomon Islands in June 1975 and in January 1976 became fully self-governing, when the Chief Minister was allowed to preside over the Council of Ministers in place of the British-appointed governor. After new Legislative Assembly elections, in June 1976, Peter Kenilorea was chosen as the new Chief Minister. He was re-designated Prime Minister, and the Legislative Assembly the National Parliament, when full independence, within the Commonwealth, was granted in July 1978. Kenilorea was re-elected in August 1980, following fresh parliamentary elections, but the following year was defeated on a motion of no-confidence in the National Parliament and replaced by former Chief Minister Solomon Mamaloni. The chief factor behind Kenilorea's downfall had been his resistance to growing pressure, which was particularly strong in the commercially developed Western District, to decentralise and devolve powers to the regions. In contrast, his successor, Mamaloni, warmly supported the idea and one of his first actions as Prime Minister was to create five ministerial posts specifically for provincial affairs.

By the time of the October 1984 general election, support for Sir Peter Kenilorea, as he had become, had risen and he was put back into office, at the head of a coalition government. He immediately abolished the five provincial ministries, restoring the balance between central and regional power. Support for the governing party soon began to wane, however. Kenilorea narrowly survived 'no-confidence' votes in parliament in September 1985 and July 1986 and was forced to reconstitute his coalition when the Solomons Ano Sagufenua (SAS) Party withdrew its support. Following allegations that he had secretly accepted US$47,000 of French aid to repair cyclone damage to his home village in Malaita province, and faced with a fresh 'no-confidence' motion, Kenilorea eventually resigned as Prime Minister, in December 1986. He was replaced, following three secret ballots in parliament, by the Deputy Prime Minister and fellow Solomon Islands United Party (SIUPA) member, Ezekiel Alebua. Kenilorea continued, however, to hold ministerial office, serving, first, as natural resources minister and, then, from February 1988, as joint foreign minister and Deputy Prime Minister, while Alebua continued to adhere to the existing policy course. However, at the general election of February 1989 support for the SIUPA slumped, its seats tally being halved, and the PAP, led by Mamaloni, re-emerged as the dominant political party. Mamaloni became head of a new coalition government which was determined to reduce the influence of 'foreign aid personnel' and which promised to reform the constitution so as to establish a republic.

Since the 1960s, the broad strategy of successive governments has been to diversify the islands' economic base, reducing dependence on copra exports, by encouraging tuna, timber, palm kernel and cocoa exports. This has been successfully achieved. Nevertheless, the country was adversely affected by the decline in world commodity prices during the early 1980s, resulting in a decline in GDP and a sharp rise both in the inflation rate and balance of payments deficit. The current rapid rate of population growth, around 3.8 per cent per annum, has not helped matters. As a consequence, the country remains heavily dependent on foreign economic aid, 15 per cent of its GDP being currently derived from this source.

In its external relations, the Solomon Islands, under the SIUPA administrations, has pursued a moderate, pro-Western course. This has contrasted with the more radical approach of the PAP between 1981 and 1984, when relations with the United States were strained by the government's refusal to allow nuclear-powered warships within Solomon Islands' territorial waters and by the seizure of an American fishing boat in June 1984, for violating its claimed 200-mile sea limit. In March 1988, the Solomon Islands, as part of a new, broader 'Pacific strategy', joined Vanuatu and Papua New Guinea to form the 'Spearhead Group'. The principal aims of this grouping are to preserve Melanesian cultural traditions and to secure independence for the French overseas territory of New Caledonia.

TONGA

Kingdom of Tonga
Pule'anga Fakatu'i 'o Tonga

Capital: Nuku'alofa

Social and economic data

Area: 751 km^2
Population: 105,000*
Pop density per km^2: 140*
Literacy rate: 99%
GDP: $70m*; per capita GDP: $667
Economy type: low income
Labour force in agriculture: 44%

*1985

Ethnic composition

Ninety-eight per cent of the population are of Tongan ethnic stock, a Polynesian group with a small mixture of Melanesian. The remainder are Europeans and part-Europeans. Tongan (Tongatabu) is the official language, with English and Polynesian sub-dialects also being widely spoken.

Religions

The population is almost entirely Christian. Forty-seven per cent and 9 per cent respectively adhere to the Methodist Free Wesleyan Church of Tonga and Church of Tonga; 15 per cent to Roman Catholicism; and 14 per cent to the Church of Jesus Christ of Latter-day Saints (Mormons).

Political features

State type: absolutist
Date of state formation: 1970
Political structure: unitary
Executive: absolute
Assembly: one-chamber
Party structure: no parties
Human rights rating: N/A

Local and regional government
For administrative purposes, the country is divided into three districts, Vava'u, Ha'apai and Tongatapu, corresponding to its three island groups. The first two districts are administered by governors who are *ex officio* members of the Privy Council. For Tongatapu, the King acts as governor. Below, there is a small network of town and district officials who have been popularly elected since 1965.

Head of state and head of government
King Taufa'ahou Tupou IV, since 1965.

Political leaders since 1970
1965– King Taufa'ahou Tupou IV.

Political system
Tonga is an independent hereditary monarchy within the Commonwealth. Its constitution dates from 1875, having been most recently revised in 1970, and provides for a monarch who is both head of state and head of government. He appoints and presides over a Privy Council, which also serves as a cabinet, and consists of himself, eight ministers and the governors, of Ha'apai and Vava'u. The cabinet is led by the Prime Minister, who is currently the King's younger brother, and includes, as *ex officio* members, the governors of Ha'apai and Vava'u. There is a single-chamber Legislative Assembly, of 29 members, who include the King, the Privy Council, nine hereditary nobles, elected by the 33 hereditary nobles of Tonga, and nine representatives of the people, elected by universal adult suffrage. The Assembly has a life of three years and meets at least once a year, usually for a session which lasts between two and four months. Legislation, in the form of ordinances passed by the executive, is subject to review by the Assembly.

Political parties
There are no political parties in Tonga, 'People's Representatives' being elected as independents. However, within the Legislative Assembly informal pro- and anti-government groupings do form from time to time.

Latest elections
In the most recent Legislative Assembly elections, held in February 1987, six of the nine 'People's Representatives' were replaced by newcomers, the majority of whom were viewed as government critics.

Political history
Tonga is an island chain in the south-west Pacific Ocean, 2,250 kilometres north east of New Zealand and 640 kilometres east of Fiji, between 18 and 22 degrees south of the equator. It comprises 133 inhabited and 36 uninhabited volcanic and coral islands divided into three main groups, Vava'u in the north, Ha'apai in the centre and Tongatapu-Eua in the south. Sixty-eight per cent of the population reside on the main island of Tongatapu, on which the capital of Nuku'alofa is situated.

The first European visitor to Tonga was the Dutch explorer, Abel Tasman, in 1643. More than a century later, in 1773, the islands were charted by Captain Cook and dubbed the 'Friendly Islands'. The contemporary Tongan dynasty was founded in 1831 by Prince Taufa'ahau Tupou, who took the name King George Tupou I when he ascended the throne. He consolidated the kingdom by conquest, encouraged the spread of Christianity, and, in 1875, granted a constitution. In 1900 his great-grandson, King George Tupou II, signed a Treaty of Friendship and Protection under which Tonga formally became a British protectorate. Tonga retained its independence and substantial internal autonomy, but handed over control of its foreign policy and defence to the United Kingdom. This position was broadly reaffirmed in revised treaties which were signed in 1958 and 1967, under which Tonga was granted increased control over its internal affairs.

Queen Salote Tupou III, who had ascended the throne in 1918, died in December 1965 and was succeeded by her son Prince Tupouto'a Tungi, who had been Prime Minister since 1949. He assumed the title King Tuafa'ahou Tupou IV and appointed his brother, Prince Fatafehi Tu'ipelehake as the new Prime Minister. Full independence, within the Commonwealth, was finally achieved in June 1970, giving the nation control over its foreign affairs. The country's foreign policy approach since independence has, however, changed little, the country remaining the strongest supporter of the Western powers in the Pacific region, particularly close links being maintained with Britain, Australia and New Zealand. Tonga remains dependent on foreign development aid for more than a fifth of its current GDP and is still heavily reliant on its traditional cash crop exports of bananas and coconuts. Although recent lucrative growth has been achieved by both the tourist and fishing industries, unemployment, exacerbated by a rapid population expansion, of more than 2 per cent per annum, remains high, resulting in substantial labour emigration.

TUVALU

South West Pacific State of Tuvalu

Capital: Funafuti (Fongafale)

Social and economic data

Area: 26 km^2
Population: 9,000*
Pop density per km^2: 330*
Literacy rate: 95%
GDP: $3.2m*; per capita GDP: $372
Economy type: low income
Labour force in agriculture: N/A

*1985

Ethnic composition

The population are almost entirely of Polynesian stock, maintaining close ties with the Samoans and Tokelauans to the south and east. Tuvaluan and English are the principal languages.

Religions
Ninety-eight per cent of the population are adherents to the Protestant Church of Tuvalu (Ekalesia Tuvalu), which was established in 1861. It is a Congregationalist body derived from the London Missionary Society.

Political features
State type: liberal democracy
Date of state formation: 1978
Political structure: unitary
Executive: parliamentary
Assembly: one-chamber
Party structure: no parties
Human rights rating: N/A

Local and regional government
For local government, each inhabited atoll has its own six-member island council, headed by a president. The councils meet in large council halls *(maneabas)*, which are also used to sleep as many as 1,000 people during the annual communal feasts, which last for several weeks.

Head of state
Queen Elizabeth II, represented by Governor-General Sir Tupua Leupena, since 1986.

Head of government
Prime Minister Dr Tomasi Puapua, since 1981.

Political leaders since 1970
1975–81 Toaripi Lauti (Ind), 1981– Dr Tomasi Puapua (Ind).

Political system
The constitution dates from October 1978 when Tuvalu became an independent state within the Commonwealth, retaining the monarch as head of state, represented by a resident Governor-General. The system of government contains elements of the British, Westminster, model, with a single-chamber parliament of twelve members and a Prime Minister and cabinet, of four additional ministers, elected by and responsible to it. The Governor-General must be a citizen of Tuvalu and is appointed on the recommendation of the Prime Minister. The Prime Minister also currently holds the portfolios of foreign minister and civil service and local government minister. Members of parliament are elected by universal adult suffrage, through a simple plurality voting system, for a four-year term. The parliament is subject to dissolution during its term. Four atolls, Nanumea, Niutao, Vaitupu and Funafuti, each send two representatives to parliament, with Niulakita being regarded, for electoral purposes, as part of Niutao. The remaining four atolls return one member each.

Political parties
There are no political parties, members being elected to parliament as independents.

Latest elections

The most recent parliamentary elections were held in September 1985, twelve independents being returned, with an average of three candidates contesting each seat.

Political history

Tuvalu is a small island grouping in the south-west Pacific, 1,050 kilometres north of Fiji and 4,020 kilometres north-east of Sydney, Australia. It comprises the low lying coral atolls of Funafuti, on which 34 per cent of the population reside, Vaitupu, with 15 per cent, Nanumea, 11 per cent, Niutao, 11 per cent, Nukufetau, 8 per cent, Nanumanga, 7 per cent, Nui, 7 per cent, Nukulailai, 4 per cent, and Niulakita, 1 per cent, and extends 560 kilometres from north to south.

The islands were invaded and occupied by Samoans during the sixteenth century. In the mid-nineteenth century, between 1850 and 1875, European slave traders visited Tuvalu and captured the indigenous Melanesians for forced labour in the guano mines and on the coffee plantations of South America. As a result of both these activities and the importation of European diseases, the islands' population fell markedly from an estimated 20,000 to barely 3,000.

In 1877, when the British established the Western Pacific High Commission (WPHC), with its headquarters on Fiji, Tuvalu, which at this time was known as the Ellice, or Lagoon, Islands, was placed under its charge. Fifteen years later, in 1892, the islands were officially declared a British Protectorate and were linked, for administrative purposes, with the larger, Micronesian-peopled, Gilbert Islands, known today as Kiribati. From 1916 the protectorate was ruled formally as a colony under the designation Gilbert and Ellice Islands Colony (GEIC), a resident commissioner being based on Tarawa Atoll in the Gilbert group.

During the Second World War, the GEIC was invaded and occupied by Japan in 1942. A year later, the Japanese were removed by American naval forces and British control re-established. After the war, a succession of advisory and legislative councils were set up, paving the way for self-government. This culminated, in May 1974, in the establishment of a House of Assembly, comprising 28 elected members, eight from the Ellice Islands, and three official members. The assembly elected a Chief Minister and between four to six cabinet ministers, one of whom had to be from the Ellice Islands. The British seemed, at this time, to be preparing the way for granting independence to the GEIC as a constituent whole. This, however, was strongly opposed by the Ellice Islanders, who feared domination by the Micronesians of the Gilbert Islands. They therefore pressed for separate status and in a referendum held on the Ellice Islands in August–September 1974 they voted overwhelmingly, by a 90 per cent majority, for this option. Thus, in October 1975, reverting to their traditional name of Tuvalu, meaning 'eight standing together', the Ellice Islands became a separate British dependency. The eight Ellice Islands' representatives of the former GEIC House of Assembly constituted themselves as a new Tuvalu House of Assembly and elected Toaripi Lauti as their first Chief Minister.

In the House of Assembly elections of August 1977, the number of elective seats was increased to twelve and a year later, in October 1978, following the framing in London of a constitution, Tuvalu became fully independent as a 'special member', of the Commonwealth. This meant that, because of its small size, it did not participate in heads of governments' meetings. Lauti became the country's Prime Minister and the House of Assembly was re-designated parliament.

In the first post-independence parliamentary elections, of September 1981, Lauti, who had been involved in an alleged investment scandal, was replaced as Prime Minister, following a seven to five parliamentary vote against him. His successor was Dr Tomasi Puapua, who was re-elected in September 1985. During 1986 constitutional changes designed to reduce the authority of the Governor-General, and in particular his right to reject the advice of the incumbent government, were mooted. However, in February 1986, in a national poll held to decide whether Tuvalu should remain a constitutional monarchy or become a republic, only one atoll supported republican status.

As a result of its scanty resource base, with much of the soil too poor to make cultivation feasible, economic development has been slow in Tuvalu. Rapid population growth, currently at 3.4 per cent per annum, and the closure of the phosphate mines in neighbouring Kiribati in 1979, where many Tuvaluans worked, have made matters worse, depressing living standards in recent years. As a consequence, the country has become highly dependent on overseas development aid, more than a quarter of its GDP being derived from this source.

In its conduct of foreign relations, the administration of Dr Puapua has maintained close links with Britain and the United States. The government has, however, been a strong opponent of the French nuclear weapons testing programme based at Mururoa Atoll, in French Polynesia, refusing permision for a French warship to visit the country on a goodwill mission in February 1986.

VANUATU

Republic of Vanuatu

Capital: Port Vila

Social and economic data
Area: 14,760 km^2
Population: 136,000*
Pop density per km^2: 9*
Literacy rate: 53%
GDP: $90m*; per capita GDP: $662
Economy type: low income
Labour force in agriculture: 77%

*1985

Ethnic composition
Ninety-five per cent of the population are Melanesian; 3 per cent European or mixed European; and 2 per cent Vietnamese, Chinese or other Pacific islanders. Bislama (ni-Vanuatu pidgin English) is the official language, with English and French also being widely understood.

Religions
Thirty-three per cent of the population are members of the Presbyterian Church of Vanuatu; 13 per cent of the Church of the Province of Melanesia; 13 per cent Roman Catholic; 10 per cent belong to other Christian Churches, including the Apostolic, Churches of Christ, Assemblies of God and Seventh-day Adventist. Nine per cent adhere to animist beliefs.

Political features
State type: liberal democracy
Date of state formation: 1980
Political structure: unitary
Executive: parliamentary
Assembly: one-chamber
Party structure: multi-party
Human rights rating: N/A

Local and regional government
The country is divided into four administrative regions, with headquarters at Lenakel (Tanna), Vila, Lamap (Malekula) and Espiritu Santo. Most islands also have their own local councils.

Head of state
President Fred Timakata, since 1989.

Head of government
Prime Minister Father Walter Hadye Lini, since 1980.

Political leaders since 1970
1978–80 Father Gerard Leymang (Ind), 1980– Father Walter Lini (VP).

Political system
Vanuatu is an independent republic within the Commonwealth. The constitution dates from independence in July 1980. It provides for a President, who functions as a ceremonial head of state and is elected for a five-year term in a secret ballot by an electoral college consisting of parliament and the presidents of the country's regional councils. Parliament consists of a single chamber of 46 members, elected by universal adult suffrage, through a system which embraces an element of proportional representation, for a four-year term. They elect a Prime Minister from among their members, who then appoints and presides over a nine- to eleven-member Council of Ministers. In the spring of 1989 the Prime Minister, Walter Lini, also held the public service, planning and information ministerial portfolios. There is a National Council of Chiefs, comprising custom chiefs elected by District Councils of Chiefs, which is empowered to make recommendations to parliament on subjects connected with the preservation and promotion of traditional culture and languages.

Political parties
The ruling Vanuaaku Pati (VP: 'Party of Our Land') was formed in 1972 as the New Hebrides National Party (NHNP). Led by Prime Minister Father

Walter Lini, it promotes a unique 'Melanesian socialist' programme, founded upon non-alignment overseas and, domestically, the transfer of lands held by non-natives to the indigenes. A faction within the VP, led by its radical Secretary-General, Barak Tame Sopé, who was dismissed from the government in May 1988 and was later imprisoned for seditious conspiracy, in March 1989, has strongly opposed recent policy initiatives, in particular, proposed reforms of traditional land ownership rights. The VP's national support, which is drawn predominantly from English-speaking Melanesian Protestant groups, has declined significantly in recent years from the 63 per cent and 56 per cent achieved in the general elections of 1979 and 1983 respectively.

Francophone opposition parties have been grouped since 1980 under the umbrella organisation, the Union of Moderate Parties (UMP), which is nominally led by Maxime Carlot. The UMP was associated with the 1980 Espiritu Santo rebellion and enjoys strong Roman Catholic support. Three other opposition groups were formed in 1986, the National Democratic Party (NDP), the New People's Party (NPP) and the Vanuatu Labour Party (VLP), each of which also favours cultivating closer ties with France and other former Pacific colonial powers. The NDP is currently led by John Naupa, a dissident founder member of the VP; the NPP by a senior civil servant, Jimmy Tasso; and the VLP by Kenneth Satungia, the former Secretary-General of the Vanuatu Trade Union Congress from which it derives the bulk of its support. Five other parties currently function: the Na-Griamel, Namaki Aute and Fren Melanesia, which represent rural interests on Santo and Malekula islands; the conservative, free enterprise, Vanuatu Independent Alliance Party (VIAP); and the regionalist, Efate Island-based, Efate Laketu Party (ELP).

Latest elections

In the most recent parliamentary elections, held in November 1987, the VP won 26 seats, on a 47 per cent share of the vote, and the opposition UMP 20 seats, on a 42 per cent poll share. Turnout was 83 per cent. Nine separate political groupings contested the election, putting forward 100 candidates.

Political history

The Republic of Vanuatu, formerly known as the New Hebrides, is an irregular Y-shaped chain of 13 volcanic islands and 70 islets in the south-west Pacific Ocean lying between Fiji and New Caledonia. Sixty per cent of the population reside on the four main islands of Efate, Espiritu Santo, Malekula and Tanna. The bulk of the inland portions of the islands are densely forested, settlements being concentrated on the coastal fringes.

The islands were first visited by the Portuguese navigator, Pedro Fernandez de Queiras, in 1606, before being charted and named the New Hebrides by the British explorer, James Cook, in 1774. During the nineteenth century they were disputed by both Britain and France until 1887, when a joint naval commission was placed in charge of their administration. From 1906, the New Hebrides (Nouvelles-Hébrides) were placed under a joint Anglo-French condominium, with each power being responsible for its own citizens, governing in its own language and having its own forces and institutions. British and French missionaries, planters and traders subsequently settled in the country, which escaped occupation by Japan during the Second World War.

After the war, an indigenous political grouping, Na-Griamel (NG) began to develop, and was formally established in 1963. It campaigned against the acquisition of native land by Europeans, more than a third of the country's land being owned by foreigners by the 1960s. Later, in 1972, the New Hebrides National Party (NHNP) was formed, enjoying the support of Protestant missions and British interests. It was opposed by the Union of New Hebrides Communities (UNHC), a body which had been established by pro-French groups. Discussions began in London, in 1974, about eventual independence and they resulted in the creation of a 42-member Representative Assembly, 29 members of which were directly elected in November 1975. This body superseded an Advisory Council which had been operating since 1957.

Negotiations for establishing a timetable for a gradual move towards independence, planned for 1980, were hampered by objections by the National Party, which changed its name to the Vanuaaku Party (VP), in January 1977, which pressed for immediate independence. Eventually, however, a Government of National Unity was formed, in December 1978, with Father Gerard Leymang as Chief Minister and the VP leader, Father Walter Lini, a former Anglican priest, as his deputy. A further delay was caused in 1980 when French settlers and pro-NG plantation workers in the island of Espiritu Santo revolted, after a sweeping victory in the Representative Assembly elections of November 1979 by the VP. Jimmy Stevens, leader of the NG, proclaimed Espiritu Santo independent under the designation 'State of Vemarana', in June 1980, allegedly receiving financial support from the Phoenix Foundation, a right-wing group in the United States. The revolt was, controversially, put down by British, French and Papua New Guinean troops after several days of fighting.

Agreement was finally reached about independence, in July 1980, with the new sovereign state remaining within the Commonwealth, and its name being changed to the Republic of Vanuatu. The first President was the former Deputy Chief Minister, George Kalkoa, who adopted the name Sokomanu, or 'leader of thousands', and the first Prime Minister was Father Lini. In the November 1983 general election the VP was re-elected, with a slightly reduced majority, and Father Lini continued as Prime Minister.

Lini proceeded to pursue a controversial left-of-centre, non-aligned foreign policy, which included support for the Kanak National Liberation Front (FLNKS), which was fighting for independence in French-ruled New Caledonia, and the possible establishment of diplomatic relations with the USSR and Libya. This soured relations with France and provoked mounting parliamentary opposition, the government's actions being viewed as likely to discourage both inward foreign investment and the expansion of the tourist industry, with consequential adverse effects on the country's economic development. During 1986 three anti-government opposition parties, the National Democratic Party (NDP), the New People's Party (NPP) and the Vanuatu Labour Party (VLP), were formed. However, in the general election of November 1987, the VP retained its assembly majority and Lini, despite ailing health, was re-elected Prime Minister.

Nevertheless, opposition to Lini's domestic and external policies continued to grow during 1988. In response, in July 1988, the Prime Minister expelled from parliament his intra-party rival Barak Sopé, together with four supporters, as well as 18 opposition MPs who had boycotted parliament in protest. Five months later, in December 1988, Lini was dismissed as Prime Minister and parliament dissolved by President Ati George Sokomanu, who appointed his nephew, Sopé, head of an interim administration. Within days, however, following a Supreme Court ruling that these actions had been unconstitutional, security forces loyal to the former Prime Minister arrested the President, Sopé and opposition leader Maxime Carlot, reinstating Lini in power. Fred Timakata, formerly the minister of health, was elected the new President in January 1989, with, two months later, Sokomanu, Sopé and Carlot each being sentenced to between five and six years' imprisonment for their seditious actions in December 1988.

Externally, Vanuatu's relations with France reached a low point in October 1987, when the French ambassador was expelled from the country for providing 'substantial financial assistance' to opposition parties. France reacted by reducing its annual provision of economic aid. Relations with the United States, however, have improved since Vanuatu's signing of a five-year fishing agreement, in October 1986, under which American trawlers have been granted licences to fish for tuna within the country's 'exclusive fishing zone'. The general thrust of Vanuatu's foreign policy since independence has, however, been to promote greater co-operation among the small states of the Pacific region. As part of this strategy, Vanuatu joined Papua New Guinea, which, was already closely bound to Vanuatu by a 'peace pact' signed at the time of independence, and the Solomon Islands in forming, in March 1988, the 'Spearhead Group', whose aim is to preserve Melanesian cultural traditions and campaign for New Caledonia's independence. Despite these departures, Vanuatu has also needed to ensure that its diplomatic relations with the Western powers remain cordial, since a fifth of its GDP is currently derived from foreign development aid.

WESTERN SAMOA

The Independent State of Samoa
Samoa i Sisifo

Capital: Apia

Social and economic data
Area: 2,840 km^2
Population: 180,000*
Pop density per km^2: 63*
Literacy rate: 98%
GDP: $110m*; per capita GDP: $611
Economy type: low income
Labour force in agriculture: 60%

*1985

Ethnic composition
Ninety per cent of the population are of Samoan, or Polynesian, ethnic stock and 10 per cent Euronesian, or mixed Europeans and Polynesians. Samoan, a Polynesian dialect, and English are the official languages.

Religions
Ninety-nine per cent of the population are Christians. Forty-five per cent are members of the Congregational Christian Church in Samoa, which was established in 1830 as the London Missionary Society; 22 per cent are Roman Catholics; 19 per cent belong to the Methodist Church in Samoa, which was founded in 1828; 8 per cent are followers of the Church of Jesus Christ of Latter-day Saints (Mormons), established in 1888; and 4 per cent belong to the Seventh-day Adventist Church, which was founded in 1895.

Political features
State type: liberal democracy
Date of state formation: 1962
Political structure: unitary
Executive: parliamentary
Assembly: one-chamber
Party structure: multi-party
Human rights rating: N/A

Local and regional government
The country is divided into 24 districts for development and law and order administration. However, the real units of local government are the villages *(nu'u)* and sub-villages *(pitonu'u)*, where extended family *(aiga)* heads *(matai)* gather in assemblies *(fonos)*, each headed by a chief *(ali'i)*. These local assemblies direct the use and distribution of family land and assets and supervise welfare provision.

Head of state
King Malietoa Tanumafili II, since 1962.

Head of government
Prime Minister Tofilau Eti Alesana, since 1988.

Political leaders since 1970
1970–73 Tupua Tamasese Lealofi (Ind), 1973–75 Fiame Mata'afa Mulinu'u (Ind), 1975–76 Tupua Tamasese Lealofi (Ind), 1976–82 Tupuola Taisi Efi (Ind), 1982–82, Va'ai Kolone (HRPP), 1982–82 Tupuola Taisi Efi (Ind.), 1982–85 Tofilau Eti Alesana (HRPP), 1985–88 Va'ai Kolone (VKG), 1988–88 Tupuola Taisi Efi (CDP), 1988– Tofilau Eti Alesana (HRPP).

Political system
Western Samoa is an independent state within the Commonwealth. The constitution dates from independence in January 1962 and provides for a parliamentary system of government, with a constitutional head of state (O le Ao o le Malo), a single-chamber Legislative Assembly (Fono), and a Prime Minister and cabinet drawn from and responsibile to the Assembly. The head of state is normally elected by the Assembly for a five-year term

from among the holders of the country's four paramount titles. However, the present holder of the office has been elected for life.

The Assembly has 47 members. Forty-five of these are Samoans, who are elected by holders of Matai titles, or elected clan chiefs. There are about 16,000 of such chiefs, representing 41 traditional territorial constituencies. The remaining two members are elected by people, mainly Europeans, who appear on the individual voters' rolls. The Assembly has a life of three years.

The head of state appoints the Prime Minister and a cabinet of up to eight further Fono members, on the basis of Assembly support. The current Prime Minister, Tofilau Eti Alesana, holds six additional ministerial portfolios: foreign affairs; labour; broadcasting; justice; police and prisons; and attorney-general. Cabinet decisions are subject to review by an Executive Council, which is composed of the head of state and cabinet. A stress on consensus and the blending of both traditional and modern representative forms, in a conservative manner, the 'Samoan Way' *(fa'a Samoa)*, permeates and distinguishes the political system.

Political parties

Prior to 1979 there were no formal political parties, all candidates for election standing as independents. Then, in February 1979, the Human Rights Protection Party (HRPP) was formed by opposition Fono deputies, led by Va'ai Kolone, a former chairman of the public accounts committee. The party opposed the rapid economic development plans of the Tupuola Efi government and emerged, under the leadership of Tofilau Eti Alesana, as the dominant party between 1982 and 1985. In 1985 it was weakened by the breakaway of a faction supporting former leader Va'ai Kolone. This breakaway group later formed what became known as the Va'ai Kolone Group (VKG), in 1988.

The principal opposition to the HRPP, which currently forms the government, comes, in addition to the VKG, from the Christian Democratic Party (CDP), a loose grouping of Assembly members formed by Tupuola Taisi Efi in 1985. This party is an ideological heir of the pre-1982 governing majority group within the Fono.

Latest elections

In the most recent Fono elections, held in February 1988, the HRPP captured 24 of the 47 available seats and the CDP-VKG coalition 23. The initial count gave each group 23 seats each, with the result in the remaining constituency a tie. After two inconclusive recounts, a judge from New Zealand was called in to preside over a third recount. He declared the CDP the winner. However, a CDP coalition deputy had, in the meantime, been induced to defect to the HRPP, giving the party a narrow Fono majority.

Political history

Western Samoa is a volcanic island grouping in the south-west Pacific Ocean, 2,575 kilometres north-east of Auckland, New Zealand, and between 13 and 15 degrees south of the equator. It comprises two large inhabited islands, Upolu and Savaii, which are 18 kilometres apart, two much smaller inhabited islands, Apolima and Manono, and four tiny uninhabited islands, Fanuatapu, Nuutele, Nuula and Nuusafee. The inland portions of the inhabited islands are mountainous, covered with extinct volcanoes, and agriculturally barren. The bulk of the population therefore live in scattered coastal villages, with 72 per cent of the total on Upolu Island.

The islands of Samoa were first discovered by Dutch and French traders during the 1720s, but had been previously inhabited by Polynesians for more than 2,000 years. During the early nineteenth century, Christian missionaries began to settle there and from that time Germany, Britain and the United States vied with each other for their control, intriguing with local paramount chiefs in a series of mid-century civil wars. Eventually, in 1899, a treaty was signed among the three Western powers, recognising American paramountcy over the islands east of 171 degrees longitude west, which were to be called American Samoa, and German supremacy over the other islands, named Western Samoa. Britain was given control of Tonga and the Solomon Islands as part of this agreement. German control lasted, however, barely a decade. On the outbreak of the First World War in 1914, New Zealand took over Western Samoa and thereafter administered the islands, first as a League of Nations mandated territory, between 1919 and 1945, and then, from 1946, as a United Nations trust territory.

During the inter-war years, New Zealand rule was challenged by a nationalist organisation, the Mau, which resorted to civil disobedience. After the Second World War, as part of its trusteeship agreement, New Zealand began to promote self-government, introducing a cabinet form of government in 1959 and a provisional constitution in October 1960. This paved the way for Western Samoa's achievement of full independence, within the Commonwealth, on 1 January 1962, after the holding of a UN-sponsored plebiscite. Initially, the office of head of state in the newly independent country was held jointly by two traditional rulers. However, on the death of one of them, in April 1963, the other, Malietoa Tanumafili II, became the sole head, for life, serving as a constitutional monarch. Effective executive power was held by the Prime Minister, who, at the time of independence, was Fiame Mata'afa Mulinu'u. He had occupied that position since 1959.

Mata'afa lost power to Tupua Tamasese Lealofi in the general election of 1970. He regained it, however, in 1973, after fresh elections, and continued to serve as Prime Minister until his death in May 1975. Tamasese briefly succeeded him, before being replaced by Tupuola Taisi Efi, the first Prime Minister not of royal blood, in the March 1976 general election. Tupuola Efi held power for six years, being re-elected by the Legislative Assembly in March 1979. At the general election of February 1982, however, the opposition groupings, who had combined in 1979 to form the Human Rights Protection Party (HRPP), won a narrow majority and their leader Va'ai Kolone became Prime Minister. Within seven months, however, he was forced to resign, after charges of electoral malpractice, including impersonation of the dead. Tupuola Efi briefly returned to power for three months, but, when his budget proposal was voted down in the Fono in December 1982, resigned to be replaced by the HRPP leader, Tofilau Eti Alesana.

The HRPP won a decisive victory in the February 1985 general election, substantially increasing its Fono majority, by securing 31 of the 47 seats, and Tofilau Eti continued as Prime Minister. At the end of the year, however, he resigned because of opposition within the Assembly to his budget plan and the defection from the HRPP grouping of supporters of Va'ai Kolone. The head of state refused to call another general election and Va'ai Kolone was appointed as the new Prime Minister, putting together a coalition of 'independents' and members of the newly formed Christian Democratic Party (CDP), led by Tupuola Taisi Efi, now known by the honorific title of Tupua Tamasese. Va'ai held power until the general election of February 1988. This resulted in a disputed 'hung parliament' after which Tupuola Efi was first chosen as Prime Minister and, then, from April 1988, the HRPP leader, Tofilau Eti.

In its external relations, Western Samoa has maintained close links with New Zealand since independence, entering into a Treaty of Friendship in 1962, under which New Zealand acts as a channel of communication with non-Pacific region powers. Western Samoa has a free-enterprise economic system, encouraging inward foreign investment, but remains predominantly subsistence based. With rapid population growth of more than two per cent per annum eating into food supplies, the nation is highly dependent on remittances sent home by its countrymen working overseas, and on foreign development aid.

PART III

TOWARDS ONE WORLD

CHAPTER 8

THE RELICS OF EMPIRE—COLONIES, DEPENDENCIES AND SEMI-SOVEREIGN STATES

8.1 The building of the colonial empires: 1492–1919

Nine-tenths of the contemporary sovereign states outside Western Europe have, at one time or another during the two centuries before 1945, been subject to external rule by the 'great' colonial powers of Europe, the United States or Japan. The notable exceptions have been Japan itself, China apart from Manchuria and the coastal 'treaty port' enclaves, Afghanistan until 1979, Iran, Saudi Arabia, North Yemen, Liberia since 1847, Thailand, Bhutan and Nepal. 'Informal' external influence was, however, strong in many of these states, Nepal and Bhutan, for example, being bound by strict treaty obligations to Britain until 1947.

The process of modern colonisation occurred in a series of distinct phases. It began in the late fifteenth and early sixteenth centuries, with the conquest of Southern and Central America, including the Caribbean, by Spain and Portugal, the indigenous Amerindian civilisation being destroyed and replaced by a new mixed, white-creole-black, plantation and mining economy. This was followed, during the seventeenth century, by the Netherlands' assertion of supremacy over the East Indies' 'spice islands', and the creation of British and French settlements in coastal North America.

The majority of the early colonies on the mainland of the Americas were, following revolts by the settlers, to secure their independence during the late eighteenth and early nineteenth centuries, as Table 66 shows. Elsewhere in the world, however, European interests multiplied, an extensive new chain of dependencies being established across South and South-East Asia, Australasia, Africa and the Caribbean during what was the dominant era of imperial expansion, between the 1770s and the 1920s. The lead in this second phase of colonialism was taken by Britain and France. Also involved in the process were the rising nations of central, eastern and southern Europe, notably Germany, Tsarist Russia and Italy, the ambitious small kingdom of Belgium, the old imperial states of the Netherlands, Spain and Portugal and the emergent world powers of the United States and Japan.

Imperial expansion during this 'mature' phase usually took the form of the imposition of a ruling body, or person, on indigenous peoples, or even indirect control, rather than the emigration and settlement of white colonists. The exceptions were the settler colonies of Australia and New Zealand, upland parts of southern and eastern Africa and the tea and rubber planter belts of South-East Asia. The expansion was at its maximum, in areal terms, at the time of the Versailles Settlement of 1919,

Table 66

THE INITIAL WAVE OF COLONIAL EXPANSION—THE AMERICAS, 1496–1903 (22 STATES)

Country	*Date of Colonisation*	*Original Colonising Power*	*Date of Independence*
Argentina	1516	Spain	1816
Bolivia	1530s	Spain	1825
Brazil	1532	Portugal	1822
Canada	1604	France & UK	1851–67*
Chile	1541	Spain	1818
Colombia	1538	Spain	1821/30†
Costa Rica	1563	Spain	1821
Cuba	1511	Spain	1899
Dominican Republic	1496	Spain	1844
Ecuador	1532	Spain	1821/30†
El Salvador	1525	Spain	1821/38‡
Guatemala	1524	Spain	1839
Haiti	1697	France	1804
Honduras	1523	Spain	1821/38‡
Mexico	1521	Spain	1821
Nicaragua	1552	Spain	1838
Panama	1513	Spain	1821/1903§
Paraguay	1537	Spain	1811
Peru	1533	Spain	1824
United States of America	1607	United Kingdom	1776
Uruguay	1624	Spain	1825
Venezuela	1567	Spain	1821/30†

*Canada was not fully freed from the supremacy of Acts of the United Kingdom parliament until 1931, while Newfoundland remained under British administration until 1949.

†These states formed part of a federation between 1821 and 1830.

‡Part of a federation of Central American States until 1838.

§Part of Colombia until 1903.

when nearly all of Africa, South and South-East Asia, Oceania and the Caribbean, as well as much of West Asia and the Middle East, had been politically incorporated into the imperial nexus.

8.2 The decolonisation process: 1920–85

During the inter-war years, the first halting steps towards decolonisation were taken, beginning in the Middle East, where, in 1922, Britain, prompted by the outbreak of serious nationalist riots, transferred full sovereignty in Egypt. It continued to maintain, however, a strategic military presence to protect its Suez Canal interests. Then in 1932 and 1944 respectively, Britain and France, which had been administering the territories under League of Nations mandates since 1920, conceded independence to Iraq and Lebanon. During the same period the 'white settler' Dominions of Canada and South Africa, which had experienced a substantial measure of self-government from as early as the mid nineteenth century, became effectively fully independent with the passage of the Statute of Westminster, in 1931. Australia and New Zealand, the other two overseas

Dominions, delayed accepting the terms of this legislation until 1942 and 1947 respectively. These cases were, however, the exceptions. Elsewhere, the 1920s and 1930s were a period of imperial consolidation, and even some further expansion by countries such as fascist Italy, militarist Japan and, finally, remotivated to imperial ambitions, Nazi Germany.

Matters changed dramatically after the Second World War, the process of decolonisation now gaining an unstoppable momentum. The initial factor behind this sea change was the strain imposed on ruler-colony relations by the war itself. For example, in the case of India, where a powerful nationalist movement had already won significant political concessions during the inter-war period, the British government was forced, in 1941, to offer the carrot of Dominion status as a means of securing civilian co-operation in the war effort. By the end of the war, however, the popular desire for full independence had become irresistible, with the result that full sovereignty, on a partitioned basis, was transferred in August 1947. The adjacent South Asian countries of Ceylon (later Sri Lanka) and Burma soon followed suit and were granted independence in 1948. The loss of the Indian sub-continent, the linchpin of the British imperial system, was to have far-reaching consequences, undermining its whole economic and strategic rationale.

Further to the east, in South-East Asia, the French and Dutch colonies in 'Indo-China' and the 'East Indies' had been even more seriously affected by the events of the Second World War. Between 1942 and 1945 both had been occupied by Japan, which had sponsored new puppet nationalist governments. The re-imposition of European colonial rule proved highly unpopular and was fiercely resisted. Full autonomy was thus granted to the Dutch 'East Indies', now Indonesia, in 1949 and substantial semi-autonomy, within the 'French Union', to France's possessions in Indo-China: Vietnam, Cambodia and Laos. They achieved full independence some five years later after a prolonged military struggle.

During the later 1940s and mid 1950s, the British- and French-administered states of North Africa and the Middle East were also granted independence: Syria in 1946, Israel, formerly Palestine, in 1948, Libya in 1951, and Sudan, Morocco and Tunisia, all in 1956. In addition, the 'informal colony' of Oman regained full sovereignty in foreign and defence affairs in 1951. It was not, however, until the Suez and Algerian crises of 1956 and 1958 that the pace of decolonisation decisively quickened. Both events had profound repercussions on the internal political dynamics of the two leading imperial nations, and on their global outlooks, resulting in the accession to power of the realistic decolonisers, Macmillan, in the United Kingdom, and de Gaulle, in France. These crises also transformed public opinion, adding a new moral imperative to a decolonisation process which had now gained an irresistible momentum.

The first indication of this changed perspective was the granting of full independence to the British West African colony of Ghana, known as the Gold Coast, in March 1957, by the handing over of power to the popular radical socialist, Kwame Nkrumah. Ushering in what the British Prime Minister, Harold Macmillan, termed a 'wind of change' across black Africa, 33 African states secured independence during the next ten years. In one year alone, 1960, 17 new African states were proclaimed. Independence was also granted during this hectic decolonisation phase, between 1957 and

1968, to nine small island states in the Caribbean, Oceania and East Asia, as Tables 67 and 68 show.

Table 67

THE CHANGING PACE OF DECOLONISATION BETWEEN 1920 AND 1985

(a) THE DISTRIBUTION OF FORMER COLONIAL POWERS IN RELATION TO THE COUNTRIES 'FREED' DURING THIS PERIOD

*(Number of Countries 'Freed' per Year)**

Period	*Under British Control*	*Under French Control*	*Under Dutch Control*	*Under Belgian Control*	*Under Portuguese Control*	*Under US Control*	*Under the Control of Other States*	*Total*
1920–45	5	1	—	—	—	—	1	7
1946–50	6	1	1	—	—	2	2	12
1951–55	1.7	3.3	—	—	—	—	—	5
1956–60	7.5	16.5	—	1	—	—	—	25
1961–65	13	1	—	2	—	—	1	17
1966–70	9	—	—	—	—	—	2	11
1971–75	5	1	1	—	5	—	2	14
1976–80	7.5	1.5	—	—	—	—	—	9
1981–85	4	—	—	—	—	—	—	4
1920–85	58.7	25.3	2	3	5	2	8†	104
% Share of Total	56.4	24.3	1.9	2.9	4.8	1.9	7	100

*Where control was shared between two or more colonial powers, the number of 'freed' countries is shown proportionately.

†Australia 2, Spain 2, China 1, New Zealand 1, Soviet Union 1, Italy 1.

(b) REGIONAL DISTRIBUTION OF 'FREED' COUNTRIES, 1920–85

Period	*Central & Southern Africa*	*Middle East & North Africa*	*Asia*	*Central America & the Caribbean*	*South America*	*North America*	*Oceania*	*Western Europe*	*Total*
1920–45	2	3	—	—	—	1	1	—	7
1946–50	—	3	8	—	—	—	1	—	12
1951–55	—	2	3	—	—	—	—	—	5
1956–60	20	2	2	—	—	—	—	1	25
1961–65	10	2	1	2	—	—	1	1	17
1966–70	5	1	—	1	1	—	3	—	11
1971–75	6	4	—	2	1	—	1	—	14
1976–80	1	1	—	3	—	—	4	—	9
1981–85	—	—	1	3	—	—	—	—	4
1920–85	44	18	15	11	2	1	11	2	104
% Share of Total	42.3	17.3	14.4	10.6	1.9	1.0	10.6	1.9	100

By the early 1970s, Britain and France, playing the leading roles in the decolonisation process, as can be seen in Table 67, had divested themselves of their principal mainland-based colonial possessions. They were now left mainly in control of small island dependencies in the Caribbean and Oceania, as well as treaty protectorates in the Gulf region. These were slowly 'set free', at an average rate of two per annum, during the 1970s and early 1980s.

Ironically, the last substantial European overseas empire was maintained during this period by Portugal, the pioneer of European imperial expansion. Comprising Guinea-Bissau in West Africa, Angola in south-western Africa, Mozambique in south-eastern Africa and the off-shore islands of Cape Verde and Sao Tome and Principe, this empire covered more than 2,000 square kilometres and had been under Portuguese rule for almost 500 years. With its still untapped mineral wealth and energy reserves, it remained moreover of considerable economic value to the colonial power, attracting extensive white settlement during the 1960s. Portuguese rule and immigration were however becoming increasingly unpopular with the indigenous population, fuelling a powerful guerrilla resistance movement, which was supplied with modern arms by the Soviet Union's Cuban and East German proxies. This eventually had calamitous repercussions for the Lisbon regime, provoking a left-wing coup by disaffected army units which succeeded in bringing down the conservative dictatorship of Marcello Caetano, in April 1974. In the immediate wake of this power change Portugal's African dependencies pressed for independence. Unable and unwilling to resist, the new Lisbon regime hastily acceded to the requests, and within the space of 14 months, between October 1974 and November 1975, the empire was dissolved.

This left only one major land-based European overseas empire which dated back to the pre-1945 period, the one established by Tsarist Russia in Central Asia between 1846 and 1895. It was an empire inherited by the 'anti-colonial' Soviet Union, but which it had firmly consolidated and incorporated within its federal structure. Since the war the Soviet Union has also established an informal hegemony over its East European neighbours, although the economic relationship by no means corresponds to a classic imperial one in terms of the nature of the goods interchanged, the USSR exporting mineral and energy products westwards and importing manufactured items. Two other major contemporary communist powers, China, in the case of Tibet, and Vietnam, in relation to Laos and Cambodia, also maintain both formal and quasi-formal imperial control over neighbouring regions.

Table 68

THE DECOLONISATION PROCESS, 1922–85

Year of Decolonisation or Sovereignty Transfer	*State*	*Last Colonising Power*	*Date of Establishment of Control*
1922	Egypt	Britain	1882
1931	Canada*	Britain (France 1604–1763)	1713–63
1932	Iraq	Britain (M)	1920
1934	South Africa*	Britain (Netherlands 1652–1795)	1795–1824
1941	Ethiopia	Italy (MO)	1936
1942	Australia*	Britain	1788
1944	Lebanon	France (M)	1920
1946	Jordan	Britain (M)	1920

Table 68—The Decolonisation Process, 1922–85 (Contd.)

Year of Decolonisation or Sovereignty Transfer	*State*	*Last Colonising Power*	*Date of Establishment of Control*
1946	Mongolia	China	1689
1946	Philippines	United States (Spain 1565–1898)	1899
1946	Syria	France (M)	1920
1947	India & Pakistan (incl E Pakistan, later Bangladesh)	Britain	late 18th–early 19th century
1947	New Zealand*	Britain	1840
1948	Burma	Britain (Japan 1942–45)	1824–86
1948	Israel (formerly W Palestine)	Britain (M)	1920
1948	North Korea	Soviet Union (OZ) (Japan 1910–45)	1945
1948	South Korea	United States (OZ) (Japan 1910–45)	1945
1948	Sri Lanka (Ceylon)	Britain	1798
1949	Indonesia	Netherlands (Japan 1942–45)	1595
1951	Libya	70% Britain & 30% France (Italy 1912–42)	1942
1951	Oman	Britain (MP)	1891
1954	Cambodia (Kampuchea)	France (Japan 1941–45)	1863
1954	Laos	France (Japan 1940–45)	1893
1954	Vietnam	France (Japan 1940–45)	1867–83
1956	Morocco	France	1912
1956	Sudan	Britain	1899
1956	Tunisia	France	1881
1957	Ghana	Britain	1901
1957	Malaysia	Britain (Portugal 1511–1641 Netherlands 1641–1795)	1795–1888
1957	Singapore	Britain	1819
1958	Guinea	France	1898
1960	Benin	France	1892
1960	Burkina Faso (Upper Volta)	France	1896
1960	Cameroon	80% France & 20% Britain (M) (Germany 1884–1916)	1919
1960	Central African Republic	France	1901
1960	Chad	France	1900
1960	Congo	France	1910
1960	Cyprus	Britain	1914
1960	Gabon	France	1890
1960	Ivory Coast	France	1893
1960	Madagascar	France	1885
1960	Mali	France	1881–99
1960	Mauritania	France	1904–12
1960	Niger	France	1901
1960	Nigeria	Britain	1861–99
1960	Senegal	France	1659–1840
1960	Somalia	Britain (Italy 1908–41)	1884–86
1960	Togo	66% France & 34% Britain (M) (Germany 1884–1914)	1914
1960	Zaire	Belgium	1885–1908
1961	Kuwait	Britain (MP)	1899
1961	Sierra Leone	Britain	1808
1961	Tanzania	Britain (M) (Germany 1885–1914)	1914

Table 68—The Decolonisation Process, 1922–85 (Contd.)

Year of Decolonisation or Sovereignty Transfer	*State*	*Last Colonising Power*	*Date of Establishment of Control*
1962	Algeria	France	1830
1962	Burundi	Belgium (M) (Germany 1895–1916)	1916
1962	Jamaica	Britain (Spain 1509–1655)	1655
1962	Rwanda	Belgium (M) (Germany 1894–1916)	1916
1962	Trinidad & Tobago	Britain (Spain 1552–1797)	1797–1820
1962	Uganda	Britain	1888
1962	Western Samoa	New Zealand (M) (Germany 1900–14)	1914
1963	Kenya	Britain (Portugal 1498–1699)	1888–95
1964	Malawi	Britain	1887–92
1964	Malta	Britain	1814
1964	Zambia	Britain	1891–1923
1965	Gambia	Britain	1816
1965	Maldives	Britain	1887
1965	Rhodesia (later Zimbabwe: UDI)	Britain	1897–1923
1966	Barbados	Britain	1624
1966	Botswana	Britain	1885
1966	Guyana	Britain (Netherlands 1616–1796)	1796–1814
1966	Lesotho	Britain	1868
1967	South Yemen	Britain	1839
1968	Equatorial Guinea	Spain (Portugal 1494–1778 Spain 1778–81 Britain 1781–1843)	1858
1968	Mauritius	Britain (Netherlands 1598–1710 France 1715–1810)	1810
1968	Nauru	Australia (M) (Germany 1888–1914 Japan 1942–45)	1914
1968	Swaziland	Britain (South Africa 1894–1902)	1881
1970	Fiji	Britain	1874
1970	Tonga	Britain	1900
1971	Bahrain	Britain (MP)	1861
1971	Qatar	Britain (MP) (Also temp 1868–72)	1916
1971	United Arab Emirates	Britain (MP)	1892
1973	Bahamas	Britain	1629
1974	Grenada	Britain (France 1674–1762)	1762
1974	Guinea-Bissau	Portugal	late 15th C
1975	Angola	Portugal	1491
1975	Cape Verde	Portugal	late 15th C
1975	Comoros	France	1912
1975	Mozambique	Portugal	1505
1975	Papua New Guinea	Australia (50% German 1885–1914 50% Britain 1885–1901)	1901
1975	Sao Tome & Principe	Portugal	1471
1975	Spanish Sahara (Western Sahara)	Spain	1912
1975	Suriname	Netherlands (Britain 1651–67, 1779–1802 & 1804–16)	1816

Table 68—The Decolonisation Process, 1922–85 (Contd.)

Year of Decolonisation or Sovereignty Transfer	*State*	*Last Colonising Power*	*Date of Establishment of Control*
1976	Seychelles	Britain (France 1768–1814)	1814
1977	Djibouti	France	1859
1978	Dominica	Britain (France 1778–83)	1763
1978	Solomon Islands	Britain (50% Germany 1885–1900)	1885
1978	Tuvalu	Britain	1875
1979	Kiribati	Britain	1892
1979	St Lucia	Britain (France 1651–1803)	1803
1979	St Vincent & the Grenadines	Britain (France 1779–83)	1783
1980	Vanuatu	Britain & France (JT)	1887
1981	Antigua & Barbuda	Britain	1632
1981	Belize	Britain	17th C–1862
1983	St Kitts & Nevis	Britain	1623
1984	Brunei	Britain	1888

*The white-settler colonies of Australia, Canada, New Zealand and South Africa achieved 'de facto' independence from British control at earlier dates than those shown. The separate Australian states, for example, enjoyed a substantial measure of autonomy as early as 1855–68; the Canadian colonies between 1851 and 1867; and New Zealand and Cape Colony in South Africa as early as 1853. These powers were extended in 1907 when Dominion status was conferred. Not until the dates shown, however, following the passage of the Statute of Westminster, 1931, were these territories fully freed from the supremacy of Acts of the United Kingdom Parliament.

ABBREVIATIONS:
JT—Joint condominium
M—League of Nations 'mandate' territory
MO—Military Occupation
MP—Independent and fully internally self-governing, but dependent on British military protection, much in the same way as Bhutan and Nepal
OZ—Occupied Zone
UDI—Unilateral Declaration of Independence

8.3 Remaining colonial possessions and dependencies in the world today

There currently exist, on the broadest count, 50 regularly inhabited colonies or dependencies, controlled by twelve colonial powers. These territories and the controlling nations are set out, in an aggregated form, in Tables 69, 70 and 71 below. They total fewer than 21 million people, a number which corresponds to less than 0.5 per cent of the global population. This compares with the situation in 1945 when almost a third of the world's population lived in colonies or dependencies or with early 1960, when the proportion stood at 5 per cent.

Included in these figures are the four 'independent' Bantustans (black homelands) of South Africa, the occupied territories of Namibia and Western Sahara, the Chinese 'Autonomous Region' of Xizang (Tibet) and the French internal 'Collective Territory' of Corsica. These areas do not always feature in textbook dependency categories. They have, however, been included in this chapter so as to provide more detailed treatments of their political structures and histories. Taken together, they embrace

Table 69

CONTEMPORARY COLONIES, DEPENDENCIES AND EXTERNAL TERRITORIES

Controlling State	*Number of Inhabited Colonies, Dependencies & External Territories*	*Area ('000 km²)*	*Population (m) (1985)*	*% Share of Total Colonial Population*
Australia	3	0.20	0.006	0.0
China	1	1221.60	1.970	9.4
Denmark	2	2177.00	0.099	0.5
France	10	128.27	1.958	9.4
Morocco	1	266.00	0.165	0.8
Netherlands	2	0.99	0.270	1.3
New Zealand	3	0.51	0.023	0.1
Norway	1	62.70	0.003	0.0
Portugal	1	0.02	0.300	1.4
South Africa	5	923.35	6.607	31.6
United Kingdom	13	15.69	5.814	27.8
United States of America	8	11.69	3.717	17.8
Total	50	4808.02	20.932	100.0

Table 70

REGIONAL DISTRIBUTION OF CONTEMPORARY COLONIES, DEPENDENCIES AND EXTERNAL TERRITORIES*

	Oceania	*Central America & Caribbean*	*North America*	*South America*	*Asia*	*Middle East & North Africa*	*Western Europe*	*Central Southern Africa*
Number	16	13	1	1	3	1	5	8
Area (km²)	26.74	104.28	0.24	12.17	1222.69	266.00	10.85	926.74
Population (m) 1985	0.677	4.526	0.006	0.002	7.726	0.165	0.522	7.240
% Share of Total Colonial Population	3.2	21.6	0.0	0.0	36.9	0.8	2.4	34.6

*Two dependencies, not shown, lie in the Arctic region.

Table 71

DISTRIBUTION OF CONTEMPORARY COLONIES, DEPENDENCIES AND EXTERNAL TERRITORIES BY POPULATION SIZE

Below 10,000	*10,000–50,000*	*50,000–100,000*	*100,000–500,000*	*500,000–1,000,000*	*1,000,000–6,000,000*	*Total*
12	11	7	12	2	6	50

9 million people, a figure which is equivalent to 43 per cent of the colonies/dependencies total.

In the remaining colonial territories and dependencies, there are fewer than 12 million people. Almost three-quarters of this total is accounted for by the two British and United States dependencies of Hong Kong and Puerto Rico, with, as Table 71 shows, the majority of the other 'colonial relics' being relatively tiny communities, with populations below 100,000. The territories still held by six of the colonial powers, Australia, Denmark, New Zealand, the Netherlands, Norway and Portugal, are particularly small. Only two of them, controlled by the Netherlands and Portugal, are the residue of earlier, and greater, empires. Instead, there are three powers, the United Kingdom, the United States and France, which dominate any record of contemporary colonial holdings, the territories still under their control embracing, respectively, 48 per cent, 31 per cent and 16 per cent of the total colonial/dependency population. The territories they administer are spread across the world. There is, however, a notable numerical concentration in Oceania and the Caribbean, many of the dependencies being island communities too small to have an independent political and economic viability. In a few cases, most notably in some of the French Oceania dependencies, colonial control has been maintained against the wishes of a significant proportion of the indigenous population. In general, however, in the bulk of the other, still dependent, territories no discernible independence movement is visible and colony-coloniser cultural and economic ties remain strong.

8.4 Profiles of existing colonies and dependencies

In the pages which now follow we shall try to sketch a profile of each of the countries which still remain within the category of colony or dependency, following a similar approach to that taken in Part II: in other words, on the bases of their political structures and recent histories.

8.4.1 Australia's dependencies

Australia's dependencies are called External Territories, of which, as Table 72 shows, there are seven. Five of them are within the Oceania region, two of which are uninhabited. The other two, both uninhabited, are within Antarctica. Details of the political structures and histories of the inhabited regions are given below.

Table 72

AUSTRALIA'S EXTERNAL TERRITORIES

Name	*Date of First Coming Under Australian Administration*	*Area (km²)*	*Population (1985)*
The Ashmore & Cartier Islands	1931	3.0	Uninhabited
The Australian Antarctic Territory	1936	6,112.4	Uninhabited
Christmas Island	1958	155.4	3,000
Cocos (Keeling) Islands	1955	14.2	579
Coral Sea Islands	1969	2.0†	Uninhabited
Heard Island & McDonald Islands	1947	409.2	Uninhabited
Norfolk Island	1913	34.5	2,400
Total	—	6,730.7	5,979

†This figure is the area of land only. The islands cover 1 million km² of ocean.

CHRISTMAS ISLAND

Location
Oceania. In the Indian Ocean 360 km south of Java.

Social and economic data
Area: 155 km^2.
Population: 3,000*.
Pop density per km^2: 19*
Literacy rate: N/A
GDP: $40m*; per capita GDP: $13,333
Economy type: high income
Labour force in agriculture: N/A

*1985

Ethnic composition
Sixty-three per cent Chinese, 25 per cent Malay and 12 per cent European.

Political system
The island, which became an Australian Territory in October 1958, is governed by an administrator appointed by the Governor-General of Australia and responsible to the Minister for Territories. There is also a nine-member advisory island council.

Political history
Discovered on Christmas Day in 1643 by Captain W. Mynars, the island, then uninhabited, was annexed by Britain in 1888, and administered as part of the Straits Settlement Crown Colony, together with Singapore, Malacca, Penang and the Cocos Islands. During the Second World War it was occupied by Japan. In 1958, following the grant of independence to Singapore, under whose direct responsibility it had been placed since 1900, Britain transferred its sovereignty to Australia. Since then it has been ruled as part of the Northern Territory. The island's economy has traditionally been dependent on the recovery of phosphates. In 1987, however, the phosphate mine was closed because of industrial unrest and efforts are now being made to develop the island for tourism.

COCOS (KEELING) ISLANDS

Location
Oceania. In the Indian Ocean, west of Christmas Island and 3,685 km west of Darwin.

Social and economic data
Area: 14 km^2
Population: 579*
Pop density per km^2: 41*
Literacy rate: N/A
GDP: $1.4m*; per capita GDP: $2,418
Economy type: middle income
Labour force in agriculture: N/A

*1985

Ethnic composition
The principal island, Home Island, is peopled by local Cocos Malays, while the other major island, West Island, is settled chiefly by Europeans.

Political system
The Australian government is represented on the islands by an administrator, appointed by the Governor-General of Australia and responsible to the Minister of Territories. Most local government functions are, however, undertaken by a Cocos Islands Council, which was established in July 1979 and whose authority was expanded in 1984. Following the islands' vote in April 1984 to become fully integrated with Australia, the islanders now enjoy the rights and privileges of ordinary Australian citizens, including voting rights in Australian parliament elections.

Political history
The Cocos Islands, a group of low-lying coral atolls thickly covered with coconut palms, were discovered in 1609 by Captain William Keeling of the East India Company. They were originally settled by Malays brought to the islands by Alexander Hare and John Clunies-Ross, in 1826–27. They were annexed to the British Crown in 1857 and incorporated in the Settlement of Singapore from 1903, although their economic interests, which were mainly the extraction of copra from coconuts, had been granted to the Clunies-Ross family in 1886. In November 1955 administration was transferred to Australia and in 1978 the Australian government bought out the Clunies-Ross family's interests and established a Cocos Malay co-operative to manage the copra plantation. In April 1984 the islands' residents voted to become part of Australia.

NORFOLK ISLAND

Capital: Kingston

Location
Oceania, in the Western Pacific 1,488 km north-east of Sydney and almost midway between Australia and New Zealand.

Social and economic data
Area: 35 km^2
Population: 2,400*
Pop density per km^2: 70*
Literacy rate: N/A
GDP: $13m*; per capita GDP: $5,417
Economy type: high income
Labour force in agriculture: N/A

*1985

Ethnic composition
The population comprises descendants of those who migrated from Pitcairn in the mid-nineteenth century, and who speak Tahitian, and more recent 'mainlander' immigrants from Australia, New Zealand and Britain.

Political system
The Australian government is represented on the island by an administrator, appointed by the Governor-General of Australia and responsible to the Minister for Territories. Since the passage of the Norfolk Island Act in 1979, there has been a progression towards a form of responsible legislative and executive self-government, founded on an elected nine-member Legislative Assembly, from which is drawn a three-member ministerial Executive Council. In 1985 the powers of the Assembly and Council were extended to cover such matters as civil defence and public works and services.

Political history
The island, which was then uninhabited, was first visited by Captain James Cook in 1774 and originally served as a British penal settlement, between 1788 and 1814, and from 1826 to 1855. After 1856 there was an influx of people from over-populated Pitcairn Island, some of them descendants of those who had settled there after the 'Mutiny on the *Bounty*', in 1789. In 1913 Norfolk Island became an Australian 'external territory', forming part of the New South Wales colony. Since 1979 it has been substantially self-governing.

8.4.2 China's dependency

China's one dependency is Xizang, or Tibet. It is one of the country's five Autonomous Regions. Details of its political structure and history are given below.

XIZANG (TIBET)

Capital: Lhasa

Location
Asia, in a mountainous region in south-west China, bordered to the south by Bhutan, India and Nepal, to the west by India, to the east by Sichuan province, China, and to the north by Xinjiang Autonomous Region, China. The country is one of immense strategic importance to China, being the site of between 50,000 and 100,000 troops, as well as having a major nuclear missile base at Nagchuka.

Social and economic data
Area: 1,221,600 km^2
Population: 1,970,000*
Pop density per km^2: 2*
GDP: N/A*
Literacy rate: N/A
Labour force in agriculture: N/A

*1985

Ethnic composition
Predominantly Tibetan, with a growing Han Chinese immigrant minority.

Principal religion
Buddhism, in the form of Lamaism. There are, however, barely 1,000 lamas, or Buddhist monks/priests today, compared with 110,000, in 6,000 monasteries and temples, prior to 1959.

Political system
Xizang constitutes one of the five Autonomous Regions of the People's Republic of China (PRC) and has its own People's Government and People's Congress. The controlling force in Tibet is the Communist Party of China (CCP), which is headed locally by First Secretary Hu Jintao, a member of the Han Chinese community. As an Autonomous Region, Xizang is allowed to conduct its government's affairs in its own language and uphold local customs and culture. It enjoys, however, little real political autonomy, being required to adhere to decisions made in Beijing (Peking) by the leadership of the ruling CCP.

Political history
Xizang was an independent kingdom from the fifth century AD, with the Dalai Lama emerging as its spiritual and temporal ruler from AD 750 onwards. The country was conquered and ruled by the Mongols between 1279 and 1368 and came under nominal Chinese sovereignty between about 1700 and 1912. However, independence was regained, under the Dalai Lama's leadership, after a revolt in 1912. China's rule over Xizang was nominally re-established in 1950–51 and the Dalai Lama was driven out of the country and the Buddhist monks, who constituted a quarter of the population, forced out of their monasteries. Between 1951 and 1959 the Chinese People's Liberation Army (PLA) controlled Xizang, although the Dalai Lama returned as nominal spiritual and temporal head of state. In 1959, a Tibetan uprising spread from bordering regions to Lhasa and was supported by the Xizang local government. The rebellion was, however, brutally suppressed by the PLA, prompting the Dalai Lama and 9,000, subsequently mounting to 100,000, Tibetans to flee to India. The Chinese proceeded to dissolve the Xizang local government, abolish serfdom, collectivise agriculture and suppress Lamaism. In 1965 Xizang became an Autonomous Region of China. Industrialisation, based on the production of textiles, chemicals and agricultural machinery, was encouraged and 200,000 Han Chinese settled in the country. Chinese rule continued to be resented, however, and the economy languished, thousands dying from famine. Since 1979 the new leadership in Beijing has adopted a more liberal and pragmatic policy towards Xizang. Traditional agriculture, livestock and trading practices have been restored, under the 1980 slogan 'relax, relax and relax again', a number of older political leaders and rebels have been rehabilitated or pardoned, and the promotion of local Tibetan cadres has been encouraged. In addition, a more tolerant attitude towards Lamaism has been adopted, temples damaged during the 1966–69 Cultural Revolution having been repaired, and attempts, so far unsuccessful, have been made to persuade the Dalai Lama to return from exile. The violent pro-independence demonstrations by Buddhist monks, which erupted in Lhasa in September and October 1987, in March and December 1988 and in March 1989 and were forcibly suppressed by Chinese troops, exhibit the continuing strength of nationalist feeling.

8.4.3 Denmark's dependencies

Denmark has two dependencies, described as Outlying Territories. Their political structures and histories are given below.

Table 73

DANISH OUTLYING TERRITORIES

Name	*Date of First Coming Under Danish Administration*	*Area (km²)*	*Population (1985)*
Faroe Islands	1380	1,399	46,000
Greenland	985†	2,175,600‡	53,000
Total	—	2,176,999	99,000

†Formally in 1917.
‡80 per cent covered by ice-cap.

FAROE ISLANDS

Capital: Torshavn

Location
Western Europe. A group of 21 volcanic islands, 18 of which are inhabited, in the North Atlantic between Iceland and the Shetland Isles, which are some 350 km to the south-east. The largest islands are Stromo and Ostero.

Social and economic data
Area: 1,399 km²
Population: 46,000*
Pop density per km²: 33*
Literacy rate: 99%
GDP: $500m*; per capita GDP: $10,870
Economy type: high income
Labour force in agriculture: 19%

*1985

Ethnic composition
The inhabitants are predominantly ethnic Faroese. Five per cent of the workforce are immigrants.

Principal religion
Christianity, in the form of the Lutheran Protestant Church.

Political system
An elected assembly (Logting) of 32 members has operated since 1852. Twenty-seven of its seats are filled by direct election under universal adult suffrage and seven by a party list system, in accordance with an equalisation

formula. A six-member cabinet (Landsstyri), headed by a chairman, or Prime Minister (Logmadur), is responsible to the chamber. This assembly has, since 1948, been devolved full authority for internal affairs, but the Danish government, which is represented on the islands by a Commissioner, has responsibility for foreign affairs and regulates education, social welfare, civil, criminal and Church affairs and currency matters. The islands elect two representatives to the Danish parliament (Folketing).

Six political parties currently operate in the Faroes. They are the Social Democratic Party (SDP or Javnaoarflokkurin), the Union Party (UP), the Republican Party (RP), the Faroese People's Party (FPP or Folkaflokkurin), the Self-Government Party (SGP) and the Progressive and Fishermen's Party (PFP).

The SDP was established in 1928, and has a membership of about 1,000. It has frequently participated in coalition governments, with the UP, RP, FPP and SGP, since 1958 and is social democratic in outlook. The UP was founded in 1906. It is a conservative party which stands for close links with the Danish Crown and dominated the Logting before 1958. The RP dates from 1948. It favours secession from Denmark and the establishment of a fully independent republic. It has participated in government coalitions, with the SGP, PFP, SDP and FPP, since the early 1960s. The FPP was established in 1940 and is a liberal-conservative party, in favour of free enterprise and greater economic autonomy. It has also participated in government coalitions, with the RP, SDP, SGP and PFP, since the early 1960s. The SGP was formed in 1906 and now has a membership of about 1,700. It is a centrist party which was originally formed to press for greater legislative devolution. It was a regular member of government coalitions between 1948 and 1970. The PFP is a minor party which favours increased internal self-government.

Following the November 1984 general election, the SDP had eight Logting seats, the FPP and UP seven each, the RP six and the SGP and PFP two each. A four-party coalition government, consisting of the SDP, SGP, RP and FPP, and headed by the SDP's leader Atli Dam, was subsequently formed. The Social Democratic coalition lost its majority, however, in the general election of November 1988, with the FPP emerging as the new dominant force.

Political history

The islands were settled by the Norse during the eighth and ninth centuries and became part of the Kingdom of Norway in the eleventh century. They passed to Denmark in 1380, when Queen Margrete inherited Norway. During the Second World War, following the German invasion of Denmark, they were temporarily occupied by British troops. Home rule was granted in 1948. Fishing is the principal industry, employing 26 per cent of the labour force, and export earner, while Danish subsidies account for a sixth of GDP. Although Denmark joined the European Community in 1973, the Faroes have remained outside.

GREENLAND

Kalaallitt Nunaat

Capital: Nuuk (Godthab)

Location
Arctic. Greenland is the second-largest island in the world, after Australia. It is situated in the North Atlantic and Arctic Oceans, north-east of Canada. The interior is covered by an ice-sheet, with only 16 per cent ice-free and 5 per cent habitable by man.

Social and economic data
Area: 2,175,600 km^2
Population: 53,000*
Pop density per km^2: 0.2†
Literacy rate: 100%
GDP: $380m*; per capita GDP: $7,170
Economy type: high income
Labour force in agriculture: 15%

*1985
†Based on ice-free area

Ethnic composition
The population is predominantly Inuit (Eskimo) with Danish admixtures.

Principal religions
Shamanism and Lutheran Christianity.

Local government
There are 19 settlement councils responsible for local affairs.

Political system
In 1979 a new parliament (Landsting) was set up to replace the existing Greenland Provincial Council. It consists of 27 members, elected by universal adult suffrage on the basis of proportional representation, from which a seven-member government (Landsstyre), headed by a Prime Minister, is formed.

There are four political parties: the Forward (Siumut) Party, the Feeling of Community (Atassut) Party, the Eskimo Brotherhood (Inuit Ataqatigiit or IA) and the Polar Party (Issitrup-partii or IP).

The Siumut is the most important of the four. It was established in 1977 and has a current membership of 5,000. It is a quasi-socialist body which spearheaded the movement for self-rule and opposed Greenland's European Community entry terms. Drawing its support from the fishing and hunting community, the Siumut, led by a Lutheran pastor, Jonathan Motzfeldt, formed Greenland's first home-rule government in 1979. Motzfeldt has subsequently remained Prime Minister, leading coalition governments since 1983 with the IA. The Atassut is a moderate, non-socialist grouping which dominated the pre-autonomy Council. The IA is a Marxist-Leninist, pro-independence party which was founded in 1978. The IP was formed as recently as 1987 and favours the privatisation of the state's trawler fleet. At the most recent, May 1987, general election the Siumut and Atassut each captured eleven Landsting seats, the IA four and the IP one, a new Siumut-IA coalition government subsequently being formed.

Greenland also sends two representatives to the Danish Folketing and used to elect one Euro-MP. The Danish government is represented on the island by a High Commissioner.

Political history

The island was settled by seal-hunting eskimos from North America about 2,500 BC and colonised by the Danish King, Eric the Red, in AD 985. The south west of the island was colonised by Danes between the twelfth and fifteenth centuries, but these colonies were later abandoned. New settlements were founded in the seventeenth century and Danish sovereignty extended over the whole island in 1917. An agreement for the joint defence of Greenland, within the North Atlantic Treaty Organisation (NATO), was signed with the United States in 1951 and an American air base and, later, a radar station, were established at Thule in the far north. In 1953 the island became fully part of Denmark, returning two members to the Danish parliament (Folketing). Following a referendum supported by 70 per cent of voters, it was granted home-rule in 1979. Denmark retains responsibility for the island's defence, monetary policy and external affairs. In 1985, after another referendum, Greenland withdrew from the European Community, which it had joined with Denmark, in 1973. There had been an overwhelming, 71 per cent to 29 per cent, vote against entering in October 1972. Fishing, especially cod, is the principal industry, but a very high proportion of the island's income is derived from annual subsidies from Denmark.

8.4.4 France's dependencies

The French dependencies consist of four Overseas Departments, two Overseas Collective Territories, four Overseas Territories and one Internal Collective Territory, as listed in Table 74.

Table 74

FRENCH OVERSEAS DEPARTMENTS, TERRITORIES AND COLLECTIVE TERRITORIES

Name	*Date of First Coming Under French Administration*	*Area (km²)*	*Population (1985)*	*French National Assembly (NA) & Senate (S) Seats*
OVERSEAS DEPARTMENTS				
French Guiana	1817	90,000	84,177	2 NA/1 S
Guadeloupe	1613	1,780	333,378	4 NA/2 S
Martinique	1635	1,100	328,281	4 NA/2 S
Réunion	1642	2,512	560,000	5 NA/3 S
OVERSEAS COLLECTIVE TERRITORIES				
Mayotte	1843	376	67,167	1 NA/1 S
Saint-Pierre et Miquelon	17thC/1816	242	6,041	1 NA/1 S

Table 74—French Overseas Departments, Territories and Collective Territories (contd.)

Name	*Date of First Coming Under French Administration*	*Area (km²)*	*Population (1985)*	*French National Assembly (NA) & Senate (S) Seats*
OVERSEAS TERRITORIES				
French Polynesia	1842	4,200	176,543	2 NA/1 S
French Southern & Antarctic Territories	—	7,567*	210†	—
New Caledonia	1853	19,103	145,368	2 NA/1 S
Wallis & Futuna Islands	1842	274	12,391	1 NA/1 S
Total	—	127,154	1,713,556	22 NA/13 S
INTERNAL COLLECTIVE TERRITORY				
Corsica	1768	8,600	244,600	—

*Excludes 500,000 km² of the uninhabited mainland of Antarctica.

†Scientific mission workers.

FRENCH OVERSEAS DEPARTMENTS

Départements d'Outre-Mer

Overseas Departments, which form integral parts of the French Republic, have an administrative structure similar to that of the Departments of metropolitan France, although the former have their own Courts of Appeal. Prior to the decentralisation reforms of 1982, each Overseas Department was administered by a central government-appointed Prefect, assisted by a directly elected General Council and an indirectly elected Regional Council. After the reforms the Prefect was renamed Commissaire de la République (Government Commissioner), his formal executive power being transferred to the General Council, while the powers of the Regional Council, which was now directly elected, were considerably increased in the social, economic and cultural spheres. An earlier plan to merge the two councils into one was blocked by a decision of the French Constitutional Council in December 1982. French Overseas Departments also send representatives to the French national parliament and participate in French presidential elections.

FRENCH GUIANA

La Guyane Française

Capital: Cayenne

Location
South America. French Guiana lies between Suriname, to the west, and Brazil, to the east and south, on the north coast of South America.

Social and economic data
Area: 90,000 km^2
Population: 84,177*
Pop density per km^2: 0.9*
Literacy rate: 83 per cent
GDP: $280m*; per capita GDP: $3,326
Economy type: middle income
Labour force in agriculture: 11%

*1985

Ethnic composition
The population is a mixture of creoles, Europeans, Amerindians and Negroes.

Principal religion
Seventy-five per cent of the population are Roman Catholics.

Local government
The country is divided into two districts of Cayenne and Saint Laurent du Maroni.

Political system
French Guiana is administered by an appointed French Government Commissioner (Commissaire de la République), who is assisted by a two-chamber body comprising the 19-member General Council (Conseil Général) and the 31-member Regional Council (Conseil de Région). Both are directly elected for six-year terms and exercise a number of local powers. Additionally, the inhabitants elect two members to the French National Assembly and send, through indirect elections, one representative to the Senate.

The principal political parties are the two conservative groups, the Rally for the Republic (RPR) and Union for French Democracy (UDF); the Guiana Socialist Party (PSG); the leftist Guyanese Democratic Action Party (ADG: Action Démocratique Guyanaise); and the separatist Guyanese Popular National Party (PNGP: Parti National Populaire Guyanais). The PNPG was established in 1985, before which it was known as the Union of Guyanese Workers (UTG).

The PSG, with 15 seats, dominated the ruling coalition in the Regional Council following the elections of March 1986, its leader Georges Othily being re-elected Council President. The RPR won nine seats, the ADG four and the UDF three. In the June 1988 French National Assembly election, both the PSG and RPR won one seat each. In the September–October (two-ballot) 1988 General Council elections, the PSG secured an increased majority.

Political history
First settled by France in 1604, the area was successively under Dutch, English and Portuguese rule during the seventeenth and eighteenth centuries before French control was re-established and recognised in 1817. It was used as a penal colony during the nineteenth century and remained

economically undeveloped, possessing few natural resources except timber. In 1946 French Guiana became an Overseas Department of the French Republic, making it subject to the same laws and system of government as France's mainland departments. Such departmental status was opposed during the 1970s by left-wing groups, led by the Guiana Socialist Party (PSG), who demanded greater internal autonomy and called for increased priority to be given to economic development. In response, the French government introduced an indirectly elected Regional Council in 1974, which became directly elected and was given increased authority in 1983. In addition, France provided substantial amounts of economic aid. French Guiana still, however, remains extremely poor and has been subject to terrorist bombing campaigns by the Guadeloupe-based Caribbean Revolutionary Alliance (ARC: Alliance Révolutionnaire Caraïbe) during recent years.

GUADELOUPE

Capital: Basse-Terre

Location

Central America. Guadeloupe consists of a group of islands in the central Lesser Antilles, of the eastern Caribbean, lying between Dominica, to the south, and Antigua and Montserrat, to the north-west. The two principal islands are Basse-Terre and Grande-Terre, on which 43 per cent and 48 per cent, respectively, of the total population live.

Social and economic data

Area: 1,780 km^2
Population: 333,378*
Pop density per km^2: 187*
Literacy rate: 90%
GDP: $1,100m*; per capita GDP: $3,300
Economy type: middle income
Labour force in agriculture: 10%

*1985

Ethnic composition

Ninety per cent of the population are blacks or mulattos, 5 per cent Caucasians and 4 per cent East Indians. French, spoken in a creole dialect, is the main language.

Principal religion

Ninety per cent of the population are Roman Catholics.

Local government

The islands are divided into three *arrondissements* (districts), which are subdivided into 34 communes.

Political system

The country is administered by an appointed French government Commissioner (Commissaire de la République), who is assisted by a two-chamber body comprising the 43-member General Council (Conseil Général) and the 41-member Regional Council (Conseil de Région). Both are elected for a period of up to six years and exercise a number of local powers. In addition, Guadeloupe elects four members to the French National Assembly and sends two, indirectly elected, representatives to the Senate.

The principal political parties are two conservative groups, Rally for the Republic (RPR) and Union for French Democracy (UDF); the centrist Guadeloupe Party (LPG); the Guadeloupe Socialist Party (FGPS: Fédération Guadeloupenne du Parti Socialiste); and the Guadeloupe Communist Party (PCG), which was established in 1944.

Felix Proto, of the FGPS, was elected, with support from the PCG, as the new leader of the Regional Council following the elections of March 1986, the FGPS and PCG having secured twelve and ten Council seats respectively, compared with the RPR's 15 and UDF's four. The FGPS also won, in alliance with the PCG, a majority in the General Council in the election of September 1988, the party's leader, Dominique Larifla, being re-elected to the chamber's presidency. In the French National Assembly elections of June 1988, the FGPS captured two seats, the PCG one and the RPR one.

Political history

Discovered by Christopher Columbus in 1493, the islands of Guadeloupe were occupied by France in 1635. They became renowned for sugar production and remained under French rule for the next three centuries, apart from brief British occupations in the eighteenth and early nineteenth centuries. The country became an Overseas Department of the French Republic in 1946. During the 1960s opposition to the monopoly of economic power by white (creole) settlers and to the restrictions imposed by the status of being a Department led to a movement for greater internal autonomy, spearheaded by the Guadeloupe Communist Party (PCG). In response to these demands, an indirectly elected Regional Council was established in 1974. This body became directly elected, with increased powers, from February 1983. A small extremist minority, led by the Popular Movement for an Independent Guadeloupe (MPGI: Mouvement populaire pour une Guadeloupe indépendante) and the outlawed Caribbean Revolutionary Alliance (ARC: Alliance Révolutionnaire Caraïbe) a left-wing extremist group, continue however to seek full independence. The ARC has resorted to terrorist bombing outrages in recent years. However, despite a deterioration in economic conditions since the 1970s, caused by the steady decline of the sugar industry, which sent the unemployment rate to above 25 per cent, electoral support for pro-independence parties has remained below 5 per cent. There has, however, been a gradual shift in support away from the parties of the right and centre towards those of the pro-autonomy 'conventional left', the Guadeloupe Socialist Party (FGPS) and PCG. In February 1988, the PCG switched to a policy of pro-independence.

MARTINIQUE

Capital: Fort-de-France

Location
Central America and the Caribbean. Martinique is one of the Windward Islands in the eastern Caribbean, situated between Dominica, to the north, and St Lucia, to the south.

Social and economic data
Area: 1,100 km^2
Population: 328,281*
Pop density per km^2: 298*
Literacy rate: 93%
GDP: $1,300m*; per capita GDP: $3,960
Economy type: middle income
Labour force in agriculture: 8%

*1985

Ethnic composition
Ninety per cent of the population are of African and African-Caucasian-Indian descent. French is the official language, with creole widely spoken.

Principal religion
Ninety per cent of the population are Roman Catholics.

Local government
The island is divided into three *arrondissements* (districts), which are subdivided into 34 communes.

Political system
Martinique is administered by an appointed French government Commissioner (Commissaire de la République), assisted by a two-chamber body comprising the 44-member General Council (Conseil Général) and the 41-member Regional Council (Conseil de Région). Both are elected for a term of up to six years and exercise a number of local powers. In addition, Martinique elects four members to the French National Assembly and sends, through indirect election, two representatives to the French Senate.

The principal political parties are the two conservative groups, the Rally for the Republic (RPR) and Union for French Democracy (UDF); the left-of-centre Progressive Party of Martinique (PPM: Parti Progressiste Martiniquais), which was established in 1936, and the Martinique Socialist Federation (FSM: Fédération Socialiste de la Martinique), which is a local branch of the mainland Socialist Party; the Martinique Communist Party (PCM), which was formed in 1957; and the, secessionist, Martinique Independence Movement (MIM: Mouvement Indépendantiste Martiniquais). In the most recent Regional Council election of March 1986, the parties of the left (PPM, FSM and PCM) joined together in a 'Union of the Left' (Union de la Gauche) and won 21 seats, compared with the RPR's eleven and UDF's nine. The PPM leader, Aimé Césaire, was re-elected

Regional Council President. The General Council, following the elections of September 1988 has a left majority but an RPR President. In contrast, since the elections of June 1988, all four French National Assembly seats are held by Socialists and various left-wing representatives.

Political history
Martinique was discovered by Spanish navigators in 1493 and became a French colony in 1635. Famed for its sugar production and as the birthplace of the Empress Josephine, the island became an Overseas Department of the French Republic in 1946. Despite the country's close cultural integration with France, a nationalist movement emerged during the 1950s and 1960s, spearheaded by the Progressive Party of Martinique (PPM) and the Martinique Communist Party (PCM), which opposed the concentration of economic power in the hands of white settler families *(békés)*. In response to this movement, consultative General and Regional Councils were created in 1960 and 1974 respectively. The Regional Council became directly elected and was granted additional powers, including greater control over taxation, local police and economic affairs, in 1983, as part of the metropolitan Socialist government's decentralisation initiative. The PPM and PCM continue to seek greater autonomy, but only a small minority of the population, less than 5 per cent, support a campaign for full independence from France.

This extreme policy is championed by the Martinique Independence Movement (MIM) and the outlawed Caribbean Revolutionary Alliance (ARC: Alliance Révolutionnaire Caraïbe) terrorist organisation. The island's economy has been in a depressed condition during recent years, the sugar industry continuing to decline and growth in new export lines, for example bananas, being disappointing. More than a quarter of the labour force are currently unemployed and emigration to France and French Guiana is now at a level of 15,000 per annum.

REUNION

Capital: Saint-Denis

Location
Central and Southern Africa. Réunion, formerly Bourbon, island lies in the Indian Ocean 800 km east of Madagascar. Thirty-five per cent of its area is under forest, and both active and dormant volcanoes are to be found in the interior.

Social and economic data
Area: 2,512 km^2
Population: 560,000*
Pop density per km^2: 223*
Literacy rate: 79%
GDP: $1,800m*; per capita GDP: $3,214
Economy type: middle income
Labour force in agriculture: 26%

*1985

Ethnic composition

The population comprises a mixture of people of European, African, Indian and Chinese descent. There are also more than 3,000 French troops based on the island, which serves as the headquarters of French military forces in the Indian Ocean.

Principal religion

Eighty-nine per cent of the population are Roman Catholics.

Local government

The island is divided into four *arrondissements* (districts), which are subdivided into 24 communes and 36 cantons.

Political system

The island is administered by an appointed French government Commissioner (Commissaire de la République), assisted by a two-chamber body consisting of the 36-member General Council (Conseil Général) and the 45-member Regional Council (Conseil de Région). Both are directly elected by proportional representation for six-year terms and exercise a number of local powers. In addition, Réunion elects five members to the French National Assembly, and sends, through indirect election, three representatives to the French Senate and one to the Economic and Social Council.

The principal political parties are the three conservative groups, the Rally for the Republic (RPR), the Union for French Democracy (UDF) and France-Réunion-Avenir (FRA), which was established in 1986; the Réunion Communist Party (PCR), which was founded in 1959; and the Socialist Party (PS). The RPR/UDF, in alliance with the recently formed FRA, control the Regional Council, after capturing, respectively, 18 and eight seats in the election of March 1986. The PCR and PS, drawing the bulk of their support from poor creole (Afro-Asian) urban and rural workers and campaigning for improved labour conditions, won 13 and six seats respectively. In the French National Assembly election of June 1988, the PCR won two seats, the RPR, UDF and 'independent right' candidates securing one seat each.

Political history

Discovered by the Portuguese in 1513, Réunion was annexed by France in 1642, serving initially as a penal colony and then, from 1665, as a post of the French East India Company. During the eighteenth century the island was developed into a major coffee exporter, this crop being replaced by sugar cane during the nineteenth century. Réunion was designated an Overseas Department of the French Republic in 1946 and was given the additional status of a region in 1974. Despite calls on the part of the Organisation of African Unity (OAU), for the island's 'liberation', there is majority support on Réunion for continued French control. The left-wing parties, however, favour enhanced autonomy. Réunion's economy, which remains heavily dependent on the sugar industry, has been depressed during recent years. As a consequence, despite growth in the tourist sector, the unemployment rate has risen to more than 30 per cent, forcing the island to draw increasingly on the mainland for development grants.

FRENCH OVERSEAS COLLECTIVE TERRITORIES

Collectivités Territoriales

The status of a Collective Territory (CT) is intermediate between that of an Overseas Department and an Overseas Territory. CTs constitute integral parts of the French Republic. They are administered by an appointed government Commissioner (Commissaire de la République), who works with an elected General Council, and they send representatives to the French parliament and participate in French presidential elections.

MAYOTTE (Mahore)

Capital: Dzaoudzi

Location
Central and Southern Africa. Mayotte consists of a volcanic island group which forms part of the Comoro archipelago, between Madagascar and the African mainland. The two main islands are Grande Terre and La Petite Terre.

Social and economic data
Area: 376 km^2
Population: 67,167*
Pop density per km^2: 179*
Literacy rate: N/A
GDP: $25m*; per capita GDP: $372
Economy type: low income
Labour force in agriculture: N/A

*1985

Principal languages
French and Mahorian, a Swahili dialect.

Principal religion
Islam, to which 98 per cent of the population adhere.

Local government
Mayotte is divided into 17 communes.

Political system
The islands are administered by an appointed French government Commissioner (Commissaire de la République), who works with the assistance of an elected 17-member General Council (Conseil Général). In addition, Mayotte elects one member to the French National Assembly and one representative to the French Senate.

Five political parties operate on the islands, including branches of the mainland Union for French Democracy (UDF), Centre of Social Democrats (CDS) and Rally for the Republic (RPR). The RPR branch is termed the

Mayotte Federation of the Rally for the Republic (FMRPR) and holds six General Council seats. The dominant political party on the island, however, currently holding nine General Council seats, is the Mayotte People's Movement (MPM: Mouvement populaire mahorais). The MPM led the movement for Mayotte's exclusion from the independent Republic of the Comoros and has since campaigned for departmental status. Its leader, Younoussa Bamana, is President of the General Council. Following the French general election of June 1988, Mayotte's National Assembly seat is held by the UDF-CDS.

Political history

The most populous of the Comoros group of islands in the Indian Ocean, Mayotte, together with its sister islands, was a French colony from 1843, and attached to Madagascar from 1914. Later, in 1947, the Comoros Islands were designated a French Overseas Territory, and granted internal autonomy within the French Republic in 1961. It was agreed, in 1973, that eventual independence would be secured in 1979. However, when the Comoran parliament declared unilateral independence in July 1975, Mayotte refused to join the new state, preferring to remain formally linked to France. The French government granted Mayotte special status as a Collective Territory of the French Republic in December 1976, a decision which was reaffirmed by the French National Assembly in December 1979 and October 1984. They rejected, however, the Mayotte People's Movement's demands for full departmental status, because of the island's economic backwardness. The Comoran government continues to claim sovereignty over Mayotte and is supported in this view by the United Nations' General Assembly and the Organisation of African Unity (OAU). The island is heavily dependent on French economic aid, benefiting recently from the launching, in 1986, of a French-funded, 100 million franc, five-year development plan.

SAINT-PIERRE AND MIQUELON

Iles Saint-Pierre-et-Miquelon

Capital: Saint-Pierre

Location

North America. It consists of a small group of eight rocky islands lying 25 km south of Newfoundland, in the North Atlantic Ocean. Ninety per cent of the population live on St Pierre Island.

Social and economic data

Area: 242 km^2
Population: 6,041*
Pop density per km^2: 25*
Literacy rate: 99%
GDP: $45m*; per capita GDP: $7,449
Economy type: high income
Labour force in agriculture: 6%

*1985

Principal language
French.

Principal religion
Ninety-nine per cent of the population are Roman Catholics.

Political system
The islands are administered by an appointed French government Commissioner (Commissaire de la République), who is assisted by a 14-member General Council (Conseil Général), which is elected for a six-year term. In addition, the islands elect one member to the French National Assembly and one representative to the French Senate and one to the Economic and Social Council.

The dominant political party is the Socialist Party (PS), which currently holds all the General Council seats. The Union for French Democracy (UDF) and Centre of Social Democrats (CDS) also operate, currently holding, following the French general election of June 1988, the islands' one National Assembly seat.

Political history
The islands, which were first visited and settled by Breton and Basque fishermen during the sixteenth and seventeenth centuries, constitute the remnants of the once extensive French Empire in North America. They were formally designated French territory in 1816 and gained departmental status in the French Republic in July 1976. This move, tying the local economy into the remote institutions of metropolitan France and the European Community, disrupted economic relations with neighbouring Canada and was opposed by local politicians and trade unionists. In 1978 and 1980 there were general strikes in protest and in the March 1982 General Council election Socialist candidates, campaigning for a change in the islands' status, swept the board. This persuaded the French government to grant them special status as a Collective Territory, in June 1985. The islands continue to serve as the centre for the French Atlantic cod fishing, although this industry has been in steady decline since the mid 1970s, seriously depressing the local economy. During recent years, a dispute has developed between the French and Canadian governments over cod quotas and territorial limits, France claiming a 200-mile 'exclusive economic zone' in the waters around Saint-Pierre and Miquelon. This conflict, which has been heightened by recent offshore gas and petroleum exploration, is to be resolved by the International Court of Justice.

FRENCH OVERSEAS TERRITORIES

Territoires d'Outre-Mer

Overseas territories, which form integral parts of the French Republic, are administered by an appointed High Commissioner or Chief Administrator, who works with an elected Territorial Assembly or Congress. They send representatives to the French parliament and participate in French presidential elections.

FRENCH POLYNESIA

Capital: Papeete, on the island of Tahiti.

Location
Oceania. French Polynesia comprises five scattered volcanic and coral island groups in the south-eastern Pacific Ocean, between the Cook Islands, to the west, and Kiribati to the north-east. The largest island, on which 70 per cent of the population live, is Tahiti.

Social and economic data
Area: 4,200 km^2
Population: 176,543*
Pop density per km^2: 42*
Literacy rate: 95%
GDP: $1,290m*; per capita GDP: $7,307
Economy type: high income
Labour force in agriculture: 17%

*1985

Ethnic composition
Seventy per cent of the population are Polynesian, 18 per cent Chinese and 12 per cent European.

Principal religion
About 55 per cent of the population are Protestants and 24 per cent Roman Catholics.

Political system
Under the terms of the 1984 constitution, an appointed French High Commissioner controls defence, foreign policy, justice and monetary affairs, while a 41-member Territorial Assembly (Assemblée Territoriale), which is directly elected for a five-year term, appoints, from its own ranks, a President and ten-member Council of Ministers (COM). The COM has considerable autonomy in internal policy matters. French Polynesia also elects two members to the French National Assembly and one each to the French Senate and Economic and Social Council.

The five principal political parties are the Rally for the Republic/Popular Union Party (RPR/Tahoeraa Huiraatira), the Pupu Here Ai'a Te Nunaa (PHA), the Ia Mana Te Nunaa (IMTN), the New Land Party (Ai'a Api) and the Polynesian Liberation Front (FLP: Front de Libération de la Polynésie).

The RPR/Tahoeraa Huiraatira was established in 1958, and is led by Gaston Flosse. It supports the maintenance of close links with France, though with enhanced internal autonomy. The PHA is a pro-autonomy party which was founded in 1965. It is led by the mayor of Papeete, Jean Juventin. The Ia Mana Te Nunaa was formed in 1976 and advocates 'socialist independence'. The New Land Party dates from 1982. The FLP campaigns for independence and is led by Oscar Temaru.

In the Territorial Assembly election of March 1986, the RPR secured the first outright assembly majority in the territory's history, capturing 24 seats to the PHA's four, IMTN's three, FLP's two and the six of the Amuitahiraa Mo Porinesia, which is a coalition of smaller parties. However, the RPR's leader, Gaston Flosse, was forced to resign as President of the COM in February 1987, following charges of corruption, and the RPR subsequently split, in December 1987, a breakaway faction, led by Alexandre Léontieff, forming a new coalition government with the support of opposition members. In the June 1988 French National Assembly election, the RPR and centre-left candidates each won one seat.

Political history

The islands of French Polynesia were visited by Spanish and Portuguese explorers in the late sixteenth century and by the French and British in the 1760s. Tahiti became a French protectorate in 1842, the remaining islands being annexed between 1880 and 1900. In 1957 French Polynesia was made an Overseas Territory of the French Republic, ruled by an appointed governor and an advisory Territorial Assembly. During the mid 1970s, a separatist movement, spearheaded by Francis Sanford, leader of the United Front Party (Te E'a Api), gained strength. France responded by devolving greater authority to the Territorial Assembly and its Council of Ministers under new constitutions of 1977 and 1984.

Mururoa Atoll, in the Tuamotu Archipelago, has been a controversial nuclear test site since 1966. However, despite the adverse environmental aspects, its use has brought an influx of French military personnel into the territory, 5,400 being stationed in French Polynesia in 1987, and provided economic opportunities in the service and construction industries.

NEW CALEDONIA

Nouvelle-Calédonie

Capital: Nouméa

Location

Oceania. New Caledonia comprises the large, mountainous island of Grande Terre, or New Caledonia, the adjacent Loyalty Islands and, 400 km to the north-west, the uninhabited Chesterfield Islands. They are situated in the South Pacific Ocean, 1,500 km east of Queensland, Australia. Forty-one per cent of the population live at the capital, Nouméa, on Grande Terre.

Social and economic data

Area: 19,103 km^2
Population: 145,368*
Pop density per km^2: 7.6*
Literacy rate: 91%
GDP: $860m*; per capita GDP: $5,916
Economy type: high income
Labour force in agriculture: 27%

*1985

Ethnic composition
Forty-three per cent of the population are Melanesian, 37 per cent European, 8 per cent Wallisian, 4 per cent Polynesian, 4 per cent Indonesian and 2 per cent Vietnamese. France maintains a force of 4,900 military personnel in New Caledonia.

Principal religion
About 65 per cent of the population are Roman Catholics.

Local government
The territory is divided into four *circonscriptions* and subdivided into 32 communes, administered by locally elected councils and mayors.

Political system
Following the 'Fabius plan' of April 1985, New Caledonia has enjoyed a considerable degree of autonomy. A High Commissioner represents the French government's interests in the islands and retains control over defence, foreign policy and justice. Since September 1985, and pending the full implementation of proposed administrative reforms, New Caledonia has been divided into four regions, North, Centre, South, or Greater Nouméa, and the Loyalty Islands, each of which has the status of a self-governing territorial unit and has its own directly elected Regional Council (Conseil de Région). These Regional Councils control economic planning, education, the social and health services, land rights, housing and transport and each is headed by a President. Members of the Regional Councils also serve on a national, 46-member Territorial Congress (Congrès Territorial), headed by an elected President, who joins the Presidents of the four Regional Councils to form a consultative Executive Council (Conseil Exécutif). From June 1989, the four existing Regional Councils will be replaced by three Regional Assemblies, based in the South, North and Outer Islands, with 32, 15 and seven members each. They will sit jointly as an Island Congress, under the French High Commissioner.

There are five principal political parties in New Caledonia. Two of them, the extreme right-wing National Front (FN) and the Rally for Caledonia within the Republic (RPCR: Rassemblement pour la Calédonie dans la République), led by Jacques Lafleur, are settler-orientated bodies which favour retaining French control over the islands. One, the Caledonian Republican Party (PRC: Parti Républicain Calédonien), campaigns for greater internal autonomy. Two, the Melanesian-orientated Kanak Socialist National Liberation Front (FLNKS: Front de libération nationale kanake socialiste), a six-party alliance led by the former Catholic priest François Burck, and the Kanak Socialist Liberation Party (LKS: Libération kanake socialiste), press for full independence.

Between 1986 and 1988, the FLNKS controlled the small seven- to nine-member Regional Councils of the North, Centre and Loyalty Islands, and the RPCR, the large, 21-member, Regional Council of Greater Nouméa. The RPCR-FN also dominated the Territorial Congress, holding 28 seats *vis-à-vis* the FLNKS-LKS's 17 and the PRC's one, and the RPCR's Dick Ukeiwe served as its President. Following the elections of April 1988, however, which were largely boycotted by the Melanesian community, the

RPCR and FN won control of all the councils, capturing 35 and eight seats respectively. New Caledonia elects two members to the French National Assembly and sends, through indirect election, one representative to both the French Senate and the Economic and Social Council. In the June 1988 French National Assembly elections, the RPCR captured both available seats.

Political history

Discovered by James Cook in 1774, New Caledonia was annexed by France in 1853, and was initially used, between 1871 and 1898, as a penal settlement. It became an Overseas Territory of the French Republic in 1946. Friction developed between the urban-based French settlers (Caldoches) and the local Melanesians (Kanaks) during the 1970s. Many of the Caldoches had been attracted to the Territory during the 1960s nickel boom, New Caledonia being the world's third-largest nickel producer. The Kanaks, however, constituted a majority in rural areas. In response to Kanak demands for self-government the authority of the locally elected Territorial Assembly, which had been established in 1956, was increased, in December 1976. Direct 'Commissioner rule' had to be imposed in 1979 when pro-independence parties gained control of the Assembly's Council of Government and in September 1981 tensions were heightened, following the assassination of Pierre Declercq, leader of the separatist movement. Further cultural and political reforms were suggested by France's socialist Mitterrand administration after 1981, including proposals, in January 1985, for independence 'in association with' France, subject to a referendum. The holding of a national referendum, planned for July 1985, was violently opposed, however, by the Kanak Socialist National Liberation Front (FLNKS), forcing the declaration of a state of emergency.

The poll was shelved and a new 'Fabius plan' of regional devolution adopted instead. Regional councils were elected in September 1985 and a referendum on independence was held in September 1987. In this poll, 98 per cent of those who voted gave approval to New Caledonia's remaining part of the French Republic. Turnout was only 59 per cent, however, with the bulk of the Melanesian community adhering to the advice of the FLNKS and boycotting the poll. Soon after the referendum, Bernard Pons, the Minister for Overseas Departments and Territories in France's conservative (RPR) Chirac administration, submitted an administrative reorganisation plan to New Caledonia's Territorial Assembly. This settler-biased scheme was accepted by Rally for Caledonia within the Republic (RPCR) Assembly members, but was strongly criticised by the FLNKS. This prompted a renewed outbreak of Kanak violence by militant factions during the run-up to the French presidential and new regional elections, in April-May 1988.

The return of the Socialists to power in Paris in June 1988 was swiftly followed by a fresh initiative by Michel Rocard, the new French Prime Minister. After a fortnight of negotiations in Paris, a compromise settlement was agreed by the FLNKS and RPCR leaders, Jean-Marie Tjibaou and Lafleur, in late June. The outcome was a decision to delay the holding of another referendum on independence until 1998, and, instead, to establish, in June 1989, a new system of local government based on the division of the territory into three self-governing provinces: one in the south for white settlers, and two, in the north and outer islands, for Kanaks. This scheme, which was planned to bring to an end a year of direct administration from Paris, was approved in a national referendum held throughout the French Republic in November 1988. It was accompanied by a generous, new economic development programme, targeted at poor Kanak rural areas. However, its long-term success in securing communal peace remains to be proven. External pressure for decolonisation has increased during recent years, particularly since the United Nations' General Assembly decision, in December 1986, to re-inscribe New Caledonia on the UN list of non-self-governing territories. Internal Kanak disquiet with the June 1988 Matignon Accord surfaced in May 1989 with the assassination of Tjibaou by a separatist extremist.

WALLIS AND FUTUNA ISLANDS

Capital: Mata-Utu, on Wallis Island.

Location
Oceania. The Territory comprises two groups of islands, the Wallis and the Futuna and Alofi. They are situated in the south-central Pacific Ocean to the north-east of Fiji and west of Western Samoa. Sixty-five per cent of the population live on Wallis Island.

Social and economic data
Area: 274 km^2
Population: 12,391*
Pop density per km^2: 45*
Literacy rate: N/A
GDP: $12m*; per capita GDP: $968
Economy type: low income
Labour force in agriculture: N/A

*1985

Ethnic composition
The population is predominantly Polynesian.

Principal religion
Roman Catholicism.

Political system
The islands are administered by an appointed French Chief Administrator, who is assisted by a 20-member Territorial Assembly (Assemblée Territoriale), which is directly elected for five-year terms on a common roll. The Territory elects one member to the French National Assembly and one representative to the Senate. The three traditional kingdoms, one in Wallis and two in Futuna, from which the territory was formed, retain a number of limited powers.

The two dominant political parties are the Rally for the Republic (RPR) and Union for French Democracy (UDF), each of which, following elections held in March 1987, holds seven seats in the Territorial Assembly.

Affiliated to the UDF is the Lua kae tahi Party, and holding six Assembly seats is the Futuna-based Local Popular Union (UPL: Union Populaire Locale). This party was formed in April 1985 by the Territorial Assembly's President, Falakiko Gata, a former member of the RPR, who wished to give greater emphasis to local issues. The RPR has formed an alliance with the UPL to retain control of the Assembly. The RPR also holds, since the French general election of June 1988, the islands' one National Assembly seat.

Political history

The Futuna island group was discovered by Dutch explorers in 1616 and the Wallis islands by the British in 1767. They were later settled by French missionaries in the early nineteenth century, becoming a French dependency in 1842 and protectorate in 1888. Following a local referendum in December 1959, the islands were designated an Overseas Territory of the French Republic in July 1961. In contrast to the French Pacific territories of French Polynesia and New Caledonia, there is no secessionist movement at present on the islands. However, there have been calls by the kings of Futuna for two separate, Wallis and Futuna, Overseas Territories to be created. Lacking natural resources, the islands export little and are heavily dependent on economic aid from France and remittances sent home by the 11,000 countrymen employed in New Caledonia and Vanuatu.

FRENCH 'INTERNAL' COLLECTIVE TERRITORY

This category is a special one, since Corsica is so close to France that it is not usually thought of as an 'overseas' dependency. Prior to the decentralisation reforms of 1982, it constituted the twenty-second region of metropolitan France. It was then, however, elevated to the status of a Collective Territory and given a parliament with substantive powers, thus distinguishing it from the other 21 regions of metropolitan France.

CORSICA

Corse

Capital: Ajaccio

Location

Western Europe. Corsica is an island in the Mediterranean Sea, west of Italy and north of Sardinia.

Social and economic data

Area: 8,680 km^2
Population: 244,600*
Pop density per km^2: 28*
GDP: N/A*

*1985

Ethnic composition
Fifty per cent of the population are native Corsicans.

Principal religion
Roman Catholicism.

Local government
The island is divided into two departments (Haute-Corse and Corse-du-Sud), five *arrondissements* (districts), 52 cantons and 360 communes.

Political system
Corsica forms an integral part of the French Republic. Since 1982, however, it has been given the special status of a Collective Territory, with its own directly elected, 61-member parliament. This has the power to scrutinise bills passed by the French National Assembly and propose amendments applicable to the island.

The principal political parties are, the moderate Radical Party, led by François Giacobbi, which is based principally in the north (Haute Corse); the Bonapartist Party, led by Charles Ornano and based in Ajaccio; the conservative Gaullist Party, led by Jean-Paul de Rocca-Serra and based in the far south (Corse du Sud); the far-right National Front; the Communist Party; the Socialist Party; the Union for the Corsican People, a moderate autonomist movement; and the Corsican Movement for Self-determination (MCA), the political wing of the banned Corsican National Liberation Front (FNLC), a separatist, extremist organisation. Political activity is clan-based and intensely localised.

Political history
The island, which had earlier been ruled by the Phocaeans of Ionia, the Etruscans, the Carthaginians, the Romans, the Vandals and the Arabs, came under Genoa's control during the fourteenth century, before being sold to France in 1768. Under French rule it remained underdeveloped, but its people made their mark in metropolitan France and the French empire as eminent soldiers and administrators. The most notable of these was Napoléon Bonaparte.

During the Second World War, Corsica was occupied by Italy between 1942 and 1943. Since 1962 French *pieds noirs* (refugees from Algeria) settled on the island, largely as vineyard owners. Their relative prosperity fuelled a radical separatist movement, involving the bombing of 'colonial targets', by the Corsican National Liberation Front (FNLC). The annual level of bombings increased from 200 in 1975 to a peak of 800 in 1982. The French socialist Mitterrand administration responded by granting considerable autonomy to the island, to be exercised through a directly elected regional parliament. Elections to this body were held in 1982, 1984 and 1986–87 but, under the proportional representation system used, failed to produce a clear party or coalition majority. Terrorism has continued since 1982 at a reduced level, although only 5 per cent of the population support the Corsican Movement for Self-determination (MCA) or the FNLC extremists. In January 1987 the MCA itself was banned and dissolved by the French government.

8.4.5 Morocco's dependency

Western Sahara, which Morocco has controlled in one way or another since the early 1950s, is in strict legality an occupied territory, rather than a colony or dependency, and its future has yet to be finally determined. Details of its political structure and history are given below.

WESTERN SAHARA

Capital: La'youn

Location
Middle East and North Africa. It is situated in north-west Africa, between Morocco, to the north, and Mauritania, to the south, with the Atlantic Ocean to the west. The bulk of the territory is desert.

Social and economic data
Area: 266,000 km^2
Population: 165,000*
Pop density per km^2: 0.6*
Literacy rate: N/A
GDP: N/A*
Labour force in agriculture: N/A

*1985

Ethnic composition
The territory is peopled predominantly by nomadic herdsmen.

Principal religion
Sunni Muslim.

Local government
For administrative purposes, the territory is divided into the provinces of La'youn, Oued Eddahab, Es-Semara and Boujdour.

Political system
Since 1976, as a result of the territory's disputed status, Western Sahara has had two competing governments, both of which claim legitimacy. The Moroccan-controlled area is divided into four provinces noted above and administered by Moroccan officials. The nationalist Polisario Front (PF), which was set up in 1973, also, however, claims to rule this territory and has its own Saharan Arab Democratic Republic (SADR), 'government in exile', headed by a President, Mohamed Abdelaziz, and Prime Minister, Mohamed Lamine Ould Ahmed. It also includes a seven-member Executive Council, a 25-member Political Bureau and a 45-member, legislative, Saharawi National Council. At its refugee camps in south-western Algeria, there is also a rudimentary form of local government, based on people's councils. The PF is a socialist organisation, campaigning for the establishment of a fully independent and non-aligned Arab-Islamic state.

Political history

The 1,000-km-long Saharan coastal region between French-dominated Morocco and Mauritania was designated a Spanish 'sphere of influence' in 1884, being situated opposite the Spanish-ruled Canary Islands. However, Morocco had long laid claim to this border region and when it secured independence from France, in 1956, re-activated it by invading Spanish Sahara, only to be repulsed by Spanish troops. From 1965, after the discovery of rich phosphate resources at Bu Craa, in the heart of the territory, Moroccan interest was rekindled, but in a peaceful manner. Meanwhile, within Spanish Sahara, nationalist sentiment began to awaken and in 1973 the Yema'a, a council of local elders and elected officials, pressed for self-determination. A more radical nationalist group, the Polisario Front (Frente Popular de Liberacion de Sakiet el Hamra y Rio de Oro), was also formed, in May 1973, to fight for independence.

These calls were rejected by neighbouring Morocco and Mauritania, who, soon after the death of the Spanish ruler, General Franco, had moved in to divide the territory between themselves. This partition was finally effected during 1975–76, when Spain withdrew completely. Morocco secured two-thirds of the land area, including the phosphate mines, and Mauritania the rest. The Polisario nationalist forces, however, refused to accept this division and, declaring the establishment of their own Saharan Arab Democratic Republic (SADR: Republica Arabe Saharaui Democratica), proceeded to wage a guerrilla war against both Morocco and Mauritania, benefiting from indirect support provided by Algeria and Libya.

Polisario was successful in its struggle with Mauritania and forced its recognition of the SADR in August 1979. The SADR was also accepted, in February 1982, as a full member of the Organisation of African Unity (OAU). However, Morocco, by establishing an 'electronic defensive wall', which was a 2,500-km-long sand barrier, 2.75 metres high, on which modern electronic surveillance devices were put, and by the receipt of American support, remained impregnable. It kept control of the key towns and phosphate mines of Western Sahara, while conceding most of the surrounding, largely unpopulated, desert interior to Polisario. It also occupied much of the Mauritania-conceded area in the south.

With an army of more than 100,000 stationed in the territory and faced with a Polisario force of barely 8,000, the Moroccans gradually began to gain the upper hand, during the mid 1980s, and progressively extended their defensive wall outwards. They were boosted by Libya's decision to end its support for Polisario, in 1984, and by a gradual calming of Algeria's socialist revolutionary ardour, culminating, in May 1988, in the formal re-establishment of Algerian-Moroccan diplomatic relations. Three months later, in August 1988, a United Nations-sponsored settlement of the 'Western Saharan dispute' was effected in Geneva, when representatives from Morocco and the Polisario Front accepted a plan to hold a referendum, based on 1974 voting rolls, in Western Sahara, to decide the territory's political future. As part of this agreement, a UN Special Representative will be appointed to serve as a temporary pro-consul to run the civil administration and ensure order and political neutrality during the run-up to the planned referendum.

8.4.6 Netherlands' dependencies

The two dependencies of the Netherlands represent the residue of what was once a considerable colonial empire, dating back to the seventeenth century, which had been built up on the basis of trade and exploration. Details of the political structures and histories of these remaining overseas possessions are given below.

ARUBA

Capital: Oranjestad

Location
Central America and the Caribbean. Aruba is the westernmost island of the Lesser Antilles group, situated in the south-eastern Caribbean, 30 km north of Venezuela.

Social and economic data
Area: 193 km^2
Population: 68,000*
Pop density per km^2: 352*
Literacy rate: N/A
GDP: $400m*; per capita GDP: $5,882
Economy type: high income
Labour force in agriculture: N/A

*In 1985

Principal languages
Dutch, Papiamento (a local form of creole), Spanish and English.

Principal religion
Roman Catholicism.

Political system
There is a 21-member single chamber assembly, termed the Island Council (Staten), elected by universal adult suffrage for a four-year term and subject to dissolution during that time. Executive authority is wielded by an eight-member Council of Ministers, headed by a Prime Minister and responsible to the Staten. Dutch interests are overseen by a crown-appointed governor, who serves as commander-in-chief of the island's armed forces.

There are two principal political parties, the People's Electoral Movement (MEP) and the Aruba People's Party (AVP). The MEP was established in 1971 and has a current membership of 1,200. It is a secular, cross-race, social democratic party which dominated the Staten until 1985. The AVP was formed in 1942 and is led by the popular Henny Eman. Like the MEP, it campaigned for separation from Curaçao during the 1970s, but boycotted the MEP-induced referendum on the subject, in 1977. With minority party support, it gained a majority in the Staten following the elections of November 1985 and Eman became the island's first Prime Minister. Among the minor parties, the Aruban Patriotic Party (PPA), which was formed in 1949, and opposes full independence, is the most influential. It draws its support from non-Aruban islanders. In the 1985 general election, the MEP captured eight Staten seats; the AVP, seven; the PPA, two; and 'other parties', four.

Political history

The island was colonised by Holland in 1636 and became a member of the Netherlands Antilles autonomous federation in 1954. The economy developed significantly from the 1930s, following the establishment of a large oil refinery, at St Nicolaas, in 1929. This created growing resentment at the island's political dominance by adjacent Curaçao and the redistributive drain of wealth to other poorer islands in the federation. During the 1970s the People's Electoral Movement (MEP) exploited this sentiment by campaigning for Aruba's secession from the federation. A referendum on the issue was forced in March 1977, 82 per cent of the electorate voting for withdrawal and independence. Formal separation from the federation was finally achieved on 1 January 1986, following the report of a commission on the subject. The Netherlands remains responsible for the defence and external relations of the island until full independence, which is planned for 1996. The island's economy in recent years has been in a depressed condition, particularly following the closure of the oil refinery in March 1985.

THE NETHERLANDS ANTILLES

Capital: Willemstad, on Curaçao

Location

Central America and the Caribbean. The Netherlands Antilles consists of two island groups, 800 km apart, in the south-eastern Caribbean. The more northerly group is the 'Leeward Islands', which include Curaçao, Bonaire and, formerly, Aruba. It is 60 km north of Venezuela. The other group is the 'Windward Islands' and consists of the three small volcanic islands of St Eustatius, Saba and St Maarten.

Social and economic data

Area: 800 km^2
Population: 202,000*
Pop density per km^2: 253*
Literacy rate: 92%
GDP: $1,100m*; per capita GDP: $5,446
Economy type: high income
Labour force in agriculture: N/A

*1985

Ethnic composition

Eighty-five per cent of the population are of mixed African descent.

Principal languages
Dutch, Papiamento (a local form of creole), Spanish and English.

Principal religions
Roman Catholicism on the 'Leeward Islands' and Saba, and Protestantism on St Eustatius and St Maarten islands.

Political system
A crown-appointed governor serves as head of state and oversees Dutch interests, having control of the islands' defence and external affairs. The governor is assisted by an Advisory Council. Executive authority for internal affairs rests with a six-member Council of Ministers, responsible to an elected assembly, the Staten. This is composed of 22 members elected by universal adult suffrage for a four-year term and subject to dissolution within this period. Each island group forms an electoral district for election purposes, Curaçao returning 14 members, Bonaire and St Maarten three each, and Saba and St Eustatius one member each. A proportional representation system is used in the cases of the multi-member districts. In addition, each island group has its own Island Council, Executive Council and Lieutenant-Governor, to manage local affairs.

The principal political party is the Curaçao-based National People's Party (PNP), which was founded in 1948. It is a 'social-Christian' body and is led by Maria Liberia-Peters, who has been Prime Minister between 1984 and 1985 and since May 1988. Following the general election of November 1985, however, a new seven-party coalition assumed power, headed by Dominico (Don) Martina, leader of the socialist New Antilles Movement (MAN), which was formed in 1979. Martina was also Prime Minister between 1979 and 1984. Other significant parties are the liberal-socialist Democratic Party (DP), which was established in 1944. It is divided among Curaçao, Bonaire and St Maarten branches. Another party is the Bonaire Patriotic Union (UPB). In the November 1985 general election the PNP captured six Staten seats; the MAN, four; the three DP branches, eight; the UPB, one; and 'other parties', three.

Political history
Originally claimed by Spain, the Netherlands Antilles were colonised by Holland during the 1630s, Curaçao developing into a prosperous entrepôt for the Caribbean trade. Sovereignty was periodically contested by France and Britain during the eighteenth century, before the islands were finally confirmed as Dutch territories in 1816.

The abolition of slavery in 1863 ushered in a period of economic depression which was ended during the 1920s only by the establishment of petroleum refineries on Aruba and Curaçao islands. In 1954 the island group was granted full autonomy over domestic affairs, while remaining within the Kingdom of Netherlands. During the 1960s and 1970s internal politics were characterised by intense inter-island rivalries, most notably between Curaçao and Aruba, and policy-making has been paralysed by the coalition nature of the governments returned. Arguments over revenue sharing, and rights to prospective offshore oil reserves, eventually led to the withdrawal of Aruba from the Netherlands Antilles federation in 1986. In recent years, the economy, which is heavily dependent on the refining of oil imported from Venezuela, for export to the USA, has been in a depressed condition, forcing unpopular budgetary retrenchment.

8.4.7 New Zealand's dependencies

New Zealand's four dependencies were acquired 'second hand', all having been British possessions but, after it had achieved full independence, being more sensibly administered by New Zealand than by the 'mother country'. Their political structures and histories are set out below.

Table 75

NEW ZEALAND'S OVERSEAS (ASSOCIATED) TERRITORIES

Name	*Date of First Coming Under New Zealand Administration*	*Area (km²)*	*Population (1985)*
Cook Islands	1901	238.0	17,754
Niue	1901	259.0	3,300
Ross Dependency	1923	414.4	Uninhabited
Tokelau	1925	10.0	1,600
Total	—	921.4	22,654

COOK ISLANDS

Capital: Avarua, on Rarotonga Island.

Location
Oceania. The islands are situated in the South Pacific Ocean, 2,600 km north-east of Auckland, New Zealand. There are six large and nine small volcanic and coral islands in the Cook group, scattered widely across almost 2 million square kilometres of the South Pacific. The highest-lying, and most important, island is Rarotonga, which is in the southern island group.

Social and economic data
Area: 238 km^2
Population: 17,754*
Pop density per km^2: 75*
Literacy rate: 92 per cent
GDP: $25m*; per capita GDP: $1,408
Economy type: middle income
Labour force in agriculture: 29%

*1985

Ethnic composition
Eighty-one per cent of the population are Polynesian; 8 per cent mixed Polynesian and European; 8 per cent mixed Polynesian and other races; and 2 per cent European. English is the official language.

Principal religion
Congregational Christian.

Political system
There is an 24-member Legislative Assembly, which is elected for a five-year term by universal adult suffrage. It selects from its ranks a Prime Minister, who oversees a six-member cabinet of his choosing. Hereditary island chiefs are represented in a second assembly chamber, the House of Ariki. This body, however, has no legislative powers. An appointed High Commissioner represents the crown as the islands' formal head of state, and the New Zealand government has a representative on Rarotonga.

There are four principal political parties, the two most important being the Cook Islands Party (CIP), which was formed in 1965 and held power continuously between 1965 and 1978; and the Democratic Party (DP), which was established in 1971. In the general election of January 1989, the CIP won twelve Legislative Assembly seats, the DP nine, and the Democratic Tumu Party (DTP) two. A CIP-DTP coalition government was subsequently formed.

Political history
The islands, which were first visited by Captain James Cook in 1773, and subsequently named after him, were annexed by Britain in 1888, but were later transferred to New Zealand, in 1901. In 1965 they became internally self-governing in 'free association' and with common citizenship with New Zealand, which retains responsibility for defence and foreign affairs. Their chief importance lies in their coconut, pineapple and citrus fruit production, fruit processing constituting the main industry, and as a tax haven and growing tourist centre. However, the islands have a huge trade deficit and rely on substantial aid to sustain their living standards. Three-quarters of this aid is supplied by New Zealand and currently amounts to $10 million, or $563 per year for each inhabitant.

NIUE

Capital: Alofi

Location
Oceania. Niue is a coral island situated in the South Pacific Ocean west of the Cook Islands and 2,140 km north-east of New Zealand. The population live in small coastal villages, with a concentration in Alofi.

Social and economic data
Area: 259 km^2
Population: 3,300*
Pop density per km^2: 13*
Literacy rate: 94%
GDP: $4m*; per capita GDP: $1,212
Economy type: middle income
Labour force in agriculture: N/A

*1985

Ethnic composition
The inhabitants are predominantly Polynesian and mixed Polynesian. English is the official language.

Principal religion
Protestantism.

Political system
There is an elected 20-member Legislative Assembly, comprising 14 village representatives and six members elected on a common roll. Government is in the hands of a cabinet of four, headed by a Prime Minister, and drawn from the Assembly's ranks. Until recently, candidates for election to the Assembly have stood as independents. To contest the general election of March 1987, however, the island's first political party, the Niue People's Action Party (NPAP), was founded. It was highly critical of the government's record of economic management and won one Assembly seat in this contest. The New Zealand government has an official representative on the island, stationed at Alofi.

Political history
The island, when visited by Captain Cook in 1774, was already inhabited. Its indigenous population, who were at first hostile to Europeans, were converted to Christianity by missionaries during the nineteenth century and, following petitioning by the islanders, a British protectorate was established in 1900. In the following year Niue was annexed by New Zealand. Full internal self-government, in 'free association' with New Zealand, was granted in October 1974, with New Zealand retaining responsibility for the island's defence and external affairs. The economy is founded upon passion fruit, copra and handicraft exports, but, despite this, is heavily dependent on foreign aid and support from New Zealand.

TOKELAU

Capital: Nukunonu

Location
Oceania. Tokelau consists of three coral atolls, Atafu, Fakaofo and Nukunonu, situated in the South Pacific Ocean, 480 km north of Western Samoa and 3,500 km north-north-east of New Zealand.

Social and economic data
Area: 10 km^2
Population: 1,600*
Pop density per km^2: 160*
Literacy rate: 97%
GDP: $1.3m*; per capita GDP: $813
Economy type: low income
Labour force in agriculture: N/A

*In 1985

Ethnic composition
The population is wholly Polynesian, enjoying close family and cultural links with Western Samoa. English is the second language. Many inhabitants have migrated to New Zealand, sending home earnings for their families.

Principal religion
The majority of people belong to the Roman Catholic or Congregational Church.

Political system
The islands are governed directly by a Resident Administrator of the New Zealand Ministry of Foreign Affairs. In practice, much of the executive work is delegated to an Official Secretary, based at Tokelau. At the local level, however, the islands are substantially self-governing. On each atoll there is a Council of Elders (COE: Taupulega), comprising the heads of family groups plus two members elected triennially by universal adult suffrage. One is the Faipule, who presides over the Council and represents the atoll in its dealings with the New Zealand administration, and the other is the Pulenuku, who is responsible for village affairs. Twice a year, 15 delegates from each atoll COE convene in a general *Fono*, or meeting, chaired by the islands' three Faipule.

Political history
The islands were made a British protectorate in 1877 and formed part of the Gilbert and Ellice Islands colony, together with Kiribati and Tuvalu, from 1916. In 1925 they were transferred to New Zealand, becoming formally part of New Zealand in 1949. Copra is the principal revenue-earning product, but 85 per cent of the island's annual budget expenditure is paid for from a subsidy provided by New Zealand.

8.4.8 Norway's dependencies

Norway has five dependencies, all situated in the Arctic or Antarctic regions, and most of them uninhabited. The one inhabited possession, Svalbard, was finally secured by an international treaty after its sovereignty had been contested by other European powers.

Table 76

NORWEGIAN DEPENDENCIES

Name	*Date of First Coming Under Norwegian Administration*	*Area (km^2)*	*Population (1985)*
Bouvet Island	1928	60	Uninhabited
Jan Mayen Island	1929	380	Uninhabited
Peter I Island	1931	180	Uninhabited
Queen Maud Land	1939	(Antarctic Territory)	Uninhabited
Svalbard	1920	62,700	3,480
Total	—	63,320	3,480

SVALBARD

Capital: Long Year City (Longyearbyen) on Spitsbergen

Location
Arctic. Svalbard is an archipelago composed of nine main islands, the most important being Spitsbergen. It is situated in the Arctic Ocean, 650 km north of Norway.

Social and economic data
Area: 62,700 km^2
Population: 3,480*
Pop density per km^2: 0.06*
Literacy rate: N/A
GDP: N/A*
Labour force in agriculture: N/A

*1985

Ethnic composition
Sixty-two per cent of the population are Russian and 36 per cent Norwegian.

Political system
The island is administered by a Norwegian governor (*sysselmann*) resident at Longyearbyen.

Political history
The island group was discovered by the Dutch seafarer Willem Barents in 1596 and briefly served as a centre for whale hunting during the seventeenth century, with its sovereignty being contested by Denmark, Norway, Britain and the Netherlands. Interest in the islands was re-awakened during the early twentieth century with the discovery of coal deposits. In 1920 Norway's sovereignty claims were upheld in an international agreement, the Svalbard Treaty, formally ratified in 1925. In return, Norway agreed to allow free scientific and economic access to other nations. Norway and the Soviet Union currently maintain permanent mining settlements on the islands, while Poland has a small research station. The Soviet Union, which unsuccessfully claimed joint sovereignty rights with Norway in 1944, also has a helicopter station and mobile radar base there.

8.4.9 Portugal's dependencies

Portugal was once one of the world's leading colonial powers, and one of the last to concede sovereignty to the local communities. It now has only one possession and that will pass to Chinese control at the end of the century.

MACAO

Macau

Capital: Macao

Location

Asia. The territory consists of the coastal peninsula of Macao and the two small islands of Taipa and Coloane, situated on the Zhujiang, or Pearl, River delta in south-east China, 64 km west of Hong Kong.

Social and economic data

Area: 17 km^2
Population: 300,000*
Pop density per km^2: 17,647*
Literacy rate: 79%
GDP: $1,000m*; per capita GDP: $3,333
Economy type: middle income
Labour force in agriculture: N/A

*1985

Ethnic composition

Ninety-nine per cent of the population are Chinese, speaking Cantonese, with Portuguese as the official language.

Principal religions

The people are predominantly Buddhists, with 7 per cent adhering to Roman Catholicism.

Political system

Designated a Special Territory of Portugal, executive power is held by a governor, appointed by the President of Portugal. He is assisted by a cabinet of five Portuguese-appointed Secretaries-Adjunct. Foreign affairs are controlled by the President of Portugal. The governor works in consultation with a local Legislative Assembly which comprises 17 members, six of whom are elected directly by universal adult suffrage, six elected indirectly by business associations and five appointed by the governor. The members serve three-year terms and elect a President from among themselves. The governor also presides over a Superior Council of Security, which includes three Legislative Assembly members, and a Consultative Council, five of whose members are indirectly elected by local administrative bodies and interest groups. There are no formal political parties in Macao. However, three civil associations are represented in the Legislative Assembly: the Electoral Union (UNE), the Pro-Macao and the Flower of Friendship and Development of Macao (FADEM).

Political history

Macao was first established as a Portuguese missionary and trading post in 1537, before being leased from China in 1557. Later, in 1849, it was annexed by Portugal and formally recognised as a colony by the Chinese government under the terms of an 1887 treaty. The colony's commercial importance steadily diminished during the later nineteenth and early twentieth centuries, as Macao harbour silted up and trade was diverted to the British entrepôt of Hong Kong and other Treaty Ports. It was forced, instead, to concentrate on the local 'country' trade, as well as on gambling and tourism.

In 1951 Macao became more closely integrated with mainland Portugal, and was designated a Portuguese Overseas Province. This entitled it to send an elected representative to the Lisbon parliament. However, after the Portuguese revolution of 1974, the colony, re-designated a 'Special Territory', was granted greater autonomy, based upon the adoption, in February 1976, of an 'organic statute' which established the present political structure.

In June 1986, the Portuguese and Chinese governments began negotiations over the question of the return of Macao's sovereignty, under similar 'one country, two systems' terms as had been agreed in 1984 by Britain and China for Hong Kong. These negotiations were successfully concluded in March 1987, when the 'Macao Pact' was signed. Under the terms of this concord, Portugal has agreed to hand over sovereignty formally to the People's Republic on 20 December 1999. In return, the People's Republic has undertaken to maintain the capitalist economic and social system of the port enclave for at least 50 years thereafter. Under Chinese rule, Macao will be re-designated a 'special administrative region' and, although subject to the appointment of a chief executive by the Chinese government, will have its own assembly which will contain 'a majority of elected members'. To oversee the transfer of power, a Joint Liaison Committee is to be established.

8.4.10 South Africa's dependencies

South Africa's dependencies consist of four so-called 'independent' Bantu homelands and the state of Namibia. The homelands were created as part of the racial separatism policy (*apartheid*), and Namibia has, in international terms, been illegally controlled by South Africa since 1946. Under the Angola peace accord, signed in 1988, South Africa agreed to Namibia's achieving full independence in 1989. The political structures and histories of the homelands and Namibia are set out below.

Table 77

SOUTH AFRICAN DEPENDENCIES

Name	*Date of Creation or of Coming Under South African Control*	*Area (km²)*	*Population (1985)*
BANTU HOMELANDS			
Bophuthatswana	1977	44,000	1,736,000
Ciskei	1981	8,500	730,000
Transkei	1976	41,002	2,530,000
Venda	1979	6,677	460,000
Total	—	100,179	5,456,000
Namibia	1920	823,168	1,151,000

THE BANTU HOMELANDS

In accordance with the apartheid, or segregated development, policy adopted by the South African government since the late 1940s, separate 'homelands' (Bantustans) have been established for the black community. These are deemed by the government in Pretoria to be self-governing, the four 'homelands' of Bophuthatswana, Ciskei, Transkei and Venda being officially declared independent states, thus depriving their inhabitants of South African citizenship. However, since their economies remain heavily dependent on the white-dominated government of South Africa, in terms of both financial subsidies and employment opportunities, two-thirds of Bantustan adult males working outside the 'homelands', and their political structures restricted by the apartheid system, these territories have not been accorded international recognition. Each of the 'independent' Bantustans has a small armed force of its own, consisting of between 850 and 2,600 men. These forces have, however, been effectively penetrated and controlled by the South African military and secret services. More substantively, the Bantustans' constitutions include the provision for joint consultation and administration in both the defence and customs and excise spheres.

BOPHUTHATSWANA

The Republic of Bophuthatswana

Capital: Mmabatho

Location

Central and Southern Africa. Bophuthatswana consists of seven separate units of land in the Cape, Orange Free State and Transvaal provinces of South Africa, close to the frontier with Botswana, which lies to the north-west.

Social and economic data

Area: 44,000 km^2
Population: 1,736,000*
Pop density per km^2: 39*
Literacy rate: N/A
GDP: N/A
Labour force in agriculture: N/A

*1985

Ethnic composition

The population is black, predominantly Setswana-speaking, with important Pedi, Shangana, Xhosa, South Sotho and Zulu minorities. A quarter are commuters or migrant workers in South Africa.

Principal religion

Most people are Christians, mainly Anglicans.

Local government
There are twelve regional authorities and 76 tribal and community authorities.

Political system
Under the terms of Bophuthatswana's 'independence' constitution, executive authority rests with a directly elected President, who appoints, and acts on the advice of, a 15-member Executive Council, or cabinet. There is a single-chamber National Assembly, comprising 72 popularly elected members, twelve appointed by the President and 24 nominated by regional authorities.

Three political parties currently function, the dominant two being the ruling, 600,000-member, Bophuthatswana Democratic Party (BDP), which was established in 1974, and is led by Chief Lucas Manyane Mangope, and the opposition People's Progressive Party (PPP), led by Rocky Metsing. In the National Assembly election of October 1987, the BDP captured 66 of the 72 elective seats and the PPP the remaining six.

Political history
Bophuthatswana was granted 'self-government' in June 1972, under the terms of South Africa's 1971 Bantu Homelands Constitution Act. It was declared independent in December 1977, assuming the designation 'The Republic of Bophuthatswana'. Since 'independence', the Republic's areal size has increased by 4,000 square kilometres as a result of a programme of territorial consolidation that has been taking place, with the support of the South African government. An attempt, in February 1988, by dissident officers in the Bophuthatswana army to overthrow the government of President Mangope, which it accused of gross corruption, and install in power the People's Progressive Party (PPP) leader, Rocky Metsing, was thwarted by the intervention of South African security forces. The PPP was subsequently banned, in October 1988.

CISKEI

The Republic of Ciskei

Capital: Bisho

Location
Central and Southern Africa. Ciskei is situated in the Eastern Cape near the western boundary of Transkei, bordered by South African territory to the west and south-west and the Indian Ocean to the south-east.

Social and economic data
Area: 8,500 km^2
Population: 730,000*
Pop density per km^2: 86*
Literacy rate: N/A
GDP: N/A
Labour force in agriculture: N/A

*1985

Ethnic composition
The population is black, the majority being Xhosa and dependent on subsistence agriculture. A sixth are commuters or migrant workers in South Africa.

Principal religion
Christianity.

Political system
Under the terms of the 1981 constitution, legislative power is vested in a National Assembly which comprises 50 deputies, directly elected for a five-year term, and 37 hereditary chiefs. After each general election, the Assembly is supposed to meet to elect a President as head of state, commander-in-chief of the armed forces and as head of an appointed 15-member Executive Council, or cabinet. In June 1983, however, the National Assembly confirmed Chief Lennox L. Sebe as President for life.

Since 'independence', Ciskei has been a one-party state, dominated by President Sebe's Ciskei National Independence Party (CNIP), which was formed in 1973. It holds all the seats in the National Assembly. Opposition parties are, theoretically, allowed to function if they are able to secure signatures from at least 10,000 members. However, when the Ciskei People's Rights Protection Party (CPRP), which was set up in 1986, and is led by Chief L. W. Maqoma, succeeded in surmounting this hurdle, immediately prior to the November 1986 election, its registration was disallowed on a technicality.

Political history
The Ciskei region was originally peopled by African tribes from the central lakes area during the mid seventeenth century. A century later, white settlers from Cape Colony penetrated the area, precipitating a series of wars between the whites and indigenous peoples, known as Xhosas, between 1779 and 1878, from which the settlers emerged victorious. Moves towards restoring self-government to the Xhosas began in 1961, with the establishment, in accordance with the Promotion of Bantu Self-Government Act, 1959, of an assembly of 84 chiefs and an executive council. In August 1972, after the passage of South Africa's 1971 Bantu Homeland's Constitution Act, 20 elected members were added to the legislative assembly and a system of ministerial government established. Subsequently, in October 1980, a new constitution was approved by referendum, becoming effective in December 1981 when the state was declared an independent republic. This grant of independence was opposed by the neighbouring Transkei government since it divided the Xhosa people of the two Bantustans.

Chief Lennox L. Sebe was made the Republic's first President. However, in July 1983, shortly after having been confirmed in his post for life by the National Assembly, he was faced with an attempted coup masterminded by his brothers General Charles Sebe, head of the Ciskei Central Intelligence Service (CIS), and Namba Sebe, minister of transport. The coup was foiled, despite suspicions of South African involvement on the side of General Sebe. General Sebe was subsequently sentenced to twelve years' imprisonment, while Namba Sebe fled to Transkei. However, in September 1986, the

General was released from jail by armed raiders and a further attempt was made to oust President Sebe. This power struggle was broadened in February 1987 when an attempt was made to assassinate the President by a military unit from Transkei. The venture failed, however, and, following mediation by South Africa's foreign affairs minister, the crisis was resolved by the signing of a tripartite, non-aggression, 'treaty of regional security and co-operation' by South Africa, Ciskei and Transkei.

TRANSKEI

The Republic of Transkei

Capital: Umtata

Location

Central and Southern Africa. Transkei extends north-east from the Great Kei River, on the coast of Cape Province, in South Africa, to the border of Natal. The Indian Ocean lies to the east.

Social and economic data

Area: 41,002 km^2
Population: 2,530,000*
Pop density per km^2: 62*
Literacy rate: N/A
GDP: N/A
Labour force in agriculture: N/A

*1985

Ethnic composition

The inhabitants are mostly black, predominantly Xhosa, with a small coloured minority. A sixth of them are commuters or migrant workers in South Africa.

Principal religion

Christianity.

Political system

Under the terms of the 1976 constitution, executive power rests with a President who is elected by the National Assembly for a seven-year term, and who works with an appointed, 15-member Executive Council, or cabinet. The National Assembly consists of 75 members, directly elected for a five-year term, and 75 chiefs or paramount chiefs, co-opted by their peers.

There are four political parties, the most important of which is the Transkei National Independence Party (TNIP), which was established in 1964, and is led by Paramount Chief Tutor Ndamase. The TNIP secured 56 of the 75 elective seats in the October 1985 National Assembly election, with the opposition, anti-apartheid and anti-South African, Democratic Progressive Party (DPP) capturing two and independents, 16. However, since a military coup in December 1987, all party political activity has been outlawed and the 1976 constitution suspended. All power is now concentrated in the hands of a Military Council, headed by Major-General Bantu Holomisa, and a Council of Ministers, which includes eight ministers from the toppled administration, pending the calling of fresh elections.

Political history

Transkei, which is the traditional territorial home for the Xhosa people, was brought under British rule between 1866 and 1894. Later, in 1903, the Transkeian Territories were formed, which, under the terms of the Native Land Act of 1913, became reserved for black occupation. The territory, under the terms of the Transkei Constitution Act, was granted 'self-government' in 1963, and an executive council, presided over by a Chief Minister elected by a legislative assembly, was established. It was declared 'independent' in October 1976, assuming the designation 'The Republic of Transkei'.

Soon after 'independence', a conflict developed between Transkei and South Africa over the former's claims to East Griqualand, a fertile agricultural tract along the northern border with Natal. This led to a severing of Transkei's diplomatic relations with South Africa, from April 1978. Transkei is reliant on South Africa for over half of its annual revenue, so that it was not difficult for the South African government to force the restoration of relations, in February 1980.

The dominant power in Transkei politics since the 1960s has been Paramount Chief Kaiser Matanzima, who served continuously as Chief Minister and then President between 1968 and 1986. A year after announcing his retirement as President, in February 1986, he attempted to resume control by resigning from the ruling Transkei National Independence Party (TNIP) and forming a new Transkei National Party (TNP). This provoked a constitutional crisis which ended with the Paramount Chief's younger brother, Prime Minister Chief George Matanzima, drafting a law to make it illegal for ex-presidents to sit in parliament, and summarily banishing Kaiser Matanzima to his rural home district of Qamata Great Place. Several months later, George Matanzima's government was overthrown in a coup led by the commander of the Transkei Defence Force, Major-General Bantu Holomisa. This followed the establishment, at South Africa's request, of a commission of inquiry to investigate allegations of serious government corruption. In March 1989 George Matanzima was sentenced to nine years' imprisonment (half suspended) for accepting bribes.

VENDA

The Republic of Venda

Capital: Thohoyandou

Location

Central and Southern Africa. Venda consists of two non-contiguous, mountainous territories in the north-east of South Africa, south-east of Messina, and near the Zimbabwean frontier.

Social and economic data

Area: 6,677 km^2
Population: 460,000*
Pop density per km^2: 69*
Literacy rate: N/A
GDP: N/A
Labour force in agriculture: N/A

*1985

Ethnic composition

The people are black, and mainly Luvenda-speaking Vhavenda. A fifth of them commute to or are migrant workers in South Africa.

Principal religion

Christianity.

Local government

Venda is divided into four regions, each with its own council. Government is carried out on traditional tribal lines at community levels below.

Political system

Under the terms of the 1979 constitution, executive power is held by a President who is elected by the National Assembly and who works with an appointed nine-member Council of Ministers, or cabinet. The President is officially elected only for the life span of the National Assembly. However, these rules were waived in the case of the late President, Chief Patrick Mphephu, who was designated President for life. The National Assembly is a single-chamber body, comprising 45 members directly elected for a five-year term, in addition to four presidential appointees, 28 chiefs (*mahosi*) and 15 members selected by Venda's regional councils. Since August 1986, Venda has become, constitutionally, a one-party state, with the Venda National Party (VNP), which was formed in 1973, constituting the sole permissible political group.

Political history

The traditional home of the Vhavenda people, Venda was first reached by Europeans in 1816, but its relative isolation meant that it was little affected by the wars of the nineteenth century between white settlers and indigenous black tribes. After the Boer War in 1902, it came under South African administration and was given a limited degree of home rule, in 1962. This was followed by more extensive self-government in 1973, before 'independence' was granted in September 1979. Chief Patrick R. Mphephu, leader of one of the 27 tribes that have historically made up the Venda nation, served continuously, first as Chief Minister, and then as President, from 1973 until his death in April 1988. He was succeeded as President by Gota Vho Frank N. Ravele.

NAMIBIA

South West Africa

Capital: Windhoek

Location
Central and Southern Africa. Namibia is bounded on the north by Angola and Zambia, on the east by Botswana and South Africa and on the west by the Atlantic Ocean. Much of the land is desert.

Social and economic data
Area: 823,168 km^2
Population: 1,151,000*
Pop density per km^2: 1*
Literacy rate: 38%
GDP: $1,247m*; per capita GDP: $1,084
Economy type: middle income
Labour force in agriculture: 46%

*1985

Ethnic composition
Eighty-five per cent of the population are black Africans, 51 per cent of them belonging to the Ovambo tribe. The rest include the pastoral Nama and Bushmen. There is a 6 per cent white minority.

Principal religions
Christianity is the main religion, practised by 90 per cent of the population. Among the Christians, 51 per cent are Lutherans, 19 per cent Roman Catholics, 6 per cent members of the Dutch Reformed Church, and 6 per cent Anglicans.

Local government
The country is divided into 22 administrative districts.

Political system
Since June 1985, following the establishment of the 'Transitional Government of National Unity' (TGNU), South Africa has controlled Namibia's defence and foreign affairs, through an appointed Administrator-General. Nominal control over its internal affairs has rested with a cabinet comprising eight ministers and eight deputy ministers, drawn from a legislative body, the 62-member National Assembly. This consisted, the Assembly being dissolved in February 1989, of members appointed from among the ranks of the six moderate parties which had formed a grouping termed the Multi-Party Conference (MPC) in 1983. In 1985, a 16-, later 18-member, Constitutional Council was also established from among the ranks of the MPC to frame a new draft constitution, whose outlines were submitted in June 1987. The authority of the TGNU has diminished since April 1988 as a result of the South African government's decision to grant the Administrator-General internal powers to curb newspapers which promote 'subversion and terrorism' and to call ethnically based local, 'second tier', elections.

Six political parties are currently represented in the TGNU: the Democratic Turnhalle Alliance (DTA), the South-West Africa National Union (SWANU), the South West Africa People's Organisation-Democrats (SWAPO-Dem), the Labour Party (LP), the National Party of South West Africa (SWANP) and the Rehoboth Free Democratic Party (RFDP).

The DTA was formed in 1977, and is a coalition of moderate African, coloured and white, parties, led by the Republican Party leader Dirk Mudge. SWANU was founded in 1959 and is a Herero-orientated body led by Moses Katjiuongua. SWAPO-Dem was formed in 1978 and is a breakaway faction from SWAPO. The LP is a coloureds-orientated grouping, SWANP a white party closely linked to the ruling National Party in South Africa, and the RFDP a conservative Afrikaner grouping.

However, the principal political party in Namibia, which draws strong support from the Ovambo majority community and which lies outside the TGNU, is the South West Africa People's Organisation of Namibia (SWAPO). It was founded in 1958 and is led by Sam Nujoma. Campaigning for full and unconditional independence for the territory and the establishment of a classless, socialist society, it was banned inside the country between 1960 and 1989 and forced to operate from bases in neighbouring Angola and Zambia.

Political history

Deterred by the coastal Namib desert, European penetration of Namibia was delayed until the eighteenth century. British and Dutch missionaries first moved into the area, before, later in 1884, Britain incorporated a small enclave around Walvis Bay in Cape Colony, while the Germans annexed the remainder of the territory. But, in 1915, during the First World War, South African forces seized control of the German colony.

Administration of the area, now designated South West Africa (SWA), was entrusted to the Union of South Africa under the terms of a League of Nations mandate in 1920 and, in 1925, a limited measure of self-government was granted to the territory's European inhabitants. After the Second World War, South Africa applied, in 1946, to the newly established United Nations (UN) for the full incorporation of the mandated lands, rich in diamonds and uranium, within its Union. This demand was rejected and, instead, South Africa was called upon to prepare a trusteeship agreement for the area.

The South Africans, however, rejected this request and, instead, proceeded to integrate SWA more closely with Pretoria, granting the territory's white voters representation in the Union's parliament in 1949, and extending to it its own apartheid laws, in October 1966. In response to these measures, the South West African People's Organisation (SWAPO) was established in 1958 by an Ovambo, Sam Nujoma, to lead a campaign for an end to racial discrimination and for the grant of full independence from South Africa. The organisation was harassed by the South African authorities and its more radical wing, led by Nujoma, was forced into exile in 1960. Later, from the mid 1960s, Nujoma's exiled party established a military wing, the People's Liberation Army of Namibia (PLAN), and, utilising bases in Angola and Zambia, proceeded to wage a guerrilla war of attrition against the South African occupying army.

South Africa's continued occupation of Namibia, as SWA was re-designated by the UN in 1968, met with increasing challenge by international bodies from the late 1960s, and was declared to be illegal by the International Court of Justice in 1971. Three years later, the UN Security Council passed a resolution requiring South Africa to begin a transfer of power to Namibians by the end of May 1975 or face UN action. South Africa's Prime Minister, Balthazar J. Vorster, responded by expressing willingness to enter into negotiations on Namibian independence, but not with SWAPO, an organisation which the UN had, in 1973, formally recognised as the 'authentic representative of the Namibian people'.

During the mid-1970s, military conflict in Namibia and the bordering region escalated as Pretoria attempted, unsuccessfully, to topple the new Marxist government which had come to power in neighbouring Angola, in 1975. Tentative moves towards a settlement were made in 1978, with the holding of tripartite talks between SWAPO, South Africa and the five Western members of the UN Security Council, the 'Contact Group'. At the conclusion of these discussions, SWAPO and the Pretoria regime conditionally accepted proposals involving a reduction in the level of South African troops and the release of political prisoners as the prelude to the holding of UN-supervised elections. These proposals were incorporated in UN Security Council Resolution 435 of September 1978. However, South Africa subsequently retracted, holding, instead, in December 1978, and under its own terms, elections which were boycotted by SWAPO and not recognised by the West. A long period of political and military stalemate followed, during which South Africa continued its armed offensive against Angola and the PLAN, while at the same time attempting to establish in Namibia a stable pro-Pretoria regime, based on a conservative coalition termed the Democratic Turnhalle Alliance (DTA). This experiment came to an end, however, in January 1983 when the DTA's leader, Dirk Mudge, resigned following disagreements with Pretoria and direct rule was reimposed.

Negotiations among Pretoria, the Western powers, neighbouring African states and Namibian political forces continued during the succeeding years, but repeatedly foundered on South Africa's insistence that any withdrawal of its military forces from both Angola and Namibia should be linked to the departure of the 50,000 Cuban troops stationed in Angola. Internally, in June 1985, South Africa established a new 'puppet regime' in Namibia, termed the 'Transitional Government of National Unity' (TGNU). It was dominated by political representatives drawn from the white and black ethnic minority communities, and contained only one minister from the dominant Ovambo tribe. The TGNU, which failed to gain recognition from the UN or Western powers, attempted to reform the apartheid system in Namibia and adopt a new draft constitution, but was seriously divided between its conservative and moderate wings. In particular, more reformist, non-white elements within the TGNU sought to move away from a political structuring based on ethnic, rather than national or geographical lines. This was firmly opposed, however, by the South African Administrator-General, Louis Pienaar, since it would destroy the safeguards, called 'minority rights', which had been established to protect white interests.

During 1987–88, as South Africa began to tire of its war of attrition in support of the National Union for the Total Independence of Angola (UNITA) resistance movement in Angola, and as pressure from the Soviet Union was exerted on Cuba, major strides towards resolving the Namibian-Angolan issues began finally to be made. After a series of fruitful talks in Geneva between United States, Angolan, Cuban and South African representatives, a path-finding agreement was signed by the South African and Angolan governments, in August 1988, at the Angola-Namibia border centre of Ruacana. This agreement provided for an immediate cease-fire in military activities, to be followed by a rapid withdrawal of South African troops from Angola and then, during 1989, a phased withdrawal of both Cuban forces from Angola and 48,500 of South Africa's 50,000 troops from Namibia.

In the case of Namibia, a 4,650-strong UN peacekeeping force was to be stationed there from April 1989, as a means of ensuring order during the run-up to free, open, UN-supervised, elections to be held later in the year. The elected assembly would then adopt and approve a new independence constitution. The initial actions taken after the signing of this agreement suggested that a real end to the Namibian crisis was in sight. However, South Africa's future reaction to the likely establishment in Namibia of a SWAPO regime, if free elections are held, remains to be seen. If independence is, however, achieved, Pretoria will still retain considerable economic influence over Namibia, since it will continue to control the former British colonial enclave of Walvis Bay, the country's only port.

8.4.11 United Kingdom's dependencies

The British Empire began when the first successful English colony was founded at Jamestown, Virginia, in 1607. At its peak, at the end of the nineteenth century, it covered a quarter of the world's land surface and included a quarter of its peoples. It had spread over every continent to every race. Now most of the greatest empire history ever recorded consists of separate, independently sovereign states, banded together as much by sentiment and history as other ties, within the Commonwealth. This global body is described, with other world and regional groupings, in Chapter 9. What is left of the British Empire today consists of a number of states which still enjoy the protection of the British Crown. Their political structures and histories are given below.

Table 78

UNITED KINGDOM CROWN DEPENDENCIES AND BRITISH DEPENDENT TERRITORIES

Name	*Date of First Coming Under British Administration*	*Area (km²)*	*Population (1985)*
UK CROWN DEPENDENCIES			
Channel Islands	1066	196	138,144
Isle of Man	1765	572	64,282

Table 78—United Kingdom Crown Dependencies and British Dependent Territories (Contd.)

Name	*Date of First Coming Under British Administration*	*Area (km²)*	*Population (1985)*
BRITISH DEPENDENT TERRITORIES			
Anguilla	1650	96	7,109
Bermuda	1612	53	57,145
British Antarctic Territory	1908	1,710,000	Uninhabited*
British Indian Ocean Territory	1965	60	Uninhabited*
British Virgin Islands	1666	153	11,858
Cayman Islands	1670	259	22,000
Falkland Islands	1765/1833	12,173	1,919
Gibraltar	1704	6	29,166
Hong Kong	1841/1860	1,069	5,456,200
Montserrat	1632	102	12,000
Pitcairn Islands	1790	5	62
St Helena & Dependencies	1659	501	6,467
South Georgia & the South Sandwich Islands†	1775	3,903	Uninhabited*
Turks & Caicos Islands	1765	500	7,413
Total	—	1,729,648	5,813,765

*With the periodic exception of scientific or military personnel.

†Dependencies of the Falkland Islands between 1908 and 1985, with the Falklands' governor continuing to serve as their administrative Commissioner.

UNITED KINGDOM CROWN DEPENDENCIES

These islands, although lying offshore, do not form integral parts of the United Kingdom. Instead they are designated as Crown Dependencies, enjoying effective self-government in internal affairs.

THE CHANNEL ISLANDS

Capitals: St Helier, on Jersey, and St Peter Port, on Guernsey

Location

Western Europe. The Channel Islands comprise the islands of Guernsey, Jersey, Alderney, Sark, Herm, Jethou, Brechou and Lihou, and lie in the English Channel off the north-west coast of France. Fifty-eight per cent of the population live on Jersey and 40 per cent on Guernsey.

Social and economic data

Area: 196 km²
Population: 138,114*
Pop density per km²: 705*
Literacy rate: 100%
GDP: $1139m*; per capita GDP: $8,247
Economy type: high income
Labour force in agriculture: 13%

*1985

Principal religion
Christianity, mainly Church of England and Roman Catholic.

Political system
The Channel Islands are internally self-governing. However, the United Kingdom is responsible for their defence and international relations, with Queen Elizabeth II serving as head of state. For the purposes of government, the islands are divided into the Bailiwick of Jersey and the Bailiwick of Guernsey, the latter embracing Guernsey island, as well as Alderney, Sark and the remaining smaller islands. In each Bailiwick the Crown is represented by a Lieutenant-Governor. He appoints, from the ranks of the local legal community, Bailiffs to serve as Presidents of the representative assemblies, termed the States of Deliberation, and the judicial bodies, or Royal Courts.

Government on the islands is conducted by Committees appointed by the States of Deliberation (SD). On Jersey, the SD comprises twelve Senators, who are elected for six-year terms, a half retiring every three years. At the local and at-large levels, respectively, there are twelve Constables and 29 Deputies, directly elected for three-year terms. On Guernsey, the SD consists of twelve Conseillers, who are indirectly elected by the States of Election, a 108-member body comprising local political and judicial officers, for six-year terms, a half retiring every three years, plus 33 directly elected People's Deputies, ten Douzaine Representatives, elected by their respective parishes, and two Alderney Representatives. On Alderney, the SD is a twelve-member body, directly elected for a three-year term. Finally, on Sark, the assembly, called the Chief Pleas, consists of twelve popularly elected members plus 40 tenants nominated by the feudal suzerain of the island, the Seigneur. Members sit in the SDs usually as independents, although the Jersey Democratic Movement has occasionally held a number of seats.

Political history
The islands were granted to the Duke of Normandy in the tenth century, being attached to the Crown of England in 1066. They are the only part of Normandy to have remained under British rule since 1204 and were the only British possession to have been occupied by Germany during the Second World War. The islands enjoy tax sovereignty and, with imports exempt from British value added tax, and local income tax levels low, they have developed into 'tax haven' finance centres in recent decades. They do not form part of the European Community.

THE ISLE OF MAN

Capital: Douglas

Location
Western Europe. The Isle of Man lies in the Irish Sea, equidistant from Scotland, to the north-east, England, to the east, and Northern Ireland, to the west.

Social and economic data
Area: 572 km^2
Population: 64,282*
Pop density per km^2: 112*
Literacy rate: 100%
GDP: $260m*; per capita GDP: $4,045
Economy type: middle income
Labour force in agriculture: 5%

*1985

Principal religion
Christianity, especially the Church of England.

Political system
Queen Elizabeth II is head of state, under the designation 'Lord of Man', and has ultimate responsibility for the island's good government, being represented on the island by an appointed Lieutenant-Governor. The Isle of Man is dependent on the United Kingdom for its defence and external relations. In internal matters, however, it is substantially self-governing, having its own legislative assembly, the Court of Tynwald, and legal and administrative systems, as well as control over direct taxation. The Court of Tynwald, which traces its roots back to Scandinavian times, is a two-chamber body, comprising the Legislative Council, or Upper House, and the House of Keys, or Lower House. The Legislative Council consists of the Lieutenant-Governor, a President, the Lord Bishop of Sodor and Man, the Attorney-General and seven members elected by the House of Keys. The House of Keys consists of 24 members who are directly elected by universal adult suffrage for five-year terms. Both chambers sit together as one body in the legislature, but vote separately. Most members sit as independents, although a number of political parties, most notably the Manx Labour Party and the Sons of Man (Mec Vannin) nationalist party, have won seats from time to time.

Political history
The Isle of Man was ruled successively by the Welsh, during the sixth to ninth centuries, the Vikings/Norwegians, from the ninth century to 1266, and the Scots, between 1266 and 1765, before being purchased by the British government, in 1765. Because of its independent fiscal policies, the island has, like the Channel Islands, become something of a tax haven in recent years and is not part of the European Community.

BRITISH DEPENDENT TERRITORIES

These are overseas territories enjoying a colonial status, with varying degrees of internal autonomy.

ANGUILLA

Capital: The Valley

Location

Central America and the Caribbean. Anguilla is an island in the Eastern Caribbean, the most northerly of the Leeward Islands, and situated 112 km north-west of St Christopher and Nevis, and 8 km north of St Maarten.

Social and economic data

Area: 96 km^2
Population: 7,019*
Pop density per km^2: 73*
Literacy rate: N/A
GDP: $8m*; per capita GDP: $1,140
Economy type: middle income
Labour force in agriculture: N/A

*1985

Principal religion

Christianity, especially Anglican, with a Roman Catholic minority.

Political system

Under the terms of the 1982 constitution, the British Crown is represented on Anguilla by an appointed Governor who is responsible for external affairs, defence, the judiciary and internal security and presides over meetings of the Executive Council and House of Assembly. The Executive Council, or cabinet, comprises a Chief Minister, with whom the Governor works closely, and three other ministers drawn from the House of Assembly, as well as two *ex officio* members, the attorney-general and the permanent secretary for finance. The House of Assembly consists of seven members directly elected for five-year terms, as well as two nominated and two *ex officio* representatives.

Currently, three political parties operate: the Anguilla National Alliance (ANA), which was formerly known as the People's Progressive Party (PPP) prior to 1980 and is led by Chief Minister Emile Gumbs; the Anguilla Democratic Party (ADP), which was known as the Anguilla People's Party (APP) prior to the resignation of Ronald Webster as party leader in 1984; and the Anguilla United Party (AUP), which is led by Webster. The ANA captured three House of Assembly seats in the February 1989 general election; the AUP two; the ADP one; and an independent one.

Political history

Anguilla was first colonised by English settlers from overcrowded St Christopher (St Kitts) in 1650. It became more closely tied with St Christopher in 1825 and was later formally incorporated in the colony of St Kitts-Nevis-Anguilla (SNA). In February 1967 this colony, together with others in the Eastern Caribbean, became an internally self-governing state in association with the United Kingdom, Britain retaining responsiblity for its defence and external affairs.

However, in May 1967, under the leadership of Ronald Webster, a local businessman and leader of the People's Progressive Party (PPP), Anguilla, alleging domination by its larger associated islands, revolted, refusing to accept rule from St Christopher. After attempts to reach a compromise had failed and Anguilla had voted to cut all ties with the UK and declare independence, British troops were sent there, in March 1969. A Crown-appointed British Commissioner was installed and a truce signed. Subsequently, in July 1971, Anguilla was designated a dependency of Britain and two months later all troops were withdrawn.

A new constitution was framed in 1976, providing for a government of elected representatives, and in December 1980 the island was formally separated from the SNA. Ronald Webster served as the island's Chief Minister between 1976 and 1977 and between 1980 and 1984, but, after being replaced as the party's leader in February 1977 by Emile Gumbs, left the PPP to form the Anguilla United Party (AUP), and the Anguilla People's Party (APP), in 1980 and 1981 respectively. In the March 1984 general election, however, Webster's APP was heavily defeated, its leader losing his seat. Gumbs, who had earlier served as Chief Minister between 1977 and 1980, returned to office and proceeded to implement a policy programme geared towards revitalising the economy, unemployment standing at 40 per cent in 1984, by encouraging tourism and foreign inward investment. Gumbs was returned to power for a second term in the February 1989 general election, his Anguilla National Alliance (ANA) relying on the support of an independent member for its assembly majority.

BERMUDA

Capital: Hamilton, on Main Island, or Great Bermuda

Location

Central America and the Caribbean. Bermuda is an archipelago consisting of 138 low-lying coral islands and islets stretching 35 km east and west and 22 km north and south, and lying in the Atlantic Ocean 917 km off the coast of South Carolina, USA. Twenty of the islands are inhabited.

Social and economic data

Area: 53 km^2
Population: 57,145*
Pop density per km^2: 1,078*
Literacy rate: 98%
GDP: $900m*; per capita GDP: $15,749
Economy type: high income
Labour force in agriculture: N/A

*1985

Ethnic composition

Two-thirds of the population are black, the remainder being of British or Portuguese stock.

Principal religion
Christianity, with 42 per cent of the people Anglicans and 16 per cent Roman Catholics.

Local government
The country is divided into nine parishes.

Political system
Bermuda is internally self-governing. However, Britain remains, under the terms of the 1968 constitution as amended in 1973 and 1979, responsible for the islands' external affairs, defence and internal security, including the police, with British interests being represented by a crown-appointed governor. The islands' assembly has two chambers: the eleven-member Senate and the 40-member House of Assembly. Three of the Senate's members are appointed by the governor, five by the Prime Minister and three by the Leader of the Opposition. The House's members are all directly elected by universal adult suffrage for five-year terms, standing in 20 two-member constituencies. From the majority grouping in the House of Assembly, the governor appoints a Prime Minister to preside over a twelve-member cabinet of his own choosing. At least six cabinet ministers must be drawn from the assembly, to which the cabinet itself is collectively responsible. There is also a governor's Council which is used by the governor and ministers for consultative purposes.

Three political parties currently operate in Bermuda. The most important is the United Bermuda Party (UBP), led by Prime Minister John W. Swan. It has held power continuously since 1968. It is liberal-conservative in outlook and supports multi-racialism and free enterprise. The main opposition party is the Progressive Labour Party (PLP), led by Frederick Wade. This is a moderate-socialist force which advocates the 'Bermudianisation' of the economy and eventual independence. The third minor party, the National Liberal Party (NLP), is a centrist grouping led by Gilbert Darrell, and was formed in August 1985 by breakaway members from the PLP. At the February 1989 general election the UBP captured 23 House of Assembly seats, and 50 per cent of the popular vote, the PLP 15 seats, the NLP one seat, and an Independent Environmentalist one seat.

Political history
The islands were discovered by and named after the Spanish mariner, Juan de Bermudez, in 1515. They were later colonised by British settlers in 1612, forming part of the Virginia Company's charter, before being transferred to the British crown, in 1684. During the seventeenth century the economy was based on tobacco growing, whaling and ship building. Bermuda also served as a penal settlement, until 1862, and a naval station, before developing into an Atlantic trading entrepôt during the nineteenth century. The islands were granted a new constitution, in 1968, conceding internal autonomy and establishing a new ministerial system.

Popular politics were to be characterised, however, by intense rivalry between the moderate, though predominantly white, United Bermuda Party (UBP) and the more radical, black-led, pro-independence Progressive Labour Party (PLP). The general election of May 1968, which was won by the UBP, was accompanied by serious race riots. This was followed by a wave of murders in 1972–73, including that of the governor, Sir Richard Sharples. Further race riots broke out in December 1977, after two blacks were hanged for complicity in the 1972–73 incidents. This forced the despatch of British troops to restore order. To investigate the causes of this racial tension, a Royal Commission was set up, in February 1978. This later recommended, in its report of August 1978, a redrawing of constituency boundaries to improve the PLP's prospects of capturing seats. However, despite implementation of this recommendation, the UDP continued to win Assembly majorities in the elections of December 1980, February 1983, October 1985, and February 1989. The 1978 Royal Commission also recommended early independence for Bermuda, but the majority of the population oppose this.

The country currently has one of the highest per capita GDP in the world, having developed, in recent decades, into a major centre for tourism and financial services, as well as as an offshore 'tax shelter' for more than 6,000 international companies. The United States has an air base on the islands at Kindley Field, held on a 99-year lease.

THE BRITISH VIRGIN ISLANDS

Capital: Road Town, on Tortola island

Location

Central America and the Caribbean. The British Virgin Islands consist of 40 mountainous islands and islets situated at the north end of the Leeward Islands, or Lesser Antilles, chain, 90 km east of Puerto Rico and adjoining the US Virgin Islands. Fifteen of the islands are inhabited, 83 per cent of the population living on Tortola island and 13 per cent on Virgin Gorda.

Social and economic data

Area: 153 km^2
Population: 11,858*
Pop density per km^2: 78*
Literacy rate: 98%
GDP: $80m*; per capita GDP: $6,747
Economy type: high income
Labour force in agriculture: 8%

*1985

Ethnic composition

The population is predominantly of Negro or mixed Negro and European descent.

Principal religion

Christianity, especially Protestant, with a Roman Catholic minority.

Political system

Under the terms of the 1977 constitution, the British crown is represented on the Virgin Islands by an appointed governor who has sole responsibility for external affairs, defence, judicial and internal security matters. The governor also serves as chairman of a six-member Executive Council, or cabinet, and possesses reserve legislative powers. There is also a Legislative Council, which comprises nine members directly elected from single-member constituencies, an appointed Speaker and one *ex officio* member, the Attorney-General. From the majority grouping in the Legislative Council is drawn a Chief Minister and three other ministers who work with the governor and Attorney-General in the Executive Council.

Two political parties currently function on the islands: the Virgin Islands Party (VIP), led by Chief Minister H. Lavity Stoutt; and the United Party (UP). Stoutt had previously served as Chief Minister during the later 1960s and between 1979 and 1983, returning to power at the general election of September 1986, when the VIP captured five Legislative Council seats, the remaining four seats being shared by the UP and independents.

Political history

Tortola was originally settled by the Dutch in 1648. It was colonised by British planters in 1666 and formally annexed by Britain in 1672. A form of constitutional government was granted in 1774 and in 1834 slavery was abolished. From 1872 the islands formed part of the British federal colony of the Leeward Islands, before later becoming a separate crown colony, in July 1956. They received their own appointed administrator, known as governor from 1971, in 1960 and a constitution was promulgated in 1967 which provided for a ministerial system. This was superseded by a new constitution in June 1977 which extended the degree of internal self-government.

Politics have been characterised since 1967 by the alternation in power of the Virgin Islands Party (VIP), led by H. Lavity Stoutt, and a coalition of United Party (UP) and independent deputies. Cyril Romney, an independent councilman, served as Chief Minister from November 1983, but lost power to Stoutt in September 1986, after his reputation had been damaged by his alleged connection with a company which was under investigation by the British police and US Drug Enforcement Administration. Since the mid-1970s, the islands' economy has developed rapidly, principally as a result of a boom in tourism, the number of annual visitors having doubled to 190,000. The tourist industry now contributes 50 per cent of GDP and 30 per cent of employment. Following the passage of the Business Companies Act by the Legislative Council in 1984, which simplified procedures for company registrations, the Virgins have also attracted much foreign 'offshore-capital', 4,450 international companies being registered between 1985 and 1987, utilising the islands as a 'tax shelter'.

CAYMAN ISLANDS

Capital: George Town, on Grand Cayman

Location

Central America and the Caribbean. The Cayman Islands consist of the islands of Grand Cayman, Cayman Brac and Little Cayman, and lie in the

Western Caribbean, 290 km north-west of Jamaica and 240 km south of Cuba. Ninety-three per cent of the population live on Grand Cayman and 6 per cent on Cayman Brac.

Social and economic data
Area: 259 km^2
Population: 22,000*
Pop density per km^2: 85*
Literacy rate: 97%
GDP: $240m*; per capita GDP: $10,909
Economy type: high income
Labour force in agriculture: N/A

*1985

Ethnic composition
Sixty per cent of the population are of mixed descent.

Principal religion
Christianity is the chief religion, predominantly of the Anglican and Baptist Churches, with a Roman Catholic minority.

Political system
Under the terms of the 1959 constitution, as revised in 1972, the British crown is represented on the Caymans by an appointed governor who has sole responsibility for external affairs, defence, judicial, public service and internal security matters. The governor also serves as chairman of the Executive Council, or cabinet, which comprises three appointed *ex officio* members and four elected representatives drawn from the Legislative Assembly. The latter four serve as ministers. The Legislative Assembly consists of three official representatives and twelve members elected by universal adult suffrage from six electoral districts for a four-year term. There are no political parties. Instead, candidates contest elections both as independents and in loose 'teams', the most important of which is the Unity team. All candidates favour the Caymans' continued dependent status and liberal-conservative economic strategy.

Political history
The Caymans were first visited by Christopher Columbus in 1503, but were never settled by the Spanish. They were subsequently ceded, with Jamaica, to Britain under the terms of the 1670 Treaty of Madrid. Grand Cayman island was later colonised by British military deserters from Jamaica, from where it was administered. The islands of Cayman Brac and Little Cayman were permanently settled only from 1833, and until 1877 were not administratively connected with Grand Cayman. On Jamaica's independence in 1962, the islands were made a separate British crown colony and have subsequently grown into an important centre for tourism, currently attracting almost half a million visitors annually, as well as for oil trans-shipment and as an offshore 'tax shelter' for foreign businesses and banking companies.

FALKLAND ISLANDS

Capital: Port Stanley, on East Falkland Island

Location

South America. The Falkland Islands consist of two large islands, East and West Falkland, and around 200 smaller islands, all situated in the South Atlantic Ocean, 770 km north-east of Cape Horn. Sixty-five per cent of the population live in the capital.

Social and economic data

Area: 12,173 km^2
Population: 1,919
Pop density per km^2: 0.2*
Literacy rate: N/A
GDP: $13m*; per capita GDP: $6,774
Economy type: high income
Labour force in agriculture: N/A

*1985

Ethnic composition

Most of the population are of British descent. In addition to the population total shown above, there were 1,500 British troops stationed on the island in 1987.

Principal religion

Christianity, based on the Anglican, Roman Catholic and United Free Churches.

Political system

Under the terms of the October 1985 constitution, the Falkland Islands are administered by a crown-appointed governor, who works with an advisory Executive Council composed of two, non-voting, *ex officio* members, a chief executive and a financial secretary, and three representatives elected by the Legislative Council. The Falkland Islands' Legislative Council comprises eight directly elected members and the two, non-voting *ex officio* representatives. There are no political parties.

Political history

The Falklands were first visited by the English navigator John Davis in 1592 and in the late seventeenth century were named after Lord Falkland, treasurer of the British navy. East Falkland was colonised by French settlers from St Malo in 1764, who gave the group the name Iles Malouines, and West Falkland by British settlers in 1765. From 1767, however, the Spanish, who took over the French settlement, gradually gained the upper hand, ejecting the British in 1774. British sovereignty was never ceded, however. During the early nineteenth century, Spanish influence waned, its garrison being withdrawn in 1811, and, following a brief period of occupation, between 1826 and 1831, by the Republic of Buenos Aires, Britain re-asserted her possession in 1833. Formal annexation of the Falkland

Islands and its dependencies took place in 1908 and 1917, a modest, sheep-raising, settler economy being established.

Argentina, however, never relinquished its claim over the islands ('Islas Malvinas') and in 1966, at the instigation of the United Nations (UN), negotiations to resolve the continuing dispute were started. During the early 1970s, relations thawed. Britain's Heath administration (1970–74) signed a communications agreement which effectively gave Argentina control over air access to the islands. Following this, the Buenos Aires government extended the Port Stanley airstrip, enabling tourists to visit the Falklands and islanders to make use of Argentinian schools and hospitals. The British government appeared anxious to foster closer socio-economic links between the Falklands and the Argentinian mainland, but consistently refused, in inter-government talks, to countenance any transfer of sovereignty against the wishes of the inhabitants, who consistently favoured maintaining their British connection.

After the accession to power, in 1976, in Buenos Aires, of a nationalist-minded military junta, led by Lieutenant-General Jorge Videla, Anglo-Argentinian relations deteriorated. In December 1977, a military invasion was threatened and, in response, the British Callaghan administration (1976–79) despatched a hunter-killer submarine to the islands. Two years later, the new Conservative Thatcher administration (1979–) recommenced negotiations with the Argentinian government. However, the two compromise options suggested to resolve the dispute, condominium, or joint sovereignty and rule, and 'lease-back', the transfer of formal sovereignty to Argentina, who would, in turn, lease back the islands' administration to Britain, were overwhelmingly rejected when put before the islands' Council. A third, Argentinian-sponsored, option, designated 'most pampered region' status, which would involve the transfer of sovereignty in return for Argentinian guarantees to retain the existing democratic form of government and local legal and education systems, was also rejected. Two years later, on 2 April 1982, soon after the accession to power in Buenos Aires of another military leader, the intransigent General Leopoldo Galtieri, Port Stanley was invaded by Argentinian troops. The British government immediately responded by despatching a naval 'task force' and a fierce conflict ensued in which 255 British, 755 Argentinian and three Falklander lives were lost, before, on 14 June, the 12,000 Argentinian troops on the islands surrendered and British control was restored.

After this war, the British government instituted a new 'Fortress Falklands' policy, based on establishing a large permanent garrison on the islands to deter future Argentinian aggression. A 278 km-wide protection and fishing zone was declared, licences being sold to foreign trawler companies seeking to fish within it. New development schemes were also promoted by the islands' newly established Falklands Islands Development Agency, resulting in a boom in the islands' once moribund economy. Despite UN calls for a re-opening of negotiations to find a peaceful solution to the 'Falklands issue' and the accession to power of a new democratic administration in Argentina, the British government has, so far, refused to enter into talks. With the islanders' right to self-determination having been guaranteed in the Falklands' new, 1985 constitution, a speedy resolution of the dispute seems remote.

GIBRALTAR

Capital: Gibraltar

Location

Western Europe. Gibraltar consists of a narrow peninsula connected to the south-west tip of Spain by an isthmus.

Social and economic data

Area: 6 km^2
Population: 29,166*
Pop density per km^2: 5,303*
Literacy rate: 66%
GDP: $120m*; per capita GDP: $4,114
Economy type: middle income
Labour force in agriculture: N/A

*1985

Ethnic composition

Sixty-nine per cent of the population are Gibraltarians and 20 per cent British. More than a thousand Moroccan labourers also work on 'The Rock'.

Principal religion

Seventy-five per cent of the population are Roman Catholics and 8 per cent members of the Church of England. Nine per cent are Muslims and 3 per cent Jewish.

Political system

Under the terms of the 1969 constitution, British interests in Gibraltar have been represented by a crown-appointed governor, who is advised by the Gibraltar Council, a body which comprises four *ex officio* and five elected members of the House of Assembly. The United Kingdom is responsible for the territory's defence and external affairs, as well as matters of internal security. Since 1969, full control over the remainder of internal affairs has been vested in the elected House of Assembly and a Council of Ministers, or cabinet, drawn from the majority grouping within the Assembly.

The House of Assembly consists of a Speaker appointed by the governor, two *ex officio* representatives, the Attorney-General and the financial and development secretary, and 15 members who are popularly elected for four-year terms. The electoral system is unique, allowing each elector to vote for a maximum of eight candidates. The Council of Ministers, which constitutes the territory's 'internal executive', has seven ministers and a Chief Minister drawn from the House.

Four political parties currently function. The two most important secured eight and seven House of Assembly seats, respectively, in the March 1988 general election, based on 58 per cent and 29 per cent shares of the popular vote. They are the moderate-socialist Gibraltar Socialist

Labour Party (GSLP), which was established in 1976 and is led by its founder, José (Joe) Bossano, and the centre-right Gibraltar Labour Party-Association for the Advancement of Civil Rights (GLP-AACR), which was formed in 1942, and is led by Adolfo Canepa. The GLP-AACR dominated political affairs in Gibraltar prior to 1988, its former leader, Sir Joshua Hasan, serving continuously as Chief Minister between 1964 and 1969 and between 1972 and 1987. However, opposition to the December 1987 Anglo-Spanish transport accord, which sanctioned joint civilian use of Gibraltar's airport, caused a split in the GLP-AACR, prompting the resignation of Hasan and the formation of the breakaway right-of-centre Independent Democratic Party (IDP), by Joe Pitaluga. This new group won 13 per cent of the popular vote in the ensuing general election. Both leading parties firmly reject any transfer of sovereignty to Spain. However, the GSLP, a strongly nationalist body, also opposes British colonial control, seeking to achieve full independence for 'The Rock'.

Political history

Gibraltar has long served as a strategic promontory, commanding the western entrance to the Mediterranean and boasting excellent port facilities. Occupied by Arabs from AD 711, it passed to the Moorish kingdom of Granada during the fifteenth century and subsequently fell under Spanish control. During the War of the Spanish Succession (1701–14), it was captured by an Anglo-Dutch force in 1704 and was formally ceded to Britain by Spain under the terms of the Treaty of Utrecht (1713). It was designated a crown colony in 1830 and, following the Second World War, during which it served as a strategic base for Allied naval forces, a Legislative Council was established in 1950. In 1963 the Franco government in Spain began to campaign for the territory's return to Spain, exerting diplomatic pressure through the United Nations (UN) and economic pressure, culminating in the closure of the frontier with Spain and the withdrawal of the Spanish labour force. In accordance with a UN resolution which called for the interests of the people of Gibraltar to be taken into account, the British government held a referendum on the sovereignty question in September 1967 in which an overwhelming (95 per cent) majority voted to retain the United Kingdom link. A new constitution was thus framed and adopted in 1969 in which full internal self-government was conceded, but in which the UK government undertook never to enter into arrangements to transfer the territory's sovereignty to another state against their freely and democratically expressed wishes. Spain remained intransigent, continuing to claim Gibraltar's sovereignty and keep the border closed, until General Franco's death in November 1975. Thereafter Anglo-Spanish relations slowly thawed, beginning with the restoration of Gibraltar-Spain telephone links in December 1977 and culminating in the reopening of the border in February 1985, a year prior to Spain's entry into the European Community. Early in 1989 the British government announced that it intended to reduce the size of its forces in Gibraltar because Spain's commitment to the EC and NATO had made the need for substantial defences unnecessary. At the same time, it reassured Gibraltarians that no change in sovereignty would be contemplated without their agreement.

HONG KONG

Xianggang
British Crown Colony of Hong Kong

Capital: Hong Kong

Location

Asia. Hong Kong lies off the south coast of China, 145 km south-east of Guangzhou or Canton, and comprises the island of Hong Kong, Stonecutter's Island, the Kowloon Peninsula and the New Territories, which are part of the Chinese mainland.

Social and economic data

Area: 1,069 km^2
Population: 5,456,200*
Pop density per km^2: 5,104*
Literacy rate: 77%
GDP: $34,225m*; per capita GDP: $6,272
Economy type: high income
Labour force in agriculture: 2%

*1985

Ethnic composition

Fifty-seven per cent of the population are Hong Kong Chinese and 40 per cent refugees from the Chinese mainland. English and Cantonese are the official languages.

Principal religion

Buddhism, mixed with Confucianism and Daoism, with a 9 per cent Christian minority.

Human rights rating

Eighty-three per cent.

Local government

Hong Kong is divided into the three regions of Hong Kong Island, Kowloon and New Territories, with 18 districts below, each having its own advisory local committee.

Political system

Hong Kong is administered by a crown-appointed governor who presides over an unelected Executive Council, or cabinet. This is composed of four *ex officio* and ten nominated, unofficial representatives and one appointed, official member. The governor also chairs a Legislative Council, comprising three *ex officio* Executive Council representatives, seven appointed, official members, 22 nominated, unofficial representatives and 24 elected members, twelve of the last 24 being chosen by an electoral college and twelve by 'functional constituencies'. From 1991, ten of the Legislative Council's members will be directly elected. The Executive Council serves as a consultative body for administrative matters, while the Legislative

Council, which has two sub-committees, scrutinises all government expenditure proposals and advises the governor on the enactment of the territory's laws. An Urban Council, composed of 15 appointed and 15 biennially elected members, is responsible for the urban areas of Hong Kong Island and Kowloon. Voting is limited to 200,000–300,000 professional and skilled people.

No political parties, as such, currently operate in Hong Kong, although a number of 'reform associations', which favour more extensive democracy, have been formed since the signing of the Sino-British Joint Declaration in 1984. The Chinese Communist Party and Kuomintang (Chinese Nationalist Party : Taiwan-based) also have organisations there.

Political history

Hong Kong Island was occupied by Britain in 1841 and ceded by the Chinese government under the terms of the 1842 Treaty of Nanking. The Kowloon Peninsula and Stonecutter's Island were acquired under the Peking (Beijing) Convention of 1860 and the New Territories secured on a 99-year lease signed in June 1898. The colony, which developed into a major entrepôt for Sino-British trade during the late nineteenth and early twentieth centuries, was occupied by Japanese forces between December 1941 and August 1945. The restored British administration promised, after 1946, to introduce a greater degree of self-government. These plans were shelved, however, after the 1949 communist revolution in mainland China.

During the 1950s almost 1 million Chinese, predominantly Cantonese, refugees fled to Hong Kong. This immigration continued during the 1960s and 1970s, raising the colony's population from 1 million in 1946 to 5 million in 1980 and forcing the imposition of strict border controls. Hong Kong's economy expanded rapidly during the corresponding period, the colony developing into one of the major commercial, financial and industrial centres in Asia. As the date for the termination of the New Territories' lease approached, negotiations on Hong Kong's future were opened between the British and Chinese governments during the early 1980s. These culminated in a unique agreement signed in Beijing, in December 1984, by which the British government agreed to transfer full sovereignty of the islands and New Territories to China in July 1997 in return for a Chinese assurance that Hong Kong's social and economic freedoms and capitalist lifestyle would be preserved for at least 50 years.

Under this 'one country, two systems' agreement, Hong Kong will, in 1997, become a special administrative region within China, with its own laws, currency, budget and tax system and retain its free port status and authority to negotiate separate international trade agreements. The existing, only partly elected, Legislative Council will be replaced by a similar, still partially elected – 25 per cent in fact – legislature, headed by a chief executive. The chief executive will replace the governor and will be selected by an appointed 600-member electoral college and subject to removal by the Chinese government.

In preparation for its future withdrawal from the colony, the British government introduced indirect elections, to select a portion of the new Legislative Council, in 1984 and direct elections for seats on lower-tier local councils, in 1985. A Sino-British joint liaison group was also established to monitor the functioning of the new agreement and a 58-member Basic Law

Drafting Committee, which included 23 representatives from Hong Kong, was formed in Beijing, in June 1985, to draft a new constitution. The first draft of this Basic Law was published in April 1988 and a 176-member Basic Law Consultative Committee was established to collect public comments on its provisions. Events in mainland China in June 1989 raised considerable doubts among the population about the value of the People's Republic's 'one country, two systems' assurances, and increased pressure on the British authorities to accelerate the pre-1997 internal democratisation process.

MONTSERRAT

Capital: Plymouth

Location

Central America and the Caribbean. Montserrat is a volcanic island lying 43 km south-west of Antigua in the Leeward Islands group of the Lesser Antilles in the Eastern Caribbean. Thirty per cent of the population live in the capital.

Social and economic data

Area: 102 km^2
Population: 12,000*
Pop density per km^2: 118*
Literacy rate: 97%
GDP: $37m*; per capita GDP: $3,083
Economy type: middle income
Labour force in agriculture: 9%

*1985

Ethnic composition

The population is predominantly of mixed African and European descent.

Principal religion

Christianity, especially Anglican, with a Roman Catholic minority.

Political system

Under the terms of the 1960 constitution, as amended in 1977, the British crown is represented on the island by an appointed governor who is responsible for defence, foreign affairs and internal security. The governor also serves as President of a seven-member Executive Council, or cabinet, which also includes a Chief Minister, three other ministers, and the Attorney-General and financial secretary, both *ex officio*. There is also a twelve-member Legislative Council, consisting of two official members, three nominated, including a Speaker, and seven directly elected members. The Executive Council's Chief Minister and ministers are chosen from the Legislative Council.

There are three political parties currently operating. The most important, the People's Liberation Movement (PLM), won four of the elective Legislative Assembly seats in the August 1987 election, and its leader, John A. Osborne, has served as Chief Minister since 1978. The National Development Party (NDP) captured two seats and the Progressive Democratic Party (PDP) one. All the parties support the island's present dependent status, although the PLM is pledged to securing eventual independence when it becomes 'economically viable'. In the meantime, it campaigns for greater development expenditure to improve the island's agricultural potential, as well as its educational and physical infrastructure.

Political history

Montserrat was first visited in 1493 by Christopher Columbus, who gave it its name. In 1632 it was colonised by English and Irish settlers who had moved from the overcrowded Caribbean island of St Christopher (St Kitts). They proceeded to establish a plantation economy based on slave labour. However, the island was not formally made a British crown colony until 1871. Between 1871 and 1956 Montserrat was administered as a division of the federal colony of the Leeward Islands. When the federation was dissolved, it became a separate colony, opting not to join the West Indies Associated States, which was established in 1967.

Since 1960 the island has had its own administrator, who was redesignated governor in 1971, and constitutional system. The dominant political party since 1978 has been the People's Liberation Movement (PLM), a moderate, nationalist body, led by John Osborne. The party has supported the development of agriculture, cotton and peppers being important export crops, light manufacturing, and the tourist industry, which currently contributes 25 per cent of Montserrat's GDP.

PITCAIRN ISLANDS

Capital: Adamstown, on Pitcairn Island

Location

Oceania. The Pitcairn Islands consist of volcanic Pitcairn Island and the uninhabited atolls of Ducie, Henderson and Oeno, all situated in the south-eastern Pacific Ocean, east of French Polynesia.

Social and economic data

Area: 5 km^2
Population: 62*
Pop density per km^2: 12*
Literacy rate: N/A
GDP: $0.4m*; per capita GDP: $6,452
Economy type: high income
Labour force in agriculture: N/A

*1985

Principal religion

Seventh Day Adventist Church.

Political system
As a crown colony, Pitcairn is administered by the British High Commissioner in New Zealand. Under the terms of the Local Government Ordinance of 1964, the High Commissioner governs in consultation with an Island Council, presided over by the Island Magistrate, who is elected for a three-year term. The Island Council consists of the Island Secretary, an *ex officio* representative, as well as five appointed and four elected members.

Political history
Pitcairn Island was discovered by the British navigator Carteret in 1767 and was settled by nine mutineers from HMS *Bounty*, in 1790. It was annexed as a British colony in 1838, but by 1856 the population had outgrown the island's resources, forcing 194 inhabitants to move to Norfolk Island, off the east coast of Australia. Forty-three Pitcairn islanders later returned home, in 1864, and since then the island has remained permanently settled. In 1898 Pitcairn was brought within the jurisdiction of the High Commissioner for the Western Pacific. It was later transferred to the governor of Fiji, in 1952, but since Fiji's independence, in 1970, it has been governed by the British High Commissioner in New Zealand.

ST HELENA AND DEPENDENCIES

Capital: Jamestown

Location
Central and Southern Africa. St Helena and its dependencies constitute a volcanic island grouping situated in the South Atlantic Ocean. St Helena lies 1,930 km off the south-west coast of Africa. The dependency of Ascension island is 1,131 km north-west of St Helena, while the dependency of Tristan da Cunha island lies 2,100 km to the north-east.

Social and economic data
Area: 501 km^2
Population: 6,467*
Pop density per km^2: 13*
Literacy rate: 97%
GDP: $8.4m*; per capita GDP: $1,299
Economy type: middle income
Labour force in agriculture: N/A

*1985

Principal religion
Christianity, principally Anglican, with a Roman Catholic minority.

Political system
Under the terms of its 1967 constitution, St Helena is administered by a crown-appointed governor, who works with a Legislative Council and an Executive Council. The Legislative Council includes the governor, the Government Secretary and Government Treasurer, as *ex officio* members,

and twelve elected members. The Executive Council, or cabinet, also includes the Government Treasurer and Government Secretary, *ex officio*, as well as the Chairmen of Council Committees, all of whom are drawn from the Legislative Council. The task of the Legislative Council is to oversee the work of government departments.

Two political parties, the St Helena Labour Party, which was established in 1975, and the St Helena Progressive Party, formed in 1973, and favouring the retention of close economic links with Britain, nominally exist, but have been inactive since 1976.

The dependencies of Ascension and Tristan da Cunha are governed by appointed administrators. Tristan da Cunha also has an advisory Council, consisting of eight elected and three nominated members.

Political history

The island of St Helena was discovered by the Portuguese navigator Joao da Nova Castella in 1502 and subsequently became a port of call for ships en route to the East Indies. It was annexed and occupied by the British East India Company in 1659 and, before being brought under direct crown rule in 1834, gained fame as the place of Napoleon's exile between 1815 and 1821.

Ascension Island was discovered in 1501, but remained uninhabited until occupied by Britain in 1815. It was made a dependency of St Helena in 1922 and today serves as an important commercial and military communications centre. During the Falklands War, of 1982, it also served as a crucial staging post for the naval 'task force' which had been sent to the South Atlantic.

Tristan da Cunha, which has been occupied since 1816, is currently the site of a small crayfish processing plant operated by a subsidiary of the South Atlantic Islands Development Corporation.

SOUTH GEORGIA AND THE SOUTH SANDWICH ISLANDS

Although both are British dependent territories in the South Atlantic, they have no permanent human inhabitants and, hence, no communities or political systems.

TURKS AND CAICOS ISLANDS

Capital: Cockburn Town, on Grand Turk island

Location

Central America and the Caribbean. The Turks and Caicos Islands consist of 30 islands, which form the south-eastern archipelago of the Bahamas chain in the West Atlantic Ocean, 144 km north of the Dominican Republic and Haiti and 920 km south-east of Miami. Forty-two per cent of the population live on Grand Turk, 19 per cent on South Caicos, 17 per cent on North Caicos, 13 per cent on Providenciales and 5 per cent on Middle Caicos island.

Social and economic data
Area: 500 km^2
Population: 7,413
Pop density per km^2: 15*
Literacy rate: 98%
GDP: $30m*; per capita GDP: $4,047
Economy type: middle income
Labour force in agriculture: 14%
*1985

Ethnic composition
The population is predominantly of African descent.

Principal religion
Christianity.

Political system
Under the terms of the 1976 constitution, later amended in March 1988, executive power is exercised by a crown-appointed governor, who is responsible for defence, external affairs, internal security and official appointments. The governor presides over an eight-member Executive Council, or cabinet, comprising three *ex officio* representatives and five chosen by the governor from among the elected members of the Legislative Council. The Legislative Council consists of three *ex officio* members, a Speaker and 13 directly elected representatives.

Four political parties currently function, the most important two of which are the People's Democratic Movement (PDM), which was formed in 1976, and is led by Chief Minister Oswald Skippings, and the Progressive National Party (PNP). In the March 1988 Legislative Council election, the PDM won eleven seats, based on a 60 per cent share of the vote, and the PNP two seats, with a 30 per cent vote share. Both parties are strong supporters of a free-enterprise economy and favour continued development of the islands' tourist and financial services industries. There are five electoral districts on the islands and thus a number of multi-member constituencies.

Political history
The Turks and Caicos Islands were first linked administratively to the Bahamas in 1765, before being made dependencies of Jamaica, in 1874. They subsequently became a unit territory within the Federation of the West Indies in 1959 and, on Jamaica's independence in 1962, were made a crown colony. Under this new arrangement, the islands were first administered from the Bahamas, but in 1972 received their own governor.

The first elections under the new 1976 constitution were won by the People's Democratic Movement (PDM), a political party which was, initially, strongly committed to achieving independence. In 1980 Britain agreed to accede to this on the condition that the PDM again won a Legislative Council majority in the general election of November. It failed to achieve this, however, being handicapped by the death of its leader and founder, J. A. G. S. McCartney, in an accident in June. Instead, the Progressive National Party (PNP), which favoured continued dependent status, secured a Legislative Council majority in both this and the subsequent May 1984 general election. As a consequence, the question of independence faded from the political agenda.

Instead, the islands' politics became dominated by a series of high-level scandals. These began in March 1985, when the Chief Minister and PNP leader, Norman Saunders, together with two senior colleagues, was forced to resign, after charges of drug smuggling into the United States. All three were later convicted and imprisoned. A year later, in July 1986, Saunders' replacement as Chief Minister, Nathaniel Francis (PNP), was also compelled to step down, after the publication of a report by a commission of inquiry found him, and two ministerial colleagues, guilty of unconstitutional behaviour and administrative malpractice. The government was immediately dissolved by the governor and a special five-member Advisory Council set up to take over the work of the Executive Council while the islands' political future was reviewed by a special constitutional commission. The recommendations subsequently made by this commission were accepted by the United Kingdom government, in March 1987, and formed the basis for an amended constitution, which came into force after the general election of March 1988.

8.4.12 United States' dependencies

The dependencies of the United States have been acquired in a variety of ways. Guam and Puerto Rico were ceded, as part of the spoils of victory after a war, the American Virgin Islands were purchased, others are held as Trust Territories, on behalf of the United Nations, and many, particularly in the Pacific, form part of what the US sees as its defensive shield. In total, including three military bases, there are eleven territories in the anti-imperialist United States' 'mini-empire'.

Table 79

UNITED STATES EXTERNAL TERRITORIES

Name	*Date of First Coming Under United States Administration*	*Area (km²)*	*Population (1985)*	*Form of Government*
FORMAL DEPENDENCIES				
American Samoa	1899/1922	199	35,000	NSGT
Guam	1899	541	125,000	SGT
Puerto Rico	1898	8,897	3,282,000	SGT
US Virgin Islands	1917	343	111,000	NSGT
FORMER UN PACIFIC TRUST TERRITORIES				
Marshall Islands	1947*	180	35,000	SIS
Federated States of Micronesia	1947	691	85,200	SIS
Northern Mariana Islands	1947*	471	19,635	CT
Republic of Palau	1947*	367	14,000	TT
MILITARY BASES				
Johnston Atoll	1898	3	327	MB
Midway Islands	1867	5	453	MB
Wake Islands	1898	8	302	MB
Total	—	11,705	3,707,917	—

KEY:

*	Held by US as trustees	SGT	Self-Governing Territory
CT	Commonwealth Territory	SIS	Semi-Independent State
MB	Military base	TT	United Nations Trust Territory
NSGT	Non-Self-Governing Territory		

FORMAL DEPENDENCIES

AMERICAN SAMOA

Capital: Pago Pago, on Tutuila

Location

Oceania. American Samoa consists of five main volcanic islands and two coral atolls situated in the central South Pacific Ocean, 3,550 km north-north-east of New Zealand. Ninety-three per cent of the population live on the westernmost island of Tutuila.

Social and economic data

Area: 199 km^2
Population: 35,000*
Pop density per km^2: 176*
Literacy rate: N/A
GDP: $190m*; per capita GDP: $5,429
Economy type: high income
Labour force in agriculture: N/A

*1985

Ethnic composition

The indigenous population are of Polynesian origin.

Principal religion

Christianity: 50 per cent Congregational and 20 per cent Roman Catholic.

Local government

The islands are divided, for administrative purposes, into 15 counties, which are grouped into Eastern, Western and Manu'a districts.

Political system

Under the terms of the 1967 constitution, executive power is exercised by a governor, who is directly elected for a four-year term, and is limited to two terms. The governor has the authority to appoint heads of government departments, subject to the approval of the assembly, and can veto legislation. The assembly, termed the Fono, is a two-chamber body, comprising an 18-member Senate, elected, according to Samoan custom, from among local chiefs (*matai*) for four-year terms, and a 20-member House of Representatives, whose members are popularly elected every two years. Swain's Island, with a population of only 27, also sends one non-voting member to the House. The Fono meets twice a year, in January and July, for a maximum of 45 days a year. American Samoa has, since 1981, also sent a non-voting delegate to the US House of Representatives. Changes to the 1967 constitution have been drafted by a constitutional convention and await ratification by the US Congress. These include increasing the size of the Senate and House of Representatives.

Political history
The islands of American Samoa were first visited by Europeans in the early eighteenth century and the London Missionary Society established a base there in 1830. They were ruled by local chiefs grouped together to form the independent Kingdom of Samoa. In 1878 the United States was given permission by the Kingdom to establish a naval base at Pago Pago and, from 1899, when the Treaty of Berlin, signed by America, Britain and Germany, recognised US rights in the area, it gradually gained dominance over the region. In 1900 and 1904 the chiefs of the western and eastern islands, respectively, accepted US sovereignty and later, in 1922, after residual German claims had been removed, the islands were officially designated an 'unincorporated territory' of the United States.

American Samoa was initially, between 1900 and 1951, placed under the administration of the US Department of the Navy and, thereafter, of the Department of the Interior, power being devolved to a resident governor. The governor was, for a long time, an American appointee, working since 1948 with an advisory two-chamber assembly. Under the terms of the 1960 constitution, which was amended in 1967, the authority of this assembly was increased and in November 1977 direct elections for the governorship were introduced. Peter Coleman became the first governor, between 1978 and 1984. The Samoan economy, which is heavily dependent on the tuna industry, is closely tied to the American. Many Samoans have emigrated to the United States in search of work during recent years and the country receives substantial economic aid from the mainland. In September 1988, its delegate to the US House of Representatives, Fofo Sunia, was forced to resign his seat after being convicted of fraud over the use of his official expense account, and sentenced to five months' imprisonment.

GUAM

Capital: Agana

Location
Oceania. Guam is the largest and southernmost of the Mariana Islands, being situated in the West Pacific Ocean, 5,920 km west of Hawaii and 2,400 km east of Manila.

Social and economic data
Area: 541 km^2
Population: 125,000*
Pop density per km^2: 231*
Literacy rate: 96%
GDP: $650m*; per capita GDP: $5,200
Economy type: high income
Labour force in agriculture: N/A

*1985

Ethnic composition

Forty-two per cent of the population are Chamorros, a mixture of Micronesian, Filipino and Spanish, 24 per cent Caucasians and 21 per cent Filipinos. Twenty-four thousand military personnel and their dependants also live on Guam.

Principal religion

Roman Catholicism is practised by about 93 per cent of the population.

Political system

Under the terms of the 1950 Guam 'Organic Act', or constitution, executive power is wielded by a governor, who is directly elected every four years. Legislative authority lies with a 21-member Legislature, whose members are elected biennially. It is empowered to pass laws regulating local affairs. A member, who may vote in committees but not on the floor, is elected to the US House of Representatives every two years. However, residents of Guam, although classed as citizens of the United States, cannot vote in US presidential elections. Two political parties operate on the island, the Republican Party and the Democratic Party, both of which are mainland party affiliates.

Political history

Guam was 'discovered' by Ferdinand Magellan in 1521 and claimed by Spain in 1565. The native Micronesian population, which was estimated to be 100,000 in 1521, declined rapidly during the later sixteenth and throughout the seventeenth and early eighteenth centuries, reaching a low of less than 5,000 in 1741, as a result of Spanish aggression and exposure to imported diseases. It later revived, however, through inter-marriage with Spaniards and Filipinos. Spain ceded Guam to the United States after the Spanish-American war of 1898 and the country became an 'unincorporated territory' of the United States.

During the Second World War, the island fell under Japanese control, between December 1941 and July 1944. When American rule was re-established greater authority was progressively devolved to local inhabitants and its administration transferred, in 1950, from the US Department of the Navy to the Department of the Interior. In 1970, the island's governor was directly elected for the first time and in September 1976 support for the maintenance of close ties with the US was re-affirmed in a referendum. More recently, in November 1987, a referendum came out in support of the island's negotiating a new relationship with the United States.

With a fine deep-water port at Apra, Guam has become one of the most important American naval and airforce bases in the Pacific. Currently, there are 11,500 US troops stationed on the island, a third of whose surface is covered by military installations. Guam is also a commercial and financial entrepôt and growing tourist centre, particularly for the Japanese. Its economy has, however, been in a depressed condition since the early 1970s.

PUERTO RICO

Commonwealth of Puerto Rico (COPR)
Estado Libre Asociado de Puerto Rico

Capital: San Juan

Location
Central America and the Caribbean. Puerto Rico is the easternmost island of the Greater Antilles, situated between the Dominican Republic to the west and the US Virgin Islands to the east, and 1,600 km south-east of Miami.

Social and economic data
Area: 8,897 km^2
Population: 3,282,000*
Pop density per km^2: 369*
Literacy rate: 89%
GDP: $20,200m*; per capita GDP: $6,155
Economy type: high income
Labour force in agriculture: 6%

*1985

Ethnic composition
The population is predominantly of European (Hispanic) descent. Spanish is the official language.

Principal religion
Roman Catholicism, practised by about 85 per cent of the population.

Local government
The island is divided into 78 'municipal districts', which include surrounding rural areas, each of which is governed by a mayor and municipal assembly, elected for a four-year term.

Political system
Under the constitution, called the 'Public Law', of 1952, Puerto Rico is a self-governing 'Commonwealth', voluntarily associated with the United States. Both states share a common currency and market, while the US is responsible for the COPR's defence. However, Puerto Rico's position differs from that of a full-member-state in that its inhabitants, while officially designated US citizens, may not vote in presidential elections and are represented in the US Congress only by a resident commissioner, who participates in House of Representatives' debates, but may vote only in committee. In addition, most US federal taxes, social security being an exception, are not levied in Puerto Rico.

Executive power is exercised by a governor, who is directly elected for a four-year term and works with a cabinet of 15 Secretaries. Legislative authority is held by a two-chamber Legislative Assembly, which is composed of a 27-member Senate and a 51-member House of Representatives, sitting each year between January and May. Assembly members are elected every four years, in November, at the same time as the US President, in accordance with an electoral procedure designed to ensure minority party representation. Sixteen senators are returned, two from each of the eight senatorial districts, and 40 representatives are elected in single-member constituencies, by a simple plurality voting system. The remaining eleven places in each chamber are 'at large' seats, reserved for minority party legislators. The legislative process is similar to that in the United States, the governor's approval being required for the enactment of bills. His veto can, however, be overridden by a two-thirds majority vote.

The principal political parties in Puerto Rico are, the liberal, pro-Commonwealth, 660,000-member, Popular Democratic Party (PPD), which was established in 1939, and is led by Governor Rafael Hernandez Colon; the 230,000-member New Progressive Party (PNP), formed in 1967, and which favours federation with the United States; the Puerto Rican Renewal Party (PRP), founded in 1983 as a breakaway group from the PNP; and the 60,000-member Puerto Rican Independence Party (PIP), dating from 1946 and with a social democratic, pro-separatist orientation. The PPD and PNP are the dominant forces, each regularly securing about 45 per cent of the popular vote in what is essentially a two-party system. The PIP and PRP attract less than 5 per cent of the state vote each.

Political history

Discovered by Christopher Columbus in 1493, when known by the Arawak Indian name of Boriquen, Puerto Rico was annexed by Spain in 1509. The Spanish exploited gold and sugar resources during the succeeding centuries, during which period the indigenous Carib and Arawak Indians, newly exposed to European diseases, were virtually wiped out, and replaced by a new mixed-race population. Following the Spanish-American war of 1898, Puerto Rico was ceded to the United States, under the terms of the Treaty of Paris, in December 1898. It was declared an 'unincorporated territory' of the USA, administered by a US-appointed governor, working with an elected local assembly.

In March 1917, under the terms of the Jones-Shafroth Act, the island's inhabitants were granted US citizenship and in 1947 direct elections for the post of Governor were introduced. In July 1952, following approval of a draft constitution in a referendum held a year earlier, the territory was given special status as a 'Commonwealth', 'freely associated' with the USA, enjoying extensive powers of self-government.

During the 1950s and 1960s, Puerto Rican politics were dominated by the Popular Democratic Party (PPD), who were strong supporters of the country's 'Commonwealth' status. A split occurred within the party's ranks, however, in 1967, leading to the formation of the New Progressive Party (PNP), following a referendum in which 60.5 per cent of voters supported continued 'Commonwealth' status. Some 38.9 per cent favoured full incorporation within the USA as a constituent state and 0.6 per cent favoured independence. The PNP, led by Carlos Romero Barcelo, held the governorship between 1977 and 1984 and pressed for Puerto Rico's inclusion as a state of the United States. This served to fan terrorist outrages by separatist extremists grouped in the Armed Forces for National Liberation (FALN) organisation. Barcelo was, however, defeated by the PDP in the November 1984 governorship contest.

Since the launching of the programme 'Operation Bootstrap' in 1948, there has been considerable industrial development on the island, most notably in the textiles and electrical equipment 'light industrial' sector. However, the pace of economic development has slowed down since the mid 1970s. As a consequence, the current unemployment rate exceeds 20 per cent, and two-thirds of Puerto Rico's population live below the official US poverty line. In such circumstances, there has been considerable migration to the US during recent years, more than 2 million Puerto Ricans now living on the American mainland.

UNITED STATES VIRGIN ISLANDS

Capital: Charlotte Amalie, on St Thomas

Location
Central America and the Caribbean. The US Virgin Islands consist of more than 50 islands in the south and west of the Virgin Islands group, situated in the Caribbean Sea, 64 km east of Puerto Rico. The two principal islands, accounting for 50 per cent and 47 per cent of the total population respectively, are St Croix and St Thomas. The island of St John is also inhabited.

Social and economic data
Area: 343 km^2
Population: 111,000*
Pop density per km^2: 324*
Literacy rate: 90%
GDP: $1,030m; per capita GDP: $9,279
Economy type: high income
Labour force in agriculture: N/A

*1985

Ethnic composition
Twenty to twenty-five per cent of the population are native-born, 35–40 per cent come from other Caribbean islands, 10 per cent from the US mainland and 5 per cent from Europe. Eighty per cent of the population are black.

Principal religion
Christianity, predominantly Protestantism, with a Roman Catholic minority.

Local government
The governor is represented on each of the three inhabited islands by an appointed administrator.

Political system
The islands have been granted a measure of self-government under the constitution of 1936, as amended in 1954, 1970 and 1973. Executive power is wielded by a directly elected governor, who serves a four-year term. The

governor appoints, on the advice of the assembly, the heads of government departments and his approval is required for legislation. The assembly, termed the Senate, is a single-chamber body, comprising 15 members, popularly elected for two-year terms, who represent two legislative districts.

The principal political parties are the Democratic Party, the Republican Party, both of which are mainland affiliates, and the Independent Citizens Movement, a breakaway group from the Democratic Party. The Democratic Party is dominant in the Senate and also provides the present governor, Alexander Farrelly. Since 1968 the US Virgin Islands have elected a non-voting delegate to the US House of Representatives. The islands' citizens are debarred, however, from voting in US presidential elections.

Political history

Originally discovered by Christopher Columbus in 1493, the islands passed, successively, into English, French and Dutch control, before the Danish West Indies Company colonised St Thomas and St John islands in 1671. To these, the Danes added St Croix, which they had acquired from France in 1733, and established sugar plantations. Following a decline in the sugar trade, the United States, recognising the islands' strategic importance in relation to the Panama Canal, took them over in 1917, purchasing them for US $25 million.

They became an 'unincorporated terrritory' of the USA and were originally placed under the administrative control of the US Department of the Navy, before being transferred to the Department of the Interior in 1931. The islanders were granted American citizenship in 1927 and have enjoyed increasing degrees of self-government since the 'Organic Law', which granted universal suffrage to all adults who could read and write English, was adopted in 1936. Popular election of the governor, who had previously been appointed by the US President, commenced in 1970. However, proposals for increased autonomy were rejected in referenda held in March 1979 and November 1981.

The islands have developed as a major centre for tourism and have attracted, in growing numbers, white 'tax shelter' immigrants. St Croix is also an important centre for petroleum refining.

UN TRUST TERRITORY OF THE PACIFIC ISLANDS (MICRONESIA)

The United Nations' Trust Territory of the Pacific Islands comprises 2,125 islands in the Micronesia region which were discovered by Spanish and Portuguese explorers during the 1520s and fell under Spanish rule soon afterwards. Germany (1885–1914) and then Japan (1914–44) became the dominant powers in the region during the late nineteenth and early twentieth centuries, exploiting the islands' natural resources, before a UN Trusteeship was established in 1947. Under the terms of this trusteeship agreement, the United States was given administrative control of the islands, but was charged with preparing them for eventual independence.

Pressures for local autonomy developed during the 1960s and 1970s. The American Carter administration (1977–80) was sympathetic to these wishes and encouraged the drafting of new constitutions, involving the principle of self-government, for the Marshall Islands, in the east, and the Federated States of Micronesia, in the centre, and for the Republic of Belau, in the west. Under 'Compacts of Free Association', which were approved in 1983 and 1986, the three states of the Trust Territory received 'semi-independence' from the United States, which remains responsible solely for the defence and security of the region. The United States retains military bases and nuclear testing grounds in the area, giving in return substantial economic aid. The Northern Marianas Islands, although they became a 'commonwealth territory' of the United States in 1978, remain legally part of the UN trusteeship.

MARSHALL ISLANDS

Republic of the Marshall Islands

Capital: Dalap-Uliga-Darrit Municipality, on Majuro Atoll

Location
Oceania. The Marshall Islands consist of two parallel groups of island chains, the Ratak and Ralik, comprising 34 atolls in the West Pacific Ocean region of north-east Micronesia, 3,200 km south-west of Hawaii and 2,100 km south-east of Guam. Thirty-seven per cent of the population live on Majuro Atoll.

Social and economic data
Area: 180 km^2
Population: 35,000*
Pop density per km^2: 194*
Literacy rate: N/A
GDP: N/A*
Labour force in agriculture: N/A

*1985

Ethnic composition
Predominantly Micronesian

Principal religion
Roman Catholicism

Political system
Under the terms of the May 1979 constitution, the islands have a parliamentary form of government. Legislative authority rests with the 33-member Nitijela, from whose ranks a President, who heads a twelve-member cabinet, is elected.

Political history
The islands were visited by the Spanish navigator, Miguel de Saavedra, in 1529 and remained under Spanish influence until being annexed and

colonised by Germany in 1885. At the start of the First World War, in 1914, the Japanese occupied the islands, afterwards administering them under the terms of a League of Nations mandate, between 1920 and 1944, when they were removed by US forces.

After the war the islands were placed under United States administration as part of the United Nations (UN) Trust Territory of the Pacific Islands. In moves towards autonomy set in train by the US Carter administration, the Marshall Islands District adopted its own constitution, in May 1979, and in October 1982 a 'Compact of Free Association' was signed by the United States. Under the terms of this Compact, the islands secured full independence, but the United States remained responsible for their defence and was allowed to retain military bases there for at least 15 years. In return, it pledged to provide annual aid of $30 million. It was also required to set up a $150 million trust fund to compensate for claims made against the US government in connection with contamination caused by nuclear tests carried out on the islands during the 1940s and 1950s. There was also a 'rent' payment for land still used for missile tracking. The Compact was approved in a plebiscite on the islands in September 1983 and, following endorsement by the UN Trusteeship Council, came into effect in October 1986.

THE FEDERATED STATES OF MICRONESIA

Capital: Kolonia, on Pohnpei

Location
Oceania. The Federated States of Micronesia consist of the four states of Yap, Truk, Pohnpei and Kosrae, which form, together with Palau, the archipelago of the Caroline Islands, situated in south-central Micronesia in the West Pacific Ocean, 800 km east of the Philippines. Fifty per cent of the population live in Truk state, 31 per cent in Pohnpei, 12 per cent in Yap and 7 per cent in Kosrae.

Social and economic data
Area: 691 km^2
Population: 85,200*
Pop density per km^2: 123*
Literacy Rate: N/A
GDP: N/A*
Labour force in agriculture: N/A

*1985

Ethnic composition
Predominantly Micronesian.

Principal religion
Roman Catholicism.

Political system
Under the terms of the May 1979 constitution, each of the constituent states of the federation has its own assembly, elected for a four-year term;

28 members in Truk, 27 in Pohnpei, 14 in Kosrae and ten in Yap. There is also a federal assembly, termed the House of Representatives, and an elected executive President, who heads a seven-member cabinet.

Political history
The islands have a similar history to the Marshall Islands, although they did not come under German control until 1898, when they were purchased, under the designation of the Caroline Islands, from Spain. After the Second World War, like the Marshall Islands, they were placed, by the United Nations, under United States administration and, until 1979, were governed by a local administrator appointed by the US President. In May 1979, however, a constitution was adopted, establishing the 'Federated States of Micronesia'. In October 1982, a 'Compact of Free Association' was signed with the United States, under which the federation became independent, though the US remained responsible for their defence and security. This Compact was approved in a plebiscite held in June 1983 and came into effect in October 1986, following its endorsement by the United Nations' Trusteeship Council. This established the federation as a 'sovereign, self-governing state'.

THE NORTHERN MARIANA ISLANDS

Commonwealth of the Northern Mariana Islands

Capital: Garapan, on Saipan

Location
Oceania. The territory consists of 16 islands and atolls in northern Micronesia in the West Pacific Ocean, 5,280 km west of Hawaii and 2,800 km east of the Philippines. Eighty-eight per cent of the population live on the island of Saipan, 7 per cent on Rota and 5 per cent on Tinian.

Social and economic data
Area: 471 km^2
Population: 19,635*
Pop density per km^2: 42*
Literacy rate: N/A
GDP: N/A*
Labour force in agriculture: N/A

*1985

Ethnic composition
Predominantly Micronesian.

Principal religion
Roman Catholicism.

Political system
Under the terms of the October 1977 constitution, the Northern Mariana Islands are internally self-governing. Executive power is exercised by a

directly elected governor and legislative authority by a bicameral assembly composed of a nine-member Senate, whose members are elected for four-year terms, and a 15-member House of Representatives, which is elected biennially. The islands' citizens also enjoy a broad range of civil and political rights within the United States. The principal political parties are the Democratic Party, led by governor Pedro Tenorio, the Republican Party and the Territorial Party.

Political history

The islands of the Northern Marianas group were discovered by European explorers during the 1520s. They fell successively under Spanish (1565–1898), German (1899–1914), Japanese (1914–21 and 1941–4) and League of Nations (1921–41) control, before being liberated by US marines in 1944–45 and becoming part of the United States' United Nations Trust Territory of the Pacific Islands, in 1947. In January 1978, following a referendum in June 1975, the Northern Marianas became a 'Commonwealth Territory' of the United States with considerable powers of internal self-government. In November 1986, the American administration conferred full US citizenship on the residents of the islands. Substantial economic aid has been provided by the US government during recent years. In return, the United States has acquired control of much land on Tinian island for military purposes.

PALAU (Belau)

Republic of Palau

Capital: Koror, on Koror Island

Location

Oceania. Palau consists of more than 350 islands, islets and atolls in the West Micronesia Caroline islands group, lying in a 650-km-long chain in the West Pacific Ocean, 960 km east of the Philippines and 7,150 km south-west of Hawaii. Fifty-eight per cent of the Republic's population live in the capital, Koror.

Social and economic data

Area: 367 km^2
Population: 14,000*
Pop density per km^2: 38*
Literacy rate: N/A
GDP: N/A*
Labour force in agriculture: N/A

*1985

Ethnic composition

Predominantly Micronesian.

Principal religion

Roman Catholicism.

Political system

Palau currently remains a United Nations Trust Territory, administered by the United States, with a High Commissioner, appointed by the US President, subject to the approval of the US Senate, serving as formal executive head. The High Commissioner works under the direction of the US Secretary of the Interior. However, under the terms of the 1981 constitution, the High Commissioner's powers are restricted and the Republic is now substantially self-governing. This constitution established a democratic, representative form of government, blending elements of the indigenous system of hereditary, female, chiefs with American democracy. Executive authority is held by a President who is directly elected and heads a six-member cabinet. The assembly, called Olbiil era Kelulau, is a two-chamber body, comprising a Senate and House of Delegates.

Political history

Palau has a similar history to the Federated States of Micronesia with which it forms part of the Caroline Islands group. A Republic was proclaimed in January 1981 when, following its approval in a referendum held in July 1979, a locally drafted constitution came into effect. Later, in August 1982, a 'Compact of Free Association' was signed with the United States, providing for Palau's independence, though the US remained responsible for the Republic's defence and security.

This Compact was approved by 60 per cent of those who voted in a referendum held in February 1983. However, fewer than the required 75 per cent supported the proposal to amend the Republic's constitution so as to allow the transit and storage of nuclear materials, which otherwise was outlawed by one of its clauses. The United States government viewed this constitutional change as essential if it was to fulfil its defence obligations and thus refused to endorse the Compact. A new Compact was framed in 1986, in which the US, anxious to make use of Palau's ports as a possible naval alternative to its Philippines' bases, agreed to provide $421 million in economic assistance to the islands. However, after the failures of plebiscites held in February 1986, October 1986 and June 1987 to secure the necessary 75 per cent majority support to change the constitution, the Compact was unratified.

Following pressure from pro-nuclear supporters of the Compact, an effort was made to break this impasse, in a new referendum held in August 1987. This proposed changing the plebiscitary majority required for amending the constitution from 75 per cent to only 51 per cent. Support for this proposed change was achieved, the required majority for both the Compact and constitutional nuclear clause change being obtained in an ensuing referendum. However, in April 1988, the Supreme Court of Palau ruled these changes unconstitutional. Five months later, in August 1988, the Republic's President, Lazarus Salii, was found dead with a gunshot wound to his head. Initial reports suggested that he had been assassinated by anti-Compact extremists. Later evidence suggested, however, that the President had committed suicide because of both policy failures and pending corruption charges.

The Republic remains the only surviving part of the Trust Territory of the Pacific Islands which has not formally achieved 'independence'. Its economy is in a depressed condition and heavily dependent on American aid, currently running at about $20 million per annum.

8.5 Semi-sovereign states

Within Western Europe there are five tiny principalities, city and theocratic states, Andorra, Liechtenstein, Monaco, San Marino, and the Vatican City. Although often listed as independent nations in general reference works, these 'micro-states' lack full and effective sovereignty, being both politically and militarily closely linked to, and heavily dependent on, much larger neighbours for their security. They have thus been termed semi-sovereign states and are treated separately, in a condensed format, below.

Survivors from an earlier era when continental Europe was composed of a patchwork quilt of small duchies, principalities and kingdoms, they have variously adapted to modern conditions by establishing themselves as picturesque and duty-free tourist centres or as prosperous tax havens. None of the states is formally a member of either the United Nations or European Community. Their current prosperity is, however, endangered by the shift towards a single European market in 1992. Table 80 sets out aggregated data for these five states.

Table 80

SEMI-SOVEREIGN STATES

State	*Area (km^2)*	*Population (m) (1985)*	*Date of State Establishment*
Andorra	468	0.035	1278
Liechtenstein	160	0.027	1342
Monaco	2	0.027	1297
San Marino	61	0.022	c 301 AD
Vatican City State	0.4	0.001	1377/1929
Total	691.4	0.112	—

ANDORRA

Co-Principality of Andorra
Principat D'Andorra

Capital: Andorre-la-Vella

Social and economic data
Area: 468 km^2
Population: 35,000*
Pop density per km^2: 75*
Literacy rate: 100%
GDP: $300m; per capita GDP: $8,571
Economy type: high income
Labour force in agriculture: N/A

*1985

Ethnic composition
Twenty-five per cent of the population are Andorrans and 75 per cent immigrant Spanish workers. Catalan is the local language.

Principal religion
Roman Catholicism.

Date of state formation
1278

Local government
Andorra is divided into seven parishes.

Co-heads of state
Episcopal Co-Prince: Monsignor Dr Juan Marti Alanis, Bishop of Seo de Urgel, Spain.
French Co-Prince: François Mitterrand, President of France, since 1981.

Head of government
Prime Minister Josep Pintat Solens, since 1984.

Political system
Andorra has no formal constitution and the government, despite the passage of administrative statutes in 1748 and 1763 and a 'Plan of Reform' in 1866, is still based on its feudal origins. Although administratively independent, it has no individual international status, its joint heads of state being the Bishop of Urgel, in Spain, and the President of the French Republic. They are represented by Permanent Delegates, the Vicar-General of the Urgel diocese, and the prefect of the French department of Pyrénées-Orientales. There is a General Council of the Valleys, consisting of 28 people, four from each of the seven parishes, elected by Andorran citizens for a four-year term. The Council, which meets periodically throughout the year, submits motions and proposals to the Permanent Delegates for approval. Until 1982 the General Council elected, as its head, someone called the First Syndic, or manager, to act as chief executive, but there is now a seven-member Executive Council, headed by a Prime Minister, who is called President of Government. This has resulted in some separation of the legislative and executive powers and marks an important step towards a more constitutional form of government. For the time being, however, any reforms are dependent on the agreement of the two co-princes, through their representatives.

Political history
Andorra's 'independence' is viewed as dating from 1278, when an agreement (*pareage*) was entered into between France and the Bishop of Seo de Urgel in Spain for the state's co-rule. Since then, possessing only an unpaid ceremonial militia, it has remained dependent upon its larger neighbours for its security and continued existence.

Until 1970 only third-generation Andorran males had the vote. Now the franchise extends to all first-generation Andorrans of foreign parentage aged 28 or over. The electorate is still small, however, in relation to the total population, up to 75 per cent of whom are foreign citizens, who are constantly demanding political and nationality rights. Immigration, controlled by a quota system, is restricted to French and Spanish nationals intending to work in Andorra. Since 1980 there have been signs of a fragile, but growing, democracy. There are loose political groupings but no direct party representation on the General Council. There is, however, a technically illegal political organisation, the liberal-reformist Democratic Party of Andorra, which was founded in 1976, which may well provide the basis for a future democratic system.

Economically, the co-principality has progressed significantly during recent decades, utilising its exemption, under the terms of an 1867 Franco-Spanish agreement, from the payment of import duties, to develop a growing tourist industry. About 10 million visitors currently pass through the state annually, purchasing low-priced consumer goods, while several thousand North Europeans use Andorra as a tax haven. This prosperity is threatened, however, by the shift towards a single market in Europe, in 1992.

LIECHTENSTEIN

Principality of Liechtenstein
Fürstentum Liechtenstein

Capital: Vaduz

Social and economic data
Area: 160 km^2
Population: 27,000*
Pop density per km^2: 169*
Literacy rate: 99%
GDP: $450m*; per capita GDP: $16,667
Economy type: high income
Labour force in agriculture: 3%

*1985

Ethnic composition
The indigenous population are of German-speaking Alemannic origin, while a third are foreign-born resident workers.

Principal religion
Roman Catholicism.

Date of state formation
1342

Local government
The Principality is divided into two districts, Oberland (Upper Country) and Unterland (Lower Country), which, in turn, comprise eleven communes.

Head of state
Prince Franz Josef II, since 1938.

Head of government
Prime Minister Hans Brunhart, since 1978.

Political system
The October 1921 constitution established an hereditary Principality, with a single-chamber parliament, the Landtag. The Prince is the formal and constitutional head of state. He may dissolve parliament at any time and his approval is required for all legislation before it may become law. The Landtag, which currently has 25 members, 15 from the Upper Country and ten from the Lower Country, is elected for a four-year term through a system of proportional representation. This is based on the use of two district-level constituencies and the rule that parties which secure less than 8 per cent of the votes cast fail to qualify for the distribution of seats. Its size was increased by ten seats following a narrow vote, of 52 per cent to 48 per cent, in a referendum held in January 1988.

Originally, only men were entitled to vote in Landtag elections, but since a referendum, in July 1984, approving the extension of the franchise to women, who constitute 67 per cent of the electorate, there has been universal suffrage for all adults aged 20 and over.

A group of five people, a Prime Minister and four Councillors, are elected by the Landtag to form the Principality's government (Collegial Board) for the duration of parliament.

There are three political parties, the two most dominant being the Fatherland Union (VU), and the Progressive Citizens' Party (FBP). The VU was founded in 1918 and remodelled in 1938. It has a firm support base in the mountainous south of the Principality and won 13 Landtag seats in the March 1989 general election. The FBP is a northern-based party which has twelve parliamentary seats. Both parties share a similar conservative ideological outlook, with the FBP predominating in the Landtag between 1928 and 1970 and the VU since 1978.

Political history
Liechtenstein was founded as a sovereign state in 1342 and has remained within its present boundaries since 1432. It did not, however, adopt its current name until 1719, when it was purchased by the present ruling family, and formed part of the Holy Roman Empire until 1806. Between 1815 and 1866 the state was a member of the German Confederation, before leaving to become a fully independent Principality.

However, because of its small size and the decision to abolish its armed forces in 1868, Liechtenstein has found it convenient, while remaining neutral in external disputes, to associate itself with larger neighbouring nations in international matters. For example, it has, since 1923, shared a customs union with Switzerland, which also represents it. Previously Austria undertook its diplomatic representation. It is, nevertheless, one of the world's richest countries, with an income per head comparable to that of Switzerland and the United States and nearly twice as great as that of the United Kingdom. High technology, precision engineering, international banking, aided by its favourable tax structure and legal system, and tourism constitute the three pillars of this successful economy.

The Principality has chosen not to be a full member of the United Nations but it is represented in some UN specialist agencies and has also, since 1978, been a member of the Council of Europe. Prince Franz Josef II, who succeeded to the throne in 1938, and was *de facto* ruler for four and a half decades, handed over executive powers to his son and heir, Prince Hans Adam, in August 1984. Prince Franz Josef II remains, however, titular head of state. Liechtenstein's political system is innately conservative in that women did not secure the right to vote in national elections until 1984 and remained debarred from voting in three of the Principality's eleven communes until April 1986.

MONACO

Principality of Monaco
Principauté de Monaco

Capital: Monaco-Ville

Social and economic data
Area: 2 km^2
Population: 27,000*
Pop density per km^2: 13,500*
Literacy rate: 100%
GDP: $280m*; per capita GDP: $10,370
Economy type: high income
Labour force in agriculture: 0%

*1985

Ethnic composition
Nineteen per cent of the population are Monégasque and 58 per cent French.

Principal religion
Roman Catholicism.

Date of state formation
1297

Local government
For administrative purposes, the Principality is divided into four districts, called communal quarters.

Head of state
Prince Rainier III, since 1949.

Head of government
Minister of State Jean Ausseil, since 1986.

Political system

The 1911 constitution was modified in 1917 and then largely rewritten in 1962. It preserves Monaco as an hereditary Principality but an earlier concept of attributing the Prince with a divine right to rule has been deleted. Legislative power is shared between the Prince and a single-chamber National Council (Conseil National), with 18 members elected by universal adult suffrage for a five-year term. Voting is restricted to Monégasque citizens aged 21 and over, and a two-ballot majoritarian system is employed. Executive power is formally vested in the Prince, but, in practice, exercised by a four-member Council of Government, headed by a Minister of State, who is a French civil servant chosen by the Prince. There are no political parties as such but the January 1988 National Council elections were contested by the National and Democratic Union (UND), which was formed in 1962, and which supports Prince Rainier. It won all 18 seats. A rival organisation, the Democratic and Socialist Union, contested the 1983 general election, but has since been dormant.

Political history

Once part of the Roman empire, Monaco became a Genoese possession during the twelfth century, later coming under the rule of the Grimaldi dynasty in 1297. The Principality, after alternate periods under Spanish, French and Sardinian control, became an independent state, under the protection of France, in 1861 and that close relationship has continued. Agreements between the two countries, made in 1918–19, state that Monaco will be incorporated in France if the reigning Prince dies without leaving a male heir. France is closely involved in the government of Monaco, providing a civil servant, of the Prince's choosing, to head its Council of Government, as well as providing its Interior Minister. The small state has developed into a prosperous centre for tourism, which attracts 1.5 million visitors a year. Banking is also an important business and there are light industries, most notably cosmetics and micro-electronics. Monaco is also attractive as a 'shelter' for tax exiles.

SAN MARINO

Most Serene Republic of San Marino
Serenissima Repubblica di San Marino

Capital: San Marino

Social and economic data

Area: 61 km^2
Population: 22,000*
Pop density per km^2: 361*
Literacy rate: 96%
GDP: $200m*; per capita GDP: $9,091
Economy type: high income
Labour force in agriculture: 3%

*1985

Ethnic composition
Predominantly Italian.

Principal religion
Roman Catholicism.

Date of state formation
c AD 301

Head of state and head of government
Two Captains-Regent, elected for a six-month period.

Political system
Because of its small size, San Marino is able to operate a uniquely intimate form of direct democracy, echoing some of the features of the ancient Greek city-states. It does not have a formal constitution, though a basic set of 'governing principles' was framed in 1600, and the system of government is derived from its early origins. The country is divided into nine 'Castles', or districts, which correspond to the original nine parishes of the republic. Each 'Castle' is governed by a Castle-Captain and an Auxiliary Council, who serve, respectively, two- and five-year terms. For the whole country there is a single-chamber Great and General Council composed of 60 members, elected by universal adult suffrage for a five-year term, through a system of proportional representation. The Council elects two of its members, one representing the capital and one the country, to serve a six-month term as Captains-Regent and together they share the duties of head of state and head of government. They preside over a cabinet of ten, elected by the Council for a five-year term, called the Congress of State.

There are a number of political parties, the two most significant being the San Marino Christian Democrat Party (PDCS) and the San Marino Communist Party (PCS). The PDCS was formed in 1948 and has 27 seats in the 1988 elected Council. Its coalition partner, the PCS, was founded in 1941, and is a moderate Euro-communist party. It currently has 18 seats. The two most significant smaller, opposition, parties are the Socialist Unity Party (PSU), formed in 1975, and the Socialist Party (PSS). The PSU has eight seats and the PSS seven. The right to vote, which was extended to women in 1960, is enjoyed by all adults born in San Marino whether continuing to reside in the state or not. To encourage expatriate voting, the state pays 75 per cent of the return fare of any Sammarinese living abroad to return home to vote. In the May 1988 election, 5,402, or about 50 per cent of those eligible, availed themselves of this opportunity.

Political history
San Marino was founded by a Christian saint, St Marinus, at the start of the fourth century AD as a refuge against religious persecution. It survived as a city-state after the unification of Italy in the late nineteenth century, thus being able to claim the distinction of being the world's oldest republic. It has a treaty of friendship with Italy, dating originally from 1862, but which was renewed in 1939 and 1971, and its multi-party system mirrors that of the larger country that surrounds it. For the past forty years it has been governed by a series of left-wing and centre-left coalitions, the current one,

termed the 'grand coalition', comprising the Communists and Christian Democrats and dating from July 1986. The state relies heavily on earnings derived from tourism, more than three million visitors passing through its borders annually, but also, in recent decades, it has developed a number of light industries, most notably cement, leather and textile production.

VATICAN CITY STATE

Temporal State of the Bishop of Rome
Stato Della Citta del Vaticano

Capital: Vatican City, Rome.

Social and economic data
Area: 0.4 km^2
Population: 700*
Pop density per km^2: 1,750*
Literacy rate: N/A
GDP: N/A*; per capita GDP: N/A
Economy type: N/A
Labour force in agriculture: N/A

*1985

Religion
Roman Catholicism.

Date of state formation
1377/1929

Head of state
His Holiness Pope John Paul II, since 1978.

Head of government
Cardinal Sebastiano Baggio, since 1984.

Political system
The Vatican City State came into being through the Lateran Treaty of February 1929, under which the King of Italy recognised the sovereignty of the Pope over the city of the Vatican. The Pope, the Supreme Pontiff of the Universal Church, is elected for life by 120 members of the Sacred College of Cardinals. He appoints a Pontifical Commission (PC), headed by a President, to administer the State's affairs on his behalf and under his direction. The PC comprises seven Cardinals, each appointed for a five-year period, served by a staff of laymen headed by a Special Delegate. Routine Vatican administration has been entrusted since April 1984 to the Secretary of State, Cardinal Agostino Casaroli.

In the Vatican, the central administration of the Roman Catholic Church throughout the world is also conducted by eleven Congregations, each under the direction of a Cardinal, three Secretariats and numerous committees, councils and commissions.

Political history

The Vatican City State is a direct successor to early papal states which had ruled much of the central Italian peninsula during the millennium between the era of Charlemagne and the unification of Italy in 1870–71. The Vatican Palace in Rome had served as the papal residence since 1377 and remained so during the period between 1871 and 1929 when the Vatican was formally absorbed within the new Italian state. Under the terms of the 1929 Lateran Agreement, signed by Benito Mussolini and Pope Pius XI, full sovereign jurisdiction over the Vatican City State was restored to the Holy See, which is the formal title of the bishopric of Rome. The new state was declared a neutral and inviolable territory.

This treaty was reaffirmed in the Italian constitution of 1947. Under the terms of a Concordat, also agreed in 1929, Roman Catholicism became the state religion in Italy, enjoying special legal privileges. This status was also reaffirmed in 1947. However, a new Concordat was signed in February 1984, and subsequently ratified in June 1985, under which Catholicism ceased to be the Italian state religion.

The present (266th) Pope, John Paul II, formerly Cardinal Karol Wojtyla, took up his office in October 1978. Born in Poland and having previously served as Archbishop of Krakow in Poland, he is the first non-Italian Pope since 1522. In May 1981 and May 1982, he survived two assassination attempts and has since established himself as a vigorous and influential leader. As head of a Church claiming more than 750 million worldwide adherents, 26 per cent of whom live in Europe, 53 per cent in the Americas and the remaining 21 per cent in Africa, Asia and Oceania, Pope John Paul II has travelled extensively, drawing large audiences wherever he visits.

RECOMMENDED READING

Cammack, P., Pool, D. and Tordoff, W., *Third World Politics: A Comparative Introduction*, Macmillan, 1988, Part 1.

Clapham, C., *Third World Politics: An Introduction*, Croom Helm, 1985, Ch 3.

Fieldhouse, D. K., *The Colonial Empires: A Comparative Study from the Eighteenth Century*, 2nd edn., Macmillan, 1982.

Holland, R. F., *European Decolonization, 1918–1981: An Introductory Survey*, Macmillan, 1985.

Taylor, P. J., *Political Geography: World Economy, Nation-State and Locality*, Longman, 1985, Ch 3.

CHAPTER 9

THE WORLD GROWS SMALLER: INTERNATIONAL CO-OPERATION

9.1 Competition or co-operation?

Ever since the birth of the nation-state, its history has been one of competition, rather than co-operation. Nations have vied with each other in trade. One state has tried to impose its own religion on another. Empires have been created by strong countries dominating the weak. Where co-operation has occurred it has nearly always been on the basis of national self-interest and rarely in any altruistic, international sense.

International alliances have often been between major powers which have temporarily joined forces, in military terms, to attack, or defend themselves against, another opposing alliance. During the nineteenth and early twentieth centuries the political maps of the world were drawn and redrawn as a result of treaties and agreements reached by victors in international disputes, the provisions of which were then imposed on the vanquished.

The two most significant examples of such international decision-taking in the present century are the treaties signed at the end of the two World Wars, in 1918 and 1945. The terms of the Treaty of Versailles, of 1919, sowed the seeds of the Second World War, 20 years later, but its lessons were partially, but not entirely, learned by the statesmen who had the responsibility of trying to secure lasting world peace after 1945.

Since 1945 there has been a virtually unending succession of regional conflicts but a global war has so far been avoided and there are encouraging prospects of greater, rather than less, international co-operation. A number of factors have contributed to this new sense of urgency and optimism in international affairs.

First, improvements in the ease and speed of communication have made the world shrink in physical terms.

Second, the complexities of production and distribution have resulted in international co-operation on a scale hitherto unknown, resulting in the growth of multi-national, rather than national, corporations.

Third, there has been a growing realisation that the economies of the major nation-states cannot be seen as discrete, separate entities, but are so intermeshed that the success or failure of one has its impact on the others.

Fourth, there has been a recognition in the years since 1945 that it is in the interests of the advanced world to assist the economic and social progress of the underdeveloped world by financial and technical means.

Fifth, the possibility of a nuclear holocaust has persuaded the major powers to step back from the brink of another global war.

The sixth, and ultimately the most significant factor in the long term, is the increasing recognition of the fragility of the world's ecology, in other words, the 'green factor'.

Seventh, and last, have been the recent encouraging moves towards more pluralistic and democratic political systems in many states, including, of course, the major changes which are taking place within the Soviet bloc and the likely effects of these changes on its relations with other nations in the world.

There are encouraging signs, therefore, that in the years ahead, running into the twenty-first century, international co-operation, rather than competition, is likely to be the prevalent force. It would be unwise, however, to be over optimistic. Political attitudes can quickly change and a regime favouring positive co-operation can easily be replaced by one based on negative self-interest. Nevertheless, there is already a widespread, and sometimes complex, array of global and regional schemes of co-operation already in being, some more successful than others, and those which have already proved their worth might well provide the foundation for yet greater future collaboration.

9.2 Global co-operation: the United Nations Organisation

The United Nations (UN) originated from a conference held at Dumbarton Oaks, Washington DC, between the Second World War allies, the Soviet Union, the United Kingdom and the United States, at the end of September and the beginning of October, 1944. The name United Nations was devised by Franklin Roosevelt and was first used in the Declaration by United Nations, on 1 January 1942, when representatives of 26 nations pledged their governments to continue fighting the Axis powers of Germany, Italy and Japan. Its forerunner was the League of Nations which had been established after the First World War but had failed to fulfil its early promise and had eventually been abandoned by the United States.

The Dumbarton Oaks conference produced a set of proposals which were put before a conference held at San Francisco on 25–26 June 1945 and, after certain amendments had been agreed, a Charter was signed by 50 of the 51 founder members, on 26 June 1945. Poland, although a founder member, did not sign it at the time but at a later date. The United Nations officially came into being on 24 October 1945, which is now celebrated annually as United Nations Day. Membership is open to all peace-loving nations and currently stands at 159. The names of member states and the dates of their admission are shown in Table 81 below.

Table 81

UNITED NATIONS MEMBERSHIP

Country	*Year of Admission*	*% Contribution to UN Budget†*	*Country*	*Year of Admission*	*% Contribution to UN Budget†*
Afghanistan	1946	0.01	Austria	1955	0.74
Albania	1955	0.01	Bahamas	1973	0.01
Algeria	1962	0.14	Bahrain	1971	0.02
Angola	1976	0.01	Bangladesh	1974	0.02
Antigua & Barbuda	1981	0.01	Barbados	1966	0.01
			*Belgium	1945	1.18
*Argentina	1945	0.62	Belize	1981	0.01
*Australia	1945	1.66	Benin	1960	0.01

Table 81—United Nations Membership (Contd.)

Country	Year of Admission	% Contribution to UN Budget†	Country	Year of Admission	% Contribution to UN Budget†
Bhutan	1971	0.01	*India	1945	0.35
*Bolivia	1945	0.01	Indonesia	1950	0.14
Botswana	1966	0.01	*Iran	1945	0.63
*Brazil	1945	1.40	*Iraq	1945	0.12
Brunei	1984	0.04	Ireland	1955	0.18
Bulgaria	1955	0.16	Israel	1949	0.22
Burkina Faso	1960	0.01	Italy	1955	3.79
Burma	1948	0.01	Jamaica	1962	0.02
Burundi	1962	0.01	Japan	1956	10.84
*Byelorussian SSR‡	1945	0.34	Jordan	1955	0.01
Cambodia	1955	0.01	Kenya	1963	0.01
Cameroon	1960	0.01	Kuwait	1963	0.29
*Canada	1945	3.06	Laos	1955	0.01
Cape Verde	1975	0.01	*Lebanon	1945	0.01
Central African Republic*	1960	0.01	Lesotho	1966	0.01
			*Liberia	1945	0.01
Chad	1960	0.01	Libya	1955	0.26
*Chile	1945	0.07	*Luxembourg	1945	0.05
*China, People's Republic§	1945	0.79	Madagascar	1960	0.01
			Malawi	1964	0.01
*Colombia	1945	0.13	Malaysia	1957	0.10
Comoros	1975	0.01	Maldives	1965	0.01
Congo	1960	0.01	Mali	1960	0.01
*Costa Rica	1945	0.02	Malta	1964	0.01
Côte d'Ivoire	1960	0.02	Mauritania	1961	0.01
*Cuba	1945	0.09	Mauritius	1968	0.01
Cyprus	1960	0.02	*Mexico	1945	0.89
*Czechoslovakia	1945	0.70	Mongolia	1961	0.01
*Denmark	1945	0.72	Morocco	1956	0.05
Djibouti	1977	0.01	Mozambique	1975	0.01
Dominica	1978	0.01	Nepal	1955	0.01
*Dominican Republic	1945	0.03	*Netherlands	1945	1.74
			*New Zealand	1945	0.24
*Ecuador	1945	0.03	*Nicaragua	1945	0.01
*Egypt	1945	0.07	Niger	1960	0.01
*El Salvador	1945	0.01	Nigeria	1960	0.19
Equatorial Guinea	1968	0.01	*Norway	1945	0.54
*Ethiopia	1945	0.01	Oman	1971	0.02
Fiji	1970	0.01	Pakistan	1947	0.06
Finland	1955	0.50	*Panama	1945	0.02
*France	1945	6.37	Papua New Guinea	1975	0.01
Gabon	1960	0.03			
The Gambia	1965	0.01	*Paraguay	1945	0.02
German Democratic Republic	1973	1.33	*Peru	1945	0.07
			*Philippines	1945	0.10
German Federal Republic	1973	8.26	*Poland	1945	0.64
			Portugal	1955	0.18
Ghana	1957	0.01	Qatar	1971	0.04
*Greece	1945	0.44	Romania	1955	0.19
Grenada	1974	0.01	Rwanda	1962	0.01
*Guatemala	1945	0.02	St Kitts-Nevis	1983	0.01
Guinea	1958	0.01			
Guinea-Bissau	1974	0.01	St Lucia	1979	0.01
Guyana	1966	0.01	St Vincent & the Grenadines	1980	0.01
*Haiti	1945	0.01			
*Honduras	1945	0.01	Sao Tome & Principe	1975	0.01
Hungary	1955	0.22			
Iceland	1946	0.03	*Saudi Arabia	1945	0.97

Table 81—United Nations Membership (Contd.)

Country	*Year of Admission*	*% Contribution to UN Budget**
Senegal	1960	0.01
Seychelles	1976	0.01
Sierra Leone	1961	0.01
Singapore	1965	0.10
Solomon Islands	1978	0.01
Somalia	1960	0.01
*South Africa	1945	0.44
Spain	1955	2.03
Sri Lanka	1955	0.01
Sudan	1956	0.01
Suriname	1975	0.01
Swaziland	1968	0.01
Sweden	1946	1.25
*Syria	1945	0.04
Tanzania	1961	0.01
Thailand	1946	0.09
Togo	1960	0.01
Trinidad & Tobago	1962	0.04
Tunisia	1956	0.03
*Turkey	1945	0.34
Uganda	1962	0.01

Country	*Year of Admission*	*% Contribution to UN Budget‡*
*Ukrainian SSR‡	1945	1.28
*USSR	1945	10.20
United Arab Emirates	1971	0.18
*United Kingdom	1945	4.86
*USA	1945	25.00
*Uruguay	1945	0.04
Vanuatu	1981	0.01
*Venezuela	1945	0.60
Vietnam	1977	0.01
Western Samoa	1976	0.01
Yemen Arab Republic	1947	0.01
Yemen, People's Democratic Republic	1967	0.01
*Yugoslavia	1945	0.46
Zaire	1960	0.01
Zambia	1964	0.01
Zimbabwe	1980	0.02

*Founder members.

†These are assessments of percentage contributions to the UN budget for the years 1986, 1987 and 1988.

‡Byelorussian SSR and Ukrainian SSR are integral parts of the Soviet Union, and not independent countries, but they have separate UN membership.

§From 1945 until 1971 China was represented by the Republic of China, now Taiwan. Since 1971 the member has been the People's Republic of China.

The sovereign countries which are not UN members are: Andorra, Kiribati, North Korea, South Korea, Liechtenstein, Monaco, Nauru, San Marino, Switzerland, Taiwan, Tonga, Tuvalu and Vatican City.

The major declared aims of the United Nations are to maintain international peace and security and to develop international co-operation in economic, social, cultural and humanitarian problems, and, in pursuit of these aims, it has erected an impressive institutional structure of councils, commissions, committees and agencies, as well as the International Court of Justice. Some institutions, such as the International Court, are developments of earlier bodies from the days of the League of Nations and before. Others are new creations.

9.2.1 Principal UN institutions

The principal UN institutions are the General Assembly, the Security Council, the Economic and Social Council, the Trusteeship Council, the International Court of Justice and the Secretariat. The permanent headquarters of the UN are in the United Nations Plaza, Lower Manhattan, New York City, USA, and meetings of its main organisations are usually held there, but they can be, and sometimes are, arranged elsewhere. The International Court of Justice is based in the Hague, in the Netherlands, and several other UN bodies have their headquarters in Geneva, Switzerland, though that country is not a member of the UN.

General Assembly
The General Assembly is the UN parliament of which all nations are members, each having one vote. It meets once a year at the UN headquarters in New York in a session beginning on the third Tuesday in September, running through to the end of the year, or into the following year if business demands it. It can be summoned to meet at any time in an emergency session and there have been over 25 such special sessions convened to date, covering such topics as peace-keeping in Lebanon, the Suez crisis, Afghanistan, Namibia and the economic situation in Africa. Below the main Assembly is a network of committees.

General Assembly decisions are made by simple majority voting but on certain important matters, such as the condemnation of an act by one of its members, a two-thirds majority is needed. If the Assembly feels that the Security Council is not fulfilling its chief responsibility of maintaining international peace satisfactorily it may take it upon itself to consider a special case, such as an act of aggression, or some other breach of the peace, and recommend action to be taken.

Security Council
The Security Council has a membership of 15. There are five permanent members, China, France, the Soviet Union, the United Kingdom and the United States, and the other ten are elected for two-year terms by a two-thirds vote of the General Assembly. Retiring members are not eligible for immediate re-election. Any UN member may be invited to participate in its discussions if they bear on its interests, but only the permanent or elected members are permitted to vote.

In pursuit of its responsibility for maintaining peace and security, the Council may call on armed forces, and other assistance, from member states. It has at its disposal a Military Staff Committee composed of the chiefs of staff of the countries of the permanent members. The presidency of the Security Council is held for a month at a time by a representative of a member-state, in English language alphabetical order. The Council has two standing committees: a Committee of Experts and a Committee on the Admission of New Members.

Economic and Social Council
The Economic and Social Council is responsible for economic, social, cultural, educational, health and related matters. It has 54 members, again elected by a two-thirds majority vote of the General Assembly. The Council has a large number of functional and regional commissions and committees working for it as well as hundreds of non-governmental agencies which have been granted consultative status.

Trusteeship Council
The Trusteeship Council is responsible for overseeing the administration of the UN Trust Territories. Its members are China, France, the Soviet Union, the United Kingdom and the United States. It holds one regular session per year but can meet in special sessions if required.

International Court of Justice
The International Court of Justice is composed of independent judges,

elected by the Security Council and the General Assembly, sitting separately, and are chosen because of their competence in international law, irrespective of their nationalities. There are 15 judges, no two of whom can be nationals of the same state. Candidates for election are nominated by national groups, and once elected, serve for nine years, and may be immediately re-elected. Only states, not individuals, may be parties to cases before the Court.

The Court is based at the Hague, in the Netherlands, but may sit elsewhere if it chooses. It sits permanently, except for customary judicial vacations. Its official languages are English and French and it reaches its decisions by a majority of votes of the judges present. The President and Vice-President are elected by the Court itself and serve three-year terms. If the votes of judges are equal, the President has a casting vote. Judgements are final, and there is no appeal.

The Court's membership, until 1991, will include judges from the following countries: Algeria, Argentina, China, France, Guyana, India, Italy, Japan, Nigeria, Norway, Poland, Senegal, the Soviet Union, the United Kingdom and the United States.

Secretariat

The United Nations Secretariat consists of the Secretary-General, who is its chief administrator, Under and Assistant Secretaries-General and a large international staff. The Secretary-General is appointed by the General Assembly for a five-year term, which can be renewed. The present occupant, Javier Perez de Cuellar, of Peru, was originally appointed in 1981 and had his term renewed, until 1991, in 1986. The first holder of the post was Trygve Lie, of Norway (1946–53), and subsequent holders, before Javier Perez, were Dag Hammarskjöld, of Sweden (1953–61), U Thant, of Burma (1961–71) and Kurt Waldheim, of Austria (1972–81).

Being UN Secretary-General is clearly an important, and prestigious, job, but experience shows that its significance depends very much on what a particular holder makes of it. Trygve Lie and Dag Hammarskjöld, who was killed in an air crash while on UN business, became well known, even to ordinary people, as did U Thant, to a lesser degree. Hammarskjöld was awarded the Nobel Peace Prize for his efforts. Kurt Waldheim, on the other hand, made a less marked impression. The present Secretary-General, Perez de Cuellar, has not only become a popular, and even famous, international figure, but by the success of his practical efforts to secure peace in troubled parts of the world has done much to revive the standing of the United Nations, which had fallen to a low ebb during the 1970s.

9.2.2 UN specialised agencies

Working directly within the United Nations organisational structure are a number of specialised agencies, financed by the UN through contributions from the 159 member states. The scale of these contributions, which are based broadly on the principle of the 'ability to pay', are shown in Table 81. The specialised agencies operate mainly from the headquarters in New York or from Geneva, in Switzerland.

International Atomic Energy Agency (IAEA)
The IAEA was established in 1957 to accelerate and enlarge the contribution of atomic energy to peace, health and prosperity throughout the world and to prevent its diversion from peaceful purposes to military ends. It negotiates safeguard agreements with individual states, 164 of such agreements currently being in force. The Agency is based in Vienna, Austria.

International Labour Organisation (ILO)
The ILO pre-dates the United Nations itself, having been originally created in 1919 by the League of Nations. It is an inter-governmental agency with a tripartite membership of government, employer and worker representatives. It seeks to improve labour conditions, raise living standards and promote productive employment through international co-operation. It became part of the UN in 1946 and in 1969 was awarded the Nobel Peace Prize. It conducts research into industrial relations and publishes Conventions and Recommendations. If a member-state ratifies a Convention it automatically agrees to bring its national law into line with it. Recommendations are not binding but all member-states have a duty to consider them.

The ILO consists of the International Labour Conference, which is its supreme deliberative body and meets annually in Geneva, and the International Labour Office, which is also in Geneva. In 1960 it established the International Institute for Labour Studies and, in 1965, a training institution in Turin, Italy, particularly concerned with the needs of developing countries. Indeed, much of the ILO's work in recent years has been orientated towards the less developed parts of the world.

Food and Agriculture Organisation (FAO)
A conference in May 1943 at Hot Springs, Virginia, USA, provided the stimulus for the setting up of the FAO in October 1945. Its aims are to raise levels of nutrition and standards of living, to improve the production and distribution of food and agricultural products, to improve the living standards of rural populations and, by accomplishing all these things, to eliminate hunger. Like many other UN agencies, the FAO tends to concentrate its efforts on the less developed parts of the world. It provides guidance on food production and can sponsor relief in emergency situations. It operates from Rome, in Italy.

United Nations Educational, Scientific and Cultural Organisation (UNESCO)
UNESCO came into being in 1946 as a result of a conference held in London, in November 1945, under the auspices of the United Kingdom and French governments. Its main purpose is to promote peace by encouraging international collaboration in education, science and culture. It attempts to do this through teacher-training programmes, the promotion of research and the dissemination of information. Its headquarters are in Paris.

World Health Organisation (WHO)
The World Health Organisation was founded in April 1948. Its main purpose is to assist all peoples in attaining the highest possible levels of

health. It does this by research, teaching and guidance through recommended standards of behaviour. For example, it has, in recent years, sponsored greater international co-operation in the prevention and treatment of AIDS and related infections. It has also made recommendations on the quality control of drugs. Its headquarters are in Geneva and it has regional offices in the Congo, Egypt, Denmark, the Philippines, India and the United States.

International Monetary Fund (IMF)

The inspiration for the IMF was the International Monetary Conference held at Bretton Woods, in New Hampshire, USA, in July 1944, under the chairmanship of the US Secretary to the Treasury, Henry Morgenthau. Conference delegates, including the British delegation led by the celebrated economist Lord Keynes, agreed to the creation of a Fund which would promote international monetary co-operation, establish a multilateral system of payments, and help remedy any serious disequilibrium in a country's balance of payments by allowing it to draw on the resources of the Fund while it took measures to correct the imbalance. The IMF was established on 27 December 1945, as an independent organisation, and began operating on 1 March 1947. It became associated with the UN, on the basis of mutual co-operation, on 15 November 1947.

IMF members subscribe to the Fund on a quota basis, determined by their ability to pay at the time of membership. The Fund itself can also borrow to supplement its resources. Most of the assistance given by the IMF is, naturally, to less developed countries but occasionally it is asked to provide temporary help to economically advanced nations. The United Kingdom, for example, had recourse to the Fund in 1976. When it is asked to assist, the IMF's representatives invariably impose conditions to ensure that the problem to be dealt with is only a temporary phenomenon. The headquarters of the IMF are in Washington, DC, and it also has offices in Paris and Geneva.

International Bank for Reconstruction and Development (IBRD)

The IBRD is often popularly known as the 'World Bank'. Like the IMF, it too, was conceived at the Bretton Woods Conference. Its purpose is to provide funds and technical assistance to help the economies of the poorer nations of the world. It obtains its own funds from capital paid in by member countries, from loans, from repayments, from income from investments and from fees paid for the technical services it provides. Its headquarters are in Washington, DC, where it also has a staff college, called the Economic Development Institute.

International Development Association (IDA)

The IDA is an agency of the World Bank, concentrating on providing financial and technical help to the poorest nations. It came into existence in 1960.

International Finance Corporation (IFC)

The IFC is affiliated to the World Bank and was established in 1956. It makes investments in companies, to assist their development, or provides loans. It is particularly active in helping new ventures or providing finance for established companies which wish to expand or diversify.

International Civil Aviation Organisation (ICAO)
The idea for creating the ICAO came from a conference on international aviation held in Chicago at the end of 1944. The Organisation was formally set up on 4 April 1947. Its objects are to establish technical standards for safety and efficiency in air navigation, to develop regional plans for ground facilities and services for civil aviation, and generally to provide advice to airline operators. Its headquarters are in Montreal, Canada.

Universal Postal Union (UPU)
The UPU was established as long ago as 1875 when the Universal Postal Convention was adopted at a Congress in Berne, Switzerland. It was originally called the General Postal Union and changed its name in 1878. Currently, 158 countries are members. Its aim is to improve the standards of postal services and promote international co-operation. Its headquarters are in Berne.

International Telecommunication Union (ITU)
The aims of the ITU are to maintain and extend international co-operation in improving telecommunications of all kinds by promoting the development of technical skills and services and harmonising national activities. It originated in 1932 when, at a conference in Madrid, it was decided to merge the Telegraph Convention of 1865 and the Radiotelegraph Convention of 1906 into a single Convention and functioning organisation. The ITU's headquarters are in Geneva.

World Meteorological Organisation (WMO)
The Directors of the International Meteorological Organisation, which had been set up in 1873, met in Washington, DC, in 1947 and adopted a convention establishing the WMO. Its main aim is to facilitate worldwide co-operation in the creation and maintenance of a network of stations for making meteorological observations and to ensure the rapid exchange of information. The headquarters of the WMO are in Geneva.

International Maritime Organisation (IMO)
Known until 1982 as the Inter-Governmental Maritime Consultative Organisation (IMCO), the IMO was established as a specialised agency of the UN in 1948. It began to operate effectively in 1959. Its aim is to promote co-operation between governments on technical matters affecting merchant shipping, with the object of improving safety at sea. It formulates and publishes conventions and regulations and has its headquarters in London.

General Agreement on Tariffs and Trade (GATT)
The GATT was negotiated in 1947 and came into force on 1 January 1948. It is a multilateral treaty which lays down a common code of conduct in international trade. It also provides a forum for discussion of trade problems, with the object of reducing trade barriers. Part of its purpose is to help less developed countries through its 'most-favoured-nation' treatment, which gives protection to 'infant economies'. The GATT is administered from Geneva.

World Intellectual Property Organisation (WIPO)
WIPO was established in 1967 as the successor to the United International Bureau for the Protection of Intellectual Property. It became a UN specialised agency in 1974. Its primary purpose is to protect intellectual property, which, in general, means patents and trade marks, throughout the world. It is based in Geneva.

International Fund for Agricultural Development (IFAD)
IFAD is the result of a recommendation of a World Food Conference which was held in 1974. The Fund began operating in 1977 with the prime object of mobilising funds for agricultural and rural development. IFAD has its headquarters in Rome.

Office of the United Nations Disaster Relief Co-ordinator (UNDRO)
UNDRO was established in 1972 to mobilise and co-ordinate international emergency relief for disaster-hit areas. It provides a 24-hour monitoring service for monitoring natural disasters and emergencies and has four main functions: relief co-ordination; disaster preparedness; disaster prevention and the provision of information and communications facilities. It operates from Geneva.

United Nations Centre for Human Settlements (UNCHS) (Habitat)
UNCHS was founded in 1978 to service the intergovernmental Commission on Human Settlements. It is particularly concerned with the shelter needs of disadvantaged people, and provides functional services in the areas of planning, construction, land and infrastructure development and finance. It is based at Nairobi, Kenya.

United Nations Children's Fund (UNICEF)
It was originally established, in 1946, as the UN International Children's Emergency Fund, to meet the emergency needs of children in post-war Europe and China. Four years later its mandate was changed to cater for children in developing countries and in 1953 it became a permanent part of the UN system. Its headquarters are in New York and it has major offices in Switzerland, Kenya, Jordan, the Ivory Coast, Colombia, Thailand, India, Australia and Japan.

United Nations Conference on Trade and Development (UNCTAD)
UNCTAD was established in 1964 to promote international trade, particularly in developing countries. It reports directly to the UN General Assembly and its headquarters are in Geneva.

United Nations Environment Programme (UNEP)
UNEP was set up in 1972 following a UN Conference on the Human Environment, which was held in Stockholm, Sweden. Its main functions are to monitor closely the state of the environment and to promote environmentally sound developments throughout the world. As the public becomes increasingly concerned about threats to the environment so the role of UNEP is likely to be enhanced. Its headquarters are in Nairobi, Kenya.

United Nations Fund for Population Activities (UNFPA)
UNFPA was created in 1967 as the Trust Fund for Population Activities. It became a Fund of the General Assembly in 1972 and operates under the umbrella of UNDP. Its function is to provide finance for projects in the areas of family planning, education, and research into population trends and the needs of particular age groups. Its headquarters are in New York.

United Nations High Commissioner for Refugees
The office of the High Commissioner was established in Geneva, Switzerland, in 1951 to provide international protection for refugees and to find solutions to their problems. The High Commissioner's services are available to anyone who has a well-founded fear of being persecuted for reason of race, religion, nationality or political opinion, and, being outside the country of his or her nationality, is fearful of returning to it. Its headquarters are in Geneva.

United Nations Institute for Training and Research (UNITAR)
UNITAR was established in 1965 to improve the effectiveness of the UN through training and research. It is based at UN headquarters in New York.

United Nations Research Institute for Social Development (UNRISD)
The Institute was founded in 1964, in Geneva, Switzerland, to conduct research, on behalf of the UN, into problems and policies of social and economic development.

World Food Council (WFC)
The WFC was established in 1974 on the recommendation of the World Food Conference, held earlier that year. Its purpose is to stimulate national and international policies and programmes for alleviating world hunger and to improve the global food system. Its headquarters are in Rome.

World Food Programme (WFP)
WFP was set up in 1963 as the food aid arm of the UN. It aims to improve economic and social development through food aid and to provide emergency relief. Like the WFC, it, too, is based in Rome.

9.2.3 UN Development Programme (UNDP)

The UN Development Programme was begun in 1961 to promote higher standards of living in the poorer nations and to try to remedy the economic imbalance between industrialised and developing countries. The first part of the Programme was the UN Development Decade (1961-70) which aimed at achieving a 5 per cent growth rate in developing countries. It was not successful, however, growth rates of only 2 per cent being achieved. The UN

General Assembly therefore decided to support another Development Decade, in the 1970s, this time with a growth target of 6 per cent. This was to be achieved mainly by the economically advanced countries providing financial and technical help and by adopting economic and commercial policies favouring the less advanced nations.

Currently UNDP has 48 members: 15 of them advanced industrial countries, including the United States; six of them communist states, including the Soviet Union and China; and the rest in varying stages of development. UNDP is headed by an administrator who is responsible to a Governing Council of the 48 member-states, and has its headquarters in New York. It operates through a number of regional commissions which are described later in this chapter.

9.3 Global co-operation: the Commonwealth

The Commonwealth is the modern successor to the British Empire. It is formally described as a free association of sovereign independent states. It has no charter, treaty or constitution, the association being based on a desire for co-operation, consultation and mutual assistance. The current membership of 48 countries is shown in Table 82.

It has been described as the world's most unusual 'club' and is a singularly British institution, still echoing the United Kingdom's imperial past. In recent years, however, the influence of the 'mother country' has shown signs of weakening and there are indications that the leadership might be taken up by states such as India, Canada or Australia. Nevertheless, it is inconceivable that the Commonwealth could survive in anything like its present form without Britain's active participation.

As the successor to the British Empire, the Commonwealth was initially based on allegiance to a common Crown. However, in 1949, India chose to become a republic and from that date the modern Commonwealth was born, based now on the concept of the British Monarch being a symbol, rather than a legal entity, and, as such, the 'Head of the Commonwealth'. At the moment 17 of the 48 members accept the British Queen as their head of state, 26 are republics and five have their own local monarchs.

Heads of government of Commonwealth countries meet every two years to discuss international affairs and areas of co-operation. Finance ministers meet annually and other ministers as and when the need arises. The Commonwealth is not a mutual defence organisation and most member countries are committed to regional treaties.

The Commonwealth is frequently criticised because it has little real power to influence world affairs. Its supporters would argue that its strength lies in its voluntary nature and that, should the need arise, its potentially immense resources could be put to considerable use. Britain's role as the originator of the Commonwealth would be crucial in this respect but as it is increasingly committed to its role in Europe its place within the wider organisation is put into some doubt.

The Commonwealth is serviced by a Secretariat which is based in Marlborough House, Pall Mall, London and headed by the Secretary-General, Shridath (Sonny) Ramphal of Guyana. The Secretariat's staff come from a wide range of member countries which also pay its operating costs.

Table 82

THE COMMONWEALTH

State	*Date of Independence*	*Type*	*Head of state*
Antigua & Barbuda	1981	Lib Dem	British Monarch
Australia	1901	Lib Dem	British Monarch
Bahamas	1973	Lib Dem	British Monarch
Bangladesh	1971	Emgt Dem	President
Barbados	1966	Lib Dem	British Monarch
Belize	1981	Lib Dem	British Monarch
Botswana	1966	Lib Dem	President
Brunei	1984	Absolutist	Local Monarch
Canada	1867	Lib Dem	British Monarch
Cyprus	1960	Emgt Dem	President
Dominica	1978	Lib Dem	President
Gambia	1965	Lib Dem	President
Ghana	1957	Mil Auth	President
Grenada	1974	Emgt Dem	British Monarch
Guyana	1966	Emgt Dem	President
India	1947	Lib Dem	President
Jamaica	1962	Lib Dem	British Monarch
Kenya	1963	Auth Nat	President
Kiribati	1979	Lib Dem	President
Lesotho	1966	Mil Auth	Local Monarch
Malawi	1964	Auth Nat	President
Malaysia	1957	Lib Dem	Local Monarch
Maldives	1965	Auth Nat	President
Malta	1964	Lib Dem	President
Mauritius	1968	Lib Dem	British Monarch
Nauru	1968	Lib Dem	President
New Zealand	1947	Lib Dem	British Monarch
Nigeria	1960	Mil Auth	President
Papua New Guinea	1975	Lib Dem	British Monarch
St Kitts-Nevis	1983	Lib Dem	British Monarch
St Lucia	1979	Lib Dem	British Monarch
St Vincent and the Grenadines	1979	Lib Dem	British Monarch
Seychelles	1976	Nat Soc	President
Sierra Leone	1961	Auth Nat	President
Singapore	1963	Lib Dem	President
Solomon Islands	1978	Lib Dem	British Monarch
Sri Lanka	1948	Lib Dem	President
Swaziland	1968	Absolutist	Local Monarch
Tanzania	1961	Nat Soc	President
Tonga	1970	Absolutist	Local Monarch
Trinidad & Tobago	1962	Lib Dem	President
Tuvalu	1978	Lib Dem	British Monarch
Uganda	1962	Emgt Dem	President
United Kingdom	—	Lib Dem	British Monarch
Vanuatu	1980	Lib Dem	President
Western Samoa	1962	Lib Dem	President
Zambia	1964	Nat Soc	President
Zimbabwe	1980	Nat Soc	President

NOTE:

Fiji was a Commonwealth member, with the British Queen as head of state, until 1987 when a military coup overthrew the elected government and declared the country a republic. Its future within the Commonwealth has yet to be decided. South Africa withdrew from membership in 1961, following criticisms of its racial policies. Pakistan withdrew in 1972, after Bangladesh had been admitted, but reapplied for membership in 1989.

ABBREVIATIONS:

State type: Auth Nat—Authoritarian Nationalist; Emgt Dem—Emergent Democratic; Lib Dem—Liberal Democratic; Nat Soc—Nationalistic Socialist

9.4 Global co-operation: the World Council of Churches (WCC)

The World Council of Churches was established on 23 August 1945 in Amsterdam by an assembly representing 147 Churches from 44 countries. By 1988 the number of member-Churches had risen to more than 300 and the number of countries to over 100. The Council's aim is to bring together diverse Christian movements. The Assembly, which is the supreme governing body, convenes every seven or eight years to frame policy. A 150-member central committee meets annually and a 22-member Executive Committee twice a year. The headquarters of the WCC is in Geneva.

9.5 Global co-operation: the Helsinki Accord

The Helsinki Accord was signed by 35 countries, including the Soviet Union and the United States, at the end of a Conference on Security and Co-operation in Europe (CSCE), in 1985. The signatories consisted of the NATO and Warsaw Pact states plus 13 neutral and non-aligned nations. The Accord registered agreement on co-operation in a number of areas such as security, economics, science, technology and human rights, and is generally regarded as marking an end to the Cold War between the Eastern bloc and the West.

9.6 Global co-operation: Organisation of the Islamic Conference (OIC)

The OIC was established in May 1971 following a conference of Muslim heads of state in Rabat, Morocco, in 1969, and meetings of Islamic foreign ministers in Jeddah and Karachi, in 1970. The main aim of the Organisation is to promote Islamic solidarity and its members include 45 countries in the Middle East and North Africa, Central and Southern Africa and Asia, plus the Palestine Liberation Organisation (PLO). The OIC has its headquarters and secretariat in Jeddah, Saudi Arabia.

9.7 Global co-operation: the Antarctic Treaty

The Antarctic Treaty was signed in 1961 by 18 countries which conduct scientific research in Antarctica. They include five Western European states, two in East Europe, including the Soviet Union, and four in South America, plus Australia, China, India, Japan, New Zealand, South Africa, the United Kingdom and the United States. The main objective of the Treaty is to prevent military activity in the region.

9.8 Inter-regional co-operation

There are several examples of mutual co-operation between countries which cut across the regions we have defined for the purposes of this book. Some are sponsored by the United Nations, some by the European Community, some are the products of Commonwealth membership, some have been inspired by the United States, on the basis of enlightened self-interest, and some are examples of self-help by states in different, but physically adjacent, regions. One is an example of co-operation between Eastern and Western Europe.

9.8.1 UN inter-regional groups

Within the United Nations organisation there are four Commissions intended to promote co-operation between under- or less-developed countries in various parts of the world.

Economic Commission for Africa (ECA)
ECA was founded by the UN in 1958. South Africa was originally a member but suspended in 1963. Namibia is an associate member and may well become a full member soon. The total current membership consists of 50 states, representing virtually the whole of north, central and southern Africa. The purpose of the Commission is to promote and facilitate concerted action for the economic and social development of Africa, and it seeks to achieve this through research and the co-ordination of national policies.

Some examples of ECA's work are the establishment of the African Development Bank, in 1964, the creation of the Association of African Central Banks, in 1969, and the setting up of the Centre for Mineral Resources Development at Dar es Salaam, Tanzania, in 1976. It is a regular publisher, largely of statistical material, and operates from Addis Ababa, in Ethiopia.

Economic and Social Commission for Asia and the Pacific (ESCAP)
ESCAP was founded in 1947 as the Economic Commission for Asia and the Far East and changed its name in 1974. It currently has 35 full members and 10 associate members. Most of the full members are states in Asia or Oceania but other countries with interests in the regions, such as the United States, the United Kingdom, the Soviet Union, France and the Netherlands also enjoy full membership. The associate members are the smaller countries of Asia and Oceania.

ESCAP performs a broadly similar role in Asia and Oceania to that of ECA in Africa. It, too, has had success in setting up a number of ventures and organisations, such as the Asian and Pacific Centre for Development Administration, the Asian Clearing Union and the Asian Development Bank. ESCAP has its headquarters in Bangkok, Thailand.

Economic Commission for Europe (ECE)
ECE was also founded in 1947 and includes all Western and Eastern European countries except East Germany and Switzerland, the latter participating in a consultative capacity. The United States is also a consultant. The Commission's role is similar to that of the other UN inter-regional commissions. It is based in Geneva, Switzerland.

Economic Commission for Latin America (ECLA)
ECLA was founded in 1948 with the object of raising the level of economic activity in Latin America, which, in the Commission's terms, includes what we have defined as Central America and the Caribbean and South America. It currently has 33 members. They include, in addition to the countries of the regions, Canada, France, the Netherlands, the United Kingdom and the United States. Its headquarters are in Santiago, Chile.

Economic Commission for Western Asia (ECWA)
ECWA was founded in 1973 and operates from the UN building in Amman, Jordan. It was set up to provide a better service for countries previously catered for by the UN Economic and Social Office in Beirut. Its objects are broadly similar to those of ECLA. The use of the term Western Asia in its title is a little misleading since its 14 members, which include 13 countries plus the Palestine Liberation Organisation (PLO), are all situated in the Middle East or North or Central Africa.

9.8.2 Commonwealth-inspired inter-regional co-operation

Colombo Plan for Co-operative Economic Development in South and South East Asia (CP)
The purpose of the Colombo Plan is to facilitate and co-ordinate economic and social development in the countries of South and South East Asia. It was set up in 1951 within the framework of the Commonwealth, on the initiative of the Commonwealth foreign ministers. Since that date it has lost much of its original Commonwealth character and most of its current members are not in the Commonwealth. They now total 26 and include, as well as the original Commonwealth states in the region, Cambodia, Canada, Iran, Japan, South Korea, the United Kingdom and the United States. The Plan's headquarters are in Colombo, Sri Lanka.

9.8.3 Western European-inspired inter-regional co-operation

The Lomé Convention
The Lomé Convention takes its name from Lomé, the capital of Togo, in Africa, where in 1975 the members of the European Community (EC) agreed to assist the less developed countries of Africa, the Caribbean and the Pacific by establishing a 'special relationship' with them so that they would not suffer unduly from the tariff policies of the EC. The countries concerned include virtually all those in Central and Southern Africa, excluding South Africa, most of those in the Caribbean and the smaller states of Oceania. Under the terms of the Convention the EC guarantees the 66 states who benefit from it virtually unrestricted access for their agricultural products to Western European markets. The 66 ACP (Asia-Caribbean-Pacific) countries, as they are called, may, for their part, operate varying degrees of protection of their own economies. Aid to the ACP nations is also provided from the European Development Fund. The original Convention was renewed in 1979 and 1985.

Organisation for Economic Co-operation and Development (OECD)
OECD is the expanded successor to the Organisation for European Economic Co-operation (OEEC) which was set up in 1948, at the instigation of the United States, to promote economic recovery in post-war Europe. The OECD now has 24 members, including the twelve EC countries, the six EFTA nations plus Australia, Canada, Japan, New Zealand, Turkey and the United States. In its expanded form its object is to promote freer trade and to stimulate Western aid to undeveloped countries.

9.8.4 Eastern European-inspired inter-regional co-operation

Danube Commission

The Danube Commission is based on a Convention controlling navigation on the River Danube, which was signed in Belgrade in 1948. The Convention confirmed that navigation from Ulm, in West Germany, to the Black Sea was open and free to people, shipping and merchandise of all states. The Commission, which ensures the Convention's enforcement, is composed of representatives of all the seven states through which the Danube flows. The Commission represents an almost unique example of co-operation between Eastern and Western European countries. Its headquarters are in Budapest, Hungary.

Council for Mutual Economic Assistance (CMEA or COMECON)

CMEA was established in 1948 with the object of promoting improved co-operation and socialist economic integration, with particular emphasis on assistance to less industrialised countries. Its founder members were the Soviet Union, Bulgaria, Czechoslovakia, Hungary, Poland and Romania. Albania joined in 1949, but ceased participating in 1961. Countries which later joined were East Germany, 1950, Mongolia, 1962, Cuba, 1972, and Vietnam, in 1978. Afghanistan, Angola, Ethiopia, Laos, Mexico, Mozambique, Nicaragua and North Yemen are observers, rather than full members.

9.8.5 Middle East-inspired inter-regional co-operation

Organisation of the Petroleum Exporting Countries (OPEC)

OPEC was formed in Baghdad, Iraq, in 1960 with five founder members: Iran, Iraq, Kuwait, Saudi Arabia and Venezuela. Its membership later expanded to include, in addition to the founder members: Algeria, Ecuador, Gabon, Indonesia, Libya, Nigeria, Qatar, and the United Arab Emirates. Its primary object is to co-ordinate the production and pricing policies of the major oil producers so as to guarantee stable prices and stable incomes, based on what the Organisation would claim to be a fair return on capital invested. Despite its existence, oil prices on world markets have often been as much affected by changing economic conditions as by OPEC policies. Since coming into existence, however, it has done much to eliminate the worst examples of the exploitation of primary producing countries by the industrialised nations. The headquarters of OPEC are in Vienna, Austria.

9.8.6 Central and Southern African-inspired inter-regional co-operation

Organisation of African Unity (OAU)

The OAU was founded in Addis Ababa in 1963, on the initiative of Emperor Haile Selassie of Ethiopia. Its main aims are to further African unity and solidarity; to co-ordinate political, economic, cultural, health, scientific and defence policies; and to eliminate colonialism in Africa. There are 50 countries in membership, representing virtually the whole of Central and Southern Africa, excluding South Africa, plus Algeria, Egypt and Tunisia, in North Africa and the Middle East. The Organisation is headed by an

Assembly of Heads of State and Government which meets annually and a Council of Ministers which meets twice a year. It also has a secretariat which is based in Addis Ababa, Ethiopia. The elected post of OAU chairman is a highly prestigious position in Black Africa.

9.8.7 United States-inspired inter-regional co-operation

As a leading industrial and military power, and as part of a strategy of mutual defence and economic development, the United States has promoted or sponsored a number of inter-regional groups with Western European and North, Central and South American countries. Military groups are described later, in paragraph 9.10.

Organisation of American States (OAS)

The OAS was founded in 1948 by a charter signed at Bogota, Colombia by representatives of 30 states in Central and South America and the Caribbean, plus the United States. Its declared purpose is: 'To achieve an order of peace and justice, promoting solidarity among the American states; to defend their sovereignty, their territorial integrity and their independence; to establish new objectives and standards for the promotion of the economic, social and cultural development of the peoples of the Hemisphere, and to speed the process of economic integration.'

The origins of the OAS go back as far as 1826 when the First Congress of American States was convened by the Venezuelan revolutionary leader, Simon Bolivar. Since those early days the Organisation has become more formally institutionalised, with a General Assembly, a Permanent Council, consisting of one representative from each of the member states, and numerous other councils, commissions and committees. Although its objectives are clearly, and impressively, stated in its charter, and although its structure appears to be democratically representative of all the signatories, the OAS has become increasingly dominated by the United States, so that, in pursuit of the Monroe Doctrine, enunciated in 1823, which effectively warned off European powers from America's 'back yard', what is regarded as 'good' for the American continent is mostly what is seen as good in the eyes of the United States, and this is an attitude often resented by many of the OAS members. It is interesting to note that, although several signatories are Commonwealth members, Canada, which, of course, shares the American continent, is not one of them. The headquarters of the OAS are in Washington, DC.

Inter-American Development Bank (IADB)

The IADB was founded in 1959, at the instigation of the OAS, to finance economic and social development, particularly in the less wealthy regions of the Americas. Its membership is wider than that of the OAS and includes Austria, Belgium, Canada, Denmark, Finland, France, West Germany, Israel, Italy, Japan, the Netherlands, Spain, Sweden, Switzerland and the United Kingdom, as well as the states of Central and Southern America, the Caribbean and the United States. Its headquarters are in Washington, DC.

9.8.8 Latin American-inspired inter-regional co-operation

In an effort to avoid over-dependence on the United States, and to come out of the shadow of living in its 'back yard', some Latin American states have sought to pursue a more independent economic policy line.

Andean Group (AG)
The Andean Group, also known as the Andean Sub-Regional Group, or the Andean Common Market, was established under the Cartagena Agreement of 1969 to promote the balanced and harmonious development of member countries through economic integration. The members include Bolivia, Colombia, Ecuador, Peru and Venezuela, with Mexico as a working partner since 1972. Chile was originally a member but left in 1976. The Group aims to harmonise policies on tariffs, the protection of intellectual property, such as patents and trade marks, and industrial and commercial development. Its institutions include a parliament and an executive commission and its headquarters are in Lima, Peru.

Latin American Economic System (Sistema Economico Latinoamericana) (LAES/SELA)
LAES was founded by treaty in 1975 as the successor to the Latin American Economic Co-ordination Commission. The aim was to have a purely Latin American organisation, with neither of the developed nations of North America involved. Its purpose is to create and promote multi-national enterprises in the region, to provide markets and to stimulate technological and scientific co-operation. LAES has 26 members, covering Central and South America and parts of the Caribbean, and its headquarters are in Caracas, Venezuela.

Latin American Integration Association (Asociacion Latino-Americana de Integration) (ALADI)
ALADI was formed in 1980 to replace the Latin American Free Trade Association (LAFTA). LAFTA encouraged trade by across-the-board tariff cuts while ALADI takes into account the different stages of economic development that individual countries have reached and so applies tariff reductions preferentially. The ultimate aim of the Association is to create a fully fledged common market. It has eleven member countries, all of them, except Mexico, in South America. ALADI is based in Montevideo, Uruguay.

9.8.9 Asian-inspired inter-regional co-operation

Asian Development Bank (ADB)
The idea of an Asian Development Bank, to foster economic growth by promoting investment and providing loan capital, was first mooted at a Conference of Asian Economic Planners in New Delhi in 1961. The ADB came into existence in 1966 and now has 28 regional members, representing most of the major countries in Asia and Oceania plus 14 non-regional members, including the United States, Canada and most of the states of Western Europe. The Bank's headquarters are in Manila, in the Philippines.

Association of South East Asian Nations (ASEAN)
ASEAN is an association of non-communist states in South East Asia which was formed in 1967 by the signing of the Bangkok Declaration. The declared aims of the Association are to foster economic and social progress and cultural development and to promote peace in the region. Its members include Indonesia, Malaysia, Philippines, Singapore and Thailand, and its headquarters are in Jakarta, Indonesia.

Asian and Pacific Council (ASPAC)
ASPAC was founded in 1966 to encourage cultural and economic co-operation throughout the regions. Its members include Australia, Japan, South Korea, Malaysia, New Zealand, Philippines, Taiwan and Thailand.

9.8.10 Oceania-inspired inter-regional co-operation

Rarotonga Treaty
The Rarotonga Treaty was signed in 1987 by Australia, Fiji, Indonesia, New Zealand and the Soviet Union. It formally declares the South Pacific a nuclear-free zone.

9.9 Intra-regional co-operation

There are many examples of co-operation within our defined regions. Some are primarily political and cultural, such as the Arab League, many are essentially economic and at least one, the Palestine Liberation Organisation, is intended to be an instrument for creating a new, independent state. To try to include every intra-regional group currently operating would be a virtually impossible task but those which are described below are seen as the most significant as well as being representative of their respective regions.

9.9.1 Western Europe

The Second World War had a profound and lasting effect on the countries of Western Europe, whether they were the 'victors' or the 'vanquished'. Above all else, it convinced the leading politicians of the countries which had experienced the war at first hand, France, Belgium, Luxembourg, the Netherlands, West Germany and Italy, that they should take steps to set up institutions which would make another war in Europe virtually impossible. The first practical step towards this end, in 1951, was the establishment of the European Coal and Steel Community (ECSC), in the belief that if the leading nations shared coal and steel-making facilities, which were seen as the basic raw materials of war, future conflicts would be avoided. The ECSC was followed, in 1955, by the European Investment Fund and then, two years later, in 1957, by the momentous signing in Rome of the treaties which established the European Economic Community (EEC) and the European Atomic Energy Community (Euratom). The preamble to the treaty setting up the EEC declared its objectives as: the establishment of the foundations of an even closer union among European peoples; the improvement of their working and living conditions; the progressive abolition of restrictions on trade between them; and the development of the prosperity of overseas countries. The founder members of the EEC were France, West Germany, Italy, Netherlands, Belgium and Luxembourg. The United Kingdom, Ireland and Denmark were admitted into membership in 1973, Greece in 1981 and Spain and Portugal in 1985. The twelve countries of the merged ECSC, Euratom and EEC, now known as the European Community (EC), have combined populations of more than 320 million, about 100 million more than the United States and 50 million more than the Soviet Union. Other forms of Western European co-operation are important but all are overshadowed by the sheer size, economic and political importance and the enormous potential of the Community.

European Community (EC)

The main EC institutions are the Commission, the Council of Ministers, the Committee of Permanent Representatives (COREPER), the Economic and Social Committee, the Court of Justice and the European Parliament.

The Commission is at the heart of the Community's decision-taking process. It consists of 16 members: two each from France, West Germany, Italy and the United Kingdom, and one each from Belgium, Denmark, Greece, Ireland, Luxembourg, Netherlands, Portugal and Spain. The members are nominated by each state for a four-year, renewable, term of office. One member is chosen as President for a two-year, renewable, term. The post of President is a mixture of head of government and head of the European civil service, and a highly respected appointment.

Although the commissioners are drawn proportionately from member-states, each takes an oath on appointment not to promote national interests. They head a comparatively large bureaucracy, with 20 directorates-general, each responsible for a particular department. Critics often complain about the size of the EC permanent machine but it is not unduly large in relation to the scope of its activities and its workload.

The Council of Ministers is the supreme decision-taking body and consists of one minister from each of the twelve member-countries. The actual representatives vary according to the subject matter under discussion. If it is economic policy it will be the finance ministers, if it is agricultural policy, the agriculture ministers. It is the foreign ministers, however, who tend to be the most active. The Presidency of the Council changes hands at six-monthly intervals, each member-state taking its turn.

The Committee of Permanent Representatives (COREPER) is a subsidiary body of officials, often called 'ambassadors', who act on behalf of the Council. The members of COREPER are senior civil servants who have been temporarily released by member-states to work for the Community.

The **Economic and Social Committee** is a consultative body consisting of representatives from member-countries and covering a wide range of interests. For example, they may include employers, members of labour unions, professional people, farmers and so on. The Committee advises the Council of Ministers and the Commission.

Membership of the **European Parliament** is determined by the populations of member-states. The total number of seats is 518, of which France, West Germany, Italy and the United Kingdom have 81 each, Spain has 60, the Netherlands 25, Belgium, Greece and Portugal 24 each, Denmark 16, Ireland 15 and Luxembourg six. Members are elected for five-year terms in large Euro-constituencies. Voting is by a system of proportional representation in all countries except the United Kingdom. The party composition of the European parliament, following the 1989 elections, is shown in Table 83.

Policy is made and carried out within the Community in the following way. The Commission makes a particular proposal which will have first been worked on by one of the 20 directorates. The proposal is sent to the Council of Ministers who will initially pass it to COREPER for further examination. At the same time it will be passed to the European Parliament for consideration. The Parliament's role is still mainly consultative, but it does have power to reject the Community budget and to dismiss the Commission if it has good grounds for doing so.

Table 83

PARTY COMPOSITION OF THE EUROPEAN PARLIAMENT: 1989

Country	Seats	Party	Seats won
Belgium	24 seats:	Socialists	(8)
		Independent Socialist	(1)
		Christian Democrats	(7)
		Liberals	(4)
		Voksunie	(1)
		Ecology	(3)
Denmark	16 seats:	Conservatives	(2)
		Anti-EC	(4)
		Social Democrats	(4)
		Liberals	(3)
		Socialist People's Party	(1)
		Centre	(2)
France	81 seats:	Socialists and Left Radicals	(22)
		Gaullists and Liberals (Combined Right)	(26)
		Communists	(7)
		National Front	(10)
		Centre	(7)
West Germany	81 seats:	Christian Democrats/CSU	(32)
		Social Democrats	(31)
		Greens	(8)
		Free Democrats	(4)
		Republicans	(6)
Greece	24 seats:	Socialists	(9)
		New Democracy	(10)
		Communist	(4)
		Democratic Renewal	(1)
Ireland	15 seats:	Fianna Fail	(6)
		Fine Gael	(4)
		Independents	(2)
		Other parties	(3)
Italy	81 seats:	Communists	(22)
		Christian Democrats	(27)
		Socialists	(12)
		Liberals/Republicans	(4)
		MSI	(4)
		Social Democrats	(2)
		Greens	(5)
		Other parties	(5)

Table 83—Party Composition of the European Parliament: 1989 (Contd.)

Luxembourg	6 seats:	Christian Democrats	(3)
		Socialists	(2)
		Liberal	(1)
Netherlands	25 seats:	Labour	(8)
		Christian Democrats	(10)
		Liberals	(3)
		GPU	(1)
		Other parties	(3)
Portugal	24 seats:	Social Democrats	(9)
		Socialists	(8)
		Centre	(3)
		Communists	(4)
Spain	60 seats:	Socialists	(27)
		People's Party	(15)
		Centre	(5)
		Communists	(4)
		Regional Lists	(7)
		Other parties	(2)
United Kingdom	81 seats:	Conservative	(32)
		Labour	(45)
		SNP	(1)
		DUP	(1)
		OUP	(1)
		SDLP	(1)
Main party groupings:	Left (260)	—Socialists	(180)
		Communists	(41)
		Rainbow (Greens)	(39)
	Centre (203)	—Christian Democrats	(123)
		Independents	(16)
		Liberals	(44)
		Gaullists (with Fianna Fail and SNP)	(20)
	Right (55)	—Conservatives	(34)
		Right	(21)

After examination by COREPER, with the addition of any views of the European Parliament, the proposal is formally considered by the Council of Ministers who decide whether or not action should be taken. Voting in the Council is weighted in favour of the larger member-states, but votes are taken only rarely. Either there is a unanimous decision or if one or more of the ministers argue that the policy would be against national interests the proposal is likely to be shelved. Once the Council has agreed a policy proposal it is passed back to the Commission for implementation.

A policy decision can take one of two forms. It can be a regulation or a directive. Both are legally binding but a regulation applies to all member-states whereas a directive relates only to one or more specific countries.

Decision-taking within the Community is only partially democratic and only marginally accountable to the electorates of the member-states but, as the European Parliament becomes more firmly established, on broad European party lines, its influence, and eventually its powers, will undoubtedly grow.

The European Court of Justice consists of judges and officials appointed by the member-states. Its task is to ensure that the Community treaties are fairly observed and that regulations and directives are followed. The Court can make rulings but it has no powers of its own to enforce them. This is the responsibility of the individual member-states in their own national courts.

The Commission, the Council of Ministers and COREPER are based in Brussels, the European Parliament meets in Luxembourg or Strasbourg, France, and the European Court of Justice sits in Luxembourg.

The Community has not yet achieved its aim of creating a single European market, when all internal barriers to trade will be removed, but all member-states have agreed that this will happen at the end of 1992. The broader objective of agreeing common economic and foreign policies, eventually leading, as pro-Europeans would hope, to political union, is a much longer-term aim and some heads of government would clearly like to postpone its implementation indefinitely, or even summarily abandon it.

Council of Europe

The Council of Europe was established in Strasbourg, France, in 1949 to secure 'a greater measure of unity between the European countries', by the discussion of common interests and problems and the discovery of new methods and areas of co-operation. Its membership is wider than that of the EC, including Austria, Cyprus, Iceland, Malta, Norway, Sweden, Switzerland and Turkey, as well as ten of the twelve European Community members, the absentees being Spain and Portugal. It has a Consultative Assembly which meets annually and a Standing Committee to represent it when it is not in session.

The Council has been particularly active, and effective, in the field of human rights. Under the European Convention of Human Rights of 1950, it established the **European Commission of Human Rights**, also based in Strasbourg, to investigate complaints by states or individuals. The findings of the Commission are then considered by the **European Court of Human Rights**, in Strasbourg, which was formed in 1959. Many European states have recognised the jurisdiction of the Court by making its decisions binding nationally, and this has resulted in ordinary citizens who feel aggrieved by judgements in their own national courts taking their cases, over the heads of governments, to Strasbourg.

Benelux

A customs union, to encourage trade between the three countries, was established by Belgium, the Netherlands and Luxembourg in 1948 and was called Benelux. It was later overtaken by the creation of the European Economic Community, and the other bodies which now form part of the EC, but in 1960, by the Benelux Treaty, the economic union of the three states was formalised. This made them, in economic terms, a single unit, while retaining their political independence and their obligations to the European Community. The organisation has a Committee of Ministers, comprising at least three ministers from each state, which meets every two months, and a Council of Economic Union which is an umbrella body with the task of co-ordinating the work of the many Benelux committees. The head of the permanent Secretariat, which is based in Brussels, is always Dutch and is assisted by two deputies from the other member-states.

European Free Trade Association (EFTA)
EFTA was originally established in 1960 as a free trade alternative to the European Economic Community. Its original members included Austria, Denmark, Norway, Portugal, Sweden and the United Kingdom. Finland became an associate member in 1961 and Iceland a full member in 1970. It soon became clear that EFTA could never supplant the EEC and several members began to apply for entry into the Community. Denmark and the United Kingdom left in 1972 and Portugal in 1985. EFTA now comprises Austria, Finland, Iceland, Norway, Sweden and Switzerland. It is essentially an economic association whereby import duties between the six member countries have been abolished. It has its headquarters in Geneva, Switzerland.

Nordic Council
The Nordic Council was founded in 1953 by Denmark, Iceland, Norway and Sweden as a consultative body to increase co-operation between them. They were joined in 1956 by Finland. Council members are elected by the parliaments of member-states, 16 each from Denmark, Finland, Norway and Sweden and five from Iceland. The Council does not have permanent headquarters.

European Space Agency (ESA)
ESA is an organisation to promote space research and technology for peaceful purposes. It was originally founded in 1975 and reorganised in 1980. Its members include Belgium, Denmark, France, West Germany, Ireland, Italy, the Netherlands, Spain, Sweden, Switzerland and the United Kingdom. ESA has developed a number of scientific and communication satellites, as well as the Ariane rocket.

European Organisation for Nuclear Research (*Centre D'Etudes de Recherches Nucléaires*) (CERN)
CERN was established in 1954 as a co-operative venture for research into nuclear energy for peaceful purposes. It members include twelve major West European countries who provide teams of scientists to work together at laboratories at Meyrin, near Geneva, Switzerland.

9.9.2 Middle East and North Africa

Co-operation within the Middle East and North Africa is generally founded on a strong, and proud, sense of a common identity among Arabs, even though the region contains many races and religions. Israel has been excluded from virtually all the co-operative groups and associations and this has undoubtedly contributed to its sense of isolation and suspicions about neighbouring states. Future harmony in the region depends greatly on whether the degree of mutual trust which has been established between Egypt and Israel can be extended to the wider Arab world.

The League of Arab States (*Al Jamia al Arabiyyah* or Arab League)
The Arab League was founded in 1945 largely on the initiative of Egypt. It now has 21 members, comprising all the states of the Middle East and North Africa except Israel. Its declared purpose is 'to strengthen the close

ties linking sovereign Arab States and to co-ordinate their policies and activities and direct them to the common good of the Arab countries'. It also acts as a mediator in disputes between Arab nations. The main body in the League is the Council, which includes representatives of all the member-states and usually meets twice a year, in March and September. Attached to it are 16 specialist, functional committees. There are a large number of agencies and bureaux operating within the League. The headquarters, with its secretariat, used to be in Cairo but when Egypt signed a peace treaty, in 1979, with Israel it was suspended from membership and the headquarters moved to Tunis. Egypt has since been re-admitted.

Arab Common Market

The Arab Common Market, providing for the abolition of customs duties on agricultural products, and reductions on other items, came into effect in 1965. Membership was open to all Arab League states but only Egypt, Iraq, Jordan and Syria have signed the treaty which set it up.

Arab Monetary Fund (AMF)

The AMF was established in 1976 by 20 Arab states plus the PLO to provide a mechanism for promoting greater stability in exchange rates and to co-ordinate Arab economic and monetary policies. The Fund's headquarters are in Abu Dhabi, in the United Arab Emirates. It operates mainly by regulating petrodollars within the Arab community to make it less dependent on the West for the handling of its surplus funds.

Organisation of Arab Petroleum Exporting Countries (OAPEC)

OAPEC was established in 1968 to safeguard the interests of its members and to encourage co-operation in economic activity within the petroleum industry. It currently has ten members: Algeria, Bahrain, Egypt, Iraq, Kuwait, Libya, Qatar, Saudi Arabia, Syria and the United Arab Emirates. Its headquarters are in Kuwait.

Palestine Liberation Organisation (PLO)

The PLO was founded in 1964 with the objective of bringing about an independent state of Palestine. It contains a number of factions, the most important being *al-Fatah*, which is led by Yasser Arafat. To achieve its main aim it has pursued a mixed policy of diplomacy and guerrilla activity. Although it has been long recognised in the Arab world as a legitimate political body, its reputation among Western nations has not been good, some political leaders referring to it as a terrorist organisation. However, in 1988, when Jordan announced its decision to relinquish its responsibility for the Israeli-occupied West Bank, and Arafat later publicly accepted the right of Israel to exist as an independent state, world opinion changed and the PLO became an organisation which could be regarded as the legitimate representative of the Palestinians and, therefore, could provide the nucleus of an independent Palestine state.

Co-operative Council for the Arab States of the Gulf (CCASG)

The CCASG was established in 1981 as an exclusively Arab organisation for promoting peace in the Persian Gulf area. Its declared purpose is 'to bring about integration, co-ordination and co-operation in economic, social, defence and political affairs among Arab Gulf states'. Its members include Bahrain, Kuwait, Oman, Qatar, Saudi Arabia and the United Arab Emirates and its headquarters are at Riyadh, Saudi Arabia.

9.9.3 Central and Southern Africa

Co-operation in economic and social matters in Central and Southern Africa has been fragmentary and sometimes duplicated. Because of this, it has been less effective than in some other regions of the world. This lack of cohesion has arisen partly because of the sheer size of the continent and the poor communications within it, particularly between the east and west coasts, and partly because of tribal and language differences. Co-operation is, therefore, frequently sub-regional and often influenced by the colonial histories of particular countries. Thus those states which used to form part of the French empire co-operate more naturally with other French-speaking countries whereas former British colonies tend to link with countries where English is the principal language.

Southern African Development Co-ordination Conference (SADCC)
SADCC was formed at its first conference in Arusha, Tanzania, in July 1979, when representatives of Angola, Botswana, Lesotho, Malawi, Mozambique, Swaziland, Tanzania, Zambia and Zimbabwe agreed to work more closely together to reduce their economic dependence on South Africa. Since then an organisation has been formed with its headquarters in Gabarone, Botswana. Annual meetings of heads of state and heads of government are held and SADCC ministers meet at least twice a year to formulate plans. The main areas that the organisation has targeted as in need of particular attention are transport and communications, energy and mining and industrial production, and a number of sector units have been set up to implement proposals.

Organisation Commune Africaine et Mauricienne (OCAM)
OCAM was founded in 1965 as the Organisation Commune Africaine et Malgache. This was itself a successor to the Union Africaine et Malgache de Co-opération Economique, which had operated between 1961 and 1965. In 1970 the name of Organisation Commune Africaine Malgache et Mauricienne was adopted but when Madagascar withdrew from the Organisation in 1975 the present name was adopted. The full membership now includes Benin, Burkina Faso, Central African Republic, Ivory Coast, Niger, Rwanda, Senegal and Togo. The declared purpose of OCAM is to strengthen the solidarity and close ties between member-states and to raise living standards and co-ordinate economic policies. Through the Organisation, members share an airline, a merchant fleet and a common postal and communications system. The headquarters of OCAM are at Bangui in the Central African Republic.

Council of the Entente (CE)
The CE was set up in 1959 by four states, Benin, Burkina Faso, Ivory Coast and Niger, to strengthen economic links and promote industrial development. Togo joined in 1966 when a Mutual Aid and Loan Guarantee Fund was established. The headquarters of the Council are in Abidjan, Ivory Coast.

Economic Community of West African States (ECOWAS)
ECOWAS was established in 1975, by the Treaty of Lagos, to promote economic co-operation and development. Its members include Benin, Burkina Faso, Cape Verde, Gambia, Ghana, Guinea, Guinea-Bissau, Ivory Coast, Liberia, Mali, Mauritania, Niger, Nigeria, Senegal, Sierra Leone and Togo. Its headquarters are in Lagos, Nigeria.

Preferential Trade Area for East and Southern Africa (PTA)
The PTA was established in 1981 with the object of increasing economic and commercial co-operation between member-states, harmonising tariffs and reducing trade barriers, with the eventual aim of creating a common market. The current members include Burundi, Comoros, Djibouti, Ethiopia, Kenya, Lesotho, Malawi, Mauritius, Rwanda, Somalia, Swaziland, Tanzania, Uganda, Zambia and Zimbabwe. The headquarters of the PTA are in Lusaka, Zambia.

9.9.4 Central America and the Caribbean

Caribbean Community and Common Market (CARICOM)
CARICOM was founded in 1973 as a successor to the Caribbean Free Trade Association, as a vehicle for increasing economic co-operation and reducing trade barriers in the area. Its members include Antigua and Barbuda, Grenada, Guyana, Jamaica, Montserrat, St Kitts-Nevis, St Lucia, St Vincent and the Grenadines and Trinidad and Tobago. The headquarters of CARICOM are at Georgetown, Guyana.

Central American Common Market (CACM)
The CACM is roughly the mainland equivalent of CARICOM. It was founded in 1961 with similar objectives and its members include Costa Rica, Guatemala, Honduras, Nicaragua and El Salvador. Its headquarters are in Guatemala City.

Organisation of Central American States (ODECA)
ODECA was founded in 1951 for the purpose of strengthening unity in Central America and fostering economic, political and social co-operation, with a view to avoiding overdependence on the United States and its dominance in the Organisation of American States (OAS). ODECA's membership includes Costa Rica, Guatemala, Honduras, El Salvador and Nicaragua. Its headquarters are in San Salvador.

9.9.5 South America

The Amazon Pact
The Amazon Pact is a treaty signed in 1978 by Bolivia, Brazil, Colombia, Ecuador, Guyana, Peru, Suriname and Venezuela to protect and control the development of the Amazon River.

The Andean Group
The Andean Group was formed in 1969 by Bolivia, Chile, Colombia, Ecuador and Peru who signed an agreement to work more closely together in economic matters and in reducing trade barriers so as to create a common market. In 1973 Venezuela joined the group and in 1977 Chile withdrew.

9.9.6 Asia

South Asian Association for Regional Co-operation (SAARC)
Established in 1985 to foster co-operation between Bangladesh, Bhutan, India, Maldives, Nepal, Pakistan and Sri Lanka.

9.9.7 Oceania

South Pacific Commission (SPC)
The SPC was established by an agreement signed in Canberra, Australia, in 1947, with the object of encouraging economic and social co-operation in the region. Its members include most of the states in Oceania, including the dependencies, plus France, the United Kingdom and the United States, who are involved because of their past and present interests in the region. The headquarters of the Commission are in Nouméa, New Caledonia.

South Pacific Forum (SPF)
The SPF was created in 1971, as an offshoot of the SPC, to provide an opportunity for member-states to discuss common interests and develop common policies. The membership includes Australia, Cook Islands, the Federated States of Micronesia, Fiji, Kiribati, the Marshall Islands, Nauru, New Zealand, Niue, Papua New Guinea, Solomon Islands, Tonga, Tuvalu, Vanuatu and Western Samoa. In 1985 the Forum adopted a treaty for creating a nuclear-free zone in the Pacific.

South Pacific Bureau for Economic Co-operation (SPEC)
SPEC was founded in 1973, following a meeting of the SPF, as a practical scheme for stimulating economic co-operation and the development of trade. The headquarters of SPEC are in Suva, Fiji.

9.10 Military co-operation

The examples of global, inter-regional and intra-regional co-operation described above are generally positive and peaceful in character. However, the world is still filled with distrust and insecurity and, because of this, a number of military pacts and organisations have been established to provide what states and regions see as vital defences against possible aggression. The hopeful signs are that nations, and groups of nations, are beginning to talk more openly with one another, across the barriers that schemes of military co-operation inevitably create.

North Atlantic Treaty Organisation (NATO)
NATO was established under the North Atlantic Treaty of 1949, which was signed by Belgium, Canada, Denmark, France, Iceland, Italy, Luxembourg, the Netherlands, Norway, Portugal, the United Kingdom and the United States. It is a mutual defence treaty by which it was agreed that 'an armed attack against one or more in Europe or North America shall be considered an attack against all'. Greece and Turkey joined the organisation in 1952, West Germany was admitted in 1955 and Spain in 1982. France withdrew from the organisation, but not the alliance, in 1966, Greece withdrew politically, but not militarily, in 1974, and its re-entry was opposed by Turkey in 1980.

NATO's supreme body is the Council of Foreign Ministers of all the participating nations and its secretariat is based in Brussels, where there is also a Military Committee composed of the chiefs of staff of the member countries. The military headquarters, Supreme Headquarters Allied Powers, Europe (SHAPE), is at Chièvres, near Mons, in Belgium. The two Supreme Allied Commanders, Europe and Atlantic are US military officers and the Allied Commander, Channel is a British Admiral. In 1960 it was agreed to form a permanent, multi-national unit, called the Allied Mobile Force (AMF), to move immediately to any NATO country which appeared to be under threat. This mobile unit is based in Heidelberg, in West Germany.

NATO was originally formed to oppose a threat from the Soviet Union and its Warsaw Pact satellites and, although it has remained the keystone of Western defence for more than 40 years, relations between its members have not always been harmonious. The main areas of contention have been the degree of US dominance, the presence of nuclear weapons on European soil and the respective levels of contribution by signatories to the organisation's upkeep. The changed climate created by the new Gorbachev regime in the Soviet Union has added another dimension to NATO's role and to future attitudes within the alliance.

Western European Union (WEU)

The WEU is based on the Brussels Treaty of 1948 and was established in 1955 as a forum for the discussion of defence issues by West European governments. Its members include Belgium, France, West Germany, Italy, Luxembourg, the Netherlands and the United Kingdom, and, since 1989, Portugal and Spain. There is an Assembly which meets twice yearly in Paris, and sometimes in the Hague, and a Council, consisting of the foreign ministers of the member-states, which normally meets quarterly. The Union is pledged, under its charter, to work closely with NATO. It has a permanent secretariat based in London, but there has been pressure from the British government to locate both the Assembly and the Secretariat in Brussels. Other EC members, who are not also in the WEU, are sometimes invited to attend Assembly meetings as observers.

Warsaw Treaty of Friendship, Co-operation and Mutual Assistance— The Warsaw Pact

On 14 May 1955 Albania, Bulgaria, Czechoslovakia, East Germany, Hungary, Poland, Romania and the Soviet Union signed a 20-year treaty of friendship and collaboration, in Warsaw, which became known as the Warsaw Pact. Under the terms of the treaty, the eight states are pledged to a policy of mutual defence, an attack on one being regarded as an attack on all. It was also agreed that there should be a joint command for their armed forces. Albania ceased to be an active member in 1962 and formally withdrew in 1968.

The Treaty's organisation includes a Political Consultative Committee (PCC), a Committee of Defence Ministers, a Military Council, a Technical Committee, a Committee of Foreign Ministers and a Joint Command. The headquarters are in Moscow.

APPENDIX

DATA SOURCES

Bogdanor, V. (ed), *The Blackwell Encyclopedia of Political Institutions*, Basil Blackwell, 1987.

Chambers World Gazetteer: An A-Z of Geographical Information, Chambers & Cambridge University Press, 1988.

Day, A. J. and Degenhardt, H. W., *Political Parties of the World: a Keesing's Reference Publication*, 2nd edn., Longman, 1987.

Delury, G. E. (ed), *World Encyclopedia of Political Systems*, Vols I-III, Facts on File, 1987.

The Economist (weekly), London

The Economist, *World Atlas of Elections*, The Economist Publications, 1987.

The Economist, *World Human Rights Guide*, The Economist Publications, 1986.

Europa Publications: *A World Survey* (annual).
Africa South of the Sahara Yearbook (annual).
Western Europe—A Political and Economic Survey.
The Far East and Australasia.
The Middle East and North Africa.
South America, Central America and the Caribbean.

Facts on File.

Financial Times (daily), London.

Guardian (daily), London.

The Hutchinson Encyclopedia, 8th edn., Hutchinson, 1987.

Independent (daily), London.

Information Please Almanac: Atlas and Yearbook, 1987, Houghton Mifflin, 1987.

Keesing's Record of World Events (monthly), London

Kidron, M. and Segal, R., *The New State of the World Atlas*, revised 1st edn., Pan Books, 1987.

Kurian, G. T., *Encyclopedia of the Third World*, Vols I-III, 3rd edn., Mansell Publishing Ltd., 1987.

Kurian, G. T., *The New Book of World Rankings*, Facts on File, 1985.

Mackie, T. T. and Rose, R., *International Almanac of Electoral History*, new edn., Macmillan, 1982.

Minority Rights Group Reports, MRG.

Newsweek (weekly).

Observer (weekly), London.

Segal, G. *Guide to the World Today*, Simon & Schuster, 1987.

South (monthly), South Publications.

Statesman's Yearbook (annual), Macmillan.

Sunday Times (weekly), London.

Taylor, C. L. and Jodice, D. A. A., *World Handbook of Political and Social Indicators*, Vols 1 and 2, 3rd edn., Yale University Press, 1983.

Time Magazine (weekly).

The Times (daily), London.

United Nations, *Statistical Yearbook* (annual).

The World Almanac and Book of Facts (annual).

The World Bank, *World Development Report*, Oxford University Press, 1987.

Yearbook of International Organisations, München.

INDEX

Index